T0180704

Lecture Notes in Computer Science 12492

More information about this subseries at http://www.springer.com/series/7410

Shiho Moriai · Huaxiong Wang (Eds.)

Advances in Cryptology – ASIACRYPT 2020

26th International Conference on the Theory
and Application of Cryptology and Information Security
Daejeon, South Korea, December 7–11, 2020
Proceedings, Part II

Springer

Editors
Shiho Moriai
Network Security Research Institute (NICT)
Tokyo, Japan

Huaxiong Wang ⓘ
Nanyang Technological University
Singapore, Singapore

ISSN 0302-9743   ISSN 1611-3349   (electronic)
Lecture Notes in Computer Science
ISBN 978-3-030-64833-6   ISBN 978-3-030-64834-3   (eBook)
https://doi.org/10.1007/978-3-030-64834-3

LNCS Sublibrary: SL4 – Security and Cryptology

This Springer imprint is published by the registered company Springer Nature Switzerland AG
The registered company address is: Gewerbestrasse 11, 6330 Cham, Switzerland

Preface

The 26th Annual International Conference on Theory and Application of Cryptology and Information Security (ASIACRYPT 2020), was originally planned to be held in Daejeon, South Korea, during December 7–11, 2020. Due to the COVID-19 pandemic, it was shifted to an online-only virtual conference.

The conference focused on all technical aspects of cryptology, and was sponsored by the International Association for Cryptologic Research (IACR).

We received a total of 316 submissions from all over the world, the Program Committee (PC) selected 85 papers for publication in the proceedings of the conference. The two program chairs were supported by a PC consisting of 66 leading experts in aspects of cryptology. Each submission was reviewed by at least three PC members (or their sub-reviewers) and five PC members were assigned to submissions co-authored by PC members. The strong conflict of interest rules imposed by the IACR ensure that papers are not handled by PC members with a close working relationship with authors. The two program chairs were not allowed to submit a paper, and PC members were limited to two submissions each. There were approximately 390 external reviewers, whose input was critical to the selection of papers.

The review process was conducted using double-blind peer review. The conference operated a two-round review system with a rebuttal phase. After the reviews and first-round discussions, the PC selected 205 submissions to proceed to the second round, including 1 submission with early acceptance. The authors of 204 papers were then invited to provide a short rebuttal in response to the referee reports. The second round involved extensive discussions by the PC members.

The three volumes of the conference proceedings contain the revised versions of the 85 papers that were selected, together with the abstracts of 2 invited talks. The final revised versions of papers were not reviewed again and the authors are responsible for their contents.

The program of ASIACRYPT 2020 featured two excellent invited talks by Shweta Agrawal and Jung Hee Cheon. The conference also featured a rump session which contained short presentations on the latest research results of the field.

The PC selected three papers to receive the Best Paper Award, via a voting-based process that took into account conflicts of interest, which were solicited to submit the full versions to the *Journal of Cryptology*: "Finding Collisions in a Quantum World: Quantum Black-Box Separation of Collision-Resistance and One-Wayness" by Akinori Hosoyamada and Takashi Yamakawa; "New results on Gimli: full-permutation distinguishers and improved collisions" by Antonio Flórez Gutiérrez, Gaëtan Leurent, María Naya-Plasencia, Léo Perrin, André Schrottenloher, and Ferdinand Sibleyras; and "SQISign: Compact Post-Quantum signatures from Quaternions and Isogenies" by Luca De Feo, David Kohel, Antonin Leroux, Christophe Petit, and Benjamin Wesolowski.

Many people contributed to the success of ASIACRYPT 2020. We would like to thank the authors for submitting their research results to the conference. We are very grateful to the PC members and external reviewers for contributing their knowledge and expertise, and for the tremendous amount of work that was done with reading papers and contributing to the discussions. We are greatly indebted to Kwangjo Kim, the general chair, for his efforts and overall organization. We thank Michel Abdalla, McCurley, Kay McKelly, and members of the IACR's emergency pandemic team for their work in designing and running the virtual format. We thank Steve Galbraith, Joo Young Lee, and Yu Sasaki for expertly organizing and chairing the rump session. We are extremely grateful to Zhenzhen Bao for checking all the latex files and for assembling the files for submission to Springer. Finally, we thank Shai Halevi and the IACR for setting up and maintaining the Web Submission and Review software, used by IACR conferences for the paper submission and review process. We also thank Alfred Hofmann, Anna Kramer, and their colleagues at Springer for handling the publication of these conference proceedings.

December 2020

Shiho Moriai
Huaxiong Wang

Organization

General Chair

Kwangjo Kim   Korea Advanced Institute of Science and Technology (KAIST), South Korea

Program Chairs

Shiho Moriai   Network Security Research Institute (NICT), Japan
Huaxiong Wang   Nanyang Technological University, Singapore

Program Committee

Shweta Agrawal   IIT Madras, India
Gorjan Alagic   University of Maryland, USA
Shi Bai   Florida Atlantic University, USA
Zhenzhen Bao   Nanyang Technological University, Singapore
Paulo Barreto   University of Washington Tacoma, USA
Lejla Batina   Radboud University, The Netherlands
Amos Beimel   Ben-Gurion University, Israel
Sonia Belaïd   CryptoExperts, France
Olivier Blazy   University of Limoges, France
Jie Chen   East China Normal University, China
Yilei Chen   Visa Research, USA
Chen-Mou Cheng   Osaka University, Japan
Jun Furukawa   NEC Israel Research Center, Israel
David Galindo   University of Birmingham, Fetch.AI, UK
Jian Guo   Nanyang Technological University, Singapore
Swee-Huay Heng   Multimedia University, Malaysia
Xinyi Huang   Fujian Normal University, China
Andreas Hülsing   TU Eindhoven, The Netherlands
Takanori Isobe   University of Hyogo, Japan
David Jao   University of Waterloo, evolutionQ, Inc., Canada
Jérémy Jean   ANSSI, France
Zhengfeng Ji   University of Technology Sydney, Australia
Hyung Tae Lee   Jeonbuk National University, South Korea
Jooyoung Lee   KAIST, South Korea
Benoît Libert   CNRS, ENS, France
Dongdai Lin   Chinese Academy of Sciences, China
Helger Lipmaa   University of Tartu, Estonia, and Simula UiB, Norway
Feng-Hao Liu   Florida Atlantic University, USA

Giorgia Azzurra Marson	University of Bern, Switzerland, and NEC Laboratories Europe, Germany
Daniel Masny	Visa Research, USA
Takahiro Matsuda	AIST, Japan
Brice Minaud	Inria, ENS, France
Shiho Moriai	NICT, Japan
Kartik Nayak	Duke University, VMware Research, USA
Khoa Nguyen	Nanyang Technological University, Singapore
Svetla Nikova	KU Leuven, Belgium
Carles Padró	UPC, Spain
Jiaxin Pan	NTNU, Norway
Arpita Patra	Indian Institute of Science, India
Thomas Peters	UCL, Belgium
Duong Hieu Phan	University of Limoges, France
Raphael C.-W. Phan	Monash University, Malaysia
Josef Pieprzyk	CSIRO, Australia, and Institute of Computer Science, Polish Academy of Sciences, Poland
Ling Ren	VMware Research, University of Illinois at Urbana-Champaign, USA
Carla Ràfols	Universitat Pompeu Fabra, Spain
Rei Safavi-Naini	University of Calgary, Canada
Yu Sasaki	NTT laboratories, Japan
Jae Hong Seo	Hanyang University, South Korea
Ron Steinfeld	Monash University, Australia
Willy Susilo	University of Wollongong, Australia
Qiang Tang	New Jersey Institute of Technology, USA
Mehdi Tibouchi	NTT laboratories, Japan
Huaxiong Wang	Nanyang Technological University, Singapore
Xiaoyun Wang	Tsinghua University, China
Yongge Wang	The University of North Carolina at Charlotte, USA
Chaoping Xing	Shanghai Jiao Tong University, China, and NTU, Singapore
Yu Yu	Shanghai Jiao Tong University, China
Mark Zhandry	Princeton University, NTT Research, USA

External Reviewers

Behzad Abdolmaleki	Marcel Armour	Saikrishna
Parhat Abla	Gilad Asharov	Badrinarayanan
Mamun Akand	Man Ho Au	Mir Ali Rezazadeh Baee
Orestis Alpos	Benedikt Auerbach	Joonsang Baek
Hiroaki Anada	Khin Mi Mi Aung	Karim Baghery
Benny Applebaum	Sepideh Avizheh	Gustavo Banegas
Diego F. Aranha	Christian Badertscher	Laasya Bangalore

Subhadeep Banik
James Bartusek
Carsten Baum
Rouzbeh Behnia
Aner Ben-Efraim
Fabrice Benhamouda
Francesco Berti
Luk Bettale
Tim Beyne
Shivam Bhasin
Nina Bindel
Nir Bitansky
Xavier Bonnetain
Katharina Boudgoust
Florian Bourse
Zvika Brakerski
Jaqueline Brendel
Olivier Bronchain
Benedikt Bunz
Seyit Camtepe
Ignacio Cascudo
Gaëtan Cassiers
Suvradip Chakraborty
Jorge Chávez Saab
Hao Chen
Hua Chen
Long Chen
Rongmao Chen
Yu Chen
Yuan Chen
Ding-Yuan Cheng
Ji-Jian Chin
Seongbong Choi
Wonseok Choi
Ashish Choudhury
Sherman S. M. Chow
Heewon Chung
Michele Ciampi
Benoît Cogliati
Craig Costello
Nicholas Courtois
Geoffroy Couteau
Alain Couvreur
Daniele Cozzo
Hongrui Cui
Edouard Cuvelier

Jan Czajkowski
João Paulo da Silva
Jan-Pieter D'anvers
Joan Daemen
Ricardo Dahab
Nilanjan Datta
Bernardo David
Gareth Davies
Yi Deng
Amit Deo
Patrick Derbez
Siemen Dhooghe
Hang Dinh
Christoph Dobraunig
Javad Doliskani
Jelle Don
Xiaoyang Dong
Dung Duong
Betül Durak
Avijit Dutta
Sabyasachi Dutta
Sébastien Duval
Ted Eaton
Keita Emura
Muhammed F. Esgin
Thomas Espitau
Xiong Fan
Antonio Faonio
Prastudy Fauzi
Hanwen Feng
Shengyuan Feng
Tamara Finogina
Apostolos Fournaris
Ashley Fraser
Philippe Gaborit
Steven Galbraith
Pierre Galissant
Chaya Ganesh
Romain Gay
Chunpeng Ge
Kai Gellert
Nicholas Genise
Alexandru Gheorghiu
Hossein Ghodosi
Satrajit Ghosh
Benedikt Gierlichs

Kristian Gjøsteen
Aarushi Goel
Huijing Gong
Junqing Gong
Zheng Gong
Alonso González
Rishab Goyal
Benjamin Grégoire
Jiaxin Guan
Cyprien de Saint Guilhem
Aldo Gunsing
Chun Guo
Fuchun Guo
Qian Guo
Felix Günther
Ariel Hamlin
Ben Hamlin
Jinguang Han
Kyoohyung Han
Keisuke Hara
Debiao He
Chloé Hébant
Javier Herranz
Shoichi Hirose
Deukjo Hong
Akinori Hosoyamada
Hector Hougaard
Qiong Huang
Shih-Han Hung
Kathrin Hövelmanns
Akiko Inoue
Tetsu Iwata
Ashwin Jha
Dingding Jia
Shaoquan Jiang
Chanyang Ju
Eliran Kachlon
Saqib A. Kakvi
Ghassan Karame
Sabyasachi Karati
Angshuman Karmakar
Shuichi Katsumata
Marcel Keller
Dongwoo Kim
Jihye Kim
Jinsu Kim

Jiseung Kim
Jongkil Kim
Minkyu Kim
Myungsun Kim
Seongkwang Kim
Taechan Kim
Elena Kirshanova
Fuyuki Kitagawa
Susumu Kiyoshima
Michael Kloss
François Koeune
Lisa Kohl
Markulf Kohlweiss
Chelsea Komlo
Yashvanth Kondi
Nishat Koti
Toomas Krips
Veronika Kuchta
Thijs Laarhoven
Jianchang Lai
Qiqi Lai
Huy Quoc Le
Byeonghak Lee
Changmin Lee
Moon Sung Lee
Liang Li
Shuaishuai Li
Shun Li
Xiangxue Li
Xinyu Li
Ya-Nan Li
Zhe Li
Bei Liang
Cheng-Jun Lin
Fuchun Lin
Wei-Kai Lin
Dongxi Liu
Fukang Liu
Guozhen Liu
Jia Liu
Joseph K. Liu
Meicheng Liu
Qipeng Liu
Shengli Liu
Yunwen Liu
Zhen Liu

Julian Loss
Yuan Lu
Zhenliang Lu
Lin Lyu
Fermi Ma
Hui Ma
Xuecheng Ma
Bernardo Magri
Monosij Maitra
Christian Majenz
Nathan Manohar
Ange Martinelli
Zdenek Martinasek
Ramiro Martínez
Pedro Maat C. Massolino
Loïc Masure
Bart Mennink
Lauren De Meyer
Peihan Miao
Kazuhiko Minematsu
Rafael Misoczki
Tarik Moataz
Tal Moran
Tomoyuki Morimae
Hiraku Morita
Travis Morrison
Pratyay Mukherjee
Sayantan Mukherjee
Pierrick Méaux
Helen Möllering
Michael Naehrig
Yusuke Naito
Maria Naya-Plasencia
Ngoc Khanh Nguyen
Jianting Ning
Ryo Nishimaki
Ariel Nof
Kazuma Ohara
Daniel Esteban Escudero
   Ospina
Giorgos Panagiotakos
Bo Pang
Lorenz Panny
Anna Pappa
Anat Paskin-Cherniavsky
Alain Passelègue

Shravani Patil
Sikhar Patranabis
Kateryna Pavlyk
Alice Pellet-Mary
Geovandro Pereira
Thomas Peyrin
Phuong Pham
Stjepan Picek
Zaira Pindado
Rafael del Pino
Rachel Player
Geong Sen Poh
David Pointcheval
Yuriy Polyakov
Ali Poostindouz
Frédéric de Portzamparc
Chen Qian
Tian Qiu
Sai Rahul Rachuri
Adrian Ranea
Divya Ravi
Jean-René Reinhard
Peter Rindal
Francisco
   Rodríguez-Henríquez
Mélissa Rossi
Partha Sarathy Roy
Ajith S.
Yusuke Sakai
Kosei Sakamoto
Amin Sakzad
Simona Samardjiska
Olivier Sanders
Partik Sarkar
Santanu Sarkar
John Schanck
André Schrottenloher
Jacob Schuldt
Mahdi Sedaghat
Ignacio Amores Sesar
Siamak Shahandashti
Setareh Sharifian
Yaobin Shen
Sina Shiehian
Kazumasa Shinagawa
Janno Siim

Javier Silva
Ricardo Dahab
Siang Meng Sim
Leonie Simpson
Daniel Slamanig
Daniel Smith-Tone
Fang Song
Yongcheng Song
Florian Speelman
Akshayaram Srinivasan
Jun Xu
Igors Stepanovs
Ling Sun
Shi-Feng Sun
Akira Takahashi
Katsuyuki Takashima
Benjamin Hong
   Meng Tan
Syh-Yuan Tan
Titouan Tanguy
Adrian Thillard
Miaomiao Tian
Ivan Tjuawinata
Yosuke Todo
Alin Tomescu
Junichi Tomida
Ni Trieu
Viet Cuong Trinh
Ida Tucker
Aleksei Udovenko
Bogdan Ursu
Damien Vergnaud
Fernando Virdia

Srinivas Vivek
Misha Volkhov
Quoc Huy Vu
Alexandre Wallet
Ming Wan
Chenyu Wang
Han Wang
Junwei Wang
Lei Wang
Luping Wang
Qingju Wang
Weijia Wang
Wenhao Wang
Yang Wang
Yuyu Wang
Zhedong Wang
Gaven Watson
Florian Weber
Man Wei
Weiqiang Wen
Thom Wiggers
Zac Williamson
Lennert Wouters
Qianhong Wu
Keita Xagawa
Zejun Xiang
Hanshen Xiao
Xiang Xie
Yanhong Xu
Haiyang Xue
Shota Yamada
Takashi Yamakawa
Sravya Yandamuri

Jianhua Yan
Zhenbin Yan
Bo-Yin Yang
Guomin Yang
Kang Yang
Rupeng Yang
Shao-Jun Yang
Wei-Chuen Yau
Kisoon Yoon
Yong Yu
Zuoxia Yu
Chen Yuan
Tsz Hon Yuen
Aaram Yun
Alexandros Zacharakis
Michal Zajac
Luca Zanolini
Arantxa Zapico
Ming Zeng
Bin Zhang
Bingsheng Zhang
Cong Zhang
Hailong Zhang
Jiang Zhang
Liang Feng Zhang
Xue Zhang
Zhenfei Zhang
Zhifang Zhang
Changan Zhao
Yongjun Zhao
Zhongxiang Zheng
Yihong Zhu
Arne Tobias Ødegaard

Contents – Part II

Isogeny-Based Cryptography

Quantum Algorithms

Authenticated Key Exchange

Public Key Cryptography

Incrementally Aggregatable Vector Commitments and Applications to Verifiable Decentralized Storage

Matteo Campanelli[1], Dario Fiore[2(✉)], Nicola Greco[4], Dimitris Kolonelos[2,3], and Luca Nizzardo[4]

[1] Aarhus University, Aarhus, Denmark
matteo@cs.au.dk
[2] IMDEA Software Institute, Madrid, Spain
{dario.fiore,dimitris.kolonelos}@imdea.org
[3] Universidad Politecnica de Madrid, Madrid, Spain
[4] Protocol Labs, San Francisco, USA
{nicola,luca}@protocol.ai

Abstract. Vector commitments with subvector openings (SVC) [Lai-Malavolta, Boneh-Bunz-Fisch; CRYPTO'19] allow one to open a committed vector at a set of positions with an opening of size independent of both the vector's length and the number of opened positions.

We continue the study of SVC with two goals in mind: improving their efficiency and making them more suitable to decentralized settings. We address both problems by proposing a new notion for VC that we call *incremental aggregation* and that allows one to merge openings in a succinct way an *unbounded* number of times. We show two applications of this property. The first one is immediate and is a method to generate openings in a distributed way. The second application is an algorithm for faster generation of openings via preprocessing.

We then proceed to realize SVC with incremental aggregation. We provide two constructions in groups of unknown order that, similarly to that of Boneh et al. (which supports aggregating only once), have constant-size public parameters, commitments and openings. As an additional feature, for the first construction we propose efficient arguments of knowledge of subvector openings which immediately yields a keyless proof of storage with compact proofs.

Finally, we address a problem closely related to that of SVC: storing a file efficiently in completely decentralized networks. We introduce and construct *verifiable decentralized storage* (VDS), a cryptographic primitive that allows to check the integrity of a file stored by a network of nodes in a distributed and decentralized way. Our VDS constructions rely on our new vector commitment techniques.

M. Campanelli—Work done while author was at IMDEA Software Institute.
A full version of this paper can be found at https://ia.cr/2020/149.

S. Moriai and H. Wang (Eds.): ASIACRYPT 2020, LNCS 12492, pp. 3–35, 2020.
https://doi.org/10.1007/978-3-030-64834-3_1

1   Introduction

Commitment schemes are one of the most fundamental cryptographic primitives. They have two basic properties. *Hiding* guarantees that a commitment reveals no information about the underlying message. *Binding* instead ensures that one cannot change its mind about the committed message; namely, it is not possible to open a commitment to two distinct values $m \neq m'$.

Vector commitments (VC) [LY10, CF13] are a special class of commitment schemes in which one can commit to a vector $\vec{v}$ of length n and to later open the commitment at any position $i \in [n]$. The distinguishing feature of VCs is that both the commitment and an opening for a position i have size independent of n. In terms of security, VCs should be *position binding*, i.e., one cannot open a commitment at position i to two distinct values $v_i \neq v'_i$.

VCs were formalized by Catalano and Fiore [CF13] who proposed two realizations based on the CDH assumption in bilinear groups and the RSA assumption respectively. Both schemes have constant-size commitments and openings but suffer from large public parameters that are $O(n^2)$ and $O(n)$ for the CDH- and RSA-based scheme respectively. Noteworthy is that Merkle trees [Mer88] are VCs with $O(\log n)$-size openings.

Two recent works [BBF19, LM19] proposed new constructions of vector commitments that enjoy a new property called *subvector openings* (also called *batch openings* in [BBF19]). A VC with subvector openings (called SVC, for short) allows one to open a commitment at a collection of positions $I = \{i_1, \ldots, i_m\}$ with a constant-size proof, namely of size independent of the vector's length n and the subvector length m. This property has been shown useful for reducing communication complexity in several applications, such as PCP/IOP-based succinct arguments [LM19, BBF19] and keyless Proofs of Retrievability (PoR) [Fis18].

In this work we continue the study of VCs with subvector openings with two main goals: (1) improving their efficiency, and (2) enabling their use in decentralized systems.

With respect to efficiency, although the most attractive feature of SVCs is the constant size of their opening proofs, a drawback of all constructions is that generating each opening takes at least time $O(n)$ (i.e., as much as committing). This is costly and may harm the use of SVCs in applications such as the ones mentioned above.

When it comes to decentralization, VCs have been proposed as a solution for integrity of a distributed ledger (e.g., blockchains in the account model [BBF19]): the commitment is a succinct representation of the ledger, and a user responsible for the i-th entry can hold the corresponding opening and use it to prove validity of v_i. In this case, though, it is not obvious how to create a succinct subvector opening for, say, m positions held by *different* users each responsible *only* of its own position/s in the vector. We elaborate more on the motivation around this problem in Sect. 1.2.

1.1 A New Notion for SVCs: Incremental Aggregation

To address these concerns, we define and investigate a new property of vector commitments with subvector openings called *incremental aggregation*. In a nutshell, aggregation means that different subvector openings (say, for sets of positions I and J) can be merged together into a single *concise* (i.e., constant-size) opening (for positions $I \cup J$). This operation must be doable *without* knowing the entire committed vector. Moreover, aggregation is incremental if aggregated proofs can be further aggregated (e.g., two openings for $I \cup J$ and K can be merged into one for $I \cup J \cup K$, and so on an unbounded number of times) and disaggregated (i.e., given an opening for set I one can create one for any $K \subset I$).

While a form of aggregation is already present in the VC of Boneh et al. [BBF19], in [BBF19] this can be performed only once. In contrast, *we define (and construct) the first VC schemes where openings can be aggregated an unbounded number of times.* This incremental property is key to address efficiency and decentralized applications of SVCs, as we detail below.

Incremental Aggregation for Efficiency. To overcome the barrier of generating each opening in linear time[1] $O_\lambda(n)$, we propose an alternative preprocessing-based method. The idea is to precompute at commitment time an auxiliary information consisting of n/B openings, one for each batch of B positions of the vector. Next, to generate an opening for an arbitrary subset of m positions, one uses the incremental aggregation property in order to disaggregate the relevant subsets of precomputed openings, and then further aggregate for the m positions. Concretely, with this method, in our construction we can do the preprocessing in time $O_\lambda(n \log n)$ and generate an opening for m positions in time roughly $O_\lambda(mB \log n)$.

With the VC of [BBF19], a limited version of this approach is also viable: one precomputes an opening for each bit of the vector in $O_\lambda(n \log n)$ time; and then, at opening time, one uses their one-hop aggregation to aggregate relevant openings in time roughly $O_\lambda(m \log n)$. This however comes with a huge drawback: one must store one opening (of size $p(\lambda) = \mathsf{poly}(\lambda)$ where λ is the security parameter) *for every bit* of the vector, which causes a prohibitive storage overhead, i.e., $p(\lambda) \cdot n$ bits in addition to storing the vector $\vec{v}$ itself.

With incremental aggregation, we can instead tune the chunk size B to obtain flexible time-memory tradeoffs. For example, with $B = \sqrt{n}$ one can use $p(\lambda)\sqrt{n}$ bits of storage to get $O_\lambda(m\sqrt{n} \log n)$ opening time. Or, by setting $B = p(\lambda)$ as the size of one opening, we can obtain a storage overhead of exactly n bits and opening time $O_\lambda(m \log n)$.

Incremental Aggregation for Decentralization. Essentially, by its definition, incremental aggregation enables generating subvector openings in a distributed fashion. Consider a scenario where different parties each hold an opening of some subvector; using aggregation they can create an opening for the union of their subvectors, moreover the incremental property allows them to perform

---

[1] We use the notation $O_\lambda(\cdot)$ to include the factor depending on the security parameter λ. Writing "$O_\lambda(t)$" essentially means "$O(t)$ cryptographic operations".

this operation in a non-coordinated and asynchronous manner, i.e. without the need of a central aggregator. We found this application of incrementally aggregatable SVCs to decentralized systems worth exploring in more detail. To fully address this application, we propose a new cryptographic primitive called verifiable decentralized storage which we discuss in Sect. 1.2.

Constructing VCs With Incremental Aggregation. Turning to realizing SVC schemes with our new incremental aggregation property, we propose two SVC constructions that work in hidden-order groups [DK02] (instantiatable using classical RSA groups, class groups [BH01] or the recently proposed groups from Hyperelliptic Curves [DG20]).

Our first SVC has constant-size public parameters and constant-size subvector openings, and its security relies on the Strong RSA assumption and an argument of knowledge in the generic group model. Asymptotically, its efficiency is similar to the SVC of Boneh et al. [BBF19], but concretely we outperform [BBF19]. We implement our new SVC and show it can obtain very fast opening times thanks to the preprocessing method described earlier: opening time reduces by several orders of magnitude for various choices of vector and opening sizes, allowing us to obtain practical opening times—of the order of seconds—that would be impossible without preprocessing—of the order of hundred of seconds. In a file of 1 Mibit (2^{20} bits), preprocessing reduces the time to open 2048 bits from one hour to less than 5 s!

For the second construction, we show how to modify the RSA-based SVC of [LM19] (which in turn extends the one of [CF13] to support subvector openings) in order to make it with *constant-size* parameters and to achieve incremental aggregation. Compared to the first construction, it is more efficient and based on more standard assumptions, in the standard model.

Efficient Arguments of Knowledge of Subvector Opening. As an additional result, we propose efficient arguments of knowledge (AoK) with *constant-size* proofs for our first VC. In particular, we can prove knowledge of the subvector that opens a commitment at a public set of positions. An immediate application of this AoK is a *keyless proof of storage* (PoS) protocol with compact proofs. PoS allows a client to verify that a server is storing intactly a file via a short-communication challenge-response protocol. A PoS is said *keyless* if no secret key is needed by clients (e.g., mutually distrustful verifiers in a blockchain) and the server may even be one of these clients. With our AoK we can obtain openings of fixed size, as short as 2KB, which is 40x shorter than those based on Merkle trees in a representative setting without relying on SNARKs (that would be unfeasible in terms of time and memory). For lack of space, these AoK results appear in the full version.

1.2 Verifiable Decentralized Storage (VDS)

We now turn our attention to the problem of preserving storage integrity in a highly decentralized context which some of the distributed features of our VCs (i.e. incremental aggregation) can help us address. We are interested in studying the security of the emerging trend of decentralized and open alternatives to traditional cloud storage and hosting services: *decentralized storage networks* (DSNs). Filecoin (built on top of IPFS), Storj, Dat, Freenet and general-purpose blockchains like Ethereum[2] are some emerging projects in this space.

Background on DSNs. Abstracting from the details of each system, a DSN consists of participants called *nodes*. These can be either storage providers (aka *storage nodes*) or simple *client nodes*. Akin to centralized cloud storage, a client can outsource[3] the storage of large data. However, a key difference with DSN is that storage is provided by, and distributed across, a collection of nodes that can enter and leave the system at will. To make these systems viable it is important to tackle certain basic security questions. DSNs can have some reward mechanism to economically incentivize storage nodes. This means, for example, that there are economic incentives to *fake* storing a file. A further challenge for security (and for obtaining it efficiently) is that these systems are *open* and *decentralized*: anyone can enter the system (and participate as either a service provider or a consumer) and the system works without any central management or trusted parties.

In this work we focus on the basic problem of ensuring that the storage nodes of the DSN are doing their job properly, namely: *How can any client node check that the whole DSN is storing correctly its data (in a distributed fashion)?*

While this question is well studied in the centralized setting where the storage provider is a single server, for decentralized systems the situation is less satisfactory.

The Problem of Verifiable Decentralized Storage in DSNs. Consider a client who outsources the storage of a large file F, consisting of blocks $(F_1, \ldots, F_N)$, to a collection of storage nodes. A storage node can store a portion of F and the network is assumed to be designed in order to self-coordinate so that the whole F is stored, and to be fault-resistant (e.g., by having the same data block stored on multiple nodes). Once the file is stored, clients can request to the network to retrieve or modify a data block F_i (or more), as well as to append (resp. delete) blocks to (resp. from) the file.

In this scenario, our goal is to formalize a cryptographic primitive that can provide clients with the guarantee of *integrity of the outsourced data and its modifications*. The basic idea of VDS is that: (i) the client retains a short *digest* δ_F that "uniquely" points to the file F; (ii) any operation performed by the network, a retrieval or a file modification, can be proven by generating a short *certificate* that is publicly verifiable given δ_F.

This problem is similar in scope to the one addressed by authenticated data structures (ADS) [Tam03]. But while ADS is centralized, VDS is not. In VDS nodes act as storage in a distributed and uncoordinated fashion. This is more challenging as VDS needs to preserve some basic properties of the DSN:

---

[2] `filecoin.io`, `storj.io`, `datproject.org`, `freenetproject.org`, `ethereum.org`.

[3] We point out that in systems like Filecoin some nodes do not effectively outsource anything. Yet they participate (for economic rewards) verifying that others are actually storing for some third party node.

Highly Local. The file is stored across multiple nodes and no node is required to hold the entire F: in VDS every node should function with only its own local view of the system, which should be much smaller than the whole F. Another challenge is dynamic files: in VDS both the digest and the local view must be *locally* updatable, possibly with the help of a short and publicly verifiable update advice from the node holding the modified data blocks.

Decentralized Keyless Clients. In a decentralized system the notion of a client who outsources the storage of a file is blurry. It may for example be a set of mutually distrustful parties (even the entire DSN), or a collection of storage nodes themselves that decide to make some data available to the network. This comes with two implications:

1. *VDS must work without any secret key* on the clients side, so that everyone in the network can delegate and verify storage. This *keyless* setting captures not only clients requiring no coordination, but also a stronger security model. Here the attacker may control both the storage node and the client, yet it must not be able to cheat when proving correctness of its storage. The latter is crucial in DSNs with economic rewards for well-behaving nodes[4].
2. *In VDS a file F exists as long as some storage nodes provide its storage* and a pointer to the file is known to the network through its digest. When a file F is modified into F' and its digest δ_F is updated into $\delta_{F'}$, both versions of the file may coexist. Forks are possible and it is left to each client (or the application) to choose which digest to track: the old one, the new one, or both.

Non-Coordinated Certificates Generation. There are multiple ways in which data retrieval queries can be answered in a DSN. In some cases (e.g., Freenet [CSWH01] or the original Gnutella protocol), data retrieval is also answered in a peer-to-peer non-coordinated fashion. When a query for blocks $i_1, \ldots, i_m$ propagates through the network, every storage node replies with the blocks that it owns and these answers are aggregated and propagated in the network until they reach the client who asked for them. To accommodate arbitrary aggregation strategies, in VDS we consider the incremental aggregation of query certificates in an arbitrary and bandwidth-efficient fashion. For example, short certificates for file blocks F_i and F_j should be mergeable into a *short* certificate for (F_i, F_j) and this aggregation process should be carried on and on. Noteworthy that having certificates that stay short after each aggregation keeps the communication overhead of the VDS integrity mechanism at a minimum.[5]

A New Cryptographic Primitive: VDS. To address the problem described above, we put forward the definition of a new cryptographic primitive called

---

[4] Since in a decentralized system a storage node may also be a client, an attacker could "delegate storage to itself" and use the client's secret key to cheat in the proof in order to steal rewards (akin to the so-called "generation attack" in Filecoin [Lab17]).

[5] The motivation of this property is similar to that of sequential aggregate signatures, see e.g., [LMRS04,BGR12].

verifiable decentralized storage (VDS). In a nutshell, VDS is a collection of algorithms that can be used by clients and storage nodes to maintain the system. The basic ideas are the following: every file F is associated to a succinct digest δ_F; a storage node can answer and certify retrieval queries for subportions of F that it stores, as well as to push updates of F that enable anyone else to update the digest accordingly. Moreover, certified retrieval results can be arbitrarily aggregated. With respect to security, VDS guarantees that malicious storage nodes (even a full coalition of them) cannot create certificates for falsified data blocks that pass verification. For efficiency, the key property of VDS is that digests and every certificate are at most $O(\log |F|)$, and that every node in the system works with storage and running time that depends at most logarithmically in F's size. We discuss our definition of VDS in Section 5.

Constructing VDS. We propose two constructions of VDS in hidden-order groups. Both our VDS schemes are obtained by extending our first and second SVC scheme respectively, in order to handle updates and to ensure that all such update operations can be performed locally. We show crucial use of the new properties of our constructions: subvector openings, incremental aggregation and disaggregation, and arguments of knowledge for sub-vector commitments (the latter for the first scheme only).

Our two VDS schemes are based on the Strong RSA [BP97] and Strong distinct-prime-product root [LM19], and Low Order [BBF18] assumptions and have similar performances. The second scheme has the interesting property that the storage node can perform and propagate updates by running in time that is independent of even its total local storage.

Finally, we note that VDS shares similarities with the notion of updatable VCs [CF13] extended with incrementally aggregatable subvector openings. There are two main differences. First, in VDS updates can be applied with the help of a short advice created by the party who created the update, whereas in updatable VC this is possible having only the update's description. The second difference is that in VDS the public parameters must be short, otherwise nodes could not afford storing them. This is not necessarily the case in VCs and in fact, to the best of our knowledge, there exists no VC construction with short parameters that is updatable (according to the updatability notion of [CF13]) and has incrementally aggregatable subvector openings. We believe this is an interesting open problem.

1.3   Concurrent Work

In very recent concurrent works, Gorbunov et al. [GRWZ20] and Tomescu et al. [TAB+20] study similar problems related to aggregation properties of vector commitments. In [TAB+20], Tomescu et al. study a vector commitment scheme based on the Kate et al. polynomial commitment [KZG10]: they show how it can be made both updatable and aggregatable, and propose an efficient Stateless Cryptocurrency based on it. In Pointproofs [GRWZ20] they propose the notion of Cross-Commitment Aggregation, which enables aggregating opening proofs for different commitments, and show how this notion is relevant to blockchain applications. The VC schemes in both [TAB+20] and [GRWZ20] work in bilinear groups and have linear-size public parameters. Also, these constructions do not support incremental aggregation or disaggregation. In contrast, our VCs work in hidden-order groups, which likely makes them concretely less efficient, but they have constant-size parameters, and they support incremental aggregation and disaggregation. Finally, we note that by using techniques similar to [GRWZ20] we can extend our constructions to support cross-commitment aggregation; we leave formalizing this extension for future work.

1.4 Preliminaries

In the paper we use rather standard cryptographic notation and definitions that for completeness are recalled in the full version. More specific to this paper we denote by $\mathsf{Primes}(\lambda)$ the set of all prime integers less than 2^λ.

Groups of Unknown Order and Computational Assumptions. Our constructions use a group $\mathbb{G}$ of unknown (aka hidden) order [DK02], in which the Low Order assumption [BBF18] and the Strong RSA assumption [BP97] hold. We let $\mathsf{Ggen}(1^\lambda)$ be a probabilistic algorithm that generates such a group $\mathbb{G}$ with order in a specific range $[\mathsf{ord}_{min}, \mathsf{ord}_{max}]$ such that $\frac{1}{\mathsf{ord}_{min}}, \frac{1}{\mathsf{ord}_{max}}, \frac{1}{\mathsf{ord}_{max} - \mathsf{ord}_{min}} \in \mathsf{negl}(\lambda)$. As discussed in [BBF18, BBF19, LM19], two concrete instantiations of $\mathbb{G}$ are class groups [BH01] and the quotient group $\mathbb{Z}_N^* / \{1, -1\}$ of an RSA group [Wes18]. See the full version for the formal definitions of the assumptions and for a recall of Shamir's trick [Sha83] that we use extensively in our constructions.

2 Vector Commitments with Incremental Aggregation

In this section, we recall vector commitments with subvector openings [CF13, LM19, BBF19] and then we formally define our new incremental aggregation property.

2.1 Vector Commitments with Subvector Openings

In our work we consider the generalization of vector commitments proposed by Lai and Malavolta [LM19] called *VCs with subvector openings*[6] (we call them SVCs for brevity) in which one can open the commitment to an ordered collection of positions with a short proof. Below is a brief recap of their definition.

Let $\mathcal{M}$ be a set, $n \in \mathbb{N}$ be a positive integer and $I = \{i_1, \ldots, i_{|I|}\} \subseteq [n]$ be an ordered index set. The I-subvector of a vector $\vec{v} \in \mathcal{M}^n$ is $\vec{v}_I := (v_{i_1}, \ldots, v_{i_{|I|}})$. Let $I, J \subseteq [n]$ be two sets, and let $\vec{v}_I, \vec{v}_J$ be two subvectors of some $\vec{v} \in \mathcal{M}^n$. The *ordered union* of $\vec{v}_I$ and $\vec{v}_J$ is the subvector $\vec{v}_{I \cup J}$, where $I \cup J$ is the ordered union of I and J.

---

[6] This is also called VCs with batchable openings in an independent work by Boneh et al. [BBF19] and can be seen as a specialization of the notion of *functional vector commitments* [LRY16].

A vector commitment scheme with subvector openings (SVC) is a tuple of algorithms VC = (VC.Setup, VC.Com, VC.Open, VC.Ver) that work as follows. The probabilistic setup algorithm, VC.Setup$(1^\lambda, \mathcal{M}) \rightarrow$ crs, which given the security parameter λ and description of a message space $\mathcal{M}$ for the vector components, outputs a common reference string crs; the committing algorithm, VC.Com$(\text{crs}, \vec{v}) \rightarrow (C, \text{aux})$, which on input crs and a vector $\vec{v} \in \mathcal{M}^n$, outputs a commitment C and an auxiliary information aux; the opening algorithm, VC.Open$(\text{crs}, I, \vec{y}, \text{aux}) \rightarrow \pi_I$ which on input the CRS crs, a vector $\vec{y} \in \mathcal{M}^m$, an ordered index set $I \subset \mathbb{N}$ and auxiliary information aux, outputs a proof π_I that $\vec{y}$ is the I-subvector of the committed message; the verification algorithm, VC.Ver$(\text{crs}, C, I, \vec{y}, \pi_I) \rightarrow b \in \{0, 1\}$, which on input the CRS crs, a commitment C, an ordered set of indices $I \subset \mathbb{N}$, a vector $\vec{y} \in \mathcal{M}^m$ and a proof π_I, accepts (i.e., it outputs 1) only if π_I is a valid proof that C was created to a vector $\vec{v} = (v_1, \ldots, v_n)$ such that $\vec{y} = \vec{v}_I$. We require three properties from a vector commitment: *correctness* (verification acts as expected on honestly generated commitments and openings); *position binding* (no adversary can produce two valid openings for different subvectors); *conciseness* (if its commitments and openings are of size independent of $|\vec{v}|$).

Vector Commitments with Specializable Universal CRS. The notion of VCs defined above slightly generalizes the previous ones in which the generation of public parameters (aka common reference string) depends on a bound n on the length of the committed vectors. In contrast, in our notion VC.Setup is length-independent. To highlight this property, we also call this primitive *vector commitments with universal CRS*.

Here we formalize a class of VC schemes that lies in between VCs with universal CRS (as defined above) and VCs with length-specific CRS (as defined in [CF13]). Inspired by the recent work of Groth et al. [GKM+18], we call these schemes VCs with *Specializable* (Universal) CRS. In a nutshell, these are schemes in which the algorithms VC.Com, VC.Open and VC.Ver work on input a length-specific CRS crs_n. However, this crs_n is generated in two steps: (i) a *length-independent, probabilistic* setup crs $\leftarrow$ VC.Setup$(1^\lambda, \mathcal{M})$, and (ii) a *length-dependent, deterministic* specialization $\text{crs}_n \leftarrow$ VC.Specialize(crs, n). The advantage of this model is that, being VC.Specialize deterministic, it can be executed by anyone, and it allows to re-use the same crs for multiple vectors lengths.

See the full version for the formal definition of VCs with specializable CRS.

2.2   Incrementally Aggregatable Subvector Openings

In a nutshell, aggregation means that different proofs of different subvector openings can be merged together into a single *short* proof which can be created *without* knowing the entire committed vector. Moreover, this aggregation is composable, namely aggregated proofs can be further aggregated. Following a terminology similar to that of aggregate signatures, we call this property *incremental aggregation* (but can also be called *multi-hop aggregation*). In addition to aggregating openings, we also consider the possibility to "disaggregate" them, namely from an opening of positions in the set I one can create an opening for positions in a set $K \subset I$.

We stress on the two main requirements that make aggregation and disaggregation non-trivial: all openings must remain short (independently of the number of positions that are being opened), and aggregation (resp. disaggregation) must be computable locally, i.e., without knowing the whole committed vector. Without such requirements, one could achieve this property by simply concatenating openings of single positions.

Definition 2.1 (Aggregatable Subvector Openings). *A vector commitment scheme* VC *with subvector openings is called* aggregatable *if there exists algorithms* VC.Agg, VC.Disagg *working as follows:*

VC.Agg$(\mathsf{crs}, (I, \vec{v}_I, \pi_I), (J, \vec{v}_J, \pi_J)) \rightarrow \pi_K$ *takes as input triples* $(I, \vec{v}_I, \pi_I), (J, \vec{v}_J, \pi_J)$ *where* I *and* J *are sets of indices,* $\vec{v}_I \in \mathcal{M}^{|I|}$ *and* $\vec{v}_J \in \mathcal{M}^{|J|}$ *are subvectors, and* π_I *and* π_J *are opening proofs. It outputs a proof* π_K *that is supposed to prove opening of values in positions* $K = I \cup J$.

VC.Disagg$(\mathsf{crs}, I, \vec{v}_I, \pi_I, K) \rightarrow \pi_K$ *takes as input a triple* $(I, \vec{v}_I, \pi_I)$ *and a set of indices* $K \subset I$, *and it outputs a proof* π_K *that is supposed to prove opening of values in positions* K.

The aggregation algorithm VC.Agg *must guarantee the following two properties:*

Aggregation Correctness. *Aggregation is (perfectly) correct if for all* $\lambda \in \mathbb{N}$, *all honestly generated* $\mathsf{crs} \leftarrow$ VC.Setup$(1^\lambda, \mathcal{M})$, *any commitment* C *and triple* $(I, \vec{v}_I, \pi_I)$ *s.t.* VC.Ver$(\mathsf{crs}, C, I, \vec{v}_I, \pi_I) = 1$, *the following two properties hold:*

1. *for any triple* $(J, \vec{v}_J, \pi_J)$ *such that* VC.Ver$(\mathsf{crs}, C, J, \vec{v}_J, \pi_J) = 1$,

$$\Pr\left[\mathsf{VC.Ver}(\mathsf{crs}, C, K, \vec{v}_K, \pi_K) = 1 \; : \; \pi_K \leftarrow \mathsf{VC.Agg}(\mathsf{crs}, (I, \vec{v}_I, \pi_I), (J, \vec{v}_J, \pi_J)) \right] = 1$$

where $K = I \cup J$ *and* $\vec{v}_K$ *is the ordered union* $\vec{v}_{I \cup J}$ *of* $\vec{v}_I$ *and* $\vec{v}_J$;

2. *for any subset of indices* $K \subset I$,

$$\Pr\left[\mathsf{VC.Ver}(\mathsf{crs}, C, K, \vec{v}_K, \pi_K) = 1 \; : \; \pi_K \leftarrow \mathsf{VC.Disagg}(\mathsf{crs}, I, \vec{v}_I, \pi_I, K) \right] = 1$$

where $\vec{v}_K = (v_{i_l})_{i_l \in K}$, *for* $\vec{v}_I = (v_{i_1}, \ldots, v_{i_{|I|}})$.

Aggregation Conciseness. *There exists a fixed polynomial* $p(\cdot)$ *in the security parameter such that all openings produced by* VC.Agg *and* VC.Disagg *have length bounded by* $p(\lambda)$.

We remark that the notion of specializable CRS can apply to aggregatable VCs as well. In this case, we let VC.Agg* (resp. VC.Disagg*) be the algorithm that works on input the specialized crs_n instead of crs.

3   Applications of Incremental Aggregation

We discuss two general applications of the SVC incremental aggregation property.

One application is generating subvector openings in a distributed and decentralized way. Namely, assume a set of parties hold each an opening of some subvector. Then it is possible to create a (concise) opening for the union of their subvectors by using the VC.Agg algorithm. Moreover, the incremental (aka multi-hop) aggregation allows these users to perform this operation in an arbitrary order, hence no coordination or a central aggregator party are needed. This application is particularly useful in our extension to verifiable decentralized storage.

The second application is to generate openings in a faster way via preprocessing. As we mentioned in the introduction, this technique is useful in the scenario where a user commits to a vector and then must generate openings for various subvectors, which is for example the use case when the VC is used for proofs of retrievability and IOPs [BBF19].

So, here the goal is to achieve a method for computing subvector openings in time sub-linear in the total size of the vector, which is the barrier in all existing constructions. To obtain this speedup, the basic idea is to (A) compute and store openings for all the positions at commitment time, and then (B) use the aggregation property to create an opening for a specific set of positions. In order to obtain efficiency using this approach it is important that both steps (A) and (B) can be computed efficiently. In particular, step (A) is challenging since typically computing one opening takes linear time, hence computing all of them would take quadratic time.

In this section, we show how steps (A) and (B) can benefit from disaggregation and aggregation respectively. As a preliminary for this technique, we begin by describing two generic extensions of (incremental) aggregation (resp. disaggregation) that support many inputs (resp. outputs). Then we show how these extended algorithms can be used for committing and opening with preprocessing.

3.1   Divide-and-Conquer Extensions of Aggregation and Disaggregation

We discuss how the incremental property of our aggregation and disaggregation can be used to define two extended versions of these algorithms. The first one is an algorithm that can aggregate many openings for different sets of positions into a single opening for their union. The second one does the opposite, namely it disaggregates one opening for a set I into many openings for partitions of I.

Aggregating Many Openings. We consider the problem of aggregating several openings for sets of positions $I_1, \ldots, I_m$ into a single opening for $\bigcup_{j=1}^{m} I_j$. Our syntax in Definition 2.1 only considers pairwise aggregation. This can be used to handle many aggregations by executing the pairwise aggregation in a sequential (or arbitrary order) fashion. Sequential aggregation might however be costly since it would require executing VC.Agg on increasingly growing sets. If $f_a(k)$ is the complexity of VC.Agg on two sets of total size k, then the complexity of the sequential method is $\sum_{j=2}^{m} f(\sum_{l=1}^{j-1} |I_l| + |I_j|)$, which for example is quadratic in m, for $f_a(k) = \Theta(k)$.

In Fig. 1, we show an algorithm, VC.AggManyToOne, that is a nearly optimal solution for aggregating m openings based on a divide-and-conquer methodology. Assuming for simplicity that all I_j's have size bounded by some s, then the complexity of VC.AggManyToOne is given by the recurrence relation $T(m) = 2T\left(\frac{m}{2}\right) + f_a(s \cdot m)$, which solves to $\Theta(s \cdot m \log m)$ if $f_a(n) \in \Theta(n)$, or to $\Theta(s \cdot m \log(sm) \log m)$ if $f_a(n) \in \Theta(n \log n)$.

VC.AggManyToOne(crs, $(I_j, \boldsymbol{v}_{I_j}, \pi_j)_{j \in [m]}$)	VC.DisaggOneToMany(crs, $B, I, \boldsymbol{v}_I, \pi_I$)
if $m = 1$ **return** π_1	**if** $n = |I| = B$ **return** π_I
$m' \leftarrow m/2$	$n' \leftarrow n/2$
$L \leftarrow \cup_{j=1}^{m'} I_j, \quad R \leftarrow \cup_{j=m'+1}^{m} I_j,$	$L \leftarrow \cup_{j=1}^{n'} i_j, \quad R \leftarrow \cup_{j=n'+1}^{m} i_j,$
$\pi_L \leftarrow$ VC.AggManyToOne(crs, $(I_j, \boldsymbol{v}_{I_j}, \pi_j)_{j=1,\ldots,m'}$)	$\pi'_L \leftarrow$ VC.Disagg(crs, $I, \boldsymbol{v}_I, \pi_I, L$)
$\pi_R \leftarrow$ VC.AggManyToOne(crs, $(I_j, \boldsymbol{v}_{I_j}, \pi_j)_{j=m'+1,\ldots,m}$)	$\pi'_R \leftarrow$ VC.Disagg(crs, $I, \boldsymbol{v}_I, \pi_I, R$)
$\pi_{L \cup R} \leftarrow$ VC.Agg(crs, $(L, \boldsymbol{v}_L, \pi_L), (R, \boldsymbol{v}_R, \pi_R)$)	$\boldsymbol{\pi}_L \leftarrow$ VC.DisaggOneToMany(crs, $B, L, \boldsymbol{v}_L, \pi'_L$)
return $\pi_{L \cup R}$	$\boldsymbol{\pi}_R \leftarrow$ VC.DisaggOneToMany(crs, $B, R, \boldsymbol{v}_R, \pi'_R$)
	return $\boldsymbol{\pi}_L \| \boldsymbol{\pi}_R$

Fig. 1. Extensions of aggregation and disaggregation

Disaggregating from One to Many Openings. We consider the problem that is dual to the one above, namely how to disaggregate an opening for a set I into several openings for sets $I_1, \ldots, I_m$ that form a partition of I. Our syntax in Definition 2.1 only considers disaggregation from I to one subset K of I. Similarly to aggregation, disaggregating from one set to many subsets can be trivially obtained via a sequential application of VC.Disagg on all pairs (I, I_j). This however can be costly if the number of partitions approaches the size of I, e.g., if we want to disaggregate to all the elements of I.

In Fig. 1, we show a divide-and-conquer algorithm, VC.DisaggOneToMany, for disaggregating an opening for a set I of size m into $m' = m/B$ openings, each for a partition of size B. For simplicity, we assume that m is a power of 2, and $B \mid m$. Let $f_d(|I|)$ be the complexity of VC.Disagg. The complexity of VC.DisaggOneToMany is given by the recurrence relation $T(m) = 2T\left(\frac{m}{2}\right) + 2f_d(m/2)$, which solves to $\Theta(m \log(m/B))$ if $f_d(n) \in \Theta(n)$, or to $\Theta(m \log m \log(m/B))$ if $f_d(n) \in \Theta(n \log n)$.

3.2 Committing and Opening with Precomputation

We present a construction of committing and opening algorithms (denoted VC.PPCom and VC.FastOpen respectively) that works generically for any SVC with incremental aggregation and that, by relying on preprocessing, can achieve fast opening time.

Our preprocessing method works with a flexible choice of a parameter B that allows for different time-memory tradeoffs. In a nutshell, ranging from 1 to n, a larger B reduces memory but increases opening time while a smaller B (e.g., $B = 1$) requires larger storage overhead but gives the fastest opening time.

Let B be an integer that divides n, and let $n' = n/B$. The core of our idea is that, during the commitment stage, one can create openings for $n' = n/B$ subvectors of $\vec{v}$ that cover the whole vector (e.g., B contiguous positions). Let $\pi_{P_1}, \ldots, \pi_{P_{n'}}$ be such openings; these elements are stored as advice information.

Next, in the opening phase, in order to compute the opening for a subvector $\vec{v}_I$ of m positions, one should: (i) fetch the subset of openings π_{P_j} such that, for some S, $I \subseteq \cup_{j \in S} P_j$, (ii) possibly disaggregate some of them and then aggregate in order to compute π_I.

The two algorithms VC.PPCom and VC.FastOpen are described in detail in Fig. 2.

VC.PPCom(crs, B, $\boldsymbol{v}$)	VC.FastOpen(crs, B, aux*, I)
$(C, \text{aux}) \leftarrow$ VC.Com(crs, $\boldsymbol{v}$)	**Let** $P_j := \{(j-1)B + i : i \in [B]\}, \forall j \in [n']$
$\pi^* \leftarrow$ VC.Open(crs, $[n]$, $\boldsymbol{v}$, aux)	**Let** $I := \{i_1, \ldots, i_m\}$
$\pi \leftarrow$ VC.DisaggOneToMany(crs, B, $[n]$, $\boldsymbol{v}$, π^*)	**Let** S minimal set s.t. $\bigcup_{j \in S} P_j \supseteq I$
aux$^* := (\pi_1, \ldots, \pi_{n'}, \boldsymbol{v})$	**for** $j \in S$ **do** :
return C, aux*	$\quad I_j \leftarrow I \cap P_j$
	$\quad \pi'_j \leftarrow$ VC.Disagg(crs, P_j, $\boldsymbol{v}_{P_j}$, π_j, I_j)
	endfor
	$\pi_I \leftarrow$ VC.AggManyToOne(crs, $((I_j, \boldsymbol{v}_{I_j}, \pi'_j))_{j \in S}$)
	return π_I

Fig. 2. Generic algorithms for committing and opening with precomputation.

In terms of auxiliary storage, in addition to the vector $\vec{v}$ itself, one needs at most $(n/B)p(\lambda)$ bits, where $p(\lambda)$ is the polynomial bounding the conciseness of the SVC scheme. In terms of time complexity, VC.PPCom requires one execution of VC.Com, one execution of VC.Open, and one execution of VC.DisaggOneToMany, which in turn depends on the complexity of VC.Disagg; VC.FastOpen requires to perform (at most) $|S|$ disaggregations (each with a set $|I_j|$ such that their sum is $|I|$)[7], and one execution of VC.AggManyToOne on $|S|$ openings. Note that VC.FastOpen's running time depends only on the size m of the set I and size B of the buckets P_j, and thus offers various tradeoffs by adjusting B.

---

[7] Note that for $B = 1$ the disaggregation step can be skipped.

More specific running times depend on the complexity of the algorithms VC.Com, VC.Open, VC.Agg, and VC.Disagg of the given SVC scheme. See Sect. 4.3 and the full version for these results for our constructions.

4   Our Realizations of Incrementally Aggregatable SVCs

In this section we describe our new SVC realizations.

4.1   Our First SVC Construction

AN OVERVIEW OF OUR TECHNIQUES. The basic idea underlying our VC can be described as a generic construction from any accumulator with union proofs. Consider a vector of bits $\vec{v} = (v_1, \ldots, v_n) \in \{0,1\}^n$. In order to commit to this vector we produce two accumulators, Acc_0 and Acc_1, on two partitions of the set $S = \{1, \ldots, n\}$. Each accumulator Acc_b compresses the set of positions i such that $v_i = b$. In other words, Acc_b compresses the set $S_{=b} := \{i \in S : v_i = b\}$ with $b \in \{0,1\}$. In order to open to bit b at position i, one can create an accumulator membership proof for the statement $i \in \tilde{S}_b$ where we denote by $\tilde{S}_b$ the alleged set of positions that have value b.

However, if the commitment to $\vec{v}$ is simply the pair of accumulators $(\mathsf{Acc}_0, \mathsf{Acc}_1)$ we do not achieve position binding as an adversary could for example include the same element i in both accumulators. To solve this issue we set the commitment to be the pair of accumulators plus a succinct non-interactive proof π_S that the two sets $\tilde{S}_0, \tilde{S}_1$ they compress constitute together a *partition* of S. Notably, this proof π_S guarantees that each index i is in either $\tilde{S}_0$ or $\tilde{S}_1$, and thus prevents an adversary from also opening the position i to the complement bit $1 - b$.

The construction described above could be instantiated with any accumulator scheme that admits an efficient and succinct proof of union. We, though, directly present an efficient construction based on RSA accumulators [Bd94,BP97,CL02,Lip12,BBF19] as this is efficient and has some nice extra properties like aggregation and constant-size parameters. Also, part of our technical contribution to construct this VC scheme is the construction of efficient and succinct protocols for proving the union of two RSA accumulators built with different generators.

Succinct AoK Protocols for Union of RSA Accumulators. Let $\mathbb{G}$ be a hidden order group as generated by Ggen, and let $g_1, g_2, g_3 \in \mathbb{G}$ be three honestly sampled random generators. We propose a succinct argument of knowledge for the following relation

$$R_{\mathsf{PoProd}_2} = \left\{ ((Y, C), (a, b)) \in \mathbb{G}^2 \times \mathbb{Z}^2 \; : \; Y = g_1^a g_2^b \wedge C = g_3^{a \cdot b} \right\}$$

Our protocol (described in Fig. 3) is inspired by a similar protocol of Boneh et al. [BBF19], PoDDH, for a similar relation in which there is only one generator (i.e., $g_1 = g_2 = g_3$, namely for DDH tuples (g^a, g^b, g^{ab})). Their protocol has a proof consisting of 3 groups elements and 2 integers of λ bits.

As we argue later PoProd_2 is still sufficient for our construction, i.e., for the goal of proving that $C = g_3^c$ is an accumulator to a set that is the union of sets represented by two accumulators $A = g_1^a$ and $B = g_2^b$ respectively. The idea is to invoke PoProd_2 on (Y, C) with $Y = A \cdot B$.

$\mathsf{Setup}(1^\lambda)$: run $\mathbb{G} \leftarrow_\$ \mathsf{Ggen}(1^\lambda)$, $g_1, g_2, g_3 \leftarrow_\$ \mathbb{G}$, set $\mathsf{crs} := (\mathbb{G}, g_1, g_2, g_3)$.
Prover's input: $(\mathsf{crs}, (Y, C), (a, b))$. Verifier's input: $(\mathsf{crs}, (Y, C))$.

$\underline{\mathsf{V} \to \mathsf{P}}$: $\ell \leftarrow_\$ \mathsf{Primes}(\lambda)$
$\underline{\mathsf{P} \to \mathsf{V}}$: $\pi := ((Q_Y, Q_C), r_a, r_b)$ computed as follows
 - $(q_a, q_b, q_c) \leftarrow (\lfloor a/\ell \rfloor, \lfloor b/\ell \rfloor, \lfloor ab/\ell \rfloor)$
 - $(r_a, r_b) \leftarrow (a \bmod \ell, b \bmod \ell)$
 - $(Q_Y, Q_C) := (g_1^{q_a} g_2^{q_b}, g_3^{q_c})$
$\underline{\mathsf{V}(\mathsf{crs}, (Y, C), \ell, \pi)}$:
 - Compute $r_c \leftarrow r_a \cdot r_b \bmod \ell$
 - Output 1 iff $r_a, r_b \in [\ell] \;\wedge\; Q_Y^\ell g_1^{r_a} g_2^{r_b} = Y \;\wedge\; Q_C^\ell g_3^{r_c} = C$

Fig. 3. PoProd_2 protocol

To prove the security of our protocol we rely on the adaptive root assumption and, in a non-black-box way, on the knowledge extractability of the PoKRep and PoKE^* protocols from [BBF19]. The latter is proven in the generic group model for hidden order groups (where also the adaptive root assumption holds), therefore we state the following theorem.

Theorem 4.1. *The PoProd_2 protocol is an argument of knowledge for R_{PoProd_2} in the generic group model.*

For space reasons the full proof is in the full version. The basic intuition is to use the extractors of PoKRep and PoKE^* to extract (a, b, c) such that $Y = g_1^a g_2^b \wedge C = g_3^{a \cdot b}$. Then $c = a \cdot b$ comes from the fact that ℓ is randomly chosen, which makes the equality $r_c = r_a \cdot r_b \bmod \ell$ happen with negligible probability if $c \neq a \cdot b$.

In the full version we also give a protocol PoProd that proves $g_1^a = A \wedge g_2^b = B$ instead of $g_1^a g_2^b = Y$ (i.e., a version of PoDDH with different generators). Despite being conceptually simpler, it is slightly less efficient than PoProd_2, and thus we use the latter in our VC construction.

HASH TO PRIME FUNCTION AND NON-INTERACTIVE PoProd_2. Our protocols can be made non-interactive by applying the Fiat-Shamir transform. For this we need an hash function that can be modeled as a random oracle and that maps arbitrary strings to prime numbers, i.e., $\mathsf{H}_{\mathsf{prime}} : \{0,1\}^* \to \mathsf{Primes}(2\lambda)$.[8] A simple

---

[8] As pointed out in [BBF18], although for the interactive version of such protocols the prime can be of size λ, the non-interactive version requires at least a double-sized prime 2λ, as an explicit square root attack was presented.

way to achieve such a function is to apply a standard hash function $H : \{0,1\}^* \to \{0,1\}^{2\lambda}$ to an input $\vec{y}$ together with a counter i, and if $p_{y,i} = H(\vec{y}, i)$ is prime then output $p_{y,i}$, otherwise continue to $H(\vec{y}, i+1)$ and so on, until a prime is found. Due to the distribution of primes, the expected running time of this method is $O(\lambda)$, assuming that H's outputs are uniformly distributed. For more discussion on hash-to-prime functions we refer to [GHR99, CMS99, CS99, BBF19, OWB19].

Our First SVC Construction. Now we are ready to describe our SVC scheme. For an intuition we refer the reader to the beginning of this section. Also, we note that while the intuition was given for the case of committing to a vector of bits, our actual VC construction generalizes this idea to vectors where each item is a *block of k bits*. This is done by creating $2k$ accumulators, each of them holding sets of indices i for specific positions inside each block v_j.

Notation and Building Blocks

- Our message space is $\mathcal{M} = \{0,1\}^k$. Then for a vector $\vec{v} \in \mathcal{M}^n$, we denote with $i \in [n]$ the vector's position, i.e., $v_i \in \mathcal{M}$, and with $j \in [k]$ the position of its j'th bit. So $v_{i,j}$ denotes the j-th bit in position i.
- We make use of a deterministic collision resistant function PrimeGen that maps integers to primes. In our construction we do not need its outputs to be random (see e.g., [BBF19] for possible instantiations).
- As a building block, we use the PoProd$_2$ AoK from the previous section.
- PartndPrimeProd$(I, \vec{y}) \to ((a_{I,1}, b_{I,1}), \dots, (a_{I,k}, b_{I,k}))$: given a set of indices $I = \{i_1, \dots, i_m\} \subseteq [n]$ and a vector $\vec{y} \in \mathcal{M}^m$, this function computes

$$(a_{I,j}, b_{I,j}) := \left(\prod_{l=1:y_{l,j}=0}^{m} p_{i_l}, \prod_{l=1:y_{l,j}=1}^{m} p_{i_l} \right) \quad \text{for } j = 1, \dots, k$$

  where $p_i \leftarrow \mathsf{PrimeGen}(i)$ for all i.
  Basically, for every bit position $j \in [k]$, the function computes the products of primes that correspond to, respectively, 0-bits and 1-bits.
  In the special case where $I = [n]$, we omit the set of indices from the notation of the outputs, i.e., PartndPrimeProd$([n], \vec{v})$ outputs a_j and b_j.
- PrimeProd$(I) \to u_I$: given a set of indices I, this function outputs the product of all primes corresponding to indices in I. Namely, it returns $u_I := \prod_{i \in I} p_i$. In the special case $I = [n]$, we denote the output of PrimeProd$([n])$ as u_n.
  Notice that by construction, for any I and $\vec{y}$, it always holds $a_{I,j} \cdot b_{I,j} = u_I$.

SVC Scheme. We describe our SVC scheme and then show its incremental aggregation.

VC.Setup$(1^\lambda, \{0,1\}^k) \to$ crs generates a hidden order group $\mathbb{G} \leftarrow \mathsf{Ggen}(1^\lambda)$ and samples three generators $g, g_0, g_1 \leftarrow \mathbb{G}$. It also determines a deterministic collision resistant function PrimeGen that maps integers to primes.
  Returns crs $= (\mathbb{G}, g, g_0, g_1, \mathsf{PrimeGen})$

VC.Specialize(crs, n) $\rightarrow$ crs$_n$ computes $u_n \leftarrow$ PrimeProd($[n]$) and $U_n = g^{u_n}$, and returns crs$_n \leftarrow$ (crs, U_n). One can think of U_n as an accumulator to the set $[n]$.

VC.Com*(crs$_n$, $\vec{v}$) $\rightarrow$ ($C^\star$, aux*) does the following:

1. Compute $((a_1, b_1), \ldots, (a_k, b_k)) \leftarrow$ PartndPrimeProd($[n], \vec{v}$); next,

$$\text{for all } j \in [k] \text{ compute } A_j = g_0^{a_j} \text{ and } B_j = g_1^{b_j}$$

   One can think of each (A_j, B_j) as a pair of RSA accumulators for two sets that constitute a partition of $[n]$ done according to the bits of $v_{1j}, \ldots, v_{nj}$. Namely A_j and B_j accumulate the sets $\{i \in [n] : v_{i,j} = 0\}$ and $\{i \in [n] : v_{i,j} = 1\}$ respectively.

2. For all $j \in [k]$, compute $C_j = A_j \cdot B_j \in \mathbb{G}$ and a proof $\pi_{\text{prod}}^{(j)} \leftarrow$ PoProd$_2$.P(crs, $(C_j, U_n), (a_j, b_j)$). Such proof ensures that the sets represented by A_j and B_j are a partition of the set represented by U_n. Since U_n is part of the CRS (i.e., it is trusted), this ensures the well-formedness of A_j and B_j.

Return $C^\star := \left(\{A_1, B_1, \ldots, A_k, B_k\}, \left\{ \pi_{\text{prod}}^{(1)}, \ldots, \pi_{\text{prod}}^{(k)} \right\} \right)$ and aux$^\star := \vec{v}$.

VC.Open*(crs$_n$, $I, \vec{y}$, aux*) $\rightarrow \pi_I$ proceeds as follows:

   – let $J = [n] \setminus I$ and compute $((a_{J,1}, b_{J,1}), \ldots, (a_{J,k}, b_{J,k})) \leftarrow$ PartndPrimeProd($J, \vec{v}_J$);
   – for all $j \in [k]$ compute $\Gamma_{I,j} := g_0^{a_{J,j}}$ and $\Delta_{I,j} := g_1^{b_{J,j}}$.

Notice that $a_{J,j} = a_j / a_{I,j}$ and $b_{J,j} = b_j / b_{I,j}$. Also $\Gamma_{I,j}$ is a membership witness for the set $\{i_l \in I : y_{l,j} = 0\}$ in the accumulator A_j, and similarly for $\Delta_{I,j}$.

Return $\pi_I := \{\pi_{I,1}, \ldots, \pi_{I,k}\} \leftarrow \{(\Gamma_{I,1}, \Delta_{I,1}), \ldots, (\Gamma_{I,k}, \Delta_{I,k})\}$

VC.Ver*(crs$_n$, $C^\star$, $I, \vec{y}, \pi_I$) $\rightarrow b$ computes $((a_{I,1}, b_{I,1}), \ldots, (a_{I,k}, b_{I,k}))$ using PartndPrimeProd($I, \vec{y}$), and then returns $b \leftarrow b_{acc} \wedge b_{prod}$ where:

$$b_{acc} \leftarrow \bigwedge_{j=1}^{k} \left(\Gamma_{I,j}^{a_{I,j}} = A_j \wedge \Delta_{I,j}^{b_{I,j}} = B_j \right) \tag{1}$$

$$b_{prod} \leftarrow \bigwedge_{j=1}^{k} \left(\text{PoProd}_2.\text{V}(\text{crs}, (A_j \cdot B_j, U_n), \pi_{\text{prod}}^{(j)}) \right) \tag{2}$$

Remark 4.1. For more efficient verification, VC.Open* can be changed to include $2k$ (non-interactive) proofs of exponentiation PoE (which using the PoKCR aggregation from [BBF19] add only k elements of $\mathbb{G}$). This reduces the exponentiations cost in VC.Ver*. As noted in [BBF19], although the asymptotic complexity is the same, the operations are in $\mathbb{Z}_{2^{2\lambda}}$ instead of $\mathbb{G}$, which concretely makes up an improvement.

The correctness of the vector commitment scheme described above is obvious by inspection (assuming correctness of $\mathsf{PoProd_2}$).

Incremental Aggregation. We show incremental aggregation of our SVC scheme.

$\mathsf{VC.Disagg}(\mathsf{crs}, I, \vec{v}_I, \pi_I, K) \to \pi_K$. Let $L := I \setminus K$, and $\vec{v}_L$ be the subvector of $\vec{v}_I$ at positions in L. Then compute $\{a_{L,j}, b_{L,j}\}_{j \in [k]} \leftarrow \mathsf{PartndPrimeProd}(L, \vec{v}_L)$, and for each $j \in [k]$ set: $\Gamma_{K,j} \leftarrow \Gamma_{I,j}^{a_{L,j}}$, $\Delta_{K,j} \leftarrow \Delta_{I,j}^{b_{L,j}}$ and return $\pi_K :=$ $\{\pi_{K,1}, \ldots, \pi_{K,k}\} := \{(\Gamma_{K,1}, \Delta_{K,1}), \ldots, (\Gamma_{K,k}, \Delta_{K,k})\}$

$\mathsf{VC.Agg}(\mathsf{crs}, (I, \vec{v}_I, \pi_I), (J, \vec{v}_J, \pi_J)) \to \pi_K := \{(\Gamma_{K,1}, \Delta_{K,1}), \ldots, (\Gamma_{K,k}, \Delta_{K,k})\}$.
1. Let $L := I \cap J$. If $L \neq \emptyset$, set $I' := I \setminus L$ and compute $\pi_{I'} \leftarrow$ $\mathsf{VC.Disagg}(\mathsf{crs}, I, \vec{v}_I, \pi_I, I')$; otherwise let $\pi_{I'} = \pi_I$.
2. Compute $\{a_{I',j}, b_{I',j}\}_{j \in [k]} \leftarrow \mathsf{PartndPrimeProd}(I', \vec{v}_{I'})$ and $\{a_{J,j}, b_{J,j}\}_{j \in [k]} \leftarrow \mathsf{PartndPrimeProd}(J, \vec{v}_J)$.
3. Parse $\pi_{I'} := \{(\Gamma_{I',j}, \Delta_{I',j})\}_{j=1}^{k}$, $\pi_J := \{(\Gamma_{J,j}, \Delta_{J,j})\}_{j=1}^{k}$, and for all $j \in [k]$, compute $\Gamma_{K,j} \leftarrow \mathbf{ShamirTrick}(\Gamma_{I',j}, \Gamma_{J,j}, a_{I',j}, a_{J,j})$ and $\Delta_{K,j} \leftarrow \mathbf{ShamirTrick}(\Delta_{I',j}, \Delta_{J,j}, b_{I',j}, b_{J,j})$.

Note that our algorithms above can work directly with the universal CRS crs, and do not need the specialized one crs_n.

Aggregation Correctness. The second property of aggregation correctness (the one about $\mathsf{VC.Disagg}$) is straightforward by construction: if we let $\{a_{K,j}, b_{K,j}\}_{j \in [k]} \leftarrow \mathsf{PartndPrimeProd}(K, \vec{v}_K)$, then $a_{I,j} = a_{L,j} \cdot a_{K,j}$, and thus $A_j = \Gamma_{I,j}^{a_{I,j}} = \Gamma_{I,j}^{a_{L,j} \cdot a_{K,j}} = \Gamma_{K,j}^{a_{K,j}}$ (and similarly for $\Delta_{K,j}$).

The first property instead follows from the correctness of Shamir's trick if the integer values provided as input are coprime; however since $I' \cap J = \emptyset$, $a_{I',j}$ and $a_{J,j}$ (resp. $b_{I',j}$ and $b_{J,j}$) are coprime unless a collision occurs in $\mathsf{PrimeGen}$.

Security. The security of our SVC scheme, i.e., position binding, can be reduced to the Strong RSA and Low Order assumptions in the hidden order group $\mathbb{G}$ used in the construction and to the knowledge extractability of $\mathsf{PoProd_2}$.

A bit more in detail the steps of the proof are as follows. Let an adversary to the position binding output $(C, I, \vec{y}, \pi, \vec{y}', \pi')$. First from knowledge extractability of $\mathsf{PoProd_2}$ it comes that $A_j B_j = g_1^{a_j} g_2^{b_j}$ and $g^{a_j b_j} = U_n = g^{u_n}$. However, this does not necessarily means that $a_j b_j = u_n$ over the integers and to prove it we need the Low Order assumptions, under which it holds. Afterwards we prove that since $A_j B_j = g_1^{a_j} g_2^{b_j}$ no different proofs π, π' for the same positions can pass the verification under the strong RSA assumption, which is the core of our proof. The main caveat of the proof is that instead of knowing that $A_j = g_1^{a_j}$ and $B_j = g_2^{b_j}$ we know only that $A_j B_j = g_1^{a_j} g_2^{b_j}$. The former case would directly reduce to RSA Accumulator's security (strong RSA assumption). For this we first need to prove an intermediate lemma which shows that specifically for our case $A_j B_j = g_1^{a_j} g_2^{b_j}$ is enough, since the choice of the primes p_i in the exponent is restricted to a polynomially bounded set.

For lack of space, the proof is in the full version. For an intuition we refer to the overview given at the beginning of this section.

Theorem 4.2 (Position-Binding). *Let* Ggen *be the generator of hidden order groups where the Strong RSA and Low Order assumptions hold, and let* PoProd$_2$ *be an argument of knowledge for* R_{PoProd_2}. *Then the subVector Commitment scheme defined above is position binding.*

On Concrete Instantiation. Our SVC construction is described generically from a hidden order group $\mathbb{G}$, an AoK PoProd$_2$, and a mapping to primes PrimeGen. The concrete scheme we analyze is the one where PoProd$_2$ is instantiated with the non-interactive version of the PoProd$_2$ protocol described in Sect. 4.1. The non-interactive version needs a hash-to-prime function H$_{\mathsf{prime}}$. We note that the same function can be used to instantiate PrimeGen, though for the sake of PrimeGen we do not need its randomness properties. One can choose a different mapping to primes for PrimeGen and even just a bijective mapping (which is inherently collision resistant) would be enough: this is actually the instantiation we consider in our efficiency analysis. Finally, see Sect. 1.4 for a discussion on possible instantiations of $\mathbb{G}$.

We note that by using the specific PoProd$_2$ protocol given in Sect. 4.1 we are assuming adversaries that are generic with respect to the group $\mathbb{G}$. Therefore, our SVC is ultimately position binding in the generic group model.

4.2   Our Second SVC Construction

In this section we propose another SVC scheme with constant-size parameters and incremental aggregation. This scheme builds on the SVC of [LM19] based on the RSA assumption, which in turn extends the VC of [CF13] to support subvector openings. Our technical contribution is twofold. First, we show that the SVC of [CF13,LM19] can be modified in order to have public parameters and verification time independent of the vector's length. Second, we propose new algorithms for (incremental) aggregation and disaggregation for this SVC.

Our Second SVC Construction. Let us start by giving a brief overview of the [CF13] VC scheme and of the basic idea to turn it into one with succinct parameters and verification time. In brief, in [CF13] a commitment to a vector $\vec{v}$ is $C = S_1^{v_1} \cdots S_n^{v_n}$, where each $S_i := g^{\prod_{j \in [n] \setminus \{i\}} e_j}$ with $g \in \mathbb{G}$ a random generator and e_j being distinct prime numbers (which can be deterministically generated using a suitable map-to-primes). The opening for position i is an element Λ_i such that $\Lambda_i^{e_i} \cdot S_i^{v_i} = C$ and the key idea is that such Λ_i is an e_i-th root that can be publicly computed as long as one does it for the correct position i and value v_i. Also, as it can be seen, the element S_i is necessary to verify an opening of position i, and thus $(S_1, \ldots, S_n)$ were included in the public parameters. Catalano and Fiore observed that one can remove the S_i-s from crs if the verifier opts for recomputing S_i at verification time *at the price of linear-time verification*. Our goal though is to obtain constant-size parameters *and* constant-time verification. To do that we let the prover compute S_i and include it in the opening for position i. To prevent adversaries from providing false S_i's, we store in the public parameters $U_n = g^{\prod_{i \in [n]} e_i}$ (i.e., an accumulator to all positions) so that the verifier can verify the correctness of S_i in constant-time by checking $S_i^{e_i} = U_n$. This technique easily generalizes to subvector openings.

In the following, we describe the scheme in details and then propose our incremental aggregation algorithms. To simplify our exposition, we use the following notation: for a set of indices $I \subseteq [n]$, $e_I := \prod_{i \in I} e_i$ denotes the product of all primes corresponding to the elements of I, and $S_I := g^{\prod_{i \in [n] \setminus I} e_i} = g^{e_{[n] \setminus I}} = U_n^{1/e_I}$ (which is a generalization of the former S_i), where, we recall, the e_i's are defined from the crs.

VC.Setup($1^\lambda, \ell, n$) $\to$ crs generates a hidden order group $\mathbb{G} \leftarrow$ Ggen(1^λ) and samples a generator $g \leftarrow_\$ \mathbb{G}$. It also determines a deterministic collision resistant function PrimeGen that maps integers to primes.
Returns crs $= (\mathbb{G}, g, \mathsf{PrimeGen})$

VC.Specialize(crs, n) $\to$ crs$_n$ computes n primes of $(\ell + 1)$ bits $e_1, \ldots, e_n$, $e_i \leftarrow$ PrimeGen(i) for each $i \in [n]$, and $U_n = g^{e_{[n]}}$ and returns crs$_n \leftarrow$ (crs, U_n). One can think of U_n as an accumulator to the set $[n]$.

VC.Com(crs, $\vec{v}$) $\to$ (C, aux) Computes for each $i \in [n]$, $S_i \leftarrow g^{e_{[n] \setminus \{i\}}}$ and then $C \leftarrow S_1^{v_1} \ldots S_n^{v_n}$ and aux $\leftarrow (v_1, \ldots, v_n)$.

VC.Open(crs, $I, \vec{y}$, aux) $\to \pi_I$ Computes for each $j \in [n] \setminus I$, $S_j^{1/e_I} \leftarrow g^{e_{[n] \setminus (I \cup \{j\})}}$ and $S_I \leftarrow g^{e_{[n] \setminus I}}$ and then

$$\Lambda_I \leftarrow \prod_{j=1, j \notin I}^{n} \left(S_j^{1/e_I} \right)^{y_j} = \left(\prod_{j=1, j \notin I}^{n} S_j^{y_j} \right)^{1/e_I}$$

Returns $\pi_I := (S_I, \Lambda_I)$

VC.Ver(crs, $C, I, \vec{y}, \pi_I$) $\to b$ Parse $\pi_I := (S_I, \Lambda_I)$, and compute $S_i = S_I^{e_{I \setminus \{i\}}} = U_n^{1/e_i}$ for every $i \in I$. Return 1 (accept) if both the following checks hold, and 0 (reject) otherwise:

$$S_I^{e_I} = U_n \ \wedge \ C = \Lambda_I^{e_I} \prod_{i \in I} S_i^{y_i}$$

The correctness of the above construction holds essentially the same as the one of the SVC of [CF13,LM19] with the addition of the S_I elements of the openings, whose correctness can be seen by inspection (and is the same as for RSA accumulators).

Incremental Aggregation. Let us now show that the SVC above has incremental aggregation. Note that our algorithms also implicitly show that the RSA-based SVC of [LM19] is incrementally aggregatable.

VC.Disagg(crs, $I, \vec{v}_I, \pi_I, K$) $\to \pi_K$ Parse $\pi_I := (S_I, \Lambda_I)$. First compute S_K from S_I, $S_K \leftarrow S_I^{e_{I \setminus K}}$, and then, for every $j \in I \setminus K$, $\chi_j = S_K^{1/e_j}$, e.g., by computing $\chi_j \leftarrow S_I^{e_{I \setminus (K \cup \{j\})}}$.

Return $\pi_K := (S_K, \Lambda_K)$ where

$$\Lambda_K \leftarrow \Lambda_I^{e_{I\setminus K}} \cdot \prod_{j \in I \setminus K} \chi_j^{v_j}$$

$\mathsf{VC.Agg}(\mathsf{crs}, (I, \vec{v}_I, \pi_I), (J, \vec{v}_J, \pi_J)) \rightarrow \pi_K$ Parse $\pi_I := (S_I, \Lambda_I)$ and similarly π_J. Also, let $K = I \cup J$, and assume for simplicity that $I \cap J = \emptyset$ (if this is not the case, one could simply disaggregate π_I (or π_J) to $\pi_{I\setminus J}$ (or $\pi_{J\setminus I}$)). First, compute $S_K \leftarrow \mathbf{ShamirTrick}(S_I, S_J, e_I, e_J)$. Next, compute $\phi_j \leftarrow S_K^{e_{J\setminus\{j\}}} = S_I^{1/e_j}$ for every $j \in J$, and similarly $\psi_i \leftarrow S_K^{e_{I\setminus\{i\}}} = S_J^{1/e_i}$ for every $i \in I$. Then compute

$$\rho_I \leftarrow \frac{\Lambda_I}{\prod_{j \in J} \phi_j^{v_j}} \qquad \text{and} \qquad \sigma_J \leftarrow \frac{\Lambda_J}{\prod_{i \in I} \psi_i^{v_i}}$$

Return $\pi_K := (S_K, \Lambda_K)$ where $\Lambda_K \leftarrow \mathbf{ShamirTrick}(\rho_I, \sigma_J, e_I, e_J)$.

Aggregation Correctness. It follows from the correctness of Shamir's trick and by construction. The details are in the full version

Security. For the security of the above SVC scheme we observe that the difference with the corresponding [LM19] lies in the generation of S_i's. In [LM19] they are generated in the trusted setup phase, thus they are considered "well-formed" in the security proof. In our case, the S_i's are reconstructed during verification time from the S_I that comes in the opening π_I which can (possibly) be generated in an adversarial way. However, in the verification it is checked that $S_I^{e_I} = U$, where $U = g^{e_{[n]}}$ is computed in the trusted setup. So under the Low Order assumption we get that S_I has the correct form, $S_I = g^{e_{[n]}/e_I} = g^{e_{[n]\setminus I}}$, with overwhelming probability. Except for this change, the rest reduces to the position binding of the [LM19] SVC. The proof of the theorem is in the full version.

Theorem 4.3 (Position-Binding). *Let* Ggen *be the generator of hidden order groups where the Low Order assumption holds and the [LM19] SVC is position binding. Then the SVC scheme defined above is position binding.*

As showed in [LM19], their SVC is position binding under the strong Distinct-Prime-Product Root assumption in the standard model. We conclude that the above SVC is position binding in hidden order groups where the Low Order and the Strong Distinct-Prime-Product Root assumptions hold.

4.3   Comparison with Related Work

We compare our two SVC schemes with the recent scheme proposed by Boneh et al. [BBF19] and the one by Lai and Malavolta [LM19], which extends [CF13] to support subvector openings.[9] We present a detailed comparison in Table 1,

---

[9] We refer to [BBF19] to see how these schemes compare with Merkle trees.

considering to work with vectors of length N of ℓ-bit elements and security parameter λ. In particular we consider an instantiation of our first SVC with $k = 1$ (and thus $n = N \cdot \ell$). A detailed efficiency analysis of our schemes is in the full version.

SETUP MODEL. [BBF19] works with a fully universal CRS, whereas our schemes have both a universal CRS with deterministic specialization, which however, in comparison to [CF13,LM19], outputs *constant-size* parameters instead of linear.

AGGREGATION. The VC of [BBF19] supports aggregation only on openings created by VC.Open (i.e., it is one-hop) and does not have disaggregatable proofs (unless in a different model where one works linearly in the length of the vector or knows the full vector). In contrast, we show the first schemes that satisfy incremental aggregation (also, our second one immediately yields a method for the incremental aggregation of [LM19]). As we mention later, incremental aggregation can be very useful to precompute openings for a certain number of vector blocks allowing for interesting time-space tradeoffs that can speedup the running time of VC.Open.

EFFICIENCY. From the table, one can see that our first SVC has: slightly worse commitments size than all the other schemes, computational asymptotic performances similar to [BBF19], and opening size slightly better than [BBF19]. Our second SVC is the most efficient among the schemes with constant-size parameters; in particular, it has faster asymptotics than our first SVC and [BBF19] for having a smaller logarithmic factor (e.g., $\log(N - m)$ vs. $\log(\ell N)$), which is due to the avoidance of using one prime per bit of the vector. In some cases, [CF13,LM19] is slightly better, but this is essentially a benefit of the linear-size parameters, namely the improvement is due to having the S_i's elements already precomputed.

When considering applications in which a user creates the commitment to a vector and (at some later points in time) is requested to produce openings for various subvectors, *our incremental aggregation property leads to use preprocessing to achieve more favorable time and memory costs*. In a nutshell, the idea of preprocessing is that one can precompute and store information that allows to speedup the generation of openings, in particular by making opening time less dependent on the total length of the vector. Our method in Sect. 3.2 works generically for any SVC that has incremental aggregation. A similar preprocessing solution can also be designed for the SVC of [BBF19] by using its one-hop aggregation; we provide a detailed description of the method in the full version. The preprocessing for [BBF19] however has no flexibility in choosing how much auxiliary storage can be used, and one must store (a portion of) a non-membership witness *for every bit* of the vector.

Even in the simplest case of $B = 1$ (shown in Table 1) both our SVCs save a factor ℓ in storage, which concretely turns into 3× less storage.

Furthermore we support flexible choices of B thus allowing to tune the amount of auxiliary storage. For instance, we can choose $B = \sqrt{N}$ so as to get $2\sqrt{N}|\mathbb{G}|$ bits of storage, and opening time about $O(\ell m \log n(\sqrt{n} + \log m))$ and $O(m(\sqrt{n} + \log^2 m))$ in the first and second scheme respectively. Our flexibility may also allow one to choose the buckets size B and their distribution according to applications-dependent heuristics; investigating its benefit may be an interesting direction for future work.

Table 1. Comparison between the SVC's of [BBF19], [LM19] and this work; our contributions are highlighted in gray. We consider committing to a vector $\vec{v} \in (\{0,1\}^\ell)^N$ of length N, and opening and verifying for a set I of m positions. By '$O(x)$ $\mathbb{G}$' we mean $O(x)$ group operations in $\mathbb{G}$; $|\mathbb{G}|$ denotes the bit length of an element of $\mathbb{G}$. An alternative algorithm for VC.Open in [LM19] costs $O(\ell \cdot (N - m) \cdot \log(N - m))$. Our precomputation is for $B = 1$.

Metric	Our First SVC	Our Second SVC	[BBF19]	[CF13, LM19]
		Setup		
VC.Setup	$O(1)$	$O(1)$	$O(1)$	$O(1)$
$\|crs\|$	$3\,\|\mathbb{G}\|$	$1\,\|\mathbb{G}\|$	$1\,\|\mathbb{G}\|$	$1\,\|\mathbb{G}\|$
VC.Specialize	$O(\ell \cdot N \cdot \log(\ell N))$ $\mathbb{G}$	$O(\ell \cdot N)$ $\mathbb{G}$	—	$O(\ell \cdot N \cdot \log N)$ $\mathbb{G}$
$\|crs_N\|$	$1\,\|\mathbb{G}\|$	$1\,\|\mathbb{G}\|$	—	$N\,\|\mathbb{G}\|$
		Commit a vector $\vec{v} \in (\{0,1\}^\ell)^N$		
VC.Com	$O(\ell \cdot N \cdot \log(\ell N))$ $\mathbb{G}$	$O(\ell \cdot N \cdot \log N)$ $\mathbb{G}$	$O(\ell \cdot N \cdot \log(\ell N))$ $\mathbb{G}$	$O(\ell \cdot N)$ $\mathbb{G}$
$\|C\|$	$4\,\|\mathbb{G}\| + 2\,\|\mathbb{Z}_{q2\lambda}\|$	$1\,\|\mathbb{G}\|$	$1\,\|\mathbb{G}\|$	$1\,\|\mathbb{G}\|$
		Opening and Verification for $\vec{v}_I$ with $\|I\| = m$		
VC.Open	$O(\ell \cdot (N - m) \cdot \log(\ell N))$ $\mathbb{G}$	$O(\ell \cdot (N - m) \cdot \log(N - m))$ $\mathbb{G}$	$O(\ell \cdot (N - m) \cdot \log(\ell N))$ $\mathbb{G}$	$O(\ell \cdot (N - m) \cdot m \log m)$ $\mathbb{G}$
$\|\pi_I\|$	$3\,\|\mathbb{G}\|$	$2\,\|\mathbb{G}\|$	$5\,\|\mathbb{G}\| + 1\,\|\mathbb{Z}_{q2\lambda}\|$	$1\,\|\mathbb{G}\|$
VC.Ver	$O(\ell \cdot m \cdot \log(\ell N))$ $\mathbb{Z}_{q2\lambda} + O(\lambda)$ $\mathbb{G}$	$O(\ell \cdot m \log m)$ $\|\mathbb{G}\|$	$O(m \cdot \ell \cdot \log(\ell N))$ $\mathbb{Z}_{q2\lambda} + O(\lambda)$ $\mathbb{G}$	$O(\ell \cdot m)$ $\mathbb{G}$
		Commitment and Opening with Precomputation		
VC.Com	$O(\ell \cdot N \cdot \log(\ell \cdot N) \cdot \log(N))$ $\mathbb{G}$	$O(\ell \cdot N \log^2(N))$ $\mathbb{G}$	$O(\ell \cdot N \cdot \log(\ell \cdot N) \cdot \log(N))$ $\mathbb{G}$	$O(\ell \cdot N \log^2(N))$ $\mathbb{G}$
$\|aux\|$	$2N\,\|\mathbb{G}\|$	$2N\,\|\mathbb{G}\|$	$2N\,\|\mathbb{G}\| + O(\ell \cdot N \log(\ell N))$	$2N\,\|\mathbb{G}\|$
VC.Open	$O(m \cdot \ell \cdot \log(m) \log(\ell N))$ $\mathbb{G}$	$O(m \cdot \ell \cdot \log^2 m)$ $\mathbb{G}$	$O(m \cdot \ell \cdot \log(m) \log(\ell N))$ $\mathbb{G}$	$O(m \cdot \ell \cdot \log^2(m))$ $\mathbb{G}$
Aggregation	Incremental	Incremental	One-hop	Incremental
Disaggregation	Yes	Yes	No	Yes

4.4 Experimental Evaluation

We have implemented in Rust our first SVC scheme of Sect. 4.1 (with and without preprocessing) and the recent SVC of [BBF19] (referred as BBF in what follows). Here we discuss an experimental evaluation of these schemes.[10] Below is a summary of the comparison, details of the experiments are in the full version.

- Our SVC construction is faster in opening and verification than BBF (up to 2.5× and 2.3× faster respectively), but at the cost of a slower commitment stage (up to 6× slower). These differences tend to flatten for larger vectors and opening sizes.

---

[10] We did not include BBF with precomputation in our experimental evaluation because this scheme has worse performances than our preprocessing construction in terms of both required storage and running time. We elaborate on this in the full version.

– Our SVC construction with preprocessing allows for extremely fast opening times compared to non-preprocessing constructions. Namely, it can reduce the running time by several orders of magnitude for various choices of vector and opening sizes, allowing to obtain practical opening times—of the order of seconds—that would be impossible without preprocessing—of the order of hundred of seconds. In a file of 1 Mibit (2^{20} bits), preprocessing reduces the time to open 2048 bits from one hour to less than 5 s! This efficient opening, however, comes at the cost of a one-time preprocessing (during commitment) and higher storage requirements. We discuss how to mitigate these space requirements by trading for opening time and/or communication complexity later in this section. We stress that it is thanks to the incremental aggregation property of our construction that allows these tradeoffs (they are not possible in BBF with preprocessing).
– Although our SVC construction with preprocessing has an expensive commitment stage, this tends to be amortized throughout very few openings[11], as few as 30 (see full version for more details). These effects are particularly significant over a higher number of openings: over 1000 openings our SVC construction with preprocessing has an amortized cost of less than 6 s, while our SVC construction and BBF have amortized openings above 90 s.

Time/Storage Tradeoffs. Our construction allows for some tradeoffs between running times and storage by selecting larger precomputed chunks or by committing to hashed blocks of the file. See the full version for a detailed discussion.

5   Verifiable Decentralized Storage

In this section we introduce verifiable decentralized storage (VDS). We recall that in VDS there are two types of parties (called nodes): the generic *client nodes* and the more specialized *storage nodes* (a storage node can also act as a client node). We refer the reader to Sect. 1.2 for a discussion on the motivation and requirements of VDS.

5.1   Syntax

Here we introduce the syntax of VDS. A VDS scheme is defined by a collection of algorithms that are to be executed by either storage nodes or client nodes. The only exception is the Bootstrap algorithm that is used to bootstrap the entire system and is assumed to be executed by a trusted party, or to be implemented in a distributed fashion (which is easy if it is public coin).

The syntax of VDS reflects its goal: guaranteeing data integrity in a highly dynamic and decentralized setting (the file can change and expand/shrink often

---

[11] Amortized opening time roughly represents how computationally expensive a scheme is "in total" throughout all its operations. *Amortized opening time for m openings is the cost of one commitment plus the cost of m openings, all averaged over the m openings.*

and no single node stores it all). In VDS we create both parameters and an initial commitment for an empty file at the beginning (through the probabilistic Bootstrap algorithm, which requires a trusted execution). From then on this commitment is changed through incremental updates (of arbitrary size). Updating is divided in two parts. A node can carry out an update and "push" it to all the other nodes, i.e. providing auxiliary information (that we call "update hint") other nodes can use to update their local certificates (if affected by the change) and a new digest[12]. These operations are done respectively through StrgNode.PushUpdate and StrgNode.ApplyUpdate. Opening and verifying are where VC (with incremental aggregation) and VDS share the same mechanism. To respond to a query, a storage node can produce (possibly partial) proofs of opening via the StrgNode.Retrieve algorithm. If these proofs need to be aggregated, any node can use algorithm AggregateCertificates. Anyone can verify a proof through ClntNode.VerRetrieve.

Some more details about our notation follow. In VDS we model the files to be stored as vectors in some message space $\mathcal{M}$ (e.g., $\mathcal{M} = \{0,1\}$ or $\{0,1\}^\ell$), i.e., $F = (F_1, \ldots, F_N)$. Given a file F, we define a *portion* of it as a pair (I, F_I) where F_I is essentially the I-subvector of F. We denote input (resp. output) states by st (resp. st'). Update operations op are modifications, additions or deletions, i.e. $\text{op} \in \{\text{mod}, \text{add}, \text{del}\}$, and Δ denotes the update description, e.g., which positions to change and the new values. We denote by Υ_Δ the *update hint* that whoever is producing the update can share with other nodes to generate a new digest from the changes. The output bit b marks acceptance/rejection. For a query Q, we mark by π_Q a certificate vouching for a response F_Q.

Definition 5.1 (Verifiable Decentralized Storage). *Algorithm to bootstrap the system:*

Bootstrap(1^λ) $\rightarrow$ (pp, δ_0, st$_0$) *which outputs a digest and storage node's local state for an empty file. All the algorithms below implicitly take the public parameters pp as input.*

The algorithms for storage nodes are:

StrgNode.AddStorage($\delta, n, \text{st}, I, F_I, Q, F_Q, \pi_Q$) $\rightarrow$ (st', J, F_J) *by which a storage node can extend its storage from (I, F_I) to $(J, F_J) := (I, F_I) \cup (Q, F_Q)$. Note: this allows anyone holding a valid certificate for a file portion F_Q to become a storage node of such portion.*

StrgNode.RmvStorage($\delta, n, \text{st}, I, F_I, K$) $\rightarrow$ (st', J, F_J) *by which a storage node can shrink its local storage to (J, F_J).*

StrgNode.PushUpdate($\delta, n, \text{st}, I, F_I, \text{op}, \Delta$) $\rightarrow$ ($\delta', n', \text{st}', J, F'_J, \Upsilon_\Delta$) *which allows a storage node to perform an update on (I, F_I) generating a corresponding new digest, length and local view, along with hint Υ_Δ others can use to update their own digests/local view.*

---

[12] One can also see this update hint as a certificate to check that a new digest is consistent with some changes. This issue does not arise in our context at all but the Bootstrap algorithms are deterministic.

StrgNode.ApplyUpdate($\delta, n, \mathsf{st}, I, \mathsf{F}_I, \mathsf{op}, \Delta, \Upsilon_\Delta$) $\rightarrow$ ($b, \delta', n', \mathsf{st}', J, \mathsf{F}'_J$) *which allows a storage node to incorporate changes in a file pushed by another node.*

StrgNode.Retrieve($\delta, n, \mathsf{st}, I, \mathsf{F}_I, Q$) $\rightarrow$ (F_Q, π_Q) *which allows a storage node to respond to a query and to create a certificate vouching for the correctness of the returned blocks.*

The algorithms for clients nodes are:

CIntNode.ApplyUpdate($\delta, \mathsf{op}, \Delta, \Upsilon_\Delta$) $\rightarrow$ (b, δ') *which updates a digest by hint Υ_Δ.*

CIntNode.VerRetrieve($\delta, Q, \mathsf{F}_Q, \pi_Q$) $\rightarrow b$ *which verifies a response to a query.*

AggregateCertificates($\delta, (I, \mathsf{F}_I, \pi_I), (J, \mathsf{F}_J, \pi_J)$) $\rightarrow \pi_K$ *which aggregates two certificates π_I and π_J into a single certificate π_K (with $K := I \cup J$). In a running VDS, any node can aggregate two (or more) incoming certified data blocks into a single certified data block.*

Remark 5.1 (On CreateFrom). For completeness, our VDS syntax also includes the functionalities (StrgNode.CreateFrom, CIntNode.GetCreate) that allow a storage node to initialize storage (and corresponding digest) for a new file that is a subset of an existing one, and a client node to verify such resulting digest. Although this feature can be interesting in some application scenarios, we still see it as an extra feature that may or may not be satisfied by a VDS construction. We refer to the full version for more discussion and a detailed description of this functionality.

5.2   Correctness and Efficiency of VDS

Intuitively, we say that a VDS scheme is *efficient* if running VDS has a "small" overhead in terms of the storage required by all the nodes and the bandwidth to transmit certificates. More formally, a VDS scheme is said efficient if there is a fixed polynomial $p(\cdot)$ such that $p(\lambda, \log n)$ (with λ the security parameter and n the length of the file) is a bound for all certificates and advices generated by the VDS algorithms as well as for digests δ and the local state st of storage nodes. Note that combining this bound with the requirement that all algorithms are polynomial time in their input, we also get that no VDS algorithm can run linearly in the size of the file (except in the trivial case that the file is processed in one shot, e.g., in the first StrgNode.AddStorage).

Efficiency essentially models that running VDS is cost-effective for all the nodes in the sense that it does not require them to store significantly more data than they would have to store without. Notice that by requiring certificates to have a fixed size implies that they do not grow with aggregation.

For correctness, intuitively speaking, we want that for any (valid) evolution of the system in which the VDS algorithms are honestly executed we get that any storage node storing a portion of a file F can successfully convince a client holding a digest of F about retrieval of any portion of F. And such (intuitive notion of) correctness is also preserved when updates, aggregations, or creations of new files are done.

Turning this intuition into a formal correctness definition turned out to be nontrivial. This is due to the distributed nature of this primitive and the fact that there could be many possible ways in which, at the time of answering a retrieval query, a storage node may have reached its state starting from the empty node state. The basic idea of our definition is that an empty node is "valid", and then any "valid" storage node that runs StrgNode.PushUpdate "transfers" such validity to both itself and to other nodes that apply such update. A bit more precisely, we model "validity" as the ability to correctly certify retrievals of any subsets of the stored portion. A formal correctness definition follows. To begin with, we define the notion of validity for the view of a storage node.

Definition 5.2 (Validity of storage node's view). *Let* pp *be public parameters as generated by* Bootstrap. *We say that a local view* $(\delta, n, \mathsf{st}, I, \mathsf{F}_I)$ *of a storage node is valid if* $\forall Q \subseteq I$: ClntNode.VerRetrieve$(\delta, Q, \mathsf{F}_Q, \pi_Q) = 1$, *where* $(\mathsf{F}_Q, \pi_Q) \leftarrow$ StrgNode.Retrieve$(\delta, n, \mathsf{st}, I, \mathsf{F}_I, Q)$

Remark 5.2. By Definition 5.2 the output of a bootstrapping algorithm $(\mathsf{pp}, \delta_0, \mathsf{st}_0) \leftarrow$ Bootstrap(1^λ) is always such that $(\mathsf{pp}, \delta_0, 0, \mathsf{st}_0, \emptyset, \emptyset)$ is valid. This provides a "base case" for Definition 5.4.

Second, we define the notion of admissible update, which intuitively models when a given update can be meaningfully processed, locally, by a storage node.

Definition 5.3 (Admissible Update). *An update* (op, Δ) *is* admissible *for* (n, I, F_I) *if:*

- *for* op = mod, $K \subseteq I$ *and* $|\mathsf{F}'_K| = |K|$, *where* $\Delta := (K, \mathsf{F}'_K)$.
- *for* op = add, $K \cap I = \emptyset$ *and* $|\mathsf{F}'_K| = |K|$ *and* $K = \{n+1, n+2, \ldots, n+|K|\}$, *where* $\Delta := (K, \mathsf{F}'_K)$.
- *for* op = del, $K \subseteq I$ *and* $K = \{n - |K| + 1, \ldots, n\}$, *where* $\Delta := K$.

In words, the above definition formalizes that: to push a modification at positions K, the storage node must store those positions; to push an addition, the new positions K must extend the currently stored length of the file; to push a deletion of position K, the storage node must store data of the positions to be deleted and those positions must also be the last $|K|$ positions of the currently stored file (i.e., the file length is reduced).

Definition 5.4 (Correctness of VDS). *A VDS scheme* VDS *is* correct *if for all honestly generated parameters* $(\mathsf{pp}, \delta_0, \mathsf{st}_0) \leftarrow$ Bootstrap(1^λ) *and any storage node's local view* $(\delta, n, \mathsf{st}, I, \mathsf{F}_I)$ *that is valid, the following conditions hold.*
Update Correctness. *For any update* (op, Δ) *that is admissible for* (n, I, F_I) *and for any* $(\delta', n', \mathsf{st}', J, \mathsf{F}'_J, \Upsilon_\Delta) \leftarrow$ StrgNode.PushUpdate$(\delta, n, \mathsf{st}, I, \mathsf{F}_I, \mathsf{op}, \Delta)$:

1. $(\mathsf{pp}, \delta', n', \mathsf{st}', J, \mathsf{F}'_J)$ *is valid;*
2. *for any valid* $(\delta, n, \mathsf{st}_s, I_s, \mathsf{F}_{I_s})$, *if* $(b_s, \delta'_s, n', \mathsf{st}'_s, I'_s, \mathsf{F}'_s) \leftarrow$ StrgNode.ApplyUpdate$(\delta, n, \mathsf{st}_s, I_s, \mathsf{F}_{I_s}, \mathsf{op}, \Delta, \Upsilon_\Delta)$ *then we have:* $b_s = 1$, $\delta'_s = \delta'$, $n'_s = n'$, *and* $(\delta'_s, n'_s, \mathsf{st}'_s, I'_s, \mathsf{F}'_s)$ *is valid;*

3. if $(b_c, \delta'_c) \leftarrow$ ClntNode.ApplyUpdate$(\delta, \text{op}, \Delta, \Upsilon_\Delta)$, *then* $\delta'_c = \delta'$ *and* $b_c = 1$.

ADD-STORAGE   CORRECTNESS.   *For   any* (Q, F_Q, π_Q) *such   that* ClntNode.VerRetrieve$(\delta, Q, \mathsf{F}_Q, \pi_Q) = 1$, *if* $(\text{st}', J, \mathsf{F}_J) \leftarrow$ StrgNode.AddStorage $(\delta, \text{st}, I, \mathsf{F}, Q, \mathsf{F}_Q, \pi_Q)$ *then* $(\delta, n, \text{st}', J, \mathsf{F}_J)$ *is valid.*

REMOVE-STORAGE   CORRECTNESS.   *For   any* $K \subseteq I$, *if* $(\text{st}', J, \mathsf{F}_J) \leftarrow$ StrgNode.RmvStorage$(\delta, \text{st}, I, \mathsf{F}, K)$ *then* $(\delta, n, \text{st}', J, \mathsf{F}_J)$ *is valid.*

CREATE CORRECTNESS. *For any* $J \subseteq I$, *if* $(\delta', n', \text{st}', J, \mathsf{F}_J, \Upsilon_J)$ *is output of* StrgNode.CreateFrom$(\delta, n, \text{st}, I, \mathsf{F}_I, J)$ *and* $(b, \delta'') \leftarrow$ ClntNode.GetCreate(δ, J, Υ_J), *then* $b = 1$, $n' = |J|$, $\delta'' = \delta'$ *and* $(\text{pp}, \delta', n', \text{st}', J, \mathsf{F}_J)$ *is valid.*

AGGREGATE CORRECTNESS. *For any pair of triples* (I, F_I, π_I) *and* (J, F_J, π_J) *such that* ClntNode.VerRetrieve$(\delta, I, \mathsf{F}_I, \pi_I) = 1$ *and* ClntNode.VerRetrieve$(\delta, J, \mathsf{F}_J, \pi_J) = 1$, *if* $\pi_K \leftarrow$ AggregateCertificates$((I, \mathsf{F}_I, \pi_I), (J, \mathsf{F}_J, \pi_J))$ *and* $(K, \mathsf{F}_K) := (I, \mathsf{F}_I) \cup (J, \mathsf{F}_J)$, *then* ClntNode.VerRetrieve$(\delta, K, \mathsf{F}_K, \pi_K) = 1$.

Remark 5.3 (Relation with Updatable VCs). Our notion of VDS is very close to the notion of updatable VCs [CF13] extended to support subvector openings and incremental aggregation. On a syntactical level, in comparison to updatable VCs, our VDS notion makes more evident the decentralized nature of the primitive, which is reflected in the definition of our algorithms where for example it is clear that no one ever needs to store/know the entire file. One major difference is that in VDS the public parameters must necessarily be *short* since no node can run linearly in the size of the file (nor it can afford such storage), whereas in VCs this may not be necessarily the case. Another difference is that in updatable VCs [CF13] updates can be received without any hint, which is instead the case in VDS. Finally, it is interesting to note that, as of today, there exists no VC scheme that is updatable, incrementally aggregatable and with subvector openings, that enjoys short parameters and has the required short verification time. So, in a way, our two VDS realizations show how to bypass this barrier of updatable VC by moving to a slightly different (and practically motivated) model.

5.3   Security of VDS

In this section we discuss the security definition of VDS schemes. For lack of space a formal definition is in the full version. Intuitively speaking, we require that a malicious storage node (or a coalition of them) cannot convince a client of a false data block in a retrieval query. To formalize this, we let the adversary fully choose a *history* of the VDS system that starts from the empty state and consists of a sequence of steps, where each step is either an update (addition, deletion, modification) or a creation (from an existing file) and is accompanied by an advice. A client's digest δ is updated following such history and using the adversarial advices, and similarly one gets a file F corresponding to such digest. At this point, the adversary's goal is to provide a tuple $(Q, \pi_Q, \mathsf{F}^*_Q)$ that is accepted by a client with digest δ but where $\mathsf{F}^*_Q \neq \mathsf{F}_Q$.

VDS Proof of Storage. As an additional security mechanism we consider the possibility to ensure a client that a given file is stored by the network at a certain point of time without having to retrieve it. To this end, we extend the VDS notion to provide a *proof of storage* mechanism in the form of a proof of retrievability (PoR) [JK07] or a proof of data possession (PDP) [ABC+07]. Our proof of storage model for VDS is such that proofs are publicly verifiable given the file's digest. Also, in order to support the decentralized and open nature of DSNs, the entire proof mechanism should not use any secret, and proofs should be generatable in a distributed fashion (this is a main distinguishing feature compared to existing PoRs/PDPs) while staying compact. The formalization of this property is in the full version.

5.4   Realizing VDS

We show two realizations of VDS in hidden-order groups, summarized below.

Theorem 5.1 (VDS$_1$). *Under the strong RSA assumption in a hidden-order group $\mathbb{G}$, there exists a VDS scheme* VDS$_1$ *in which, for a file* F*: a digest δ_F is $2|\mathbb{G}| + \log|F|$ bits-long; a storage node holding (I, F_I) keeps a state* st$_I$ *of $2|\mathbb{G}|$ bits, answers retrieval of portion Q with a certificate of $2|\mathbb{G}|$ bits in time $O(\ell \cdot (|I| - |Q|) \log|F|)$, and pushes an update Δ in time $O(\ell \cdot |I| \log|F|)$ for* op = mod*, $O(\ell \cdot |\Delta| \log|F|)$ for* op = add*, and $O(\ell \cdot (|I| - |\Delta|) \log|F|)$ for* op = del*; a client verifies a query for positions in Q (resp. an update Δ) in time $O(\ell \cdot |Q| \log|F|)$ (resp. $O(\ell \cdot |\Delta| \log|F|)$).*

Theorem 5.2 (VDS$_2$). *Under the strong distinct-prime-product root and the Low Order assumptions in a hidden-order group $\mathbb{G}$, there exists a VDS scheme* VDS$_2$ *in which, for a file* F*: a digest δ_F is $2|\mathbb{G}| + \log|F|$ bits-long; a storage node holding (I, F_I) keeps a state* st$_I$ *of $2|\mathbb{G}|$ bits, answers retrieval of portion Q with a certificate of $2|\mathbb{G}|$ bits in time $O(\ell \cdot (|I| - |Q|) \log(|I| - |Q|))$, and pushes an update Δ in time $O(\ell \cdot |\Delta| \log|\Delta|)$ for* op = mod, add*, and $O(\ell \cdot (|I| + |\Delta| \log|\Delta|))$ for* op = del*; a client verifies a query for positions in Q (resp. an update Δ) in time $O(\ell \cdot |Q| \log|Q|)$ (resp. $O(\ell \cdot |\Delta| \log|\Delta|)$).*

In terms of assumptions, VDS$_1$ is based on a weaker assumption than VDS$_2$ (although the assumptions are equivalent when $\mathbb{G}$ is instantiated with RSA groups).

In terms of performances, as one can see, VDS$_1$ and VDS$_2$ do similarly, with VDS$_2$ being slightly more efficient. In VDS$_1$ the complexity of all operations includes a factor $\alpha = \log|F|$, whereas in VDS$_2$ operations are affected by a factor logarithmic only in the number of positions involved in the given operation (e.g., how many are updated), which is typically much smaller than the entire file. Also, VDS$_2$ has the interesting feature that storage nodes can add and modify values in time which depends only on the update size but not on the size of the local storage.

Finally, VDS$_1$ has the additional feature of being compatible with our succinct arguments of knowledge, which enable the StrgNode.CreateFrom functionality and compact Proofs of Data Possession (see next section for an intuition and the full version for the details).

The main ideas of the two constructions are described in the following paragraphs; full constructions are in the full version.

Our First VDS Construction. Our first VDS VDS_1 is obtained by extending the techniques used for our SVC of Sect. 4.1.

Let us assume for a moment that a digest for file F is a commitment to F. Then, a storage node holding a portion (I, F_I) keeps as local state $\mathsf{st}_I = \pi_I = (\Gamma_I, \Delta_I)$, and this clearly enables it to certify retrieval queries for any portion $Q \subseteq I$ by using disaggregation in order to create π_Q from π_I. Moreover, such certificates of retrieval queries can be arbitrarily aggregated over the network.

In order to support updates, the main obstacle is that our commitment cannot be publicly updated without knowing the entire vector due to the presence of the AoK of union of Acc_0 and Acc_1. To solve this, we exploit the fact that in the VDS security model the digest provided by the adversary must be compatible with the claimed history of changes. So we can remove the AoK. Then, updating the digest boils down to updating the two RSA accumulators $(\mathsf{Acc}_0, \mathsf{Acc}_1)$ appropriately. For instance, changing the i-th bit from 0 to 1 requires to remove p_i from Acc_0 (i.e., $\mathsf{Acc}_0' = \mathsf{Acc}_0^{1/p_i}$ computable through π_I) and adding it to Acc_1 (i.e., $\mathsf{Acc}_1' = \mathsf{Acc}_1^{p_i}$). This can be performed by a storage node holding positions in the set I such that $i \in I$, and verified by anyone having previous and new digest. As we show in the full description of the scheme, by using similar ideas other storage nodes holding other positions, say J, can also update their local state st_J accordingly.

Finally, in this VDS we take advantage of our efficient AoK protocols to support two additional features. The first one is a compact proof of data possession by which the storage node can convince a verifier that it stores a certain subset of positions without sending the data at those positions. The second one is what we call "CreateFrom": a storage node holding a prefix F' of F can publish a new digest $\delta_{\mathsf{F}'}$ corresponding to F' as a new file, and to convince any client about its correctness without the need for them to know neither F' nor F.

Our Second VDS Construction. Our second scheme VDS_2 is obtained by modifying our second SVC scheme from Sect. 4.2 and makes key use of its aggregation/disaggregation properties.

As in our first VDS scheme, a storage node holding (I, F_I) keeps an opening π_I as local state, and uses our disaggregation and aggregation methods to certify retrieval queries for $Q \subset I$.

Let us now turn to how we can support updates. Let us consider an update on a subset K of the vector. First, the commitment is updatable as $C' \leftarrow C \cdot \prod_{i \in K} S_i^{\mathsf{F}_i' - \mathsf{F}_i}$. To update the opening proof, which we recall is $\pi_I := (S_I, \Lambda_I)$, we note that the Λ_I-part is updatable without the need of hint as $\Lambda_I' \leftarrow \Lambda_I \cdot \left(\prod_{j \in K \setminus I} S_j^{1/\prod_{i \in I} e_i} \right)^{\mathsf{F}_j' - \mathsf{F}_j}$. This part works as in [CF13] with some additional techniques that let a node do this in time $O(|I|+|K|\log|K|)$ and without having to store all the S_j values. The S_I-part resembles an RSA accumulator witness as observed in Sect. 4.2, and thus we can use techniques similar to those of our first VDS construction to update it. That is, upon update on K, S_K is sufficient for any node to update S_I (more details are in the full version).

A remaining problem is that the SVC scheme works with a specialized CRS, $U_n = g^{e_{[n]}}$, which depends on the vector's length. In the SVC schemes, this CRS is generated (deterministically) only once, but in VDS the vector's length evolves according to the updates, i.e., for each addition or deletion U_n should also be updated. To solve this problem, in our VDS_2 scheme we make U_n part of the digest together with C, and each node is responsible to verifiably update U_n. Technically, U_n is an RSA accumulator to the vector positions, and thus it can be updated by using techniques similar to our first scheme.

Acknowledgements. We thank Ben Fisch for valuable clarifications about the notions of Proof of Retrievable Commitment and Proof of Replication, and Justin Drake for pointing out the need (due to the attack discussed in [BBF18]) of using a hash function mapping into $\mathsf{Primes}(2\lambda)$ in the Fiat-Shamir transformation when making our succinct arguments of knowledge non-interactive.

Research leading to these results has been partially supported by the Spanish Government under projects SCUM (ref. RTI2018-102043-B-I00), CRYPTOEPIC (refs. ERC2018-092822, EUR2019-103816), and SECURITAS (ref. RED2018-102321-T), by the Madrid Regional Government under project BLOQUES (ref. S2018/TCS-4339), and by research gifts from Protocol Labs.

References

[ABC+07] Ateniese, R.C., et al.: Provable data possession at untrusted stores. In: Ning, P., De Capitani di Vimercati, S., Syverson, P.F. (eds.) ACM CCS 2007, pp. 598–609. ACM Press, October 2007

[BBF18] Boneh, D., Bünz, B., Fisch, B.: A Survey of Two Verifiable Delay Functions. Cryptology ePrint Archive, Report 2018/712 (2018). https://eprint.iacr.org/2018/712

[BBF19] Boneh, D., Bünz, B., Fisch, B.: Batching techniques for accumulators with applications to IOPs and stateless blockchains. In: Boldyreva, A., Micciancio, D. (eds.) CRYPTO 2019. LNCS, vol. 11692, pp. 561–586. Springer, Cham (2019). https://doi.org/10.1007/978-3-030-26948-7_20

[Bd94] Benaloh, J., de Mare, M.: One-way accumulators: a decentralized alternative to digital signatures (Extended Abstract). In: Helleseth, T. (ed.) EUROCRYPT 1993. LNCS, vol. 765, pp. 274–285. Springer, Heidelberg (1994). https://doi.org/10.1007/3-540-48285-7_24

[BGR12] Brogle, K., Goldberg, S., Reyzin, L.: Sequential aggregate signatures with lazy verification from trapdoor permutations (Extended Abstract). In: Wang, X., Sako, K. (eds.) ASIACRYPT 2012. LNCS, vol. 7658, pp. 644–662. Springer, Heidelberg (2012). https://doi.org/10.1007/978-3-642-34961-4_39

[BH01]   Buchmann, J., Hamdy, S.: A Survey on IQ Cryptography (2001)

[BP97]   Barić, N., Pfitzmann, B.: Collision-free accumulators and fail-stop signature schemes without trees. In: Fumy, W. (ed.) EUROCRYPT 1997. LNCS, vol. 1233, pp. 480–494. Springer, Heidelberg (1997). https://doi.org/10.1007/3-540-69053-0_33

[CF13]   Catalano, D., Fiore, D.: Vector commitments and their applications. In: Kurosawa, K., Hanaoka, G. (eds.) PKC 2013. LNCS, vol. 7778, pp. 55–72. Springer, Heidelberg (2013). https://doi.org/10.1007/978-3-642-36362-7_5

[CL02]   Camenisch, J., Lysyanskaya, A.: Dynamic accumulators and application to efficient revocation of anonymous credentials. In: Yung, M. (ed.) CRYPTO 2002. LNCS, vol. 2442, pp. 61–76. Springer, Heidelberg (2002). https://doi.org/10.1007/3-540-45708-9_5

[CMS99] Cachin, C., Micali, S., Stadler, M.: Computationally private information retrieval with polylogarithmic communication. In: Stern, J. (ed.) EUROCRYPT 1999. LNCS, vol. 1592, pp. 402–414. Springer, Heidelberg (1999). https://doi.org/10.1007/3-540-48910-X_28

[CS99]   Cramer, R., Shoup, V.: Signature schemes based on the strong RSA assumption. In: Motiwalla, J., Tsudik, G. (eds.) ACM CCS 1999, pp. 46–51. ACM Press, November 1999

[CSWH01] Clarke, I., Sandberg, O., Wiley, B., Hong, T.W.: Freenet: a distributed anonymous information storage and retrieval system. In: Federrath, H. (ed.) Designing Privacy Enhancing Technologies. LNCS, vol. 2009, pp. 46–66. Springer, Heidelberg (2001). https://doi.org/10.1007/3-540-44702-4_4

[DG20]   Dobson, S., Galbraith, S.D.: Trustless Groups of Unknown Order with Hyperelliptic Curves. Cryptology ePrint Archive, Report 2020/196 (2020). https://eprint.iacr.org/2020/196

[DK02]   Damgård, I., Koprowski, M.: Generic lower bounds for root extraction and signature schemes in general groups. In: Knudsen, L.R. (ed.) EUROCRYPT 2002. LNCS, vol. 2332, pp. 256–271. Springer, Heidelberg (2002). https://doi.org/10.1007/3-540-46035-7_17

[Fis18] Fisch, B.: PoReps: Proofs of Space on Useful Data. Cryptology ePrint Archive, Report 2018/678 (2018). https://eprint.iacr.org/2018/678

[GHR99] Gennaro, R., Halevi, S., Rabin, T.: Secure hash-and-sign signatures without the random oracle. In: Stern, J. (ed.) EUROCRYPT 1999. LNCS, vol. 1592, pp. 123–139. Springer, Heidelberg (1999). https://doi.org/10.1007/3-540-48910-X_9

[GKM+18] Groth, J., Kohlweiss, M., Maller, M., Meiklejohn, S., Miers, I.: Updatable and universal common reference strings with applications to zk-SNARKs. In: Shacham, H., Boldyreva, A. (eds.) CRYPTO 2018. LNCS, vol. 10993, pp. 698–728. Springer, Cham (2018). https://doi.org/10.1007/978-3-319-96878-0_24

[GRWZ20] Gorbunov, S., Reyzin, L., Wee, H., Zhang, Z.: Pointproofs: Aggregating Proofs for Multiple Vector Commitments. Cryptology ePrint Archive, Report 2020/419 (2020). https://eprint.iacr.org/2020/419

[JK07]   Juels, A., Kaliski Jr, B.S.: PORs: proofs of retrievability for large files. In: Ning, P., De Capitani di Vimercati, S., Syverson, P.F. (eds.) ACM CCS 2007, pp. 584–597. ACM Press, October 2007

[KZG10]   Kate, A., Zaverucha, G.M., Goldberg, I.: Constant-size commitments to polynomials and their applications. In: Abe, M. (ed.) ASIACRYPT 2010. LNCS, vol. 6477, pp. 177–194. Springer, Heidelberg (2010). https://doi.org/10.1007/978-3-642-17373-8_11

[Lab17]   Labs, P.: Filecoin: A Decentralized Storage Network (2017). https://filecoin.io/filecoin.pdf

[Lip12]   Lipmaa, H.: Secure accumulators from Euclidean rings without trusted setup. In: Bao, F., Samarati, P., Zhou, J. (eds.) ACNS 2012. LNCS, vol. 7341, pp. 224–240. Springer, Heidelberg (2012). https://doi.org/10.1007/978-3-642-31284-7_14

[LM19]   Lai, R.W.F., Malavolta, G.: Subvector commitments with application to succinct arguments. In: Boldyreva, A., Micciancio, D. (eds.) CRYPTO 2019. LNCS, vol. 11692, pp. 530–560. Springer, Cham (2019). https://doi.org/10.1007/978-3-030-26948-7_19

[LMRS04]   Lysyanskaya, A., Micali, S., Reyzin, L., Shacham, H.: Sequential aggregate signatures from trapdoor permutations. In: Cachin, C., Camenisch, J.L. (eds.) EUROCRYPT 2004. LNCS, vol. 3027, pp. 74–90. Springer, Heidelberg (2004). https://doi.org/10.1007/978-3-540-24676-3_5

[LRY16]   Libert, B., Ramanna, S.C., Yung, M.: Functional commitment schemes: from polynomial commitments to pairing-based accumulators from simple assumptions. In: Chatzigiannakis, I., Mitzenmacher, M., Rabani, Y., Sangiorgi, D. (eds.) ICALP 2016, LIPIcs, vol. 55, pp. 30:1–30:14. Schloss Dagstuhl, July 2016

[LY10]   Libert, B., Yung, M.: Concise mercurial vector commitments and independent zero-knowledge sets with short proofs. In: Micciancio, D. (ed.) TCC 2010. LNCS, vol. 5978, pp. 499–517. Springer, Heidelberg (2010). https://doi.org/10.1007/978-3-642-11799-2_30

[Mer88]   Merkle, R.C.: A digital signature based on a conventional encryption function. In: Pomerance, C. (ed.) CRYPTO 1987. LNCS, vol. 293, pp. 369–378. Springer, Heidelberg (1988). https://doi.org/10.1007/3-540-48184-2_32

[OWB19]   Ozdemir, A., Wahby, R.S., Boneh, D.: Scaling Verifiable Computation Using Efficient Set Accumulators. Cryptology ePrint Archive, Report 2019/1494 (2019). https://eprint.iacr.org/2019/1494

[Sha83]   Shamir, A.: On the generation of cryptographically strong pseudorandom sequences. ACM Trans. Comput. Syst. 1(1), 38–44 (1983)

[TAB+20]   Tomescu, A., Abraham, I., Buterin, V., Drake, J., Feist, D., Khovratovich, D.: Aggregatable Subvector Commitments for Stateless Cryptocurrencies. Cryptology ePrint Archive, Report 2020/527 (2020). https://eprint.iacr.org/2020/527

[Tam03]   Tamassia, R.: Authenticated data structures. In: Di Battista, G., Zwick, U. (eds.) ESA 2003. LNCS, vol. 2832, pp. 2–5. Springer, Heidelberg (2003). https://doi.org/10.1007/978-3-540-39658-1_2

[Wes18]   Wesolowski, B.: Efficient verifiable delay functions. Cryptology ePrint Archive, Report 2018/623 (2018). https://eprint.iacr.org/2018/623

Non-committing Encryption
with Constant Ciphertext Expansion
from Standard Assumptions

Yusuke Yoshida[1]($\boxtimes$), Fuyuki Kitagawa[2], Keita Xagawa[2], and Keisuke Tanaka[1]

[1] Tokyo Institute of Technology, Tokyo, Japan
yoshida.y.aw@m.titech.ac.jp, keisuke@is.titech.ac.jp
[2] NTT Secure Platform Laboratories, Tokyo, Japan
fuyuki.kitagawa.yh@hco.ntt.co.jp, keita.xagawa.zv@hco.ntt.co.jp

Abstract. Non-committing encryption (NCE) introduced by Canetti et al. (STOC '96) is a central tool to achieve multi-party computation protocols secure in the adaptive setting. Recently, Yoshida et al. (ASIACRYPT '19) proposed an NCE scheme based on the hardness of the DDH problem, which has ciphertext expansion $\mathcal{O}(\log \lambda)$ and public-key expansion $\mathcal{O}(\lambda^2)$.

In this work, we improve their result and propose a methodology to construct an NCE scheme that achieves *constant* ciphertext expansion. Our methodology can be instantiated from the DDH assumption and the LWE assumption. When instantiated from the LWE assumption, the public-key expansion is $\lambda \cdot \text{poly}(\log \lambda)$. They are the first NCE schemes satisfying constant ciphertext expansion without using iO or common reference strings.

Along the way, we define a weak notion of NCE, which satisfies only weak forms of correctness and security. We show how to amplify such a weak NCE scheme into a full-fledged one using wiretap codes with a new security property.

Keywords: Non-committing encryption · Wiretap codes · Learning with errors

1 Introduction

1.1 Background

In secure multi-party computation (MPC) protocols, a group of parties can compute some function of their private inputs by communicating with each other. Depending on when corrupted parties are determined, two types of adversarial settings called static and adaptive have been considered for MPC. In the static setting, an adversary is required to declare which parties it corrupts before the protocol starts. On the other hand, in the adaptive setting, an adversary can choose which parties to corrupt on the fly, and thus the corruption pattern can

S. Moriai and H. Wang (Eds.): ASIACRYPT 2020, LNCS 12492, pp. 36–65, 2020.
https://doi.org/10.1007/978-3-030-64834-3_2

depend on the messages exchanged during the protocol. Security guarantee in the adaptive setting is more desirable than that in the static setting since the former naturally captures adversarial behaviors in the real world while the latter is somewhat artificial.

Beaver and Haber [3] showed if honest parties are assumed to be able to erase sensitive local information completely, then adaptively secure MPC can be obtained efficiently. However, as discussed by Canetti et al. [8], such trusted erasure may be unrealistic in many scenarios.

If private channels are provided between each pair of parties, information-theoretically secure MPC protocols such as those proposed by Ben-Or et al. [7] and Chaum et al. [12] are secure against adaptive adversaries.[1] In order to use those protocols in the actual usage scenarios, we have to simulate private channels by using encryption primitives. For this aim, *non-committing encryption (NCE)* was introduced by Canetti et al. [8]. Informally, an encryption scheme is said to be non-committing if it can generate a dummy ciphertext that is indistinguishable from real ones but can later be opened to any message by producing a secret key and encryption randomness that "explain" the ciphertext as an encryption of the message. Canetti et al. showed that the information-theoretically secure MPC protocols are still adaptively secure if private channels are replaced by NCE over insecure channels (assumed they are authenticated). Canetti, Lindell, Ostrovsky, and Sahai [9] also showed a slightly augmented version of NCE is useful to achieve adaptive security in the universally composable (UC) setting.

Prior Works on Non-committing Encryption. The ability to open a dummy ciphertext to any message is generally achieved at the price of efficiency. This is in contrast to the ordinary public-key encryption for which we can easily obtain schemes the size of whose ciphertext is $n + \mathsf{poly}(\lambda)$ by using hybrid encryption methodology, where n is the length of an encrypted message and λ is the security parameter. Thus, many previous works have focused on constructing efficient NCE schemes. Especially, they tried to improve *ciphertext expansion* which is the ratio of ciphertext length and message length since ciphertext length dominates the online communication complexity.

In literature, the term NCE was also used to indicate 3-round message transmission protocols which have the non-committing property [2,15]. In this work, we only focus on 2-round schemes, that is, public-key encryption with the non-committing property.

Canetti et al. [8] constructed the first NCE scheme, based on common-domain trapdoor permutations which can be instantiated from the computational Diffie-Hellman (CDH) or RSA problem. Ciphertext expansion of their scheme is $\mathcal{O}(\lambda^2)$.

Choi, Dachman-Soled, Malkin, and Wee [13] constructed an NCE scheme with ciphertext expansion $\mathcal{O}(\lambda)$ from trapdoor simulatable PKE. Their construction

---

[1] On the other hand, for the MPC protocols relying on complexity assumption such as the one proposed by Goldreich et al. [20], the security proof fails against an adaptive adversary as observed by Damgård and Nielsen [15].

can be instantiated under many computational problems including factoring problem, since many existing (ordinary) PKE schemes satisfy trapdoor simulatability.

The first NCE scheme with sub-linear ciphertext expansion was proposed by Hemenway, Ostrovsky, and Rosen [23]. They proposed an NCE scheme with ciphertext expansion $\mathcal{O}(\log n)$ for n-bit messages based on the Φ-hiding problem, which we can easily modify its ciphertext expansion to $\mathcal{O}(\log \lambda)$ by dividing long messages to λ-bit blocks. Hemenway, Ostrovsky, Richelson, and Rosen [22] also showed constructions of NCE with ciphertext expansion $\mathsf{poly}(\log \lambda)$ from the learning with errors (LWE) and Ring-LWE problems.

Canetti, Poburinnaya, and Raykova [10] studied the construction of NCE in the common reference strings (CRS) model. They achieved optimal ciphertext expansion $1 + o(1)$ assuming the existence of indistinguishability obfuscation (iO) and one-way function.

Recently, Yoshida, Kitagawa, and Tanaka [31] constructed an NCE scheme with ciphertext expansion $\mathcal{O}(\log \lambda)$ from a primitive called chameleon encryption (CE), which additionally satisfies oblivious sampleability. They showed an instantiation of obliviously sampleable CE based on the decisional Diffie-Hellman (DDH) problem.

1.2   Our Contribution

We propose the first NCE schemes with constant ciphertext expansion without the use of iO or CRS.

We construct such an NCE scheme based on the construction paradigm using obliviously sampleable CE proposed by Yoshida et al. [31]. Yoshida et al. showed obliviously sampleable CE can be realized based on the DDH problem. In this work, we also show that it can be realized based on the LWE problem for super-polynomially large modulus. As a result, we obtain constant ciphertext expansion NCE schemes based on the DDH problem and LWE problem.

One of the disadvantage of the NCE scheme proposed by Yoshida et al. is its relatively large public-key size. The size of public key for each message bit of their scheme is $\mathcal{O}(\lambda^2)$. In addition to the ciphertext expansion, our LWE based NCE scheme also improves public-key size compared to Yoshida et al.'s scheme. The size of the public key for each message bit of our LWE based scheme is $\lambda \cdot \mathsf{poly}(\log \lambda)$. This is the same as that of NCE scheme proposed by Hemenway et al. [22], which is also based on the LWE problem for super-polynomially large modulus. We provide a comparison between our NCE schemes and existing NCE schemes in Table 1.

1.3   Overview

Weak Non-committing Encryption. Our starting point is the observation that by adjusting the parameters of an intermediate version of Yoshida et al. 's NCE scheme, its ciphertext expansion can be reduced to a constant, at the cost of its perfect form of correctness and security.

Table 1. Comparison of existing (2-round) NCE schemes in terms of their ciphertext and public-key expansion. The security parameter is denoted by λ. [*] This scheme uses common reference strings.

	CT expansion	PK expansion	Assumption
Canetti et al. [8]	$\mathcal{O}(\lambda^2)$	$\mathcal{O}(\lambda^2)$	Common-Domain TDP (CDH, RSA)
Choi et al. [13]	$\mathcal{O}(\lambda)$	$\mathcal{O}(\lambda)$	Trapdoor Simulatable PKE (DDH etc.)
Hemenway et al. [23]	$\mathcal{O}(\log \lambda)$	$\lambda \cdot \mathrm{poly}(\log \lambda)$	Φ-hiding
Hemenway et al. [22]	$\mathrm{poly}(\log \lambda)$	$\lambda \cdot \mathrm{poly}(\log \lambda)$	LWE
Hemenway et al. [22]	$\mathrm{poly}(\log \lambda)$	$\mathrm{poly}(\log \lambda)$	Ring-LWE
Canetti et al. [10] [*]	$1 + o(1)$	$1 + o(1)$	Indistinguishability Obfuscation
Yoshida et al. [31]	$\mathcal{O}(\log \lambda)$	$\mathcal{O}(\lambda^2)$	Obliviously Sampleable CE (DDH)
This work	$\mathcal{O}(1)$	$\mathcal{O}(\lambda^2)$	Obliviously Sampleable CE (DDH)
This work	$\mathcal{O}(1)$	$\lambda \cdot \mathrm{poly}(\log \lambda)$	Obliviously Sampleable CE (LWE)

Specifically, the scheme only satisfies *weak correctness*, which means that each bit of decrypted plaintext is flipped with constant probability. Moreover, the scheme only satisfies *weak security* that only guarantees the secrecy of some part of encrypted plaintexts. In Sect. 3, we formally define weak correctness and weak security for NCE and introduce the notion of *weak NCE* as NCE satisfying only those weak correctness and weak security.

In Sect. 5, we give the description of the above scheme and its building block, obliviously sampleable CE. Then we prove that the scheme is indeed a weak NCE scheme.

Amplification for Non-committing Encryption. Next, we show that we can amplify a weak NCE scheme into a full-fledged NCE scheme in Sect. 4. As a tool of amplification, we use a coding scheme called *wiretap codes*. More specifically, we define a new security property, *conditional invertibility* for wiretap codes. We show an instantiation of wiretap codes constructed from randomness extractor and linear error-correcting codes satisfies the conditional invertibility.

This amplification increases the ciphertext expansion by only a constant factor. Thus, by applying this transformation to the weak NCE scheme shown in Sect. 5, we obtain an NCE scheme with a constant ciphertext expansion.

Lattice-Based Instantiation. We propose a lattice-based instantiation of obliviously sampleable CE in Sect. 6. The construction is a natural composition of the lattice-based hash encryption by Döttling et al. [17] and the lattice-based chameleon hash functions by Cash et al. [11].

One caveat of our construction is that we need the modulus of lattices to be super-polynomially large for the correctness of it. This seems unavoidable since the chameleon encryption implies non-interactive key exchange, which is considered difficult to be realized from lattice problems for polynomially large modulus as discussed by Guo et al. [21].

1.4   Related Works on Amplification for Public-Key Encryption

Studies on security amplification have asked and answered the question: "How far can we weaken a security definition so that schemes satisfying the definition can still be transformed into those satisfying full-fledged security?" Dwork, Naor, and Reingold [18] first studied the amplification of public-key encryption. They showed that a public-key encryption scheme that satisfies weak forms of one-wayness and correctness can be transformed into one satisfies the ordinary correctness and IND-CPA security. Holenstein and Renner [24] showed a more efficient amplification method, starting from a scheme satisfying weak forms of IND-CPA security and correctness. Lin and Tessaro [26] provided an amplification method for schemes with IND-CCA security. In this work, we show an amplification method for NCE, which can be seen as one of this line of research.

2   Preliminaries

Notations. In this paper, PPT denotes probabilistic polynomial time. $x \leftarrow X$ denotes an element x is sampled from uniform distribution over a set X. $y \leftarrow A(x; r)$ denotes A given input x, using internal randomness r, outputs y. $f(\lambda) = \mathsf{negl}(\lambda)$ denotes function f is negligible, that is, $f(\lambda) = 2^{-\omega(\log \lambda)}$ holds.

For an integer n, $[n]$ denotes a set $\{1, \ldots, n\}$. For a subset $\mathcal{I} \subset [n]$ and a vector $x = (x_i)_{1 \leq i \leq n} \in \{0,1\}^n$, $x_{\mathcal{I}}$ denotes $(x_i)_{i \in \mathcal{I}}$. For a matrix $M = (m_i)_{1 \leq i \leq n} \in \{0,1\}^{k \times n}$, $M_{\mathcal{I}} \in \{0,1\}^{k \times |\mathcal{I}|}$ denotes the matrix composed from column vectors m_i of M for $i \in \mathcal{I}$.

$h_2(\cdot)$ denotes the binary entropy function, $h_2(p) = -p \log p - (1-p) \log(1-p)$. $H(Y|X)$ denotes the conditional entropy.

Lemma 1 (Chernoff Bound). *Let X be a binomial random variable. If* $\mathbb{E}[X] \leq \mu$, *then for all $\delta > 0$*, $\Pr[X \geq (1+\delta)\mu)] \leq e^{-\frac{\delta^2}{2+\delta}\mu}$ *holds.*

Lemma 2 (Leftover hash lemma). *Let $\mathcal{H} := \{h : \{0,1\}^n \to \{0,1\}^\ell\}$ be a universal hash family. If $\ell \leq \mathbf{H}_\infty(x) - \omega(\log \lambda)$, $(h, h(x))$ and (h, u) are statistically indistinguishable where $u \leftarrow \{0,1\}^\ell$.*

Channel Model. When a sender transmits a message $x \in \{0,1\}^n$ through a channel ChR, the receiver gets a noisy version of the message $\tilde{x} \in \{0,1,\perp\}^n$. We define the procedure of such channels as probabilistic functions, $\tilde{x} \leftarrow \mathsf{ChR}(x; r_{ch})$. We review two channel models, Binary Erasure Channel (BEC) and Binary Symmetric Channel (BSC).

Let $\mathcal{B}_p^n$ be the n-bit Bernoulli distribution with parameter p. In other words, $r_{ch} \leftarrow \mathcal{B}_p^n$ is an n-bit string where for each $i \in [n]$, $\Pr[r_{ch_i} = 1] = p$ and $\Pr[r_{ch_i} = 0] = 1 - p$.

Definition 1 (Binary Erasure Channel (BEC)). *Through a binary erasure channel BEC_p, each bit of input $x \in \{0,1\}^n$ is erased with probability p.*

$\mathsf{BEC}_p(x; r_{ch})$ samples randomness $r_{ch} \leftarrow \mathcal{B}_p^n$. Output of the channel is $\tilde{x}$ where $\tilde{x}_i = \perp$ if $r_{ch_i} = 1$ and $\tilde{x}_i = x_i$ if $r_{ch_i} = 0$.

We also denote the output of BEC by $x_{\mathcal{I}} \leftarrow \mathsf{BEC}_p(x; r_{\mathsf{ch}})$ where $\mathcal{I} = \{i \in [n] \mid r_{\mathsf{ch}i} = 0\}$ is the set of non-erased indices.

Definition 2 (Binary Symmetric Channel (BSC)). *Through a binary symmetric channel* BSC_p, *each bit of input* $x \in \{0,1\}^n$ *is flipped with probability* p. BSC_p *samples randomness* $r_{\mathsf{ch}} \leftarrow \mathcal{B}_p^n$. *Output of the channel is* $\tilde{x} = x \oplus r_{\mathsf{ch}}$.

We denote by $\mathsf{BEC}_{\leq p}$, a binary symmetric channel with parameter $p' \leq p$.

3 (Weak) Non-committing Encryption

A non-committing encryption (NCE) scheme is a public-key encryption (PKE) scheme that has efficient simulator algorithms $(\mathsf{Sim}, \mathsf{Open})$ satisfying the following properties. The simulator Sim can generate a simulated public key pk and a simulated ciphertext CT. Later Open can explain the ciphertext CT as encryption of any message. Concretely, given a message m, Open can output a pair of randomness for key generation r_{Gen} and encryption r_{Enc}, as if pk was generated by the key generation algorithm with the randomness r_{Gen}, and CT is an encryption of m with the randomness r_{Enc}.

Some previous works proposed NCE schemes that are three-round protocols [2,15]. In this work, we focus on NCE that needs only two rounds, which is also called non-committing public-key encryption, and we use the term NCE to indicate it unless stated otherwise.

In this work, we abstract the intermediate construction of NCE by Yoshida et al. [31] and formalize it as weak NCE. Specifically, we introduce weak correctness and weak security for NCE.

Syntax. Since an NCE scheme is public-key encryption, we recall its syntax.

Definition 3 (Public-Key Encryption). *A PKE scheme consists of the following PPT algorithms* $(\mathsf{Gen}, \mathsf{Enc}, \mathsf{Dec})$.

- $\mathsf{Gen}\left(1^\lambda; r_{\mathsf{Gen}}\right)$: *Given the security parameter* 1^λ, *using a randomness* r_{Gen}, *it outputs a public key* pk *and a secret key* sk.
- $\mathsf{Enc}\left(pk, m; r_{\mathsf{Enc}}\right)$: *Given a public key* pk *and a plaintext* $m \in \{0,1\}^\mu$, *using a randomness* r_{Enc}, *it outputs a ciphertext* CT.
- $\mathsf{Dec}\left(sk, CT\right)$: *Given a secret key* sk *and a ciphertext* CT, *it outputs* m *or* $\perp$.

Public-Key/Ciphertext Expansion. Public-key expansion and ciphertext expansion of a public-key encryption scheme are defined by $|pk|/|m|$ and $|CT|/|m|$, respectively, for $|m| = \mathsf{poly}(\lambda)$.

Correctness. Since the ordinary correctness can be seen as a special case of weak correctness, we first introduce the notion of weak correctness and then define correctness. Informally, we say that a PKE scheme is weakly correct if it has decryption error for each message bit as defined below.

Definition 4 ((Weak) Correctness). *We say that a PKE scheme* NCE = (Gen, Enc, Dec) *is weakly correct if it has non-negligible decryption error for each plaintext bit. Specifically, we say that* NCE *has ϵ-decryption error if for all plaintext $m \in \{0,1\}^\mu$ and $i \in [\mu]$,*

$$\Pr\left[m_i \neq \mathsf{Dec}\left(sk, \mathsf{Enc}\left(pk, m; r_{\mathsf{Enc}}\right)\right)_i\right] \leq \epsilon$$

holds, where $(pk, sk) \leftarrow \mathsf{Gen}\left(1^\lambda; r_{\mathsf{Gen}}\right)$ and the probability is taken over the choice of r_{Gen} and r_{Enc}. In other words, the procedure of encryption and decryption works as the binary symmetric channel

$$\mathsf{Dec}(sk, \mathsf{Enc}(pk, \cdot\,)) = \mathsf{BSC}_{\leq \epsilon}(\cdot).$$

Furthermore, we say that NCE *satisfies correctness if $\epsilon = \mathsf{negl}(\lambda)$.*

Security. We first introduce the notion of weak security. We then recall the ordinary security of NCE.

Weak security allows an adversary to learn some partial information of a plaintext $\mathsf{Leak}(m)$. Still, it guarantees that other information of m remains hidden. Furthermore, in the security experiment of weak security, the challenge message is fixed in advance independently of the public key.

Definition 5 (Weak Security for NCE). *For a PKE scheme* NCE = (Gen, Enc, Dec) *and a probabilistic function* Leak, *consider the following PPT simulators* (SimGen, SimEnc, Open):

- SimGen $\left(1^\lambda\right)$: *Given the security parameter 1^λ, it outputs a simulated public key pk and its internal state information st_1.*
- SimEnc($\tilde{m} \leftarrow \mathsf{Leak}(m; r), st_1$): *Given a partial information of a plaintext $\tilde{m}$ which is computed by the probabilistic function* Leak *with randomness r, and a state st_1, it outputs a simulated ciphertext CT and a state st_2.*
- Open(m, r, st_2): *Given a plaintext m, randomness r used by* Leak, *and a state st_2, it outputs randomness for key generation r_{Gen} and encryption r_{Enc}.*

For an adversary $\mathcal{A}$ and a message m, define two experiments as follows.

$\mathsf{Exp}_{\mathsf{NCE}, \mathcal{A}}^{Weak\ Real}$	$\mathsf{Exp}_{\mathsf{NCE}, \mathcal{A}}^{Weak\ Ideal}$
$(pk, sk) \leftarrow \mathsf{Gen}\left(1^\lambda; r_{\mathsf{Gen}}\right)$	$(pk, st_1) \leftarrow \mathsf{SimGen}\left(1^\lambda\right)$
$CT \leftarrow \mathsf{Enc}\left(pk, m; r_{\mathsf{Enc}}\right)$	$(CT, st_2) \leftarrow \mathsf{SimEnc}(\mathsf{Leak}(m; r), st_1)$
	$(r_{\mathsf{Gen}}, r_{\mathsf{Enc}}) \leftarrow \mathsf{Open}(m, r, st_2)$
$\mathsf{out} \leftarrow \mathcal{A}\left(pk, CT, r_{\mathsf{Gen}}, r_{\mathsf{Enc}}\right)$	$\mathsf{out} \leftarrow \mathcal{A}\left(pk, CT, r_{\mathsf{Gen}}, r_{\mathsf{Enc}}\right)$

We say that NCE *is weakly secure with respect to* Leak *if there exist PPT simulators* (SimGen, SimEnc, Open) *such that for any PPT adversary* $\mathcal{A}$ *and any message* m,

$$\mathsf{Adv}_{\mathrm{NCE},\mathcal{A}}^{Weak}(\lambda) := \left| \Pr\left[\mathsf{out} = 1 \ in \ \mathsf{Exp}_{\mathrm{NCE},\mathcal{A}}^{Weak \ Real} \right] - \Pr\left[\mathsf{out} = 1 \ in \ \mathsf{Exp}_{\mathrm{NCE},\mathcal{A}}^{Weak \ Ideal} \right] \right|$$
$$= \mathsf{negl}(\lambda)$$

holds.

Weak security with respect to Leak $= \bot$ in which the target message is chosen by the adversary is exactly the same notion as the full-fledged security for NCE which we recall below.

Definition 6 (Security for NCE). *For a PKE scheme* NCE $=$ (Gen, Enc, Dec), *consider the following PPT simulators* (Sim, Open):

- Sim (1^λ): *Given the security parameter* 1^λ, *it outputs a simulated public key* pk, *a simulated ciphertext* CT *and its state* st.
- Open(m, st): *Given a message* m *and a state* st, *it outputs randomness for key generation* r_{Gen} *and encryption* r_{Enc}.

For a stateful adversary $\mathcal{A}$, *we define two experiments as follows.*

$\mathsf{Exp}_{\mathrm{NCE},\mathcal{A}}^{Real}$	$\mathsf{Exp}_{\mathrm{NCE},\mathcal{A}}^{Ideal}$
$(pk, sk) \leftarrow \mathsf{Gen}\left(1^\lambda; r_{\mathsf{Gen}}\right)$	$(pk, CT, st) \leftarrow \mathsf{Sim}\left(1^\lambda\right)$
$m \leftarrow \mathcal{A}(pk)$	$m \leftarrow \mathcal{A}(pk)$
$CT \leftarrow \mathsf{Enc}(pk, m; r_{\mathsf{Enc}})$	$(r_{\mathsf{Gen}}, r_{\mathsf{Enc}}) \leftarrow \mathsf{Open}(m, st)$
$\mathsf{out} \leftarrow \mathcal{A}(CT, r_{\mathsf{Gen}}, r_{\mathsf{Enc}})$	$\mathsf{out} \leftarrow \mathcal{A}(CT, r_{\mathsf{Gen}}, r_{\mathsf{Enc}})$

We say that NCE *is secure if there exist PPT simulators* (Sim, Open) *such that for all PPT adversary* $\mathcal{A}$,

$$\mathsf{Adv}_{\mathrm{NCE},\mathcal{A}}(\lambda) := \left| \Pr\left[\mathsf{out} = 1 \ in \ \mathsf{Exp}_{\mathrm{NCE},\mathcal{A}}^{Real} \right] - \Pr\left[\mathsf{out} = 1 \ in \ \mathsf{Exp}_{\mathrm{NCE},\mathcal{A}}^{Ideal} \right] \right| = \mathsf{negl}(\lambda)$$

holds.

Definition 7 ((Weak) Non-Committing Encryption). *Let* NCE *be a PKE scheme.* NCE *is said to be NCE if it satisfies the above correctness and security for NCE. Also,* NCE *is said to be weak NCE if it satisfies the above weak correctness and weak security for NCE.*

4   Amplification for Non-committing Encryption

When weak NCE is used to communicate, roughly speaking, the receiver gets a noisy version of the transmitted message x, and the adversary can see some partial information of x. In fact, such a situation is very natural and studied as physical layer security in the Information and Coding (I&C) community since the wiretap channel model was proposed by Wyner [30]. Based on this observation, in this section, we show how to amplify a weak NCE scheme into a full-fledged one by using *wiretap codes*.[2]

4.1   Wiretap Codes

As described in Fig. 1, when the sender transmits a message x over the wiretap channel, on one hand, the receiver gets the message affected by noise over receiver channel $\mathsf{ChR}(x)$. On the other hand, an adversary can interrupt the transmission and gets a noisier version of the message $\mathsf{ChA}(x)$.

In such a model, using the difference in the amount of noise the receiver and the adversary are affected, wiretap codes WC enable us to transmit a message m correctly to the receiver while keeping it information-theoretically secure against the adversary.

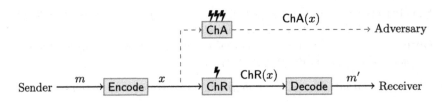

Fig. 1. Wiretap channel model.

Wiretap codes have an encoding and a decoding algorithm similar to error-correcting codes. Wiretap codes satisfy two properties. One is correctness, which ensures that the receiver can decode codewords even if they are affected by some amount of noise. The other is security, which guarantees that the adversary can get no information about the message given some part of the codeword. It is known that the encoding algorithm must use randomness to satisfy security.

Originally in the I&C community, the security of wiretap codes was defined by mutual information. Bellare et al. [4–6] proposed several equivalent definitions in a cryptographic manner. Among them, we recall one adopting the distinguishing style of security below. Then we proposed a new security property, *conditional invertibility* for wiretap codes, which we need in the security proof of our amplification for NCE.

Note that the following definition adopts the seeded version of wiretap codes also proposed by Bellare et al. [6]. In the seeded wiretap channel, the sender, receiver, and an adversary can see a public random seed. We adopt the seeded wiretap codes to give a simple construction of the codes. The seed can be removed without increasing the rate of the codes by a transformation shown in [4]. In this work, we put the seed into a part of the public key when constructing NCE.

---

[2] In literature, wiretap codes sometimes appeared in the name of "encryption" or "one-way secret-key agreement". It can be also interpreted as a kind of secret sharing scheme.

Definition 8 (Wiretap Codes). *(Seeded) wiretap codes* WC *consist of the following PPT algorithms* (WC.Setup, WC.Encode, WC.Decode).

- WC.Setup(1^λ): Given the security parameter 1^λ, it samples a public seed p.
- WC.Encode($p, m; s$): It encodes a message $m \in \{0,1\}^\mu$ with a public seed p and randomness $s \leftarrow \mathbf{S}$, and outputs a codeword $x \in \{0,1\}^n$.
- WC.Decode(p, x): On input a noisy codeword $x \in \{0,1\}^n$ and a public seed p, it outputs a message m.

Rate of Wiretap Codes. The rate of WC is the length of messages over the length of codewords $\mu/n \in (0,1)$. The rate of WC is at most the secrecy capacity of the wiretap channel. The secrecy capacity of wiretap channel, defined with symmetric channels ChR and ChA, is equal to $H(U|\mathsf{ChA}(U)) - H(U|\mathsf{ChR}(U))$ for a uniformly random bit U [25], where $H(Y|X)$ denotes the conditional entropy.

Usually, wiretap codes are required to satisfy the following correctness and security.

As a security property, we present a definition of distinguishing security adopted for seeded wiretap codes. This is a natural extension of the distinguishing security for seedless wiretap codes proposed by Bellare et al. [6].

Correctness: WC is correct over the receiver's channel ChR if for all message $m \in \{0,1\}^\mu$ and public seed p, we have

$$\Pr[\mathsf{WC.Decode}(p, \mathsf{ChR}(\mathsf{WC.Encode}(p, m))) \neq m] = \mathsf{negl}(\lambda) \ .$$

Security: WC is DS-secure against adversary's channel ChA if for any unbounded stateful adversary $\mathcal{A}$, we have

$$\left| \Pr\left[b = b' \ \middle| \ \begin{array}{l} p \leftarrow \mathsf{WC.Setup}(1^\lambda), (m_0, m_1) = \mathcal{A}(p), \\ b \leftarrow \{0,1\}, x \leftarrow \mathsf{WC.Encode}(p, m_b), \\ \tilde{x} \leftarrow \mathsf{ChA}(x; r_{\mathsf{ch}}), \\ b' = \mathcal{A}(\tilde{x}) \end{array} \right] - \frac{1}{2} \right| = \mathsf{negl}(\lambda) \ .$$

Next, we introduce a new security property for wiretap codes, *conditional invertibility*.

Intuitively, this security notion states that after the adversary sees the partial information $\tilde{x} \leftarrow \mathsf{ChA}(x)$ resulted from the codeword x of a message m', we can efficiently explain that $\tilde{x}$ has resulted from another message m. The security definition involves a PPT inversion algorithm WC.Invert, which on inputs seed p, a condition $\tilde{x}$, and a message m, outputs randomness s' and r_{ch}' such that $\mathsf{ChA}(\mathsf{WC.Encode}(p, m; s'); r_{\mathsf{ch}}')$ is equal to the condition $\tilde{x}$.

Conditional invertibility implies the ordinary distinguishing security. It can be seen as non-committing security for wiretap codes. Note that wiretap codes are inherently non-committing in the sense that they usually required to statistically lose the information of messages. Thus, the only point conditional invertibility additionally requires is that the inversion can be computed efficiently.

Definition 9 (Conditional Invertibility). *For an unbounded stateful adversary $\mathcal{A}$ and a PPT algorithm* WC.Invert, *define two experiments as follows:*

$\mathsf{Exp}_{\mathsf{WC},\mathcal{A}}^{Real}$	$\mathsf{Exp}_{\mathsf{WC},\mathcal{A}}^{Ideal}$
$p \leftarrow \mathsf{WC.Setup}(1^\lambda)$	$p \leftarrow \mathsf{WC.Setup}(1^\lambda)$
$(m, m') = \mathcal{A}(p)$	$(m, m') = \mathcal{A}(p)$
$x \leftarrow \mathsf{WC.Encode}(p, m; s)$	$x \leftarrow \mathsf{WC.Encode}(p, m'; s)$
$\tilde{x} \leftarrow \mathsf{ChA}(x; r_{\mathsf{ch}})$	$\tilde{x} \leftarrow \mathsf{ChA}(x; r_{\mathsf{ch}})$
	$(s', r_{\mathsf{ch}}') \leftarrow \mathsf{WC.Invert}(p, \tilde{x}, m)$
$\mathsf{out} = \mathcal{A}(\tilde{x}, s, r_{\mathsf{ch}})$	$\mathsf{out} = \mathcal{A}(\tilde{x}, s', r_{\mathsf{ch}}')$

We say that WC *is invertible conditioned on* ChA *if there exists a PPT inverter* WC.Invert *such that for any unbounded adversary $\mathcal{A}$,*

$$\left| \Pr\left[\mathsf{out} = 1 \ in \ \mathsf{Exp}_{\mathsf{WC},\mathcal{A}}^{Real} \right] - \Pr\left[\mathsf{out} = 1 \ in \ \mathsf{Exp}_{\mathsf{WC},\mathcal{A}}^{Ideal} \right] \right| = \mathsf{negl}(\lambda)$$

holds.

4.2 Instantiation of Wiretap Codes

Overview. We recall a modular construction of wiretap codes proposed by Bellare et al. [6] called Invert-then-Encode construction. The building blocks are error-correcting codes and invertible extractors. This idea of composing error-correcting codes and extractors can be found also in the construction of a linear secret sharing scheme proposed by Cramer et al. [14].

Consider an seeded extractor $\mathsf{Ext} : \{0, 1\}^k \to \{0, 1\}^\mu$ which on inputs $X \in \{0, 1\}^k$ and a seed p, outputs $m \in \{0, 1\}^\mu$. The extractor is *invertible* if there is an efficient inverter Inv, which on inputs $m \in \{0, 1\}^\mu$ and seed p, samples a preimage $X \in \{0, 1\}^k$ using randomness s. The Invert-then-Encode construction takes input m with seed p, first inverts the extractor $X \leftarrow \mathsf{Inv}(m, p; s)$, then encodes X by the error-correcting code as $x = \mathsf{Encode}(X)$.

For a concrete instantiation, Bellare et al. suggested to use the polar codes [1] as error-correcting codes to achieve the optimal rate. Note that we can compute the encoding of input m by mG where G is a generator matrix of the linear error-correcting code. Invertible extractors can be instantiated using multiplication over $\mathrm{GF}(2^k)$. Concretely, the extractor takes inputs $x \in \{0, 1\}^k$ and seed $p \in \mathrm{GF}(2^k)$, and outputs the first μ bit of $x \odot p$, where $\odot$ denotes multiplication over $\mathrm{GF}(2^k)$. The inverter Inv for this extractor is obtained by $\mathsf{Inv}(m, p; s) = (m\|s) \odot p^{-1}$.

Construction. We describe the construction of wiretap codes for $\mu = \mathcal{O}(\lambda)$ bit messages. For a longer message, we can encode it by first dividing it into blocks of μ bit and then encoding each block by the following codes (see [4]).

Let $\mu, k, n = \mathcal{O}(\lambda)$. Let $G \in \{0,1\}^{k \times n}$ be a generator matrix of a linear error-correcting code, and ECC.Decode a corresponding decoding algorithm. Choose a constant $\epsilon > 0$ such that the error-correcting code can be correct over $\mathsf{ChR} = \mathsf{BSC}_{\leq \epsilon}$. We construct wiretap codes which is correct over $\mathsf{ChR} = \mathsf{BSC}_{\leq \epsilon}$ and invertible conditioned on $\mathsf{ChA} = \mathsf{BEC}_{0.5}$. Thus, in this construction, the wiretap decoding algorithm takes as input $x' \leftarrow \mathsf{BSC}_\epsilon(x)$, and the wiretap inverter algorithm takes as input $x_\mathcal{I} \leftarrow \mathsf{BEC}_{0.5}(x; r_{\mathsf{ch}})$ where $\mathcal{I} \in [n]$ is the set of non-erased indices determined by a uniformly random n-bit string r_{ch}.

- WC.Setup(1^λ): Sample and output $p \leftarrow \mathsf{GF}(2^k) \backslash \{0\}$.
- WC.Encode$(p, m; s)$: For input $m \in \{0,1\}^\mu$, sample $s \leftarrow \{0,1\}^{k-\mu}$, output $x = ((m \| s) \odot p)G \in \{0,1\}^n$.
- WC.Decode(p, x'): Output the first μ bits of ECC.Decode$(x') \odot p^{-1}$.
- WC.Invert$(p, x_\mathcal{I}, m)$: On input a condition $x_\mathcal{I} \leftarrow \mathsf{BEC}_{0.5}(x; r_{\mathsf{ch}})$, sample and output s' which satisfies $x_\mathcal{I} = ((m \| s') \odot p)G_\mathcal{I}$.
  Concretely, let $\sum_i z_i c_i + c_0$ $(c_i \in \{0,1\}^k, z_i \in \{0,1\})$ be the general solution of linear equation $x_\mathcal{I} = y G_\mathcal{I}$. Then, uniformly sample a solution $\{z_i\}_i$ of linear equation $m = \sum_i z_i (c_i \odot p^{-1})_{\{1,\ldots,\mu\}} + (c_0 \odot p^{-1})_{\{1,\ldots,\mu\}}$. Finally, output $s' = \sum_i z_i (c_i \odot p^{-1})_{\{\mu+1,\ldots,k\}} + (c_0 \odot p^{-1})_{\{\mu+1,\ldots,k\}}$.
  It also outputs randomness for the channel $r_{\mathsf{ch}}' = r_{\mathsf{ch}}$, which is a uniformly random n-bit string representing the non-erased indices $\mathcal{I}$.

Rate of the Scheme. The rate μ/n of the scheme can be set to a constant smaller than $(\frac{k}{n} - \frac{1}{2})$. If the rate k/n of the error-correcting codes is close to its capacity $1 - h_2(\epsilon)$, the rate of WC can be close to its secrecy capacity $1/2 - h_2(\epsilon)$, which is the optimal rate of wiretap codes.

Correctness. The correctness of the wiretap codes directly follows from the correctness of the underlying error-correcting codes.

Conditional Invertibility. To show the invertibility conditioned on $\mathsf{BEC}_{0.5}$, we need to show that distributions of $(\tilde{x}, s, r_{\mathsf{ch}})$ are statistically indistinguishable in the real and ideal experiments of the definition. We introduce the hybrid experiment defined as follows:

$\mathsf{Exp}_{\mathsf{WC},\mathcal{A}}^{\mathrm{Real}}$	$\mathsf{Exp}_{\mathsf{WC},\mathcal{A}}^{\mathrm{Hybrid}}$	$\mathsf{Exp}_{\mathsf{WC},\mathcal{A}}^{\mathrm{Ideal}}$
$p \leftarrow$ WC.Setup(1^λ)	$p \leftarrow$ WC.Setup(1^λ)	$p \leftarrow$ WC.Setup(1^λ)
$(m, m') = \mathcal{A}(p)$	$(m, m') = \mathcal{A}(p)$	$(m, m') = \mathcal{A}(p)$
$x \leftarrow$ WC.Encode$(p, m; s)$	$x \leftarrow$ WC.Encode$(p, m; s')$	$x \leftarrow$ WC.Encode$(p, m'; s)$
$\tilde{x} \leftarrow \mathsf{ChA}(x; r_{\mathsf{ch}})$	$\tilde{x} \leftarrow \mathsf{ChA}(x; r_{\mathsf{ch}})$	$\tilde{x} \leftarrow \mathsf{ChA}(x; r_{\mathsf{ch}})$
	$(s', r_{\mathsf{ch}}') \leftarrow$ WC.Invert$(p, \tilde{x}, m)$	$(s', r_{\mathsf{ch}}') \leftarrow$ WC.Invert$(p, \tilde{x}, m)$
$\mathsf{out} = \mathcal{A}(\tilde{x}, s, r_{\mathsf{ch}})$	$\mathsf{out} = \mathcal{A}(\tilde{x}, s', r_{\mathsf{ch}}')$	$\mathsf{out} = \mathcal{A}(\tilde{x}, s', r_{\mathsf{ch}}')$

Claim. The distribution of output in the real and hybrid experiments are same.

Proof. In general, for a function $f : \mathcal{X} \to \mathcal{Y}$,

$$\{(x,y) \mid x \leftarrow \mathcal{X}, y = f(x)\} \equiv \{(x',y) \mid x \leftarrow \mathcal{X}, y = f(x), x' \leftarrow f^{-1}(y)\}$$

holds, where $f^{-1}(y)$ denotes the set of pre-images of y.

By applying the above fact to $f_{p,m}(s, r_{\mathsf{ch}}) = \mathsf{ChA}(\mathsf{WC.Encode}(p, m; s); r_{\mathsf{ch}})$, what we need to show is that $\mathsf{WC.Invert}$ implements sampling $(s', r_{\mathsf{ch}}') \leftarrow f_{p,m}^{-1}(\tilde{x})$.

Since we consider $\mathsf{ChA} = \mathsf{BEC}_{0.5}$, $\mathsf{WC.Invert}$ can uniquely determine $r_{\mathsf{ch}}' = r_{\mathsf{ch}}$ from the representation of $\tilde{x} = x_{\mathcal{I}}$. Recall that $\mathsf{WC.Invert}$ samples s' satisfying $x_{\mathcal{I}} = ((m\|s') \odot p)G_{\mathcal{I}} = \mathsf{BEC}_{0.5}(\mathsf{WC.Encode}(p, m; s'); r_{\mathsf{ch}})$ uniformly at random. Hence, the claim follows.   □

Claim. The hybrid and ideal experiments are statistically close if the wiretap codes are secure in the ordinarily sense.

Proof. Consider the adversary $\mathcal{A}$ that distinguished the two experiments. We can construct another adversary $\mathcal{A}'$ against the security of the wiretap codes as follows: Given p, run $\mathcal{A}'$ on p and obtain m, m'; send them to its challenger and receive $\tilde{x}$; compute $(s, r_{\mathsf{ch}}) \leftarrow \mathsf{WC.Invert}(p, \tilde{x}, m)$; run $\mathcal{A}'$ on $\tilde{x}, s, r_{\mathsf{ch}}$ and receive out; output out. The claim is proven, since the simulation by $\mathcal{A}$ is perfect.   □

Claim. The wiretap codes are secure in the ordinarily sense.

Bellare et al. [6] show a detailed security proof of the wiretap codes for general ChA. Below, we show a specific security proof for $\mathsf{ChA} = \mathsf{BEC}_{0.5}$.

Proof. Recall that the parameter is selected to satisfy $\mu/n < (k/n - 1/2)$. Let $2\delta := ((k - \mu)/n - 1/2) > 0$ be a constant.

Since $\mathsf{ChA} = \mathsf{BEC}_{0.5}$, the input for the adversary is $x_{\mathcal{I}} = ((m\|s) \odot p)G_{\mathcal{I}}$. By the Chernoff bound, $|\mathcal{I}| < (\frac{1}{2} + \delta)n$ holds except negligible probability.

Let us decompose the submatrix of the generator $G_{\mathcal{I}} = PDQ$, where $P \in \{0, 1\}^{k \times k}$ and $Q \in \{0, 1\}^{|\mathcal{I}| \times |\mathcal{I}|}$ are invertible. Furthermore $D = (d_{i,j}) \in \{0, 1\}^{k \times |\mathcal{I}|}$ satisfies $d_{i,i} = 1$ for $1 \le i \le r := \mathsf{Rank}(G_{\mathcal{I}})$ and $d_{i,j} = 0$ for other elements. We interpret the multiplication by D as getting the first r bits and concatenating $0^{|\mathcal{I}|-r}$. Thus $x_{\mathcal{I}} = ((((m\|s) \odot p)P)_{[r]}\|0^{|\mathcal{I}|-r})Q$.

For input $m\|s$ and seed p, $h_p(m\|s) := ((m\|s \odot p)P)_{[r]}$ forms a universal hash family. Note that the input has min-entropy $\mathbf{H}_\infty(m\|s) = k - \mu$.

Since $r \le |\mathcal{I}| \le (\frac{1}{2} + \delta)n \le k - \mu - \delta n < \mathbf{H}_\infty(m\|s) - \omega(\log \lambda)$ holds, by the left over hash lemma, $(p, h_p(m\|s))$ is statistically indistinguishable from (p, u) where $u \leftarrow \{0, 1\}^r$. Therefore $x_{\mathcal{I}}$ is statistically indistinguishable from $(u\|0^{|\mathcal{I}|-r})Q$, which is independent of m. Thus, the claim is proven.   □

By combining the above three claims, conditional invertibility of the wiretap codes follows.

4.3   Full-Fledged NCE from Weak NCE

In this section, we amplify a weak NCE scheme into a full-fledged one using conditionally invertible wiretap codes.

Construction. Let $\mathsf{NCE} = (\mathsf{Gen}, \mathsf{Enc}, \mathsf{Dec})$ be a weak NCE scheme which has ϵ-decryption error and weak security with respect to $\mathsf{BEC}_{0.5}$, and wiretap codes $\mathsf{WC} = (\mathsf{WC.Setup}, \mathsf{WC.Encode}, \mathsf{WC.Decode})$ which is correct over receiver channel $\mathsf{BSC}_{\leq \epsilon}$ and conditionally invertible against the adversary channel $\mathsf{BEC}_{0.5}$. We construct a full-fledged NCE scheme $\mathsf{NCE'} = (\mathsf{Gen'}, \mathsf{Enc'}, \mathsf{Dec'})$ as follows.

$\mathsf{Gen'}(1^\lambda)$:
 - Sample a public seed of the wiretap codes $p \leftarrow \mathsf{WC.Setup}(1^\lambda)$.
 - Generate a key pair of weak NCE $(pk, sk) \leftarrow \mathsf{Gen}\left(1^\lambda; r_{\mathsf{Gen}}\right)$.
 - Output $(pk', sk') := ((p, pk), sk)$.

The randomness for key generation r_{Gen}' is r_{Gen}.

$\mathsf{Enc'}(pk', m)$:
 - Sample a key for one-time pad $k \leftarrow \{0,1\}^\mu$.[3]
 - Encode the key as $x \leftarrow \mathsf{WC.Encode}(p, k; s) \in \{0,1\}^n$.
 - Compute $CT \leftarrow \mathsf{Enc}(pk, x; r_{\mathsf{Enc}})$.
 - Output ciphertext $CT' = (CT, m \oplus k)$.

The randomness for encryption r_{Enc}' is (r_{Enc}, k, s).

$\mathsf{Dec'}(sk', CT')$:
 - Parse CT' as (c_1, c_2).
 - Compute $k = \mathsf{WC.Decode}(p, \mathsf{Dec}(sk, c_1))$.
 - Output $m = c_2 \oplus k$.

Ciphertext Expansion. The ciphertext expansion of $\mathsf{NCE'}$ is

$$\frac{\text{ciphertext expansion of NCE}}{\text{rate of WC}} + 1. \tag{1}$$

Since the rate of the wiretap codes is constant, this amplification increases ciphertext expansion only by a constant factor. Combining the ciphertext expansion given in Sect. 5, we will estimate its concrete value for our scheme in Sect. 7.

Correctness. Due to the decryption error of NCE, each bit of the decrypted codeword x is flipped with probability at most ϵ. The wiretap codes correct this error as shown below.

Theorem 1 (Correctness). *If NCE has ϵ-decryption error, and WC is correct over $\mathsf{BSC}_{\leq\epsilon}$, then $\mathsf{NCE'}$ is correct.*

Proof. The probability of $\mathsf{NCE'}$ fails to decrypt is evaluated as

$$\Pr[k \neq \mathsf{WC.Decode}(p, \mathsf{Dec}(sk, \mathsf{Enc}(pk, x)))]$$
$$= \Pr[k \neq \mathsf{WC.Decode}(p, \mathsf{BSC}_{\leq\epsilon}(\mathsf{WC.Encode}(p, k; s)))]$$
$$= \mathsf{negl}(\lambda).$$

Thus $\mathsf{NCE'}$ is correct.

---

[3] Note that weak security of NCE requires the challenge message to be independent of the public key. To address this issue, we use one-time pad in this amplification.

Security. We now show the security of NCE′.

Theorem 2 (Security). *If* NCE *is weakly secure with respect to* $\mathsf{BEC}_{0.5}$, *and* WC *is invertible conditioned on* $\mathsf{BEC}_{0.5}$, *then* NCE′ *is secure.*

Proof. We first construct a simulator of NCE′ (Sim′, Open′) from the simulator (SimGen, SimEnc, Open) of NCE, and the inverter WC.Invert of WC.

$\mathsf{Sim}'(1^\lambda)$:
- Sample $p \leftarrow \mathsf{WC.Setup}(1^\lambda)$.
- Generate $(pk, st_1) \leftarrow \mathsf{SimGen}\left(1^\lambda\right)$.
- Sample $k \leftarrow \{0,1\}^\mu$.
- Compute $\tilde{x} \leftarrow \mathsf{BEC}_{0.5}(\mathsf{WC.Encode}(p, 0^\mu; s'); r_{\mathsf{ch}}')$.
- Compute $(CT, st_2) \leftarrow \mathsf{SimEnc}(\tilde{x}, st_1)$.
- Set $pk' = (p, pk), CT' = (CT, k), st' = (st_2, p, k, \tilde{x})$.
- Output (pk', CT', st').

$\mathsf{Open}'(m, st')$:
- Parse st' as $(st_2, p, k, \tilde{x})$.
- $(s, r_{\mathsf{ch}}) \leftarrow \mathsf{WC.Invert}(p, \tilde{x}, m \oplus k)$.
- $(r_{\mathsf{Gen}}, r_{\mathsf{Enc}}) \leftarrow \mathsf{Open}(\mathsf{WC.Encode}(p, m \oplus k; s), r_{\mathsf{ch}}, st_2)$.
- Output $(r_{\mathsf{Gen}}', r_{\mathsf{Enc}}') = (r_{\mathsf{Gen}}, (r_{\mathsf{Enc}}, m \oplus k, s))$.

Let $\mathcal{A}$ be an adversary against the security of NCE′. We then define the following experiments:

Exp 0: This experiment is the same as $\mathsf{Exp}_{\mathsf{NCE}', \mathcal{A}}^{\mathrm{Real}}$. Specifically,
   1. Sample $p \leftarrow \mathsf{WC.Setup}(1^\lambda)$.
   2. Generate the key pair $(pk, sk) \leftarrow \mathsf{Gen}\left(1^\lambda; r_{\mathsf{Gen}}\right)$.
   3. Run the adversary to output plaintext $m \leftarrow \mathcal{A}(p, pk)$.
   4. Sample $k \leftarrow \{0,1\}^\mu$ and encoded it as $x \leftarrow \mathsf{WC.Encode}(p, k; s)$.
   5. Encrypt the codeword as $CT \leftarrow \mathsf{Enc}(pk, x; r_{\mathsf{Enc}})$.
   6. Output this experiment is out $\leftarrow \mathcal{A}((CT, m \oplus k), r_{\mathsf{Gen}}, (r_{\mathsf{Enc}}, k, s))$.

Exp 1: In this experiment, we use the simulator (SimGen, SimEnc, Open) for NCE. The ciphertext CT is simulated by SimEnc only given partial information of the message $\tilde{x} \leftarrow \mathsf{Leak}(x)$, where $\mathsf{Leak} = \mathsf{BEC}_{0.5}$ and $x \leftarrow \mathsf{WC.Encode}(p, k; s)$ now. Specifically,
   1. Sample $p \leftarrow \mathsf{WC.Setup}(1^\lambda)$.
   2. Simulate the public key as $(pk, st_1) \leftarrow \mathsf{SimGen}\left(1^\lambda\right)$.
   3. Run the adversary to output plaintext $m \leftarrow \mathcal{A}(p, pk)$.
   4. Sample $k \leftarrow \{0,1\}^\mu$ and encoded it as $x \leftarrow \mathsf{WC.Encode}(p, k; s)$.
   5. Compute partial information $\tilde{x} \leftarrow \mathsf{BEC}_{0.5}(x; r_{\mathsf{ch}})$.
   6. Simulate the ciphertext as $(CT, st_2) \leftarrow \mathsf{SimEnc}(\tilde{x}, st_1)$.
   7. Explain the randomness for key generation and encryption as $(r_{\mathsf{Gen}}, r_{\mathsf{Enc}}) \leftarrow \mathsf{Open}(\mathsf{WC.Encode}(p, k; s), r_{\mathsf{ch}}, st_2)$.
   8. Output of this experiment is out $\leftarrow \mathcal{A}((CT, m \oplus k), r_{\mathsf{Gen}}, (r_{\mathsf{Enc}}, k, s))$.

Exp 2: In this experiment, we completely eliminate the information of k from the input of SimEnc to simulate the ciphertext. Later WC.Invert determines the randomness s used in the encode. Specifically,

1. Sample $p \leftarrow$ WC.Setup(1^λ).
2. Simulate the public key as $(pk, st_1) \leftarrow$ SimGen (1^λ).
3. Run the adversary to output plaintext $m \leftarrow \mathcal{A}(p, pk)$.
4. Sample $k \leftarrow \{0, 1\}^\mu$, but the codeword is $x \leftarrow$ WC.Encode($p, 0^\mu; s'$).
5. Compute partial information $\tilde{x} \leftarrow$ BEC$_{0.5}(x; r_{\mathsf{ch}}')$.
6. Simulate the ciphertext as $(CT, st_2) \leftarrow$ SimEnc($\tilde{x}, st_1$).
7. Invert the randomness for encode as $(s, r_{\mathsf{ch}}) \leftarrow$ WC.Invert($p, \tilde{x}, k$).
8. Explain the randomness for key generation and encryption as $(r_{\mathsf{Gen}}, r_{\mathsf{Enc}}) \leftarrow$ Open(WC.Encode($p, k; s$), r_{ch}, st_2).
9. Output of this experiment is out $\leftarrow \mathcal{A}((CT, m \oplus k), r_{\mathsf{Gen}}, (r_{\mathsf{Enc}}, k, s))$.

Exp 3: In this experiment, we completely eliminate m from the ciphertext by switching k to $m \oplus k$. Specifically,

1. Sample $p \leftarrow$ WC.Setup(1^λ).
2. Simulate the public key as $(pk, st_1) \leftarrow$ SimGen (1^λ).
3. Run the adversary to output plaintext $m \leftarrow \mathcal{A}(p, pk)$.
4. Sample $k \leftarrow \{0, 1\}^\mu$, but the codeword is $x \leftarrow$ WC.Encode($p, 0^\mu; s'$).
5. Compute partial information $\tilde{x} \leftarrow$ BEC$_{0.5}(x; r_{\mathsf{ch}}')$.
6. Simulate the ciphertext as $(CT, st_2) \leftarrow$ SimEnc($\tilde{x}, st_1$).
7. Invert the randomness for encoding as $(s, r_{\mathsf{ch}}) \leftarrow$ WC.Invert($p, \tilde{x}, m \oplus k$).
8. Explain the randomness for key generation and encryption as $(r_{\mathsf{Gen}}, r_{\mathsf{Enc}}) \leftarrow$ Open(WC.Encode($p, m \oplus k; s$), r_{ch}, st_2).
9. Output of this experiment is out $\leftarrow \mathcal{A}((CT, k), r_{\mathsf{Gen}}, (r_{\mathsf{Enc}}, m \oplus k, s))$.

Note that the last experiment Exp 3 is identical to Exp$_{\mathsf{NCE}', \mathcal{A}}^{\mathsf{Ideal}}$.

We show the difference between each experiments are negligible.

Lemma 3. *If* NCE *is weakly secure with respect to* BEC$_{0.5}$, *the difference of* Pr[out $= 1$] *in* Exp 0 *and* Exp 1 *is negligible.*

This lemma directly follows from the weak security of NCE. Note that the message encrypted by NCE is the key of one-time pad k, which is independent of the public key.

Lemma 4. *If* WC *is invertible conditioned on* BEC$_{0.5}$, *the difference of* Pr[out $= 1$] *in* Exp 1 *and* Exp 2 *is negligible.*

By the conditional invertibility of WC, the following items are statistically indistinguishable.

- (BEC$_{0.5}$(WC.Encode($p, k; s$); r_{ch}), (s, r_{ch}))
- (BEC$_{0.5}$(WC.Encode($p, 0^\mu; s'$); r_{ch}'), (s, r_{ch})) where (s, r_{ch}) is output of WC.Invert(p, BEC$_{0.5}$(WC.Encode($p, 0^\mu; s'$); r_{ch}'), k)

The lemma follows because $(CT', r_{\mathsf{Gen}}', r_{\mathsf{Enc}}')$, and hence out in Exp 1 are computed from the former item, while those in Exp 2 are computed from the latter item.

Lemma 5. Pr[out $= 1$] *is identical in* Exp 2 *and* Exp 3.

This lemma holds unconditionally, because $(k, m \oplus k)$ and $(m \oplus k, k)$ distribute identically when k is sampled uniformly at random.

Combining the above lemmas, we complete the proof of Theorem 2.

5   Construction of Weak NCE

In this section, we show an intermediate version of the NCE scheme in Yoshida et al. [31] is a weak NCE scheme. Their scheme is constructed from obliviously sampleable CE. We first recall the definition of obliviously sampleable CE. We then describe the construction of weak NCE, show that it has $1/2^{\ell+1}$-decryption error, where ℓ is a constant which appears in the chameleon encryption, and prove its weak security with respect to $\mathsf{BEC}_{0.5}$. The ciphertext expansion of the resulting weak NCE is $2\ell + o(1)$.

5.1   Obliviously Sampleable Chameleon Encryption

Chameleon encryption (CE) was proposed by Döttling and Garg [16]. We recall its obliviously sampleable variant, introduced by Yoshida et al. [31] as a building block of their NCE scheme. They showed an instantiation of obliviously sampleable CE from the DDH problem. We also show an instantiation from the LWE problem in Sect. 6.

Definition 10 (Obliviously Sampleable Chameleon Encryption). *An obliviously sampleable chameleon encryption scheme* CE *consists of PPT algorithms for hash functionality* $(\mathsf{G}, \mathsf{H}, \mathsf{H}^{-1})$, *those for encryption functionality* $(\mathsf{E}_1, \mathsf{E}_2, \mathsf{D})$, *and those for oblivious sampling* $(\widehat{\mathsf{G}}, \widehat{\mathsf{E}_1})$. *We first introduce algorithms for the first two functionality. Below, we let* $\mathcal{R}_\mathsf{H}$ *(and* $\mathcal{R}_\mathsf{E}$, *resp.) be the randomness space of* H *(and that of* E_1 *and* E_2, *resp.). We let* $\{0,1\}^\ell$ *be the key space.*

- $\mathsf{G}\left(1^\lambda, 1^n\right)$: Given the security parameter 1^λ and the length of inputs to the hash function 1^n, it outputs a hash key hk and a trapdoor td.
- $\mathsf{H}\left(\mathsf{hk}, x; r\right)$: Given a hash key hk and an input $x \in \{0,1\}^n$, using randomness $r \in \mathcal{R}_\mathsf{H}$, it outputs a hash value y.
- $\mathsf{H}^{-1}\left(\mathsf{td}, (x, r), x'\right)$: Given a trapdoor td, an input to the hash function x, randomness for the hash function r, and another input to the hash function x', it outputs randomness r'.
- $\mathsf{E}_1\left(\mathsf{hk}, (i, b); \rho\right)$: Given a hash key hk, an index $i \in [n], b \in \{0,1\}$, using randomness $\rho \in \mathcal{R}_\mathsf{E}$, it outputs a ciphertext ct.
- $\mathsf{E}_2\left(\mathsf{hk}, (i, b), y; \rho\right)$: Given a hash key hk, an index $i \in [n], b \in \{0,1\}$, and a hash value y, using randomness $\rho \in \mathcal{R}_\mathsf{E}$, it outputs $K \in \{0,1\}^\ell$.
- $\mathsf{D}\left(\mathsf{hk}, (x, r), \mathsf{ct}\right)$: Given a hash key hk, a pre-image of the hash function (x, r), and a ciphertext ct, it outputs $K \in \{0,1\}^\ell$.

We then introduce algorithms for oblivious sampling.

- $\widehat{\mathsf{G}}\left(1^\lambda, 1^n\right)$: Given the security parameter 1^λ, it outputs only a hash key $\widehat{\mathsf{hk}}$ without using any randomness other than $\widehat{\mathsf{hk}}$ itself.
- $\widehat{\mathsf{E}_1}\left(\widehat{\mathsf{hk}}, (i, b)\right)$: Given a hash key $\widehat{\mathsf{hk}}$, an index $i \in [n]$, and $b \in \{0,1\}$, it outputs a ciphertext $\widehat{\mathsf{ct}}$ without using any randomness except $\widehat{\mathsf{ct}}$ itself.

An obliviously sampleable CE scheme satisfies the following trapdoor collision property, correctness, oblivious sampleability of hash keys, and security with oblivious sampleability.

Trapdoor Collision: For a chameleon encryption scheme and a stateful adversary $\mathcal{A}$, we define two experiments as follows.

$\mathsf{Exp}^{\mathrm{Real}}$	$\mathsf{Exp}^{\mathrm{Ideal}}$
$(\mathsf{hk},\mathsf{td}) \leftarrow \mathsf{G}\left(1^\lambda,1^n\right)$	$(\mathsf{hk},\mathsf{td}) \leftarrow \mathsf{G}\left(1^\lambda,1^n\right)$
$(x,x') = \mathcal{A}(\mathsf{hk})$	$(x,x') = \mathcal{A}(\mathsf{hk})$
$y \leftarrow \mathsf{H}\left(\mathsf{hk},x;r\right)$	$y \leftarrow \mathsf{H}(\mathsf{hk},x';r')$
	$r \leftarrow \mathsf{H}^{-1}(\mathsf{td},(x',r'),x)$
$\mathsf{out} = \mathcal{A}\left(y,r\right)$	$\mathsf{out} = \mathcal{A}\left(y,r\right)$

We say the chameleon encryption scheme satisfies trapdoor collision if for any unbounded stateful adversary $\mathcal{A}$,

$$\left| \Pr\left[\mathsf{out} = 1 \text{ in } \mathsf{Exp}^{\mathrm{Real}}\right] - \Pr\left[\mathsf{out} = 1 \text{ in } \mathsf{Exp}^{\mathrm{Ideal}}\right] \right| = \mathsf{negl}(\lambda)$$

holds.

Correctness: For all $x \in \{0,1\}^n, r \in \mathcal{R}_\mathsf{H}, i \in [n]$, hk output by either $\mathsf{G}\left(1^\lambda,1^n\right)$ or $\widehat{\mathsf{G}}\left(1^\lambda,1^n\right)$, we have

$$\Pr[\mathsf{E}_2(\mathsf{hk},(i,x_i),y;\rho) = \mathsf{D}\left(\mathsf{hk},(x,r),\mathsf{ct}\right)] = 1 - \mathsf{negl}(\lambda)$$

where $\rho \leftarrow \mathcal{R}_\mathsf{E}$, $y \leftarrow \mathsf{H}\left(\mathsf{hk},x;r\right), \mathsf{ct} \leftarrow \mathsf{E}_1(\mathsf{hk},(i,x_i);\rho)$, and x_i denotes the i-th bit of x.

Oblivious Sampleability of Hash Keys: $\mathsf{hk} \leftarrow \mathsf{G}\left(1^\lambda,1^n\right)$ and $\widehat{\mathsf{hk}} \leftarrow \widehat{\mathsf{G}}\left(1^\lambda,1^n\right)$ are computationally indistinguishable.

Security with Oblivious Sampleability: For any $x \in \{0,1\}^n, r \in \mathcal{R}_\mathsf{H}, i \in [n]$, and PPT adversary $\mathcal{A}$, define two experiments as follows.

$\mathsf{Exp}^{\mathrm{real}}_{\mathrm{CE},\mathcal{A}}$	$\mathsf{Exp}^{\mathrm{os}}_{\mathrm{CE},\mathcal{A}}$
$(\mathsf{hk},\mathsf{td}) \leftarrow \mathsf{G}\left(1^\lambda,1^n\right)$	$(\mathsf{hk},\mathsf{td}) \leftarrow \mathsf{G}\left(1^\lambda,1^n\right)$
$\mathsf{ct} \leftarrow \mathsf{E}_1(\mathsf{hk},(i,1-x_i);\rho)$	$\mathsf{ct} \leftarrow \widehat{\mathsf{E}}_1(\mathsf{hk},(i,1-x_i))$
$K \leftarrow \mathsf{E}_2(\mathsf{hk},(i,1-x_i),\mathsf{H}(\mathsf{hk},x;r);\rho)$	$K \leftarrow \{0,1\}^\ell$
$\mathsf{out} \leftarrow \mathcal{A}\left(\mathsf{hk},\mathsf{ct},K\right)$	$\mathsf{out} \leftarrow \mathcal{A}\left(\mathsf{hk},\mathsf{ct},K\right)$

Then, we have

$$\mathsf{Adv}_{\mathrm{CE},\mathcal{A}}\left(\lambda\right) := \left| \Pr\left[\mathsf{out} = 1 \text{ in } \mathsf{Exp}^{\mathrm{real}}_{\mathrm{CE},\mathcal{A}}\right] - \Pr\left[\mathsf{out} = 1 \text{ in } \mathsf{Exp}^{\mathrm{os}}_{\mathrm{CE},\mathcal{A}}\right] \right| = \mathsf{negl}(\lambda) \ .$$

Remark 1. In the original definition of Yoshida et al. [31], security of an obliviously sampleable CE scheme and its oblivious sampleability of ciphertexts are defined separately. In the above definition, we combine them into a single notion, security with oblivious sampleability. This yields a clean and simple security proof of obliviously sampleable CE based on the LWE assumption and that of NCE scheme based on obliviously sampleable CE.

5.2   Construction

We show a construction of weak NCE scheme NCE for message space $\{0,1\}^n$ based on an obliviously sampleable CE scheme CE below. NCE has constant ciphertext expansion and ϵ-decryption error, and satisfies weak security with respect to Leak $=$ BEC$_{0.5}$. We can set ϵ to be arbitrarily small constant by appropriately selecting the constant parameter ℓ of CE; we require that $\epsilon \geq 2^{-\ell-1} + \mathsf{negl}(\lambda)$.

Gen $(1^\lambda; r_{\mathsf{Gen}})$:
- Generate $\widehat{\mathsf{hk}} \leftarrow \widehat{\mathsf{G}}(1^\lambda, 1^n)$, and sample $z \leftarrow \{0,1\}^n$.
- For all $i \in [n]$, sample $\rho_i \leftarrow \mathcal{R}_{\mathsf{E}}$.
- For all $i \in [n]$ and $b \in \{0,1\}$, compute

$$\mathsf{ct}_{i,b} \leftarrow \begin{cases} \mathsf{E}_1\left(\widehat{\mathsf{hk}}, (i,b); \rho_i\right) & (\text{if } b = z_i) \\ \widehat{\mathsf{E}_1}\left(\widehat{\mathsf{hk}}, (i,b)\right) & (\text{otherwise}) \end{cases}.$$

- Output

$$pk := \left(\widehat{\mathsf{hk}}, \begin{pmatrix} \mathsf{ct}_{1,0}, \ldots, \mathsf{ct}_{n,0} \\ \mathsf{ct}_{1,1}, \ldots, \mathsf{ct}_{n,1} \end{pmatrix}\right) \quad \text{and} \quad sk := (z, (\rho_1, \ldots, \rho_n)). \tag{2}$$

The key generation randomness r_{Gen} is $\left(\widehat{\mathsf{hk}}, z, \{\rho_i\}_{i \in [n]}, \{\mathsf{ct}_{i,1-z_i}\}_{i \in [n]}\right)$.

Enc$(pk, x \in \{0,1\}^n; r_{\mathsf{Enc}})$:
- Parse public key pk as the Eq. 2.
- Sample randomness $r \leftarrow \mathcal{R}_{\mathsf{H}}$ and compute $y \leftarrow \mathsf{H}(\widehat{\mathsf{hk}}, x; r)$.
- For all $i \in [n]$ and $b \in \{0,1\}$, compute

$$K_{i,b} \leftarrow \begin{cases} \mathsf{D}\left(\widehat{\mathsf{hk}}, (x,r), \mathsf{ct}_{i,b}\right) & (\text{if } b = x_i) \\ \{0,1\}^\ell & (\text{otherwise}) \end{cases}.$$

- Output

$$CT := \left(y, \begin{pmatrix} K_{1,0}, \ldots, K_{n,0} \\ K_{1,1}, \ldots, K_{n,1} \end{pmatrix}\right). \tag{3}$$

The encryption randomness r_{Enc} is $\left(r, \{K_{i,1-x_i}\}_{i \in [n]}\right)$.

Dec (sk, CT):
- Parse sk and CT as the Eqs. 2 and 3, respectively.
- For all $i \in [n]$, compute

$$x_i := \begin{cases} z_i & \left(\text{if } K_{i,z_i} = \mathsf{E}_2\left(\widehat{\mathsf{hk}}, (i,z_i), y; \rho_i\right)\right) \\ 1 - z_i & (\text{otherwise}) \end{cases}$$

- Output x.

Ciphertext Expansion. Ciphertext length of this scheme is $|CT| = |y| + 2n\ell$, where length of the output of the chameleon hash $|y|$ does not depend on n. Therefore ciphertext expansion of this scheme is

$$|CT|/n = 2\ell + o(1).$$

Next, we show that NCE is weak NCE. More concretely, we show that NCE has ϵ-decryption error and satisfies weak security with respect to $\mathsf{BEC}_{0.5}$.

Theorem 3 (Weak Correctness). *Let ℓ be a constant noticeably larger than $\log(1/\epsilon) - 1$. If CE satisfies correctness, then NCE has ϵ-decryption error.*

Proof. Let $x \in \{0,1\}^n$ be a message encrypted by NCE and $z \in \{0,1\}^n$ a random string sampled when generating a key pair of NCE.

We fail to decrypt x_i if the underlying chameleon encryption causes correctness error when $z_i = x_i$, or $K_{i,1-z_i} \leftarrow \{0,1\}^\ell$ accidentally coincides with $\mathsf{E}_2(\mathsf{hk}, (i, z_i), y; \rho_i)$ when $z_i \neq x_i$. The probability of the former is negligible since CE is correct, and that of the later is $1/2^\ell$. Notice that correctness of CE holds for obliviously sampled hash key $\widehat{\mathsf{hk}}$. Thus, the probability of failure to decrypt x_i is evaluated as

$$\Pr[x_i \neq (\mathsf{Dec}(sk, CT))_i]$$
$$= \Pr \left[\begin{array}{c} \left(z_i = x_i \wedge \mathsf{D}(\widehat{\mathsf{hk}}, (x, r), \mathsf{ct}_{i, x_i}) \neq \mathsf{E}_2(\widehat{\mathsf{hk}}, (i, z_i), y; \rho_i) \right) \\ \vee \left(z_i \neq x_i \wedge K_{i,1-x_i} = \mathsf{E}_2(\widehat{\mathsf{hk}}, (i, z_i), y; \rho_i) \right) \end{array} \right]$$
$$= \frac{1}{2} \left(\mathsf{negl}(\lambda) + \frac{1}{2^\ell} \right) \leq \epsilon \ .$$

$\square$

Theorem 4 (Weak Security). *If CE is an obliviously sampleable CE scheme, then NCE is weakly secure with respect to $\mathsf{Leak} = \mathsf{BEC}_{0.5}$.*

Proof. We construct a tuple of simulators as follows.

$\mathsf{SimGen}(1^\lambda)$:
  - Generate $(\mathsf{hk}, \mathsf{td}) \leftarrow \mathsf{G}(1^\lambda, 1^n)$.
  - For all $i \in [n]$ and $b \in \{0,1\}$, compute $\mathsf{ct}_{i,b} \leftarrow \mathsf{E}_1(\mathsf{hk}, (i, b); \rho_{i,b})$.
  - Output a simulated public key $pk := \left(\mathsf{hk}, \begin{pmatrix} \mathsf{ct}_{1,0}, \ldots, \mathsf{ct}_{n,0} \\ \mathsf{ct}_{1,1}, \ldots, \mathsf{ct}_{n,1} \end{pmatrix} \right)$ and state
    $st_1 = (\mathsf{hk}, \mathsf{td}, \{\rho_{i,b}\}_{i \in [n], b \in \{0,1\}})$.
$\mathsf{SimEnc}(x_\mathcal{I} \leftarrow \mathsf{BEC}_{0.5}(x; r_{\mathsf{ch}}), st_1)$:
  - Sample $r' \leftarrow \mathcal{R}_\mathsf{H}$ and compute $y \leftarrow \mathsf{H}(\mathsf{hk}, 0; r')$.
  - For all $i \notin \mathcal{I}$, compute $K_{i,b} \leftarrow \mathsf{E}_2(\mathsf{hk}, (i, b), y; \rho_{i,b})$ for $b \in \{0,1\}$. For all $i \in \mathcal{I}$, compute

$$K_{i,b} \leftarrow \begin{cases} \mathsf{E}_2(\mathsf{hk}, (i, b), y; \rho_{i,b}) & (\text{if } b = x_i) \\ \{0,1\}^\ell & (\text{otherwise}) \end{cases} .$$

- Output a simulated ciphertext $CT := \left(y, \begin{pmatrix} K_{1,0}, \ldots, K_{n,0} \\ K_{1,1}, \ldots, K_{n,1} \end{pmatrix} \right)$ and state $st_2 = (st_1, r', \{K_{i,b}\}_{i \in [n], b \in \{0,1\}})$.

Open(x, r_{ch}, st_2):
- Sample $r \leftarrow H^{-1} (td, (0, r'), x)$.
- Set $z = x \oplus 1^n \oplus r_{ch}$.
- Output the following simulated randomness

$$r_{Gen} := \left(hk, z, \{\rho_{i,z_i}\}_{i \in [n]}, \{ct_{i,1-z_i}\}_{i \in [n]} \right) \quad \text{and}$$

$$r_{Enc} := \left(r, \{K_{i,1-x_i}\}_{i \in [n]} \right).$$

Let $\mathcal{A}$ be a PPT adversary against weak security of NCE and $x \in \{0,1\}^n$. We define the following sequence of experiments.[4]

Exp 0: This experiment is exactly the same as $\mathsf{Exp}_{\mathsf{NCE},\mathcal{A}}^{\mathsf{Real}}$. Specifically;
1. Generate $\widehat{hk} \leftarrow \widehat{G}(1^\lambda, 1^n)$ and $z \leftarrow \{0,1\}^n$.
2. For all $i \in [n]$, sample $\rho_i \leftarrow \mathcal{R}_E$.
3. For all $i \in [n]$ and $b \in \{0,1\}$, compute

$$ct_{i,b} \leftarrow \begin{cases} E_1 \left(\widehat{hk}, (i,b); \rho_i \right) & (\text{if } b = z_i) \\ \widehat{E_1} \left(\widehat{hk}, (i,b) \right) & (\text{otherwise}) \end{cases}.$$

4. Set

$$pk := \left(\widehat{hk}, \begin{pmatrix} ct_{1,0}, \ldots, ct_{n,0} \\ ct_{1,1}, \ldots, ct_{n,1} \end{pmatrix} \right) \quad \text{and} \quad r_{Gen} := \left(\widehat{hk}, z, \{\rho_i\}_{i \in [n]}, \{ct_{i,1-z_i}\}_{i \in [n]} \right).$$

5. Sample $r \leftarrow \mathcal{R}_H$ and compute $y \leftarrow H(\widehat{hk}, x; r)$.
6. For all $i \in [n]$ and $b \in \{0,1\}$, compute

$$K_{i,b} \leftarrow \begin{cases} D \left(\widehat{hk}, (x,r), ct_{i,b} \right) & (\text{if } b = x_i) \\ \{0,1\}^\ell & (\text{otherwise}) \end{cases}.$$

7. Set

$$CT := \left(y, \begin{pmatrix} K_{1,0}, \ldots, K_{n,0} \\ K_{1,1}, \ldots, K_{n,1} \end{pmatrix} \right) \quad \text{and} \quad r_{Enc} := \left(r, \{K_{i,1-x_i}\}_{i \in [n]} \right).$$

8. Output of this experiment is $\mathsf{out} \leftarrow \mathcal{A}(pk, CT, r_{Gen}, r_{Enc})$.

---

[4] The flow of the hybrids is slightly different from the proof given by Yoshida et al. [31] as the security definition of obliviously sampleable CE is reorganized.

Exp 1: In this experiment, instead of sampling $z \leftarrow \{0,1\}^n$, we first compute $x_{\mathcal{I}} \leftarrow \mathsf{BEC}_{0.5}(x; r_{\mathsf{ch}})$ and set $z = x \oplus 1^n \oplus r_{\mathsf{ch}}$.

Notice that z distributes uniformly at random over $\{0,1\}^n$ also in Exp 1 since $r_{\mathsf{ch}} \leftarrow \mathcal{B}_{0.5}^n$. Thus, $\Pr[\mathsf{out} = 1]$ in Exp 1 is identical to that in Exp 0. Also notice that $i \in \mathcal{I}$ iff $z_i \neq x_i$ holds by the setting of z.

Exp 2: In this experiment, we run $(\mathsf{hk}, \mathsf{td}) \leftarrow \mathsf{G}\left(1^\lambda, 1^n\right)$ instead of $\widehat{\mathsf{hk}} \leftarrow \widehat{\mathsf{G}}\left(1^\lambda, 1^n\right)$.

From the oblivious sampleability of hash keys of CE, the difference of $\Pr[\mathsf{out} = 1]$ between Exp 1 and Exp 2 is negligible.

In subsequent experiments, we eliminate information of x_i for $i \notin \mathcal{I}$ from the ciphertext $CT = (y, \{K_{i,b}\}_{i \in [n], b \in \{0,1\}})$.

Exp 3.j: This experiment is defined for $j = 0, \ldots, n$. Exp 3.j is the same experiment as Exp 2 except that we modify the procedures 3 and 6 as follows.
  3. For all $i \leq j$, compute $\mathsf{ct}_{i,b}$ for $b \in \{0,1\}$ as $\mathsf{ct}_{i,b} \leftarrow \mathsf{E}_1(\mathsf{hk}, (i,b); \rho_{i,b})$. For all $i > j$, compute them in the same way as Exp 2.
  6. For all $i \leq j$, if $i \notin \mathcal{I}$, compute $K_{i,0}, K_{i,1}$ as $K_{i,x_i} \leftarrow \mathsf{D}(\mathsf{hk}, (x,r), \mathsf{ct}_{i,x_i})$ and $K_{i,1-x_i} \leftarrow \mathsf{E}_2(\mathsf{hk}, (i, 1-x_i), y; \rho_{i,1-x_i})$. For all $i \leq j$, if $i \in \mathcal{I}$, compute them in the same way as Exp 2. Also, for all $i > j$, compute them in the same way as Exp 2 regardless of whether $i \in \mathcal{I}$ or not.
Note that Exp 3.0 is exactly the same as Exp 2.

Lemma 6. *If* CE *satisfies security with oblivious sampleability, the difference of* $\Pr[\mathsf{out} = 1]$ *between* Exp 3.$(j-1)$ *and* Exp 3.j *is negligible for every* $j \in [n]$.

Proof. Using $\mathcal{A}$, we construct a reduction algorithm $\mathcal{A}'$ which attacks the security with oblivious sampleability of CE with respect to x, r, and j.

What differ in Exp 3.$(j-1)$ and Exp 3.j are $\mathsf{ct}_{i,1-x_i}$, K_{j,x_j}, and $K_{j,1-x_j}$.

K_{j,x_j} is the same in both experiments except negligible probability due to the correctness of CE. We consider the following two cases.

Case 1. $z_j = x_j$: $\mathsf{ct}_{j,1-x_j}$ is output of $\widehat{\mathsf{E}}_1(\mathsf{hk}, (j, 1-x_j))$ or $\mathsf{E}_1\left(\mathsf{hk}, (j, 1-x_j); \rho_{j,1-x_j}\right)$. $K_{j,1-x_j}$ is uniform random or output of $\mathsf{E}_2\left(\mathsf{hk}, y; \rho_{i,1-x_j}\right)$. In this case, the reduction algorithm $\mathcal{A}'$, given $(\mathsf{hk}^*, \mathsf{ct}^*, K^*)$, embed $\mathsf{ct}_{i,1-x_i} = \mathsf{ct}^*$, $K_{j,1-x_j} = K^*$.

Case 2. $z_j \neq x_j$: $\mathsf{ct}_{j,1-x_j}$ is output of $\widehat{\mathsf{E}}_1(\mathsf{hk}, (j, 1-x_j))$ or $\mathsf{E}_1\left(\mathsf{hk}, (j, 1-x_j); \rho_{j,1-x_j}\right)$.
$K_{j,1-x_j}$ is uniform random in both experiments.
In this case, the reduction algorithm $\mathcal{A}'$, given $(\mathsf{hk}^*, \mathsf{ct}^*, K^*)$, embed $\mathsf{ct}_{i,1-x_i} = \mathsf{ct}^*$, set $K_{j,1-x_j} \leftarrow \{0,1\}^\ell$.

In both cases, $\mathcal{A}'$ returns output out $\leftarrow \mathcal{A}(pk, CT, r_{\mathsf{Gen}}, r_{\mathsf{Enc}})$.

Depending on $\mathcal{A}'$ playing in either $\mathsf{Exp}^{\mathrm{real}}_{\mathsf{CE},\mathcal{A}'}$ or $\mathsf{Exp}^{\mathrm{os}}_{\mathsf{CE},\mathcal{A}'}$, $\mathcal{A}'$ perfectly simulates $\mathsf{Exp}^{\mathrm{Weak\ Real}}_{\mathsf{NCE},\mathcal{A}}$ or $\mathsf{Exp}^{\mathrm{Weak\ Ideal}}_{\mathsf{NCE},\mathcal{A}}$ except correctness error on K_{j,x_j}, which occurs with negligible probability.

Hence assuming the CE satisfies security with oblivious sampleability, the difference of $\Pr[\mathsf{out} = 1]$ in Exp $3.(j-1)$ and Exp $3.j$ is negligible.

Exp 4: This experiment is the same as Exp $3.n$ except that K_{i,x_i} is generated by $K_{i,x_i} \leftarrow \mathsf{E}_2\left(\mathsf{hk}, (i, x_i), y; \rho_{i,x_i}\right)$ instead of $K_{i,x_i} \leftarrow \mathsf{D}\left(\mathsf{hk}, (x, r), \mathsf{ct}_{i,b}\right)$ for every $i \in [n]$.

From the correctness of CE, the difference of $\Pr[\mathsf{out} = 1]$ between Exp $3.n$ and Exp 4 is negligible.

Exp 5: In this experiment, we compute y as $y \leftarrow \mathsf{H}\left(\mathsf{hk}, 0; r'\right)$, where $r' \leftarrow \mathcal{R}_{\mathsf{H}}$. Later, we compute r as $r \leftarrow \mathsf{H}^{-1}\left(\mathsf{td}, (0, r'), x\right)$. Note that this experiment is exactly the same as $\mathsf{Exp}^{\mathrm{Weak\ Ideal}}_{\mathsf{NCE},\mathcal{A}}$ in which $\mathsf{Leak} = \mathsf{BSC}_{0.5}$ is used. In detail, the experiment proceeds as follows.

1. Generate $(\mathsf{hk}, \mathsf{td}) \leftarrow \mathsf{G}\left(1^\lambda, 1^n\right)$ and $z \leftarrow \{0,1\}^n$. For all $i \in [n], b \in \{0,1\}$, compute $\mathsf{ct}_{i,b} \leftarrow \mathsf{E}_1\left(\mathsf{hk}, (i, b); \rho_{i,b}\right)$. Set

$$pk := \left(\mathsf{hk}, \begin{pmatrix} \mathsf{ct}_{1,0}, \ldots, \mathsf{ct}_{n,0} \\ \mathsf{ct}_{1,1}, \ldots, \mathsf{ct}_{n,1} \end{pmatrix}\right).$$

Note that this pk does not depend on z.

2. Compute $y \leftarrow \mathsf{H}\left(\mathsf{hk}, 0; r'\right)$,

$$K_{i,b} \leftarrow \begin{cases} \mathsf{E}_2\left(\mathsf{hk}, y; \rho_{i,b}\right) & (b = x_i \vee z_i = x_i) \\ \{0,1\}^\ell & (b \neq x_i \wedge z_i \neq x_i) \end{cases}$$

for all $i \in [n], b \in \{0,1\}$, and

$$CT := \left(y, \begin{pmatrix} K_{1,0}, \ldots, K_{n,0} \\ K_{1,1}, \ldots, K_{n,1} \end{pmatrix}\right).$$

Note that this CT can be computed only from $x_\mathcal{I}$, where $\mathcal{I} = \{i \in [n] \mid z_i \neq x_i\}$. Moreover, we can regard $x_\mathcal{I} \leftarrow \mathsf{BEC}_{0.5}(x; r_{\mathsf{ch}} = x \oplus z \oplus 1^n)$, since $z \leftarrow \{0,1\}^n$ has not appeared elsewhere in this experiment.

3. Sample $r \leftarrow \mathsf{H}^{-1}\left(\mathsf{td}, (0, r'), x\right)$. Set the randomness as

$$r_{\mathsf{Gen}} := \left(\mathsf{hk}, z, \{\rho_{i,z_i}\}_{i \in [n]}, \{\mathsf{ct}_{i,1-z_i}\}_{i \in [n]}\right)$$

$$r_{\mathsf{Enc}} := \left(r, \{K_{i,1-x_i}\}_{i \in [n]}\right).$$

4. out $\leftarrow \mathcal{A}(pk, CT, r_{\mathsf{Gen}}, r_{\mathsf{Enc}})$

Lemma 7. *If the obliviously sampleable CE satisfies trapdoor collision, the difference of* $\Pr[\mathsf{out} = 1]$ *in* Exp 4 *and* Exp 5 *is negligible.*

From the above arguments, we see that NCE satisfies weak security with respect to $\mathsf{Leak} = \mathsf{BSC}_{0.5}$. This completes the proof of Theorem 4.   □

6 Obliviously Sampleable Chameleon Encryption from Lattices

We propose a lattice-based construction of obliviously sampleable CE. The ciphertext length of the proposed scheme is $\lambda \cdot \mathsf{poly}(\log \lambda)$, which is smaller than $\mathcal{O}(\lambda^2)$ of the construction from the DDH problem [31].

The construction is similar to the construction of hash encryption from LWE proposed by Döttling et al. [17]. However we need a super-polynomially large modulus $\mathbb{Z}_q$ for the scheme to satisfy correctness. Although security of the hash encryption is claimed to be proved from a valiant of the LWE assumption, called extended-LWE, we prove the security directly from the LWE assumption.

Before describing our construction, we recall preliminaries on lattices.

6.1 Preliminaries on Lattices

Notations. Let $\boldsymbol{A}, \boldsymbol{B}$ be matrices or vectors. $[\boldsymbol{A}|\boldsymbol{B}]$ and $[\boldsymbol{A}; \boldsymbol{B}]$ denotes concatenation of columns and rows respectively. $\boldsymbol{A}_{\backslash i}$ denotes the matrix obtained by removing the i-th column of $\boldsymbol{A}$.

The n-dimensional Gaussian function with parameter s is defined as $\rho_s(\boldsymbol{x}) := \exp(-\pi \|\boldsymbol{x}\|^2 / s^2)$. For positive real s and countable set A, the discrete Gaussian distribution $D_{A,s}$ is defined by $D_{A,s}(\boldsymbol{x}) = \rho_s(\boldsymbol{x}) / \sum_{\boldsymbol{y} \in A} \rho_s(\boldsymbol{y})$. We note that, if $s = \omega(\log m)$,

$$\Pr_{r \leftarrow D_{\mathbb{Z}^m, s}} [\|\boldsymbol{r}\| \leq s\sqrt{m}] \geq 1 - 2^{-m+1}.$$

(See [28].)

Parameters. We let $n = \lambda$, $m = \mathcal{O}(n \log q)$ (e.g., $m = 2n \log q$), $q = 2^{\mathsf{poly}(\log \lambda)}$. Let χ be the discrete Gaussian distribution over $\mathbb{Z}$ with parameter $s = \omega(\sqrt{m \log n})$, that is, $D_{\mathbb{Z},s}$. Rounding function $\mathsf{round} : \mathbb{Z}_q \to \{0, 1\}$ is defined as $\mathsf{round}(v) = \lfloor 2v/q \rfloor$. If input for round is a vector $\boldsymbol{v} \in \mathbb{Z}_q^\ell$, the rounding is applied to each component. ℓ be a constant.

Definition 11 ((Decisional) Learning with Errors [29]). *The LWE assumption with respect to n dimension, m samples, modulus q, and error distribution χ over $\mathbb{Z}_q$ states that for all PPT adversary $\mathcal{A}$, we have*

$$\left| \Pr[\mathcal{A}(\boldsymbol{A}, \boldsymbol{S}^{\mathrm{T}} \boldsymbol{A} + \boldsymbol{E}) = 1] - \Pr[\mathcal{A}(\boldsymbol{A}, \boldsymbol{B}) = 1] \right| = \mathsf{negl}(\lambda),$$

where $\boldsymbol{A} \leftarrow \mathbb{Z}_q^{n \times m}, \boldsymbol{S} \leftarrow \mathbb{Z}_q^{n \times \ell}, \boldsymbol{E} \leftarrow \chi^{m \times \ell}, \boldsymbol{B} \leftarrow \mathbb{Z}_q^{m \times \ell}$.

Definition 12 (Lattice Trapdoor [19,27]). *There exists following PPT algorithms* TrapGen *and* Sample.

TrapGen(1^λ): *Output a matrix* $\boldsymbol{A}_T \in \mathbb{Z}_q^{n \times m}$ *together with its trapdoor* $\boldsymbol{T}$.
Sample($\boldsymbol{A}_T, \boldsymbol{T}, \boldsymbol{u}, s$): *Given a matrix* $\boldsymbol{A}_T$ *with its trapdoor* $\boldsymbol{T}$, *a vector* $\boldsymbol{u} \in \mathbb{Z}_q^n$,
  and a parameter s, *output a vector* $\boldsymbol{r} \in \mathbb{Z}^m$.

These algorithms satisfy the following two properties.

1. $\boldsymbol{A}_T$ *is statistically close to uniform in* $\mathbb{Z}_q^{n \times m}$.
2. *If* $s \geq \omega(\sqrt{m \cdot \log n})$, *then* $\boldsymbol{r} \in \mathbb{Z}^m$ *output by* Sample($\boldsymbol{A}_T, \boldsymbol{T}, \boldsymbol{u}, s$) *is statistically close to* $D_{\mathbb{Z}^m, s}$ *conditioned on* $\boldsymbol{r} \in \Lambda_{\boldsymbol{u}}(\boldsymbol{A}_T) := \{\boldsymbol{r} \in \mathbb{Z}^m \mid \boldsymbol{A}_T \boldsymbol{r} \equiv \boldsymbol{u} \pmod{q}\}$.

6.2 Construction

We construct an obliviously sampleable CE scheme from the LWE problem for super-polynomially large modulus.

G($1^\lambda, 1^N$):
  - Sample $\boldsymbol{R} \leftarrow \mathbb{Z}_q^{n \times N}$ and $(\boldsymbol{A}_T \in \mathbb{Z}_q^{n \times m}, \boldsymbol{T}) \leftarrow$ TrapGen(1^λ).
  - Output

$$\mathsf{hk} := \boldsymbol{A} = [\boldsymbol{R} \mid \boldsymbol{A}_T] \text{ and } \mathsf{td} := \boldsymbol{T}.$$

H ($\mathsf{hk}, x; r$):
  - Sample $\boldsymbol{r} \in \mathbb{Z}_q^m$ according to distribution $\mathcal{R}_{\mathsf{H}} = \chi^m$.
  - Output

$$\boldsymbol{y} := \boldsymbol{A} \cdot [\boldsymbol{x}; \boldsymbol{r}] \bmod q.$$

H^{-1} ($\mathsf{td}, (x, r), x'$):
  - Set $\boldsymbol{y}' = \boldsymbol{R}(\boldsymbol{x} - \boldsymbol{x}') + \boldsymbol{A}_T \boldsymbol{r} \bmod q$. Sample and output a short collision by the sampling algorithm of the lattice trapdoor

$$\boldsymbol{r}' \leftarrow \mathsf{Sample}(\boldsymbol{A}_T, \boldsymbol{T}, \boldsymbol{y}', s).$$

E_1 ($\mathsf{hk}, (i, b); \rho$):
  - Sample $\rho = (\boldsymbol{S}, \boldsymbol{E})$ where $\boldsymbol{S} \leftarrow \mathbb{Z}_q^{n \times \ell}, \boldsymbol{E} \leftarrow \chi^{\ell \times (N+m)}$.
  - Output

$$\mathsf{ct} := \boldsymbol{S}^{\mathsf{T}} \boldsymbol{A}_{\backslash i} + \boldsymbol{E}_{\backslash i} \in \mathbb{Z}_q^{\ell \times (N+m-1)}.$$

E_2($\mathsf{hk}, (i, b), y; \rho$):
  - Compute $\boldsymbol{v} = \boldsymbol{S}^{\mathsf{T}}(\boldsymbol{y} - b \cdot \boldsymbol{a}_i) + \boldsymbol{e}_i$ and output $K := \mathsf{round}(\boldsymbol{v})$, where $\boldsymbol{a}_i$ and $\boldsymbol{e}_i$ are the i-th rows of $\boldsymbol{A}$ and $\boldsymbol{E}$.

D ($\mathsf{hk}, (x, r), \mathsf{ct}$):
  - Compute $\boldsymbol{v}' = \mathsf{ct} \cdot [\boldsymbol{x}_{\backslash i}; \boldsymbol{r}]$ and output $K := \mathsf{round}(\boldsymbol{v}')$.

$\widehat{\mathsf{G}}(1^\lambda, 1^N)$:
  - Sample and output

$$\widehat{\mathsf{hk}} \leftarrow \mathbb{Z}_q^{n \times (N+m)}.$$

$\widehat{\mathsf{E}_1}\left(\widehat{\mathsf{hk}}, (i, b)\right)$:
  - Sample and output

$$\widehat{\mathsf{ct}} \leftarrow \mathbb{Z}_q^{\ell \times (N+m-1)}.$$

Trapdoor Collision. For all x, x', $\mathsf{H}(\mathsf{hk}, x; r) = \mathsf{H}(\mathsf{hk}, x'; r')$ holds, because the lattice trapdoor samples r such that $A_T r' \equiv y' \pmod{q}$ where $y' = R(x - x') + A_T r \bmod q$. Moreover, if $r \leftarrow \chi^m$, $A_T r \bmod q$ is statistically close to uniform over $\mathbb{Z}_q^n$ [19, Cor. 5.4], hence y' is also statistically close to uniform. Thus, the distribution of r' is statistically close to χ^m (conditioned on $Rx' + A_T r' \equiv Rx + A_T r \pmod{q}$).

Correctness. Let $\Delta := |v_j - v'_j|$, where v_j and v'_j are the j-th component of the inputs to the rounding function in the computation of E_2 and D respectively.

$$
\begin{aligned}
\Delta &= \left| \left(s_j^{\mathrm{T}}(y - x_i \cdot a_i) + e_{i,j} \right) - \left(\mathsf{ct}_j \cdot [x_{\backslash i}; r] \right) \right| \\
&= \left| s_j^{\mathrm{T}} (A \cdot [x; r] - x_i \cdot a_i) + e_{i,j} - \left(s_j^{\mathrm{T}} A_{\backslash i} + e_{\backslash i,j} \right) [x_{\backslash i}; r] \right| \\
&= \left| e_{i,j} - e_{\backslash i,j} [x_{\backslash i}; r] \right| \\
&\leq \| e_j \| \cdot \| [x; r] \| \\
&\leq s\sqrt{N + m} \cdot \sqrt{N + s^2 m} \leq s^2(N + m),
\end{aligned}
$$

holds with overwhelming probability. The probability of decryption error on j-th bit is bounded by

$$
\Pr[\mathsf{round}(v_j) \neq \mathsf{round}(v'_j)] \leq 2\Delta/q = \mathsf{negl}(\lambda),
$$

which is negligible since the modulus q is super-polynomially large. Thus, by taking the union bound for all $|v| = \ell$ bits, the probability of decryption error is bounded by

$$
\Pr[\mathsf{round}(v) \neq \mathsf{round}(v')] \leq 2\ell\Delta/q = \mathsf{negl}(\lambda).
$$

Oblivious Sampleability of Hash Keys. R distributes uniformly at random. The distribution of A_T output by $\mathsf{TrapGen}(1^\lambda)$ is also statistically close to uniform. Thus, A output by $\mathsf{G}(1^\lambda, 1^n)$ is statistically indistinguishable from the output of $\widehat{\mathsf{G}}(1^\lambda, 1^n)$.

Security with Oblivious Sampleability. Let $\mathcal{A}$ be an adversary that distinguishes experiments $\mathsf{Exp}_{\mathsf{CE},\mathcal{A}}^{\mathsf{real}}$ and $\mathsf{Exp}_{\mathsf{CE},\mathcal{A}}^{\mathsf{os}}$.

We construct a reduction algorithm $\mathcal{A}'$ that breaks the LWE assumption with $(N + m)$ samples by using $\mathcal{A}$ as follows:

1. $\mathcal{A}'$ receives $\left(A = [R \mid A_T] \in \mathbb{Z}_q^{n \times (N+m)}, B \in \mathbb{Z}_q^{\ell \times (N+m)} \right)$, where B is either $S^{\mathrm{T}} A + E$ or uniformly random.
2. $\mathcal{A}'$ sets

$$
\begin{aligned}
a' &:= (2x_i - 1)\left(a_i - A_{\backslash i}[x_{\backslash i}; r] \right), \\
R' &:= [a_1 \mid \cdots \mid a_{i-1} \mid a' \mid a_{i+1} \mid \cdots \mid a_N].
\end{aligned}
$$

and set

$$
\mathsf{hk} := [R' \mid A_T], \mathsf{ct} := B_{\backslash i}, \text{ and } K := \mathsf{round}(b_i).
$$

3. Finally, $\mathcal{A}'$ returns $\mathcal{A}(\mathsf{hk}, \mathsf{ct}, K)$.

In the LWE case, that is, $\boldsymbol{B} = \boldsymbol{S}^{\mathrm{T}}\boldsymbol{A} + \boldsymbol{E}$ and $\boldsymbol{b}_i = \boldsymbol{S}^{\mathrm{T}}\boldsymbol{a}_i + \boldsymbol{e}_i$, $\mathcal{A}'$ statistically simulates $\mathsf{Exp}_{\mathsf{CE},\mathcal{A}}^{\mathrm{real}}$: (1) The distribution of $\mathsf{hk} = [\boldsymbol{R} \mid \boldsymbol{A}_T]$ is the uniform one and statistically close to the real distribution of hk, in which $\boldsymbol{A}_T$ is one of output of $\mathsf{TrapGen}(1^\lambda)$; (2) The distribution of ct is perfectly correct; (3) The distribution of $K = \mathsf{round}(\boldsymbol{b}_i)$ is also perfectly correct: By our reduction algorithm, we have $\boldsymbol{y} = \mathsf{H}(\mathsf{hk}, \boldsymbol{x}; \boldsymbol{r}) = \mathsf{hk} \cdot [\boldsymbol{x}; \boldsymbol{r}] = \boldsymbol{A}_{\backslash i}[\boldsymbol{x}_{\backslash i}; \boldsymbol{r}] + x_i \boldsymbol{a}'$. Thus, in the computation of $K \leftarrow \mathsf{E}_2(\mathsf{hk}, (i, 1 - x_i), \boldsymbol{y}; \rho)$, we compute

$$
\begin{aligned}
\boldsymbol{v}_i &= \boldsymbol{S}^{\mathrm{T}}(\boldsymbol{y} - (1 - x_i) \cdot \boldsymbol{a}') + \boldsymbol{e}_i \\
&= \boldsymbol{S}^{\mathrm{T}}(\boldsymbol{A}_{\backslash i}[\boldsymbol{x}_{\backslash i}; \boldsymbol{r}] + x_i \boldsymbol{a}' - (1 - x_i) \cdot \boldsymbol{a}') + \boldsymbol{e}_i \\
&= \boldsymbol{S}^{\mathrm{T}}(\boldsymbol{A}_{\backslash i}[\boldsymbol{x}_{\backslash i}; \boldsymbol{r}] + (2x_i - 1)\boldsymbol{a}') + \boldsymbol{e}_i \\
&= \boldsymbol{S}^{\mathrm{T}}\left(\boldsymbol{A}_{\backslash i}[\boldsymbol{x}_{\backslash i}; \boldsymbol{r}] + (2x_i - 1)(2x_i - 1)\left(\boldsymbol{a}_i - \boldsymbol{A}_{\backslash i}[\boldsymbol{x}_{\backslash i}; \boldsymbol{r}]\right)\right) + \boldsymbol{e}_i \\
&= \boldsymbol{S}^{\mathrm{T}}\left(\boldsymbol{A}_{\backslash i}[\boldsymbol{x}_{\backslash i}; \boldsymbol{r}] + \left(\boldsymbol{a}_i - \boldsymbol{A}_{\backslash i}[\boldsymbol{x}_{\backslash i}; \boldsymbol{r}]\right)\right) + \boldsymbol{e}_i \\
&= \boldsymbol{S}^{\mathrm{T}}\boldsymbol{a}_i + \boldsymbol{e}_i = \boldsymbol{b}_i,
\end{aligned}
$$

where we use the fact $(2x_i - 1)(2x_i - 1) = 1$ for $x_i \in \{0, 1\}$ to move forth line to fifth line. Therefore, $K = \mathsf{round}(\boldsymbol{v}_i) = \mathsf{round}(\boldsymbol{b}_i)$ has the correct distribution.

In the random case, $\mathcal{A}'$ statistically simulates $\mathsf{Exp}_{\mathsf{CE},\mathcal{A}}^{\mathrm{os}}$.

Therefore, assuming the LWE assumption, we obtain $\mathsf{Adv}_{\mathsf{CE},\mathcal{A}}(\lambda) = \mathsf{negl}(\lambda)$.

Public-Key Size of the Resulting NCE. The ciphertext space of this chameleon encryption is $\mathbb{Z}_q^{\ell \times (N+m)}$, where $q = 2^{\mathsf{poly}(\log \lambda)}$, $\ell = \mathcal{O}(1)$, $N = \mathcal{O}(\lambda)$, $m = \mathcal{O}(n \log q) = \lambda \cdot \mathsf{poly}(\log \lambda)$. Thus the length of ciphertexts is

$$|\mathsf{ct}| = \mathsf{poly}(\log \lambda) \cdot \mathcal{O}(1) \cdot (\mathcal{O}(\lambda) + \lambda \cdot \mathsf{poly}(\log \lambda)) = \lambda \cdot \mathsf{poly}(\log \lambda).$$

The length of the hash key is

$$|\mathsf{hk}| = \mathsf{poly}(\log \lambda) \cdot \lambda \cdot (\mathcal{O}(\lambda) + \lambda \cdot \mathsf{poly}(\log \lambda)) = \lambda^2 \cdot \mathsf{poly}(\log \lambda).$$

The length of seed for the wiretap codes is $|p| = \mathcal{O}(\lambda)$. Public key expansion of the resulting NCE scheme is

$$\frac{|p| + |\mathsf{hk}| + 2N |\mathsf{ct}|}{N} = \lambda \cdot \mathsf{poly}(\log \lambda).$$

7   Conclusion

In this work, we constructed NCE schemes with constant ciphertext expansion from the DDH or LWE problem.

Along the way, we defined weak NCE. Given that the full-fledged NCE is a tool to establish private channels in adaptively secure MPC, weak NCE can be interpreted as a tool to establish wiretap channels in adaptively secure MPC.

Through wiretap channels, we can securely transmit a message by encoding with wiretap codes that satisfy conditional invertibility.

We showed instantiation of weak NCE that has constant ciphertext expansion and amplified it by using constant rate wiretap codes. Finally, we roughly estimate the ciphertext expansion of the resulting NCE scheme. As we see in Sect. 5, ciphertext expansion of our weak NCE scheme is 2ℓ asymptotically. Suppose the wiretap codes used in the amplification achieve the secrecy rate $1/2 - h_2(\epsilon)$ where $\epsilon = 1/2^{\ell+1}$. Then, the ciphertext expansion in Eq. 1 has minimum value ≈ 27 when $\ell = 5$.

We also showed the public-key expansion of our NCE scheme can be reduced to $\lambda \cdot \text{poly}(\log \lambda)$ if it is instantiated from the LWE problem. One may think that the use of the ring-LWE problem may further reduce public-key expansion similar to the LWE based NCE scheme by Hemenway et al. [22]. However, unfortunately, it seems that the ring-LWE problem is not helpful to reduce the public-key size asymptotically. Constructing an NCE scheme with constant ciphertext expansion and better public-key expansion is a natural future direction.

Acknowledgments. A part of this work was supported by NTT Secure Platform Laboratories, JST OPERA JPMJOP1612, JST CREST JPMJCR14D6, JSPS KAKENHI JP16H01705, JP17H01695, JP19J22363.

References

1. Arikan, E.: Channel polarization: a method for constructing capacity-achieving codes for symmetric binary-input memoryless channels. IEEE Trans. Inf. Theory **55**(7), 3051–3073 (2009)
2. Beaver, D.: Plug and play encryption. In: Kaliski, B.S. (ed.) CRYPTO 1997. LNCS, vol. 1294, pp. 75–89. Springer, Heidelberg (1997). https://doi.org/10.1007/BFb0052228
3. Beaver, D., Haber, S.: Cryptographic protocols provably secure against dynamic adversaries. In: Rueppel, R.A. (ed.) EUROCRYPT 1992. LNCS, vol. 658, pp. 307–323. Springer, Heidelberg (1993). https://doi.org/10.1007/3-540-47555-9_26
4. Bellare, M., Tessaro, S.: Polynomial-time, semantically-secure encryption achieving the secrecy capacity. Cryptology ePrint Archive, Report 2012/022 (2012)
5. Bellare, M., Tessaro, S., Vardy, A.: A cryptographic treatment of the wiretap channel. Cryptology ePrint Archive, Report 2012/015 (2012)
6. Bellare, M., Tessaro, S., Vardy, A.: Semantic security for the wiretap channel. In: Safavi-Naini, R., Canetti, R. (eds.) CRYPTO 2012. LNCS, vol. 7417, pp. 294–311. Springer, Heidelberg (2012). https://doi.org/10.1007/978-3-642-32009-5_18
7. Ben-Or, M., Goldwasser, S., Wigderson, A.: Completeness theorems for non-cryptographic fault-tolerant distributed computation (extended abstract). In: 20th Annual ACM Symposium on Theory of Computing, Chicago, IL, USA, pp. 1–10 (1988)
8. Canetti, R., Feige, U., Goldreich, O., Naor, M.: Adaptively secure multi-party computation. In: 28th Annual ACM Symposium on Theory of Computing, Philadephia, PA, USA, pp. 639–648 (1996)

9. Canetti, R., Lindell, Y., Ostrovsky, R., Sahai, A.: Universally composable two-party and multi-party secure computation. In 34th Annual ACM Symposium on Theory of Computing, Montréal, Québec, Canada, pp. 494–503 (2002)

10. Canetti, R., Poburinnaya, O., Raykova, M.: Optimal-rate non-committing encryption. In: Takagi, T., Peyrin, T. (eds.) ASIACRYPT 2017. LNCS, vol. 10626, pp. 212–241. Springer, Cham (2017). https://doi.org/10.1007/978-3-319-70700-6_8

11. Cash, D., Hofheinz, D., Kiltz, E., Peikert, C.: Bonsai trees, or how to delegate a lattice basis. In: Gilbert, H. (ed.) EUROCRYPT 2010. LNCS, vol. 6110, pp. 523–552. Springer, Heidelberg (2010). https://doi.org/10.1007/978-3-642-13190-5_27

12. Chaum, D., Crépeau, C., Damgård, I.: Multiparty unconditionally secure protocols (extended abstract). In: 20th Annual ACM Symposium on Theory of Computing, Chicago, IL, USA, pp. 11–19 (1988)

13. Choi, S.G., Dachman-Soled, D., Malkin, T., Wee, H.: Improved non-committing encryption with applications to adaptively secure protocols. In: Matsui, M. (ed.) ASIACRYPT 2009. LNCS, vol. 5912, pp. 287–302. Springer, Heidelberg (2009). https://doi.org/10.1007/978-3-642-10366-7_17

14. Cramer, R., Damgård, I.B., Döttling, N., Fehr, S., Spini, G.: Linear secret sharing schemes from error correcting codes and universal hash functions. In: Oswald, E., Fischlin, M. (eds.) EUROCRYPT 2015. LNCS, vol. 9057, pp. 313–336. Springer, Heidelberg (2015). https://doi.org/10.1007/978-3-662-46803-6_11

15. Damgård, I., Nielsen, J.B.: Improved non-committing encryption schemes based on a general complexity assumption. In: Bellare, M. (ed.) CRYPTO 2000. LNCS, vol. 1880, pp. 432–450. Springer, Heidelberg (2000). https://doi.org/10.1007/3-540-44598-6_27

16. Döttling, N., Garg, S.: Identity-based encryption from the Diffie-Hellman assumption. In: Katz, J., Shacham, H. (eds.) CRYPTO 2017. LNCS, vol. 10401, pp. 537–569. Springer, Cham (2017). https://doi.org/10.1007/978-3-319-63688-7_18

17. Döttling, N., Garg, S., Hajiabadi, M., Masny, D.: New constructions of identity-based and key-dependent message secure encryption schemes. In: Abdalla, M., Dahab, R. (eds.) PKC 2018. LNCS, vol. 10769, pp. 3–31. Springer, Cham (2018). https://doi.org/10.1007/978-3-319-76578-5_1

18. Dwork, C., Naor, M., Reingold, O.: Immunizing encryption schemes from decryption errors. In: Cachin, C., Camenisch, J.L. (eds.) EUROCRYPT 2004. LNCS, vol. 3027, pp. 342–360. Springer, Heidelberg (2004). https://doi.org/10.1007/978-3-540-24676-3_21

19. Gentry, C., Peikert, C., Vaikuntanathan, V.: Trapdoors for hard lattices and new cryptographic constructions. In: 40th Annual ACM Symposium on Theory of Computing, Victoria, BC, Canada, pp. 197–206 (2008)

20. Goldreich, O., Micali, S., Wigderson, A.: How to play any mental game or a completeness theorem for protocols with honest majority. In: 19th Annual ACM Symposium on Theory of Computing, New York City, NY, USA, pp. 218–229 (1987)

21. Guo, S., Kamath, P., Rosen, A., Sotiraki, K.: Limits on the efficiency of (ring) LWE based non-interactive key exchange. In: Kiayias, A., Kohlweiss, M., Wallden, P., Zikas, V. (eds.) PKC 2020. LNCS, vol. 12110, pp. 374–395. Springer, Cham (2020). https://doi.org/10.1007/978-3-030-45374-9_13

22. Hemenway, B., Ostrovsky, R., Richelson, S., Rosen, A.: Adaptive security with quasi-optimal rate. In: Kushilevitz, E., Malkin, T. (eds.) TCC 2016. LNCS, vol. 9562, pp. 525–541. Springer, Heidelberg (2016). https://doi.org/10.1007/978-3-662-49096-9_22

23. Hemenway, B., Ostrovsky, R., Rosen, A.: Non-committing encryption from Φ-hiding. In: Dodis, Y., Nielsen, J.B. (eds.) TCC 2015. LNCS, vol. 9014, pp. 591–608. Springer, Heidelberg (2015). https://doi.org/10.1007/978-3-662-46494-6_24

24. Holenstein, T., Renner, R.: One-way secret-key agreement and applications to circuit polarization and immunization of public-key encryption. In: Shoup, V. (ed.) CRYPTO 2005. LNCS, vol. 3621, pp. 478–493. Springer, Heidelberg (2005). https://doi.org/10.1007/11535218_29

25. Leung-Yan-Cheong, S.K.: On a special class of wiretap channels (corresp.). IEEE Trans. Inf. Theory **23**(5), 625–627 (1977)

26. Lin, H., Tessaro, S.: Amplification of chosen-ciphertext security. In: Johansson, T., Nguyen, P.Q. (eds.) EUROCRYPT 2013. LNCS, vol. 7881, pp. 503–519. Springer, Heidelberg (2013). https://doi.org/10.1007/978-3-642-38348-9_30

27. Micciancio, D., Peikert, C.: Trapdoors for lattices: simpler, tighter, faster, smaller. In: Pointcheval, D., Johansson, T. (eds.) EUROCRYPT 2012. LNCS, vol. 7237, pp. 700–718. Springer, Heidelberg (2012). https://doi.org/10.1007/978-3-642-29011-4_41

28. Micciancio, D., Regev, O.: Worst-case to average-case reductions based on Gaussian measures. SIAM J. Comput. **37**(1), 267–302 (2007)

29. Regev, O.: On lattices, learning with errors, random linear codes, and cryptography. In: 37th Annual ACM Symposium on Theory of Computing, Baltimore, MA, USA, pp. 84–93 (2005)

30. Wyner, A.D.: The wire-tap channel. Bell Syst. Tech. J. **54**(8), 1355–1387 (1975)

31. Yoshida, Y., Kitagawa, F., Tanaka, K.: Non-committing encryption with quasi-optimal ciphertext-rate based on the DDH problem. In: Galbraith, S.D., Moriai, S. (eds.) ASIACRYPT 2019. LNCS, vol. 11923, pp. 128–158. Springer, Cham (2019). https://doi.org/10.1007/978-3-030-34618-8_5

Collusion Resistant Trace-and-Revoke for Arbitrary Identities from Standard Assumptions

Sam Kim[1(✉)] and David J. Wu[2(✉)]

[1] Stanford University, Stanford, CA, USA
skim13@cs.stanford.edu
[2] University of Virginia, Charlottesville, VA, USA
dwu4@virginia.edu

Abstract. A traitor tracing scheme is a multi-user public-key encryption scheme where each user in the system holds a decryption key that is associated with the user's identity. Using the public key, a content distributor can encrypt a message to all of the users in the system. At the same time, if a malicious group of users combine their respective decryption keys to build a "pirate decoder," there is an efficient tracing algorithm that the content distributor can use to identify at least one of the keys used to construct the decoder. A *trace-and-revoke* scheme is an extension of a standard traitor tracing scheme where there is an additional key-revocation mechanism that the content distributor can use to disable the decryption capabilities of compromised keys. Namely, during encryption, the content distributor can encrypt a message with respect to a list of revoked users such that only non-revoked users can decrypt the resulting ciphertext.

Trace-and-revoke schemes are challenging to construct. Existing constructions from standard assumptions can only tolerate bounded collusions (i.e., there is an *a priori* bound on the number of keys an adversary obtains), have system parameters that scale *exponentially* in the bit-length of the identities, or satisfy weaker notions of traceability that are vulnerable to certain types of "pirate evolution" attacks. In this work, we provide the first construction of a trace-and-revoke scheme that is fully collusion resistant and capable of supporting arbitrary identities (i.e., the identities can be drawn from an exponential-size space). Our scheme supports public encryption and secret tracing, and can be based on the sub-exponential hardness of the LWE problem (with a super-polynomial modulus-to-noise ratio). The ciphertext size in our construction scales logarithmically in the size of the identity space and linearly in the size of the revocation list. Our scheme leverages techniques from both combinatorial and algebraic constructions for traitor tracing.

The full version of this paper is available at https://eprint.iacr.org/2019/984.pdf.

S. Moriai and H. Wang (Eds.): ASIACRYPT 2020, LNCS 12492, pp. 66–97, 2020.
https://doi.org/10.1007/978-3-030-64834-3_3

1   Introduction

Traitor tracing schemes [CFN94] provide content distributors a way to identify malicious receivers and pirates. Specifically, a traitor tracing scheme is a public-key encryption scheme that is defined over a set of global public parameters pp and many secret decryption keys $\{sk_{id}\}$. Each of the decryption keys sk_{id} is associated with an identifier id (e.g., a user's name or profile picture). Anyone is able to encrypt a message using the public parameters pp and any user who holds a valid decryption key sk_{id} can decrypt the resulting ciphertext. The main security property is *traceability*, which says that if a coalition of users combine their respective decryption keys to create a new decryption algorithm (i.e., a "pirate decoder"), there is an efficient tracing algorithm that, given (black-box) access to the decoder, will successfully identify at least one of the secret keys that was used to construct the pirate decoder. As such, traitor tracing schemes provide an effective way for content distributors to combat piracy.

In practice, simply identifying the keys that went into a pirate decoder is not enough; we also require a way for the content distributor to disable the decryption capabilities of a compromised key. Traitor tracing schemes that support efficient key-revocation mechanisms are called *trace-and-revoke* schemes [NP00]. In a trace-and-revoke scheme, the encryption algorithm additionally takes in a list of revoked users $\mathcal{L}$. A ciphertext that is generated with respect to a revocation list $\mathcal{L}$ can only be decrypted by keys for identities id $\notin \mathcal{L}$. Furthermore, the revocation mechanism should remain compatible with tracing: namely, if an adversary builds a pirate decoder that can still decrypt ciphertexts encrypted with respect to a revocation list $\mathcal{L}$, the tracing algorithm should successfully identify at least one of the non-revoked decryption keys (i.e., some id $\notin \mathcal{L}$) that went into the construction of the pirate decoder. We give the formal definition in Sect. 4.

Properties of Trace-and-Revoke Schemes. There are a number of possible properties that a trace-and-revoke scheme could provide. We enumerate several important ones below:

- **Collusion resistance:** A trace-and-revoke scheme is t-collusion resistant if tracing works as long as the pirate obtains fewer than t decryption keys, and the scheme parameters are allowed to depend on t. When t can be an arbitrary polynomial, the scheme is *fully collusion resistant*.
- **A priori unbounded revocation:** Some trace-and-revoke schemes support bounded revocation where at setup time, there is an *a priori* bound r on the maximum number of revoked users the scheme supports. A scheme supports *a priori unbounded revocation* if the number of revoked users can be an arbitrary polynomial. We note here that while we can require an even stronger property that supports revoking a super-polynomial number of users, the scheme we develop in this work does not support this stronger property (except in certain restricted settings; see Sect. 1.1).
- **Black box tracing:** A trace-and-revoke scheme supports black box tracing if the tracing algorithm only requires oracle access to the pirate decoder.

This means we do not need to impose any restrictions on the structure of the adversary's decoder. Tracing must work on *any* decoder that is able to decrypt (or even better, *distinguish*) ciphertexts.

- **Identity-based:** A trace-and-revoke scheme is "identity-based" or supports *arbitrary* identities if the set of possible identities $\mathcal{ID}$ the scheme supports can be exponential in size [NWZ16]. In most trace-and-revoke schemes, the set of possible identities is assumed to have polynomial size (i.e., identities are represented by an element of the set $[N] = \{1, \ldots, N\}$). This means that there is an a priori bound on the maximum number of users supported by the system, and moreover, in practical scenarios, the tracing authority needs to separately maintain a database mapping from a numeric index id $\in [N]$ to a user's actual identifier (which may not fit into a string of length $\log N$). In addition, as noted in [NWZ16], an added benefit of trace-and-revoke schemes that support arbitrary identities is *anonymity*: namely, a user can obtain a decryption key for their identity without needing to reveal their identity to the key issuer.

Our Results. In this work, we focus on constructing trace-and-revoke schemes that provide each of the above guarantees. Namely, we seek schemes that are flexible (e.g., can support arbitrary identities of polynomial length and an arbitrary polynomial number of revocations) while providing strong security (i.e., full collusion resistance and security against arbitrary adversarial strategies). We achieve these properties assuming sub-exponential hardness of the learning with errors (LWE) assumption [Reg05]. Specifically, we show the following:

Theorem 1.1 (informal). *Let λ be a security parameter and $\mathcal{ID} = \{0,1\}^n$ be the set of possible identities. Assuming sub-exponential hardness of LWE, there exists a fully collusion resistant trace-and-revoke scheme where the secret key for an identity* id $\in \{0,1\}^n$ *has size* $n \cdot \mathsf{poly}(\lambda, \log n)$ *and a ciphertext encrypting a message m with respect to a revocation list* $\mathcal{L} \subseteq \{0,1\}^n$ *has size* $|m| + |\mathcal{L}| \cdot \mathsf{poly}(\lambda, \log n)$. *Encryption in our scheme is a public operation while tracing requires knowledge of a secret key.*

Previous trace-and-revoke constructions were either not collusion resistant [NWZ16, ABP+17], could only support a polynomial-size identity space [BW06, GKSW10, GQWW19], achieved weaker models of tracing [NNL01, DF02], or relied on strong assumptions such as indistinguishability obfuscation [NWZ16] or (positional) witness encryption [GVW19]. We refer to Sect. 1.2 for a more detailed comparison of our construction with existing ones.

Open Questions. Before giving an overview of our construction, we highlight several interesting directions to further improve upon our trace-and-revoke scheme:

- *Public tracing:* Our tracing algorithm requires a secret key. It is an interesting open problem to obtain fully collusion resistant trace-and-revoke for arbitrary identities with public tracing from standard assumptions. In fact, even obtaining a collusion resistant traitor tracing scheme with succinct keys and public tracing from standard assumptions is currently open.

- *Succinct broadcast:* The length of the ciphertexts in our construction scales *linearly* in the size of the revocation list, and as such, our scheme only supports revocation for a polynomial number of users. It is an open question is to develop an scheme that supports arbitrary identities and where the ciphertext size scales *sublinearly* in the number of revoked users (and more generally, where the ciphertext size scales with the *description length* of the revocation list rather than its size). Schemes with these properties are often called "broadcast, trace, and revoke" schemes [BW06] as they combine both the succinctness of a "broadcast encryption" [FN93] with the tracing capability of a traitor tracing scheme. Existing broadcast, trace, and revoke constructions [BW06, GKSW10, GQWW19] from standard assumptions can only handle a polynomial number of users. We provide a more thorough comparison in Sect. 1.2.
- *Polynomial hardness:* Security of our tracing construction relies on the *subexponential* hardness of LWE. Our reliance on sub-exponential hardness assumptions is due to our use of complexity leveraging [BB04] to instantiate *adaptively-secure* variants of the underlying cryptographic primitives we require in our construction. An important open problem is to base security on polynomial hardness. The work of Goyal et al. [GKW19] show how to obtain traitor tracing for an exponential-size identity space from a polynomial hardness assumption, but their scheme does not support revocation.

1.1 Construction Overview

In this section, we provide a high-level overview of our construction. Our approach combines an identity-based traitor tracing scheme based on the techniques developed in [NWZ16, GKW18] with the combinatorial revocation scheme from [NNL01]. We describe each of these components below.

Traitor Tracing from Private Linear Broadcast. Boneh et al. [BSW06] showed how to construct a collusion resistant traitor tracing scheme from a private linear broadcast encryption (PLBE) scheme. A PLBE scheme is an encryption scheme where decryption keys are associated with an index $i \in [N]$, and ciphertexts are associated with a secret index $j \in [N]$ and a message m. The correctness property guarantees that a decryption key sk_i for index i can decrypt all ciphertexts encrypted to indices j where $i \leq j$. There are two ways to generate a ciphertext. The *public* encryption algorithm allows anyone to encrypt to the index N, which can be decrypted by secret keys sk_i for all $i \in [N]$. The *secret* encryption algorithm allows the tracing authority who holds a tracing key to encrypt to indices $j \leq N$. The "index-hiding" requirement guarantees that an adversary who does not have a key for index j cannot distinguish an encryption to index j from an encryption to index $j + 1$. Finally, the "message-hiding" requirement says that ciphertexts encrypted to index 0 are semantically secure (given any subset of decryption keys for indices $1 \leq j \leq N$). These properties form the basis of the tracing algorithm described in [BSW06]. Boneh et al. showed how to construct

PLBE from pairing-based assumptions where the ciphertexts have size $O(\sqrt{N})$. Hence their scheme only supports a polynomial-size identity space.

Recently, Goyal et al. [GKW18] gave a new construction of a PLBE scheme from the LWE assumption by combining a new cryptographic notion called mixed functional encryption (mixed FE) with an attribute-based encryption (ABE) scheme [SW05,GPSW06]. Their construction has the appealing property that the size of all of the system parameters (e.g., the public parameters, decryption keys, and ciphertexts) scale with $\mathsf{poly}(\lambda, \log N)$. Thus, the construction of Goyal et al. [GKW18] can in principle support arbitrary set of identities. However, the tracing algorithm in the PLBE framework runs in time that scales *linearly* with the size of the identity space. As a result, the [GKW18] construction does not support tracing over an exponential space of identities.

Identity-Based Traitor-Tracing from Functional Encryption. In [NWZ16], Nishimaki et al. introduced a more general tracing algorithm for PLBE that supports an exponential identity space (by abstracting the tracing problem as an "oracle jump-finding" problem). Their construction relies on a PLBE scheme that satisfies a more general notion of index-hiding security. Namely a ciphertext encrypted to index j_1 should be indistinguishable from a ciphertext encrypted to index j_2 as long as the adversary does not have any keys in the interval $(j_1, j_2]$.[1] A limitation of this construction is that the ciphertexts scale linearly in the bit-length of the identities. Nishimaki et al. then show how to construct a traitor tracing scheme with *short* ciphertexts (i.e., one where the ciphertext size scales with $\mathsf{poly}(\log \log N)$) from a private broadcast encryption scheme that support slightly more general broadcast sets. Finally, they note that private broadcast is just a special case of general-purpose functional encryption which can be instantiated using indistinguishability obfuscation [GGH+13], or, in the bounded-collusion setting, from LWE [GKP+13] or even just public-key encryption [SS10,GVW12].

A More General View of [GKW18]. In this work, we take a more general view of the PLBE construction in [GKW18] and show that the construction in fact gives a *secret-key predicate encryption scheme with a broadcast functionality*. In turn, PLBE can be viewed as a specific instantiation of the predicate encryption scheme for the particular class of threshold predicates. This view will enable our generalization to identity-based traitor tracing with short ciphertexts (by following the approach of [NWZ16]) as well as enable an efficient mechanism for key revocation. Note that the "broadcast functionality" considered here refers to a method to *publicly* encrypt a message that can be decrypted by *all* secret keys in the system (i.e., broadcasting a message to all users in the system). We are not requiring the ability to succinctly broadcast messages to subsets of users (as in the setting of broadcast encryption [FN93]).

---

[1] This property follows from the usual index-hiding security game by a standard hybrid argument when the indices are drawn from a polynomial-size space, but not when the indices are drawn from an exponentially-large one.

Specifically, in a secret-key (ciphertext-policy) predicate encryption scheme, ciphertexts are associated with a predicate f and a message m, while decryption keys are associated with an attribute x. Decrypting a ciphertext $\mathsf{ct}_{f,m}$ associated with a predicate f and a message m with a function key for an attribute x yields m if $f(x) = 1$ and $\perp$ otherwise. Moreover, the policy f associated with a ciphertext is hidden irrespective of whether decryption succeeds or not—this property is the analog of the "strong" attribute-hiding property considered in the study of key-policy predicate encryption [BW07, KSW08, SBC+07]. Finally, while the predicate encryption scheme is secret-key, there exists a *public* encryption algorithm that allows anyone to encrypt a message with respect to the "always-accept" policy (i.e., $f(x) = 1$ for all inputs x). In Sect. 3.1, we show how to combine mixed FE (for general circuits) and attribute-based encryption (for general circuits) to obtain a secret-key ciphertext-policy predicate encryption scheme with broadcast. This construction is a direct analog of the [GKW18] construction of PLBE from the same set of underlying primitives. Next, we note that this type of predicate encryption directly implies a fully collusion resistant traitor tracing scheme with short ciphertexts via [NWZ16]. The one difference, however, is that since the predicate encryption scheme is in the secret-key setting, only the tracing authority who holds the master secret key is able to run the tracing algorithm. Thus in contrast to [NWZ16], our scheme only supports *secret tracing*. We note that working in the secret-key setting introduces some new challenges in the security analysis of the [NWZ16] construction. These can be handled using similar techniques as those developed in [GKW18], and we discuss this in greater detail in Sect. 4.1.

Trace-and-Revoke via Revocable Predicate Encryption. Thus far, we have shown how to combine ideas from [GKW18] and [NWZ16] to obtain a collusion resistant traitor tracing scheme for arbitrary identities. The next step is to develop a mechanism for key revocation. Previously, Nishimaki et al. showed how to use a revocable functional encryption scheme to construct a trace-and-revoke scheme. In this work, we show that a revocable variant of our secret-key predicate encryption scheme with broadcast also suffices for this general transformation. Namely, in a revocable predicate encryption scheme, each decryption key is additionally tagged with an identity id, and at encryption time (both secret and public), the encrypter provides both the decryption policy f and the revocation list $\mathcal{L}$. The resulting ciphertext can then be decrypted by all keys $\mathsf{sk}_{\mathsf{id},x}$ associated with an identity id and an attribute x such that $f(x) = 1$ and $\mathsf{id} \notin \mathcal{L}$.

A natural approach to support revocation is to include the revocation list $\mathcal{L}$ as part of the ciphertext policy in the predicate encryption scheme. We would then embed the identity id as part of the decryption key, and the final decryption policy would first check that $\mathsf{id} \notin \mathcal{L}$ and then check that $f(x) = 1$. While this basic approach seems straightforward, it unfortunately does not apply in our setting. As noted above, the predicate encryption scheme we construct is a *secret-key* scheme, and the only public operation it supports is the broadcast functionality.[2] Obtaining a public-key analog of collusion resistant, strong attribute-hiding predicate encryption seems quite challenging (and in fact, implies public-key functional encryption). But as we note in Remark 3.3, even in the bounded-collusion setting (where we can construct public-key predicate encryption from standard assumptions), this basic approach seems to run into a barrier, and any such instantiation from standard assumptions would likely have to assume a bound on the maximum number of revoked users. In this work, we seek solutions from standard assumptions that are collusion resistant and support unbounded revocation.

Revocable Predicate Encryption via Subset Cover Set Systems. As we described above, constructing a collusion resistant trace-and-revoke scheme for arbitrary identities reduces to constructing a secret-key revocable predicate encryption scheme with a broadcast functionality. To build the necessary revocable predicate encryption scheme, we leverage ideas from combinatorial constructions of traitor tracing. We note that while we rely on combinatorial ideas in our construction, we do not provide a generic transformation of any predicate encryption scheme into a revocable analog. Rather, our construction relies on a careful integration of the algebraic approach from [GKW18] with the combinatorial approach from [NNL01].

The core combinatorial ingredient that we use for our construction is a subset-cover set system, a notion that has featured in several traitor tracing constructions [NNL01,DF02,HS02]. Let $[N]$ be the identity space. A subset-cover set system for $[N]$ is a set of indices $[K]$ with the following two properties. Each identity $\mathsf{id} \in [N]$ is associated with a small number of indices $\mathcal{I}_{\mathsf{id}} \subseteq [K]$. Moreover, given a revocation list $\mathcal{L} \subseteq [N]$, there is an efficient algorithm to compute a "covering" set of indices $\mathcal{J}_{\mathcal{L}} \subseteq [K]$ with the property that $\mathsf{id} \in \mathcal{L}$ if and only if $\mathcal{I}_{\mathsf{id}} \cap \mathcal{J}_{\mathcal{L}} = \varnothing$. If we instantiate using the subset-cover set system from [NNL01], then $K = O(N)$, $|\mathcal{I}_{\mathsf{id}}| = O(\log N)$, and $|\mathcal{J}_{\mathcal{L}}| = O(|\mathcal{L}| \log(N/|\mathcal{L}|))$.

Given a subset-cover set system, a first attempt to construct a revocable predicate encryption scheme is as follows. We associate a set of public parameters pp_i and master secret key msk_i with each index $i \in [K]$. A key for an identity $\mathsf{id} \in [N]$ and an attribute x would consist of predicate encryption keys $\mathsf{sk}_{\mathsf{id},x} \leftarrow \mathsf{KeyGen}(\mathsf{msk}_i, x)$ for all the predicate encryption schemes $i \in \mathcal{I}_{\mathsf{id}}$ associated with id. Finally, an encryption of a message m with respect to the revocation list $\mathcal{L} \subseteq [N]$ would consist of a collection of ciphertexts $\{\mathsf{ct}_i\}_{i \in \mathcal{J}_{\mathcal{L}}}$ where each ct_i is an encryption of m with respect to pp_i for $i \in \mathcal{J}_{\mathcal{L}}$. By the property described above, if $\mathsf{id} \notin \mathcal{L}$, then $\mathcal{I}_{\mathsf{id}} \cap \mathcal{J}_{\mathcal{L}} \neq \varnothing$. This means that all non-revoked users $\mathsf{id} \notin \mathcal{L}$ will possess a key $\mathsf{sk}_{i,x}$ for some $i \in \mathcal{J}_{\mathcal{L}}$, and therefore, will be able to decrypt (provided that $f(x) = 1$). For a revoked user, it will be the case that $i \notin \mathcal{J}_{\mathcal{L}}$ for

---

[2] The recent work of Goyal et al. [GQWW19] introduces a notion of *broadcast mixed FE* that supports a *succinct* public broadcast to a restricted set of identities (of polynomial size). The notion we develop in this work supports an exponential-sized identity space, but in a *non-succinct* manner (i.e., the ciphertext size scales linearly with the size of the revocation list).

all $i \in \mathcal{I}_{\mathsf{id}}$, and they will be unable to decrypt. The problem though is that the size of the public parameters now scale *linearly* with K (which is as large as N). As such, this scheme only supports a polynomial number of identities. Thus, we need a different approach. We describe two candidate ideas below:

- If the underlying predicate encryption scheme has the property where the master secret key msk can be sampled *after* the public parameters pp, then in principle, the construction above would suffice. Namely, we would use a single set of public parameters for all of the predicate encryption schemes, and derive the master secret key msk_i for each $i \in [K]$ from a pseudorandom function (PRF). Unfortunately, such a predicate encryption scheme cannot be secure since the adversary can always generate for itself a master secret key and use it to decrypt.
- If the scheme supports a *public* encryption algorithm, then we can support revocation by including the index $i \in [K]$ as part of the policy associated with the ciphertext as well as the attribute in the decryption key. Then, the decryption policy would additionally check that the index associated with the key matched the index associated with the ciphertext. Essentially, we ensure that a decryption key for i can only be used to decrypt ciphertexts encrypted to index i. However, this revocation approach also does not seem to apply in our setting because our predicate encryption scheme is in the secret-key setting, and it is not clear how to generalize to a public-key encryption algorithm that can support more general policies (while retaining the same security properties).[3]

While neither of these approaches directly apply in our setting, we can combine *both* ideas in our construction to obtain a revocable predicate encryption scheme. As noted above, our basic secret-key predicate encryption scheme with broadcast combines a mixed FE scheme with an ABE scheme. Without getting into too many details, the construction has the following properties. Each ciphertext in the scheme consists of a mixed FE ciphertext and an ABE ciphertext, and analogously, each decryption key consists of a mixed FE decryption key and an ABE decryption key. The mixed FE scheme is a secret-key scheme that supports a broadcast mechanism while the ABE scheme is a standard public-key scheme. The key observation is that if *both* the underlying mixed FE scheme and the ABE scheme support revocation, then the resulting predicate encryption scheme also supports revocation. For our construction it is critical that both schemes support revocation as we rely on the mixed FE scheme to hide the ciphertext policy and the ABE scheme to hide the message. If only one of the underlying schemes

---

[3] While the notion of attribute-based mixed FE from [CVW+18] seems like it would also provide this functionality, this revocation approach only preserves the message hiding property and not the mixed FE attribute hiding property of the underlying attribute-based mixed FE scheme. For our trace-and-revoke scheme, we require both message hiding and attribute hiding (which we refer to as "function hiding"). Obtaining the latter property seemingly requires a way to revoke mixed FE decryption keys.

supports revocation, then one or both of these security properties become incompatible with revocation. We now describe how we implement revocation for the underlying mixed FE and ABE schemes:

- The mixed FE scheme is a secret-key scheme that supports public broadcast. Unlike standard predicate encryption, the security properties of mixed FE can be satisfied by schemes where the master secret key is sampled *after* the public parameters, and this property is satisfied by existing constructions [GKW18, CVW+18]. This means that we can associate a different mixed FE scheme with each index $i \in [K]$ where the master secret key associated with each instance is derived from a PRF. All of the mixed FE schemes share a common set of public parameters. We can now use the first revocation idea described above to implement revocation for the mixed FE scheme.
- Next, the ABE scheme is a public-key encryption scheme, and thus, we can use the second type of revocation described above. Namely, we require a single set of ABE parameters and simply include the index $i \in [K]$ in both the decryption key and the ciphertext to identity which index is being targeted.

By combining these two approaches for revocation, we show in Sect. 3.1 how to construct a secret-key revocable predicate encryption with broadcast scheme from the sub-exponential hardness of LWE. Notably, our final revocation mechanism relies critically on both the combinatoric properties of the subset-cover set system as well as the specific algebraic nature of the predicate encryption construction. Together, this yields the first collusion resistant trace-and-revoke scheme for arbitrary identities from the same underlying assumptions (Theorem 1.1).

A Simple Extension: More General Revocation Policies. While the basic scheme we described above supports revoking any polynomial number of identities, it naturally extends to support any revocation policy supported by the underlying subset-cover set system. Specifically, if we use the prefix-based subset-cover set system by Naor et al. [NNL01], our scheme supports revoking any number of identities that can be specified by a polynomial number of *prefix-based patterns*. For instance, we can revoke all users whose identity starts with a fixed prefix—which may consist of an *exponential* number of identities. In a concrete application, if the first few bits of a user's identity specifies a region, then we can use prefix-based policies to efficiently revoke all of the users from one or more regions. We provide more discussion in Remark 3.10.

1.2   Related Work

In this section, we survey some of the related work on traitor tracing and trace-and-revoke schemes and compare our results to existing notions.

Traitor Tracing and Trace-and-Revoke. Numerous works have studied constructions of both traitor tracing and trace-and-revoke schemes from a wide range of assumptions and settings. Very broadly, most existing constructions can be categorized into two main categories: *combinatorial* approaches [CFN94, NP98, SSW01, CFNP00, NNL01, HS02, DF02, SSW01, BN08] and *algebraic* approaches [KD98, NP00, BSW06, BW06, GKSW10, LPSS14, KT15, NWZ16, ABP+17, GKW18, CVW+18, GVW19, GQWW19]. We refer to these works and the references therein for a survey of the field.

Many existing traitor-tracing and trace-and-revoke schemes (from standard assumptions) are only secure against bounded collusions [CFN94, KD98, NP00, SSW01, LPSS14, KT15, NWZ16, ABP+17]. Other schemes are fully collusion resistant, but can only handle a polynomial-size identity space [BSW06, BW06, GKSW10, GKW18, CVW+18, GQWW19]. In this work, we focus on schemes that are fully collusion resistant and support arbitrary identity spaces. While there are schemes that are both collusion resistant and support a super-polynomial identity space [NWZ16, GVW19], these construction require strong assumptions such as indistinguishability obfuscation [BGI+12] or positional witness encryption and cannot currently be based on standard intractability assumptions.

Several of the aforementioned schemes from standard assumptions [BW06, GKSW10, GQWW19] additionally provide a *succinct* broadcast mechanism where anyone can encrypt a message to any subset of the users with a ciphertext whose size scales with $N^{1/2}$ [BW06, GKSW10] or with N^{ε} [GQWW19] for any constant $\varepsilon > 0$, where N is the total number of users in the system. Such schemes are commonly referred to as "broadcast, trace, and revoke" schemes. Notably, the ciphertext size in these constructions is *independent* of the number of revoked users and only depends on the total number of users. In our trace-and-revoke construction (Theorem 1.1), the ciphertext size scales *linearly* with the number of revoked users (which can be $\Omega(N)$ in the worst case). Thus, in the setting where we have a polynomial-size identity space and when the number of revoked users is a sufficiently-large fraction of the total number of users, existing broadcast, trace, and revoke constructions will have shorter ciphertexts. In the setting where there is an exponential identity space, the ciphertexts in these existing constructions are also exponential, and they do not provide a compelling solution.

Several works [NP98, CFNP00, BN08] consider a threshold notion of traitor tracing where the tracing algorithm is only guaranteed to work for decoders that succeed with probability at least $\delta = 1/\text{poly}(\lambda)$ (and the scheme parameters are allowed to depend on the parameter δ). In this work, we focus on schemes that work for any decoder that succeeds with non-negligible probability.

Some combinatorial constructions [NNL01, HS02, DF02] are fully collusion resistant, but they only satisfy a weaker notion of traceability where the tracing algorithm either succeeds in extracting a pirated key *or* identifies an encryption strategy that disables the pirate decoder (this latter strategy increases the ciphertext size). This weaker traceability notion has led to pirate evolution [KP07] and Pirate 2.0 attacks [BP09] on schemes satisfying this weaker security notion. In this work, we focus on the strong notion of traceability where the tracing algorithm always succeeds in extracting at least one pirate key from any functional decoder. This notion is not affected by the pirate evolution attacks.

Cryptographic Watermarking. A closely-related notion to traitor tracing is cryptographic watermarking [BGI+12, CHN+16]. Very briefly, a cryptographic watermarking scheme allows an authority to embed arbitrary data into the secret key of a cryptographic function such that the marked program preserves the original functionality, and moreover, it is difficult to remove the watermark from the program without destroying its functionality. A collusion resistant watermarking scheme for a public-key encryption scheme would imply a collusion resistant traitor tracing scheme. Existing constructions [KW17, QWZ18, KW19b] of watermarking from standard assumptions are not collusion resistant and they are also limited to watermarking PRFs, which are not sufficient for traitor tracing. The recent construction of watermarking for public-key primitives [GKM+19] does imply a traitor tracing scheme for general identities (with public tracing), but only provides bounded collusion resistance (in fact, in this setting, their construction precisely coincides with the bounded collusion resistant traitor tracing construction from [NWZ16]). Moreover, it is not clear that existing constructions of watermarking can be extended to support key revocation.

Concurrent Work. In a recent and concurrent work, Goyal et al. [GKW19] also study the problem of identity-based traitor tracing for arbitrary identities (i.e., which they call "traitor tracing with embedded identities"). Their focus is on traitor tracing (without revocation) and achieving security based on *polynomial* hardness assumptions. In contrast, our focus is on supporting both tracing *and* revocation while still supporting arbitrary identities. Security of our construction, however, does rely on making a stronger sub-exponential hardness assumption.

2 Preliminaries

We begin by introducing some notation. We use λ (often implicitly) to denote the security parameter. We write $\mathsf{poly}(\lambda)$ to denote a quantity that is bounded by a fixed polynomial in λ and $\mathsf{negl}(\lambda)$ to denote a function that is $o(1/\lambda^c)$ for all $c \in \mathbb{N}$. We say that an event occurs with overwhelming probability if its complement occurs with negligible probability. We say an algorithm is efficient if it runs in probabilistic polynomial time in the length of its input. For two families of distributions $\mathcal{D}_1 = \{\mathcal{D}_{1,\lambda}\}_{\lambda \in \mathbb{N}}$ and $\mathcal{D}_2 = \{\mathcal{D}_{2,\lambda}\}_{\lambda \in \mathbb{N}}$, we write $\mathcal{D}_1 \overset{c}{\approx} \mathcal{D}_2$ if the two distributions are computationally indistinguishable (i.e., no efficient algorithm can distribution $\mathcal{D}_1$ from $\mathcal{D}_2$ except with negligible probability).

For an integer $n \geq 1$, we write $[n]$ to denote the set of integers $\{1, \ldots, n\}$. For integers $1 \leq m \leq n$, we write $[m, n]$ to denote the set of integers $\{m, m + 1, \ldots, n\}$, and $[m, n]_{\mathbb{R}}$ to denote the closed interval between m and n (inclusive) over the real numbers. For a distribution $\mathcal{D}$, we write $x \leftarrow \mathcal{D}$ to denote that x is drawn from $\mathcal{D}$. For a finite set S, we write $x \overset{\mathrm{R}}{\leftarrow} S$ to denote that x is drawn uniformly at random from S.

Cryptographic Primitives. We now recall the standard definition of pseudorandom functions and collision-resistant hash functions.

Definition 2.1 (Pseudorandom Function [GGM84]). *A pseudorandom function (PRF) with key-space $\mathcal{K} = \{\mathcal{K}_\lambda\}_{\lambda \in \mathbb{N}}$, domain $\mathcal{X} = \{\mathcal{X}_\lambda\}_{\lambda \in \mathbb{N}}$, and range $\mathcal{Y} = \{\mathcal{Y}_\lambda\}_{\lambda \in \mathbb{N}}$ is an efficiently-computable function $F \colon \mathcal{K} \times \mathcal{X} \to \mathcal{Y}$ such that for all efficient adversaries $\mathcal{A}$,*

$$\Pr[k \xleftarrow{\text{R}} \mathcal{K} : \mathcal{A}^{F(k,\cdot)}(1^\lambda) = 1] - \Pr[f \xleftarrow{\text{R}} \mathsf{Funs}[\mathcal{X}, \mathcal{Y}] : \mathcal{A}^{f(\cdot)}(1^\lambda) = 1] = \mathsf{negl}(\lambda).$$

Definition 2.2 (Keyed Collision-Resistant Hash Function). *A keyed collision-resistant hash function with key-space $\mathcal{K} = \{\mathcal{K}_\lambda\}_{\lambda \in \mathbb{N}}$, domain $\mathcal{X} = \{\mathcal{X}_\lambda\}_{\lambda \in \mathbb{N}}$, and range $\mathcal{Y} = \{\mathcal{Y}_\lambda\}_{\lambda \in \mathbb{N}}$ is an efficiently-computable function $H \colon \mathcal{K} \times \mathcal{X} \to \mathcal{Y}$ such that for all efficient adversaries $\mathcal{A}$ and sampling $k \xleftarrow{\text{R}} \mathcal{K}$,*

$$\Pr[(x_0, x_1) \leftarrow \mathcal{A}(1^\lambda, k) : x_0 \neq x_1 \text{ and } H(k, x_0) = H(k, x_1)] = \mathsf{negl}(\lambda).$$

Subset-Cover Set Systems. As discussed in Sect. 1.1, the subset-cover framework introduced by Naor et al. [NNL01] is the basis for many *combinatorial* trace-and-revoke schemes. We provide the formal definition below:

Definition 2.3 (Subset-Cover Set System [NNL01]). *Let N be a positive integer. A subset-cover set system for $[N]$ is a set of indices $[K]$ where $K = \mathsf{poly}(N)$ together with a pair of algorithms $(\mathsf{Encode}, \mathsf{ComputeCover})$ satisfying the following properties:*

- $\mathsf{Encode}(x) \to \mathcal{I}_x$: *On input an element $x \in [N]$, the encoding algorithm outputs a set of indices $\mathcal{I}_x \subseteq [K]$.*
- $\mathsf{ComputeCover}(\mathcal{L}) \to \mathcal{J}_\mathcal{L}$: *On input a revocation list $\mathcal{L} \subseteq [N]$, the cover-computation algorithm outputs a collection of indices $\mathcal{J}_\mathcal{L} \subseteq [K]$.*

We require the following efficiency and security requirements for a subset-cover set system.

- **Efficiency:** *Take any element $x \in [N]$ and any revocation list $\mathcal{L} \subseteq [N]$. Then, $\mathsf{Encode}(x)$ runs in time $\mathsf{poly}(\log N)$ and $\mathsf{ComputeCover}(\mathcal{L})$ runs in time $\mathsf{poly}(|\mathcal{L}|, \log N)$.*
- **Correctness:** *Take any element $x \in [N]$ and revocation list $\mathcal{L} \subseteq [N]$, and let $\mathcal{I}_x \leftarrow \mathsf{Encode}(x)$, $\mathcal{J}_\mathcal{L} \leftarrow \mathsf{ComputeCover}(\mathcal{L})$. Then, $x \in \mathcal{L}$ if and only if $\mathcal{I}_x \cap \mathcal{J}_\mathcal{L} = \varnothing$.*

In this work, we will use the "complete subtree" system from [NNL01, §3.1]. The details of this construction are not essential to our construction, so we omit them and just summarize the main properties below:

Fact 2.4 (Subset-Cover Set System [NNL01, §3.1]). Let N be a positive integer. Then there exists a subset-cover set system $[K]$ for $[N]$ where $K = 2N - 1$, and where the algorithms $(\mathsf{Encode}, \mathsf{ComputeCover})$ satisfy the following properties:

- For all elements $x \in [N]$, if $\mathcal{I}_x \leftarrow \mathsf{Encode}(x)$, then $|\mathcal{I}_x| = \log N + 1$.
- For all revocation lists $\mathcal{L} \subseteq [N]$, if $\mathcal{J}_\mathcal{L} \leftarrow \mathsf{ComputeCover}(\mathcal{L})$, then $|\mathcal{J}_\mathcal{L}| = O(|\mathcal{L}| \log(N/|\mathcal{L}|))$.

The Generalized Jump-Finding Problem. Next, we recall the generalized jump-finding problem introduced by Nishimaki et al. [NWZ16, §3.1] for constructing identity-based traitor tracing schemes with succinct ciphertexts. We note that [NWZ16] also introduced a simpler variant of the jump-finding problem that essentially abstracts out the algorithmic core of the traitor tracing construction from private linear broadcast. Here, we consider the generalized version because it enables shorter ciphertexts (where the ciphertext size scales logarithmically with the bit-length of the identities).

Definition 2.5 (Generalized Jump-Finding Problem [NWZ16, Definition 3.9]**).** *For positive integers $N, r, q \in \mathbb{N}$ and $\delta, \varepsilon > 0$, the $(N, r, q, \delta, \varepsilon)$ generalized jump-finding problem is defined as follows. An adversary begins by choosing a set C of up to q tuples $(s, b_1, \ldots, b_r) \in [N] \times \{0, 1\}^r$ where all of the s are distinct. Each tuple $(s, b_1, \ldots, b_r)$ describes a curve between grid points from the top to bottom of the grid $[1, r] \times [0, 2N]$, which oscillates about the column at position $2s - 1$, with $b = (b_1, \ldots, b_r)$ specifying which side of the column the curve is on in each row. The curves divide the grid into $|C| + 1$ contiguous regions. For each pair $(i, x) \in [1, r] \times [0, 2N]$, the adversary chooses a probability $p_{i,x} \in [0, 1]_{\mathbb{R}}$ with the following properties:*

- *For any two pairs $(i, 2x), (j, 2x) \in [1, r] \times [0, 2N]$, it holds that $|p_{i,2x} - p_{j,2x}| < \delta$.*
- *Let $C_i = \{(s, b_1, \ldots, b_r) \in C : 2s - b_i\}$ be the set of values $2s - b_i$ for tuples in C. For any two pairs $(i, x), (i, y) \in [1, r] \times [0, 2N]$ such that $(x, y] \cap C_i = \varnothing$, then $|p_{i,x} - p_{i,y}| < \delta$.*
- *For all $i, j \in [r]$, it holds that $p_{i,0} = p_{j,0}$ and $p_{i,2N} = p_{j,2N}$. Define $p_0 = p_{i,0}$ and $p_{2N} = p_{i,2N}$.*
- *Finally, $|p_{2N} - p_0| > \varepsilon$.*

Next, define the oracle $Q \colon [1, r] \times [0, 2N] \to \{0, 1\}$ to be a randomized oracle that on input (i, x) outputs 1 with probability $p_{i,x}$. Repeated calls to Q on the same input (i, x) will yield a fresh and independently-sampled bit. The $(N, r, q, \delta, \varepsilon)$ generalized jump-finding problem is to output some element in C given oracle access to Q.

Theorem 2.6 (Generalized Jump-Finding Algorithm [NWZ16, Theorem 3.10]**).** *There is an efficient algorithm $\mathsf{QTrace}^Q(\lambda, N, r, q, \delta, \varepsilon)$ that runs in time $t = \mathrm{poly}(\lambda, \log N, r, q, 1/\delta)$ and makes at most t queries to Q that solves the $(N, r, q, \delta, \varepsilon)$ generalized jump-finding problem with probability $1 - \mathrm{negl}(\lambda)$ whenever $\varepsilon \geq \delta(9 + 4(\lceil \log N \rceil - 1)q)$. Moreover, any element $(s, b_1, \ldots, b_r) \in [N] \times \{0, 1\}^r$ output by QTrace^Q satisfies the following property (with overwhelming probability):*

- *For all $i \in [r]$, $|P(i, 2s - b_i) - P(i, 2s - 1 - b_i)| \geq \delta$, where $P(i, x) := \Pr[Q(i, x) = 1]$.*

Remark 2.7 (Cheating Oracles [NWZ16, Remark 3.8]). The algorithm QTrace^Q from Theorem 2.6 succeeds in solving the $(N, r, q, \delta, \varepsilon)$ generalized jump-finding problem even if the oracle Q does not satisfy all of the requirements in Definition 2.5. As long as the first two properties hold for all pairs (i, x) and (j, y) queried by QTrace^Q, the algorithm succeeds in outputting an element in C.

2.1   Functional Encryption

In this section, we recall the notions of attribute-based encryption (ABE) and mixed functional encryption (mixed FE) that we use in this work.

Mixed FE. A mixed FE scheme [GKW18] is a secret-key FE scheme (i.e., a secret key is needed to encrypt) where ciphertexts are associated with binary-valued functions $f \colon \mathcal{X} \to \{0, 1\}$ and decryption keys are associated with inputs $x \in \mathcal{X}$. When a secret key sk_x associated with an input x is used to decrypt a ciphertext encrypting a message f, the decryption algorithm outputs $f(x)$. The special property in a mixed FE scheme is that there additionally exists a *public-key* encryption algorithm that can be used to encrypt to the "always-accept" function (i.e., the function f where $f(x) = 1$ for all $x \in \mathcal{X}$). Moreover, ciphertexts encrypted using the public key are computationally indistinguishable from ciphertexts produced by using the secret key to encrypt the "always-accept" function. Finally, for our constructions, we require an additional property where the master public key and the master secret key for the mixed FE scheme can be generated *independently.* This means that we can have a family of mixed FE schemes sharing a common set of public parameters. As we discuss in the full version of this paper [KW19a], all existing mixed FE schemes satisfy this requirement.

Definition 2.8 (Mixed Functional Encryption [GKW18]). *A mixed functional encryption scheme Π_{MFE} with domain $\mathcal{X}$ and function family $\mathcal{F} = \{f \colon \mathcal{X} \to \{0, 1\}\}$ is a tuple of algorithms $\Pi_{\mathsf{MFE}} = (\mathsf{PrmsGen}, \mathsf{MSKGen}, \mathsf{KeyGen}, \mathsf{PKEnc}, \mathsf{SKEnc}, \mathsf{Dec})$ with the following properties:*

- $\mathsf{PrmsGen}(1^\lambda) \to \mathsf{pp}$: *On input the security parameter λ, the parameter generation algorithm outputs the public parameters pp.*
- $\mathsf{MSKGen}(\mathsf{pp}) \to \mathsf{msk}$: *On input the public parameters pp, the master secret key generation algorithm outputs a master secret key msk.*
- $\mathsf{KeyGen}(\mathsf{msk}, x) \to \mathsf{sk}_x$: *On input the master secret key msk and an input $x \in \mathcal{X}$, the key-generation algorithm outputs a secret key sk_x.*
- $\mathsf{PKEnc}(\mathsf{pp}) \to \mathsf{ct}$: *On input the public parameters pp, the public encryption algorithm outputs a ciphertext ct.*
- $\mathsf{SKEnc}(\mathsf{msk}, f) \to \mathsf{ct}_f$: *On input the master secret key msk and a function $f \in \mathcal{F}$, the secret encryption algorithm outputs a ciphertext ct_f.*
- $\mathsf{Dec}(\mathsf{sk}, \mathsf{ct}) \to b$: *On input a secret key sk and a ciphertext ct, the decryption algorithm outputs a bit $b \in \{0, 1\}$.*

A *mixed FE scheme* should satisfy the following properties:

- **Correctness:** For all functions $f \in \mathcal{F}$ and all inputs $x \in \mathcal{X}$, and setting pp $\leftarrow$ PrmsGen(1^λ), msk $\leftarrow$ MSKGen(pp), sk$_x \leftarrow$ KeyGen(msk, x), ct $\leftarrow$ PKEnc(pp), ct$_f \leftarrow$ SKEnc(msk, f), it follows that

$$\Pr[\mathsf{Dec}(\mathsf{sk}_x, \mathsf{ct}) = 1] = 1 - \mathsf{negl}(\lambda) \quad and \quad \Pr[\mathsf{Dec}(\mathsf{sk}_x, \mathsf{ct}_f) = f(x)] = 1 - \mathsf{negl}(\lambda).$$

- **Semantic security:** For a bit $b \in \{0,1\}$, we define the security experiment $\mathsf{ExptMFE}_{\mathsf{SS}}[\lambda, \mathcal{A}, b]$ between a challenger and an adversary $\mathcal{A}$. The challenger begins by sampling pp $\leftarrow$ PrmsGen(1^λ), msk $\leftarrow$ MSKGen(pp), and gives pp to $\mathcal{A}$. The adversary is then given access to the following oracles:
  - **Key-generation oracle:** On input $x \in \mathcal{X}$, the challenger replies with sk$_x \leftarrow$ KeyGen(msk, x).
  - **Encryption oracle:** On input $f \in \mathcal{F}$, the challenger replies with ct$_f \leftarrow$ SKEnc(msk, f).
  - **Challenge oracle:** On input two functions $f_0, f_1 \in \mathcal{F}$, the challenger replies with ct $\leftarrow$ SKEnc(msk, f_b).
  At the end of the game, the adversary outputs a bit $b' \in \{0,1\}$, which is also the output of the experiment. An adversary $\mathcal{A}$ is admissible for the mixed FE semantic security game if it makes one challenge query (f_0, f_1), and for all inputs $x \in \mathcal{X}$ the adversary submits to the key-generation oracle, $f_0(x) = f_1(x)$. The mixed FE scheme satisfies (adaptive) semantic security if for all efficient and admissible adversaries $\mathcal{A}$,

$$|\Pr[\mathsf{ExptMFE}_{\mathsf{SS}}[\lambda, \mathcal{A}, 0] = 1] - \Pr[\mathsf{ExptMFE}_{\mathsf{SS}}[\lambda, \mathcal{A}, 1] = 1]| = \mathsf{negl}(\lambda).$$

- **Public/secret key indistinguishability:** For a bit $b \in \{0,1\}$, we define the security experiment $\mathsf{ExptMFE}_{\mathsf{PK/SK}}[\lambda, \mathcal{A}, b]$ between a challenger and an adversary $\mathcal{A}$. The challenger begins by sampling pp $\leftarrow$ PrmsGen(1^λ), msk $\leftarrow$ MSKGen(pp), and gives pp to $\mathcal{A}$. The adversary is then given access to the following oracles:
  - **Key-generation oracle:** On input $x \in \mathcal{X}$, the challenger replies with sk$_x \leftarrow$ KeyGen(msk, x).
  - **Encryption oracle:** On input $f \in \mathcal{F}$, the challenger replies with ct$_f \leftarrow$ SKEnc(msk, f).
  - **Challenge oracle:** On input a function $f \in \mathcal{F}$, the challenger computes ct$_0 \leftarrow$ PKEnc(pp) and ct$_1 \leftarrow$ SKEnc(msk, f) and gives sk$_b$ to the adversary.
  At the end of the game, the adversary outputs a bit $b' \in \{0,1\}$, which is also the output of the experiment. An adversary $\mathcal{A}$ is admissible for the public/secret key indistinguishability game if it makes a single challenge query $f \in \mathcal{F}$ and for all inputs $x \in \mathcal{X}$ the adversary submits to the key-generation oracle, $f(x) = 1$. The mixed FE scheme satisfies (adaptive) public/secret key indistinguishability if for all efficient and admissible adversaries $\mathcal{A}$, it holds that

$$\left|\Pr[\mathsf{ExptMFE}_{\mathsf{PK/SK}}[\lambda, \mathcal{A}, 0] = 1] - \Pr[\mathsf{ExptMFE}_{\mathsf{PK/SK}}[\lambda, \mathcal{A}, 1] = 1]\right| = \mathsf{negl}(\lambda).$$

We include additional preliminaries and discussion about mixed FE (e.g., imposing a bound on the number of encryption oracle queries the adversary can make in the security games) in the full version of this paper [KW19a].

3   Revocable Predicate Encryption

In this section, we introduce our notion of a secret-key revocable predicate encryption scheme that supports a public broadcast functionality (i.e., a public-key encryption algorithm that outputs ciphertexts that can be decrypted by all secret keys in the system). This will be the primary primitive we use to construct our identity-based trace-and-revoke scheme (described in Sect. 4). Our definitions can be viewed as a special case of the more general notion of (public-key) revocable functional encryption from [NWZ16]. The advantage of considering this relaxed notion is that it enables constructions from standard assumptions (whereas we only know how to construct fully secure revocable functional encryption from indistinguishability obfuscation). We introduce our notion below and then show how to construct it by combining mixed FE, ABE, and a subset-cover set system in Sect. 3.1.

Definition 3.1 (Secret-Key Revocable Predicate Encryption with Broadcast).   *A secret-key revocable predicate encryption scheme (RPE) scheme with broadcast for an identity space $\mathcal{ID}$, an attribute space $\mathcal{X}$, a function family $\mathcal{F} = \{f\colon \mathcal{X} \to \{0,1\}\}$, and a message space $\mathcal{M}$ is a tuple of algorithms $\Pi_{\mathsf{RPE}} = (\mathsf{Setup}, \mathsf{KeyGen}, \mathsf{Broadcast}, \mathsf{Enc}, \mathsf{Dec})$ defined as follows:*

- $\mathsf{Setup}(1^\lambda) \to (\mathsf{pp}, \mathsf{msk})$: *On input the security parameter λ, the setup algorithm outputs the public parameters pp and the master secret key msk.*
- $\mathsf{KeyGen}(\mathsf{msk}, \mathsf{id}, x) \to \mathsf{sk}_{\mathsf{id},x}$: *On input the master secret key msk, an identity $\mathsf{id} \in \mathcal{ID}$, and an attribute $x \in \mathcal{X}$, the key-generation algorithm outputs a decryption key $\mathsf{sk}_{\mathsf{id},x}$.*
- $\mathsf{Broadcast}(\mathsf{pp}, m, \mathcal{L}) \to \mathsf{ct}_{m,\mathcal{L}}$: *On input the public key, a message m, and a revocation list $\mathcal{L} \subseteq \mathcal{ID}$, the broadcast algorithm outputs a ciphertext $\mathsf{ct}_{m,\mathcal{L}}$.*
- $\mathsf{Enc}(\mathsf{msk}, f, m, \mathcal{L}) \to \mathsf{ct}_{f,m,\mathcal{L}}$: *On input the master secret key msk, a function $f \in \mathcal{F}$, a message $m \in \mathcal{M}$, and a revocation list $\mathcal{L} \subseteq \mathcal{ID}$, the encryption algorithm outputs a ciphertext $\mathsf{ct}_{f,m,\mathcal{L}}$.*
- $\mathsf{Dec}(\mathsf{sk}, \mathsf{ct}) \to m/\bot$: *On input a decryption key sk and a ciphertext ct, the decryption algorithm either outputs a message $m \in \mathcal{M}$ or a special symbol $\bot$.*

A secret-key RPE scheme with broadcast should satisfy the following properties:

- **Correctness:** *For all functions $f \in \mathcal{F}$, all identities $\mathsf{id} \in \mathcal{ID}$, all attributes $x \in \mathcal{X}$ where $f(x) = 1$, all messages $m \in \mathcal{M}$, and all revocation lists $\mathcal{L} \subseteq \mathcal{ID}$ where $\mathsf{id} \notin \mathcal{L}$, if we set $(\mathsf{pp}, \mathsf{msk}) \leftarrow \mathsf{Setup}(1^\lambda)$, $\mathsf{sk}_{\mathsf{id},x} \leftarrow \mathsf{KeyGen}(\mathsf{msk}, \mathsf{id}, x)$, the following holds:*
  - **Broadcast correctness:** *If $\mathsf{ct}_{m,\mathcal{L}} \leftarrow \mathsf{Broadcast}(\mathsf{pp}, m, \mathcal{L})$, then*

$$\Pr[\mathsf{Dec}(\mathsf{sk}_{\mathsf{id},x}, \mathsf{ct}_{m,\mathcal{L}}) = m] = 1 - \mathsf{negl}(\lambda).$$

  - **Encryption correctness:** *If $\mathsf{ct}_{f,m,\mathcal{L}} \leftarrow \mathsf{Enc}(\mathsf{msk}, f, m, \mathcal{L})$, then*

$$\Pr[\mathsf{Dec}(\mathsf{sk}_{\mathsf{id},x}, \mathsf{ct}_{f,m,\mathcal{L}}) = m] = 1 - \mathsf{negl}(\lambda).$$

- **Message hiding:** For a bit $b \in \{0,1\}$, we define the experiment $\mathsf{ExptRPE}_{\mathsf{MH}}[\lambda, \mathcal{A}, b]$ between a challenger and an adversary $\mathcal{A}$. The challenger begins by sampling $(\mathsf{pp}, \mathsf{msk}) \leftarrow \mathsf{Setup}(1^\lambda)$ and gives pp to $\mathcal{A}$. The adversary is then given access to the following oracles:
  - **Key-generation oracle:** On input an identity $\mathsf{id} \in \mathcal{ID}$ and an attribute $x \in \mathcal{X}$, the challenger replies with $\mathsf{sk}_{\mathsf{id},x} \leftarrow \mathsf{KeyGen}(\mathsf{msk}, \mathsf{id}, x)$.
  - **Encryption oracle:** On input a function $f \in \mathcal{F}$, a message $m \in \mathcal{M}$, and a revocation list $\mathcal{L} \subseteq \mathcal{ID}$, the challenger replies with $\mathsf{ct}_{f,m,\mathcal{L}} \leftarrow \mathsf{Enc}(\mathsf{msk}, f, m, \mathcal{L})$.
  - **Challenge oracle:** On input a function $f \in \mathcal{F}$, two messages $m_0, m_1 \in \mathcal{M}$, and a revocation list $\mathcal{L} \subseteq \mathcal{ID}$, the challenger computes $\mathsf{ct}_b \leftarrow \mathsf{Enc}(\mathsf{msk}, f, m_b, \mathcal{L})$ and gives ct_b to the adversary.
  At the end of the game, the adversary outputs a bit $b' \in \{0,1\}$, which is the output of the experiment. An adversary $\mathcal{A}$ is admissible for the message hiding game if it makes a single challenge query $(f, m_0, m_1, \mathcal{L})$ such that for all pairs (id, x) the adversary submitted to the key-generation oracle, it holds that $f(x) = 0$ or $\mathsf{id} \in \mathcal{L}$. We say that Π_{RPE} satisfies (adaptive) message hiding if for all efficient and admissible adversaries $\mathcal{A}$,

$$|\Pr[\mathsf{ExptRPE}_{\mathsf{MH}}[\lambda, \mathcal{A}, 0] = 1] - \Pr[\mathsf{ExptRPE}_{\mathsf{MH}}[\lambda, \mathcal{A}, 1] = 1]| = \mathsf{negl}(\lambda).$$

- **Function hiding:** For a bit $b \in \{0,1\}$, we define the experiment $\mathsf{ExptRPE}_{\mathsf{FH}}[\lambda, \mathcal{A}, b]$ between a challenger and an adversary $\mathcal{A}$ exactly as $\mathsf{ExptRPE}_{\mathsf{MH}}[\lambda, \mathcal{A}, b]$, except the challenge oracle is replaced with the following:
  - **Challenge oracle:** On input two functions $f_0, f_1 \in \mathcal{F}$, a message $m \in \mathcal{M}$, and a revocation list $\mathcal{L} \subseteq \mathcal{ID}$, the challenger computes $\mathsf{ct}_b \leftarrow \mathsf{Enc}(\mathsf{msk}, f_b, m, \mathcal{L})$ and gives ct_b to the adversary.
  We say an adversary $\mathcal{A}$ is admissible for the function-hiding game if it makes a single challenge query $(f_0, f_1, m, \mathcal{L})$ such that for all pairs (id, x) the adversary submitted to the key-generation oracle, either $f_0(x) = f_1(x)$ or $\mathsf{id} \in \mathcal{L}$. We say that Π_{RPE} satisfies (adaptive) function hiding if for all efficient and admissible adversaries $\mathcal{A}$,

$$|\Pr[\mathsf{ExptRPE}_{\mathsf{FH}}[\lambda, \mathcal{A}, 0] = 1] - \Pr[\mathsf{ExptRPE}_{\mathsf{FH}}[\lambda, \mathcal{A}, 1] = 1]| = \mathsf{negl}(\lambda).$$

- **Broadcast security:** For a bit $b \in \{0,1\}$, we define the security experiment $\mathsf{ExptRPE}_{\mathsf{BC}}[\lambda, \mathcal{A}, b]$ between a challenger and an adversary $\mathcal{A}$ exactly as $\mathsf{ExptRPE}_{\mathsf{MH}}[\lambda, \mathcal{A}, b]$, except the challenge oracle is replaced with the following:
  - **Challenge oracle:** On input a message $m \in \mathcal{M}$ and a revocation list $\mathcal{L} \subseteq \mathcal{ID}$, the challenger computes $\mathsf{ct}_0 \leftarrow \mathsf{Broadcast}(\mathsf{pp}, m, \mathcal{L})$ and $\mathsf{ct}_1 \leftarrow \mathsf{Enc}(\mathsf{msk}, f, m, \mathcal{L})$ where f_{accept} is the "always-accept" function (i.e., $f_{\mathsf{accept}}(x) = 1$ for all $x \in \mathcal{X}$). It gives ct_b to the adversary.
  At the end of the game, the adversary outputs a bit $b' \in \{0,1\}$, which is the output of the experiment. We say that Π_{RPE} satisfies (adaptive) broadcast security if for all efficient adversaries $\mathcal{A}$ that make at most one challenge query,

$$|\Pr[\mathsf{ExptRPE}_{\mathsf{BC}}[\lambda, \mathcal{A}, b] = 1] - \Pr[\mathsf{ExptRPE}_{\mathsf{BC}}[\lambda, \mathcal{A}, 1]]| = \mathsf{negl}(\lambda).$$

Remark 3.2 (Non-Adaptive q-Query Security). For each of the security notions in Definition 3.1 (message hiding, function hiding, and broadcast security), we define a notion of *non-adaptive q-query security* where the corresponding security notion only holds against all adversaries that make at most $q \in \mathbb{N}$ queries to the encryption oracle, and moreover, all of the non-encryption queries occur *before* the encryption queries. Achieving this notion is easier and suffices for our main construction (*adaptively-secure* trace-and-revoke).

Remark 3.3 (Embedding the Revocation List in the Attribute). A natural approach for constructing a revocable predicate encryption scheme from any vanilla predicate encryption scheme is to include the revocation list $\mathcal{L}$ as part of the function in the predicate encryption scheme. A decryption key for an identity id would then check that id is not contained in the revocation list $\mathcal{L}$ associated with the ciphertext. This is the approach suggested in [NWZ16, Remark 6.2] in the context of constructing a revocable functional encryption scheme. While this approach may seem straightforward, it has a significant drawback in most settings. In existing predicate encryption schemes from standard assumptions, the decryption functionality is represented as a *circuit*, which takes *fixed-size* inputs. Thus, if the revocation list is embedded as part of the ciphertext, then a predicate encryption scheme for circuit-based predicates would only be able to support an *a priori* bounded number of revocations. In contrast, the our construction allows for revoking an *arbitrary* polynomial number of users (Sect. 3.1). Of course, if we can construct predicate or functional encryption for Turing machine or RAM computations, then this natural revocation approach would suffice. Existing constructions of functional encryption for Turing machine computations all rely on indistinguishability obfuscation [KLW15, AJS17, AS16, GS18].

3.1 Constructing Secret-Key Revocable Predicate Encryption with Broadcast

In this section, we describe our construction of a secret-key revocable predicate encryption with broadcast scheme for general predicates by combining a mixed FE scheme, an ABE scheme, and a subset-cover set system. As discussed in Sect. 1.1, our core construction (without revocation) can be viewed as a direct generalization of the construction of private linear broadcast encryption from mixed FE and ABE from [GKW18]. We next augment our construction with a subset cover set system to support revocation. Our techniques allow revoking an arbitrary number of users (in contrast to previous trace-and-revoke schemes from standard assumptions that could only handle bounded revocations [NWZ16, ABP+17]). We give our full construction and its analysis below:

Construction 3.4 (Secret-Key Revocable Predicate Encryption with Broadcast). Fix an identity space $\mathcal{ID} = \{0,1\}^n$, attribute space $\mathcal{X}$, function family $\mathcal{F} = \{f \colon \mathcal{X} \to \{0,1\}\}$ and message space $\mathcal{M}$, where $n = n(\lambda)$.

- Let $[K]$ be the subset-cover set system for the set $\mathcal{ID} = \{0,1\}^n$. Let $\Pi_{\mathsf{SC}} = (\mathsf{Encode}, \mathsf{ComputeCover})$ be the algorithms associated with the set system.

- Let Π_{MFE} = (MFE.PrmsGen, MFE.MSKGen, MFE.KeyGen, MFE.PKEnc, MFE.SKEnc, MFE.Dec) be a mixed FE scheme with domain $\mathcal{X}$ and function family $\mathcal{F}$. Let $\rho = \rho(\lambda)$ be the randomness complexity of the master secret key generation algorithm MFE.MSKGen, let $\mathcal{CT}$ denote the ciphertext space of Π_{MFE} (i.e., the range of MFE.PKEnc and MFE.SKEnc), and let $\mathcal{SK}$ denote the secret key space of Π_{MFE} (i.e., the range of MFE.KeyGen). We will require that Π_{MFE} be sub-exponentially secure, so let $\varepsilon > 0$ be a constant such that $2^{-\Omega(\lambda^\varepsilon)}$ bounds the advantage of any efficient adversary $\mathcal{A}$ for the security of Π_{MFE}.
- For a secret key $\mathsf{mfe.sk} \in \mathcal{SK}$ and an index $i^* \in [K]$, define the function $g_{\mathsf{mfe.sk},i^*} : \mathcal{CT} \times [K] \to \{0,1\}$ to be the function

$$g_{\mathsf{mfe.sk},i^*}(\mathsf{ct},i) = \begin{cases} 1 & \mathsf{MFE.Dec}(\mathsf{mfe.sk},\mathsf{ct}) = 1 \text{ and } i = i^* \\ 0 & \text{otherwise.} \end{cases}$$

- Let Π_{ABE} = (ABE.Setup, ABE.KeyGen, ABE.Enc, ABE.Dec) be an attribute-based encryption scheme over message space $\mathcal{M}$, attribute space $\mathcal{X}' = \mathcal{CT} \times [K]$ and function family $\mathcal{F}' = \{\mathsf{mfe.sk} \in \mathcal{SK}, i^* \in [K] : g_{\mathsf{mfe.sk},i^*}\}$.
- Let $F : \mathcal{K} \times [K] \to \{0,1\}^\rho$ be a pseudorandom function.

We construct a secret-key revocable predicate encryption scheme as follows:

- Setup(1^λ): On input the security parameter λ, the setup algorithm sets $\lambda' = \max(\lambda, (\log K)^{2/\varepsilon})$. It then generates mixed FE public parameters $\mathsf{mfe.pp} \leftarrow \mathsf{MFE.PrmsGen}(1^{\lambda'})$. It also instantiates an attribute-based encryption scheme $(\mathsf{abe.pp}, \mathsf{abe.msk}) \leftarrow \mathsf{ABE.Setup}(1^\lambda)$, samples a PRF key $k \xleftarrow{\text{R}} \mathcal{K}$, and outputs

$$\mathsf{pp} = (\mathsf{mfe.pp}, \mathsf{abe.pp}) \quad \text{and} \quad \mathsf{msk} = (\mathsf{pp}, \mathsf{abe.msk}, k).$$

- KeyGen($\mathsf{msk}, \mathsf{id}, x$): On input a master secret key msk, an identity $\mathsf{id} \in \mathcal{ID}$, and an attribute $x \in \mathcal{X}$, the key-generation algorithm does the following:
  1. Compute a subset-cover encoding of the identity $\mathcal{I}_{\mathsf{id}} \leftarrow \mathsf{Encode}(\mathsf{id})$.
  2. For each index $i \in \mathcal{I}_{\mathsf{id}}$, the algorithm samples randomness $r_i \leftarrow F(k,i)$. It then generates a mixed FE master secret key $\mathsf{mfe.msk}_i \leftarrow \mathsf{MFE.MSKGen}(\mathsf{mfe.pp}; r_i)$ and a mixed FE decryption key $\mathsf{mfe.sk}_{i,x} \leftarrow \mathsf{MFE.KeyGen}(\mathsf{mfe.msk}_i, x)$.
  3. Finally, for each $i \in \mathcal{I}_{\mathsf{id}}$, it constructs an ABE decryption key with respect to the function $g_{\mathsf{mfe.msk}_{i,x},i}$ as follows: $\mathsf{abe.sk}_{i,x} \leftarrow \mathsf{ABE.KeyGen}(\mathsf{abe.msk}, g_{\mathsf{mfe.sk}_{i,x},i})$.
  4. It outputs the collection of keys $\mathsf{sk}_{\mathsf{id},x} = \{(i, \mathsf{abe.sk}_{i,x})\}_{i \in \mathcal{I}_{\mathsf{id}}}$.
- Broadcast($\mathsf{pp}, m, \mathcal{L}$): On input the public parameters $\mathsf{pp} = (\mathsf{mfe.pp}, \mathsf{abe.pp})$, a message m, and a revocation list $\mathcal{L} \subseteq \mathcal{ID}$, the broadcast algorithm does the following:
  1. Obtain a cover for $\mathcal{ID} \backslash \mathcal{L}$ by computing $\mathcal{J}_\mathcal{L} \leftarrow \mathsf{ComputeCover}(\mathcal{L})$.
  2. For each $i \in \mathcal{J}_\mathcal{L}$, it generates a mixed FE ciphertext $\mathsf{mfe.ct}_i \leftarrow \mathsf{MFE.PKEnc}(\mathsf{mfe.pp})$ and an ABE ciphertext $\mathsf{abe.ct}_i \leftarrow \mathsf{ABE.Enc}(\mathsf{abe.pp}, (\mathsf{mfe.ct}_i, i), m)$.

3. It outputs the ciphertext $\mathsf{ct}_{m,\mathcal{L}} = \{(i, \mathsf{abe.ct}_i)\}_{i \in \mathcal{J}_\mathcal{L}}$.

– $\mathsf{Enc}(\mathsf{msk}, f, m, \mathcal{L})$: On input the master secret key $\mathsf{msk} = (\mathsf{pp}, \mathsf{abe.msk}, k)$, a function $f \in \mathcal{F}$, a message $m \in \mathcal{M}$, and a revocation list $\mathcal{L} \subseteq \mathcal{ID}$, where $\mathsf{pp} = (\mathsf{mfe.pp}, \mathsf{abe.pp})$, the encryption algorithm does the following:
  1. Obtain a cover for $\mathcal{ID} \backslash \mathcal{L}$ by computing $\mathcal{J}_\mathcal{L} \leftarrow \mathsf{ComputeCover}(\mathcal{L})$.
  2. Then,

    for each $i \in \mathcal{J}_\mathcal{L}$, it computes $r_i \leftarrow F(k, i)$ and derives the corresponding mixed FE master secret key $\mathsf{mfe.msk}_i \leftarrow \mathsf{MFE.MSKGen}(\mathsf{mfe.pp}; r_i)$. It then encrypts $\mathsf{mfe.ct}_i \leftarrow \mathsf{MFE.SKEnc}(\mathsf{mfe.msk}_i, f)$.
  3. For each $i \in \mathcal{J}_\mathcal{L}$, it computes $\mathsf{abe.ct}_i \leftarrow \mathsf{ABE.Enc}(\mathsf{abe.pp}, (\mathsf{mfe.ct}_i, i), m)$, and outputs the ciphertext $\mathsf{ct}_{f,m,\mathcal{L}} = \{(i, \mathsf{abe.ct}_i)\}_{i \in \mathcal{J}_\mathcal{L}}$.

– $\mathsf{Dec}(\mathsf{sk}, \mathsf{ct})$: On input a key $\mathsf{sk} = \{(i, \mathsf{abe.sk}_i)\}_{i \in \mathcal{I}}$ and a ciphertext $\mathsf{ct} = \{(i, \mathsf{abe.ct}_i)\}_{i \in \mathcal{J}}$, the decryption algorithm first checks if $\mathcal{I} \cap \mathcal{J} = \varnothing$. If so, it outputs $\bot$. Otherwise, it chooses an arbitrary index $i \in \mathcal{I} \cap \mathcal{J}$ and outputs $m \leftarrow \mathsf{ABE.Dec}(\mathsf{abe.sk}_i, \mathsf{abe.ct}_i)$.

Correctness and Security Analysis. We state our main theorems on the properties of Construction 3.4 below, but defer their analysis to the full version of this paper [KW19a].

Theorem 3.5 (Correctness). *Suppose that Π_{MFE}, Π_{ABE}, and Π_{SC} are correct. Then, the predicate encryption scheme Π_{RPE} from Construction 3.4 is correct.*

Theorem 3.6 (Message Hiding). *Suppose that Π_{MFE} and Π_{SC} are correct, and Π_{ABE} satisfies semantic security. Then, the predicate encryption scheme Π_{RPE} from Construction 3.4 satisfies message hiding.*

Theorem 3.7 (Function Hiding). *Suppose that Π_{MFE} satisfies subexponential non-adaptive q-query (resp., adaptive) semantic security. Specifically, suppose that the advantage of any adversary running in time $\mathsf{poly}(\lambda)$ in the semantic security game is bounded by $2^{-\Omega(\lambda^\varepsilon)}$. In addition, suppose that Π_{ABE} is secure, F is a secure PRF, and Π_{SC} is correct. Then, the predicate encryption scheme in Construction 3.4 satisfies non-adaptive q-query (resp., adaptive) function hiding security.*

Theorem 3.8 (Broadcast Security). *Suppose that Π_{MFE} satisfies subexponential non-adaptive q-query (resp., adaptive) public/secret key indistinguishability. Specifically, suppose that the advantage of any adversary running in time $\mathsf{poly}(\lambda)$ in the public/secret key indistinguishability game is bounded by $2^{-\Omega(\lambda^\varepsilon)}$. In addition, suppose that F is a secure PRF. Then the predicate encryption scheme Π_{RPE} in Construction 3.4 satisfies non-adaptive q-query (resp., adaptive) broadcast security.*

3.2 Instantiating Secret-Key Revocable Predicate Encryption with Broadcast

In this section, we describe one possible instantiation of secret-key revocable predicate encryption with broadcast from Construction 3.4. In particular, combining Construction 3.4 with Theorems 3.5 through 3.8 yields the following corollary:

Corollary 3.9 (Secret-Key Revocable Predicate Encryption from LWE). *Take an identity-space $\mathcal{ID} = \{0,1\}^n$, attribute space $\mathcal{X} = \{0,1\}^\ell$, and message space $\mathcal{M} = \{0,1\}^t$ where $n = n(\lambda)$, $\ell = \ell(\lambda)$, and $t = t(\lambda)$. Let $\mathcal{F} = \{f\colon \mathcal{X} \to \{0,1\}\}$ be a function family where every function $f \in \mathcal{F}$ can be specified by a string of length $z = z(\lambda)$ and computed by a Boolean circuit of depth $d = d(\lambda)$. Then, assuming sub-exponential hardness of LWE (with a super-polynomial modulus-to-noise ratio), there exists a non-adaptive 1-key secure secret-key revocable predicate encryption scheme with broadcast Π_{RPE} over the identity space $\mathcal{ID}$, attribute space $\mathcal{X}$, and function family $\mathcal{F}$. Moreover, Π_{RPE} satisfies the following properties:*

- **Public parameter size:** $|\mathsf{pp}| = \ell \cdot \mathsf{poly}(\lambda, d, n, z)$.
- **Secret key size:** *The secret key* $\mathsf{sk}_{\mathsf{id},x}$ *for an identity* $\mathsf{id} \in \{0,1\}^n$ *and an attribute* $x \in \{0,1\}^\ell$ *has size* $|\mathsf{sk}_{\mathsf{id},x}| = \ell + \mathsf{poly}(\lambda, d, n, z)$.
- **Ciphertext size:** *An encryption* $\mathsf{ct}_{m,\mathcal{L}}$ *of a message* $m \in \{0,1\}^t$ *with revocation list* $\mathcal{L}$ *has size* $|\mathsf{ct}_{m,\mathcal{L}}| = t + |\mathcal{L}| \cdot \mathsf{poly}(\lambda, d, n, z)$.

Proof. We instantiate Construction 3.4 using the subset-cover set system from Fact 2.4, the mixed FE scheme using the construction of Chen et al. [CVW+18], the ABE scheme using the construction of Boneh et al. [BGG+14], and the PRF from any one-way function [GGM84]. We describe the exact instantiations in greater detail in the full version of this paper [KW19a]. The mixed FE scheme is instantiated with domain $\mathcal{X} = \{0,1\}^\ell$ and function family $\mathcal{F}$, while the ABE scheme is instantiated with message space $\mathcal{M}$, attribute space $\mathcal{X}' = \mathcal{CT} \times [K]$ and function family $\mathcal{F}' = \{\mathsf{mfe.sk} \in \mathcal{SK}, i^* \in [K] : g_{\mathsf{mfe.sk},i^*}\}$. We will use the following bounds in our analysis:

- From Fact 2.4, we have that $K = O(N)$, and correspondingly, $\log K = O(\log N) = O(n)$.
- We have that the length of a mixed FE ciphertext $\mathsf{mfe.ct} \in \mathcal{CT}$ is bounded by $|\mathsf{mfe.ct}| = \mathsf{poly}(\lambda, d, z)$. Correspondingly, this means that the length ℓ_{ABE} of an ABE attribute is bounded by $\ell_{\mathsf{ABE}} = \mathsf{poly}(\lambda, d, z) + \log K = \mathsf{poly}(\lambda, d, n, z)$.
- Each function $g_{\mathsf{mfe.sk},i^*}$ can be implemented by a circuit with depth at most $\mathsf{poly}(\lambda, d) + \log \log K = \mathsf{poly}(\lambda, d, \log n)$. Specifically, the mixed FE decryption circuit can be evaluated by a circuit of depth $\mathsf{poly}(\lambda', d) = \mathsf{poly}(\lambda, d, n, z)$ and the equality-check circuit can be evaluated by a circuit of depth $\log \log K$ (since each input to the equality-check circuit is a $(\log K)$-bit value). Thus, the functions in $\mathcal{F}'$ can be computed by Boolean circuits with depth at most $d_{\mathsf{ABE}} \leq \mathsf{poly}(\lambda, d, n, z)$. The description length of functions in $\mathcal{F}'$ is $|\mathsf{mfe.sk}| + \log K = \ell + \mathsf{poly}(\lambda, n, z)$.

Putting all the pieces together, we now have the following:

- **Public parameter size:** The public parameters pp consist of the ABE public parameters $\mathsf{abe.pp}$ and the mixed FE public parameters $\mathsf{mfe.pp}$. Then,

$$|\mathsf{abe.pp}| = \mathsf{poly}(\lambda, d_{\mathsf{ABE}}, \ell_{\mathsf{ABE}}) = \mathsf{poly}(\lambda, d, n, z),$$

and correspondingly,

$$|\text{mfe.pp}| = \ell \cdot \text{poly}(\lambda', d, z) = \ell \cdot \text{poly}(\lambda, d, n, z),$$

since $\lambda' = \text{poly}(\lambda, \log K) = \text{poly}(\lambda, n)$. Thus, $|\text{pp}| = \ell \cdot \text{poly}(\lambda, d, n, z)$.

- **Secret key size:** The secret key $\text{sk}_{\text{id},x} = \{(i, \text{abe.sk}_{i,x})\}_{i \in \mathcal{I}_{\text{id}}}$ for an identity id and attribute x consists of $|\mathcal{I}_{\text{id}}|$ ABE secret keys, where $|\mathcal{I}_{\text{id}}| \leftarrow \text{Encode}(\text{id})$. By Fact 2.4, $|\mathcal{I}_{id}| = \log N + 1 = \text{poly}(n)$. Finally,

$$\left|\text{abe.sk}_{i,x}\right| = \left|g_{\text{mfe.sk}_{i,x},i}\right| + \text{poly}(\lambda, d_{\text{ABE}}, \ell_{\text{ABE}}) = \ell + \text{poly}(\lambda, d, n, z).$$

Thus, $|\text{sk}_{\text{id},x}| = |\mathcal{I}_{\text{id}}| \cdot |\text{abe.sk}_{i,x}| = \ell + \text{poly}(\lambda, d, n, z)$.

- **Ciphertext size:** Without loss of generality, we can always use hybrid encryption for the ciphertexts. Namely, the encryption algorithm samples a symmetric key k to encrypt the message and then encrypts k using the secret-key revocable predicate encryption scheme. The final ciphertext $\text{ct}_{m,\mathcal{L}}$ then consists of a symmetric encryption of the message m (which has size $|m| + \text{poly}(\lambda)$) and a revocable predicate encryption ciphertext $\widehat{\text{ct}}$ of the key k. In this case, $|k| = \text{poly}(\lambda)$, and the overall ciphertext size is $|\text{ct}| = |m| + \text{poly}(\lambda) + |\widehat{\text{ct}}|$, where $\widehat{\text{ct}} = \{(i, \text{abe.ct}_i)\}_{i \in \mathcal{J}_{\mathcal{L}}}$ is an encryption of k using Π_{RPE}. By construction, $\widehat{\text{ct}}$ consists of $|\mathcal{J}_{\mathcal{L}}|$ ABE ciphertexts, where $\mathcal{J}_{\mathcal{L}} \leftarrow \text{ComputeCover}(\mathcal{L})$. By Fact 2.4, $|\mathcal{L}| = O(|\mathcal{L}| \log(N/|\mathcal{L}|)) = |\mathcal{L}| \cdot \text{poly}(n)$. Finally, $|\text{abe.ct}_i| = |k| + \ell_{\text{ABE}} \cdot \text{poly}(\lambda, d_{\text{ABE}}, \ell_{\text{ABE}}) = \text{poly}(\lambda, d, n, z)$, and so

$$|\text{ct}_{m,\mathcal{L}}| = |m| + \text{poly}(\lambda) + |\widehat{\text{ct}}| = t + |\mathcal{L}| \cdot \text{poly}(\lambda, d, n, z). \qquad \square$$

Remark 3.10 (Handling More General Revocation Policies). Construction 3.4 naturally supports any revocation policy that can be described by a polynomial-size cover in the underlying subset-cover set system. In particular, the prefix-based subset-cover set system by Naor et al. [NNL01] from Fact 2.4 can compute a cover that excludes any polynomial number of *prefixes* (in addition to full identities). For instance, we can use the set system to revoke all users whose identities start with "000" or "01" (i.e., revoke all identities of the form 000∗∗∗ and 01∗∗∗∗). This way, the number of revoked users in the set $\mathcal{L}$ can be *exponential*, as long as they can be described by a polynomial-number of prefix-based clusters. Correspondingly, the traitor tracing scheme we construct in Sect. 4 will also support these types of revocation policies.

4   Identity-Based Trace-and-Revoke

In this section, we describe how to construct an identity-based trace-and-revoke scheme using a secret-key revocable predicate encryption scheme with broadcast (Definition 3.1). We begin by recalling the formal definition of a trace-and-revoke scheme. Our definitions are adapted from the corresponding ones in [BW06, NWZ16]. As we discuss in greater detail in Remark 4.2, our definition combines aspects of both definitions and is strictly stronger than both of the previous notions.

Definition 4.1 (Trace-and-Revoke [NWZ16, adapted]). *A trace-and-revoke scheme for a set of identities* $\mathcal{ID}$ *and a message space* $\mathcal{M}$ *is a tuple of algorithms* $\Pi_{\mathsf{TR}} = (\mathsf{Setup}, \mathsf{KeyGen}, \mathsf{Enc}, \mathsf{Dec}, \mathsf{Trace})$ *defined as follows:*

- $\mathsf{Setup}(1^\lambda) \rightarrow (\mathsf{pp}, \mathsf{msk})$*: On input the security parameter* λ*, the setup algorithm outputs the public parameters* pp *and the master secret key* msk*.*
- $\mathsf{KeyGen}(\mathsf{msk}, \mathsf{id}) \rightarrow \mathsf{sk_{id}}$*: On input the master secret key* msk *and an identity* $\mathsf{id} \in \mathcal{ID}$*, the key-generation algorithm outputs a secret key* $\mathsf{sk_{id}}$*.*
- $\mathsf{Enc}(\mathsf{pp}, m, \mathcal{L}) \rightarrow \mathsf{ct}_{m,\mathcal{L}}$*: On input the public parameters* pp*, a message* $m \in \mathcal{M}$*, and a list of revoked users* $\mathcal{L} \subseteq \mathcal{ID}$*, the encryption algorithm outputs a ciphertext* $\mathsf{ct}_{m,\mathcal{L}}$*.*
- $\mathsf{Dec}(\mathsf{sk}, \mathsf{ct}) \rightarrow m/\bot$*: On input a decryption key* sk *and a ciphertext* ct*, the decryption algorithm either outputs a message* $m \in \mathcal{M}$ *or a special symbol* $\bot$*.*
- $\mathsf{Trace}^{\mathcal{D}}(\mathsf{msk}, m_0, m_1, \mathcal{L}, \varepsilon) \rightarrow \mathsf{id}/\bot$*: On input the master secret key* msk*, two messages* $m_0, m_1 \in \mathcal{M}$*, a revocation list* $\mathcal{L} \subseteq \mathcal{ID}$*, a decoder-success parameter* $\varepsilon > 0$*, and assuming oracle access to a decoder algorithm* $\mathcal{D}$*, the tracing algorithm either outputs an identity* $\mathsf{id} \in \mathcal{ID}$ *or* $\bot$*.*

Moreover, a trace-and-revoke scheme should satisfy the following properties:

- **Correctness:** *For all messages* $m \in \mathcal{M}$*, all identities* $\mathsf{id} \in \mathcal{ID}$*, and all revocation lists* $\mathcal{L} \subseteq \mathcal{ID}$ *where* $\mathsf{id} \notin \mathcal{L}$*, if we set* $(\mathsf{pp}, \mathsf{msk}) \leftarrow \mathsf{Setup}(1^\lambda)$*,* $\mathsf{sk_{id}} \leftarrow \mathsf{KeyGen}(\mathsf{msk}, \mathsf{id})$*, and* $\mathsf{ct}_{m,\mathcal{L}} \leftarrow \mathsf{Enc}(\mathsf{pp}, m, \mathcal{L})$*, then*

$$\Pr[\mathsf{Dec}(\mathsf{sk_{id}}, \mathsf{ct}_{m,\mathcal{L}}) = m] = 1 - \mathsf{negl}(\lambda).$$

- **Semantic Security:** *For a bit* $b \in \{0, 1\}$*, we define the security experiment* $\mathsf{ExptTR_{SS}}[\lambda, \mathcal{A}, b]$ *between a challenger and an adversary* $\mathcal{A}$*. The challenger begins by sampling* $(\mathsf{pp}, \mathsf{msk}) \leftarrow \mathsf{Setup}(1^\lambda)$ *and gives* pp *to* $\mathcal{A}$*. The adversary is then given access to the following oracles:*
  - **Key-generation oracle.** *On input an identity* $\mathsf{id} \in \mathcal{ID}$*, the challenger replies with* $\mathsf{sk_{id}} \leftarrow \mathsf{KeyGen}(\mathsf{msk}, \mathsf{id})$*.*
  - **Challenge oracle.** *On input two messages* $m_0, m_1 \in \mathcal{M}$ *and a revocation list* $\mathcal{L} \subseteq \mathcal{ID}$*, the challenger replies with* $\mathsf{ct}_b \leftarrow \mathsf{Enc}(\mathsf{pp}, m_b, \mathcal{L})$*.*

  At the end of the game, the adversary outputs a bit $b' \in \{0, 1\}$*, which is the output of the experiment. An adversary* $\mathcal{A}$ *is admissible for the semantic security game if it makes a single challenge query* $(m_0, m_1, \mathcal{L})$*, and moreover, for all key-generation queries* id *the adversary makes,* $\mathsf{id} \in \mathcal{L}$*. We say that* Π_{TR} *is semantically secure if for all efficient and admissible adversaries* $\mathcal{A}$*,*

$$|\Pr[\mathsf{ExptTR_{SS}}[\lambda, \mathcal{A}, 0] = 1] - \Pr[\mathsf{ExptTR_{SS}}[\lambda, \mathcal{A}, 1] = 1]| = \mathsf{negl}(\lambda).$$

- **Traceability:** *We define the experiment* $\mathsf{ExptTR_{TR}}[\lambda, \mathcal{A}]$ *between a challenger and an adversary* $\mathcal{A}$*. The challenger begins by sampling* $(\mathsf{pp}, \mathsf{msk}) \leftarrow \mathsf{Setup}(1^\lambda)$ *and gives* pp *to* $\mathcal{A}$*. The adversary is then given access to the key-generation oracle:*
  - **Key-generation oracle.** *On input an identity* $\mathsf{id} \in \mathcal{ID}$*, the challenger replies with* $\mathsf{sk_{id}} \leftarrow \mathsf{KeyGen}(\mathsf{msk}, \mathsf{id})$*.*

At the end of the game, the adversary outputs a decoder algorithm $\mathcal{D}$, two messages $m_0, m_1 \in \mathcal{M}$, a revocation list $\mathcal{L} \subseteq \mathcal{ID}$, and a non-negligible decoder-success probability $\varepsilon > 0$. Let $\mathcal{R} \subseteq \mathcal{ID}$ be the set of identities the adversary submitted to the key-generation oracle and let $\mathsf{id}^* \leftarrow \mathsf{Trace}^{\mathcal{D}}(\mathsf{msk}, m_0, m_1, \mathcal{L}, \varepsilon)$. Then the output of the experiment is 1 if $\mathsf{id}^* \notin \mathcal{R} \backslash \mathcal{L}$ and 0 otherwise. We say that an adversary $\mathcal{A}$ is admissible for the traceability game if the decoder algorithm output by $\mathcal{A}$ satisfies

$$\Pr[b \xleftarrow{\mathrm{R}} \{0,1\} : \mathcal{D}(\mathsf{Enc}(\mathsf{pp}, m_b, \mathcal{L})) = b] \geq 1/2 + \varepsilon.$$

Finally, we say that Π_{TR} satisfies traceability security if for all efficient and admissible adversaries $\mathcal{A}$,

$$\Pr[\mathsf{ExptTR}_{\mathsf{TR}}[\lambda, \mathcal{A}] = 1] = \mathsf{negl}(\lambda).$$

Remark 4.2 (Comparison to Previous Traceability Notions). Our notion of traceability in Definition 4.1 combines aspects of the notions considered in [BW06] and [NWZ16] and is stronger than both of these previous definitions. First, similar to [NWZ16], we only require that the decoder $\mathcal{D}$ output by $\mathcal{A}$ to be able to distinguish the encryptions of two adversarially-chosen messages. The previous notion in [BW06] made the more stringent requirement that the adversary's decoder must correctly decrypt a noticeable fraction of ciphertexts. Thus, our definitions enable tracing for much weaker decoders. Next, and similar to [BW06], our tracing definition naturally incorporates revocation. Namely, if an adversary constructs a decoder that is able to distinguish encryptions of two messages with respect to a revocation list $\mathcal{L}$, then the tracing algorithm must identify a compromised key that is outside $\mathcal{L}$. In contrast, the definition in [NWZ16] only considered tracing in a standalone setting: namely, while the scheme supports revocation, the tracing definition only considered decoders that can decrypt ciphertexts encrypted to an empty revocation list. Overall, our definition is stronger than the previous definitions and we believe provides a more realistic modeling of the security demands in applications of trace-and-revoke systems.

Remark 4.3 (Adaptive Security). We note that all of the security requirements in Definition 4.1 are adaptive: namely, the adversary chooses its challenge messages and revocation list after seeing the public parameters and (adaptively-chosen) secret decryption keys. Our final construction is fully adaptive (Construction 4.4, Corollary 4.8), but we do rely on complexity leveraging and subexponential hardness assumptions. We remark here that a selective notion of security where the adversary commits to its revocation list ahead of time does not seem to directly imply adaptive security by the usual complexity leveraging technique [BB04] unless we additionally impose an a priori bound on the size of the revocation list (which we do not require in our analysis). It is an interesting problem to construct a fully collusion resistant trace-and-revoke scheme for arbitrary identities from standard polynomial hardness assumptions.

4.1   Constructing an Identity-Based Trace-and-Revoke Scheme

Our construction follows the general high-level schema as that by Nishimaki et al. [NWZ16], except our construction is secretly-traceable (but will provide *full* collusion resistance). Very briefly, we use a secret-key revocable predicate encryption scheme to embed an instance of the generalized jump-finding problem (Definition 2.5) where the position of the "jumps" correspond to non-revoked keys. The tracing algorithm relies on the generalized jump-finding algorithm (Theorem 2.6) to identify the compromised keys. We give our construction below.

Construction 4.4 (Identity-Based Trace-and-Revoke). Let $\mathcal{ID} = \{0,1\}^n$ be the identity space and let $\mathcal{M}$ be a message space. We additionally rely on the following primitives:

- Let $H: \mathcal{K} \times \mathcal{ID} \to [2^\ell]$ be a keyed collision-resistant hash function.
- Let $\mathcal{ID}_0 = [2^{\ell+1}]$. For a pair $(i, u) \in [n] \times [0, 2^{\ell+1}]$, define the function $f_{i,u}: \mathcal{ID}_0^n \to \{0,1\}$ to be the function that takes as input $v = (v_1, \ldots, v_n)$, where each $v_i \in \mathcal{ID}_0$, and outputs 1 if $v_i \le u$ and 0 otherwise. When $u = 0$, $f_{i,u}(v) = 0$ for all $i \in [n]$ and $v \in \mathcal{ID}_0^n$. Similarly, when $u = 2^{\ell+1}$, $f_{i,u}(v) = 1$ for all $i \in [n]$ and $v \in \mathcal{ID}_0^n$. We will use a canonical "all-zeroes" function to represent $f_{i,0}$ and a canonical "all-ones" function to represent $f_{i,2^{\ell+1}}$ for all $i \in [n]$.
- Let $\Pi_{\mathsf{RPE}} = (\mathsf{RPE.Setup}, \mathsf{RPE.KeyGen}, \mathsf{RPE.Broadcast}, \mathsf{RPE.Enc}, \mathsf{RPE.Dec})$ be a secret-key revocable predicate encryption scheme with broadcast with attribute space $\mathcal{ID}_0^n$, label space $[2^\ell]$, message space $\mathcal{M}$, and function space $\mathcal{F} = \{i \in [n], u \in [0, 2^{\ell+1}] : f_{i,u}\}$.

We construct a trace-and-revoke scheme $\Pi_{\mathsf{TR}} = (\mathsf{Setup}, \mathsf{KeyGen}, \mathsf{Enc}, \mathsf{Dec}, \mathsf{Trace})$ with identity space $\mathcal{ID}$ and message space $\mathcal{M}$ as follows:

- $\mathsf{Setup}(1^\lambda)$: On input the security parameter λ, the setup algorithm samples a key $\mathsf{hk} \xleftarrow{\text{R}} \mathcal{K}$, parameters $(\mathsf{rpe.pp}, \mathsf{rpe.msk}) \leftarrow \mathsf{RPE.Setup}(1^\lambda)$, and outputs

$$\mathsf{pp} = (\mathsf{hk}, \mathsf{rpe.pp}) \quad \text{and} \quad \mathsf{msk} = (\mathsf{hk}, \mathsf{rpe.msk}).$$

- $\mathsf{KeyGen}(\mathsf{msk}, \mathsf{id})$: On input the master secret key $\mathsf{msk} = (\mathsf{hk}, \mathsf{rpe.msk})$ and an identity $\mathsf{id} = (\mathsf{id}_1, \ldots, \mathsf{id}_n) \in \mathcal{ID}$, the key-generation algorithm computes $s_{\mathsf{id}} \leftarrow H(\mathsf{hk}, \mathsf{id})$ and defines the vector $v_{\mathsf{id}} = (2s_{\mathsf{id}} - \mathsf{id}_1, \ldots, 2s_{\mathsf{id}} - \mathsf{id}_n) \in \mathcal{ID}_0^n$. It outputs $\mathsf{sk}_{\mathsf{id}} \leftarrow \mathsf{RPE.KeyGen}(\mathsf{rpe.msk}, s_{\mathsf{id}}, v_{\mathsf{id}})$.
- $\mathsf{Enc}(\mathsf{pp}, m, \mathcal{L})$: On input the public parameters $\mathsf{pp} = (\mathsf{hk}, \mathsf{rpe.pp})$, a message m, and a revocation list $\mathcal{L} \subseteq \mathcal{ID}$, the encryption algorithm first constructs a new list $\mathcal{L}' \subseteq \{0,1\}^\ell$ where $\mathcal{L}' = \{\mathsf{id} \in \mathcal{L} : H(\mathsf{hk}, \mathsf{id})\}$. Then, it outputs $\mathsf{ct}_{m,\mathcal{L}} \leftarrow \mathsf{RPE.Broadcast}(\mathsf{rpe.pp}, m, \mathcal{L}')$.
- $\mathsf{Dec}(\mathsf{sk}, \mathsf{ct})$: On input a secret key sk and a ciphertext ct, the decryption algorithm outputs $m \leftarrow \mathsf{RPE.Dec}(\mathsf{sk}, \mathsf{ct})$.
- $\mathsf{Trace}^{\mathcal{D}}(\mathsf{msk}, m_0, m_1, \mathcal{L}, \varepsilon)$: On input the decryption oracle $\mathcal{D}$, the master secret key $\mathsf{msk} = (\mathsf{hk}, \mathsf{rpe.msk})$, messages $m_0, m_1 \in \mathcal{M}$, a revocation list

$\mathcal{L} \subseteq \mathcal{ID}$, and a success probability ε, the tracing algorithm begins by constructing the set $\mathcal{L}' \subseteq \{0,1\}^\ell$ where $\mathcal{L}' = \{\mathsf{id} \in \mathcal{L} : H(\mathsf{hk}, \mathsf{id})\}$. It then defines the following *randomized* oracle Q (Fig. 1):

On input a pair $(i, u) \in [n] \times [0, 2^{\ell+1}]$:

1. Sample a random bit $b \xleftarrow{\text{R}} \{0,1\}$, and construct the ciphertext $\mathsf{ct}_b \leftarrow$ RPE.Enc($\mathsf{rpe.msk}, f_{i,u}, m_b, \mathcal{L}'$).
2. Run the decoder algorithm $\mathcal{D}$ on the ciphertext ct_b to obtain a bit $b' \leftarrow \mathcal{D}(\mathsf{ct}_b)$.
3. Output 1 if $b = b'$ and 0 otherwise.

Fig. 1. The randomized oracle Q used for tracing.

Let $q = 1$, set $\delta_q = \varepsilon/(9 + 4(\ell - 1)q)$, and compute $\mathcal{T}_q \leftarrow \mathsf{QTrace}^Q(\lambda, 2^\ell, n, q, \delta_q, \varepsilon)$. If $\mathcal{T}_q$ is non-empty, take any element $(s_{\mathsf{id}}, \mathsf{id}_1, \ldots, \mathsf{id}_n) \in \mathcal{T}_q$, and output $\mathsf{id} = (\mathsf{id}_1, \ldots, \mathsf{id}_n) \in \mathcal{ID}$. Otherwise, update $q \leftarrow 2q$ and repeat this procedure.[4]

Correctness and Security Analysis. We now show that Π_{TR} from Construction 4.4 satisfies correctness, semantic security, and traceability. We state the main theorems below, but defer their formal proofs to the full version of this paper [KW19a]. The analysis proceeds similarly to the corresponding analysis from [NWZ16], except we operate in the secret-traceability setting. The main challenge in the secret-key setting is that when the adversary in the traceability game outputs a pirate decoder, the reduction algorithm cannot easily tell whether the decoder is "useful" or not (where a "useful" decoder is one that can be leveraged to break the security of the underlying secret-key revocable predicate encryption scheme). The analysis in [NWZ16] solves this problem by having the reduction algorithm sample ciphertexts of its own and observe the decoder's behavior on those ciphertexts. In this way, the reduction is able to estimate the decoder's distinguishing advantage and identify whether the adversary produced a good decoder or not. In the secret-key setting, the reduction *cannot* sample ciphertexts of its own and as such, it cannot estimate the decoder's success probability. To solve this problem, we adopt the approach taken in [GKW18] and

---

[4] We will argue in the proof of Theorem 4.7 that this algorithm will terminate with overwhelming probability. Alternatively, we can set an upper bound on the maximum number of iterations q_{max}. In this case, the tracing algorithm succeeds as long as the total number of keys issued is bounded by $2^{q_{\mathsf{max}}}$. Note that this is not an *a priori* bound on the number of keys that can be issued, just a bound on the number of iterations on which to run the tracing algorithm, which can be a flexible parameter (independent of other scheme parameters).

allow the reduction algorithm to make a *single* encryption query to the secret-key predicate encryption scheme. Using the same type of analysis as in [GKW18], we then show that with just a single encryption query, the reduction can leverage the decoder output by the traceability adversary to break security of the underlying predicate encryption scheme. The full analysis is provided in the full version of this paper [KW19a].

Theorem 4.5 (Correctness). *If H is collision-resistant and Π_{RPE} is correct, then Π_{TR} from Construction 4.4 is correct.*

Theorem 4.6 (Semantic Security). *If Π_{RPE} satisfies broadcast security and message hiding (without encryption queries), then Π_{TR} from Construction 4.4 is semantically secure.*

Theorem 4.7 (Traceability). *If H is collision-resistant and Π_{RPE} satisfies non-adaptive 1-query message hiding security, non-adaptive 1-query function hiding, and non-adaptive 1-query broadcast security, then Π_{TR} is traceable. In particular, the tracing algorithm Trace is efficient.*

4.2 Instantiating the Trace-and-Revoke Scheme

In this section, we describe our instantiation of our resulting trace-and-revoke scheme using the secret-key revocable predicate encryption scheme from Sect. 3.1 (Construction 3.4, Corollary 3.9). In particular, combining Construction 4.4 with Theorems 4.5 through 4.7 yields the following corollary:

Corollary 4.8 (Identity-Based Trace-and-Revoke from LWE). *Assuming sub-exponential hardness of LWE (with a super-polynomial modulus-to-noise ratio), there exists a fully secure identity-based trace-and-revoke scheme with identity space $\mathcal{ID} = \{0,1\}^n$ and message space $\mathcal{M} = \{0,1\}^t$ with the following properties:*

- ***Public parameter size:** $|\mathsf{pp}| = n \cdot \mathsf{poly}(\lambda, \log n)$.*
- ***Secret key size:** The secret key $\mathsf{sk}_{\mathsf{id}}$ for an identity $\mathsf{id} \in \{0,1\}^n$ has size $\mathsf{sk}_{\mathsf{id}} = n \cdot \mathsf{poly}(\lambda, \log n)$.*
- ***Ciphertext size:** An encryption $\mathsf{ct}_{m,\mathcal{L}}$ of a message $m \in \{0,1\}^t$ with respect to a revocation list $\mathcal{L}$ has size $\mathsf{ct}_{m,\mathcal{L}} = t + |\mathcal{L}| \cdot \mathsf{poly}(\lambda, \log n)$.*

Proof. The claim follows by instantiating Construction 4.4 with the following primitives:

- We can instantiate the collision-resistant hash function H with the standard SIS-based collision-resistant hash function [Ajt96, GGH96]. In this case, the hash key hk has size $|\mathsf{hk}| = \mathsf{poly}(\lambda)$ and the output length of the hash function is also $\ell = \mathsf{poly}(\lambda)$.

- We instantiate the secret-key revocable predicate encryption scheme with broadcast Π_{RPE} with the construction from Corollary 3.9. For $i \in [n]$ and $u \in [0, 2^{\ell+1}]$, the description length z of the functions $f_{i,u} \in \mathcal{F}$ satisfies

$$z = |i| + |u| \leq \log n + \ell + 3 = \mathsf{poly}(\lambda, \log n).$$

Moreover, each function $f_{i,u}$ is computing a comparison on ℓ-bit values and selecting one out of the n components of the vector. This can be computed by a Boolean circuit with depth $d = \mathsf{poly}(\lambda, \log n)$—$\mathsf{poly}(\lambda)$ for the comparison and $\mathsf{poly}(\log n)$ to select the element to compare. Finally, the identity-space for the underlying revocable predicate encryption scheme is $\mathcal{ID}_0 = [2^{\ell+1}]$ and the attribute space is $\mathcal{ID}_0^n$.

We now verify the parameter sizes for the resulting construction:

- **Public parameters size:** The public parameters pp consists of the hash key hk and the public parameters rpe.pp for the revocable predicate encryption scheme. Thus,

$$|\mathsf{pp}| = |\mathsf{hk}| + |\mathsf{rpe.pp}| = \mathsf{poly}(\lambda) + n\ell \cdot \mathsf{poly}(\lambda, d, \ell, z) = n \cdot \mathsf{poly}(\lambda, \log n).$$

- **Secret key size:** The secret key $\mathsf{sk}_{\mathsf{id}}$ for an identity $\mathsf{id} \in \{0,1\}^n$ consists of a secret key for the underlying revocable predicate encryption scheme. By Corollary 3.9, we have that $|\mathsf{sk}_{\mathsf{id}}| = n\ell + \mathsf{poly}(\lambda, d, \ell, z) = n \cdot \mathsf{poly}(\lambda, \log n)$.
- **Ciphertext size:** The ciphertext $\mathsf{ct}_{m,\mathcal{L}}$ for a message $m \in \{0,1\}^t$ with respect to a revocation list $\mathcal{L}$ consists of a ciphertext for the underlying revocable predicate encryption scheme. By Corollary 3.9,

$$|\mathsf{ct}_{m,\mathcal{L}}| = t + |\mathcal{L}| \cdot \mathsf{poly}(\lambda, d, \ell, z) = t + |\mathcal{L}| \cdot \mathsf{poly}(\lambda, \log n). \qquad \square$$

Acknowledgments. We thank Ahmadreza Rahimi for helpful discussions on this work and the anonymous reviewers for useful suggestions on improving the exposition. S. Kim is supported by NSF, DARPA, a grant from ONR, and the Simons Foundation. D. J. Wu is supported by NSF CNS-1917414 and a University of Virginia SEAS Research Innovation Award. Opinions, findings and conclusions or recommendations expressed in this material are those of the authors and do not necessarily reflect the views of DARPA.

References

[ABP+17] Agrawal, S., Bhattacherjee, S., Phan, D.H., Stehlé, D., Yamada, S.: Efficient public trace and revoke from standard assumptions: extended abstract. In: ACM CCS, pp. 2277–2293 (2017)

[AJS17] Ananth, P., Jain, A., Sahai, A.: Indistinguishability obfuscation for turing machines: constant overhead and amortization. In: Katz, J., Shacham, H. (eds.) CRYPTO 2017. LNCS, vol. 10402, pp. 252–279. Springer, Cham (2017). https://doi.org/10.1007/978-3-319-63715-0_9

[Ajt96]   Ajtai, M.: Generating hard instances of lattice problems (extended abstract). In: STOC, pp. 99–108 (1996)

[AS16]   Ananth, P., Sahai, A.: Functional encryption for turing machines. In: Kushilevitz, E., Malkin, T. (eds.) TCC 2016. LNCS, vol. 9562, pp. 125–153. Springer, Heidelberg (2016). https://doi.org/10.1007/978-3-662-49096-9_6

[BB04]   Boneh, D., Boyen, X.: Efficient selective-id secure identity-based encryption without random oracles. In: Cachin, C., Camenisch, J.L. (eds.) EUROCRYPT 2004. LNCS, vol. 3027, pp. 223–238. Springer, Heidelberg (2004). https://doi.org/10.1007/978-3-540-24676-3_14

[BGG+14]   Boneh, D., et al.: Fully key-homomorphic encryption, arithmetic circuit ABE and compact garbled circuits. In: Nguyen, P.Q., Oswald, E. (eds.) EUROCRYPT 2014. LNCS, vol. 8441, pp. 533–556. Springer, Heidelberg (2014). https://doi.org/10.1007/978-3-642-55220-5_30

[BGI+12]   Barak, B., et al.: On the (im)possibility of obfuscating programs. J. ACM 59(2), 6:1–6:48 (2012)

[BN08]   Boneh, D., Naor, M.: Traitor tracing with constant size ciphertext. In: ACM CCS, pp. 501–510 (2008)

[BP09]   Billet, O., Phan, D.H.: Traitors collaborating in public: pirates 2.0. In: Joux, A. (ed.) EUROCRYPT 2009. LNCS, vol. 5479, pp. 189–205. Springer, Heidelberg (2009). https://doi.org/10.1007/978-3-642-01001-9_11

[BSW06]   Boneh, D., Sahai, A., Waters, B.: Fully collusion resistant traitor tracing with short ciphertexts and private keys. In: Vaudenay, S. (ed.) EUROCRYPT 2006. LNCS, vol. 4004, pp. 573–592. Springer, Heidelberg (2006). https://doi.org/10.1007/11761679_34

[BW06]   Boneh, D., Waters, B.: A fully collusion resistant broadcast, trace, and revoke system. In: ACM CCS, pp. 211–220 (2006)

[BW07]   Boneh, D., Waters, B.: Conjunctive, subset, and range queries on encrypted data. In: Vadhan, S.P. (ed.) TCC 2007. LNCS, vol. 4392, pp. 535–554. Springer, Heidelberg (2007). https://doi.org/10.1007/978-3-540-70936-7_29

[CFN94]   Chor, B., Fiat, A., Naor, M.: Tracing traitors. In: Desmedt, Y.G. (ed.) CRYPTO 1994. LNCS, vol. 839, pp. 257–270. Springer, Heidelberg (1994). https://doi.org/10.1007/3-540-48658-5_25

[CFNP00]   Chor, B., Fiat, A., Naor, M., Pinkas, B.: Tracing traitors. IEEE Trans. Inf. Theory 46(3), 893–910 (2000)

[CHN+16]   Cohen, A., Holmgren, J., Nishimaki, R., Vaikuntanathan, V., Wichs, D.: Watermarking cryptographic capabilities. In: STOC, pp. 1115–1127 (2016)

[CVW+18]   Chen, Y., Vaikuntanathan, V., Waters, B., Wee, H., Wichs, D.: Traitor-tracing from LWE made simple and attribute-based. In: Beimel, A., Dziembowski, S. (eds.) TCC 2018. LNCS, vol. 11240, pp. 341–369. Springer, Cham (2018). https://doi.org/10.1007/978-3-030-03810-6_13

[DF02]   Dodis, Y., Fazio, N.: Public key broadcast encryption for stateless receivers. In: Feigenbaum, J. (ed.) DRM 2002. LNCS, vol. 2696, pp. 61–80. Springer, Heidelberg (2003). https://doi.org/10.1007/978-3-540-44993-5_5

[FN93]   Fiat, A., Naor, M.: Broadcast encryption. In: Stinson, D.R. (ed.) CRYPTO 1993. LNCS, vol. 773, pp. 480–491. Springer, Heidelberg (1994). https://doi.org/10.1007/3-540-48329-2_40

[GGH96]   Goldreich, O., Goldwasser, S., Halevi, S.: Collision-free hashing from lattice problems. IACR Cryptology ePrint Archive 1996/9 (1996)

[GGH+13]   Garg, S., Gentry, C., Halevi, S., Raykova, M., Sahai, A., Waters, B.: Candidate indistinguishability obfuscation and functional encryption for all circuits. In: FOCS, pp. 40–49 (2013)

[GGM84]   Goldreich, O., Goldwasser, S., Micali, S.: How to construct random functions (extended abstract). In: FOCS, pp. 464–479 (1984)

[GKM+19]   Goyal, R., Kim, S., Manohar, N., Waters, B., Wu, D.J.: Watermarking public-key cryptographic primitives. In: Boldyreva, A., Micciancio, D. (eds.) CRYPTO 2019. LNCS, vol. 11694, pp. 367–398. Springer, Cham (2019). https://doi.org/10.1007/978-3-030-26954-8_12

[GKP+13]   Goldwasser, S., Kalai, Y.T., Popa, R.A., Vaikuntanathan, V., Zeldovich, N.: Reusable garbled circuits and succinct functional encryption. In: STOC, pp. 555–564 (2013)

[GKSW10]   Garg, S., Kumarasubramanian, A., Sahai, A., Waters, B.: Building efficient fully collusion-resilient traitor tracing and revocation schemes. In: ACM CCS, pp. 121–130 (2010)

[GKW18]   Goyal, R., Koppula, V., Waters, B.: Collusion resistant traitor tracing from learning with errors. In: STOC, pp. 660–670 (2018)

[GKW19]   Goyal, R., Koppula, V., Waters, B.: New approaches to traitor tracing with embedded identities. In: Hofheinz, D., Rosen, A. (eds.) TCC 2019. LNCS, vol. 11892, pp. 149–179. Springer, Cham (2019). https://doi.org/10.1007/978-3-030-36033-7_6

[GPSW06]   Goyal, V., Pandey, O., Sahai, A., Waters, B.: Attribute-based encryption for fine-grained access control of encrypted data. In: ACM CCS, pp. 89–98 (2006)

[GQWW19]   Goyal, R., Quach, W., Waters, B., Wichs, D.: Broadcast and trace with N^ε ciphertext size from standard assumptions. In: Boldyreva, A., Micciancio, D. (eds.) CRYPTO 2019. LNCS, vol. 11694, pp. 826–855. Springer, Cham (2019). https://doi.org/10.1007/978-3-030-26954-8_27

[GS18]   Garg, S., Srinivasan, A.: A simple construction of iO for turing machines. In: Beimel, A., Dziembowski, S. (eds.) TCC 2018. LNCS, vol. 11240, pp. 425–454. Springer, Cham (2018). https://doi.org/10.1007/978-3-030-03810-6_16

[GVW12]   Gorbunov, S., Vaikuntanathan, V., Wee, H.: Functional encryption with bounded collusions via multi-party computation. In: Safavi-Naini, R., Canetti, R. (eds.) CRYPTO 2012. LNCS, vol. 7417, pp. 162–179. Springer, Heidelberg (2012). https://doi.org/10.1007/978-3-642-32009-5_11

[GVW19]   Goyal, R., Vusirikala, S., Waters, B.: Collusion resistant broadcast and trace from positional witness encryption. In: Lin, D., Sako, K. (eds.) PKC 2019. LNCS, vol. 11443, pp. 3–33. Springer, Cham (2019). https://doi.org/10.1007/978-3-030-17259-6_1

[HS02]   Halevy, D., Shamir, A.: The LSD broadcast encryption scheme. In: Yung, M. (ed.) CRYPTO 2002. LNCS, vol. 2442, pp. 47–60. Springer, Heidelberg (2002). https://doi.org/10.1007/3-540-45708-9_4

[KD98]   Kurosawa, K., Desmedt, Y.: Optimum traitor tracing and asymmetric schemes. In: Nyberg, K. (ed.) EUROCRYPT 1998. LNCS, vol. 1403, pp. 145–157. Springer, Heidelberg (1998). https://doi.org/10.1007/BFb0054123

[KLW15]   Koppula, V., Lewko, A.B., Waters, B.: Indistinguishability obfuscation for turing machines with unbounded memory. In: STOC, pp. 419–428 (2015)

[KP07]   Kiayias, A., Pehlivanoglu, S.: Pirate evolution: how to make the most of your traitor keys. In: Menezes, A. (ed.) CRYPTO 2007. LNCS, vol. 4622, pp. 448–465. Springer, Heidelberg (2007). https://doi.org/10.1007/978-3-540-74143-5_25

[KSW08] Katz, J., Sahai, A., Waters, B.: Predicate encryption supporting disjunctions, polynomial equations, and inner products. In: Smart, N. (ed.) EUROCRYPT 2008. LNCS, vol. 4965, pp. 146–162. Springer, Heidelberg (2008). https://doi.org/10.1007/978-3-540-78967-3_9

[KT15]   Kiayias, A., Tang, Q.: Traitor deterring schemes: using bitcoin as collateral for digital content. In: ACM CCS, pp. 231–242 (2015)

[KW17]   Kim, S., Wu, D.J.: Watermarking cryptographic functionalities from standard lattice assumptions. In: Katz, J., Shacham, H. (eds.) CRYPTO 2017. LNCS, vol. 10401, pp. 503–536. Springer, Cham (2017). https://doi.org/10.1007/978-3-319-63688-7_17

[KW19a] Kim, S., David, J.W.: Collusion resistant trace-and-revoke for arbitrary identities from standard assumptions. IACR Cryptol. ePrint Arch. 2019/984 (2019)

[KW19b] Kim, S., Wu, D.J.: Watermarking PRFs from lattices: stronger security via extractable PRFs. In: Boldyreva, A., Micciancio, D. (eds.) CRYPTO 2019. LNCS, vol. 11694, pp. 335–366. Springer, Cham (2019). https://doi.org/10.1007/978-3-030-26954-8_11

[LPSS14] Ling, S., Phan, D.H., Stehlé, D., Steinfeld, R.: Hardness of k-LWE and applications in traitor tracing. In: Garay, J.A., Gennaro, R. (eds.) CRYPTO 2014. LNCS, vol. 8616, pp. 315–334. Springer, Heidelberg (2014). https://doi.org/10.1007/978-3-662-44371-2_18

[NNL01] Naor, D., Naor, M., Lotspiech, J.: Revocation and tracing schemes for stateless receivers. In: Kilian, J. (ed.) CRYPTO 2001. LNCS, vol. 2139, pp. 41–62. Springer, Heidelberg (2001). https://doi.org/10.1007/3-540-44647-8_3

[NP98]   Naor, M., Pinkas, B.: Threshold traitor tracing. In: Krawczyk, H. (ed.) CRYPTO 1998. LNCS, vol. 1462, pp. 502–517. Springer, Heidelberg (1998). https://doi.org/10.1007/BFb0055750

[NP00]   Naor, M., Pinkas, B.: Efficient trace and revoke schemes. In: Frankel, Y. (ed.) FC 2000. LNCS, vol. 1962, pp. 1–20. Springer, Heidelberg (2001). https://doi.org/10.1007/3-540-45472-1_1

[NWZ16] Nishimaki, R., Wichs, D., Zhandry, M.: Anonymous traitor tracing: how to embed arbitrary information in a key. In: Fischlin, M., Coron, J.-S. (eds.) EUROCRYPT 2016. LNCS, vol. 9666, pp. 388–419. Springer, Heidelberg (2016). https://doi.org/10.1007/978-3-662-49896-5_14

[QWZ18] Quach, W., Wichs, D., Zirdelis, G.: Watermarking PRFs under standard assumptions: public marking and security with extraction queries. In: Beimel, A., Dziembowski, S. (eds.) TCC 2018. LNCS, vol. 11240, pp. 669–698. Springer, Cham (2018). https://doi.org/10.1007/978-3-030-03810-6_24

[Reg05] Regev, O.: On lattices, learning with errors, random linear codes, and cryptography. In: STOC, pp. 84–93 (2005)

[SBC+07] Shi, E., Bethencourt, J., Chan, H.T.-H., Song, D.X., Perrig, A.: Multidimensional range query over encrypted data. In: IEEE S&P, pp. 350–364 (2007)

[SS10]   Sahai, A., Seyalioglu, H.: Worry-free encryption: functional encryption with public keys. In: ACM CCS, pp. 463–472 (2010)

[SSW01] Staddon, J., Stinson, D.R., Wei, R.: Combinatorial properties of frame-proof and traceability codes. IEEE Trans. Inf. Theory **47**(3), 1042–1049 (2001)

[SW05] Sahai, A., Waters, B.: Fuzzy identity-based encryption. In: Cramer, R. (ed.) EUROCRYPT 2005. LNCS, vol. 3494, pp. 457–473. Springer, Heidelberg (2005). https://doi.org/10.1007/11426639_27

Subvert KEM to Break DEM: Practical Algorithm-Substitution Attacks on Public-Key Encryption

Rongmao Chen[1], Xinyi Huang[2(✉)], and Moti Yung[3,4]

[1] College of Computer, National University of Defense Technology, Changsha, China
chromao@nudt.edu.cn
[2] Fujian Provincial Key Laboratory of Network Security and Cryptology, College of Mathematics and Informatics, Fujian Normal University, Fuzhou, China
xyhuang@fjnu.edu.cn
[3] Google LLC, New York, NY, USA
[4] Columbia University, New York City, USA
moti@cs.columbia.edu

Abstract. Motivated by the currently widespread concern about mass surveillance of encrypted communications, Bellare *et al.* introduced at CRYPTO 2014 the notion of Algorithm-Substitution Attack (ASA) where the legitimate encryption algorithm is replaced by a subverted one that aims to undetectably exfiltrate the secret key via ciphertexts. Practically implementable ASAs on various cryptographic primitives (Bellare *et al.*, CRYPTO'14 & ACM CCS'15; Ateniese *et al.*, ACM CCS'15; Berndt and Liśkiewicz, ACM CCS'17) have been constructed and analyzed, leaking the secret key successfully. Nevertheless, in spite of much progress, the practical impact of ASAs (formulated originally for symmetric key cryptography) on public-key (PKE) encryption operations remains unclear, primarily since the encryption operation of PKE does not involve the secret key, and also previously known ASAs become relatively inefficient for leaking the plaintext due to the logarithmic upper bound of exfiltration rate (Berndt and Liśkiewicz, ACM CCS'17).

In this work, we formulate a practical ASA on PKE encryption algorithm which, perhaps surprisingly, turns out to be much more efficient and robust than existing ones, showing that ASAs on PKE schemes are far more effective and dangerous than previously believed. We mainly target PKE of hybrid encryption which is the most prevalent way to employ PKE in the literature and in practice. The main strategy of our ASA is to subvert the underlying key encapsulation mechanism (KEM) so that the session key encapsulated could be efficiently extracted, which, in turn, breaks the data encapsulation mechanism (DEM) enabling us to learn the plaintext itself. Concretely, our non-black-box yet quite general attack enables recovering the plaintext from only two successive ciphertexts and minimally depends on a short state of previous internal randomness. A widely used class of KEMs is shown to be subvertible by our powerful attack.

Our attack relies on a novel identification and formalization of certain properties that yield practical ASAs on KEMs. More broadly,

© International Association for Cryptologic Research 2020
S. Moriai and H. Wang (Eds.): ASIACRYPT 2020, LNCS 12492, pp. 98–128, 2020.
https://doi.org/10.1007/978-3-030-64834-3_4

it points at and may shed some light on exploring structural weaknesses of other "composed cryptographic primitives," which may make them susceptible to more dangerous ASAs with effectiveness that surpasses the known logarithmic upper bound (i.e., reviewing composition as an attack enabler).

Keywords: Algorithm-substitution attacks · Public-key encryption · Key encapsulation mechanism

1 Introduction

Provable security provides strong guarantees for deploying cryptographic tools in the real world to achieve security goals. Nevertheless, it has been shown that even provably secure cryptosystems might be problematic in practice. Such a security gap—between the ideal and the real world—lies in the fact that the robustness of provable security closely depends on the adopted adversarial model which, however, often makes idealized assumptions that are not always fulfilled in actual implementations.

An implicit and common assumption—in typical adversarial models for provable security—is that cryptographic algorithms should behave in the way specified by their *specifications*. In the real world, unfortunately, such an assumption may turn out to be invalid due to a variety of reasons such as software/hardware bugs and even malicious tampering attacks. In particular, attackers (manufacturers and supply-chain intermediaries), in reality, may be able to modify the algorithm implementation so that the subverted one remains indistinguishable—in black-box testing—from the specification, while leaking private information (e.g., secret keys) during its subsequent runs. The threat was originally identified as *kleptography* by Young and Yung [30,31] over two decades ago, while the Snowden revelations of actual deployments of such attacks (in 2013) attracted renewed attention of the research community [3–9,11,12,14,15,17,18,24,25,27–29].

1.1 Algorithm-Substitution Attacks

In Crypto 2014, Bellare, Paterson, and Rogaway [7] initiated the formal study of *algorithm-substitution attack* (ASA), which was defined broadly, against symmetric encryption. In the ASA model, the encryption algorithm is replaced by an altered version created by the adversary. Such a substitution is said to be undetectable if the detector—who knows the secret key—cannot differentiate subverted ciphertexts from legitimate ones. The subversion goal of an ASA adversary is to gain the ability to recover the secret key from (sequential) subverted ciphertexts. Concretely, [7] proposed actual substitution attacks against certain symmetric encryption schemes.

Subsequently, Degabriele, Farshim and Poettering [14] further justified Bellare *et al.*'s ASA model [7] from an increased practical perspective, and redefined the security notion by relaxing the assumption that any subverted ciphertext produced by the altered algorithm should be decryptable. Bellare, Jaeger and Kane [6] strengthened the undetectability notion of [7] by considering stronger detectors which are able to adaptively feed the encryption code with some specified inputs and see all outputs written to memory, including the current state of the encryption code. They then designed stateless ASAs against all randomized symmetric encryption schemes. In [3], Ateniese, Magri and Venturi extended the ASA model and studied signature schemes in the setting of fully-adaptive and continuous subversion. Berndt and Liśkiewicz [8], in turn, rigorously investigated the relationship between ASAs and steganography—a well-known concept of hiding information in unsuspicious communication. By modeling encryption schemes as steganographic channels, they showed that successful ASAs correspond to secure stegosystems on the channels and vice versa. This indicates a general result that there exist *universal* ASAs—*work with no knowledge on the internal implementation of the underlying cryptographic primitive*—for any cryptographic algorithm with sufficiently large min-entropy, and in fact almost all known ASAs [3,6,7] are universal ASAs.

In this work, we turn to another fundamental cryptographic primitives, i.e., public-key encryption (PKE), aiming at better understanding the impact of ASAs on PKE systems. Indeed, Bellare, Paterson and Rogaway mentioned in [7] that:

> "...one can consider subversion for public-key schemes or for other cryptographic goals, like key exchange. There are possibilities for algorithms-substitution attacks (ASAs) in all these settings...the extensions to cover additional schemes is an obvious and important target for future research."

At first glance, the general result by Berndt and Liśkiewicz [8] has already illustrated the feasibility of ASAs on randomized PKE algorithms, and, further, a concrete attack was indeed exhibited on the CPA-secure PKE by Russell *et al.* [28] (where their main result was a concrete architectural setting and construction to prevent such attacks). However, as we will explain below, the impact of such univerisal ASAs on PKE encryption algorithm turns out to be much weaker (i.e., much less efficient) than those on symmetric encryption [6,7]. We concentrate in this work on subverting the system via the content of its ciphertexts.

Limited Efficiency and Impact of Previously Known ASAs on PKE. It is proved that the exfiltration rate of universal ASAs—the number of embedded bits per ciphertext—suffers a logarithmic upper bound [8]. Concretely, for the case of encryption schemes, no universal and consistent ASA is able to embed more than $\log(\kappa)$ (κ is the key length) bits of information into a single ciphertext in the random oracle model. Although this upper bound is somewhat limited, it does not significantly weaken the impact of universal ASAs on secret-key algorithms [3,6,7], since given sufficient ciphertexts—or sufficient signatures in the case of signature schemes—the adversary can extract the whole secret key, and afterwards can completely break the security of these algorithms, as long as the underlying secret key remains unchanged. However, when it comes to the case of PKE, the impact of universal ASAs turns out to be quite impractical as the encryption procedure of PKE has only access to the public key, and thus it is impossible to leak the secret key via subverting the PKE encryption algorithm itself (via the ciphertexts). Hence, as we see it, the best possible goal for ASAs on PKE encryption procedure is to recover plaintexts. For legitimate users, this seems somewhat positive as different from the (fixed) secret key, the plaintext is usually much longer, and thus the adversary needs to collect much more ciphertexts—due to the logarithmic upper bound of universal ASAs—to recover the whole plaintext successfully. Note that although gaining one-bit information of plaintext suffices for the adversary to win the indistinguishibility-based security game (e.g., IND-CPA), such a bit-by-bit recovery of plaintext is rather inefficient and thus not desirable from the point of view of the adversary, especially given the fact that plaintexts are usually fresh across various encryption sessions in reality.

CONCRETE EXAMPLES. We apply Bellare et al.'s ASAs [6,7] to PKE to give a more intuitive picture. Precisely, the *biased ciphertext attack* [7]—using rejection sampling of randomness—could be also mounted on PKE and it has been indeed proposed by Russell et al. [28] to leak the plaintext bit from the subverted PKE ciphertext. However, such an attack could only leak one bit of information per subverted ciphertext, and thus fully recovering a plaintext would (at least) require as many ciphertexts as the length of a plaintext. This concretely shows that existing ASAs are relatively inefficient on PKE. Moreover, such an attack is stateful with a large state, as it needs to maintain a global counter that represents which bit(s) of the plaintext it is trying to exfiltrate in each run. This weakens the robustness of attacks in practice as it depends on a state related to a long system history, in order to successfully leak the whole plaintext of PKE encryption. Note also that the strong ASA proposed in [6]—although being stateless—is much less efficient on PKE due to the application of the coupon collector's problem.

Our Concrete Question: Efficient and Robust ASAs on PKE? The aforementioned observations and the importance of better understanding of the impact of ASAs, motivated us to consider the following question:

> Are there ASAs that could be efficiently mounted on a wide range of PKE schemes and only have much limited (i.e., constant length) dependency on the system history?

In particular, we mainly consider the possibility of practical ASAs on PKE that *enable the plaintext recovery with a constant number—independent of the plaintext length—of ciphertexts* while *only depending on a short system history*. Generally, a stateful attack is more robust if its state depends on just a small history. For example, in the backdoored Dual EC DRBG (Dual Elliptic Curve Deterministic Random Bit Generator) [10], an attack which apparently was successfully employed, there is a dependency on prior public randomness and learning the current seed. Nevertheless, it turned out to be deployed and the limited dependency does not weaken its impacts on practical systems. This is mainly due to the fact that an implementation of pseudo-random generators (PRGs), in fact, needs to maintain some states and the state of generators always persists for a while at least in systems (hence, some limited dependency on the past is natural, whereas long history dependency is not that typical and creates more complicated state management).

REMARK: *Young and Yung's Kleptography* [30–32]. In the line of kleptography, subversions of PKE have been studied (primarily of key generation procedures of PKE) by Young and Yung [30–32]. They introduced the notion of *secretly embedded trapdoor with universal protection* (SETUP) mechanism, which enables the attacker to exclusively and efficiently recover the user private information. Young and Yung showed how SETUP can be embedded in several concrete cryptosystems including RSA, ElGamal key generation and Diffie-Hellman key exchange [30–32]. Our motivation may be viewed as a modern take on Young and Yung's kleptographic attacks on PKE key generation, but in the ASA model against the encryption operation itself, and particularly we ask: *to what extent their type of attacks may be extended to cover PKE encryption algorithms (and composed methods like hybrid encryption) more generally?*

1.2   Our Results

In this work, we provide an affirmative answer to the above question by proposing a practical ASA that is generically applicable to a wide range of PKE schemes, demonstrating that ASAs on PKE could be much more dangerous than previously thought. Our idea is initially inspired by the observation that almost all primary PKE constructions adopt the hybrid encryption: a public key cryptosystem (the *key encapsulation mechanism* or KEM) is used to encapsulate the so-called *session key* which is subsequently used to encrypt the plaintext by a symmetric encryption algorithm (the *data encapsulation mechanism* or DEM). Specifically, we turn to consider the possibility of substituting the underlying KEM stealthily so that the attacker is able to recover the session key to break the DEM (and thereafter recover the plaintext). The idea behind our attack strategy is somewhat intuitive as compared with the plaintext that might be of arbitrary length, the session key is usually much shorter and thus easier to recover. However, this does not immediately gain much efficiency improvement in subverting PKE encryption, mainly due to the fact that the underlying KEM produces fresh session keys in between various encryption invocations. Hence, we further explore the feasibility of efficient ASA on KEMs that could successfully recover a session key from a constant number of ciphertexts. Given the logarithmic upper bound of universal ASAs [8], we turn to study the possibility of non-black-box yet still general ASAs.

   To the end, due to the successful identification of a general structural weakness in existing KEM constructions, we manage to mount a much more efficient ASA on KEMs that could recover a session key from only two successive ciphertexts, which means that the state required by the attack is much smaller than the generic one. In fact, the state relation (as we will discuss below) in our proposed ASA is similar to that of the well-known Dual EC DRBG attack, and thus it is similar to typical state cryptosystems keep in operation, which indicates that the attack is very robust in actual systems. Our proposed attack relies on the novel identification of non-black-box yet general enough properties that yield practical ASAs on KEMs. Also, it is a fundamental property that turns out to be conceptually easy to explain after we formulate the non-black-box assumption. However, we remark that the exact formulations and analysis are challenging. In particular, we are able to prove that the attack works only assuming that the underlying KEM satisfies some special properties, and we formally define them, rigorously showing a wide range of KEMs suffering from our ASA. This new finding explains why the attack was not considered before, even though the rationale behind our attack (as briefly shown below) was implicitly informally already hinted about if one considers the cases given in [30]. In fact, our attack could be regarded as a general extension of Young and Yung's kleptographic attacks in the ASA model against the modern encryption procedures of PKE schemes. More broadly, our work may shed some light on further exploring the non-black-box but quite general structural weaknesses of other composed cryptographic primitives (which the KEM/ DEM paradigm is an example of), that may make them susceptible to more efficient and effective ASAs surpassing the logarithmic upper bound of universal ASAs [8].

Our Contributions. To summarize, we make the following contributions.

1. We formalize an asymmetric ASA model for KEMs. Compared with previous works that mainly studied symmetric ASAs [3,6,7,14], in this work we consider a stronger setting where revealing the hard-wired subversion key does not provide users with the same cryptographic capabilities as the subverter.
2. We redefine the KEM syntax in a module level with two new properties—namely *universal decryptability* and *key-pseudo-randomness*—that are vital to our proposed ASA. We then introduce a generic ASA and rigorously prove its session-key-recoverability and undetectability in our ASA model.
3. We show that our attack works on a wide range of KEMs including the generic construction from hash proof system [20,23]; and concrete KEMs derived from popular PKE schemes such as the Cramer-Shoup scheme [13], the Kurosawa-Desmedt scheme [23], and the Hofheinz-Kiltz scheme [20].

Below we further elaborate on the results presented in this work.

ASYMMETRIC ASA MODEL. We start with briefly introducing the adopted ASA model in our work. Current ASA models [3,6–8,14] are in the symmetric setting where the subversion key hard-wired in the (subverted) algorithm is the same with the one used for secret key recovery. Such a symmetric setting would enable anyone who reverse-engineers the subversion key from the subverted algorithm to have the same cryptographic ability as the subverter. In this work, we turn to the asymmetric ASA setting advocated by kleptograhic attacks [31], and we carefully formalize an asymmetric ASA model specifically for KEMs. In our model, the subverted KEM contains the public subversion key while the corresponding secret subversion key is only known to the subverter. The session key recovery requires the secret subversion key and thus the attacking ability is exclusive to the subverter (and is not acquired by reverse engineering the subverted device). Also, we further enhance the notion of undetectability in the sense that the detector is allowed to know the public subversion key in the detection game. We note that in [7], an asymmetric ASA model is also discussed in the context of symmetric encryption, whereas all the proposed ASAs are symmetric. In fact, as we will show later, the asymmetric setting essentially enables our proposed effective ASAs.

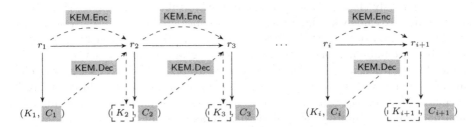

Fig. 1. The sketc.h map of our ASA on (simplified) KEMs. The dashed line at the top represents that in the subverted encapsulation algorithm, r_{i+1} is derived from r_i (i starts with "1") via running the legitimate algorithm KEM.Enc. The dashed diagonal line indicates that the attacker recovers r_{i+1} (and K_{i+1}) from C_i via running KEM.Dec.

A SKETCH MAP OF OUR ASA (SIMPLIFIED VERSION). We now informally describe our identified non-black-box structural weakness in existing KEM constructions and show how it enables our efficient attack. We remark that here we only take the case of simplified KEM as an example to illustrate our basic idea. For more details and formal analysis we refer the reader to Sect. 4.2 where we present our ASA on more general KEMs. We first roughly recall the syntax of (simplified) KEM. Informally, a KEM is defined by a tuple of algorithms (KEM.Setup, KEM.Gen, KEM.Enc, KEM.Dec). The key generation algorithm KEM.Gen generates the public/secret key pair (pk, sk). The encapsulation algorithm KEM.Enc takes as input pk and output the session key K with the key ciphertext C. The decapsulation algorithm KEM.Dec uses sk to decrypt C for computing K. Our proposed ASA is essentially inspired by the observation that many popular KEM constructions, in fact, produce "public-key-independent" ciphertexts which only depend on the internal random coins generated by KEM.Enc while is independent of the public key. Consequently, such kind of key ciphertexts are "decryptable" with any key pair honestly generated by KEM.Gen (formalized as *universal decryptability* in our work). Relying on this fact, we manage to mount a substitution attack on KEM.Enc via manipulating the internal random coin. Specifically, the subverter runs the legitimate algorithm KEM.Gen—with the public parameter—to generate the subversion key pair (psk, ssk) of which psk is hard-wired in the subverted KEM.Enc (denoted by ASA.Enc in our ASA model), while ssk is exclusively held by the subverter.

Note that KEM.Enc would be run repeatedly in an ongoing encryption procedure of PKE and let r_i denote the random coin generated by KEM.Enc in its i-th invocation. Ideally, it is expected that random coins from different invocations are generated independently. However, in our designed ASA.Enc, as roughly depicted in Fig. 1, the random coin r_{i+1} is actually derived via KEM.Enc taking psk and r_i (maintained as an internal state) as inputs. Consequently, due to the universal decryptability of KEM, the subverter is able to recompute r_{i+1} (and thereafter recover the session key K_{i+1}) by running KEM.Dec to decrypt C_i using ssk. In this way, our attack enables the subverter to recover the session key of a subverted ciphertext with the help of the previous subverted ciphertext.

On the Robustness of Our Stateful Attacks. As pointed out by Bellare *et al.* [6], stateful ASAs may become detectable upon the system reboot (e.g., resetting the state). However, we argue below that the state in our attack is practically acceptable, and our attack could still be very robust and meaningful in cryptographic implementation practices nowadays. The state relation (i.e., only the previous randomness) in our proposed ASA is similar to that of Dual EC DRBG, and is much more limited than the stateful ASA on symmetric encryption [7], which needs to maintain a global counter that represents which bit(s) of the secret is trying to exfiltrate in each run. More broadly, modern cryptosystems in the cloud services are implemented typically in secure hardware modules that are rented to cloud customers. This has become a popular configuration in recent years. It is inconceivable that such service cannot be temporarily non-volatile and stateful. Even if it happens or all relevant tools are reinitiated at system initiation, our attack persists since we do not really need a state depending on the entire system history, but only the randomness generated in the previous session. Therefore, we categorically see no practical weakness with our configuration, primarily in view of modern secure hardware modules as cryptographic implementations, and the successful large scale attack on Dual EC DRBG [10].

2 Preliminaries

Notations. For any randomized algorithm $\mathcal{F}$, $y := \mathcal{F}(x; r)$ denotes the output of $\mathcal{F}$ on the fixed randomness r and $y \leftarrow_s \mathcal{F}(x)$ denotes the random output of $\mathcal{F}$. We write $\mathcal{A}^{\mathcal{O}_1, \mathcal{O}_2, \cdots}(x, y, \cdots)$ to indicate that $\mathcal{A}$ is an algorithm with inputs $x, y, \cdots$ and access to oracle $\mathcal{O}_1, \mathcal{O}_2, \cdots$. Let $z \leftarrow \mathcal{A}^{\mathcal{O}_1, \mathcal{O}_2, \cdots}(x, y, \cdots)$ denote the outputs of running $\mathcal{A}$ with inputs $(x, y, \cdots)$ and access to oracles $\mathcal{O}_1, \mathcal{O}_2, \cdots$.

2.1 Entropy Smoothing Hash Functions

Let $\mathcal{H} = \{H_{\hat{k}}\}_{\hat{k} \in \hat{\mathcal{K}}}$ ($\hat{\mathcal{K}}$ is the key space) be a family of keyed hash functions, where every function $H_{\hat{k}}$ maps an element of group X to another element of group Y. Let $\mathcal{D}$ be a PPT algorithm that takes as input an element of $\hat{\mathcal{K}}$, and an element from Y, and outputs a bit. The ES-advantage of $\mathcal{D}$ is defined as

$$\mathsf{Adv}_{\mathcal{H},\mathcal{D}}^{\mathsf{es}}(n) := |\Pr\left[\mathcal{D}(\hat{k}, H_{\hat{k}}(x)) = 1 | \hat{k} \leftarrow_{\$} \hat{\mathcal{K}}, x \leftarrow_{\$} X\right]$$
$$- \Pr\left[\mathcal{D}(\hat{k}, y) = 1 | \hat{k} \leftarrow_{\$} \hat{\mathcal{K}}, y \leftarrow_{\$} Y\right]|.$$

We say $\mathcal{H}$ is $\epsilon_{\mathsf{es}}(n)$-*entropy smoothing* if for any PPT algorithm $\mathcal{D}$, $\mathsf{Adv}_{\mathcal{H},\mathcal{D}}^{\mathsf{es}}(n) \leq \epsilon_{\mathsf{es}}(n)$. It has been shown in [16] that the CBC-MAC, HMAC and Merkle-Damgård constructions meet the above definition on certain conditions.

2.2 Key Encapsulation Mechanism (KEM)

Syntax. A key encapsulation mechanism $\mathcal{KEM}$ consists of algorithms (KEM.Setup, KEM.Gen, KEM.Enc, KEM.Dec) which are formally defined as below.

- KEM.Setup(1^n). Takes as input the security parameter $n \in \mathbb{N}$ and outputs the public parameter pp. We assume pp is taken by all other algorithms as input (except of KEM.Gen where it is explicitly given).
- KEM.Gen(pp). Takes as input pp, and outputs the key pair (pk, sk).
- KEM.Enc(pk). Takes as input the public key pk, and outputs (K, ψ) where K is the session key and ψ is the ciphertext.
- KEM.Dec(sk, ψ). Takes as input the secret key sk and the ciphertext ψ, and outputs the session key K or $\bot$.

Correctness. We say $\mathcal{KEM}$ satisfies (perfect) correctness if for any $n \in \mathbb{N}$, for any pp $\leftarrow_{\$}$ KEM.Setup(1^n), for any $(pk, sk) \leftarrow_{\$}$ KEM.Gen(pp) and for any $(K, \psi) \leftarrow_{\$}$ KEM.Enc(pk), we have KEM.Dec(sk, ψ) = K.

Security. Let $\mathcal{KEM}$ = (KEM.Setup, KEM.Gen, KEM.Enc, KEM.Dec) be a KEM. We say $\mathcal{KEM}$ is IND-CCA-secure if for any PPT adversary $\mathcal{A}$,

$$\mathsf{Adv}_{\mathsf{kem},\mathcal{A}}^{\mathsf{cca}}(n) := \left| \Pr\left[b = b' : \begin{array}{l} \mathsf{pp} \leftarrow_{\$} \mathsf{KEM.Setup}(1^n) \\ (pk, sk) \leftarrow_{\$} \mathsf{KEM.Gen(pp)} \\ (K_0, \psi^*) \leftarrow_{\$} \mathsf{KEM.Enc}(pk) \\ K_1 \leftarrow_{\$} \mathcal{K}_{\mathsf{kem}}, b \leftarrow_{\$} \{0, 1\} \\ b' \leftarrow \mathcal{A}^{\mathcal{O}_{\mathsf{Dec}}(\cdot)}(pk, K_b, \psi^*) \end{array} \right] - \frac{1}{2} \right| \leq \mathsf{negl}(n),$$

where $\mathcal{K}_{\mathsf{kem}}$ is the key space of $\mathcal{KEM}$, and $\mathcal{O}_{\mathsf{Dec}}$ is a decryption oracle that on input any ciphertext ψ, returns $K := $ KEM.Dec(sk, ψ) on the condition that $\psi \neq \psi^*$. As a weak security definition, we say $\mathcal{KEM}$ is IND-CPA-secure if in the above definition, the adversary is restricted not to query $\mathcal{O}_{\mathsf{Dec}}$.

3 Asymmetric ASA Model for KEMs

In this section, we extend the notion of ASA model by Bellare *et al.* [7] to the asymmetric setting for KEMs. Here we mainly consider substitution attacks against the encapsulation algorithm while assuming that the key generation and decapsulation algorithm are not subverted. It is worth noting that via subverting the decapsulation algorithm it is possible to exfiltrate decapsulation key. Particularly, Armour and Poettering [1] demonstrated the feasibility of exfiltrating secret keys by subverting the decryption algorithm of AEAD.

3.1   Asymmetric ASA on KEMs

An ASA on KEM is that in the real-world implementation, the attacker replaces the legitimate algorithm KEM.Enc by a subverted one denoted by ASA.Enc, which hard-wires some auxiliary information chosen by the subverter. The goal of subverter is to gain some advantages in breaking the security of the subverted KEM. The algorithm ASA.Enc could be arbitrary. Particularly, the randomness space in ASA.Enc could be different from that of KEM.Enc, and the subverted ciphertext space is not necessarily equal to the valid ciphertext space of KEM.Enc[1]. Also, ASA.Enc may be *stateful* by maintaining some internal state, even in the case that KEM.Enc is not.

Syntax. Let $\mathcal{KEM} = $ (KEM.Setup, KEM.Gen, KEM.Enc, KEM.Dec) be a KEM which generates pp $\leftarrow_\$$ KEM.Setup(1^n) and $(pk, sk) \leftarrow_\$$ KEM.Gen(pp). An asymmetric ASA on $\mathcal{KEM}$ is denoted by $\mathcal{ASA} = $ (ASA.Gen, ASA.Enc, ASA.Rec).

- $(psk, ssk) \leftarrow_\$$ ASA.Gen(pp). The subversion key generation algorithm takes as input pp, and outputs the subversion key pair (psk, ssk). *This algorithm is run by the subverter. The public subversion key psk is hard-wired in the subverted algorithm while the secret subversion key ssk is hold by the attacker.*
- $(K, \psi) \leftarrow_\$$ ASA.Enc(pk, psk, τ). The subverted encapsulation algorithm takes as input pk, psk, and the (possible) internal state τ, outputs (K, ψ) and updates the state τ (if exists). *This algorithm is created by the subverter and run by the legitimate user. The state τ is never revealed to the outside.*
- $K \leftarrow_\$$ ASA.Rec(pk, ssk, ψ, Φ_ψ). The key recovery algorithm takes as input pk, ssk, ψ, the associated ciphertext set Φ_ψ, and outputs K or $\bot$. *This algorithm is run by the subverter to recover the session key K encapsulated in ψ.*

REMARK. The algorithm ASA.Rec is run by the subverter to "decrypt" the subverted ciphertext ψ—output by ASA.Enc—using the secret subversion key ssk that is associated with psk hard-wired in ASA.Enc. However, due to the information-theoretic reasons, it might be impossible for the subverter to recover the key given the subverted ciphertext only. Therefore, we generally assume that the subverter needs some *associated ciphertexts* (e.g., a tuple of previous ciphertexts) to successfully run ASA.Rec. More details are provided in Sect. 4.2.

Below we define the notion of *decryptability* which says that the subverted ciphertext—produced by ASA.Enc—is still decryptable to the legitimate receiver. In fact, decryptability could be viewed as the basic form of undetectability notion defined in Sect. 3.3.

---

[1] For example, the subverted algorithm ASA.Enc may directly output the key as its ciphertext.

Definition 1 (Decryptability). *Let* $\mathcal{ASA} = (\mathsf{ASA.Gen}, \mathsf{ASA.Enc}, \mathsf{ASA.Rec})$ *be an ASA on* $\mathcal{KEM} = (\mathsf{KEM.Setup}, \mathsf{KEM.Gen}, \mathsf{KEM.Enc}, \mathsf{KEM.Dec})$. *We say* $\mathcal{ASA}$ *preserves* **decryptability** *for* $\mathcal{KEM}$ *if for any* $n \in \mathbb{N}$, *any* $\mathsf{pp} \leftarrow_\$ \mathsf{KEM.Setup}(1^n)$, *and any* $(pk, sk) \leftarrow_\$ \mathsf{KEM.Gen}(\mathsf{pp})$, *for any* $(psk, ssk) \leftarrow_\$ \mathsf{ASA.Gen}(\mathsf{pp})$, *and all state* $\tau \in \{0,1\}^*$,

$$\Pr\left[\mathsf{Dec}(sk, \psi) \neq K : (K, \psi) \leftarrow_\$ \mathsf{ASA.Enc}(pk, psk, \tau)\right] \leq \mathsf{negl}(n),$$

where the probability is taken over the randomness of algorithm $\mathsf{ASA.Enc}$.

3.2   Session Key Recovery

Generally, the goal of the subverter is to gain some advantages in attacking the scheme. In the ASA model for symmetric encryption and signature schemes, the notion of *key recovery* is defined as a strong goal [3,6]. However, for KEMs, the encapsulation algorithm has no access to the secret (decapsulation) key and thus it is impossible to exfiltrate the long-term secret of a subverted encapsulation algorithm. Alternatively, we define another notion which captures the ability of the subverter—who has the secret subversion key ssk—to recover the session key from the subverted ciphertext. In the following definition, we let Γ denote the internal state space of ASA.

Definition 2 (Session-Key-Recoverability). *Let* $\mathcal{ASA} = (\mathsf{ASA.Gen}, \mathsf{ASA.Enc}, \mathsf{ASA.Rec})$ *be an ASA on* $\mathcal{KEM} = (\mathsf{KEM.Setup}, \mathsf{KEM.Gen}, \mathsf{KEM.Enc}, \mathsf{KEM.Dec})$. *We say that* $\mathcal{ASA}$ *is* **session-key-recoverable** *if for any* $n \in \mathbb{N}$, *any* $\mathsf{pp} \leftarrow_\$ \mathsf{KEM.Setup}(1^n)$, *any* $(pk, sk) \leftarrow_\$ \mathsf{KEM.Gen}(\mathsf{pp})$, *any* $(psk, ssk) \leftarrow_\$ \mathsf{ASA.Gen}(\mathsf{pp})$, *and any* $\tau \in \Gamma$,

$$\Pr[\mathsf{ASA.Rec}(pk, ssk, \psi, \Phi_\psi) \neq K : (K, \psi) \leftarrow_\$ \mathsf{ASA.Enc}(pk, psk, \tau)] \leq \mathsf{negl}(n).$$

Here we implicitly assume that for every state $\tau \in \Gamma$, *the subverted ciphertext* ψ *and the associated ciphertext set* Φ_ψ *exist, i.e.,* $\Phi_\psi \neq \emptyset$.

3.3   Undetectability

The notion of undetectability denotes the inability of ordinary users to tell whether the ciphertext is produced by a subverted encapsulation algorithm $\mathsf{ASA.Enc}$ or the legitimate encapsulation algorithm $\mathsf{KEM.Enc}$. Different from conventional security games, here the challenger is the subverter who aims to subvert the encapsulation algorithm without being detected, while the detector (denoted by $\mathcal{U}$) is the legitimate user who aims to detect the subversion via a black-box access to the algorithm.

Note that our undetectability notion does not cover all possible detection strategies in the real world, such as comparing the (possibly subverted) code execution time with that of a legitimate code. In fact, as argued by Bellare *et al.* [6], it is impossible for an ASA to evade all forms of detection and there is usually a tradeoff between detection effort and attack success.

Definition 3 (Secret Undetectability). *Let $\mathcal{ASA}$ = (ASA.Gen, ASA.Enc, ASA.Rec) be an ASA on $\mathcal{KEM}$ = (KEM.Setup, KEM.Gen, KEM.Enc, KEM.Dec). For a user $\mathcal{U}$, we define the advantage function*

$$\mathsf{Adv}_{\mathsf{asa},\mathcal{U}}^{u\text{-det}}(n) := \left| \Pr \left[b = b' : \begin{array}{l} \mathsf{pp} \leftarrow_{\$} \mathsf{KEM.Setup}(1^n) \\ \{(pk_\ell, sk_\ell)\}_{\ell=1}^{u} \leftarrow_{\$} \mathsf{KEM.Gen(pp)} \\ (psk, ssk) \leftarrow_{\$} \mathsf{ASA.Gen(pp)} \\ \tau := \varepsilon,\ b \leftarrow_{\$} \{0,1\} \\ b' \leftarrow \mathcal{U}^{\mathcal{O}_{\mathsf{Enc}}} \left(\{(pk_\ell, sk_\ell)\}_{\ell=1}^{u}, psk \right) \end{array} \right] - \frac{1}{2} \right|,$$

where $\mathcal{O}_{\mathsf{Enc}}$ is an encapsulation oracle that for each query of input $pk_\ell(\ell \in [1, u])$ by user $\mathcal{U}$, returns (K, ψ) which are generated depending on the bit b:

- *if $b = 1$, $(K, \psi) \leftarrow_{\$} \mathsf{KEM.Enc}(pk_\ell)$;*
- *if $b = 0$, $(K, \psi) \leftarrow_{\$} \mathsf{ASA.Enc}(pk_\ell, psk, \tau)$.*

*We say $\mathcal{ASA}$ is **secretly** (u, q, ϵ)-**undetectable** w.r.t. $\mathcal{KEM}$ if for all PPT users $\mathcal{U}$ that make $q \in \mathbb{N}$ queries with $u \in \mathbb{N}$ key pairs, $\mathsf{Adv}_{\mathsf{asa},\mathcal{U}}^{u\text{-det}}(n) \leq \epsilon$.*

Alternatively, we say $\mathcal{ASA}$ is *publicly* (u, q, ϵ)-*undetectable* w.r.t. $\mathcal{KEM}$ if in the above definition of advantage function, user $\mathcal{U}$ is only provided with pk but not sk. Such an undetectability notion may still make sense in the real world as when the user is the encryptor, it may only know the public key. Nevertheless, since that secret undetectability clearly implies public undetectability, we only consider secret undetectability for ASAs on KEMs in this work.

Strong Undetectability. The notion of *strong undetectability* was introduced by Bellare *et al.* [6] for the case of subverting symmetric encryption. In the definition of strong undetectability, the challenger also returns the state to the user. This mainly considers a strong detection where the detector may be able to see all outputs written to the memory of the machine when the subverted code is running. Meeting such a strong notion naturally limits the ASA to be stateless otherwise it would be detectable to the user.

Multi-user Undetectability. Here we only consider the case of a single user in Definition 3 for simplicity. One could extend our notion to the more general setting of multi-user. Precisely, in the undetectability definition for the multi-user setting, user $\mathcal{U}$ also receives multiple key pairs from the challenger and is allowed to make polynomially many queries to ν identical encapsulation oracles independently and adaptively (ν denotes the user number).

4   Mounting ASAs on KEMs

We present an ASA on KEMs that enables the subverter to recover the session key efficiently while the attack is undetectable to the user. We first revisit the KEM syntax in the module level so that it has some notational advantages in describing our proposed ASA. New properties with respect to the module-level KEM are then explicitly defined for the formal analysis of the proposed attack.

4.1   A Module-Level Syntax of KEM

The module-level KEM syntax is mainly depicted in Fig. 2.

- pp $\leftarrow$ KEM.Setup(1^n). Takes as input the security parameter $n \in \mathbb{N}$ and outputs the public parameter pp which includes the descriptions of the session key space $\mathcal{K}_{\mathsf{kem}}$ and the randomness space $\mathcal{R}_{\mathsf{kem}}$.
- $(pk = (ek, tk), sk = (dk, vk)) \leftarrow$ KEM.Gen(pp). Takes as input the public parameter and runs the following sub-algorithms.
  - $(ek, dk) \leftarrow$ KEM.Ek(pp). The encapsulation key generation algorithm generates the key pair (ek, dk) for key encapsulation and decapsulation.
  - $(tk, vk) \leftarrow$ KEM.Tk(pp). The tag key generation algorithm generates the key pair (tk, vk) for tag generation and verification. *This algorithm is usually required only for KEM of strong security, e.g.., IND-CCA security.*
- $(K, \psi = (C, \pi)) \leftarrow$ KEM.Enc(pk). Takes as input the public key and runs the following sub-algorithms.
  - $r \leftarrow$ KEM.Rg(pp). The randomness generation algorithm picks $r \leftarrow_\$ \mathcal{R}_{\mathsf{kem}}$.
  - $K \leftarrow$ KEM.Kg(ek, r). The encapsulated key generation algorithm takes as input ek and randomness r, and outputs key K.
  - $C \leftarrow$ KEM.Cg(r). The key ciphertext generation algorithm takes as input randomness r, and outputs key ciphertext C.
  - $\pi \leftarrow$ KEM.Tg(tk, r). The tag generation algorithm takes as input tk and r, and outputs the ciphertext tag π.
- $K/\bot \leftarrow$ KEM.Dec$(sk, \psi = (C, \pi))$. Takes as input the secret key and the ciphertext, and runs the following sub-algorithms.
  - $K \leftarrow$ KEM.Kd(dk, C). The ciphertext decapsulation algorithm takes as input dk and C, and outputs key K.
  - $\pi' \leftarrow$ KEM.Vf(vk, C) . The tag re-generation algorithm takes as input vk and C, and outputs tag π'.

  The key K is finally output if $\pi' = \pi$. Otherwise, $\bot$ is output.

KEM.Gen(pp)	KEM.Enc(pk)	KEM.Dec($sk, \psi = (C, \pi)$)
$(ek, dk) \leftarrow_\$$ KEM.Ek(pp)	$r \leftarrow_\$$ KEM.Rg(pp)	$K' := $ KEM.Kd(dk, C)
$(tk, vk) \leftarrow_\$$ KEM.Tk(pp)	$K := $ KEM.Kg(ek, r)	$\pi' := $ KEM.Vf(vk, C)
$pk := (ek, tk)$	$C := $ KEM.Cg(r)	If $\pi' = \pi$ then $K := K'$
$sk := (dk, vk)$	$\pi := $ KEM.Tg(tk, r)	Else $K := \bot$
Return (pk, sk)	Return $(K, \psi = (C, \pi))$	Return K

Fig. 2. Module-level Syntax of KEM. The boxed algorithms are optional.

REMARK. Our syntax mainly covers KEMs of the following features. First, the generation of key ciphertext (KEM.Cg) is independent of the public key. Although this is quite general for most KEM constructions, it fails to cover KEMs that require public key for ciphertext generation. For example, the lattice-based KEM in [26] produces ciphertexts depending on the encapsulation key and thus it is not captured by our framework. Second, the separation of ciphertext and tag clearly indicates *explicit-rejection* KEMs, i.e., all inconsistent ciphertexts get immediately rejected by the decapsulation algorithm. Although explicit-rejection variants are generally popular, some special setting requires implicit-rejection KEMs, where inconsistent ciphertexts yield one uniform key and hence will be rejected by the authentication module of the encryption scheme. Concrete examples could be found in [20]. Nevertheless, in Sect. 5.2, we show that our defined KEM framework already covers many known KEM constructions derived from popular schemes, such as the Cramer-Shoup scheme [13], the Kurosawa-Desmedt scheme [23], and the Hofheinz-Kiltz scheme [20].

4.2 Our Non-Black-Box ASA on KEMs

Following the above module-level syntax, we first identify and formalize two new non-black-box properties for KEMs, which essentially enable our extremely efficient ASA against KEMs.

Non-Black-Box Properties Formulations. Our notions, namely *universal decryptability* and *key-pseudo-randomness*, are actually met by all known KEMs that could be interpreted using our module-level syntax. Here we explicitly define them as they are vital to our proposed ASA.

The first non-black-box assumption, i.e., universal decryptability, says that any key ciphertext C output by KEM.Cg is decryptable via KEM.Kd with any dk output by KEM.Ek.

Definition 4 (Universal Decryptability). *Let* $\mathcal{KEM}$ = (KEM.Setup, KEM.Gen, KEM.Enc, KEM.Dec) *be a KEM defined in Fig. 2. We say* $\mathcal{KEM}$ *is* **universally decryptable** *if for any* $n \in \mathbb{N}$, pp $\leftarrow_\$ $KEM.Setup$(1^n)$, *for any* $r \leftarrow_\$ $KEM.Rg(pp)$ *and* $C := $KEM.Cg$(r)$, *we have*

$$\text{KEM.Kd}(dk, C) = \text{KEM.Kg}(ek, r)$$

holds for any $(ek, dk) \leftarrow_\$ $KEM.Ek(pp)$.

The second notion, i.e., key-pseudo-randomness, indicates that the key produced by KEM.Kg is computationally indistinguishable from a random key.

Definition 5 (Key-Pseudo-Randomness). *Let* $\mathcal{KEM}$ = (KEM.Setup, KEM.Gen, KEM.Enc, KEM.Dec) *be a KEM as defined in Fig. 2. We say* $\mathcal{KEM}$ *is* ϵ_{prk}-**key-pseudo-random** *if for any PPT adversary* $\mathcal{A}$, *we have*

$$\text{Adv}_{\text{kem},\mathcal{A}}^{\text{prk}}(n) := \left| \Pr \left[b = b' : \begin{array}{l} \text{pp} \leftarrow_\$ \text{KEM.Setup}(1^n) \\ r \leftarrow_\$ \text{KEM.Rg(pp)} \\ C := \text{KEM.Cg}(r) \\ (ek, dk) \leftarrow_\$ \text{KEM.Ek(pp)} \\ b \leftarrow_\$ \{0,1\}, K_0 \leftarrow_\$ \mathcal{K}_{\text{kem}} \\ K_1 := \text{KEM.Kg}(ek, r) \\ b' \leftarrow \mathcal{A}(ek, K_b, C) \end{array} \right] - \frac{1}{2} \right| \leq \epsilon_{\text{prk}}.$$

REMARK. One may note that for those KEMs that are only IND-CPA-secure (i.e., no tag generation/verification is involved in key encapsulation/decapsulation), our formalized notions of *universal decryptability* and *key-pseudo-randomness* are actually the typical properties of "perfect correctness" and "IND-CPA security" respectively for KEMs that follows the above module-level syntax. Here we explicitly redefine them for generality consideration since we are also interested in exploring effective ASAs on IND-CCA-secure KEMs.

The Proposed Attack. We now describe our proposed (asymmetric) ASA. Let $\mathcal{KEM} = (\mathsf{KEM.Setup}, \mathsf{KEM.Gen}, \mathsf{KEM.Enc}, \mathsf{KEM.Dec})$ be a KEM. Consider a sequential execution of KEM.Enc. Suppose $\mathsf{pp} \leftarrow_\$ \mathsf{KEM.Setup}(1^n)$ and

$$(pk = (ek, tk), sk = (dk, vk)) \leftarrow_\$ \mathsf{KEM.Gen}(\mathsf{pp}).$$

Let $(K_i, \psi_i = (C_i, \pi_i))$ denote the output of the i-th execution of KEM.Enc, for which the internal randomness is denoted as $r_i \leftarrow_\$ \mathsf{KEM.Rg}(\mathsf{pp})$. That is, $K_i := \mathsf{KEM.Kg}(ek, r_i)$, $C_i := \mathsf{KEM.Cg}(r_i)$, and $\pi_i := \mathsf{KEM.Tg}(tk, r_i)$.

Our ASA on $\mathcal{KEM}$ is depicted in Fig. 3. Below are more details.

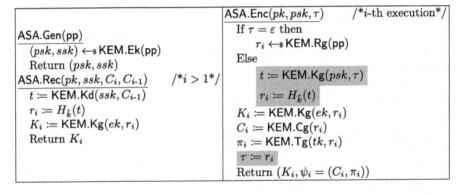

Fig. 3. The generic ASA on KEMs. The grey background highlights the difference between ASA.Enc and KEM.Enc.

Subversion Key Generation (ASA.Gen). The subversion key generation algorithm runs $(psk, ssk) \leftarrow_\$ \mathsf{KEM.Ek}(\mathsf{pp})$. Note that psk is hard-wired in the subverted key encapsulation algorithm ASA.Enc while ssk is kept by the subverter. Our ASA also makes use of a family of keyed hash function $\mathcal{H} := \{H_{\hat{k}}\}_{\hat{k} \in \hat{\mathcal{K}}}$, where each $H_{\hat{k}}$ maps $\mathcal{K}_{\mathsf{kem}}$ to $\mathcal{R}_{\mathsf{kem}}$ (both $\mathcal{K}_{\mathsf{kem}}$ and $\mathcal{R}_{\mathsf{kem}}$ are defined by pp). Therefore, the hash function key $\hat{k}$ is also hard-wired in the subverted algorithm ASA.Enc.

Subverted Encapsulation (ASA.Enc). As depicted in the right of Fig. 3, the subverted encapsulation algorithm ASA.Enc takes the public key pk, the hard-wired key psk and the internal state τ as input. The initial value of τ is set as $\tau := \varepsilon$. Then for the i-th execution ($i \geq 1$), ASA.Enc executes the same as KEM.Enc does except of:

- For algorithm KEM.Enc, the randomness r_i is generated via running KEM.Rg to sample $r_i \leftarrow_\$ \mathcal{R}_{\mathsf{kem}}$ uniformly.
- For algorithm ASA.Enc, if $\tau = \varepsilon$, the randomness r_i is generated via running KEM.Rg; otherwise, r_i is generated via firstly running $t := \mathsf{KEM.Kg}(psk, \tau)$ and then computing $r_i := H_{\hat{k}}(t)$. The internal state τ is then updated to r_i.

The generation of ciphertext C_i and the session key K_i still follow the legitimate procedure, i.e., by running algorithm KEM.Cg and KEM.Kg respectively.

Session Key Recovery (ASA.Rec). The left down part of Fig. 3 depicts the encapsulated key recovery algorithm ASA.Rec run by the subverter. To recover the session key encapsulated in the subverted ciphertext C_i ($i > 1$), the subverter first uses ssk to decrypt the ciphertext $C_{i\text{-}1}$ to recover t and then computes r_i, based on which the key K_i—encapsulated in C_i—could be trivially computed. It is worth noting that the subverted ciphertext C_i is in fact not used in the running of ASA.Rec to recover the underlying key K_i. The core idea of the session key recovery is to recover the randomness r_i by using ssk to decapsulate $C_{i\text{-}1}$ which is actually the associated ciphertext of C_i.

4.3   Formal Analysis

Let $\mathcal{KEM} = (\mathsf{KEM.Setup}, \mathsf{KEM.Gen}, \mathsf{KEM.Enc}, \mathsf{KEM.Dec})$ be a KEM and $\mathcal{ASA} = (\mathsf{ASA.Gen}, \mathsf{ASA.Enc}, \mathsf{ASA.Rec})$ be an ASA on $\mathcal{KEM}$ described in Fig. 3. Then we have the following results.

Theorem 1. *The $\mathcal{ASA}$ depicted in Fig. 3 preserves the decryptability of $\mathcal{KEM}$.*

Proof. This clearly holds as ASA.Enc is the same as the original algorithm KEM.Enc except of the internal randomness generation. Particularly, the generation of ciphertext and key essentially remain unchanged in ASA.Enc.

Theorem 2. *The $\mathcal{ASA}$ depicted in Fig. 3 is session-key-recoverable if $\mathcal{KEM}$ is universally decryptable.*

Proof. Note that the notion of session-key-recoverability is defined for the subverted ciphertext ψ which has the associated ciphertexts Φ, i.e., $\Phi_\psi \neq \emptyset$. That is, here we consider the session-key-recoverability for all subverted ciphertext C_i where $i \geq 2$. By the fact that $\mathcal{KEM}$ is universally decryptable, we have that $\mathsf{KEM.Kd}(ssk, C_{i\text{-}1}) = \mathsf{KEM.Kg}(psk, r_{i\text{-}1})$ holds for all $r_{i\text{-}1} \in \mathcal{R}_{\mathsf{kem}}$ ($i \geq 2$) and $C_{i\text{-}1} := \mathsf{KEM.Cg}(r_{i\text{-}1})$, and for all $(psk, ssk) \leftarrow_\$ \mathsf{KEM.Ek}$. Note that the randomness recovered in ASA.Rec equals to that from ASA.Enc. Therefore, for any $(pk, sk) \leftarrow_\$ \mathsf{KEM.Gen}$ and any $(K_i, \psi_i = (C_i, \pi_i)) \leftarrow_\$ \mathsf{ASA.Enc}(pk, psk, r_{i\text{-}1})$, we have $\mathsf{ASA.Rec}(pk, ssk, C_i, C_{i\text{-}1}) = K_i$.

Theorem 3. *Assume $\mathcal{KEM}$ is $\epsilon_{\mathsf{prk}}(n)$-key-pseudo-random and $\mathcal{H}$ is $\epsilon_{\mathsf{es}}(n)$-entropy smoothing, then our $\mathcal{ASA}$ depicted in Fig. 3 satisfies (u, q, ϵ)-undetectability where q is the query number by the adversary in the detection game and*

$$\epsilon \leq (q - 1)(\epsilon_{\mathsf{prk}}(n) + \epsilon_{\mathsf{es}}(n)).$$

GAME $\mathbf{G}_0(n)$
> $pp \leftarrow_\$ \mathsf{KEM.Setup}(1^n)$
> $\{(pk_\ell, sk_\ell)\}_{\ell=1}^u \leftarrow_\$ \mathsf{KEM.Gen}(pp)$, $(psk, ssk) \leftarrow_\$ \mathsf{KEM.Ek}(pp)$
> $\tau := \varepsilon$, $b \leftarrow_\$ \{0,1\}$, $b' \leftarrow \mathcal{A}^{\mathcal{O}_{\mathsf{Enc}}}\left(\{(pk_\ell, sk_\ell)\}_{\ell=1}^u, psk\right)$
> Return $(b = b')$

$\mathcal{O}_{\mathsf{Enc}}(pk_\ell = (ek_\ell, tk_\ell))$
> If $(b = 1)$ then
> > $(K, \psi) \leftarrow_\$ \mathsf{KEM.Enc}(pk_\ell)$
>
> Else
> > If $\tau = \varepsilon$ then
> > > $r \leftarrow_\$ \mathsf{KEM.Rg}(pp)$
> >
> > Else
> > > $t := \mathsf{KEM.Kg}(psk, \tau)$
> > > $r := H_{\hat{k}}(t)$
> >
> > $K := \mathsf{KEM.Kg}(ek_\ell, r)$, $C := \mathsf{KEM.Cg}(r)$, $\pi := \mathsf{KEM.Tg}(tk_\ell, r)$
> > $\tau := r$, $\psi := (C, \pi)$
>
> Return (K, ψ)

Fig. 4. Games $\mathbf{G}_0$ in the proof of Theorem 3

GAME $\mathbf{G}_{j\text{-}1,1}(n)$, $\boxed{\mathbf{G}_{j\text{-}1,2}(n)}$ $(j \in [2, q])$
> $pp \leftarrow_\$ \mathsf{KEM.Setup}(1^n)$
> $\{(pk_\ell, sk_\ell)\}_{\ell=1}^u \leftarrow_\$ \mathsf{KEM.Gen}(pp)$
> $(psk, ssk) \leftarrow_\$ \mathsf{KEM.Ek}(pp), \tau := \varepsilon$, $\boxed{i := 0}$
> $b \leftarrow_\$ \{0,1\}$, $b' \leftarrow \mathcal{A}^{\mathcal{O}_{\mathsf{Enc}}}\left(\{(pk_\ell, sk_\ell)\}_{\ell=1}^u, psk\right)$
> Return $(b = b')$

$\mathcal{O}_{\mathsf{Enc}}(pk_\ell = (ek_\ell, tk_\ell))$
> $\boxed{i := i + 1}$
> If $(b = 1)$ then
> > $(K, \psi) \leftarrow_\$ \mathsf{KEM.Enc}(pk_\ell)$
>
> Else
> > If $i < j$ then
> > > $r \leftarrow_\$ \mathsf{KEM.Rg}(pp)$
> >
> > Else
> > > If $i = j$ then
> > > > $t \leftarrow_\$ \mathcal{K}_{\mathsf{kem}}, \; r := H_{\hat{k}}(t)$
> > > > $\boxed{r \leftarrow_\$ \mathsf{KEM.Rg}(pp)}$
> > >
> > > Else
> > > > $t := \mathsf{KEM.Kg}(psk, \tau)$, $r := H_{\hat{k}}(t)$
> > >
> > > $K := \mathsf{KEM.Kg}(ek_\ell, r)$, $C := \mathsf{KEM.Cg}(r)$, $\pi := \mathsf{KEM.Tg}(tk_\ell, r)$
> > > $\tau := r$, $\psi := (C, \pi)$
>
> Return (K, ψ)

Fig. 5. Games $\mathbf{G}_{1,1}, \mathbf{G}_{1,2}, \mathbf{G}_{2,1}, \mathbf{G}_{2,2}, \cdots, \mathbf{G}_{q\text{-}1,1}, \mathbf{G}_{q\text{-}1,2}$ in the proof of Theorem 3. Game $\mathbf{G}_{j\text{-}1,2}$ contains the corresponding boxed statements, but game $\mathbf{G}_{j\text{-}1,1}$ does not.

Proof. We prove this theorem via a sequence of games. Suppose that the adversary $\mathcal{A}$ makes q queries in total to the oracle $\mathcal{O}_{\mathsf{Enc}}$ in the security game. We define a game sequence: $\{\mathbf{G}_0, \mathbf{G}_{1,1}, \mathbf{G}_{1,2}, \mathbf{G}_{2,1}, \mathbf{G}_{2,2}, \cdots, \mathbf{G}_{q\text{-}1,1}, \mathbf{G}_{q\text{-}1,2}\}$. $\mathbf{G}_0$ is the real game and depicted in Fig. 4 while $\{\mathbf{G}_{1,1}, \mathbf{G}_{1,2}, \mathbf{G}_{2,1}, \mathbf{G}_{2,2}, \cdots, \mathbf{G}_{q\text{-}1,1}, \mathbf{G}_{q\text{-}1,2}\}$ are described in Fig. 5. Note that in the following illustrations, we also let $\mathbf{G}_{0,2}$ denote the game $\mathbf{G}_0$ for the consideration of notational consistency. Let Adv_x be the advantage function with respect to $\mathcal{A}$ in Game $\mathbf{G}_x$. Below we provide more details of $\mathbf{G}_0$, $\mathbf{G}_{j-1,1}$ and $\mathbf{G}_{j-1,2}$ for all $j \in [2, q]$. Note that in all games $\mathbf{G}_{j-1,1}$ and $\mathbf{G}_{j-1,2}$ ($j \in [2, q]$), an internal counter i (initialized to 0) is set for the encapsulation oracle and increments upon each query by the adversary.

- GAME $\mathbf{G}_0$ (i.e., $\mathbf{G}_{0,2}$): This game is the real game and thus we have

$$\mathsf{Adv}_{\mathsf{asa},\mathcal{U}}^{u\text{-det}}(n) = \mathsf{Adv}_0.$$

- GAME $\mathbf{G}_{j-1,1}$ is identical to $\mathbf{G}_{j-2,2}$ except that for the case of $b = 0$, to generate the response for the j-th query of $\mathcal{A}$, the challenger picks $t \leftarrow_{\$} \mathcal{K}_{\mathsf{kem}}$ instead of computing $t := \mathsf{KEM}.\mathsf{Kg}(psk, \tau)$. We claim that from the view of $\mathcal{A}$, $\mathbf{G}_{j-1,1}$ is indistinguishable from $\mathbf{G}_{j-2,2}$ if $\mathcal{KEM}$ is key-pseudo-random. That is, $|\mathsf{Adv}_{j-2,2} - \mathsf{Adv}_{j-1,1}| \leq \epsilon_{\mathsf{prk}}(n)$. See Lemma 1 for more details.
- GAME $\mathbf{G}_{j-1,2}$ is identical to $\mathbf{G}_{j-1,1}$ except that for the case of $b = 0$, to generate the response for the j-th query of $\mathcal{A}$,r is derived by $r \leftarrow_{\$} \mathsf{KEM}.\mathsf{Rg}(\mathsf{pp})$ (i.e., $r \leftarrow_{\$} \mathcal{R}_{\mathsf{kem}}$) instead of $r := H_{\hat{k}}(t)$. We claim that from the view of $\mathcal{A}$, $\mathbf{G}_{j-1,2}$ is indistinguishable from $\mathbf{G}_{j-1,1}$ if $\mathcal{H}$ is entropy smoothing. That is, $|\mathsf{Adv}_{j-1,2} - \mathsf{Adv}_{j-1,1}| \leq \epsilon_{\mathsf{es}}(n)$. See Lemma 2 for more details.

Lemma 1 ($\mathbf{G}_{j-1,1} \approx_c \mathbf{G}_{j-2,2}$). *For all $j \in [2, q]$ and all PPT adversary $\mathcal{A}$,*

$$|\mathsf{Adv}_{j-2,2} - \mathsf{Adv}_{j-1,1}| \leq \epsilon_{\mathsf{prk}}(n).$$

Proof. To prove this transition, we construct an adversary $\mathcal{B}_{j-1}$ attacking the property of key-pseudo-randomness of $\mathcal{KEM}$. Suppose that $\mathcal{B}_{j-1}$ receives $(\mathsf{pp}^*, ek^*, K^*, C^*)$ from the challenger in the game defined in Definition 5. Its goal is to tell whether K^* is the key encapsulated in C^* or a random value.

$\mathcal{B}_{j-1}$ then simulates the detection game to interact with $\mathcal{A}$ via the procedure depicted in Fig. 6. $\mathcal{B}_{j-1}$ first sets $psk = ek^*$ as the public subversion key and simulates the encapsulation oracle (denoted by $O_{\mathsf{Enc}}^{\mathsf{sim}}$) for $\mathcal{A}$. Precisely, if $b = 0$, for each query with input $pk_\ell = (ek_\ell, tk_\ell)$, $O_{\mathsf{Enc}}^{\mathsf{sim}}$ performs depending on the internal counter i as follows.

- CASE 1: $i = (j - 1)$. $\mathcal{B}_{j-1}$ sets $C = C^*$, computes $K := \mathsf{KEM}.\mathsf{Kd}(dk_\ell, C^*)$ and $\pi := \mathsf{KEM}.\mathsf{Vf}(C^*, vk_\ell)$, and returns (K, C, π).
- CASE 2: $i < (j-1)$. $\mathcal{B}_{j-1}$ runs the algorithm $\mathsf{KEM}.\mathsf{Enc}$, i.e., $\mathsf{KEM}.\mathsf{Rg}, \mathsf{KEM}.\mathsf{Cg}$ and $\mathsf{KEM}.\mathsf{Tg}$ sequentially, updates τ and returns the output.
- CASE 3: $i = j$. $\mathcal{B}_{j-1}$ sets $t = K^*$, computes $r := H_{\hat{k}}(t)$, $K := \mathsf{KEM}.\mathsf{Kg}(ek_\ell, r)$, $C := \mathsf{KEM}.\mathsf{Cg}(r)$ and $\pi := \mathsf{KEM}.\mathsf{Tg}(tk_\ell, r)$, updates τ and returns (K, C, π).

$$\begin{array}{l} \hline \mathcal{B}_{j\text{-}1}(pp^*, ek^*, K^*, C^*) \\ \hline \qquad pp := pp^*, \; psk := ek^*, \; \tau := \varepsilon, i := 0, \; \{(pk_\ell, sk_\ell)\}_{\ell=1}^u \leftarrow_\$ \mathsf{KEM.Gen}(pp) \\ \qquad b \leftarrow_\$ \{0,1\}, \; b' \leftarrow \mathcal{A}^{\mathcal{O}_{\mathsf{Enc}}^{\mathsf{sim}}} \left(\{(pk_\ell, sk_\ell)\}_{\ell=1}^u, psk\right) \\ \qquad \text{Return } (b = b') \\ \hline \mathcal{O}_{\mathsf{Enc}}^{\mathsf{sim}} \left(pk_\ell = (ek_\ell, tk_\ell)\right) \\ \hline \qquad i := i+1 \\ \qquad \text{If } (b=1) \text{ then} \\ \qquad\qquad (K, \psi) \leftarrow_\$ \mathsf{KEM.Enc}(pk_\ell) \\ \qquad \text{Else} \\ \qquad\qquad \text{If } i = (j-1) \text{ then} \\ \qquad\qquad\qquad C := C^*, \; K := \mathsf{KEM.Kd}(dk_\ell, C^*) \\ \qquad\qquad\qquad \pi := \mathsf{KEM.Vf}(C^*, vk_\ell), \; \psi := (C, \pi) \\ \qquad\qquad \text{Else} \\ \qquad\qquad\qquad \text{If } i < (j-1) \text{ then} \\ \qquad\qquad\qquad\qquad r \leftarrow_\$ \mathsf{KEM.Rg}(pp) \\ \qquad\qquad\qquad \text{Else} \\ \qquad\qquad\qquad\qquad \text{If } i = j \text{ then} \\ \qquad\qquad\qquad\qquad\qquad t := K^*, \; r := H_{\hat{k}}(t) \\ \qquad\qquad\qquad\qquad \text{Else} \\ \qquad\qquad\qquad\qquad\qquad t := \mathsf{KEM.Kg}(psk, \tau), r := H_{\hat{k}}(t) \\ \qquad\qquad\qquad\qquad K := \mathsf{KEM.Kg}(ek_\ell, r), \; C := \mathsf{KEM.Cg}(r), \; \pi := \mathsf{KEM.Tg}(tk, r) \\ \qquad\qquad\qquad\qquad \tau := r, \; \psi := (C, \pi) \\ \qquad \text{Return } (K, \psi) \\ \hline \end{array}$$

Fig. 6. Adversary $\mathcal{B}$ attacking the key-pseudo-randomness of $\mathcal{KEM}$ in the proof of Lemma 1.

- CASE 4: $i > j$. $\mathcal{B}_{j\text{-}1}$ sets $t := \mathsf{KEM.Kg}(psk, \tau)$, computes $r := H_{\hat{k}}(t)$, runs $K := \mathsf{KEM.Kg}(ek_\ell, r)$, $C := \mathsf{KEM.Cg}(r)$ and $\pi := \mathsf{KEM.Tg}(tk_\ell, r)$, updates τ and returns (K, C, π).

Finally, $\mathcal{B}_{j\text{-}1}$ outputs 1 if $\mathcal{A}$ outputs $b' = b$ otherwise outputs 0.

One could note that if K^* is the key encapsulated in C^*, then the game simulated by $\mathcal{B}_{j\text{-}1}$ is exactly the game $\mathbf{G}_{j\text{-}2,2}$ from the view of $\mathcal{A}$. Otherwise, the simulated game is $\mathbf{G}_{j\text{-}1,1}$ from the view of $\mathcal{A}$. Therefore, we have $|\mathsf{Adv}_{j\text{-}2,2} - \mathsf{Adv}_{j\text{-}1,1}| \leq \epsilon_{\mathsf{prk}}(n)$.

Lemma 2 ($\mathbf{G}_{j\text{-}1,2} \approx_c \mathbf{G}_{j\text{-}1,1}$)**.** *For all $j \in [2, q]$ and all PPT adversary $\mathcal{A}$,*

$$|\mathsf{Adv}_{j\text{-}1,1} - \mathsf{Adv}_{j\text{-}1,2}| \leq \epsilon_{\mathsf{es}}(n).$$

Proof. To prove this transition, we construct an adversary $\mathcal{D}_{j\text{-}1}$ attacking the entropy smoothing hash function $H_{\hat{k}} : \mathcal{K}_{\mathsf{kem}} \to \mathcal{R}_{\mathsf{kem}}$. Suppose that $\mathcal{D}_{j\text{-}1}$ receives $(\hat{k}, y^*)$ from the challenger. Its goal is to tell whether $y^* = H_{\hat{k}}(x)$ where $x \leftarrow_\$ \mathcal{K}_{\mathsf{kem}}$, or $y^* \leftarrow_\$ \mathcal{R}_{\mathsf{kem}}$.

$\mathcal{D}_{j\text{-}1}$ then simulates the detection game to interact with $\mathcal{A}$ via the procedure depicted in Fig. 7. $\mathcal{D}_{j\text{-}1}$ simulates the encapsulation oracle (denoted by $\mathcal{O}_{\mathsf{Enc}}^{\mathsf{sim}}$)

$\mathcal{D}_{j\text{-}1}(\hat{k}, y^*)$

    $\mathsf{pp} \leftarrow_\$ \mathsf{KEM.Setup}(1^n)$

    $\{(pk_\ell, sk_\ell)\}_{\ell=1}^u \leftarrow_\$ \mathsf{KEM.Gen(pp)},\ (psk, ssk) \leftarrow_\$ \mathsf{KEM.Ek(pp)}$

    $\tau := \varepsilon,\ i := 0,\ b \leftarrow_\$ \{0,1\},\ b' \leftarrow \mathcal{A}^{\mathcal{O}_{\mathsf{Enc}}^{\mathsf{sim}}}\left(\{(pk_\ell, sk_\ell)\}_{\ell=1}^u, psk\right)$

    Return $(b = b')$

$\mathcal{O}_{\mathsf{Enc}}^{\mathsf{sim}}\ (pk_\ell = (ek_\ell, tk_\ell))$

    $i := i + 1$

    If $(b = 1)$ then

        $(K, \psi) \leftarrow_\$ \mathsf{KEM.Enc}(pk_\ell)$

    Else

        If $i < j$ then

            $r \leftarrow_\$ \mathsf{KEM.Rg(pp)}$

        Else

            If $i = j$ then

                $r := y^*$

            Else

                $t := \mathsf{KEM.Kg}(psk, \tau),\ r := H_{\hat{k}}(t)$

        $K := \mathsf{KEM.Kg}(ek_\ell, r),\ C := \mathsf{KEM.Cg}(r),\ \pi := \mathsf{KEM.Tg}(tk_\ell, r)$

        $\tau := r,\ \psi := (C, \pi)$

    Return (K, ψ)

Fig. 7. Adversary $\mathcal{D}$ attacking the entropy smoothing hash function $H_{\hat{k}}$ in the proof of Lemma 2.

for $\mathcal{A}$. Precisely, if $b = 0$, for each query with input $pk_\ell = (ek_\ell, tk_\ell)$, $\mathcal{O}_{\mathsf{Enc}}^{\mathsf{sim}}$ performs depending on the internal counter i as follows.

- CASE 1: $i < j$. $\mathcal{D}_{j\text{-}1}$ runs the algorithm KEM.Enc, i.e., runs KEM.Rg, KEM.Cg and KEM.Tg sequentially, updates τ and returns the output.
- CASE 2: $i = j$. $\mathcal{D}_{j\text{-}1}$ sets $r := y^*$, runs $K := \mathsf{KEM.Kg}(ek_\ell, r)$, $C := \mathsf{KEM.Cg}(r)$ and $\pi := \mathsf{KEM.Tg}(tk_\ell, r)$, updates τ and returns (K, C, π).
- CASE 3: $i > j$. $\mathcal{D}_{j\text{-}1}$ sets $t := \mathsf{KEM.Kg}(psk, \tau)$, computes $r := H_{\hat{k}}(t)$, runs $K := \mathsf{KEM.Kg}(ek_\ell, r)$, $C := \mathsf{KEM.Cg}(r)$ and $\pi := \mathsf{KEM.Tg}(tk_\ell, r)$, updates τ and returns (K, C, π).

Finally, $\mathcal{D}_{j\text{-}1}$ outputs 1 if $\mathcal{A}$ outputs $b' = b$ otherwise outputs 0.

One could note that from the view of $\mathcal{A}$, if $y^* = H_{\hat{k}}(x)$ where $x \leftarrow_\$ \mathcal{K}_{\mathsf{kem}}$, then the game simulated by $\mathcal{D}_{j\text{-}1}$ is exactly the game $\mathbf{G}_{j\text{-}1,1}$. Otherwise, the simulated game is $\mathbf{G}_{j\text{-}1,2}$. Hence, we have $|\mathsf{Adv}_{j\text{-}1,2} - \mathsf{Adv}_{j\text{-}1,1}| \le \epsilon_{\mathsf{es}}(n)$.

Summary. Note that in GAME $\mathbf{G}_{q\text{-}1,2}$, for all queries to $\mathcal{O}_{\mathsf{Enc}}$, the challenger always runs the algorithm KEM.Enc to generate the response and thus the view of the detector $\mathcal{A}$ actually does not depend on the chosen bit b. Therefore,

$$\mathsf{Adv}_{q\text{-}1,2} \le \mathsf{negl}(n).$$

Putting all the above together, we have

$$
\begin{aligned}
\mathsf{Adv}_{\mathsf{asa},\mathcal{U}}^{u\text{-det}}(n) &= \mathsf{Adv}_0 \\
&= |\mathsf{Adv}_0 - \mathsf{Adv}_{1,1} + \mathsf{Adv}_{1,1} - \mathsf{Adv}_{1,2} + \mathsf{Adv}_{1,2} - \mathsf{Adv}_{2,1} + \cdots \\
&\quad + \mathsf{Adv}_{q\text{-}2,2} - \mathsf{Adv}_{q\text{-}1,1} + \mathsf{Adv}_{q\text{-}1,1} - \mathsf{Adv}_{q\text{-}1,2} + \mathsf{Adv}_{q\text{-}1,2}| \\
&\leq |\mathsf{Adv}_0 - \mathsf{Adv}_{1,1}| + |\mathsf{Adv}_{1,1} - \mathsf{Adv}_{1,2}| + |\mathsf{Adv}_{1,2} - \mathsf{Adv}_{2,1}| + \cdots \\
&\quad + |\mathsf{Adv}_{q\text{-}2,2} - \mathsf{Adv}_{q\text{-}1,1}| + |\mathsf{Adv}_{q\text{-}1,1} - \mathsf{Adv}_{q\text{-}1,2}| + \mathsf{Adv}_{q\text{-}1,2}| \\
&\leq (q-1)(\epsilon_{\mathsf{prk}}(n) + \epsilon_{\mathsf{es}}(n)).
\end{aligned}
$$

This completes the proof of Theorem 3.

5   Instantiations

In this section, we describe some popular KEM constructions that are subvertible to our proposed generic ASA.

5.1   KEMs from Hash Proof Systems

Syntax of HPS [13]. Let $\mathcal{X}, Y$ be sets and $\mathcal{L} \subset X$ be a language. Let $\Lambda_{hk} : \mathcal{X} \to Y$ be a hash function indexed with $hk \in \mathcal{HK}$ where $\mathcal{HK}$ is a set. We say a hash function Λ_{hk} is projective if there exists a projection $\varphi : \mathcal{HK} \to \mathcal{HP}$ such that, (1) for every $x \in \mathcal{L}$, the value of $\Lambda_{hk}(x)$ is uniquely determined by $\varphi(hk)$ and x; and (2) for any $x \in \mathcal{X} \setminus \mathcal{L}$, it is infeasible to compute $\Lambda_{hk}(x)$ from $\varphi(hk)$ and x. Formally, a hash proof system $\mathcal{HPS}$ consists of (HPS.Setup, HPS.Gen, HPS.Pub, HPS.Priv):

- HPS.Setup(1^n). The parameter generation algorithm takes as input 1^n, and outputs $\mathsf{pp} = (\mathcal{X}, \mathcal{Y}, \mathcal{L}, \mathcal{HK}, \mathcal{HP}, \Lambda_{(.)} : \mathcal{X} \to \mathcal{Y}, \varphi : \mathcal{HK} \to \mathcal{HP})$.
- HPS.Gen(pp). The key generation algorithm takes as input pp. It outputs the secret hashing key $hk \twoheadleftarrow \mathcal{HK}$ and the public key $hp := \varphi(hk) \in \mathcal{HP}$.
- HPS.Pub(hp, x, w). The public evaluation algorithm takes as input $hp = \varphi(hk)$, a language element $x \in \mathcal{L}$ with the witness w of the fact that $x \in \mathcal{L}$. It outputs the hash value $y = \Lambda_{hk}(x)$.
- HPS.Priv(hk, x). The private evaluation algorithm takes as input hk, an element $x \in \mathcal{X}$. It outputs the hash value $y = \Lambda_{hk}(x)$.

It is generally assumed that one could efficiently sample elements from $\mathcal{X}$. In this work, for sampling $x \in \mathcal{L}$, we explicitly define the following algorithms.

- HPS.Wit(pp). The witness sampling algorithm takes as input pp. It outputs a witness w as $w \twoheadleftarrow \mathcal{W}$ where $\mathcal{W}$ is the witness space included in pp.
- HPS.Ele(w). The language element generation algorithm takes as input w. It outputs the language element $x \in \mathcal{L}$.

Note that here we require the language element generation only takes as input the witness (and public parameter) and mainly consider the HPS where the projection key is independent from the language element, which is also known as KV-type HPS [22].

Correctness. For all $pp \leftarrow_s \mathsf{HPS.Setup}$, all $(hk, hp) \leftarrow_s \mathsf{HPS.Gen}$, all $w \leftarrow_s \mathsf{HPS.Wit(pp)}$ and $x := \mathsf{HPS.Ele}(w)$, it holds that $\mathsf{HPS.Pub}(hp, x, w) = \Lambda_{hk}(x) = \mathsf{HPS.Priv}(hk, x)$.

Subset Membership Problem. We say the *subset membership problem* is hard in $\mathcal{HPS}$ if it is computationally hard to distinguish a random element $\mathcal{L}$ from a random element from $\mathcal{X} \setminus \mathcal{L}$. A formal definition appears in Appendix A.1.

Computational Smoothness. We say $\mathcal{HPS}$ satisfies *computational smoothness* if the hash value of a random element from $\mathcal{X} \setminus \mathcal{L}$ looks random to an adversary only knowing the projection key. A formal definition appears in Appendix A.1.

KEMs from HPS [20,23]. Kurosawa and Desmedt [23] proposed a generic KEM based on HPS. Their paradigm is later explicitly given by Hofheinz and Kiltz in [20]. Let $\mathcal{HPS} = (\mathsf{HPS.Setup}, \mathsf{HPS.Gen}, \mathsf{HPS.Pub}, \mathsf{HPS.Priv}, \mathsf{HPS.Wit}, \mathsf{HPS.Ele})$ be an HPS. The constructed KEM $\mathcal{KEM} = (\mathsf{KEM.Setup}, \mathsf{KEM.Gen}, \mathsf{KEM.Enc}, \mathsf{KEM.Dec})$ is as follows.

- $\mathsf{KEM.Setup}(1^n)$. Run $pp \leftarrow_s \mathsf{HPS.Setup}(1^n)$, output the public parameter pp.
- $\mathsf{KEM.Gen}(pp)$. Run $(hk, hp) \leftarrow_s \mathsf{HPS.Gen}(pp)$, set $ek := hp$, $dk := hk$, output $(pk = ek, sk = dk)$.
- $\mathsf{KEM.Enc}(pk)$. Run the following sub-algorithms.
    - $\mathsf{KEM.Rg}(pp)$: Run $w \leftarrow_s \mathsf{HPS.Wit}(pp)$, and return $r := w$;
    - $\mathsf{KEM.Cg}(r)$: Run $x := \mathsf{HPS.Ele}(r)$, and return $C := x$;
    - $\mathsf{KEM.Kg}(ek, r)$: Run $y := \mathsf{HPS.Pub}(ek, C, r)$, and return $K := y$.
  Output (K, C).
- $\mathsf{KEM.Dec}(sk, C)$. Run $y := \mathsf{HPS.Priv}(dk, C)$, output $K := y$.

For their generic construction, we have the following result.

Theorem 4. *The above generic construction $\mathcal{KEM}$ is universally decryptable and key-pseudo-random if $\mathcal{HPS}$ is of computational smoothness and the subset membership problem is hard in $\mathcal{HPS}$.*

We defer the detailed proof to Appendix A.2.

5.2 Concrete KEMs

Below we present some known KEM constructions subvertible by our ASA.

Cramer-Shoup KEMs [13]. In [13], Cramer and Shoup designed a hybrid encryption framework based on KEMs and provided instantiations based on various hardness assumptions.

The DDH-Based. Let $\mathbb{G}$ be a cyclic group of prime order p, and g_1, g_2 are generators of $\mathbb{G}$. Figure 8 shows the DDH-based KEM proposed in [13]. The public

KEM.Gen		KEM.Enc				KEM.Dec	
KEM.Ek	KEM.Tk	KEM.Rg	KEM.Kg	KEM.Cg	KEM.Tg	KEM.Kd	KEM.Vf
$(x_1, x_2) \leftarrow\$$ $\mathbb{Z}_p^2$; $h = g_1^{x_1} g_2^{x_2}$; $ek = h$; $dk = (x_1, x_2)$	(y_1, y_2, z_1, z_2) $\leftarrow\$ \mathbb{Z}_p^4$; $c = g_1^{y_1} g_2^{y_2}$; $d = g_1^{z_1} g_2^{z_2}$; $tk = (c, d)$; $vk = (y_1, y_2, z_1, z_2)$	$r \leftarrow\$ \mathbb{Z}_p^*$	$K = h^r$	$C = (u_1, u_2)$ $= (g_1^r, g_2^r)$	$t = H(C)$; $\pi = (cd^t)^r$	$K = u_1^{x_1} u_2^{x_2}$	$t = H(C)$; $\pi' = u_1^{y_1 + z_1 t}$ $\cdot u_2^{y_2 + z_2 t}$

Fig. 8. The DDH-Based KEM from Cramer-Shoup Encryption Scheme [13]

parameter is $pp = (\mathbb{G}, p, g_1, g_2)$. The key space $\mathcal{K}_{kem}$ is $\mathbb{G}$ and the randomness space $\mathcal{R}_{kem}$ is $\mathbb{Z}_p^*$. $H : \mathbb{G}^2 \to \mathbb{Z}_p^*$ is a collision resistant hash function.

The DCR-Based. Let p, q, p', q' denote distinct odd primes with $p = 2p' + 1$ and $q = 2q' + 1$. Let $N = pq$ and $N' = p'q'$. The group $\mathbb{Z}_{N^2}^* = \mathbb{G}_N \cdot \mathbb{G}_{N'} \cdot \mathbb{G}_2 \cdot \mathbb{G}$ where each group $\mathbb{G}_\rho$ is a cyclic group of order ρ, and $\mathbb{G}$ is the subgroup of $\mathbb{Z}_{N^2}^*$ generated by $(-1 \bmod N^2)$. Let $\eta \leftarrow\$ \mathbb{Z}_{N^2}^*$ and $g = -\eta^{2N}$. Figure 9 shows the DCR-based KEM proposed in [13]. The public parameter is $pp = (N, g)$. The key space $\mathcal{K}_{kem}$ is $\mathbb{Z}_{N^2}^*$ and the randomness space $\mathcal{R}_{kem}$ is $\{0, \cdots, \lfloor N/2 \rfloor\}$. $H : \mathbb{Z}_{N^2}^* \to \mathcal{R}_{kem}$ is a target collision resistant hash function.

KEM.Gen		KEM.Enc				KEM.Dec	
KEM.Ek	KEM.Tk	KEM.Rg	KEM.Kg	KEM.Cg	KEM.Tg	KEM.Kd	KEM.Vf
$x \leftarrow\$$ $\{0, \cdots, \lfloor N^2/2 \rfloor\}$; $h = g^x$; $ek = h; dk = x$	$y \leftarrow\$ \{0, \cdots, \lfloor N^2/2 \rfloor\}$; $z \leftarrow\$ \{0, \cdots, \lfloor N^2/2 \rfloor\}$; $c = g^y; d = g^z$; $tk = (c, d)$; $vk = (y, z)$	$r \leftarrow\$ \{0, \cdots, \lfloor N/2 \rfloor\}$	$K = h^r$	$C = g^r$	$t = H(C)$; $\pi = (cd^t)^r$	$K = C^x$	$t = H(C)$; $\pi' = C^{y + zt}$

Fig. 9. The DCR-Based KEM from Cramer-Shoup Encryption Scheme [13]

The QR-Based. Let p, q, p', q' be distinct odd primes with $p = 2p' + 1$ and $q = 2q' + 1$. Let $N = pq$ and $N' = p'q'$. Group $\mathbb{Z}_N^* = \mathbb{G}_{N'} \cdot \mathbb{G}_2 \cdot \mathbb{G}$ where each group $\mathbb{G}_\rho$ is a cyclic group of order ρ, and $\mathbb{G}$ is the subgroup of $\mathbb{Z}_N^*$ generated by $(-1 \bmod N)$. Let $\eta \leftarrow\$ \mathbb{Z}_N^*$ and $g = \eta^2$. Figure 10 describes the QR-based KEM proposed in [13]. The public parameter is $pp = (N, g, k, \hat{k})$. The key space $\mathcal{K}_{kem}$ is $(\mathbb{Z}_N^*)^k$ and the randomness space $\mathcal{R}_{kem}$ is $\{0, \cdots, \lfloor N/4 \rfloor\}$. Let $\Omega = \{0, \ldots, \lfloor N/2 \rfloor\}$. $H : \mathbb{Z}_N^* \to \{0, 1\}$ is an efficiently computable injective map.

Kurosawa-Desmedt KEM [23]. In [23], Kurosawa and Desmedt designed a KEM that is not CCA-secure whereas the resulting hybrid encryption scheme is CCA secure. In [20], Hofheinz and Kiltz generalized the Kurosawa-Desmedt KEM to be based on the k-linear assumption. Here we show the generalized Kurosawa-Desmedt KEM in its implicit-rejection variant. Let $\mathbb{G}$ be a cyclic group of prime order p, and $g_1, \cdots, g_k, \hat{g}$ are randomly chosen generators of $\mathbb{G}$. Figure 11

KEM.Gen		KEM.Enc				KEM.Dec	
KEM.Ek	KEM.Tk	KEM.Rg	KEM.Kg	KEM.Cg	KEM.Tg	KEM.Kd	KEM.Vf
$\mathbf{x} \leftarrow_\$ \Omega^k$; $\mathbf{h} = g^{\mathbf{x}}$; $ek = \mathbf{h}$; $dk = \mathbf{x}$	$\mathbf{y} \leftarrow_\$ \Omega^k$ $\mathbf{z} \leftarrow_\$ \Omega^k$ $\mathbf{c} = g^{\mathbf{y}}$; $\mathbf{d} = g^{\mathbf{z}}$; $tk = (\mathbf{c},\mathbf{d})$; $vk = (\mathbf{y},\mathbf{z})$	$r \leftarrow_\$ \{0, \cdots, \lfloor N/4 \rfloor\}$	$\forall i \in [1,k]:$ $K_i = h_i^r$; $K = \{K_1, \cdots, K_k\}$	$C = g^r$	$t = H(C)$; $\forall i \in [1,\hat{k}]:$ $\pi_i = c_i^r \cdot d_i^{t \cdot r}$; $\pi = \{\pi_1, \cdots, \pi_{\hat{k}}\}$	$\forall i \in [1,k]:$ $K_i = C^{x_i}$; $K = \{K_1, \cdots, K_k\}$	$t = H(C)$; $\forall i \in [1,\hat{k}]:$ $\pi'_i = C^{y_i} \cdot C^{t \cdot z_i}$; $\pi' = \{\pi'_1, \cdots, \pi'_{\hat{k}}\}$

Fig. 10. The QR-Based KEM from Cramer-Shoup Encryption Scheme [13]. $\mathbf{x} = \{x_1, \cdots, x_k\}, \mathbf{h} = \{h_1, \cdots, h_k\}, \mathbf{y} = \{y_1, \cdots, y_{\hat{k}}\}, \mathbf{z} = \{z_1, \cdots, z_{\hat{k}}\}, \mathbf{c} = \{c_1, \cdots, c_{\hat{k}}\}, \mathbf{d} = \{d_1, \cdots, d_{\hat{k}}\}$.

depicts the generalized Kurosawa-Desmedt KEM based on k-linear assumption. The public parameter is $\mathsf{pp} = (\mathbb{G}, p, k, g_1, \cdots, g_k, \hat{g})$. The key space $\mathcal{K}_{\mathsf{kem}}$ is $\mathbb{G}$ and the randomness space $\mathcal{R}_{\mathsf{kem}}$ is $\mathbb{Z}_p^k$. $H : \mathbb{G}^{k+1} \to \mathbb{Z}_p^*$ is a target collision resistant hash function. Note that DDH assumption is equivalent to the 1-linear assumption, and the scheme instantiated with $k = 1$ precisely reproduces the Kurosawa-Desmedt KEM [23].

KEM.Gen		KEM.Enc				KEM.Dec	
KEM.Ek	KEM.Tk	KEM.Rg	KEM.Kg	KEM.Cg	KEM.Tg	KEM.Kd	KEM.Vf
$(z,\hat{z}) \leftarrow_\$ (\mathbb{Z}_p^*)^2$; $\forall i \in [1,k]:$ $(x_i, y_i) \leftarrow_\$ (\mathbb{Z}_p^*)^2$; $h_i = g_i^{x_i} \hat{g}^z$; $\hat{h}_i = g_i^{y_i} \hat{g}^{\hat{z}}$; $ek = (\mathbf{h},\hat{\mathbf{h}})$; $dk = (\mathbf{x},\mathbf{y},z,\hat{z})$	-	$\forall i \in [1,k]:$ $r_i \leftarrow_\$ \mathbb{Z}_p^*$;	$t = H(C)$; $K = \prod_{i=1}^k (h_i^t \hat{h}_i)^{r_i}$	$C = (u_1, \cdots, u_k, u)$ $= (g_1^{r_1}, \cdots, g_k^{r_k}, \hat{g}^{r_1 + \cdots + r_k})$	-	$t = H(C)$ $K = u^{zt+\hat{z}}$ $\prod_{i=1}^k u_i^{x_i t + y_i}$	-

Fig. 11. Generalized Kurosawa-Desmedt KEM based on k-Linear Assumption [20,23]. $\mathbf{x} = \{x_1, \cdots, x_k\}, \mathbf{y} = \{y_1, \cdots, y_k\}, \mathbf{h} = \{h_1, \cdots, h_k\}, \hat{\mathbf{h}} = \{\hat{h}_1, \cdots, \hat{h}_k\}\}$

Hofheinz-Kiltz KEMs [20]. In [20], Hofheinz and Kiltz formalized a new notion of CCCA (constrained chosen-ciphertext security) security for KEM and designed a new CCCA-secure KEM from the DDH assumption. As depicted by Fig. 12, the construction (the public parameter is $\mathsf{pp} = (\mathbb{G}, p, g)$) is almost the same as the DDH-based one by Cramer and Shoup [13] except that the ciphertext consists of only one group element. Therefore, the DDH-based KEM by Hofheinz and Kiltz is also subvertible by our ASA.

KEM.Gen		KEM.Enc				KEM.Dec	
KEM.Ek	KEM.Tk	KEM.Rg	KEM.Kg	KEM.Cg	KEM.Tg	KEM.Kd	KEM.Vf
$x \leftarrow_\$ \mathbb{Z}_p$; $h = g^x$; $ek = h$; $dk = x$	$(y,z) \leftarrow_\$ \mathbb{Z}_p^2$; $c = g^y$; $d = g^z$; $tk = (c,d), vk = (y,z)$	$r \leftarrow_\$ \mathbb{Z}_p^*$	$K = h^r$	$C = g^r$	$t = H(C)$; $\pi = (cd^t)^r$	$K = C^x$	$t = H(C)$; $\pi' = C^{y+zt}$

Fig. 12. Hofheinz-Kiltz KEM based on k-Linear Assumption [20]

REMARK. In [21], Hofheinz and Kiltz generalized their DDH-based KEM to the k-linear based one. We remark that their k-linear version is not subvertible by our ASA as all the group generators must be parts of the public key and thus the public subversion key cannot be generated before the public key is generated by the user. Moreover, an implicit-rejection variant of the above DDH-based KEM (Fig. 12) is also proposed in [21], we claim that it is not subvertible to our ASA either as the key ciphertext depends on the public key and thus is not of universal decryptability. For more details we refer the reader to [21].

6   Discussions on Countermeasures

In this section, we mainly discuss how to design KEMs secure against ASAs. Indeed, as we have discussed previously, there exist several KEMs that are not subvertible by our ASA [21,26]. Nevertheless, we generally consider the security of KEMs against a wider range of possible subversion attacks in the real world. Noting that almost all known ASAs are mainly due to the free choice of randomness in the cryptographic algorithm, current defense approaches could be roughly classified as two types, depending on whether the randomness is permitted.

6.1   Abandoning Randomized Algorithms

Some prior works [3,5–7,14] have suggested to use deterministic schemes that produce unique output (e.g., unique ciphertext for encryption). For such schemes, any subversion attack could be detected via comparing the output of the (possibly) subverted algorithm with the expected output of the legitimate one at running time. The notion of unique-ciphertext public-key encryption has been proposed by Bellare and Hoang [5] as a useful primitive to resist undetectable subversion attacks. Unfortunately, although abandoning randomized algorithms could well resist subversions, it naturally makes some desirable security notions unachievable. In particular, it is a common wisdom that the conventional IND-CPA security is impossible for deterministic encryption.

6.2   Permitting Randomized Algorithms with Further Assumptions

Some other approaches permitting randomized algorithms have been proposed to defeat subversions. Note that it is generally impossible for randomized algorithms to resist subversion attacks without making further assumptions (regarding trusted component assumptions and architectural requirements). Indeed, all current generic approaches that permit randomized algorithms require various assumptions. Here we mainly introduce three generic techniques using which one could possibly secure KEM against subversion. Note that all these defensive techniques rely on different assumptions and thus are generally incomparable.

(1) **Split-program methodology** [2,12,27–29]. The split-program methodology is introduced by Russell *et al.* [27,28] where an algorithm is decomposed into

several functional components that are executed independently (as in threshold cryptography or multiparty computation elements is often assumed, and as can be implemented based on well isolated enclaves architecturally). It mainly relies on a so-called watchdog that is trustworthy for detecting subversions of each individual component of the randomized algorithm. Particularly, in the split-program model, the adversary is required to supply implementations of all components to the watchdog who has the specification of these components. The watchdog's goal is to test whether the (possibly subverted) implementation of each individual component is compliant with the specification via black-box testing. The split-program methodology is generally applicable for every randomized algorithm and has nice properties in resisting the complete subversion including subverted key generation. Note that Russell *et al.*'s PKE construction [28] trivially implies an IND-CPA-secure KEM with subversion resilience in the offline watchdog model. However, it remains unknown how to achieve stronger security (e.g., IND-CCA security) for KEMs in the subversion setting.

(2) Cryptographic reverse firewall [11,17,25]. Cryptographic reverse firewall was firstly introduced by Mironov and Stephens-Davidowitz [25] to secure arbitrary two-party protocol that are run on possibly subverted machines. The reverse firewall model requires an on-line external party to re-randomize all incoming/outgoing communication of the randomized algorithm. This model is quite powerful in the sense that it could secure the fully black-box use of (possibly subverted) algorithms without complex detection mechanisms. However, it requires a source of trusted randomness, and may not be readily applicable to every existing protocol as it requires some "re-randomizable" structure of the cryptographic scheme. In [17], Dodis *et al.* showed how to design secure message transmission protocols on corrupted machines. Their CPA-secure rerandomizable PKE trivially implies IND-CPA-secure KEMs with reverse firewalls. However, as pointed out by Dodis *et al.*, such a construction usually requires the computation of public-key operations on the entire plaintext and thus is inefficient.

(3) Self-guarding mechanism [18]. The self-guarding mechanism, introduced by Fischlin and Mazaheri [18], assumes the existence of a good initial phase when the randomized algorithm is not subverted. It could be viewed as an alternative approach to reverse firewall, but does not depend on external parties and applies more smoothly to some primitives like symmetric encryption. The core idea is to use *samples* gathered from its underlying primitives during their good initial phase in addition to basic operations to resist subversion attacks that are later on mounted on the primitives. That is, self-guarding mechanism mainly counter subversion attacks that are triggered to wake up at a later point in time. Here we roughly discuss how to construct self-guarding KEMs. Once a set of fresh samples are gathered at the good initial phase, for each output (K, ψ) of the possibly subverted encapsulation algorithm, a sample $(K_\$, \psi_\$)$ is first randomly chosen (and deleted) from the set, and then $K_\$$ is used to mask ψ while $\psi_\$$ is appended to the updated ciphertext. To decapsulate the key K, $K_\$$ is first recovered to remove the mask in the ciphertext and thereafter the recovered ciphertext is decrypted. Note that the security of KEM in this setting is inherently bounded by the number of samples collected during the good initial phase.

Note that in [19], Giacon *et al.* introduced the notion of *KEM combiners* as an approach to garner trust from different KEM constructions instead of relying on a single one. We remark that their proposed combiners could be potentially used to restore security against subversion attacks by assuming at least one of the underlying KEMs is not subverted. Further, there are several other approaches for protecting specific primitives against subversions, e.g., anonymous attestation protocols by Camenisch *et al.* [9], and backdoored pseudorandom generators by Dodis *et al.* [15].

Acknowledgement. We would like to thank all anonymous reviewers for their valuable comments. Part of this work was done while Rongmao Chen was visiting COSIC in KU Leuven, Belgium. This work is supported in part by the National Natural Science Foundation of China (Grant No. 62032005, Grant No. 61702541, and Grant No. 61872087), Science Foundation of Fujian Provincial Science and Technology Agency (Grant No. 2020J02016) and the Young Elite Scientists Sponsorship Program by China Association for Science and Technology.

A   Omitted Definitions and Proof

A.1   Hash Proof System

Below we formally define the subset membership problem and computational smoothness for HPSs.

(1). *Subset membership problem.* We say the *subset membership problem* is hard in $\mathcal{HPS}$ if it is computationally hard to distinguish a random element $\mathcal{L}$ from a random element from $\mathcal{X} \setminus \mathcal{L}$. Formally, for any PPT algorithm $\mathcal{A}$,

$$\mathsf{Adv}^{\mathsf{smp}}_{\mathsf{hps},\mathcal{A}}(n) := |\Pr[\mathcal{A}(\mathcal{X}, L, x) = 1 | x \leftarrow_\$ \mathcal{L}] - \Pr[\mathcal{A}(\mathcal{X}, L, x) = 1 | x \leftarrow_\$ \mathcal{X} \setminus \mathcal{L}]| \leq \mathsf{negl}(n).$$

(2). *Computational smoothness.* We say $\mathcal{HPS}$ is of *computational smoothness* if the hash value of a random element from $\mathcal{X} \setminus \mathcal{L}$ looks random to an adversary only knowing the projection key. Formally, for any PPT algorithm $\mathcal{A}$, its advantage $\mathsf{Adv}^{\mathsf{smooth}}_{\mathsf{hps},\mathcal{A}}(n)$ defined as below is negligible.

$$\mathsf{Adv}^{\mathsf{smooth}}_{\mathsf{hps},\mathcal{A}}(n) := \left| \Pr \left[b' = b : \begin{array}{l} \mathsf{pp} \leftarrow_\$ \mathsf{HPS.Setup}(1^n); \\ (hp, hk) \leftarrow_\$ \mathsf{HPS.Gen(pp)}; \\ x \leftarrow_\$ \mathcal{X} \setminus \mathcal{L}; b \leftarrow_\$ \{0,1\}; \\ y_0 \leftarrow_\$ \mathcal{Y}; \\ y_1 := \mathsf{HPS.Priv}(hk, x); \\ b' \leftarrow \mathcal{A}(\mathsf{pp}, hp, x, y_b) \end{array} \right] - \frac{1}{2} \right|.$$

A.2   Proof of Theorem 4

Theorem 4. *The generic construction of* $\mathcal{KEM}$ *depicted in Sect. 5.1 is universally decryptable and key-pseudo-random if* $\mathcal{HPS}$ *is computationally smooth and the subset membership problem is hard in* $\mathcal{HPS}$.

Proof. The property of universal decryptability clearly holds due to the projection property of $\mathcal{HPS}$. We now prove the key-pseudo-randomness via games: $\{\mathbf{G}_0, \mathbf{G}_1, \mathbf{G}_2, \mathbf{G}_3\}$. Let Adv_x be the advantage of $\mathcal{A}$ in Game $\mathbf{G}_x$. Below we provide more details of each game.

- GAME $\mathbf{G}_0$: This is the real game and thus $\mathsf{Adv}^{\mathsf{prk}}_{\mathsf{kem},\mathcal{A}}(n) = \mathsf{Adv}_0$.
- GAME $\mathbf{G}_1$: Same as $\mathbf{G}_0$ except that instead of computing $K_1 := \mathsf{KEM.Kg}(ek, r)$, the challenger computes $K_1 := \mathsf{KEM.Kd}(dk, C)$. One can see that from the view of the adversary, $\mathbf{G}_1$ is identical to $\mathbf{G}_0$ due to the property of universal decryptability. Therefore, we have $\mathsf{Adv}_1 = \mathsf{Adv}_0$.
- GAME $\mathbf{G}_2$: Same as $\mathbf{G}_1$ except that the challenger chooses $C \leftarrow_\$ \mathcal{X} \setminus \mathcal{L}$. One can see that from the view of the adversary, $\mathbf{G}_2$ is indistinguishable from $\mathbf{G}_1$ due to the hard subset membership problem in $\mathcal{HPS}$. Therefore, we have $|\mathsf{Adv}_2 - \mathsf{Adv}_1| \leq \mathsf{Adv}^{\mathsf{smp}}_{\mathsf{hps},\mathcal{A}}(n)$.
- GAME $\mathbf{G}_3$: Same as $\mathbf{G}_2$ except that the challenger chooses $K_1 \leftarrow_\$ \mathcal{K}_{\mathsf{kem}}$ instead of computing $K_1 := \mathsf{KEM.Kd}(dk, C)$. Below we show that a distinguisher between both games could be turned into an attacker $\mathcal{A}'$ against the smoothness of $\mathcal{KEM}$. Precisely, when $\mathcal{A}'$ receives $(\mathsf{pp}, hp, x^*, y^*)$ from its challenger, it sets $ek := hp$, $C := x$ and $K_1 := y^*$. One can note that if $y^* := \mathsf{HPS.Priv}(hk, x^*)$, then the simulation is GAME $\mathbf{G}_2$, otherwise it is GAME $\mathbf{G}_3$. This yields $|\mathsf{Adv}_3 - \mathsf{Adv}_2| \leq \mathsf{Adv}^{\mathsf{smooth}}_{\mathsf{hps},\mathcal{A}}(n)$.

In GAME $\mathbf{G}_3$, the view of the adversary actually does not depend on the chosen bit b and thus we have $\mathsf{Adv}_3 = 0$. Putting all the above together,

$$
\begin{aligned}
\mathsf{Adv}^{\mathsf{prk}}_{\mathsf{kem},\mathcal{A}}(n) &= \mathsf{Adv}_0 \\
&= |\mathsf{Adv}_0 - \mathsf{Adv}_1 + \mathsf{Adv}_1 - \mathsf{Adv}_2 + \mathsf{Adv}_2 - \mathsf{Adv}_3 + \mathsf{Adv}_3| \\
&\leq |\mathsf{Adv}_0 - \mathsf{Adv}_1| + |\mathsf{Adv}_1 - \mathsf{Adv}_2| + |\mathsf{Adv}_2 - \mathsf{Adv}_3| + \mathsf{Adv}_3 \\
&\leq \mathsf{Adv}^{\mathsf{smp}}_{\mathsf{hps},\mathcal{A}}(n) + \mathsf{Adv}^{\mathsf{smooth}}_{\mathsf{hps},\mathcal{A}}(n).
\end{aligned}
$$

This completes the proof of the theorem.

References

1. Armour, M., Poettering, B.: Subverting decryption in AEAD. In: Albrecht, M. (ed.) IMACC 2019. LNCS, vol. 11929, pp. 22–41. Springer, Cham (2019). https://doi.org/10.1007/978-3-030-35199-1_2
2. Ateniese, G., Francati, D., Magri, B., Venturi, D.: Public immunization against complete subversion without random oracles. In: Deng, R.H., Gauthier-Umaña, V., Ochoa, M., Yung, M. (eds.) ACNS 2019. LNCS, vol. 11464, pp. 465–485. Springer, Cham (2019). https://doi.org/10.1007/978-3-030-21568-2_23

3. Ateniese, G., Magri, B., Venturi, D.: Subversion-resilient signature schemes. In: Ray, I., Li, N., Kruegel: C. (eds.) ACM CCS, vol. 15, pp. 364–375. ACM Press, October 2015. https://doi.org/10.1145/2810103.2813635
4. Auerbach, B., Bellare, M., Kiltz, E.: Public-key encryption resistant to parameter subversion and its realization from efficiently-embeddable groups. In: Abdalla, M., Dahab, R. (eds.) PKC 2018. LNCS, vol. 10769, pp. 348–377. Springer, Cham (2018). https://doi.org/10.1007/978-3-319-76578-5_12
5. Bellare, M., Hoang, V.T.: Resisting randomness subversion: fast deterministic and hedged public-key encryption in the standard model. In: Oswald, E., Fischlin, M. (eds.) EUROCRYPT 2015. LNCS, vol. 9057, pp. 627–656. Springer, Heidelberg (2015). https://doi.org/10.1007/978-3-662-46803-6_21
6. Bellare, M., Jaeger, J., Kane, D.: Mass-surveillance without the state: strongly undetectable algorithm-substitution attacks. In: Ray, I., Li, N., Kruegel: C. (eds.) ACM CCS, vol. 15, pp. 1431–1440. ACM Press, October 2015. https://doi.org/10.1145/2810103.2813681
7. Bellare, M., Paterson, K.G., Rogaway, P.: Security of symmetric encryption against mass surveillance. In: Garay, J.A., Gennaro, R. (eds.) CRYPTO 2014. LNCS, vol. 8616, pp. 1–19. Springer, Heidelberg (2014). https://doi.org/10.1007/978-3-662-44371-2_1
8. Berndt, S., Liskiewicz, M.: Algorithm substitution attacks from a steganographic perspective. In: Thuraisingham, B.M., Evans, D., Malkin, T., Xu, D. (eds.) ACM CCS, vol. 17, pp. 1649–1660. ACM Press, October/November 2017. https://doi.org/10.1145/3133956.3133981
9. Camenisch, J., Drijvers, M., Lehmann, A.: Anonymous attestation with subverted TPMs. In: Katz, J., Shacham, H. (eds.) CRYPTO 2017. LNCS, vol. 10403, pp. 427–461. Springer, Cham (2017). https://doi.org/10.1007/978-3-319-63697-9_15
10. Checkoway, S., et al.: On the Practical Exploitability of Dual EC in TLS Implementations, pp. 319–335 (2014)
11. Chen, R., Mu, Y., Yang, G., Susilo, W., Guo, F., Zhang, M.: Cryptographic reverse firewall via malleable smooth projective hash functions. In: Cheon, J.H., Takagi, T. (eds.) ASIACRYPT 2016. LNCS, vol. 10031, pp. 844–876. Springer, Heidelberg (2016). https://doi.org/10.1007/978-3-662-53887-6_31
12. Chow, S.S.M., Russell, A., Tang, Q., Yung, M., Zhao, Y., Zhou, H.-S.: Let a non-barking watchdog bite: cliptographic signatures with an offline watchdog. In: Lin, D., Sako, K. (eds.) PKC 2019. LNCS, vol. 11442, pp. 221–251. Springer, Cham (2019). https://doi.org/10.1007/978-3-030-17253-4_8
13. Cramer, R., Shoup, V.: Universal hash proofs and a paradigm for adaptive chosen ciphertext secure public-key encryption. In: Knudsen, L.R. (ed.) EUROCRYPT 2002. LNCS, vol. 2332, pp. 45–64. Springer, Heidelberg (2002). https://doi.org/10.1007/3-540-46035-7_4
14. Degabriele, J.P., Farshim, P., Poettering, B.: A more cautious approach to security against mass surveillance. In: Leander, G. (ed.) FSE 2015. LNCS, vol. 9054, pp. 579–598. Springer, Heidelberg (2015). https://doi.org/10.1007/978-3-662-48116-5_28
15. Dodis, Y., Ganesh, C., Golovnev, A., Juels, A., Ristenpart, T.: A formal treatment of backdoored pseudorandom generators. In: Oswald, E., Fischlin, M. (eds.) EUROCRYPT 2015. LNCS, vol. 9056, pp. 101–126. Springer, Heidelberg (2015). https://doi.org/10.1007/978-3-662-46800-5_5

16. Dodis, Y., Gennaro, R., Håstad, J., Krawczyk, H., Rabin, T.: Randomness extraction and key derivation using the CBC, cascade and HMAC modes. In: Franklin, M. (ed.) CRYPTO 2004. LNCS, vol. 3152, pp. 494–510. Springer, Heidelberg (2004). https://doi.org/10.1007/978-3-540-28628-8_30

17. Dodis, Y., Mironov, I., Stephens-Davidowitz, N.: Message transmission with reverse firewalls—secure communication on corrupted machines. In: Robshaw, M., Katz, J. (eds.) CRYPTO 2016. LNCS, vol. 9814, pp. 341–372. Springer, Heidelberg (2016). https://doi.org/10.1007/978-3-662-53018-4_13

18. Fischlin, M., Mazaheri, S.: Self-guarding cryptographic protocols against algorithm substitution attacks. In: 31st IEEE Computer Security Foundations Symposium, CSF 2018, Oxford, United Kingdom, 9–12 July 2018, pp. 76–90 (2018). https://doi.org/10.1109/CSF.2018.00013

19. Giacon, F., Heuer, F., Poettering, B.: KEM combiners. In: Abdalla, M., Dahab, R. (eds.) PKC 2018. LNCS, vol. 10769, pp. 190–218. Springer, Cham (2018). https://doi.org/10.1007/978-3-319-76578-5_7

20. Hofheinz, D., Kiltz, E.: Secure hybrid encryption from weakened key encapsulation. In: Menezes, A. (ed.) CRYPTO 2007. LNCS, vol. 4622, pp. 553–571. Springer, Heidelberg (2007). https://doi.org/10.1007/978-3-540-74143-5_31

21. Hofheinz, D., Kiltz, E.: Secure hybrid encryption from weakened key encapsulation. Cryptology ePrint Archive, Report 2007/288 (2007). http://eprint.iacr.org/2007/288

22. Katz, J., Vaikuntanathan, V.: Round-optimal password-based authenticated key exchange. In: Ishai, Y. (ed.) TCC 2011. LNCS, vol. 6597, pp. 293–310. Springer, Heidelberg (2011). https://doi.org/10.1007/978-3-642-19571-6_18

23. Kurosawa, K., Desmedt, Y.: A new paradigm of hybrid encryption scheme. In: Franklin, M. (ed.) CRYPTO 2004. LNCS, vol. 3152, pp. 426–442. Springer, Heidelberg (2004). https://doi.org/10.1007/978-3-540-28628-8_26

24. Kwant, R., Lange, T., Thissen, K.: Lattice klepto. In: Adams, C., Camenisch, J. (eds.) SAC 2017. LNCS, vol. 10719, pp. 336–354. Springer, Cham (2018). https://doi.org/10.1007/978-3-319-72565-9_17

25. Mironov, I., Stephens-Davidowitz, N.: Cryptographic reverse firewalls. In: Oswald, E., Fischlin, M. (eds.) EUROCRYPT 2015. LNCS, vol. 9057, pp. 657–686. Springer, Heidelberg (2015). https://doi.org/10.1007/978-3-662-46803-6_22

26. Peikert, C.: Lattice cryptography for the internet. In: Mosca, M. (ed.) PQCrypto 2014. LNCS, vol. 8772, pp. 197–219. Springer, Cham (2014). https://doi.org/10.1007/978-3-319-11659-4_12

27. Russell, A., Tang, Q., Yung, M., Zhou, H.-S.: Cliptography: clipping the power of kleptographic attacks. In: Cheon, J.H., Takagi, T. (eds.) ASIACRYPT 2016. LNCS, vol. 10032, pp. 34–64. Springer, Heidelberg (2016). https://doi.org/10.1007/978-3-662-53890-6_2

28. Russell, A., Tang, Q., Yung, M., Zhou, H.S.: Generic semantic security against a kleptographic adversary. In: Thuraisingham, B.M., Evans, D., Malkin, T., Xu, D. (eds.) ACM CCS, vol. 17, pp. 907–922. ACM Press, October/November 2017. https://doi.org/10.1145/3133956.3133993

29. Russell, A., Tang, Q., Yung, M., Zhou, H.-S.: Correcting subverted random oracles. In: Shacham, H., Boldyreva, A. (eds.) CRYPTO 2018. LNCS, vol. 10992, pp. 241–271. Springer, Cham (2018). https://doi.org/10.1007/978-3-319-96881-0_9

30. Young, A., Yung, M.: The dark side of "black-box" cryptography or: should we trust capstone? In: Koblitz, N. (ed.) CRYPTO 1996. LNCS, vol. 1109, pp. 89–103. Springer, Heidelberg (1996). https://doi.org/10.1007/3-540-68697-5_8

31. Young, A., Yung, M.: Kleptography: using cryptography against cryptography. In: Fumy, W. (ed.) EUROCRYPT 1997. LNCS, vol. 1233, pp. 62–74. Springer, Heidelberg (1997). https://doi.org/10.1007/3-540-69053-0_6
32. Young, A., Yung, M.: The prevalence of kleptographic attacks on discrete-log based cryptosystems. In: Kaliski, B.S. (ed.) CRYPTO 1997. LNCS, vol. 1294, pp. 264–276. Springer, Heidelberg (1997). https://doi.org/10.1007/BFb0052241

Unbounded HIBE with Tight Security

Roman Langrehr[1]([✉]) and Jiaxin Pan[2]

[1] ETH Zurich, Zurich, Switzerland
`roman.langrehr@inf.ethz.ch`
[2] Department of Mathematical Sciences, NTNU – Norwegian University of Science
and Technology, Trondheim, Norway
`jiaxin.pan@ntnu.no`

Abstract. We propose the first tightly secure and *unbounded* hierarchical identity-based encryption (HIBE) scheme based on standard assumptions. Our main technical contribution is a novel proof strategy that
allows us to tightly randomize user secret keys for identities with arbitrary hierarchy depths using low entropy hidden in a small and hierarchy-
independent master public key.

The notion of unbounded HIBE is proposed by Lewko and Waters
(Eurocrypt 2011). In contrast to most HIBE schemes, an unbounded
scheme does not require any maximum depth to be specified in the setup
phase, and user secret keys or ciphertexts can be generated for identities
of arbitrary depths with hierarchy-independent system parameters.

While all the previous unbounded HIBE schemes have security loss
that grows at least linearly in the number of user secret key queries,
the security loss of our scheme is only dependent on the security parameter, even in the multi-challenge setting, where an adversary can ask
for multiple challenge ciphertexts. We prove the adaptive security of
our scheme based on the Matrix Decisional Diffie-Hellman assumption
in prime-order pairing groups, which generalizes a family of standard
Diffie-Hellman assumptions such as k-Linear.

Keywords: Unbounded hierarchical identity-based encryption · Tight
security · Multi-challenge security

1 Introduction

1.1 Motivation

Hierarchical identity-based encryption (HIBE) [16,26] is a generalization of
identity-based encryption (IBE) [36]. It offers more flexibility in sharing sensitive data than IBE or classical public-key encryption (PKE).

In an HIBE scheme, users' identities are arranged in an organizational hierarchy and, more precisely, a hierarchical identity is a vector of identities of some

R. Langrehr—Part of the work done at Karlsruhe Institute of Technology, Karlsruhe,
Germany. Supported in part by ERC CoG grant 724307.

S. Moriai and H. Wang (Eds.): ASIACRYPT 2020, LNCS 12492, pp. 129–159, 2020.
https://doi.org/10.1007/978-3-030-64834-3_5

length $p > 0$. As in an IBE scheme, anyone can encrypt a message with respect to an identity id := $(\text{id}_1, ..., \text{id}_p)$ by access to only the public parameters. To decrypt this encrypted message, one of id's ascendants at level p' where $0 < p' < p$ can delegate a user secret key for id, in addition to asking the trusted authority for id's user secret key as in the IBE setting. Furthermore, a user at level p is not supposed to decrypt any ciphertext for a recipient who is not among its descendants.

The security we focus on in this paper is adaptive security, where an adversary is allowed to declare a fresh challenge identity id* adaptively and obtain a challenge ciphertext of id* after seeing user secret keys for arbitrary chosen identities and (master) public keys. It is a widely accepted security notion for both HIBE and IBE schemes. Most of the existing HIBE schemes in the standard model have a security loss of at least Q_e (such as [6,9]) or even Q_e^L [39], where Q_e is the maximum number of user secret key queries and L is the maximum hierarchy depth. Constructions from recent work of Langrehr and Pan (LP) [29,30] are the known exceptions. Their security loss depends only on the security parameter, but not Q_e. However, their master public key size[1] depends on L. As L grows, the master public key becomes larger.

In particular, the maximum hierarchy depth L needs to be fixed in the setup phase. Once it is fixed and master public keys are generated, there is no way to add new levels into the hierarchy. This can be an undesirable burden to deploy HIBE in practice since institutions grow rapidly nowadays. Hence, it is more desirable to construct a tightly secure HIBE scheme whose master public keys are independent of the maximum hierarchy depth.

We note that the limitation mentioned above exists not only in the LP schemes but also in almost all the HIBE schemes even with non-tight security in the standard model. The notion of unbounded HIBE from Lewko and Waters [33] is proposed to overcome this limitation. In an unbounded HIBE, the whole scheme is not bounded to the maximum depth L. In particular, its master public keys, user secret keys and ciphertexts are all independent of L. (Though the user secret keys and ciphertexts can still depend on the actual hierarchy depth of the identity.) They and the follow-up work [18,31] give constructions of unbounded HIBE in composite- and prime-order pairing groups, respectively, to implement this notion. Unfortunately, none of these constructions is tight.

OUR GOAL: TIGHTLY SECURE UNBOUNDED HIBE. In this paper, we aim at constructing unbounded HIBE with tight reductions based on standard assumptions. We start recalling tight security and then give some reasons about why it is technically challenging to achieve this goal.

A security reduction is usually used to prove the security of a cryptographic scheme S by reducing any attacker $\mathcal{A}$ against S to an attacker $\mathcal{R}$ against a corresponding computational hard problem P in an efficient way. After that, we can conclude that breaking the security of S is at least as hard as solving P. More precisely, we establish a relation that states $\varepsilon_{\mathcal{A}} \leq \ell \cdot \varepsilon_{\mathcal{R}}$. Here $\varepsilon_{\mathcal{A}}$ and $\varepsilon_{\mathcal{R}}$

---

[1] We measure the size of the master public key in terms of the number of group elements.

are success probability of $\mathcal{A}$ and $\mathcal{R}$, respectively, and for simplicity we ignore the additive negligible terms and assume that the running time of $\mathcal{R}$ is approximately the same as that of $\mathcal{A}$.

Ideally, we want a reduction to be *tight*, namely, ℓ to be a small constant. Recent works are also interested in "almost tight security", where ℓ may be (for instance, linearly or logarithmically) dependent on the security parameter, but not the size of $\mathcal{A}$. We will not distinguish these two tightness notions, but state the precise security loss in security proofs and comparison of schemes. A tight security reduction means the security of S is tightly coupled with the hardness of P. A scheme with tight reductions is more desirable since it provides the same level of security regardless of the application size. Moreover, we can implement it with smaller parameters and do not need to compensate for the security loss. As a result, tightly secure schemes drew a lot of attention in the last few years, from basic primitives, such as PKE [13,14,21] and signature [1,15] schemes, to more advanced ones, such as (non-interactive) key exchange [10,17,22], zero-knowledge proof [2,3], IBE [6,9,20,23] and functional encryption [37] schemes. Currently, research is carried out to reduce the cost for tight security. For instance, for PKE, the public key size is shortened from being linear [13] (in the security parameter) to constant [14,21]. In particular, the scheme in [14] only has one element more in the ciphertext overhead than its non-tight counterpart [28] asymptotically. By taking the concrete security loss into account, we are optimistic that scheme in [14] will have shorter ciphertext length in terms of bits.

DIFFICULTIES IN ACHIEVING OUR GOAL. Given the existing research, it is quite challenging to construct a tightly secure HIBE, even for a bounded one. Firstly, the potential difficulty of this task has been shown by Lewko and Waters [34], namely, it is hard to prove an HIBE scheme with security loss less than exponential in L, if its user secret keys are rerandomizable over all "functional" keys. Secondly, the work of Blazy, Kiltz, and Pan (BKP) [6] is the first that claimed to have solved this challenge by proposing a bounded tightly secure HIBE. Their scheme has indeed bypassed the impossibility result of [34] by having its user secret keys only rerandomizable in a subspace of all "functional" keys, which is similar to schemes based on the dual system technique [9,32]. Unfortunately, shortly after its publication, a technical flaw was found in their proof, which shows that their proof strategy is insufficient for HIBE with flexible identity depth.

Recently, Langrehr and Pan have proposed the first tightly secure HIBE in the standard model [29]. A very recent and concurrent work [30] improves this HIBE and proposes a tightly secure HIBE in the multi-challenge setting. Core techniques in both papers crucially require their master public key size depend on the maximum hierarchy, L. More precisely, they need to know L in advance so that they can choose independent master secret keys for different levels, which will be turned into master public keys. With these relatively large master secret keys, they can apply their independent randomization to isolate randomization for identities with different maximum levels. As a result, their scheme is bounded to the maximum level L of the whole HIBE scheme and its master public key size is dependent on L.

1.2   Our Contribution

We construct the *first* tightly secure unbounded HIBE based on standard assumptions. Our scheme is furthermore tightly multi-challenge secure. The multi-challenge security is a more realistic notion for (H)IBE, where an adversary is allowed to query multiple challenge identities adaptively and obtain the corresponding ciphertexts. It has comparable efficiency to its non-tight counterparts [18,31], and, in particular, it has shorter ciphertext and user secret key than the scheme of [31]. At the core of our construction is a novel technique that allows us to prove tight adaptive security of HIBE with "small", hierarchy-independent master public keys.

More precisely, the identity space for our scheme $\mathcal{ID} := \mathcal{S}^*$ has unbounded depth and the base set $\mathcal{S}$ can be arbitrary. In this section, we consider $\mathcal{S} := \{0,1\}^n$ for simplicity, where n is the security parameter. The master public key of our scheme is independent of L and contains only $\mathbf{O}(n)$-many group elements, which is the same as the existing tightly secure IBE schemes [6,9,20,23].

All our security proofs are in the standard model and based on the Matrix Decisional Diffie-Hellman (MDDH) assumption [11] in prime-order asymmetric pairing groups. The MDDH assumption is a generalization of a class of Decisional Diffie-Hellman assumptions, such as the k-Lin [24] and aSymmetric eXternal Diffie-Hellman (SXDH) (for $k = 1$) assumptions. The security of our MAC requires an additional assumption on the existence of collision-resistant hash functions. There exist collision-resistant hash functions in the standard model that maps arbitrary-length bit-strings to fixed-length ones using fixed-length keys. For instance, one can use the Merkle-Damgård construction with hash functions from the SHA familiy or the less efficient but completely provably secure one from the discrete logarithm assumption.

EFFICIENCY COMPARISON. We compare the efficiency of bounded and unbounded HIBE schemes in the standard model with prime-order pairings in Table 1. We note that [35] achieves a weaker notion of unbounded HIBE in the sense that their master public key is independent of L, but the size of the user secret key is dependent on L. More precisely, their user secret key contains $\mathbf{\Omega}(L - p)$-many group elements for an identity $\mathsf{id} := (\mathsf{id}_1, \ldots, \mathsf{id}_p)$.

According to Table 1, our scheme has shorter ciphertexts and user secret keys than Lew12, which is comparable to GCTC16. We note that both Lew12 and GCTC16 are unbounded HIBE with non-tight reductions, while ours are tight. Thus, when accounting for a larger security loss in the reduction with larger groups, our scheme may have shorter ciphertexts and user secret keys than GCTC16 at the concrete level. We want to emphasize that our scheme is not fully practical yet, but it lays down a theoretical foundation for more efficient unbounded HIBE with tight security in the future.

EXTENSIONS. Our unbounded HIBE scheme directly implies a tightly secure unbounded identity-based signature by the Naor transformation. Furthermore, our HIBE is compatible with the Quasi-Adaptive NIZK (QANIZK) for linear subspaces and thus, similar to [23] it can be combined with a tightly simulation-sound QANIZK to construct a tightly CCA-secure unbounded HIBE in the multi-challenge setting. We give a detailed treatment in the full version for completeness.

Table 1. Comparison of bounded and unbounded HIBEs in prime-order pairing groups with adaptive security in the standard model based on static assumptions. The second column indicates whether an HIBE is bounded (✗) or unbounded (✓). The identity space for bounded HIBE is $(\{0,1\}^n)^{\leq L}$ and that for unbounded HIBE is $(\{0,1\}^n)^*$. γ is the bit length of the range of a collision-resistant hash function. '$|\mathsf{mpk}|$,' '$|\mathsf{usk}|$,' and '$|\mathsf{C}|$' stand for the size of the master public key, a user secret key and a ciphertext, respectively. We count the number of group elements in $\mathbb{G}_1$, $\mathbb{G}_2$, and $\mathbb{G}_T$. For a scheme that works in symmetric pairing groups, we write $\mathbb{G}(:= \mathbb{G}_1 = \mathbb{G}_2)$. In the '$|\mathsf{usk}|$' and '$|\mathsf{C}|$' columns p stands for the hierarchy depth of the identity vector. In bounded HIBEs, L denotes the maximum hierarchy depth. In the security loss, Q_e denotes the number of user secret key queries by the adversary. MC stands for multi-challenge and this column indicates whether the adversary is allowed to query multiple challenge ciphertexts (✓) or just one (✗). Lew12 is the prime-order variant of the unbounded scheme in [33].

Scheme	U	$|\mathsf{mpk}|$	$|\mathsf{usk}|$	$|\mathsf{C}|$	Loss	MC	Assumption
Wat05 [39]	✗	$\mathbf{O}(nL)|\mathbb{G}|$	$\mathbf{O}(nL)|\mathbb{G}|$	$(1+p)|\mathbb{G}|$	$\mathbf{O}(nQ_e)^L$	✗	DBDH
Wat09 [38]	✗	$\mathbf{O}(L)|\mathbb{G}|$	$\mathbf{O}(p)(|\mathbb{G}|+|\mathbb{Z}_q|)$	$\mathbf{O}(p)(|\mathbb{G}|+|\mathbb{Z}_q|)$	$\mathbf{O}(Q_e)$	✗	2-LIN
Lew12[31]	✓	$60|\mathbb{G}|+2|\mathbb{G}_T|$	$(60+10p)|\mathbb{G}|$	$10p|\mathbb{G}|$	$\mathbf{O}(Q_e)$	✗	2-LIN
OT12 [35]	✗	$160|\mathbb{G}|$	$\mathbf{O}(p^2 L)|\mathbb{G}|$	$3+6p|\mathbb{G}|$	$\mathbf{O}(Q_e L^2)$	✗	2-LIN
CW13 [9]	✗	$\mathbf{O}(L)(|\mathbb{G}_1|+|\mathbb{G}_2|)$	$\mathbf{O}(L)|\mathbb{G}_2|$	$4|\mathbb{G}_1|$	$\mathbf{O}(Q_e)$	✗	SXDH
BKP14 [6]	✗	$\mathbf{O}(L)(|\mathbb{G}_1|+|\mathbb{G}_2|)$	$\mathbf{O}(L)|\mathbb{G}_2|$	$4|\mathbb{G}_1|$	$\mathbf{O}(Q_e)$	✗	SXDH
GCTC16 [18]	✓	$18(|\mathbb{G}_1|+|\mathbb{G}_2|)+3|\mathbb{G}_T|$	$(18\lceil p/3\rceil - 3p+18)|\mathbb{G}_2|$	$9\lceil p/3\rceil|\mathbb{G}_1|$	$\mathbf{O}(QL)$	✗	SXDH
LP19$_1^{\mathcal{H}}$ [29]	✗	$\mathbf{O}(\gamma L)(|\mathbb{G}_1|+|\mathbb{G}_2|)$	$\mathbf{O}(\gamma L)|\mathbb{G}_2|$	$5|\mathbb{G}_1|$	$\mathbf{O}(\gamma L)$	✗	SXDH
LP19$_2^{\mathcal{H}}$ [29]	✗	$\mathbf{O}(\gamma L)(|\mathbb{G}_1|+|\mathbb{G}_2|)$	$(3p+2)|\mathbb{G}_2|$	$(3p+2)|\mathbb{G}_1|$	$\mathbf{O}(\gamma)$	✗	SXDH
LP20$_1^{\mathcal{H}}$ [30]	✗	$\mathbf{O}(\gamma L)(|\mathbb{G}_1|+|\mathbb{G}_2|)$	$\mathbf{O}(\gamma L)|\mathbb{G}_2|$	$5|\mathbb{G}_1|$	$\mathbf{O}(\gamma L)$	✓	SXDH
LP20$_2^{\mathcal{H}}$ [30]	✗	$\mathbf{O}(\gamma L)(|\mathbb{G}_1|+|\mathbb{G}_2|)$	$(3p+2)|\mathbb{G}_2|$	$(3p+2)|\mathbb{G}_1|$	$\mathbf{O}(\gamma L)$	✓	SXDH
Ours (Fig. 14)	✓	$\mathbf{O}(\gamma)(|\mathbb{G}_1|+|\mathbb{G}_2|)$	$(7p+2)|\mathbb{G}_2|$	$(7p+2)|\mathbb{G}_1|$	$\mathbf{O}(\gamma)$	✓	SXDH

1.3 Technical Overview

To achieve our goal, we develop a novel tight method that uses (limited) entropy hidden in hierarchy-independent master public key to generate enough entropy to randomize user secret keys of identities with unbounded hierarchy depths (in a computational manner). As a bonus, our technique naturally give us tight multi-challenge security.

A MODULAR TREATMENT: FROM MAC TO HIBE. We follow the modular approach of Blazy, Kiltz, and Pan (BKP) [6] to construct our unbounded HIBE. The basis of our construction is a novel tightly secure message authentication code (MAC). Our MAC has *suitable algebraic structures* and thus can be turned into an unbounded HIBE tightly by adapting the BKP framework.

The BKP framework [6] tightly reduces constructing an (H)IBE to a suitable affine MAC. As a result, we only need to focus on constructing the suitable MAC. Affine MACs are algebraic MACs that have affine structures, and such structures allow transformation to (H)IBEs. This framework abstracts the first tightly secure IBE from Chen and Wee (CW) [9] and can be viewed as extending the "MAC → Signature" framework of Bellare and Goldwasser [5] to the IBE setting by using the affine structure and pairings. Most of the tightly secure IBE and HIBE schemes are related to this framework, such as [19,20,23,25,29,30].

PREPARATION: SHRINKING THE MESSAGE SPACE VIA HASHING. We first apply a collision-resistant hash function to shrink the message space which the "bit-by-bit" argument applies on. More precisely, let $H : \{0,1\}^* \to \{0,1\}^n$ be a collision-resistant hash function. For an (unbounded) hierarchical message $\mathsf{m} := (\mathsf{m}_1, \ldots, \mathsf{m}_p) \in (\{0,1\}^n)^p$, we hash every i-th prefix $(1 \leq i \leq p)$ and have the hashed message $\mathsf{hm} := (\mathsf{hm}_1, \mathsf{hm}_2, \ldots, \mathsf{hm}_p)$ where $\mathsf{hm}_i := H(\mathsf{m}_1, \ldots, \mathsf{m}_i) \in \{0,1\}^n$. The collision-resistance guarantees that it is hard for an adversary to find two distinct m and $\mathsf{m}^\star$ messages with $H(\mathsf{m}) = H(\mathsf{m}^\star)$. In particular, after hashing every prefixes of a message, if a hierarchical message m is not a prefix of $\mathsf{m}^\star$, then the last hash value of m is different to every hash value of $\mathsf{m}^\star$. As a result, our argument is only applied on the last hash value.

OUR STRATEGY: "INJECT-AND-PACK". Our strategy contains two steps: (1) injecting enough randomness into MAC tags locally and (2) packing the local randomness and lift it up to the global level. Both steps are compatible with each other, and they only rely on the limited entropy in the hierarchy-independent MAC keys and can provide tight security even in the multi-challenge setting.

Our MAC has the following structures that enable our "inject-and-pack" strategy. This is captured by our MAC scheme MAC_u in Sect. 3.2.

For a hierarchical message $\mathsf{m} := (\mathsf{m}_1, \ldots, \mathsf{m}_p)$, our MAC tag $\tau_\mathsf{m} := (([\mathbf{t}_i]_2, [\tilde{\mathbf{t}}_i]_2, [\mathbf{u}_i]_2)_{1 \leq i \leq p}, [\tilde{\mathbf{u}}]_2)$ has the following form:

$$\mathbf{t}_i := \mathbf{B}\mathbf{s}_i \in \mathbb{Z}_q^{n_1} \text{ and } \tilde{\mathbf{t}}_i := \tilde{\mathbf{B}}\tilde{\mathbf{s}}_i \in \mathbb{Z}_q^{n_2} \quad \text{for} \quad \mathbf{s}_i, \tilde{\mathbf{s}}_i \xleftarrow{\$} \mathbb{Z}_q^{n_3}$$

$$\mathbf{u}_i := \boxed{\textstyle\sum_{j=1}^n \mathbf{X}_{j,\mathsf{hm}_i[\![j]\!]}\mathbf{t}_i} + \boxed{\tilde{\mathbf{X}}_1\tilde{\mathbf{t}}_i} \in \mathbb{Z}_q^{n_4} \tag{1}$$

$$\tilde{\mathbf{u}} := \boxed{\textstyle\sum_{j=1}^p \tilde{\mathbf{X}}_2\tilde{\mathbf{t}}_j} + \boxed{\mathbf{x}'} \,,$$

where $\mathbf{B} \xleftarrow{\$} \mathbb{Z}_q^{n_1 \times n_3}$, $\tilde{\mathbf{B}} \xleftarrow{\$} \mathbb{Z}_q^{n_2 \times n_3 2}$, $\mathbf{X}_{j,b} \xleftarrow{\$} \mathbb{Z}_q^{n_4 \times n_1}$ for $1 \leq j \leq n, b \in \{0,1\}$ and $\tilde{\mathbf{X}}_1, \tilde{\mathbf{X}}_2 \xleftarrow{\$} \mathbb{Z}_q^{n_4 \times n_2}$ and $\mathbf{x}' \xleftarrow{\$} \mathbb{Z}_q^{n_4}$ and they are all contained in the secret key of our MAC, namely, $\mathsf{sk}_{\mathsf{MAC}} := (\mathbf{B}, \tilde{\mathbf{B}}, (\mathbf{X}_{j,b})_{\text{for } 1 \leq j \leq n, b \in \{0,1\}}, \tilde{\mathbf{X}}_1, \tilde{\mathbf{X}}_2, \mathbf{x}')$. Here the (hierarchical) message space of a MAC is the identity space of the resulting HIBE.

We highlight different purposes of different parts in our MAC tags:

- randomizing $\boxed{\mathbf{x}'}$ is our end goal. In the resulting HIBE, once $\mathbf{x}'$ is randomized, it will further randomize challenge ciphertexts;
- the linear part, $\boxed{\textstyle\sum_{j=1}^n \mathbf{X}_{j,\mathsf{hm}_i[\![j]\!]}\mathbf{t}_i}$, is used to inject randomness;

---

[2] For simplicity, we choose $\mathbf{B}$ and $\tilde{\mathbf{B}}$ uniformly at random here, while in the actual scheme we choose them based on the underlying assumption.

- with the packing helpers, $\boxed{\tilde{\mathbf{X}}_1 \tilde{\mathbf{t}}_i}$ and $\boxed{\sum_{j=1}^{p} \tilde{\mathbf{X}}_2 \tilde{\mathbf{t}}_j}$, we can transfer the injected randomness in $\mathbf{u}_p$ to randomize $\boxed{\mathbf{x}'}$.

We will discuss how to choose the dimensions of these random matrices and vectors to enable our strategy.

Before that, we stress that it is crucial to generate $([\mathbf{t}_i]_2, [\tilde{\mathbf{t}}_i]_2, [\mathbf{u}_i]_2)$ for all $1 \leq i \leq p$ and $\mathsf{hm}_i := H(\mathsf{m}_1, ..., \mathsf{m}_i)$ so that we can delegate and randomize MAC tags for further levels by publishing $([\mathbf{B}]_2, [\tilde{\mathbf{B}}]_2, ([\mathbf{X}_{j,b}\mathbf{B}]_2)_{j,b}, [\tilde{\mathbf{X}}_1\tilde{\mathbf{B}}]_2, [\tilde{\mathbf{X}}_2\tilde{\mathbf{B}}]_2)$. Details about public delegation can be found in Remark 1 and the full version.

INTERLUDE: SECURITY REQUIREMENT. The MAC security we need for the "MAC-to-HIBE" transformation is pseudorandomness against adaptive chosen message attacks, which is a decisional version of the EUF-CMA security of MAC. To simplify our discussion, we use the EUF-CMA notion only in this chapter, but in the main body we prove the decisional one. In the EUF-CMA security game, an adversary can adaptively ask many MAC tag queries and at some point it will submit one forgery. For the multi-challenge security, we allow the adversary submit multiple forgeries. Here we only consider one forgery for simplicity. Note that our technique works tightly for multiple forgeries.

LOCAL STEP: INJECTING RANDOMNESS. Here we only focus terms in the solid box of Eq. (1) and find a right way to define the dimensions to implement the injection strategy. We note that one cannot use the idea of BKP MAC here, since it uses a square full-rank matrix $\mathbf{B} \in \mathbb{Z}_q^{k \times k}$ and there is no room to hide $\mathbf{X}_{j,b}$ from the published terms $[\mathbf{X}_{j,b}\mathbf{B}]_2$. These terms have to be public to delegate secret keys, while it is not a problem for IBE. Moreover, the same $(\mathbf{X}_{j,b})_{1 \leq j \leq n, b \in \{0,1\}}$ is re-used for all $\mathbf{u}_i$ and the injected randomness will be leaked along them, which is another issue we encounter with the BKP MAC.

To have control on where to inject randomness, we increase the number of row vectors in $\mathbf{B} \overset{\$}{\leftarrow} \mathbb{Z}_q^{3k \times k}$, namely, $n_1 := 3k$, as the LP method in [29], where $\mathbf{X}_{j,b} \overset{\$}{\leftarrow} \mathbb{Z}_q^{1 \times 3k}$ are row vectors. Now the column space of $\mathbf{B}$, $\mathsf{Span}(\mathbf{B}) := \{\mathbf{v} \mid \exists \mathbf{w} \in \mathbb{Z}_q^k \text{ s.t. } \mathbf{v} = \mathbf{B} \cdot \mathbf{w}\}$, is a subspace of $\mathbb{Z}_q^{3k}$ and there is a non-zero kernel matrix $\mathbf{B}^{\perp} \in \mathbb{Z}_q^{3k \times 2k}$ such that $(\mathbf{B}^{\perp})^{\top}\mathbf{B} = \mathbf{0} \in \mathbb{Z}_q^{2k \times k}$. $\mathsf{Span}(\mathbf{B}^{\perp})$ is orthogonal to $\mathsf{Span}(\mathbf{B})$.

We introduce a random function "inside" $\mathsf{Span}(\mathbf{B}^{\perp})$ by tight reductions to the MDDH assumption and all $\mathbf{u}_i$ $(1 \leq i \leq p)$ in Eq. (1) will distribute according to the following new form:

$$\mathbf{u}_i := \left(\sum_{j=1}^{n} \mathbf{X}_{j, \mathsf{hm}_i \llbracket j \rrbracket}^{\top} + \mathsf{RF}(\mathsf{hm}_i) \cdot (\mathbf{B}^{\perp})^{\top} \right) \mathbf{t}_i + \tilde{\mathbf{X}}_1 \tilde{\mathbf{t}}_i \in \mathbb{Z}_q . \qquad (2)$$

Now $\mathsf{RF}(\mathsf{hm}_i)$ is multiplied by $\mathbf{B}^{\perp}$ and we can control where it gets introduced by choose $\mathbf{t}_i \notin \mathsf{Span}(\mathbf{B})$. More precisely, we only introduce the random function, RF, in $\mathbf{u}_p$ at level p for a hierarchical identity $\mathsf{m} := (\mathsf{m}_1, ..., \mathsf{m}_p)$.

The above idea is borrowed from [29], but it is still not enough to correctly inject randomness: It only helps us to hide RF in MAC tag queries, but we still have issue in answering the verification query for an adversary's forgery.

The issue described below does not happen in the BKP and LP [29] schemes, since our MAC has more expressive structure. More precisely, on a forgery of message $m^\star := (m_1^\star, ..., m_p^\star)$, we need to verify whether the forgery satisfies Eq. (1), which form an explicit hierarchy. Since we have no control of how an adversary computes its random $t_i^\star$, in answering one verification query, we compute RF on p many distinct messages, $hm_1^\star, ..., hm_p^\star$. This leaks too much information about RF.

Our solution is to increase the number of row vectors in $X_{j,b}$ from 1 to k, namely, $n_4 := k$. As a result, there is room for us to use an assumption (namely, the MDDH assumption [11]) to tightly inject randomness into these row vectors. Thus, in the end, verification equations defined by Eq. (1) get randomized and the information about RF is properly hidden. We refer Lemma 4 for technical details. The whole core step is formally captured by the Randomness Injection Lemma (cf. Lemma 4). Furthermore, this lemma abstracts the core ideas of [30].

GLOBAL STEP: PACKING RANDOMNESS. After the randomness is injected in u_i at the local level, we pack and move it into the global level to randomize x' which will be use to randomize the challenge ciphertexts. Implicitly, we pack the randomness firstly in $\tilde{t}_p$ for an identity has p levels via the packing helper $\tilde{X}_1\tilde{t}_p$. Secondly, via another packing helper $\tilde{X}_2\tilde{t}_p$, we move the randomness into $\tilde{u}$.

We choose $\tilde{B} \xleftarrow{\$} \mathbb{Z}_q^{2k \times k}$, namely, $n_2 := 2k$, so that there is enough room to implement the above packing steps. Although the randomness is successfully injected, it may be leaked from MAC tag and verification queries during the packing process. In particular, we have small MAC secret keys. To accomplish the task, we carefully design several intermediate hybrid steps and apply the MDDH assumption several times. We refer Lemma 5 for details. The whole core step is formally captured by the Randomness Packing Lemma (cf. Lemma 5).

AN ALTERNATIVE INTERPRETATION: LOCALIZING HIBEs INTO IBEs, TIGHTLY. In contrast to the methods of Langrehr and Pan [29,30], our overall idea can be viewed as localizing a p-level HIBE into p IBE pieces which share the same master public and secret keys, and p is an arbitrary integer. In the security proof, we generate enough entropy locally and then extract it to the global level to argue the security of HIBE. Such an idea is borrowed from [18,31,33], where some variants of Boneh-Boyen's IBE [7] are used at the local level and all these IBE pieces are connected via a secret sharing method. However, implementing this idea with tight reductions is rather challenging, even with the existing tightly secure (H)IBEs (such as [6,9,20,29,30]). We observed that these techniques either fail to introduce local entropy or cannot collect the local randomness to argue the security of the (global) HIBE.

1.4   More Discussion on Related Work

THE FAMILY OF LP HIBE SCHEMES. To implement the "level-by-level" argument, the LP HIBEs [29,30] require the size of master public keys dependent on the maximum hierarchy depth, L, so that they have enough entropy to randomize corresponding MAC tags.

Our approach provides an economic, tightly secure technique to do the randomization with more compact and hierarchy-independent master keys. Our technique uses and abstracts the core technique in a very recent and concurrent work [30] to inject randomness. As we showed above, injecting randomness is not enough for our goal and we require an additional suitable randomness packing technique. [30] achieves tight multi-challenge security for bounded HIBE, while ours is for unbounded HIBE.

OTHER TECHNIQUES FOR TIGHT MULTI-CHALLENGE SECURITY. Over the last few years, several techniques have been proposed for tightly secure IBE in the multi-challenge setting, such as [4, 19, 20, 23, 25], where [4, 19] are based on strong and non-standard assumptions and [25] requires a composite-order group. Motivated by [25], the work of [20, 23] construct the tightly multi-challenge secure IBE schemes in the prime-order group and they both follow the BKP method. They have the same limitation as discussed in the "LOCAL STEP: INJECTING RANDOMNESS" section and cannot be used for our goal, since their $\mathbf{B}$ is also full-rank square matrix. The same kind of information about $\mathbf{X}_{j,b}$ is leaked.

Furthermore, in the work of Hofheinz, Jia, and Pan [23] (also in [20] and BKP), they randomize their MAC by developing a random function, RF, in the $\mathbb{Z}_q$ full space gradually. This is problematic in the unbounded HIBE setting: When we "plug" their MAC into our framework, there is no room to hide RF and by a "mix-and-match" approach an adversary can learn $\mathsf{RF}(\mathsf{hm}^*)$, where $\mathsf{hm}^* := H(\mathsf{m}^*)$. Imagine a challenge message $\mathsf{m}^* \in \{0,1\}^n$. By asking a MAC tag of $(\mathsf{m}^*, \mathsf{m})$, an adversary can easily learn $\mathsf{RF}(\mathsf{hm}^*)$ from $\mathbf{u}_1$. Finally, [29] has discussed why these multi-challenge security techniques cannot be used for HIBEs.

OTHER UNBOUNDED TECHNIQUE. Chen et al. [8] proposes a variant of the bilinear entropy expansion lemma [27] in prime-order groups, which can be used to transform a (bounded) attribute-based encryption (ABE) scheme to an unbounded one in a tight manner. However, we note that their lemma requires a certain algebraic structure of the underlying scheme, which the LP schemes [29, 30] do not have. Moreover, they only prove their scheme in the single-challenge setting, and it is not clear for us whether their single-challenge security tightly implies multi-challenge security.

OPEN PROBLEMS. It is interesting to consider if we can extend our "inject-and-pack" strategy in a more general setting, such as predicate encryption schemes. Another open problem is to consider the Master-Key-KDM security [12] for HIBEs. Garg et al. [12] proposed a Master-Key-KDM secure IBE based on a tightly multi-challenge secure IBE. We are optimistic that our unbounded HIBE can be adapted to achieve the KDM security by following the approach of Garg et al., since our scheme has tight multi-challenge security as well. However, we leave a formal treatment of it as an open problem.

2   Preliminaries

NOTATIONS. We use $x \xleftarrow{\$} \mathcal{S}$ to denote the process of sampling an element x from $\mathcal{S}$ uniformly at random if $\mathcal{S}$ is a set and to denote the process of running $\mathcal{S}$ with its internal randomness and assign the output to x if $\mathcal{S}$ is an algorithm. The expression $a \overset{?}{=} b$ stands for comparing a and b on equality and returning the result in Boolean value. For positive integers $k, \eta \in \mathbb{N}_+$ and a matrix $\mathbf{A} \in \mathbb{Z}_q^{(k+\eta) \times k}$, we denote the upper square matrix of $\mathbf{A}$ by $\overline{\mathbf{A}} \in \mathbb{Z}_q^{k \times k}$ and the lower η rows of $\mathbf{A}$ by $\underline{\mathbf{A}} \in \mathbb{Z}_q^{\eta \times k}$. Similarly, for a column vector $\mathbf{v} \in \mathbb{Z}_q^{k+\eta}$, we denote the upper k elements by $\overline{\mathbf{v}} \in \mathbb{Z}_q^k$ and the lower η elements of $\mathbf{v}$ by $\underline{\mathbf{v}} \in \mathbb{Z}_q^\eta$. We use $\mathbf{A}^{-\top}$ as shorthand for $\left(\mathbf{A}^{-1}\right)^{\top}$. $\mathsf{GL}_k(\mathbb{Z}_q)$ denotes the set of invertible $k \times k$ matrices in $\mathbb{Z}_q$. $\mathbf{I}_k$ is the $k \times k$ identity matrix. For a matrix $\mathbf{A} \in \mathbb{Z}_q^{n \times m}$, we use $\mathsf{Span}(\mathbf{A}) := \left\{ \mathbf{Av} \mid \mathbf{v} \in \mathbb{Z}_q^m \right\}$ to denote the linear span of $\mathbf{A}$ and – unless state otherwise – $\mathbf{A}^{\perp}$ denotes an arbitrary matrix with $\mathsf{Span}\left(\mathbf{A}^{\perp}\right) = \left\{ \mathbf{v} \mid \mathbf{A}^{\top}\mathbf{v} = \mathbf{0} \right\}$.

For a set $\mathcal{S}$ and $n \in \mathbb{N}_+$, $\mathcal{S}^n$ denotes the set of all n-tuples with components in $\mathcal{S}$ and $\mathcal{S}^* := \bigcup_{n=1}^{\infty} \mathcal{S}^n$. For an n-tuple or string $\mathsf{m} \in \mathcal{S}^n$, $\mathsf{m}_i \in \mathcal{S}$ and $\mathsf{m}[\![i]\!] \in \mathcal{S}$ both denote the i-th component of m ($1 \leq i \leq n$) and $\mathsf{m}_{|i} \in \mathcal{S}^i$ denotes the prefix of length i of m.

All algorithms in this paper are probabilistic polynomial-time unless we state otherwise. If $\mathcal{A}$ is an algorithm, then we write $a \xleftarrow{\$} \mathcal{A}(b)$ to denote the random variable outputted by $\mathcal{A}$ on input b.

GAMES. Following [6], we use code-based games to define and prove security. A game G contains procedures INIT and FINALIZE, and some additional procedures $P_1, \ldots, P_n$, which are defined in pseudo-code. Initially all variables in a game are undefined (denoted by $\bot$), all sets are empty (denote by $\emptyset$), and all partial maps (denoted by $f : A \dashrightarrow B$) are totally undefined. An adversary $\mathcal{A}$ is executed in game G (denote by $\mathsf{G}^{\mathcal{A}}$) if it first calls INIT, obtaining its output. Next, it may make arbitrary queries to P_i (according to their specification), again obtaining their output. Finally, it makes one single call to FINALIZE$(\cdot)$ and stops. We use $\mathsf{G}^{\mathcal{A}} \Rightarrow d$ to denote that G outputs d after interacting with $\mathcal{A}$, and d is the output of FINALIZE. $T(\mathcal{A})$ denotes the running time of $\mathcal{A}$.

2.1   Pairing Groups and Matrix Diffie-Hellman Assumptions

Let GGen be a probabilistic polynomial-time (PPT) algorithm that on input 1^λ returns a description $\mathcal{G} := (\mathbb{G}_1, \mathbb{G}_2, \mathbb{G}_T, q, P_1, P_2, e)$ of asymmetric pairing groups where $\mathbb{G}_1$, $\mathbb{G}_2$, $\mathbb{G}_T$ are cyclic groups of order q for a λ-bit prime q. The group elements P_1 and P_2 are generators of $\mathbb{G}_1$ and $\mathbb{G}_2$, respectively. The function $e : \mathbb{G}_1 \times \mathbb{G}_2 \to \mathbb{G}_T$ is an efficient computable (non-degenerated) bilinear map. Define $P_T := e(P_1, P_2)$, which is a generator in $\mathbb{G}_T$. In this paper, we only consider Type III pairings, where $\mathbb{G}_1 \neq \mathbb{G}_2$ and there is no efficient homomorphism between them. All constructions in this paper can be easily instantiated with Type I pairings by setting $\mathbb{G}_1 = \mathbb{G}_2$ and defining the dimension k to be greater than 1.

We use the implicit representation of group elements as in [11]. For $s \in \{1, 2, T\}$ and $a \in \mathbb{Z}_q$ define $[a]_s = aP_s \in \mathbb{G}_s$ as the implicit representation of a in $\mathbb{G}_s$. Similarly, for a matrix $\mathbf{A} = (a_{ij}) \in \mathbb{Z}_q^{n \times m}$ we define $[\mathbf{A}]_s$ as the implicit representation of $\mathbf{A}$ in $\mathbb{G}_s$. $\mathsf{Span}(\mathbf{A}) := \{\mathbf{Ar} | \mathbf{r} \in \mathbb{Z}_q^m\} \subset \mathbb{Z}_q^n$ denotes the linear span of $\mathbf{A}$, and similarly $\mathsf{Span}([\mathbf{A}]_s) := \{[\mathbf{Ar}]_s | \mathbf{r} \in \mathbb{Z}_q^m\} \subset \mathbb{G}_s^n$. Note that it is efficient to compute $[\mathbf{AB}]_s$ given $([\mathbf{A}]_s, \mathbf{B})$ or $(\mathbf{A}, [\mathbf{B}]_s)$ with matching dimensions. We define $[\mathbf{A}]_1 \circ [\mathbf{B}]_2 := e([\mathbf{A}]_1, [\mathbf{B}]_2) = [\mathbf{AB}]_T$, which can be efficiently computed given $[\mathbf{A}]_1$ and $[\mathbf{B}]_2$.

Next we recall the definition of the matrix Diffie-Hellman (MDDH) and related assumptions [11].

Definition 1 (Matrix distribution). *Let* $k, \ell \in \mathbb{N}$ *with* $\ell > k$. *We call* $\mathcal{D}_{\ell,k}$ *a matrix distribution if it outputs matrices in* $\mathbb{Z}_q^{\ell \times k}$ *of full rank* k *in polynomial time.*

Without loss of generality, we assume the first k rows of $\mathbf{A} \xleftarrow{\$} \mathcal{D}_{\ell,k}$ form an invertible matrix. The $\mathcal{D}_{\ell,k}$-matrix Diffie-Hellman problem is to distinguish the two distributions $([\mathbf{A}], [\mathbf{Aw}])$ and $([\mathbf{A}], [\mathbf{u}])$ where $\mathbf{A} \xleftarrow{\$} \mathcal{D}_{\ell,k}$, $\mathbf{w} \xleftarrow{\$} \mathbb{Z}_q^k$ and $\mathbf{u} \xleftarrow{\$} \mathbb{Z}_q^\ell$.

Definition 2 ($\mathcal{D}_{\ell,k}$-matrix Diffie-Hellman assumption). *Let* $\mathcal{D}_{\ell,k}$ *be a matrix distribution and* $s \in \{1, 2, T\}$. *We say that the* $\mathcal{D}_{\ell,k}$-*matrix Diffie-Hellman ($\mathcal{D}_{\ell,k}$-MDDH) assumption holds relative to* PGGen *in group* $\mathbb{G}_s$ *if for all PPT adversaries* $\mathcal{A}$, *it holds that*

$$\mathsf{Adv}_{\mathcal{D}_{\ell,k}, \mathsf{PGGen}, s}^{\mathsf{mddh}}(\mathcal{A}) := |\Pr[\mathcal{A}(\mathcal{PG}, [\mathbf{A}]_s, [\mathbf{Aw}]_s) = 1] - \Pr[\mathcal{A}(\mathcal{PG}, [\mathbf{A}]_s, [\mathbf{u}]_s) = 1]|$$

is negligible where the probability is taken over $\mathcal{PG} \xleftarrow{\$} \mathsf{PGGen}(1^\lambda)$, $\mathbf{A} \xleftarrow{\$} \mathcal{D}_{\ell,k}$, $\mathbf{w} \xleftarrow{\$} \mathbb{Z}_q^k$ *and* $\mathbf{u} \xleftarrow{\$} \mathbb{Z}_q^\ell$.

The uniform distribution is a particular matrix distribution that deserves special attention, as an adversary breaking the $\mathcal{U}_{\ell,k}$ assumption can also distinguish between real MDDH tuples and random tuples for all other possible matrix distributions. For uniform distributions, they stated in [13] that $\mathcal{U}_k$-MDDH and $\mathcal{U}_{\ell,k}$-MDDH assumptions are equivalent.

Definition 3 (Uniform distribution). *Let* $k, \ell \in \mathbb{N}_+$ *with* $\ell > k$. *We call* $\mathcal{U}_{\ell,k}$ *a uniform distribution if it outputs uniformly random matrices in* $\mathbb{Z}_q^{\ell \times k}$ *of rank* k *in polynomial time. Let* $\mathcal{U}_k := \mathcal{U}_{k+1,k}$.

Lemma 1 ($\mathcal{U}_{\ell,k}$-MDDH $\Leftrightarrow$ $\mathcal{U}_k$-MDDH [13]). *Let* $\ell, k \in \mathbb{N}_+$ *with* $\ell > k$. *An* $\mathcal{U}_{\ell,k}$-MDDH *instance is as hard as an* $\mathcal{U}_k$-MDDH *instance. More precisely, for each adversary* $\mathcal{A}$ *there exists an adversary* $\mathcal{B}$ *and vice versa with*

$$\mathsf{Adv}_{\mathcal{U}_{\ell,k}, \mathsf{PGGen}, s}^{\mathsf{mddh}}(\mathcal{A}) = \mathsf{Adv}_{\mathcal{U}_k, \mathsf{PGGen}, s}^{\mathsf{mddh}}(\mathcal{B})$$

and $T(\mathcal{A}) \approx T(\mathcal{B})$.

Lemma 2 ($\mathcal{D}_{\ell,k}$-MDDH $\Rightarrow$ $\mathcal{U}_k$-MDDH [11]). *Let $\ell, k \in \mathbb{N}_+$ with $\ell > k$ and let $\mathcal{D}_{\ell,k}$ be a matrix distribution. A $\mathcal{U}_k$-MDDH instance is at least as hard as an $\mathcal{D}_{\ell,k}$ instance. More precisely, for each adversary $\mathcal{A}$ there exists an adversary $\mathcal{B}$ with*

$$\mathsf{Adv}^{\mathsf{mddh}}_{\mathcal{U}_k,\mathsf{PGGen},s}(\mathcal{A}) \leq \mathsf{Adv}^{\mathsf{mddh}}_{\mathcal{D}_{\ell,k},\mathsf{PGGen},s}(\mathcal{B})$$

and $T(\mathcal{A}) \approx T(\mathcal{B})$.

For $Q \in \mathbb{N}_+$, $\mathbf{W} \xleftarrow{\$} \mathbb{Z}_q^{k \times Q}$, $\mathbf{U} \xleftarrow{\$} \mathbb{Z}_q^{\ell \times Q}$, consider the Q-fold $\mathcal{D}_{\ell,k}$-MDDH problem which is distinguishing the distributions $(\mathcal{PG}, [\mathbf{A}], [\mathbf{AW}])$ and $(\mathcal{PG}, [\mathbf{A}], [\mathbf{U}])$. That is, the Q-fold $\mathcal{D}_{\ell,k}$-MDDH problem contains Q independent instances of the $\mathcal{D}_{\ell,k}$-MDDH problem (with the same $\mathbf{A}$ but different $\mathbf{w}_i$). By a hybrid argument, one can show that the two problems are equivalent, where the reduction loses a factor Q. The following lemma gives a tight reduction.

Lemma 3 (Random self-reducibility [11]). *For $\ell > k$ and any matrix distribution $\mathcal{D}_{\ell,k}$, the $\mathcal{D}_{\ell,k}$-MDDH assumption is random self-reducible. In particular, for any $Q \in \mathbb{N}_+$ and any adversary $\mathcal{A}$ there exists an adversary $\mathcal{B}$ with*

$$(\ell - k)\mathsf{Adv}^{\mathsf{mddh}}_{\mathcal{D}_{\ell,k},\mathsf{PGGen},s}(\mathcal{B}) + \frac{1}{q-1} \geq \mathsf{Adv}^{Q\text{-mddh}}_{\mathcal{D}_{\ell,k},\mathsf{PGGen},s}(\mathcal{A}) :=$$

$$\left| \Pr[\mathcal{A}(\mathcal{PG}, [\mathbf{A}], [\mathbf{AW}] \Rightarrow 1)] - \Pr[\mathcal{A}(\mathcal{PG}, [\mathbf{A}], [\mathbf{U}] \Rightarrow 1)] \right|,$$

where $\mathcal{PG} \xleftarrow{\$} \mathsf{PGGen}(1^\lambda)$, $\mathbf{A} \xleftarrow{\$} \mathcal{D}_{\ell,k}$, $\mathbf{W} \xleftarrow{\$} \mathbb{Z}_q^{k \times Q}$, $\mathbf{U} \xleftarrow{\$} \mathbb{Z}_q^{(k+1) \times Q}$, and $T(\mathcal{B}) \approx T(\mathcal{A}) + Q \cdot \mathsf{poly}(\lambda)$, where poly is a polynomial independent of $\mathcal{A}$.

To reduce the Q-fold $\mathcal{U}_{\ell,k}$-MDDH assumption to the $\mathcal{U}_k$-MDDH assumption we have to apply Lemma 3 to get from Q-fold $\mathcal{U}_{\ell,k}$-MDDH to standard $\mathcal{U}_{\ell,k}$-MDDH and then Lemma 1 to get from $\mathcal{U}_{\ell,k}$-MDDH to $\mathcal{U}_k$-MDDH. Thus for every adversary $\mathcal{A}$ there exists an adversary $\mathcal{B}$ with

$$\mathsf{Adv}^{Q\text{-mddh}}_{\mathcal{U}_{\ell,k},\mathsf{PGGen},s}(\mathcal{A}) \leq (\ell - k)\mathsf{Adv}^{\mathsf{mddh}}_{\mathcal{U}_k,\mathsf{PGGen},s}(\mathcal{B}) + \frac{1}{q-1}.$$

Formal definitions of collision-resistant hash functions (CRHF) and message authentication codes (MACs) can be found in the full version.

3   Unbounded Affine MAC

3.1   Core Lemmata

The following two core Lemmata contain the main ingredient for the security proof of our new unbounded MAC. They form the main technical novelty of this work. Lemma 4 abstracts the technique used in [30]. It shows that the prototypic MAC $\mathsf{MAC}_{\mathsf{lin}}$ allows the injection of randomness in the tags.

We give a brief overview of how MAC_u is constructed from $\mathsf{MAC}_{\mathsf{lin}}$: For a p-level hierarchical message $\mathsf{m} := (\mathsf{m}_1, \ldots, \mathsf{m}_p) \in (\{0,1\}^\gamma)^p$, we divide it into

p pieces $\mathsf{hm}_1, \ldots, \mathsf{hm}_p$ and each $\mathsf{hm}_i := H(m_1, \ldots, m_i)$ where H is a collision-resistant hash function (CRHF). For each hm_i we apply $\mathsf{MAC}_{\mathsf{lin}}$ on it and the purpose of $\mathsf{MAC}_{\mathsf{lin}}$ is to inject suitable randomness at the local level.

Lemma 5 is then used to move the entropy from $\mathbf{u}_p$ to the vector $\tilde{\mathbf{u}}$ and randomize it. This makes the user secret keys information-theoretically independent from the secret $\mathbf{x}'$ and allows us to randomize h_K in the CHAL queries.

$\mathsf{Gen}_{\mathsf{MAC}}(1^\lambda)$:

$\mathcal{PG} \stackrel{\$}{\leftarrow} \mathsf{PGGen}(1^\lambda)$
parse $\mathcal{PG} =: (\mathbb{G}_1, \mathbb{G}_2, \mathbb{G}_T, q, P_1, P_2, e)$
$\mathbf{B} \stackrel{\$}{\leftarrow} \mathcal{U}_{3k,k}$
for $j \in \{1, \ldots, \gamma\}$, $b \in \{0,1\}$ **do**
$\quad \lfloor \mathbf{X}_{j,b} \stackrel{\$}{\leftarrow} \mathbb{Z}_q^{k \times 3k}$
return $\mathsf{sk}_{\mathsf{MAC}} := (\mathbf{B}, (\mathbf{X}_{j,b})_{1 \le j \le \gamma, b \in \{0,1\}})$

$\mathsf{Tag}(\mathsf{sk}_{\mathsf{MAC}}, \mathsf{hm} \in \{0,1\}^\gamma)$:

parse $\mathsf{sk}_{\mathsf{MAC}} =: (\mathbf{B}, (\mathbf{X}_{j,b})_{1 \le j \le \gamma, b \in \{0,1\}})$
$\mathbf{s} \stackrel{\$}{\leftarrow} \mathbb{Z}_q^k$; $\mathbf{t} := \mathbf{Bs}$
$\mathbf{u} := \sum_{j=1}^\gamma \mathbf{X}_{j, \mathsf{hm}[j]} \mathbf{t} \in \mathbb{Z}_q^k$
return $\tau := ([\mathbf{t}]_2, [\mathbf{u}]_2)$

$\mathsf{Ver}_{\mathsf{MAC}}(\mathsf{sk}_{\mathsf{MAC}}, \mathsf{hm} \in \{0,1\}^\gamma, \tau)$:

parse $\mathsf{sk}_{\mathsf{MAC}} =: (\mathbf{B}, (\mathbf{X}_{j,b})_{1 \le j \le \gamma, b \in \{0,1\}})$
parse $\tau =: ([\mathbf{t}]_2, [\mathbf{u}]_2)$
$\mathbf{h} \stackrel{\$}{\leftarrow} \mathbb{Z}_q^k$
$\mathbf{h}_0 := \sum_{j=1}^\gamma \mathbf{X}_{j, \mathsf{hm}^*[j]}^\top \mathbf{h}$
return $e([\mathbf{h}^\top]_1, [\mathbf{u}]_2) \stackrel{?}{=} e([\mathbf{h}_0^\top]_1, [\mathbf{t}]_2)$

Fig. 1. Our linear MAC $\mathsf{MAC}_{\mathsf{lin}}$ for the message space $\{0,1\}^\gamma$

RANDOMNESS INJECTION LEMMA. We start our exposition with a message authentication code (MAC) with linear structure[3] in Fig. 1, $\mathsf{MAC}_{\mathsf{lin}}$. This MAC scheme is abstracted from [30]. The tags of this MAC can be verified by checking whether $\mathbf{u} = \sum_{j=1}^\gamma \mathbf{X}_{j, \mathsf{hm}[j]} \mathbf{t}$, but we require the more sophisticated randomized verification procedure as in Fig. 1 for the transformation to an unbounded HIBE later.

The MAC $\mathsf{MAC}_{\mathsf{lin}}$ is correct, since

$$e([\mathbf{h}^\top]_1, [\mathbf{u}]_2) => \mathbf{h}^\top \sum_{j=1}^\gamma \mathbf{X}_{j, \mathsf{hm}[j]} \mathbf{t} = e([\mathbf{h}_0^\top]_1, [\mathbf{t}]_2).$$

Our $\mathsf{MAC}_{\mathsf{lin}}$ is a stepping stone for our unbounded MAC for constructing HIBEs. For the transformation to unbounded HIBE our $\mathsf{MAC}_{\mathsf{lin}}$ satisfies a special security notion which is captured by Lemma 4. This security notion needs to combine with Lemma 5 to get a secure MAC for the unbounded HIBE (cf. Sect. 3.2).

In the security experiment (defined in Fig. 2), the adversary gets values in dk_1 that allow her to rerandomize tags. These values also allows her to forge

---

[3] We call it "linear" since it matches the affine MAC definition from [6] without using the affine part, i.e. the message dependent part $\mathbf{u}$ of the tags depends linear on the randomness $\mathbf{t}$ of the tags.

INIT$_{ri}$:	EVAL$_{ri}$(hm $\in \{0,1\}^\gamma$):
$\mathbf{B} \overset{\$}{\leftarrow} \mathcal{U}_{3k,k}$	**if** hm $\in \mathcal{Q}_{hm}$ **then return** $\perp$
for $j \in \{1,\ldots,\gamma\}$, $b \in \{0,1\}$ **do**	$\mathcal{Q}_{hm} := \mathcal{Q}_{hm} \cup \{hm\}$
$\quad \left\lfloor \mathbf{X}_{j,b} \overset{\$}{\leftarrow} \mathbb{Z}_q^{k\times 3k} \right.$	$\mathbf{s} \overset{\$}{\leftarrow} \mathbb{Z}_q^k$; $\mathbf{t} := \mathbf{B}\mathbf{s}$
$dk_1 := \left([\mathbf{X}_{j,b}\mathbf{B}]_2 \right)_{1 \le j \le \gamma, b \in \{0,1\}}$	$\boxed{\mathbf{t} \overset{\$}{\leftarrow} \mathbb{Z}_q^{3k}}$
return $\left([\mathbf{B}]_2, dk_1 \right)$	$\mathbf{u} := \sum_{j=1}^{\gamma} \mathbf{X}_{j,hm[j]}\mathbf{t} \in \mathbb{Z}_q^k$
	$\boxed{\mathbf{u} \overset{\$}{\leftarrow} \mathbb{Z}_q^k}$
CHAL$_{ri}$(hm$^\star \in \{0,1\}^\gamma$):	**return** $\tau := \left([\mathbf{t}]_2, [\mathbf{u}]_2 \right)$
$\mathcal{C}_{hm} := \mathcal{C}_{hm} \cup \{hm^\star\}$	
$\mathbf{h} \overset{\$}{\leftarrow} \mathbb{Z}_q^k$	FINALIZE$_{ri}$($\beta \in \{0,1\}$):
$\mathbf{h}_0 := \sum_{j=1}^{\gamma} \mathbf{X}_{j,hm^\star[j]}^\top \mathbf{h}$	**return** $\left(\mathcal{C}_{hm} \cap \mathcal{Q}_{hm} \overset{?}{=} \emptyset \right) \wedge \beta$
$\boxed{\mathbf{h}_0 := \mathbf{h}_0 + \mathbf{B}^\perp \mathsf{RF}(hm^\star)^\top \mathbf{h}}$	
return $\left([\mathbf{h}]_1, [\mathbf{h}_0]_1 \right)$	

Fig. 2. Games RI$_{real}$ and $\boxed{\text{RI}_{rand}}$ that define the security of MAC$_{lin}$. The function RF : $\{0,1\}^\gamma \to \mathbb{Z}_q^{k \times 2k}$ is a random function, defined on-the-fly.

arbitrary tags. This is the reason why it is not a secure MAC, but the goal of the adversary here is not to forge a tag, but to distinguish two games RI$_{real}$ and RI$_{rand}$. More precisely, $\mathcal{A}$ gets access to two oracles, EVAL$_{ri}$ that gives her a tag for a message, and CHAL$_{ri}$ that gives her necessary values to check validity of a tag. She can query these two oracles arbitrary times in an adaptive manner, but for each message $\mathcal{A}$ can query it for either EVAL$_{ri}$ or CHAL$_{ri}$, but not both. $\mathcal{A}$ wins if she can distinguish game RI$_{real}$ from RI$_{rand}$. For technical reasons the verification tokens are also randomized over Span($\mathbf{B}^\perp$) when the tags are random. The formal security game can be found in Fig. 2. Interestingly, Lemma 4 can be used to prove the security of LP HIBEs in [30] in a black-box manner. Essentially, Lemma 4 has a similar purpose as the core lemma in [15], namely, to inject randomness.

Lemma 4 (Randomness Injection Lemma). *For all adversaries $\mathcal{A}$ there exist adversaries $\mathcal{B}_1$ and $\mathcal{B}_2$ with*

$$\left| \Pr\left[\text{RI}_{real}^{\mathcal{A}} \Rightarrow 1 \right] - \Pr\left[\text{RI}_{rand}^{\mathcal{A}} \Rightarrow 1 \right] \right| \le (8k\gamma + 2k)\mathsf{Adv}_{\mathcal{U}_k,\mathsf{PGGen},2}^{\mathsf{mddh}}(\mathcal{B}_1)$$

$$+ k\gamma \mathsf{Adv}_{\mathcal{U}_k,\mathsf{PGGen},1}^{\mathsf{mddh}}(\mathcal{B}_2) + \frac{\gamma Q_c + 6\gamma + 1}{q-1} + \frac{Q_e}{q^{2k}}$$

and $T(\mathcal{B}_1) \approx T(\mathcal{B}_2) \approx T(\mathcal{A}) + (Q_e + Q_c) \cdot \mathsf{poly}(\lambda)$, where Q_e resp. Q_c denotes the number of EVAL$_{ri}$ resp. CHAL$_{ri}$ queries of $\mathcal{A}$ and poly is a polynomial independent of $\mathcal{A}$. RI$_{real}$ and RI$_{rand}$ are defined as in Fig. 2.

We give the overall hybrids used to prove this Lemma in Fig. 3. The proof can be found in the full version.

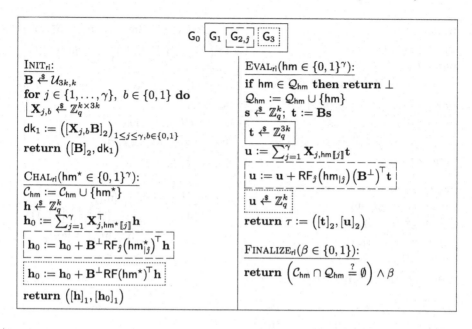

Fig. 3. Hybrids for the security proof of Lemma 4.

RANDOMNESS PACKING LEMMA. We will use a tight variant of the Lewko-Waters approach [33] to tie these local, linear tags together and move entropy from the local to the global part. Lemma 5 captures this approach.

Lemma 5 (Randomness Packing Lemma). *For all adversaries $\mathcal{A}$ there exist adversaries $\mathcal{B}_1$ and $\mathcal{B}_2$ with*

$$\left| \Pr\left[\mathsf{RP}_{\mathsf{real}}^{\mathcal{A}} \Rightarrow 1 \right] - \Pr\left[\mathsf{RP}_{\mathsf{rand}}^{\mathcal{A}} \Rightarrow 1 \right] \right| \leq 2k\mathsf{Adv}_{\mathcal{U}_k,\mathsf{PGGen},2}^{\mathsf{mddh}}(\mathcal{B}_1)$$

$$+ k\mathsf{Adv}_{\mathcal{U}_k,\mathsf{PGGen},1}^{\mathsf{mddh}}(\mathcal{B}_2) + \frac{6}{q-1}$$

and $T(\mathcal{B}_1) \approx T(\mathcal{B}_2) \approx T(\mathcal{A}) + (Q_e + Q_c) \cdot \mathsf{poly}(\lambda)$, where Q_e resp. Q_c denotes the number of $\mathrm{EVAL}_{\mathsf{rp}}$ resp. $\mathrm{CHAL}_{\mathsf{rp}}$ queries of $\mathcal{A}$ and poly is a polynomial independent of $\mathcal{A}$. $\mathsf{RP}_{\mathsf{real}}$ and $\mathsf{RP}_{\mathsf{rand}}$ are defined as in Fig. 5.

Proof. The proof uses a hybrid argument with hybrids G_0 (the $\mathsf{RP}_{\mathsf{real}}$ game), G_1, G_2, and G_3 (the $\mathsf{RP}_{\mathsf{rand}}$ game). The hybrids are given in Fig. 6. A summary can be found in Table 2.

Lemma 6. $(\mathsf{G}_0 \rightsquigarrow \mathsf{G}_1)$. *For all adversaries $\mathcal{A}$ there exists an adversary $\mathcal{B}$ with*

$$\left| \Pr[\mathsf{G}_0^{\mathcal{A}} \Rightarrow 1] - \Pr[\mathsf{G}_1^{\mathcal{A}} \Rightarrow 1] \right| \leq k\mathsf{Adv}_{\mathcal{U}_k,\mathsf{PGGen},2}^{\mathsf{mddh}}(\mathcal{B}) + \frac{1}{q-1}$$

and $T(\mathcal{B}) \approx T(\mathcal{A}) + (Q_e + Q_c) \cdot \mathsf{poly}(\lambda)$.

$\underline{\mathsf{Gen_{MAC}}(1^\lambda):}$

$\mathcal{PG} \xleftarrow{\$} \mathsf{PGGen}(1^\lambda)$
parse $\mathcal{PG} =: (\mathbb{G}_1, \mathbb{G}_2, \mathbb{G}_T, q, P_1, P_2, e)$
$H \xleftarrow{\$} \mathcal{H}(1^\lambda);\ \mathbf{B} \xleftarrow{\$} \mathcal{U}_{3k,k};\ \tilde{\mathbf{B}} \xleftarrow{\$} \mathcal{U}_{2k,k}$

for $j \in \{1, \ldots, \gamma\},\ b \in \{0,1\}$ **do**
$\quad \mathbf{X}_{j,b} \xleftarrow{\$} \mathbb{Z}_q^{k \times 3k}$

$\tilde{\mathbf{X}}_1 \xleftarrow{\$} \mathbb{Z}_q^{k \times 2k};\ \tilde{\mathbf{X}}_2 \xleftarrow{\$} \mathbb{Z}_q^{k \times 2k};\ \mathbf{x}' \xleftarrow{\$} \mathbb{Z}_q^k$
return $\mathsf{sk_{MAC}}$

$\underline{\mathsf{Tag}(\mathsf{sk_{MAC}}, \mathsf{m} = (\mathsf{m}_1, \ldots, \mathsf{m}_p) \in \mathcal{S}^*):}$
for $i \in \{1, \ldots, p\}$ **do**
$\quad \mathbf{s}_i \xleftarrow{\$} \mathbb{Z}_q^k;\ \mathbf{t}_i := \mathbf{B}\mathbf{s}_i$
$\quad \tilde{\mathbf{s}}_i \xleftarrow{\$} \mathbb{Z}_q^k;\ \tilde{\mathbf{t}}_i := \tilde{\mathbf{B}}\tilde{\mathbf{s}}_i$
$\quad \mathsf{hm}_i := H(\mathsf{m}_1, \ldots, \mathsf{m}_i)$
$\quad \mathbf{u}_i := \sum_{j=1}^{\gamma} \mathbf{X}_{j,\mathsf{hm}_i[j]}\mathbf{t}_i + \tilde{\mathbf{X}}_1 \tilde{\mathbf{t}}_i$

$\tilde{\mathbf{u}} := \sum_{i=1}^p \tilde{\mathbf{X}}_2 \tilde{\mathbf{t}}_i + \mathbf{x}'$
return $\left(([\mathbf{t}_i]_2, [\tilde{\mathbf{t}}_i]_2, [\mathbf{u}_i]_2)_{1 \le i \le p}, [\tilde{\mathbf{u}}]_2 \right)$

$\underline{\mathsf{Ver_{MAC}}(\mathsf{sk_{MAC}}, \mathsf{m} = (\mathsf{m}_1, \ldots, \mathsf{m}_p) \in \mathcal{S}^*, \tau):}$

$\tau =: \left(([\mathbf{t}_i]_2, [\tilde{\mathbf{t}}_i]_2, [\mathbf{u}_i]_2)_{1 \le i \le p}, [\tilde{\mathbf{u}}]_2 \right)$
$\tilde{\mathbf{h}} \xleftarrow{\$} \mathbb{Z}_q^k$
for $i \in \{1, \ldots, p\}$ **do**
$\quad \mathbf{h}_i \xleftarrow{\$} \mathbb{Z}_q^k$
$\quad \mathsf{hm}_i := H(\mathsf{m}_1, \ldots, \mathsf{m}_i)$
$\quad \mathbf{h}_{0,i} := \sum_{j=1}^{\gamma} \mathbf{X}_{j,\mathsf{hm}_i[j]}^\top \mathbf{h}_i$
$\quad \tilde{\mathbf{h}}_{0,i} := \tilde{\mathbf{X}}_1^\top \mathbf{h}_i + \tilde{\mathbf{X}}_2^\top \tilde{\mathbf{h}}$
$h_K := (\mathbf{x}')^\top \tilde{\mathbf{h}}$
return $\sum_{i=1}^p \big(e([\mathbf{h}_i^\top]_1, [\mathbf{u}_i]_2)$
$\quad - e([\mathbf{h}_{0,i}^\top]_1, [\mathbf{t}_i]_2) - e([\tilde{\mathbf{h}}_{0,i}^\top]_1, [\tilde{\mathbf{t}}_i]_2) \big)$
$\quad + e([\tilde{\mathbf{h}}]_1, [\tilde{\mathbf{u}}]_2) \stackrel{?}{=} [h_K]_T$

Fig. 4. Our unbounded affine MAC MAC_u. It uses a CRHF $\mathcal{H}$ with domain $\mathcal{S}^*$ and range $\{0,1\}^\gamma$. Throughout the scheme, $\mathsf{sk_{MAC}} := \big(H, \mathbf{B}, \tilde{\mathbf{B}}, (\mathbf{X}_{j,b})_{1 \le j \le \gamma, b \in \{0,1\}}, \tilde{\mathbf{X}}_1, \tilde{\mathbf{X}}_2, \mathbf{x}' \big)$ with values generated in $\mathsf{Gen_{MAC}}$. The linear MAC components are highlighted in gray.

Proof. The only difference between these two games is, that the EVAL queries pick the vectors $\tilde{\mathbf{t}}$ uniformly random from $\mathbb{Z}_q^{2k}$ instead of only from $\mathsf{Span}(\tilde{\mathbf{B}})$. This leads to a straightforward reduction to the Q_e-fold $\mathcal{U}_{2k,k}$-MDDH assumption on $\tilde{\mathbf{B}}$. $\qquad \square$

Lemma 7 ($\mathsf{G}_1 \rightsquigarrow \mathsf{G}_2$). *For all adversaries $\mathcal{A}$ there exists an adversary $\mathcal{B}$ with*

$$\big| \Pr[\mathsf{G}_1^{\mathcal{A}} \Rightarrow 1] - \Pr[\mathsf{G}_2^{\mathcal{A}} \Rightarrow 1] \big| \le k\mathsf{Adv}_{\mathcal{U}_k,\mathsf{PGGen},1}^{\mathsf{mddh}}(\mathcal{B}) + \frac{2}{q-1}$$

and $T(\mathcal{B}) \approx T(\mathcal{A}) + (Q_e + Q_c) \cdot \mathsf{poly}(\lambda)$.

Proof. In game G_2 the $\bar{\mathbf{B}}^\perp$-part of $\tilde{\mathbf{h}}_0$ (for all $i \in \{1, \ldots, p\}$) is uniformly random. To switch to this game, pick a Q_c-fold $\mathcal{U}_{2k,k}$-MDDH challenge and use the reduction in Fig. 7.

Assume that $\bar{\mathbf{D}}$ is invertible. This happens with probability at least $(1 - 1/(q-1))$. The INIT, EVAL, and FINALIZE oracles are identical in both games. The reduction correctly simulates INIT because the summand $\bar{\mathbf{D}}^{-\top} \underline{\mathbf{D}}^\top (\tilde{\mathbf{B}}^\perp)^\top$ cancels out in public key.

INIT_{rp}:
$\tilde{\mathbf{B}} \xleftarrow{\$} \mathcal{U}_{2k,k}$
$\tilde{\mathbf{X}}_1 \xleftarrow{\$} \mathbb{Z}_q^{k \times 2k}; \ \tilde{\mathbf{X}}_2 \xleftarrow{\$} \mathbb{Z}_q^{k \times 2k}$
$\text{dk}_2 := \left(\left[\tilde{\mathbf{X}}_1\tilde{\mathbf{B}}\right]_2, \left[\tilde{\mathbf{X}}_2\tilde{\mathbf{B}}\right]_2\right)$
$\textbf{return } \left(\left[\tilde{\mathbf{B}}\right]_2, \text{dk}_2\right)$

$\text{CHAL}_{\text{rp}}\left(\tilde{\mathbf{h}} \in \mathbb{Z}_q^k\right)$:
$\mathbf{h} \xleftarrow{\$} \mathbb{Z}_q^k$
$\tilde{\mathbf{h}}_0 := \tilde{\mathbf{X}}_1^\top \mathbf{h} + \tilde{\mathbf{X}}_2^\top \tilde{\mathbf{h}}$
$\boxed{\mathbf{r} \xleftarrow{\$} \mathbb{Z}_q^k; \ \tilde{\mathbf{h}}_0 := \tilde{\mathbf{h}}_0 + \tilde{\mathbf{B}}^\perp \mathbf{r}}$
$\textbf{return } \left([\mathbf{h}]_1, \left[\tilde{\mathbf{h}}_0\right]_1\right)$

EVAL_{rp}:
$\tilde{\mathbf{s}} \xleftarrow{\$} \mathbb{Z}_q^k; \ \tilde{\mathbf{t}} := \tilde{\mathbf{B}}\tilde{\mathbf{s}}$
$\boxed{\tilde{\mathbf{t}} \xleftarrow{\$} \mathbb{Z}_q^{2k}}$
$\tilde{\mathbf{u}} := \tilde{\mathbf{X}}_2\tilde{\mathbf{t}}$
$\boxed{\tilde{\mathbf{u}} \xleftarrow{\$} \mathbb{Z}_q^k}$
$\textbf{return } \left([\tilde{\mathbf{t}}]_2, [\tilde{\mathbf{u}}]_2\right)$

$\text{FINALIZE}_{\text{rp}}(\beta \in \{0,1\})$:
$\textbf{return } \beta$

Fig. 5. Games RP_{real} and $\boxed{\text{RP}_{\text{rand}}}$ for Lemma 5.

Table 2. Summary of the hybrids in Fig. 6. EVAL_{rp} queries draw $\tilde{\mathbf{t}}$ from the set described by the second column and add a uniform random element from the set $r_{\tilde{\mathbf{u}}}$ to $\tilde{\mathbf{u}}$. The CHAL_{rp} queries add a uniform random element from $r_{\tilde{\mathbf{h}}_0}$ to each $\tilde{\mathbf{h}}_0$. The background color indicates repeated transitions.

Hybrid	$\tilde{\mathbf{t}}$ drawn from	$r_{\tilde{\mathbf{u}}}$	$r_{\tilde{\mathbf{h}}_0}$	Transition
G_0	$\text{Span}(\tilde{\mathbf{B}})$	$\{0\}$	$\{0\}$	—
G_1	$\mathbb{Z}_q^{2k}$	$\{0\}$	$\{0\}$	$\mathcal{U}_k$-MDDH in $\mathbb{G}_2$
G_2	$\mathbb{Z}_q^{2k}$	$\{0\}$	$\text{Span}(\tilde{\mathbf{B}}^\perp)$	$\mathcal{U}_k$-MDDH in $\mathbb{G}_1$
G_3	$\mathbb{Z}_q^{2k}$	$\mathbb{Z}_q^k$	$\text{Span}(\tilde{\mathbf{B}}^\perp)$	$\mathcal{U}_k$-MDDH in $\mathbb{G}_2$

To analyze the CHAL queries define $\mathbf{f}_c =: \begin{pmatrix} \overline{\mathbf{D}}\mathbf{w}_c \\ \underline{\mathbf{D}}\mathbf{w}_c + \mathbf{r}_c \end{pmatrix}$ where $\mathbf{w}_c$ is uniform random in $\mathbb{Z}_q^k$ and $\mathbf{r}_c$ is $\mathbf{0} \in \mathbb{Z}_q^k$ or uniform random in $\mathbb{Z}_q^k$. The reduction defines $\mathbf{h} := \overline{\mathbf{f}_c}$, which is a uniform random vector.

The vector $\tilde{\mathbf{h}}_0$ is then computed as

$$\begin{aligned}
\tilde{\mathbf{h}}_0 &:= \tilde{\mathbf{J}}_1^\top \mathbf{h} + \tilde{\mathbf{X}}_2^\top \tilde{\mathbf{h}} + \tilde{\mathbf{B}}^\perp \underline{\mathbf{f}_c} \\
&= \tilde{\mathbf{J}}_1^\top \mathbf{h} + \tilde{\mathbf{X}}_2^\top \tilde{\mathbf{h}} + \tilde{\mathbf{B}}^\perp \underline{\mathbf{D}} \, \overline{\mathbf{D}}^{-1} \mathbf{h} + \tilde{\mathbf{B}}^\perp \mathbf{r}_c \\
&= \tilde{\mathbf{X}}_1^\top \mathbf{h} + \tilde{\mathbf{X}}_2^\top \tilde{\mathbf{h}} + \tilde{\mathbf{B}}^\perp \mathbf{r}_c
\end{aligned}$$

If $\mathbf{r}_c = \mathbf{0}$, the reduction is simulating game G_1 and if $\mathbf{r}_c$ is uniform, the reduction is simulating G_2. $\qquad \square$

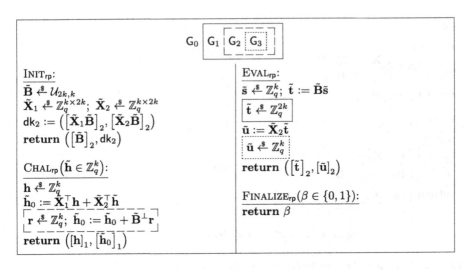

Fig. 6. Hybrids for the security proof of Lemma 5.

Lemma 8 ($G_2 \rightsquigarrow G_3$). *For all adversaries $\mathcal{A}$ there exists an adversary $\mathcal{B}$ with*

$$\left|\Pr\left[G_2^{\mathcal{A}} \Rightarrow 1\right] - \Pr\left[G_3^{\mathcal{A}} \Rightarrow 1\right]\right| \leq k\mathsf{Adv}_{\mathcal{U}_k,\mathsf{PGGen},2}^{\mathsf{mddh}}(\mathcal{B}) + \frac{3}{q-1}$$

and $T(\mathcal{B}) \approx T(\mathcal{A}) + (Q_e + Q_c) \cdot \mathsf{poly}(\lambda)$.

Proof. In game G_3 the vector $\tilde{\mathbf{u}}$ is chosen uniformly random. For the transition to this game, we need a Q_e-fold $\mathcal{U}_{2k,k}$-MDDH challenge. The reduction is given in Fig. 8.

The reduction aborts if the upper or lower $k \times k$-submatrix of $\tilde{\mathbf{B}}$ does not have full rank. This happens only with probability at most $2/(q-1)$. Assume in the following, that the reduction does not abort. Furthermore assume $q > 2$.

The way we defined $\tilde{\mathbf{B}}^\perp$ and $\tilde{\mathbf{B}}'$ we get the following three properties:

$$\left(\tilde{\mathbf{B}}^\perp\right)^\top \tilde{\mathbf{B}} = \overline{\tilde{\mathbf{B}}}^{-1}\overline{\tilde{\mathbf{B}}} - \underline{\tilde{\mathbf{B}}}^{-1}\underline{\tilde{\mathbf{B}}} = \mathbf{I}_k - \mathbf{I}_k = \mathbf{0} \tag{3}$$

$$\left(\tilde{\mathbf{B}}^\perp\right)^\top \tilde{\mathbf{B}}' = \frac{1}{2}\left(\overline{\tilde{\mathbf{B}}}^{-1}\overline{\tilde{\mathbf{B}}} + \underline{\tilde{\mathbf{B}}}^{-1}\underline{\tilde{\mathbf{B}}}\right) = \frac{1}{2}(\mathbf{I}_k + \mathbf{I}_k) = \mathbf{I}_k \tag{4}$$

$\text{INIT}_{rp}:$	$\text{EVAL}_{rp}:$
$\tilde{\mathbf{B}} \xleftarrow{\$} \mathcal{U}_{2k,k}$	$\tilde{\mathbf{t}} \xleftarrow{\$} \mathbb{Z}_q^{2k}$
$\tilde{\mathbf{J}}_1 \xleftarrow{\$} \mathbb{Z}_q^{k \times 2k}; \ \tilde{\mathbf{X}}_2 \xleftarrow{\$} \mathbb{Z}_q^{k \times 2k}$	$\tilde{\mathbf{u}} := \tilde{\mathbf{X}}_2 \tilde{\mathbf{t}}$
// Implicit: $\tilde{\mathbf{X}}_1 := \tilde{\mathbf{J}}_1 + \overline{\mathbf{D}}^{-\top} \underline{\mathbf{D}}^{\top} (\tilde{\mathbf{B}}^{\perp})^{\top}$	return $\left([\tilde{\mathbf{t}}]_2, [\tilde{\mathbf{u}}]_2 \right)$
$\mathsf{dk}_2 := \left([\tilde{\mathbf{J}}_1 \tilde{\mathbf{B}}]_2, [\tilde{\mathbf{X}}_2 \tilde{\mathbf{B}}]_2 \right)$	
return $\left([\tilde{\mathbf{B}}]_2, \mathsf{dk}_2 \right)$	$\text{CHAL}_{rp}(\tilde{\mathbf{h}} \in \mathbb{Z}_q^k):$
	Let this be the c-th CHAL query.
	$\mathbf{h} := \overline{\mathbf{f}_c}$
$\text{FINALIZE}_{rp}(\beta \in \{0,1\}):$	$\tilde{\mathbf{h}}_0 := \tilde{\mathbf{J}}_1^\top \tilde{\mathbf{h}} + \tilde{\mathbf{X}}_2^\top \tilde{\mathbf{h}} + \tilde{\mathbf{B}}^\perp \underline{\mathbf{f}_c}$
return β	return $\left([\mathbf{h}]_1, [\tilde{\mathbf{h}}_0]_1 \right)$

Fig. 7. Reduction for the transition from G_1 to G_2 to the Q_c-fold $\mathcal{U}_{2k,k}$-MDDH challenge $\left([\mathbf{D}]_1, [\mathbf{f}_1]_1, \ldots, [\mathbf{f}_{Q_c}]_1 \right)$.

$\text{INIT}_{rp}:$	$\text{EVAL}_{rp}:$
$\tilde{\mathbf{B}} \xleftarrow{\$} \mathcal{U}_{2k,k}$	Let this be the c-th EVAL query.
if $\text{rank}(\underline{\tilde{\mathbf{B}}}) \neq k \lor \text{rank}(\overline{\tilde{\mathbf{B}}}) \neq k$ then	$\tilde{\mathbf{s}} \xleftarrow{\$} \mathbb{Z}_q^k; \ \tilde{\mathbf{t}} := \tilde{\mathbf{B}}\tilde{\mathbf{s}} + \tilde{\mathbf{B}}'\overline{\mathbf{f}_c}$
$\quad \lfloor$ abort	$\tilde{\mathbf{u}} := \sum_{i=1}^p \tilde{\mathbf{J}}_2 \tilde{\mathbf{t}} + \underline{\mathbf{f}_c}$
$\tilde{\mathbf{B}}^\perp := \begin{pmatrix} \overline{\tilde{\mathbf{B}}}^{-\top} \\ -\underline{\tilde{\mathbf{B}}}^{-\top} \end{pmatrix}; \ \tilde{\mathbf{B}}' := \frac{1}{2} \begin{pmatrix} \overline{\tilde{\mathbf{B}}} \\ -\underline{\tilde{\mathbf{B}}} \end{pmatrix}$	return $\left([\tilde{\mathbf{t}}]_2, [\tilde{\mathbf{u}}]_2 \right)$
$\tilde{\mathbf{X}}_1 \xleftarrow{\$} \mathbb{Z}_q^{k \times 2k}; \ \tilde{\mathbf{J}}_2 \xleftarrow{\$} \mathbb{Z}_q^{k \times 2k}$	$\text{CHAL}_{rp}(\tilde{\mathbf{h}} \in \mathbb{Z}_q^k):$
// Implicit: $\tilde{\mathbf{X}}_2 := \tilde{\mathbf{J}}_2 + \underline{\mathbf{D}}\overline{\mathbf{D}}^{-1}(\tilde{\mathbf{B}}^\perp)^\top$	$\mathbf{h} \xleftarrow{\$} \mathbb{Z}_q^k$
$\mathsf{dk}_2 := \left([\tilde{\mathbf{X}}_1 \tilde{\mathbf{B}}]_2, [\tilde{\mathbf{J}}_2 \tilde{\mathbf{B}}]_2 \right)$	$\mathbf{r} \xleftarrow{\$} \mathbb{Z}_q^k; \ \tilde{\mathbf{h}}_0 := \tilde{\mathbf{X}}_1^\top \mathbf{h} + \tilde{\mathbf{J}}_2^\top \tilde{\mathbf{h}} + \tilde{\mathbf{B}}^\perp \mathbf{r}$
return $\left([\tilde{\mathbf{B}}]_2, \mathsf{dk}_2 \right)$	return $\left([\mathbf{h}]_1, [\tilde{\mathbf{h}}_0]_1 \right)$
	$\text{FINALIZE}_{rp}(\beta \in \{0,1\}):$
	return β

Fig. 8. Reduction for the transition from G_2 to G_3 to the Q_e-fold $\mathcal{U}_{2k,k}$-MDDH challenge $\left([\mathbf{D}]_2, [\mathbf{f}_1]_2, \ldots, [\mathbf{f}_{Q_e}]_2 \right)$.

$$\tilde{\mathbf{B}}, \tilde{\mathbf{B}}' \text{ is a basis of } \mathbb{Z}_q^{2k} \tag{5}$$

To see Eq. (5), note that this is equivalent to the column vectors $\mathbf{b}_1, \ldots, \mathbf{b}_{2k}$ of

$$(\tilde{\mathbf{B}} | 2\tilde{\mathbf{B}}') = \begin{pmatrix} \overline{\tilde{\mathbf{B}}} & \overline{\tilde{\mathbf{B}}} \\ \underline{\tilde{\mathbf{B}}} & -\underline{\tilde{\mathbf{B}}} \end{pmatrix}$$

being linear independent. Assume there exist $\mu_1, \ldots, \mu_{2k} \in \mathbb{Z}_q$ with

$$\mu_1 \mathbf{b}_1 + \cdots + \mu_{2k} \mathbf{b}_{2k} = \mathbf{0}.$$

Looking at the first k entries in each vector and using that $\overline{\tilde{\mathbf{B}}}$ has full rank we get

$$\mu_1 = -\mu_{k+1}, \ldots, \mu_k = -\mu_{2k}.$$

Now looking at the remaining lower k entries and using that the column vectors of $\tilde{\underline{B}}$ can not be $\mathbf{0}$ (because we already assumed that $\tilde{\underline{B}}$ has full rank) we get that

$$\mu_1 = 0, \ldots, \mu_{2k} = 0.$$

The INIT oracle is identically distributed in both games and correctly simulated by the reduction, because the $\underline{D}\overline{D}^{-1}(\tilde{B}^{\perp})^{\top}$ cancels out in the public key.

The CHAL oracle is also distributed identically in both games and simulated correctly since the $\tilde{B}^{\perp}$-part of $\tilde{h}_0$ is uniform random. More precisely, $\mathbf{r}$ is identically distributed to $\mathbf{r} + \overline{D}^{-\top}\underline{D}^{\top}\tilde{h}$. Thus $\tilde{h}_0$ as computed by the reduction:

$$\tilde{h}_0 := \tilde{X}_1^{\top}\mathbf{h} + \tilde{J}_2^{\top}\tilde{h} + \tilde{B}^{\perp}\mathbf{r}$$

is identically distributed to

$$\tilde{X}_1^{\top}\mathbf{h} + \tilde{J}_2^{\top}\tilde{h} + \tilde{B}^{\perp}\left(\mathbf{r} + \overline{D}^{-\top}\underline{D}^{\top}\tilde{h}\right)$$
$$= \tilde{X}_1^{\top}\mathbf{h} + \tilde{X}_2^{\top}\tilde{h} + \tilde{B}^{\perp}\mathbf{r},$$

which is the real $\tilde{h}_0$.

To analyze the EVAL queries, define $\mathbf{f}_c =: \begin{pmatrix} \overline{D}\mathbf{w}_c \\ \underline{D}\mathbf{w}_c + \mathbf{r}_c \end{pmatrix}$ where $\mathbf{w}_c$ is uniform random in $\mathbb{Z}_q^k$ and $\mathbf{r}_c$ is $\mathbf{0} \in \mathbb{Z}_q^k$ or uniform random in $\mathbb{Z}_q^k$. In the EVAL queries the reduction computes $\tilde{t}$ as $\tilde{t} := \tilde{B}\tilde{s} + \tilde{B}'\overline{f_c}$, but this is distributed identically to a uniform random vector, because $\tilde{s}$ and $\overline{f_c}$ are uniform random and $\tilde{B}, \tilde{B}'$ are a basis of $\mathbb{Z}_q^{2k}$ (see Eq. (5)).

The vector $\tilde{u}$ is computed as

$$\tilde{u} := \sum_{i=1}^{p} \tilde{J}_2\tilde{t} + \underline{f_c}$$
$$= \sum_{i=1}^{p} \tilde{J}_2\tilde{t} + \underline{D}\overline{D}^{-1}\overline{f_c} + \mathbf{r}_c$$
$$= \sum_{i=1}^{p} \tilde{J}_2\tilde{t} + \underline{D}\overline{D}^{-1}\underbrace{(\tilde{B}^{\perp})^{\top}\tilde{B}'}_{=\mathbf{I}_k \text{ (Eq. (4))}}\overline{f_c} + \mathbf{r}_c$$
$$\overset{\text{Eq. (3)}}{=} \sum_{i=1}^{p} \tilde{J}_2\tilde{t} + \underline{D}\overline{D}^{-1}(\tilde{B}^{\perp})^{\top}\underbrace{(\tilde{B}\tilde{s} + \tilde{B}'\overline{f_c})}_{=\tilde{t}} + \mathbf{r}_c$$
$$= \sum_{i=1}^{p} \tilde{X}_2\tilde{t} + \mathbf{r}_c.$$

If $\mathbf{r}_c = \mathbf{0}$, the reduction is simulating game G_2 and if $\mathbf{r}_c$ is uniform, the reduction is simulating G_3. □

SUMMARY. To prove Lemma 5, we combine Lemmata 6–8. □

3.2   An Unbounded Affine MAC

Our next step is to construct an unbounded affine MAC as in Fig. 4. Again, our idea is to divide a hierarchical message $(m_1, \ldots, m_p)$ into p pieces $hm_i :=$

<table>
<tr><td>

INIT_{MAC}:

$\text{sk}_{\text{MAC}} \xleftarrow{\$} \text{Gen}_{\text{MAC}}(1^\lambda)$

parse $\text{sk}_{\text{MAC}} =: \left(H, \mathbf{B}, \tilde{\mathbf{B}}, (\mathbf{X}_{j,b})_{1 \le j \le \gamma, b \in \{0,1\}},\right.$
$\left. \tilde{\mathbf{X}}_1, \tilde{\mathbf{X}}_2, \mathbf{x}'\right)$

$\text{dk}_1 := \left([\mathbf{X}_{j,b}\mathbf{B}]_2\right)_{1 \le j \le \gamma, b \in \{0,1\}}$

$\text{dk}_2 := \left([\tilde{\mathbf{X}}_1\tilde{\mathbf{B}}]_2, [\tilde{\mathbf{X}}_2\tilde{\mathbf{B}}]_2\right)$

return $\left(\mathcal{PG}, H, [\mathbf{B}]_2, [\tilde{\mathbf{B}}]_2, \text{dk}_1, \text{dk}_2\right)$

$\text{EVAL}(\mathsf{m} = (\mathsf{m}_1, \ldots, \mathsf{m}_p) \in \mathcal{S}^*)$:

$\mathcal{Q}_{\mathcal{M}} := \mathcal{Q}_{\mathcal{M}} \cup \{\mathsf{m}\}$

return $\text{Tag}(\text{sk}_{\text{MAC}}, \mathsf{m})$

$\text{FINALIZE}_{\text{MAC}}(\beta \in \{0,1\})$:

return $\left(\bigcup_{\mathsf{m}^\star \in \mathcal{C}_{\mathcal{M}}} \text{Prefix}(\mathsf{m}^\star) \cap \mathcal{Q}_{\mathcal{M}} = \emptyset\right) \wedge \beta$

</td><td>

$\text{CHAL}\left(\mathsf{m}^\star = (\mathsf{m}_1^\star, \ldots, \mathsf{m}_p^\star) \in \mathcal{S}^\star\right)$:

$\mathcal{C}_{\mathcal{M}} := \mathcal{C}_{\mathcal{M}} \cup \{\mathsf{m}^\star\}$

$\tilde{\mathbf{h}} \xleftarrow{\$} \mathbb{Z}_q^\eta$

for $i \in \{1, \ldots, p\}$ **do**

$\quad \mathbf{h}_i \xleftarrow{\$} \mathbb{Z}_q^\eta$

$\quad \text{hm}_i^\star := H(\mathsf{m}_1^\star, \ldots, \mathsf{m}_i^\star)$

$\quad \mathbf{h}_{0,i} := \sum_{j=1}^\gamma \mathbf{X}_{j, \text{hm}_i^\star[j]}^\top \mathbf{h}_i$

$\quad \tilde{\mathbf{h}}_{0,i} := \tilde{\mathbf{X}}_1^\top \mathbf{h}_i + \tilde{\mathbf{X}}_2^\top \tilde{\mathbf{h}}$

$h_K := (\mathbf{x}')^\top \tilde{\mathbf{h}}$

$\boxed{h_K \xleftarrow{\$} \mathbb{Z}_q}$

$\mathbf{H} := \left([\mathbf{h}_i]_1, [\mathbf{h}_{0,i}]_1, [\tilde{\mathbf{h}}_{0,i}]_1\right)_{1 \le i \le p}$

return $\left([\tilde{\mathbf{h}}]_1, \mathbf{H}, [h_K]_T\right)$

</td></tr>
</table>

Fig. 9. Games $\text{uMAC}_{\text{real}}$ and $\boxed{\text{uMAC}_{\text{rand}}}$ for defining security for MAC_u.

$H(\mathsf{m}_1 \| \ldots \| \mathsf{m}_i)$ $(1 \le i \le p)$ by using a CRHF H. In stark contrast to methods in [29, 30], we generate a MAC tag for each hm_i with the same secret key. More precisely, we apply MAC_{lin} on each hm_i, and additionally we have a wrapper, namely, $\tilde{\mathbf{X}}_1 \cdot \tilde{\mathbf{t}}_i$ to connect all these p pieces together.

One can show MAC_u is a secure MAC according to the (standard) UF-CMA security (cf. the full version). Our MAC_u has stronger security which is formally stated in Theorem 1.[4] It is not a standard security for a MAC scheme, but it is exactly what we need for the transformation to unbounded HIBE. As in the security game for linear MACs, values in dk_1 and dk_2 can be used to rerandomize tags (cf. Remark 1). Oracle EVAL is available to an adversary $\mathcal{A}$ for a tag on any message of her choice. Moreover, oracle CHAL provides $\mathcal{A}$ necessary values to check validity of a tag. She can query these two oracles arbitrary many times in an adaptive manner. In the end, $\mathcal{A}$ needs to distinguish during the experiment CHAL always gives her the real values or the random ones. Of course, we exclude the case where $\mathcal{A}$ trivially wins by asking EVAL for any prefix of a challenge message $\mathsf{m}^\star$. The formal security game can be found in Fig. 9.

Remark 1 (Delegation). The tags of MAC_u are delegatable in the following sense: Given a tag $\tau = \left(([\mathbf{t}_i]_2, [\tilde{\mathbf{t}}]_2, [\mathbf{u}_i]_2)_{1 \le i \le p}, [\tilde{\mathbf{u}}]_2\right)$ for a message $\mathsf{m} = (\mathsf{m}_1, \ldots, \mathsf{m}_p)$, one can compute a fresh tag τ'' for a message $\mathsf{m}' := (\mathsf{m}_1, \ldots, \mathsf{m}_p, \mathsf{m}_{p+1})$ for arbitrary $\mathsf{m}_{p+1} \in \mathcal{S}$ using only the "public key" returned from the INIT_{MAC} oracle in the $\text{uMAC}_{\text{real}}$ game. We call the tag τ'' *fresh*, because its distribution is independent of τ.

---

[4] Our security notion is stronger than UF-CMA since a forged tag could be used to distinguish the real from the random CHAL queries.

First, we define the tag τ' for m' as $\tau' := \left(\left([\mathbf{t}'_i]_2, [\tilde{\mathbf{t}}']_2, [\mathbf{u}'_i]_2 \right)_{1 \leq i \leq p+1}, [\tilde{\mathbf{u}}']_2 \right)$.
This tag is identical to τ on the first p levels, i.e., for all $i \in \{1, \ldots, p\}$ we define
$\mathbf{t}'_i := \mathbf{t}_i$, $\tilde{\mathbf{t}}' := \tilde{\mathbf{t}}$ and $\mathbf{u}'_i := \mathbf{u}_i$. Furthermore we define $\mathbf{t}'_{p+1} := \mathbf{0}$, $\tilde{\mathbf{t}}' := \mathbf{0}$, $\mathbf{u}'_{p+1} = \mathbf{0}$
and $\tilde{\mathbf{u}}' := \tilde{\mathbf{u}}$. The resulting tag τ is indeed a valid tag for m', but it is not fresh.

To get a fresh tag $\tau'' := \left(\left([\mathbf{t}''_i]_2, [\tilde{\mathbf{t}}'']_2, [\mathbf{u}''_i]_2 \right)_{1 \leq i \leq p+1}, [\tilde{\mathbf{u}}'']_2 \right)$, we rerandomize
the tag τ'. That is, for all $i \in \{1, \ldots, p+1\}$ we define $\mathbf{t}''_i := \mathbf{t}'_i + \mathbf{B}\mathbf{s}'_i$ and
$\tilde{\mathbf{t}}''_i := \tilde{\mathbf{t}}' + \mathbf{B}\tilde{\mathbf{s}}'$ for uniform random $\mathbf{s}'_i \overset{\$}{\leftarrow} \mathbb{Z}_q^{n'}$ and $\tilde{\mathbf{s}} \overset{\$}{\leftarrow} \mathbb{Z}_q^{\tilde{n}'}$. Moreover, we adapt
$\mathbf{u}_i$ and $\tilde{\mathbf{u}}$ to the new $\mathbf{t}''_i$ and $\tilde{\mathbf{t}}''_i$ in the following way:

$$\mathbf{u}''_i := \mathbf{u}'_i + \sum\nolimits_{j=1}^{\gamma} \mathbf{X}_{j,b} \mathbf{B}\mathbf{s}'_i + \tilde{\mathbf{X}}_1 \mathbf{B}\tilde{\mathbf{s}}'_i$$

$$\tilde{\mathbf{u}}'' := \tilde{\mathbf{u}}' + \sum\nolimits_{i=1}^{p} \tilde{\mathbf{X}}_2 \mathbf{B}\tilde{\mathbf{s}}'_i$$

Theorem 1 (Security of MAC_u). MAC_u *is tightly secure under the $\mathcal{U}_k$-MDDH
assumption for $\mathbb{G}_1$, the $\mathcal{U}_k$-MDDH assumption for $\mathbb{G}_2$ and the collision resistance
of $\mathcal{H}$. More precisely, for all adversaries $\mathcal{A}$ there exist adversaries $\mathcal{B}_1$, $\mathcal{B}_2$ and
$\mathcal{B}_3$ with*

$$\left| \Pr\left[\mathsf{uMAC}^{\mathcal{A}}_{\mathsf{real}} \Rightarrow 1 \right] - \Pr\left[\mathsf{uMAC}^{\mathcal{A}}_{\mathsf{rand}} \Rightarrow 1 \right] \right| \leq (8k + 16k\gamma) \mathsf{Adv}^{\mathsf{mddh}}_{\mathcal{U}_k, \mathsf{PGGen}, 2}(\mathcal{B}_1)$$

$$+ (1 + 2k(\gamma + 1)) \mathsf{Adv}^{\mathsf{mddh}}_{\mathcal{U}_k, \mathsf{PGGen}, 1}(\mathcal{B}_2) + 2\mathsf{Adv}^{\mathsf{cr}}_{\mathcal{H}}(\mathcal{B}_3) + \frac{16 + (12 + 2Q_c L)\gamma}{q - 1} + \frac{2Q_e}{q^{2k}}$$

*and $T(\mathcal{B}_1) \approx T(\mathcal{B}_2) \approx T(\mathcal{B}_3) \approx T(\mathcal{A}) + (Q_e + Q_c)L \cdot \mathsf{poly}(\lambda)$, where Q_e resp. Q_c
denotes the number of EVAL resp. CHAL queries of $\mathcal{A}$, L denotes the maximum
length of the messages for which the adversary queried a tag or a challenge, and
poly is a polynomial independent of $\mathcal{A}$.*

Proof. The proof uses a hybrid argument with hybrids G_0–G_5, where G_0 is the
$\mathsf{uMAC}_{\mathsf{real}}$ game. The hybrids are given in Fig. 10. They make use of the random
function $\mathsf{RF} : \{0,1\}^\gamma \rightarrow \mathbb{Z}_q^{k \times 2k}$, defined on-the-fly.

Lemma 9 ($\mathsf{G}_0 \rightsquigarrow \mathsf{G}_1$).

$$\Pr\left[\mathsf{G}_0^{\mathcal{A}} \Rightarrow 1 \right] = \Pr\left[\mathsf{G}_1^{\mathcal{A}} \Rightarrow 1 \right]$$

Proof. In game G_1 each time the adversary queries a tag for a message m, where
she queried a tag for m before, the adversary will get a rerandomized version of
the first tag she queried. The $\mathsf{RerandTag}$ algorithm chooses $\mathbf{t}'_i := \mathbf{t}_i + \mathbf{B}\mathbf{s}'_i$ and
$\tilde{\mathbf{t}}' := \tilde{\mathbf{t}} + \tilde{\mathbf{B}}\tilde{\mathbf{s}}'$, which is uniformly random in $\mathsf{Span}(\mathbf{B})$ resp. $\mathsf{Span}(\tilde{\mathbf{B}})$, independent
of $\mathbf{t}_i$ and $\tilde{\mathbf{t}}$, because $\mathbf{s}'_i$ and $\tilde{\mathbf{s}}'$ are uniform random in $\mathbb{Z}_q^k$. The $\mathsf{RerandTag}$ algorithm
then computes $\mathbf{u}'_i$ and $\tilde{\mathbf{u}}'$ such to get another valid tag for m, that is distributed
like a fresh tag, independent of the input tag. Thus the games are equivalent.

Note that the rerandomization uses only the "public key" returned by the
INIT oracle so that it could be carried out by the adversary herself. In the
following, we will ignore these duplicated EVAL queries.   □

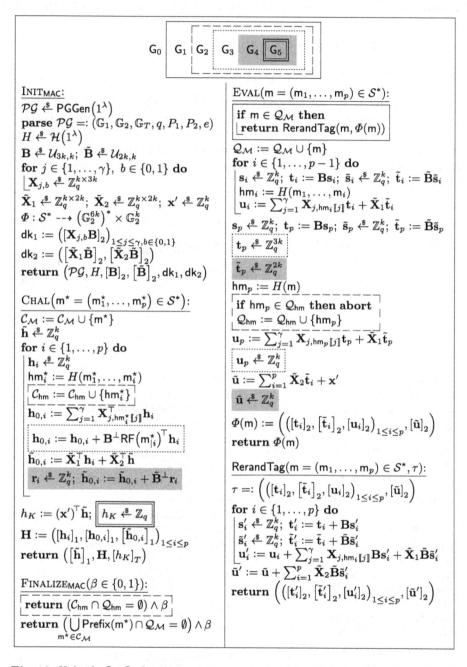

Fig. 10. Hybrids G_0–G_5 for the security proof of MAC_u. The algorithm RerandTag is only helper function and not an oracle for the adversary. The partial map Φ is initially totally undefined.

Lemma 10 ($G_1 \rightsquigarrow G_2$). *For all adversaries $\mathcal{A}$ there exist adversaries $\mathcal{B}_1$ and $\mathcal{B}_2$ with*

$$\left| \Pr\left[G_1^{\mathcal{A}} \Rightarrow 1\right] - \Pr\left[G_2^{\mathcal{A}} \Rightarrow 1\right] \right| \leq \mathsf{Adv}_{\mathcal{H}}^{\mathsf{cr}}(\mathcal{B})$$

and $T(\mathcal{B}) \approx T(\mathcal{A}) + (Q_e + Q_c)L \cdot \mathrm{poly}(\lambda)$.

Proof. Compared to G_1, the hybrid G_2 aborts if two different messages, for which the adversary queried a tag, have the same hash value. Furthermore, in G_2 the adversary looses (i.e., the output of $\mathrm{FINALIZE}_{\mathsf{MAC}}$ is always 0), if the hash of a prefix of a message sent to the CHAL oracle is identical to the hash of a message send to the EVAL oracle. So the two games are identical, except when a hash function collision occurs. $\qquad\square$

Lemma 11 ($G_2 \rightsquigarrow G_3$). *For all adversaries $\mathcal{A}$ there exists an adversary $\mathcal{B}$ with*

$$\left| \Pr\left[G_2^{\mathcal{A}} \Rightarrow 1\right] - \Pr\left[G_3^{\mathcal{A}} \Rightarrow 1\right] \right| \leq (8k\gamma + 2k)\mathsf{Adv}_{\mathcal{U}_k,\mathsf{PGGen},2}^{\mathsf{mddh}}(\mathcal{B}_1)$$

$$+ k\gamma\mathsf{Adv}_{\mathcal{U}_k,\mathsf{PGGen},1}^{\mathsf{mddh}}(\mathcal{B}_2) + \frac{\gamma Q_c L + 6\gamma + 1}{q - 1} + \frac{Q_e}{q^{2k}}$$

and $T(\mathcal{B}) \approx T(\mathcal{A}) + (Q_e + Q_c)L \cdot \mathrm{poly}(\lambda)$.

$\mathrm{INIT}_{\mathsf{MAC}}$:
$H \xleftarrow{\$} \mathcal{H}(1^\lambda); \; \tilde{\mathbf{B}} \xleftarrow{\$} \mathcal{U}_{2k,k}$
$\left(\mathcal{PG}, [\mathbf{B}]_2, \mathsf{dk}_1\right) \xleftarrow{\$} \mathrm{INIT}_{\mathsf{ri}}$
parse $\mathsf{dk}_1 =: \left([\mathbf{D}_{j,b}]_2\right)_{1 \leq j \leq \gamma, b \in \{0,1\}}$
$\tilde{\mathbf{X}}_1 \xleftarrow{\$} \mathbb{Z}_q^{k \times 2k}; \; \tilde{\mathbf{X}}_2 \xleftarrow{\$} \mathbb{Z}_q^{k \times 2k}; \; \mathbf{x}' \xleftarrow{\$} \mathbb{Z}_q^k$
$\Phi : \mathcal{S}^* \dashrightarrow \left(\mathbb{G}_2^{6k}\right)^* \times \mathbb{G}_2^k$
$\mathsf{dk}_2 := \left(\left[\tilde{\mathbf{X}}_1\tilde{\mathbf{B}}\right]_2, \left[\tilde{\mathbf{X}}_2\tilde{\mathbf{B}}\right]_2\right)$
return $\left(\mathcal{PG}, H, [\mathbf{B}]_2, \left[\tilde{\mathbf{B}}\right]_2, \mathsf{dk}_1, \mathsf{dk}_2\right)$

$\mathrm{CHAL}\left(m^* = (m_1^\star, \ldots, m_p^\star) \in \mathcal{S}^*\right)$:
$\mathcal{C}_\mathcal{M} := \mathcal{C}_\mathcal{M} \cup \{m^*\}$
$\tilde{\mathbf{h}} \xleftarrow{\$} \mathbb{Z}_q^k; \; h_K := (\mathbf{x}')^\top \tilde{\mathbf{h}}$
for $i \in \{1, \ldots, p\}$ **do**
$\quad \mathsf{hm}_i^* := H(m_1^\star, \ldots, m_i^\star)$
$\quad \mathcal{C}_{\mathsf{hm}} := \mathcal{C}_{\mathsf{hm}} \cup \{\mathsf{hm}_i^*\}$
$\quad (\mathbf{h}_i, \mathbf{h}_{0,i}) \xleftarrow{\$} \mathrm{CHAL}_{\mathsf{ri}}(\mathsf{hm}_i^*)$
$\quad \tilde{\mathbf{h}}_{0,i} := \tilde{\mathbf{X}}_1^\top \mathbf{h}_i + \tilde{\mathbf{X}}_2^\top \tilde{\mathbf{h}}$
$\mathbf{H} := \left(([\mathbf{h}_i]_1, [\mathbf{h}_{0,i}]_1, [\tilde{\mathbf{h}}_{0,i}]_1\right)_{1 \leq i \leq p}$
return $\left([\tilde{\mathbf{h}}]_1, \mathbf{H}, [h_K]_T\right)$

$\mathrm{EVAL}(m = (m_1, \ldots, m_p) \in \mathcal{S}^*)$:
if $m \in \mathcal{Q}_\mathcal{M}$ **then**
$\quad$**return** $\mathrm{RerandTag}(m, \Phi(m))$
$\mathcal{Q}_\mathcal{M} := \mathcal{Q}_\mathcal{M} \cup \{m\}$
for $i \in \{1, \ldots, p - 1\}$ **do**
$\quad \mathbf{s}_i \xleftarrow{\$} \mathbb{Z}_q^k; \; \mathbf{t}_i := \mathbf{B}\mathbf{s}_i; \; \tilde{\mathbf{s}}_i \xleftarrow{\$} \mathbb{Z}_q^k; \; \tilde{\mathbf{t}}_i := \tilde{\mathbf{B}}\tilde{\mathbf{s}}_i$
$\quad \mathsf{hm}_i := H(m_1, \ldots, m_i)$
$\quad \mathbf{u}_i := \sum_{j=1}^\gamma \mathbf{D}_{j,\mathsf{hm}_i[j]}\mathbf{s}_i + \tilde{\mathbf{X}}_1\tilde{\mathbf{t}}_i$
$\mathsf{hm}_p := H(m)$
if $\mathsf{hm}_p \in \mathcal{Q}_{\mathsf{hm}}$ **then abort**
$\mathcal{Q}_{\mathsf{hm}} := \mathcal{Q}_{\mathsf{hm}} \cup \{\mathsf{hm}_p\}$
$\left([\mathbf{t}_p]_2, [\mathbf{u}_p']_2\right) \xleftarrow{\$} \mathrm{EVAL}_{\mathsf{ri}}(\mathsf{hm}_p)$
$\tilde{\mathbf{s}}_p \xleftarrow{\$} \mathbb{Z}_q^k; \; \tilde{\mathbf{t}}_p := \tilde{\mathbf{B}}\tilde{\mathbf{s}}_p$
$\mathbf{u}_p := \mathbf{u}_p' + \tilde{\mathbf{X}}_1\tilde{\mathbf{t}}_p$
$\tilde{\mathbf{u}} := \sum_{i=1}^p \tilde{\mathbf{X}}_2\tilde{\mathbf{t}}_i + \mathbf{x}'$
$\Phi(m) := \left(\left(([\mathbf{t}_i]_2, [\tilde{\mathbf{t}}_i]_2, [\mathbf{u}_i]_2\right)_{1 \leq i \leq p}, [\tilde{\mathbf{u}}]_2\right)$
return $\Phi(m)$

$\mathrm{FINALIZE}_{\mathsf{MAC}}(\beta \in \{0,1\})$:
return $\mathrm{FINALIZE}_{\mathsf{ri}}(\beta)$

Fig. 11. Reduction for the transition from G_2 to G_3 to the Randomness Injection Lemma.

Proof. In game G_3 the value $\mathbf{u}_p$ is chosen uniformly random (and some side-effect changes are made). For the transition to this game, we use the security of the underlying linear MAC. The reduction is given in Fig. 11.

We use the Randomness Injection Lemma to compute the components $\mathbf{h}$ and $\mathbf{h}_{0,i}$ for all levels i in the CHAL oracle and to compute $\mathbf{t}_p$ and $\mathbf{u}'_p$, i.e. the last-level components of the tags. For the other components, we use the public key returned from INIT_{ri}. This is important to avoid asking both the EVAL_{ri} and CHAL_{ri} oracles on common prefixes of EVAL_{ri}-messages and CHAL_{ri}-messages.

If the reduction is accessing the RI_{real} game, it simulates G_2. Otherwise, it simulates G_3.   □

Lemma 12 ($G_3 \rightsquigarrow G_4$). *For all adversaries $\mathcal{A}$ there exists an adversary $\mathcal{B}$ with*

$$\left|\Pr\left[G_3^{\mathcal{A}} \Rightarrow 1\right] - \Pr\left[G_4^{\mathcal{A}} \Rightarrow 1\right]\right| \leq 2k\text{Adv}_{\mathcal{U}_k,\text{PGGen},2}^{\text{mddh}}(\mathcal{B}_1) + k\text{Adv}_{\mathcal{U}_k,\text{PGGen},1}^{\text{mddh}}(\mathcal{B}_2) + \frac{6}{q-1}$$

and $T(\mathcal{B}) \approx T(\mathcal{A}) + (Q_e + Q_c)L \cdot \text{poly}(\lambda)$.

Proof. In game G_4 the value $\tilde{\mathbf{u}}$ is chosen uniformly random (and some side-effect changes are made). For the transition to this game, we use the Randomness Packing Lemma (Lemma 5). The reduction is given in Fig. 12.

$\underline{\text{INIT}_{\text{MAC}}:}$
$H \stackrel{\$}{\leftarrow} \mathcal{H}(1^\lambda)$; $\mathbf{B} \stackrel{\$}{\leftarrow} \mathcal{U}_{3k,k}$
for $j \in \{1, \ldots, \gamma\}$, $b \in \{0,1\}$ **do**
$\quad\lfloor \mathbf{X}_{j,b} \stackrel{\$}{\leftarrow} \mathbb{Z}_q^{k \times 3k}$
$\text{dk}_1 := \left([\mathbf{X}_{j,b}\mathbf{B}]_2\right)_{1 \leq j \leq \gamma, b \in \{0,1\}}$
$\left([\tilde{\mathbf{B}}]_2, \text{dk}_2\right) \stackrel{\$}{\leftarrow} \text{INIT}_{\text{rp}}$
parse $\text{dk}_2 =: \left([\tilde{\mathbf{D}}_1]_2, [\tilde{\mathbf{D}}_2]_2\right)$
$\Phi : \mathcal{S}^* \dashrightarrow \left(\mathbb{G}_2^{6k}\right)^* \times \mathbb{G}_2^k$
return $\left(\mathcal{PG}, H, [\mathbf{B}]_2, [\tilde{\mathbf{B}}]_2, \text{dk}_1, \text{dk}_2\right)$

$\underline{\text{CHAL}\left(\mathbf{m}^\star = (\mathbf{m}_1^\star, \ldots, \mathbf{m}_p^\star) \in \mathcal{S}^*\right):}$
$\mathcal{C}_\mathcal{M} := \mathcal{C}_\mathcal{M} \cup \{\mathbf{m}^\star\}$
$\tilde{\mathbf{h}} \stackrel{\$}{\leftarrow} \mathbb{Z}_q^k$; $h_K := (\mathbf{x}')^\top \tilde{\mathbf{h}}$
for $i \in \{1, \ldots, p\}$ **do**
$\quad$ $\text{hm}_i^\star := H(\mathbf{m}_1^\star, \ldots, \mathbf{m}_i^\star)$
$\quad$ $\mathcal{C}_{\text{hm}} := \mathcal{C}_{\text{hm}} \cup \{\text{hm}_i^\star\}$
$\quad$ $\left(\mathbf{h}_i, \tilde{\mathbf{h}}_{0,i}\right) \stackrel{\$}{\leftarrow} \text{CHAL}_{\text{rp}}\left(\tilde{\mathbf{h}}\right)$
$\quad\lfloor \mathbf{h}_{0,i} := \sum_{j=1}^\gamma \mathbf{X}_{j,\text{hm}_i^\star[j]}^\top \mathbf{h}_i$
$\mathbf{H} := \left([\mathbf{h}_i]_1, [\mathbf{h}_{0,i}]_1, [\tilde{\mathbf{h}}_{0,i}]_1\right)_{1 \leq i \leq p}$
return $\left([\tilde{\mathbf{h}}]_1, \mathbf{H}, [h_K]_T\right)$

$\underline{\text{EVAL}(\mathbf{m} = (\mathbf{m}_1, \ldots, \mathbf{m}_p) \in \mathcal{S}^*):}$
if $\mathbf{m} \in \mathcal{Q}_\mathcal{M}$ **then**
$\quad\lfloor$ **return** $\text{RerandTag}(\mathbf{m}, \Phi(\mathbf{m}))$
$\mathcal{Q}_\mathcal{M} := \mathcal{Q}_\mathcal{M} \cup \{\mathbf{m}\}$
for $i \in \{1, \ldots, p-1\}$ **do**
$\quad$ $\mathbf{s}_i \stackrel{\$}{\leftarrow} \mathbb{Z}_q^k$; $\mathbf{t}_i := \mathbf{Bs}_i$; $\tilde{\mathbf{s}}_i \stackrel{\$}{\leftarrow} \mathbb{Z}_q^k$; $\tilde{\mathbf{t}}_i := \tilde{\mathbf{B}}\tilde{\mathbf{s}}_i$
$\quad$ $\text{hm}_i := H(\mathbf{m}_1, \ldots, \mathbf{m}_i)$
$\quad\lfloor \mathbf{u}_i := \sum_{j=1}^\gamma \mathbf{X}_{j,\text{hm}_i[j]} \mathbf{t}_i + \tilde{\mathbf{D}}_1 \tilde{\mathbf{s}}_i$
$\text{hm}_p := H(\mathbf{m})$
if $\text{hm}_p \in \mathcal{Q}_{\text{hm}}$ **then abort**
$\mathcal{Q}_{\text{hm}} := \mathcal{Q}_{\text{hm}} \cup \{\text{hm}_p\}$
$\mathbf{t}_p \stackrel{\$}{\leftarrow} \mathbb{Z}_q^{3k}$
$\mathbf{u}_p \stackrel{\$}{\leftarrow} \mathbb{Z}_q^k$
$\left([\tilde{\mathbf{t}}_p]_2, [\tilde{\mathbf{u}}']_2\right) \stackrel{\$}{\leftarrow} \text{EVAL}_{\text{ri}}(\text{hm}_p)$
$\tilde{\mathbf{u}} := \sum_{i=1}^{p-1} \tilde{\mathbf{D}}_2 \tilde{\mathbf{s}}_i + \tilde{\mathbf{u}}' + \mathbf{x}'$
$\Phi(\mathbf{m}) := \left(\left([\mathbf{t}_i]_2, [\tilde{\mathbf{t}}_i]_2, [\mathbf{u}_i]_2\right)_{1 \leq i \leq p}, [\tilde{\mathbf{u}}]_2\right)$
return $\Phi(\mathbf{m})$

$\underline{\text{FINALIZE}_{\text{MAC}}(\beta \in \{0,1\}):}$
return $\text{FINALIZE}_{\text{ri}}(\beta)$

Fig. 12. Reduction for the transition from G_3 to G_4 to the Randomness Packing Lemma.

We use the Randomness Packing Lemma to compute the components $\mathbf{h}$ and $\tilde{\mathbf{h}}_0$ for all levels i in the CHAL oracle and to compute $\tilde{\mathbf{t}}$ and $\tilde{\mathbf{u}}'$. Everything else can be computed with the delegation key returned from INIT_{rp}.

If the reduction is accessing the RP_{real} game, it simulates G_3. Otherwise, it simulates G_4.   □

Lemma 13 ($\mathsf{G}_4 \rightsquigarrow \mathsf{G}_5$). *For all adversaries $\mathcal{A}$ there exists an adversary $\mathcal{B}$ with*

$$\left|\Pr\left[\mathsf{G}_4^{\mathcal{A}} \Rightarrow 1\right] - \Pr\left[\mathsf{G}_5^{\mathcal{A}} \Rightarrow 1\right]\right| \leq \mathsf{Adv}_{\mathcal{U}_k,\text{PGGen},1}^{\text{mddh}}(\mathcal{B}) + \frac{2}{q-1}$$

and $T(\mathcal{B}) \approx T(\mathcal{A}) + (Q_e + Q_c)L \cdot \text{poly}(\lambda)$.

$\underline{\text{INIT}_{\text{MAC}}:}$

$H \xleftarrow{\$} \mathcal{H}(1^\lambda)$; $\mathbf{B} \xleftarrow{\$} \mathcal{U}_{3k,k}$; $\tilde{\mathbf{B}} \xleftarrow{\$} \mathcal{U}_{2k,k}$

for $j \in \{1,\dots,\gamma\}$, $b \in \{0,1\}$ **do**

$\quad \left\lfloor \mathbf{X}_{j,b} \xleftarrow{\$} \mathbb{Z}_q^{k \times 3k} \right.$

$\tilde{\mathbf{X}}_1 \xleftarrow{\$} \mathbb{Z}_q^{k \times 2k}$; $\tilde{\mathbf{X}}_2 \xleftarrow{\$} \mathbb{Z}_q^{k \times 2k}$; $\mathbf{j}' \xleftarrow{\$} \mathbb{Z}_q^k$

// Implicit: $\tilde{\mathbf{x}}' := \mathbf{j}' + \left(\underline{\mathbf{D}}\overline{\mathbf{D}}^{-1}\right)^\top$

$\Phi : \mathcal{S}^* \dashrightarrow \left(\mathbb{G}_2^{6k}\right)^* \times \mathbb{G}_2^k$

$\mathsf{dk}_1 := \left([\mathbf{X}_{j,b}\mathbf{B}]_2\right)_{1 \leq j \leq \gamma, b \in \{0,1\}}$

$\mathsf{dk}_2 := \left([\tilde{\mathbf{X}}_1\tilde{\mathbf{B}}]_2, [\tilde{\mathbf{J}}_2\tilde{\mathbf{B}}]_2\right)$

return $\left(\mathcal{PG}, H, [\mathbf{B}]_2, [\tilde{\mathbf{B}}]_2, \mathsf{dk}_1, \mathsf{dk}_2\right)$

$\underline{\text{CHAL}\left(\mathsf{m}^* = (\mathsf{m}_1^*,\dots,\mathsf{m}_p^*) \in \mathcal{S}^*\right):}$

$\mathcal{C}_{\mathcal{M}} := \mathcal{C}_{\mathcal{M}} \cup \{\mathsf{m}^*\}$

Let this be the c-th CHAL query.

$\tilde{\mathbf{h}} := \mathbf{f}_c$; $h_K := (\mathbf{j}')^\top \tilde{\mathbf{h}} + \underline{\mathbf{f}_c}$

for $i \in \{1,\dots,p\}$ **do**

$\quad \mathbf{h}_i \xleftarrow{\$} \mathbb{Z}_q^k$

$\quad \mathsf{hm}_i^* := H(\mathsf{m}_1^*,\dots,\mathsf{m}_i^*)$

$\quad \mathbf{h}_{0,i} := \left(\sum_{j=1}^{\gamma} \mathbf{X}_{j,\mathsf{hm}_i^*[\![j]\!]}^\top + \mathbf{B}^\perp \mathsf{RF}\left(\mathsf{m}_{|i}^*\right)^\top\right)\mathbf{h}_i$

$\quad \left\lfloor \mathbf{r}_i \xleftarrow{\$} \mathbb{Z}_q^k \right.$; $\tilde{\mathbf{h}}_{0,i} := \tilde{\mathbf{X}}_1^\top \mathbf{h}_i + \tilde{\mathbf{X}}_2^\top \tilde{\mathbf{h}} + \tilde{\mathbf{B}}^\perp \mathbf{r}_i$

$\mathbf{H} := \left([\tilde{\mathbf{h}}]_1, \left([\mathbf{h}_i]_1, [\mathbf{h}_{0,i}]_1, [\tilde{\mathbf{h}}_{0,i}]_1\right)_{1 \leq i \leq p}\right)$

return $\left(\mathbf{H}, [h_K]_T\right)$

$\underline{\text{EVAL}(\mathsf{m} = (\mathsf{m}_1,\dots,\mathsf{m}_p) \in \mathcal{S}^*):}$

if $\mathsf{m} \in \mathcal{Q}_{\mathcal{M}}$ **then**

$\quad \lfloor$ **return** $\mathsf{RerandTag}(\mathsf{m}, \Phi(\mathsf{m}))$

$\mathcal{Q}_{\mathcal{M}} := \mathcal{Q}_{\mathcal{M}} \cup \{\mathsf{m}\}$

for $i \in \{1,\dots,p-1\}$ **do**

$\quad \mathbf{s}_i \xleftarrow{\$} \mathbb{Z}_q^k$; $\mathbf{t}_i := \mathbf{B}\mathbf{s}_i$

$\quad \tilde{\mathbf{s}}_i \xleftarrow{\$} \mathbb{Z}_q^k$; $\tilde{\mathbf{t}}_i := \tilde{\mathbf{B}}\tilde{\mathbf{s}}_i$

$\quad \mathsf{hm}_i := H(\mathsf{m}_1,\dots,\mathsf{m}_i)$

$\quad \mathbf{u}_i := \sum_{j=1}^{\gamma} \mathbf{X}_{j,\mathsf{hm}_i[\![j]\!]}\mathbf{t}_i + \tilde{\mathbf{X}}_1\tilde{\mathbf{t}}_i$

$\mathbf{t}_p \xleftarrow{\$} \mathbb{Z}_q^{3k}$

$\tilde{\mathbf{t}}_p \xleftarrow{\$} \mathbb{Z}_q^{2k}$

$\mathbf{u}_p \xleftarrow{\$} \mathbb{Z}_q^k$

$\tilde{\mathbf{u}} \xleftarrow{\$} \mathbb{Z}_q^k$

$\Phi(\mathsf{m}) := \left(([\mathbf{t}_i]_2, [\tilde{\mathbf{t}}_i]_2, [\mathbf{u}_i]_2)_{1 \leq i \leq p}, [\tilde{\mathbf{u}}]_2\right)$

return $\Phi(\mathsf{m})$

$\underline{\text{FINALIZE}_{\text{MAC}}(\beta \in \{0,1\}):}$

return $\left(\bigcup_{\mathsf{m}^* \in \mathcal{C}_{\mathcal{M}}} \mathsf{Prefix}(\mathsf{m}^*) \cap \mathcal{Q}_{\mathcal{M}} = \emptyset\right) \wedge \beta$

Fig. 13. Reduction for the transition from G_4 to G_5 to the Q_c-fold $\mathcal{U}_k$-MDDH challenge $\left([\mathbf{D}]_1, [\mathbf{f}_1]_1, \dots, [\mathbf{f}_{Q_c}]_1\right)$.

Proof. In game G_5 the value h_K is chosen uniformly random. For the transition to this game, we need a Q_c-fold $\mathcal{U}_k$-MDDH challenge $\left([\mathbf{D}]_1, [\mathbf{f}_1]_1, \ldots, [\mathbf{f}_{Q_c}]_1\right)$. The reduction is given in Fig. 13.

Assume that $\overline{\mathbf{D}}$ is invertible. This happens with probability at least $(1 - 1/(q-1))$. The INIT and EVAL oracles are identical in both games and simulated correctly by the reduction, because they do not return anything depending on $\mathbf{x}'$. Write $\mathbf{f}_c =: \begin{pmatrix} \overline{\mathbf{D}}\mathbf{w}_c \\ \underline{\mathbf{D}}\mathbf{w}_c + r_c \end{pmatrix}$ where $\mathbf{w}_c$ is uniform random in $\mathbb{Z}_q^k$ and r_c is 0 or uniform random in $\mathbb{Z}_q$. In the CHAL queries the reduction picks $\tilde{\mathbf{h}} := \overline{\mathbf{f}_c}$. Since $\overline{\mathbf{f}_c}$ is a uniform random vector, $\tilde{\mathbf{h}}$ is distributed correctly. Furthermore, h_K is computed as

$$h_K := (\mathbf{j}')^\top \tilde{\mathbf{h}} + \underline{\mathbf{f}_c} = (\mathbf{j}')^\top \tilde{\mathbf{h}} + \underline{\mathbf{D}}\,\overline{\mathbf{D}}^{-1}\overline{\mathbf{f}_c} + r_c = (\mathbf{x}')^\top \tilde{\mathbf{h}} + r_c \,.$$

If $r_c = 0$, we are simulating game G_4. If r_c is uniform random we are simulating game G_5.   □

SUMMARY. To prove Theorem 1, we combine Lemmata 9–13 to change h_K from real to random and then apply all Lemmata (except Lemma 13) in reverse order to get to the uMAC$_{\mathsf{rand}}$ game.   □

4   Transformation to Unbounded HIBE

Our unbounded affine MAC can be tightly transformed to an unbounded HIBE under the $\mathcal{U}_k$-MDDH assumption in $\mathbb{G}_1$. The transformation follows the same idea as [6]. It can be found in the full version.

The unbounded HIBE obtained from our unbounded affine MAC can be instantiated with any MDDH assumption. The result for the SXDH assumption can be found in Fig. 14.

$\underline{\mathsf{Gen}(1^\lambda):}$

$\mathcal{PG} \stackrel{\$}{\leftarrow} \mathsf{PGGen}(1^\lambda); \; H \stackrel{\$}{\leftarrow} \mathcal{H}(1^\lambda)$

$\mathbf{parse}\ \mathcal{PG} =: (\mathbb{G}_1, \mathbb{G}_2, \mathbb{G}_T, q, P_1, P_2, e)$

$\mathbf{B} \stackrel{\$}{\leftarrow} \mathcal{U}_{3,1}; \; \tilde{\mathbf{B}} \stackrel{\$}{\leftarrow} \mathcal{U}_{2,1}; \; \mathbf{A} \stackrel{\$}{\leftarrow} \mathcal{U}_1$

$\mathbf{for}\ j \in \{1,\dots,\gamma\},\ b \in \{0,1\}\ \mathbf{do}$

$\quad \left| \begin{array}{l} \mathbf{X}_{j,b} \stackrel{\$}{\leftarrow} \mathbb{Z}_q^{1\times 3}; \; \mathbf{Y}_{j,b} \stackrel{\$}{\leftarrow} \mathbb{Z}_q^{1\times 3} \\ \mathbf{Z}_{j,b} := (\mathbf{Y}_{j,b}^\top \mid \mathbf{X}_{j,b}^\top)\mathbf{A} \\ \mathbf{D}_{j,b} := \mathbf{X}_{j,b}\mathbf{B}; \; \mathbf{E}_{j,b} := \mathbf{Y}_{j,b}\mathbf{B} \end{array} \right.$

$\mathbf{for}\ \delta \in \{1,2\}\ \mathbf{do}$

$\quad \left| \begin{array}{l} \tilde{\mathbf{X}}_\delta \stackrel{\$}{\leftarrow} \mathbb{Z}_q^{1\times 2}; \; \tilde{\mathbf{Y}}_\delta \stackrel{\$}{\leftarrow} \mathbb{Z}_q^{1\times 2} \\ \tilde{\mathbf{Z}}_\delta := (\tilde{\mathbf{Y}}_\delta^\top \mid \tilde{\mathbf{X}}_\delta^\top)\mathbf{A} \\ \tilde{\mathbf{D}}_\delta := \tilde{\mathbf{X}}_\delta\tilde{\mathbf{B}}; \; \tilde{\mathbf{E}}_\delta := \tilde{\mathbf{Y}}_\delta\tilde{\mathbf{B}} \end{array} \right.$

$\mathbf{x}' \stackrel{\$}{\leftarrow} \mathbb{Z}_q; \; \mathbf{y}' \stackrel{\$}{\leftarrow} \mathbb{Z}_q; \; \mathbf{z}' := (\mathbf{y}' \mid \mathbf{x}') \cdot \mathbf{A}$

$\mathsf{pk} := \left(\mathcal{PG}, H, [\mathbf{A}]_1, ([\mathbf{Z}_{j,b}]_1)_{1\le j\le\gamma, b\in\{0,1\}}, \right.$
$\qquad\qquad \left. [\tilde{\mathbf{Z}}_1]_1, [\tilde{\mathbf{Z}}_2]_1, [\mathbf{z}']_1 \right)$

$\mathsf{dk} := \left([\mathbf{B}]_2, [\tilde{\mathbf{B}}]_2, ([\mathbf{D}_{j,b}]_2, [\mathbf{E}_{j,b}]_2)_{\substack{1\le j\le\gamma,\\ b\in\{0,1\}}}, \right.$
$\qquad\qquad \left. [\tilde{\mathbf{D}}_1]_2, [\tilde{\mathbf{D}}_2]_2, [\tilde{\mathbf{E}}_1]_2, [\tilde{\mathbf{E}}_2]_2 \right)$

$\mathsf{sk} := \left(\mathsf{sk}_{\mathsf{MAC}}, (\mathbf{Y}_{j,b})_{\substack{1\le j\le\gamma\\ b\in\{0,1\}}}, \tilde{\mathbf{Y}}_1, \tilde{\mathbf{Y}}_2, \mathbf{y}' \right)$

$\mathbf{return}\ (\mathsf{pk}, \mathsf{dk}, \mathsf{sk})$

$\underline{\mathsf{Ext}(\mathsf{sk}, \mathsf{id} = (\mathsf{id}_1,\dots,\mathsf{id}_p) \in \mathcal{S}^*):}$

$\mathbf{for}\ i \in \{1,\dots,p\}\ \mathbf{do}$

$\quad \left| \begin{array}{l} \mathbf{s}_i \stackrel{\$}{\leftarrow} \mathbb{Z}_q; \; \mathbf{t}_i := \mathbf{B}\mathbf{s}_i; \; \tilde{\mathbf{s}}_i \stackrel{\$}{\leftarrow} \mathbb{Z}_q; \; \tilde{\mathbf{t}}_i := \tilde{\mathbf{B}}\tilde{\mathbf{s}}_i \\ \mathsf{hid}_i := H(\mathsf{id}_1,\dots,\mathsf{id}_i) \\ \mathbf{u}_i := \sum_{j=1}^{\gamma} \mathbf{X}_{j,\mathsf{hid}_i[\![j]\!]}\mathbf{t}_i + \tilde{\mathbf{X}}_1\tilde{\mathbf{t}}_i \\ \mathbf{v}_i := \sum_{j=1}^{\gamma} \mathbf{Y}_{j,\mathsf{hid}_i[\![j]\!]}\mathbf{t}_i + \tilde{\mathbf{Y}}_1\tilde{\mathbf{t}}_i \end{array} \right.$

$\tilde{\mathbf{u}} := \sum_{i=1}^{p} \tilde{\mathbf{X}}_2\tilde{\mathbf{t}}_i + \mathbf{x}'; \; \tilde{\mathbf{v}} := \sum_{i=1}^{p} \tilde{\mathbf{Y}}_2\tilde{\mathbf{t}}_i + \mathbf{y}'$

$\mathbf{return}\ \left(([\mathbf{t}_i]_2, [\tilde{\mathbf{t}}_i]_2, [\mathbf{u}_i]_2, [\mathbf{v}_i]_2)_{1\le i\le p}, \right.$
$\qquad\qquad\quad \left. [\tilde{\mathbf{u}}]_2, [\tilde{\mathbf{v}}]_2 \right)$

$\underline{\mathsf{Enc}(\mathsf{pk}, \mathsf{id} = (\mathsf{id}_1,\dots,\mathsf{id}_p) \in \mathcal{S}^*):}$

$\mathbf{r} \stackrel{\$}{\leftarrow} \mathbb{Z}_q; \; \mathbf{c}_4 := \mathbf{A}\mathbf{r}; \; K := \mathbf{z}' \cdot \mathbf{r}$

$\mathbf{for}\ i \in \{1,\dots,p\}\ \mathbf{do}$

$\quad \left| \begin{array}{l} \mathbf{r}_i \stackrel{\$}{\leftarrow} \mathbb{Z}_q; \; \mathbf{c}_{2,i} := \mathbf{A}\mathbf{r}_i \\ \mathsf{hid}_i := H(\mathsf{id}_1,\dots,\mathsf{id}_i) \\ \mathbf{c}_{1,i} := \sum_{j=1}^{\gamma} \mathbf{Z}_{j,\mathsf{hid}_i[\![j]\!]}\mathbf{r}_i \\ \mathbf{c}_{3,i} := \tilde{\mathbf{Z}}_1\mathbf{r}_i + \tilde{\mathbf{Z}}_2\mathbf{r} \end{array} \right.$

$\mathbf{C} := \left(([\mathbf{c}_{1,i}]_1, [\mathbf{c}_{2,i}]_1, [\mathbf{c}_{3,i}]_1)_{1\le i\le p}, [\mathbf{c}_4]_1 \right)$

$\mathbf{return}\ ([K]_T, \mathbf{C})$

$\underline{\mathsf{Del}(\mathsf{dk}, \mathsf{usk}[\mathsf{id}], \mathsf{id} \in \mathcal{S}^p, \mathsf{id}_{p+1} \in \mathcal{S}):}$

$\mathbf{parse}\ \mathsf{usk}[\mathsf{id}] =: \Big(([\mathbf{t}_i]_2, [\tilde{\mathbf{t}}_i]_2, [\mathbf{u}_i]_2, $
$\qquad\qquad\qquad [\mathbf{v}_i]_2)_{1\le i\le p}, [\tilde{\mathbf{u}}]_2, [\tilde{\mathbf{v}}]_2 \Big)$

$\mathbf{t}_{p+1} := \mathbf{0}; \; \tilde{\mathbf{t}}_{p+1} := \mathbf{0}$

$\mathbf{u}_{p+1} := \mathbf{0}; \; \mathbf{v}_{p+1} := \mathbf{0}$

$\mathsf{id}' := (\mathsf{id}_1,\dots,\mathsf{id}_p, \mathsf{id}_{p+1})$

$\mathsf{usk}[\mathsf{id}'] := \Big(([\mathbf{t}_i]_2, [\mathbf{u}_i]_2, [\mathbf{v}_i]_2)_{1\le i\le p+1}, $
$\qquad\qquad\qquad\qquad [\tilde{\mathbf{u}}]_2, [\tilde{\mathbf{v}}]_2 \Big)$

$\mathbf{return}\ \mathsf{RerandUSK}(\mathsf{dk}, \mathsf{id}', \mathsf{usk}[\mathsf{id}'])$

$\underline{\mathsf{RerandUSK}(\mathsf{dk}, \mathsf{id} \in \mathcal{S}^p, \mathsf{usk}[\mathsf{id}]):}$

$\mathbf{parse}\ \mathsf{usk}[\mathsf{id}] =: \Big(([\mathbf{t}_i]_2, [\tilde{\mathbf{t}}_i]_2, [\mathbf{u}_i]_2, $
$\qquad\qquad\qquad [\mathbf{v}_i]_2)_{1\le i\le p}, [\tilde{\mathbf{u}}]_2, [\tilde{\mathbf{v}}]_2 \Big)$

$\mathbf{for}\ i \in \{1,\dots,p\}\ \mathbf{do}$

$\quad \left| \begin{array}{l} \mathbf{s}'_i \stackrel{\$}{\leftarrow} \mathbb{Z}_q; \; \mathbf{t}'_i := \mathbf{t}_i + \mathbf{B}\mathbf{s}'_i \\ \tilde{\mathbf{s}}'_i \stackrel{\$}{\leftarrow} \mathbb{Z}_q; \; \tilde{\mathbf{t}}'_i := \tilde{\mathbf{t}}_i \stackrel{\$}{\leftarrow} \tilde{\mathbf{B}}\tilde{\mathbf{s}}'_i \\ \mathsf{hid}_i := H(\mathsf{id}_1,\dots,\mathsf{id}_i) \\ \mathbf{u}'_i := \mathbf{u}_i + \sum_{j=1}^{\gamma} \mathbf{D}_{j,\mathsf{hid}_i[\![j]\!]}\mathbf{s}'_i + \tilde{\mathbf{D}}_1\tilde{\mathbf{s}}'_i \\ \mathbf{v}'_i := \mathbf{v}_i + \sum_{j=1}^{\gamma} \mathbf{E}_{j,\mathsf{hid}_i[\![j]\!]}\mathbf{s}'_i + \tilde{\mathbf{E}}_1\tilde{\mathbf{s}}'_i \end{array} \right.$

$\tilde{\mathbf{u}}' := \tilde{\mathbf{u}} + \sum_{i=1}^{p} \tilde{\mathbf{D}}_2\tilde{\mathbf{s}}'_i$

$\tilde{\mathbf{v}}' := \tilde{\mathbf{v}} + \sum_{i=1}^{p} \tilde{\mathbf{E}}_2\tilde{\mathbf{s}}'_i$

$\mathbf{return}\ \left(([\mathbf{t}'_i]_2, [\tilde{\mathbf{t}}'_i]_2, [\mathbf{u}'_i]_2, [\mathbf{v}'_i]_2)_{1\le i\le p}, \right.$
$\qquad\qquad\quad \left. [\tilde{\mathbf{u}}']_2, [\tilde{\mathbf{v}}']_2 \right)$

$\underline{\mathsf{Dec}(\mathsf{usk}[\mathsf{id}], \mathsf{id} = (\mathsf{id}_1,\dots,\mathsf{id}_p) \in \mathcal{S}^*, \mathbf{C}):}$

$\mathbf{parse}\ \mathsf{usk}[\mathsf{id}] =: \Big(([\mathbf{t}_i]_2, [\tilde{\mathbf{t}}_i]_2, [\mathbf{u}_i]_2, $
$\qquad\qquad\qquad [\mathbf{v}_i]_2)_{1\le i\le p}, [\tilde{\mathbf{u}}]_2, [\tilde{\mathbf{v}}]_2 \Big)$

$\mathbf{parse}\ \mathbf{C} =: \Big(([\mathbf{c}_{1,i}]_1, [\mathbf{c}_{2,i}]_1, $
$\qquad\qquad\qquad [\mathbf{c}_{3,i}]_1)_{1\le i\le p}, [\mathbf{c}_4]_1 \Big)$

$[K]_T := \sum_{i=1}^{p} \left(e\left([\mathbf{c}_{2,i}^\top]_1, \begin{bmatrix} \mathbf{v}_i \\ \mathbf{u}_i \end{bmatrix}_2 \right) \right.$
$\qquad\qquad \left. - e([\mathbf{c}_{1,i}^\top]_1, [\mathbf{t}_i]_2) - e([\mathbf{c}_{3,i}^\top]_1, [\tilde{\mathbf{t}}_i]_2) \right)$
$\qquad\qquad + e\left([\mathbf{c}_4^\top]_1, \begin{bmatrix} \tilde{\mathbf{v}} \\ \tilde{\mathbf{u}} \end{bmatrix}_2 \right)$

$\mathbf{return}\ [K]_T$

Fig. 14. The scheme obtained from MAC_u instantiated with the SXDH assumption.

References

1. Abe, M., Hofheinz, D., Nishimaki, R., Ohkubo, M., Pan, J.: Compact structure-preserving signatures with almost tight security. In: Katz, J., Shacham, H. (eds.) CRYPTO 2017. LNCS, vol. 10402, pp. 548–580. Springer, Cham (2017). https://doi.org/10.1007/978-3-319-63715-0_19
2. Abe, M., Jutla, C.S., Ohkubo, M., Pan, J., Roy, A., Wang, Y.: Shorter QA-NIZK and SPS with tighter security. In: Galbraith, S.D., Moriai, S. (eds.) ASIACRYPT 2019. LNCS, vol. 11923, pp. 669–699. Springer, Cham (2019). https://doi.org/10.1007/978-3-030-34618-8_23
3. Abe, M., Jutla, C.S., Ohkubo, M., Roy, A.: Improved (almost) tightly-secure simulation-sound QA-NIZK with applications. In: Peyrin, T., Galbraith, S. (eds.) ASIACRYPT 2018. LNCS, vol. 11272, pp. 627–656. Springer, Cham (2018). https://doi.org/10.1007/978-3-030-03326-2_21
4. Attrapadung, N., Hanaoka, G., Yamada, S.: A framework for identity-based encryption with almost tight security. In: Iwata, T., Cheon, J.H. (eds.) ASIACRYPT 2015. LNCS, vol. 9452, pp. 521–549. Springer, Heidelberg (2015). https://doi.org/10.1007/978-3-662-48797-6_22
5. Bellare, M., Goldwasser, S.: New paradigms for digital signatures and message authentication based on non-interactive zero knowledge proofs. In: Brassard, G. (ed.) CRYPTO 1989. LNCS, vol. 435, pp. 194–211. Springer, Heidelberg (1990). https://doi.org/10.1007/0-387-34805-0_19
6. Blazy, O., Kiltz, E., Pan, J.: (Hierarchical) identity-based encryption from affine message authentication. In: Garay, J.A., Gennaro, R. (eds.) CRYPTO 2014. LNCS, vol. 8616, pp. 408–425. Springer, Heidelberg (2014). https://doi.org/10.1007/978-3-662-44371-2_23
7. Boneh, D., Boyen, X.: Efficient selective identity-based encryption without random oracles. J. Cryptol. **24**(4), 659–693 (2011)
8. Chen, J., Gong, J., Kowalczyk, L., Wee, H.: Unbounded ABE via bilinear entropy expansion, revisited. In: Nielsen, J.B., Rijmen, V. (eds.) EUROCRYPT 2018. LNCS, vol. 10820, pp. 503–534. Springer, Cham (2018). https://doi.org/10.1007/978-3-319-78381-9_19
9. Chen, J., Wee, H.: Fully, (almost) tightly secure IBE and dual system groups. In: Canetti, R., Garay, J.A. (eds.) CRYPTO 2013. LNCS, vol. 8043, pp. 435–460. Springer, Heidelberg (2013). https://doi.org/10.1007/978-3-642-40084-1_25
10. Cohn-Gordon, K., Cremers, C., Gjøsteen, K., Jacobsen, H., Jager, T.: Highly efficient key exchange protocols with optimal tightness. In: Boldyreva, A., Micciancio, D. (eds.) CRYPTO 2019. LNCS, vol. 11694, pp. 767–797. Springer, Cham (2019). https://doi.org/10.1007/978-3-030-26954-8_25
11. Escala, A., Herold, G., Kiltz, E., Ràfols, C., Villar, J.: An algebraic framework for diffie-hellman assumptions. In: Canetti, R., Garay, J.A. (eds.) CRYPTO 2013. LNCS, vol. 8043, pp. 129–147. Springer, Heidelberg (2013). https://doi.org/10.1007/978-3-642-40084-1_8
12. Garg, S., Gay, R., Hajiabadi, M.: Master-key KDM-secure IBE from pairings. In: Kiayias, A., Kohlweiss, M., Wallden, P., Zikas, V. (eds.) PKC 2020. LNCS, vol. 12110, pp. 123–152. Springer, Cham (2020). https://doi.org/10.1007/978-3-030-45374-9_5
13. Gay, R., Hofheinz, D., Kiltz, E., Wee, H.: Tightly CCA-secure encryption without pairings. In: Fischlin, M., Coron, J.-S. (eds.) EUROCRYPT 2016. LNCS, vol. 9665, pp. 1–27. Springer, Heidelberg (2016). https://doi.org/10.1007/978-3-662-49890-3_1

14. Gay, R., Hofheinz, D., Kohl, L.: Kurosawa-desmedt meets tight security. In: Katz, J., Shacham, H. (eds.) CRYPTO 2017. LNCS, vol. 10403, pp. 133–160. Springer, Cham (2017). https://doi.org/10.1007/978-3-319-63697-9_5

15. Gay, R., Hofheinz, D., Kohl, L., Pan, J.: More efficient (almost) tightly secure structure-preserving signatures. In: Nielsen, J.B., Rijmen, V. (eds.) EUROCRYPT 2018. LNCS, vol. 10821, pp. 230–258. Springer, Cham (2018). https://doi.org/10.1007/978-3-319-78375-8_8

16. Gentry, C., Silverberg, A.: Hierarchical ID-based cryptography. In: Zheng, Y. (ed.) ASIACRYPT 2002. LNCS, vol. 2501, pp. 548–566. Springer, Heidelberg (2002). https://doi.org/10.1007/3-540-36178-2_34

17. Gjøsteen, K., Jager, T.: Practical and tightly-secure digital signatures and authenticated key exchange. In: Shacham, H., Boldyreva, A. (eds.) CRYPTO 2018. LNCS, vol. 10992, pp. 95–125. Springer, Cham (2018). https://doi.org/10.1007/978-3-319-96881-0_4

18. Gong, J., Cao, Z., Tang, S., Chen, J.: Extended dual system group and shorter unbounded hierarchical identity based encryption. Designs, Codes and Cryptography **80**(3), 525–559 (2015). https://doi.org/10.1007/s10623-015-0117-z

19. Gong, J., Chen, J., Dong, X., Cao, Z., Tang, S.: Extended nested dual system groups, revisited. In: Cheng, C.M., Chung, K.M., Persiano, G., Yang, B.Y. (eds.) PKC 2016, Part I. LNCS, vol. 9614, pp. 133–163. Springer, Heidelberg (2016)

20. Gong, J., Dong, X., Chen, J., Cao, Z.: Efficient IBE with tight reduction to standard assumption in the multi-challenge setting. In: Cheon, J.H., Takagi, T. (eds.) ASIACRYPT 2016. LNCS, vol. 10032, pp. 624–654. Springer, Heidelberg (2016). https://doi.org/10.1007/978-3-662-53890-6_21

21. Han, S., Liu, S., Lyu, L., Gu, D.: Tight leakage-resilient CCA-security from quasi-adaptive hash proof system. In: Boldyreva, A., Micciancio, D. (eds.) CRYPTO 2019, Part II. LNCS, vol. 11693, pp. 417–447. Springer, Heidelberg (2019)

22. Hesse, J., Hofheinz, D., Kohl, L.: On tightly secure non-interactive key exchange. In: Shacham, H., Boldyreva, A. (eds.) CRYPTO 2018, Part II. LNCS, vol. 10992, pp. 65–94. Springer, Heidelberg (2018)

23. Hofheinz, D., Jia, D., Pan, J.: Identity-based encryption tightly secure under chosen-ciphertext attacks. In: Peyrin, T., Galbraith, S. (eds.) ASIACRYPT 2018. LNCS, vol. 11273, pp. 190–220. Springer, Cham (2018). https://doi.org/10.1007/978-3-030-03329-3_7

24. Hofheinz, D., Kiltz, E.: Secure hybrid encryption from weakened key encapsulation. In: Menezes, A. (ed.) CRYPTO 2007. LNCS, vol. 4622, pp. 553–571. Springer, Heidelberg (2007). https://doi.org/10.1007/978-3-540-74143-5_31

25. Hofheinz, D., Koch, J., Striecks, C.: Identity-based encryption with (almost) tight security in the multi-instance, multi-ciphertext setting. In: Katz, J. (ed.) PKC 2015. LNCS, vol. 9020, pp. 799–822. Springer, Heidelberg (2015). https://doi.org/10.1007/978-3-662-46447-2_36

26. Horwitz, J., Lynn, B.: Toward hierarchical identity-based encryption. In: Knudsen, L.R. (ed.) EUROCRYPT 2002. LNCS, vol. 2332, pp. 466–481. Springer, Heidelberg (2002). https://doi.org/10.1007/3-540-46035-7_31

27. Kowalczyk, L., Lewko, A.B.: Bilinear entropy expansion from the decisional linear assumption. In: Gennaro, R., Robshaw, M. (eds.) CRYPTO 2015. LNCS, vol. 9216, pp. 524–541. Springer, Heidelberg (2015). https://doi.org/10.1007/978-3-662-48000-7_26

28. Kurosawa, K., Desmedt, Y.: A new paradigm of hybrid encryption scheme. In: Franklin, M. (ed.) CRYPTO 2004. LNCS, vol. 3152, pp. 426–442. Springer, Heidelberg (2004). https://doi.org/10.1007/978-3-540-28628-8_26

29. Langrehr, R., Pan, J.: Tightly secure hierarchical identity-based encryption. In: Lin, D., Sako, K. (eds.) PKC 2019. LNCS, vol. 11442, pp. 436–465. Springer, Cham (2019). https://doi.org/10.1007/978-3-030-17253-4_15

30. Langrehr, R., Pan, J.: Hierarchical identity-based encryption with tight multi-challenge security. In: Kiayias, A., Kohlweiss, M., Wallden, P., Zikas, V. (eds.) PKC 2020. LNCS, vol. 12110, pp. 153–183. Springer, Cham (2020). https://doi.org/10.1007/978-3-030-45374-9_6

31. Lewko, A.: Tools for simulating features of composite order bilinear groups in the prime order setting. In: Pointcheval, D., Johansson, T. (eds.) EUROCRYPT 2012. LNCS, vol. 7237, pp. 318–335. Springer, Heidelberg (2012). https://doi.org/10.1007/978-3-642-29011-4_20

32. Lewko, A., Waters, B.: New techniques for dual system encryption and fully secure HIBE with short ciphertexts. In: Micciancio, D. (ed.) TCC 2010. LNCS, vol. 5978, pp. 455–479. Springer, Heidelberg (2010). https://doi.org/10.1007/978-3-642-11799-2_27

33. Lewko, A., Waters, B.: Unbounded HIBE and attribute-based encryption. In: Paterson, K.G. (ed.) EUROCRYPT 2011. LNCS, vol. 6632, pp. 547–567. Springer, Heidelberg (2011). https://doi.org/10.1007/978-3-642-20465-4_30

34. Lewko, A., Waters, B.: Why proving HIBE systems secure is difficult. In: Nguyen, P.Q., Oswald, E. (eds.) EUROCRYPT 2014. LNCS, vol. 8441, pp. 58–76. Springer, Heidelberg (2014). https://doi.org/10.1007/978-3-642-55220-5_4

35. Okamoto, T., Takashima, K.: Fully secure unbounded inner-product and attribute-based encryption. In: Wang, X., Sako, K. (eds.) ASIACRYPT 2012. LNCS, vol. 7658, pp. 349–366. Springer, Heidelberg (2012). https://doi.org/10.1007/978-3-642-34961-4_22

36. Shamir, A.: Identity-based cryptosystems and signature schemes. In: Blakley, G.R., Chaum, D. (eds.) CRYPTO 1984. LNCS, vol. 196, pp. 47–53. Springer, Heidelberg (1985). https://doi.org/10.1007/3-540-39568-7_5

37. Tomida, J.: Tightly secure inner product functional encryption: multi-input and function-hiding constructions. In: Galbraith, S.D., Moriai, S. (eds.) ASIACRYPT 2019. LNCS, vol. 11923, pp. 459–488. Springer, Cham (2019). https://doi.org/10.1007/978-3-030-34618-8_16

38. Waters, B.: Dual system encryption: realizing fully secure IBE and HIBE under simple assumptions. In: Halevi, S. (ed.) CRYPTO 2009. LNCS, vol. 5677, pp. 619–636. Springer, Heidelberg (2009). https://doi.org/10.1007/978-3-642-03356-8_36

39. Waters, B.: Efficient identity-based encryption without random oracles. In: Cramer, R. (ed.) EUROCRYPT 2005. LNCS, vol. 3494, pp. 114–127. Springer, Heidelberg (2005). https://doi.org/10.1007/11426639_7

Multi-client Oblivious RAM
with Poly-logarithmic Communication

Sherman S. M. Chow[1]($\boxtimes$) $\text{\textcircled{iD}}$, Katharina Fech[2], Russell W. F. Lai[2],
and Giulio Malavolta[3]

[1] The Chinese University of Hong Kong, Shatin, Hong Kong
sherman@ie.cuhk.edu.hk
[2] Friedrich-Alexander-Universität Erlangen-Nürnberg, Erlangen, Germany
{fech,lai}@cs.fau.de
[3] UC Berkeley & Carnegie Mellon University, Pittsburgh, USA
giulio.malavolta@hotmail.it

Abstract. Oblivious RAM enables oblivious access to memory in the
single-client setting, which may not be the best fit in the network setting.
Multi-client oblivious RAM (MCORAM) considers a collaborative but
untrusted environment, where a database owner selectively grants read
access and write access to different entries of a confidential database to
multiple clients. Their access pattern must remain oblivious not only to
the server but also to fellow clients. This upgrade rules out many techniques for constructing ORAM, forcing us to pursue new techniques.
MCORAM not only provides an alternative solution to private anonymous data access (Eurocrypt 2019) but also serves as a promising building block for equipping oblivious file systems with access control and
extending other advanced cryptosystems to the multi-client setting.

Despite being a powerful object, the current state-of-the-art is unsatisfactory: The only existing scheme requires $O(\sqrt{n})$ communication and
client computation for a database of size n. Whether it is possible to
reduce these complexities to $\mathsf{polylog}(n)$, thereby matching the upper
bounds for ORAM, is an open problem, *i.e.*, can we enjoy access control
and client-obliviousness under the same bounds?

Our first result answers the above question affirmatively by giving
a construction from fully homomorphic encryption (FHE). Our main
technical innovation is a new technique for cross-key trial evaluation of
ciphertexts. We also consider the same question in the setting with N
non-colluding servers, out of which at most t of them can be corrupt. We
build multi-server MCORAM from distributed point functions (DPF),
and propose new constructions of DPF via a virtualization technique

S. S. M. Chow—This work is supported in parts by General Research Funds (CUHK
14209918 and 14210217) and Germany/Hong Kong Joint Research Scheme G-
CUHK406/17 of the Research Grants Council, University Grant Committee, Hong
Kong, and German Academic Exchange Service under Grant No.: PPP-HK 57391915.
The authors would like to thank Brice Minaud and anonymous reviewers for their
helpful comments.

S. Moriai and H. Wang (Eds.): ASIACRYPT 2020, LNCS 12492, pp. 160–190, 2020.
https://doi.org/10.1007/978-3-030-64834-3_6

with bootstrapping, assuming the existence of homomorphic secret sharing and pseudorandom generators in NC0, which are not known to imply FHE.

Keywords: Multi-client oblivious RAM · Access control · Homomorphic encryption · Distributed point function · Homomorphic secret sharing

1   Introduction

Oblivious RAM (ORAM) [22] allows random accesses to physical memory locations without revealing the logical read/write access patterns. The original motivation considers a software accessing the local memory, where the latter is modeled as a machine that can only perform read and write operations but no computation (known as the "balls and bins" model). Later, ORAM was also considered in a network setting, where a client wishes to obliviously access its data outsourced to a remote server, where computation might be allowed. Besides direct applications in local and remote storage, ORAM techniques have been shown useful for many other cryptographic goals.

In a realistic setting, a database can be accessed by hundreds of mutually untrusted clients. The security of ORAM or even its parallel variant (OPRAM) [3,13] becomes insufficient as all clients (processors in the same machine in OPRAM) share the same secret key. To remedy this, Maffei *et al.* [29] considered multi-client ORAM (MCORAM), which aims to capture the following natural scenario: A database owner encodes an array of data M and outsources the encoded database to a server. Clients can dynamically join the system and request access rights to individual entries of M. After the permission is granted, a client can obliviously perform random access to the permitted entries of M, without communicating with the database owner or other clients.

For privacy, MCORAM expects two strengthened requirements against an adversary who can *corrupt an arbitrary subset of clients* and the server:

- Read and write accesses are anonymous.
- Read and write accesses are indistinguishable, except when the adversary has read access to the address being written.

Integrity is another interesting security feature needed in a multi-client scenario – legitimately written entries should be retrievable by any permitted clients and cannot be overwritten by malicious clients, assuming an honest server.

After three decades of development, the complexities of ORAM schemes are well-understood. Unfortunately, many techniques for constructing ORAM break down completely when the client can be corrupt. This forces us to pursue new techniques in building MCORAM, regardless of the many ORAM constructions.

The only (fully-oblivious) MCORAM by Maffei *et al.* [30] requires $O(n)$ server computation and $O(\sqrt{n})$ communication and client computation. They also show $\Omega(n)$ server computation is *necessary* (in the balls-and-bins model),

Table 1. Comparison of MCORAM schemes for storing n messages in the following criteria: security against malicious clients (MC), support of multiple data owners (MD), security against t out of N corrupt servers, server computation, client computation, and communication of the access protocol (factors of $\mathsf{poly}(\lambda)$ are omitted.)

Scheme	MC	MD	(t, N)	S Comp	C Comp	Comm
[29]	✗	✗	$(1,1)$	$O(\log n)$	$O(\log n)$	$O(\log n)$
[30]	✓	✓	$(1,1)$	$O(n)$	$O(\sqrt{n})$	$O(\sqrt{n})$
This work	✓	✓	$(1,1)$	$O(n)$	$O(\log n)$	$O(\log n)$
This work	✓	✓	$(N'-1, N'^2), N' \in \{2,3,4\}$	$O(n)$	$\mathsf{polylog}(n)$	$\mathsf{polylog}(n)$

in contrast to $\mathsf{polylog}(n)$ computation of ORAM. For communication, no non-trivial lower bound for MCORAM is known, while the upper bounds for ORAM and MCORAM are $\mathsf{polylog}(n)$ and $O(\sqrt{n})$, respectively. The inherent complexities of MCORAM are still poorly understood. We are thus motivated to ask:

Is multi-client ORAM with $\mathsf{polylog}(n)$ communication possible?

Our Results. We answer the above question affirmatively. Our main contribution is a single-server MCORAM construction with $O(\log n)$ communication and client computation, and $O(n)$ server computation (omitting factors of $\mathsf{poly}(\lambda)$). This scheme relies on a new usage of key-indistinguishable FHE, in which ciphertexts encrypted under an unknown key are evaluated under non-matching keys. When instantiated with a rate-1 FHE [8,19], the communication complexity is optimal ($\log n$) up to an additive fixed polynomial factor. In other words:

Theorem 1 (Informal). *Assuming FHE, there exists a multi-client ORAM scheme with poly-logarithmic communication complexity.*

We also consider the setting with multiple (non-colluding) servers, in which we propose an N^2-server MCORAM scheme resilient against the corruption of t servers, with $\mathsf{polylog}(n)$ communication and client computation. The scheme assumes the existence of a (t, N) distributed point function (DPF) [21], where N is the number of parties and t is the corruption threshold. We then show new constructions of DPFs for parameters $(t, N) \in \{(2,3),(3,4)\}$, respectively, assuming homomorphic secret sharing (HSS) and constant-depth pseudorandom generators (PRGs), which are not known to imply FHE. Together with the existing $(1,2)$-DPF [21], we show the following theorem.

Theorem 2 (Informal). *Assuming HSS and PRG in NC0, there exist multi-client $\{4,9,16\}$-servers ORAM schemes with poly-logarithmic communication complexity, resilient against the corruption of $\{1,2,3\}$ servers respectively.*

As summarized in Table 1, we made clear contributions in communication and client computation complexities. One may further ask for an even better construction as (i) the computation of the servers is linear in the database size and (ii) the client storage is proportional to the number of entries with access granted. While the former is inherent to some extent (as shown in [30]) and the latter appears to be natural for fine-grained access control allowing $O(2^n)$ possible policies for each user, we show how to reduce the client storage by constrained PRFs [2]. For simple access structures (such as prefix predicates), known constrained PRFs (*e.g.*, [24]) do not add any extra assumption.

2 Technical Overview

2.1 MCORAM with Poly-log Communication: Initial Attempts

A first attempt to construct MCORAM with poly-logarithmic communication is to extend an ORAM with the same complexity. Simply sharing the same ORAM secret key among all clients (*e.g.*, [25]) fails. The *secret state* kept by each client is the root issue. For obliviousness against the server and fellow clients, they must be kept confidential from others. To ensure consistency of the operations across all clients, they must be correlated. These *contradicting* requirements seem to forbid the adoption of many ORAM techniques. Another idea is to secret-share the ORAM secret key to all clients, and emulate the ORAM accesses using secure multi-party computation. This requires interactions between many clients for each access and is clearly undesirable when the number of clients is large.

We note that a database can be privately accessed without a persistent secret client state in (single-server) private-information retrieval (PIR) [14], in which a *stateless* client can *read* an entry while hiding its address. For the discussion below, it is useful to recall the standard FHE-based PIR scheme, which achieves poly-logarithmic communication. Recall that FHE allows homomorphic evaluations of any circuits over ciphertexts. To read the entry $M[a]$ of a database M at address a, the client samples a fresh FHE key pair $(\mathsf{pk}, \mathsf{sk})$ and sends $(\mathsf{pk}, \mathsf{Enc}(\mathsf{pk}, a))$ to the server. The server homomorphically evaluates the following circuit Read_M parameterized by M over $\mathsf{Enc}(\mathsf{pk}, a)$:

$\mathsf{Read}_M(\mathsf{addr})$: Return $M[\mathsf{addr}]$.

This results in a ciphertext encrypting $M[a]$ to be sent to the client.

We can extend a PIR scheme to the multi-client setting and yield a read-only MCORAM. More concretely, the data owner encrypts each database entry with a different key. Granting read access means delegating the decryption key of the corresponding address. To read, recall that PIR clients are stateless, the client first performs PIR, and then decrypts the retrieved encrypted entry locally.

Challenge: Write Access. Towards supporting write access, a rough idea is as follows. First, each database entry $M[a]$ is encrypted under FHE, so the server cannot just see which entries have changed after a write access. Next, when writing data m^* to address a^*, the client encrypts its update instruction (a^*, m^*) using FHE, so that the server could "somehow" update the database entries homomorphically by evaluating a Write function over the ciphertexts of (a^*, m^*)

and (each entry of) M. This raises the question of – Under which key should (1) each entry $M[a]$, and (2) the update instruction (a^*, m^*) be encrypted?

Using the same key across all $M[a]$ fails as we discussed – all clients need to hold the same decryption key to access their data. Now we need to encrypt each $M[a]$ under a key pk_a independently generated for each a. With $O(n)$ communication and client computation, the client can just create n FHE-ciphertexts, each using a different key, and sends them to the server. With the polylogarithmic constraint, we face a *dilemma*: Either the client informs the server about (a^*, pk_{a^*}) so that the latter knows which ciphertext it should update, which violates obliviousness; or the server would need to somehow evaluate Write over a^*, m^*, and $M[a]$, where the first two are encrypted under pk_{a^*}, and the last is under pk_a, for $a \in [n]$, and then it is unclear if correctness would hold. Multi-key FHE does not seem to be useful in this context because its homomorphic evaluation results in a ciphertext under a new combined key, which creates a complicated key-management problem and suffers from the problem of high interaction similar to the secure multi-party computation solution.

2.2 FHE-Based Construction

Our insight into resolving the dilemma is that some meaningful operations can actually be done over FHE ciphertexts encrypted under *different* keys. Specifically, we introduce a *cross-key trial evaluation* technique that interprets a ciphertext as one encrypted under a possibly mismatching key.[1] Below, we illustrate our technique with a simplified setting that is sufficient to capture the essence.

Cross-Key Trial Evaluation. Recall that the server database stores $(a, \mathsf{Enc}(\mathsf{pk}_a, M[a]))$ for $a \in [n]$. To write, a client sends the encrypted instruction $(\mathsf{Enc}(\mathsf{pk}_{a^*}, a^*), \mathsf{Enc}(\mathsf{pk}_{a^*}, m^*))$ to the server, which evaluates for each $a \in [n]$ the following simplified writing circuit, parameterized by a, over $\mathsf{Enc}(\mathsf{pk}_{a^*}, a^*)$ and $\mathsf{Enc}(\mathsf{pk}_{a^*}, m^*)$ from the client, and $\mathsf{Enc}(\mathsf{pk}_a, M[a])$ from the server storage, by treating as if all of them were created under pk_a:

$\mathsf{SimpleWrite}_a(\mathsf{addr}, \mathsf{data}', \mathsf{data})$: If $\mathsf{addr} = a$, return data'; else return data.

For each $a \in [n]$, the server overwrites the a-th ciphertext it stored with the ciphertext output by evaluating $\mathsf{SimpleWrite}_a$. Let us examine what happens depending on whether a matches a^* from the update instruction. If $a = a^*$, all three ciphertexts are encrypted under the same key; the server would get a ciphertext of m^* under pk_{a^*}, i.e., $M[a^*]$ is correctly overwritten with m^*.

If $a \neq a^*$, it seems paradoxical that this evaluation gives us anything meaningful since there is no correctness guarantee when homomorphic evaluations are performed under a *wrong public key* $\mathsf{pk}_{a^*} \neq \mathsf{pk}_a$. However, as a

---

[1] This technique is reminiscent of *decrypting* a *random* string interpreted as an FHE ciphertext in the surprising result of Canetti, Lombardi, and Wichs [12], which constructs non-interactive zero-knowledge from any circular-secure FHE.

matter of fact, the homomorphic evaluation still proceeds as if everything is encrypted under pk_a. Namely, it interprets its input, particularly the first ciphertext $\mathsf{Enc}(\mathsf{pk}_{a^*}, a^*)$, as if it is encrypted under pk_a. With this treatment, it is very unlikely that $\mathsf{Enc}(\mathsf{pk}_{a^*}, a^*)$ is also a ciphertext of a under pk_a. More precisely, $\mathsf{Dec}(\mathsf{sk}_a, \mathsf{Enc}(\mathsf{pk}_{a^*}, a^*))$ should be "independent" of a (we will revisit this shortly), and therefore the check $\mathsf{addr} = a$ would most likely fail. Then, by the correctness of FHE, the evaluation would result in a new ciphertext encrypting $\mathsf{data} = M[a]$ under pk_a, i.e., entries $M[a]$ with $a \neq a^*$ remain unchanged.

The critical insight here is that the random outcomes of operating on a "wrong" ciphertext, with overwhelming probability, "match" with the desired behavior we expect as if *cross-key evaluation* is possible. Note that after each write operation, the entries are left in a consistent state, i.e., each entry $M[a]$ is still encrypted under pk_a, and the database size stays the same. For this to be true, our FHE scheme must satisfy a strong variant of correctness, where the evaluation algorithm must be well-defined and correct over the entire ciphertext space (and not necessarily in the support of a particular public key). In Sect. 4.2, we show how to generically transform any FHE scheme to satisfy this notion, provided that it meets some weak structural requirements.

Finally, the FHE scheme here needs to be *key-private*, i.e., ciphertexts under different keys are indistinguishable. Fortunately, essentially all known FHE schemes are key-private, as their ciphertexts are typically indistinguishable from uniformly sampled elements from the ciphertext space.

Achieving Integrity and a Formal Reduction. The above approach can provide writing functionality, *but not integrity* as everyone can encrypt using the keys pk_a. Furthermore, we relied on the heuristic that $\mathsf{Dec}(\mathsf{sk}_a, \mathsf{Enc}(\mathsf{pk}_{a^*}, a^*)) \neq a$ with high probability, which is difficult to guarantee formally.

We propose a technique that resolves both issues simultaneously using any signature scheme Σ. Clients with writing rights to a are granted an address-dependent signing key sk_a^Σ. Instead of encrypting (a^*, m^*), the client computes $\mathsf{Enc}(\mathsf{pk}_{a^*}, \sigma^*)$ and $\mathsf{Enc}(\mathsf{pk}_{a^*}, m^*)$, where σ^* is a signature of (r, m^*) under $\mathsf{pk}_{a^*}^\Sigma$, and r is a random nonce chosen by the server for each access. Correspondingly, the server homomorphically evaluates for each a the circuit $\mathsf{Write}_{\mathsf{pk}_a^\Sigma, r}$, parameterized by $(\mathsf{pk}_a^\Sigma, r)$, over the ciphertexts of $\mathsf{Enc}(\mathsf{pk}_{a^*}, \sigma^*)$, $\mathsf{Enc}(\mathsf{pk}_{a^*}, m^*)$, and $\mathsf{Enc}(\mathsf{pk}_a, M[a])$, again as if they are all ciphertexts under pk_a:

$\mathsf{Write}_{\mathsf{pk}_a^\Sigma, r}(\mathsf{sig}, \mathsf{data}', \mathsf{data})$: If sig is a valid signature of (r, data') under pk_a^Σ, return data'; else return data.

With a similar argument as above, $M[a]$ would be overwritten by m^* if $a^* = a$ and σ^* is a valid signature, which can only be generated by clients having writing rights to a^*. Unlike using $\mathsf{SimpleWrite}_a$, we can further argue about the converse without relying on heuristics. Concretely, if $a \neq a^*$ but $\mathsf{Dec}(\mathsf{sk}_a, \mathsf{Enc}(\mathsf{pk}_{a^*}, \sigma^*))$ is a valid signature of $(r, \mathsf{Dec}(\mathsf{sk}_a, \mathsf{Enc}(\mathsf{pk}_{a^*}, m^*)))$ under pk_a^Σ, we can extract a signature forgery with respect to the verification key pk_a^Σ, violating the unforgeability of the signature scheme. Consequently, it holds that when $a \neq a^*$, $M[a]$ would not be overwritten except with negligible probability.

Applications. The above technique can be generalized to enable *(key-dependent) conditional evaluations* of FHE ciphertexts, with the condition depends on not only the messages encrypted within but also the keys used to generate the ciphertexts. This feature is useful in (outsourced) access-control applications such as an *"oblivious whitelisting firewall"* that only allows incoming ciphertexts encrypted under one of the whitelisted keys to pass through without the firewall keeping any secret key.

Reducing Secret Key Size. So far, we have assumed that the data owner generates address-dependent secret keys, and grants clients reading and writing rights by delegating the keys for the corresponding addresses. In the worst case, data owner and client keys are of size linear in the size of the database.

A common technique to reduce the data-owner key size is to generate those address-dependent secret keys by a pseudorandom function (PRF). Towards reducing the client key size, a constrained PRF (cPRF) can be used. Recall that cPRF can create a constrained key K_X that constrains the PRF key K within some subset X of the domain. Given K_X, one can evaluate the PRF on all inputs $x \in X$, while the PRF values of all $x \notin X$ remain pseudorandom. That means the data owner can delegate to the clients cPRF keys that allow derivation of the address-dependent secret keys. If the cPRF keys are succinct, *e.g.*, of size sublinear in the size of X, the client key size is also short. For example, the well-known PRF construction by Goldreich, Goldwasser, and Micali [24] is a cPRF for prefix constraints with logarithmic-size keys.

On Sublinear Server Computation. The focus of our work is to minimize the communication complexity of the protocol. We note that recent works [7,11] have investigated the possibility of sublinear server computation (with preprocessing) in PIR (essentially a read-only MCORAM with no access control) in the *single-client* setting, and have proposed a solution based on new hardness assumptions on permuted Reed-Solomon codes. They also consider the *public-key* setting, which does not require any secret state to read the database, *i.e.*, multiple clients are allowed to query the database obliviously. Unfortunately, the only proposed solutions build on a strong notion of virtual black-box obfuscation. We consider constructing an MCORAM with sublinear server computation (from standard assumption) as a fascinating open problem.

2.3 DPF-Based Multi-server Construction

The scheme described above resolves the open question of communication efficiency for MCORAM using FHE schemes, which are yet to become efficient in a practical sense, and are only known to be realizable from lattices. Towards finding more practical solutions, to broaden the spectrum of assumptions, and to get a larger variety of MCORAM schemes, we turn our attention to the multi-server setting, in which we leverage the non-collusion between different servers. We restrict to the three-message setting where *the servers do not talk to each other.* This motivates the non-collusion assumption and rules out trivial constructions.[2]

In this direction, we rely on another tool known as distributed point functions (DPF), which were shown to be useful in constructing PIR and in complexity theory [21], as well as private queries on public data [32]. A DPF allows a client to split a given point function into keys $(k_1, \ldots, k_N)$. Given k_i, one can locally evaluate the shared function at some input point to obtain a value z_i. Computing $z_1 + \cdots + z_N$ reconstructs the function output at the evaluated point. If the point function is *hidden* even if t-out-of-N shares are leaked, we call it a (t, N)-DPF. The main efficiency measure for a DPF is the size of the shares, which can be as small as $\log n$, where n is the size of the truth table of the point function.

We are going to build DPFs for new values of (t, N) not achieved before. In particular, the existing query system [32] was only instantiated by $(1, 2)$-DPF.

From DPF to Multi-server MCORAM. There is a folklore N^2-server ORAM construction (a.k.a. distributed ORAM [9]) assuming only a (t, N)-DPF. Using a DPF with polylog(n) communication, the construction achieves polylog(n) communication. While its server computation complexity is $O(n)$, it has been shown to outperform other optimized competitors in practice [16]. More importantly, we observe that we can adopt this DPF-based scheme to the multi-client setting in a relatively simple manner.

On a very high level, the construction arranges a set of N^2 servers in a square matrix according to some (*e.g.*, lexicographical) ordering. The database M is split into N shares such that $\bar{M}_1 + \cdots + \bar{M}_N = M$, and all servers belonging to the i-th row are given the i-th share $\bar{M}_i$. Clients can read the a-th location $M[a]$ by sharing a point function (which evaluates to a bit-string with the a-th bit being 1) to each server in some i-th row. The responses from a server allow the client to decode the i-th share of $M[a]$. Repeating this for all N rows, the client could recover all shares and hence $M[a]$. Writing can be done similarly, except that shares of the DPF are distributed row-wise to keep the share of the databases consistent (see Sect. 7 for more details).

New DPF Constructions. With the generic transformation, we can focus on constructing DPFs. The *only known* DPF with (poly)logarithmic-size shares from non-lattice assumptions is due to Boyle *et al.* [4]. They show how to construct a $(1, 2)$-DPF with logarithmic-size shares, assuming only the existence of

---

[2] In the three-message setting, the accessing client sends one message to each of the servers, each server sends one message back to the client, and the client sends one final message back to each server. Thus, the servers cannot communicate with each other (even through the client) in coming up with the responses to the client. Not letting the servers communicate also ruled out any straightforward adaption that evaluates an ORAM under the hood of secure two/multi-party computation.

PRGs, which is equivalent to the existence of one-way functions. This yields a $(1, 4)$-MCORAM resilient against a single server.

For improving resilience against a higher number of faulty servers, we investigate new constructions of DPFs with different parameters. In this work, we build a $(2, 3)$-DPF and a $(3, 4)$-DPF with poly-logarithmic communication. These new constructions give us a $(2, 9)$-MCORAM and a $(3, 16)$-MCORAM, respectively.

The design blueprint is as follows. We start with a crucial observation that the evaluation algorithm of the existing $(1, 2)$-DPF [4] can be run in an NC1 circuit by instantiating the underlying PRG appropriately. Our key insight into increasing the number of parties is *a virtualization technique* for emulating the execution of the DPF evaluation algorithm of each party by 2 servers. To realize such *bootstrapping*, we leverage another tool called homomorphic-secret sharing [6]. By applying our techniques to one or two parties, we obtain a $(2, 3)$-DPF and a $(3, 4)$-DPF, respectively. Both schemes rely on a PRG that can be computed in NC0 (*e.g.*, Goldreich PRG [23]) and either the decisional Diffie-Hellman (DDH) or the decisional composite residuosity (DCR) assumption.

3   Related Work

ORAM has been extensively studied for more than three decades, but mostly in the single client setting, with drastically different research challenges compared to the multi-client setting. For example, S^3ORAM [27] is a *single-client* ORAM that splits the server-side computation across 3 servers via secure multiparty computation, which we aim to avoid. Recent works [3,13] considered how to preserve obliviousness when a large number of clients access the database in parallel, without considering security against *malicious* clients or *access control*. These works require the clients to *synchronize* with each other and periodically *interact* with the data owner, which is not needed by our MCORAM constructions.

ORAM and similar cryptographic techniques such as private information retrieval (PIR) [14,28] have been utilized in building oblivious file systems (*e.g.*, TaoStore [31] and prior works cited by [30,31]). These systems do not support access control, and their obliviousness does not hold against malicious clients. (Also see [30, Table 1].) Oblivious transfer (OT) can be considered as an ORAM without writing. Camenisch *et al.* [10] proposed OT with access control. Seeing a valid zero-knowledge proof of the client credential, the "server" helps the client *decrypt* one (randomized) entry of the encrypted database previously sent to the client. Since the decryption key is needed, the *data owner should remain online*.

Also relying on zero-knowledge proofs, group ORAM [29] allows the client to access the database according to a predefined policy without any interaction with the data owner. Yet, the obliviousness does not hold against *malicious* clients.

Blass, Mayberry, and Noubir [1] proposed "multi-client ORAM" in a model different from ours, in which all the clients trust each other. Their focus is security against a server that is actively malicious and may rewind the state information shared by multiple clients (and stored by the server).

A recent work of Hamlin *et al.* [26] considered a closely related problem called private anonymous data access (PANDA), yet with some crucial differences. PANDA can be considered as combining the best of PIR and ORAM. It focuses on achieving sublinear server computation, leveraging assumptions such as only t out of the N clients can be corrupt for some *predefined threshold t*, and the set of clients are fixed at setup. In contrast, MCORAM allows any subset of the clients to be corrupt, and clients can dynamically join the system. All PANDA schemes have both communication and computation complexities *scale multiplicatively* in t. One of their schemes (Secret-Writes PANDA) achieves the closest functionality aimed by MCORAM. However, writing is append-only, meaning that their server storage grows linearly in the total number of writes performed by all clients. Reads and writes are also distinguishable. While one could hide the access type by performing dummy reads and writes, the append-only nature makes *the server storage grows linearly in the number of reads and writes*. In short, MCORAM with polylog(n) communication provides a better alternative with no reliance on the client corruption threshold for security or communication efficiency.

4 Preliminaries

Let PPT denote probabilistic polynomial time. The security parameter is denoted by $\lambda \in \mathbb{N}$. We say that a function negl($\cdot$) is negligible if it vanishes faster than any inverse polynomial. We write the set $\{1, \ldots, N\}$ as $[N]$.

4.1 Constrained Pseudorandom Functions

A constrained PRF (cPRF) [2] is a PRF equipped with the additional algorithms Constrain and cEval. Let $\mathcal{X}$ be the domain of the PRF. For any subset $X \subseteq \mathcal{X}$, Constrain produces a constrained key K_X from the secret key K. Given K_X, cEval can evaluate the PRF over any input $x \in X$, yet the PRF values for $x' \notin X$ remain pseudorandom. We focus on polynomial-size domains, so the membership $x \in X$ for any $X \subseteq \mathcal{X}$ can be checked in polynomial time.

Definition 1 (Constrained Pseudorandom Functions). *A constrained pseudorandom function family with domain $\mathcal{X}$ and range $\mathcal{Y}$ is defined as a tuple of* PPT *algorithms* (KGen, Eval, Constrain, cEval) *such that:*

KGen(1^λ): *On input the security parameter 1^λ, the key generation algorithm returns a secret key K.*

Eval(K, x): *On input the secret key K and a value $x \in \mathcal{X}$, the deterministic evaluation algorithm returns a (pseudorandom) value $y \in \mathcal{Y}$.*

Constrain(sk, X): *On input the secret key and a set $X \subseteq \mathcal{X}$, the constrain algorithm returns a constrained secret key K_X.*

cEval(K_X, x): *On input a constrained key K_X and a value $x \in \mathcal{X}$, the deterministic constrained evaluation algorithm returns a value $y \in \mathcal{Y}$ or $\bot$.*

Correctness$_{\mathcal{A},\mathsf{cPRF}}(1^\lambda)$	Pseudorandom$^b_{\mathcal{A},\mathsf{cPRF}}(1^\lambda)$
$\mathsf{ChSet} \leftarrow \mathcal{A}(1^\lambda)$	$\mathsf{ChSet} \leftarrow \mathcal{A}(1^\lambda)$
$K \leftarrow \mathsf{KGen}(1^\lambda)$	$K \leftarrow \mathsf{KGen}(1^\lambda)$
$(x, X) \leftarrow \mathcal{A}^{\mathsf{EvalO},\mathsf{ConstrainO}}(1^\lambda)$	$f \leftarrow \mathcal{Y}^{\mathcal{X}}$ /\!/ the set of all functions from $\mathcal{X}$ to $\mathcal{Y}$
$K_X \leftarrow \mathsf{Constrain}(K, X)$	$Y_0 := \{ f(x) : x \in \mathsf{ChSet} \}$
$b_0 := (x \in X)$	$Y_1 := \{ \mathsf{cPRF.Eval}(K, x) : x \in \mathsf{ChSet} \}$
$b_1 := (\mathsf{Eval}(K, x) \neq \mathsf{cEval}(K_X, x))$	$b' \leftarrow \mathcal{A}^{\mathsf{EvalO},\mathsf{ConstrainO}}(Y_b)$
return $b_0 \wedge b_1$	**return** b

EvalO(x)	ConstrainO(X)
ensure $x \notin \mathsf{ChSet}$	**ensure** $X \cap \mathsf{ChSet} = \emptyset$
$y := \mathsf{cPRF.Eval}(K, x)$	$K_X := \mathsf{cPRF.Constrain}(K, X)$
return y	**return** K_X

Fig. 1. Correctness and Pseudorandomness Experiments for Constrained PRFs

We only require a cPRF to satisfy weak selective-input variants of correctness and pseudorandomness, where the adversary first commits to a set ChSet before given access to the evaluation and constrain oracles. The adversary promises not to query the oracles over inputs which has any intersection with ChSet.

Definition 2. *A constrained PRF* cPRF *with domain* $\mathcal{X}$ *and range* $\mathcal{Y}$ *is said to be selective-input correct if, for all* PPT *algorithms* $\mathcal{A}$, *it holds that*

$$\Pr \left[\mathsf{Correctness}_{\mathcal{A},\mathsf{cPRF}}(1^\lambda) = 1 \right] \leq \mathsf{negl}(\lambda)$$

where Correctness$_{\mathcal{A},\mathsf{cPRF}}$ *is defined in Fig. 1.*

Definition 3. *A constrained PRF* cPRF *with domain* $\mathcal{X}$ *and range* $\mathcal{Y}$ *is said to be selective-input pseudorandom if, for all* PPT *algorithms* $\mathcal{A}$, *it holds that*

$$\left| \Pr \left[\mathsf{Pseudorandom}^0_{\mathcal{A},\mathsf{cPRF}}(1^\lambda) = 1 \right] - \Pr \left[\mathsf{Pseudorandom}^1_{\mathcal{A},\mathsf{cPRF}}(1^\lambda) = 1 \right] \right| \leq \mathsf{negl}(\lambda)$$

where Pseudorandom$^b_{\mathcal{A},\mathsf{cPRF}}$ *is defined in Fig. 1.*

4.2 Fully Homomorphic Encryption

Definition 4 (Fully Homomorphic Encryption). *Let* $\mathcal{K} = \mathcal{K}_\lambda$ *be a secret key space,* $\mathcal{M} = \mathcal{M}_\lambda$ *be a plaintext space, and* $\mathcal{C} = \mathcal{C}_\lambda$ *be a ciphertext space. For each* $n \in \mathbb{N}$, *let* $\mathbb{C}_n$ *be the set of all polynomial-size circuits from* $\mathcal{M}^n \to \mathcal{M}$. *A homomorphic encryption scheme is defined as a tuple of* PPT *algorithms below.*

$\underline{\mathsf{KGen}(1^\lambda)}$: *On input the security parameter* $\lambda \in \mathbb{N}$, *this key generation algorithm returns a pair of public and secret keys* $(\mathsf{pk}, \mathsf{sk})$ *where* $\mathsf{sk} \in \mathcal{K}$.

$\underline{\mathsf{Enc}(\mathsf{pk}, m)}$: *On input* pk *and a message* $m \in \mathcal{M}$, *this encryption algorithm returns a ciphertext* $c \in \mathcal{C}$.

$\underline{\mathsf{Dec}(\mathsf{sk}, c)}$: *On input* $\mathsf{sk} \in \mathcal{K}$ *and a ciphertext* $c \in \mathcal{C}$, *this decryption algorithm returns the plaintext* $m \in \mathcal{M}$.

$\underline{\mathsf{Eval}(\mathsf{pk}, \mathsf{C}, (c_1, \ldots, c_n))}$: *On input a public key* pk, *a polynomial-size circuit* $\mathsf{C} \in \mathbb{C}_n$, *and a set of ciphertexts* $(c_1, \ldots, c_n) \in \mathcal{C}^n$ *for some* $n \in \mathbb{N}$, *this evaluation algorithm returns an evaluation output* $c' \in \mathcal{C}$.

Fix $\lambda \in \mathbb{N}$. For each $(\mathsf{pk}, \mathsf{sk}) \in \mathsf{KGen}(1^\lambda)$, we recursively define $\mathcal{C}_{\mathsf{pk}} :=$

$$\left\{ c : \begin{array}{c} (\exists m \in \mathcal{M} \text{ s.t. } c \in \mathsf{Enc}(\mathsf{pk}, m)) \\ \vee \left(\exists n \in \mathbb{N}, \mathsf{C} \in \mathbb{C}_n, (c_1, \ldots, c_n) \in \mathcal{C}_{\mathsf{pk}}^n \text{ s.t. } c \in \mathsf{Eval}(\mathsf{pk}, \mathsf{C}, (c_1, \ldots, c_n)) \right) \end{array} \right\}$$

to be the space of "well-formed" ciphertexts under the key pk, *i.e.*, all ciphertexts produced by $\mathsf{Enc}(\mathsf{pk}, \cdot)$ and $\mathsf{Eval}(\mathsf{pk}, \cdot, \cdot)$. Apparently, $\mathcal{C} \supseteq \bigcup_{\mathsf{pk}:(\mathsf{pk},\mathsf{sk})\in\mathsf{KGen}(1^\lambda)} \mathcal{C}_{\mathsf{pk}}$.

Typically, the decryption algorithm $\mathsf{Dec}(\mathsf{sk}, \cdot)$ is only required to be well-defined over $\mathcal{C}_{\mathsf{pk}}$ for $(\mathsf{pk}, \mathsf{sk}) \in \mathsf{KGen}(1^\lambda)$, but not necessarily over the entire ciphertext space $\mathcal{C}$ (which includes ciphertexts produced under other public keys).

Correspondingly, evaluation correctness is defined upon "valid" ciphertexts.

In this work, we explicitly require the decryption algorithm $\mathsf{Dec}(\cdot, \cdot)$ of an FHE to be *well-defined over the entirety of* $\mathcal{K} \times \mathcal{C}$, in the sense that it always outputs something in the message space $\mathcal{M}$ (albeit the message obtained when decrypting with a wrong key might be unpredictable). We also require the scheme to satisfy a stronger variant of evaluation correctness over all ciphertexts in $\mathcal{C}$. We bundle these extra requirements into *the strong correctness property*.

CORRECTNESS. An FHE scheme is correct if the following are satisfied.

- (Decryption Correctness) For any $\lambda \in \mathbb{N}$, any $(\mathsf{pk}, \mathsf{sk}) \in \mathsf{KGen}(1^\lambda)$, and any message $m \in \mathcal{M}$, we have that

$$\Pr[\mathsf{Dec}(\mathsf{sk}, \mathsf{Enc}(\mathsf{pk}, m)) = m] \geq 1 - \mathsf{negl}(\lambda)$$

  where the probability is taken over the random coins of Enc.
- (Evaluation Correctness) For any $\lambda \in \mathbb{N}$, any $(\mathsf{pk}, \mathsf{sk}) \in \mathsf{KGen}(1^\lambda)$, any positive integer $n \in \mathsf{poly}(\lambda)$, any polynomial-size circuit $\mathsf{C} \in \mathbb{C}_n$, any ciphertexts $(c_1, \ldots, c_n) \in \mathcal{C}_{\mathsf{pk}}^n$, if there exists $m_i = \mathsf{Dec}(\mathsf{sk}, c_i) \in \mathcal{M}$ for all $i \in \{1, \ldots, n\}$, then

$$\Pr[\mathsf{Dec}(\mathsf{sk}, c) = \mathsf{C}(m_1, \ldots, m_n) : c \leftarrow \mathsf{Eval}(\mathsf{pk}, \mathsf{C}, (c_1, \ldots, c_n))] \geq 1 - \mathsf{negl}(\lambda)$$

  where the probability is taken over the random coins of Enc and Eval.

The scheme is *perfectly correct* if the above probabilities are exactly 1.

STRONG CORRECTNESS. A strongly-correct FHE scheme satisfies all below.

IND-CPA$_{\mathcal{E},\mathcal{A}}^{b}(1^{\lambda})$	IK-IND-CPA$_{\mathcal{E},\mathcal{A}}^{b}(1^{\lambda})$	IND-CIRC-CPA$_{\mathcal{E},\mathcal{A}}^{b}(1^{\lambda})$
$(\mathsf{pk},\mathsf{sk}) \leftarrow \mathsf{KGen}(1^{\lambda})$	$(\mathsf{pk}_0,\mathsf{sk}_0) \leftarrow \mathsf{KGen}(1^{\lambda})$	$(\mathsf{pk},\mathsf{sk}) \leftarrow \mathsf{KGen}(1^{\lambda})$
$(m_0,m_1,\mathsf{st}) \leftarrow \mathcal{A}_1(\mathsf{pk})$	$(\mathsf{pk}_1,\mathsf{sk}_1) \leftarrow \mathsf{KGen}(1^{\lambda})$	$c_{\mathsf{sk}} \leftarrow \mathsf{Enc}(\mathsf{pk},\mathsf{sk})$
$c \leftarrow \mathsf{Enc}(\mathsf{pk},m_b)$	$(m_0,m_1,\mathsf{st}) \leftarrow \mathcal{A}_1(\mathsf{pk}_0,\mathsf{pk}_1)$	$(m_0,m_1,\mathsf{st}) \leftarrow \mathcal{A}_1(\mathsf{pk})$
$b' \leftarrow \mathcal{A}_2(\mathsf{st},c)$	$c \leftarrow \mathsf{Enc}(\mathsf{pk}_b,m_b)$	$c_b \leftarrow \mathsf{Enc}(\mathsf{pk},m_b)$
return b'	$b' \leftarrow \mathcal{A}_2(\mathsf{st},c)$	$b' \leftarrow \mathcal{A}_2(\mathsf{st},c_{\mathsf{sk}},c_b)$
	return b'	**return** b'

Fig. 2. Security Experiments of FHE (st is the state information of $(\mathcal{A}_1,\mathcal{A}_2)$)

- (Decryption Correctness) Same as in the (usual) correctness definition above.
- (Well-Defined Decryption) $\mathsf{Dec}(\cdot,\cdot)$ is well-defined over $\mathcal{K} \times \mathcal{C}$, i.e., for any $(\mathsf{sk},c) \in \mathcal{K} \times \mathcal{C}$, there exists $m \in \mathcal{M}$ such that $m = \mathsf{Dec}(\mathsf{sk},c)$.
- (Strong Evaluation Correctness) Evaluation correctness holds even for ciphertexts taken in $\mathcal{C}$. Formally, for any $\lambda \in \mathbb{N}$, any $(\mathsf{pk},\mathsf{sk}) \in \mathsf{KGen}(1^{\lambda})$, any positive integer $n \in \mathsf{poly}(\lambda)$, any polynomial-size circuit $\mathsf{C} \in \mathbb{C}_n$, any ciphertexts $(c_1,\ldots,c_n) \in \mathcal{C}^n$ (possibly with $c_i \notin \mathcal{C}_{\mathsf{pk}}$), if there exists $m_i = \mathsf{Dec}(\mathsf{sk},c_i) \in \mathcal{M}$ for all $i \in \{1,\ldots,n\}$, then

$$\Pr[\mathsf{Dec}(\mathsf{sk},c) = \mathsf{C}(m_1,\ldots,m_n) : c \leftarrow \mathsf{Eval}(\mathsf{pk},\mathsf{C},(c_1,\ldots,c_n))] \geq 1 - \mathsf{negl}(\lambda)$$

where the probability is taken over the random coins of Enc and Eval.

The scheme is *perfectly strongly correct* if the above probabilities are exactly 1.

SECURITY. We recall the standard IND-CPA-security and define a new notion called IK-IND-CPA-security, which combines key privacy and message indistinguishability. We also recall the notion of circular security.

Definition 5 (IND-CPA). *An FHE scheme $\mathcal{E}$ is IND-CPA-secure (has indistinguishable messages under chosen-plaintext attack) if for any PPT adversary $\mathcal{A} = (\mathcal{A}_1,\mathcal{A}_2)$, it holds that*

$$\left| \Pr\left[\mathsf{IND\text{-}CPA}_{\mathcal{E},\mathcal{A}}^{0}(1^{\lambda}) = 1\right] - \Pr\left[\mathsf{IND\text{-}CPA}_{\mathcal{E},\mathcal{A}}^{1}(1^{\lambda}) = 1\right] \right| \leq \mathsf{negl}(\lambda)$$

where $\mathsf{IND\text{-}CPA}_{\mathcal{E},\mathcal{A}}^{b}$ is defined in Fig. 2.

Definition 6 (IK-IND-CPA). *An FHE scheme $\mathcal{E}$ is IK-IND-CPA-secure (has indistinguishable keys and indistinguishable messages under chosen-plaintext attack) if for any PPT adversary $\mathcal{A} = (\mathcal{A}_1,\mathcal{A}_2)$, it holds that*

$$\left| \Pr\left[\mathsf{IK\text{-}IND\text{-}CPA}_{\mathcal{E},\mathcal{A}}^{0}(1^{\lambda}) = 1\right] - \Pr\left[\mathsf{IK\text{-}IND\text{-}CPA}_{\mathcal{E},\mathcal{A}}^{1}(1^{\lambda}) = 1\right] \right| \leq \mathsf{negl}(\lambda)$$

where $\mathsf{IK\text{-}IND\text{-}CPA}_{\mathcal{E},\mathcal{A}}^{b}$ is defined in Fig. 2.

Definition 7 (Circular Security). *Let $\mathcal{E}$ be an FHE scheme such that $\mathcal{K} = \mathcal{M}$. $\mathcal{E}$ is circular secure if for any* PPT *adversary $\mathcal{A} = (\mathcal{A}_1, \mathcal{A}_2)$, it holds that*

$$\left| \Pr\left[\mathsf{IND\text{-}CIRC\text{-}CPA}^0_{\mathcal{E},\mathcal{A}}(1^\lambda) = 1 \right] - \Pr\left[\mathsf{IND\text{-}CIRC\text{-}CPA}^1_{\mathcal{E},\mathcal{A}}(1^\lambda) = 1 \right] \right| \leq \mathsf{negl}(\lambda)$$

where $\mathsf{IND\text{-}CIRC\text{-}CPA}^b_{\mathcal{E},\mathcal{A}}$ *is defined in Fig. 2.*

INSTANTIATIONS. While IND-CPA security is the *de facto* standard of FHE schemes, virtually all of them satisfy the stronger notion of IK-IND-CPA security. This is because FHE ciphertexts are typically indistinguishable from elements uniformly sampled from the ciphertext space (see, *e.g.* [20]).

Typically, FHE schemes are proven to satisfy the standard correctness notion. Below, we show how these schemes can be transformed into one with strong correctness, assuming circular security and the decryption algorithm $\mathsf{Dec}(\cdot, \cdot)$ is well-defined over $\mathcal{K} \times \mathcal{C}$. The former assumption is "for free" as it is already needed for bootstrapping the FHE scheme [18]. The latter is already satisfied by most existing FHE schemes and can be otherwise obtained by artificially extending the decryption algorithm to be well-defined over any input. For the case of FHE schemes based on learning with errors (LWE), $\mathsf{Dec}(\cdot, \cdot)$ typically consists of an inner product of two vectors in $\mathbb{Z}_q^\ell$, followed by rounding. Thus $\mathsf{Dec}(\cdot, \cdot)$ is well defined for *any* pair of vectors in $\mathbb{Z}_q^\ell$ if we set $\mathcal{C} := \mathcal{K} := \mathbb{Z}_q^\ell$.

Let $\mathcal{E}$ be such an FHE scheme. A public key in our transformed scheme $\mathcal{E}'$ is of the form $\mathsf{pk}' = (\mathsf{pk}, c_{\mathsf{sk}})$ where $c_{\mathsf{sk}} = \mathcal{E}.\mathsf{Enc}(\mathsf{pk}, \mathsf{sk})$ is an encryption of the secret key sk under pk. The secret key sk' is identical to sk. The encryption (with input pk) and decryption algorithms of $\mathcal{E}$ and $\mathcal{E}'$ are identical.

The evaluation algorithm $\mathcal{E}'.\mathsf{Eval}$, on input pk', a circuit $\mathsf{C} \in \mathbb{C}_n$, and (not necessarily well-formed) ciphertexts $(c_1, \ldots, c_n) \in \mathcal{C}^n$ works as follows:

- homomorphically decrypts c_i using c_{sk} for each $i \in [n]$, *i.e.*, compute

$$c'_i \leftarrow \mathcal{E}.\mathsf{Eval}(\mathsf{pk}, \mathcal{E}.\mathsf{Dec}(\cdot, c_i), c_{\mathsf{sk}}),$$

- then, evaluates C homomorphically over $(c'_1, \ldots, c'_n)$, *i.e.*, output

$$c' \leftarrow \mathcal{E}.\mathsf{Eval}(\mathsf{pk}, \mathsf{C}, (c'_1, \ldots, c'_n)).$$

Clearly, if $\mathcal{E}$ is IK-IND-CPA-secure and circular secure, then $\mathcal{E}'$ is IK-IND-CPA-secure. To see why $\mathcal{E}'$ has strong correctness, we note that $c_{\mathsf{sk}} \in \mathcal{C}_{\mathsf{pk}}$ by construction and $\mathsf{Dec}(\cdot, c_i)$ is well-defined over $\mathcal{K} = \mathcal{M}$ for all $i \in [n]$ by assumption. Therefore, by the (standard) correctness of $\mathcal{E}$, for all $i \in [n]$, $\mathcal{E}.\mathsf{Dec}(\mathsf{sk}, c'_i) = \mathcal{E}.\mathsf{Dec}(\mathsf{sk}, c_i)$. Next, since $c'_i \in \mathcal{C}_{\mathsf{pk}}$ for all $i \in [n]$, we have $c' \in \mathcal{C}_{\mathsf{pk}}$. Using the (standard) correctness of $\mathcal{E}$ again, if $m_i = \mathcal{E}'.\mathsf{Dec}(\mathsf{sk}', c_i) = \mathcal{E}.\mathsf{Dec}(\mathsf{sk}, c_i)$ for all $i \in [n]$, then $\mathcal{E}'.\mathsf{Dec}(\mathsf{sk}', c') = \mathcal{E}.\mathsf{Dec}(\mathsf{sk}, c') = \mathsf{C}(m_1, \ldots, m_n)$ as we desired.

To draw an analogy to LWE-based schemes, even though $(c_1, \ldots, c_n)$ might have very large noise (with respect to pk), $\mathcal{E}.\mathsf{Eval}$ is executed over c_{sk}, which is well-formed (has small noise) and $(c_1, \ldots, c_n)$ are just constants in the description of the circuits $\mathcal{E}.\mathsf{Dec}(\cdot, c_i)$. This is analogous to Gentry's bootstrapping procedure [18] and works for exactly the same reason.

Our modification essentially introduces an additional bootstrapping step before every homomorphic evaluation. Thus, fast bootstrapping techniques can be applied to make the overhead we added minimal when compared to the cost of the homomorphic evaluation. As the communication complexity of our scheme depends on the rate (message-to-ciphertext size ratio) of the FHE scheme, one can achieve optimal communication (for large enough data blocks) by using the rate-1 FHE [8,19]. It is not hard to see that those schemes also satisfy the notion of IK-IND-CPA security (since ciphertexts are identical to those of [20]).

4.3   Distributed Point Functions

A point function is a function whose images are zero at all points except one.

Definition 8 (Point Function). *A point function* $F_{a,b} : \{0,1\}^d \rightarrow \{0,1\}^r$, *for* $a \in \{0,1\}^d$ *and* $b \in \{0,1\}^r$, *is defined by* $F_{a,b}(a) = b$, *and* $F_{a,b}(c) = 0^r$ *if* $c \neq a$.

Unless differently specified, we interpret the output domain $\{0,1\}^r$ of F as an Abelian group $\mathbb{G}$ with respect to the group operator $\oplus$.

A distributed point function (DPF) allows secret-sharing a point function f to multiple servers. The servers can locally evaluate the shared function at any point x and produce output shares, which can be combined to recover $f(x)$.

Definition 9 (Distributed Point Function [4]). *For* $N \in \mathbb{N}$ *and* $t \in [N]$, *a* (t, N)-*DPF is a tuple of* PPT *algorithms* DPF.(Gen, Eval, Dec) *defined as follows.*

DPF.Gen($1^\lambda, F_{a,b}$): *On input the security parameter* 1^λ *and the description of a point function* $F_{a,b}$, *the key generation algorithm returns* N *keys* $(k_1, \ldots, k_N)$.

DPF.Eval(i, k_i, x): *On input a party index* i, *a key* k_i, *and a string* $x \in \{0,1\}^d$, *the evaluation algorithm returns a share* s_i.

DPF.Dec($s_1, \ldots, s_N$): *On input a set of shares* $(s_1, \ldots, s_N)$, *the decoding algorithm returns the function output* y.

We consider an N-party additive output decoder for an Abelian group $(\mathbb{G}, +)$ that returns $y = \sum_{i=1}^{N} s_i$ on input $(s_1, \ldots, s_N) \in \mathbb{G}^N$. We state a relaxed correctness notion that allows the evaluation algorithm to have an error Δ, and recall the standard notion of security.

Definition 10 (Δ-Correctness). *A* (t, N)-*DPF* = (DPF.Gen, DPF.Eval, DPF.Dec) *is correct if there exists an inverse polynomial error bound* Δ *such that for all* $\lambda \in \mathbb{N}$, $x \in \{0,1\}^d$, *and point functions* $F_{a,b}$,

$$\Pr\left[\begin{array}{l} (k_1, \ldots, k_N) \leftarrow \mathsf{DPF.Gen}(1^\lambda, F_{a,b}) \\ \{s_i \leftarrow \mathsf{DPF.Eval}(i, k_i, x)\}_{i \in [N]} \end{array} : \mathsf{DPF.Dec}(s_1, \ldots, s_N) \neq F_{a,b}(x) \right] \leq \Delta.$$

If $\Delta = 0$ *then we say that the scheme is perfectly correct.*

Definition 11 (Security). *A* (t, N)-DPF $=$ DPF.(Gen, Eval, Dec) *is secure if there exists a negligible function* negl$(\cdot)$ *such that for all* $\lambda \in \mathbb{N}$, *subsets* $T \subseteq [N]$ *such that* $|T| = t$, *all* PPT *non-uniform distinguishers* $\mathcal{A}$, *it holds that*

$$\Pr \left[\begin{array}{l} ((a^0, b^0), (a^1, b^1)) \leftarrow \mathcal{A}(1^\lambda) \\ \beta \leftarrow \{0, 1\} \\ (k_1, \ldots, k_N) \leftarrow \mathsf{DPF.Gen}(1^\lambda, F_{a^\beta, b^\beta}) \end{array} : \beta = \mathcal{A}(\{k_i\}_{i \in T}) \right] \leq \mathsf{negl}(\lambda).$$

Boyle *et al.* [4] showed that $(1, 2)$-DPF can be built from one-way functions.

Theorem 3 ([4]). *A perfectly-correct* $(1, 2)$-DPF *of* poly $(d(\lambda + \log(|\mathbb{G}|)))$-*size key can be built from one-way functions.*

We also observe that the complexity of the DPF.Eval algorithm in their construction [4] is dominated by d-many sequential evaluations of a length-doubling PRG. This fact is going to be useful for our later construction.

4.4 Homomorphic Secret Sharing

Homomorphic secret sharing (HSS) can be seen as generalizing a distributed point function where the evaluation algorithm supports the evaluation of more complex circuits. We focus on single-client HSS. In such a scheme, a single client secret shares an input x to multiple servers. These servers can then locally evaluate any circuit C in the supported class of circuits to produce some output shares. The value $C(x)$ can then be recovered by combining these output shares.

Definition 12 (Homomorphic Secret Sharing [6]). *For* $N \in \mathbb{N}$, $t \in [N]$, *a* (t, N)-HSS *for a circuit family* $\mathcal{C}$ *is defined by the following* PPT *algorithms:*

HSS.Gen$(1^\lambda, x)$: *On input the security parameter* 1^λ *and an input* x, *the share generation algorithm returns a set of shares* $(s_1, \ldots, s_N)$.

HSS.Eval(i, s_i, C): *On input a party index* i, *a share* s_i, *and a circuit* $C \in \mathcal{C}$, *the evaluation algorithm returns an evaluated share* z_i.

HSS.Dec$(z_1, \ldots, z_N)$: *On input a set of shares* $(z_1, \ldots, z_N)$, *the decoding algorithm returns the output* y.

We say that an HSS scheme is *compact* if the size of the output shares does not grow with the size of the circuit given as input to the HSS.Eval algorithm. We define correctness where the evaluation algorithm may incur an error with probability at most Δ, for some inverse polynomial function Δ.

Definition 13 (Δ-Correctness). *A* (t, N)-HSS $=$ HSS.(Gen, Eval, Dec) *is correct if there exists an inverse polynomial error bound* Δ *such that for all* $\lambda \in \mathbb{N}$, *inputs* x, *and circuits* $C \in \mathcal{C}$, *we have that*

$$\Pr \left[\begin{array}{l} (s_1, \ldots, s_N) \leftarrow \mathsf{HSS.Gen}(1^\lambda, x) \\ \{z_i \leftarrow \mathsf{HSS.Eval}(i, s_i, C)\}_{i \in [N]} \end{array} : \mathsf{HSS.Dec}(z_1, \ldots, z_N) \neq C(x) \right] \leq \Delta.$$

Security is defined canonically.

Definition 14 (Security). *A* (t, N)-*HSS* = *HSS*.(Gen, Eval, Dec) *is secure if there exists a negligible function* negl$(\cdot)$ *such that for all* $\lambda \in \mathbb{N}$, *subsets* $T \subseteq [N]$ *such that* $|T| = t$, *all* PPT *non-uniform distinguishers* $\mathcal{A}$, *it holds that*

$$\Pr\left[\begin{array}{l} (x^0, x^1) \leftarrow \mathcal{A}(1^\lambda) \\ \beta \leftarrow \{0, 1\} \\ (s_1, \ldots, s_N) \leftarrow \text{HSS.Gen}(1^\lambda, x^\beta) \end{array} : \beta = \mathcal{A}(\{s_i\}_{i \in T}) \right] \leq \text{negl}(\lambda).$$

It is useful to recall a theorem from Boyle *et al.* [5], where they propose an HSS scheme for NC1 circuits assuming the hardness of the DDH problem. There also exists a similar construction based on the hardness of the DCR problem [17].

Theorem 4 ([5]). *If the DDH problem is hard, there exists a compact* Δ-*correct* $(1, 2)$-*HSS for circuits in NC1, for any inverse polynomial* Δ.

5 Multi-client ORAM and Its Simulation-Based Security

5.1 Syntax

MCORAM was introduced by Maffei *et al.* [29] and later extended to the malicious client setting [30]. Existing MCORAM definitions are mostly verbal, which left many subtleties. We recall (a slightly rephrased version of) its definition.

Definition 15. *An MCORAM scheme for message space* $\mathcal{M} \not\supseteq \{\epsilon\}$ *consists of a* PPT *algorithm* Setup *and protocols* (ChMod, Access) *executed between a data owner* D, *polynomially many independent instances of client* C, *and a server* S:

$(pp, msk, \bar{M}) \leftarrow \text{Setup}(1^\lambda, 1^n, M)$: *The setup algorithm is run by the database owner* D. *It inputs the security parameter* λ, *a size parameter* n, *and an array* $M \in \mathcal{M}^n$ *of initial data. It outputs the public parameter* pp *(an implicit input of all other algorithms), the master secret key* msk *(to be kept secret by the owner* D), *and a database* $\bar{M}$ *(to be forwarded to the server* S).

$\langle \epsilon; sk'; \bar{M}' \rangle \leftarrow \text{ChMod}\langle D(msk, A_R, A_W); C(sk, A_R, A_W); S(\bar{M}) \rangle$: *The data owner* D *grants access rights to a client* C, *possibly with the help of the server* S, *using the change-mode protocol. If* C *has not joined the system yet, it is assumed that* $sk = \epsilon$. *The basic model only allows granting additional rights.*

To run ChMod, D *inputs the master (owner) secret key* msk, *a client identifier* id $\in \{0, 1\}^*$, *and two sets* $A_R, A_W \subseteq [n]$ *of addresses.* C *inputs his secret key* sk, *and the same sets of addresses* A_R *and* A_W. *The server* S *inputs the database* $\bar{M}$. *Supposedly,* C *will be granted reading rights to* A_R, *and writing rights to* A_W.

At the end of ChMod, D *outputs a the empty string* ϵ. C *outputs an updated secret key* sk'. S *outputs a possibly updated database* $\bar{M}'$.

$\langle m'; \bar{M}' \rangle \leftarrow \text{Access}\langle C(sk, a, m); S(\bar{M}) \rangle$: *To access a certain address of the memory, client* C *engages in the access protocol with the server. The client* C *inputs its secret key* sk, *an address* $a \in [n]$, *and some data* $m \in \mathcal{M} \cup \{\epsilon\}$. *Read access is* *indicated by $m = \epsilon$. Otherwise, the data $m \neq \epsilon$ is to be written to the address a. The server S inputs $\bar{M}$. Regardless of the type of access, the client outputs some data m' read from the address a, while the server updates its database to $\bar{M}'$.*

It is straightforward to extend the MCORAM syntax and security definitions to the *multi-server setting*. Setup outputs multiple encoded databases $\bar{M}_1, \ldots, \bar{M}_N$ to be maintained by the respective servers. ChMod becomes an $(N + 2)$-party protocol between the database owner D, the client C, and the servers $S_1, \ldots, S_N$. The outputs of D and C remain unchanged, while S_i outputs an updated database $\bar{M}'_i$. Similarly, Access becomes an $(N + 1)$-party protocol between the client C and $S_1, \ldots, S_N$. Their outputs are defined analogously.

Although our model allows ChMod and Access to be general multi-party protocols, we are primarily interested in constructions where the servers do not communicate with each other to better justify the non-colluding assumption.

5.2   Correctness and Integrity

An MCORAM scheme should not only be correct but satisfy an even stronger property called integrity (*subsuming correctness*): The database entry at the address a can only be changed by clients having write access to a, other clients who might attempt to maliciously tamper with the data of the honest clients will fail. It is a unique property here and is absent in the single-client setting.

More formally, integrity is modeled by an experiment involving an adversary $\mathcal{A}$. The experiment acts as an honest MCORAM server, provides the interface of an MCORAM instance to $\mathcal{A}$, *i.e.*, $\mathcal{A}$ can request to corrupt a client, request for access permissions on behalf of a client, and access the data. To capture the notion of correctness, $\mathcal{A}$ maintains a plaintext copy of the MCORAM-encoded database, *i.e.*, all accesses are *mirrored to the plaintext copy*. The winning condition of $\mathcal{A}$ is to make the maintained plaintext copy of the database ends up inconsistent with the one encoded in the MCORAM.

Definition 16 (Integrity of MCORAM). *An MCORAM Θ has integrity if, for all PPT adversaries $\mathcal{A}$, size parameters $n = \mathsf{poly}(\lambda)$, and arrays $M \in \mathcal{M}^n$, with experiment Int as defined in Fig. 3, we have*

$$\Pr\left[\mathsf{Int}_{\Theta,\mathcal{A}}(1^\lambda, 1^n, M) = 1\right] \leq \mathsf{negl}(\lambda).$$

Integrity in the multi-server setting is almost identical, except that all oracles now return the views of all servers, which reflects that they are all honest but curious. However, integrity in this setting seems challenging to achieve, especially if we assume that the servers do not communicate with each other. Instead, one may consider a weaker notion known as *accountable integrity* (defined in the single-server setting [29]), which requires that any violation of integrity can be caught after-the-fact. Extending it to the multi-server setting is straightforward.

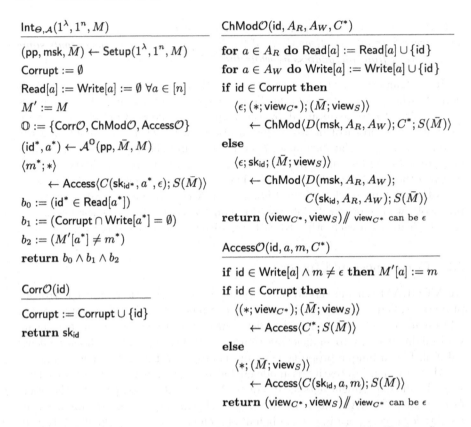

$\underline{\mathsf{Int}_{\Theta,\mathcal{A}}(1^\lambda, 1^n, M)}$

$(\mathsf{pp}, \mathsf{msk}, \bar{M}) \leftarrow \mathsf{Setup}(1^\lambda, 1^n, M)$
$\mathsf{Corrupt} := \emptyset$
$\mathsf{Read}[a] := \mathsf{Write}[a] := \emptyset \ \forall a \in [n]$
$M' := M$
$\mathbb{O} := \{\mathsf{Corr}\mathcal{O}, \mathsf{ChMod}\mathcal{O}, \mathsf{Access}\mathcal{O}\}$
$(\mathsf{id}^*, a^*) \leftarrow \mathcal{A}^{\mathbb{O}}(\mathsf{pp}, \bar{M}, M)$
$\langle m^*; * \rangle$
$\quad \leftarrow \mathsf{Access}\langle C(\mathsf{sk}_{\mathsf{id}^*}, a^*, \epsilon); S(\bar{M})\rangle$
$b_0 := (\mathsf{id}^* \in \mathsf{Read}[a^*])$
$b_1 := (\mathsf{Corrupt} \cap \mathsf{Write}[a^*] = \emptyset)$
$b_2 := (M'[a^*] \neq m^*)$
return $b_0 \wedge b_1 \wedge b_2$

$\underline{\mathsf{Corr}\mathcal{O}(\mathsf{id})}$

$\mathsf{Corrupt} := \mathsf{Corrupt} \cup \{\mathsf{id}\}$
return $\mathsf{sk}_{\mathsf{id}}$

$\underline{\mathsf{ChMod}\mathcal{O}(\mathsf{id}, A_R, A_W, C^*)}$

for $a \in A_R$ **do** $\mathsf{Read}[a] := \mathsf{Read}[a] \cup \{\mathsf{id}\}$
for $a \in A_W$ **do** $\mathsf{Write}[a] := \mathsf{Write}[a] \cup \{\mathsf{id}\}$
if $\mathsf{id} \in \mathsf{Corrupt}$ **then**
$\quad \langle \epsilon; (*; \mathsf{view}_{C^*}); (\bar{M}; \mathsf{view}_S)\rangle$
$\quad\quad \leftarrow \mathsf{ChMod}\langle D(\mathsf{msk}, A_R, A_W); C^*; S(\bar{M})\rangle$
else
$\quad \langle \epsilon; \mathsf{sk}_{\mathsf{id}}; (\bar{M}; \mathsf{view}_S)\rangle$
$\quad\quad \leftarrow \mathsf{ChMod}\langle D(\mathsf{msk}, A_R, A_W);$
$\quad\quad\quad\quad C(\mathsf{sk}_{\mathsf{id}}, A_R, A_W); S(\bar{M})\rangle$
return $(\mathsf{view}_{C^*}, \mathsf{view}_S) /\!\!/ \ \mathsf{view}_{C^*}$ can be ϵ

$\underline{\mathsf{Access}\mathcal{O}(\mathsf{id}, a, m, C^*)}$

if $\mathsf{id} \in \mathsf{Write}[a] \wedge m \neq \epsilon$ **then** $M'[a] := m$
if $\mathsf{id} \in \mathsf{Corrupt}$ **then**
$\quad \langle (*; \mathsf{view}_{C^*}); (\bar{M}; \mathsf{view}_S)\rangle$
$\quad\quad \leftarrow \mathsf{Access}\langle C^*; S(\bar{M})\rangle$
else
$\quad \langle *; (\bar{M}; \mathsf{view}_S)\rangle$
$\quad\quad \leftarrow \mathsf{Access}\langle C(\mathsf{sk}_{\mathsf{id}}, a, m); S(\bar{M})\rangle$
return $(\mathsf{view}_{C^*}, \mathsf{view}_S) /\!\!/ \ \mathsf{view}_{C^*}$ can be ϵ

Fig. 3. MCORAM's Integrity against Malicious Clients and Honest-but-Curious Server

5.3   Obliviousness

Access in MCORAM is fully specified by (id, a, m), meaning that client id is reading address a (if $m = \epsilon$) or writing m to address a. Obliviousness mandates that such information would not be leaked to any other parties, unless the access is write access and the parties have read access to a.

More formally, (*indistinguishability-based*) obliviousness is modeled by a pair of experiments, labeled by $b = 0, 1$ respectively, involving an adversary $\mathcal{A}$. As in the integrity experiment, the experiments provide the interface of an instance of MCORAM to $\mathcal{A}$, with some differences. First, $\mathcal{A}$ has to provide malicious server codes to the interfaces, which models the setting where the server is always trying to compromise clients' obliviousness. Second, the interface for the access protocol is parameterized by the bit b (which specifies the experiment) and takes as input *two* access instructions $(\mathsf{id}_\beta, a_\beta, m_\beta)$ for $\beta \in \{0, 1\}$. The interface would execute instruction labeled with $\beta = b$. After some interactions with the interface, $\mathcal{A}$ would output a bit b', which can be interpreted as a guess of b. An MCORAM is said to be (indistinguishably) oblivious against malicious clients if the probabilities of $\mathcal{A}$ outputting 1 in either experiment are negligibly close.

$\mathsf{Obl}^b_{\Theta,\mathcal{A}}(1^\lambda, 1^n, M)$

$(\mathsf{pp}, \mathsf{msk}, \bar{M}) \leftarrow \mathsf{Setup}(1^\lambda, 1^n, M)$

$\mathsf{Corrupt} := \mathsf{ChAddr} := \emptyset$

$\mathsf{Read}[a] := \emptyset \; \forall a \in [n]$

$\mathbb{O} := \{\mathsf{Corr}\mathcal{O}, \mathsf{ChMod}\mathcal{O}, \mathsf{Access}\mathcal{O}_b\}$

$b' \leftarrow \mathcal{A}^{\mathbb{O}}(\mathsf{pp}, \bar{M}, M)$

return b'

$\mathsf{Corr}\mathcal{O}(\mathsf{id})$

---

ensure $\forall \, a \in \mathsf{ChAddr}, \; \mathsf{id} \notin \mathsf{Read}[a]$

$\mathsf{Corrupt} := \mathsf{Corrupt} \cup \{\mathsf{id}\}$

return $\mathsf{sk}_{\mathsf{id}}$

$\mathsf{ChMod}\mathcal{O}(\mathsf{id}, A_R, A_W, C^*, S^*)$

---

for $a \in A_R$ **do** $\mathsf{Read}[a] := \mathsf{Read}[a] \cup \{\mathsf{id}\}$

if $\mathsf{id} \in \mathsf{Corrupt}$ **then**

  ensure $\mathsf{ChAddr} \cap A_R = \emptyset$

  $\langle \epsilon; (*; \mathsf{view}_{C^*}); (*; \mathsf{view}_{S^*}) \rangle$

    $\leftarrow \mathsf{ChMod}\langle D(\mathsf{msk}, A_R, A_W); C^*; S^* \rangle$

else

  $\langle \epsilon; \mathsf{sk}_{\mathsf{id}}; (*; \mathsf{view}_{S^*}) \rangle$

    $\leftarrow \mathsf{ChMod}\langle D(\mathsf{msk}, A_R, A_W);$

        $C(\mathsf{sk}_{\mathsf{id}}, A_R, A_W); S^* \rangle$

return $(\mathsf{view}_{C^*}, \mathsf{view}_S)$ // view_{C^*} can be ϵ

$\mathsf{Access}\mathcal{O}_b((\mathsf{id}_0, a_0, m_0), (\mathsf{id}_1, a_1, m_1), S^*)$

$\beta_0 := \big(\mathsf{Corrupt} \cap \{\mathsf{id}_0, \mathsf{id}_1\} = \emptyset\big)$

$\beta_1 := \big((a_0, m_0) \neq (a_1, m_1)\big) \wedge (m_0 \neq \epsilon)$

$\beta_1 := \beta_1 \wedge (\mathsf{Read}[a_0] \cap \mathsf{Corrupt} \neq \emptyset)$

$\beta_2 := \big((a_0, m_0) \neq (a_1, m_1)\big) \wedge (m_1 \neq \epsilon)$

$\beta_2 := \beta_2 \wedge (\mathsf{Read}[a_1] \cap \mathsf{Corrupt} \neq \emptyset)$

if $\beta_0 \vee \beta_1 \vee \beta_2$ **then return** $\bot$

$\mathsf{ChAddr} := \mathsf{ChAddr} \cup \{a_0, a_1\}$

$\langle *; (*; \mathsf{view}_{S^*}) \rangle \leftarrow \mathsf{Access}\langle C(\mathsf{sk}_{\mathsf{id}_b}, a_b, m_b); S^* \rangle$

return view_{S^*}

Fig. 4. Obliviousness Experiment of MCORAM against Malicious Clients and Server

Definition 17 (Indistinguishability-based Obliviousness). *An MCO-RAM scheme Θ is indistinguishably oblivious against malicious clients if, for all PPT $\mathcal{A}$, all λ and $n = \mathsf{poly}(\lambda)$, all arrays $M \in \mathcal{M}^n$, with Obl as in Fig. 4,*

$$\left| \Pr\left[\mathsf{Obl}^0_{\Theta,\mathcal{A}}(1^\lambda, 1^n, M) = 1\right] - \Pr\left[\mathsf{Obl}^1_{\Theta,\mathcal{A}}(1^\lambda, 1^n, M) = 1\right] \right| \leq \mathsf{negl}(\lambda).$$

So far, we followed Maffei *et al.* [29] and defined an indistinguishability-based obliviousness definition. However, when constructing higher-level protocols, it is often more convenient to prove security based on simulation-based security notions of the building blocks. We thus propose a new simulation-based obliviousness definition for MCORAM, which turns out to be an equivalent one.

Our *simulation-based obliviousness* notion is also modeled by a pair of experiments involving an adversary $\mathcal{A}$, called the real and ideal experiment, respectively. Both experiments provide the interface of an MCORAM instance to $\mathcal{A}$. However, the way that queries to the interface are answered varies greatly.

In the real experiment, the interface is backed by a real execution of the MCORAM instance (as in the integrity experiment), where $\mathcal{A}$ needs to pro-

Real-Obl$_{\Theta,\mathcal{A}}(1^{\lambda}, 1^n, M)$

$(pp, msk, \bar{M}) \leftarrow \mathsf{Setup}(1^{\lambda}, 1^n, M)$

Corrupt := ChAddr := $\emptyset$

Read$[a]$:= $\emptyset$ $\forall a \in [n]$

$\mathbb{O}$:= $\{\mathsf{Corr}\mathcal{O}, \mathsf{ChMod}\mathcal{O}, \mathsf{Access}\mathcal{O}\}$

$b' \leftarrow \mathcal{A}^{\mathbb{O}}(pp, \bar{M}, M)$

return b'

ChMod$\mathcal{O}(id, A_R, A_W, C^*, S^*)$

---

for $a \in A_R$ **do** Read$[a]$:= Read$[a] \cup \{id\}$

if id $\in$ Corrupt **then**

  ensure ChAddr $\cap$ $A_R = \emptyset$

  $\langle \epsilon; (*; \mathsf{view}_{C^*}); (*; \mathsf{view}_{S^*}) \rangle$

    $\leftarrow \mathsf{ChMod}\langle D(msk, A_R, A_W); C^*; S^* \rangle$

else

  $\langle \epsilon; sk_{id}; (*; \mathsf{view}_{S^*}) \rangle$

    $\leftarrow \mathsf{ChMod}\langle D(msk, A_R, A_W);$

        $C(sk_{id}, A_R, A_W); S^* \rangle$

return $(\mathsf{view}_{C^*}, \mathsf{view}_S)$ // view_{C^*} can be ϵ

Corr$\mathcal{O}(id)$

---

ensure $\forall$ $a \in$ ChAddr, id $\notin$ Read$[a]$

Corrupt := Corrupt $\cup \{id\}$

return sk_{id}

Access$\mathcal{O}(id \notin \mathsf{Corrupt}, a, m, S^*)$

---

if Read$[a] \cap \mathsf{Corrupt} = \emptyset \wedge m \neq \epsilon$ **then**

  ChAddr := ChAddr $\cup \{a\}$

$\langle *; (*; \mathsf{view}_{S^*}) \rangle \leftarrow \mathsf{Access}\langle C(sk_{id}, a, m); S^* \rangle$

return view_{S^*}

Fig. 5. Real Experiment for Obliviousness against Malicious Clients and Server

vide the malicious server code (as in the indistinguishability-based obliviousness experiment). Answering a query in the ideal experiment generally invokes a simulator $\mathcal{S}$ with the leakage of the query as the input. For example, upon receiving a query (id, a, m) to the interface for the access protocol, if $\mathcal{A}$ has read access to a and $m \neq \epsilon$, then $\mathcal{S}$ is given (a, m). Otherwise, $\mathcal{S}$ is given no information (other than the fact that the query is issued to the access interface). In any case, given such a leakage, $\mathcal{S}$ is supposed to simulate the response of a real execution. After some interactions, $\mathcal{A}$ would output a bit b', which can be interpreted as a guess of whether it has interacted with the real experiment or the ideal experiment. An MCORAM is said to be *semantically oblivious* against malicious clients if the probabilities of $\mathcal{A}$ outputting 1 in either experiment are negligibly close.

Definition 18 (Semantic Obliviousness). *An MCORAM scheme Θ is semantically oblivious against malicious clients if, for all* PPT *adversaries $\mathcal{A}$, all λ and $n = \mathrm{poly}(\lambda)$, and all arrays $M \in \mathcal{M}^n$, there exists a* PPT *simulator $\mathcal{S}$, with* Real-Obl *and* Ideal-Obl *as defined in Figs. 5 and 6 respectively, such that*

$$\left| \Pr\left[\mathsf{Real\text{-}Obl}_{\Theta,\mathcal{A}}(1^{\lambda}, 1^n, M) = 1\right] - \Pr\left[\mathsf{Ideal\text{-}Obl}_{\Theta,\mathcal{A},\mathcal{S}}(1^{\lambda}, 1^n, M) = 1\right] \right| \leq \mathsf{negl}(\lambda).$$

The above two definitions can be shown equivalent using arguments for proving similar statements in encryption. See the full version for formal treatment.

Extending obliviousness to the multi-server setting where at most t of the N servers are corrupt is slightly more complicated. To model this, we modify the

$\text{Ideal-Obl}_{\Theta,\mathcal{A},\mathcal{S}}(1^\lambda,1^n,M)$	$\text{ChMod}\mathcal{O}(\text{id}, A_R, A_W, C^*, S^*)$
$(\text{pp},\text{td},\bar{M}) \leftarrow \mathcal{S}(\text{'Setup'}, 1^\lambda, 1^n, M)$	**for** $a \in A_R$ **do** $\text{Read}[a] := \text{Read}[a] \cup \{\text{id}\}$
$\text{Corrupt} := \text{ChAddr} := \emptyset$	**if** $\text{id} \in \text{Corrupt}$ **then**
$\mathbb{O} := \{\text{Corr}\mathcal{O}, \text{ChMod}\mathcal{O}, \text{Access}\mathcal{O}\}$	$\quad$ **ensure** $\text{ChAddr} \cap A_R = \emptyset$
$\text{Read} := \text{Empty dictionaries}$	$\quad (\text{view}_{C^*}, \text{view}_{S^*}, \text{td})$
$b' \leftarrow \mathcal{A}^{\mathbb{O}}(\text{pp}, \bar{M}, M)$	$\quad\quad \leftarrow \mathcal{S}^{C^*,S^*}(\text{'CorrChMod'}, \text{td}, \text{id}, A_R, A_W)$
return b'	$\quad$ **return** $(\text{view}_{C^*}, \text{view}_{S^*})$
	else
$\underline{\text{Corr}\mathcal{O}(\text{id})}$	$\quad (\text{view}_{S^*}, \text{td}) \leftarrow \mathcal{S}^{S^*}(\text{'ChMod'}, \text{td}, \text{id}, A_R, A_W)$
ensure $\forall\, a \in \text{ChAddr},\ \text{id} \notin \text{Read}[a]$	**return** $(\text{view}_{C^*}, \text{view}_S)$ // view_{C^*} can be ϵ
$\text{Corrupt} := \text{Corrupt} \cup \{\text{id}\}$	
$(\text{sk}_\text{id}, \text{td}) \leftarrow \mathcal{S}(\text{'Corrupt'}, \text{td}, \text{id})$	$\underline{\text{Access}\mathcal{O}(\text{id} \notin \text{Corrupt}, a, m, S^*)}$
return sk_id	**if** $\text{Read}[a] \cap \text{CorrAddr} \neq \emptyset \wedge m \neq \epsilon$ **then**
	$\quad (\text{view}_{S^*}, \text{td}) \leftarrow \mathcal{S}^{S^*}(\text{'CorrAccess'}, \text{td}, a, m)$
	else
	$\quad$ **if** $m \neq \epsilon$ **then** $\text{ChAddr} := \text{ChAddr} \cup \{a\}$
	$\quad (\text{view}_{S^*}, \text{td}) \leftarrow \mathcal{S}^{S^*}(\text{'Access'}, \text{td})$
	return view_{S^*}

Fig. 6. Ideal Experiment for Obliviousness against Malicious Clients and Server

security experiments such that all N servers are initially honest, and at most t of them can be corrupted using a modified $\text{Corr}\mathcal{O}$ oracle. Correspondingly, the inputs of the modified $\text{ChMod}\mathcal{O}$ oracle and $\text{Access}\mathcal{O}$ oracle now include at most t pieces of malicious codes $\{S_j^*\}$ for the respective servers, such that S_j^* will be used to generate the communication transcript if server j is corrupt.

6   FHE-based Single-Server Construction

6.1   Formal Description

Fix a database size $n \in \mathbb{N}$ with $n = \text{poly}(\lambda)$. Let cPRF be a constrained PRF family (Sect. 4.1) with domain $[n] \cup \{0\}$. Let $\mathcal{E}.(\text{KGen}, \text{Enc}, \text{Dec}, \text{Eval})$ be an FHE scheme (Sect. 4.2) with message space $\mathcal{M}_\mathcal{E}$. Let $\Sigma.(\text{KGen}, \text{Sig}, \text{Verify})$ be a signature scheme with message space $\mathcal{M}_\Sigma := \{0,1\}^\lambda \times \mathcal{M}_\mathcal{E}$. For any array $\bar{M}$, nonce $r \in \{0,1\}^\lambda$, and public key pk of Σ, we define the following circuits:

$$\text{Read}_{\bar{M}}(\text{addr}) := \bar{M}[\text{addr}]$$

$$\text{Write}_{\text{pk},r}(\text{sig}, \text{data}', \text{data}) := \begin{cases} \text{data}' & \text{if } \Sigma.\text{Verify}(\text{pk}, (r, \text{data}'), \text{sig}) = 1 \\ \text{data} & \text{otherwise} \end{cases}$$

$\underline{\text{Setup}(1^\lambda, 1^n, M = (m_1, \ldots, m_n))}$

$\text{msk} \leftarrow \text{cPRF.KGen}(1^\lambda)$

$(\text{pk}_0^{\mathcal{E}}, \text{sk}_0^{\mathcal{E}}) := \mathcal{E}.\text{KGen}(1^\lambda)$

for $k \in [n]$ **do**

  $r_{R,k} := \text{cPRF.Eval}(\text{msk}, (0, k))$

  $r_{W,k} := \text{cPRF.Eval}(\text{msk}, (1, k))$

  $(\text{pk}_k^{\mathcal{E}}, \text{sk}_k^{\mathcal{E}}) := \mathcal{E}.\text{KGen}(1^\lambda; r_{R,k})$

  $(\text{pk}_k^{\Sigma}, \text{sk}_k^{\Sigma}) := \Sigma.\text{KGen}(1^\lambda; r_{W,k})$

  $\bar{M}[k] := \bar{m}_k \leftarrow \mathcal{E}.\text{Enc}(\text{pk}_k^{\mathcal{E}}, m_k)$

$\text{pp} := \left\{ \text{pk}_0^{\mathcal{E}}, (\text{pk}_k^{\mathcal{E}}, \text{pk}_k^{\Sigma}) \right\}_{k=1}^n$

return $(\text{pp}, \text{msk}, \bar{M})$

$\underline{\text{ChMod}\langle D, C, S \rangle}$

$\underline{D(\text{msk}, A_R, A_W)}$

  ensure $A_R, A_W \subseteq [n]$

  $X := (\{0\} \times A_R) \cup (\{1\} \times A_W)$

  $\text{sk}' := \text{cPRF.Constrain}(\text{msk}, X)$

  send K **to** C

  return ϵ

$\underline{C(\text{sk}, A_R, A_W)}$

  receive sk' **from** D

  return sk'

$\underline{S(\bar{M})}$

  return $\bar{M}' := \bar{M}$

$\underline{\text{Access}\langle C, S \rangle}$

$\underline{C(\text{sk}_{\text{id}}, a, m)}$

  receive r **from** S

  $r_{R,a} := \text{cPRF.cEval}(\text{sk}, (0, a))$

  $r_{W,a} := \text{cPRF.cEval}(\text{sk}, (1, a))$

  $(\text{pk}_a^{\mathcal{E}}, \text{sk}_a^{\mathcal{E}}) := \mathcal{E}.\text{KGen}(1^\lambda; r_{R,a})$

  $(\text{pk}_a^{\Sigma}, \text{sk}_a^{\Sigma}) := \Sigma.\text{KGen}(1^\lambda; r_{W,k})$

  $(\tilde{\text{pk}}^{\mathcal{E}}, \tilde{\text{sk}}^{\mathcal{E}}) \leftarrow \mathcal{E}.\text{KGen}(1^\lambda)$

  $\sigma \leftarrow \Sigma.\text{Sig}(\text{sk}_a^{\Sigma}, (r, m))$

  $\tilde{c}_0 \leftarrow \mathcal{E}.\text{Enc}(\tilde{\text{pk}}^{\mathcal{E}}, a)$

  if $m \neq \epsilon$ **then**

    $c_1 \leftarrow \mathcal{E}.\text{Enc}(\text{pk}_a^{\mathcal{E}}, \sigma), c_2 \leftarrow \mathcal{E}.\text{Enc}(\text{pk}_a^{\mathcal{E}}, m)$

  else

    $c_1 \leftarrow \mathcal{E}.\text{Enc}(\text{pk}_0^{\mathcal{E}}, 0), c_2 \leftarrow \mathcal{E}.\text{Enc}(\text{pk}_0^{\mathcal{E}}, 0)$

  send $(\tilde{\text{pk}}^{\mathcal{E}}, \tilde{c}_0, c_1, c_2)$ **to** S

  receive $\tilde{c}_0'$ **from** S

  $\bar{m}' \leftarrow \mathcal{E}.\text{Dec}(\tilde{\text{sk}}^{\mathcal{E}}, \tilde{c}_0')$

  return $m' \leftarrow \mathcal{E}.\text{Dec}(\text{sk}_a^{\mathcal{E}}, \bar{m}')$

$\underline{S(\bar{M})}$

  send $r \leftarrow_{\$} \{0, 1\}^\lambda$ **to** C

  receive $(\tilde{\text{pk}}^{\mathcal{E}}, \tilde{c}_0, c_1, c_2)$ **from** C

  send $\tilde{c}_0' \leftarrow \mathcal{E}.\text{Eval}(\tilde{\text{pk}}^{\mathcal{E}}, \text{Read}_{\bar{M}}, \tilde{c}_0)$ **to** C

  for $k \in [n]$ **do**

    $\bar{m}_k' \leftarrow \mathcal{E}.\text{Eval}(\text{pk}_k^{\mathcal{E}}, \text{Write}_{\text{pk}_k^{\Sigma}, r}, (c_1, c_2, \bar{m}_k))$

    $\bar{M}'[k] := \bar{m}_k'$

  return $\bar{M}'$

Fig. 7. FHE-based Single-Server MCORAM Construction

With the above, Fig. 7 presents an MCORAM Θ for the message space $\mathcal{M}_{\mathcal{E}}$. We highlight some key steps. We assume for now that the data owner D generates the keys $(\text{pk}_k^{\mathcal{E}}, \text{sk}_k^{\mathcal{E}})$ and $(\text{pk}_k^{\Sigma}, \text{sk}_k^{\Sigma})$ for $k \in [n] \cup \{0\}$ during setup, and publishes all public keys as public parameters. Naturally, the keys indexed by $k \in [n]$ corresponds to the n addresses of the database, while the keys indexed by 0 are reserved for other purposes. The database at the server S is $\bar{M} = \{\bar{m}_k\}_{k \in [n]}$, where $\bar{m}_k = \mathcal{E}.\text{Enc}(\text{pk}_k^{\mathcal{E}}, m_k)$. Reading and writing rights to an address $a \in [n]$ is granted to a client C by simply sending to C the key $\text{sk}_a^{\mathcal{E}}$ and sk_a^{Σ}, respectively.

To obliviously access an address $a \in [n]$, the client C first requests a nonce r from the server S. C then generates a fresh FHE key $\tilde{\text{pk}}^{\mathcal{E}}$, and uses it to encrypt a in c_0. Then, for a write access, C uses sk_a^{Σ} to sign r and the data m to be stored, and encrypts the resulting signature σ in c_1 and m in c_2. For a read operation, C sets both σ and m to 0, and uses $\mathsf{pk}_0^{\mathcal{E}}$ to generate c_1 and c_2 instead.

As S is supposedly oblivious to the address, it homomorphically evaluates the reading circuit $\mathsf{Read}_{\bar{M}}$ parameterized by the entire database $\bar{M}$ over c_0. This results in a ciphertext encrypting m_a under $\tilde{\mathsf{pk}}^{\mathcal{E}}$, whose secret key is only known by C. S also evaluates the writing circuit $\mathsf{Write}_{\mathsf{pk}_k^{\Sigma},r}$ over $(c_1, c_2, \bar{m}_k)$ for each address $k \in [n]$. Under the hood of FHE, $\mathsf{Write}_{\mathsf{pk}_k^{\Sigma},r}$ checks if σ is a valid signature of (r, m) w.r.t. pk_k^{Σ}, and if so (C has writing rights to k and intends to write m there), returns a ciphertext $\bar{m}_k'$ encrypting the new m under $\mathsf{pk}_k^{\mathcal{E}}$. If not, $\bar{m}_k'$ would be encrypting m_k (the original data) under $\mathsf{pk}_k^{\mathcal{E}}$. Regardless of the result (which S is oblivious to), S updates the k-th entry of the database to $\bar{m}_k'$.

To reduce the size of the master secret key, D can derive the $\mathcal{E}$ and Σ keys using the pseudorandomness generated by cPRF. Correspondingly, D sends the appropriately constrained PRF keys, so that the clients can re-derive the $\mathcal{E}$ and Σ secret keys. If cPRF features succinct constrained keys (of size sublinear in the description size of the constraining set), then the MCORAM features succinct client keys (of size sublinear in the number of permitted addresses).

6.2 Security

Integrity requires that data written honestly can be successfully read by honest clients, which largely follows from the correctness of the building blocks. The more challenging requirement is to ensure the adversary can not overwrite entries without write access. We first use the correctness of FHE and the signature scheme to argue that, unless a valid signature of a random nonce is given, an entry would never be overwritten, then we argue for its unforgeability.

Obliviousness is intuitive, too, because a client always sends a fresh public key and three FHE ciphertexts during access, regardless of the access type. Although the ciphertexts are generated using keys that may depend on the access, we can rely on the key privacy of FHE and argue that they are still indistinguishable. The proofs for our theorems can be found in the full version.

Theorem 5. *If* cPRF *is selective-input correct and pseudorandom,* $\mathcal{E}$ *is strongly correct,* Σ *is correct, and* Σ *is EUF-CMA-secure, then* Θ *has integrity.*

Theorem 6. *If* cPRF *is selective-input pseudorandom, and* $\mathcal{E}$ *is IND-CPA-secure and IK-IND-CPA-secure, then* Θ *is oblivious.*

6.3 Access Rights Revocation

Generic techniques for revocation are compatible with our construction. First of all, the data owner could always re-encrypt database entries and/or re-generate the corresponding signature verification keys. However, this requires the data owner to re-grant the access rights of the refreshed entries from scratch. Using a constrained PRF for a powerful enough class of constraints, we can save the data owner from some troubles in always re-granting the keys to the clients.

Recall that cPRF is used for deriving the address-dependent secret keys. To support revocation, we consider an equivalent formulation of cPRF, where the PRF key is constrained by a predicate P, such that the constrained key allows evaluations of the PRF over the inputs x satisfying $P(x) = 1$. The core idea is to put the latest client revocation list as an input of P for deriving the latest keys.

In more detail, the data owner publishes (*e.g.*, via the server) the client revocation lists $\mathcal{L}_{\text{Read},a}$ and $\mathcal{L}_{\text{Write},a}$ for each $a \in [n]$, which contain the identifiers of clients whose read access and respectively write access to address a have been revoked. Suppose client id is entitled to read access to addresses $a \in A_R$ and write access to addresses $a \in A_W$, respectively. The data owner delegates to client id a PRF key constrained with respect to the following predicate $P_{A_R, A_W, \text{id}}$ parameterized by A_R, A_W, and id (*i.e.*, they are embedded in the constraint key):

$P_{A_R, A_W, \text{id}}(\text{op}, \text{addr}, \text{CRL})$: If $(\text{id} \notin \text{CRL}) \wedge ((\text{op} = \text{Read} \wedge \text{addr} \in A_R) \vee (\text{op} = \text{Write} \wedge \text{addr} \in A_W))$, return 1; else return 0.

The last input CRL can be changing ($\mathcal{L}_{\text{Read}}$ or $\mathcal{L}_{\text{Write}}$). We still use the PRF output to generate the signing and verification keys for the address a, but it would be the PRF value on $(\text{Write}, a, \mathcal{L}_{\text{Write},a})$ for write access, for example. If $a \in A_W$ and id $\notin \mathcal{L}_{\text{Write},a}$, client id can evaluate the PRF on $(\text{Write}, a, \mathcal{L}_{\text{Write},a})$, and hence derive the signing key needed for write access to a.

To revoke (more) clients their write access to a, the data owner informs the server of a new verification key (which is a PRF value of the new blacklist). Read access can be revoked similarly, except that the data owner would need to re-encrypt those database entries whose revocation policies have been changed.

7   DPF-based Multi-server Construction

7.1   Our Distributed Point Function

Let $(\text{DPF}'.\text{Gen}, \text{DPF}'.\text{Eval}, \text{DPF}'.\text{Dec})$ be a $(1, 2)$-DPF such that $\text{DPF}'.\text{Eval}$ is in NC1, and let $(1, 2)$-HSS $= (\text{HSS.Gen}, \text{HSS.Eval}, \text{HSS.Dec})$ be a homomorphic secret sharing as defined in Sect. 4.4 for NC1 circuits. Figure 8 shows our $(3, 4)$-DPF construction. The $(2, 3)$-DPF follows a straightforward modification, which we include in the full version.

Theorem 7 (Correctness). *Let $\hat{\Delta}$ and $\tilde{\Delta}$ be inverse polynomials. Let $(1, 2)$-DPF$'$ be a $\hat{\Delta}$-correct distributed point function and let $(1, 2)$-HSS be a $\tilde{\Delta}$-correct homomorphic secret sharing. Our construction in Fig. 8 is a Δ-correct $(3, 4)$-DPF, for some inverse polynomial Δ.*

Theorem 8 (Security). *Let $(1, 2)$-DPF$'$ be a secure distributed point function and let $(1, 2)$-HSS be a secure homomorphic secret sharing. The construction in Fig. 8 is a secure $(3, 4)$-DPF.*

The proofs of Theorems 7 and 8 can be found in the full version.

$\mathsf{DPF.Gen}(1^\lambda, F_{a,b})$	$\mathsf{DPF.Eval}(i, k_i, x)$	$\mathsf{DPF.Dec}(z_1, z_2, z_3, z_4)$
$(k_1, k_2) \leftarrow \mathsf{DPF'.Gen}(1^\lambda, F_{a,b})$	**if** $i \in \{1,3\}$ **then** $j := 1$	$y_1 \leftarrow \mathsf{HSS.Dec}(z_1, z_2)$
$(s_1, s_2) \leftarrow \mathsf{HSS.Gen}(1^\lambda, k_1)$	**if** $i \in \{2,4\}$ **then** $j := 2$	$y_2 \leftarrow \mathsf{HSS.Dec}(z_3, z_4)$
$(s_3, s_4) \leftarrow \mathsf{HSS.Gen}(1^\lambda, k_2)$	$\ell := 2$	$z \leftarrow \mathsf{DPF'.Dec}(y_1, y_2)$
return (s_1, s_2, s_3, s_4)	**if** $i \leq 2$ **then** $\ell := 1$	**return** z
	$C \leftarrow \mathsf{DPF'.Eval}(\ell, \cdot, a)$	
	$z \leftarrow \mathsf{HSS.Eval}(j, k_i, C)$	
	return z	

Fig. 8. $(3,4)$-DPF Construction

INSTANTIATIONS. By Theorem 4, there exists a $(1,2)$-HSS for NC1 circuits with share size $\mathsf{poly}(\lambda|a|)$, which is Δ-correct for any inverse polynomial Δ, assuming the hardness of the DDH (or DCR) problem. By Theorem 3, there exists a perfectly-correct $(1,2)$-DPF$'$ with $\mathsf{poly}(d(\lambda + \log(|\mathbb{G}|)))$ key size, where $\{0,1\}^d$ is the domain of the point function, assuming the existence of one-way functions. What is left to be shown is that our $(3,4)$-DPF is efficient when plugging in these two building blocks. More precisely, we will show that DPF$'$.Eval of the $(1,2)$-DPF$'$ is computable by an NC1 circuit. Recall that the complexity of the algorithm of [4] is dominated by d calls for a length-doubling PRG. For a point function with a polynomial-size domain, we can set $d = c\log(\lambda)$, for some constant c, then implementing the length-doubling PRG with a construction in NC0 (such as Goldreich PRG [23]) gives us an evaluation algorithm computable by an NC1 circuit. The size of the resulting keys of our $(3,4)$-DPF is $\mathsf{poly}(\lambda d \cdot (\lambda + \log(|\mathbb{G}|))) = \mathsf{poly}(\lambda c \log(\lambda) \cdot (\lambda + \log(|\mathbb{G}|)))$. We thus obtain:

Corollary 1. *If the DDH or DCR problem is hard and there exists a PRG in NC0, there exists a Δ-correct $(3,4)$-DPF for any inverse polynomial Δ, for functions with polynomial-size domain $\{0,1\}^d$ with key size $\mathsf{poly}(\lambda d \cdot (\lambda + \log(|\mathbb{G}|)))$.*

7.2 Multi-client ORAM from Distributed Point Functions

As described in the introduction, there exists a folklore way (*e.g.*, [9]) to construct distributed ORAM (DORAM) with stateless client from any (t, N)-DPF with linear reconstruction. Such a DORAM can be further transformed into a multi-server MCORAM by equipping it with access control. Incorporating reading rights (while achieving obliviousness) is straightforward via encryption. Granting meaningful writing rights and achieving integrity, however, seems impossible in the setting where the servers cannot communicate (even indirectly).

To show the legitimacy of an update, the client needs to prove the knowledge of a witness for a statement about the database, which is secret-shared among the servers. As any single server has no information about the statement, the

$\text{Setup}(1^\lambda, 1^n, 1^N, M = (m_1, \ldots, m_n))$

for $k \in [n]$ **do**

  $(\text{pk}_k^{\mathcal{E}}, \text{sk}_k^{\mathcal{E}}) \leftarrow \mathcal{E}.\text{KGen}(1^\lambda)$

  $\bar{m}_k' \leftarrow \mathcal{E}.\text{Enc}(\text{pk}_k^{\mathcal{E}}, m_k)$

$\bar{M}' := (\bar{m}_1', \ldots, \bar{m}_n')$

for $k \in [N]$

  sample $\bar{M}_k$ s.t. $\bar{M}' = \sum_{i \in [N]} \bar{M}_i$

for $(i, j) \in [N]^2$ **do** $\bar{M}_{i,j} := \bar{M}_i$

$\text{pp} := (\text{pk}_1^{\mathcal{E}}, \ldots, \text{pk}_n^{\mathcal{E}})$

$\text{msk} := (\text{sk}_1^{\mathcal{E}}, \ldots, \text{sk}_n^{\mathcal{E}})$

return $(\text{pp}, \text{msk}, \bar{M}_{1,1}, \ldots, \bar{M}_{N,N})$

$\text{Join}(\text{msk}, \text{id})$

return $\text{sk}_{\text{id}} := \epsilon$

$\text{ChMod}\langle D, C_{\text{id}}, (S_{1,1}, \ldots, S_{N,N})\rangle$

$D(\text{msk}, \text{id}, A \subseteq [n])$

  $\tilde{\text{sk}}_{\text{id}} := \emptyset$

  for $a \in A$ **do**

    $\tilde{\text{sk}}_{\text{id}} := \tilde{\text{sk}}_{\text{id}} \cup \{(a, \text{sk}_a^{\mathcal{E}})\}$

  send $\tilde{\text{sk}}_{\text{id}}$ to C_{id}

  return ϵ

$C_{\text{id}}(\text{sk}_{\text{id}}, A \subseteq [n])$

  receive $\tilde{\text{sk}}_{\text{id}}$

  return $\text{sk}_{\text{id}}' := \text{sk}_{\text{id}} \cup \tilde{\text{sk}}_{\text{id}}$

$S_{i,j}(\bar{M}_{i,j}), (i, j) \in [N]^2$

  return $\bar{M}_{i,j}' := \bar{M}_{i,j}$

$\text{Access}\langle C_{\text{id}}, (S_{1,1}, \ldots, S_{N,N})\rangle$

$C_{\text{id}}(\text{sk}_{\text{id}}, a, m)$

  $(k_1, \ldots, k_N) \leftarrow \text{DPF.Gen}(1^\lambda, F_{a,1})$

  for $(i, j) \in [N]^2$ **send** k_j to $S_{i,j}$

$S_{i,j}(\bar{M}_{i,j}), (i, j) \in [N]^2$

  receive k_j

  for $a' \in [n]$ **do**

    $z_{a'} \leftarrow \text{DPF.Eval}(j, k_j, a')$

  send $c_{i,j} = \sum_{a' \in [n]} \bar{M}_{i,j}[a'] \cdot z_{a'}$ to C_{id}

$C_{\text{id}}(\text{sk}_{\text{id}}, a, m)$

  receive $(c_{1,1}, \ldots, c_{N,N})$

  $\bar{m}' := \sum_{(i,j) \in [N]^2} c_{i,j}$

  if $(x, \text{sk}_a^{\mathcal{E}}) \in \text{sk}_{\text{id}}$ **then**

    $m' \leftarrow \mathcal{E}.\text{Dec}(\text{sk}_a^{\mathcal{E}}, \bar{m}')$

  if $m = \epsilon$ **then** $b := 0$

  else $\bar{m} \leftarrow \mathcal{E}.\text{Enc}(\text{pk}_a^{\mathcal{E}}, m), b := \bar{m} - \bar{m}'$

  $(k_1, \ldots, k_N) \leftarrow \text{DPF.Gen}(1^\lambda, F_{a,b})$

  for $(i, j) \in [N]^2$ **send** k_i to $S_{i,j}$

  return m'

$S_{i,j}(\bar{M}_{i,j}), (i, j) \in [N]^2$

  receive k_i

  for $a' \in [n]$ **do**

    $z_{a'} \leftarrow \text{DPF.Eval}(i, k_i, a')$

    $\bar{M}_{i,j}'[a'] := \bar{M}_{i,j}[a'] + z_{a'}$

  return $\bar{M}_{i,j}'$

Fig. 9. DPF-based Multi-Server MCORAM Construction

proof cannot be verified during the access. (We discuss an alternative later). In Fig. 9, we propose a transformation in a simplified setting where all clients have writing rights to all addresses by default, so the ChMod protocol is used only for granting reading rights (via decryption keys). In this setting, the syntax of ChMod can be simplified, which inputs a set of addresses A (cf. A_R and A_W).

Figure 9 assumes N^2 servers, indexed by $(i, j) \in [N]^2$, with at most t of them collude. Each entry $M[a]$ of the initial data array M is first encrypted with an independent public key pk_a of a public-key encryption scheme $\mathcal{E}$, and then secret-shared using the additive N-out-of-N secret sharing scheme. The (i, j)-th server gets the i-th share $\bar{M}_i$ of the ciphertext. We use independent encryption and decryption keys for each address for simplicity. The master and client secret key sizes can be reduced using constrained PRFs as in the FHE-based construction.

To access address a, the client generates fresh DPF keys $(k_1, \ldots, k_N)$ for the point function $F_{a,1}$, and sends k_j to server (i, j) for $(i, j) \in [N]^2$. Using the additive reconstruction property of the DPF, the (i, j)-th server can compute the j-th share of $\bar{M}_i[a] = \sum_{a' \in [n]} F_{a,1}(a') \bar{M}_i[a]$. Collecting all N^2 shares, the client can recover $\bar{M}[a]$, and decrypt it using sk_a to get $M[a]$. Regardless of whether logical access is a read or a write, the client must write something to ensure obliviousness. In case of a write access, the client encrypts the new data item as $\bar{m}$, and sets $b := \bar{m} - \bar{M}[a]$; in case of a read access, the client sets $b := 0$. The client then generates another fresh tuple of DPF keys $(k_1, \ldots, k_N)$ for the point function $F_{a,b}$, and sends k_i to server (i, j) for $(i, j) \in [N]^2$. Using the reconstruction property again, the i-th row of servers can obtain, for each $a' \in [n]$, the same i-th share of $\bar{M}'[a']$ being $\bar{M}[a']$ for $a' \neq a$, $\bar{m}$ otherwise.

PROPERTIES OF THE RESULTING MULTI-SERVER MCORAM. Since the DPF is resilient against the disclosure of any $t < N$ shares, the multi-server (MC)ORAM scheme is secure against a t/N^2 fraction of corruptions. One can show that the scheme is oblivious with a simple reduction to the security of DPF.

Meaningful selective writing rights can be granted by settling for accountable integrity. The techniques for it are rather standard [29]. Roughly, assuming there is an underlying versioning system (as in a typical storage system) that stores each (encrypted) update instruction, we additionally require the client to anonymously sign the update with traceable signatures (*e.g.*, [15]). The data owner can then trace the misbehaving party via the anonymity revocation mechanism.

Consistency is another issue. Due to the underlying HSS [5], our DPF might fail with a certain probability. This is undesirable, especially for write operations, as it would leave the database in a corrupted state. Fortunately, the same HSS [5] allows the servers to detect potential errors; thus, they can abort accordingly.

Finally, note that we can even use different DPF algorithms of different parameters for read and write. This allows some tunable trade-offs, *e.g.*, using a (t, N)-DPF for write and a (t', N')-DPF for read brings the threshold/server-ratio to $\min\{t, t'\}/(NN')$. Specifically, using a (t, N)-DPF for write and a $(1, 1)$-DPF (*i.e.*, a PIR scheme) for read brings the threshold/server-ratio down to t/N.

8   Concluding Remarks

Since many techniques for constructing single-client ORAM break down completely when the client can be corrupt, it was unclear whether the poly-logarithmic communication complexity of ORAM can be attained by MCORAM with an access control mechanism and obliviousness against fellow clients. We devise a cross-key trial evaluation technique and two new distributed point functions for building (multi-server) MCORAM with poly-logarithmic communication complexity. Besides, existing MCORAM definitions are indistinguishability based and may not be readily applicable in higher cryptographic applications. This paper also filled in this gap. Our study benefits the applications of MCORAM for building higher cryptographic primitives and enriches our understanding of homomorphic secret sharing. Application-wise, our MCORAM is especially useful for private anonymous data access in an outsourced setting.

References

1. Blass, E.-O., Mayberry, T., Noubir, G.: Multi-client oblivious RAM secure against malicious servers. In: Gollmann, D., Miyaji, A., Kikuchi, H. (eds.) ACNS 2017. LNCS, vol. 10355, pp. 686–707. Springer, Cham (2017). https://doi.org/10.1007/978-3-319-61204-1_34
2. Boneh, D., Waters, B.: Constrained pseudorandom functions and their applications. In: Sako, K., Sarkar, P. (eds.) ASIACRYPT 2013, Part II. LNCS, vol. 8270, pp. 280–300. Springer, Heidelberg (2013). https://doi.org/10.1007/978-3-642-42045-0_15
3. Boyle, E., Chung, K.-M., Pass, R.: Oblivious parallel RAM and applications. In: Kushilevitz, E., Malkin, T. (eds.) TCC 2016, Part II. LNCS, vol. 9563, pp. 175–204. Springer, Heidelberg (2016). https://doi.org/10.1007/978-3-662-49099-0_7
4. Boyle, E., Gilboa, N., Ishai, Y.: Function secret sharing. In: Oswald, E., Fischlin, M. (eds.) EUROCRYPT 2015, Part II. LNCS, vol. 9057, pp. 337–367. Springer, Heidelberg (2015). https://doi.org/10.1007/978-3-662-46803-6_12
5. Boyle, E., Gilboa, N., Ishai, Y.: Breaking the circuit size barrier for secure computation under DDH. In: Robshaw, M., Katz, J. (eds.) CRYPTO 2016, Part I. LNCS, vol. 9814, pp. 509–539. Springer, Heidelberg (2016). https://doi.org/10.1007/978-3-662-53018-4_19
6. Boyle, E., Gilboa, N., Ishai, Y., Lin, H., Tessaro, S.: Foundations of homomorphic secret sharing. In: ITCS, pp. 21:1–21:21 (2018)
7. Boyle, E., Ishai, Y., Pass, R., Wootters, M.: Can we access a database both locally and privately? In: Kalai, Y., Reyzin, L. (eds.) TCC 2017, Part II. LNCS, vol. 10678, pp. 662–693. Springer, Cham (2017). https://doi.org/10.1007/978-3-319-70503-3_22
8. Brakerski, Z., Döttling, N., Garg, S., Malavolta, G.: Leveraging linear decryption: rate-1 fully-homomorphic encryption and time-lock puzzles. In: Hofheinz, D., Rosen, A. (eds.) TCC 2019, Part II. LNCS, vol. 11892, pp. 407–437. Springer, Cham (2019). https://doi.org/10.1007/978-3-030-36033-7_16
9. Bunn, P., Katz, J., Kushilevitz, E., Ostrovsky, R.: Efficient 3-party distributed ORAM. In: Galdi, C., Kolesnikov, V. (eds.) SCN 2020. LNCS, vol. 12238, pp. 215–232. Springer, Cham (2020). https://doi.org/10.1007/978-3-030-57990-6_11
10. Camenisch, J., Dubovitskaya, M., Neven, G.: Oblivious transfer with access control. In: CCS, pp. 131–140 (2009)
11. Canetti, R., Holmgren, J., Richelson, S.: Towards doubly efficient private information retrieval. In: Kalai, Y., Reyzin, L. (eds.) TCC 2017, Part II. LNCS, vol. 10678, pp. 694–726. Springer, Cham (2017). https://doi.org/10.1007/978-3-319-70503-3_23

12. Canetti, R., Lombardi, A., Wichs, D.: Non-interactive zero knowledge and correlation intractability from circular-secure FHE. Cryptology ePrint Archive, Report 2018/1248 (2018)
13. Chen, B., Lin, H., Tessaro, S.: Oblivious parallel RAM: improved efficiency and generic constructions. In: Kushilevitz, E., Malkin, T. (eds.) TCC-A 2016, Part II. LNCS, vol. 9563, pp. 205–234. Springer, Heidelberg (2016). https://doi.org/10.1007/978-3-662-49099-0_8
14. Chor, B., Kushilevitz, E., Goldreich, O., Sudan, M.: Private information retrieval. J. ACM **45**(6), 965–981 (1998)
15. Chow, S.S.M.: Real traceable signatures. In: Jacobson, M.J., Rijmen, V., Safavi-Naini, R. (eds.) SAC 2009. LNCS, vol. 5867, pp. 92–107. Springer, Heidelberg (2009). https://doi.org/10.1007/978-3-642-05445-7_6
16. Doerner, J., Shelat, A.: Scaling ORAM for secure computation. In: CCS, pp. 523–535 (2017)
17. Fazio, N., Gennaro, R., Jafarikhah, T., Skeith III, W.E.: Homomorphic secret sharing from paillier encryption. In: Okamoto, T., Yu, Y., Au, M.H., Li, Y. (eds.) ProvSec 2017. LNCS, vol. 10592, pp. 381–399. Springer, Cham (2017). https://doi.org/10.1007/978-3-319-68637-0_23
18. Gentry, C.: A fully homomorphic encryption scheme. Ph.D. thesis, Stanford University (2009)
19. Gentry, C., Halevi, S.: Compressible FHE with applications to PIR. In: Hofheinz, D., Rosen, A. (eds.) TCC 2019, Part II. LNCS, vol. 11892, pp. 438–464. Springer, Cham (2019). https://doi.org/10.1007/978-3-030-36033-7_17
20. Gentry, C., Sahai, A., Waters, B.: Homomorphic encryption from learning with errors: conceptually-simpler, asymptotically-faster, attribute-based. In: Canetti, R., Garay, J.A. (eds.) CRYPTO 2013, Part I. LNCS, vol. 8042, pp. 75–92. Springer, Heidelberg (2013). https://doi.org/10.1007/978-3-642-40041-4_5
21. Gilboa, N., Ishai, Y.: Distributed point functions and their applications. In: Nguyen, P.Q., Oswald, E. (eds.) EUROCRYPT 2014. LNCS, vol. 8441, pp. 640–658. Springer, Heidelberg (2014). https://doi.org/10.1007/978-3-642-55220-5_35
22. Goldreich, O.: Towards a theory of software protection and simulation by oblivious RAMs. In: STOC, pp. 182–194 (1987)
23. Goldreich, O.: A primer on Pseudorandom Generators, vol. 55. American Mathematical Society (2010)
24. Goldreich, O., Goldwasser, S., Micali, S.: How to construct random functions. J. ACM **33**(4), 792–807 (1986)
25. Goodrich, M.T., Mitzenmacher, M., Ohrimenko, O., Tamassia, R.: Privacy-preserving group data access via stateless oblivious RAM simulation. In: SODA, pp. 157–167 (2012)
26. Hamlin, A., Ostrovsky, R., Weiss, M., Wichs, D.: Private anonymous data access. In: Ishai, Y., Rijmen, V. (eds.) EUROCRYPT 2019. LNCS, vol. 11477, pp. 244–273. Springer, Cham (2019). https://doi.org/10.1007/978-3-030-17656-3_9
27. Hoang, T., Ozkaptan, C.D., Yavuz, A.A., Guajardo, J., Nguyen, T.: S³ORAM: a computation-efficient and constant client bandwidth blowup ORAM with Shamir secret sharing. In: CCS, pp. 491–505 (2017)
28. Kushilevitz, E., Ostrovsky, R.: Replication is not needed: single database, computationally-private information retrieval. In: FOCS, pp. 364–373 (1997)
29. Maffei, M., Malavolta, G., Reinert, M., Schröder, D.: Privacy and access control for outsourced personal records. In: S&P, pp. 341–358 (2015)

30. Maffei, M., Malavolta, G., Reinert, M., Schröder, D.: Maliciously secure multi-client ORAM. In: Gollmann, D., Miyaji, A., Kikuchi, H. (eds.) ACNS 2017. LNCS, vol. 10355, pp. 645–664. Springer, Cham (2017). https://doi.org/10.1007/978-3-319-61204-1_32
31. Sahin, C., Zakhary, V., Abbadi, A.E., Lin, H., Tessaro, S.: TaoStore: overcoming asynchronicity in oblivious data storage. In: S&P, pp. 198–217 (2016)
32. Wang, F., Yun, C., Goldwasser, S., Vaikuntanathan, V., Zaharia, M.: Splinter: practical private queries on public data. In: NSDI, pp. 299–313 (2017)

Privacy-Preserving Pattern Matching
on Encrypted Data

Anis Bkakria[1(✉)], Nora Cuppens[1,2], and Frédéric Cuppens[1,2]

[1] IMT Atlantique, Rennes, France
{anis.bkakria,nora.cuppens,frederic.cuppens}@imt-atlantique.fr
[2] Polytechnique Montréal, Montréal, Canada
{nora.cuppens,frederic.cuppens}@polymtl.ca

Abstract. Pattern matching is one of the most fundamental and important paradigms in several application domains such as digital forensics, cyber threat intelligence, or genomic and medical data analysis. While it is a straightforward operation when performed on plaintext data, it becomes a challenging task when the privacy of both the analyzed data and the analysis patterns must be preserved. In this paper, we propose new provably correct, secure, and relatively efficient (compared to similar existing schemes) public and private key based constructions that allow arbitrary pattern matching over encrypted data while protecting both the data to be analyzed and the patterns to be matched. That is, except the pattern provider (resp. the data owner), all other involved parties in the proposed constructions will learn nothing about the patterns to be searched (resp. the data to be inspected). Compared to existing solutions, the constructions we propose have some interesting properties: (1) the size of the ciphertext is linear to the size of plaintext and independent of the sizes and the number of the analysis patterns; (2) the sizes of the issued trapdoors are constant on the size of the data to be analyzed; and (3) the search complexity is linear on the size of the data to be inspected and is constant on the sizes of the analysis patterns. The conducted evaluations show that our constructions drastically improve the performance of the most efficient state of the art solution.

Keywords: Searchable encryption · Pattern Matching

1 Introduction

In several application domains such as deep-packet inspection and genomic data analysis, learning the presence of specific patterns as well as their positions in the data are essential. In the previous two use cases, pattern searches are often performed by entities that are not fully trusted by data owners. For instance, in the case of deep-packet inspection (DPI), a company that aims to outsource its network traces to a third party forensic scientist to find indictors of compromise might not be comfortable revealing the full contents of its traces to the forensic scientist. Similarly, in the case of genomic data analysis, a patient that wants

© International Association for Cryptologic Research 2020
S. Moriai and H. Wang (Eds.): ASIACRYPT 2020, LNCS 12492, pp. 191–220, 2020.
https://doi.org/10.1007/978-3-030-64834-3_7

to check whether its genome contains particular patterns representing a genetic predisposition to specific diseases might not be comfortable revealing the full contents of its genome to the laboratory that performs the analysis.

Existing solutions that may be used to overcome the previous problem rely mainly on searchable encryption based techniques [1–6]. Unfortunately, these techniques suffer from at least one of the following limitations. First, the lack of support for pattern-matching with evolving patterns, such as virus signatures which are updated frequently (case of symmetric searchable encryption [2–4]); second, the lack of support for variable pattern lengths (e.g., tokenization-based techniques such as BlindBox [5]); third, the incompleteness of pattern detection methods which yield false negatives (case of BlindIDS [6]); and fourth, the disclosure of detection patterns (case of searchable encryption with shiftable trapdoors [1]). We provide a full comparison with related literature in Sect. 2.

In this paper, we propose two technically sound constructions: S^4E supporting pattern matching of adaptively chosen and variable (upper bounded) lengths patterns on secret key encrypted streams, and AS^3E supporting pattern matching of adaptively chosen and variable (upper bounded) lengths patterns on public key encrypted streams. Both S^4E and AS^3E ensure that (1) both the data owner and the third-party entity performing pattern matching operations will learn nothing about the searched patterns except their lengths, (2) both the pattern provider and the third-party entity that is going to perform pattern matching will learn nothing about the data to be analyzed except the presence or the absence of the set of unknown patterns (i.e., the third-party entity will not have access to patterns plaintexts), (3) the third-party entity will be able to perform pattern matching correctly over the data to be analyzed. From a practical point of view, our construction has some interesting properties. First, the size of the ciphertext depends only on the size of the plaintext (it is independent of the sizes and the number of analysis patterns). Second, the size of the issued trapdoors is independent of the size of the data to be analyzed. Third, the search complexity depends only on the size of the data to be analyzed and is constant on the size of the analysis patterns. The two constructions we propose in this paper are – to our knowledge – the first constructions to provide all previously mentioned properties without using costly and complex cryptographic scheme such as fully homomorphic encryption. The conducted evaluations show that the two proposed constructions improve by up to four orders of magnitude the performance of the most efficient state of the art solution SEST [1].

The paper is organized as follows. Section 2 reviews related work and details the main contributions of our work. Section 3 presents the assumptions under which our schemes achieve provable security. The intuition behind the proposed constructions is presented in Sect. 4. Section 5 and 6 formalize our S^4E and AS^3E primitives and provide their security results. In Sects. 7 and 8, we discuss the complexity of our constructions and provide experimental results. Finally, Sect. 9 concludes.

2 Related Work

One possible solution for pattern matching over encrypted traffic is to use techniques that allow evaluation of functions over encrypted data. Generic approaches such as fully homomorphic encryption (FHE) [7,9] and functional encryption (FE) [8] are currently impractical due to their very high complexities.

Several searchable encryption (SE) techniques have been proposed for keyword searching over encrypted data [2–4]. The main idea is to associate a trapdoor with each keyword to allow searching for these keywords within a given encrypted data. Ideally, an entity which does not have access to the plaintext and encryption key should learn nothing about the plaintext except the presence or the absence of the keyword. For most existing SE techniques, searches are performed on keywords that have been pre-chosen by the entity encrypting the data. Such approaches are more suitable for specific types of searches, such as database searches in which records are already indexed by keywords, or in the case of emails filtering in which flags such as "urgent" are used. Unfortunately, SE techniques become useless when the set of keywords cannot be known before encryption. This is usually the case for messaging application and Internet browsing traffic where keywords can include expressions that are not sequences of words *per se* (e.g., /chamjavanv.inf?aapf/login.jsp?=). The two constructions we propose in this paper offer better search flexibility as, even after the plaintext has been encrypted, they can allow arbitrarily chosen keywords to be searched without re-encryption.

To overcome the previous limitations, tokenization-based approaches have been proposed. In [5], the authors propose BlindBox, an approach that splits the data to be encrypted into fragments of the same size l and encrypts each of those fragments using a searchable encryption scheme where each fragment will represent a keyword. Nevertheless, this solution suffers from two limitations: (1) it is useful only if all the searchable keywords have the same length l. Obviously the previous condition is seldom satisfied in real-world applications that requires pattern matching (e.g., DPI). If we want to use this approach with keyword of different lengths $\mathcal{L}$, we should for each $l_i \in \mathcal{L}$, split the data to be encrypted into fragments of size l_i and encrypt them, which quickly becomes bulky. (2) The proposed approach may easily cause false negatives since, even if the keyword is of size l (the size of each fragment), it cannot be detected if it straddles two fragments. Recently, in [6], Canard et al. proposed BlindIDS – a public key variant of the BlindBox approach [5] that additionally ensures keywords indistinguishability. That is, the entity that is going to search over the encrypted data will lean nothing about the keywords. Unfortunately, BlindIDS suffers from the same limitations as BlindBox. The two constructions we propose in this paper address the main drawbacks of these tokenization-based techniques since they allow for arbitrary trapdoors to be matched against the encrypted data, without false negatives or false positives.

Several approaches [10–12] proposed solutions for substring search over encrypted data based on secure multi-party computation. Unfortunately, to offer pattern matching operation, these solutions require often several interactions between the searcher and the data encrypter.

As pointed out in [1], anonymous predicate encryption (e.g., [13]) or hidden vector encryption [14] may provide a convenient solution for pattern matching over encrypted data. However, in order to search a pattern p of length l on a data of length n, the searcher should obtain $n - l$ keys to be able to check the presence of p on every possible offset of the data, which is clearly a problem when dealing with large datasets.

One of the most interesting techniques for pattern matching over encrypted traffic is the searchable encryption with shiftable trapdoor (SEST) [1]. The proposed construction relies on public-key encryption and bilinear pairings to overcome most of the limitations of previously mentioned techniques. It allows for patterns of arbitrary lengths to be matched against the encrypted data, without false negatives or false positives. This improvement comes at the cost of the practicability of the technique. In fact, the proposed schema requires a public key of size linear to the size of the data to be encrypted (a public key of $\simeq 8000$ GB is required for encrypting 1GB of data). Moreover, the trapdoor generation technique used by the SEST leaks many information (such as, the number of different characters, the maximum number of occurrences of a character) about the patterns to be searched. Furthermore, the number of pairings needed for testing the presence of a keyword in an offset of the data depends on the maximum number of occurrences of the characters contained in the keyword. This makes the proposed technique quite inefficient when used for bit level matching. By contrast, for testing the presence of a pattern in encrypted data, our constructions require a constant number of pairings in the size of the pattern (see Sect. 7 for more details). This makes our constructions more efficient when matching long keywords at bit level.

As we have seen, many different approaches can be used to address pattern matching over encrypted data. To give better understanding of the benefits of the two approaches we propose in this paper compared to existing ones, we provide in Table 1 a comparative overview of their asymptotic complexities, and their ability to ensure the security properties we are aiming to provide. Note that we only consider BlindBox (a symmetric searchable encryption-based solution), BlindIDS (an asymmetric searchable encryption-based solution), Predicate Encryption/Hidden Vector Encryption and the SEST approach. Other approaches, as explained before, require data re-encryption each time a new keyword is considered [2–4], induce higher complexity [7–9], require interactivity [10–12] or ensure weaker privacy level [4].

According to the Table 1, the two constructions we propose in this paper (S^4E and AS^3E) are the only primitives that simultaneously enable arbitrary trapdoors (with upper bounded keyword size), provides a correct keyword detection, and ensures the privacy of the used trapdoors.

In Table 1, ($\checkmark$) is used to denote that a property is provided under specific conditions. AS^3E ensures trapdoor's privacy for patterns of high-min entropy (see Sect. 6 for more details). In addition, both S^4E and AS^3E support pattern

Table 1. Complexity and ensured security properties comparison between related work and our primitive. The scalars n, q, l_i, L, s denotes respectively the length of the traffic to encrypt, the number of pattern to be searched, the length of each pattern, the number of different lengths among the q patterns to be searched and the number of data encrypters. We used ($\checkmark$) to denote that the property is provided under specific conditions.

	Primitives					
	BlindBox	BlindIDS	PE/HVE	SEST	S^4E	AS^3E
Number of Trapdoors	$O(s \cdot q)$	$O(q)$	$O(n \cdot q)$	$O(q)$	$O(q)$	$O(q)$
Public Parameters size	$O(1)$	$O(1)$	$O(1)$	$O(1)$	$O(l_i)$	$O(1)$
Encryption keys size	$O(1)$	$O(1)$	$O(n)$	$O(n)$	$O(l_i)$	$O(l_i)$
Ciphertext size	$O(n \cdot L)$	$O(n \cdot L)$	$O(n)$	$O(n)$	$O(n)$	$O(n)$
Number of trapdoors	$O(q)$	$O(q)$	$O(n \cdot q)$	$O(q)$	$O(q)$	$O(q)$
Search complexity	$q \cdot \log(q)$ comparisons	q pairings	$q \cdot n$ pairings	$2 \times \prod_1^q l_i \cdot n$ pairings	$2 \cdot q \cdot n$ pairings	$2 \cdot q \cdot n$ pairings
Arbitrary trapdoors	✗	✗	$\checkmark$	$\checkmark$	($\checkmark$)	($\checkmark$)
Trapdoor's privacy	✗	($\checkmark$)	✗	✗	$\checkmark$	($\checkmark$)
Correctness (no false positives)	✗	✗	$\checkmark$	$\checkmark$	$\checkmark$	$\checkmark$

matching of arbitrary but upper bounded lengths patterns. As we show in Sect. 7, we stress that in both S^4E and AS^3E, increasing the upper bound size of patterns affects only the size of the trapdoor generated for each pattern. The size of later increases linearly with the increase of the size of the former.

The two constructions we propose do not require very large public parameters, secret key or very large public keys as SEST and PE/HVE. Moreover, their search complexities is lower than SEST by a factor of l_i (the length of the pattern w_i to be searched), since they are constant in the size of the pattern to be searched. Therefore, the proposed constructions are an interesting middle way which provides the best of PE/HVE and SEST while ensuring patterns' privacy. Their only limitation compared to PE/HVE and SEST is the upper bounded size of patterns to be searched that should be fixed before the data encryption, which we believe to be a reasonable price to pay to achieve all the other features.

3   Security Assumption

In this section, we describe the security assumptions under which our two constructions S^4E and AS^3E achieve provable security.

Definition 1 (Bilinear Maps). *Let $\mathbb{G}_1, \mathbb{G}_2, \mathbb{G}_T$ be three finite cyclic groups of large prime order p. We assume that there is an asymmetric bilinear map $e : \mathbb{G}_1 \times \mathbb{G}_2 \to \mathbb{G}_T$ such that, for all $a, b \in \mathbb{Z}_p$ the following conditions hold:*

- *For all $g \in \mathbb{G}_1, \widetilde{g} \in \mathbb{G}_2, e(g^a, \widetilde{g}^b) = e(g, \widetilde{g})^{a \cdot b}$*
- *For all $g \in \mathbb{G}_1, \widetilde{g} \in \mathbb{G}_2, e(g^a, \widetilde{g}^b) = 1$ iff $a = 0$ or $b = 0$*
- *$e(\cdot, \cdot)$ is efficiently computable*

As in [1], the security of the proposed constructions hold as long as $\mathbb{G}_1 \neq \mathbb{G}_2$ and no efficiently computable homomorphism exists between $\mathbb{G}_1$ and $\mathbb{G}_2$ in either directions. In the sequel, the tuple $(\mathbb{G}_1, \mathbb{G}_2, \mathbb{G}_T, p, e(\cdot, \cdot))$ is refereed to as a bilinear environment.

Some of the security proofs of the proposed constructions, given in the full version of this paper [22], rely partially on showing that given a number of pattern trapdoors, the adversary will be unable to distinguish a new valid trapdoor from a random element. Thus, the leakage can be bounded only by considering the adversary's query to the issuing oracle. Hence, either we considerably reduce the maximum length of the patterns to be searched (≤ 30), which allow to define a GDH instance providing all public parameters, the trapdoors for all possible patterns, and the challenge elements. Or we use an interactive variant of the GDH assumption to offer flexibility to the simulator by allowing the elements $g^{R^{(i)}(x_1, \cdots, x_c)}$, $\widetilde{g}^{S^{(i)}(x_1, \cdots, x_c)}$, and $e(g, \widetilde{g})^{T^{(i)}(x_1, \cdots, x_c)}$ of the GDH assumption [19] to be queried to specific oracles.

So, we prove the security of the proposed constructions under an interactive assumption. That is, we use a slightly modified General Diffie-Hellman (GDH) problem assumption [19] to allow the adversary to request the set of values on which the reduction will break the GDH assumption. This interactive aspect of the GDH instance we are considering reduces slightly the security of the construction we are proposing. However, this interactive assumption makes possible the definition of quite efficient constructions with interesting properties. First, the size of the ciphertext depends only on the size of the plaintext (it is independent of the sizes and the number of the analysis patterns). Second, the size of the issued trapdoors is independent of the size of the data to be searched. Third, the search complexity depends only on the size of the data and is constant on the sizes of the patterns to be matched. Attaining all previously mentioned properties while protecting both the data to be analyzed and the patterns to be matched and being able to handle arbitrary analysis pattern query is not obvious and may justify the use of such an interactive assumption.

Definition 2 (independence [19]). *Let p be some large prime, r, s, t, c, and k be five positive integers and $R \in \mathbb{F}_p[X_1, \cdots, X_c]^r$, $S \in \mathbb{F}_p[X_1, \cdots, X_c]^s$, and $T \in \mathbb{F}_p[X_1, \cdots, X_c]^t$ be three tuples of multivariate polynomials over $\mathbb{F}_p$. Let $R^{(i)}$, $S^{(i)}$ and $T^{(i)}$ denote respectively the i-th polynomial contained in R, S, and T. For any polynomial $f \in \mathbb{F}_p[X_1, \cdots, X_c]$, we say that f is dependent on $<R, S, T>$ if there exist constants $\{\vartheta_j^{(a)}\}_{j=1}^s$, $\{\vartheta_{i,j}^{(b)}\}_{i=1,j=1}^{i=r,j=s}$, $\{\vartheta_k^{(c)}\}_{k=1}^t$ such that*

$$f \cdot \left(\sum_j \vartheta_j^{(a)} \cdot S^{(j)} \right) = \sum_{i,j} \vartheta_{i,j}^{(b)} \cdot R^{(i)} \cdot S^{(j)} + \sum_k \vartheta_k^{(c)} T^{(k)}$$

We say that f is independent of $<R, S, T>$ if f is not dependent on $<R, S, T>$.

Definition 3 (i-GDH assumption). *Let p be some large prime, r, s, t, c, and k be five positive integers and $R \in \mathbb{F}_p[X_1, \cdots, X_c]^r$, $S \in \mathbb{F}_p[X_1, \cdots, X_c]^s$, and $T \in \mathbb{F}_p[X_1, \cdots, X_c]^t$ be three tuples of multivariate polynomials over $\mathbb{F}_p$.*

Let $\mathcal{O}^r$, (resp. $\mathcal{O}^s$ and $\mathcal{O}^t$) be oracle that, on input $\{\{a_{i_1,\cdots,i_c}^{(k)}\}_{i_j=0}^{d_k}\}_k$, adds the polynomials $\{\sum_{i_1,\cdot,i_c} a_{i_1,\cdot,i_c}^{(k)} \prod_j X_j^{i_j}\}_k$ to R (resp. S and T).

Let $(x_1,\cdots,x_c)$ be secret vector and q_r (resp. q_s) (resp. q_t) be the number of queries to $\mathcal{O}^r$ (resp. $\mathcal{O}^s$) (resp. $\mathcal{O}^t$). The i-GDH assumption states that, given $\{g^{R^{(i)}(x_1,\cdots,x_c)}\}_{i=1}^{r+k\cdot q_r}$, $\{\widetilde{g}^{S^{(i)}(x_1,\cdots,x_c)}\}_{i=1}^{s+k\cdot q_s}$, and $\{e(g,\widetilde{g})^{T^{(i)}(x_1,\cdots,x_c)}\}_{i=1}^{t+k\cdot q_t}$, it is hard to decide whether (i) $U = g^{f(x_1,\cdots,x_c)}$ or U is random and (ii) $U' = \widetilde{g}^{f(x_1,\cdots,x_c)}$ or U' is random if f is independent of $<R,S,T>$.

As argued in [1], the hardness of the i-GDH problem depends on the same argument as the GDH problem which has already been proven in the generic group model [19]. That is, as long as the challenge polynomial that we denote f is independent of $<R,S,T>$, an adversary cannot distinguish $g^{f(x_1,\cdots,x_c)}$ (resp. $\widetilde{g}^{f(x_1,\cdots,x_c)}$) from a random element of $\mathbb{G}_1$ (resp. $\mathbb{G}_2$). The definition method of the content of the sets R,S, and T (by assumption or by the queries to oracles) does not fundamentally change the proof.

4   The Intuition

The intuition behind the proposed constructions relies on two observations. First, the number of analysis patterns is often very small compared to the quantity of data that are going to be analyzed, e.g., in a deep packet inspection scenario, the number of patterns provided by the SNORT intrusion detection system is 3734 [20]. Second, the sizes of the detection patterns are also very small compared to the size of the traces to be analyzed (e.g., the largest pattern size used by SNORT is 364 Bytes).

For a data with alphabet Σ, the proposed constructions associate each element σ of Σ with a secret encoding $(\alpha'_\sigma, \alpha_\sigma)$. They fragment the sequence of symbols that represents the data $\mathcal{B}$ as described in the Fig. 1 in which Φ represents the number of symbols (i.e., the size) of each fragment and p_{max} represents the largest number of symbols in a pattern. To allow the matching of patterns at any possible offset of the data to be searched, in the proposed constructions, we require that $\Phi \geq 2\cdot(p_{max}-1)$. In the rest of the paper, we will use $\{x_i\}_{i=a}^{i=b}$ to denote the set of elements x_i, $i \in [a,b]$ and $|\mathcal{B}|$ to denote the number of symbol (i.e., the size) that compose $|\mathcal{B}|$.

As illustrated by the Fig. 1, the sequence of symbols $\mathcal{B}$ is fragmented into $2 \times \eta - 1$ fragments $\{F_i, \overline{F}_j\}_{i=0,j=0}^{i=\eta-1,j=\eta-2}$ where $\eta = |\mathcal{B}|/\Phi$ (for simplicity we will suppose that $|\mathcal{B}|$ is a multiple of Φ). Each $F_i, i \in [0,\eta-1]$, contains the symbols at indexes $[i\cdot\Phi, (i+1)\cdot\Phi - 1]$, while $\overline{F}_i, i \in [0,\eta-2]$, contains the symbols at indexes $[(i+1)\cdot\Phi - p_{max} - 1, (i+1)\cdot\Phi + p_{max} - 1]$ of $\mathcal{B}$.

Given an $i \in [0,|\mathcal{B}|-1]$, in the rest of this paper, we will denote by i_F the index of i inside the fragment F where $F \in \{F_0,\cdots,F_{\eta-1},\overline{F}_0,\cdots,\overline{F}_{\eta-2}\}$. If $i \notin F$, i_F is not defined. Formally, assuming that $F = [a,b]$:

$$i_F = \begin{cases} i \bmod a & \text{if } i \in F \\ \text{not defined} & \text{otherwise} \end{cases}$$

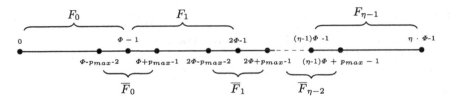

Fig. 1. Fragmentation approach

A trapdoor for a pattern $w = \sigma_{w,0} \cdots \sigma_{w,l-1}$ will be associated with a set of polynomials $\{V_i = v_i \sum_{k=0}^{l-1} \alpha'_{\sigma_{w,k}} \cdot \alpha^{k+i}_{\sigma_{w,k}} \cdot z^k\}_{i=0}^{i=\Phi-l}$ where v_i is a random secret scalar used to prevent new trapdoor forgeries and z a random scalar belonging to the secret key $\mathcal{K}_s$. The trapdoor generated for w consists then in the elements $\{\widetilde{g}^{V_i}, \widetilde{g}^{v_i}\}_{i=0}^{i=\Phi-l}$. Each of the previous elements will be used to check the presence of w at a specific index of the previously constructed fragments.

Meanwhile, the encryption of each symbol σ_i is the tuple $\mathcal{C}_i = \{C_i, C'_i, \overline{C}_i, \overline{C}'_i\}$ that depends on the fragment in which the index i of σ_i in $\mathcal{B}$ belongs. If it belongs to F_ϵ (resp. $\overline{F}_\epsilon$) then C_i and C'_i (resp. $\overline{C}_i$ and $\overline{C}'_i$) contain the encryption of σ_i regarding the index i_{F_ϵ} of i in F_ϵ (resp. the index $i_{\overline{F}_\epsilon}$ of i in $\overline{F}_\epsilon$).

Then, if we want to test the presence of w at the index i, if i belongs to F_ϵ (resp. $\overline{F}_\epsilon$), then we compare the bilinear mapping results of the elements $C_{i_{F_\epsilon}}$, $\widetilde{g}^{v_{i_{F_\epsilon}}}$ (resp. $\overline{C}_{i_{\overline{F}_\epsilon}}$, $\widetilde{g}^{v_{i_{\overline{F}_\epsilon}}}$) and $C'_{i_{F_\epsilon}}$, $\widetilde{g}^{V_{i_{F_\epsilon}}}$ (resp. $\overline{C}'_{i_{\overline{F}_\epsilon}}$, $\widetilde{g}^{V_{i_{\overline{F}_\epsilon}}}$). If w is not present, then the bilinear mapping results will be random-looking elements of $\mathbb{G}_T$ which will be useless to the adversary for learning any information about the plaintext and/or the content of the tested pattern.

5 S^4E Construction

In this section, we propose S^4E, a construction that supports pattern matching of adaptively chosen and variable (upper bounded) lengths patterns on secret key encrypted streams. Before formalizing S^4E, we present a use-case scenario on which S^4E can be useful.

5.1 Usage Scenario

To cope with new and sophisticated cybercrime threats, new threat intelligence platforms such as [18] are relying on the collaboration between different involved entities that include, on one side, companies, organizations, and individuals that are targeted by cyber attacks, and on the other, security editors that are in charge of defining and providing strategies for effectively detect and prevent cyber attacks. To be useful, such platforms should, on one hand, be fueled by data owners, i.e., companies, organizations, and individuals that agree to share the traces (e.g., network and operating system traces) of the cyber attacks that they have suffered. On the other hand, the platform should allow the security editors to analyze (e.g., search specific patterns) and correlate the traces that are shared by the data owners. The considered threat intelligence platform is often managed by non-fully trusted third-party service provider (SP) which provides the required storage space and computation power with affordable cost.

Unfortunately, both data owners (i.e., attack traces owners) and security editors are still very reluctant for adopting such kind of threat intelligence platforms because of two main reasons. First, the traces to be shared contain often highly sensitive information that may raise serious security and/or business threats when disclosed to non-fully trusted third parties (e.g., SP). Second, the shared traces analysis rely mainly on techniques that use pattern matching for inspecting and detecting malicious behaviors. Those analysis patterns are the result of extensive threat intelligence conducted by security editors. They are often put forward as a key competitive differentiator arguing that they can cover a wider set of malicious behaviors. Thus, security editors are typically reluctant to share their analysis patterns with non-fully trusted third-parties.

The S^{4}E construction can be used to overcome the previous two limitations by building a platform that is (1) market compliant meaning that both the data owner and the third-party entity performing the pattern matching operations will learn nothing about the patterns to be used by security editors for analyzing the shared traces (as proved by Theorem 4), and (2) privacy-friendly, signifying that (2.1) the third-party entity performing pattern matching will learn nothing about the shared data except the presence or the absence of a set of unknown analysis patterns, and (2.2) the pattern provider will learn no more than the indexes on which the searched pattern exists (as proved by Theorem 2).

5.2   Architecture

The architecture considered for the S^{4}E construction involves three parties: the data owner (DO) representing the entity that holds the data to be analyzed (e.g., the network traces in the case of DPI), the pattern provider (PP) representing the entity that supplies the patterns that will be matched, and the service provider (SP) are stakeholders that offer computation infrastructures that will be used to perform the pattern matching operations on the data to be analyzed. To test the presence of a pattern on DO's data, PP starts by generating collaboratively with DO a trapdoor for the pattern to be matched. Then, PP sends the generated trapdoor to SP who performs the matching operation and notifies the PP with the results (i.e., the presence of the patterns as well as their corresponding positions in the DO's data).

5.3   Security Requirements and Hypothesis

PP, DO, and SP are considered in S^{4}E as *Honest-but-curious* entities. First, we expect PP to provide valid patterns allowing an effective analysis of DO's shared data. This a fairly reasonable assumption since a pattern provider (e.g., a security editor in the case of DPI or a laboratory in the case of genomic data analysis) will not defile its reputation by issuing incorrect or misleading analysis patterns. Otherwise, this will result in many false positives, which may considerably degrade the quality of the analyses that will be provided to the DO. Nevertheless, we expect the PP to be curious: it may try to derive information about the analyzed data by accessing the data analyzed by the SP and/or the pattern matching results returned by the SP.

Second, we suppose that SP will perform the pattern matching operations honestly over the DO's data using the analysis patterns provided by PP. However, we suppose that SP may try to learn additional information about either or both the DO's outsourced data and the analysis patterns provided by PP. In addition, we assume that the SP that may try to create values by analyzing other third-parties data using the set of patterns provided by PP for the analysis of DO's outsourced data.

Third, we suppose DO to follow honestly the S^4E protocol. However, we expect that he/she may try to learn additional information about the patterns provided by PP for analyze his/her data.

In addition, we suppose that (i) SP and PP will not collude to learn more information about the traffic, and (ii) SP and DO will not collude to learn more information about the patterns to be searched. We believe that these two last assumptions are fairly reasonable since, in a free market environment, an open dishonest behavior will result in considerable damages for involved entities.

Finally, we require S^4E to provide correct results. That is, (1) any part of DO's data that matches one of PP's patterns when not encrypted must be matched by S^4E (no false negatives), and (2) we require that for any traffic that does not match any of the PP's analysis patterns when not encrypted, the probability that S^4E returns a false positive is negligible.

5.4 Definition of S^4E

S^4E is defined using five algorithms that we denote **Setup, Keygen, Encrypt, Issue,** and **Test**. The first three algorithms are performed by DO, the **Issue** algorithm is performed collaboratively by DO and PP, and the **Test** algorithm is performed by SP.

- **Setup**$(1^\lambda, \Phi, p_{max})$ is a probabilistic algorithm that takes an input a security parameter λ, the fragmentation size to be used Φ, and the maximum size of a pattern p_{max}. It returns the public parameters $params$.
- **Keygen**$(params, \Sigma)$ is a probabilistic key generation algorithm that takes as input the public parameters $params$ and a finite set Σ representing the alphabet to be used for representing the data to be searched and the pattern to be matched. It outputs a secret key $\mathcal{K}_s$ and a trapdoor generation key $\mathcal{K}_t$. The latter will be sent to PP using a secure channel.
- **Encrypt**$(params, \mathcal{K}_s, \mathcal{B})$ is a probabilistic algorithm that takes as input the public parameters $params$, the secret key $\mathcal{K}_s$, and a finite sequence (string) of elements $\mathcal{B}$ of Σ of size n. It returns a ciphertext $\mathcal{C}$.

- **Issue**$(params, \mathcal{K}_s, \mathcal{K}_t, w)$ is a probabilistic algorithm executed interactively between PP and DO. It takes as input the public parameters $params$, the secret key $\mathcal{K}_s$, the trapdoor generation key $\mathcal{K}_t$, and w – a sequence of elements of Σ of length smaller or equal to p_{max}, and returns a trapdoor td_w.

- **Test**$(params, \mathcal{C}, td_w)$ is a deterministic algorithm that takes as input the public parameters $params$, a ciphertext $\mathcal{C}$ encrypting a sequence of m elements $\mathcal{B} = \sigma_0 \cdots \sigma_{m-1}$ of Σ, and the trapdoor td_w for the sequence of Σ's elements of length l, $w = \sigma_{w,0} \cdots \sigma_{w,l-1}$. This algorithm is executed interactively between PP and SP. The former provides the trapdoor td_w and the latter executes the algorithm and returns the set of indexes $\mathcal{I} \subset \{0, m-l-1\}$ where for each $i \in \mathcal{I}$, $\sigma_i \cdots \sigma_{i+l-1} = \sigma_{w,0} \cdots \sigma_{w,l-1}$ to PP.

We note that the sizes of the elements defined in the previous algorithms, i.e., the size of the data to be analyzed $\mathcal{B}$, the size of the pattern to be searched w, and the largest analysis pattern size p_{max} refer to the number of symbols of Σ that compose each element. In addition, we note that S⁴E does not consider a decryption algorithm since there is no need for decrypting the outsourced data. However, we stress that a decryption feature can be straightforwardly performed by issuing a trapdoor for all characters $\sigma \in \Sigma$ and running the Test algorithm on the encrypted data for each of them.

5.5 S⁴E's Security Requirements

As said in Sect. 5.3, there are mainly 4 security requirements that should be satisfied by our construction: Trace indistinguishability for both PP and SP, pattern indistinguishability for both DO and SP, trapdoor usefulness (i.e., the trapdoors are useful only to search DO's data), and the correctness property.

In the following, we use the game-based security definition proposed in [1] for trace indistinguishability by adapting the standard notion of IND-CPA which requires that no adversary $\mathcal{A}$ (e.g., PP or SP), even with an access to an oracle $\mathcal{O}^s$ that issues a trapdoor td_{p_i} for any adaptively chosen pattern p_i, can decide whether an encrypted trace contains T_0 or T_1 as long as the trapdoors $\{td_{p_i}\}$ issued by $\mathcal{O}^s$ do not allow trivial distinction of the traces T_0 and T_1. We note that we consider the quite standard *selective* security notion [16]. This notion requires the adversary to choose and commit T_0 and T_1 at the beginning of the experiment, before seeing $params$.

Definition 4 (Data indistinguishability). *Let λ be the security parameter, Σ be the alphabet to be used, $\mathcal{A}$ be the adversary and $\mathcal{C}$ be the challenger. We consider the following game that we denote $Exp_{\mathcal{A},\beta}^{S^4E\text{-}D\text{-}IND\text{-}CPA}$:*

(1) Setup: $\mathcal{C}$ executes $Setup(1^\lambda, \Phi, p_{max})$ to generate $params$ and the algorithm $Keygen(params, \Sigma)$ to generate the keys $\mathcal{K}_s$ and $\mathcal{K}_t$. Then it sends $params$ to the adversary.

(2) Query: $\mathcal{A}$ can adaptively ask $\mathcal{O}^s$ for the trapdoor td_{w_i} for any pattern $w_i = \sigma_{i,0} \cdots \sigma_{i,l_i-1}$ where $\sigma_{i,j} \in \Sigma$. We denote $\mathcal{W}$ the set of patterns submitted by $\mathcal{A}$ to $\mathcal{O}^s$ in this phase.

(3) *Challenge: Once $\mathcal{A}$ decides that Phase (2) is over, it chooses two data streams $T_0 = \sigma_{0,0}^* \cdots \sigma_{0,m-1}^*$ and $T_1 = \sigma_{1,0}^* \cdots \sigma_{1,m-1}^*$ and sends them to $\mathcal{C}$.*
    (a) *If $\exists w = \sigma_0 \cdots \sigma_{l_i} \in \mathcal{W}$, $k \in \{0,1\}$, and j such that:*

$$\sigma_{k,j}^* \cdots \sigma_{k,j+l_i}^* = \sigma_0 \cdots \sigma_{l_i} \neq \sigma_{1-k,j}^* \cdots \sigma_{1-k,j+l_i}^* \quad \text{then return } 0.$$

   (b) *$\mathcal{C}$ chooses a random $\beta \in \{0,1\}$, creates $C = Encrypt(param, \mathcal{K}_s, T_\beta)$, and sends it to $\mathcal{A}$.*
(4) *Guess. $\mathcal{A}$ outputs the guess β'.*
(5) *Return $(\beta = \beta')$.*

We define $\mathcal{A}$'s advantage by $Adv^{Exp_{\mathcal{A},\beta}^{S^4E\_D\_IND\_CPA}}(\lambda) = |Pr[\beta = \beta'] - 1/2|$. S^4E is said to be data indistinguishable if $Adv^{Exp_{\mathcal{A},\beta}^{S^4E\_D\_IND\_CPA}}(\lambda)$ is negligible.

We note that in the previous definition, the restriction used in phase (3)(a) ensures that if one of the data streams T_k contains a pattern $w_i \in \mathcal{W}$ in the position j, then this is also the case for T_{1-k}. If such a restriction is not used, $\mathcal{A}$ will trivially win the game by running $Test(params, C, td_{w_i})$.

We want to be able to evaluate the advantage of the SP for using the issued trapdoors to analyze other third-parties' data (i.e., data that are not provided and encrypted by DO). Since encrypted data and trapdoors should be created using the same secret key $\mathcal{K}_s$ (the trapdoor generation key $\mathcal{K}_t$ is created using $\mathcal{K}_s$), such an advantage is equivalent to the ability of the SP to forge valid DO's encrypted data.

Definition 5 (Encrypted Data Forgery). *Let λ be a security parameter, Σ be the alphabet to be used, $\mathcal{A}$ be the adversary, $\mathcal{C}$ be the challenger, $\mathcal{O}^s$ be an oracle that issues a trapdoor for any adaptively chosen pattern, and $\mathcal{O}^r$ be an oracle that encrypts any adaptively chosen data. We consider the following $Exp_{\mathcal{A}}^{S^4E\_EDF}$ game:*

(1) *Setup: $\mathcal{C}$ executes $Setup(1^\lambda, \Phi, p_{max})$ to generate params and the algorithm $Keygen(params, \Sigma)$ to generate the keys $\mathcal{K}_s$ and $\mathcal{K}_t$. Then it sends params to the adversary.*
(2) *Query:*
    - *$\mathcal{A}$ can ask $\mathcal{O}^s$ for issuing the trapdoor td_{w_i} for any adaptively chosen pattern $w_i = \sigma_{i,1} \cdots \sigma_{i,l_i}$ where $\sigma_{i,j} \in \Sigma$. We denote $\mathcal{W}$ the set of patterns submitted by $\mathcal{A}$ to $\mathcal{O}^s$ in this phase.*
    - *$\mathcal{A}$ can adaptively ask $\mathcal{O}^r$ to create $C^T = Encrypt(params, \mathcal{K}_s, T)$. We denote $\mathcal{T}$ the set of datasets encrypted by the $\mathcal{O}^r$.*
(3) *Forgery: The adversary chooses the dataset $T^* \notin \mathcal{T}$ such that T^* contains w ($w \in \mathcal{W}$) at index i and forges the encrypted dataset C^{T^*} of T^*.*

We define $\mathcal{A}$'s advantage of winning the game $Exp_{\mathcal{A}}^{S^4E\_EDF}$ by $Adv^{Exp_{\mathcal{A}}^{S^4E\_EDF}}(\lambda) = Pr[i \in Test(params, C^{T^*}, td_w)]$. S^4E is said to be encrypted data forgery secure if $Adv^{Exp_{\mathcal{A}}^{S^4E\_EDF}}(\lambda)$ is negligible.

The following definition formalizes the patterns indistinguishability property for SP. That is, we evaluate the advantage of the SP to decide whether a trapdoor encrypts the pattern w_0^* or w_1^* even with an access to an oracle $\mathcal{O}^s$ that issues a trapdoor for any adaptively chosen pattern.

Definition 6 (Pattern Indistinguishability to SP). *Let λ be the security parameter, Σ be the alphabet to be used, $\mathcal{A}$ be the adversary and $\mathcal{C}$ the challenger. We consider the following game that we denote $Exp_{\mathcal{A}_{SP},\beta}^{S^4E\_P\_IND\_CPA}$:*

(1) Setup: $\mathcal{C}$ executes $Setup(1^\lambda, \Phi, p_{max})$ to generate params and the algorithm $Keygen(params, \Sigma)$ to generate the keys $\mathcal{K}_s$ and $\mathcal{K}_t$. Then it sends params to the adversary.

(2) Observation: $\mathcal{A}$ may observe the ciphertext C^{T_i} of a set of (unknown) traces $T_i \in \mathcal{T}$.

(3) Query: $\mathcal{A}$ can adaptively ask $\mathcal{O}^s$ for the trapdoor td_{w_i} for any pattern $w_i = \sigma_{i,1} \cdots \sigma_{i,l_i}$ where $\sigma_{i,j} \in \Sigma$. We denote by $\mathcal{W}$ the set of patterns submitted by $\mathcal{A}$ to $\mathcal{O}^s$ in this phase.

(4) Challenge: Once $\mathcal{A}$ decides that Phase (2) is over, it chooses two patterns $w_0^* = \sigma_{0,0}^* \cdots \sigma_{0,l}^*$ and $w_1^* = \sigma_{1,0}^* \cdots \sigma_{1,l}^*$ such that $w_0^*, w_1^* \notin \mathcal{W}$ and sends them to $\mathcal{C}$. If $\exists T \in \mathcal{T}$ such that $w_0^* \in T$ or $w_1^* \in T$ then return 0. Otherwise, $\mathcal{C}$ chooses a random $\beta \in \{0,1\}$, creates $td_{w_\beta^*}$, and sends it to $\mathcal{A}$.

(5) Guess:
  – $\mathcal{A}$ may try to forge the ciphertext of chosen date and uses the Test algorithm to try to find out the chosen value of β.
  – $\mathcal{A}$ outputs the guess β'.

(6) Return $(\beta = \beta')$.

We define the advantage of the adversary $\mathcal{A}$ for winning $Exp_{\mathcal{A}_{SP},\beta}^{S^4E\_P\_IND\_CPA}$ by $Adv^{Exp_{\mathcal{A}_{SP},\beta}^{S^4E\_P\_IND\_CPA}}(\lambda) = |Pr[\beta' = \beta] - 1/2|$. S^4E is said to be pattern indistinguishable to SP if $Adv^{Exp_{\mathcal{A}_{SP},\beta}^{S^4E\_P\_IND\_CPA}}(\lambda)$ is negligible.

In addition, we aim to evaluate the advantage of DO for deciding whether a trapdoor encrypts the patterns w_0^* or w_1^* even with an access to an oracle $\mathcal{O}^s$ that plays the role of PP and perform the issue algorithm for any adaptively chosen pattern. The following definition formalizes the pattern indistinguishably property for DO.

Definition 7 (Pattern Indistinguishability to DO). *Let λ be the security parameter, Σ be the alphabet to be used, $\mathcal{A}$ be the adversary and $\mathcal{C}$ the challenger. We consider the following game that we denote $Exp_{\mathcal{A}_{DO},\beta}^{S^4E\_P\_IND\_CPA}$:*

(1) Setup: $\mathcal{C}$ executes $Setup(1^\lambda, \Phi, p_{max})$ to generate params and the algorithm $Keygen(params, \Sigma)$ to generate the keys $\mathcal{K}_s$ and $\mathcal{K}_t$. Then it sends params to the adversary.

(2) Query: $\mathcal{A}$ can ask $\mathcal{O}^s$ to play the role of PP in the issue algorithm for any adaptively chosen pattern $w_i = \sigma_{i,1} \cdots \sigma_{i,l_i}$ where $\sigma_{i,j} \in \Sigma$. We denote by $\mathcal{W}$ the set of patterns chosen by $\mathcal{A}$ in this phase.

(3) Challenge: Once $\mathcal{A}$ decides that Phase (2) is over, it chooses two patterns $w_0^* = \sigma_{0,0}^* \cdots \sigma_{0,l}^*$ and $w_1^* = \sigma_{1,0}^* \cdots \sigma_{1,l}^*$ such that $w_0^*, w_1^* \notin \mathcal{W}$ and sends them to $\mathcal{C}$. The latter chooses a random $\beta \in \{0,1\}$, and plays the role of PP in the issue algorithm to generate a trapdoor for w_β^*.
(4) Guess: $\mathcal{A}$ outputs the guess β'.
(5) Return $(\beta = \beta')$.

We define the advantage of the adversary $\mathcal{A}$ for winning $Exp_{\mathcal{A}_{DO},\beta}^{S^4E\_P\_IND\_CPA}$ by $Adv^{Exp_{\mathcal{A}_{DO},\beta}^{S^4E\_P\_IND\_CPA}}(\lambda) = |Pr[\beta' = \beta] - 1/2|$. S^4E is said to be pattern indistinguishable to DO if $Adv^{Exp_{\mathcal{A}_{DO},\beta}^{S^4E\_P\_IND\_CPA}}(\lambda)$ is negligible.

We say that S^4E provides pattern indistinguishability if it is pattern indistinguishable to both DO and SP.

Definition 8 (S^4E Correctness). *Let $\mathcal{B} = \sigma_0, \cdots \sigma_{m-1}$ and $w = \sigma_{w,0}, \cdots \sigma_{w,l-1}$ be respectively the data to be analyzed and the pattern to be matched. S^4E is correct iff the following conditions hold:*

(i) $Pr[i \in Test(params, Encrypt(params, \mathcal{B}, \mathcal{K}_s), Issue(params, \mathcal{K}_s, \mathcal{K}_t, w))] = 1$ if $\mathcal{B}$ contains p at index i.
(ii) $Pr[i \in Test(params, Encrypt(params, \mathcal{B}, \mathcal{K}_s), Issue(params, \mathcal{K}_s, \mathcal{K}_t, w))]$ is negligible if $\mathcal{B}$ does not contain w at index i.

Condition (i) of the previous definition ensures that the Test algorithm used by S^4E produces no false negatives. Condition (ii) ensures that false positives (i.e., the case in which Test algorithm returns i notwithstanding the fact that $\sigma_i \cdots \sigma_{i+l-1} \neq \sigma_{w,0} \cdots \sigma_{w,l-1}$) only occur with negligible probability.

5.6   A Trivial Protocol

A trivial attempt for defining a construction that ensures all of the security requirements we defined in Sect. 5.3 would consist of modifying the most efficient state of the art solution SEST [1] towards a secret key based-construction as described in the following algorithms. The Setup, Keygen, and Encrypt algorithms are to be performed by the DO. The Issue algorithm will be performed collaboratively by the DO and the PP, while the Test algorithm will be performed by the SP.

- **Setup$(1^\lambda, n)$**: Let $(\mathbb{G}_1, \mathbb{G}_2, \mathbb{G}_T, p, e(\cdot, \cdot))$ be a bilinear environment. This algorithm selects $g \xleftarrow{\$} \mathbb{G}_1, \tilde{g} \xleftarrow{\$} \mathbb{G}_2$ and returns $params \leftarrow (\mathbb{G}_1, \mathbb{G}_2, \mathbb{G}_T, p, e(\cdot, \cdot), g, \tilde{g}, n)$.
- **Keygen$(params, \Sigma)$**: On input of the alphabet Σ, this algorithm selects $z \xleftarrow{\$} \mathbb{Z}_p$ and $\{\alpha_\sigma \xleftarrow{\$} \mathbb{Z}_p\}_{\sigma \in \Sigma}$, computes and adds $\{g^{z^i}\}_{i=0}^{i=n-1}$ to $params$ (required for proving the trace indistinguishability property). It returns the secret key $\mathcal{K}_s = \{z, \{\alpha_\sigma\}_{\sigma \in \Sigma}\}$.

- **Encrypt**$(params, \mathcal{B}, \mathcal{K}_s)$: To encrypt $\mathcal{B} = \sigma_1 \cdots \sigma_n$, this algorithm chooses $a \xleftarrow{\$} \mathbb{Z}_p$ and returns $\mathcal{C} = \{C_i, C_i'\}_{i=0}^{n-1}$ where $C_i = g^{a \cdot z^i}$ and $C_i' = g^{a \cdot \alpha_{\sigma_i} \cdot z^i}$.
- **Issue**$(params, w, \mathcal{K}_s)$ issues a trapdoor td_w for a pattern $w = \sigma_{w,0}, \cdots, \sigma_{w,l-1}$ of length $l \leq n$ as described in Algorithm 1. We denote by L the array that will be used to store random scalars that will be used to encode each symbol of the pattern w, and by $\mathcal{I}$ the array of sets representing the indices of symbols in w that are encoded using the same random scalar. Actually, a random scalar can be re-used as long as it has not been used to encode the same symbol. That is, $L[i]$ is the random scalar to use with the (imperatively distinct) symbols at indices $\mathcal{I}_i$ of w.
- **Test**$(params, \mathcal{C}, td_w)$ checks whether the encrypted data $\mathcal{C}$ contains w by parsing td_w as $\{c, \{\mathcal{I}_j\}_{j=0}^{j=c-1}, \{\tilde{g}^{L[j]}\}_{j=0}^{j=c-1}, \tilde{g}^V\}$ and $\mathcal{C}$ as $\{C_i, C_i'\}_{i=0}^{n-1}$, and checking for all $j \in [0, n-l]$ if the following equation holds:

$$\prod_{t=0}^{c-1} e(\prod_{i \in \mathcal{I}_t} C_{j+i}', \tilde{g}^{L[t]}) = e(C_j, \tilde{g}^V)$$

Input: $\mathcal{K}_s, params, w = \sigma_{w,0}, \cdots \sigma_{w,l-1}$
Output: td_w
$td_w = \emptyset, V = 0, c = 0$
$L[i] = 0$ for all $i \in [0, l-1]$
$Ind[\sigma] = 0$ for all $\sigma \in \Sigma$
foreach $i \in [0, l-1]$ **do**
  if $L[Ind[\sigma_{w,i}]] = 0$ **then**
    $\big|\ L[c] \xleftarrow{\$} \mathbb{Z}_p, \mathcal{I}_c = \{i\}, c = c+1$
  else
    $\big|\ \mathcal{I}_{Ind[\sigma_{w,i}]} = \mathcal{I}_{Ind[\sigma_{w,i}]} \cup \{i\}$
  end
  $V = V + z^i \cdot \alpha_{\sigma_{w,i}} \cdot L[Ind[\sigma_{w,i}]]$
  $Ind[\sigma_{w,i}] = Ind[\sigma_{w,i}] + 1$
end
$td_w = \{c, \{\mathcal{I}_j\}_{j=0}^{j=c-1}, \{\tilde{g}^{L[j]}\}_{j=0}^{j=c-1}, \tilde{g}^V\}$

Algorithm 1: Issue

We can prove the correctness, the data indistinguishability, and encrypted data unforgeability properties by following the same strategies as in [22] (Sections A.1, A.2, and A.3). Unfortunately, this construction inherits the three main limitations of the SEST construction. First, the size of the public parameters *params* is linear to the size of the data to be analyzed (which may be very large). Second, the pattern indistinguishability requirement cannot be satisfied since the Issue algorithm (Algorithm 1) leaks many information (such as, the number of different symbols and the maximum number of occurrences of a symbol) about the pattern to be matched. Third, searching the presence of a pattern w is linear to the maximum number of occurrences of each symbol in w, which makes this construction impractical for matching small alphabet based patterns (e.g., bit, or hexadecimal patterns).

5.7 The S⁴E's Protocol

- **Setup**$(1^\lambda, \Phi, p_{max})$: Let $(\mathbb{G}_1, \mathbb{G}_2, \mathbb{G}_T, p, e(\cdot, \cdot))$ be a bilinear environment. This algorithm selects $g \xleftarrow{\$} \mathbb{G}_1, \tilde{g} \xleftarrow{\$} \mathbb{G}_2$, chooses Φ such that $\Phi \geq 2 \cdot (p_{max} - 1)$, and returns $params \leftarrow (\mathbb{G}_1, \mathbb{G}_2, \mathbb{G}_T, p, e(\cdot, \cdot), g, \tilde{g}, p_{max}, \Phi)$.

- **Keygen**$(params, \Sigma)$: On input of the alphabet Σ, this algorithm selects $z \xleftarrow{\$} \mathbb{Z}_p, \{\alpha'_\sigma \xleftarrow{\$} \mathbb{Z}_p, \alpha_\sigma \xleftarrow{\$} \mathbb{Z}_p\}_{\sigma \in \Sigma}, r \xleftarrow{\$} \mathbb{Z}_p$, and computes and adds $\{g^{z^i}\}_{i=0}^{i=\Phi-1}$ to $params$. It returns the secret key $\mathcal{K}_s = \{r, z, \{\alpha'_\sigma, \alpha_\sigma\}_{\sigma \in \Sigma}\}$ and the trapdoor generation key $\mathcal{K}_t = \{\tilde{g}^{r \cdot \alpha'_\sigma \cdot \alpha_\sigma^i \cdot z^j}\}_{i=0,j=0,\sigma \in \Sigma}^{i=\Phi-1,j=p_{max}-1}$ which will be sent to PP using a secure channel.

- **Encrypt**$(params, \mathcal{B}, \mathcal{K}_s)$: it starts by fragmenting $\mathcal{B} = \sigma_0, \cdots \sigma_{m-1}$ into $\{F_i, \overline{F}_j\}_{i=0,j=0}^{i=\eta-1,j=\eta-2}$ where $F_i = [i \cdot \Phi, (i+1) \cdot \Phi - 1]$ and $\overline{F}_j = [(j+1) \cdot \Phi - p_{max} - 2, (j+1) \cdot \Phi + p_{max} - 1]$. It chooses $a_k \xleftarrow{\$} \mathbb{Z}_p$ for each $k \in [0, \eta-1]$ and $\overline{a}_k \xleftarrow{\$} \mathbb{Z}_p$ for each $k \in [0, \eta-2]$ and returns $\mathcal{C} = \{C_i, \overline{C}_i, C'_i, \overline{C}'_i\}_{i=0}^{m-1}$ as described in the following algorithm.

Input: $params, \mathcal{B} = \sigma_0, \cdots \sigma_{m-1}, \mathcal{K}_s,$
$\{F_i, a_i, \overline{F}_j, \overline{a}_j\}_{i=0,j=0}^{i=\eta-1,j=\eta-2}$
Output: $\mathcal{C} = \{C_i, \overline{C}_i, C'_i, \overline{C}'_i\}_{i=0}^{m-1}$
$\mathcal{C} \leftarrow \emptyset$
foreach $i \in [0, m-1]$ **do**
  $\quad \epsilon \leftarrow i/\Phi$ #find the fragment F_ϵ to which i belongs
  $\quad C_i \leftarrow g^{a_\epsilon \cdot \alpha'_{\sigma_i} \cdot (\alpha_{\sigma_i} \cdot z)^{i F_\epsilon}}, \quad C'_i \leftarrow g^{a_\epsilon \cdot z^{i F_\epsilon}}$
  $\quad$ **if** $\epsilon > 0$ **and** $i \in \overline{F}_{\epsilon-1}$ **then**
  $\quad \quad \mid \overline{C}_i \leftarrow g^{\overline{a}_{\epsilon-1} \cdot \alpha'_{\sigma_i} \cdot (\alpha_{\sigma_i} \cdot z)^{i \overline{F}_{\epsilon-1}}}, \quad \overline{C}'_i \leftarrow g^{\overline{a}_{\epsilon-1} \cdot z^{i \overline{F}_{\epsilon-1}}}$
  $\quad$ **else if** $\epsilon < \eta - 1$ **and** $i \in \overline{F}_\epsilon$ **then**
  $\quad \quad \mid \overline{C}_i \leftarrow g^{\overline{a}_\epsilon \cdot \alpha'_{\sigma_i} \cdot (\alpha_{\sigma_i} \cdot z)^{i \overline{F}_\epsilon}}, \quad \overline{C}'_i \leftarrow g^{\overline{a}_\epsilon \cdot z^{i \overline{F}_\epsilon}}$
  $\quad$ **else**
  $\quad \quad \mid \overline{C}_i \leftarrow$ Null, $\overline{C}'_i \leftarrow$ Null
  $\quad$ **end**
  $\quad \mathcal{C} \leftarrow \mathcal{C} \cup \{C_i, C'_i, \overline{C}_i, \overline{C}'_i\}$
end

Algorithm 2: Encrypt

- **Issue**$(params, \mathcal{K}_s, \mathcal{K}_t, w)$ issues a trapdoor td_w for the sequence of symbols $w = \sigma_{w,0}, \cdots, \sigma_{w,l-1}$ of length $l < p_{max}$ as described in the following:
  - PP generates $\{v_i \xleftarrow{\$} \mathbb{Z}_p\}_{i=0}^{i=\Phi-l-1}$, uses $\mathcal{K}_t$ to compute

$$\left\{ \left(\prod_{j=0}^{l-1} \tilde{g}^{r \cdot \alpha'_{\sigma_{w,j}} \cdot \alpha_{\sigma_{w,j}}^{i+j} \cdot z^j} \right)^{v_i} \right\}_{i=0}^{\Phi-l-1} = \left\{ \tilde{g}^{v_i \cdot r \sum_{j=0}^{l-1} \alpha'_{\sigma_{w,j}} \cdot \alpha_{\sigma_{w,j}}^{i+j} \cdot z^j} \right\}_{i=0}^{\Phi-l-1}$$

and sends it to DO.

- DO computes

$$\left\{ \left(\widetilde{g}^{\,v_i \cdot r \sum\limits_{j=0}^{l-1} \alpha'_{\sigma_{w,j}} \cdot \alpha^{i+j}_{\sigma_{w,j}} \cdot z^j} \right)^{-r} \right\}_{i=0}^{\Phi-l-1} = \left\{ \widetilde{g}^{\,v_i \sum\limits_{j=0}^{l-1} \alpha'_{\sigma_{w,j}} \cdot \alpha^{i+j}_{\sigma_{w,j}} \cdot z^j} \right\}_{i=0}^{\Phi-l-1}$$

and sends it to PP.

- PP computes $td_w = \{\widetilde{g}^{V_i}, \widetilde{g}^{v_i}\}_{i=0}^{\Phi-l-1}$ with $V_i = v_i \sum\limits_{j=0}^{l-1} \alpha'_{\sigma_{w,j}} \cdot \alpha^{i+j}_{\sigma_{w,j}} \cdot z^j$

– **Test**$(params, C, td_w)$ tests whether the encrypted data C contains w using the following algorithm. It returns the set $\mathcal{I}$ of indexes i in which w exists in C.

Input: $C = \{C_i, \overline{C}_i, C'_i, \overline{C'}_i\}_{i=0}^{m-1}, td_w = \{V_i, v_i\}_{i=0}^{i=\Phi-l-1}$
Output: $\mathcal{I}$
$\mathcal{I} \leftarrow \emptyset$
foreach $i \in [0, m-1]$ **do**
    $\epsilon \leftarrow i/\Phi$ #find the fragment F_ϵ to which i belongs
    if $i \in F_\epsilon \cap \overline{F}_\epsilon$ **then**
        if $e(\prod_{j=0}^{l-1} \overline{C}_{i+j}, \widetilde{g}^{v_i_{\overline{F}_\epsilon}}) = e(\overline{C'}_i, \widetilde{g}^{V_i_{\overline{F}_\epsilon}})$ **then**
        | $\mathcal{I} \leftarrow \mathcal{I} \cup i$
        end
    else
        if $e(\prod_{j=0}^{l-1} C_{i+j}, \widetilde{g}^{v_i_{F_\epsilon}}) = e(C'_i, \widetilde{g}^{V_i_{F_\epsilon}})$ **then**
        | $\mathcal{I} \leftarrow \mathcal{I} \cup i$
        end
    end
end

Algorithm 3: Test

We note here that the size of the ciphertext produced by the Encrypt algorithm does not depend on the set of patterns to be used but depends only on the size of data to be encrypted. In addition, our Issue and Test algorithms allow to search an arbitrary (upper bounded size) and unforgeable (without the knowledge of the secret key $\mathcal{K}_s$) patterns. The sizes of those trapdoors do not depend on the size of the data to be encrypted but only on the size of the data fragment (around the double of the maximum size of a pattern). Finally, we underline that the elements $\{\widetilde{g}^{v_i}\}_{i=0}^{\Phi-l-1}$ of a trapdoor td_w will not be accessible to the DO, since the trapdoor is to be used only between PP and SP in the Test algorithm to match the pattern w on the encrypted data.

5.8   S⁴E's Security Results

In this section, we prove that the S^4E construction described in Sect. 5.7 provides the security requirements we described in Sect. 5.3. The proofs of the following theorems are provided in the full version [22].

Theorem 1. *S^4E is correct.*

Theorem 2. *S^4E is trace indistinguishable under the i-GDH assumption.*

Theorem 3. *S^4E is encrypted data forgery secure under the i-GDH assumption.*

Theorem 4. *S^4E is pattern indistinguishable under the i-GDH assumption.*

6   AS³E Construction

The S^4E construction, introduced in Sect. 5, allows for pattern matching on symmetrically encrypted data. In this section we show that the data fragmentation approach we propose in Sect. 4 can also be used to build AS^3E: a pattern matching of upper bounded length keywords on asymmetrically encrypted stream. In particular, we show in Sect. 7 that considering the same system and threat model as the most efficient state of the art solution SEST [1], AS^3E is far more practical than SEST as it reduces (1) considerably the size of public keys and (2) slightly the search complexity while increasing the size of ciphertext only by a factor of 2.

6.1   Architecture

AS^3E involves four roles: Pattern Provider (PP), Service Provider (SP), a *sender*, and a *receiver*. PP and SP are the same two entities we used in the S^4E construction. That is, PP is the entity that supplies the patterns that will be searched, and the Service Provider SP are stakeholders that offer computation infrastructures that will be used to perform pattern matching operations on the data to be analyzed. The role *sender* is used to represent the entities that are going to generate the data that is going to be analyzed (e.g., a website that provides web contents). The role *receiver* represents the entities that will receive and process the traffic sent by the *sender*. The *receiver* and the *sender* roles are interchangeable. That is, within the same secure network connection session, each end-point may play both the *sender* and the *receiver* roles. In this context, we suppose that the *receiver* want to analyze the data (e.g., to detect malicious contents) to be sent by the *sender* before using it. In AS^3E, we require that the *sender* and the *receiver* will not collaborate together, otherwise, they could use a secure channel that is out of reach for the SP. This scenario should not be considered as a limitation of AS^3E since, in such scenario pattern matching cannot be provided by SP even in the context of a plaintext traffic.

6.2   Security Requirements and Hypothesis

We consider the same hypothesis for the two entities PP and SP as in our S^4E construction. That is, PP and SP are considered to be *honest-but-curious* entities. Specifically, PP is supposed to provide valid patterns that allow SP to effectively analyze the data generated by the *sender* while SP is supposed to perform correctly the matching between the patterns provided by PP and the *sender*'s data. Nevertheless, we expect PP and SP to be curious as the former may try to learn information about the sender's data and the latter may try to get additional information about both the patterns provided by PP and the sender's data.

Moreover, we expect the *receiver* to be *honest-but-curious*. That is, he/she will correctly follow AS^3E's protocol. However, he/she may try to learn more information about the patterns that are provided by PP.

In addition, we suppose that the *receiver* and SP will not collude to learn more information about the patterns provided by PP. Otherwise, they could easily mount a dictionary attack. Again, we believe that this last assumption is fairly reasonable since an open dishonest behavior will result in considerable damages for both entities.

Finally, as in S^4E, the pattern matching functionality provided by AS^3E should be correct in a way that (1) any traffic that matches a least one of the analysis patterns provided by PP when not encrypted must be detected as malicious traffic by our construction, and (2) the probability that our construction returns a false positive for any traffic that does not match any of the PP's analysis patterns when not encrypted is negligible.

6.3   Definition of AS^3E

Similarly to the S^4E construction, we used five algorithms to define our construction: **Setup**, **Keygen**, **Encrypt**, **Issue**, and **Test**. The algorithms Setup and Keygen are performed by the entity playing *receiver* role. The Issue algorithm is performed collaboratively by the *receiver* and the PP. The Encrypt algorithm is performed by the *sender* while the Test algorithm is performed by SP.

- **Setup**(1^λ, Φ, p_{max}) is a probabilistic algorithm that takes as input a security parameter λ, the fragmentation size to be used Φ, and the maximum size of a pattern p_{max}. It returns the public parameters *params* which will be an implicit input to all other algorithms.
- **Keygen**(Σ) is a probabilistic algorithm that takes as input a finite set of symbols Σ representing the alphabet (e.g., bit symbols, byte symbols) used to represent the data to be analyzed. It returns the keys $\mathcal{K}_s$, $\mathcal{K}_p$, and $\mathcal{K}_t$, where $\mathcal{K}_s$ is private and known only to the *receiver*, $\mathcal{K}_t$ is know only to PP, and $\mathcal{K}_p$ is public.
- **Encrypt**($\mathcal{B}, \mathcal{K}_p$) is a probabilistic algorithm that takes as input the data to be encrypted $\mathcal{B}$ along with the public key $\mathcal{K}_p$ and returns a ciphertext $\mathcal{C}$.

- **Issue**$(\mathcal{K}_s, \mathcal{K}_t, w)$ is a probabilistic algorithm performed collaboratively by the *receiver* and the PP. It takes as input the *receiver*'s private key $\mathcal{K}_s$, the trapdoor generation key $\mathcal{K}_t$, and a pattern w of length l ($l \leq p_{max}$) and returns a trapdoor td_w.
- **Test**$(\mathcal{C}, td_w)$ is a deterministic algorithm that takes as input a ciphertext $\mathcal{C}$ encrypting a data stream $\mathcal{B}$ along with a trapdoor td_w for a pattern w and returns the set of indexes at which the pattern w occurs in $\mathcal{B}$.

Similarly to the S^4E construction, we omit the decryption algorithm in the previous description since we focus mainly on providing arbitrary universal[1] pattern matching over encrypted traffic. The decryption functionality can be easily added by encrypting the data stream $\mathcal{B}$ under a conventional encryption scheme.

6.4   Security Model

For the AS^3E construction, there are mainly three security requirements that should be satisfied: the traffic indistinguishability to SP and PP, the pattern indistinguishability to SP and the *receiver*, and the correct detection requirements. We note that, similarly to our S^4E construction, we consider the *selective* security notion [16]. In the following, we denote by $\mathcal{O}^s$ a trapdoor-issuing oracle that can be queried to create a trapdoor for any pattern.

The following definition states that it is not feasible for the SP or PP to learn any information about the content of the traffic more than the presence or the absence of the patterns to be matched.

Definition 9 (Trace indistinguishability). *Let λ be the security parameter, Σ be the alphabet to be used, $\mathcal{A}$ be the adversary and $\mathcal{C}$ be the challenger. We consider the following game that we denote $Exp_{\mathcal{A},\beta}^{AS^3\_E\_T\_IND\_CPA}$:*

(1) Setup: $\mathcal{C}$ executes $Setup(1^\lambda, \Phi, p_{max})$ to generate params and $Keygen(\Sigma)$ to generate $\mathcal{K}_s$, $\mathcal{K}_t$, and $\mathcal{K}_p$. Then it sends params, $\mathcal{K}_p$, and $\mathcal{K}_t$ to $\mathcal{A}$.

(2) Query: $\mathcal{A}$ can adaptively query $\mathcal{O}^s$ to create a trapdoor td_{w_i} for any adaptively chosen pattern $w_i = \sigma_{i,0} \cdots \sigma_{i,l_i-1}$ where $\sigma_{i,j} \in \Sigma$. We denote $\mathcal{W}$ the set of patterns submitted by $\mathcal{A}$ to $\mathcal{O}^s$ in this phase.

(3) Challenge: Once $\mathcal{A}$ decides that Phase (2) is over, it chooses two data streams $T_0 = \sigma_{0,0}^* \cdots \sigma_{0,m-1}^*$ and $T_1 = \sigma_{1,0}^* \cdots \sigma_{1,m-1}^*$ and sends them to $\mathcal{C}$.

(a) If $\exists w = \sigma_0 \cdots \sigma_l \in \mathcal{W}$, $k \in \{0,1\}$, and j such that:

$$\sigma_{k,j}^* \cdots \sigma_{k,j+l}^* = \sigma_0 \cdots \sigma_l \neq \sigma_{1-k,j}^* \cdots \sigma_{1-k,j+l}^* \quad \text{then return } 0.$$

(b) $\mathcal{C}$ chooses a random $\beta \in \{0,1\}$, creates $\mathcal{C} = Encrypt(T_\beta, \mathcal{K}_p)$, and sends it to $\mathcal{A}$.

(4) Guess. $\mathcal{A}$ outputs the guess β'.

(5) Return $(\beta = \beta')$.

---

[1] The trapdoor generated collaboratively by the *receiver* and PP can be used to analyze any *sender*'s data that is sent to the *receiver*.

We define $\mathcal{A}$'s advantage by $Adv^{Exp_{\mathcal{A},\beta}^{AS^3E\_T\_IND\_CPA}}(\lambda) = |Pr[\beta = \beta'] - 1/2|$. AS^3E is data indistinguishable if $Adv^{Exp_{\mathcal{A},\beta}^{AS^3E\_T\_IND\_CPA}}(\lambda)$ is negligible.

The pattern indistinguishability property informally requires that it is not feasible for an adversary (the SP or the *receiver*) to learn any information about the detection patterns. Since our construction is a public-key based scheme, we need to take into consideration the fact that an adversary can create any traffic of its choice using the public key $\mathcal{K}_p$. In this case, an adversary can mount a brute force attack on PP's patterns by adaptively creating as much traffic as needed to understand the logic behind them. However, a pattern matching-based solution over plaintext or public-key encryption ciphertext cannot resist such an attack, and therefore, it should not be considered in the security model of AS^3E. Hence, for AS^3E, the pattern indistinguishability property requires that the adversary $\mathcal{A}$ will not learn more information than what is provided as output to the Test algorithm. Formally, we use the high-min entropy property [17] which informally states that $\mathcal{A}$ cannot obtain the patterns "by chance".

Definition 10 (min-entropy). *Given a set of detection patterns $\mathcal{W}$, and a random bit $\beta \in \{0,1\}$. A probabilistic adversary $\mathcal{A} = (\mathcal{A}_f, \mathcal{A}_g)$ has min-entropy μ if*

$$\forall \lambda \in \mathbb{N}, \forall w \in \mathcal{W}, \forall \beta : Pr[w' \leftarrow \mathcal{A}(\lambda, \beta) : w = w'] \leq 2^{-\mu(\lambda)}$$

$\mathcal{A}$ is said to have high-min entropy if it has min-entropy μ with $\mu(\lambda) \in \omega(\log(\lambda))$.

In the experiment $Exp_{\mathcal{A}_{SP}=(\mathcal{A}_f,\mathcal{A}_g),\beta}^{AS^3E\_P\_IND}$ (Definition 11), we define the security notion $AS^3E\_P\_IND$ for an adversary $\mathcal{A}_{SP} = (\mathcal{A}_f, \mathcal{A}_g)$ ($\mathcal{A}_f$ and $\mathcal{A}_g$ are non colluding entities, as in e.g., [6,17]) with high-min entropy, that can create any traffic of its choice.

Definition 11 (Pattern indistinguishability to SP). *Let λ be the security parameter, Σ be the alphabet to be used, $\mathcal{A}_{SP} = (\mathcal{A}_f, \mathcal{A}_g)$ be the adversary and $\mathcal{C}$ be the challenger. We consider the following game that we denote $Exp_{\mathcal{A}_{SP}=(\mathcal{A}_f,\mathcal{A}_g),\beta}^{AS^3E\_P\_IND}$:*

(1) Setup: $\mathcal{C}$ executes $Setup(1^\lambda, \Phi, p_{max})$ to generate params and $Keygen(\Sigma)$ to generate $\mathcal{K}_s$, $\mathcal{K}_t$, and $\mathcal{K}_p$. Then it sends params and $\mathcal{K}_p$ to $\mathcal{A}_{SP}$.

(2) Query: $\mathcal{A}_{SP}$ can adaptively query $\mathcal{O}^s$ to create a trapdoor td_{w_i} for any pattern $w_i = \sigma_{i,1} \cdots \sigma_{i,l_i}$ where $\sigma_{i,j} \in \Sigma$. We denote by $\mathcal{W}$ the set of patterns submitted by $\mathcal{A}_{SP}$ to $\mathcal{O}^s$ in this phase.

(3) Challenge: Once $\mathcal{A}_{SP}$ decides that Phase (2) is over, $\mathcal{A}_f$ chooses two patterns $w_0^* = \sigma_{0,0}^* \cdots \sigma_{0,l}^*$ and $w_1^* = \sigma_{1,0}^* \cdots \sigma_{1,l}^*$ such that $w_0^*, w_1^* \notin \mathcal{W}$ and sends them to $\mathcal{C}$. $\mathcal{C}$ chooses a random $\beta \in \{0,1\}$, creates $td_{w_\beta^*}$, and sends it to $\mathcal{A}_g$.

(4) Guess: $\mathcal{A}_g$ outputs the guess β'.

(5) Return $(\beta = \beta')$.

We define $\mathcal{A}$'s advantage by $Adv^{Exp^{AS^3E\_P\_IND}_{\mathcal{A}SP=(\mathcal{A}_f,\mathcal{A}_g),\beta}}(\lambda) = |Pr[\beta = \beta'] - 1/2|$. AS^3E is said to be pattern indistinguishable to SP if for any probabilistic polynomial-time $\mathcal{A}_{SP} = (\mathcal{A}_f, \mathcal{A}_g)$ having high-min entropy, $Adv^{Exp^{AS^3E\_P\_IND}_{\mathcal{A}SP=(\mathcal{A}_f,\mathcal{A}_g),\beta}}(\lambda)$ is negligible.

In addition, since the Issue algorithm is performed interactively between the **receiver** and PP, we aim to evaluate the advantage of the *receiver* to decide whether a trapdoor encrypts w_0^* or w_1^* even with an access to an oracle $\mathcal{O}^s$ that plays the role of a PP and performs the Issue algorithm for any adaptively chosen pattern. The following definition formalizes the pattern indistinguishability property for the *receiver*.

Definition 12 (Pattern Indistinguishability to the receiver). *Let λ be the security parameter, Σ be the alphabet to be used, $\mathcal{A}$ be the adversary and $\mathcal{C}$ the challenger. We consider the following game that we denote $Exp^{AS^3E\_P\_IND\_CPA}_{\mathcal{A}R,\beta}$:*

(1) Setup: $\mathcal{C}$ executes $Setup(1^\lambda, \Phi, p_{max})$ to generate params and $Keygen(\Sigma)$ to generate $\mathcal{K}_s$, $\mathcal{K}_p$, and $\mathcal{K}_t$. Then it sends params, $\mathcal{K}_s$, $\mathcal{K}_p$, and $\mathcal{K}_t$ to the adversary.

(2) Query: $\mathcal{A}$ can use $\mathcal{O}^s$ as a PP in the Issue algorithm to create a trapdoor for any adaptively chosen pattern $w_i = \sigma_{i,1} \cdots \sigma_{i,l_i}$ where $\sigma_{i,j} \in \Sigma$. We denote by $\mathcal{W}$ the set of patterns chosen by $\mathcal{A}$ in this phase.

(3) Challenge: Once $\mathcal{A}$ decides that Phase (2) is over, it chooses two patterns $w_0^* = \sigma_{0,0}^* \cdots \sigma_{0,l}^*$ and $w_1^* = \sigma_{1,0}^* \cdots \sigma_{1,l}^*$ such that $w_0^*, w_1^* \notin \mathcal{W}$ and sends them to $\mathcal{C}$. $\mathcal{C}$ chooses a random $\beta \in \{0,1\}$, and plays the role of PP in the issue algorithm to generate collaboratively with $\mathcal{A}$ a trapdoor for w_β^*.

(4) Guess: $\mathcal{A}$ outputs the guess β'

(5) Return $(\beta = \beta')$.

We define the advantage of the adversary $\mathcal{A}$ for winning $Exp^{AS^3E\_P\_IND\_CPA}_{\mathcal{A}R,\beta}$ by $Adv^{Exp^{AS^3E\_P\_IND\_CPA}_{\mathcal{A}R,\beta}}(\lambda) = |Pr[\beta' = \beta] - 1/2|$. AS^3E is said to be pattern indistinguishable for the receiver if $Adv^{Exp^{AS^3E\_P\_IND\_CPA}_{\mathcal{A}R\beta}}(\lambda)$ is negligible.

Finally, the pattern matching correctness property is formally defined in the following Definition.

Definition 13 (Correctness). *Given a data stream T and a pattern w. AS^3E is correct iff the following conditions hold:*

(i) $Pr[i \in Test(Encrypt(T, \mathcal{K}_p), Issue(\mathcal{K}_s, \mathcal{K}_t, w))] = 1$ if T contains w at index i.

(ii) $Pr[i \in Test(Encrypt(T, \mathcal{K}_p), Issue(\mathcal{K}_s, \mathcal{K}_t, w))]$ is negligible if T does not contain w at index i.

6.5   The Protocol

- **Setup**$(1^\lambda, \Phi, p_{max})$: Let $(\mathbb{G}_1, \mathbb{G}_2, \mathbb{G}_T, p, e(\cdot, \cdot))$ be a bilinear environment. This algorithm selects $g \xleftarrow{\$} \mathbb{G}_1, \widetilde{g} \xleftarrow{\$} \mathbb{G}_2$ and returns $params \leftarrow (\mathbb{G}_1, \mathbb{G}_2, \mathbb{G}_T, p, e(\cdot, \cdot), g, \widetilde{g}, \Phi, p_{max})$.

- **Keygen**(Σ): On input of the alphabet Σ, this algorithm chooses Φ such that $\Phi \geq 2 \cdot (p_{max} - 1)$, selects $z \xleftarrow{\$} \mathbb{Z}_p, \{\alpha'_\sigma \xleftarrow{\$} \mathbb{Z}_p, \alpha_\sigma \xleftarrow{\$} \mathbb{Z}_p\}_{\sigma \in \Sigma}$, and $r \xleftarrow{\$} \mathbb{Z}_p$, computes and sets the public key $\mathcal{K}_p = \{g^{z^i}, g^{\alpha'_\sigma \cdot (\alpha_\sigma \cdot z)^i}\}_{i=0, \sigma \in \Sigma}^{i=\Phi-1}$, the private key $\mathcal{K}_s = \{r, \alpha_\sigma, \alpha'_\sigma, z\}_{\sigma \in \Sigma}$, and the trapdoor generation key $\mathcal{K}_t = \{\widetilde{g}^{r \cdot \alpha'_\sigma \cdot \alpha_\sigma^i \cdot z^j}\}_{i=0, j=0, \sigma \in \Sigma}^{i=\Phi-1, j=p_{max}-1}$. It sends $\mathcal{K}_t$ to PP.

- **Encrypt**$(\mathcal{B}, \mathcal{K}_p)$ fragments $\mathcal{B} = \sigma_1, \cdots \sigma_m$ into $\{F_i, \overline{F}_j\}_{i=0, j=0}^{i=\eta-1, j=\eta-2}$ where $F_i = [i \cdot \Phi + 1, (i+1) \cdot \Phi]$ and $\overline{F}_j = [(j+1) \cdot \Phi - p_{max} - 1, (j+1) \cdot \Phi + p_{max}]$. It chooses $a_k \xleftarrow{\$} \mathbb{Z}_p$ for each $k \in [0, \eta-1]$ and $\overline{a}_k \xleftarrow{\$} \mathbb{Z}_p$ for each $k \in [0, \eta-2]$ and returns $\mathcal{C} = \{C_i, \overline{C}_i, C'_i, \overline{C'}_i\}_{i=1}^m$ as described in the following algorithm.

Input: $\mathcal{B} = \sigma_1, \cdots \sigma_m, \mathcal{K}_p, \{F_i, a_i, \overline{F}_j, \overline{a}_j\}_{i=0, j=0}^{i=\eta-1, j=\eta-2}$
Output: $\mathcal{C} = \{C_i, \overline{C}_i, C'_i, \overline{C'}_i\}_{i=1}^m$
$\mathcal{C} \leftarrow \emptyset$
foreach $i \in [1, m]$ **do**
    $\epsilon \leftarrow i/\Phi$ #find the fragment F_ϵ to which i belongs
    $C_i \leftarrow g^{a_\epsilon \cdot \alpha'_{\sigma_i} \cdot (\alpha_{\sigma_i} \cdot z)^{iF_\epsilon}}$, $C'_i \leftarrow g^{a_\epsilon \cdot z^{iF_\epsilon}}$
    # $g^{\alpha'_{\sigma_i} \cdot (\alpha_{\sigma_i} \cdot z)^{iF_\epsilon}}$ and $g^{z^{iF_\epsilon}}$ are retrieved from $\mathcal{K}_p$
    if $\epsilon > 0$ **and** $i \in \overline{F}_{\epsilon-1}$ **then**
        $\overline{C}_i \leftarrow g^{\overline{a}_{\epsilon-1} \cdot \alpha'_{\sigma_i} \cdot (\alpha_{\sigma_i} \cdot z)^{i\overline{F}_{\epsilon-1}}}$, $\overline{C'}_i \leftarrow g^{\overline{a}_{\epsilon-1} \cdot z^{i\overline{F}_{\epsilon-1}}}$
    else if $\epsilon < \eta - 1$ **and** $i \in \overline{F}_\epsilon$ **then**
        $\overline{C}_i \leftarrow g^{\overline{a}_\epsilon \cdot \alpha'_{\sigma_i} \cdot (\alpha_{\sigma_i} \cdot z)^{i\overline{F}_\epsilon}}$, $\overline{C'}_i \leftarrow g^{\overline{a}_\epsilon \cdot z^{i\overline{F}_\epsilon}}$
    else
        $\overline{C}_i \leftarrow \text{Null}, \overline{C'}_i \leftarrow \text{Null}$
    end
    $\mathcal{C} \leftarrow \mathcal{C} \cup \{C_i, C'_i, \overline{C}_i, \overline{C'}_i\}$
end

Algorithm 4: Encrypt

- **Issue**$(\mathcal{K}_s, \mathcal{K}_t, w)$ issues a trapdoor td_w for the sequence of symbols $w = \sigma_{w,0}, \cdots, \sigma_{w,l-1}$ of length $l < p_{max}$. AS³E uses the same Issue algorithm as S⁴E except that DO will be replaced by the *receiver*.

- **Test**$(\mathcal{C}, td_w)$ tests whether the encrypted traces $\mathcal{C}$ contains the sequence of symbols w. It returns the set $\mathcal{I}$ of indexes i in which w exists in $\mathcal{C}$. The Test algorithm is the same as described for the S⁴E construction (Algorithm 3).

6.6   AS³E Security Results

This section presents the security results of AS³E. The proofs of the following theorems are given in the full version of this paper [22].

Theorem 5. AS^3E *is correct.*

Theorem 6. AS^3E *is trace indistinguishable under the i-GDH assumption.*

Theorem 7. AS^3E *is pattern-indistinguishable to SP for patterns of high min-entropy under the i-GDH assumption.*

Theorem 8. AS^3E *is pattern-indistinguishable to the receiver under the i-GDH assumption.*

7   The Complexity

We evaluate the practicability of S^{4}E and AS^{3}E regarding several properties: the sizes of the public parameters for S^{4}E, public keys for AS^{3}E, the trapdoor generation key, the ciphertext, the trapdoor, and the encryption and search complexities. Let Φ be the size of a fragment, p_{max} be the maximum size of a pattern, n be the total number of symbols in the data to be analyzed. Note that S^{4}E and AS^{3}E share the same sizes for the ciphertext, the trapdoor generation key, the trapdoors, and the same complexities for trapdoor generation, encryption, and search operations.

The Size of the Public Parameters Used in S^{4}E: The public parameters *params* used in the S^{4}E construction contain Φ elements of $\mathbb{G}_1$ which represents $32 \times \Phi$ bytes using Barreto-Naehrig (BN) [15].

The Size of the Public Keys Used in AS^{3}E: The public key $\mathcal{K}_p$ used in the S^{4}E construction contains $2 \times \Phi$ elements of $\mathbb{G}_1$ which represents $64 \times \Phi$ bytes using BN. We underline that the size of the required public key is independent of the size of the data to be analyzed n and depends only on the maximum size of a pattern p_{max} ($n \gg \Phi \geq 2 \times (p_{max} - 1)$). Hence, compared to the most efficient state of the art solution SEST, AS^{3}E reduces considerably the size of the required public key. To illustrate, if we suppose that 1G of data is to be analyzed using a set of patterns, each composed of at most 10000 bytes, SEST requires a public key of size $32 \times (1 + 256) \times 10^9$ bytes $\simeq$ 8000 GB while AS^{3}E requires a public key of size 20000×64 bytes $\simeq$ 1.20 MB.

The Size of the Pattern Generation Key $\mathcal{K}_t$: For both S^{4}E and AS^{3}E, $\mathcal{K}_t$ contains $\Phi \times p_{max} \times |\Sigma|$ elements of $\mathbb{G}_2$. A key allowing to generate trapdoors for a binary pattern of length $l \leq 1000$ will have a size equals to 128 MB.

The Size of the Ciphertext: In the worst case (i.e., $\Phi = 2 \times (p_{max} - 1)$), each symbol is represented by 4 elements of $\mathbb{G}_1$. Thus, encrypting n symbols requires $128 \times n$ bytes, while SEST produces a ciphertext of size $64 \times n$ bytes using BN.

Trapdoor's Size: A trapdoor is composed of $2 \times (\Phi - p_{max})$ elements of $\mathbb{G}_2$ which represents $64 \times (\Phi - p_{max})$ bytes using BN.

Trapdoor Generation Complexity. Generating a trapdoor for a pattern of length l ($l \leq p_{max}$), as described in the Issue algorithm, requires $(\Phi - l) \times (2l + 2)$ exponentiations and $4l(\Phi - l)$ multiplications in $\mathbb{G}_2$.

The Upper Bound Size of Patterns: The upper bound size p_{max} of the patterns that can be searched by S^4E and AS^3E depends Φ ($p\_max = \Phi/2 - 1$). Increasing p_max will increase linearly the trapdoor's sizes and generation complexity. However, it will not affect any of the other properties of S^4E and AS^3E.

Encryption Complexity: According to the Encrypt algorithm (Algorithm 2), in the worst case (i.e., $\Phi = 2 \times (p_{max} - 1)$), encrypting a sequence of n symbols using S^4E requires $10 \times n$ exponentiations in $\mathbb{G}_1$. In case in which n is large (i.e., $n \gg \Phi$ and $n \gg |\Sigma|$), the previous complexity can be reduced by pre-computing $\{g^{\alpha'_\sigma \cdot (\alpha_\sigma \cdot z)^i}, g^{z^i}\}_{i=0,\sigma \in \Sigma}^{i=\Phi-1}$. Then for each symbol to encrypt, the encryptor needs only to perform four exponentiations: $(g^{\alpha'_\sigma \cdot (\alpha_\sigma \times z)^{i F_\epsilon}})^{a_\epsilon}$, $(g^{z^{i F_\epsilon}})^{a_\epsilon}$, $(g^{\alpha'_\sigma \cdot (\alpha_\sigma \times z)^{i \overline{F}_\epsilon}})^{\overline{a}_\epsilon}$, and $(g^{z^{i \overline{F}_\epsilon}})^{\overline{a}_\epsilon}$ which reduces the overall complexity to $\Phi \times |\Sigma| + 4 \times n$ exponentiations in $\mathbb{G}_1$. As for AS^3E, encrypting a sequence of n symbols requires $2 \times n$ exponentiations in $\mathbb{G}_1$.

Search Complexity: According to the Test algorithm (Algorithm 3), searching a pattern of size l on a sequence of symbols of size n requires $nl - l^2$ multiplications on the group $\mathbb{G}_1$ and $2 \times (n-l)$ pairings. In fact, the Test algorithm verifies the presence of a pattern (using its associated trapdoor) in each possible offset in the data to be analyzed. Let us denote by s_0 and s_1 the two sequences of symbols of length l to be analyzed to check the presence of a pattern in offsets 0 and 1 respectively of the fragment F_i (resp. $\overline{F}_i$). Checking the presence of the pattern in the offset 0 requires the computation of $\prod_{i=0}^{l-1} C_i$ (resp. $\prod_{i=0}^{l-1} \overline{C}_i$) while checking the presence of the pattern in offset 1 requires the computation of $\prod_{i=0}^{l-1} C_{i+1}$ (resp. $\prod_{i=0}^{l-1} \overline{C}_{i+1}$). Obviously, for the offset 1, we can avoid the recomputation of $\prod_{i=1}^{l-1} C_i$ since it has already been computed for the offset 0. Following the previous observation, searching a pattern of length l on a sequence of symbols of length n requires only n multiplications and n divisions on the group $\mathbb{G}_1$, and $2 \times (n-l)$ pairings. Considering the fact that $l \ll n$, we can upper bound the search complexity by n multiplications, n divisions and $2n$ pairings. Finally, we note that pairing operations can be implemented very efficiently [21] and that our Test procedure is highly parallelizable.

8 Empirical Evaluation

In this section, we experimentally evaluate the performance of S^4E and AS^3E^2. We implement the two constructions using the RELIC cryptographic library [21] over the 254-bits BN curve[3]. For all conducted experiments, we used real

---

[2] We note that the goals of this section is to (1) provide a more concrete estimations of the different operations used by S^4E and AS^3E and (2) show that S^4E and AS^3E are more practical than SEST. Particularly, we do not claim that S^4E and AS^3E are practical enough to perform pattern matching on very large data streams.

[3] The objective behind the usage of the 254-bits BN is to consider the same elliptic curve as in the implementation of the SEST construction. We note that the pairings over the 254-bits BN curve provides almost 100-bit security level.

network traces as the data to be encrypted and analyzed, and we (pseudo) randomly generated the analysis patterns to be searched. In addition, since in both S^4E and AS^3E, the encryption and the trapdoor generation algorithms are to be performed by entities (data owners in case of S^4E or data sender in case of AS^3E) which may not have a large computation power, we run both the trapdoor generation and the encryption algorithms tests on an Amazon EC2 instance (a1.2xlarge) running Linux with an Intel Xeon E5-2680 v4 Processor with 8 vCPU and 16 GB of RAM. In contrast, as the search operations are performed by SP which is supposed to have a large computation power, we run search experiments on an Amazon EC2 instance (m5.24xlarge) running Linux with an Intel Xeon E5-2680 v4 Processor with 96 vCPU and 64 GB of RAM.

In our empirical evaluation, we aim to quantify the following characteristics of the proposed constructions:

- The time required to generate a trapdoor and its corresponding size as a function of the size of the largest analysis pattern p_{max} that can be searched.
- The time taken to encrypt a data stream as a function of its size (i.e. the size of the sequence of symbols that composed the data to be encrypted), the fragmentation size Φ and the size of the considered alphabet.
- The time needed to perform a pattern matching query as a function of the size of the data to be queried and the size of the patterns to be searched.

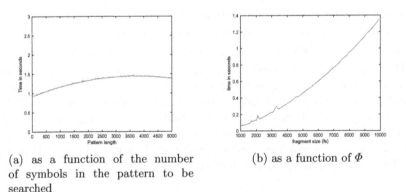

(a) as a function of the number of symbols in the pattern to be searched

(b) as a function of Φ

Fig. 2. Trapdoor generation time

Trapdoor Generation. Figure 2 describes the time required for issuing a trapdoor for a pattern w as a function of its length (Fig. 2 (a)) as well as the size Φ of data a data fragment (Fig. 2 (b)). According to our experiments, issuing a trapdoor for a pattern of 5000 symbols take 1.4 s. In addition, the sizes of the generated trapdoors are relatively small (256 KB for a pattern of 4000 symbols and a fragmentation size of 10000 symbols).

Encryption Time. According to Sect. 7, the duration of an encryption operation depends mainly on the number of symbols in the data to be encrypted n but also on the fragmentation size Φ and the size $|\Sigma|$ of the considered alphabet Σ. Table 2 reports the time needed to encrypt a data stream fragmented in chunks, each containing 1000 bits ($\Phi = 1000$ and $\Sigma = \{0, 1\}$), as a function of the data stream length n.[4].

Table 2. Encrypting time as a function of n

Data length (bytes)	Time (seconds)
1000	0.031
3000	0.097
5000	0.158
10000	0.371
30000	1.01
100000	3.0355

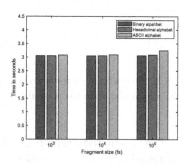

Fig. 3. Time required for encrypting 10^5 symbols as a function of Φ and Σ

As we noted in Sect. 4, the fragmentation size Φ and the considered alphabets are important parameters in our construction. The former directly influences the size of the largest analysis pattern that can be searched over the encrypted data since the bigger the size of the fragments are, the bigger the size of the supported analysis patterns could be. The latter parameter determines the type of search that can be performed by our construction. In Fig. 3, we compute the time required for the encryption of a data stream composed of 10^5 symbols as a function of the fragmentation size Φ and the type of the considered symbols. We consider three types of alphabets: binary, hexadecimal, and base 256 (i.e., ASCII alphabet) where each symbol is represented respectively in 1, 4 and 8 bits. For Φ, we consider 3 different fragment sizes: 10^3, 10^4, and 10^5 symbols.

As illustrated in Fig. 3, the time required for encrypting a dataset composed of 10^5 symbols increases only by a factor of 0.02 (from 3,04 to 3,2 s) when increasing the size of the fragments by a factor of 100 (from 10^3 to 10^5) and increasing the size of the considered alphabet by a factor of 128 (from a base 2 alphabet where $\Sigma = \{0, 1\}$ to a base 256 alphabet where $\Sigma = \{0, 1, \cdots, 255\}$). The previous results show that the increase of the size of supported patterns and the size of the considered alphabet affects very little the encryption time required by the proposed constructions.

Search Time. As shown in Sect. 7, the complexity of the search operation depends mainly on the number of encrypted symbols n that compose the data to be analyzed. Figure 4 describes the time required for searching a pattern as a function of the number of encrypted symbols in the data to be analyzed.

---

[4] Encryption time would be roughly 8 times slower with a single-threaded execution.

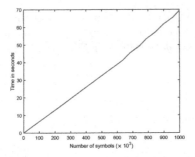

Fig. 4. Time required for searching a pattern as a function of the number of encrypted symbols in the data to be analyzed

The conducted evaluations show that the average search throughput of our construction is 139078 symbols per second with a multi-threaded implementation[5]. Thus, if an ASCII (resp. binary) alphabet is considered, the search throughput is 139 KB (resp. Kb) per second.

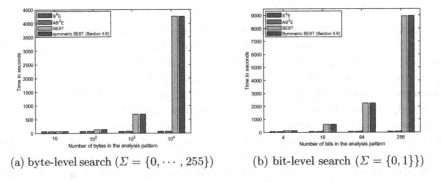

(a) byte-level search ($\Sigma = \{0, \cdots, 255\}$)   (b) bit-level search ($\Sigma = \{0, 1\}\}$)

Fig. 5. Timing comparison for testing the presence of a pattern in a string of 10^7 symbols as a function of the pattern size

Figure 5 (a) (resp. Fig. 5 (b)) compares the time needed for both our and the SEST (both its asymmetric [1] and symmetric (Sect. 5.6) variants) constructions to test the presence of a pattern of bytes (resp. of bits) in a 10 MB (resp. Mb) dataset as a function of the length of the pattern to be searched. In both bit and byte searches, our construction drastically reduces the search time compared to SEST. This is because that our Test algorithm is constant on the size and on the content of the searched pattern which is not the case for SEST.

---

[5] Search time would be roughly 96 times slower with a single-threaded execution.

9   Conclusion

In this work, we introduced two new provably correct and secure constructions S^4E and AS^3E. S^4E (resp. AS^3E) supporting pattern matching of adaptively chosen and variable (upper bounded) lengths patterns on secret key (resp. public key) encrypted streams. The proposed constructions have several interesting properties. First, they ensure data and pattern indistinguishability meaning that the entity that is going to perform pattern matching will learn nothing about the patterns to be searched as well as the data to be inspected, except the presence or the absence of a set of "unknown" patterns (since the entity charged to perform pattern matching will not have access to the patterns plaintexts). Second, the size of the ciphertext is linear to the size of the plaintext and is constant on the sizes and the number of analysis patterns. Third, the size of the issued trapdoors is constant on the size of the data to be analyzed. Finally, the search complexity is linear to the size of the trace and is constant on the size of the analysis patterns. The proposed constructions can be useful for other application scenarios such as subtrees search and searching of structured data.

To prove the security of the two proposed schemes, we used a slightly modified GDH assumption where the adversary is allowed to choose on which input to play the GDH instance. This relatively minor modification of the GDH assumption allow to define constructions that offer an interesting compromise between the secure and quite costly solutions and the fast and unsecure solution where the data has to be decrypted by the third-party entity that performs the pattern matching.

References

1. Desmoulins, N., Fouque, P.-A., Onete, C., Sanders, O.: Pattern matching on encrypted streams. In: Peyrin, T., Galbraith, S. (eds.) ASIACRYPT 2018. LNCS, vol. 11272, pp. 121–148. Springer, Cham (2018). https://doi.org/10.1007/978-3-030-03326-2_5
2. Curtmola, R., Garay, J., Kamara, S., Ostrovsky, R.: Searchable symmetric encryption: improved definitions and efficient constructions. J. Comput. Secur. **19**(5), 895–934 (2011)
3. Kamara, S., Moataz, T., Ohrimenko, O.: Structured encryption and leakage suppression. In: Shacham, H., Boldyreva, A. (eds.) CRYPTO 2018. LNCS, vol. 10991, pp. 339–370. Springer, Cham (2018). https://doi.org/10.1007/978-3-319-96884-1_12
4. Chase, M., Shen, E.: Substring-searchable symmetric encryption. In: Proceedings on Privacy Enhancing Technologies, no. 2, pp. 263–281 (2015)
5. Sherry, J., Lan, C., Popa, R.A., Ratnasamy, S.: Blindbox: deep packet inspection over encrypted traffic. ACM SIGCOMM Comput. Commun. Rev. **45**(4), 213–226 (2015)
6. Canard, S., Diop, A., Kheir, N., Paindavoine, M., Sabt, M.: Blindids: market-compliant and privacy-friendly intrusion detection system over encrypted traffic. In: Proceedings of the 2017 ACM on Asia Conference on Computer and Communications Security, pp. 561–574. ACM, April 2017

7. Gentry, C., Boneh, D.: A fully homomorphic encryption scheme, vol. 20, no. 09. Stanford University, Stanford (2009)
8. Boneh, D., Sahai, A., Waters, B.: Functional encryption: definitions and challenges. In: Ishai, Y. (ed.) TCC 2011. LNCS, vol. 6597, pp. 253–273. Springer, Heidelberg (2011). https://doi.org/10.1007/978-3-642-19571-6_16
9. Lauter, K., López-Alt, A., Naehrig, M.: Private computation on encrypted genomic data. In: Aranha, D.F., Menezes, A. (eds.) LATINCRYPT 2014. LNCS, vol. 8895, pp. 3–27. Springer, Cham (2015). https://doi.org/10.1007/978-3-319-16295-9_1
10. Hazay, C., Lindell, Y.: Efficient protocols for set intersection and pattern matching with security against malicious and covert adversaries. J. Cryptol. 23(3), 422–456 (2010)
11. Gennaro, R., Hazay, C., Sorensen, J.S.: Automata evaluation and text search protocols with simulation-based security. J. Cryptol. 29(2), 243–282 (2016)
12. Troncoso-Pastoriza, J.R., Katzenbeisser, S., Celik, M.: Privacy preserving error resilient DNA searching through oblivious automata. In: Proceedings of the 14th ACM Conference on Computer and Communications Security, pp. 519–528. ACM, October 2007
13. Katz, J., Sahai, A., Waters, B.: Predicate encryption supporting disjunctions, polynomial equations, and inner products. J. Cryptol. 26(2), 191–224 (2013)
14. Boneh, D., Waters, B.: Conjunctive, subset, and range queries on encrypted data. In: Vadhan, S.P. (ed.) TCC 2007. LNCS, vol. 4392, pp. 535–554. Springer, Heidelberg (2007). https://doi.org/10.1007/978-3-540-70936-7_29
15. Barreto, P.S.L.M., Naehrig, M.: Pairing-friendly elliptic curves of prime order. In: Preneel, B., Tavares, S. (eds.) SAC 2005. LNCS, vol. 3897, pp. 319–331. Springer, Heidelberg (2006). https://doi.org/10.1007/11693383_22
16. Canetti, R., Halevi, S., Katz, J.: A forward-secure public-key encryption scheme. In: Biham, E. (ed.) EUROCRYPT 2003. LNCS, vol. 2656, pp. 255–271. Springer, Heidelberg (2003). https://doi.org/10.1007/3-540-39200-9_16
17. Bellare, M., Boldyreva, A., O'Neill, A.: Deterministic and efficiently searchable encryption. In: Menezes, A. (ed.) CRYPTO 2007. LNCS, vol. 4622, pp. 535–552. Springer, Heidelberg (2007). https://doi.org/10.1007/978-3-540-74143-5_30
18. MISP - Open Source Threat Intelligence Platform & Open Standards For Threat Information Sharing (2011). https://www.misp-project.org/
19. Boyen, X.: The uber-assumption family. In: Galbraith, S.D., Paterson, K.G. (eds.) Pairing 2008. LNCS, vol. 5209, pp. 39–56. Springer, Heidelberg (2008). https://doi.org/10.1007/978-3-540-85538-5_3
20. Snort Rules. https://www.snort.org/. Accessed 31 Aug 2019
21. Aranha, D.F., Gouvêa, C.P.L.: RELIC is an Efficient LIbrary for Cryptography. https://github.com/relic-toolkit/relic
22. Bkakria, A., Cuppens, N., Cuppens, F.: Pattern matching on encrypted data. Cryptology ePrint Archive, Report 2020/422 (2020). https://eprint.iacr.org/2020/422

Efficient Homomorphic Comparison Methods with Optimal Complexity

Jung Hee Cheon[1,2], Dongwoo Kim[1], and Duhyeong Kim[1(✉)]

[1] Department of Mathematical Sciences, Seoul National University,
Seoul, Republic of Korea
{jhcheon,dwkim606,doodoo1204}@snu.ac.kr
[2] Crypto Lab Inc., Seoul, Republic of Korea

Abstract. Comparison of two numbers is one of the most frequently used operations, but it has been a challenging task to efficiently compute the comparison function in homomorphic encryption (HE) which basically supports addition and multiplication. Recently, Cheon et al. (Asiacrypt 2019) introduced a new approximate representation of the comparison function with a rational function, and showed that this rational function can be evaluated by an iterative algorithm. Due to this iterative feature, their method achieves a logarithmic computational complexity compared to previous polynomial approximation methods; however, the computational complexity is still not optimal, and the algorithm is quite slow for large-bit inputs in HE implementation.

In this work, we propose new comparison methods with *optimal* asymptotic complexity based on *composite polynomial* approximation. The main idea is to systematically design a constant-degree polynomial f by identifying the *core properties* to make a composite polynomial $f \circ f \circ \cdots \circ f$ get close to the sign function (equivalent to the comparison function) as the number of compositions increases. We additionally introduce an acceleration method applying a mixed polynomial composition $f \circ \cdots \circ f \circ g \circ \cdots \circ g$ for some other polynomial g with different properties instead of $f \circ f \circ \cdots \circ f$. Utilizing the devised polynomials f and g, our new comparison algorithms only require $\Theta(\log(1/\epsilon)) + \Theta(\log \alpha)$ computational complexity to obtain an approximate comparison result of $a, b \in [0, 1]$ satisfying $|a - b| \geq \epsilon$ within $2^{-\alpha}$ error.

The asymptotic optimality results in substantial performance enhancement: our comparison algorithm on 16-bit encrypted integers for $\alpha = 16$ takes $1.22\,\text{ms}$ in amortized running time based on an approximate HE scheme HEAAN, which is 18 times faster than the previous work.

1 Introduction

Homomorphic Encryption (HE) is a primitive of cryptographic computing, which allows computations over encrypted data without any decryption process. With HE, clients who sent encrypted data to an untrusted server are guaranteed data privacy, and the server can perform any operations over the encrypted data. In recent years, HE has gained worldwide interest from various fields related to data

© International Association for Cryptologic Research 2020
S. Moriai and H. Wang (Eds.): ASIACRYPT 2020, LNCS 12492, pp. 221–256, 2020.
https://doi.org/10.1007/978-3-030-64834-3_8

privacy issues including genomics [37–39] and finances [3,31]. In particular, HE is emerging as one of the key tools to protect data privacy in machine learning tasks, which now became a necessary consideration due to public awareness of data breaches and privacy violation.

The comparison function comp(a, b), which outputs 1 if $a > b$, 0 if $a < b$ and 1/2 if $a = b$, is one of the most prevalent operations along with addition and multiplication in various real-world applications. For example, many of the machine learning algorithms such as cluster analysis [17,33], gradient boosting [25,26], and support-vector machine [19,40] require a number of comparison operations. Therefore, it is indispensable to find an efficient method to compute the comparison function in an encrypted state for HE applications.

Since HE schemes [7,11,24] basically support homomorphic addition and multiplication, to compute non-polynomial operations including the comparison function in an encrypted state, we need to exploit polynomial approximations on them. The usual polynomial approximation methods such as minimax find approximate polynomials with minimal degree on a target function for given a certain error bound. However, the computational complexity to evaluate these polynomials is so large that it is quite inefficient to obtain approximate results with high-precision by these methods. Recently, to resolve this problem, Cheon et al. [12] introduced a new identity comp(a, b) = $\lim_{k \to \infty} a^k / (a^k + b^k)$, and showed that the identity can be computed by an iterative algorithm. Due to this iterative feature, their algorithm achieves a logarithmic computational complexity compared to usual polynomial approximation methods. However, the algorithm only achieves quasi-optimal computational complexity, and it is quite slow in HE implementation; more than 20 min is required to compute a single homomorphic comparison of 16-bit integers.

In this work, we propose new comparison methods using composite polynomial approximation on the sign function, which is equivalent to the comparison function. Starting from the analysis on the behavior of a composite polynomial $f^{(d)} := f \circ f \circ \cdots \circ f$, we identify the *core properties* of f that make $f^{(d)}$ get close to the sign function as d increases. We additionally introduce a novel acceleration method by applying a *mixed composition* of f and some other polynomial g with different properties instead of a simple composition of f. Applying these systematically devised polynomials f and g, we construct new comparison algorithms which firstly achieve the *optimal* computational complexity *among all polynomial evaluations* to obtain an approximate value of the comparison result within a certain error bound.

Our composite polynomial methods can be directly applied to evaluate piecewise polynomials with two sub-polynomials including the absolute function: For example, the function p such that $p(x) = p_1(x)$ if $x \in [0, 1]$ and $p(x) = p_2(x)$ if $x \in [-1, 0)$ for polynomials p_1 and p_2 can be represented by $p_1(x) \cdot (1 + \text{sgn}(x))/2 + p_2(x) \cdot (1 - \text{sgn}(x))/2$. Furthermore, our method is potentially applicable to more general piecewise polynomials including step functions (see Remark 1).

1.1   Our Idea and Technical Overview

Our key idea to identify several core properties of the basic function f essentially comes from a new interpretation of the previous work [12]. To be precise, [12] exploits the following identity to construct a comparison algorithm:

$$\lim_{k \to \infty} \frac{a^k}{a^k + b^k} = \left\{ \begin{array}{ll} 1 & \text{if } a > b \\ 1/2 & \text{if } a = b \\ 0 & \text{if } a < b \end{array} \right\} = \text{comp}(a, b)$$

for positive numbers $a, b \in [1/2, 3/2]$. Since very large exponent $k = 2^d$ is required to obtain a comparison result within small error, they suggest to iteratively compute $a \leftarrow a^2/(a^2 + b^2)$ and $b \leftarrow b^2/(a^2 + b^2)$ with an initial step $a \leftarrow a/(a + b)$ and $b \leftarrow b/(a + b)$, which results in $a^{2^d}/(a^{2^d} + b^{2^d}) \simeq \text{comp}(a, b)$ after d iterations. The inverse operation $1/(a^2 + b^2)$ in each iteration is computed by Goldschmidt's division algorithm [30].

The computational inefficiency of the comparison algorithm in [12] mainly comes from that inverse operation which should be done at least d times. Then, the natural question would be

"How can we construct an efficient comparison algorithm
without inverse operation?"

To do this, we analyze the comparison algorithm in [12] with a new perspective. Let $f_0(x) = x^2/(x^2 + (1 - x)^2)$, then each iteration $a \leftarrow a^2/(a^2 + b^2)$ and $b \leftarrow b^2/(a^2 + b^2)$ can be interpreted as an evaluation of $f_0(a)$ and $f_0(b) = 1 - f_0(a)$ for $0 \leq a, b \leq 1$, respectively. Indeed, the d iterations correspond to the d-time composition of the basic function f_0 denoted by $f_0^{(d)} := f_0 \circ f_0 \circ \cdots \circ f_0$, and the comparison algorithm can be interpreted as approximating $(\text{sgn}(2x - 1) + 1)/2$ by a composite polynomial $f_0^{(d)}$ (Fig. 1).

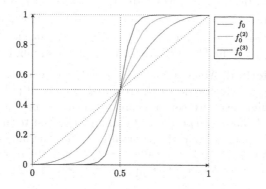

Fig. 1. Illustration of $f_0^{(d)}$ for $d = 1, 2, 3$

Our key observation on the basic function f_0 is that we actually do not need the exact formula of $f_0(x) = x^2/(x^2 + (1 - x)^2)$. Instead, it suffices to use other polynomials with *similar shape* to f_0: convex in $[0, 0.5]$, concave in $[0.5, 1]$, symmetric to the point $(0.5, 0.5)$, and have a value 1 at $x = 1$. For example, the composition $h_1^{(d)}$ of our devised polynomial $h_1(x) = -2x^3 + 3x^2$, which has similar shape to f_0, gets close to $(\text{sgn}(2x - 1) + 1)/2$ as d increases. As a result, we can approximate the comparison function by a composite polynomial $f^{(d)}$ for some constant-degree polynomial f with several *core properties*, and identifying these core properties is the most important step in our algorithm construction.

Core Properties of f. Since the sign function is equivalent to the comparison function, via $\text{sgn}(x) = 2 \cdot \text{comp}(x, 0) - 1$ and $\text{comp}(a, b) = (\text{sgn}(a - b) + 1)/2$, it is enough to find a polynomial f such that $f^{(d)}(x)$ *gets close to* $\text{sgn}(x)$ over $[-1, 1]$ for some proper d. The core properties of f are as following:

Prop I. $f(-x) = -f(x)$

Prop II. $f(1) = 1$, $f(-1) = -1$

Prop III. $f'(x) = c(1 - x)^n(1 + x)^n$ for some constant $c > 0$

The first property is necessary from the origin symmetry of the sign function, and the second property is required to achieve $\lim_{d \to \infty} f^{(d)}(x) = 1$ for $0 < x \leq 1$. The last property makes f to be concave in $[0, 1]$ and convex in $[-1, 0]$, and the multiplicity n of ± 1 in $f'(x)$ accelerates the convergence of $f^{(d)}$ to the sign function. Interestingly, for each $n \geq 1$, a polynomial f_n satisfying above three properties is uniquely determined as

$$f_n(x) = \sum_{i=0}^{n} \frac{1}{4^i} \cdot \binom{2i}{i} \cdot x(1 - x^2)^i.$$

Since $\text{sgn}(x)$ is a discontinuous function at $x = 0$, the closeness of a polynomial $f(x)$ to $\text{sgn}(x)$ should be considered carefully. Namely, we do not consider a small neighborhood $(-\epsilon, \epsilon)$ of zero when measuring the difference between $f(x)$ and $\text{sgn}(x)$ (if not, the infinite norm is always ≥ 1). In Sect. 3.2, we prove that the infinite norm of $f_n^{(d)}(x) - \text{sgn}(x)$ over $[-1, -\epsilon] \cup [\epsilon, 1]$ is smaller than $2^{-\alpha}$ if $d \geq d_n$ for some $d_n > 0$. Then, $(f_n^{(d_n)}(a - b) + 1)/2$ outputs an approximate value of $\text{comp}(a, b)$ within $2^{-\alpha}$ error for $a, b \in [0, 1]$ satisfying $|a - b| \geq \epsilon$.

Acceleration Method. Along with $\{f_n\}_{n \geq 1}$, we provide another family of odd polynomials $\{g_n\}_{n \geq 1}$ which reduces the required number of polynomial compositions d_n. At a high-level, we can interpret d_n as $d_n := d_\epsilon + d_\alpha$ where each of the terms d_ϵ and d_α has distinct aim as following: The first term d_ϵ is a required number of compositions to map the interval $[\epsilon, 1]$ into the interval $[1 - \tau, 1]$ for some fixed constant $0 < \tau < 1$ (typically, $\tau = 1/4$), and the second term d_α is a required number of compositions to map $[1 - \tau, 1]$ into $[1 - 2^{-\alpha}, 1]$, i.e.,

$$f_n^{(d_\epsilon)}([\epsilon, 1]) \subseteq [1 - \tau, 1],$$
$$f_n^{(d_\alpha)}([1 - \tau, 1]) \subseteq [1 - 2^{-\alpha}, 1].$$

In this perspective, our idea is to reduce d_ϵ by substituting $f_n^{(d_\epsilon + d_\alpha)}$ with $f_n^{(d_\alpha)} \circ g_n^{(d_\epsilon)}$ for some other $(2n + 1)$-degree polynomial g_n with *weaker properties* than the core properties of f_n. Since the first d_ϵ compositions only need to map $[\epsilon, 1]$ into $[1 - \tau, 1]$, Prop II & III are *unnecessary* in this part. Instead, the following property along with Prop I is required:

Prop IV. $\exists\, 0 < \delta < 1$ s.t. $x < g_n(x) \leq 1$ for $x \in (0, \delta]$ and $g_n([\delta, 1]) \subseteq [1 - \tau, 1]$

For g_n satisfying Prop I & IV, the composition $g_n^{(d)}$ does not get close to the sign function as d increases; however, we can guarantee that $g_n^{(d_\epsilon)}([\epsilon, 1]) \subseteq [1 - \tau, 1]$ for some $d_\epsilon > 0$ which is exactly the aim of first d_ϵ compositions. With some heuristic properties on g_n obtained by Algorithm 2, the required number of the first-part compositions d_ϵ is reduced by nearly half (see Sect. 3.5).

1.2   Our Results

New Comparison Methods with Optimal Complexity. We first propose a family of polynomials $\{f_n\}_{n \geq 1}$ whose composition $f_n^{(d)}$ gets close to the sign function (in terms of (α, ϵ)-closeness) as d increases. Based on the approximation

$$\frac{f_n^{(d)}(a - b) + 1}{2} \simeq \frac{\mathrm{sgn}(a - b) + 1}{2} = \mathrm{comp}(a, b),$$

we construct a new comparison algorithm $\texttt{NewComp}(a, b; n, d)$ which achieves *optimal asymptotic complexity* among the polynomial evaluations obtaining an approximate value of comparison within a certain level of error. The following theorem is the first main result of our work:

Theorem 1. *If* $d \geq \frac{2 + o(1)}{\log n} \cdot \log(1/\epsilon) + \frac{1}{\log n} \cdot \log \alpha + O(1)$, *the comparison algorithm* $\texttt{NewComp}(a, b; n, d)$ *outputs an approximate value of* $\mathrm{comp}(a, b)$ *within* $2^{-\alpha}$ *error for* $a, b \in [0, 1]$ *satisfying* $|a - b| \geq \epsilon$.

The theorem implies that one can obtain an approximate value of $\mathrm{comp}(a, b)$ within $2^{-\alpha}$ error for $a, b \in [0, 1]$ satisfying $|a - b| \geq \epsilon$ with $\Theta(\log(1/\epsilon)) + \Theta(\log \alpha) + O(1)$ complexity and depth with $\texttt{NewComp}$.

We also provide another family of polynomials $\{g_n\}_{n \geq 1}$, which enables to reduce the number of polynomial compositions by substituting $f_n^{(d)}$ with $f_n^{(d_f)} \circ g_n^{(d_g)}$. From the mixed polynomial composition, we construct another comparison algorithm $\texttt{NewCompG}$ with the following result:

Theorem 2 (Heuristic). *If* $d_g \geq \frac{1 + o(1)}{\log n} \cdot \log(1/\epsilon) + O(1)$ *and* $d_f \geq \frac{1}{\log n} \cdot \log \alpha + O(1)$, *the comparison algorithm* $\texttt{NewCompG}(a, b; n, d_f, d_g)$ *outputs an approximate value of* $\mathrm{comp}(a, b)$ *within* $2^{-\alpha}$ *error for* $a, b \in [0, 1]$ *satisfying* $|a - b| \geq \epsilon$.

Since g_n and f_n have the same degree, the total depth and computational complexity of $\texttt{NewCompG}$ are strictly smaller than those of $\texttt{NewComp}$.

The variety on choosing n in our comparison algorithms provides flexibility in complexity-depth tradeoff. For instance, one can choose $n = 4$ to achieve the minimal computational complexity (see Sect. 3.4). On the other hand, if one wants to obtain comparison results with larger complexity but smaller depth, one can choose n larger than 4. Assuming some heuristic properties of g_n, the total depth of $\texttt{NewCompG}(\cdot, \cdot; n, d_f, d_g)$ gets close to the theoretical minimal depth as n increases (see Sect. 3.5).

Improved Performance. For two 8-bit integers which are encrypted by an approximate HE scheme HEAAN [11], the comparison algorithm NewComp (for $\epsilon = 2^{-8}$ and $\alpha = 8$) takes 0.9 ms in amortized running time, and the performance is twice accelerated by applying the other comparison algorithm NewCompG. The implementation result on NewCompG is about 8 times faster than that on the comparison algorithm of the previous work [12] based on HEAAN. Note that this performance gap grows up as the bit-length of input integers increases: For two encrypted 20-bit integers, our algorithm NewCompG is about 30 times faster than the previous work.

Application to Max. Since the max function is expressed by the sign function as $\max(a, b) = \frac{a+b}{2} + \frac{a-b}{2} \cdot \text{sgn}(a-b)$, we can directly obtain max algorithms from the family of polynomials $\{f_n\}_{n \geq 1}$ (and hence $\{g_n\}_{n \geq 1}$). Our max algorithms NewMax and NewMaxG outperform the max algorithm in the previous work [12] in terms of both computational complexity and depth. To be precise, the max algorithm in [12] requires $4\alpha + O(1)$ depth and $6\alpha + O(1)$ complexity to obtain an approximate value of min/max of two numbers in $[0, 1]$ within $2^{-\alpha}$ error. In our case, the max algorithm NewMax applying f_4 only require $3.08\alpha + O(1)$ depth and complexity, and it can be even reduced to $1.54\alpha + 1.72 \log \alpha + O(1)$ by using the other max algorithm NewMaxG. In practice, for encrypted 20-bit integers our NewMaxG algorithm is 4.5 times faster than the max algorithm in [12].

Moreover, our max algorithms fundamentally solve a potential problem of the max algorithm in [12] when inputs are encrypted by HEAAN. When two input numbers are too close so that the difference is even smaller than approximate errors of HEAAN, then the max algorithm in [12] may output a totally wrong result; in contrast, our max algorithms works well for any inputs from $[0, 1]$.

1.3 Related Works

Numerical Analysis on the Sign Function. In the literature of numerical analysis, to the best of our knowledge, there exist two main approaches on the polynomial approximation of the sign function. One is to naively apply general polynomial approximation methods (Taylor, least squares, minimax, etc.), and the other is to apply Newton's root-finding algorithm on a function which has ± 1 as roots.

General polynomial approximation methods provide an approximate polynomial with *minimal degree* under a certain upper bound of the approximate error. However, the evaluation of such approximate polynomial requires at least $\Theta(\sqrt{degree})$ multiplications, which yields *super-large computational complexity* when we aim to obtain a high-precision approximation. For example, when we want to obtain an approximate polynomial of the sign function with α-bit precision over $[-1, -2^{-\alpha}] \cup [2^{-\alpha}, 1]$ via general polynomial approximation methods, the required computational complexity is at least $\Theta(\sqrt{\alpha} \cdot 2^{\alpha/2})$ which is exponential to α (see Sect. 2.2 for more details). There have been recent works [8,32] applying Chebyshev polynomial approximation (on the sine function) instead of the minimax polynomial approximation for better efficiency. However, the Chebyshev polynomial approximation method still requires exponential computational complexity with respect to α when it is applied to the sign function.

Newton's root-finding algorithm outputs an approximate value of roots of a function $r(x)$ by iteratively computing $x_{n+1} = x_n - \frac{r(x_n)}{r'(x_n)}$ for an initial point x_0. That is, an iterative computation of the function $f(x) = x - \frac{r(x)}{r'(x)}$ gives an approximate value to one of the roots of r. The most simple choice of r to compute the sign function is $r(x) = 1 - x^2$ which derives $f(x) = \frac{1}{2} \cdot \left(x + \frac{1}{x}\right)$ so-called Newton's method [34,36]. There have also been several attempts to improve the convergence rate of this iterative method to the sign function by changing f to $f(x) = \frac{3x+x^3}{1+3x^2}$ (Halley's method [42]), $f(x) = \frac{5x+10x^3+x^5}{1+10x^2+5x^4}$ [18], and $f(x) = \frac{10x+98x^3+126x^5+22x^7}{1+42x^2+140x^4+70x^6+3x^8}$ [46].[1] However, all these methods commonly require the inverse operation, and additional polynomial approximation on inverse is required to apply these methods in HE as the previous work [12]. Consequently, these methods are much less efficient than our methods for the evaluation of the sign function in HE due to a number of expensive inverse operations.

There has been proposed another choice of r that makes f a polynomial as in this paper, so-called Newton-Schulz method [34,36]. When we take $r(x) = 1 - 1/x^2$, the function f is expressed as $f(x) = \frac{x}{2} \cdot (3 - x^2)$ and we can obtain an approximate value of the sign function by the iterative computation of f. Interestingly, this function is one of our devised polynomials f_1. However, we note that the design rationale of our methods, setting core properties of f that makes $f^{(d)}$ get close to the sign function as d increases, is totally different from that of the Newton's root-finding method. With Newton's method it is not clear at all how to generalize f_1 to f_n for $n > 1$ or how to obtain the intuition for devising other polynomials $\{g_n\}_{n \geq 1}$ for convergence acceleration. Our methods applying $\{f_n\}_{n>1}$ and $\{g_n\}_{n \geq 1}$ achieve much less computational complexity and depth than the previous numerical method (see Sect. 3.4 and Sect. 3.5).

HE-Based Comparison Methods. There have been several works on comparison algorithms for HE schemes [7,11,24] basically supporting addition and multiplication. The most recent work was proposed by Cheon et al. [12] which exploits the identity $\text{comp}(a, b) = \lim_{k \to \infty} \frac{a^k}{a^k + b^k}$ for $a, b > 0$ with an iterative inverse algorithm. Their comparison algorithm requires $\Theta(\alpha \log \alpha)$ complexity, which is quasi-optimal, to obtain an approximate value of $\text{comp}(a, b)$ within $2^{-\alpha}$ error for $a, b \in [1/2, 3/2]$ satisfying $\max(a, b)/\min(a, b) \geq 1 + 2^{-\alpha}$.

---

[1] In fact, this line of work in numerical analysis aims to compute the matrix sign function [36] which is a more general object than the sign function in our context. An inverse operation is not much more costly than a multiplication in their (asymptotic) cost analysis and experiments, which is a crucial difference from HE which requires an additional costly polynomial approximation for inverse [12].

There have been several approaches to approximate the sign function by polynomials to obtain a comparison algorithm. In 2018, Boura et al. [5] proposed an analytic method to compute the sign function by approximating it via Fourier series over a target interval which has an advantage on numerical stability. In this method, one should additionally consider the error induced by the polynomial approximation on e^{ix}. Another approach is to approximate the sign function by $\tanh(kx) = \frac{e^{kx}-e^{-kx}}{e^{kx}+e^{-kx}}$ for sufficiently large $k > 0$ [14]. In order to efficiently compute $\tanh(kx)$, they repeatedly apply the double-angle formula $\tanh(2x) = \frac{2\tanh(x)}{1+\tanh^2(x)} \approx \frac{2x}{1+x^2}$ where the inverse operation is substituted by a low-degree minimax approximate polynomial. This procedure can be interpreted as a composition of polynomial f which is the low-degree minimax approximation polynomial of $\frac{2x}{1+x^2}$. However, their method does not catch core properties of the basic polynomial f (e.g., $f(1) = 1$), so the error between $f^{(d)}$ and $\text{sgn}(x)$ cannot be reduced below a certain bound even if we increase d to ∞. As an independent work, Bajard et al. [4] recently proposed a new approach to approximately compute the sign function by applying the Newton's root-finding method on the function $r(x) = 1 - 1/x^2$, which corresponds to one of our devised polynomials f_1.

When each bit of message is encrypted separately [13, 16, 20], one can perform a comparison operation of two α-bit integers with $O(\log \alpha)$ depth and $O(\alpha)$ complexity. The bit-by-bit encryption method was recently generalized to encrypt an integer a after decomposing it as $a = \sum a_i b^i$ for a power of small prime $b = p^r$ [47]. However, since these encryption methods are quite inefficient for addition and multiplication, they are not desirable when comparison operations are mixed with a number of polynomials such as cluster analysis and gradient tree boosting.

2   Preliminaries

2.1   Notations

All logarithms are of base 2 unless otherwise indicated, and e denotes the Euler's constant. $\mathbb{Z}$, $\mathbb{R}$ and $\mathbb{C}$ denote the integer ring, the real number field and complex number field, respectively. For a finite set X, we denote the uniform distribution over X by $U(X)$. For a real-valued function f defined over $\mathbb{R}$ and a compact set $I \subset \mathbb{R}$, we denote the infinity norm of f over the domain I by $||f||_{\infty,I} := \max_{x \in I} |f(x)|$. The d-times composition of f is denoted by $f^{(d)} := f \circ f \circ \cdots \circ f$. We denote the sign function and the comparison function by

$$\text{sgn}(x) := \begin{cases} 1 & \text{if } x > 0 \\ 0 & \text{if } x = 0 \\ -1 & \text{if } x < 0 \end{cases}, \quad \text{comp}(a,b) := \begin{cases} 1 & \text{if } a > b \\ 1/2 & \text{if } a = b \\ 0 & \text{if } a < b \end{cases}$$

which are in fact equivalent to each other by $\text{comp}(a,b) = (\text{sgn}(a-b)+1)/2$.

For $\alpha > 0$ and $0 < \epsilon < 1$, we say a polynomial f is (α, ϵ)-*close* to $\text{sgn}(x)$ over $[-1, 1]$ if it satisfies

$$||f(x) - \text{sgn}(x)||_{\infty,[-1,-\epsilon]\cup[\epsilon,1]} \leq 2^{-\alpha}.$$

For $a, b \in \mathbb{R}$, we denote the complexity $a \cdot \log(1/\epsilon) + b \cdot \log \alpha + O(1)$ by $L(a, b)$. The O notation in this paper regards to α and $1/\epsilon$. In the rest of this paper, we only consider the (non-scalar) multiplicative depth and (non-scalar) multiplicative computational complexity, i.e., we do not count the number of additions nor scalar multiplications in computational complexity.

2.2   Minimax Polynomial Approximation Method

In this paper, we measure the accuracy of polynomial approximation methods by the maximal error between the target function and an approximate polynomial over a predetermined domain. In this respect, the minimax approximation method provides the best approximate polynomials among general polynomial approximation methods. For a positive odd integer k, let us denote by $p_{k,\epsilon}$ the degree-k polynomial p which minimizes $||\text{sgn}(x) - p(x)||_{\infty,[-1,-\epsilon]\cup[\epsilon,1]}$. For the sign function $\text{sgn}(x)$, there exists a tight lower bound on the approximation error:

$$\lim_{k\to\infty} \sqrt{\frac{k-1}{2}} \cdot \left(\frac{1+\epsilon}{1-\epsilon}\right)^{\frac{k-1}{2}} \cdot ||\text{sgn}(x) - p_{k,\epsilon}(x)||_{\infty,[-1,-\epsilon]\cup[\epsilon,1]} = \frac{1-\epsilon}{\sqrt{\pi\epsilon}}$$

for $0 < \epsilon < 1$, which was proved by Eremenko and Yuditskii [23]. More general works on minimax polynomial approximation of piecewise analytic function have been proposed [2,44], but [23] provides more tight and accurate results on error analysis for the sign function.

Assume that k is large enough so that the left-hand side $\sqrt{\frac{k-1}{2}} \cdot \left(\frac{1+\epsilon}{1-\epsilon}\right)^{\frac{k-1}{2}} \cdot$ $||\text{sgn}(x) - p_{k,\epsilon}(x)||_{\infty,[-1,-\epsilon]\cup[\epsilon,1]}$ is sufficiently close to the limit value. To bound the approximation error by $2^{-\alpha}$ for $\text{sgn}(x)$ over $[-1, -\epsilon] \cup [\epsilon, 1]$, the degree k should be chosen to satisfy

$$\sqrt{\frac{k-1}{2}} \cdot \left(\frac{1+\epsilon}{1-\epsilon}\right)^{\frac{k-1}{2}} \cdot \frac{\sqrt{\pi\epsilon}}{1-\epsilon} > 2^{\alpha},$$

which implies that k should be at least $\Theta(\alpha/\epsilon)$ from the fact $\log\left(\frac{1+\epsilon}{1-\epsilon}\right) \approx \frac{\epsilon}{2}$ for small ϵ. Then, the evaluation of the polynomial $p_{k,\epsilon}$ requires at least $\log \alpha + \log(1/\epsilon) + O(1)$ depth and $\Theta\left(\sqrt{\alpha/\epsilon}\right)$ complexity applying the Paterson-Stockmeyer method [43] which is asymptotically optimal.

There exists a well-known theorem called the equioscillation theorem attributed to Chebychev, which specifies the *shape* of the minimax approximate polynomial $p_{k,\epsilon}$.

Lemma 1 (Equioscillation Theorem for sign function [23]). *Let $sgn(x)$ be the sign function (Sect. 2.1). For $k \geq 1$ and $0 < \epsilon < 1$, an odd polynomial $p_{k,\epsilon}$ of degree $(2k + 1)$ minimizes the infinity norm $\|sgn - p_{k,\epsilon}\|_{\infty,[-1,-\epsilon]\cup[\epsilon,1]}$ if and only if there are $k + 2$ points $\epsilon = x_0 < x_1 < \cdots < x_{k+1} = 1$ such that $sgn(x_i) - p_{k,\epsilon}(x_i) = (-1)^i \|sgn - p_{k,\epsilon}\|_\infty$. Here, $x_1, x_2, \ldots, x_k$ are critical points.*

Note that the if-and-only-if statement of the above lemma also implies the *uniqueness* of the minimax polynomial approximation of $sgn(x)$ on $[-1, -\epsilon]\cup[\epsilon, 1]$ for given ϵ and degree $2k + 1$. In the rest of paper, we will use the fact that $p_{k,\epsilon}$ is concave and increasing in the interval $[0, x_0]$ (in fact it holds for $[0, x_1]$).

2.3   Homomorphic Encryption

HE is a cryptographic primitive which allows arithmetic operations including addition and multiplication over encrypted data without decryption process. HE is regarded as a promising solution which prevents leakage of private information during analyses on sensitive data (e.g., genomic data, financial data). A number of HE schemes [6,7,11,15,22,24,28] have been suggested following Gentry's blueprint [27], and achieving successes in various applications [5,9,29,37].

In this paper, we mainly focus on word-wise HE schemes, i.e., the HE schemes whose basic operations are addition and multiplication of encrypted message vectors over $\mathbb{Z}/p\mathbb{Z}$ for $p \geq 2$ [7,24,28] or the complex number field $\mathbb{C}$ [11]. An HE scheme consists of the following algorithms:

- $\underline{\mathsf{KeyGen}(\mathsf{params})}$. For parameters params determined by a level parameter L and a security parameter λ, output a public key pk, a secret key sk, and an evaluation key evk.
- $\underline{\mathsf{Enc}_{\mathsf{pk}}(m)}$. For a message m, output the ciphertext ct of m.
- $\underline{\mathsf{Dec}_{\mathsf{sk}}(\mathsf{ct})}$. For a ciphertext ct of m, output the message m.
- $\underline{\mathsf{Add}_{\mathsf{evk}}(\mathsf{ct}_1, \mathsf{ct}_2)}$. For ciphertexts ct_1 and ct_2 of m_1 and m_2, output the ciphertext $\mathsf{ct}_{\mathsf{add}}$ of $m_1 + m_2$.
- $\underline{\mathsf{Mult}_{\mathsf{evk}}(\mathsf{ct}_1, \mathsf{ct}_2)}$. For ciphertexts ct_1 and ct_2 of m_1 and m_2, output the ciphertext $\mathsf{ct}_{\mathsf{mult}}$ of $m_1 \cdot m_2$.

Though any arithmetic circuit can be computed by HE theoretically, the number of multiplications and multiplicative depth of the circuit are major factors affecting the practical performance and feasibility in real-world applications.

3   Our New Comparison Method

Since the comparison function and the sign function are equivalent, it suffices to find a nice approximate polynomial (with one variable) of the sign function instead of the comparison function (with two variables). In this section, we will introduce new polynomial approximation methods for the sign function which we call *composite polynomial approximation*, and analyze their computational efficiency. As in [12], we assume that the input numbers are contained in the bounded interval $[0, 1]$, since $x \in [c_1, c_2]$ for known constants $c_1 < c_2$ can be scaled down into $[0, 1]$ via mapping $x \mapsto (x - c_1)/(c_2 - c_1)$. Therefore, the domain of $sgn(x)$ we consider in this paper is $[-1, 1]$.

3.1 Composite Polynomial Approximation of Sign Function

As described in [12], approximating a non-polynomial function by composite polynomials has an advantage in computational complexity: A composite function F of a constant-degree polynomial f, i.e., $F := f \circ f \circ \cdots \circ f$, can be computed within $O(\log(\deg F))$ complexity, while the evaluation of an arbitrary polynomial G requires at least $\Theta(\sqrt{\deg G})$ [43]. However, even if this methodology achieves a log-degree computational complexity, it would be meaningless if the total degree of F is extremely large (e.g., $\deg F = 2^{\deg G}$). Therefore, it is very important to *well-design* a constant polynomial f so that it requires small d to make $f^{(d)}$ sufficiently close to $\mathrm{sgn}(x)$ over $[-1, 1]$. Since $\mathrm{sgn}(x)$ is discontinuous at $x = 0$, we are not able to obtain a nice polynomial approximation of $\mathrm{sgn}(x)$ over $(-\epsilon, \epsilon)$ for any $0 < \epsilon < 1$. As a result, we set our goal to find f whose composition $f^{(d)}$ is (α, ϵ)-*close* to the sign function for $\alpha > 0$ and $0 < \epsilon < 1$ with small d.

The key observation for designing such polynomial f is as follows: For $x_0 \in [-1, 1]$, let x_i be the i-time composition value $f^{(i)}(x_0)$. Then, the behavior of x_i's can be easily estimated with the graph of f. For example, given x_0 on the x-coordinate, x_1 can be identified by the x-coordinate of the intersection point of the graph $y = x$ and the horizontal line $y = f(x_0)$. Note that we can iteratively estimate x_{i+1} with the previous point x_i (see Fig. 2).

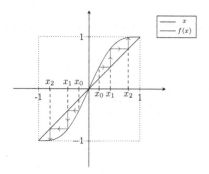

Fig. 2. Behavior of $x_i = f^{(i)}(x_0)$ for $f(x) = -\frac{5}{16}x^7 + \frac{21}{16}x^5 - \frac{35}{16}x^3 + \frac{35}{16}x$

In this perspective, the basic polynomial f should be constructed so that x_i gets close to 1 if $x_0 \in (0, 1]$ and -1 if $x_0 \in [-1, 0)$ as i increases. We can formally identify three properties of f as follows: Firstly, since the sign function is an odd function, we also set f to be an odd function. Secondly, we set $f(1) = 1$ and $f(-1) = -1$ to make $f^{(d)}(x)$ point-wise converge to $\mathrm{sgn}(x)$ whose value is ± 1 for $x \neq 0$. More precisely, if $f^{(d)}(x)$ for some $x \in [-1, 1]$ converges to y as d increases, it must hold that $f(y) = f\left(\lim_{d\to\infty} f^{(d)}(x)\right) = \lim_{d\to\infty} f^{(d)}(x) = y$. Lastly, f should be considered as a *better* polynomial if it is *more concave* over $[0, 1]$ (hence *more convex* over $[-1, 0]$), which will accelerate the convergence of $f^{(d)}$ to the sign function. In order to increase convexity, we set the derivative function f' of f to have maximal multiple roots at 1 and -1. These properties are summarized as following.

Core Properties of f:

Prop I. $f(-x) = -f(x)$ (Origin Symmetry)

Prop II. $f(1) = 1, f(-1) = -1$ (Convergence to ± 1)

Prop III. $f'(x) = c(1-x)^n(1+x)^n$ for some $c > 0$ (Fast convergence)

For a fixed $n \geq 1$, a polynomial f of the degree $(2n+1)$ satisfying those three properties is uniquely determined, and we denote this polynomial by f_n (and the uniquely determined constant c by c_n): From Prop I and III, we get $f_n(x) = c_n \int_0^x (1-t^2)^n dt$, and the constant c_n is determined by Prop II. By applying the following identity

$$\int_0^x \cos^m t \, dt = \frac{1}{m} \cdot \cos^{m-1} x \cdot \sin x + \frac{m-1}{m} \cdot \int_0^x \cos^{m-2} t \, dt$$

which holds for any $m \geq 1$, we obtain

$$f_n(x) = \sum_{i=0}^{n} \frac{1}{4^i} \cdot \binom{2i}{i} \cdot x(1-x^2)^i.$$

See Appendix A for more details. Hence, we can easily compute f_n as following:

- $f_1(x) = -\frac{1}{2}x^3 + \frac{3}{2}x$
- $f_2(x) = \frac{3}{8}x^5 - \frac{10}{8}x^3 + \frac{15}{8}x$
- $f_3(x) = -\frac{5}{16}x^7 + \frac{21}{16}x^5 - \frac{35}{16}x^3 + \frac{35}{16}x$
- $f_4(x) = \frac{35}{128}x^9 - \frac{180}{128}x^7 + \frac{378}{128}x^5 - \frac{420}{128}x^3 + \frac{315}{128}x$

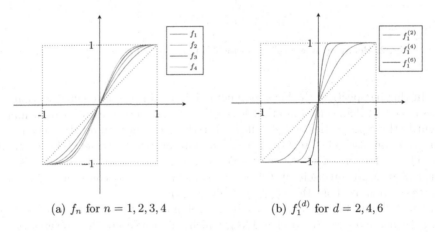

(a) f_n for $n = 1, 2, 3, 4$ (b) $f_1^{(d)}$ for $d = 2, 4, 6$

Fig. 3. Illustration of $f_n^{(d)}$

Since $\binom{2i}{i} = 2 \cdot \binom{2i-1}{i-1}$ is divisible by 2 for $i \geq 1$, every coefficient of f_n can be represented as $m/2^{2n-1}$ for $m \in \mathbb{Z}$ (Fig. 3).

Size of the Constant c_n. The constant c_n takes an important role on the convergence of $f_n^{(d)}$ (on d) to the sign function. Informally, since the coefficient of x term is exactly c_n, we can regard f_n as $f_n(x) \simeq c_n \cdot x$ for small $x > 0$, and then it holds that $1 - f_n(x) \simeq 1 - c_n \cdot x \simeq (1-x)^{c_n}$. In the next subsection, we will present a rigorous proof of the inequality $1 - f_n(x) \leq (1-x)^{c_n}$ for $0 < x < 1$. (see Sect. 3.2). From a simple computation, we obtain c_n as a linear summation of binomial coefficients

$$c_n = \sum_{i=0}^{n} \frac{1}{4^i} \binom{2i}{i},$$

which is simplified by the following lemma.

Lemma 2. *It holds that* $c_n = \sum_{i=0}^{n} \frac{1}{4^i} \binom{2i}{i} = \frac{2n+1}{4^n} \binom{2n}{n}$.

Proof. We prove the statement by induction. It is easy to check for $n = 1$. Assume that $c_n = \frac{2n+1}{4^n} \binom{2n}{n}$ for some $n \geq 1$. Then, it holds that

$$c_{n+1} = c_n + \frac{1}{4^{n+1}} \binom{2n+2}{n+1} = \frac{1}{4^{n+1}} \cdot \left(\frac{2 \cdot (2n+2)!}{(n+1)!n!} + \frac{(2n+2)!}{(n+1)!(n+1)!} \right)$$

$$= \frac{2n+3}{4^{n+1}} \binom{2n+2}{n+1}.$$

Therefore, the lemma is proved by induction.   □

To measure the size of c_n, we apply Wallis's formula [35] which gives us very tight lower and upper bound:

$$\frac{1}{\sqrt{\pi}} \cdot \frac{2n+1}{\sqrt{n+\frac{1}{2}}} < \frac{2n+1}{4^n} \binom{2n}{n} < \frac{1}{\sqrt{\pi}} \cdot \frac{2n+1}{\sqrt{n}}.$$

From the inequality, we can check that $c_n = \Theta(\sqrt{n})$, which diverges as $n \to \infty$.

Remark 1. Our method can be naturally generalized to the composite polynomial approximation on *step functions*. For example, if we substitute Prop III by $f'(x) = cx^{2m}(1-x^2)^n$ for $m, n \geq 1$, then $f^{(d)}$ would get close to a step function F (as d increases) such that $F(x) = -1$ if $x \in [-1, -t)$, $F(x) = 0$ if $x \in [-t, t]$ and $F(x) = 1$ if $x \in (t, 1]$, for some $0 < t < 1$ as d increases.

3.2   Analysis on the Convergence of $f_n^{(d)}$

In this subsection, we analyze the convergence of $f_n^{(d)}$ to the sign function as d increases. To be precise, we give a lower bound of d which makes $f_n^{(d)}$ (α, ϵ)-close to the sign function. The following lemma gives a nice upper bound on $1 - f_n(x)$, which is even tighter than the Bernoulli's inequality [41]: This well-known inequality implies $1 - c_n x \leq (1-x)^{c_n}$, but since $1 - c_n x \leq 1 - f_n(x)$ we cannot directly obtain the upper bound of $1 - f_n(x)$ from this inequality.

Lemma 3. *It holds that $0 \leq 1 - f_n(x) \leq (1-x)^{c_n}$ for $x \in [0,1]$.*

Proof. It is trivial that $f_n(x) \leq f_n(1) = 1$ for $x \in [0,1]$. We will prove $G(x) := (1-x)^{c_n} - (1 - f_n(x)) \geq 0$ for $x \in [0,1]$ by showing

1. $G(0) = G(1) = 0$,
2. there exists $x_0 \in (0,1)$ s.t. $G(x_0) > 0$,
3. there exists a unique $y_0 \in (0,1)$ s.t. $G'(y_0) = 0$.

We first check why these three conditions derive the result $G(x) \geq 0$. Assume that there exists $x_1 \in (0,1)$ such that $G(x_1) < 0$. Since G is continuous, there exists a root x_2 of G between x_0 and x_1. Then by the mean value theorem, there exist $y_1 \in (0, x_2)$ and $y_2 \in (x_2, 1)$ satisfying $G'(y_1) = G'(y_2) = 0$, which contradicts to the third condition.

Now we prove the three conditions. The first condition is trivial. To show the second condition, we observe $G(0) = 0$, $G'(0) = 0$ and $G''(0) > 0$ which can be easily checked. Since G'' is continuous, $G'(0) = 0$ and $G''(0) > 0$ imply that $G'(x) > 0$ for $x \in (0, \delta)$ for some $\delta > 0$. Combining with $G(0) = 0$, we obtain $G(x) > 0$ for $x \in (0, \delta)$ which implies the second condition.

To show the uniqueness, let $G'(x) = c_n(1 - x^2)^n - c_n(1-x)^{c_n-1} = 0$. Then it holds that $(1-x)^{n-c_n+1} \cdot (1+x)^n = 1$ for $x \in (0,1)$ which is equivalent to

$$\frac{\log(1+x)}{\log(1-x)} = -\frac{n - c_n + 1}{n}.$$

Since $\log(1+x)/\log(1-x)$ is a strictly increasing function, there should exist a unique $y_0 \in (0,1)$ satisfying the equation which implies $G'(y_0) = 0$. □

We give another inequality on $1 - f_n(x)$ which is tighter than the inequality in the previous lemma when x is close to 1.

Lemma 4. *It holds that $0 \leq 1 - f_n(x) \leq 2^n \cdot (1-x)^{n+1}$ for $x \in [0,1]$.*

Proof. Let $y = 1 - x$, and set

$$H(y) = \frac{c_n \cdot 2^n}{n+1} \cdot y^{n+1} - (1 - f_n(1 - y)).$$

Then $H'(y) = c_n \cdot 2^n \cdot y^n - f_n'(1 - y) = c_n \cdot 2^n \cdot y^n - c_n \cdot y^n(2 - y)^n \geq 0$ for $y \in [0,1]$. Since $H(0) = 0$, it holds that $H(y) \geq 0$. Therefore, we obtain

$$1 - f_n(x) \leq \frac{c_n \cdot 2^n}{n+1} \cdot (1-x)^{n+1} \leq 2^n \cdot (1-x)^{n+1}$$

for $x \in [0,1]$, where the second inequality comes from $c_n < n + 1$. □

Now we obtain the theorem on the convergence of $f_n^{(d)}$ to the sign function.

Theorem 3 (Convergence of $f_n^{(d)}$). *If $d \geq \frac{1}{\log c_n} \cdot \log(1/\epsilon) + \frac{1}{\log(n+1)} \cdot \log(\alpha - 1) + O(1)$, then $f_n^{(d)}(x)$ is an (α, ϵ)-close polynomial to $\mathrm{sgn}(x)$ over $[-1, 1]$.*

Proof. Since f_n is an odd function, it suffices to consider the case that the input x is non-negative. We analyze the lower bound of d for the convergence of $f_n^{(d)}$ by applying Lemma 3 and Lemma 4. Note that Lemma 3 is tighter than Lemma 4 if x is close to 0 while the reverse holds if x is close to 1. To this end, to obtain a tight lower bound of d, our analysis is divided into two steps:

Step 1. Since f_n is an odd function, it suffices to consider the case $x \in [\epsilon, 1]$ instead of $[-1, -\epsilon] \cup [\epsilon, 1]$. Let $d_\epsilon = \left\lceil \frac{1}{\log(c_n)} \cdot \log\left(\log\left(\frac{1}{\tau}\right)/\epsilon\right) \right\rceil$ for some constant $0 < \tau < 1$. Then applying Lemma 3, we obtain following inequality for $x \in [\epsilon, 1]$.

$$1 - f_n^{(d_\epsilon)}(x) \leq (1 - x)^{c_n^{d_\epsilon}}$$

$$\leq (1 - \epsilon)^{\log(\frac{1}{\tau})/\epsilon} < \left(\frac{1}{e}\right)^{\log(\frac{1}{\tau})} < \tau.$$

Step 2. Now let $d_\alpha = \left\lceil \frac{1}{\log(n+1)} \cdot \log\left((\alpha - 1)/\log\left(\frac{1}{2\tau}\right)\right) \right\rceil$. Applying previous result and Lemma 4, we obtain following inequality for $x \in [\epsilon, 1]$.

$$2 \cdot \left(1 - f_n^{(d_\epsilon + d_\alpha)}(x)\right) \leq \left(2 \cdot \left(1 - f_n^{(d_\epsilon)}(x)\right)\right)^{(n+1)^{d_\alpha}}$$

$$\leq (2\tau)^{(n+1)^{d_\alpha}} \leq (2\tau)^{(\alpha-1)/\log(\frac{1}{2\tau})} = 2^{-\alpha+1}.$$

Therefore, if $d \geq d_\epsilon + d_\alpha$, we obtain $1 - f_n^{(d)}(x) \leq 2^{-\alpha}$ for $x \in [\epsilon, 1]$.

Note that the choice of the constant τ is independent to ϵ and α. When $\tau = 1/4$, then we get $d_\epsilon + d_\alpha = \frac{1}{\log(c_n)} \cdot \log(1/\epsilon) + \frac{1}{\log(n+1)} \cdot \log(\alpha - 1) + \frac{1}{\log(c_n)} + O(1)$. Since $\frac{1}{\log(c_n)} \leq 2$, the theorem is finally proved.   □

Remark 2. In Appendix D, we also described the *erroneous version* of the convergence of $f_n^{(d)}$ considering the approximate error induced by HEAAN evaluation.

3.3   New Comparison Algorithm NewComp

Now we introduce our new comparison algorithm based on the previous composite function approximation (Theorem 3) of the sign function. From the identity $\text{comp}(a, b) = (\text{sgn}(a - b) + 1)/2$ and approximation $f_n^{(d)}(x) \simeq \text{sgn}(x)$, we get

$$\text{comp}(a, b) \simeq \frac{f_n^{(d)}(a - b) + 1}{2},$$

which results in our new comparison algorithm NewComp (Algorithm 1).

It is quite natural that the larger d gives more accurate result. Since the comparison algorithm $\text{NewComp}(\cdot, \cdot; n, d)$ is obtained from the evaluation of $f_n^{(d)}$, Theorem 3 is directly transformed into the context of NewComp as Corollary 1, which informs us how large d is sufficient to get the result in certain accuracy.

Algorithm 1. NewComp($a, b; n, d$)

Input: $a, b \in [0, 1]$, $n, d \in \mathbb{N}$
Output: An approximate value of 1 if $a > b$, 0 if $a < b$ and $1/2$ otherwise
1: $x \leftarrow a - b$
2: **for** $i \leftarrow 1$ **to** d **do**
3:     $x \leftarrow f_n(x)$ // compute $f_n^{(d)}(a - b)$
4: **end for**
5: **return** $(x + 1)/2$

Corollary 1. *If* $d \geq \frac{1}{\log c_n} \cdot \log(1/\epsilon) + \frac{1}{\log(n+1)} \cdot \log(\alpha - 2) + O(1)$, *then the error of the output of* NewComp($a, b; n, d$) *compared to the true value is bounded by* $2^{-\alpha}$ *for any* $a, b \in [0, 1]$ *satisfying* $|a - b| \geq \epsilon$.

Remark 3. One can substitute non-integer scalar multiplications in the evaluation of f_n with integer scalar multiplications by linearly transforming f_n to an integer-coefficient polynomial h_n as

$$h_n(x) := \frac{f_n(2x - 1) + 1}{2} = \sum_{i=0}^{n} \frac{1}{4^i} \cdot \binom{2i}{i} \cdot (2x - 1) \cdot (4x - 4x^2)^i$$

$$= \sum_{i=0}^{n} \binom{2i}{i} \cdot (2x - 1) \cdot (x - x^2)^i.$$

Note that it is easily proved that $h_n^{(d)}(x) = \frac{f^{(d)}(2x-1)+1}{2}$ by induction, so we can express the comparison functions as

$$\text{comp}(a, b) \simeq \frac{f_n^{(d)}(a - b) + 1}{2} = h_n^{(d)}\left(\frac{(a - b) + 1}{2}\right).$$

Therefore, Algorithm 1 can be naturally converted into the context of h_n which does not require non-integer scalar multiplications that consume level in HE.

3.4 Computational Complexity of NewComp and Its Asymptotic Optimality

In this subsection, we analyze the computational complexity of our new comparison method, and compare the result with the previous methods. Note that the (multiplicative) computational complexity of NewComp($\cdot, \cdot; n, d$) equals to that of evaluating $f_n^{(d)}$, so it suffices to focus on this composite polynomial.

For each $n \geq 1$, let C_n be the required number of multiplications (hence the computational complexity) of f_n using some polynomial evaluation algorithm, and denote the lower bound of d in Theorem 3 by $d_n := \frac{1}{\log c_n} \cdot \log(1/\epsilon) + \frac{1}{\log(n+1)} \cdot \log(\alpha - 1) + O(1)$. Then the total computational complexity of $f_n^{(d_n)}$ is $TC_n := d_n \cdot C_n$ which varies on the choice of n. When n becomes larger, then

d_n becomes smaller but C_n becomes larger. Namely, there is a trade-off between d_n and C_n, so we need to find the best choice of n which minimizes the total computational complexity TC_n of $f_n^{(d_n)}$.

Table 1. Depth/Computational complexity of f_n and $f_n^{(d_n)}$

n	D_n	C_n	d_n	TD_n	TC_n
1	2	2	$L(1.71, 1)$	$L(3.42, 2)$	$L(3.42, 2)$
2	3	3	$L(1.1, 0.63)$	$L(3.3, 1.89)$	$L(3.3, 1.89)$
3	3	4	$L(0.89, 0.5)$	$L(2.67, 1.5)$	$L(3.56, 2)$
4	4	4	$L(0.77, 0.43)$	$L(3.08, 1.72)$	$\mathbf{L(3.08, 1.72)}$
5	4	5	$L(0.7, 0.39)$	$L(2.8, 1.56)$	$L(3.5, 2.45)$
6	4	6	$L(0.64, 0.36)$	$L(2.56, 1.44)$	$L(3.84, 2.16)$
7	4	7	$L(0.61, 0.33)$	$L(2.44, 1.32)$	$L(4.27, 2.31)$

We assume that each polynomial f_n is computed by the Paterson-Stockmeyer method [43] which achieves an optimal computational complexity upto constant. Then, the depth is $D_n := \log(\deg f_n) + O(1) = \log n + O(1)$, and the computational complexity is $C_n := \Theta(\sqrt{\deg f_n}) = \Theta(\sqrt{n})^2$. The total depth of $f_n^{(d_n)}$ is $TD_n := d_n \cdot D_n = L\left(\frac{\log n + O(1)}{\log c_n}, \frac{\log n + O(1)}{\log(n+1)}\right)$ (see Sect. 2.1 for L notation). Since $c_n = \Theta(\sqrt{n})$ by Lemma 2, the total depth TD_n gets close to $L(2, 1)$ as n increases[3]. On the other hand, the total computational complexity of $f_n^{(d_n)}$ is

$$TC_n := d_n \cdot C_n = L\left(\frac{1}{\log c_n} \cdot \Theta(\sqrt{n}), \frac{1}{\log(n+1)} \cdot \Theta(\sqrt{n})\right),$$

which diverges as n increases, contrary to the total depth TD_n. Therefore, the optimal choice of n which minimize the total complexity TC_n exists. The exact number of multiplications C_n of f_n and the exact value of TC_n for small n's are described in Table 1. From simple computations, we can check that $n = 4$ gives the minimal computational complexity TC_4.

Asymptotic Optimality. As described in Sect. 2.2, the minimal degree of an (α, ϵ)-close approximate polynomial of the sign function over $[-1, 1]$ is $\Theta(\alpha/\epsilon)$. Since the sign function and the comparison function are equivalent, this implies that any comparison algorithm on inputs $a, b \in [0, 1]$ whose output is within $2^{-\alpha}$ error when $|a - b| \geq \epsilon$ requires at least $\Theta(\log \alpha) + \Theta(\log(1/\epsilon))$ complexity. As described above, the computational complexity of $\mathtt{NewComp}(\cdot, \cdot; n, d_n)$ is

---

[2] The complexity notations in D_n and C_n only depend on n, not α and ϵ.

[3] It does *not* mean the "convergence" to $L(2, 1)$ as $n \to \infty$, since the equation $TD_n = L\left(\frac{\log n + O(1)}{\log c_n}, \frac{\log n + O(1)}{\log(n+1)}\right)$ only holds when $n = O(1)$ with respect to α and $1/\epsilon$.

$\Theta(\log \alpha) + \Theta(\log(1/\epsilon))$ for each n. Therefore, our method achieves an *optimality in asymptotic computational complexity* upto constant, while the previous method [12] only achieves quasi-optimality with an additional $\log \alpha$ factor.

For several settings of α and ϵ, we compare the computational complexity of our method to the minimax approximation and the method in [12] as Table 2.

Table 2. Asymptotic computational complexity for each comparison method

Parameters	Minimax approx	[12] Method	Our method
$\log(1/\epsilon) = \Theta(1)$	$\Theta(\sqrt{\alpha})$	$\Theta(\log^2 \alpha)$	$\boldsymbol{\Theta(\log \alpha)}$
$\log(1/\epsilon) = \Theta(\alpha)$	$\Theta(\sqrt{\alpha} \cdot 2^{\alpha/2})$	$\Theta(\alpha \cdot \log \alpha)$	$\boldsymbol{\Theta(\alpha)}$
$\log(1/\epsilon) = 2^{\alpha}$	$\Theta\left(\sqrt{\alpha} \cdot 2^{2^{\alpha-1}}\right)$	$\Theta(\alpha \cdot 2^{\alpha})$	$\boldsymbol{\Theta\left(2^{\alpha}\right)}$

3.5   Heuristic Methodology of Convergence Acceleration

In this subsection, we introduce a heuristic methodology to reduce the *constants* a and b in $L(a,b)$ of the computational complexity TC_n, which accelerates NewComp in practice.

The intuition of our acceleration method can be found in the proof of Theorem 3. The proof is divided into two steps: Step 1 is to make $f_n^{(d_\epsilon)}([\epsilon, 1]) \subseteq [1 - \tau, 1]$ for some constant $0 < \tau < 1$ (applying Lemma 3), and Step 2 is to make $f_n^{(d_\alpha)}([1 - \tau, 1]) \subseteq [1 - 2^{-\alpha}, 1]$ (applying Lemma 4). Our key observation is that we can accelerate Step 1 by using another function g rather than f_n. The convergence of $f_n^{(d)}$ ($1 \le d \le d_\epsilon$) in Step 1 mainly depends on the constant c_n, the derivative of f_n at zero. Therefore, we may expect that the required number of polynomial compositions d_ϵ in Step 1 can be reduced if we substitute f_n by some other odd polynomial g which satisfies $g'(0) > f_n'(0)$.

However, we cannot take any g with large derivative at 0, since the range of $g^{(d)}$ over the domain $[\epsilon, 1]$ must be contained in $[1 - \tau, 1]$ when d is large enough. In particular, the polynomial g must satisfy following properties (compare it with the Core Properties of f in Sect. 3.1):

Prop I. $g(-x) = -g(x)$ (Origin Symmetry)

Prop IV. $\exists\, 0 < \delta < 1$ s.t. $x < g(x) \le 1$ for all $x \in (0, \delta]$,   (Toward $[1 - \tau, 1]$)

$\qquad\qquad$ and $g([\delta, 1]) \subseteq [1 - \tau, 1]$ (Keep in $[1 - \tau, 1]$)

For each g, we denote the minimal δ in Prop IV by δ_0 in the rest of paper.

Note that Prop IV is necessary to make $g^{(d)}(x) \in [1 - \tau, 1]$ for $x \in [\epsilon, 1]$ when $d \ge d_0$ for some sufficiently large $d_0 > 0$. Intuitively, among all g of the same degree satisfying above properties, a smaller d is required for $g^{(d)}([\epsilon, 1]) \subseteq [1 - \tau, 1]$ if g satisfies Prop IV with smaller δ_0 and has bigger value on the interval $(0, \delta_0)$ (hence $g'(0)$ is bigger).

We introduce a novel algorithm (Algorithm 2) which outputs a degree-$(2n+1)$ polynomial denoted by $g_{n,\tau}$ having *minimal* δ_0 of Prop IV among all degree-$(2n + 1)$ polynomials satisfying Prop I & IV. In a certain condition, we can additionally show that $g_{n,\tau}(x) > g(x)$ on $x \in (0, \delta)$ (hence larger derivative at zero) for any other polynomials g satisfying Prop I & IV (see Theorem 4 and Corollary 2). It implies that $g_{n,\tau}$ is the best polynomial among all same-degree polynomials achieving our goal, i.e., $g_{n,\tau}^{(d)}([\epsilon, 1]) \subseteq [1 - \tau, 1]$ with minimal d.

Algorithm 2. FindG(n, τ)

Input: $n \geq 1$, $0 < \tau < 1$
Output: A degree-$(2n + 1)$ polynomial $g_{n,\tau}$ satisfying Prop I & IV with minimal δ of Prop IV.

1: $g_{n,\tau} \leftarrow x$ // Initialize $g_{n,\tau}(x) = x$
2: **repeat**
3:    $\delta_0 \leftarrow$ minimal δ s.t. $g_{n,\tau}([\delta, 1]) \subseteq [1 - \tau, 1]$ // Initial δ_0 is $1 - \tau$
4:    $g_{min} \leftarrow$ degree-$(2n + 1)$ minimax approx. poly. of $(1 - \frac{\tau}{2})\cdot\text{sgn}(x)$ over $[-1, -\delta_0]\cup$
      $[\delta_0, 1]$
5:    $g_{n,\tau} \leftarrow g_{min}$
6:    $S \leftarrow \|g_{n,\tau} - (1 - \frac{\tau}{2})\|_{\infty,[\delta_0,1]}$
7: **until** $S == \frac{\tau}{2}$
8: **return** $g_{n,\tau}$

In Algorithm 2, the equality check $S == \frac{\tau}{2}$ on line 7 is done with a certain precision in practice (e.g., 2^{-10} or 2^{-53}). Note that S converges (increases) to $\frac{\tau}{2}$, δ_0 converges (decreases) to some $\delta_{conv} > 0$, and hence $g_{n,\tau}$ converges to some polynomial $g_{n,\tau}^{conv}$ (see Appendix B). From this, we obtain two facts: First, Algorithm 2 terminates in finite iterations given a finite precision for the equality check. Second, the algorithm output satisfies Prop I & IV[4].

We provide a theoretical analysis on $g_{n,\tau}^{conv}$ to which $g_{n,\tau}$ converges, which we call *the ideal output polynomial* of Algorithm 2. Note that the ideal output polynomial $g_{n,\tau}^{conv}$ satisfies $\|g_{n,\tau}^{conv} - (1 - \frac{\tau}{2})\|_{\infty,[\delta_0,1]} = \frac{\tau}{2}$. The following theorem shows the optimality of $g_{n,\tau}^{conv}$, which implies that the real output of Algorithm 2 with a certain precision is nearly optimal.

Theorem 4 (Optimality of $g_{n,\tau}^{conv}$). *The ideal output polynomial $g_{n,\tau}^{conv}$ of Algorithm 2 satisfies Prop I & IV with minimal δ_0 among all degree-$(2n + 1)$ polynomials satisfying Prop I & IV. Let $x_2 > 0$ be the smallest positive x-coordinate of local minimum points of $g_{n,\tau}$ following the notation in Lemma 1 (If local minimum does not exist, set $x_2 = 1$). If $x_2 \geq 1 - \tau$, then $g_{n,\tau}(x) > g(x)$ for $x \in (0, \delta_0)$ for any other degree-$(2n + 1)$ polynomial g satisfying Prop I & IV.*

---

[4] In every iteration of Algorithm 2, the minimax approximate polynomial g_{min} of $(1 - \frac{\tau}{2}) \cdot \text{sgn}(x)$ over $[-1, \delta_0] \cup [\delta_0, 1]$ satisfies Prop I & IV. Prop I is trivial, and $g_{min}([\delta_0, 1]) \subset [1 - \tau, 1]$ by Lemma 1. Since $g_{min}(\delta_0) > 1 - \tau \geq \delta_0$ and g_{min} is concave & increasing in $[0, \delta_0]$, it holds that $x < g_{min}(x) < 1$ for $x \in (0, \delta_0]$.

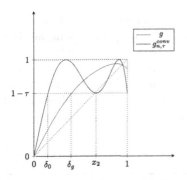 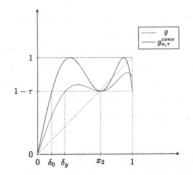

(a) Intersections without multiplicity   (b) Intersection with multiplicity at x_2

Fig. 4. Example description of intersections of g and $g_{n,\tau}^{conv}$ for $n = 3$

Proof. Let δ_{conv} be the minimal δ such that $g_{n,\tau}^{conv}([\delta, 1]) \subseteq [1 - \tau, 1]$. Assume that there exists a degree-$(2n + 1)$ polynomial g satisfying Prop I & IV with $\delta \leq \delta_{conv}$. By Prop IV, we get $\|g - (1 - \frac{\tau}{2})\|_{\infty, [\delta, 1]} \leq \frac{\tau}{2}$, and then it trivially holds that $\|g - (1 - \frac{\tau}{2})\|_{\infty, [\delta_{conv}, 1]} \leq \frac{\tau}{2} = \|g_{n,\tau}^{conv} - (1 - \frac{\tau}{2})\|_{\infty, [\delta_{conv}, 1]}$. Therefore, $g = g_{n,\tau}^{conv}$ by Lemma 1 which implies the minimality of δ_{conv}.

Now we prove the second statement. Let g be a degree-$(2n + 1)$ polynomial satisfying Prop I & IV which is distinct from $g_{n,\tau}^{conv}$, and δ_g be the minimal δ such that $g([\delta, 1]) \subseteq [1 - \tau, 1]$. From the minimality of δ_{conv} and Prop IV, it holds that $\delta_{conv} < \delta_g \leq 1 - \tau \leq x_2$. By Lemma 1, $g_{n,\tau}^{conv}$ oscillates on $[\delta_{conv}, 1]$ with 1 and $1 - \tau$ as maximum and minimum, respectively, and it has n critical points in $(\delta_{conv}, 1)$. Since $g([\delta_g, 1]) \subseteq [1 - \tau, 1]$ and $\delta_g \leq x_2$, the polynomial g intersects with $g_{n,\tau}^{conv}$ on at least n points in $[\delta_g, 1]$: when $g(x) = g_{n,\tau}^{conv}(x)$ and $g'(x) = g_{n,\tau}^{conv'}(x)$, then x is counted as two points (see Fig. 4). Now our second argument is proved as following: If $g(x) \geq g_{n,\tau}^{conv}(x)$[5] on some $x \in (0, \delta_{conv}) \subset (0, \delta_g)$, then g and $g_{n,\tau}^{conv}$ intersect on at least one point in $(0, \delta_g)$ by intermediate value theorem since there exists $y \in (\delta_{conv}, \delta_g)$ such that $g(y) < 1 - \tau \leq g_{n,\tau}^{conv}(y)$ by the definition of δ_g. This leads to a contradiction since g and $g_{n,\tau}^{conv}$ intersect on $2(n + 1) + 1 = 2n + 3$ points (the factor 2 comes from the fact that both are odd polynomials) including the origin while the degree of both g and $g_{n,\tau}^{conv}$ is $2n + 1 < 2n + 3$. Therefore, $g_{n,\tau}^{conv}(x) > g(x)$ for all $x \in (0, \delta_{conv})$.   □

Corollary 2. *Let $g_{n,\tau}^{conv}$ be the ideal output polynomial of Algorithm 2, and δ_0 be the corresponding minimal δ satisfying Prop IV. If $n = 1$, $(n, \tau) = (2, 0.25)$, or $(n, \tau) = (3, 0.35)$, then $\delta_0 < \delta_g$ and $g_{n,\tau}^{conv}(x) > g(x)$ on $x \in (0, \delta_0)$ for any other degree-$(2n + 1)$ polynomial g satisfying Prop I & IV.*

Though $g_{n,\tau}$ is hard to be expressed in closed form contrary to f_n, we can find it with a certain precision (e.g., 2^{-10}) by running Algorithm 2 in MATLAB. For

---

[5] If $g(x) = g_{n,\tau}^{conv}(x)$ on some $x \in (0, \delta_0)$, it is the point of intersection in $(0, \delta_g)$, and proof continues.

example, we provide explicit descriptions of the polynomials $g_{n,\tau}$ for $n = 1, 2, 3, 4$ and $\tau = \frac{1}{4}$ (Fig. 5). In this case, the equality check in Algorithm 2 was done with 10^{-4} precision. We omit the subscript τ of $g_{n,\tau}$ for $\tau = \frac{1}{4}$ for convenience.

- $g_1(x) = -\frac{1359}{2^{10}} \cdot x^3 + \frac{2126}{2^{10}} \cdot x$
- $g_2(x) = \frac{3796}{2^{10}} \cdot x^5 - \frac{6108}{2^{10}} \cdot x^3 + \frac{3334}{2^{10}} \cdot x$
- $g_3(x) = -\frac{12860}{2^{10}} \cdot x^7 + \frac{25614}{2^{10}} \cdot x^5 - \frac{16577}{2^{10}} \cdot x^3 + \frac{4589}{2^{10}} \cdot x$
- $g_4(x) = \frac{46623}{2^{10}} \cdot x^9 - \frac{113492}{2^{10}} \cdot x^7 + \frac{97015}{2^{10}} \cdot x^5 - \frac{34974}{2^{10}} \cdot x^3 + \frac{5850}{2^{10}} \cdot x$

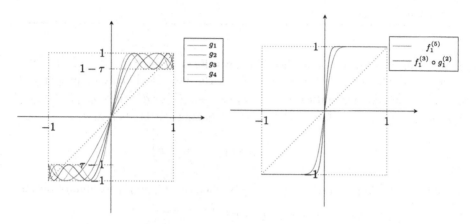

Fig. 5. Illustration of g_n and the comparison of $f_1^{(d_f + d_g)}$ and $f_1^{(d_f)} \circ g_1^{(d_g)}$

We can empirically check that g_n also satisfies the following two heuristic properties. The first property shows how large $g_n'(0)$ is when it compared to $f_n'(0)$, and the second property shows how fast $g_n(x)$ gets close to ± 1, i.e., the g_n-version of Lemma 3.

Heuristic Properties of g_n:

1. $g_n'(0) \simeq 0.98 \cdot f_n'(0)^2$ (Hence, $\log g_n'(0) \simeq 2 \cdot \log c_n$)
2. $1 - g_n(x) \leq (1 - x)^{g_n'(0)}$ for $x \in [0, \delta_0]$ where δ_0 is the minimal δ in Prop IV

Experimental results supporting above heuristic properties are described in Appendix C. Applying these g_n polynomials, we can provide a new comparison algorithm (Algorithm 3), which is a modified version of Algorithm 1 and offers the same functionality with the reduced computational complexity and depth. We can also estimate the number of compositions d_f and d_g required for this modified algorithm to achieve a certain accuracy as Corollary 3.

Corollary 3 (*With Heuristic Properties*). *If* $d_g \geq \frac{1}{\log g_n'(0)} \cdot \log(1/\epsilon) + O(1) = \frac{1/2 + o(1)}{\log c_n} \cdot \log(1/\epsilon) + O(1)$ *and* $d_f \geq \frac{1}{\log n} \cdot \log(\alpha - 2) + O(1)$, *then the error of the output of* NewCompG$(a, b; n, d_f, d_g)$ *compared to the true value is bounded by* $2^{-\alpha}$ *for any* $a, b \in [0, 1]$ *satisfying* $|a - b| \geq \epsilon$.

Algorithm 3. NewCompG$(a, b; n, d_f, d_g)$

Input: $a, b \in [0, 1]$, $n, d_f, d_g \in \mathbb{N}$
Output: An approximate value of 1 if $a > b$, 0 if $a < b$ and 1/2 otherwise
 1: $x \leftarrow a - b$
 2: **for** $i \leftarrow 1$ **to** d_g **do**
 3:     $x \leftarrow g_n(x)$ // compute $g_n^{(d_g)}(a - b)$
 4: **end for**
 5: **for** $i \leftarrow 1$ **to** d_f **do**
 6:     $x \leftarrow f_n(x)$ // compute $f_n^{(d_f)} \circ g_n^{(d_g)}(a - b)$
 7: **end for**
 8: **return** $(x + 1)/2$

Proof. Following the proof of Theorem 3, it suffices to show that $1 - g_n^{(d_g)}(x) \leq \tau$ for $x \in [\epsilon, 1]$ where $\tau = 1/4$. Let $e_n := g_n'(0)$. By the second heuristic property of g_n, we obtain two inequalities: $1 - g_n^{(d)}(x) \leq (1 - x)^{e_n^d}$ for d satisfying $g_n^{(d-1)}(x) \leq \delta_0$, and $1 - g_n^{(d)}(x) \leq \tau$ for $g_n^{(d-1)}(x) > \delta_0$. Therefore, it holds that

$$1 - g_n^{(d)}(x) \leq \max\left((1 - x)^{e_n^d}, \tau\right)$$

for any $d > 0$. Applying $d = d_g := \left\lceil \frac{1}{\log e_n} \cdot \log\left(\log\left(\frac{1}{\tau}\right)/\epsilon\right)\right\rceil$, we finally obtain $1 - g_n^{(d_g)}(x) \leq \tau$ since $(1 - x)^{e_n^{d_g}} \leq (1 - \epsilon)^{\log(\frac{1}{\tau})/\epsilon} < \tau$. $\square$

The important point is that d_g is reduced as approximately *half* (applying the first heuristic property of g_n) compared to the previous case that only uses f_n to approximate the sign function. Since g_n and f_n requires same number of non-scalar multiplications, we can conclude that the computational complexity of $f_n^{(d_f)} \circ g_n^{(d_g)}$ is $L\left(\frac{a_n}{2}, b_n\right)$ where a_n and b_n are defined from $TC_n = L(a_n, b_n)$.

The total depth of $f_n^{(d_f)} \circ g_n^{(d_g)}$ is $L\left(\frac{\log n + O(1)}{2 \cdot \log c_n}, \frac{\log n + O(1)}{\log(n+1)}\right)$ which gets close to $L(1, 1)$ as n increases[6]. Note that $L(1, 1)$ is theoretically the minimal depth obtained by minimax polynomial approximation (see Sect. 2.2).

4   Application to Min/Max

As described in [12], min/max functions correspond to the absolute function as

$$\min(a, b) = \frac{a + b}{2} - \frac{|a - b|}{2} \quad \text{and} \quad \max(a, b) = \frac{a + b}{2} + \frac{|a - b|}{2}.$$

Therefore, an approximate polynomial of $|x|$ directly gives us the approximate polynomial of min/max functions. Since $|x| = x \cdot \text{sgn}(x)$, we can consider the

---

[6] It does *not* mean the "convergence" to $L(1, 1)$ as $n \to \infty$, since n should be $O(1)$ with respect to α and $1/\epsilon$.

convergence of $x \cdot f_n^{(d)}(x)$ to $|x|$ as an analogue. As $\min(a, b)$ is directly computed from $\max(a, b)$, we only describe an algorithm of max for convenience.

Contrary to $\text{sgn}(x)$, the absolute function $|x|$ is continuous so that the parameter ϵ is unnecessary. The following theorem provides the convergence rate of $x \cdot f_n^{(d)}(x)$ to $|x|$.

Theorem 5 (Convergence of $x \cdot f_n^{(d)}$). If $d \geq \frac{1}{\log c_n} \cdot (\alpha - 1)$, then the error of $x \cdot f_n^{(d)}(x)$ compared to $|x|$ is bounded by $2^{-\alpha}$ for any $x \in [-1, 1]$.

Proof. Since $|x| = x \cdot \text{sgn}(x)$, the error is upper bounded as

$$\left| x \cdot f_n^{(d)}(x) - |x| \right| = |x| \cdot \left| f_n^{(d)}(x) - \text{sgn}(x) \right| \leq |x| \cdot |1 - |x||^{c_n^d}.$$

Let $y = |x| \in [0, 1]$ and $k = c_n^d$, then the error upper bound is expressed as $E(y) = y \cdot (1 - y)^k$. By a simple computation, one can check that $E(y)$ has the maximal value at $y = 1/(k + 1)$. Therefore, k should satisfy

$$E\left(\frac{1}{k+1} \right) = \frac{k^k}{(k+1)^{k+1}} \leq 2^{-\alpha}.$$

Since $2 \leq (1 + 1/k)^k \leq e$ for $k \geq 1$, setting $k \geq 2^{\alpha-1}$ implies $d \geq \frac{1}{\log c_n} \cdot (\alpha - 1)$. □

We denote an algorithm which evaluates $\frac{a+b}{2} + \frac{a-b}{2} \cdot f_n^{(d)}(a - b)$ by NewMax (see Algorithm 4), and Theorem 5 is naturally transformed into the context of min/max as Corollary 4.

Algorithm 4. NewMax$(a, b; n, d)$

Input: $a, b \in [0, 1]$, $n, d \in \mathbb{N}$
Output: An approximate value of $\max(a, b)$
1: $x \leftarrow a - b$, $y \leftarrow \frac{a+b}{2}$
2: **for** $i \leftarrow 1$ to d **do**
3:     $x \leftarrow f_n(x)$ // compute $f_n^{(d)}(a - b)$
4: **end for**
5: $y \leftarrow y + \frac{a-b}{2} \cdot x$
6: **return** y

Corollary 4. If $d \geq \frac{1}{\log c_n} \cdot (\alpha - 2)$, then the error of the output of *NewMax*$(a, b; n, d)$ compared to the true value is bounded by $2^{-\alpha}$ for any $a, b \in [0, 1]$.

Our Max v.s. Previous Max. In [12], Cheon et al. introduced a max algorithm exploiting the same identity $\max(a, b) = \frac{a+b}{2} + \frac{|a-b|}{2}$, but they interpret the absolute function as $|x| = \sqrt{x^2}$ which is different with our our interpretation $|x| = x \cdot \text{sgn}(x)$. To compute $\sqrt{(a-b)^2}$, they exploit Wilkes's algorithm [48] denoted by $\text{Sqrt}(y; d)$ which approximately computes $\sqrt{y}$ for $y \in [0, 1]$: Let $a_0 = y$ and $b_0 = y - 1$, and iteratively compute $a_{n+1} = a_n \left(1 - \frac{b_n}{2}\right)$ and $b_{n+1} = b_n^2 \left(\frac{b_n-3}{4}\right)$ for $0 \le n \le d - 1$, where the final output is a_d.

We note that the output of $\text{Sqrt}(x^2; d)$ equals to $x \cdot f_1^{(d)}(x)$, which means our max algorithm $\text{NewMax}(a, b; 1, d)$ (in the case of $n = 1$) gives the same output to the max algorithm in [12]. However, there are several significant advantages to use our max algorithm instead of the max algorithm in [12].

- $\text{Sqrt}(x^2; d)$ requires 3 multiplications including 1 square multiplication for each iteration, while $f_1(x)$ can be computed by only 2 multiplications. Therefore, $\text{NewMax}(\cdot, \cdot; 1, d_1)$ is faster than the max algorithm in [12].
- We can further optimize our max algorithm by substituting $f_1(x)$ with $f_n(x)$ for some $n > 1$. As an analogue of Sect. 3.4, we can select an optimal n which minimizes $d \cdot C_n$ where $d = \frac{1}{\log c_n} \cdot (\alpha - 2)$, where $n = 4$ is optimal.
- Applying the approximate HE scheme HEAAN [10,11], the max algorithm in [12] is unstable when two inputs a and b are too close. To be precise, if the input $(a - b)^2$ is close to zero and even smaller than an error accompanied by HEAAN, then the input attached with the error can be a negative value. However, the output of $\text{Sqrt}(y; d)$ for $y < 0$ diverges as d increases. In contrary, $f_n^{(d)}$ is stable over the interval $[-1, 1]$, so our max algorithm still works well even if two inputs are very close.

Applying $\{g_n\}_{n \ge 1}$ to Max. As a construction of NewCompG, we can also apply the family of polynomials $\{g_n\}_{n \ge 1}$ with heuristic properties to accelerate our NewMax algorithm. We denote an algorithm which evaluates $\frac{a+b}{2} + \frac{a-b}{2} \cdot f^{(d_f)} \circ g^{(d_g)}(a - b)$ by $\text{NewMaxG}(a, b; n, d_f, d_g)$. Applying $\epsilon = 2^{-\alpha}$ to Corollary 3, one can easily obtain the following result on NewMaxG.

Corollary 5. *If $d_g \ge \frac{1}{\log g_n'(0)} \cdot \alpha + O(1)$ and $d_f \ge \frac{1}{\log n} \cdot \log(\alpha - 2) + O(1)$, then the error of the output of $\text{NewMaxG}(a, b; n, d_f, d_g)$ compared to the true value is bounded by $2^{-\alpha}$.*

5   Experimental Results

We measured the performance of our algorithms with comparison to Comp or Max of [12]. The experiments are divided into two categories: 1. Running algorithms on plain inputs, 2. Running algorithms on encrypted inputs. All experiments were conducted on Linux with Intel Xeon CPU at 2.10GHz processor with 8 threads. For experiments in an encrypted state, we used HEAAN library [11,45].

5.1   Approximate HE Scheme HEAAN

Cheon et al. [11] proposed an HE scheme HEAAN which supports approximate computations of real/complex numbers. Let N be a power-of-two integer and

L be the bit-length of initial ciphertext modulus, and define $q_\ell = 2^\ell$ for $1 \leq \ell \leq L$. For $R = \mathbb{Z}[X]/(X^N + 1)$ and $R_q := R/qR$, let χ_{key}, χ_{err} and χ_{enc} be distributions over R. A (field) isomorphism $\tau : \mathbb{R}[X]/(X^N+1) \to \mathbb{C}^{N/2}$ is applied for encoding/decoding of plaintexts.

- $\underline{\text{KeyGen}(N, L, D)}$.
    - Sample $s \leftarrow \chi_{\text{key}}$. Set the secret key as $\text{sk} \leftarrow (1, s)$.
    - Sample $a \leftarrow U(R_{q_L})$ and $e \leftarrow \chi_{\text{err}}$. Set $\text{pk} \leftarrow (-a \cdot s + e, a) \in R_{q_L}^2$.
    - Sample $a' \leftarrow U(R_{q_L^2})$ and $e' \leftarrow \chi_{\text{err}}$, and set $\text{evk} \leftarrow (b' = -a' \cdot s + e' + q_L \cdot s^2, a') \in R_{q_L^2}^2$.
- $\underline{\text{Enc}_{\text{pk}}(\boldsymbol{m}; \Delta)}$.
    - For a plaintext $\boldsymbol{m} = (m_0, ..., m_{N/2-1})$ in $\mathbb{C}^{N/2}$ and a scaling factor $\Delta = 2^p > 0$, compute a polynomial $\mathfrak{m} \leftarrow \lfloor \Delta \cdot \tau^{-1}(\boldsymbol{m}) \rceil \in R$
    - Sample $v \leftarrow \chi_{\text{enc}}$ and $e_0, e_1 \leftarrow \chi_{\text{err}}$. Output $\text{ct} = [v \cdot \text{pk} + (\mathfrak{m} + e_0, e_1)]_{q_L}$.
- $\underline{\text{Dec}_{\text{sk}}(\text{ct}; \Delta)}$.
    - For a ciphertext $\text{ct} = (c_0, c_1) \in R_{q_\ell}^2$, compute $\mathfrak{m}' = [c_0 + c_1 \cdot s]_{q_\ell}$.
    - Output a plaintext vector $\boldsymbol{m}' = \Delta^{-1} \cdot \tau(\mathfrak{m}') \in \mathbb{C}^{N/2}$.
- $\underline{\text{Add}(\text{ct}, \text{ct}')}$. For $\text{ct}, \text{ct}' \in R_{q_\ell}^2$, output $\text{ct}_{\text{add}} \leftarrow [\text{ct} + \text{ct}']_{q_\ell}$.
- $\underline{\text{Mult}_{\text{evk}}(\text{ct}, \text{ct}')}$. For $\text{ct} = (c_0, c_1), \text{ct}' = (c_0', c_1') \in \mathcal{R}_{q_\ell}^2$, let $(d_0, d_1, d_2) = (c_0 c_0', c_0 c_1' + c_1 c_0', c_1 c_1')$. Compute $\text{ct}_{\text{mult}}' \leftarrow [(d_0, d_1) + \lfloor q_L^{-1} \cdot d_2 \cdot \text{evk} \rceil]_{q_\ell}$, and output $\text{ct}_{\text{mult}} \leftarrow [\lfloor \Delta^{-1} \cdot \text{ct}_{\text{mult}}' \rceil]_{q_{\ell-p}}$.

The secret key distribution χ_{key} is set to be $\mathcal{HWT}_N(256)$, which uniformly samples an element with ternary coefficients in R that has 256 non-zero coefficients.

5.2   Parameter Selection

We have two parameters α and ϵ which measure the quality of our comparison algorithms. In our experiments, we set $\epsilon = 2^{-\alpha}$, which is the case expecting that input and output of algorithms have the same precision bits.

HEAAN Parameters. We fix the dimension $N = 2^{17}$, then we can set the initial ciphertext modulus q_L upto 2^{1700} to achieve 128-bit security estimated by Albrecht's LWE estimator [1] (Refer to Appendix E for the script). In each experiment, we set the initial modulus such that the modulus bit after each algorithm is $\log \Delta + 10$. For example, on our comparison algorithm $\text{NewComp}(\cdot, \cdot; n, d)$, we set the initial modulus bit as

$$\log q_L = (\log \Delta \cdot \lceil \log(2n + 1) \rceil + 2n - 1) \cdot d + \log \Delta + 10.$$

Note that each coefficient of f_n is of the form $m/2^{2n-1}$ for $m \in \mathbb{Z}$ (Sect. 3.1). We progress the scalar multiplication of $m/2^{2n-1}$ in an encrypted state by multiplying m and scaling $(2n - 1)$ bits down which results in the factor $(2n - 1)$ in the above equation. In the case of $\text{NewCompG}(\cdot, \cdot; n, d_f, d_g)$, we similarly set

$$\log q_L = \log \Delta \cdot \lceil \log(2n + 1) \rceil \cdot (d_f + d_g) + (2n - 1) \cdot d_f + 10 \cdot d_g + \log \Delta + 10.$$

The bit-length of the scaling factor Δ is set to be around 40 as in [12].

Note that one can evaluate $N/2$ comparison functions simultaneously in a single homomorphic comparison. In this sense, an amortized running time of our algorithm is obtained by dividing the total running time by $N/2 = 2^{16}$.

Choice of n in $\{f_n\}_{n\geq 1}$ and $\{g_n\}_{n\geq 1}$. One should consider a different cost model other than TC_n in the case of experiments in an encrypted state. When running our algorithms with HEAAN, not only the complexity TC_n but also the depth TD_n is an important factor affecting the running time, since the computational cost of a homomorphic multiplication is different for each level. Instead of TC_n, we take another cost model $TD_n \cdot TC_n$ considering that a multiplication in R_q takes (quasi-)linear time with respect to $\log q$. Under the setting $\epsilon = 2^{-\alpha}$, one can check by simple computation that $n = 4$ also minimizes $TD_n \cdot TC_n$ as well as TC_n, and we used f_n and g_n with $n = 4$ for the experiments.

5.3   Performance of NewComp and NewCompG

We compare the performance of our new comparison algorithms NewComp and NewCompG with the previous comparison algorithm Comp proposed in [12]. The following experimental results show that NewComp is much faster than Comp in practice, and applying g_n polynomials (NewCompG) substantially improves the performance of NewComp.

Plain State Experiment. For "plain inputs" $a, b \in [0,1]$ satisfying $|a - b| \geq \epsilon = 2^{-\alpha}$, we measured the required computational complexity and depth of each comparison algorithm to obtain an approximate value of $\mathrm{comp}(a, b)$ within $2^{-\alpha}$ error. The parameters d, d_f and d_g are chosen as the lower bounds described in Corollary 1 and Corollary 3, and we checked that these theoretical lower bounds are indeed very close to those obtained experimentally.

From Fig. 6, we can see that NewComp requires much less depth and complexity than Comp, and those of NewCompG are even smaller. Note that the gap between these algorithms in terms of both depth and complexity grows up as α increases. For example, when $\alpha = 8$, the required complexity is $\times 3$–4 less in NewComp and NewCompG; when $\alpha = 32$, it is over $\times 7$ less in NewCompG.

Table 3. Running time (amortized running time) of Comp, NewComp and NewCompG on HEAAN for various α and $\epsilon = 2^{-\alpha}$; an asterisk (*) means that the parameter for HEAAN does not achieve 128-bit security due to large $\log q_L \geq 1700$.

α	Comp	NewComp	NewCompG
8	238 s (3.63 ms)*	59 s (0.90 ms)	31 s (0.47 ms)
12	572 s (8.73 ms)*	93 s (1.42 ms)	47 s (0.72 ms)
16	1429 s (21.8 ms)*	151 s (2.30 ms)*	80 s (1.22 ms)
20	2790 s (42.6 ms)*	285 s (4.35 ms)*	94 s (1.43 ms)*

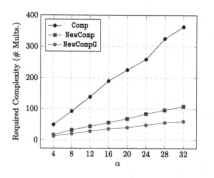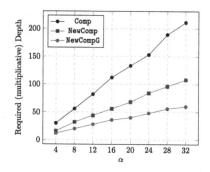

Fig. 6. Comp, NewComp and NewCompG on various α with $\epsilon = 2^{-\alpha}$ in a plain state

Encrypted State Experiment. We also measured the performance of our algorithms which output an approximate value of $\mathrm{comp}(a, b)$ within $2^{-\alpha}$ error for "encrypted inputs" $a, b \in [0, 1]$ satisfying $|a - b| \geq \epsilon$. Note that parameters d, d_f and d_g are chosen as the lower bounds in Corollary 1 and 3. We checked through 100 experiments that our algorithms with chosen parameters give accurate results in spite of errors accompanied by HEAAN.

In Table 3, we can see the running time (and amortized running time) of our algorithms NewComp, NewCompG, and that of Comp [12] for various α. Note that our new algorithms NewComp and NewCompG provide outstanding performance in terms of amortized running time: NewComp takes 0.9 ms for 8-bit comparison, and NewCompG only takes about 1 ms to compare up to 20-bit inputs. It is a significant improvement over the previous algorithm Comp. For example, NewCompG is about $\times 8$ faster than Comp when $\alpha = 8$, about $\times 18$ faster when $\alpha = 16$, and the ratio increases as α increases.

Note that the required depth of Comp is much larger than that of our algorithms as described in Fig. 6. Consequently, to run Comp for $\alpha \geq 10$ in an encrypted state with 128-bit security, one must increase the HEAAN parameter from $N = 2^{17}$ to $N = 2^{18}$, or use bootstrapping techniques [10], both of which yields more than twice performance degradation, especially in total running time.

5.4 Performance of NewMax and NewMaxG

We also compared the performance of NewMax and NewMaxG in an encrypted state to that of the max algorithm Max in the previous work [12]. The parameters d, d_f and d_g were chosen from the theoretical lower bounds described in Corollary 4 and Corollary 5, and were confirmed that they are very close to those obtained experimentally. In Fig. 7, we can see the running time of our new algorithms NewMax, NewMaxG, and that of Max in [12]. Our algorithms improve the Max considerably in running time (and depth), and the gap increases for larger α: when $\alpha = 8$, our NewMax and NewMaxG algorithms are $\times 1.6$ and $\times 2$ faster than Max, respectively; when $\alpha = 20$, our NewMaxG algorithm is $\times 4.5$ faster than Max.

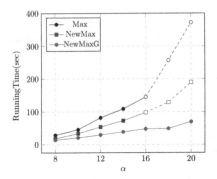

Fig. 7. Running Time of `Max`, `NewMax` and `NewMaxG` on HEAAN for various α. Hollow marker implies that the parameter does not achieve 128-bit security due to $\log q_L \geq 1700$.

Acknowledgement. We thank Kyoohyung Han for useful discussions in the early stage of this work, anonymous reviewers of Eurocrypt 2020 for suggesting us to investigate the line of work in numerical analysis, and those of Asiacrypt 2020 for valuable comments. This work was supported by the Institute for Information & Communications Technology Promotion (IITP) Grant through the Korean Government (MSIT), (Development and Library Implementation of Fully Homomorphic Machine Learning Algorithms supporting Neural Network Learning over Encrypted Data), under Grant 2020-0-00840.

A   Derivation of f_n from Core Properties

Given $f_n(x) = c_n \int_0^x (1 - s^2)^n ds$, we use substitution $s = \sin t$ to get $\frac{f_n(x)}{c_n} = \int_0^{\sin^{-1} x} \cos^{2n+1} t\, dt$. Applying the following identity (which holds for any $m \geq 2$)

$$\int_0^x \cos^m t\, dt = \frac{1}{m} \cdot \cos^{m-1} x \cdot \sin x + \frac{m-1}{m} \cdot \int_0^x \cos^{m-2} t\, dt,$$

we obtain

$$\frac{f_n(x)}{c_n} = \frac{1}{2n+1}(1 - x^2)^n x + \frac{2n}{2n+1} \frac{f_{n-1}(x)}{c_{n-1}}$$

for $n \geq 2$, and $\frac{f_1(x)}{c_1} = \frac{1}{3}(1 - x^2)x + \frac{2}{3} \cdot x$. By induction, we can obtain f_n as

$$\frac{f_n(x)}{c_n} = \frac{1}{2n+2} \cdot \sum_{i=0}^{n} \prod_{k=i}^{n} \frac{2k+2}{2k+1} \cdot (1 - x^2)^i x \tag{1}$$

Now, since $f_n(1) = 1$, evaluating above equation at $x = 1$ gives,

$$c_n = \prod_{k=1}^{n} \frac{2k+1}{2k} = \frac{1}{4^n} \binom{2n}{n} (2n+1).$$

Substituting this c_n into Eq. (1) and arranging, we get

$$f_n(x) = \sum_{i=0}^{n} \frac{1}{4^i} \cdot \binom{2i}{i} \cdot x(1 - x^2)^i.$$

B   Convergence of δ_0, S and $g_{n,\tau}$

It is trivial that $S \leq \frac{\tau}{2}$. Let us denote S, δ_0 and $g_{n,\tau}$ updated in the i-th iteration by S_i, $\delta_{0,i}$ and $g_{n,\tau,i}$ respectively. Assume that $S_i < \frac{\tau}{2}$ for some $i \geq 1$. Then it holds that $g_{n,\tau,i}(x) \geq (1 - \frac{\tau}{2}) - S_i > 1 - \tau$ for $x \in [\delta_{0,i}, 1]$. Therefore, $\delta_{0,i+1}$ should be smaller than $\delta_{0,i}$, and hence S_{i+1} is larger than S_i. Since $\delta_{0,i}$ has a lower bound 0, $\delta_{0,i}$ converges to some constant $\delta_{conv} > 0$ as i increases. Hence, $g_{n,\tau,i}$ converges to some $g_{n,\tau}^{conv}$, and S_i converges to some $S_{conv} \leq \frac{\tau}{2}$.

Now, assume that $S_{conv} < \frac{\tau}{2}$ and let $\rho = \frac{\tau}{2} - S_{conv} > 0$. Since $\delta_{0,i}$ converges (and decreases) to δ_{conv}, there exists some $i \geq 1$ such that $\delta_{0,i} < \frac{1-\tau+\rho}{1-\tau} \cdot \delta_{conv}$. Note that $g_{n,\tau,i}$ is concave in $[0, \delta_{0,i}]$ as noted in Sect. 2.2. Therefore, it holds that $\frac{g_{n,\tau,i}(\delta_{0,i}) - (1-\tau)}{\delta_{0,i} - \delta_{0,i+1}} < \frac{g_{n,\tau,i}(\delta_{0,i})}{\delta_{0,i}}$ where $g_{n,\tau,i}(\delta_{0,i+1}) = 1 - \tau$. Since $g_{n,\tau,i}(\delta_{0,i}) - (1 - \tau) \geq \rho$, we obtain

$$\delta_{0,i} - \delta_{0,i+1} > \frac{g_{n,\tau,i}(\delta_{0,i}) - (1-\tau)}{g_{n,\tau,i}(\delta_{0,i})} \delta_{0,i} = \delta_{0,i} - \frac{1-\tau}{g_{n,\tau,i}(\delta_{0,i})} \delta_{0,i}$$

$$\geq \delta_{0,i} - \frac{1-\tau}{1-\tau+\rho} \delta_{0,i} = \frac{\rho}{1-\tau+\rho} \delta_{0,i}.$$

Hence, we get $\delta_{0,i} > \frac{1-\tau+\rho}{1-\tau} \cdot \delta_{0,i+1} \geq \frac{1-\tau+\rho}{1-\tau} \cdot \delta_{conv}$, which is a contradiction.

C   Heuristic Properties on g_n

We provide experimental results validating the heuristic properties in Sect. 3.5:

1. $g_n'(0) \simeq 0.98 \cdot f_n'(0)^2$ (Hence, $\log g_n'(0) \simeq 2 \cdot \log c_n$)
2. $1 - g_n(x) \leq (1 - x)^{g_n'(0)}$ for $x \in [0, \delta_0]$ where δ_0 is the minimal δ in Prop IV

On the First Heuristic. Using MATLAB, we computed $g_n'(0)$ and compared it with $f_n'^2(0)$ derived from Lemma 2. See Fig. 8 for $1 \leq n \leq 20$.

On the Second Heuristic. Let $G_n(x) := 1 - (1 - x)^{g_n'(0)}$, then we can experimentally check that $G_n(x) \leq g_n(x)$ when $x \in (0, \delta_0]$, which is equivalent to $1 - g_n(x) \leq (1 - x)^{g_n'(0)}$. Let δ_1 be the largest δ such that $G_n(x) \leq g_n(x)$ for all $x \in [0, \delta]$ (see Fig. 9a). The experiment results show that $1/\delta_0 > 1/\delta_1$ which is equivalent to $\delta_0 < \delta_1$ (see Fig. 9b for $1 \leq n \leq 20$).

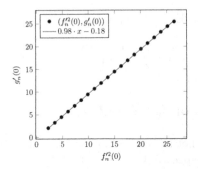

Fig. 8. $f_n'^2(0)$ and $g_n'(0)$ ($R^2 = 0.9999$); $n = 1, 2, ..., 20$ from the left to the right

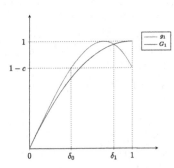

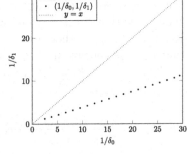

(a) Description of δ_0, δ_1, G_1, and g_1 (b) $1/\delta_0$ and $1/\delta_1$; $n = 1, 2, ..., 20$ from the
left to the right

Fig. 9. Experimental evidence on $1 - g_n(x) \leq (1 - x)^{g_n'(0)}$ when $x \in (0, \delta_0]$

D   Convergence of $f_n^{(d)}$ in Erroneous Case

Due to the approximate nature of HEAAN, the evaluation of f_n on an input x
in an encrypted stated output an approximate value of $f_n(x)$ rather than the
exact value. In this section, we analyze the convergence of $f_n^{(d)}$ considering errors
induced by HEAAN evaluation, and show that the convergence is still valid in
some sense under some conditions on parameters.

Les us denote by $\hat{f}_n(x)$ an approximate value of $f_n(x)$ obtained from HEAAN
evaluation, i.e., $|\hat{f}_n(x) - f_n(x)| \approx 0$. For a fixed $n \geq 1$, let us assume that an
approximate error $|\hat{f}_n(x) - f_n(x)|$ is bounded by $0 < B \ll 1$ (e.g.., $B \approx 2^{-20}$).
Then it holds that

$$|1 - \hat{f}_n(x)| \leq |1 - f_n(x)| + B.$$

Note that B can be easily controlled by changing the scaling factor Δ of HEAAN.

Now we provide some variants of Lemma 3 and Lemma 4 considering the
approximation errors. To simplify the proofs, we assume that $n \geq 3$ so that
$c_n > 2$.

Lemma 5. *Let* $B \leq \left(\frac{1}{2^n+1}\right)^{\frac{c_n-1}{n}} - \left(\frac{1}{2^n+1}\right)^{\frac{c_n}{n}}$. *For* $\left(\frac{c_n}{c_n-1}\right)^{c_n-1} \cdot B \leq x \leq$ $1 - \left(\frac{1}{2^n+1}\right)^{\frac{1}{n}}$, *it holds that* $-B < 1 - \hat{f}_n(x) < (1-x)^{c_n-1}$.

Proof. The first inequality is trivial since $\hat{f}_n(x) \leq f_n(x) + B \leq 1 + B$. For $K(x) = (1-x)^{c_n-1} - (1-x)^{c_n}$, it is easy to check that K has a unique local maximal point $\left(x_0 = \frac{1}{c_n}, K(x_0) = \frac{1}{c_n} \cdot \left(1 - \frac{1}{c_n}\right)^{c_n-1}\right)$ over $[0,1]$ and is convex in $[0, x_0]$. As a result, for $\frac{x_0}{K(x_0)} \cdot B = \left(\frac{c_n}{c_n-1}\right)^{c_n-1} \cdot B \leq x \leq \frac{1}{c_n}$, it holds that $B \leq K(x)$. Since $B \leq \left(\frac{1}{2^n+1}\right)^{\frac{c_n-1}{n}} - \left(\frac{1}{2^n+1}\right)^{\frac{c_n}{n}} = K\left(1 - \left(\frac{1}{2^n+1}\right)^{\frac{1}{n}}\right)$ and K decreases in $\left[\frac{1}{c_n}, 1 - \left(\frac{1}{2^n+1}\right)^{\frac{1}{n}}\right]$, the inequality $B \leq K(x)$ also holds for $\frac{1}{c_n} \leq x \leq 1 - \left(\frac{1}{2^n+1}\right)^{\frac{1}{n}}$. Therefore, we get $1 - \hat{f}_n(x) \leq 1 - f_n(x) + B \leq (1-x)^{c_n} + K(x) = (1-x)^{c_n-1}$. □

Lemma 6. *For* $0 \leq x \leq 2 \left(\frac{n+1}{c_n}\right)^{\frac{1}{n}} - 1$, *it holds that* $|1 - \hat{f}_n(x)| < (2^n + 1) \cdot$ $\max\left\{|1 - x|^{n+1}, B\right\}$.

Proof. We first observe that Lemma 4 can be extended from the domain $[0,1]$ to the larger domain $\left[0, 2\left(\frac{n+1}{c_n}\right)^{\frac{1}{n}} - 1\right]$ when we consider $|1 - f_n(x)|$ and $|1 - x|$ instead of $1 - f_n(x)$ and $1 - x$ respectively. Assume that $1 < x \leq 2\left(\frac{n+1}{c_n}\right)^{\frac{1}{n}} - 1$, and let $H(x) = 2^n \cdot |1 - x|^{n+1} - |1 - f_n(x)| = 2^n \cdot (x-1)^{n+1} + (-1)^n \cdot (1 - f_n(x))$. Then $H'(x) = (n+1)2^n \cdot (x-1)^n - (-1)^n \cdot c_n(1-x^2)^n = (x-1)^n \left((n+1)2^n - c_n(1+x)^n\right)$, so there exists a unique local maximal point of H at $x = 2\left(\frac{n+1}{c_n}\right)^{\frac{1}{n}} - 1$. Since $H(1) = 0$, it holds that $H(x) \geq 0$ for $1 \leq x \leq 2\left(\frac{n+1}{c_n}\right)^{\frac{1}{n}} - 1$. As a result, we obtain

$$|1 - f_n(x)| < 2^n \cdot |1 - x|^{n+1}$$

for $0 \leq x \leq 2\left(\frac{n+1}{c_n}\right)^{\frac{1}{n}} - 1$. Now we get the result from $|1 - \hat{f}_n(x)| \leq |1 - f_n(x)| + B < 2^n \cdot |1 - x|^{n+1} + B \leq (2^n + 1) \cdot \max\left\{|1 - x|^{n+1}, B\right\}$. □

Lemma 7. *Assume that* $B < \frac{1}{2^n+1} \cdot \min\left\{\left(\frac{1}{2^n+1}\right)^{\frac{1}{n}}, 2\left(\left(\frac{n+1}{c_n}\right)^{\frac{1}{n}} - 1\right)\right\}$. *If* $|1 - x| < (2^n + 1) \cdot B$, *then it holds that* $|1 - \hat{f}_n(x)| < (2^n + 1) \cdot B$.

Proof. Since $B < \frac{2}{2^n+1} \cdot \left(\left(\frac{n+1}{c_n}\right)^{\frac{1}{n}} - 1\right)$, if $|1 - x| < (2^n + 1) \cdot B$, then it holds that $0 < x < 1 + (2^n+1) \cdot B < 2\left(\frac{n+1}{c_n}\right)^{\frac{1}{n}} - 1$. Therefore, we can apply Lemma 6 as following:

$$|1 - \hat{f}_n(x)| < (2^n + 1) \cdot \max\left\{(2^n + 1)^{n+1} \cdot B^{n+1}, B\right\} = (2^n + 1) \cdot B,$$

where the equality comes from $B < \left(\frac{1}{2^n+1}\right)^{\frac{n+1}{n}}$. $\square$

Theorem 6. *Let* $B < \frac{1}{2^n+1} \cdot \min\left\{\left(\frac{1}{2^n+1}\right)^{\frac{1}{n}}, 2\left(\left(\frac{n+1}{c_n}\right)^{\frac{1}{n}} - 1\right)\right\}$, *and* $B < \left(\frac{1}{2^n+1}\right)^{\frac{c_n-1}{n}} - \left(\frac{1}{2^n+1}\right)^{\frac{c_n}{n}}$. *For* $\epsilon, \alpha > 0$ *satisfying* $\epsilon \geq \left(\frac{c_n}{c_n-1}\right)^{c_n-1} \cdot B$ *and* $\alpha \leq \log(1/B) - \log(2^n+1)$, *if* $d \geq \frac{1}{\log(c_n-1)} \cdot \log(1/\epsilon) + \frac{1}{\log(n+1)} \cdot \log(\alpha-1) + O(1)$, *then* $\|\hat{f}_n^{(d)}(x) - sgn(x)\|_{[-1,-\epsilon]\cup[\epsilon,1]} \leq 2^{-\alpha}$.

Proof. The proof follows the flow of the proof of Theorem 3.

Step 1. It suffices to consider the case $x \in [\epsilon, 1]$ instead of $[-1, -\epsilon] \cup [\epsilon, 1]$. Let $0 < \tau = \left(\frac{1}{2^n+1}\right)^{\frac{1}{n}} < 1$. Our claim is, for any $x \in [\epsilon, 1]$ the inequality $-B < 1 - \hat{f}_n^{(d_\epsilon)}(x) < \tau$ holds for some $0 \leq d_\epsilon \leq d' := \left\lceil \frac{1}{\log(c_n-1)} \cdot \log\left(\log\left(\frac{1}{\tau}\right)/\epsilon\right)\right\rceil$.

Assume that there exists some $x_0 \in [\epsilon, 1]$ that does not satisfy this claim. Since $\epsilon \leq x_0 \leq 1 - \tau$, we obtain $-B < 1 - \hat{f}_n(x_0) < (1 - x_0)^{c_n-1}$ by applying Lemma 5 on x_0. Then we obtain $\epsilon < x_0 < 1 - (1 - x_0)^{c_n-1} < \hat{f}_n(x_0) < 1 + B < 1 + \tau$. Since $|1 - \hat{f}_n(x_0)| \geq \tau$ by the assumption, it holds that $\epsilon < \hat{f}_n(x_0) \leq 1 - \tau$, so we can apply Lemma 5 on $\hat{f}_n(x_0)$ again which implies $-B < 1 - \hat{f}_n^{(2)}(x_0) < \left(1 - \hat{f}_n(x_0)\right)^{c_n-1}$. By induction, we obtain

$$-B < 1 - \hat{f}_n^{(d')}(x_0) \leq (1 - x_0)^{(c_n-1)^{d'}}$$
$$\leq (1 - \epsilon)^{\log\left(\frac{1}{\tau}\right)/\epsilon} < \left(\frac{1}{e}\right)^{\log\left(\frac{1}{\tau}\right)} < \tau,$$

which contradict to the assumption.

Step 2. Similarly to *Step 1*, we can set our second claim as following: for any $x \in [1 - \tau, 1 + B]$ the inequality $|1 - \hat{f}_n^{(d_\alpha)}(x)| \leq 2^{-\alpha}$ holds for some $0 \leq d_\alpha \leq d'' := \left\lceil \frac{1}{\log(n+1)} \cdot \log\left((\alpha-1)/\log\left(\frac{1}{(2^n+1)^{\frac{1}{n}} \cdot \tau}\right)\right)\right\rceil$.

Assume that there exists some $x_1 \in [1 - \tau, 1 + B]$ that does not satisfy this claim: $\left|1 - \hat{f}_n^{(d''')}(x_1)\right| \geq 2^{-\alpha} \geq (2^n + 1) \cdot B$ for all $0 \leq d''' \leq d''$. By the assumption, we can say that $x_1 \in [1 - \tau, 1 - (2^n + 1) \cdot B]$, and by applying Lemma 6 on x_1, we get $|1 - \hat{f}_n(x_1)| \leq (2^n + 1) \cdot (1 - x_1)^{n+1} \leq (2^n + 1) \cdot \tau^{n+1} = \tau$. Therefore, we obtain $1 - \tau \leq \hat{f}_n(x_1) \leq \hat{f}_n(x_1) + B \leq 1 + B$ so that we can apply

Lemma 6 on $\hat{f}_n(x_1)$. By induction, it holds that

$$(2^n + 1)^{\frac{1}{n}} \cdot \left| 1 - \hat{f}_n^{(d'')}(x_1) \right| \leq \left((2^n + 1)^{\frac{1}{n}} \cdot (1 - x_1) \right)^{(n+1)^{d''}}$$

$$\leq \left((2^n + 1)^{\frac{1}{n}} \cdot \tau \right)^{(n+1)^{d''}} \leq 2^{-\alpha+1},$$

which contradicts to the assumption.

Combining *Step 1*, *Step 2* and Lemma 7, the proof is completed.   □

Corollary 6 (Special Case of Theorem 6 ($n = 4$)). *Let $B < 0.02282$. For $\epsilon \geq 2.15B$ and $\alpha \leq log(1/B) - 4.09$, if $d \geq 1.83 \log(1/\epsilon) + 0.431 \log(\alpha-1) + O(1)$, then $\|\hat{f}_4^{(d)}(x) - sgn(x)\|_{[-1,-\epsilon] \cup [\epsilon,1]} \leq 2^{-\alpha}$.*

Remark 4. We only addressed about the erroneous evaluation of f_n, but the same logic can be applied to that of g_n: Substituting all c_n's in Lemma 5 by $g'_n(0)$, then it holds that $-B < 1 - \hat{g}_n(x) < (1 - x)^{g'_n(0)-1}$. As an analogue, by substituting all c_n's in Theorem 6 by $g'_n(0)$, we can directly convert the theorem into the context of $\hat{f}_n^{(d_f)} \circ \hat{g}_n^{(d_g)}$ instead of $\hat{f}_n^{(d)}$ for $d_g \geq \frac{1}{\log(g'_n(0)-1)} \cdot \log(1/\epsilon) + O(1)$ and $d_f \geq \frac{1}{\log(n+1)} \cdot \log(\alpha - 1) + O(1)$.

One can check that ϵ and α have lower and upper bounds in terms of B, respectively, and this is quite natural: If an input $x > 0$ is so small so that $f_n(x) < B$, then its approximate value $\hat{f}_n(x)$ may be negative due to B-bounded approximation error. Furthermore, if $|x-1| \ll B$, then $f_n(x)$ should be also very close (even closer) to 1, but a B-bounded approximation error accompanied to $\hat{f}_n(x)$ would disrupt this closeness. In this sense, those lower/upper bounds on ϵ and α with respect to B is actually inevitable.

In fact, Theorem 6 is a *worst-case* analysis on the convergence of $f_n^{(d)}$ in erroneous case by regarding the HEAAN error size in f_n evaluation as B. We also note that inequalities in Lemma 5, 6 and 7 are not as tight as those in Lemma 3 and Lemma 4. In practice, as noted in Sect. 5, even in experiments based on HEAAN, the number of compositions can still be chosen very close to the theoretical lower bounds in Corollary 1 and 3 which are based on the convergence analysis in errorless case.

E   Script for Security Estimation

We specified the parameter with security level $\lambda \geq 128$ using the latest LWE estimator [1][7]. We excluded dec estimates which might not be accurate and often not competitive [21]. The script for checking our parameter is as follows.

---

[7] Available on https://bitbucket.org/malb/lwe-estimator.

```
load("estimator.py")
n = 2**17; q = 2**3400; alpha = 8/q
duald = partial(drop_and_solve, dual_scale)
primald = partial(drop_and_solve, primal_usvp)
duald(n, alpha, q, secret_distribution=((-1,1), 256),
    reduction_cost_model=BKZ.sieve)
primald(n, alpha, q, secret_distribution=((-1,1), 256),
    rotations=False, reduction_cost_model=BKZ.sieve,
    postprocess=False)
```

References

1. Albrecht, M.R., Player, R., Scott, S.: On the concrete hardness of learning with errors. J. Math. Cryptol. **9**(3), 169–203 (2015)
2. Andrievskii, V.: Polynomial approximation of piecewise analytic functions on a compact subset of the real line. J. Approx. Theory **161**(2), 634–644 (2009)
3. Armknecht, F., et al.: A guide to fully homomorphic encryption. Cryptology ePrint Archive, Report 2015/1192 (2015)
4. Bajard, J.-C., Martins, P., Sousa, L., Zucca, V.: Improving the efficiency of SVM classification with FHE. IEEE Trans. Inf. Forensics Secur. **15**, 1709–1722 (2019)
5. Boura, C., Gama, N., Georgieva, M.: Chimera: a unified framework for B/FV, TFHE and HEAAN fully homomorphic encryption and predictions for deep learning. Accepted to Number-Theoretic Methods in Cryptology (NuTMiC) (2019)
6. Brakerski, Z.: Fully homomorphic encryption without modulus switching from classical GapSVP. In: Safavi-Naini, R., Canetti, R. (eds.) CRYPTO 2012. LNCS, vol. 7417, pp. 868–886. Springer, Heidelberg (2012). https://doi.org/10.1007/978-3-642-32009-5_50
7. Brakerski, Z., Gentry, C., Vaikuntanathan, V.: (Leveled) fully homomorphic encryption without bootstrapping. In: Proceedings of ITCS, pp. 309–325. ACM (2012)
8. Chen, H., Chillotti, I., Song, Y.: Improved bootstrapping for approximate homomorphic encryption. In: Ishai, Y., Rijmen, V. (eds.) EUROCRYPT 2019. LNCS, vol. 11477, pp. 34–54. Springer, Cham (2019). https://doi.org/10.1007/978-3-030-17656-3_2
9. Cheon, J.H., et al.: Toward a secure drone system: flying with real-time homomorphic authenticated encryption. IEEE Access **6**, 24325–24339 (2018)
10. Cheon, J.H., Han, K., Kim, A., Kim, M., Song, Y.: Bootstrapping for approximate homomorphic encryption. In: Nielsen, J.B., Rijmen, V. (eds.) EUROCRYPT 2018. LNCS, vol. 10820, pp. 360–384. Springer, Cham (2018). https://doi.org/10.1007/978-3-319-78381-9_14
11. Cheon, J.H., Kim, A., Kim, M., Song, Y.: Homomorphic encryption for arithmetic of approximate numbers. In: Takagi, T., Peyrin, T. (eds.) ASIACRYPT 2017. LNCS, vol. 10624, pp. 409–437. Springer, Cham (2017). https://doi.org/10.1007/978-3-319-70694-8_15
12. Cheon, J.H., Kim, D., Kim, D., Lee, H.H., Lee, K.: Numerical method for comparison on homomorphically encrypted numbers. In: Galbraith, S.D., Moriai, S. (eds.) ASIACRYPT 2019. LNCS, vol. 11922, pp. 415–445. Springer, Cham (2019). https://doi.org/10.1007/978-3-030-34621-8_15

13. Cheon, J.H., Kim, M., Kim, M.: Search-and-compute on encrypted data. In: Brenner, M., Christin, N., Johnson, B., Rohloff, K. (eds.) FC 2015. LNCS, vol. 8976, pp. 142–159. Springer, Heidelberg (2015). https://doi.org/10.1007/978-3-662-48051-9_11

14. Chialva, D., Dooms, A.: Conditionals in homomorphic encryption and machine learning applications. Cryptology ePrint Archive, Report 2018/1032 (2018)

15. Chillotti, I., Gama, N., Georgieva, M., Izabachène, M.: Faster fully homomorphic encryption: bootstrapping in less than 0.1 seconds. In: Cheon, J.H., Takagi, T. (eds.) ASIACRYPT 2016. LNCS, vol. 10031, pp. 3–33. Springer, Heidelberg (2016). https://doi.org/10.1007/978-3-662-53887-6_1

16. Chillotti, I., Gama, N., Georgieva, M., Izabachène, M.: Faster packed homomorphic operations and efficient circuit bootstrapping for TFHE. In: Takagi, T., Peyrin, T. (eds.) ASIACRYPT 2017. LNCS, vol. 10624, pp. 377–408. Springer, Cham (2017). https://doi.org/10.1007/978-3-319-70694-8_14

17. Comaniciu, D., Meer, P.: Mean shift: a robust approach toward feature space analysis. IEEE Trans. Pattern Anal. Mach. Intell. 24(5), 603–619 (2002)

18. Cordero, A., Soleymani, F., Torregrosa, J.R., Ullah, M.Z.: Numerically stable improved Chebyshev-Halley type schemes for matrix sign function. J. Comput. Appl. Math. 318, 189–198 (2017)

19. Cortes, C., Vapnik, V.: Support-vector networks. Mach. Learn. 20(3), 273–297 (1995)

20. Crawford, J.L., Gentry, C., Halevi, S., Platt, D., Shoup, V.: Doing real work with FHE: the case of logistic regression (2018)

21. Curtis, B.R., Player, R.: On the feasibility and impact of standardising sparse-secret LWE parameter sets for homomorphic encryption. In: Proceedings of the 7th ACM Workshop on Encrypted Computing & Applied Homomorphic Cryptography, pp. 1–10 (2019)

22. Ducas, L., Micciancio, D.: FHEW: bootstrapping homomorphic encryption in less than a second. In: Oswald, E., Fischlin, M. (eds.) EUROCRYPT 2015. LNCS, vol. 9056, pp. 617–640. Springer, Heidelberg (2015). https://doi.org/10.1007/978-3-662-46800-5_24

23. Eremenko, A., Yuditskii, P.: Uniform approximation of sgn x by polynomials and entire functions. Journal d'Analyse Mathématique 101(1), 313–324 (2007)

24. Fan, J., Vercauteren, F.: Somewhat practical fully homomorphic encryption. IACR Cryptology ePrint Archive, 2012:144 (2012)

25. Friedman, J.H.: Greedy function approximation: a gradient boosting machine. Ann. Stat. 29, 1189–1232 (2001)

26. Friedman, J.H.: Stochastic gradient boosting. Comput. Stat. Data Anal. 38(4), 367–378 (2002)

27. Gentry, C.: A fully homomorphic encryption scheme. Ph.D. thesis, Stanford University (2009). http://crypto.stanford.edu/craig

28. Gentry, C., Sahai, A., Waters, B.: Homomorphic encryption from learning with errors: conceptually-simpler, asymptotically-faster, attribute-based. In: Canetti, R., Garay, J.A. (eds.) CRYPTO 2013. LNCS, vol. 8042, pp. 75–92. Springer, Heidelberg (2013). https://doi.org/10.1007/978-3-642-40041-4_5

29. Gilad-Bachrach, R., Dowlin, N., Laine, K., Lauter, K., Naehrig, M., Wernsing, J.: Cryptonets: applying neural networks to encrypted data with high throughput and accuracy. In: International Conference on Machine Learning (2016)

30. Goldschmidt, R.E.: Applications of division by convergence. Ph.D. thesis, Massachusetts Institute of Technology (1964)

31. Han, K., Hong, S., Cheon, J.H., Park, D.: Logistic regression on homomorphic encrypted data at scale. In: The AAAI Conference on Innovative Applications of Artificial Intelligence (2019)
32. Han, K., Ki, D.: Better bootstrapping for approximate homomorphic encryption. Cryptology ePrint Archive, Report 2019/688 (2019). To Appear in CT-RSA 2020
33. Hartigan, J.A., Wong, M.A.: Algorithm as 136: a k-means clustering algorithm. J. Royal Stat. Soc. Ser. C (Appl. Stat.) **28**(1), 100–108 (1979)
34. Higham, N.J.: Functions of matrices: theory and computation. SIAM (2008)
35. Kazarinoff, D.K.: On Wallis' formula. Edinb. Math. Notes **40**, 19–21 (1956)
36. Kenney, C.S., Laub, A.J.: The matrix sign function. IEEE Trans. Autom. Control **40**(8), 1330–1348 (1995)
37. Kim, A., Song, Y., Kim, M., Lee, K., Cheon, J.H.: Logistic regression model training based on the approximate homomorphic encryption. BMC Med. Genomics **11**(4), 83 (2018)
38. Kim, D., Son, Y., Kim, D., Kim, A., Hong, S., Cheon, J.H.: Privacy-preserving approximate GWAS computation based on homomorphic encryption. Cryptology ePrint Archive, Report 2019/152 (2019)
39. Kim, M., Song, Y., Li, B., Micciancio, D.: Semi-parallel logistic regression for GWAS on encrypted data. Cryptology ePrint Archive, Report 2019/294 (2019)
40. Lin, Y.: A note on margin-based loss functions in classification. Stat. Probab. Lett. **68**(1), 73–82 (2004)
41. Mitrinović, D.S., Pečarić, J.E., Fink, A.: Bernoulli's inequality. In: Mitrinović, D.S., Pečarić, J.E., Fink, A. (eds.) Classical and New Inequalities in Analysis, pp. 65–81. Springer, Dordrecht (1993). https://doi.org/10.1007/978-94-017-1043-5
42. Nakatsukasa, Y., Bai, Z., Gygi, F.: Optimizing Halley's iteration for computing the matrix polar decomposition. SIAM J. Matrix Anal. Appl. **31**(5), 2700–2720 (2010)
43. Paterson, M.S., Stockmeyer, L.J.: On the number of nonscalar multiplications necessary to evaluate polynomials. SIAM J. Comput. **2**(1), 60–66 (1973)
44. Saff, E., Totik, V.: Polynomial approximation of piecewise analytic functions. J. London Math. Soc. **2**(3), 487–498 (1989)
45. Snucrypto. HEAAN (2017). https://github.com/snucrypto/HEAAN
46. Soheili, A.R., Toutounian, F., Soleymani, F.: A fast convergent numerical method for matrix sign function with application in SDEs. J. Comput. Appl. Math. **282**, 167–178 (2015)
47. Tan, B.H.M., Lee, H.T., Wang, H., Ren, S.Q., Khin, A.M.M.: Efficient private comparison queries over encrypted databases using fully homomorphic encryption with finite fields. IEEE Trans. Dependable Secure Comput. (2020)
48. Wilkes, M.V.: The Preparation of Programs for an Electronic Digital Computer: With special reference to the EDSAC and the Use of a Library of Subroutines. Addison-Wesley Press (1951)

Lattice-Based Cryptography

Practical Exact Proofs from Lattices: New Techniques to Exploit Fully-Splitting Rings

Muhammed F. Esgin[1,2], Ngoc Khanh Nguyen[3,4(✉)], and Gregor Seiler[3,4]

[1] Monash University, Melbourne, Australia
[2] Data61, CSIRO, Eveleigh, Australia
[3] IBM Research, Zurich, Switzerland
nkn@zurich.ibm.com
[4] ETH Zurich, Zurich, Switzerland

Abstract. We propose a very fast lattice-based zero-knowledge proof system for exactly proving knowledge of a ternary solution $\vec{s} \in \{-1, 0, 1\}^n$ to a linear equation $A\vec{s} = \vec{u}$ over $\mathbb{Z}_q$, which improves upon the protocol by Bootle, Lyubashevsky and Seiler (CRYPTO 2019) by producing proofs that are shorter by a factor of 8.

At the core lies a technique that utilizes the module-homomorphic BDLOP commitment scheme (SCN 2018) over the fully splitting cyclotomic ring $\mathbb{Z}_q[X]/(X^d + 1)$ to prove scalar products with the NTT vector of a secret polynomial.

1 Introduction

Zero-knowledge proofs[1] of knowledge are a central building-block in many cryptographic schemes, especially in privacy-preserving protocols (e.g. group signatures). In these protocols there are often underlying basic public-key primitives, such as encryption and signature schemes, and one has to prove certain statements about the ciphertexts and signatures produced by the underlying primitives. In addition to their usefulness in privacy-preserving protocols, zero-knowledge proof systems have also gained a lot of attention in recent years due to their applications in blockchain protocols.

For post-quantum security the underlying public-key primitives have to be built based on quantum-safe computational hardness assumptions, and lattice-based primitives are a leading choice in this regard. Now, when proving statements related to lattice-based primitives, one always ends up proving knowledge

---

[1] We use the term "proof" instead of the slightly more precise "argument", and mean computationally sound zero-knowledge proof when we just write zero-knowledge proof.

This research was supported by the SNSF ERC starting transfer grant FELICITY. M. F. Esgin—Work done while at IBM Research – Zurich.

S. Moriai and H. Wang (Eds.): ASIACRYPT 2020, LNCS 12492, pp. 259–288, 2020.
https://doi.org/10.1007/978-3-030-64834-3_9

of a short solution to a linear system of equations over some prime field $\mathbb{Z}_q$. More precisely, we want to be able to prove knowledge of a ternary solution $\vec{s} \in \{-1, 0, 1\}^n$ to the equation

$$A\vec{s} = \vec{u}, \tag{1}$$

where the matrix $A \in \mathbb{Z}_q^{m \times n}$ and the right hand side $\vec{u} \in \mathbb{Z}_q^m$ are public. There is no loss of generality in Eq. (1) in the sense that it encompasses the situations when the secret vector $\vec{s}$ has coefficients from a larger interval, or when the equation in fact describes linear relations between polynomials in some polynomial ring $\mathcal{R}_q$ of higher rank over $\mathbb{Z}_q$, which arise in important so-called ring-based constructions. In the first situation the secret coefficients can be expanded in base 3 and thereby the equation transformed to the above form. In the second situation the matrix A has a certain structure that describes the linear relations over $\mathcal{R}_q$ with respect to some $\mathbb{Z}_q$-basis of $\mathcal{R}_q$. Then the equation is equivalent to an equation

$$\boldsymbol{A}\vec{\boldsymbol{s}} = \vec{\boldsymbol{u}} \tag{2}$$

with polynomial matrix $\boldsymbol{A}$, polynomial vector $\vec{\boldsymbol{u}}$ and short polynomial vector $\vec{\boldsymbol{s}}$ with coefficients that are ternary polynomials.

We call a proof system that exactly proves knowledge of a ternary vector $\vec{s}$ as in Eq. (1), and hence does not have any knowledge gap, an *exact* proof system. The goal of this paper is to construct an efficient exact lattice-based proof system.

Currently the most efficient lattice-based protocols that include zero-knowledge proofs utilize so-called *approximate* proof systems which are based on the rejection sampling technique by Lyubashevsky [Lyu09, Lyu12]. Examples are the signature schemes [Lyu12, BG14, DKL+18], the group signature schemes [dPLS18, YAZ+19, EZS+19], and the ring signatures [ESLL19, EZS+19]. Efficient approximate proofs work over polynomial rings $\mathcal{R}_q$ and the prover ends up proving knowledge of a vector $\vec{\boldsymbol{s}}^*$ over $\mathcal{R}_q$ fulfilling only the perturbed equation

$$\boldsymbol{A}\vec{\boldsymbol{s}}^* = \bar{c}\vec{\boldsymbol{u}},$$

where $\bar{c}$ is a short polynomial. Moreover, the coefficients of the polynomials in $\vec{\boldsymbol{s}}^*$ are from a much larger range then the ternary coefficients in the vector $\vec{\boldsymbol{s}}$ that the prover actually knows. The most important reason for the practical efficiency of approximate proofs is that they achieve negligible soundness error with only one repetition.

While approximate proofs are sufficient for many applications, their biggest drawback is that one has to account for the longer vector $\vec{\boldsymbol{s}}^*$ when setting parameters for the underlying schemes so that these schemes are still secure with respect to $\vec{\boldsymbol{s}}^*$. Concretely, suppose that as part of a larger protocol one has to encrypt some message and prove linear relations on the message. Then, when using an approximate proof system, one cannot choose a standard and vetted lattice-based encryption scheme such as Kyber [BDK+18], NTRU, or another scheme in round 2 of the NIST PQC standardization effort. This is problematic for both theoretical and practical reasons. Moreover, if some part of the protocol does not require zero-knowledge proofs, then the efficiency of this part still suffers from the other parts involving zero-knowledge proofs because of the described effect on parameters.

Finally, there are applications for which approximate proof systems are not sufficiently expressive. Natural examples are range proofs for integers and proofs of integer relations, which have applications in blockchain protocols. In these protocols one wants to commit to integers, prove that they lie in certain intervals, and prove additive and multiplicative relations between them. All these problems can be directly solved with an exact proof system that is capable of proving linear equations as above [LLNW18], but approximate proof systems alone are not sufficient for this task. One reason is that one has to commit to the integers in their binary or some other small-base representation and then prove that the committed message really is a binary vector, i.e. that it does not have coefficients from a larger set. This cannot directly be achieved with approximate proofs.

Coming back to exact proof systems, there is a long line of research using Stern's protocol [Ste93] in a lattice setting to exactly prove Equations as in (1) [LLNW17]. But even for the smallest equations, which for example arise when proving a Ring-LWE sample, the proofs produced by this approach have several Megabytes in size and hence are not really practical. The reason behind this is that a single protocol execution has a very large soundness error of $2/3$, and thus many protocol repetitions (in the order of hundreds) are required to reach a negligible soundness error.

In [BLS19, YAZ+19], the authors use the BDLOP commitment scheme [BDL+18] to construct an exact proof system and achieve proof sizes of several hundred Kilobytes for proving Ring-LWE samples. The results in the present paper can be seen as an extension of the results of [BLS19].

Now, for post-quantum security, even when relying on underlying lattice-based primitives, it is of course not necessary to also built the zero-knowledge proof system with lattice techniques, as long as the proof system does not introduce computational assumptions that are known to be insecure against quantum computers. In fact, there are PCP-type proof systems using Kilian's framework [Kil92], such as Ligero [AHIV17] or Aurora [BCR+19], that are capable of exactly proving linear equations as above, and that are secure assuming only the security of a hash function. These proof systems are even succinct and produce proofs with sizes that are sublinear or even logarithmic in the size of the witness $\vec{s}$, but they have a base cost in the order of 100 KB for Ligero and around 70 KB for Aurora.

The proof system that we present in this paper scales linearly in the witness size but produces proofs of only 47 KB for proving a Ring-LWE sample. So there is a regime of interesting statements where linear-sized proof systems can beat the best logarithmic PCP-type systems in terms of proof size.

For larger equations where we cannot quite achieve proof sizes as small as the PCP-type systems, lattice-based systems still have one big advantage. Namely, they are very computationally lightweight. Implementations of lattice-based cryptography are generally known to be very fast. For example, the fastest lattice-based CCA-secure KEMs have encapsulation and decapsulation times in the order of a few microseconds on standard laptop processors [LS19] and are thus about one order of magnitude faster than a single elliptic curve scalar multiplication. The reason for this very high speed is essentially twofold. Firstly, there is usually no multi-precision arithmetic needed since efficient lattice-based schemes use finite field moduli q that are below 2^{32}. And secondly, the required arithmetic has a high degree of data-level parallelism that is favourable to modern CPUs, which is especially true for schemes whose arithmetic natively supports the Number Theoretic Transform (NTT). The protocols that we present in this paper are no exception to this; they use single-precision 32-bit moduli, are NTT-friendly, and don't introduce any computational tasks that are not also present in standard lattice-based basic encryption or signature schemes. We demonstrate the fast speed of our protocols with an optimized implementation for Intel CPUs that achieves prover and verifier running times of 3.52 and 0.4 ms, respectively, for the case of proving a ternary solution to a linear equation of dimensions 1024×2048 (see [ENS20, Appendix C] for more details).

Contrary to this, existing studies of using logarithmic PCP-type proof systems for proving the linear equations (1) that arise in lattice-based privacy-preserving protocols show that one ends up with prover runtimes in the order of several tens of seconds even for the smallest instances and on very powerful processors [BCOS20]. This also seems to be the case for the logarithmic but not quantum-safe Bulletproofs proof system [dPLS19]. For example, in [BCOS20] the authors construct a lattice-based group signature scheme using Aurora as the proof system. They found that proving a Ring-LWE sample takes 40 s on a laptop computer. Even worse, they could not successfully run the full signing algorithm, due to very large memory requirements, even with the help of Google Cloud large-memory compute instances. This is especially problematic since for privacy-preserving protocols to be used in practice, the prover would often need to be run on constraint devices, possibly down to smart cards or TPM chips. We summarize the above comparison in Table 1.

Table 1. Proof length comparison for proving knowledge of a Ring-LWE sample in dimension 1024 modulo a prime $q \approx 2^{32}$. Here the dimensions of the corresponding Equation as in (1) are $m = 1024$ and $n = 2048$. The sizes for the Stern-type proof is taken from [BLS19]. The sizes for Ligero and the scheme from [Beu20] are taken from [Beu20] and are for the parameter $m = 512$.

Stern-type proofs	3522 KB
[BLS19]	384 KB
[Beu20]	233 KB
Ligero [AHIV17]	157 KB
Aurora [BCR+19, BCOS20]	72 KB
Our work	**47 KB**

1.1 Our Approach

The proof system in the present work extends the system from [BLS19]. On a high level, the approach entails committing to a polynomial $\check{s} \in \mathcal{R}_q$ whose NTT basis representation is equal to the secret vector $\vec{s}$, $\mathsf{NTT}(\check{s}) = \vec{s}$. Then, using a product proof protocol that allows to prove multiplicative relations between committed polynomials, the prover shows that $\check{s}(1 - \check{s})(1 + \check{s}) = 0$. This implies that $\vec{s}$ has ternary coefficients since the polynomial product is component-wise in the NTT basis,

$$\mathsf{NTT}(\check{s}(1 - \check{s})(1 + \check{s})) = \vec{s} \circ (\vec{1} - \vec{s}) \circ (\vec{1} + \vec{s}),$$

where $\vec{1} = (1, \ldots, 1)^T$ is the all-ones vector and $\circ$ denotes the component-wise product. What remains is the linear part where the prover needs to show that $\vec{s}$ is a solution to Eq. (1). The linear part was the biggest obstacle to smaller proof sizes in [BLS19]. The reason is that while the BDLOP commitment scheme makes it very easy to prove linear relations over the polynomial ring $\mathcal{R}_q$, one needs to be able to prove linear relations between the NTT coefficients corresponding to the committed polynomials when using the above encoding of the secret vector.

Essentially there are two ways to commit to vectors using the BDLOP commitment scheme. Either one commits to polynomials whose coefficient vectors are equal to the secret vectors, or one commits to polynomials whose NTT vectors are the secret vectors. The first way makes it easy to prove structured linear equations as in (2) by directly using the homomorphic property of the commitment scheme. The second way allows for efficient range proofs with the help of an efficient product proof. But we need to prove a linear equation and conduct a range proof at the same time.

In [BLS19] the problem is side-stepped by reusing a masked opening z of the committed polynomial $\check{s}$ with scalar challenge $c \in \mathbb{Z}_q$,

$$z = y + c\check{s},$$

which is sent as part of the product proof. The verifier can apply the NTT to get a masked opening of the secret vector $\vec{s}$, $\mathsf{NTT}(z) = \hat{y} + c\vec{s}$, and then check that $A\mathsf{NTT}(z) = \vec{w} + c\vec{u}$, where $\vec{w} = A\hat{y}$ is sent by the prover before seeing the challenge c. This approach crucially requires that the challenge c is an integer from $\mathbb{Z}_q$ and not a proper polynomial. Otherwise the masked opening $\mathsf{NTT}(z)$ of $\vec{s}$ would include a component-wise product that is incompatible with the linear equation. But with only an integer challenge c the protocol is restricted to soundness error $1/q$ and hence needs to be repeated multiple times.

The main new technique in this paper is a more efficient method to directly prove linear relations among NTT coefficients of the message polynomials in the BDLOP commitment scheme. Then the product proof can make use of proper polynomial challenges and our proof system profits from further improvements in the product proof presented recently in [ALS20].

We now go a bit more into detail and describe our method for the linear proof. For concreteness, let us define $\mathcal{R}_q = \mathbb{Z}_q[X]/(X^d + 1)$, where d is a power of two and $X^d + 1$ splits fully into linear factors over $\mathbb{Z}_q$. Then the i-th NTT coefficient of a polynomial $\check{s} \in \mathcal{R}_q$ is equal to the evaluation of $\check{s}$ at the i-th primitive $2d$-th root of unity r_i. Therefore, if $\vec{s} = \mathsf{NTT}(\check{s})$ and $\vec{\gamma} \xleftarrow{\$} \mathbb{Z}_q^d$ is a random vector, we have

$$
\begin{aligned}
\langle A\vec{s} - \vec{u}, \vec{\gamma} \rangle &= \langle A\vec{s}, \vec{\gamma} \rangle - \langle \vec{u}, \vec{\gamma} \rangle = \langle \vec{s}, A^T \vec{\gamma} \rangle - \langle \vec{u}, \vec{\gamma} \rangle \\
&= \sum_{i=0}^{d-1} \check{s}(r_i) \left(\mathsf{NTT}^{-1}(A^T \vec{\gamma}) \right)(r_i) - \langle \vec{u}, \vec{\gamma} \rangle \\
&= \frac{1}{d} \sum_{i=0}^{d-1} \boldsymbol{f}(r_i) = f_0,
\end{aligned}
$$

where $\boldsymbol{f} = \mathsf{NTT}^{-1}(dA^T \vec{\gamma})\check{s} - \langle \vec{u}, \vec{\gamma} \rangle \in \mathcal{R}_q$ and $f_0 \in \mathbb{Z}_q$ is the constant coefficient of $\boldsymbol{f}$. The last equality follows from Lemma 2.1. The idea is then to prove that f_0, the constant coefficient of $\boldsymbol{f}$, is zero. This proves that $\langle A\vec{s} - \vec{u}, \vec{\gamma} \rangle = 0$. For a uniformly random $\vec{\gamma} \in \mathbb{Z}_q^d$, the probability that $\langle A\vec{s} - \vec{u}, \vec{\gamma} \rangle = 0$ when $A\vec{s} \neq \vec{u}$ is $1/q$. Therefore, allowing the verifier to choose a random $\vec{\gamma} \in \mathbb{Z}_q^d$ as a challenge, proving $f_0 = 0$ proves that $A\vec{s} = \vec{u}$ with a soundness error $1/q$.

To prove that $\boldsymbol{f}$ has vanishing constant coefficient, the prover initially commits to $\check{s}$ and a polynomial $\boldsymbol{g}$ with vanishing constant coefficient. The polynomial $\boldsymbol{g}$ will be used to mask $\boldsymbol{f}$. Upon receiving a challenge $\vec{\gamma} \in \mathbb{Z}_q^d$, the prover computes $\boldsymbol{f}$ and sets $\boldsymbol{h} = \boldsymbol{f} + \boldsymbol{g}$. Using the given information, we show that the verifier can compute a commitment to $\boldsymbol{f}$ (without requiring it to be sent by the prover). This allows to prove that $\boldsymbol{h}$ is of the correct form and the verifier can simply observe that $\boldsymbol{h}$ has a zero constant coefficient.

The above proof system has a soundness error of $1/q$, which is not negligibly small for typical choices of q. We show in Sect. 3.2 how to amplify the soundness of this protocol at a low cost using Galois automorphisms. Informally, consider k uniformly random vectors $\vec{\gamma}_0, \ldots, \vec{\gamma}_{k-1}$ such that $1/q^k$ is negligible. Similarly as before, we can write

$$
\boldsymbol{f}_i := d\mathsf{NTT}^{-1}(A^T \vec{\gamma}_i)\check{s} - \langle \vec{u}, \vec{\gamma}_i \rangle
$$

and thus the constant coefficient of $\boldsymbol{f}_i$ is $\langle A\vec{s} - \vec{u}, \vec{\gamma}_i \rangle$. For each $i = 0, \ldots, k-1$, we will define maps $\mathsf{L}_i \colon \mathcal{R}_q \to \mathcal{R}_q$ which satisfies the following property. Denote $\boldsymbol{p} = \mathsf{L}_i(\boldsymbol{f}_i)$ and $(p_0, \ldots, p_{d-1})$ to be the coefficient vector of $\boldsymbol{p}$. Then, $p_0 = \ldots = p_{i-1} = p_{i+1} = \ldots = p_{k-1} = 0$ and $p_i = \langle A\vec{s} - \vec{u}, \vec{\gamma}_i \rangle$. We can observe that if $A\vec{s} = \vec{u}$ then $\boldsymbol{f}$ defined now as

$$
\boldsymbol{f} = \mathsf{L}_0(\boldsymbol{f}_0) + \ldots + \mathsf{L}_{k-1}(\boldsymbol{f}_{k-1})
$$

has the first k coefficients equal to 0. Therefore, we can construct a protocol for proving this similarly as above. On the other hand, when $A\vec{s} \neq \vec{u}$ then the probability that all the first k coefficients of $\boldsymbol{f}$ are equal to zero is $1/q^k$. The advantage of this approach over the standard way of having k-parallel repetitions is that the size of the commitment part of the non-interactive proof remains the same as that of a single protocol run. Therefore, the overall cost is significantly reduced.

We believe that this protocol can be useful in other settings, where one wants to switch from the the coefficient basis to the NTT basis.

Another obstacle against practical efficiency (as encountered in [BLS19, YAZ+19]) is that a proof of such a non-linear relation as in (1) requires communication of "garbage terms". These garbage terms end up being a substantial cost in the proofs in [BLS19, YAZ+19]. In [ALS20], a better product proof is presented that reduces the cost of the garbage terms, also using Galois automorphisms.

Applications. Having an efficient proof system to prove knowledge of $\vec{s} \in \{-1, 0, 1\}^n$ satisfying (1) paves the way for various efficient zero-knowledge proofs that can be used in many applications. In order to show the effectiveness of our new techniques, we present two example applications with concrete parameters in the full version of our paper [ENS20]. The first one is to prove knowledge of secrets in LWE samples. This is an important proof system to be used, for example, with fully homomorphic encryption (FHE) schemes. The goal here is to prove that $\vec{u}$ is a proper LWE sample such that $\vec{u} = A'\vec{s}' + \vec{e} \bmod q$ for $\vec{s}', \vec{e} \in \{-1, 0, 1\}^k$, which is equivalent to proving $\vec{u} = (A' \parallel I_k) \cdot \vec{s} \bmod q$ for $\vec{s} = (\vec{s}', \vec{e}) \in \{-1, 0, 1\}^{2k}$. As shown in Table 1, our proof system achieves an improvement of $8\times$ in terms of proof length over the state-of-the-art result by Bootle, Lyubashevsky and Seiler [BLS19], and is dramatically shorter than the Stern-based proofs.

Our other example application is a proof of plaintext knowledge. In this case, the goal is to create a ciphertext and a zero-knowledge proof to prove that the ciphertext is a proper encryption of a message known by the prover. Proofs of plaintext knowledge have applications, for example, in the settings of verifiable encryption, verifiable secret sharing and group signatures.

Being a very core proof system, there are many other applications beyond the two examples above, where our main protocol and our new techniques can be useful. For example, one can apply our unstructured linear proof to prove that one vector is a NTT representation of a polynomial (written as a vector of coefficients). Indeed, the matrix A in (1) simply becomes a Vandermonde matrix. Furthermore, one can see [YAZ+19] for various applications that all build on a similar core proof system.

2 Preliminaries

2.1 Notation

Table 2 summarizes the notation and parameters that will appear in this paper.

Let q be an odd prime, and $\mathbb{Z}_q$ denote the ring of integers modulo q. We write $[a, b[= \{a, a + 1, \ldots, b - 1\} \subset \mathbb{Z}$ for the half-open interval of integers between a and b. For $r \in \mathbb{Z}$, we define $r \bmod q$ to be the unique element in the interval $[-\frac{q-1}{2}, \frac{q-1}{2}]$ that is congruent to r modulo q. We write $\vec{v} \in \mathbb{Z}_q^m$ to denote vectors

Table 2. Overview of parameters and notation

Parameter	Explanation
d	Degree of the polynomial $X^d + 1$, power of two
q	Rational prime modulus
$\mathbb{Z}_q = \mathbb{Z}/q\mathbb{Z}$	The field over which the linear system is defined
$m \in \mathbb{Z}$	The number of rows in the linear system
$n \in \mathbb{Z}$	The number of columns in the linear system
$\mathcal{R} = \mathbb{Z}[X]/(X^d + 1)$	The ring of integers in the $2d$-th cyclotomic number field
$\mathcal{R}_q = \mathbb{Z}_q[X]/(X^d + 1)$	The ring of integers $\mathcal{R}$ modulo q
$k \in \mathbb{Z}$	Repetition rate
$\sigma = \sigma_{2d/k+1}$	Automorphism in $\mathsf{Aut}(\mathcal{R}_q)$ of order k
$\mathcal{C} \subset \mathcal{R}$	Challenge set
C	Probability distribution over $\mathcal{C}$ for challenges
T	Bound for honest prover's $c\vec{r}$ in the infinity norm
δ_1	Width of the uniform distribution for sampling $\vec{y}$
λ	M-LWE dimension
κ	M-SIS dimension
χ	Error distribution on $\mathcal{R}$ in the M-LWE problem

over $\mathbb{Z}_q$ and matrices over $\mathbb{Z}_q$ will be written as regular capital letters M. By default, all vectors are column vectors. We write $\vec{v} \parallel \vec{w}$ for the concatenation of $\vec{v}$ and $\vec{w}$ (which is still a column vector).

Let d be a power of two and denote $\mathcal{R}$ and $\mathcal{R}_q$ to be the rings $\mathbb{Z}[X]/(X^d+1)$ and $\mathbb{Z}_q[X]/(X^d+1)$, respectively. Bold lower-case letters $\boldsymbol{p}$ denote elements in $\mathcal{R}$ or $\mathcal{R}_q$ and bold lower-case letters with arrows $\vec{\boldsymbol{b}}$ represent column vectors with coefficients in $\mathcal{R}$ or $\mathcal{R}_q$. We also use bold upper-case letters for matrices $\boldsymbol{B}$ over $\mathcal{R}$ or $\mathcal{R}_q$. For a polynomial denoted as a bold letter, we write its i-th coefficient as the corresponding regular font letter with subscript i, e.g. $f_0 \in \mathbb{Z}_q$ is the constant coefficient of $\boldsymbol{f} \in \mathcal{R}_q$.

We write $x \xleftarrow{\$} S$ when $x \in S$ is sampled uniformly at random from the finite set S and similarly $x \xleftarrow{\$} D$ when x is sampled according to the distribution D.

Norms and Sizes. For an element $w \in \mathbb{Z}_q$, we write $|w|$ to mean $|w \bmod q|$. Define the ℓ_∞ and ℓ_2 norms for $\boldsymbol{w} \in \mathcal{R}_q$ as follows,

$$\|\boldsymbol{w}\|_\infty = \max_i |w_i| \quad \text{and} \quad \|\boldsymbol{w}\|_2 = \sqrt{|w_0|^2 + \ldots + |w_{d-1}|^2}.$$

Similarly, for $\vec{\boldsymbol{w}} = (\boldsymbol{w}_1, \ldots, \boldsymbol{w}_k) \in \mathcal{R}^k$, we define

$$\|\vec{\boldsymbol{w}}\|_\infty = \max_i \|\boldsymbol{w}_i\|_\infty \quad \text{and} \quad \|\vec{\boldsymbol{w}}\|_2 = \sqrt{\|\boldsymbol{w}_1\|_2^2 + \ldots + \|\boldsymbol{w}_k\|_2^2}.$$

2.2   Prime Splitting and Galois Automorphisms

Let l be a power of two dividing d and suppose $q - 1 \equiv 2l \pmod{4l}$. Then, $\mathbb{Z}_q$ contains primitive $2l$-th roots of unity but no elements with order a higher power of two, and the polynomial $X^d + 1$ factors into l irreducible binomials $X^{d/l} - \zeta$ modulo q where ζ runs over the $2l$-th roots of unity in $\mathbb{Z}_q$ [LS18, Theorem 2.3].

The ring $\mathcal{R}_q$ has a group of automorphisms $\mathsf{Aut}(\mathcal{R}_q)$ that is isomorphic to $\mathbb{Z}_{2d}^\times$,

$$i \mapsto \sigma_i \colon \mathbb{Z}_{2d}^\times \to \mathsf{Aut}(\mathcal{R}_q),$$

where σ_i is defined by $\sigma_i(X) = X^i$. In fact, these automorphisms come from the Galois automorphisms of the $2d$-th cyclotomic number field which factor through $\mathcal{R}_q$.

The group $\mathsf{Aut}(\mathcal{R}_q)$ acts transitively on the prime ideals $(X^{d/l} - \zeta)$ in $\mathcal{R}_q$ and every σ_i factors through field isomorphisms

$$\mathcal{R}_q/(X^{d/l} - \zeta) \to \mathcal{R}_q/(\sigma^i(X^{d/l} - \zeta)).$$

Concretely, for $i \in \mathbb{Z}_{2d}^\times$ it holds that

$$\sigma_i(X^{d/l} - \zeta) = (X^{id/l} - \zeta) = (X^{d/l} - \zeta^{i^{-1}})$$

To see this, observe that the roots of $X^{d/l} - \zeta^{i^{-1}}$ (in an appropriate extension field of $\mathbb{Z}_q$) are also roots of $X^{id/l} - \zeta$. Then, for $f \in \mathcal{R}_q$,

$$\sigma_i\left(f \bmod (X^{d/l} - \zeta)\right) = \sigma_i(f) \bmod (X^{d/l} - \zeta^{i^{-1}}).$$

The cyclic subgroup $\langle 2l + 1 \rangle < \mathbb{Z}_{2d}^\times$ has order d/l [LS18, Lemma 2.4] and stabilizes every prime ideal $(X^{d/l} - \zeta)$ since ζ has order $2l$. The quotient group $\mathbb{Z}_{2d}^\times/\langle 2l + 1 \rangle$ has order l and hence acts simply transitively on the l prime ideals. Therefore, we can index the prime ideals by $i \in \mathbb{Z}_{2d}^\times/\langle 2l + 1 \rangle$ and write

$$\left(X^d + 1\right) = \prod_{i \in \mathbb{Z}_{2d}^\times/\langle 2l+1 \rangle} \left(X^{d/l} - \zeta^i\right)$$

Now, the product of the $k \mid l$ prime ideals $(X^{d/l} - \zeta^i)$ where i runs over $\langle 2l/k + 1 \rangle/\langle 2l + 1 \rangle$ is given by the ideal $(X^{kd/l} - \zeta^k)$. So, we can partition the l prime ideals into l/k groups of k ideals each, and write

$$\left(X^d + 1\right) = \prod_{j \in \mathbb{Z}_{2d}^\times/\langle 2l/k+1 \rangle} \left(X^{kd/l} - \zeta^{jk}\right) = \prod_{j \in \mathbb{Z}_{2d}^\times/\langle 2l/k+1 \rangle} \prod_{i \in \langle 2l/k+1 \rangle/\langle 2l+1 \rangle} \left(X^{\frac{d}{l}} - \zeta^{ij}\right).$$

Another way to write this, which we will use in our protocols, is to note that $\mathbb{Z}_{2d}^\times/\langle 2l/k + 1 \rangle \cong \mathbb{Z}_{2l/k}^\times$ and the powers $(2l/k + 1)^i$ for $i = 0, \ldots, k - 1$ form a complete set of representatives for $\langle 2l/k + 1 \rangle/\langle 2l + 1 \rangle$. So, if $\sigma = \sigma_{2l/k+1} \in \mathsf{Aut}(\mathcal{R}_q)$, then

$$\left(X^d + 1\right) = \prod_{j \in \mathbb{Z}_{2l/k}^\times} \prod_{i=0}^{k-1} \sigma^i\left(X^{\frac{d}{l}} - \zeta^j\right),$$

and the prime ideals are indexed by $(i, j) \in I = \{0, \ldots, k - 1\} \times \mathbb{Z}_{2l/k}^\times$.

The Fully Splitting Case. In this paper our main attention lies on the setup where $q \equiv 1 \pmod{2d}$ and hence q splits completely. In this case there is a primitive $2d$-th root of unity $\zeta \in \mathbb{Z}_q$ and

$$(X^d + 1) = \prod_{i \in \mathbb{Z}_{2d}^\times} (X - \zeta^i).$$

Then, for a divisor k of d and $\sigma = \sigma_{2d/k+1}$ of order k, we have the partitioning

$$(X^d + 1) = \prod_{j \in \mathbb{Z}_{2d}^\times / \langle 2d/k+1 \rangle} \prod_{i \in \langle 2d/k+1 \rangle} (X - \zeta^{ij}) = \prod_{j \in \mathbb{Z}_{2d/k}^\times} \prod_{i=0}^{k-1} \sigma^i (X - \zeta^j)$$

2.3   The Number Theoretic Transform

The Number Theoretic Transform (NTT) of a polynomial $\boldsymbol{f} \in \mathcal{R}_q$ is defined by

$$\mathsf{NTT}(\boldsymbol{f}) = (\hat{\boldsymbol{f}}_i)_{i \in \mathbb{Z}_{2l}^\times} \in \prod_{i \in \mathbb{Z}_{2l}^\times} \mathbb{Z}_q[X]/(X^{d/l} - \zeta^i) \cong (\mathbb{F}_{q^{d/l}})^l$$

where $\hat{\boldsymbol{f}}_i = \boldsymbol{f} \bmod (X^{d/l} - \zeta^i)$. We write $\mathsf{NTT}^{-1}(\hat{\boldsymbol{f}}) = \boldsymbol{f}$ for the inverse map, which exists due to the Chinese remainder theorem. Note that for $\boldsymbol{f}, \boldsymbol{g} \in \mathcal{R}_q$, $\mathsf{NTT}(\boldsymbol{fg}) = \mathsf{NTT}(\boldsymbol{f}) \circ \mathsf{NTT}(\boldsymbol{g})$ where $\circ$ denotes the coefficient-wise multiplication of vectors.

The (scaled) sum of the NTT coefficients of a polynomial $\boldsymbol{f} \in \mathcal{R}_q$ is equal to its first d/l coefficients. This will be later used when proving unstructured linear relations over $\mathbb{Z}_q$.

Lemma 2.1. *Let $\boldsymbol{f} \in \mathcal{R}_q$. Then $\frac{1}{l} \sum_{i \in \mathbb{Z}_{2l}^\times} \hat{\boldsymbol{f}}_i = f_0 + f_1 X + \cdots + f_{d/l-1} X^{d/l-1}$, when we lift the $\hat{\boldsymbol{f}}_i$ to $\mathbb{Z}_q[X]$.*

Proof. Write $\boldsymbol{f}(X) = \boldsymbol{f}_0(X^{d/l}) + \boldsymbol{f}_1(X^{d/l})X + \cdots + \boldsymbol{f}_{d/l-1}(X^{d/l})X^{d/l-1}$ Then, it suffices to prove

$$\frac{1}{l} \sum_{i \in \mathbb{Z}_{2l}^\times} \boldsymbol{f}_j(\zeta^i) = f_j$$

for all $j = 0, \ldots, d/l - 1$, which is the sum over the coefficients of a fully splitting length-l NTT. We find

$$\sum_{i \in \mathbb{Z}_{2l}^\times} \boldsymbol{f}_j(\zeta^i) = \sum_{i \in \mathbb{Z}_{2l}^\times} \sum_{\nu=0}^{l-1} f_{\nu d/l+j} \zeta^{i\nu} = \sum_{\nu=0}^{l-1} f_{\nu d/l+j} \sum_{i \in \mathbb{Z}_{2l}^\times} \zeta^{i\nu}$$

and it remains to show that for every $\nu \in \{1, \ldots, l-1\}$, $\sum_{i \in \mathbb{Z}_{2l}^\times} \zeta^{i\nu} = 0$. Indeed,

$$\sum_{i \in \mathbb{Z}_{2l}^\times} \zeta^{i\nu} = \sum_{i=0}^{l-1} \zeta^{(2i+1)\nu} = \zeta^\nu \sum_{i=0}^{l-1} \zeta^{2i\nu} = \zeta^\nu \frac{\zeta^{2l\nu} - 1}{\zeta^{2\nu} - 1} = 0$$

since $\zeta^{2l\nu} = 1$. □

2.4   Challenge Space

Let $\mathcal{C} = \{-1, 0, 1\}^d \subset \mathcal{R}_q$ be the set of ternary polynomials, which have coefficients in $\{-1, 0, 1\}$. We define $C \colon \mathcal{C} \to [0, 1]$ to be the probability distribution on $\mathcal{C}$ such that the coefficients of a challenge $c \xleftarrow{\$} C$ are independently identically distributed with $\Pr(0) = 1/2$ and $\Pr(1) = \Pr(-1) = 1/4$.

In [ALS20] it is shown that if $c \xleftarrow{\$} C$ then the distribution of $c \bmod X^{kd/l} - \zeta^k$ is almost uniform.

Lemma 2.2. *Let $c \xleftarrow{\$} C$. The coefficients of $c \bmod X^{kd/l} - \zeta^k$ are independently identically distributed, say with distribution X. Then, for $x \in \mathbb{Z}_q$,*

$$\Pr(X = x) \leq \frac{1}{q} + \frac{2l/k}{q} \sum_{j \in \mathbb{Z}_q^*/\langle \zeta^k \rangle} \prod_{i=0}^{l/k-1} \left| \frac{1}{2} + \frac{1}{2} \cos(2\pi j \zeta^{ki}/q) \right|. \tag{3}$$

For example, by numerical computing the probability in Lemma 2.2, one finds for $d = 128$, $q \approx 2^{32}$ fully splitting, i.e. $l = d$, and $k = 4$, that the maximum probability for the coefficients of $c \bmod X^4 - \zeta^4$ is bounded by $2^{-31.4}$.

2.5   Module-SIS and Module-LWE Problems

We employ the computationally binding and computationally hiding commitment scheme from [BDL+18] in our protocols, and rely on the well-known Module-LWE (MLWE) and Module-SIS (MSIS) [PR06, LPR10, LS15] problems to prove the security of our constructions. Both problems are defined over a ring $\mathcal{R}_q$ for a positive modulus $q \in \mathbb{Z}^+$. For the Module-SIS problem we use the variant with respect to the infinity norm.

Definition 2.3 (MSIS$_{n,m,\beta_{\mathrm{SIS}}}$). *The goal in the Module-SIS problem with parameters $n, m > 0$ and $\beta_{\mathrm{SIS}} > q$ is to find, for a given matrix $\boldsymbol{A} \xleftarrow{\$} \mathcal{R}_q^{n \times m}$, $\vec{\boldsymbol{x}} \in \mathcal{R}_q^m$ such that $\boldsymbol{A}\vec{\boldsymbol{x}} = \vec{\boldsymbol{0}}$ over $\mathcal{R}_q$ and $0 < \|\vec{\boldsymbol{x}}\|_\infty \leq \beta_{\mathrm{SIS}}$. We say that a PPT adversary $\mathcal{A}$ has advantage ϵ in solving MSIS$_{n,m,\beta_{\mathrm{SIS}}}$ if*

$$\Pr\left[0 < \|\vec{\boldsymbol{x}}\|_\infty \leq \beta_{\mathrm{SIS}} \wedge \boldsymbol{A}\vec{\boldsymbol{x}} = \vec{\boldsymbol{0}} \text{ over } \mathcal{R}_q \;\middle|\; \boldsymbol{A} \xleftarrow{\$} \mathcal{R}_q^{n \times m}; \vec{\boldsymbol{x}} \leftarrow \mathcal{A}(\boldsymbol{A}) \right] \geq \epsilon.$$

Definition 2.4 (MLWE$_{n,m,\chi}$). *In the Module-LWE problem with parameters $n, m > 0$ and an error distribution χ over $\mathcal{R}$, the PPT adversary $\mathcal{A}$ is asked to distinguish $(\boldsymbol{A}, \vec{\boldsymbol{t}}) \xleftarrow{\$} \mathcal{R}_q^{m \times n} \times \mathcal{R}_q^m$ from $(\boldsymbol{A}, \boldsymbol{A}\vec{\boldsymbol{s}} + \vec{\boldsymbol{e}})$ for $\boldsymbol{A} \xleftarrow{\$} \mathcal{R}_q^{m \times n}$, a secret vector $\vec{\boldsymbol{s}} \xleftarrow{\$} \chi^n$ and error vector $\vec{\boldsymbol{e}} \xleftarrow{\$} \chi^m$. We say that $\mathcal{A}$ has advantage ϵ in solving MLWE$_{n,m,\chi}$ if*

$$\left| \Pr\left[b = 1 \;\middle|\; \boldsymbol{A} \xleftarrow{\$} \mathcal{R}_q^{m \times n}; \vec{\boldsymbol{s}} \xleftarrow{\$} \chi^n; \vec{\boldsymbol{e}} \xleftarrow{\$} \chi^m; b \leftarrow \mathcal{A}(\boldsymbol{A}, \boldsymbol{A}\vec{\boldsymbol{s}} + \vec{\boldsymbol{e}}) \right] \right. \tag{4}$$
$$\left. - \Pr\left[b = 1 \;\middle|\; \boldsymbol{A} \xleftarrow{\$} \mathcal{R}_q^{m \times n}; \vec{\boldsymbol{t}} \xleftarrow{\$} \mathcal{R}_q^m; b \leftarrow \mathcal{A}(\boldsymbol{A}, \vec{\boldsymbol{t}}) \right] \right| \geq \epsilon.$$

For our practical security estimations of these two problems against known attacks, the parameter m in both of the problems does not play a crucial role. Therefore, we sometimes simply omit m and use the notations $\mathsf{MSIS}_{n,B}$ and $\mathsf{MLWE}_{n,\chi}$. The parameters κ and λ denote the *module ranks* for MSIS and MLWE, respectively.

2.6   Error Distribution, Discrete Gaussians and Rejection Sampling

For sampling randomness in the commitment scheme that we use, and to define the particular variant of the Module-LWE problem that we use, we need to specify the error distribution χ^d on $\mathcal{R}$. In general any of the standard choices in the literature is fine. So, for example, χ can be a narrow discrete Gaussian distribution or the uniform distribution on a small interval. In the numerical examples in Sect. 4.2 we assume that χ is the computationally simple centered binomial distribution on $\{-1, 0, 1\}$ where ± 1 both have probability $5/16$ and 0 has probability $6/16$. This distribution is chosen (rather than the more "natural" uniform one) because it is easy to sample given a random bitstring by computing $a_1 + a_2 - b_1 - b_2 \bmod 3$ with uniformly random bits a_i, b_i.

Rejection Sampling. In our zero-knowledge proof, the prover will want to output a vector $\vec{z}$ whose distribution should be independent of a secret randomness vector $\vec{r}$, so that $\vec{z}$ cannot be used to gain any information on the prover's secret. During the protocol, the prover computes $\vec{z} = \vec{y} + c\vec{r}$ where $\vec{r}$ is the randomness used to commit to the prover's secret, $c \xleftarrow{\$} C$ is a challenge polynomial, and $\vec{y}$ is a "masking" vector. To remove the dependency of $\vec{z}$ on $\vec{r}$, we use the rejection sampling technique by Lyubashevsky [Lyu08, Lyu09, Lyu12]. In the two variants of this technique the masking vector is either sampled uniformly from some bounded region or using a discrete Gaussian distribution.

Although the Gaussian variant allows to sample $\vec{y}$ from narrower distributions for acceptable rejection rates, we use the uniform variant in this paper. The reasons for this are that, firstly, uniform sampling is much faster in implementations and much easier to protect against side-channel attacks, and, secondly, uniform sampling allows to be combined with the compression techniques from [BG14, DKL+18], which make up for the disadvantage concerning the width of the distribution.

The gist of uniform rejection sampling is the following. Let T be a bound on the infinity norm of $c\vec{r}$ and let the coefficients of the polynomials of $\vec{y}$ be sampled from the interval $[-\delta_1, \delta_1[$. Then, the conditioned distribution of the coefficients of $\vec{z}$ given that $\|\vec{z}\|_\infty < \delta_1 - T$ is the uniform distribution on $]-(\delta_1 - T), \delta_1 - T[$, independent of $c\vec{r}$.

2.7   Commitment Scheme

In our protocol, we use a variant of the commitment scheme from [BDL+18], which allows to commit to a vector of messages in $\mathcal{R}_q$. Suppose that we want to commit to a message vector $\vec{m} = (m_1, \ldots, m_l)^T \in \mathcal{R}_q^l$ and that module ranks of κ and λ are required for MSIS and MLWE security, respectively. Then, in the key generation, a uniformly random matrix $\boldsymbol{B}_0 \overset{\$}{\leftarrow} \mathcal{R}_q^{\kappa \times (\lambda+\kappa+l)}$ and vectors $\vec{b}_1, \ldots, \vec{b}_l \overset{\$}{\leftarrow} \mathcal{R}_q^{\lambda+\kappa+l}$ are generated and output as public parameters. In practice, one may choose to generate $\boldsymbol{B}_0, \vec{b}_1, \ldots, \vec{b}_l$ in a more structured way as in [BDL+18] since it saves some computation. However, for readability, we write the commitment matrices in the "Knapsack" form as above. In our case, the hiding property of the commitment scheme is established via the duality between the Knapsack and MLWE problems. We refer to [EZS+19, Appendix C] for a more detailed discussion.

To commit to the message $\vec{m}$, we first sample $\vec{r} \overset{\$}{\leftarrow} \chi^{(\lambda+\kappa+l)d}$. Now, there are two parts of the commitment scheme; the binding part and the message encoding part. Particularly, we compute

$$\vec{t}_0 = \boldsymbol{B}_0 \vec{r},$$
$$t_i = \langle \vec{b}_i, \vec{r} \rangle + m_i \quad \text{for } i = 1, \ldots, l,$$

where $\vec{t}_0$ forms the binding part and each t_i encodes a message polynomial m_i. The commitment scheme is computationally hiding under the Module-LWE assumption and computationally binding under the Module-SIS assumption; see [BDL+18].

The utility of the commitment scheme for zero-knowledge proof systems stems from the fact that one can compute module homomorphisms on committed messages. For example, let a_1 and a_2 be from $\mathcal{R}_q$. Then

$$a_1 t_1 + a_2 t_2 = \langle a_1 \vec{b}_1 + a_2 \vec{b}_2, \vec{r} \rangle + a_1 m_1 + a_2 m_2$$

is a commitment to the message $a_1 m_1 + a_2 m_2$ with matrix $a_1 \vec{b}_1 + a_2 \vec{b}_2$. This module homomorphic property together with a proof that a commitment is a commitment to the zero polynomial allows to prove linear relations among committed messages over $\mathcal{R}_q$.

2.8 Opening and Product Proof

We use the opening proof from [ALS20, Fig. 2] that we sketch now. Suppose that the prover knows an opening to the commitment

$$\vec{t}_0 = \boldsymbol{B}_0 \vec{r},$$
$$t_1 = \langle \vec{b}_1, \vec{r} \rangle + m_1.$$

As in previous opening proofs the prover gives an approximate proof for the first equation. To this end, the prover and verifier engage in k parallel executions of a sigma protocol with challenges $\sigma^i(c)$, $i = 0, \ldots, k-1$, that are the rotations of a global challenge $c \overset{\$}{\leftarrow} C$. Concretely, in the first flow, the prover samples k short masking vectors $\vec{y}_i$ from the discrete Gaussian distribution $D_s^{(\lambda+\kappa+1)d}$

and sends commitments $\vec{w}_i = B_0 \vec{y}_i$ over to the verifier. The verifier replies with the challenge c. Then the prover applies rejection sampling, and, if this does not reject, sends $\vec{z}_i = \vec{y}_i + \sigma^i(c)\vec{r}$. The verifier checks that the $\vec{z}_i$ are short and the equations $B_0 \vec{z}_i = \vec{w}_i + \sigma^i(c)\vec{t}_0$.

Now, unlike in previous protocols, the algebraic setup is such that it is not possible to extract a pair of accepting transcript with invertible challenge difference $\bar{c} = c - c'$. Instead, extraction works by piecing together l/k accepting transcripts where for each ideal $(X^{kd/l} - \zeta^{kj})$, there is a transcript pair with challenge difference $\bar{c}_j \bmod (X^{kd/l} - \zeta^{kj}) \neq 0$. For this to work out it is required that the maximum probability p over $\mathbb{Z}_q$ of the coefficients of $c \bmod (X^{kd/l} - \zeta^k)$, as given by Lemma 2.2, is such that $p^{kd/l}$ is negligible. For example, if $d = 128$, $q \approx 2^{32}$ fully splits so that $l = d$, and $k = 4$, then $p^{kd/l} = p^4 \approx 2^{-128}$.

Next, the analysis of the protocol given in [ALS20, Theorem 4.4] shows that it is possible to extract a weak opening from a prover with non-negligible high success probability, as given in the following definition.

Definition 2.5. *A weak opening for the commitment $\vec{t} = \vec{t}_0 \parallel t_1$ consists of l polynomials $\sigma^i(\bar{c}_j) \in \mathcal{R}_q$, a randomness vector $\vec{r}^*$ over $\mathcal{R}_q$ and a message $m_1^* \in \mathcal{R}_q$ such that*

$$\left\| \sigma^i(\bar{c}_j) \right\|_1 \leq 2d \text{ and } \sigma^i(\bar{c}_j) \bmod \sigma^i(X^{d/l} - \zeta^j) \neq 0 \text{ for all } (i,j) \in I,$$

$$\left\| \sigma^i(\bar{c}_j)\vec{r}^* \right\|_2 \leq 2\beta \text{ for all } (i,j) \in I,$$

$$B_0 \vec{r}^* = \vec{t}_0,$$

$$\langle \vec{b}_1, \vec{r}^* \rangle + m_1^* = t_1.$$

The commitment scheme is binding with respect to weak openings, c.f. [ALS20, Lemma 4.3]. Furthermore, in the extraction it is also possible to obtain vectors $\vec{y}_i^*$ such that every accepting transcript satisfies the following

$$\vec{z}_i = \vec{y}^* + \sigma^i(c)\vec{r}^*,$$

when it contains the same prover commitments $\vec{w}_i$ that were used in the extraction.

We also apply the product proof from [ALS20, Fig. 4], adapted to the case of a cubic relation, to prove that our secret vector has ternary coefficients. In addition to the opening proof, the product proof only requires two additional commitments to garbage terms.

3   Proving Unstructured Linear Relations over $\mathbb{Z}_q^n$

Our goal for this section is to construct an efficient protocol for proving unstructured linear relations among committed $\mathbb{Z}_q$-elements. By this we mean that we want to be able to commit to a vector $\vec{s} \in \mathbb{Z}_q^n$ and prove that it fulfills an arbitrary linear equation $A\vec{s} = \vec{u}$ for a public matrix $A \in \mathbb{Z}_q^{m \times n}$ and vector

$\vec{u} \in \mathbb{Z}_q^m$. We borrow LWE terminology and call the linear equation "unstructured" to highlight the fact that A can be an arbitrary matrix over $\mathbb{Z}_q$ that does not necessarily express linear relations over some ring of higher rank.

Proofs of linear relations are useful for applications in lattice cryptography only if it is possible to amend them by a proof of shortness. So, we will also want to be able to prove that the vector $\vec{s}$ is short. As opposed to the so-called *approximate* proofs that are ubiquitous in lattice cryptography and where the prover only proves knowledge of a vector that is much longer than the one it actually knows, we are interested in *exact* proofs of shortness. These have the advantage that the parameters of underlying cryptographic schemes do not have to account for the longer vectors that can be extracted from a prover, i.e. the schemes do not need to be secure with respect to the longer vectors. This results in more efficient schemes. For example, one interesting goal of this line of research is to construct a proof of plaintext knowledge or a verifiable encryption scheme for a standard unmodified lattice-based public-key encryption scheme. In particular, for one of the schemes submitted to the NIST PQC standardization effort.

The most efficient lattice-based exact proofs of shortness work by encoding the vector $\vec{s}$ in the NTT representations $\mathsf{NTT}(\check{s}_i)$ of possibly several polynomials $\check{s}_i \in \mathcal{R}_q$. In the first step, we restrict to the case where q splits completely in $\mathcal{R}$. Then $\mathsf{NTT}(\check{s}_i)$ is a vector in $\mathbb{Z}_q^d$.

Now, for simplicity, assume that n is divisible by d. Suppose the prover $\mathcal{P}$ knows an opening to a commitment $\vec{t} = \vec{t}_0 \parallel t_1 \parallel \cdots \parallel t_{n/d}$ to n/d secret polynomials $\check{s}_1, \ldots, \check{s}_{n/d} \in \mathcal{R}_q$. More precisely,

$$\vec{t}_0 = \boldsymbol{B}_0 \vec{r},$$
$$t_i = \langle \vec{b}_i, \vec{r} \rangle + \check{s}_i \text{ for } i \in \{1, \ldots, n/d\}.$$

Then, the goal of $\mathcal{P}$ is to prove that the vector

$$\vec{s} = \mathsf{NTT}(\check{s}_1) \parallel \cdots \parallel \mathsf{NTT}(\check{s}_{n/d}) \in \mathbb{Z}_q^n$$

satisfies the linear equation $A\vec{s} = \vec{u}$ over $\mathbb{Z}_q$ where $A \in \mathbb{Z}_q^{m \times n}$ and $\vec{u} \in \mathbb{Z}_q^m$ are public.

Firstly, we describe the main ideas and present a protocol which achieves soundness error $1/q$. Then, in Sect. 3.2 and [ENS20, Appendix A] we present two methods to efficiently decrease the soundness error to negligible quantities. The latter one, however, is only interesting when the secret vector $\vec{s}$ is strictly shorter than d. In that case, we make use of non-fully splitting rings $\mathcal{R}_q$.

Although we present all of our protocols so that only *non-aborting* protocol transcripts are simulatable, there is a standard generic method to simulate aborts of an *interactive* protocol as given in [BCK+14], which is also used, e.g., in [ESS+19]. In particular, for all but the last move of the prover, the prover sends $\mathsf{aCom}(M)$ instead of the transmitted text M for an auxiliary commitment aCom. In the last move, all of these committed texts are revealed unless aborted. In the case of abort, the prover just sends an error message $\perp$. The abort can easily

be simulated in this case by relying on the hiding property of aCom. We refer
to [BCK+14, ESS+19] for more details. Also, note that the simulation of aborts
is not important for most of the practical applications as the protocol is made
non-interactive and the simulation of aborts is not needed in that case.

3.1   Basic Protocol

Let us assume that $n = d$ and denote $\check{s} := \check{s}_1$. We show how to deal with the case
$n > d$ in Sect. 3.3. The first protocol relies on the following simple observation.
Suppose that $A\vec{s} = \vec{u}$. This means that for all $\vec{\gamma} \in \mathbb{Z}_q^m$, we have $\langle A\vec{s} - \vec{u}, \vec{\gamma} \rangle = 0$.
On the contrary, if $A\vec{s} \neq \vec{u}$, then for a uniformly random $\vec{\gamma} \in \mathbb{Z}_q^m$, $\langle A\vec{s} - \vec{u}, \vec{\gamma} \rangle = 0$
only with probability $1/q$. Hence, $\vec{\gamma}$ will become a challenge generated from the
verifier. Using Lemma 2.1, we rewrite the inner product,

$$\langle A\vec{s} - \vec{u}, \vec{\gamma} \rangle = \langle A\vec{s}, \vec{\gamma} \rangle - \langle \vec{u}, \vec{\gamma} \rangle = \langle \vec{s}, A^T\vec{\gamma} \rangle - \langle \vec{u}, \vec{\gamma} \rangle$$

$$= \sum_{j \in \mathbb{Z}_{2d}^\times} s(\zeta^j)\left(\mathsf{NTT}^{-1}(A^T\vec{\gamma})\right)(\zeta^j) - \langle \vec{u}, \vec{\gamma} \rangle = \frac{1}{d}\sum_{j \in \mathbb{Z}_{2d}^\times} f(\zeta^j) = f_0,$$

where $f \in \mathcal{R}_q$ is the polynomial defined by $f := \mathsf{NTT}^{-1}(dA^T\vec{\gamma})\check{s} - \langle \vec{u}, \vec{\gamma} \rangle$ and
$f_0 \in \mathbb{Z}_q$ is the constant coefficient of f. So, by utilizing the polynomial product
in $\mathcal{R}_q$, it is possible to compute a scalar product over $\mathbb{Z}_q$ with a vector encoded
in the NTT representation of the polynomial. We observe that the verifier can
compute a commitment to f. Indeed, note that

$$\mathsf{NTT}^{-1}(dA^T\vec{\gamma})t_1 - \langle \vec{u}, \vec{\gamma} \rangle = \langle \mathsf{NTT}^{-1}(dA^T\vec{\gamma})\vec{b_1}, \vec{r} \rangle + f.$$

Hence, $\mathcal{V}$ can compute the commitment

$$\tau = \mathsf{NTT}^{-1}(dA^T\vec{\gamma})t_1 - \langle \vec{u}, \vec{\gamma} \rangle. \tag{5}$$

Now, $\mathcal{P}$ needs to prove that f has a zero constant coefficient. The idea is to first
send a commitment t_2 to a random polynomial g with a zero constant coefficient
before $\vec{\gamma}$ is generated. Intuitively, g is introduced to mask f. After getting $\vec{\gamma}$, $\mathcal{P}$
sends $h = f + g$ and the verifier can check that $h_0 = 0$. Note that by knowing
τ, t_2 and h, the verifier can compute a commitment $\tau + t_2 - h$ to the zero
polynomial $\mathbf{0}$. Hence, in the final stage, $\mathcal{P}$ needs to prove that this polynomial
is indeed a commitment to $\mathbf{0}$ in the usual way.

The full protocol is presented as follows. First, the prover $\mathcal{P}$ generates a
random polynomial $g \in \mathcal{R}_q$ with zero constant coefficient and computes a commitment to g defined as $t_2 = \langle \vec{b}_2, \vec{r} \rangle + g$. The prover also starts the opening
proof with soundness error $1/q$ for the commitments and samples a vector of
small polynomials $\vec{y}$ and computes the commitment $\vec{w} = B_0\vec{y}$. Then, $\mathcal{P}$ sends
t_2 and $\vec{w}$ to the verifier. Next, $\mathcal{V}$ generates and sends a uniformly random vector
$\vec{\gamma} \in \mathbb{Z}_q^m$. $\mathcal{P}$ can then compute the polynomial f defined above and $h = f + g$.

Furthermore, it sets $v = \langle \mathsf{NTT}^{-1}(dA^T\vec{\gamma})\vec{b_1} + \vec{b_2}, \vec{y}\rangle$ and sends h, v to $\mathcal{V}$. Then, the verifier generates a challenge $c \xleftarrow{\$} C$ and sends it to the prover. Eventually, $\mathcal{P}$ sends a response $\vec{z} = \vec{y} + c\vec{r}$.

The verifier $\mathcal{V}$ first checks that $\vec{z}$ consists of small polynomials and that h has constant coefficient equal to 0. Also, $\mathcal{V}$ checks that $B_0\vec{z} = \vec{w} + c\vec{t_0}$ and

$$\langle \mathsf{NTT}^{-1}(dA^T\vec{\gamma})\vec{b_1} + \vec{b_2}, \vec{z}\rangle = v + c\,(\tau + t_2 - h)$$

where τ is computed as in Eq. (5).

One can observe that if $A\vec{s} \neq \vec{u}$ then the constant coefficient of f becomes a uniformly random element of $\mathbb{Z}_q$, outside the control of the prover. Thus, also the constant coefficient of $h = f + g$ will be uniformly random because the constant coefficient of g is independent of the constant coefficient of f. In particular, it will be non-zero with probability $1 - 1/q$ and this can be detected by the verifier. Therefore, the probability that a malicious prover manages to cheat is essentially $1/q$.

3.2 Boosting Soundness by Mapping Down

More abstractly, in the above protocol we checked $\langle A\vec{s} - \vec{u}, \vec{\gamma}\rangle = 0$ by investigating whether $\mathsf{L}(\vec{\gamma})$ has a zero constant coefficient where $\mathsf{L} : \mathbb{Z}_q^m \to \mathcal{R}_q$ is defined as

$$\mathsf{L}(\vec{\gamma}) := \mathsf{NTT}^{-1}(dA^T\vec{\gamma})\check{s} - \langle \vec{u}, \vec{\gamma}\rangle. \tag{6}$$

As we observed earlier, the constant coefficient of $\mathsf{L}(\vec{\gamma})$ is indeed $\langle A\vec{s} - \vec{u}, \vec{\gamma}\rangle$.

Now, suppose we can define k functions $\mathsf{L}_0, \ldots, \mathsf{L}_{k-1}$ with the following property. For any $0 \leq \mu < k$ and $\vec{\gamma}_\mu \in \mathbb{Z}_q^m$, $p = \mathsf{L}_\mu(\vec{\gamma}_\mu) \in \mathcal{R}_q$ is a polynomial such that $p_0 = \ldots = p_{\mu-1} = p_{\mu+1} = \ldots = p_{k-1} = 0$ and $p_\mu = \langle A\vec{s} - \vec{u}, \vec{\gamma}_\mu\rangle$. This would mean that for $0 \leq \mu < k$, the μ-th coefficient related to X^μ of the polynomial

$$f = \mathsf{L}_0(\vec{\gamma}_0) + \mathsf{L}_1(\vec{\gamma}_1) + \ldots + \mathsf{L}_{k-1}(\vec{\gamma}_{k-1})$$

is equal to $\langle A\vec{s} - \vec{u}, \vec{\gamma}_\mu\rangle$. In particular, if $A\vec{s} = \vec{u}$, then $f_0 = f_1 = \ldots = f_{k-1} = 0$. Thus, in order to decrease the soundness error, we can let the verifier $\mathcal{V}$ send k independently uniformly random vectors $\vec{\gamma}_0, \ldots, \vec{\gamma}_{k-1}$ and then $\mathcal{P}$ proves that $f \in \mathcal{R}_q$ has the first k coefficients equal to zero. Note that we still need to find a way for $\mathcal{V}$ to compute a commitment to f from $\vec{t_1}$ and $\vec{\gamma}_0, \ldots, \vec{\gamma}_{k-1}$.

Constructing L_μ. Let $\mathcal{S}_q$ be the $\mathbb{Z}_q$-submodule of $\mathcal{R}_q$ generated by X^k, i.e.

$$\mathcal{S}_q = \{p_0 + p_1 X^k + \cdots + p_{d/k-1} X^{d-k} \in \mathcal{R}_q\} \subset \mathcal{R}_q.$$

We have $\mathcal{S}_q \cong \mathbb{Z}_q[X]/(X^{d/k} + 1)$. From Galois theory, there is a corresponding subgroup H of $\mathsf{Aut}(\mathcal{R}_q)$ of order k such that $\sigma(p) = p$ for all $\sigma \in H$ if and only if $p \in \mathcal{S}_q$. It is easy to see that this group is generated by $\sigma = \sigma_{2d/k+1} \in \mathsf{Aut}(\mathcal{R}_q)$, which is the same automorphism that we use in the automorphism opening proof. In fact, this follows from the fact that $\mathrm{ord}(\sigma) = k$ and $\sigma(X^k) = X^{k(2d/k+1)} = X^k$.

We have the trace map $\mathsf{Tr}\colon \mathcal{R}_q \to \mathcal{S}_q$ given by

$$\mathsf{Tr}(\boldsymbol{p}) = \sum_{\nu=0}^{k-1} \sigma^\nu(\boldsymbol{p}).$$

Notice that the constant coefficient of $\mathsf{Tr}(\boldsymbol{p})$ is equal to kp_0. Now define L_μ by

$$\mathsf{L}_\mu(\vec{\gamma}) = \frac{1}{k} X^\mu \mathsf{Tr}(\mathsf{L}(\vec{\gamma})) = \frac{1}{k} X^\mu \sum_{\nu=0}^{k-1} \sigma^\nu \left(\mathsf{NTT}^{-1}(dA^T\vec{\gamma})\check{s} - \langle \vec{u}, \vec{\gamma} \rangle \right).$$

If $\boldsymbol{p} = \mathsf{L}_\mu(\vec{\gamma})$, then $\boldsymbol{p}$ is of the form

$$\boldsymbol{p} = p_\mu X^\mu + p_{k+\mu} X^{k+\mu} + \cdots + p_{d-k+\mu} X^{d-k+\mu}$$

and thus has the property that the first k coefficients except the μ-th coefficient are zero. Moreover, it is clear from above that $p_\mu = \langle A\vec{s} - \vec{u}, \vec{\gamma} \rangle$.

Finally, given the commitment $\boldsymbol{t}_1$ to $\boldsymbol{s}$, the verifier can compute a commitment to $\boldsymbol{f} = \mathsf{L}_0(\vec{\gamma}_0) + \cdots + \mathsf{L}_{k-1}(\vec{\gamma}_{k-1})$ via

$$
\begin{aligned}
\boldsymbol{\tau} &= \sum_{\mu=0}^{k-1} \frac{1}{k} X^\mu \sum_{\nu=0}^{k-1} \sigma^\nu \left(\mathsf{NTT}^{-1}(dA^T\vec{\gamma}_\mu)\boldsymbol{t}_1 - \langle \vec{u}, \vec{\gamma}_\mu \rangle \right) \\
&= \sum_{\mu=0}^{k-1} \frac{1}{k} X^\mu \sum_{\nu=0}^{k-1} \sigma^\nu \left(\langle \mathsf{NTT}^{-1}(dA^T\vec{\gamma}_\mu)\vec{b}_1, \vec{r} \rangle \right) + \boldsymbol{f}.
\end{aligned}
\tag{7}
$$

The Protocol. We present the full protocol in Fig. 1 with the verification algorithm given in Fig. 2.

It is natural to separate the commitment $(\vec{t}_0, \boldsymbol{t}_1)$ to the secret polynomial $\check{s}$ from our protocol for proving the linear relation. Then, $(\vec{t}_0, \boldsymbol{t}_1)$ is given as input to the protocol, which also proves knowledge of an opening to the external commitment. Now, for efficiency reasons, one wants to avoid sending a completely fresh commitment to the masking polynomial $\boldsymbol{g}$ and instead reuse the top part $\vec{t}_0$ of the commitment to $\check{s}$, but this creates a problem with the standard notion of a zero-knowledge proof. Namely, with this approach it is required that the randomness vector $\vec{r}$, which is a part of the witness, is really random so that the commitment to $\boldsymbol{g}$ is hiding, but the zero-knowledge definition demands simulatability for any (fixed) witness. Hence, we don't take this approach and also send the commitment to $\check{s}$ as part of our protocol. Then, our protocol only shows knowledge of a solution $\vec{s}$ to the linear equation $A\vec{s} = \vec{u}$. This in itself is not a solution to a hard problem but our protocol is still useful because it can be combined with a shortness proof that simultaneously shows that $\vec{s}$ is short (see Sect. 4). In isolation our protocol is best viewed as a so-called commit-and-proof protocol [CLOS02], which is interesting even without involving a hard problem because of the commitment that can later be used outside of the protocol.

The Prover $\mathcal{P}$ starts by generating a uniformly random polynomial g satisfying $g_0 = \ldots = g_{k-1} = 0$ and then computes the commitment

$$\vec{t}_0 = B_0 \vec{r}$$
$$t_1 = \langle \vec{b}_1, \vec{r} \rangle + \check{s}$$
$$t_2 = \langle \vec{b}_2, \vec{r} \rangle + g.$$

Now the prover needs to start an opening proof with soundness $1/q^k$. Also, it is going to prove a relation which involves the k automorphisms σ^i. Therefore, it uses the automorphism opening proof from [ALS20] and samples vectors $\vec{y}_0, \ldots, \vec{y}_{k-1}$ of short polynomials that are going to be used to mask $\vec{r}$ k times with challenges of the form $\sigma^i(c)$. Also, $\mathcal{P}$ computes $\vec{w}_i = B_0 \vec{y}_i$. The prover sends $\vec{t}_0$, t_1, t_2 and $\vec{w}_i$ to $\mathcal{V}$.

Next, the verifier selects uniformly random vectors $\vec{\gamma}_0, \ldots, \vec{\gamma}_{k-1} \in \mathbb{Z}_q^m$ and sends them to $\mathcal{P}$. Then, the prover computes

$$f = \sum_{\mu=0}^{k-1} L_\mu(\vec{\gamma}_\mu) = \sum_{\mu=0}^{k-1} \frac{1}{k} X^\mu \sum_{\nu=0}^{k-1} \sigma^\nu \left(\mathsf{NTT}^{-1}(dA^T \vec{\gamma}_\mu)\check{s} - \langle \vec{u}, \vec{\gamma}_\mu \rangle \right).$$

By construction, $f_0 = \ldots = f_{k-1} = 0$. Note that $\mathcal{V}$ can compute a commitment τ to f as explained above. Now the prover sets $h = f + g$ and computes for $i = 0, \ldots, k-1$,

$$v_i = \sum_{\mu=0}^{k-1} \frac{1}{k} X^\mu \sum_{\nu=0}^{k-1} \sigma^\nu \left(\langle \mathsf{NTT}^{-1}(dA^T \vec{\gamma}_\mu)\vec{b}_1, \vec{y}_{i-\nu \bmod k} \rangle \right) + \langle \vec{b}_2, \vec{y}_i \rangle.$$

It sends h and $v_0, \ldots, v_{k-1}$. The verifier sends a random challenge polynomial $c \xleftarrow{\$} C$. Eventually, $\mathcal{P}$ computes $\vec{z}_i = \vec{y}_i + \sigma^i(c)\vec{r}$ for $i = 0, \ldots, k-1$ and sends $\vec{z}_0, \ldots, \vec{z}_{k-1}$.

The Verifier $\mathcal{V}$ first checks that for all $i = 0, \ldots, k-1$, $\vec{z}_i$ is short, and

$$B_0 \vec{z}_i = \vec{w}_i + \sigma^i(c)\vec{t}_0.$$

Then, $\mathcal{V}$ checks that $h_0, \ldots, h_{k-1}$ are all equal to zero and computes τ as in (7). Finally, the verifier checks whether for all $i = 0, \ldots, k-1$,

$$\sum_{\mu=0}^{k-1} \frac{1}{k} X^\mu \sum_{\nu=0}^{k-1} \sigma^\nu \left(\langle \mathsf{NTT}^{-1}(dA^T \vec{\gamma}_\mu)\vec{b}_1, \vec{z}_{i-\nu \bmod k} \rangle \right) + \langle \vec{b}_2, \vec{z}_i \rangle$$
$$= v_i + \sigma^i(c)(\tau + t_2 - h)$$

to test whether $\tau + t_2 - h$ really is a commitment to zero.

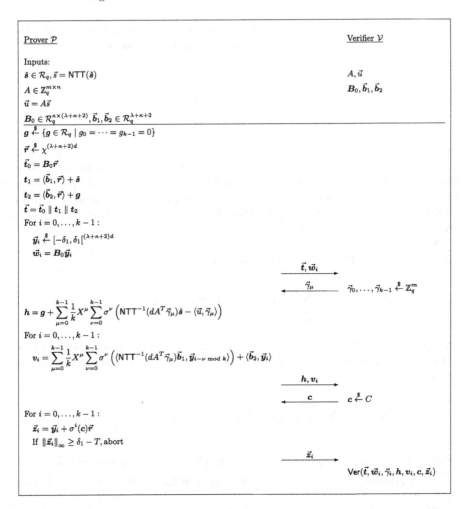

Fig. 1. Automorphism proof of knowledge of a solution to an unstructured linear equation over $\mathbb{Z}_q$. Verification equations are described in Fig. 2.

Security Analysis

Theorem 3.1. *The protocol in Fig. 1 is complete, computational honest verifier zero-knowledge under the Module-LWE assumption and computational special sound under the Module-SIS assumption. More precisely, let p be the maximum probability over $\mathbb{Z}_q$ of the coefficients of c mod $X^k - \zeta^k$ as in Lemma 2.2.*

Then, for completeness, unless the honest prover $\mathcal{P}$ aborts due to the rejection sampling, it always convinces the honest verifier $\mathcal{V}$.

For zero-knowledge, there exists a simulator $\mathcal{S}$, that, without access to secret information, outputs a simulation of a non-aborting transcript of the protocol between $\mathcal{P}$ and $\mathcal{V}$ for every statement $A\vec{s} = \vec{u}$. Then for every algorithm $\mathcal{A}$ that has advantage ε in distinguishing the simulated transcript from an actual tran-

$$\begin{array}{l}
\hline
\mathsf{Ver}(\vec{t}, \vec{w}_i, \vec{\gamma}_i, h, v_i, c, \vec{z}_i) \\
\hline
01 \ \text{For } i = 0, \ldots, k-1: \\
02 \quad \|\vec{z}_i\|_\infty \overset{?}{<} \beta = \delta_1 - T \\
03 \quad B_0\vec{z}_i \overset{?}{=} \vec{w}_i + \sigma^i(c)\vec{t}_0 \\
04 \ h_0 \overset{?}{=} \ldots \overset{?}{=} h_{k-1} \overset{?}{=} 0 \\
05 \ \tau = \sum_{\mu=0}^{k-1} \frac{1}{k} X^\mu \sum_{\nu=0}^{k-1} \sigma^\nu \left(\mathsf{NTT}^{-1}(dA^T\vec{\gamma}_\mu)t_1 - \langle \vec{u}, \vec{\gamma}_\mu \rangle\right) \\
06 \ \text{For } i = 0, \ldots, k-1: \\
07 \quad \sum_{\mu=0}^{k-1} \frac{1}{k} X^\mu \sum_{\nu=0}^{k-1} \sigma^\nu \left((\mathsf{NTT}^{-1}(dA^T\vec{\gamma}_\mu)b_1, \vec{z}_{i-\nu \bmod k})\right) + \langle \vec{b}_2, \vec{z}_i \rangle \overset{?}{=} v_i + \sigma^i(c)(\tau + t_2 - h) \\
\hline
\end{array}$$

Fig. 2. Verification equations for Fig. 1.

script, there is an algorithm $\mathcal{A}'$ with the same running time that has advantage ε in distinguishing $\mathsf{MLWE}_{\lambda,\chi}$.

For soundness, there is an extractor $\mathcal{E}$ with the following properties. When given rewindable black-box access to a deterministic prover $\mathcal{P}^*$ that sends the commitment $\vec{t}$ in the first round and convinces $\mathcal{V}$ with probability $\varepsilon \geq q^{-k} + p^k$, $\mathcal{E}$ either outputs a weak opening for $\vec{t}$ with message $\check{s}^*$ such that $\mathsf{ANTT}(\check{s}^*) = \vec{u}$, or a $\mathsf{MSIS}_{\kappa, 8d\beta}$ solution for B_0 in expected time at most $1/\varepsilon + (d/k)(\varepsilon - p^k)^{-1}$ when running $\mathcal{P}^*$ once is assumed to take unit time.

Proof. Completeness. It follows by careful inspection that the verification equations are always true for the messages sent by $\mathcal{P}$.

Zero-Knowledge. We can simulate a non-aborting transcript between the honest prover and the honest verifier in the following way. First, in a non-aborting transcript the vectors $\vec{z}_i$ are independently uniformly random in $] - (\delta_1 - T), \delta_1 - T[^{(\lambda+\kappa+2)d}$ and also independent from $c\vec{r}$. So the simulator can just sample $\vec{z}_i \overset{\$}{\leftarrow}] - (\delta_1 - T), \delta_1 - T[^{(\lambda+\kappa+2)d}$ and $c \overset{\$}{\leftarrow} C$. The polynomial h is such that $h_0 = \cdots = h_{k-1} = 0$ in honest transcripts and the other coefficients are uniformly random because of the additive term g. Hence, the simulator samples $h \overset{\$}{\leftarrow} \{h \in \mathcal{R}_q \mid h_0 = \cdots = h_{k-1} = 0\}$. Then, the challenges $\vec{\gamma}_\mu \in \mathbb{Z}_q^m$ are independently uniformly random and the simulator samples them in this way. Now, we turn to the commitment $\vec{t}$. In the honest execution the randomness vector $\vec{r}$ is statistically independent from the $\vec{z}_i$ and the other messages already handled, i.e. $c, h, \vec{\gamma}_\mu$. So, it follows that the additive term $B_0\vec{r} \parallel \langle \vec{b}_1, \vec{r} \rangle \parallel \langle \vec{b}_2, \vec{r} \rangle$ is indistinguishable from uniform given $\vec{z}_i, c, h, \vec{\gamma}_\mu$ if MLWE_λ is hard. Hence $\vec{t}$ is indistinguishable from uniform since the committed polynomials $\check{s}$ and g are also independent from $\vec{r}$ in the honest execution. Therefore, we let the simulator sample a uniformly random $\vec{t} \in \mathcal{R}_q^{\kappa+2}$. Now, in an honest transcript, the remaining messages $\vec{w}_i$ and v_i are all uniquely determined from the already handled messages and the verification equations because of completeness. We see that if the simulator computes these messages so that the verification equations become true, then the resulting transcript is indistinguishable from the honest transcript. More precisely, if there exists some distinguisher that is able to distinguish a simulated transcript from an honest transcript, then it must be able to distinguish the MLWE samples in the commitment $\vec{t}$ from uniform with the same advantage.

Soundness. First, the extractor opens the commitments t_1 and t_2. From [ALS20, Theorem 4.4], unless $\mathcal{E}$ finds an $\mathsf{MSIS}_{\kappa,8d\beta}$ solution, the extractor can compute vectors $\vec{y}^*$ and $\vec{r}^*$ such that for every accepting transcript with first messages t_2 and $\vec{w}_i$,

$$z_i = \vec{y}_i^* + \sigma^i(c)\vec{r}^*.$$

The expected runtime for this equals the runtime in the theorem statement. Then let $\check{s}^* \in \mathcal{R}_q$ and $g^* \in \mathcal{R}_q$ be the extracted messages, which are defined by

$$t_1 = \langle \vec{b}_1, \vec{r}^* \rangle + \check{s}^* \text{ and } t_2 = \langle \vec{b}_2, \vec{r}^* \rangle + g^*.$$

Now substituting these expressions into τ gives

$$\tau = \sum_{\mu=0}^{k-1} \frac{1}{k} X^\mu \sum_{\nu=0}^{k-1} \sigma^\nu \left(\langle \mathsf{NTT}^{-1}(dA^T \vec{\gamma}_\mu)\vec{b}_1, \vec{r}^* \rangle \right) + f^*,$$

where

$$f^* = \sum_{\mu=0}^{k-1} \frac{1}{k} X^\mu \sum_{\nu=0}^{k-1} \sigma^\nu \left(\mathsf{NTT}^{-1}(dA^T \vec{\gamma}_\mu)\check{s}^* - \langle \vec{u}, \vec{\gamma}_\mu \rangle \right).$$

From the discussion in this section we know that $f_\mu^* = \langle A\vec{s}^* - \vec{u}, \vec{\gamma}_\mu \rangle$ for $\mu = 0, \ldots, k-1$, $\vec{s}^* = \mathsf{NTT}(\check{s}^*)$. Next we find from the last verification equations,

$$\left(\sum_{\mu=0}^{k-1} \frac{1}{k} X^\mu \sum_{\nu=0}^{k-1} \sigma^\nu \left(\langle \mathsf{NTT}^{-1}(dA^T \vec{\gamma}_\mu)\vec{b}_1, \vec{y}_{i-\nu \bmod k}^* \rangle \right) + \langle \vec{b}_2, \vec{y}^* \rangle - v_i \right)$$
$$= \sigma^i(c) \left(f^* + g^* - h \right). \tag{8}$$

for all $i = 0, \ldots, k-1$. The coefficients of these linear polynomials in $\sigma^i(c)$ are independent from c in a random accepting transcript. We bound the success probability ε of the prover under the assumption $A\vec{s}^* \neq \vec{u}$. In this case the coefficients f_μ^* for $\mu = 0, \ldots, k-1$ are uniformly random elements in $\mathbb{Z}_q$ in a random transcript. Hence, $f_\mu^* + g_\mu^*$ is uniformly random since g^* is independent from the $\vec{\gamma}_\mu$. Also we know that $h_\mu = 0$ in every accepting transcript. So, suppose $f_\mu^* + g_\mu^* - h_\mu^* = f_\mu^* + g_\mu^* \neq 0$ for some μ. Then there exists some $j \in \mathbb{Z}_{2d}^\times$ with $f^* + g^* - h \bmod (X - \zeta^j) \neq 0$. Therefore, there is only one possible value modulo $(X^k - \zeta^{jk})$ for the challenge in such a transcript, otherwise Eq. 8 cannot be true for all i. Since the maximum probability of every coefficient of $c \bmod (X^k - \zeta^{jk})$ is less than p we see that the success probability is bounded by

$$\varepsilon = \Pr[\text{accepting}] < \left(\frac{1}{q} \right)^k + \Pr\left[\text{accepting} \mid f_\mu^* + g_\mu^* \neq 0 \text{ for some } \mu\right]$$
$$\leq \left(\frac{1}{q} \right)^k + p^k.$$

This is in contradiction to the bound in the theorem statement and thus it must hold $A\vec{s}^* = \vec{u}$. $\qquad\square$

3.3   General Case

Previously, we assumed that $n = d$ so that $\vec{s} = \mathsf{NTT}(\check{s}) = \mathsf{NTT}(\check{s}_1)$. When $n > d$, we slightly modify our approach. We have $\vec{s} = \mathsf{NTT}(\check{s}_1) \parallel \cdots \parallel \mathsf{NTT}(\check{s}_{n/d})$ and now also define polynomials ψ_j such that

$$A^T \vec{\gamma} = \mathsf{NTT}(\psi_1) \parallel \cdots \parallel \mathsf{NTT}(\psi_{n/d}).$$

Then the inner product $\langle A\vec{s}, \vec{\gamma} \rangle = \langle \vec{s}, A^T\vec{\gamma} \rangle$ can be written as a sum of smaller inner products. We find

$$\langle A\vec{s} - \vec{u}, \vec{\gamma} \rangle = \sum_{j=1}^{n/d} \langle \mathsf{NTT}(\check{s}_j), \mathsf{NTT}(\psi_j) \rangle - \langle \vec{u}, \vec{\gamma} \rangle$$

$$= \sum_{j=1}^{n/d} \sum_{i \in \mathbb{Z}_{2d}^\times} \check{s}_j(\zeta^i) \psi_j(\zeta^i) - \langle \vec{u}, \vec{\gamma} \rangle = \frac{1}{d} \sum_{i \in \mathbb{Z}_{2d}^\times} \left(\sum_{j=1}^{n/d} d\check{s}_j \psi_j - \langle \vec{u}, \vec{\gamma} \rangle \right) (\zeta^i).$$

Next, similarly as before, we incorporate more challenges. So, for $\vec{\gamma}_0, \ldots, \vec{\gamma}_{k-1} \in \mathbb{Z}_q^m$ we write

$$A^T \vec{\gamma}_\mu = \mathsf{NTT}(\psi_1^{(\mu)}) \parallel \cdots \parallel \mathsf{NTT}(\psi_{n/d}^{(\mu)})$$

and then set

$$f = \sum_{\mu=0}^{k-1} \frac{1}{k} X^\mu \sum_{\nu=0}^{k-1} \sigma^\nu \left(\sum_{j=1}^{n/d} d\psi_j^{(\mu)} s_j - \langle \vec{u}, \vec{\gamma}_\mu \rangle \right).$$

It holds that for $\mu = 0, \ldots, k-1$, $f_\mu = \langle A\vec{s} - \vec{u}, \vec{\gamma}_\mu \rangle$. Now, note that τ defined as

$$\tau = \sum_{\mu=0}^{k-1} \frac{1}{k} X^\mu \sum_{\nu=0}^{k-1} \sigma^\nu \left(\sum_{j=1}^{n/d} d\psi_j^{(\mu)} t_j - \langle \vec{u}, \vec{\gamma}_\mu \rangle \right)$$

$$= \sum_{\mu=0}^{k-1} \frac{1}{k} X^\mu \sum_{\nu=0}^{k-1} \sigma^\nu \left(\sum_{j=1}^{n/d} \langle d\psi_j^{(\mu)} \vec{b}_j, \vec{r} \rangle + d\psi_j^{(\mu)} \check{s}_j - \langle \vec{u}, \vec{\gamma} \rangle \right)$$

$$= \sum_{\mu=0}^{k-1} \frac{1}{k} X^\mu \sum_{\nu=0}^{k-1} \sigma^\nu \left(\left\langle \sum_{j=1}^{n/d} d\psi_j^{(\mu)} \vec{b}_j, \vec{r} \right\rangle \right) + f$$

is indeed a commitment to f and can be computed by the verifier.

4   Main Protocol

In this section we present our main protocol for proving knowledge of a ternary solution $\vec{s} \in \{-1, 0, 1\}^n$ to an arbitrary linear equation $A\vec{s} = \vec{u}$ over $\mathbb{Z}_q$. The protocol is essentially an amalgamation of the linear proof from Sect. 3 and the product proof from [ALS20]. We use a fully splitting prime q and automorphisms to boost the soundness. So, at a high level the prover commits to n/d polynomials $\check{s}_j$ whose NTT coefficients are the coefficients of $\vec{s}$. That is,

$$\vec{s} = \begin{pmatrix} \mathsf{NTT}(\check{s}_1) \\ \vdots \\ \mathsf{NTT}(\check{s}_{n/d}) \end{pmatrix}.$$

Then the prover uses a generalization of the product proof to many cubic relations to show that

$$\check{s}_j(\check{s}_j + 1)(\check{s}_j - 1) = 0$$

for all j. This shows that $\mathsf{NTT}(\check{s}_j) \in \{-1, 0, 1\}^d$ since the polynomial product in $\mathcal{R}_q$ is coefficient-wise in the NTT representation. This is the technique that was used in [BLS19].

In parallel, the prover uses the linear proof for the general case from Sect. 3.3, to show that the polynomials $\check{s}_j$ really give a solution to the linear equation. The complete protocol is given in Fig. 3 and it is proven secure in Theorem 4.1.

4.1   Security Analysis

Theorem 4.1. *The protocol in Fig. 3 is complete, computational honest verifier zero-knowledge under the Module-LWE assumption and computational special sound under the Module-SIS assumption. More precisely, let p be the maximum probability over $\mathbb{Z}_q$ of the coefficients of $\mathbf{c} \bmod X^k - \zeta^k$ as in Lemma 2.2.*

Then, for completeness, in case the honest prover $\mathcal{P}$ does not abort due to rejection sampling, it always convinces the honest verifier $\mathcal{V}$.

For zero-knowledge, there exists a simulator $\mathcal{S}$, that, without access to secret information, outputs a simulation of a non-aborting transcript of the protocol between $\mathcal{P}$ and $\mathcal{V}$ for every statement $A\vec{s} = \vec{u}$, $\vec{s} \in \{-1, 0, 1\}^n$. Then for every algorithm $\mathcal{A}$ that has advantage ε in distinguishing the simulated transcript from an actual transcript, there is an algorithm $\mathcal{A}'$ with the same running time that also has advantage ε in distinguishing $\mathsf{MLWE}_{\lambda,\chi}$.

For soundness, there is an extractor $\mathcal{E}$ with the following properties. When given rewindable black-box access to a deterministic prover $\mathcal{P}^*$ that convinces $\mathcal{V}$ with probability $\varepsilon > (3p)^k$, $\mathcal{E}$ either outputs a solution $\vec{s}^* \in \{-1, 0, 1\}^n$ to $A\vec{s}^* = \vec{u}$, or a $\mathsf{MSIS}_{\kappa, 8d\beta}$ solution for $\mathbf{B}_0$ in expected time at most $1/\varepsilon + (\varepsilon - p^k)^{-1}$ when running $\mathcal{P}^*$ once is assumed to take unit time.

We provide the proof of this theorem in the full version of this paper [ENS20].

4.2   Proof Size

We now look at the size of the non-interactive proof outputs via the Fiat-Shamir transform of the protocol in Fig. 3. First, note that for the non-interactive proof

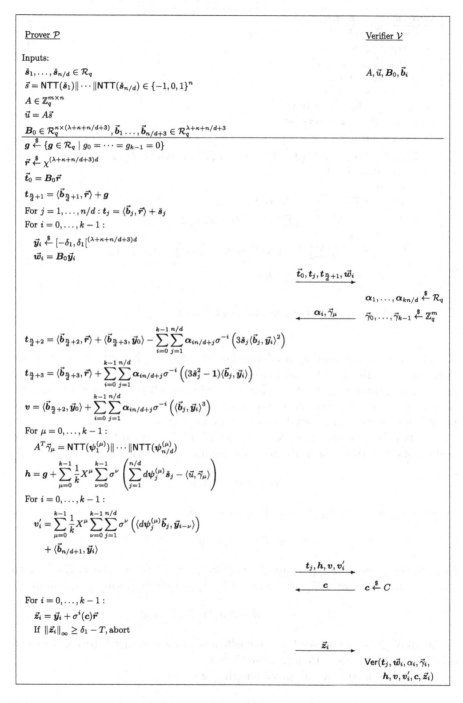

Fig. 3. Proof of knowledge of a ternary solution to an unstructured linear equation over $\mathbb{Z}_q$. Verification equations are defined in Fig. 4.

$$
\begin{array}{ll}
\multicolumn{2}{l}{\mathsf{Ver}(t_j, \vec{w}_i, \alpha_i, \vec{\gamma}_i, h, v, v'_i, c, \vec{z}_i)} \\
\hline
01 & \text{For } i = 0, \ldots, k-1: \\
02 & \quad \|\vec{z}_i\|_2 \stackrel{?}{<} \beta = \delta_1 - T \\
03 & \quad B_0 \vec{z}_i \stackrel{?}{=} \vec{w}_i + \sigma^i(c)\vec{t}_0 \\
04 & \text{For } i = 0, \ldots, k-1: \\
05 & \quad \text{For } j = 1, \ldots, n/d: \\
06 & \quad\quad f_j^{(i)} = \langle \vec{b}_j, \vec{z}_i \rangle - \sigma^i(c)t_j \\
07 & f_{\frac{n}{d}+2} = \langle \vec{b}_{\frac{n}{d}+2}, \vec{z}_0 \rangle - ct_{\frac{n}{d}+2} \\
08 & f_{\frac{n}{d}+3} = \langle \vec{b}_{\frac{n}{d}+3}, \vec{z}_0 \rangle - ct_{\frac{n}{d}+3} \\
09 & \sum_{i=0}^{k-1} \sum_{j=1}^{n/d} \alpha_{in/d+j} \sigma^{-i} \left(f_j^{(i)} (f_j^{(i)} + \sigma^i(c))(f_j^{(i)} - \sigma^i(c)) \right) + f_{\frac{n}{d}+2} + c f_{\frac{n}{d}+3} \stackrel{?}{=} v \\
10 & \text{For } \mu = 0, \ldots, k-1: \\
11 & \quad h_\mu \stackrel{?}{=} 0 \\
12 & \quad A^T \vec{\gamma}_\mu = \mathsf{NTT}(\psi_1^{(\mu)}) \| \cdots \| \mathsf{NTT}(\psi_{n/d}^{(\mu)}) \\
13 & \tau = \sum_{\mu=0}^{k-1} \frac{1}{k} X^\mu \sum_{\nu=0}^{k-1} \sigma^\nu \left(\sum_{j=1}^{n/d} d\psi_j^{(\mu)} t_j - \langle \vec{u}, \vec{\gamma}_\mu \rangle \right) \\
14 & \text{For } i = 0, \ldots, k-1: \\
15 & \quad \sum_{\mu=0}^{k-1} \frac{1}{k} X^\mu \sum_{\nu=0}^{k-1} \sum_{j=1}^{n/d} \sigma^\nu \left(d\psi_j^{(\mu)} \langle \vec{b}_j, \vec{z}_{i-\nu \bmod k} \rangle \right) + \langle \vec{b}_{n/d+1}, \vec{z}_i \rangle \\
16 & \quad \stackrel{?}{=} v'_i + \sigma^i(c)(\tau + t_{n/d+1} - h)
\end{array}
$$

Fig. 4. Verification equations for Fig. 3.

the messages w_i, v and v_i need not be included in the output as they are uniquely determined by the remaining components. Further, the challenges can be generated from a small seed of 256 bits, which itself is generated as the hash of some components. Therefore, the contribution of the challenges to the total proof length is extremely small and thus we neglect it.

As "full-sized" elements of $\mathcal{R}_q$, we have $\vec{t}_0$, t_j, and h (in fact, h is missing k coefficients, but that is a negligible consideration). Therefore, we have in total

$$
\kappa + n/d + 3 + 1
$$

full-sized elements of $\mathcal{R}_q$, which altogether costs

$$
(\kappa + n/d + 4)\, d\lceil \log q \rceil \quad \text{bits.}
$$

Now, the only remaining part are the vectors $\vec{z}_i$. Since the k vectors $\vec{z}_i$ of length $(\lambda + \kappa + n/d + 3)d$ over $\mathbb{Z}_q$ are bounded by δ_1 in infinity norm, they require

$$
k(\lambda + \kappa + n/d + 3)d\lceil \log 2\delta_1 \rceil \quad \text{bits}
$$

in the proof. It is easy to see that no coefficient of the product $\sigma^i(c)\vec{r}$ can exceed d for any $0 \le i \le k - 1$. Hence, we set $T = d$.

In conclusion, the overall proof length is about

$$
(\kappa + n/d + 4)\, d\lceil \log q \rceil + k\,(\lambda + \kappa + n/d + 3)\, d\lceil \log 2\delta_1 \rceil \quad \text{bits,} \tag{9}
$$

Proof Length Optimizations. The size of the non-interactive proof can be reduced with a number of standard techniques. The first techniques are the two compression techniques from the Bai-Galbraith [BG14] and Dilithium [DKL+18] signature schemes. They reduce the size of the masked openings $\vec{z}_i$ and the top part $\vec{t}_0$ of the commitment. As we have mentioned in Sect. 2.7, the commitment matrix $\boldsymbol{B}_0$ can be decomposed as $\boldsymbol{B}_0 = (\boldsymbol{B}_0', \boldsymbol{I})$, where $\boldsymbol{I}$ is the identity matrix of dimension κ. Then we can similarly decompose $\vec{r} = \vec{r}_1 \parallel \vec{r}_2$ and write

$$\vec{t}_0 = \boldsymbol{B}_0 \vec{r} = \boldsymbol{B}_0' \vec{r}_1 + \vec{r}_2.$$

Now, we see that when we give an approximate proof for this equation that proves $\bar{c}\vec{t}_0 = \boldsymbol{B}_0' \vec{z}_1 + \vec{z}_2$, we are essentially proving knowledge of a short vector $\vec{z}_1$ such that $\boldsymbol{B}_1 \vec{z}_1$ is close to $\bar{c}\vec{t}_0$. But this can be achieved in zero-knowledge without sending both masked openings $\vec{z}_1$ and $\vec{z}_2$ as follows. Let $\vec{y}$ be the masking vector for $\vec{r}_1$, $\vec{z} = \vec{y} + c\vec{r}_1$, and $\vec{w} = \boldsymbol{B}_0' \vec{y}$. Then decompose $\vec{w}$ as quotient and remainder modulo $\alpha = 2\delta_2 \approx \delta_1$,

$$\vec{w} = \alpha \vec{w}_1 + \vec{w}_0$$

where $\|\vec{w}_0\|_\infty \leq \delta_2$. It follows that

$$\boldsymbol{B}_0' \vec{z} - c\vec{t}_0 = \alpha \vec{w}_1 + \vec{w}_0 - c\vec{r}_2.$$

Hence, when we keep the remainder $\vec{w}_0$ secret, it can serve as the masking vector for $\vec{r}_2$. Moreover, by rejecting if $\|\vec{w}_0 - c\vec{r}_2\|_\infty \geq \delta_2 - T$, this doesn't leak information about $\vec{r}_2$ and the equation can be checked by the verifier by decomposing $\boldsymbol{B}_0' \vec{z} - c\vec{t}_0$. The second compression technique starts with the same observation that it suffices to prove knowledge of a preimage of $\boldsymbol{B}_0'$ that is close to $\bar{c}\vec{t}_0$. When we decompose

$$\vec{t}_0 = \vec{t}_{0,1} 2^D + \vec{t}_{0,0},$$

then it is actually sufficient to only send the high bits $\vec{t}_{0,1}$, because the low bits only introduce an additional noise term $\bar{c}\vec{t}_{0,0}$ in the verification equation that can be handled with sending a few hint bits. We defer to the Dilithium paper for the details.

Another optimization we employ is in the calculation of a maximum absolute coefficient in $\sigma^i(c)\vec{r}$. In our applications, we aim to minimize d and set $d = 128$. Now in this case, a coefficient of $\sigma^i(c)\vec{r}$ is the sum of 128 coefficients with i.i.d. $P(-1) = P(1) = 5/32$ and $P(0) = 22/32$.[2] If we calculate the convolution of this distribution, we find that a coefficient is bigger than 78 in absolute value with probability less than 2^{-114}. Hence, by a union bound the probability that any of the coefficients in $(\sigma^0(c)\vec{r}, \ldots, \sigma^{k-1}(c)\vec{r})$ is bigger than 78 will still be negligibly small. Therefore, we can set $T = 78$ instead of $T = d = 128$.

---

[2] Recall that a coefficient of c is zero with probability $1/2$ and a coefficient of $\vec{r}$ is zero with probability $6/16$. The probabilities of ± 1 are always equal to each other.

The previous optimization can be combined with the following optimization. Instead of using the k rotations $\sigma^i(c)$ of one dense challenge for the masked openings $\vec{z}_i$, we can write c in the subring generated by X^k and fixed by σ, i.e. $c = c_0 + c_1 X + \cdots + c_{k-1} X^{k-1}$ where the polynomials c_j are sparse with only at most d/k nonzero coefficients. Then all the images $\sigma^i(c)$ are just different linear combinations of the c_j. So it suffices to use these sparse challenges c_j in the masked openings that are transmitted and the verifier can then recombine them to obtain the masked openings with challenges $\sigma^i(c)$ as needed in the protocols.

References

[AHIV17] Ames, S., Hazay, C., Ishai, Y., Venkitasubramaniam, M.: Ligero: lightweight sublinear arguments without a trusted setup. In: ACM Conference on Computer and Communications Security, pp. 2087–2104. ACM (2017)

[ALS20] Attema, T., Lyubashevsky, V., Seiler, G.: Practical product proofs for lattice commitments. In: Micciancio, D., Ristenpart, T. (eds.) CRYPTO 2020, Part II. LNCS, vol. 12171, pp. 470–499. Springer, Cham (2020). https://doi.org/10.1007/978-3-030-56880-1_17

[BCK+14] Benhamouda, F., Camenisch, J., Krenn, S., Lyubashevsky, V., Neven, G.: Better zero-knowledge proofs for lattice encryption and their application to group signatures. In: Sarkar, P., Iwata, T. (eds.) ASIACRYPT 2014. LNCS, vol. 8873, pp. 551–572. Springer, Heidelberg (2014). https://doi.org/10.1007/978-3-662-45611-8_29

[BCOS20] Boschini, C., Camenisch, J., Ovsiankin, M., Spooner, N.: Efficient post-quantum SNARKs for RSIS and RLWE and their applications to privacy. In: Ding, J., Tillich, J.-P. (eds.) PQCrypto 2020. LNCS, vol. 12100, pp. 247–267. Springer, Cham (2020). https://doi.org/10.1007/978-3-030-44223-1_14

[BCR+19] Ben-Sasson, E., Chiesa, A., Riabzev, M., Spooner, N., Virza, M., Ward, N.P.: Aurora: transparent succinct arguments for R1CS. In: Ishai, Y., Rijmen, V. (eds.) EUROCRYPT 2019. LNCS, vol. 11476, pp. 103–128. Springer, Cham (2019). https://doi.org/10.1007/978-3-030-17653-2_4

[BDK+18] Bos, L., Ducas, J.W., et al.: CRYSTALS - kyber: a CCA-secure module-lattice-based KEM. In: 2018 IEEE European Symposium on Security and Privacy, EuroS&P, pp. 353–367 (2018)

[BDL+18] Baum, C., Damgård, I., Lyubashevsky, V., Oechsner, S., Peikert, C.: More efficient commitments from structured lattice assumptions. In: Catalano, D., De Prisco, R. (eds.) SCN 2018. LNCS, vol. 11035, pp. 368–385. Springer, Cham (2018). https://doi.org/10.1007/978-3-319-98113-0_20

[Beu20] Beullens, W.: Sigma protocols for MQ, PKP and SIS, and fishy signature schemes. In: Canteaut, A., Ishai, Y. (eds.) EUROCRYPT 2020. LNCS, vol. 12107, pp. 183–211. Springer, Cham (2020). https://doi.org/10.1007/978-3-030-45727-3_7

[BG14] Bai, S., Galbraith, S.D.: An improved compression technique for signatures based on learning with errors. In: Benaloh, J. (ed.) CT-RSA 2014. LNCS, vol. 8366, pp. 28–47. Springer, Cham (2014). https://doi.org/10.1007/978-3-319-04852-9_2

[BLS19]   Bootle, J., Lyubashevsky, V., Seiler, G.: Algebraic techniques for short(er) exact lattice-based zero-knowledge proofs. In: Boldyreva, A., Micciancio, D. (eds.) CRYPTO 2019. LNCS, vol. 11692, pp. 176–202. Springer, Cham (2019). https://doi.org/10.1007/978-3-030-26948-7_7

[CLOS02]   Canetti, R., Lindell, Y., Ostrovsky, R., Sahai, A.: Universally composable two-party and multi-party secure computation. In: STOC, pp. 494–503. ACM (2002)

[DKL+18]   Ducas, L., Kiltz, E., Lepoint, T., Lyubashevsky, V., Schwabe, P., Seiler, G., Stehlé, D.: Crystals-dilithium: a lattice-based digital signature scheme. IACR Trans. Cryptogr. Hardw. Embed. Syst. **2018**(1), 238–268 (2018)

[dPLS18]   del Pino, R., Lyubashevsky, V., Seiler, G.: Lattice-based group signatures and zero-knowledge proofs of automorphism stability. In: ACM CCS, pp. 574–591. ACM (2018)

[dPLS19]   del Pino, R., Lyubashevsky, V., Seiler, G.: Short discrete log proofs for FHE and ring-LWE ciphertexts. In: Lin, D., Sako, K. (eds.) PKC 2019. LNCS, vol. 11442, pp. 344–373. Springer, Cham (2019). https://doi.org/10.1007/978-3-030-17253-4_12

[ENS20]   Esgin, M.F., Nguyen, N.K., Seiler, G.: Practical exact proofs from lattices: new techniques to exploit fully-splitting rings (2020). https://eprint.iacr.org/2020/518

[ESLL19]   Esgin, M.F., Steinfeld, R., Liu, J.K., Liu, D.: Lattice-based zero-knowledge proofs: new techniques for shorter and faster constructions and applications. In: Boldyreva, A., Micciancio, D. (eds.) CRYPTO 2019. LNCS, vol. 11692, pp. 115–146. Springer, Cham (2019). https://doi.org/10.1007/978-3-030-26948-7_5

[ESS+19]   Esgin, M.F., Steinfeld, R., Sakzad, A., Liu, J.K., Liu, D.: Short lattice-based one-out-of-many proofs and applications to ring signatures. In: Deng, R.H., Gauthier-Umaña, V., Ochoa, M., Yung, M. (eds.) ACNS 2019. LNCS, vol. 11464, pp. 67–88. Springer, Cham (2019). https://doi.org/10.1007/978-3-030-21568-2_4

[EZS+19]   Esgin, M.F., Zhao, R.K., Steinfeld, R., Liu, J.K., Liu, D.: MatRiCT: efficient, scalable and post-quantum blockchain confidential transactions protocol. In: CCS, pp. 567–584. ACM (2019). https://eprint.iacr.org/2019/1287.pdf

[Kil92]   Kilian, J.: A note on efficient zero-knowledge proofs and arguments (extended abstract). In: STOC, pp. 723–732. ACM (1992)

[LLNW17]   Libert, B., Ling, S., Nguyen, K., Wang, H.: Zero-knowledge arguments for lattice-based prfs and applications to E-cash. In: Takagi, T., Peyrin, T. (eds.) ASIACRYPT 2017. LNCS, vol. 10626, pp. 304–335. Springer, Cham (2017). https://doi.org/10.1007/978-3-319-70700-6_11

[LLNW18]   Libert, B., Ling, S., Nguyen, K., Wang, H.: Lattice-based zero-knowledge arguments for integer relations. In: Shacham, H., Boldyreva, A. (eds.) CRYPTO 2018. LNCS, vol. 10992, pp. 700–732. Springer, Cham (2018). https://doi.org/10.1007/978-3-319-96881-0_24

[LPR10]   Lyubashevsky, V., Peikert, C., Regev, O.: On ideal lattices and learning with errors over rings. In: Gilbert, H. (ed.) EUROCRYPT 2010. LNCS, vol. 6110, pp. 1–23. Springer, Heidelberg (2010). https://doi.org/10.1007/978-3-642-13190-5_1

[LS15]   Langlois, A., Stehlé, D.: Worst-case to average-case reductions for module lattices. Des. Codes Cryptogr. **75**(3), 565–599 (2015)

[LS18] Lyubashevsky, V., Seiler, G.: Short, invertible elements in partially splitting cyclotomic rings and applications to lattice-based zero-knowledge proofs. In: Nielsen, J.B., Rijmen, V. (eds.) EUROCRYPT 2018. LNCS, vol. 10820, pp. 204–224. Springer, Cham (2018). https://doi.org/10.1007/978-3-319-78381-9_8

[LS19] Lyubashevsky, V., Seiler, G.: NTTRU: truly fast NTRU using NTT. IACR Trans. Cryptogr. Hardw. Embed. Syst. **2019**(3), 180–201 (2019)

[Lyu08] Lyubashevsky, V.: Lattice-based identification schemes secure under active attacks. In: Cramer, R. (ed.) PKC 2008. LNCS, vol. 4939, pp. 162–179. Springer, Heidelberg (2008). https://doi.org/10.1007/978-3-540-78440-1_10

[Lyu09] Lyubashevsky, V.: Fiat-Shamir with aborts: applications to lattice and factoring-based signatures. In: Matsui, M. (ed.) ASIACRYPT 2009. LNCS, vol. 5912, pp. 598–616. Springer, Heidelberg (2009). https://doi.org/10.1007/978-3-642-10366-7_35

[Lyu12] Lyubashevsky, V.: Lattice signatures without trapdoors. In: Pointcheval, D., Johansson, T. (eds.) EUROCRYPT 2012. LNCS, vol. 7237, pp. 738–755. Springer, Heidelberg (2012). https://doi.org/10.1007/978-3-642-29011-4_43

[PR06] Peikert, C., Rosen, A.: Efficient collision-resistant hashing from worst-case assumptions on cyclic lattices. In: Halevi, S., Rabin, T. (eds.) TCC 2006. LNCS, vol. 3876, pp. 145–166. Springer, Heidelberg (2006). https://doi.org/10.1007/11681878_8

[Ste93] Stern, J.: A new identification scheme based on syndrome decoding. In: Stinson, D.R. (ed.) CRYPTO 1993. LNCS, vol. 773, pp. 13–21. Springer, Heidelberg (1993). https://doi.org/10.1007/3-540-48329-2_2

[YAZ+19] Yang, R., Au, M.H., Zhang, Z., Xu, Q., Yu, Z., Whyte, W.: Efficient lattice-based zero-knowledge arguments with standard soundness: construction and applications. In: Boldyreva, A., Micciancio, D. (eds.) CRYPTO 2019. LNCS, vol. 11692, pp. 147–175. Springer, Cham (2019). https://doi.org/10.1007/978-3-030-26948-7_6

Towards Classical Hardness
of Module-LWE: The Linear Rank Case

Katharina Boudgoust$^{(\boxtimes)}$, Corentin Jeudy, Adeline Roux-Langlois,
and Weiqiang Wen

Univ Rennes, CNRS, IRISA, Rennes, France
katharina.boudgoust@irisa.fr

Abstract. We prove that the *module learning with errors* (M-LWE)
problem with arbitrary polynomial-sized modulus p is *classically* at least
as hard as standard worst-case lattice problems, as long as the module
rank d is not smaller than the number field degree n. Previous publications only showed the hardness under quantum reductions. We achieve
this result in an analogous manner as in the case of the *learning with
errors* (LWE) problem. First, we show the classical hardness of M-LWE
with an exponential-sized modulus. In a second step, we prove the hardness of M-LWE using a binary secret. And finally, we provide a modulus
reduction technique. The complete result applies to the class of power-
of-two cyclotomic fields. However, several tools hold for more general
classes of number fields and may be of independent interest.

Keywords: Lattice-based cryptography · Module learning with
errors · Classical hardness · Binary secret

1 Introduction

The *learning with errors* (LWE) problem, introduced by Regev [Reg05], is used
as a core computational problem in lattice-based cryptography. Given positive
integers n (the dimension) and q (the modulus), and a secret vector $\mathbf{s} \in \mathbb{Z}_q^n$,
an $\text{LWE}_{n,q,\psi}$ sample is defined as $(\mathbf{a}, b = \frac{1}{q}\langle \mathbf{a}, \mathbf{s}\rangle + e)$, where $\mathbf{a}$ is sampled from
the uniform distribution on $\mathbb{Z}_q^n$ and e (the error), is sampled from a probability
distribution ψ on the torus $\mathbb{T} = \mathbb{R}/\mathbb{Z}$. In many cases, the error distribution is
given by a Gaussian distribution D_α of width α, for a positive real α. The *search*
version of LWE asks to recover the secret $\mathbf{s}$, given arbitrarily many samples
of the LWE distribution. Its *decision* variant asks to distinguish between LWE
samples and samples drawn from the uniform distribution on $\mathbb{Z}_q^n \times \mathbb{T}$.

The LWE problem is fundamental in lattice-based cryptography as it allows
to construct a wide range of cryptographic primitives, from the basic ones,
as public-key encryption (e.g. [Reg05, MP12]), to the most advanced ones, as
fully homomorphic encryption (e.g. [BGV12, BV14, DM15]) or non-interactive
zero-knowledge proof systems (e.g. [PS19]). A very appealing aspect of LWE is
its connection to well-studied lattice problems. Lattices are discrete additive

© International Association for Cryptologic Research 2020
S. Moriai and H. Wang (Eds.): ASIACRYPT 2020, LNCS 12492, pp. 289–317, 2020.
https://doi.org/10.1007/978-3-030-64834-3_10

subgroups of $\mathbb{R}^n$ and arise in many different areas of mathematics, such as number theory, geometry and group theory. There are several lattice problems that are conjectured to be computationally hard to solve, for instance, the problem of finding a set of *shortest independent vectors* (SIVP) or the decisional variant of finding a *shortest vector* (GapSVP). A standard relaxation of those two problems consists in solving them only up to a factor γ, denoted by SIVP$_\gamma$ and GapSVP$_\gamma$, respectively. In the seminal work of Regev [Reg05,Reg09], a worst-case to average-case quantum reduction from GapSVP$_\gamma$ or SIVP$_\gamma$ to LWE was established. In other words, if there exists an efficient algorithm that solves LWE, then there also exists an efficient *quantum* algorithm that solves GapSVP$_\gamma$ and SIVP$_\gamma$ in the worst-case. Later, Peikert [Pei09] showed a *classical* reduction from GapSVP$_\gamma$ to LWE, but requiring the resulting modulus q to be exponentially large in the dimension n. With the help of a modulus reduction, Brakerski et al. [BLP+13] proved the hardness of LWE via a classical reduction from GapSVP$_\gamma$, for any polynomial-sized modulus q.

Structured Variants. Cryptographic protocols, whose security proofs rely on the hardness of LWE, inherently suffer from large public keys, usually consisting of m elements of $\mathbb{Z}_q^n$, where $m \in O(n \log_2 n)$. To improve their efficiency, structured variants of LWE have been proposed, e.g., [SSTX09,LPR10,LS15]. Within this paper, we focus on the *module learning with errors* (M-LWE) problem, first defined by Brakerski et al. [BGV12] and thoroughly studied by Langlois and Stehlé [LS15]. Instead of working over integers, it uses a more algebraic setting. Let K be a number field of degree n and R its ring of integers with dual $R^\vee$. Further, let q and d be positive integers. Let ψ be a distribution on the torus $\mathbb{T}_{R^\vee} = K_\mathbb{R}/R^\vee$, where $K_\mathbb{R} = K \otimes_\mathbb{Q} \mathbb{R}$, and let $\mathbf{s} \in (R_q^\vee)^d$ be a secret vector. An M-LWE$_{n,d,q,\psi}$ sample is given by $(\mathbf{a}, b = \frac{1}{q}\langle \mathbf{a}, \mathbf{s}\rangle + e)$, where $\mathbf{a} \leftarrow U((R_q)^d)$ and $e \leftarrow \psi$. Again, usually ψ is a Gaussian distribution D_α of width α. We refer to the special case of $d = 1$ as the *ring learning with errors* (R-LWE) problem.

Similar to its unstructured counterpart, M-LWE also enjoys worst-case to average-case connections from lattice problems such as SIVP$_\gamma$ [LS15]. Whereas the hardness results for LWE start from the lattice problem in the class of general lattices, the set has to be restricted to *module lattices* in the case of M-LWE. These module lattices correspond to modules in the ring R and we refer to the related lattice problem as Mod-SIVP$_\gamma$ and Mod-GapSVP$_\gamma$, respectively. Whereas both problems are conjectured to be hard to solve for γ polynomial in the lattice dimension, the problem Mod-GapSVP$_\gamma$ becomes easy in the special case of module lattices of rank 1 as their minimum can also be bounded below [PR07].

Since its introduction, the M-LWE problem has enjoyed more and more popularity as it offers a fine-grained trade-off between concrete security and efficiency. Within the NIST standardization process[1], several third round candidates rely on the hardness of M-LWE, e.g., the signature scheme Dilithium [DKL+18] and the key encapsulation mechanism Kyber [BDK+18] from the CRYSTALS suite.

---

[1] https://csrc.nist.gov/Projects/Post-Quantum-Cryptography.

Binary Secret. Several variants of LWE have been introduced during the last 15 years. One very interesting and widely-used version is the *binary secret learning with errors* (bin-LWE) problem, where the secret vector $\mathbf{s}$ is chosen from $\{0,1\}^n$. Besides gaining in efficiency, this variant also plays an important role in some applications like fully homomorphic encryption schemes, e.g., [DM15]. A first study of this problem was provided by Goldwasser et al. [GKPV10] in the context of leakage-resilient cryptography. Whereas their proof structure has the advantage of being easy to follow, their result suffers from a large error increase. Informally, they showed a reduction from $\text{LWE}_{\ell,q,D_\alpha}$ to bin-LWE_{n,q,D_β}, where $\frac{\alpha}{\beta} = \text{negl}(n)$ and $n \geq \ell \log_2 q + \omega(\log_2 n)$. Later, Brakerski et al. [BLP+13] improved the state of the art in order to show the classical hardness of LWE with a polynomial-sized modulus. Micciancio [Mic18] published another reduction from LWE to its binary version. Whereas the two reduction techniques differ, both paper achieved similar results. The dimension is still increased roughly by a factor $\log_2 q$, but the error only by a factor of $\sqrt{n}$, where n is the resulting LWE dimension. More concretely, in [BLP+13] a reduction from $\text{LWE}_{\ell,q,D_\alpha}$ to bin-LWE_{n,q,D_β} is shown, where $\frac{\alpha}{\beta} \leq \frac{1}{\sqrt{10n}}$ and $n \geq (\ell+1)\log_2 q + \omega(\log_2 n)$. The increase in dimension from ℓ to roughly $\ell \log_2 q$ is reasonable, as it essentially preserves the number of possible secrets. As stated by Micciancio [Mic18], an important open problem is whether similar results carry over to the structured variants, in particular to M-LWE, which seems to be an interesting problem to use in practice.

Our Contributions. Our first main contribution is a reduction from M-LWE to its binary secret version, bin-M-LWE, if the module rank d is at least of size $\log_2 q + \omega(\log_2 n)$, where n denotes the degree of the underlying number field and q the modulus. To the best of our knowledge, this is the first result on the hardness of a structured variant of LWE with binary secret. We then use this new result to show our second main contribution, the classical hardness of M-LWE for any polynomial-sized modulus p and module rank d at least $2n + \omega(\log_2 n)$, assuming the hardness of Mod-GapSVP$_\gamma$ with module rank at least 2. This was stated as an open problem by Langlois and Stehlé [LS15], as only quantum hardness of M-LWE for any polynomial-sized modulus p was known.

Technical Overview. At a high level, we follow the structure of the classical hardness proof of LWE from Brakerski et al. [BLP+13]. Overall, we need three ingredients: First, the classical hardness of M-LWE with an exponential-sized modulus. As a second component, we need the hardness of M-LWE using a binary secret, and finally, a modulus reduction technique.

We begin with the hardness of bin-M-LWE in Sect. 3. We follow the original proof structure of Goldwasser et al. [GKPV10], while achieving much better parameters by using the Rényi divergence instead of the statistical distance. The improvement on the noise rate compared to [GKPV10] stems from the fact that the Rényi divergence only needs to be constant for the reduction to work, compared to negligibly close to 0 for the statistical distance. Using the Rényi divergence as a tool for distance measurement requires to move to the search variants of M-LWE and its binary version, respectively. Additionally, it asks to fix the number of samples m a priori, which we denote by a suffix m, i.e., M-LWE$_{n,d,q,\psi}^m$. Throughout the paper, we assume that m is polynomial in the security parameter. At the core of the hardness proof of bin-M-LWE lies a lossy argument, where the public matrix $\mathbf{A}$ is replaced by a lossy matrix $\mathbf{B} \cdot \mathbf{C} + \mathbf{Z}$, which corresponds to the second part of some multiple-secrets M-LWE sample. To argue that an adversary cannot distinguish between the two cases, we need the hardness of the decisional M-LWE problem as well. However, prior to our work, the hardness of decisional M-LWE was only proven for polynomial-sized modulus, see [LS15]. For our purpose, we need the hardness of decisional M-LWE with an exponential-sized modulus. We solve this problem by adapting the main result of Peikert et al. [PRS17] to the module setting (Lemma 12).

This leads us to the first ingredient, the classical hardness of M-LWE with an exponential-sized modulus. In their introduction, Langlois and Stehlé [LS15] claimed that Peikert's dequantization [Pei09] carries over to the module case. In this paper, we prove this claim in Theorem 4. The proof idea is the same as the one from Peikert, but with two novelties. First, we look at the structured variants of the corresponding problems, i.e., GapSVP over module lattices and M-LWE, where the underlying ring R is the ring of integers of a number field K. Second, we replace the main component, a reduction from the *bounded distance decoding* (BDD) problem to the search version of LWE, by the reduction from the *gaussian decoding problem* (GDP) over modules to the decisional version of M-LWE (Lemma 12, adapted from [PRS17]). Thus, we also generalize the hardness of the decisional variant of M-LWE to all number fields K, not only cyclotomic fields as in [LS15].

Finally, we provide a modulus reduction technique, the last required ingredient, where the rank of the underlying module is preserved. This corresponds to the modulus reduction for LWE shown by Brakerski et al. [BLP+13, Cor. 3.2]. Prior to this paper, Albrecht and Deo [AD17] adapted the more general result from [BLP+13, Thm. 3.1], from which the necessary Corollary 3.2 is deduced. Thus, in Sect. 4.1, we first recall their general result [AD17, Thm. 1] and then derive Corollary 1, that we need, from it. The quality of the latter depends on the underlying ring structure and how the binary secret distribution behaves. For the case of power-of-two cyclotomics, we provide concrete bounds. This involves the computation of lower and upper bounds of the singular values of the rotation matrix. Note that Langlois and Stehlé [LS15] proved a modulus switching result from modulus q to modulus p, but the error increases at least by a multiplicative factor $\frac{q}{p}$, which is exponential if q is exponential-sized and p only polynomial-sized. Further note that the reason why we need to go through the binary variant of M-LWE is because we want to keep the noise amplification during the modulus switching part as small as possible.

Putting the Ingredients Together. We now explain how to complete the proof of our second main contribution, the classical hardness of M-LWE for any polynomial-sized modulus p and module rank d at least $2n + \omega(\log_2 n)$, as stated in Theorem 2. See Fig. 1 for an overview of the full proof.

Step 1: Classical worst-case to average-case reduction. Our result holds for any number field K of degree n with ring of integers R. Let $\ell \geq 2$ denote the rank of the R-module. Informally, Theorem 4 shows a reduction from Mod-GapSVP$_\gamma$

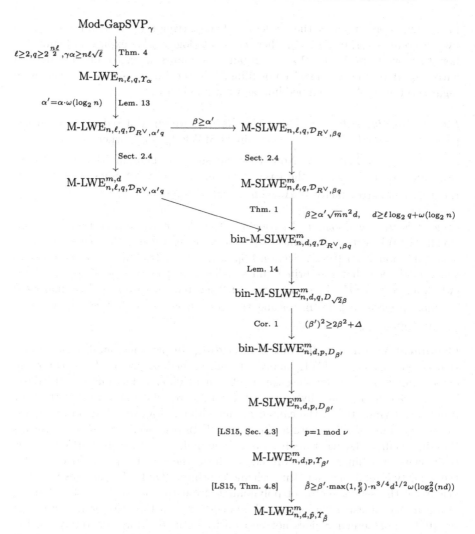

Fig. 1. Overview of the complete classical hardness proof of M-LWE for linear rank d and arbitrary polynomially large modulus $\hat{p}$, as stated in Theorem 2 for K the ν-th cyclotomic number field of degree n. The parameter Δ is determined by the underlying ring R and is poly(n) for the case of power-of-two cyclotomics.

to M-LWE$_{n,\ell,q,\Upsilon_\alpha}$, where $\alpha \in (0,1)$, $\gamma\alpha \geq n\ell\sqrt{\ell}$ and the modulus $q \geq 2^{\frac{n\ell}{2}}$. Here, Υ_α defines a distribution on some special elliptical Gaussian distributions in the canonical embedding, which we define properly later.

Step 2: Hardness of the binary secret variant. Theorem 1 shows a reduction from M-LWE$^{m,d}_{n,\ell,q,\mathcal{D}_{R^\vee,\alpha'q}}$ and M-SLWE$^m_{n,\ell,q,\mathcal{D}_{R^\vee,\beta q}}$ to bin-M-SLWE$^m_{n,d,q,\mathcal{D}_{R^\vee,\beta q}}$, where the underlying number field $K = \mathbb{Q}(\zeta)$ is a cyclotomic field, $d \geq \ell \cdot \log_2 q + \omega(\log_2 n)$ and $\beta \geq \alpha' \cdot \sqrt{m}n^2d$. Further, the modulus q has to be prime and is preserved by the reduction. The starting error distribution is given by a discrete Gaussian $\mathcal{D}_{R^\vee,\alpha'q}$, where $\alpha' = \alpha \cdot \omega(\log_2 n)$. We explain in Lemma 13 how to move from Υ_α to $\mathcal{D}_{R^\vee,\alpha'q}$. Again, the Gaussian distribution is defined with regard to the canonical embedding, but the binary secret is taken with regard to the coefficient embedding as we argue below.

Step 3: Modulus reduction. Using Corollary 1, we show a reduction from the problem bin-M-SLWE$_{n,d,q,D_{\sqrt{2}\beta}}^m$ to bin-M-SLWE$_{n,d,p,D_{\beta'}}^m$, where $q \geq p \geq 1$ and $(\beta')^2 \geq (\sqrt{2}\beta)^2 + \Delta$. Note that we show in Lemma 14 how to move from $\mathcal{D}_{R^\vee,\beta q}$ to $D_{\sqrt{2}\beta}$. In the case of power-of-two cyclotomics (Corollary 2) the additional error factor is $\Delta = 2dr^2$, with r polynomial in n.

Step 4: Search to decision. To conclude the classical hardness result of decisional M-LWE with polynomial-sized modulus p, we use the search to decision reduction from [LS15, Section 4.3], which is restricted to any ν-th cyclotomic field such that p is prime and satisfies $p = 1 \bmod \nu$. Adding a modulus switching step [LS15, Thm. 4.8], we can then reduce to *any* polynomial-sized modulus $\hat{p}$ close to p by increasing the noise from β' to $\hat{\beta} \geq \beta' \cdot \max(1, \frac{p}{\hat{p}}) \cdot n^{3/4}d^{1/2}\omega(\log_2^2(nd))$.

Canonical Versus Coefficient Embedding. In previous publications about structured variants of LWE, many authors argued in praise of the canonical embedding $\sigma \colon K \to H$ for the sake of achieving tighter reductions, e.g. [LPR10]. That is also the reason why most of the former results that we use within our proofs are formulated in the canonical embedding. However, it should be questioned again for M-LWE with a binary secret. In practice, a *small* secret means that its coefficients, when seen as a polynomial, are small. In particular, the coefficients of a binary secret are chosen from the set $\{0,1\}$. For instance, for the security level 3, the signature scheme Dilithium [DKL+18] samples the coefficients of the secret vector of polynomials from the set $\{-3,\ldots,3\}$. One big disadvantage of using the canonical embedding σ is that the preimage of the set $\{0,1\}^n \cap H$ under σ does not necessarily lie in R. More concretely, for the case of power-of-two cyclotomics, one can show that the only elements in R that have binary coefficients under the canonical embedding are the elements 0 and 1. Going from the coefficient to the canonical representation can be done by the linear transformation defined by the Vandermonde matrix. Thus, the distortion between the two embeddings depends on the norm of the Vandermonde matrix. Even though there are nice classes where the perturbation is relatively small, see [RSW18], in general, the problem of a binary secret with regard to the canonical embedding does not translate to a binary secret in the coefficient embedding. That is why we keep the definition of the binary secret in Theorem 1 with regard to the coefficient embedding. In order to keep the parameters as small as possible, this implies that the whole classical hardness proof then needs to be restricted to the class of power-of-two cyclotomics, where both embeddings are nearly isometric. Furthermore, the leftover hash lemma over rings (Lemma 7) asks for the coefficient embedding. Note that elements sampled from a Gaussian distribution are still sampled with respect to the canonical embedding.

Classical Hardness of R-LWE. The first result about the classical hardness of R-LWE with exponential-sized modulus has been informally mentioned in [BLP+13]. It can be achieved in two steps. First, by a dimension-modulus switching as in [BLP+13], LWE in dimension d and modulus q can be reduced to LWE in dimension 1 and modulus q^d with a slightly increased error rate. Then, by a ring switching technique as in [GHPS12], the latter one can be reduced to R-LWE over a ring of any degree n and modulus q^d, while keeping the same error rate. For more details on the second step, we refer to [AD17, App. B].

On the other hand, as a direct application of our classical hardness result of M-LWE, we can provide an alternative solution for the classical hardness result of R-LWE with exponential-sized modulus. The idea is that, using a rank-modulus switching as in [WW19], we can instead reduce from M-LWE over d-rank modules of n-degree ring and modulus q, to R-LWE with n-degree ring and modulus q^d, with a slightly increased error rate. However, we remark that the underlying worst-case lattice problems are different for these two results. Suppose that we consider the classical hardness of R-LWE over n-degree ring and q^d modulus where $d = \mathcal{O}(n)$. Then, the underlying problem is the standard GapSVP over general lattices of dimension $\mathcal{O}(\sqrt{n})$ for the first result, while it is Mod-GapSVP over rank-2 modules of $\mathcal{O}(n)$-degree ring for the second one.

Related Work. We now compare the results of Theorem 1 with the former results on LWE. The LWE problem can be seen as a special case of M-LWE, where the ring is $\mathbb{Z}$ and the degree n equals 1. In this case, the rank ℓ of the module corresponds to the dimension of the LWE problem and should be polynomial in the security parameter. Hence, the error-ratio is given by $\beta \geq \alpha\sqrt{m} \cdot d$ and $d \geq \ell \log_2 q + \omega(\log_2 \ell)$. Asymptotically, we lose a factor of $\sqrt{d}$ in the error-ratio in our reduction compared to the former results for LWE [BLP+13, Mic18]. However, our proof is as direct and short as the original one in [GKPV10]. We don't need to define intermediate problems such as *First-is-errorless* LWE and *Extended*-LWE as in [BLP+13] and no gadget matrix construction as in [Mic18]. Note that adapting the proof of [Mic18] asks to define a corresponding gadget matrix, which does not seem to work in an obvious way and that adapting the proof of [BLP+13] asks to define a corresponding notion of (a constant) quality for binary secrets, which is not straightforward. By replacing the statistical distance by the Rényi divergence and switching to the search variants we obtain a much better result than in the original paper from Goldwasser et al. [GKPV10].

Open Problems. In the course of this paper, we incurred several restrictions on the class of number fields we look at. Lemma 10 restricts the hardness proof of bin-M-SLWE (Theorem 1) to cyclotomic fields, in order to bound the norm of the Vandermonde matrix. The hardness of bin-M-SLWE for a rank which is smaller than $\log_2 q + \omega(\log_2 n)$, in particular for binary R-LWE, is still an open problem. In practice, we usually chose a small constant rank

(<10), as for instance in the submission to the NIST standardization process Kyber [BDK+18]. Furthermore, adapting the techniques of Brakerski et al. [BLP+13] and Micciancio [Mic18] to the module setting may help to further improve the error-ratio by a factor of $\sqrt{nd}$. Further, quantifying the error increase in the modulus reduction from Sect. 4.1 for other number fields than power-of-two cyclotomics may be interesting. The current bounds heavily depend on the singular values of the secret's rotation matrix, which further depend on the underlying number field.

2   Preliminaries

Let q be a positive integer, then $\mathbb{Z}_q$ denotes the ring of integers modulo q. For any $n \in \mathbb{N}$, we represent the set $\{1, \dots, n\}$ by $[n]$. Vectors are denoted in bold lowercase and matrices in bold capital letters. By $\mathbf{a}^T$ (resp. $\mathbf{a}^\dagger$) and $\mathbf{A}^T$ (resp. $\mathbf{A}^\dagger$) we denote the transpose (resp. conjugate transpose) of the vector $\mathbf{a}$ and the matrix $\mathbf{A}$. The standard basis of $\mathbb{C}^n$ is identified by $\{\mathbf{e}_i\}_{i \in [n]}$. For $\mathbf{a} \in \mathbb{C}^n$, we define $\mathrm{diag}(\mathbf{a}) = (a_i \delta_{ij})_{i,j \in [n]}$ to be the diagonal matrix whose diagonal entries are the entries of $\mathbf{a}$, where δ_{ij} denotes the Kronecker delta. The identity matrix of order n is denoted by $\mathbf{I}_n$. For any $\mathbf{a} \in \mathbb{R}^n$, we set $\|\mathbf{a}\|_\infty$ and $\|\mathbf{a}\|_2$ as the infinity and the Euclidean norm, respectively. For any matrix $\mathbf{A} = (a_{ij})_{i \in [m], j \in [n]}$, we define the norm $\|\mathbf{A}\| = \max_{j \in [n]} \|\mathbf{a}_j\|_2$, where $\mathbf{a}_j$ is the j-th column vector of $\mathbf{A}$ for $j \in [n]$. Further, we denote by $\|\mathbf{A}\|_F$ the Frobenius norm given by $\|\mathbf{A}\|_F^2 = \sum_{i \in [m]} \sum_{j \in [n]} a_{ij}^2$ and, by $\mathrm{GS}(\mathbf{A}) = (\mathrm{GS}(\mathbf{a}_j))_{j \in [n]}$ the Gram–Schmidt orthogonalization of $\mathbf{A}$ from left to right.

2.1   Algebraic Number Theory

A number field $K = \mathbb{Q}(\zeta)$ of degree n is a finite extension of the rational number field $\mathbb{Q}$ obtained by adjoining an algebraic number ζ. We define the tensor field $K_\mathbb{R} = K \otimes_\mathbb{Q} \mathbb{R}$ which can be seen as the finite field extension of the reals by adjoining ζ. The set of all algebraic integers of K defines a ring, called the ring of integers which we denote R. It is always true that $\mathbb{Z}[\zeta] \subseteq R$, where this inclusion can be strict. Lemma 7 is restricted to the class of number fields where the equality $R = \mathbb{Z}[\zeta]$ holds. This is the case for some quadratic extensions (i.e., when $\zeta = \sqrt{d}$ with d square-free and $d \neq 1 \bmod 4$), cyclotomic fields (i.e., when ζ is a primitive root of the unity) and number fields with a defining polynomial f of square-free discriminant Δ_f.

A subset $M \subseteq K^d$ is an R-module of rank d if it is closed under addition by elements of M and under multiplication by elements of R. It is a finitely generated module if there exists a finite family $\{b_k\}_k$ of vectors in K^d such that $M = \sum_k R \cdot b_k$.

Space H. We introduce the space $H \subseteq \mathbb{R}^{t_1} \times \mathbb{C}^{2t_2}$, where $n = t_1 + 2t_2$, as

$$H = \left\{ \mathbf{x} = (x_1, \dots, x_n)^T \in \mathbb{R}^{t_1} \times \mathbb{C}^{2t_2} : x_{t_1+t_2+j} = \overline{x_{t_1+j}}, \forall j \in [t_2] \right\}.$$

For $j \in [t_1]$, we set $\mathbf{h}_j = \mathbf{e}_j$, and for $j \in \{t_1+1, \ldots, t_1+t_2\}$, we set $\mathbf{h}_j = \frac{1}{\sqrt{2}}(\mathbf{e}_j + \mathbf{e}_{j+t_2})$ and $\mathbf{h}_{j+t_2} = \frac{i}{\sqrt{2}}(\mathbf{e}_j - \mathbf{e}_{j+t_2})$. The set $\{\mathbf{h}_j\}_{j \in [n]}$ forms an orthonormal basis of H as a real vector space, showing that H is isomorphic to $\mathbb{R}^n$. The change of basis is given by the unitary matrix

$$\mathbf{U}_H = \begin{bmatrix} \mathbf{I}_{t_1} & 0 & 0 \\ 0 & \frac{1}{\sqrt{2}}\mathbf{I}_{t_2} & \frac{i}{\sqrt{2}}\mathbf{I}_{t_2} \\ 0 & \frac{1}{\sqrt{2}}\mathbf{I}_{t_2} & \frac{-i}{\sqrt{2}}\mathbf{I}_{t_2} \end{bmatrix}.$$

Canonical Embedding. Any number field $K = \mathbb{Q}(\zeta)$ of degree n has exactly n field homomorphisms $\sigma_i \colon K \to \mathbb{C}$ fixing each element of $\mathbb{Q}$, where $i \in [n]$. Let $\sigma_1, \ldots, \sigma_{t_1}$ be the real embeddings and $\sigma_{t_1+1}, \ldots, \sigma_{t_1+2t_2}$ the complex embeddings. The complex ones come in conjugate pairs, thus $\sigma_i = \overline{\sigma_{i+t_2}}$ for $i \in \{t_1+1, \ldots, t_1+t_2\}$. In the particular case of cyclotomic fields, all n embeddings are complex. The *canonical embedding* σ is defined as the map $\sigma \colon K \to H$, where $\sigma(x) = (\sigma_i(x))_{i \in [n]}$. It describes a field homomorphism, where multiplication and addition in H are component-wise. By abuse of notation, for an $\mathbf{x} \in K^d$, we also write $\sigma(\mathbf{x})$ to denote the vector $(\sigma(x_i))_{i \in [d]} \in \mathbb{C}^{nd}$. We can represent $\sigma(x)$ via the real vector $\sigma_H(x) \in \mathbb{R}^n$ through the change of basis described above, i.e., $\sigma_H(x) = (\mathbf{U}_H)^\dagger \cdot \sigma(x)$. Note that multiplication is not component-wise for σ_H. More concretely, in the basis $\{\mathbf{e}_i\}_{i \in [n]}$, multiplication by $x \in K$ can be described as the left multiplication by the matrix $\mathbf{X} = (x_{ij})_{i,j \in [n]}$, where $x_{ij} = \sigma_i(x) \cdot \delta_{ij}$. Hence, changing to the basis $\{\mathbf{h}_i\}_{i \in [n]}$ leads to the corresponding matrix of multiplication $\mathbf{X}_H = (\mathbf{U}_H)^\dagger \mathbf{X} \mathbf{U}_H$, having the same singular values as $\mathbf{X}$, given by $|\sigma_i(x)|$ for $i \in [n]$.

The trace $\mathrm{Tr} \colon K \to \mathbb{Q}$ is defined as the sum of the embeddings, i.e., for any $x \in K$, we have $\mathrm{Tr}(x) = \sum_{i \in [n]} \sigma_i(x)$. For any fractional ideal $\mathcal{I} \subset K$, we define the dual $\mathcal{I}^\vee$ of $\mathcal{I}$ as $\mathcal{I}^\vee = \{x \in K \colon \mathrm{Tr}(x\mathcal{I}) \subseteq \mathbb{Z}\}$. In the case of $R = \mathbb{Z}[\zeta]$, it yields $R^\vee = \frac{1}{f'(\zeta)}R$, where f is the defining polynomial of K. In particular, for $K \cong \mathbb{Q}[x]/\langle x^n + 1\rangle$ the ν-th cyclotomic field, where ν is a power of two and $n = \nu/2$, it holds $R^\vee = \frac{1}{n}R$.

Coefficient Embedding. Every number field $K = \mathbb{Q}(\zeta)$ of degree n defines an n-dimensional vector space over $\mathbb{Q}$ with basis $\{1, \zeta, \ldots, \zeta^{n-1}\}$. Thus, every element $x \in K$ can be written as $x = \sum_{i=0}^{n-1} x_i \zeta^i$, where $x_i \in \mathbb{Q}$. The *coefficient embedding* $\tau \colon K \to \mathbb{R}^n$ is the map that sends every element $x \in K$ to its coefficient vector $\tau(x) = (x_0, \ldots, x_{n-1})^T$. Multiplication by x in the coefficient embedding can be represented by a matrix multiplication, where we denote the corresponding matrix by $\mathrm{Rot}(x) \in \mathbb{R}^{n \times n}$. Note that the matrix $\mathrm{Rot}(x)$ is invertible in K for every $x \neq 0$ and that its concrete form depends on the field K. Again, looking at the example, where $K = \mathbb{Q}(\zeta)$ is the ν-th cyclotomic field, with ν a power of two and thus $K \cong \mathbb{Q}[x]/\langle x^n + 1 \rangle$ with $n = \nu/2$, it yields

$$\mathrm{Rot}(x) = \begin{bmatrix} x_0 & -x_{n-1} & - & -x_1 \\ x_1 & x_0 & \searrow & | \\ | & | & \searrow & -x_{n-1} \\ x_{n-1} & x_{n-2} & - & x_0 \end{bmatrix}.$$

As both embeddings play an important role in this paper, we recall how to go from one to the other. For any $x \in K$, the embeddings $\sigma(x)$ and $\tau(x)$ are linked through the Vandermonde matrix $\mathbf{V}$ of the roots of the defining polynomial f. For $i \in [n]$, we let $\alpha_i = \sigma_i(\zeta)$ be the i-th root of f. Then, $\sigma(x) = \mathbf{V} \cdot \tau(x)$, where

$$\mathbf{V} = \begin{bmatrix} 1 & \alpha_1 & - & \alpha_1^{n-1} \\ 1 & \alpha_2 & - & \alpha_2^{n-1} \\ | & | & & | \\ 1 & \alpha_n & - & \alpha_n^{n-1} \end{bmatrix}.$$

2.2 Lattices

An n-dimensional lattice $\Lambda \subseteq \mathbb{R}^n$ is a discrete additive subgroup of $\mathbb{R}^n$. Within this work, we assume Λ to be of full rank n, i.e., $\mathrm{span}_{\mathbb{Q}}(\Lambda) = \mathbb{R}^n$. It can be seen as the set of all linear integer combinations of some n linearly independent vectors $\mathbf{B} = \{\mathbf{b}_i\}_{i \in [n]} \subseteq \mathbb{R}^n$, thus $\Lambda = \left\{ \sum_{i \in [n]} z_i \mathbf{b}_i : z_i \in \mathbb{Z} \right\}$. We call $\mathbf{B}$ a basis of Λ. The minimum $\lambda_1(\Lambda)$ of a lattice Λ is the Euclidean norm of any of its shortest nonzero vectors. The dual lattice Λ^* is defined by $\Lambda^* = \{\mathbf{x} \in \mathbb{R}^n : \langle \mathbf{x}, \mathbf{y} \rangle \in \mathbb{Z}, \forall \mathbf{y} \in \Lambda\}$. If $\mathbf{B}$ is basis of Λ, then $\mathbf{B}^* = (\mathbf{B}^T)^{-1}$ is a basis of Λ^*. The fundamental parallelepiped $\mathcal{P}(\mathbf{B})$ of the lattice Λ generated by the basis $\mathbf{B} = \{\mathbf{b}_i\}_{i \in [n]}$ is defined as $\mathcal{P}(\mathbf{B}) = \left\{ \sum_{i \in [n]} z_i \mathbf{b}_i : z_i \in \left[-\frac{1}{2}, \frac{1}{2}\right), \forall i \in [n] \right\}$. For any $\mathbf{w} \in \mathbb{R}^n$, we write $\mathbf{x} = \mathbf{w} \bmod \mathbf{B}$ to denote the unique point $\mathbf{x} \in \mathcal{P}(\mathbf{B})$ such that $\mathbf{w} - \mathbf{x} \in \Lambda$. One of the most studied lattice problems is the *shortest vector problem* (SVP). It exists in both search and decisional versions, but within this paper we are only using the approximation variant of the latter.

Definition 1 (Shortest vector problem). *Let $\gamma = \gamma(n) \geq 1$ be a function in the dimension n. An input to the shortest vector problem GapSVP_γ is a pair $(\mathbf{B}, \delta)$, where $\mathbf{B}$ is a basis of an n-dimensional lattice Λ and $\delta > 0$ is a real number. It is a YES instance if $\lambda_1(\Lambda) \leq \delta$, and it is a NO instance if $\lambda_1(\Lambda) > \gamma \cdot \delta$. The problem asks to distinguish whether a given instance is a YES or a NO instance. If $\lambda_1(\Lambda)$ falls in $(\delta, \gamma \cdot \delta]$, we can return anything.*

Let R be of degree n. Any rank d module $M \subseteq K^d$ of R is mapped by the canonical embedding $(\sigma_H, \ldots, \sigma_H): K^d \to \mathbb{R}^{nd}$ to a lattice in $\mathbb{R}^{nd}$. By abuse of notation, we simply write σ_H. Such lattices are called *module lattices*. The GapSVP_γ restricted to module lattices is denoted by $\mathrm{Mod\text{-}GapSVP}_\gamma$. For any $\mathbf{x} \in K^d$, we define three different norms $\|\mathbf{x}\|_2 = \|(\sigma_H(x_k))_{k \in [d]}\|_2$, $\|\mathbf{x}\|_\infty = \|(\sigma_H(x_k))_{k \in [d]}\|_\infty$ and $\|\mathbf{x}\|_{2,\infty} = \max_{i \in [n]} (\sum_{k \in [d]} |\sigma_i(x_k)|^2)^{1/2}$. Within this paper, we further need two intermediate lattice problems, presented in the setting of module lattices.

Definition 2 (Bounded distance decoding). *Let K be a number field with R its ring of integers of degree n and $M \subseteq K^d$ be a module of R of rank d. Further, let δ be a positive real number. An input to the bounded distance decoding problem $\mathrm{BDD}_{M,\delta}$ is a point $\mathbf{y} \in K^d$ of the form $\mathbf{y} = \mathbf{x} + \mathbf{e}$, where $\mathbf{x} \in M$ and $\|\mathbf{e}\|_{2,\infty} \leq \delta$. The problem asks to find $\mathbf{x}$.*

By D_g we denote the continuous Gaussian distribution of width g on $K_{\mathbb{R}}^d$, which we define properly in the next subsection.

Definition 3 (Gaussian decoding problem). *Let K be a number field with R its ring of integers of degree n and $M \subseteq K^d$ be a module of R of rank d. Further, let $g > 0$ be a Gaussian parameter. An input to the gaussian decoding problem $\mathrm{GDP}_{M,g}$ is a coset $\mathbf{y} + M$, where $\mathbf{y} \leftarrow D_g$. The goal is to find $\mathbf{y}$.*

Every $\mathrm{GDP}_{M,g}$ instance defines a $\mathrm{BDD}_{M,\delta}$ one with $\delta = g \cdot \sqrt{d} \cdot \omega(\sqrt{\log_2 n})$. Note that GapSVP, BDD and GDP can also be defined with regard to other norms.

Lemma 1 ([LLL82], [Bab85]). *There exists a polynomial-time algorithm that solves $\mathrm{BDD}_{M,\delta}$ for $\delta = 2^{-\frac{N}{2}} \cdot \lambda_1(M)$, where $N = nd$.*

2.3   Probabilities

For a set S and a distribution χ on S, we denote by $x \leftarrow \chi$ the process of sampling $x \in S$ according to χ. By $U(S)$ we denote the uniform distribution on S. For $s > 0$ and a vector $\mathbf{c} \in \mathbb{R}^n$, the Gaussian function $\rho_{s,\mathbf{c}}$ is defined by $\rho_{s,\mathbf{c}}(\mathbf{x}) = \exp\left(-\frac{\pi \|\mathbf{x}-\mathbf{c}\|_2^2}{s^2}\right)$. By normalizing the Gaussian function, we obtain the density function of the n-dimensional continuous Gaussian distribution $D_{s,\mathbf{c}}$ of width s and center $\mathbf{c}$. If the center is the zero vector $\mathbf{0}$, we simply omit the index $\mathbf{c}$ and write D_s. For an n-dimensional lattice $\Lambda \subseteq \mathbb{R}^n$, the discrete Gaussian distribution $\mathcal{D}_{\Lambda,s,\mathbf{c}}$ of width s and center $\mathbf{c}$ for Λ is defined by its density function $\mathcal{D}_{\Lambda,s,\mathbf{c}}(\mathbf{x}) = \frac{D_{s,\mathbf{c}}(\mathbf{x})}{D_{s,\mathbf{c}}(\Lambda)}$, where $D_{s,\mathbf{c}}(\Lambda) = \sum_{\mathbf{y} \in \Lambda} D_{s,\mathbf{c}}(\mathbf{y})$. Again, if the center is $\mathbf{0}$, we simply omit the index $\mathbf{c}$ and write $\mathcal{D}_{\Lambda,s}$.

Using the identification of H as $\mathbb{R}^n$, we can extend the definition of the continuous Gaussian distribution to an elliptical Gaussian distribution in the basis $\{\mathbf{h}_i\}_{i \in [n]}$ as follows. Let $\mathbf{r} = (r_1, \ldots, r_n)^T \in \mathbb{R}^n$ be a vector such that $r_i > 0$ for all $i \in [n]$ and $r_{t_1+j} = r_{t_1+t_2+j}$ for all $j \in [t_2]$, where $n = t_1 + 2t_2$. A sample from $D_{\mathbf{r}}$ on H is given by $\sum_{i \in [n]} x_i \mathbf{h}_i$, where $x_i \leftarrow D_{r_i}$ over $\mathbb{R}$ for $i \in [n]$. By applying the inverse of the canonical embedding σ, this provides Gaussian distributions on $K_{\mathbb{R}}^d$ for any d. For $0 \leq \alpha < \alpha'$, we define $\Psi_{[\alpha,\alpha']}$ to be the set of Gaussian distributions $D_{\mathbf{r}}$ with $\alpha < r_i \leq \alpha'$ for all $i \in [n]$. If $\alpha = 0$, we simply write $\Psi_{\leq \alpha'}$. Further, for any positive real α, we define the distribution Υ_α on distributions on H as done by Peikert et al. [PRS17]. Fix an arbitrary $f(n) = \omega(\sqrt{\log_2 n})$. A distribution sampled from Υ_α is an elliptical Gaussian $D_{\mathbf{r}}$, where $\mathbf{r}$ is sampled as follows: For $i \in [t_1]$, sample $x_i \leftarrow D_1$ and set $r_i^2 = \alpha^2(x_i^2 + f^2(n))/2$.

For $i \in \{t_1 + 1, \ldots, t_1 + t_2\}$, sample $x_i, y_i \leftarrow D_{1/\sqrt{2}}$ and set $r_i^2 = r_{i+t_2}^2 = \alpha^2(x_i^2 + y_i^2 + f^2(n))/2$. Additionally, we define the smoothing parameter $\eta_\varepsilon(\Lambda)$ of a lattice Λ which was first introduced by Micciancio and Regev [MR07]. Informally, this gives a threshold above which many properties of the continuous Gaussian distribution also hold for its discrete counterpart.

Definition 4 (Smoothing parameter). *Let Λ be an n-dimensional lattice and ε be a positive real number, the* smoothing parameter $\eta_\varepsilon(\Lambda)$ *is defined as the smallest positive real s such that $\rho_{1/s}(\Lambda^* \setminus \{0\}) \leq \varepsilon$.*

In particular, we need the following bounds on the smoothing parameter.

Lemma 2 (Lem. 1.5 [Ban93] and Claim 2.13 [Reg05]). *Let Λ be an n-dimensional lattice and $\varepsilon = \exp(-n)$, it holds $\frac{\sqrt{n}}{\sqrt{\pi}\lambda_1(\Lambda^*)} \leq \eta_\varepsilon(\Lambda) \leq \frac{\sqrt{n}}{\lambda_1(\Lambda^*)}$.*

The statistical distance is a widely used measure of distribution closeness.

Definition 5 (Statistical distance). *Let P and Q be two discrete probability distributions on a discrete domain E. The* statistical distance *is defined as $\Delta(P, Q) = \frac{1}{2}\sum_{x \in E} |P(x) - Q(x)|$.*

The statistical distance fulfills the probability preservation property.

Lemma 3. *Let P, Q be two probability distributions with $\mathrm{Supp}(P) \subseteq \mathrm{Supp}(Q)$ and $E \subseteq \mathrm{Supp}(Q)$ be an arbitrary event. Then, $P(E) \leq \Delta(P, Q) + Q(E)$.*

Within the paper, we need the following two results about the statistical distance of two Gaussian distributions.

Lemma 4 (Thm. 1.2 [DMR18]). *Let D_g denote the continuous Gaussian distribution on $K_\mathbb{R}$ and let $z \in K$. The statistical distance between D_g and $D_{g,z}$ is bounded above by $\frac{\sqrt{2\pi}\|z\|_2}{g}$.*

Lemma 5 (Claim 2.2 [Reg05]). *Let α and β be positive reals such that $\alpha < \beta$. The statistical distance between D_α and D_β is bounded above by $10 \cdot \left(\frac{\beta}{\alpha} - 1\right)$.*

The following lemma describes the behavior of the sum of a continuous Gaussian and a discrete one.

Lemma 6 (Claim. 3.9 [Reg09]). *Let Λ be an n-dimensional lattice, $s > 0$, $r > 0$ and $t = \sqrt{r^2 + s^2}$. Assume that $\frac{rs}{t} \geq \eta_\varepsilon(\Lambda)$ for some $\varepsilon \in (0, \frac{1}{2})$. Consider the distribution Y on $\mathbb{R}^n$ obtained by sampling from $\mathcal{D}_{\Lambda,r}$ and then adding a vector taken from D_s. Then, it yields $\Delta(Y, D_t) \leq 2\varepsilon$.*

Further, we need a ring version of the leftover hash lemma, where the secret vector contains binary polynomials. For this purpose, we adapt a result from Micciancio [Mic07]. A proof can be found in the full version [BJRW20].

Lemma 7. *Let n, m, d, q be positive integers, with q prime. Further, let f be the defining polynomial of degree n of the number field $K \cong \mathbb{Q}[x]/\langle f \rangle$ such that its ring of integers is $R = \mathbb{Z}[x]/\langle f \rangle$. We set $R_q = R/qR$ and $R_2 = R/2R$. Then,*

$$\Delta\left((\mathbf{A}, \mathbf{Ax}), (\mathbf{A}, \mathbf{v})\right) \leq \frac{1}{2}\sqrt{\left(1 + \frac{q^d}{2^m}\right)^n - 1},$$

where $\mathbf{A} \leftarrow U((R_q)^{d \times m})$, $\mathbf{x} \leftarrow U((R_2)^m)$ and $\mathbf{v} \leftarrow U((R_q)^d)$.

In order to guarantee a statistical distance negligibly small in n for a fixed rank d, we require $m \geq d \log_2 q + \omega(\log_2 n)$. Note that the requirement $\Omega(\log_2 n)$ is not strong enough as $\lim_{n \to \infty} \left(1 + \frac{1}{c \cdot n}\right)^n = e^{\frac{1}{c}}$, for any positive constant c.

The Rényi divergence [R61, vEH14] defines another measure of distribution closeness and was thoroughly studied for its use in cryptography as a powerful alternative for the statistical distance measure by Bai et al. [BLL+15]. In this paper, it suffices to use the Rényi divergence of order 2.

Definition 6 (Rényi divergence of order 2). *Let P and Q be two discrete probability distributions such that $\mathrm{Supp}(P) \subseteq \mathrm{Supp}(Q)$. The Rényi divergence of order 2 is defined as $\mathrm{RD}_2(P\|Q) = \sum_{x \in \mathrm{Supp}(P)} \frac{P(x)^2}{Q(x)}$.*

The Rényi divergence is multiplicative and fulfills the probability preservation property, as proved by van Erven and Harremoës [vEH14].

Lemma 8. *Let P, Q be two discrete probability distributions with $\mathrm{Supp}(P) \subseteq \mathrm{Supp}(Q)$ and $E \subseteq \mathrm{Supp}(Q)$ be an arbitrary event. Further, let $(P_n)_{n \in \mathbb{N}}$, $(Q_n)_{n \in \mathbb{N}}$ be two families of independent discrete probability distributions with $\mathrm{Supp}(P_n) \subseteq \mathrm{Supp}(Q_n)$ for all $n \in \mathbb{N}$. Then, the following properties are fulfilled:*

$$\mathrm{RD}_2\left(\prod_{n \in \mathbb{N}} P_n \middle\| \prod_{n \in \mathbb{N}} Q_n\right) = \prod_{n \in \mathbb{N}} \mathrm{RD}_2(P_n\|Q_n), \text{ and } Q(E) \cdot \mathrm{RD}_2(P\|Q) \geq P(E)^2.$$

In Sect. 3, we need the Rényi divergence of two shifted discrete Gaussians.

Lemma 9 (Adapted from Lem. 4.2 [LSS14]). *Let s and ε be positive real numbers with $\varepsilon \in (0, 1)$, $\mathbf{c}$ be a vector of $\mathbb{R}^n$ and Λ be a full-rank lattice in $\mathbb{R}^n$. We assume that $s \geq \eta_\varepsilon(\Lambda)$. Then,*

$$\mathrm{RD}_2(\mathcal{D}_{\Lambda,s,\mathbf{c}}\|\mathcal{D}_{\Lambda,s}) \leq \left(\frac{1+\varepsilon}{1-\varepsilon}\right)^2 \cdot \exp\left(\frac{2\pi\|\mathbf{c}\|^2}{s^2}\right).$$

2.4 The Module Learning with Errors Problem

The module variant of LWE was first defined by Brakerski et al. [BGV12] and thoroughly studied by Langlois and Stehlé [LS15]. It describes the following problem. Let K be a number field of degree n and R its ring of integers with dual $R^\vee$. Further, let d denote the rank and let ψ be a distribution on $K_\mathbb{R}$ and $\mathbf{s} \in (R_q^\vee)^d$ be a vector. We let $A_{\mathbf{s},\psi}^{(R^d)}$ denote the distribution on $(R_q)^d \times \mathbb{T}_{R^\vee}$ obtained by choosing a vector $\mathbf{a} \leftarrow U((R_q)^d)$, an element $e \leftarrow \psi$ and returning $(\mathbf{a}, \frac{1}{q}\langle \mathbf{a}, \mathbf{s}\rangle + e \bmod R^\vee)$.

Definition 7. *Let q, d be positive integers with $q \geq 2$. Let Ψ be a family of distributions on $K_\mathbb{R}$. The search version M-SLWE$_{n,d,q,\Psi}$ of the module learning with errors problem is as follows: Let $\mathbf{s} \in (R_q^\vee)^d$ be secret and $\psi \in \Psi$. Given arbitrarily many samples from $A_{\mathbf{s},\psi}^{(R^d)}$, the goal is to find $\mathbf{s}$. Let Υ be a distribution on a family of distributions on $K_\mathbb{R}$. Its decision version M-LWE$_{n,d,q,\Upsilon}$ is as follows: Choose $\mathbf{s} \leftarrow U((R_q^\vee)^d)$ and $\psi \leftarrow \Upsilon$. The goal is to distinguish between arbitrarily many independent samples from $A_{\mathbf{s},\psi}^{(R^d)}$ and the same number of independent samples from $U((R_q)^d \times \mathbb{T}_{R^\vee})$.*

Fixed Number of Samples. When using the Rényi divergence as a tool to measure the distance of two given probability distributions, we need to fix the number of requested samples a priori. Let m be the number of requested M-LWE samples $(\mathbf{a}_i, \frac{1}{q}\langle \mathbf{a}_i, \mathbf{s}\rangle + e_i)$ for $i \in [m]$, then we consider the matrix $\mathbf{A} \in R_q^{m \times d}$ whose rows are the $\mathbf{a}_i$'s and we set $\mathbf{e} = (e_1, \ldots, e_m)^T$. We obtain the representation $(\mathbf{A}, \frac{1}{q}\mathbf{A} \cdot \mathbf{s} + \mathbf{e})$, where $\mathbf{s} \in (R_q^\vee)^d$. We denote this problem by M-LWE$_{n,d,q,\Upsilon}^m$.

Multiple Secrets. Let k, m be natural numbers, where m denotes the number of requested samples of $A_{\mathbf{s},\psi}^{(R^d)}$. In the multiple secrets version, the secret vector $\mathbf{s} \in (R_q^\vee)^d$ is replaced by a secret matrix $\mathbf{S} \in (R_q^\vee)^{d \times k}$ and the error vector $\mathbf{e} \leftarrow \psi^m$ by an error matrix $\mathbf{E} \leftarrow \psi^{m \times k}$. There is a simple polynomial-time reduction from M-LWE using a secret vector to M-LWE using a secret matrix for any k polynomially large in d via a hybrid argument, as given for instance in [Mic18, Lem. 2.9]. We denote the corresponding problem by M-LWE$_{n,d,q,\Upsilon}^{m,k}$.

Binary Secret. Another possibility is to choose a *small* secret. We are interested in the case where the secret vector $\mathbf{s}$ is a binary vector, thus chosen from the set $(R_2^\vee)^d$. We denote the corresponding problem by bin-M-LWE$_{n,d,q,\Upsilon}$. Note that $R_2^\vee$ is defined with regard to the coefficient embedding τ, see Sect. 2.1.

Discrete Version. As pointed out by Lyubashevsky et al. [LPR10], sometimes it can be more convenient to work with a discrete variant, where the second component b of each sample $(\mathbf{a}, b)$ is taken from a finite set, and not from the continuous domain $\mathbb{T}_{R^\vee}$. Indeed, for the case of M-LWE, if the rounding function $\lfloor \cdot \rceil : K_\mathbb{R} \to R^\vee$ is chosen in a suitable way, see Lyubashevsky et al. [LPR13, Sec. 2.6] for more details, then every sample $(\mathbf{a}, b = \frac{1}{q}\langle \mathbf{a}, \mathbf{s}\rangle + e) \in (R_q)^d \times \mathbb{T}_{R^\vee}$ of the distribution $A_{\mathbf{s},\psi}^{(R^d)}$ can be transformed to $(\mathbf{a}, \lfloor q \cdot b \rceil) = (\mathbf{a}, \langle \mathbf{a}, \mathbf{s}\rangle + \lfloor q \cdot e \rceil \bmod qR^\vee) \in (R_q)^d \times R_q^\vee$. For technical reasons, we use the latter representation in Sect. 3.

3   Hardness of Binary M-LWE

In the following, we show a reduction from M-LWE to its binary secret version, if the module rank d is at least of size $\log_2 q + \omega(\log_2 n)$, where q is the modulus and n is the degree of the underlying number field.

Our proof follows the proof structure of Goldwasser et al. [GKPV10], but achieves better parameters by using the Rényi divergence, while being as direct and short as the original proof. The improvement on the noise rate $\frac{\alpha}{\beta}$ compared to [GKPV10] stems from the fact that the Rényi divergence only needs to be constant for the reduction to work and not necessarily negligibly close to 1 (compared to negligibly close to 0 for the statistical distance). However, using the Rényi divergence as a tool for distance measurement requires to move to the search variants of M-LWE and its binary version, respectively.

Within the proof of Theorem 1 we need to apply the leftover hash lemma over rings (Lemma 7), and thus need to require that the modulus q is prime. Further, we need Lemma 10, which only holds for cyclotomic number fields $K = \mathbb{Q}(\zeta)$, where ζ is a primitive root of unity. As stated in Sect. 2.1, in this case it holds $R_q^\vee = \frac{1}{f'(\zeta)} R_q$ for all $q \in \mathbb{Z}$. In order to ease notation, we set $\lambda = f'(\zeta)$ and write $x = \frac{1}{\lambda} \cdot \tilde{x}$ for every $x \in R_q^\vee$, where $\tilde{x} \in R_q$.

In the following, we study the M-LWE problem in its discrete version, as introduced in Sect. 2.4. This is convenient as we replace in the course of the proof the public matrix $\mathbf{A} \in (R_q)^{m \times d}$ by the second part of some multiple-secret M-LWE sample. Thus, we need to ensure that the second part is also an element of $(R_q)^{m \times d}$. Hence, we represent m samples by $(\mathbf{A}, \mathbf{A} \cdot \mathbf{s} + \mathbf{e} \bmod qR^\vee) \in (R_q)^{m \times d} \times (R_q^\vee)^m$, with $\mathbf{s} \in (R_2^\vee)^d$ and $\mathbf{e} \leftarrow \psi$, where ψ is a distribution on $R^\vee$. The theorem uses the discrete Gaussian distribution $\psi = \mathcal{D}_{R^\vee, \alpha q}$, for some positive real α.

Theorem 1. *Let K be a cyclotomic number field of degree n with R its ring of integers. Let ℓ, d, m and q be positive integers with q prime and m polynomial in n. Further, let α and β be positive real numbers such that $\frac{\alpha}{\beta} \leq \frac{1}{\sqrt{m} \cdot n^2 d}$. Let ε be a positive real number with $\varepsilon \in [0, 1)$ such that $\beta q \geq \eta_\varepsilon(R^\vee)$. and $\varepsilon = O(\frac{1}{m})$. Then, for any $d \geq \ell \cdot \log_2 q + \omega(\log_2 n)$, there is a probabilistic polynomial-time reduction from M-SLWE$^m_{n,\ell,q,\mathcal{D}_{R^\vee,\beta q}}$ and M-LWE$^{m,d}_{n,\ell,q,\mathcal{D}_{R^\vee,\alpha q}}$ to bin-M-SLWE$^m_{n,d,q,\mathcal{D}_{R^\vee,\beta q}}$.*

The degree n of the number field K and the number of samples m are preserved. The reduction increases the rank of the module from ℓ to $\ell \cdot \log_2 q + \omega(\log_2 n)$ and the Gaussian width from αq to $\alpha q \cdot \sqrt{m} \cdot n^2 d$. Further, M-LWE$^m_{n,\ell,q,\mathcal{D}_{R^\vee,\alpha q}}$ trivially reduces to M-SLWE$^m_{n,\ell,q,\mathcal{D}_{R^\vee,\beta q}}$, as $\beta \geq \alpha$.

Proof. Fix any $n, \ell, d, m, q, \alpha, \beta$ and ε as in the statement of the theorem. Given a bin-M-SLWE$^m_{n,d,q,\mathcal{D}_{R^\vee,\beta q}}$ sample $(\mathbf{A}, \mathbf{A} \cdot \mathbf{s} + \mathbf{e}) \in (R_q)^{m \times d} \times (R_q^\vee)^m$, with $\mathbf{s} \in (R_2^\vee)^d$ and $\mathbf{e} \leftarrow (\mathcal{D}_{R^\vee,\beta q})^m$, the search problem asks to find $\mathbf{s}$ and $\mathbf{e}$. In order to prove the statement, we define different hybrid distributions:

- $H_0 : (\mathbf{A}, \mathbf{A} \cdot \mathbf{s} + \mathbf{e})$, as in bin-M-SLWE$_{n,d,q,\mathcal{D}_{R^\vee,\beta q}}^m$,
- $H_1 : (\mathbf{A}' = \lambda(\mathbf{BC} + \mathbf{Z}), \mathbf{A}' \cdot \mathbf{s} + \mathbf{e})$, where $\mathbf{B} \leftarrow U((R_q)^{m \times \ell})$, $\mathbf{C} \leftarrow U((R_q^\vee)^{\ell \times d})$, and $\mathbf{Z} \leftarrow (\mathcal{D}_{R^\vee,\alpha q})^{m \times d}$ and $\mathbf{s}, \mathbf{e}$ as in H_0,
- $H_2 : (\mathbf{B}, \mathbf{C}, \mathbf{Z}, \mathbf{B}(\lambda \mathbf{Cs}) + \mathbf{Z}(\lambda \mathbf{s}) + \mathbf{e})$, where $\mathbf{B}, \mathbf{C}, \mathbf{Z}, \mathbf{s}, \mathbf{e}$ as in H_1,
- $H_3 : (\mathbf{B}, \mathbf{C}, \mathbf{Z}, \mathbf{B}(\lambda \mathbf{Cs}) + \mathbf{e}')$, where $\mathbf{e}' \leftarrow (\mathcal{D}_{R^\vee,\beta q})^m$ and $\mathbf{B}, \mathbf{C}, \mathbf{Z}, \mathbf{s}$ as in H_2,
- $H_4 : (\mathbf{B}, \mathbf{C}, \mathbf{Z}, \mathbf{Bs}' + \mathbf{e}')$, where $\mathbf{s}' \leftarrow U((R_q^\vee)^\ell)$ and $\mathbf{B}, \mathbf{C}, \mathbf{Z}, \mathbf{e}'$ as in H_3.

For $i \in \{0, \ldots, 4\}$, we denote by P_i the problem of finding the secret $\mathbf{s}$ (resp. $\mathbf{s}'$ in H_4), given a sample of the distribution H_i. We say that problem P_i is hard if for any probabilistic polynomial-time attacker $\mathcal{A}$ the advantage of solving P_i is negligible, thus $\mathrm{Adv}_{P_i}[\mathcal{A}(H_i) = \mathbf{s}] \leq n^{-\omega(1)}$, where n is the degree of K. The overall idea is to show that if P_4 is hard, then P_0 is hard as well.

Problem P_4 is hard: By the hardness assumption of M-SLWE$_{n,\ell,q,\mathcal{D}_{R^\vee,\beta q}}^m$, it yields

$$\mathrm{Adv}_{P_4}[\mathcal{A}(H_4) = \mathbf{s}'] \leq n^{-\omega(1)}.$$

From P_4 to P_3: By the probability preservation property of the statistical distance (Lemma 3), we have

$$\mathrm{Adv}_{P_3}[\mathcal{A}(H_3) = \mathbf{s}] \leq \mathrm{Adv}_{P_4}[\mathcal{A}(H_4) = \mathbf{s}'] + \Delta(H_3, H_4).$$

The only difference between the distributions H_3 and H_4 is that the element $\lambda \mathbf{Cs}$ in H_3 is replaced by $\mathbf{s}'$ in H_4. Our aim is to show that $\lambda \mathbf{Cs}$ is statistically close to the uniform distribution on $(R_q^\vee)^\ell$. We set $\tilde{\mathbf{C}} = \lambda \mathbf{C} \in (R_q)^{\ell \times d}$ and $\mathbf{s} = \frac{1}{\lambda} \tilde{\mathbf{s}}$, where $\tilde{\mathbf{s}} \in (R_2)^d$. By the leftover hash lemma (Lemma 7) it yields that the distribution $(\tilde{\mathbf{C}}, \tilde{\mathbf{C}}\tilde{\mathbf{s}})$ is statistically close to the distribution $(\tilde{\mathbf{C}}, \tilde{\mathbf{s}}')$, where $\tilde{\mathbf{s}}' \leftarrow U((R_q)^\ell)$, as $d \geq \ell \log_2 q + \omega(\log_2 n)$. Dividing the first and the second part of both distributions by λ preserves the statistical distance and yields that the distribution $(\mathbf{C}, \lambda \mathbf{Cs})$ is statistically close to the distribution $(\mathbf{C}, \mathbf{s}')$, where $\mathbf{s}' \leftarrow U((R_q^\vee)^\ell)$. Overall, it yields $\Delta(H_3, H_4) \leq \frac{1}{2}\sqrt{(1 + q^\ell/2^d)^n - 1}$. As we require $d \geq \ell \log_2 q + \omega(\log_2 n)$, we obtain $\Delta(H_3, H_4) \leq n^{-\omega(1)}$.

From P_3 to P_2: By the probability preservation property of the Rényi divergence (Lemma 8), we have

$$\mathrm{Adv}_{P_2}[\mathcal{A}(H_2) = \mathbf{s}]^2 \leq \mathrm{Adv}_{P_3}[\mathcal{A}(H_3) = \mathbf{s}] \cdot \mathrm{RD}(H_2 \| H_3).$$

In order to compute the Rényi divergence of H_2 and H_3, we need to compute the Rényi divergence of $\mathbf{Z}(\lambda \mathbf{s}) + \mathbf{e}$ and $\mathbf{e}'$. We claim that each of the m coefficients of $\mathbf{Z}(\lambda \mathbf{s})$ is bounded above by $\alpha q d n^2$ with probability $1 - 2^{-\Omega(n)}$, and provide a detailed proof below in Lemma 10. Thus, it suffices to compute the Rényi divergence of $(\mathcal{D}_{R^\vee,\beta q,c})^m$ and $(\mathcal{D}_{R^\vee,\beta q})^m$, where $c \in R^\vee$ with norm bounded above by $\alpha q d n^2$. Using that $\beta q \geq \eta_\varepsilon(R^\vee)$, the multiplicativity of the Rényi divergence (Lemma 8) and the result of Lemma 9 about the Rényi divergence of shifted discrete Gaussians, we deduce

$$\mathrm{RD}_2\left((\mathcal{D}_{R^\vee,\beta q,c})^m \| (\mathcal{D}_{R^\vee,\beta q})^m\right) = \mathrm{RD}_2\left(\mathcal{D}_{R^\vee,\beta q,c} \| \mathcal{D}_{R^\vee,\beta q}\right)^m$$

$$\leq \left(\frac{1+\varepsilon}{1-\varepsilon}\right)^{2m} \cdot \exp\left(\frac{2\pi\|c\|^2}{(\beta q)^2}\right)^m$$

$$\approx \left(\frac{1+\varepsilon}{1-\varepsilon}\right)^{2m} \cdot \left(1 + \frac{2\pi\|c\|^2}{(\beta q)^2}\right)^m.$$

The last approximation comes from considering the function $f(x) = \exp(x)$, developing its first-order Taylor expansion at the point 0, i.e. $f(x) \approx 1 + x$, and evaluating the function f at the small point $\frac{2\pi\|c\|^2}{(\beta q)^2}$. By setting $\frac{2\pi\|c\|^2}{(\beta q)^2} \leq \frac{2\pi}{m}$, which leads to $\frac{\alpha}{\beta} \leq \frac{1}{\sqrt{m \cdot n^2 d}}$, we get $\exp\left(\frac{2\pi\|c\|^2}{(\beta q)^2}\right)^m \approx e^{2\pi}$.

For the Rényi divergence to be bounded by a constant, we also need $\varepsilon = O(\frac{1}{m})$. Indeed, we have $\left(\frac{1+\varepsilon}{1-\varepsilon}\right)^2 = \left(1 + \frac{4\varepsilon/1-\varepsilon}{2}\right)^2 < \exp\left(\frac{4\varepsilon}{1-\varepsilon}\right)$ as $\left(1 + \frac{x}{y}\right)^y < \exp(x)$ for any $x, y > 0$. Without loss of generality, assume $\varepsilon < \frac{1}{2}$, then $\frac{1}{1-\varepsilon} < 2$ and thus, we get $\left(\frac{1+\varepsilon}{1-\varepsilon}\right)^{2m} < \exp(8m\varepsilon)$ and therefore $\varepsilon = O(\frac{1}{m})$ suffices.

From P_2 to P_1: Since more information is given in distribution H_2 than in distribution H_1, the problem P_1 is harder than P_2 and hence

$$\mathrm{Adv}_{P_1}[\mathcal{A}(H_1) = \mathbf{s}] \leq \mathrm{Adv}_{P_2}[\mathcal{A}(H_2) = \mathbf{s}].$$

From P_1 to P_0: By the hardness assumption of M-LWE$^{m,d}_{n,\ell,q,\mathcal{D}_{R^\vee,\alpha q}}$, the distributions H_0 and H_1 are computationally indistinguishable. More concretely,

$$\mathrm{Adv}_{P_0}[\mathcal{A}(H_0) = \mathbf{s}] \leq \mathrm{Adv}_{P_1}[\mathcal{A}(H_1) = \mathbf{s}] + d \cdot \mathrm{Adv}_{\text{M-LWE}}$$

$$\leq \mathrm{Adv}_{P_1}[\mathcal{A}(H_1) = \mathbf{s}] + d \cdot n^{-\omega(1)}$$

where d is the number of secret vectors, represented as the columns of the matrix $\mathbf{C}$. Putting all equations from above together, we obtain

$$\mathrm{Adv}_{P_0}[\mathcal{A}(H_0) = \mathbf{s}] \leq \mathrm{Adv}_{P_1}[\mathcal{A}(H_1) = \mathbf{s}] + d \cdot \mathrm{Adv}_{\text{M-LWE}}$$

$$\leq \mathrm{Adv}_{P_2}[\mathcal{A}(H_2) = \mathbf{s}] + d \cdot \mathrm{Adv}_{\text{M-LWE}}$$

$$\leq \sqrt{\mathrm{Adv}_{P_3}[\mathcal{A}(H_3) = \mathbf{s}] \cdot \mathrm{RD}_2(H_2 \| H_3)} + d \cdot \mathrm{Adv}_{\text{M-LWE}}$$

$$\leq \sqrt{(\mathrm{Adv}_{P_4}[\mathcal{A}(H_4) = \mathbf{s}'] + \Delta(H_3, H_4)) \cdot \mathrm{RD}_2(H_2 \| H_3)}$$
$$+ d \cdot \mathrm{Adv}_{\text{M-LWE}}$$

$$\leq n^{-\omega(1)}.$$

$\square$

To complete the proof above, we now show the following bound on the norm of the product of some discrete Gaussian matrix (in the canonical embedding) and a binary vector in the dual ring (in the coefficient embedding).

Lemma 10. *Let K be a cyclotomic number field with R its ring of integers of degree n. Let $\mathbf{Z} \leftarrow (\mathcal{D}_{R^\vee, \alpha q})^{m \times d}$ and $\mathbf{s} \leftarrow U((R_2^\vee)^d)$, where $R_2^\vee = \lambda R_2$ as in the statement of Theorem 1 above. We set $\tilde{\mathbf{s}} = \lambda \mathbf{s}$. Then, with overwhelming probability $\|\mathbf{Z}\tilde{\mathbf{s}}\|_2 \leq \alpha q n^2 d \sqrt{m}$. In particular, the Euclidean norm of each coefficient $(\mathbf{Z}\tilde{\mathbf{s}})_i$ for $i \in [m]$ is bounded above by $\alpha q n^2 d$.*

Proof. We want to bound the norm $\|\mathbf{Z}\tilde{\mathbf{s}}\|_2 = \|\sigma_H(\mathbf{Z}\tilde{\mathbf{s}})\|_2$, where the latter norm is taken in $\mathbb{R}^{nm}$. Since σ and σ_H only differ by a unitary transformation, we can consider σ instead of σ_H. For all $i \in [m]$ it yields

$$\sigma((\mathbf{Z}\tilde{\mathbf{s}})_i) = \sigma\left(\sum_{j \in [d]} z_{ij} \cdot \tilde{s}_j\right) = \sum_{j \in [d]} \mathrm{diag}(\sigma(z_{ij})) \cdot \sigma(\tilde{s}_j).$$

Let θ denote the ring homomorphism from $K^{m \times d} \to \mathbb{C}^{nm \times nd}$, where

$$\theta(\mathbf{Z}) = \begin{bmatrix} \mathbf{Z}_{11} & - & \mathbf{Z}_{1d} \\ | & \searize & | \\ \mathbf{Z}_{m1} & - & \mathbf{Z}_{md} \end{bmatrix}, \text{ with } \mathbf{Z}_{ij} = \mathrm{diag}(\sigma(z_{ij})) \in \mathbb{C}^{n \times n}.$$

Then, $\sigma(\mathbf{Z}\tilde{\mathbf{s}}) = \theta(\mathbf{Z})\sigma(\tilde{\mathbf{s}})$ and thus $\|\sigma(\mathbf{Z}\tilde{\mathbf{s}})\|_2 \leq \|\theta(\mathbf{Z})\|_2 \cdot \|\sigma(\tilde{\mathbf{s}})\|_2$. Using the Vandermonde matrix $\mathbf{V}$ to switch from the coefficient embedding τ to the canonical embedding σ, we can bound $\|\sigma(\tilde{\mathbf{s}})\|_2 \leq \|\mathbf{V}\|_2 \cdot \|\tau(\tilde{\mathbf{s}})\|_2 \leq n \cdot \sqrt{nd}$, where we use that for cyclotomic number fields it yields $\|\mathbf{V}\|_2 \leq \|\mathbf{V}\|_F = \left(\sum_{i,j \in [n]} |\alpha_i^{j-1}|^2\right)^{1/2} \leq n$ (as α is a unit) and that $\tau(\tilde{\mathbf{s}})$ is a binary vector of dimension nd. Further, for each $i \in [m]$ and $j \in [d]$ it holds $\|\sigma(z_{ij})\|_2 \leq \alpha q \sqrt{n}$ with probability $1 - 2^{-\Omega(n)}$. Hence,

$$\|\theta(\mathbf{Z})\|_2 \leq \|\theta(\mathbf{Z})\|_F = \sqrt{\sum_{i \in [m]} \sum_{j \in [d]} \sum_{k \in [n]} |\sigma_k(z_{ij})|^2}$$

$$= \sqrt{\sum_{i \in [m]} \sum_{j \in [d]} \|\sigma(z_{ij})\|_2^2} \leq \alpha q \sqrt{nd}\sqrt{m}.$$

Combining both bounds proves the claim.   □

4   Classical Hardness for Linear Rank Modules

In the following, we use the result from Sect. 3 to prove a classical reduction from Mod-GapSVP to M-LWE for any polynomial-sized modulus $\hat{p}$ and module rank d at least $2n + \omega(\log_2 n)$, for the case of power-of-two cyclotomics.

Theorem 2. *Let ν be a power of 2, defining the ν-th cyclotomic number field with R its ring of integers of degree $n = \nu/2$. Let $d, \hat{p}, m$ be positive integers and $\hat{\beta}$ and γ be positive reals. Fix $\varepsilon \in (0, \frac{1}{2})$ such that $\hat{\beta} \geq \sqrt{2} \cdot 2^{-n} \cdot \eta_\varepsilon(R^\vee)$*

and $\varepsilon = O\left(\frac{1}{m}\right)$. *There is a* classical *probabilistic polynomial-time reduction from* Mod-GapSVP$_\gamma$ *to* M-LWE$^m_{n,d,\hat{p},\Upsilon_{\hat{\beta}}}$, *where* $d \geq 2n + \omega(\log_2 n)$ *and*

$$\hat{\beta} = \tilde{\Theta}\left(\frac{\sqrt{m} \cdot n^{\frac{21}{4}}}{\gamma}\right).$$

We quickly recall the proof structure for Theorem 2 as pictured in Fig. 1 in the introduction:

1. A reduction from Mod-GapSVP to M-LWE with an exponential-sized modulus q in Theorem 4, Sect. 4.2,
2. A reduction from M-LWE and M-SLWE to bin-M-SLWE in Theorem 1, Sect. 3, still with an exponential-sized modulus q,
3. A modulus reduction from bin-M-SLWE with exponential-sized modulus q to bin-M-SLWE with polynomial-sized modulus p in Corollary 1, Sect. 4.1 (Corollary 2 for the power-of-two cyclotomic case),
4. A trivial reduction from bin-M-SLWE to M-SLWE,
5. A reduction from M-SLWE to M-LWE with polynomial-sized prime modulus p, satisfying $p = 1 \bmod \nu$, using [LS15, Sec. 4.3],
6. A reduction from M-LWE with prime modulus p satisfying $p = 1 \bmod \nu$ to M-LWE with arbitrary polynomially large modulus $\hat{p}$.

We first provide a modulus reduction in Sect. 4.1, using the results of Albrecht and Deo [AD17]. Finally, we adapt in Sect. 4.2 the classical reduction from Peikert [Pei09] to the module setting. In Sect. 4.3, we explain how to switch between different error distributions.

4.1   Modulus Switching

In order to prove the classical hardness of M-LWE, we provide a modulus reduction, where the rank of the underlying module is preserved. This corresponds to the modulus reduction for LWE shown by Brakerski et al. [BLP+13, Cor. 3.2]. Note that Langlois and Stehlé [LS15] proved a modulus switching result from M-LWE$_{n,d,q,\Upsilon_\beta}$ to M-LWE$_{n,d,p,\Upsilon_{\beta'}}$, but the error increases at least by a multiplicative factor $\frac{q}{p}$, which is exponential if q is exponential-sized and p only polynomial-sized.

Prior to this paper, Albrecht and Deo [AD17] adapted the more general result from [BLP+13, Thm. 3.1], from which Corollary 3.2 is deduced. Thus, we first recall their general result [AD17, Thm. 1] and then derive the corollary we need from it. Let K be a number field and let R be its ring of integers.

Theorem 3 (Thm. 1 [AD17]). *Let* d, d', q, p *be positive integers,* $\varepsilon \in (0, \frac{1}{2})$ *and* $\mathbf{G} \in R^{d' \times d}$. *Fix a vector* $\mathbf{s} = (s_1, \ldots, s_d)^T \in (R_q^\vee)^d$. *Further, let* Λ *be the lattice given by* $\Lambda = \frac{1}{p}\mathbf{G}_H^T R^{d'} + R^d$ *with known basis* $\mathbf{B}_\Lambda$ *in the canonical embedding, let* $\mathbf{B}_R$ *be some known basis of* R *in* H *and let* $\mathbf{B}_{s_j R}$ *be a known basis* *of $s_j R$ in the canonical embedding for $j \in [d]$. Let further be r a real number such that*

$$r \geq \max \begin{cases} \|\tilde{\mathbf{B}}_\Lambda\| \cdot \sqrt{2\ln(2nd(1+1/\varepsilon))/\pi} \\ \frac{1}{q}\|\tilde{\mathbf{B}}_R\| \cdot \sqrt{2\ln(2nd(1+1/\varepsilon))/\pi} \\ \frac{1}{q}\max_{j\in[d]} \left(\|\tilde{\mathbf{B}}_{s_j R}\| \cdot \frac{1}{\min_{i\in[n]} |\sigma_i(s_j)|} \right) \sqrt{2\ln(2n(1+1/\varepsilon))/\pi} \end{cases}.$$

There exists an efficient mapping $\mathcal{F}\colon (R_q)^d \times \mathbb{T}_{R^\vee} \to (R_p)^{d'} \times \mathbb{T}_{R^\vee}$ such that:

1. *The output distribution $\mathcal{F}(U((R_q)^d \times \mathbb{T}_{R^\vee}))$ given uniform input is within statistical distance 4ε of the uniform distribution on $(R_p)^{d'} \times \mathbb{T}_{R^\vee}$.*

2. *Set $B = \max_{i\in[n],j\in[d]} |\sigma_i(s_j)|$. The output distribution $\mathcal{F}(A_{q,s,D_\beta}^{(R^d)})$ is within statistical distance $(4d+6)\varepsilon$ of $A_{p,\mathbf{G}s,D_{\beta'}}^{(R^{d'})}$, where*

$$(\beta'_i)^2 = \beta^2 + r^2(\gamma^2 + \sum_{j\in[d]} |\sigma_i(s_j)|^2),$$

for $i \in [n]$ and γ satisfying $\gamma^2 \geq B^2 d$.

4.1.1   General Case

Whereas Albrecht and Deo [AD17] proved a rank-modulus trade-off, defining a map from M-LWE in module rank d to d/k and from modulus q to q^k for any divisor k of d, we are interested in another particular instance of Theorem 3 where the rank of the module is preserved. The following corollary specializes the general result to the case of $\mathbf{G} = \mathbf{I}_d \in R^{d\times d}$ and its proof is essentially the same as in [AD17]. Overall, we obtain a modulus reduction, where the rank d is preserved.

Corollary 1. *Let d, q, p be positive integers with $q \geq p$, ε and β be real numbers with $\varepsilon \in (0, \frac{1}{2})$ and $\beta > 0$ and $\mathbf{G} = \mathbf{I}_d \in R^{d\times d}$. Let χ be a distribution on $R_q^\vee$ satisfying*

$$\Pr_{s\leftarrow \chi} \left[\max_{i\in[n]} |\sigma_i(s)| > B \right] \leq \delta \text{ and } \Pr_{s\leftarrow \chi} \left[\max_{i,j\in[n]} \frac{|\sigma_i(s)|}{|\sigma_j(s)|} > B' \right] \leq \delta',$$

for some non-negative real numbers B, B', δ, δ'. By χ^d we denote the distribution on $(R_q^\vee)^d$, where every coefficient is sampled from χ independently. Let further be r a real number such that

$$r \geq \max \begin{cases} \frac{1}{p}\|\tilde{\mathbf{B}}_R\| \cdot \sqrt{2\ln(2nd(1+1/\varepsilon))/\pi} \\ \frac{1}{q}B'\|\tilde{\mathbf{B}}_R\| \cdot \sqrt{2\ln(2n(1+1/\varepsilon))/\pi} \end{cases}.$$

Then, there is a polynomial-time reduction from M-SLWE$_{n,d,q,D_\beta}^m(\chi^d)$ to the problem M-SLWE$_{n,d,p,D_{\beta'}}^m(\chi^d)$ for $(\beta')^2 \geq \beta^2 + 2r^2 B^2 d$. This reduction reduces the advantage by at most $1 - (1 - \delta - \delta')^d + (4d+6)\varepsilon m$.

Proof. We use the transformation from Theorem 3 by taking $\gamma^2 = B^2 d$ and replacing $\sum_{j\in[d]} |\sigma_i(s_j)|$ for every $i \in [n]$ by B. For all $j \in [d]$ it holds $\|\tilde{\mathbf{B}}_{s_j R}\| \leq \max_{i\in[n]} |\sigma_i(s_j)| \cdot \|\tilde{\mathbf{B}}_R\|$. Thus, we can replace the maximum in the third condition on r of Theorem 3 by $B' \|\tilde{\mathbf{B}}_R\|$. We can write $\mathbf{G}$ in the coefficient embedding as $\hat{\mathbf{G}} = \mathbf{I}_d \otimes \mathbf{I}_n = \mathbf{I}_{dn}$, defining the corresponding lattice $\hat{\Lambda} = \frac{1}{p}\hat{\mathbf{G}}^T \mathbb{Z}^{dn} + \mathbb{Z}^{dn}$ with basis $\mathbf{B}_{\hat{\Lambda}} = \frac{1}{p}\mathbf{I}_{dn}$. To move from the coefficient embedding to the canonical embedding, we can simply multiply the basis by the matrix $\mathbf{B}_{R^d} = \mathbf{I}_d \otimes \mathbf{B}_R$. The basis for $\Lambda = \frac{1}{p}\mathbf{G}_H^T R^d + R^d$ given in the canonical embedding is thus given by

$$\mathbf{B}_\Lambda = (\frac{1}{p}\mathbf{I}_d \otimes \mathbf{I}_n) \cdot (\mathbf{I}_d \otimes \mathbf{B}_R) = \frac{1}{p}\mathbf{I}_d \otimes \mathbf{B}_R,$$

using the mixed product property of the Kronecker product. Orthogonalizing from left to right gives $\|\tilde{\mathbf{B}}_\Lambda\| = \frac{1}{p}\|\tilde{\mathbf{B}}_R\|$. As $q \geq p$, we have $\frac{1}{q}\|\tilde{\mathbf{B}}_R\| \leq \frac{1}{p}\|\tilde{\mathbf{B}}_R\| = \|\tilde{\mathbf{B}}_\Lambda\|$ and we can thus merge the first and second condition on r of Theorem 3. The loss in advantage is the result of a simple probability calculus. Let E be the event that $\max_{i\in[n]} |\sigma_i(s)| \leq B$, which happens with probability greater than $1 - \delta$, and F be the event that $\max_{i,j\in[n]} \frac{|\sigma_i(s)|}{|\sigma_j(s)|} \leq B'$, which happens with probability greater than $1 - \delta'$ for any $s \leftarrow \chi$. It yields $\Pr(E \cap F) = \Pr(E) + \Pr(F) - \Pr(E \cup F) \geq \Pr(E) + \Pr(F) - 1 \geq 1 - \delta - \delta'$. As the secret vector $\mathbf{s} = (s_1,\ldots,s_d)^T \in (R_q^\vee)^d$ is chosen by drawing d times independently from χ, we have to add the advantage loss of $1 - (1 - \delta - \delta')^d$ to the one coming from Theorem 3. $\qquad\square$

4.1.2 Power-of-two Cyclotomic Rings

The quality of Corollary 1 depends on the factor $\Delta = 2r^2 B^2 d$, that we have to add to the error β^2. This factor is determined by the rank d, the first bound B on the secret distribution χ and the number r, which itself is quantified by the second bound B' on the secret distribution χ, the field degree n, the starting modulus q, the reduced modulus p and the norm $\|\tilde{\mathbf{B}}_R\|$. In the following, we give a concrete calculation example for those parameters in the case of power-of-two cyclotomic rings and where χ^d is the uniform distribution on $(R_2^\vee)^d$, denoted by $U((R_2^\vee)^d)$. Let ν be a power of two, defining the ring of integers of the ν-th cyclotomic field, given by $R = \mathbb{Z}[\zeta] \cong \mathbb{Z}[x]/\langle f \rangle$, where $f(x) = x^n + 1$ and $n = \nu/2$.

Corollary 2. *Let R be the ring of integers of degree n, where n is a power of 2. Let d, q, p be positive integers with $q \geq p$, ε and β be real numbers with $\varepsilon \in (0, \frac{1}{2})$ and $\beta > 0$ and $\mathbf{G} = \mathbf{I}_d \in R^{d\times d}$. Let further be r a real number such that*

$$r \geq \max \begin{cases} \frac{1}{p}\sqrt{n} \cdot \sqrt{2\ln(2nd(1+1/\varepsilon))/\pi} \\ \frac{1}{q} \cdot n^{5/2} \cdot 2^{(n-2)/2} \cdot \sqrt{2\ln(2n(1+1/\varepsilon))/\pi} \end{cases}.$$

For $(\beta')^2 \geq \beta^2 + 2dr^2$, there is a probabilistic polynomial-time reduction from the problem M-SLWE$_{n,d,q,D_\beta}^m(U((R_2^\vee)^d))$ *to* M-SLWE$_{n,d,p,D_{\beta'}}^m(U((R_2^\vee)^d))$. *This reduction reduces the advantage by at most $1 - (1 - \frac{1}{2^n})^d + (4d+6)\varepsilon m$.*

In order to guarantee a negligible loss in advantage, we require n and d to be polynomial in the security parameter and ε negligibly small. If q is exponentially large, as it is the case in the classical hardness result of Sect. 4.2, say $q \geq 2^n$, then we know that r is polynomial in n.

Proof. Let R be the ring of integers of degree n, where n is a power of 2. Its dual $R^\vee = \frac{1}{n}R$ is just a scaling of the ring R itself. Further, the map that takes the vector of an element in R defined by its canonical embedding to the vector corresponding to the coefficient embedding is a scaled isometry with scaling factor $\frac{1}{\sqrt{n}}$. A basis $\mathbf{B}_R$ for R in H is given by $\sqrt{n} \cdot \mathbf{U}$, where $\mathbf{U}$ is unitary.

For any element $s \in R$, let $\mathbf{S}_H$ be the matrix of multiplication by s in the canonical embedding written in the basis $\{\mathbf{h}_i\}_{i \in [n]}$ of H. Let $\text{Rot}(s)$ be the matrix of multiplication by s in the coefficient embedding. As mentioned above, going from the coefficient embedding to the canonical embedding is a scaled isometry of scaling factor $\sqrt{n}$. Thus,

$$\mathbf{S}_H = (\mathbf{B}_R)^{-1} \cdot \text{Rot}(s) \cdot \mathbf{B}_R = \frac{1}{\sqrt{n}} \cdot \mathbf{U}^\dagger \cdot \text{Rot}(s) \cdot \sqrt{n} \cdot \mathbf{U} = \mathbf{U}^\dagger \cdot \text{Rot}(s) \cdot \mathbf{U},$$

where $\mathbf{U}$ is unitary. As explained in the preliminaries, the singular values of $\mathbf{S}_H$ are given by $|\sigma_i(s)|$ for $i \in [n]$. It yields

$$(\mathbf{S}_H)^\dagger \mathbf{S}_H = (\mathbf{U}^\dagger \cdot \text{Rot}(s) \cdot \mathbf{U})^\dagger (\mathbf{U}^\dagger \cdot \text{Rot}(s) \cdot \mathbf{U})$$
$$= \mathbf{U}^{-1} \cdot \text{Rot}(s)^T \cdot \text{Rot}(s) \cdot \mathbf{U}.$$

As a conclusion, the singular values of $\text{Rot}(s)$ are exactly the values given by $|\sigma_i(s)|$ for $i \in [n]$. The smallest (resp. largest) singular value of $\text{Rot}(s)$ thus determines the minimum (resp. maximum) of the set $\{|\sigma_i(s)|\}_{i \in [n]}$.

We use this observation to compute the bounds B and B' of Corollary 1 for the case where χ equals $U((R_2^\vee)^d)$. Note that we provide new bounds, as the ones calculated by Albrecht and Deo [AD17] hold for a Gaussian, and not a binary secret distribution.

Using the identity $R_2^\vee = \frac{1}{n}R_2$, we know that $\text{Rot}(s) = \frac{1}{n}\text{Rot}(\tilde{s})$, where $\tilde{s} \in R_2$ and $\text{Rot}(\tilde{s})$ only has entries from the set $\{0, 1\}$. Let $\text{Rot}(\tilde{s}) = \mathbf{U} \cdot \boldsymbol{\Sigma} \cdot \mathbf{V}^\dagger$ be the singular value decomposition of $\text{Rot}(\tilde{s})$, where $\mathbf{U}$ and $\mathbf{V}$ are unitary matrices over $\mathbb{R}$ and $\boldsymbol{\Sigma}$ is a diagonal matrix with the singular values of $\text{Rot}(\tilde{s})$ on its diagonal. The singular value decomposition of $\text{Rot}(s)$ is thus given by $\text{Rot}(s) = \mathbf{U} \cdot \frac{1}{n}\boldsymbol{\Sigma} \cdot \mathbf{V}^\dagger$ and we can deduce that the singular values of $\text{Rot}(s)$ are just the singular values of $\text{Rot}(\tilde{s})$, shrank by a factor of $\frac{1}{n}$.

The largest singular value $\mathfrak{s}_1(\text{Rot}(\tilde{s}))$ of $\text{Rot}(\tilde{s})$ is bounded above by its Frobenius norm $\|\text{Rot}(\tilde{s})\|_F$ and hence

$$\mathfrak{s}_1(\text{Rot}(\tilde{s})) \leq \|\text{Rot}(\tilde{s})\|_F = \left(\sum_{i,j \in [n]} |\text{Rot}(\tilde{s})_{ij}|^2\right)^{1/2} \leq n.$$

It follows $\mathfrak{s}_1(\text{Rot}(s)) \leq 1$.

The smallest singular value $\mathfrak{s}_n(\mathrm{Rot}(\tilde{s}))$ of $\mathrm{Rot}(\tilde{s})$ is bounded below by the following formula given in [PP02]:

$$\mathfrak{s}_n(\mathrm{Rot}(\tilde{s})) \geq \frac{|\det(\mathrm{Rot}(\tilde{s}))|}{2^{(n-2)/2}\|\mathrm{Rot}(\tilde{s})\|_F} \geq \frac{|\det(\mathrm{Rot}(\tilde{s}))|}{2^{(n-2)/2} \cdot n} \geq \frac{1}{2^{(n-2)/2} \cdot n}.$$

The last equation stems from the fact that every entry of $\mathrm{Rot}(\tilde{s})$ is an integer and $\mathrm{Rot}(\tilde{s})$ is invertible (in K) for every nonzero $\tilde{s}$, thus $|\det(\mathrm{Rot}(\tilde{s}))| \geq 1$ for every $\tilde{s} \neq 0$. It follows $\mathfrak{s}_n(\mathrm{Rot}(s)) \geq \frac{1}{2^{(n-2)/2} \cdot n^2}$. We can thus set $B = 1$ with $\delta = 0$ and $B' = n^2 \cdot 2^{(n-2)/2}$ with $\delta' = \frac{1}{2^n}$ as

$$\max_{i,j \in [n]} \frac{|\sigma_i(s)|}{|\sigma_j(s)|} = \frac{\mathfrak{s}_1(\mathrm{Rot}(s))}{\mathfrak{s}_n(\mathrm{Rot}(s))} \leq n^2 \cdot 2^{(n-2)/2},$$

for every $s \neq 0$, which happens with probability $1 - \frac{1}{2^n}$.   □

As the bound on the smallest singular value of [PP02] does not take the nega-cyclic structure of $\mathrm{Rot}(\tilde{s})$ for power-of-two cyclotomics into account, we conjecture that it is very loose. Experiments in dimensions up to 2^{10} show that $\mathrm{Rot}(\tilde{s})$ behaves as a random binary matrix and the smallest singular value $\mathfrak{s}_n(\mathrm{Rot}(\tilde{s}))$ can thus with high probability be bounded below by $\frac{1}{10\sqrt{n}}$.[2] With this heuristic bound and requiring p to be large enough, we can achieve $\Delta = \beta^2$. Overall, this leads to an error increase from $\sqrt{2}\beta$ to $\sqrt{3}\beta$ in *Step 3* of Figure 1, as explained in the introduction. We refer to [vNG47] for more details on heuristic bounds on the smallest singular values of random sub-Gaussian matrices.

4.2 Classical Reduction for M-LWE

In this section, we adapt the classical hardness reduction of LWE from Peikert [Pei09, Thm. 3.1] to the module setting. In their introduction, Langlois and Stehlé [LS15] claimed that Peikert's dequantization [Pei09] carries over to the module case. We prove this claim in the following. By using the more recent results of Peikert et al. [PRS17], our reduction directly reduces Mod-GapSVP to the decisional variant M-LWE and holds for any number field K.

Throughout this section, let K be a number field of degree n with R its ring of integers. Any module $M \subseteq K^\ell$ of R of rank $\ell \geq 2$ can be identified with a module lattice Λ of dimension $N = n\ell$. First, we recall the following results about sampling discrete Gaussians over lattices and about reducing the decisional variant of M-LWE from the GDP problem over modules.

Lemma 11 (Thm. 4.1 [GPV08] and Lem. 2.3 [BLP+13]). *There exists a probabilistic polynomial-time algorithm $\mathcal{D}$ that, given a basis $\mathbf{B}$ of a lattice Λ of dimension N, $r \geq \|\mathrm{GS}(\mathbf{B})\| \cdot \sqrt{\ln(2N+4)/\pi}$ and a center $\mathbf{c} \in \mathbb{R}^N$, outputs a sample whose distribution is $D_{\Lambda,r,\mathbf{c}}$.*

---

[2] The Python code is publicly available on https://github.com/KatinkaBou/Probabilistic-Bounds-On-Singular-Values-Of-Rotation-Matrices.

Let $n = t_1 + 2t_2$. As in [PRS17], for any $r > 0, \zeta > 0$, and $T \geq 1$, we define the set of non-spherical parameter vectors $W_{r,\zeta,T}$ as the set of cardinality $(t_1 + t_2) \cdot (T + 1)$, containing for each $i \in [t_1 + t_2]$ and $j \in \{0, \dots, T\}$ the vector $\mathbf{r}_{i,j}$ which is equal to r in all coordinates except in the i-th (and the $(i + t_2)$-th if $i > t_1$), where it is equal to $r \cdot (1 + \zeta)^j$.

Lemma 12 (Adapted from Lem. 6.6 [PRS17]). *There exists a probabilistic polynomial-time algorithm that, given an oracle that solves M-LWE$_{q,\Upsilon_\alpha}$, a real $\alpha \in (0,1)$ and an integer $q \geq 2$ together with its factorization, a rank ℓ module $M \subseteq K^\ell$, a parameter $r \geq \sqrt{2}q \cdot \eta_\varepsilon(M)$ for $\varepsilon = \exp(-\ell n)$, and polynomially many samples from the discrete Gaussian distribution $\mathcal{D}_{M,\mathbf{r}}$ for each $\mathbf{r} \in W_{r,\zeta,T}$ (for some $\zeta = 1/\mathsf{poly}(n)$ and $T = \mathsf{poly}(n)$), solves GDP$_{M^\vee,g}$, for $g = \alpha q/(\sqrt{2}\ell r)$.*

A proof can be found in the full version [BJRW20].

Using these results, we are able to adapt the classical hardness result of LWE from Peikert [Pei09, Thm. 3.1] to modules.

Theorem 4. *Let α, γ be positive real numbers such that $\alpha \in (0,1)$. Let n, ℓ and q be positive integers and set $N = n\ell$. Further, assume that $\ell \geq 2$, $q \geq 2^{\frac{N}{2}}$ and $\gamma \geq \frac{N\sqrt{\ell}}{\alpha}$. Let $M \subseteq K^\ell$ be a rank-ℓ module. There exists a probabilistic polynomial-time reduction from solving Mod-GapSVP$_\gamma$ in the worst-case to solving the problem M-LWE$_{n,\ell,q,\Upsilon_\alpha}$, using $\mathsf{poly}(N)$ samples.*

The proof idea is the same as the one from Peikert, but with two novelties. First, we look at the structured variants of the corresponding problems, i.e., GapSVP over module lattices (of rank ≥ 2) and M-LWE, where the underlying ring R is the ring of integers of a number field K. Second, we replace the main component, a reduction from the BDD problem to the search version of LWE ([Pei09, Prop. 3.4], originally from [Reg05, Lem. 3.4]), by the reduction from the GDP problem over modules to the decisional version of M-LWE (Lemma 12).

Proof. Let $M \subseteq K^\ell$ be a rank-ℓ module over R, such that the corresponding module lattice of dimension N has basis $\mathbf{B} = (\mathbf{b}_i)_{i \in [N]}$. Further, let δ be a positive real. The Mod-GapSVP$_\gamma$ problem asks to decide whether $\lambda_1(M) \leq \delta$ (YES instance) or $\lambda_1(M) > \gamma\delta$ (NO instance). Without loss of generality, we assume that the basis $\mathbf{B}$ is LLL-reduced (Lemma 1) and appropriately scaled, thus the following three conditions hold:

C1) $\lambda_1(M) \leq 2^{\frac{N}{2}}$,
C2) $\min_{i \in [N]} \|\mathrm{GS}(\mathbf{b}_i)\|_2 \geq 1$,
C3) $1 \leq \gamma\delta \leq 2^{\frac{N}{2}}$.

Note for C3, that Mod-GapSVP$_\gamma$ becomes trivial if δ lies outside this range. The reduction executes the following procedure $\mathsf{poly}(N)$ many times:

- Choose $\mathbf{w} \leftarrow D_{g'}$ with $g' = \frac{\delta}{2} \cdot \sqrt{N}$,
- Compute $\mathbf{w} + M$,

- Run the GDP_g oracle from Lemma 12 with $\mathbf{w} + M$, $r = \frac{q\sqrt{2N}}{\gamma\delta}$, $g = \frac{\alpha q}{\sqrt{2\ell}r}$, and using the Gaussian sampler from Lemma 11,
- Compare the output of the oracle with $\mathbf{w}$.

If the oracle's answer is always correct, output NO, otherwise YES.

First, we show that the Gaussian sampler from Lemma 11 always succeeds to provide polynomially many samples from the discrete Gaussian distribution $\mathcal{D}_{M^\vee, \mathbf{r}}$ for each $\mathbf{r} \in W_{r,\varsigma,T}$ (for some $\varsigma = 1/\mathsf{poly}(n)$ and $T = \mathsf{poly}(n)$), needed in Lemma 12. Note that for every $\mathbf{r} = (r_i)_{i \in [n]} \in W_{r,\varsigma,T}$ it yields $r_i \geq r$ for every $i \in [n]$. Thus, it suffices to show that the Gaussian sampler succeeds for r. Let $\mathbf{D} = (\mathbf{B}^{-1})^T$ denote the basis of the dual $M^\vee$, where we denote by $\mathbf{d}_i$ its column vectors for $i \in [N]$. It yields for the ℓ_2-norm that $\|GS(\mathbf{D})\|_2 = \|GS(\mathbf{B})\|_2^{-1}$. As we require in condition C2 that $\min_{i \in [N]} \|GS(\mathbf{b}_i)\|_2 \geq 1$, it follows $\max_{i \in [N]} \|GS(\mathbf{d}_i)\|_2 \leq 1$. Using the condition C3 and that $q \geq 2^{\frac{N}{2}}$, it yields

$$r = \frac{q\sqrt{2N}}{\gamma\delta} \geq \sqrt{2N} \geq 1 \cdot \sqrt{\ln(2N+4)/\pi},$$

and thus the Gaussian sampler always succeeds.

Now, we assume that the reduction is given a NO instance, i.e., $\lambda_1(M) > \gamma\delta$. We claim that in this case, all requirements from Lemma 12 are fulfilled and thus the oracle always outputs the correct answer. Using Lemma 2 it yields $\eta_\varepsilon(M^\vee) \leq \sqrt{N}/\lambda_1(M)$ for $\varepsilon = \exp(-N)$. Thus,

$$r = \frac{q\sqrt{2N}}{\gamma\delta} > \frac{q\sqrt{2N}}{\lambda_1(M)} \geq \sqrt{2}q \cdot \eta_\varepsilon(M^\vee).$$

Further, $\mathbf{w}$ is sampled from $D_{g'}$ with

$$g' = \frac{\delta}{2} \cdot \sqrt{N} \leq \frac{\alpha\gamma\delta}{2\sqrt{n\ell}} = \frac{\alpha q}{\sqrt{2\ell}r} = g.$$

Additionally, $\mathbf{w}$ is the unique solution to this problem as with high probability

$$2 \cdot \|\mathbf{w}\|_2 \leq 2 \cdot g'\sqrt{n\ell} = 2 \cdot \frac{\delta}{2} \cdot \sqrt{N} \cdot \sqrt{n\ell} \leq \frac{\alpha\gamma\delta}{\sqrt{\ell}} < \gamma\delta < \lambda_1(M).$$

If, on the other hand, the reduction is given a YES instance, i.e., $\lambda_1(M) \leq \delta$, we can consider the following alternate experiment. Let $\mathbf{z}$ be a shortest vector in M with $\|\mathbf{z}\|_2 = \lambda_1(M) \leq \delta$. Now, we replace $\mathbf{w}$ by $\mathbf{w}' = \mathbf{w} + \mathbf{z}$ in the second step of the reduction and thus hand in $\mathbf{w}' + M$ to the GDP oracle. Using the statistical distance of $\mathbf{w}$ and $\mathbf{w}'$, it yields

$$\Pr[\mathcal{R}(\mathbf{w} + M) = \mathbf{w}] \leq \Delta(\mathbf{w}, \mathbf{w}') + \Pr[\mathcal{R}(\mathbf{w}' + M) = \mathbf{w}']$$
$$\leq \Delta(\mathbf{w}, \mathbf{w}') + 1 - \Pr[\mathcal{R}(\mathbf{w}' + M) = \mathbf{w}],$$

where $\mathcal{R}$ denotes the GDP oracle. Note that $\mathbf{w}' + M = \mathbf{w} + M$, so in the real experiment we have $\Pr[\mathcal{R}(\mathbf{w}' + M) = \mathbf{w}] = \Pr[\mathcal{R}(\mathbf{w} + M) = \mathbf{w}]$ and thus

$$\Pr[\mathcal{R}(\mathbf{w} + M) = \mathbf{w}] \leq \frac{1 + \Delta(\mathbf{w}, \mathbf{w}')}{2}.$$

Using the statistical distance of two Gaussian distributions with the same width but different means, Lemma 4, we obtain

$$\Delta(\mathbf{w}, \mathbf{w}') \leq \frac{\sqrt{2\pi}\|\mathbf{z}\|_2}{g'} \leq 2\frac{\sqrt{2\pi}}{\sqrt{N}},$$

and thus $\Pr[\mathcal{R}(\mathbf{w} + M) = \mathbf{w}] \leq \frac{1}{2} + \frac{\sqrt{2\pi}}{\sqrt{N}}$. For sufficiently many iterations, the oracle gives a wrong answer in at least one iteration and the reduction outputs YES. $\qquad\square$

4.3   Adapting the Error Distribution

In order to complete our classical hardness result for M-LWE, Theorem 2, we need to adapt twice the error distribution.

First, we have to move from the distribution Υ_α on elliptical Gaussian distributions, as used within Sect. 4.2, to a discrete Gaussian distribution $\mathcal{D}_{R^\vee, \alpha' q}$, as used in Sect. 3. To achieve this, we use the techniques of [LS15, Sec. 4.4].

Lemma 13. *Let n, ℓ, q be positive integers and α be a positive real. There exists a probabilistic polynomial-time reduction from* M-LWE$_{n,\ell,q,\Upsilon_\alpha}$ *to* M-LWE$_{n,\ell,q,\phi}$, *where $\phi = \mathcal{D}_{R^\vee, \alpha' q}$ with $\alpha' = \alpha \cdot \omega(\log_2 n)$.*

Proof. First, we reduce M-LWE$_{n,\ell,q,\Upsilon_\alpha}$ to M-LWE$_{n,\ell,q,\Psi_{\leq\alpha'}}$, where α' is given by $\alpha \cdot \omega(\log_2 n)$. Recall, that Υ_α is a distribution on elliptical Gaussian distributions $D_\mathbf{r}$, where r_i^2 is distributed as a shifted chi-squared distribution for the real embeddings ($i \in [t_1]$) and as a shifted chi-squared distribution with two degrees of freedom for complex embeddings ($i \in \{t_1 + 1, \ldots, t_1 + t_2\}$). Using properties about chi-squared distributions (see for instance [LM00, Lem. 1]), it yields that $r_i \leq \frac{\alpha}{\sqrt{2}} \cdot \omega(\log_2 n) \leq \alpha \cdot \omega(\log_2 n) = \alpha'$ with probability negligible close to 1. Thus, M-LWE$_{n,\ell,q,\Psi_{\leq\alpha'}}$ is not easier than M-LWE$_{n,\ell,q,\Upsilon_\alpha}$. Second, we use the error re-randomization from Peikert [Pei10] to reduce the continuous version M-LWE$_{n,\ell,q,\Psi_{\leq\alpha'}}$ to the discrete version M-LWE$_{n,\ell,q,\phi}$, where $\phi = \mathcal{D}_{R^\vee, \alpha' q}$. Let $D_\mathbf{r}$ be arbitrarily chosen from $\Psi_{\leq\alpha'}$, thus $\mathbf{r} = (r_i)_{i\in[n]}$ with $r_i \leq \alpha'$ for all $i \in [n]$. For any $e \leftarrow D_\mathbf{r}$, we sample $e' \leftarrow e + D_{\frac{1}{q}R^\vee - e, \mathbf{r}'}$, where $\mathbf{r}' = (r_i')_{i\in[n]}$ with $r_i' = \sqrt{(\alpha')^2 - (r_i)^2}$. Following Theorem 1 of [Pei10], the new error e' is statistically close to $\mathcal{D}_{\frac{1}{q}R^\vee, \alpha'}$. Multiplying by q completes the claim. $\qquad\square$

Second, we need to move from the discrete Gaussian $\mathcal{D}_{R^\vee, \beta q}$, as used in Sect. 3, back to the continuous Gaussian $D_{\sqrt{2}\beta}$, as used in Sect. 4.1. To achieve this, we add a continuous noise of the same width and use Lemma 6.

Lemma 14. *Let n, d, q be positive integers and β be a positive real such that $\beta \geq \sqrt{2} \cdot \eta_\varepsilon(\frac{1}{q}R^\vee)$ for some $\varepsilon \in (0, \frac{1}{2})$. There is a probabilistic polynomial-time reduction from* M-SLWE$_{n,\ell,q,\phi}$ *to* M-SLWE$_{n,\ell,q,D_{\sqrt{2}\beta}}$, *where $\phi = \mathcal{D}_{R^\vee, \beta q}$.*

Proof. Given a sample of M-SLWE$_{n,\ell,q,\phi}$ with $\phi = \mathcal{D}_{R^\vee,\beta q}$, we first divide the second part of the instance by q, thus the noise is distributed as a vector drawn from $\mathcal{D}_{\frac{1}{q}R^\vee,\beta}$. Then, we add to the second part of the instance a vector drawn from D_β. Now, we apply Lemma 6 with $\sigma = r = \beta$ to obtain that this new sample is statistically close to a sample of M-SLWE$_{n,\ell,q,D_{\sqrt{2}\beta}}$. □

Acknowledgments. This work was supported by the European Union PROMETH-EUS project (Horizon 2020 Research and Innovation Program, grant 780701). It has also received a French government support managed by the National Research Agency in the "Investing for the Future" program, under the national project RISQ P141580-2660001/DOS0044216. Katharina Boudgoust is funded by the Direction Générale de l'Armement (Pôle de Recherche CYBER). We also thank our anonymous referees for their helpful and constructive feedback.

References

[AD17]   Albrecht, M.R., Deo, A.: Large modulus ring-LWE ≥ module-LWE. In: Takagi, T., Peyrin, T. (eds.) ASIACRYPT 2017. LNCS, vol. 10624, pp. 267–296. Springer, Cham (2017). https://doi.org/10.1007/978-3-319-70694-8_10

[Bab85]   Babai, L.: On Lovász' lattice reduction and the nearest lattice point problem. In: Mehlhorn, K. (ed.) STACS 1985. LNCS, vol. 182, pp. 13–20. Springer, Heidelberg (1985). https://doi.org/10.1007/BFb0023990

[Ban93]   Banaszczyk, W.: New bounds in some transference theorems in the geometry of numbers. Math. Ann. **296**(4), 625–635 (1993)

[BDK+18]   Bos, J.W.: CRYSTALS - kyber: a CCA-secure module-lattice-based KEM. In: 2018 IEEE European Symposium on Security and Privacy, EuroS&P 2018, London, United Kingdom, 24–26 April 2018, pp. 353–367 (2018)

[BGV12]   Brakerski, Z., Gentry, C., Vaikuntanathan, V.: (Leveled) fully homomorphic encryption without bootstrapping. In: Innovations in Theoretical Computer Science 2012, Cambridge, MA, USA, 8–10 January 2012, pp. 309–325 (2012)

[BJRW20]   Boudgoust, K., Jeudy, C., Roux-Langlois, A., Wen, W.: Towards classical hardness of module-lwe: The linear rank case. IACR Cryptol. ePrint Arch. 2020:1020 (2020)

[BLL+15]   Bai, S., Langlois, A., Lepoint, T., Stehlé, D., Steinfeld, R.: Improved security proofs in lattice-based cryptography: using the rényi divergence rather than the statistical distance. In: Iwata, T., Cheon, J.H. (eds.) ASIACRYPT 2015. LNCS, vol. 9452, pp. 3–24. Springer, Heidelberg (2015). https://doi.org/10.1007/978-3-662-48797-6_1

[BLP+13]   Brakerski, Z., Langlois, A., Peikert, C., Regev, O., Stehlé, D.: Classical hardness of learning with errors. In: Symposium on Theory of Computing Conference, STOC 2013, Palo Alto, CA, USA, 1–4 June 2013, pp. 575–584 (2013)

[BV14]   Brakerski, Z., Vaikuntanathan, V.: Efficient fully homomorphic encryption from (standard) LWE. SIAM J. Comput. **43**(2), 831–871 (2014)

[DKL+18]   Ducas, L., Kiltz, E., Lepoint, T., Lyubashevsky, V., Schwabe, P., Seiler, G., Stehlé, D.: Crystals-dilithium: A lattice-based digital signature scheme. IACR Trans. Cryptogr. Hardw. Embed. Syst. **2018**(1), 238–268 (2018)

[DM15] Ducas, L., Micciancio, D.: FHEW: bootstrapping homomorphic encryption in less than a second. In: Oswald, E., Fischlin, M. (eds.) EUROCRYPT 2015. LNCS, vol. 9056, pp. 617–640. Springer, Heidelberg (2015). https://doi.org/10.1007/978-3-662-46800-5_24

[DMR18] Devroye, L., Mehrabian, A., Reddad, T.: The Total Variation Distance Between High-dimensional Gaussians (2018)

[GHPS12] Gentry, C., Halevi, S., Peikert, C., Smart, N.P.: Ring switching in BGV-style homomorphic encryption. In: Visconti, I., De Prisco, R. (eds.) SCN 2012. Ring switching in bgv-style homomorphic encryption, vol. 7485, pp. 19–37. Springer, Heidelberg (2012). https://doi.org/10.1007/978-3-642-32928-9_2

[GKPV10] Goldwasser, S., Kalai, Y.T., Peikert, C., Vaikuntanathan, V.: Robustness of the learning with errors assumption. In: Innovations in Computer Science - ICS 2010, Tsinghua University, Beijing, China, 5–7 January 2010. Proceedings, pp. 230–240. Tsinghua University Press (2010)

[GPV08] Gentry, C., Peikert, C., Vaikuntanathan, V.: Trapdoors for hard lattices and new cryptographic constructions. In: Proceedings of the 40th Annual ACM Symposium on Theory of Computing, Victoria, British Columbia, Canada, 17–20 May 2008, pp. 197–206. ACM (2008)

[LLL82] Lenstra, A.K., Lenstra Jr., H.W., Lovász, L.: Factoring polynomials with rational coefficients. Math. Ann. 261(4), 515–534 (1982)

[LM00] Laurent, B., Massart, P.: Adaptive estimation of a quadratic functional by model selection. Ann. Statist. 28(5), 1302–1338 (2000)

[LPR10] Lyubashevsky, V., Peikert, C., Regev, O.: On ideal lattices and learning with errors over rings. In: Gilbert, H. (ed.) EUROCRYPT 2010. LNCS, vol. 6110, pp. 1–23. Springer, Heidelberg (2010). https://doi.org/10.1007/978-3-642-13190-5_1

[LPR13] Lyubashevsky, V., Peikert, C., Regev, O.: On ideal lattices and learning with errors over rings. J. ACM 60(6), 43:1–43:35 (2013)

[LS15] Langlois, A., Stehlé, D.: Worst-case to average-case reductions for module lattices. Des. Codes Cryptogr. 75(3), 565–599 (2015)

[LSS14] Langlois, A., Stehlé, D., Steinfeld, R.: GGHLite: more efficient multilinear maps from ideal lattices. In: Nguyen, P.Q., Oswald, E. (eds.) EUROCRYPT 2014. LNCS, vol. 8441, pp. 239–256. Springer, Heidelberg (2014). https://doi.org/10.1007/978-3-642-55220-5_14

[Mic07] Micciancio, D.: Generalized compact knapsacks, cyclic lattices, and efficient one-way functions. Comput. Complex. 16(4), 365–411 (2007)

[Mic18] Micciancio, D.: On the hardness of learning with errors with binary secrets. Theory Comput. 14(1), 1–17 (2018)

[MP12] Micciancio, D., Peikert, C.: Trapdoors for lattices: simpler, tighter, faster, smaller. In: Pointcheval, D., Johansson, T. (eds.) EUROCRYPT 2012. LNCS, vol. 7237, pp. 700–718. Springer, Heidelberg (2012). https://doi.org/10.1007/978-3-642-29011-4_41

[MR07] Micciancio, D., Regev, O.: Worst-case to average-case reductions based on gaussian measures. SIAM J. Comput. 37(1), 267–302 (2007)

[Pei09] Peikert, C.: Public-key cryptosystems from the worst-case shortest vector problem: extended abstract. In Proceedings of the 41st Annual ACM Symposium on Theory of Computing, STOC 2009, Bethesda, MD, USA, 31 May–2 June 2009, pp. 333–342 (2009)

[Pei10] Peikert, C.: An efficient and parallel Gaussian sampler for lattices. In: Rabin, T. (ed.) CRYPTO 2010. An efficient and parallel gaussian sampler for lattices, vol. 6223, pp. 80–97. Springer, Heidelberg (2010). https://doi.org/10.1007/978-3-642-14623-7_5

[PP02] Piazza, G., Politi, T.: An upper bound for the condition number of a matrix in spectral norm. J. Comput. Appl. Math. **143**(1), 141–144 (2002)

[PR07] Peikert, C., Rosen, A.: Lattices that admit logarithmic worst-case to average-case connection factors. In: Proceedings of the 39th Annual ACM Symposium on Theory of Computing, San Diego, California, USA, 11–13 June 2007, pp. 478–487 (2007)

[PRS17] Peikert, C., Regev, O., Stephens-Davidowitz, N.: Pseudorandomness of ring-LWE for any ring and modulus. In: Proceedings of the 49th Annual ACM SIGACT Symposium on Theory of Computing, STOC 2017, Montreal, QC, Canada, 19–23 June 2017, pp. 461–473 (2017)

[PS19] Peikert, C., Shiehian, S.: Noninteractive zero knowledge for NP from (Plain) learning with errors. In: Boldyreva, A., Micciancio, D. (eds.) CRYPTO 2019. LNCS, vol. 11692, pp. 89–114. Springer, Cham (2019). https://doi.org/10.1007/978-3-030-26948-7_4

[R61] Rényi, A.: On measures of entropy and information. In: Proceedings of 4th Berkeley Symposium on Mathematical Statistics and Probability, vol. I, pp. 547–561. University of California Press, Berkeley, California (1961)

[Reg05] Regev, O.: On lattices, learning with errors, random linear codes, and cryptography. In: Proceedings of the 37th Annual ACM Symposium on Theory of Computing, Baltimore, MD, USA, 22–24 May 2005, pp. 84–93 (2005)

[Reg09] Regev, O.: On lattices, learning with errors, random linear codes, and cryptography. J. ACM **56**(6), 34:1–34:40 (2009)

[RSW18] Rosca, M., Stehlé, D., Wallet, A.: On the ring-LWE and polynomial-LWE problems. In: Nielsen, J.B., Rijmen, V. (eds.) EUROCRYPT 2018. On the ring-lwe and polynomial-lwe problems, vol. 10820, pp. 146–173. Springer, Cham (2018). https://doi.org/10.1007/978-3-319-78381-9_6

[SSTX09] Stehlé, D., Steinfeld, R., Tanaka, K., Xagawa, K.: Efficient public key encryption based on ideal lattices. In: Matsui, M. (ed.) ASIACRYPT 2009. LNCS, vol. 5912, pp. 617–635. Springer, Heidelberg (2009). https://doi.org/10.1007/978-3-642-10366-7_36

[vEH14] van Erven, T., Harremoës, P.: Rényi divergence and kullback-leibler divergence. IEEE Trans. Inf. Theory **60**(7), 3797–3820 (2014)

[vNG47] von Neumann, J., Goldstine, H.H.: Numerical inverting of matrices of high order. Bull. Amer. Math. Soc. **53**, 1021–1099 (1947)

[WW19] Wang, Y., Wang, M.: Module-lwe versus ring-lwe, revisited. IACR Cryptology ePrint Archive 2019:930 (2019)

Lattice-Based E-Cash, Revisited

Amit Deo[1,3], Benoît Libert[1,2], Khoa Nguyen[4], and Olivier Sanders[5(✉)]

[1] ENS de Lyon, Laboratoire LIP (U. Lyon, CNRS, ENSL, Inria, UCBL),
Lyon, France
[2] CNRS, Laboratoire LIP, Lyon, France
[3] Inria, Lyon, France
[4] School of Physical and Mathematical Sciences, Nanyang Technological University,
Singapore, Singapore
[5] Orange Labs, Applied Crypto Group, Cesson-Sévigné, France
`olivier.sanders@orange.com`

Abstract. Electronic cash (e-cash) was introduced 40 years ago as the digital analogue of traditional cash. It allows users to withdraw electronic coins that can be spent anonymously with merchants. As advocated by Camenisch *et al.* (Eurocrypt 2005), it should be possible to store the withdrawn coins compactly (i.e., with logarithmic cost in the total number of coins), which has led to the notion of *compact* e-cash. Many solutions were proposed for this problem but the security proofs of most of them were invalidated by a very recent paper by Bourse *et al.* (Asiacrypt 2019). The same paper describes a generic way of fixing existing constructions/proofs but concrete instantiations of this patch are currently unknown in some settings. In particular, compact e-cash is no longer known to exist under quantum-safe assumptions. In this work, we resolve this problem by proposing the first secure compact e-cash system based on lattices following the result from Bourse *et al.* Contrarily to the latter work, our construction is not only generic, but we describe two concrete instantiations. We depart from previous frameworks of e-cash systems by leveraging lossy trapdoor functions to construct our coins. The indistinguishability of lossy and injective keys allows us to avoid the very strong requirements on the involved pseudo-random functions that were necessary to instantiate the generic patch proposed by Bourse *et al.*

Keywords: Lattice-based cryptography · e-cash · Anonymity · Exculpability · Provable security

1 Introduction

The last decades have witnessed major changes in consumer habits, with a gradual shift to credit/debit cards for payments. Since 2016, the total amount of card payment transactions worldwide has indeed exceeded that of cash transactions,[1] as card transactions simply make spending easier and enable online purchases.

---

[1] https://avpsolutions.com/blog/payment-cards-now-set-to-surpass-cash/.

© International Association for Cryptologic Research 2020
S. Moriai and H. Wang (Eds.): ASIACRYPT 2020, LNCS 12492, pp. 318–348, 2020.
https://doi.org/10.1007/978-3-030-64834-3_11

However, the benefits of electronic payments come at a price. Each transaction indeed leaks very sensitive information (at least to the entity managing the payment system), such as the identity of the recipient, the amount, the location of the spender, etc. For example, a patient paying his cardiologist with his card implicitly reveals to his bank that he probably has a heart condition, which is far from insignificant.

One could argue that, in some cases, the users' or recipients' identities can be masked through pseudonyms, but the concrete privacy benefits of this solution are questionable. Indeed, even for systems without central authority such as Bitcoin, pseudonymity only provides limited anonymity guarantees as shown for example by Ron and Shamir [32]. A natural question in this context is whether we can achieve the best of the two worlds. Namely, can we combine the features of electronic payments together with the anonymity of traditional cash?

Related Work. A first answer to this question was provided by Chaum in 1982 [13] when he introduced the notion of electronic cash (e-cash). Concretely, an electronic coin is the digital analogue of a standard coin/banknote that is issued by an authority, called a bank, to users. The authenticity of coins can be checked publicly, which allows users to spend them anonymously with any merchant who knows the bank public key. Unfortunately, the comparison stops there, as there is a major difference between physical and electronic coins. In the first case, the physical support is assumed to be unclonable, unless for extremely powerful adversaries. Obviously, the same assumption does not hold for digital data, and it is thus necessary to deter multiple spendings of the same coin.

However, detecting multiple uses of the same coin without affecting the anonymity of honest users is challenging. Chaum achieved this using blind signatures [13], by associating each coin with a serial number that remains hidden until the coin is spent. At this time, the serial number is added to a register that can be public, preluding crypto-currency ledgers. Using this register, anyone can detect the reuse of a coin, which leads to two families of e-cash systems.

The first one allows detecting frauds but does not enable the identification of perpetrators. In this case, detection must be performed before accepting payments. These systems are thus inherently *online*, as any recipient must be able to check the ledger at any time. This entails incompressible latencies to process payments that can be prohibitive in some situations, such as payments at tollgates, or at turnstiles for public transport.

The second family allows for the identification of defrauders. In this case, it is no longer necessary to check the coin upfront, as the defrauders know that they will ultimately be identified and then prosecuted. This simplifies the whole payment process as the e-cash system can now work *offline*. In 2020, the ability to process transactions offline might seem less appealing but it is still necessary today as mentioned in recent Visa [33] or Mastercard [28] technical documentations. Indeed, offline payments are inevitable in situations with no (or very limited) internet connections (aboard a plane, a boat, etc) and are still preferred in some regions. For example, a study by the french central bank [15] shows that, in 2013, less than 10 % of credit/debit cards in use in France are exclusively online (such cards being usually attributed to financially fragile persons); for the other cards, online checks are only performed on a random basis of for relatively large amounts.

It is hard today to discuss e-cash without mentioning crypto-currencies such as Bitcoin, or even post-quantum ones such as MatRiCT [19]. The distinction between the two families above highlights the first difference between such systems. Crypto-currencies are indeed necessarily online whereas e-cash can be offline. However the main difference between these two systems rather lies in the trust model. The main strength of crypto-currencies is probably the absence of a central authority. This helps them circumvent the traditional reluctance of banks to novelties because a crypto-currency can be launched (almost) from scratch. In contrast, an e-cash system requires the support of a financial institution. Nevertheless, the absence of a central authority is also the main drawback of crypto-currencies. It indeed means that, in case of theft or loss of secret keys, the users lose everything, which is a major issue that we believe to be unacceptable for the general public. In the e-cash setting, where some authority manages the system, handling these situations is quite easy (corresponding procedures already exist for current payments systems such as debit/credit cards). There are also differences such as compliance with legislation, etc. In all cases, the very different features of both systems mean that they cannot be opposed. The reality is in fact the opposite and we should rather see crypto-currencies and e-cash systems as complementary solutions for privacy-preserving payments. From now on, we will only consider offline e-cash.

Following Chaum's seminal work, blind signatures were the first cornerstone of e-cash systems. Unfortunately, this design strategy comes with some limitations, such as the need to withdraw and store coins one by one, which quickly becomes cumbersome (see, e.g., [9]). This problem was addressed by Camenisch *et al.* [11] who proposed the notion of *compact* e-cash, where users withdraw and store N coins (that constitute a wallet) with constant, or at least logarithmic, complexity. The core idea of their construction – which has become the blueprint of most following works – is to associate each wallet with two seeds k and t for a pseudo-random function (PRF) family. These two seeds are then used to generate N pairs of pseudo-random values $(\mathsf{PRF}_k(i), \mathsf{PRF}_t(i))$. The former (i.e., $\mathsf{PRF}_k(i)$) serves as the coin serial number whereas $\mathsf{PRF}_t(j)$ essentially acts as a one-time pad on the spender's identity, resulting in a so-called double-spending tag. In case a coin is spent more than once, the same mask $\mathsf{PRF}_t(j)$ is used twice and can thus be cancelled out to reveal the defrauder's identity.

This elegant construction underlies many subsequent systems, including a candidate based on lattices [26]. Unfortunately, a recent result by Bourse *et al.* [9] has shown the limitations of this framework. In particular, they highlighted that systems based on it may fail to provably achieve exculpability, i.e., the property that honest users cannot be wrongly accused of double-spending a coin, even when the bank and other users conspire against them. As this issue underlies most of our design choices, we need to recall some details on it.

In the CHL construction [11], the serial number and the double-spending tag are constructed from the PRF outputs mentioned above but also from the spender's public key and some public data that can be seen as the unique identifier of a transaction. In case of double-spendings, it can be shown that the perpetrator will necessarily be identified. Unfortunately, Bourse *et al.* pointed out that the opposite is not true, except in some very specific settings excluding lattices, as carefully crafted serial numbers and double-spending tags might lead the identification process to output a public key that was not even involved in the fraudulent transactions. Actually, two spendings from different users may even be considered as a double-spending by the system. As a consequence, the security proofs of the e-cash construction of Libert *et al.* [26] and of a subsequent improvement by Yang *et al.* [35] (the only schemes relying on quantum-resistant computational assumptions) are invalid and there is no known simple fix.

Before accusing a user, it is therefore necessary to perform additional verifications on the serial number occurring in a double-spending, in particular to ensure that it was constructed from the same seed and the same identity. This unfortunately seems infeasible given only $\mathsf{PRF}_k(i)$, as in [11]. To overcome this problem, the authors of [9] extended the serial number with new elements, each one being protected by a fresh PRF output. To ensure exculpability, it is then necessary to exclude collisions that could result from the PRF, leading to strong and non-standard requirements on the latter in [9]. Indeed, Bourse *et al.* need a notion of collision-resistance where, given the public parameters of a PRF family, the adversary should be unable to output two seeds k, k' and inputs x, x' such that $\mathsf{PRF}_k(x) = \mathsf{PRF}_{k'}(x')$. This might seem achievable by using a PRF based on symmetric primitives or by applying the techniques of Farshim *et al.* [20] to key-injective PRFs [24]. However, this would result in extremely inefficient e-cash constructions. Indeed, achieving security against cheating spenders requires to have them prove in zero-knowledge that they behaved honestly and correctly evaluated these PRFs, using certified seeds with valid inputs, etc. Such complex relations hardly coexist with the two solutions above. In particular, the Kim-Wu PRF [24] relies on a complex encoding of inputs into matrices which is hardly compatible with zero-knowledge techniques in lattices (recall that the PRF inputs should be part of witnesses). These rather require PRFs with a simpler algebraic structure, in the spirit of [3,4,7]. Unfortunately, the latter are not known to achieve collision-resistance. As of today, instantiating the Bourse *et al.* framework [9] from lattices would thus require to translate all statements to be proved into Boolean circuits. This would be much more expensive (by several orders of magnitude) than what we can hope for by leveraging the most efficient zero-knowledge techniques in standard lattices [8,35].

Our Contribution. In this paper, we show that we can dispense with the need for strong collision-resistance requirements by significantly departing from previous frameworks [9,11]. Our core idea is to perform only one standard PRF evaluation and use the resulting output to mask all the components of the serial number and double-spending tag, thanks to the use of a lossy trapdoor function F_{LTF} [30]. Recall that these are function families where injective evaluation keys are computationally indistinguishable from lossy evaluation keys, for which image elements reveal very little information on their preimages. In our construction, during a spending, we reveal $F_{LTF}(PRF_k(i))$ instead of $PRF_k(i)$ and then extract randomness from the remaining entropy of $PRF_k(i)$ in order to mask the spender's public key. This masked public key constitutes the second part of our serial number. When F_{LTF} is set up in its lossy mode in the proof of anonymity, we can show that the resulting serial number is indistinguishable from random and does not leak any sensitive information on the spender. Moreover, as F_{LTF} can be generated in injective mode in the real scheme, in case of colliding serial numbers, we are guaranteed that the same value $PRF_k(i)$ is used in all the corresponding transactions. Together with the equality of serial numbers, this implies that the involved public keys necessarily coincide.

At this stage, we are ensured that a double-spending alert can only be generated by two transactions involving the same user. Then, it only remains to adapt the same technique to our double-spending tags, which is fairly simple. We can then prove security of our construction based only on the standard security properties of the pseudo-random function and the lossy trapdoor function.

However, as we intend to provide concrete constructions and not just frameworks, we still have to realise the missing component of the coin, namely the non-interactive zero-knowledge (NIZK) proofs that both the serial number and the double-spending tag are well-formed. Indeed, NIZK proofs are notoriously hard to produce in the lattice setting, at least compared to their counterparts in cyclic groups. We start from a very recent result by Yang et al. [35] which provides a protocol capturing many interesting lattice-related relations and show that it can be used to prove the statements required by our e-cash system. This is far from trivial as, in particular, spenders need to prove their correct composed evaluation of a pseudo-random function and a lossy trapdoor function using different parameters for the two primitives. We nevertheless manage to propose such NIZK arguments for two different PRF constructions [4,7], leading to two different instantiations. Notably, the GGM-based PRF [23] of Banerjee et al. [4] allows for the use of a polynomial modulus.

However, despite this nice asymptotic complexity, one should keep realistic expectations about the concrete performances of our scheme according to the current lattices state-of-the-art. We indeed note that, as of writing, most of our building blocks (zero-knowledge proofs, PRFs, etc) remain complex tools that can hardly compete with their pairing-based counterparts. This is highlighted by the recent paper by Yang et al. [35] showing that existing (insecure) lattice e-cash constructions [26,35], which use building blocks similar to ours, generate transactions ranging from 260 MB to 720 TB. Fortunately, any future improvements of these tools could easily be leveraged by our construction. This is particularly true for our zero-knowledge proofs that we manage to represent as a standard instance of the powerful framework from [35].

Eventually, we propose the first concrete e-cash systems based on quantum-resistant hardness assumptions, following the reset of the state-of-the art resulting from [9]. Unlike [9] that modifies the CHL framework [11] by requiring stronger properties on the original building blocks, we upgrade it by considering alternative building blocks that are instantiable from standard lattice assumptions. Our work does not only lead to concrete constructions, but it also sheds new lights on e-cash by implicitly relying on a new framework which differs from [9,11] and does not require PRFs with non-standard security properties.

2   Preliminaries

We use lower-case bold characters (e.g. $\mathbf{x}$) to denote vectors and upper-case bold characters (e.g. $\mathbf{M}$) to denote matrices. The $(n \times n)$ identity matrix is denoted by $\mathbf{I}_n$. A superscript $\top$ for a vector or matrix denotes its transpose (e.g. $\mathbf{M}^\top$ is the transpose of $\mathbf{M}$). For any integer $q > 0$, $\mathbb{Z}_q$ denotes the integers modulo q. For integers $a < b$, $[a, b]$ denotes the set $\{a, a + 1, \ldots, b\}$. Alternatively if $b > 1$, we define $[b] := \{1, \ldots, b\}$. For any real x, we denote by $\lfloor x \rfloor$ the greatest integer smaller than or equal to x. In addition, for positive integers n, p, q such that $q > p$, we define the rounding operation $\lfloor \cdot \rceil_p : \mathbb{Z}_q^n \to \mathbb{Z}_p^n$ as $\lfloor \mathbf{x} \rceil_p := \lfloor (p/q) \cdot \mathbf{x} \rceil$. For probability distribution $\mathcal{D}$, we write $s \hookleftarrow \mathcal{D}$ to denote that s is a sample of the distribution $\mathcal{D}$. If X is a set, then $s \hookleftarrow U(X)$ represents the sampling of a uniform element of X. We also define the min-entropy of a discrete distribution $\mathcal{D}$ as $\mathsf{H}_\infty(\mathcal{D}) := -\log \max_{x'} \Pr_{x \hookleftarrow \mathcal{D}}[x = x']$. The statistical distance between two distributions $\mathcal{D}_1$ and $\mathcal{D}_2$ is denoted $\Delta(\mathcal{D}_1, \mathcal{D}_2)$. Throughout, we let λ denote a security parameter and use standard asymptotic notation $\mathcal{O}, \Theta, \Omega, \omega$ etc. We also use the standard notion of a pseudo-random function (PRF) and a zero-knowledge argument of knowledge (ZKAoK).

Binary Decompositions. We use the same decompositions as those in [26] as explained next. Firstly, for any positive integer B and $\delta_B := \lfloor \log(B) \rfloor + 1$, we define the sequence $B_1, \ldots, B_{\delta_B}$ where $B_j := \lfloor \frac{B + 2^{j-1}}{2^j} \rfloor$ for $j \in [1, \delta_B]$. It can be verified that $\sum_{j \in [1, \delta_B]} B_j = B$. For any integer $x \in [0, B]$, there is an efficiently computable deterministic function $\mathsf{idec}_B : [0, B] \to \{0, 1\}^{\delta_B}$ outputting a vector $\mathsf{idec}_B(x) =: \mathbf{y} \in \{0, 1\}^{\delta_B}$ satisfying $\sum_{j \in [1, \delta_B]} B_j \cdot y_j = x$. The function idec_B can be extended to handle vector inputs, resulting in $\mathsf{vdec}_{m,B} : [0, B]^m \to \{0, 1\}^{m \cdot \delta_B}$, for any integer $m > 0$. Explicitly, for any $\mathbf{x} \in [0, B]^m$, $\mathsf{vdec}_{m,B}(\mathbf{x}) := (\mathsf{idec}_B(x_1)^\top, \ldots, \mathsf{idec}_B(x_m)^\top)^\top$. In order to invert $\mathsf{vdec}_{m,B}$, we define the matrix $\mathbf{H}_{m,B} := (B_1, \ldots, B_{\delta_B}) \otimes \mathbf{I}_m$. It is easy to see that $\mathbf{H}_{m,B} \cdot \mathsf{vdec}_{m,B}(\mathbf{y}) = \mathbf{x}$. In addition, for any $x \in [0, B]$, we denote by $\mathsf{ibin}_B(x)$ the *standard* binary decomposition of x that fits into $\lfloor \log(B) \rfloor + 1$ bits. We define the binary representation of a vector to be the concatenation of the binary representations of its entries. Concretely, for any vector $\mathbf{x} \in [0, B]^m$, we define its binary representation to be $\mathsf{bin}_B(\mathbf{x})^\top := (\mathsf{ibin}(x_1), \ldots, \mathsf{ibin}(x_m))$.

2.1   Lattice Preliminaries

An m-dimensional lattice is a discrete subgroup of $\mathbb{R}^m$. For any integers n and q, $\mathbf{A} \in \mathbb{Z}_q^{n \times m}$ and $\mathbf{u} \in \mathbb{Z}_q^n$ we define the full-rank lattice $\Lambda_q^\perp(\mathbf{A}) := \{\mathbf{x} \in \mathbb{Z}^m :$

$\mathbf{A} \cdot \mathbf{x} = 0 \bmod q\}$ and the lattice coset $\Lambda_q^{\mathbf{u}}(\mathbf{A}) := \{\mathbf{x} \in \mathbb{Z}^m : \mathbf{A} \cdot \mathbf{x} = \mathbf{u} \bmod q\}$. Defining $\rho_\sigma : \mathbb{R}^m \to \mathbb{R}$ as $\rho_\sigma(\mathbf{x}) := \exp(-\pi\|\mathbf{x}\|^2/\sigma^2)$, the discrete Gaussian distribution over a lattice coset L with parameter σ (denoted as $D_{L,\sigma}$) is the distribution with support L and mass function proportional to ρ_σ.

Hardness Assumptions. We will be assuming that both the learning with errors (LWE) and short integer solution (SIS) problems (as defined next) are hard for appropriate parameter settings.

Definition 1. *Let $m, n, q \in \mathbb{N}$ with $m > n$ and $\beta > 0$. The short integer solution problem $\mathsf{SIS}_{n,m,q,\beta}$ is, given $\mathbf{A} \hookleftarrow U(\mathbb{Z}_q^{n \times m})$, find a non-zero $\mathbf{x} \in \Lambda_q^\perp(\mathbf{A})$ with $0 < \|\mathbf{x}\| \le \beta$.*

Definition 2. *Let q, α be functions of a parameter n. For a secret $\mathbf{s} \in \mathbb{Z}_q^n$, the distribution $A_{q,\alpha,\mathbf{s}}$ over $\mathbb{Z}_q^n \times \mathbb{Z}_q$ is obtained by sampling $\mathbf{a} \hookleftarrow U(\mathbb{Z}_q^n)$ and a noise $e \hookleftarrow D_{\mathbb{Z},\alpha q}$, and returning $(\mathbf{a}, \langle \mathbf{a}, \mathbf{s} \rangle + e)$. The learning with errors problem $\mathsf{LWE}_{n,m,q,\alpha}$ is, for $\mathbf{s} \hookleftarrow U(\mathbb{Z}_q^n)$, to distinguish between m independent samples from $U(\mathbb{Z}_q^n \times \mathbb{Z}_q)$ and the same number of samples from $A_{q,\alpha,\mathbf{s}}$.*

If m is omitted in the LWE problem, it is assumed that $m = \mathsf{poly}(n)$. If $q \ge \beta n^\delta$ for any constant $\delta > 0$ and $m, \beta = \mathsf{poly}(n)$, then standard worst-case lattice problems with approximation factors $\gamma = \max\{1, \beta^2/q\} \cdot \tilde{\mathcal{O}}(\beta\sqrt{n})$ reduce to $\mathsf{SIS}_{n,m,q,\beta}$ [29]. Alternatively, if $q \ge \sqrt{n}\beta$ and $m, \beta = \mathsf{poly}(n)$, then standard worst-case lattice problems with approximation factors $\gamma = \mathcal{O}(\beta\sqrt{n})$ reduce to $\mathsf{SIS}_{m,q,\beta}$ (see, e.g., [22, Sec. 9]). Similarly, if $\alpha q = \Omega(\sqrt{n})$, standard worst-case lattice problems with approximation factors $\gamma = \tilde{\mathcal{O}}(n/\alpha)$ reduce to $\mathsf{LWE}_{n,q,\alpha}$ [10,31].

2.2 Lossy Trapdoor Functions

We will be using the notion of lossy trapdoor function (LTF) families from [30]. Informally, a lossy trapdoor function family can be used in one of two modes: a lossy mode and an injective mode. In the lossy mode, functions lose information on their inputs and cannot be inverted whereas in the injective mode, a trapdoor enables efficient inversion. In addition, there are generation algorithms that sample functions in either the lossy or injective mode. A crucial requirement is that no efficient adversary can distinguish whether a generation algorithm is outputting lossy functions or injective functions. We now recall the formal syntax and definition of an LTF family.

Definition 3. *An (m, k) lossy trapdoor function family with security parameter λ is a 4-tuple of PPT algorithms $(\mathsf{G}_0, \mathsf{G}_1, \mathsf{F}, \mathsf{F}^{-1})$ such that:*

- **(Injective Mode)** $\mathsf{G}_0(1^\lambda)$ *outputs a function index u and trapdoor τ. For any pair (u, τ) output by G_0, $\mathsf{F}(u, \cdot)$ computes an injective function $f_u : \{0,1\}^m \to \{0,1\}^*$ and $\mathsf{F}^{-1}(\tau, \mathsf{F}(u, x)) = x$.*

- **(Lossy Mode)** $G_1(1^\lambda)$ *outputs a function index* u. *For any* u *output by* G_1, $F(u, \cdot)$ *computes a lossy function* $f_u : \{0, 1\}^m \to \{0, 1\}^*$, *whose image is of size at most* 2^{m-k}.
- **(Indistinguishability)** *Let* $(u, \tau) \leftarrow G_0(1^\lambda)$ *and* $u' \leftarrow G_1(1^\lambda)$. *Then the distributions of* u *and* u' *are computationally indistinguishable.*

We will use the algorithms of the LTF family given in [30]. This family was reconstructed by Wee [34] where n, m, q, α are functions of λ, $p \leq q/(4n)$ and $\bar{n} = m/\log p$. In the following, $\mathbf{G} \in \mathbb{Z}_q^{m \times \bar{n}}$ is a special public matrix that allows to efficiently solve the bounded error decoding problem [30].

- $G_0(n, m, q, \alpha)$: Sample $\mathbf{A} \hookleftarrow U(\mathbb{Z}_q^{n \times m}), \mathbf{S} \hookleftarrow U(\mathbb{Z}_q^{n \times \bar{n}}), \mathbf{E} \hookleftarrow (\bar{\Psi}_\alpha)^{m \times \bar{n}}$ and output the index $(\mathbf{A}, \mathbf{B} := \mathbf{S}^\top \mathbf{A} + \mathbf{E}^\top + \mathbf{G}^\top)$ along with trapdoor $\mathbf{S}$.
- $G_1(n, m, q, \beta)$: Sample $\mathbf{A} \hookleftarrow U(\mathbb{Z}_q^{n \times m}), \mathbf{S} \hookleftarrow U(\mathbb{Z}_q^{n \times \bar{n}}), \mathbf{E} \hookleftarrow (\bar{\Psi}_\alpha)^{m \times \bar{n}}$ and output the index $(\mathbf{A}, \mathbf{B} := \mathbf{S}^\top \mathbf{A} + \mathbf{E}^\top)$
- F: On input $((\mathbf{A}, \mathbf{B}), \mathbf{x})$ where $\mathbf{A} \in \mathbb{Z}_q^{n \times m}, \mathbf{B} \in \mathbb{Z}_q^{\bar{n} \times m}$ and $\mathbf{x} \in \{0, 1\}^m$, output $(\mathbf{Ax}, \mathbf{Bx})$
- F^{-1}: On input $(\mathbf{S}, (\mathbf{y}_1, \mathbf{y}_2))$ where $\mathbf{S} \in \mathbb{Z}_q^{n \times \bar{n}}, \mathbf{y}_1 \in \mathbb{Z}_q^n$ and $\mathbf{y}_2 \in \mathbb{Z}_q^{\bar{n}}$, compute $\mathbf{y} := \mathbf{y}_2 - \mathbf{S}^\top \mathbf{y}_1$. Use the efficient bounded-error decoder with respect to $\mathbf{G}$ on $\mathbf{y}$ to recover a vector $\mathbf{x}^* \in \{0, 1\}^m$ such that $\mathbf{e}^* + \mathbf{G}^\top \mathbf{x}^* = \mathbf{y}$ for some small $\mathbf{e}^*$ with $\|\mathbf{e}^*\|_\infty \leq q/p$. Output $\mathbf{x}^*$.

Lemma 1 ([34]). *For any constant* $\gamma < 1$ *and* n, *take* $q = \Theta(n^{1+1/\gamma})$, $p = \Theta(n^{1/\gamma})$ *such that* $p \leq q/(4n)$. *Further, take* $m = \mathcal{O}(n \log q), \alpha = \Theta(\sqrt{n}/q)$ *and* $\bar{n} = m/\log p$. *Assuming that the* $\mathsf{LWE}_{n,m,q,\alpha}$ *problem is hard, the above construction is an* (m, k)-LTF *family where* $k = (1 - \gamma)m - n \log q$.

The following instantiation of the generalized Leftover Hash Lemma of [17, Lemma 2.4] will be particularly useful:

Lemma 2. *Choose* γ, n, q, p, α *as in Lemma 1, arbitrary integers* $n', q' > 2$ *and an arbitrary distribution* $\mathcal{X}$ *over* $\{0, 1\}^m$. *Then, for* $\mathbf{A} \hookleftarrow U(\mathbb{Z}_{q'}^{n' \times m})$, $(\bar{\mathbf{A}}, \bar{\mathbf{B}}) \hookleftarrow G_1(n, m, q, \alpha)$, $\mathbf{x} \hookleftarrow U(\mathcal{X})$ *and* $\mathbf{u} \hookleftarrow U(\mathbb{Z}_{q'}^{n'})$, *we have*

$$\Delta\left((\mathbf{Ax}, \mathbf{A}, (\bar{\mathbf{A}}, \bar{\mathbf{B}}, \bar{\mathbf{A}}\mathbf{x}, \bar{\mathbf{B}}\mathbf{x})), (\mathbf{u}, \mathbf{A}, (\bar{\mathbf{A}}, \bar{\mathbf{B}}, \bar{\mathbf{A}}\mathbf{x}, \bar{\mathbf{B}}\mathbf{x}))\right)$$
$$\leq \frac{1}{2} \cdot \sqrt{2^{-(\mathsf{H}_\infty(\mathcal{X}) - (m\gamma + n \log q + n' \log q'))}}.$$

2.3   Witness Extraction and Forking Lemma

Recall that the transcript of a Σ-protocol consists of three messages starting with a message from a prover to a verifier. The Fiat-Shamir transform [21] provides a well-known method to remove interaction from a Σ-protocol. In particular, the second message (which is a uniformly chosen "challenge" value from the verifier to the prover) is replaced by the evaluation of a random oracle on input given by the first message. When adopting this method, it is important to carefully argue that the resulting non-interactive protocol is still an argument of knowledge.

That is, if a prover convinces the verifier to accept with non-negligible probability, then replaying the prover allows for the extraction of a witness to the statement in question. This is usually achieved by applying a "forking lemma".

We will focus on the argument system of Yang et al.[35] which takes the three-message form of a Σ-protocol. The witness extraction for the interactive ZKAoK of Yang et al. requires any $\ell = 3$ accepting transcripts, all with the same first prover message but distinct challenge values. We refer to ℓ such accepting transcripts as an ℓ-fork.

When using a random oracle to remove interaction with our chosen argument system, a forking lemma that considers the probability of producing an ℓ-fork for $\ell = 3$ should be used. The extended/generalised forking lemma of El Kaafarani and Katsumata [18, Lemma 1] provides a forking lemma for any $\ell \geq 2$. For simplicity, we state their result in the special case that $\ell = 3$.

Lemma 3 ([18]). *Fix some input $x \in \{0,1\}^*$ and take some arbitrary set* accept. *Let $\mathcal{A}$ be an efficient algorithm outputting triples (m_1, m_2, m_3) on input x that has oracle access to a random oracle $H : \{0,1\}^* \to [h]$ and let Q be an upper bound on the number of queries that $\mathcal{A}$ makes to H. Denote*

$$\mathsf{acc} := \Pr\left[(m_1, m_2, m_3) \leftarrow \mathcal{A}^{H(\cdot)}(x) : \begin{smallmatrix}(m_1, m_2, m_3) \in \mathsf{accept} \, \land \\ m_2 \text{ is the result of an } H\text{-query}\end{smallmatrix}\right]$$

$$\mathsf{frk}_3 := \Pr\left[((m_1, m_{2,i}, m_{3,i}))_{i=1}^3 \leftarrow F^{\mathcal{A}}(x) : \begin{smallmatrix}\forall i \in \{1,2,3\} \, : \, (m_1, m_{2,i}, m_{3,i}) \in \mathsf{accept} \\ \land \, (m_{2,i})_{i=1}^3 \text{ are pairwise distinct}\end{smallmatrix}\right]$$

for any efficient algorithm $F^{\mathcal{A}}$ that runs $\mathcal{A}$ at most 3 times. Then, for a particular choice of $F^{\mathcal{A}}$,

$$\mathsf{frk}_3 \geq \mathsf{acc} \cdot \left(\left(\frac{\mathsf{acc}}{Q}\right)^2 - \frac{3}{h}\right).$$

2.4   E-Cash Security Definitions

E-cash systems involve three types of parties: banks denoted $\mathcal{B}$, users denoted $\mathcal{U}$ and merchants denoted $\mathcal{M}$. The syntax of an offline compact e-cash system consists of the following algorithms/protocols:

ParGen $(1^\lambda, 1^L)$: On input a security parameter λ and wallet size $L = \log(\mathrm{poly}(\lambda))$, outputs public parameters par containing L (amongst other things).
BKeyGen$(1^\lambda, \mathsf{par})$: On input par, outputs a key pair $(PK_\mathcal{B}, SK_\mathcal{B})$ for the bank, which allows $\mathcal{B}$ to issue wallets of size 2^L.
UKeyGen $(1^\lambda, \mathsf{par})$: On input par, generates a key pair $(PK_\mathcal{U}, SK_\mathcal{U})$ for the user.
MKeyGen$(1^\lambda, \mathsf{par})$: On input par, generates $(PK_\mathcal{M}, SK_\mathcal{M})$ for the merchant.

We henceforth assume that all algorithms implicitly take par as input.

Withdraw $(\mathcal{U}(PK_\mathcal{B}, SK_\mathcal{U}), \mathcal{B}(PK_\mathcal{U}, SK_\mathcal{B}))$: An interactive protocol that allows $\mathcal{U}$ to obtain a wallet $\mathcal{W}$ consisting of 2^L coins or an error message $\bot$. The bank $\mathcal{B}$ obtains tracing information $\mathsf{T}_\mathcal{W}$.

Spend $(\mathcal{U}(\mathcal{W}, PK_{\mathcal{B}}, PK_{\mathcal{M}}), \mathcal{M}(SK_{\mathcal{M}}, PK_{\mathcal{U}}, PK_{\mathcal{B}}, \text{info}))$: A protocol allowing a user $\mathcal{U}$ to give a coin from $\mathcal{W}$ to merchant $\mathcal{M}$ with respect to transaction metadata info. The user outputs an updated wallet $\mathcal{W}'$ whereas the output of $\mathcal{M}$ is a coin coin consisting of info, a serial number, a security tag and a proof of validity or an error symbol $\bot$.

VerifyCoin $(PK_{\mathcal{B}}, \text{coin})$: Outputs 1 if the proof of validity in coin verifies correctly with respect to $PK_{\mathcal{B}}$ and 0 otherwise.

VerifyDeposit $(PK_{\mathcal{B}}, PK_{\mathcal{M}}, \text{coin}, \mu)$: Outputs 1 if the proof of validity in coin verifies correctly with respect to $PK_{\mathcal{B}}$ and if the data μ verifies correctly with respect to $PK_{\mathcal{M}}$. Else, outputs 0.

Deposit $(\mathcal{M}(SK_{\mathcal{M}}, \text{coin}, PK_{\mathcal{B}}), \mathcal{B}(PK_{\mathcal{M}}, SK_{\mathcal{B}}, \text{state}_{\mathcal{B}}))$: This is a protocol allowing $\mathcal{M}$ to deposit coin (containing some metadata info) in its account with $\mathcal{B}$. In the protocol, $\mathcal{M}$ sends coin along with some data μ. Then, $\mathcal{B}$ uses a list $\text{state}_{\mathcal{B}}$ of previously deposited coins to proceed as follows. If VerifyCoin $(PK_{\mathcal{B}}, \text{coin}) = 0$ or VerifyDeposit $(PK_{\mathcal{B}}, PK_{\mathcal{M}}, \text{coin}, \mu) = 0$, $\mathcal{B}$ outputs $\bot$. If info and $PK_{\mathcal{M}}$ exist in the same entry of $\text{state}_{\mathcal{B}}$, then $\mathcal{B}$ returns this entry $(\text{coin}, PK_{\mathcal{M}}, \mu')$. If the serial number $\mathbf{y}_S$ derived from coin is not in $\text{state}_{\mathcal{B}}$, then $\mathcal{B}$ adds the tuple $(\text{coin}, PK_{\mathcal{M}}, \mu, \mathbf{y}_S)$ to $\text{state}_{\mathcal{B}}$. If there is some tuple $(\text{coin}', PK'_{\mathcal{M}}, \mu', \mathbf{y}_S)$ in $\text{state}_{\mathcal{B}}$, then $\mathcal{B}$ outputs such a tuple.

Identify $(PK_{\mathcal{B}}, \text{coin}_1, \text{coin}_2)$: An algorithm allowing to identify a double spender $\mathcal{U}$ whenever coin_1 and coin_2 share the same serial number. The output of this algorithm is a public key $PK_{\mathcal{U}}$ and a proof that this public key corresponds to a double spender Π_G.

E-cash systems should provide the following properties whose formal definitions, adapted from [9, 26], are provided below.

- **Anonymity:** no coalition of banks and merchants can identify the wallet that a coin originates from.
- **Traceability:** the bank is always able to identify at least one member of a coalition that has spent more than it has withdrawn. This property introduced by Canard *et al.* [12] simultaneously captures the balance and identification properties considered in [6,11].
- **Strong exculpability:** no coalition of banks and merchants can convincingly accuse an innocent user of double-spending.
- **Clearing:** an honest merchant is always able to deposit the received coins. In particular, no coalition of bank, merchants and users can generate a convincing proof that the latter have already been deposited.

Definition 4. *An e-cash system provides* **anonymity** *if there exists an efficient simulator* $\mathcal{S} = (\text{SimParGen}, \text{SimSpend})$ *such that no PPT adversary* $\mathcal{A}$ *has non-negligible advantage in the* **anonymity** *game described below:*

1. *The challenger flips a fair coin* $d \hookleftarrow U(\{0, 1\})$ *and runs* par $\leftarrow$ ParGen$(1^{\lambda}, 1^L)$ *if* $d = 1$ *and* (par, τ_{sim}) $\hookleftarrow$ SimParGen$(1^{\lambda}, 1^L)$ *otherwise. In either case, it gives* par *to* $\mathcal{A}$.
2. $\mathcal{A}$ *outputs some public key* $PK_{\mathcal{B}}$ *and adaptively invokes the following oracles:*

- $\mathcal{Q}_{GetKey}(i)$: this oracle generates $(SK_{\mathcal{U}_i}, PK_{\mathcal{U}_i}) \hookleftarrow$ UKeygen(par) if it does not exist yet and returns $PK_{\mathcal{U}_i}$.
- $\mathcal{Q}_{Withdraw}(PK_{\mathcal{B}}, i)$: this oracle plays the role of user $\mathcal{U}_i$ – and creates their key pair if it does not exist yet – in an execution of the withdrawal protocol Withdraw$(\mathcal{U}(\text{par}, PK_{\mathcal{B}}, SK_{\mathcal{U}_i}), \mathcal{A}(\text{state}))$, with the adversary $\mathcal{A}$ playing the role of the bank. At the j-th query, we denote by $\mathcal{W}_j$ the user's output which may be a valid wallet or an error message $\bot$.
- $\mathcal{Q}_{Spend}(PK_{\mathcal{B}}, i, j, PK_{\mathcal{M}}, \text{info})$: the oracle first checks if the wallet $\mathcal{W}_j$ has been issued to $\mathcal{U}_i$ by the bank $\mathcal{B}$ via an invocation of $\mathcal{Q}_{Withdraw}(PK_{\mathcal{B}}, i)$. If not, the oracle outputs $\bot$. Otherwise, $\mathcal{Q}_{Spend}$ checks if the internal counter J of $\mathcal{W}_j$ satisfies $J < 2^L - 1$. If $J = 2^L - 1$, it outputs $\bot$. Otherwise, $\mathcal{Q}_{Spend}$ responds as follows:
    - If $d = 1$, it runs Spend$(\mathcal{U}_i(\mathcal{W}_j, PK_{\mathcal{B}}, PK_{\mathcal{M}}), \mathcal{A}(\text{state}, \text{info}))$ with the merchant-executing $\mathcal{A}$ in order to spend a coin from $\mathcal{W}_j$.
    - If $d = 0$, $\mathcal{Q}_{Spend}$ runs SimSpend$(\text{par}, \tau_{sim}, PK_{\mathcal{B}}, PK_{\mathcal{M}}, \text{info})$.

3. When $\mathcal{A}$ halts, it outputs a bit $d' \in \{0, 1\}$ and wins if $d' = d$. The adversary's advantage is the distance $\mathbf{Adv}_{\mathcal{A}}^{\text{anon}}(\lambda) := |\Pr[d' = d] - 1/2|$, where the probability is taken over all coin tosses.

Definition 5. An e-cash system ensures **traceability** if, for any PPT adversary $\mathcal{A}$, the experiment below outputs 1 with negligible probability:

1. The challenger generates public parameters par $\hookleftarrow$ ParGen$(1^\lambda, 1^L)$ and a public key $(PK_{\mathcal{B}}, SK_{\mathcal{B}}) \hookleftarrow$ BKeyGen(par). It gives par and $PK_{\mathcal{B}}$ to $\mathcal{A}$.
2. $\mathcal{A}$ is granted access to the oracle $\mathcal{Q}_{Withdraw}(PK_{\mathcal{U}})$ that plays the role of the bank $\mathcal{B}$ in an execution of Withdraw$(\mathcal{A}(\text{state}), \mathcal{B}(\text{par}, PK_{\mathcal{U}}, SK_{\mathcal{B}}))$ with $\mathcal{A}$, acting as a cheating user. After each query, the challenger stores in a database T the information $T_{\mathcal{W}} = PK_{\mathcal{U}}$, or $\bot$ if the protocol fails.
3. After Q_w polynomially many queries, $\mathcal{A}$ outputs coins $\{\text{coin}_i\}_{i=1}^N$ which are parsed as $(\text{info}_i, PK_{\mathcal{M}_i}, S_i, \pi_i)$. The experiment returns 1, unless (at least) one of the following conditions holds (in which case, it returns 0):
    - $N \le 2^L \cdot Q_w$;
    - $\exists (i, j) \in \{1, \ldots, N\}^2$ such that $(\text{info}_i, PK_{\mathcal{M}_i}) = (\text{info}_j, PK_{\mathcal{M}_j})$;
    - $\exists i \in \{1, \ldots, N\}$ such that VerifyCoin$(PK_{\mathcal{B}}, \text{coin}_i) = 0$;
    - $\exists (i, j) \in \{1, \ldots, N\}^2$ such that Identify$(\text{par}, PK_{\mathcal{B}}, \text{coin}_i, \text{coin}_j)$ returns a public key $PK_{\mathcal{U}}$ that belongs to the database T.

Definition 6. An e-cash system provides **strong exculpability** if no PPT adversary $\mathcal{A}$ has noticeable success probability in the game below:

1. The challenger runs par $\leftarrow$ ParGen$(1^\lambda, 1^L)$, gives par to $\mathcal{A}$ and initializes empty sets of honest users $\mathcal{HU}$, wallets T_{FW} and double spent coins T_{ds}.
2. $\mathcal{A}$ generates $PK_{\mathcal{B}}$ on behalf of the bank and interacts with these oracles:
    - $\mathcal{Q}_{GetKey}(i)$: this oracle generates $(SK_{\mathcal{U}_i}, PK_{\mathcal{U}_i}) \hookleftarrow$ UKeygen(par) if it does not exist yet and returns $PK_{\mathcal{U}_i}$, which is added to $\mathcal{HU}$.

- $Q_{\mathsf{Withdraw}}(PK_{\mathcal{B}}, i)$: *this oracle plays the role of* $\mathcal{U}_i$ – *and creates* $(SK_{\mathcal{U}_i}, PK_{\mathcal{U}_i})$ *if it does not exist yet – in an execution of* $\mathsf{Withdraw}(\mathcal{U}(\mathsf{par}, PK_{\mathcal{B}}, SK_{\mathcal{U}_i}), \mathcal{A}(\mathsf{state}))$ *where* $\mathcal{A}$ *plays the role of the bank. At the* j-*th such query, we denote by* $\mathcal{W}_j$ *the user's output. If the protocol succeeds* $(\mathcal{W}_j = \perp)$, *then* $(j, \mathcal{W}_j)$ *is added to* T_{FW}.
- $Q_{\mathsf{Spend}}(PK_{\mathcal{B}}, i, j, PK_{\mathcal{M}}, \mathsf{info})$: *the oracle first checks if the wallet* $\mathcal{W}_j$ *was provided to* $\mathcal{U}_i$ *via an invocation of* $Q_{\mathsf{Withdraw}}(\mathsf{par}, PK_{\mathcal{B}}, i)$ *using* T_{FW}. *If not, the oracle outputs* $\perp$. *If the internal counter of* $\mathcal{W}_j$ *satisfies* $J = 2^\ell - 1$, *then* $\mathcal{W}_j$ *is reset to its original state, where* $J = 0$. *Then,* Q_{Spend} *spends a coin from* $\mathcal{W}_j$ *by running* $\mathsf{Spend}(\mathcal{U}_i(\mathcal{W}_j, PK_{\mathcal{B}}, PK_{\mathcal{M}}), \mathcal{A}(\mathsf{state}, \mathsf{info}))$ *with* $\mathcal{A}$. *If the resulting coin has the same serial number* S *as a previous query* $Q_{\mathsf{Spend}}(PK_{\mathcal{B}}, i, j, \cdot, \cdot)$ *then add* (i, j, S) *to* T_{ds}.
3. *When adversary* $\mathcal{A}$ *halts, it outputs two coins* $\mathsf{coin}_1, \mathsf{coin}_2$. *It is declared successful if* $\mathsf{Identify}(\mathsf{par}, PK_{\mathcal{B}}, \mathsf{coin}_1, \mathsf{coin}_2) \in \mathcal{HU}$ *and* $\forall(i, j), (i, j, S) \notin T_{ds}$ *where* S *is the common serial number shared by* coin_1 *and* coin_2.

Definition 7. *An e-cash system ensures* **clearing** *if for any PPT adversary* $\mathcal{A}$, *the probability of* $\mathcal{A}$ *winning the* **clearing** *game below is negligible:*

1. *The challenger runs* $\mathsf{par} \leftarrow \mathsf{ParGen}(1^\lambda, 1^L)$, *gives* par *to* $\mathcal{A}$ *and initializes a set of honest merchants* $\mathcal{HM}$ *which is initially empty.*
2. $\mathcal{A}$ *generates* $PK_{\mathcal{B}}$ *on behalf of the bank and interacts with these oracles:*

   - $Q_{\mathsf{GetKey}}(i)$: *this oracle generates* $(SK_{\mathcal{M}_i}, PK_{\mathcal{M}_i}) \hookleftarrow \mathsf{MKeygen}(\mathsf{par})$ *if it does not exist yet and returns* $PK_{\mathcal{M}_i}$, *which is added in* $\mathcal{HM}$.
   - $Q_{\mathsf{Receive}}(PK_{\mathcal{B}}, i)$: *this oracle plays the role of a merchant – and creates* $(SK_{\mathcal{M}_i}, PK_{\mathcal{M}_i})$ *if it does not exist yet – in an execution of* $\mathsf{Spend}(\mathcal{A}(\mathsf{state}), \mathcal{M}_i(SK_{\mathcal{M}}, PK_{\mathcal{U}}, \mathsf{info}))$ *where* $\mathcal{A}$ *plays the role of the user. At the* j-*th query, we denote by* coin_j *the merchant's output.*
   - $Q_{\mathsf{Deposit}}(PK_{\mathcal{B}}, i, j)$: *this oracle plays the role of the merchant in an execution of* $\mathsf{Deposit}(\mathcal{M}_i(SK_{\mathcal{M}_i}, \mathsf{coin}_j, PK_{\mathcal{B}}), \mathcal{A}(\mathsf{state}))$ *with* $\mathcal{A}$ *playing the role of* $\mathcal{B}$. *It however aborts if* $PK_{\mathcal{M}_i} \notin \mathcal{HM}$, *if* coin_j *has not been received by merchant* i *or if it has already been deposited.*
3. *When* $\mathcal{A}$ *halts, it outputs a tuple* $(PK_{\mathcal{M}}, \mathsf{coin}, \mu)$. *The adversary wins if* $PK_{\mathcal{M}} \in \mathcal{HM}$, $\mathsf{VerifyDeposit}(PK_{\mathcal{B}}, PK_{\mathcal{M}}, \mathsf{coin}, \mu) = 1$ *and* coin *has not been involved in a previous* Q_{Deposit} *query.*

3   Intuition

The core of an e-cash system is the pair constituted by the serial number $\mathbf{y}_S$ and the double-spending tag $\mathbf{y}_T$ of a coin. Besides zero-knowledge proofs, they are essentially the only elements made public during a spending and therefore must comply with very strong anonymity requirements while allowing the identification of double-spenders. In addition, it should be possible to (efficiently) prove that they are well-formed, which rules out most simple constructions.

Designing such elements is thus far from trivial which partially explains why most e-cash systems have followed the elegant idea proposed by Camenisch *et al.* [11]. It relies on a pseudo-random function PRF as follows. For a wallet of $N = 2^L$ coins, a first seed **k** is used to generate N pseudo-random values $\mathsf{PRF_k}(i)$, for $i \in [1, N]$, acting as the coins' serial numbers. Meanwhile, a second seed **t** allows generating independent values $\mathsf{PRF_t}(i)$ acting as one-time pads on the spender's identity. The concealed identity constitutes the double-spending tag.

Any user can generate at most N fresh pairs $(\mathsf{PRF_k}(i), \mathsf{PRF_t}(i))$ per wallet. In case of double-spending, a pair must have been re-used, meaning that a serial number $\mathsf{PRF_k}(i)$ will appear twice in the bank database, thus making frauds easy to detect. Moreover, in such a case, the spender's identity will be masked using the same value $\mathsf{PRF_t}(i)$. An appropriate combination of the corresponding double-spending tags thus allows to remove $\mathsf{PRF_t}(i)$ and so to identify the defrauder. Some adjustments are necessary in the lattice setting [26], but the high-level principle remains the same.

However, Bourse *et al.* [9] recently showed that this approach may fail to provide a sound proof of exculpability in many cases. Indeed, the identity returned by the identification algorithm is a complex mix of PRF outputs, public keys and random values, most of them being totally controlled by the adversary. It is therefore impossible to guarantee that the returned identity corresponds to the author of these fraudulent payments nor even to guarantee that both payments have been performed by the same user.

In [9], Bourse *et al.* point out that this problem is partially due to a misidentification of the properties that must be satisfied by the pseudo-random function PRF. They therefore propose to strengthen the requirements on PRF, introducing in particular a notion of collision resistance that essentially states the difficulty of finding $(\mathbf{s}, \mathbf{s}', i, i')$ such that $\mathsf{PRF_s}(i) = \mathsf{PRF_{s'}}(i')$. Assuming that the PRF satisfies such suitable properties, they prove security of generic constructions that are reminiscent of the seminal scheme proposed by Camenisch *et al.* An interesting aspect of [9] is thus the rehabilitation of the original intuition of compact e-cash [11] that has been common to all following works.

Unfortunately, this is done by relying on unconventional security notions for PRFs that have not been considered by designers of such functions. Bourse *et al.* show that, under suitable assumptions, these notions are actually already satisfied by some PRFs in cyclic groups, but similar results are not known in the lattice setting. Indeed, existing lattice-based PRFs are not known to provide collision-resistance in this strong sense, which prevents instantiation of their frameworks in this setting. Concretely, this means that secure lattice-based e-cash systems are not known to exist for the time being.

In this work, we choose a very different strategy that we believe to be better suited for the lattice setting as it does not rely on collision-resistant PRFs.

Our first step is to modify the construction of the serial numbers to ensure that collisions only occur for spendings performed by the same user. In [9], this is achieved by using the same seed (but different public parameters) to generate all the pseudo-random values used during a spending. Assuming that pseudo-randomness still holds in this context and that collision resistance is achieved by some of the PRFs, they prove that a collision only occurs for spendings involving the same seed. They are then able to prove that the use of the same seed implies the involvement of the same user, and so on until proving exculpability of their construction. Here, we still use a PRF as a source of pseudo-random values but our serial numbers are not simply the outputs of such a function. We indeed want to reuse the same pseudo-random values for different parts of our serial numbers and double-spending tags to rule out the adversarial strategy pointed out in [9]. To achieve this while retaining anonymity, we use the notion of a lossy trapdoor function F_{LTF} introduced in [30] and more specifically, the elegant instantiation based on LWE proposed in [34] related to the original construction in [30].

The first element of $\mathbf{y}_S$ is now $F_{\mathsf{LTF}}(\mathsf{PRF_k}(i))$, which still allows to extract random bits from $\mathsf{PRF_k}(i)$ using a universal hash function H_{UH}, as proved in [30]. We can thus incorporate $PK_{\mathcal{U}} + H_{\mathsf{UH}}(\mathsf{PRF_k}(i))$ in $\mathbf{y}_S$ while ensuring anonymity of the user $\mathcal{U}$ that owns the public key $PK_{\mathcal{U}}$. In the exculpability proof, we will generate F_{LTF} in the injective mode, thus ensuring that a collision $\mathbf{y}_S = \mathbf{y}_{S'}$ can only occur when the same value $\mathsf{PRF_k}(i)$ is used for both transactions. Together with $PK_{\mathcal{U}} + H_{\mathsf{UH}}(\mathsf{PRF_k}(i)) = PK_{\mathcal{U}'} + H_{\mathsf{UH}}(\mathsf{PRF_k}(i))$, this implies $PK_{\mathcal{U}} = PK_{\mathcal{U}'}$.

We then adapt this idea to double-spending tags. We similarly extract random bits from $\mathsf{PRF_k}(i)$ using a different universal hash function H'_{UH} to define $\mathbf{y}_T = PK_{\mathcal{U}} + \mathsf{FRD}(R) \cdot H'_{\mathsf{UH}}(\mathsf{PRF_k}(i))$, where $\mathsf{FRD}(R)$ is some public matrix specific to the transaction. As $\mathsf{PRF_k}(i)$ and the public key $PK_{\mathcal{U}}$ are the same for both transactions, the formula $\mathbf{y}_T - \mathsf{FRD}(R) \cdot [(\mathsf{FRD}(R) - \mathsf{FRD}(R'))^{-1} \cdot (\mathbf{y}_T - \mathbf{y}_{T'})]$ necessarily returns such a public key whose owner is guilty of double-spendings.

As far as efficiency goes, we essentially add some matrix-vector products to the construction of [26]. Moreover, since all of these matrices are public, a NIZK proof of correct computations can be produced using the framework provided in [26] or the more efficient techniques in Sect. 5.

4 Construction

We present a new e-cash system that overcomes the aforementioned issues in the proof of exculpability. We use the PRF from [7] that allows for a simpler description of our system. We nevertheless explain in Sect. 7 how to improve efficiency by using the alternative PRF from [4]. While the Withdraw protocol is a simplification of [26], the Spend protocol is very different in the way to construct coin serial numbers and security tags. Additional details on the zero-knowledge arguments of knowledge used in our construction are given in Sect. 5.

ParGen $(1^{\lambda}, 1^{L})$: Given security parameter λ and integer $L > 0$ such that 2^{L} is the desired number of coins per wallet issued, perform the following:

1. Choose secure public parameters $\mathsf{par_{PRF}} = (m, n, p, q, \mathbf{P}_0, \mathbf{P}_1)$ for the BLMR PRF family [7]. Namely,

   a. For $n = \mathcal{O}(\lambda)$, set $\alpha = 2^{-\omega(\log^{1+c}(n))}$ for some constant $c > 0$; a prime $p = 2^{\log^{1+c}(n)}$; a prime power $q = \mathcal{O}(\sqrt{n}/\alpha)$ such that p divides q; and $m = n \cdot \lceil \log q \rceil$.

    b. Sample $\mathbf{P}_0, \mathbf{P}_1 \hookleftarrow U(\{0,1\}^{m \times m})$ over $\mathbb{Z}_q$-invertible matrices.

2. Choose parameters $\mathsf{par}_{sig} = (q_s, \ell, \sigma, (m_i)_{i=0}^3, m_s, m_f)$ for a signature scheme allowing to sign committed values [25]. Namely,

    a. Choose a prime power modulus $q_s = \tilde{\mathcal{O}}(n^3)$ dividing q, an integer $\ell = \Theta(\lambda)$ and a Gaussian parameter $\sigma = \Omega(\sqrt{n \log q_s} \log n)$. Set $\delta_{q_s-1} = \lceil \log_2(q_s) \rceil$, $\delta_{q-1} = \lceil \log_2(q) \rceil$ and $\delta_{p-1} = \lceil \log_2(p) \rceil$. Define the message block lengths $m_0 = m_s := 2n\delta_{q_s-1}$, as well as $m_1 = m$ and $m_2 = \bar{m} := m\delta_{q-1}$.

    b. Sample $\mathbf{D}_0', \mathbf{D}_0'' \hookleftarrow U(\mathbb{Z}_{q_s}^{n \times m_0})$ and $\mathbf{D}_i \hookleftarrow U(\mathbb{Z}_{q_s}^{n \times m_i})$, for $i \in \{1, 2\}$, and define the commitment key to be $CK := (\mathbf{D}_0 := [\mathbf{D}_0' | \mathbf{D}_0''], \mathbf{D}_1, \mathbf{D}_2)$.

    c. Sample $\mathbf{F} \hookleftarrow U(\mathbb{Z}_p^{n \times m})$.

3. Choose parameters $\mathsf{par}_{\mathsf{LTF}}$ for the lossy trapdoor function of [30]. In terms of $n_{\mathsf{LTF}} = \tilde{\mathcal{O}}(\lambda)$ for constant $c > 0$, these consist of moduli $q_{\mathsf{LTF}} = \Theta(n_{\mathsf{LTF}}^{1+1/\gamma})$ that divides q and $p_{\mathsf{LTF}} = \Theta(n_{\mathsf{LTF}}^{1/\gamma})$ for some constant $\gamma < 1$; matrix dimensions n_{LTF} and $m_{\mathsf{LTF}} = \Theta(n_{\mathsf{LTF}} \log q_{\mathsf{LTF}})$ and $\bar{n}_{\mathsf{LTF}} = \bar{m}_{\mathsf{LTF}} / \log p_{\mathsf{LTF}}$ such that $p_{\mathsf{LTF}} < q_{\mathsf{LTF}}/4n_{\mathsf{LTF}}$; and an LWE error rate $\alpha_{\mathsf{LTF}} = \Theta(\sqrt{n}/q_{\mathsf{LTF}})$. We additionally require that $m_{\mathsf{LTF}} = m \cdot \lceil \log p \rceil$. Then, select an evaluation key ek_{LTF} for a lossy trapdoor function in injective mode $F_{\mathsf{LTF}} : \{0,1\}^{m_{\mathsf{LTF}}} \rightarrow \mathbb{Z}_{q_{\mathsf{LTF}}}^{n_{\mathsf{LTF}} + \bar{n}_{\mathsf{LTF}}}$, meaning that $ek_{\mathsf{LTF}} = (\mathbf{A}_{\mathsf{LTF}}, \mathbf{U}_{\mathsf{LTF}})$ consists of a random $\mathbf{A}_{\mathsf{LTF}} \hookleftarrow U(\mathbb{Z}_q^{n_{\mathsf{LTF}} \times m_{\mathsf{LTF}}})$ and a matrix

$$\mathbf{U}_{\mathsf{LTF}} = \mathbf{S}_{\mathsf{LTF}}^\top \cdot \mathbf{A}_{\mathsf{LTF}} + \mathbf{E}_{\mathsf{LTF}}^\top + \mathbf{G}_{\mathsf{LTF}}^\top \in \mathbb{Z}_{q_{\mathsf{LTF}}}^{\bar{n}_{\mathsf{LTF}} \times m_{\mathsf{LTF}}},$$

for some $\mathbf{S}_{\mathsf{LTF}} \hookleftarrow U(\mathbb{Z}_{q_{\mathsf{LTF}}}^{n_{\mathsf{LTF}} \times \bar{n}_{\mathsf{LTF}}})$, $\mathbf{E}_{\mathsf{LTF}} \hookleftarrow D_{\mathbb{Z}^{m_{\mathsf{LTF}} \times \bar{n}_{\mathsf{LTF}}}, \alpha_{\mathsf{LTF}} q_{\mathsf{LTF}}}$ and $\mathbf{G}_{\mathsf{LTF}}$ referred to in the preliminaries.

4. Choose an integer $\bar{p} > 0$ such that $\bar{p} < p/2$ which will define a challenge space $\{-\bar{p}, \ldots, \bar{p}\}$ for the argument system of [35]. Choose a hash function $H_{\mathsf{FS}} : \{0,1\}^* \rightarrow \{-\bar{p}, \ldots, \bar{p}\}^\kappa$, for some $\kappa = \mathcal{O}(\lambda/\log \bar{p})$, which will be modelled as a random oracle in the security analysis.

5. Choose a full-rank difference function $\mathsf{FRD} : \mathbb{Z}_p^n \rightarrow \mathbb{Z}_p^{n \times n}$ such as the one in [1]; two universal hash functions $H_{\mathsf{UH}} : \mathbb{Z}_p^{m_{\mathsf{LTF}}} \rightarrow \mathbb{Z}_p^n, H_{\mathsf{UH}}' : \mathbb{Z}_p^{m_{\mathsf{LTF}}} \rightarrow \mathbb{Z}_p^n$ keyed by two uniformly random matrices $\mathbf{U}_{\mathsf{UH}}, \mathbf{U}_{\mathsf{UH}}' \hookleftarrow U(\mathbb{Z}_p^{n \times m_{\mathsf{LTF}}})$; and a collision resistant hash function $H_0 : \{0,1\}^* \rightarrow \mathbb{Z}_p^n \setminus \{\mathbf{0}^n\}$.

6. Select a digital signature algorithm[2] Σ able to sign any bitstring.

The final output is $\mathsf{par} = (\mathsf{par}_{\mathsf{PRF}}, \mathsf{par}_{sig}, \mathsf{par}_{\mathsf{LTF}}, \mathbf{F}, \mathsf{FRD}, \mathbf{U}_{\mathsf{UH}}, \mathbf{U}_{\mathsf{UH}}', H_0, ek_{\mathsf{LTF}}, H_{\mathsf{FS}}, CK, \Sigma)$.

BKeyGen$(1^\lambda, \mathsf{par})$: The bank $\mathcal{B}$ generates a key pair for the signature scheme by conducting the following steps.

1. Sample $(\mathbf{A}, \mathbf{T_A}) \hookleftarrow \mathsf{TrapGen}(1^n, 1^{m_s}, q_s)$ (details are provided in the full version of this work [16]) so that $\mathbf{T_A}$ is a short basis of $\Lambda_{q_s}^\perp(\mathbf{A})$ that allows $\mathcal{B}$ to sample Gaussian vectors in $\Lambda_{q_s}^\perp(\mathbf{A})$ with parameter σ.

2. Choose uniform $\mathbf{A}_0, \ldots, \mathbf{A}_\ell \hookleftarrow U(\mathbb{Z}_{q_s}^{n \times m_s})$.

---

[2] Any EUF-CMA secure scheme Σ can be selected here.

3. Choose $\mathbf{D} \hookleftarrow U(\mathbb{Z}_{q_s}^{n \times m_s/2})$ and $\mathbf{u} \hookleftarrow U(\mathbb{Z}_{q_s}^n)$.

The key pair consists of $PK_{\mathcal{B}} := \left(\mathbf{A}, \{\mathbf{A}_j\}_{j=0}^{\ell}, \mathbf{D}, \mathbf{u}\right)$ and $SK_{\mathcal{B}} := \mathbf{T}_A$.

UKeyGen $(1^\lambda, \mathsf{par})$: Choose a secret key $SK_{\mathcal{U}} := \mathbf{e}_u \hookleftarrow U(\{0,1\}^m)$ and set the public key to be $PK_{\mathcal{U}} := \mathbf{F} \cdot \mathbf{e}_u \in \mathbb{Z}_p^n$.

MKeyGen $(1^\lambda, \mathsf{par})$: Generate and output $(SK_{\mathcal{M}}, PK_{\mathcal{M}}) \leftarrow \Sigma.\mathsf{Keygen}(1^\lambda)$.

Withdraw $(\mathcal{U}(PK_{\mathcal{B}}, SK_{\mathcal{U}}, 2^L), \mathcal{B}(PK_{\mathcal{U}}, SK_{\mathcal{B}}, 2^L))$: A user $\mathcal{U}$ withdraws a wallet with 2^L coins from a bank $\mathcal{B}$ by engaging in the following protocol:

1. $\mathcal{U}$ picks a PRF key $\mathbf{k} \hookleftarrow U(\mathbb{Z}_q^m)$ and computes its binary decomposition $\tilde{\mathbf{k}} = \mathsf{vdec}_{m,q-1}(\mathbf{k}) \in \{0,1\}^{\tilde{m}}$. Then, $\mathcal{U}$ commits to the 2-block message $(\mathbf{e}_u, \tilde{\mathbf{k}}) \in \{0,1\}^m \times \{0,1\}^{\tilde{m}}$ by sampling $\mathbf{r}_0 \hookleftarrow D_{\mathbb{Z}^{m_s}, \sigma}$ and sending

$$\mathbf{c}_{\mathcal{U}} = \mathbf{D}_0' \cdot \mathbf{r}_0 + \mathbf{D}_1 \cdot \mathbf{e}_u + \mathbf{D}_2 \cdot \tilde{\mathbf{k}} \in \mathbb{Z}_{q_s}^n$$

   to $\mathcal{B}$. In addition, $\mathcal{U}$ generates an interactive zero-knowledge argument of knowledge of an opening $(\mathbf{r}_0, \mathbf{e}_u, \tilde{\mathbf{k}})$ such that $PK_{\mathcal{U}} = \mathbf{F} \cdot \mathbf{e}_u$ with $\mathcal{B}$. This argument of knowledge can be instantiated using the methods of [35] by applying the technique of [14] to parallel repetitions.[3]

2. If the argument of $\mathcal{U}$ verifies, then $\mathcal{B}$ extends the commitment $\mathbf{c}_{\mathcal{U}}$ by sampling $\mathbf{r}_1 \hookleftarrow D_{\mathbb{Z}^{m_s}, \sigma}$, and computing $\mathbf{c}_{\mathcal{U}}' = \mathbf{c}_{\mathcal{U}} + \mathbf{D}_0' \cdot \mathbf{r}_1$. Next $\mathcal{B}$ chooses $\tau \hookleftarrow U(\{0,1\}^\ell)$, defines $\mathbf{u}_{\mathcal{U}} = \mathbf{u} + \mathbf{D} \cdot \mathsf{vdec}_{n,q_s-1}(\mathbf{c}_{\mathcal{U}}')$, sets

$$\mathbf{A}_\tau := [\mathbf{A}|\mathbf{A}_0 + \sum_{j=1}^{\ell} \tau[j] \cdot \mathbf{A}_j] \in \mathbb{Z}_{q_s}^{n \times 2m_s}$$

   and computes a short basis $\mathbf{T}_\tau$ of $\Lambda_{q_s}^{\perp}(\mathbf{A}_\tau)$ using $\mathbf{T}_A$. Using $\mathbf{T}_\tau$, it then samples a short vector $\mathbf{v} \hookleftarrow D_{\Lambda_{q_s}^{\mathbf{u}_{\mathcal{U}}}(\mathbf{A}_\tau), \sigma}$ and sends $(\tau, \mathbf{v}, \mathbf{r}_1)$ to $\mathcal{U}$.

3. $\mathcal{U}$ verifies that $\|\mathbf{v}\| \leq \sigma\sqrt{2m_s}$, $\|\mathbf{r}_1\| \leq \sigma\sqrt{m_s}$ and

$$\mathbf{A}_\tau \cdot \mathbf{v} = \mathbf{u} + \mathbf{D} \cdot \mathsf{vdec}_{n,q_s-1}(\mathbf{c}_{\mathcal{U}} + \mathbf{D}_0'' \cdot \mathbf{r}_1) \in \mathbb{Z}_{q_s}^n.$$

   If so, $\mathcal{U}$ sets $\mathbf{r} = (\mathbf{r}_0^\top \mid \mathbf{r}_1^\top)^\top \in \mathbb{Z}_{q_s}^{2m_s}$ and stores the wallet $\mathcal{W} := \left(\mathbf{e}_u, \mathbf{k}, \mathsf{Sig}_{\mathcal{B}} = (\tau, \mathbf{v}, \mathbf{r}), J = 0\right)$ whereas $\mathcal{B}$ records a debit of 2^L for the account associated to $PK_{\mathcal{U}}$.

Spend $(\mathcal{U}(\mathcal{W}, PK_{\mathcal{B}}, PK_{\mathcal{M}}), \mathcal{M}(SK_{\mathcal{M}}, PK_{\mathcal{B}}, \mathsf{info}))$: A user $\mathcal{U}$ in possession of a wallet $\mathcal{W} = \left(\mathbf{e}_u, \mathbf{k}, \mathsf{Sig}_{\mathcal{B}} = (\tau, \mathbf{v}, \mathbf{r}), J\right)$ wants to spend a coin with $\mathcal{M}$. If $J > 2^L - 1$, $\mathcal{U}$ outputs $\bot$. Otherwise, they run the following protocol:

1. $\mathcal{U}$ generates a digital coin by first hashing the transaction information to $R = H_0(PK_{\mathcal{M}}, \mathsf{info}) \in \mathbb{Z}_p^n$ before conducting the following steps.

   a. Compute a BLMR PRF evaluation on the standard binary representation of J in $\{0,1\}^L$ using key $\mathbf{k} \in \mathbb{Z}_q^m$; i.e., set

$$\mathbf{y_k} = \left\lfloor \prod_{i=1}^{L} \mathbf{P}_{J[L+1-j]} \cdot \mathbf{k} \right\rceil_p$$

   and let $\tilde{\mathbf{y}}_\mathbf{k} = \mathsf{bin}_p(\mathbf{y_k}) \in \{0,1\}^{m_{\mathsf{LTF}}}$ its standard bit-decomposition.

---

[3] Technically, we should add a CRS to par but we leave this implicit for simplicity.

b. Using ek_{LTF}, compute $\mathbf{y}_1 = F_{\mathsf{LTF}}(\tilde{\mathbf{y}}_{\mathbf{k}})$ and $\mathbf{y}_2 = PK_{\mathcal{U}} + H_{\mathsf{UH}}(\tilde{\mathbf{y}}_{\mathbf{k}})$ to form the serial number $\mathbf{y}_S := (\mathbf{y}_1, \mathbf{y}_2) \in \mathbb{Z}_{q_{\mathsf{LTF}}}^{n_{\mathsf{LTF}}+\bar{n}_{\mathsf{LTF}}} \times \mathbb{Z}_p^n$.

c. Compute the security tag $\mathbf{y}_T = PK_{\mathcal{U}} + \mathsf{FRD}(R) \cdot H'_{\mathsf{UH}}(\tilde{\mathbf{y}}_{\mathbf{k}}) \in \mathbb{Z}_p^n$.

d. Generate a non-interactive argument of knowledge π_K to show knowledge of $(J, \mathbf{k}, \mathbf{e}_u, (\tau, \mathbf{v}, \mathbf{r}))$ such that:
   - The vector $\mathbf{k}$ and secret key $\mathbf{e}_u$ associated with $\mathcal{W}$ and $PK_{\mathcal{U}}$ have been certified by $\mathcal{B}$ through the signature $(\tau, \mathbf{v}, \mathbf{r})$.
   - $\mathbf{y}_S$ and $\mathbf{y}_T$ were computed correctly using par, the secret key $\mathbf{e}_u$, the PRF seed $\mathbf{k}$ and a valid $J \in \{0, \ldots, 2^{L-1}\}$.

More precisely, letting $\mathbf{y}_S = (\mathbf{y}_1, \mathbf{y}_2)$, π_K argues knowledge of $(J, \mathbf{k}, \mathbf{e}_u, (\tau, \mathbf{v}, \mathbf{r}))$ where $J \in \{0,1\}^L$, $\mathbf{k} \in \mathbb{Z}_q^m$, $\mathbf{e}_u \in \{0,1\}^m$, $\tau \in \{0,1\}^\ell$, $\mathbf{v} \in \mathbb{Z}^{2m_s}$ s.t. $\|\mathbf{v}\|_\infty \le \sigma\sqrt{2m_s}$ and $\mathbf{r} \in \mathbb{Z}^{m_s}$ s.t. $\|\mathbf{r}\|_\infty \le \sigma\sqrt{2m_s}$, satisfying the relations

$$[\mathbf{A} \mid \mathbf{A}_0 + \sum_{j=1}^{\ell} \tau[j] \cdot \mathbf{A}_j] \cdot \mathbf{v}$$

$$= \mathbf{u} + \mathbf{D} \cdot \mathsf{vdec}_{n,q_s-1}\left([\mathbf{D}'_0 | \mathbf{D}''_0] \cdot \mathbf{r} + \mathbf{D}_1 \cdot \mathbf{e}_u + \mathbf{D}_2 \cdot \mathsf{vdec}_{m,q-1}(\mathbf{k}) \right)$$

$$\mathbf{y}_1 = F_{\mathsf{LTF}}\left(\mathsf{bin}_p\left(\left\lfloor \prod_{i=1}^{L} \mathbf{P}_{J[L+1-j]} \cdot \mathbf{k} \right\rceil_p \right) \right) \in \mathbb{Z}_{q_{\mathsf{LTF}}}^{n_{\mathsf{LTF}}+\bar{n}_{\mathsf{LTF}}}$$

$$\mathbf{y}_2 = \mathbf{F} \cdot \mathbf{e}_u + H_{\mathsf{UH}}\left(\mathsf{bin}_p\left(\left\lfloor \prod_{i=1}^{L} \mathbf{P}_{J[L+1-j]} \cdot \mathbf{k} \right\rceil_p \right) \right) \in \mathbb{Z}_p^n$$

$$\mathbf{y}_T = \mathbf{F} \cdot \mathbf{e}_u + \mathsf{FRD}(R) \cdot H'_{\mathsf{UH}}\left(\mathsf{bin}_p\left(\left\lfloor \prod_{i=1}^{L} \mathbf{P}_{J[L+1-j]} \cdot \mathbf{k} \right\rceil_p \right) \right) \in \mathbb{Z}_p^n$$

The non-interactive argument π_K is produced by running the proof described in Sect. 5.2 $\kappa = \mathcal{O}(\lambda/\log\bar{p})$ times in parallel and using the Fiat-Shamir heuristic with random oracle H_{FS}. We may write

$$\pi_K = \left(\{\mathsf{Comm}_{K,j}\}_{j=1}^{\kappa}, \mathsf{Chall}_K, \{\mathsf{Resp}_{K,j}\}_{j=1}^{\kappa} \right)$$

where $\mathsf{Chall}_K = H_{\mathsf{FS}}(\mathsf{par}, R, \mathbf{y}_S, \mathbf{y}_T, \{\mathsf{Comm}_{K,j}\}_{j=1}^{\kappa})$.

$\mathcal{U}$ sends $\mathsf{coin} = (\mathsf{info}', PK_{\mathcal{M}}, \mathbf{y}_S, \mathbf{y}_T, \pi_K)$ to $\mathcal{M}$.

2. If $\mathsf{info}' = \mathsf{info}$ and $\mathsf{VerifyCoin}\,(\mathsf{par}, PK_{\mathcal{B}}, \mathsf{coin})$ outputs 1, then $\mathcal{M}$ outputs coin. Otherwise, $\mathcal{M}$ outputs $\perp$. In either case, $\mathcal{U}$ outputs an updated wallet $\mathcal{W}'$ where J is increased by 1.

VerifyCoin $(PK_{\mathcal{B}}, \mathsf{coin})$: Parse the coin as $\mathsf{coin} = (\mathsf{info}, PK_{\mathcal{M}}, \mathbf{y}_S, \mathbf{y}_T, \pi_K)$ and output 1 if and only if π_K verifies.

VerifyDeposit $(PK_{\mathcal{B}}, PK_{\mathcal{M}}, \mathsf{coin}, \mu)$: If $\mathsf{VerifyCoin}\,(PK_{\mathcal{B}}, \mathsf{coin}) = 0$, return 0. Otherwise, return 1 if and only if μ is a valid signature on coin with respect to $PK_{\mathcal{M}}$: i.e., $\Sigma.\mathsf{Verify}(PK_{\mathcal{M}}, \mu, \mathsf{coin}) = 1$.

Deposit $(\mathcal{M}(SK_\mathcal{M}, \mathsf{coin}, PK_\mathcal{B}), \mathcal{B}(PK_\mathcal{M}, SK_\mathcal{B}, \mathsf{state}_\mathcal{B}))$: $\mathcal{M}$ and $\mathcal{B}$ interact in the following way.

1. $\mathcal{M}$ sends $\mathsf{coin} = (\mathsf{info}, PK_\mathcal{M}, \mathbf{y}_S, \mathbf{y}_T, \pi_K)$ to $\mathcal{B}$ along with a signature $\mu = \Sigma.\mathsf{Sign}(SK_\mathcal{M}, \mathsf{coin})$.
2. If $\mathsf{VerifyDeposit}\,(PK_\mathcal{B}, PK_\mathcal{M}, \mathsf{coin}, \mu) = 0$ or $\mathsf{VerifyCoin}\,(PK_\mathcal{B}, \mathsf{coin}) = 0$, then $\mathcal{B}$ outputs $\bot$. If info and $PK_\mathcal{M}$ are found in $\mathsf{state}_\mathcal{B}$, then $\mathcal{B}$ outputs the corresponding entry $(\mathsf{coin}', PK_\mathcal{M}, \mu', \mathbf{y}'_S)$. If the serial number $\mathbf{y}_S$ contained in coin is not found in $\mathsf{state}_\mathcal{B}$, then $\mathcal{B}$ accepts the coin, adds the tuple $(\mathsf{coin}, PK_\mathcal{M}, \mu, \mathbf{y}_S)$ to $\mathsf{state}_\mathcal{B}$ and credits $\mathcal{M}$'s account. If there exists a tuple $(\mathsf{coin}, PK'_\mathcal{M}, \mu', \mathbf{y}_S)$ in $\mathsf{state}_\mathcal{B}$, then $\mathcal{B}$ outputs such a tuple.

Identify $(PK_\mathcal{B}, \mathsf{coin}_1, \mathsf{coin}_2)$: Parse $\mathsf{coin}_i = (\mathsf{info}_i, PK_{\mathcal{M}_i}, \mathbf{y}_{S,i}, \mathbf{y}_{T,i}, \pi_{K,i})$ for each $i \in \{1, 2\}$. If any of the following conditions hold, output $\bot$:

- $\mathbf{y}_{S,1} \neq \mathbf{y}_{S,2}$,
- $\mathsf{VerifyCoin}\,(\mathsf{par}, PK_\mathcal{B}, \mathsf{coin}_1)$ or $\mathsf{VerifyCoin}\,(\mathsf{par}, PK_\mathcal{B}, \mathsf{coin}_2) \neq 1$,
- $(\mathsf{info}_1, PK_{\mathcal{M}_1}) = (\mathsf{info}_2, PK_{\mathcal{M}_2})$.

Otherwise, compute $\mathbf{y}'_T = (\mathsf{FRD}(R_1) - \mathsf{FRD}(R_2))^{-1} \cdot (\mathbf{y}_{T,1} - \mathbf{y}_{T,2}) \in \mathbb{Z}_p^n$ with $R_i = H_0(PK_{\mathcal{M}_i}, \mathsf{info}_i)$ and set $PK_\mathcal{U} = \mathbf{y}_{T,1} - \mathsf{FRD}(R_1) \cdot \mathbf{y}'_T \in \mathbb{Z}_p^n$. Note that this calculation is performed using publicly known values, so the proof of guilt of a double spender is simply $\Pi_G = (\mathsf{coin}_1, \mathsf{coin}_2)$. The output of this algorithm is then the pair $(PK_\mathcal{U}, \Pi_G)$.

5   Zero-Knowledge Arguments with Soundness Error $1/\mathsf{poly}(\lambda)$ in Standard Lattices

We proceed in two steps to describe the ZKAoK used to spend a coin. We first describe an argument of knowledge of a (seed,input) pair generating a given BLMR evaluation. We then extend this to capture the whole statement proved by a user during a spending. For the ZKAoK in the withdrawal protocol, we directly rely on results of [35]. Throughout our construction, we use the argument system of Yang *et al.* [35] which was originally proved computationally honest-verifier ZK (HVZK) with polynomial soundness error. However, we can use known techniques to transform parallel repetitions of this protocol into a 3-round, malicious verifier ZK protocol with negligible soundness error in the CRS model [14]. This is how we instantiate the *interactive* ZKAoK in the withdrawal protocol. In the spend protocol, we use the standard result that the Fiat-Shamir transform [21] applied to parallel repetitions of an HVZK protocol yields a NIZK argument in the ROM. We also note that one may use a statistically hiding configuration of the commitment scheme from [5] instead of the more efficient computationally hiding configuration chosen in [35] to obtain *statistical* ZK arguments.

5.1   Zero-Knowledge Arguments for the BLMR PRF

We extend the protocol of Yang *et al.* [35] to build a ZKAoK of a (seed,input) pair producing a given BLMR evaluation. A similar result for the GGM-based PRF implied by [4] is provided in the full version [16], leading to a more efficient instantiation.

In [35], Yang *et al.* provide an argument of knowledge for the "instance-relation" set given by

$$\mathcal{R}^* = \left\{ ((\mathbf{M}', \mathbf{y}', \mathcal{M}), \mathbf{x}') : \begin{array}{c} \mathbf{M}' \cdot \mathbf{x}' = \mathbf{y}' \bmod q \ \wedge \\ \forall (h,i,j) \in \mathcal{M}, \mathbf{x}'[h] = \mathbf{x}'[i] \cdot \mathbf{x}'[j] \bmod q \end{array} \right\}. \tag{1}$$

where $\mathbf{M}' \in \mathbb{Z}_q^{m' \times n'}, \mathbf{y}' \in \mathbb{Z}_q^{m'}$ and $\mathcal{M} \subseteq [n'] \times [n'] \times [n']$, for some prime power q. The tuple $(\mathbf{M}', \mathbf{y}', \mathcal{M})$ is the instance whereas $\mathbf{x}' \in \mathbb{Z}_q^{n'}$ is the witness. By carefully crafting each of these elements, we show that a proof of correct evaluation of the BLMR PRF is an instance of this argument of knowledge.

Indeed, recall that, for any seed $\mathbf{k}$ and input $x \in \{0,1\}^L$, the PRF output is defined as $\mathbf{y} = \left\lfloor \prod_{i=1}^{L} \mathbf{P}_{x_{L+1-i}} \cdot \mathbf{k} \right\rfloor_p$, where $\mathbf{P}_0, \mathbf{P}_1 \in \{0,1\}^{m \times m}$ are public parameters and p is a prime power dividing q. If we write $\mathbf{y}_j = \prod_{i=L+1-j}^{L} \mathbf{P}_{x_{L+1-i}} \cdot \mathbf{k}$ for $j \in [L]$, we can represent a PRF evaluation using the linear system over $\mathbb{Z}_q$:

$$\mathbf{y}_1 - \mathbf{P}_0 \cdot (1 - x_1)\mathbf{k} - \mathbf{P}_1 \cdot x_1 \mathbf{k} = \mathbf{0}$$
$$\mathbf{y}_2 - \mathbf{P}_0 \cdot (1 - x_2)\mathbf{y}_1 - \mathbf{P}_1 \cdot x_2 \mathbf{y}_1 = \mathbf{0}$$
$$\vdots$$
$$\mathbf{y}_L - \mathbf{P}_0 \cdot (1 - x_L)\mathbf{y}_{L-1} - \mathbf{P}_1 \cdot x_L \mathbf{y}_{L-1} = \mathbf{0}$$
$$\mathbf{y}_L - \mathbf{e} = \frac{q}{p} \cdot \mathbf{y}$$

where $\mathbf{e} \in [0, q/p]^m$. This system is a linear system in the (quadratic) unknowns $(1 - x_1)\mathbf{k}, x_1\mathbf{k}, (1 - x_2)\mathbf{y}_1, x_2\mathbf{y}_1, \ldots, (1 - x_L)\mathbf{y}_{L-1}, x_L\mathbf{y}_{L-1}, \mathbf{y}_L, \mathbf{e}$. As a first step towards transforming our system into one captured by $\mathcal{R}^*$, we can embed the above system in a larger system whose solution is given by

$$(\mathbf{x}')^\top = ((\mathbf{x}_1')^\top, (\mathbf{x}_2')^\top, (\mathbf{x}_3')^\top, \tilde{\mathbf{e}}^\top) \tag{2}$$

where

- $(\mathbf{x}_1')^\top = ((1 - x_1), x_1, \ldots, (1 - x_L), x_L) \in \{0,1\}^{2L}$,
- $(\mathbf{x}_2')^\top = (\mathbf{y}_0^\top, \mathbf{y}_1^\top, \ldots, \mathbf{y}_L^\top) \in \mathbb{Z}_q^{(L+1) \cdot m}$, with $\mathbf{y}_0 := \mathbf{k}$,
- $\mathbf{x}_3' \in \mathbb{Z}_q^{2L \cdot m}$ is of the form

$$(\mathbf{x}_3')^\top = ((1 - x_1)\mathbf{y}_0, x_1\mathbf{y}_0, (1 - x_2)\mathbf{y}_1, x_2\mathbf{y}_1, \ldots, (1 - x_L)\mathbf{y}_{L-1}, x_L\mathbf{y}_{L-1}),$$

- $\tilde{\mathbf{e}} = \mathsf{vdec}_{m, \frac{q}{p}-1}(\mathbf{e}) \in \{0,1\}^{m \cdot (\lfloor \log(\frac{q}{p}-1)\rfloor + 1)}$, which ensures that $\|\mathbf{e}\|_\infty < q/p$.

One aspect of this extended solution is that every consecutive pair of entries of $\mathbf{x}_1'$ is either $(0,1)$ or $(1,0)$. In other words, each consecutive pair of entries of $\mathbf{x}_1'$ sums to 1 and is binary. The fact that consecutive pairs add to 1 can be captured by a linear constraint that will constitute the first block of our matrix $\mathbf{M}'$. Next, the fact that the entries of $\mathbf{x}_1'$ are binary may be captured by the set of equations $\mathbf{x}_1'[i] = \mathbf{x}_1'[i] \cdot \mathbf{x}_1'[i]$. In fact, proving this relation only for even i is sufficient as $\mathbf{x}_1'[2i] \in \{0,1\}$ and $\mathbf{x}_1'[2i] + \mathbf{x}_1'[2i-1] = 1$ implies $\mathbf{x}_1'[2i-1] \in \{0,1\}$.

The next part of a valid solution's structure is that entries of $\mathbf{x}_3'$ are the result of multiplying entries of $\mathbf{x}_1'$ and $\mathbf{x}_2'$. This can be written as $\mathbf{x}_3'[h'] = \mathbf{x}_1'[i'] \cdot \mathbf{x}_2'[j']$ for appropriate choices of h', i', j'. It then only remains to prove that the entries of $\tilde{\mathbf{e}}$ are binary, which is captured by the equations $\tilde{\mathbf{e}}[i] = \tilde{\mathbf{e}}[i] \cdot \tilde{\mathbf{e}}[i]$.

Following the details outlined above, we may represent a BLMR evaluation as the system $\mathbf{M}' \cdot \mathbf{x}' = \mathbf{y}' \bmod q$ for

- $\mathbf{x}' \in \mathbb{Z}_q^{2L+(L+1)\cdot m+2L\cdot m+(\lfloor \log(q/p-1)\rfloor+1)\cdot m}$ which is subject to the following constraints, when parsed as in Eq. 2:
  - for $i \in [L]$: $\mathbf{x}_1'[2i] = \mathbf{x}_1'[2i] \cdot \mathbf{x}_1'[2i]$
  - for $(i,j) \in [m] \times [L]$: $\mathbf{x}_3'[2m(j-1)+i] = \mathbf{x}_1'[2j-1] \cdot \mathbf{x}_2'[m(j-1)+i]$ and $\mathbf{x}_3'[2m(j-1)+m+i] = \mathbf{x}_1'[2j] \cdot \mathbf{x}_2'[m(j-1)+i]$
  - for $i \in [(\lfloor \log(q/p-1)\rfloor+1)\cdot m]$: $\tilde{\mathbf{e}}[i] = \tilde{\mathbf{e}}[i] \cdot \tilde{\mathbf{e}}[i]$

- $(\mathbf{y}')^\top = (\overbrace{1,\ldots,1}^{L},\overbrace{0,\ldots,}^{m\cdot L},0,(q/p)\mathbf{y}^\top)$

-

$$\mathbf{M}' = \begin{bmatrix} \mathbf{I}_L \otimes (1,1) & & \\ \hline & 0^{mL\times m}\|\mathbf{I}_{m\cdot L} & -\mathbf{I}_L \otimes [\mathbf{P}_0\|\mathbf{P}_1] & \\ \hline & 0^{m\times L\cdot m}\|\mathbf{I}_m & & -H_{m,q/p-1} \end{bmatrix} \quad (3)$$

where all blank blocks consist of 0 entries.

5.2 Zero-Knowledge Arguments for the Spend Protocol

The previous protocol enables to prove correct evaluation of the BLMR PRF but is not sufficient to produce the proof π_K expected by the merchant during the Spend protocol. In particular, we also need to prove

- knowledge of (short) solutions to linear systems (e.g., the user's secret key);
- knowledge of solutions to an equation involving a subset sum of known-matrix and secret vector multiplications (i.e. the computation of $\mathbf{A}_\tau$);
- correct evaluation of the lossy trapdoor function F_{LTF}.

All these statements can be captured by the relation $\mathcal{R}^*$ from [35], as explained below. Together with our proof of correct PRF evaluation, this means that π_K can be instantiated using only the Yang *et al.* framework. We can then achieve inverse-polynomial soundness error $1/\bar{p}$ in one ZKAoK protocol run. To achieve a soundness error of $2^{-\lambda}$, we only need $\mathcal{O}(\lambda/\log \bar{p})$ repetitions. This clearly improves upon the Stern-type protocols used in [26], which require $\mathcal{O}(\lambda)$ repetitions.

Remark 1. It should be noted that we have different equations over various moduli in our Spend protocol. However, as long as q is a prime power and all remaining moduli divide q, we may lift all equations to use the modulus q. For example, to lift an equation over $\mathbb{Z}_{q'}$ to an equation over $\mathbb{Z}_q$ where q' divides q, we simply multiply by $q/q' \in \mathbb{Z}$. We will use this trick in what follows.

The Explicit Linear System. Transforming the argument of knowledge produced by a user during the Spend protocol into an instance of the Yang *et al.* protocol is far from trivial as there are several details to address. Besides the moduli issue mentioned above, we indeed need to juggle with two different types of binary decomposition in order to ensure security of the whole system.

We use the notation from the Spend protocol specification in Sect. 4. We further parse $\mathbf{v}$ as $(\mathbf{v}_1, \mathbf{v}_2)$, where $\mathbf{v}_1, \mathbf{v}_2 \in \mathbb{Z}^{m_s}$. Also, we define $\sigma' := \lfloor \sigma \sqrt{m_s} + 1 \rfloor$ and $\mathbf{v}_i^+ = \mathbf{v}_i + \sigma' \cdot \mathbf{1}$ for $i \in \{1, 2\}$, where $\mathbf{1}$ denotes the all-one vector. This implies that valid values of $\mathbf{v}_i$ (i.e., such that $\|\mathbf{v}_i\|_\infty \leq \sigma'$) give rise to $\mathbf{v}_i^+ \in [0, 2\sigma']^{m_s}$. We also set $\mathbf{r}^+ := \mathbf{r} + \sqrt{2}\sigma' \cdot \mathbf{1}$ so that $\mathbf{r}^+ \in [0, 2\sqrt{2}\sigma']^{2m_s}$ for valid choices of $\mathbf{r}$ (i.e. values such that $\|\mathbf{r}\|_\infty \leq \sqrt{2}\sigma'$). We can then define $\tilde{\mathbf{v}}_i := \mathsf{vdec}_{m_s, 2\sigma'} \left(\mathbf{v}_i^+ \right)$ for $i \in \{1, 2\}$, $\tilde{\mathbf{r}} := \mathsf{vdec}_{2m_s, 2\sqrt{2}\sigma'} \left(\mathbf{r}^+ \right)$, $\tilde{\mathbf{k}} := \mathsf{vdec}_{m, q-1} \left(\mathbf{k} \right)$ and

$$
\tilde{\mathbf{w}} := \mathsf{vdec}_{n, q_s - 1} \Big([\mathbf{D}_0' | \mathbf{D}_0''] \cdot \mathbf{r} + \mathbf{D}_1 \cdot \mathbf{e}_u + \mathbf{D}_2 \cdot \tilde{\mathbf{k}} \Big).
$$

We begin by considering the equation associated to the signature. We can express it as the following linear system over $\mathbb{Z}_q$

$$
\frac{q}{q_s} \bigg[\mathbf{A} \left(\mathbf{H}_{m_s, 2\sigma'} \cdot \tilde{\mathbf{v}}_1 - \sigma' \mathbf{1} \right) +
$$
$$
\mathbf{A}_0 \left(\mathbf{H}_{m_s, 2\sigma'} \cdot \tilde{\mathbf{v}}_2 - \sigma' \mathbf{1} \right) +
$$
$$
\sum_{j=1}^{\ell} \mathbf{A}_j \left(\mathbf{H}_{m_s, 2\sigma'} \cdot (\tau[j] \cdot \tilde{\mathbf{v}}_2) - \sigma' \tau[j] \cdot \mathbf{1} \right) - \mathbf{D} \cdot \tilde{\mathbf{w}} \bigg] = \frac{q}{q_s} \mathbf{u}
$$
$$
\frac{q}{q_s} \bigg[\mathbf{H}_{n, q_s - 1} \cdot \tilde{\mathbf{w}} - \bigg([\mathbf{D}_0' | \mathbf{D}_0''] \left(\mathbf{H}_{2m_s, 2\sqrt{2}\sigma'} \cdot \tilde{\mathbf{r}} - \sqrt{2}\sigma' \mathbf{1} \right) +
$$
$$
\mathbf{D}_1 \cdot \mathbf{e}_u + \mathbf{D}_2 \cdot \tilde{\mathbf{k}} \bigg) \bigg] = \mathbf{0}
$$
$$
\mathbf{H}_{m, q-1} \cdot \tilde{\mathbf{k}} - \mathbf{k} = \mathbf{0},
$$

whose solution is $\mathbf{x}_1 := \left(\tau, \tilde{\mathbf{v}}_1, \tilde{\mathbf{v}}_2, \tau[1] \cdot \tilde{\mathbf{v}}_2, \ldots, \tau[\ell] \cdot \tilde{\mathbf{v}}_2, \tilde{\mathbf{w}}, \tilde{\mathbf{r}}, \mathbf{e}_u, \mathbf{k}, \tilde{\mathbf{k}} \right)$, with some quadratic constraints amongst unknowns.

We next consider the evaluation of $\mathbf{y}_1$, as written in the Spend protocol. Here a subtlety arises as we need to use two different types of binary decomposition. So far, we have only used the $\mathsf{vdec}_{m, p-1}$ function because it allows achieving exact soundness with the proofs of Yang *et al.* Unfortunately, the decomposition of an integer according to the sequences $B_1, \ldots, B_{\delta_p - 1}$ implicitly defined by $\mathsf{vdec}_{m,p-1}$ (see Sect. 2) may not be unique, which might lead to undetected frauds in our system. We will then also use the *standard* binary decomposition (that is unique) to ensure that the user is not evaluating F_{LTF} on two different decompositions of the same PRF output. It then remains to prove consistency of both decompositions, which is explained below.

Concretely, let $\tilde{\mathbf{y}}_\mathbf{k}$ denote the standard binary decomposition of the PRF output $\mathbf{y}_\mathbf{k} = \left\lfloor \prod_{i=1}^{L} \mathbf{P}_{J[L+1-j]} \cdot \mathbf{k} \right\rceil_p$. Importantly, we must ensure that $\tilde{\mathbf{y}}_\mathbf{k}$ does really correspond to binary decomposition of a vector in $[0, p-1]^m$ rather than some larger space. Alternatively, we need to ensure that $\mathbf{y}_\mathbf{k}$ (which is unknown) has entries in $[0, p-1]$. We achieve this by considering $\tilde{\mathbf{y}}_\mathbf{k}' = \mathsf{vdec}_{m,p-1}(\mathbf{y}_\mathbf{k})$. By multiplying the evaluation equation of $\mathbf{y}_1$ by q/q_{LTF} and denoting the LTF key ek_{LTF} as $\mathbf{B}_{\mathsf{LTF}} \in \mathbb{Z}_{q_{\mathsf{LTF}}}^{(n_{\mathsf{LTF}}+\bar{n}_{\mathsf{LTF}}) \times m_{\mathsf{LTF}}}$, we can derive the following equations over $\mathbb{Z}_q$:

$$
\boxed{
\begin{array}{c}
\dfrac{q}{q_{\mathsf{LTF}}} \mathbf{B}_{\mathsf{LTF}} \cdot \tilde{\mathbf{y}}_\mathbf{k} = \dfrac{q}{q_{\mathsf{LTF}}} \cdot \mathbf{y}_1 \\[2mm]
\mathbf{y}_\mathbf{k} - \mathbf{H}_{m,p-1} \cdot \tilde{\mathbf{y}}_\mathbf{k}' = \mathbf{0} \\[2mm]
\mathbf{y}_\mathbf{k} - \mathbf{I}_m \otimes \left(1, 2, \dots, 2^{\lceil \log p \rceil}\right) \cdot \tilde{\mathbf{y}}_\mathbf{k} = \mathbf{0}
\end{array}
}
$$

Conveniently, the restriction that the entries of $\tilde{\mathbf{y}}_\mathbf{k}$ and $\tilde{\mathbf{y}}_\mathbf{k}'$ are binary is easily captured using quadratic constraints. Therefore all boxed equations so far constitute a linear system whose solution is $\mathbf{x_2} := (\mathbf{x}_1 \| \tilde{\mathbf{y}}_\mathbf{k}, \tilde{\mathbf{y}}_\mathbf{k}', \mathbf{y}_\mathbf{k})$, subject to some quadratic constraints that can easily be handled with the Yang *et al.* framework. However, we still need some equations to ensure that $\mathbf{y}_\mathbf{k}$ is computed correctly as a BLMR PRF output. In order to describe these equations, we will use the observations from Sect. 5.1 and the matrix $\mathbf{M}'$ given in Equation (3). In particular, we set the unknown vector

$$
\begin{aligned}
\mathbf{x_k} =& (1 - J[1], J[1], \dots, 1 - J[L], J[L], \mathbf{yk}_0, \dots, \mathbf{yk}_L, \\
& (1 - J[1])\mathbf{yk}_0, J[1]\mathbf{yk}_0, \dots, (1 - J[L])\mathbf{yk}_{L-1}, J[L]\mathbf{yk}_{L-1}, \mathbf{e_k})
\end{aligned}
$$

where $\mathbf{yk}_i \in \mathbb{Z}_q^m$ for $i \in [0, L]$ and $\mathbf{e_k} \in \{0, 1\}^{m \cdot (\lfloor \log(\frac{q}{p}-1) \rfloor + 1)}$. As noted in Sect. 5.1 (and shown by the form of $\mathbf{x_k}$), the constraints on these unknown vectors are quadratic as required. To capture the PRF computation, we extend the vector of unknowns by defining $\mathbf{x_3} := (\mathbf{x_2} \| \mathbf{x_k})$. We then add the following to the boxed linear equations over $\mathbb{Z}_q$ above (where $\mathbf{M}'$ is defined in Equation (3)):

$$
\boxed{
\begin{array}{c}
\mathbf{yk}_0 - \mathbf{k} = \mathbf{0} \\[2mm]
\mathbf{M}' \cdot \mathbf{x_k} - \left(\mathbf{0}^{(m+1) \cdot L}, \dfrac{q}{p}\mathbf{y}_\mathbf{k}^\top\right)^\top = (\mathbf{1}^L, \mathbf{0}^{m \cdot (L+1)})^\top
\end{array}
}
$$

Finally, it remains to prove that $\mathbf{y}_2$ and $\mathbf{y}_T$ are well-formed. This consists in proving the following relation over $\mathbb{Z}_q$:

$$\frac{q}{p}\mathbf{F} \cdot \mathbf{e}_u + \frac{q}{p}\mathbf{U}_{\mathsf{UH}} \cdot \tilde{\mathbf{y}}_{\mathbf{k}} = \frac{q}{p}\mathbf{y}_2$$

$$\frac{q}{p}\mathbf{F} \cdot \mathbf{e}_u + \frac{q}{p}\mathsf{FRD}(R) \cdot \mathbf{U}'_{\mathsf{UH}} \cdot \tilde{\mathbf{y}}_{\mathbf{k}} = \frac{q}{p}\mathbf{y}_T,$$

where the witnesses are already included in $\mathbf{x}_3$.

We have shown that the whole statement proved during the Spend protocol can be expressed as the collection of the boxed linear systems with a vector $\mathbf{x}_3$ of unknowns subject to quadratic constraints supported by the protocol of [35].

6   Security Proofs

In this section and the full version [16], we prove Theorem 1, which states that our construction provides all the required security properties.

Theorem 1. *Our construction is a secure e-cash system in the random oracle model assuming that the following conditions hold:*

- *The* $\mathsf{SIS}_{n,m_s,q_s,\beta'}$ *for* $\beta' = \mathcal{O}\left(\sigma^2 m_s^{1/2}(m_s + m \log q)\right)$ *and* $\mathsf{SIS}_{n,m,p,2\sqrt{m}}$ *problems are hard;*
- *Parameters are chosen so that the interactive AoK* Π_1 *in the withdrawal protocol is zero-knolwedge (ZK) and that the non-interactive AoK* Π_2 *in the spend protocol is honest-verifier zero-knowledge (HVZK);*
- *Parameters* m, n, q, p *are chosen so that the BLMR PRF is pseudo-random;*
- *The* $\mathsf{LWE}_{n_{\mathsf{LTF}},m_{\mathsf{LTF}},q_{\mathsf{LTF}},\alpha}$ *problem is hard;*
- Σ *is an EUF-CMA secure signature scheme.*

Proof of Exculpability. Suppose the lossy trapdoor function is sampled in its injective mode. The proof of exculpability relies on the fact that an adversary producing two valid coins with the same serial number must produce at least one fresh proof of knowledge of a secret key underlying an honestly produced public key. In particular, our construction guarantees that this public key is the one that Identify points to. The ability to produce fresh arguments of knowledge for an honest public key can be used to solve the SIS problem. We first present a lemma about collision probabilities on PRFs with randomly sampled seeds and polynomial-size domain.

Lemma 4. *Let* $\mathsf{PRF} = \{\mathsf{PRF}_{\mathbf{k}} : \{0,1\}^L \to \{0,1\}^M \mid \mathbf{k} \in \mathcal{K}\}$ *be a family of pseudo-random functions where* $2^L = \mathsf{poly}(\lambda)$ *and* $M = \mathsf{poly}(\lambda)$. *Take any* $N = \mathsf{poly}(\lambda)$ *and sample* $\mathbf{k}_1, \ldots, \mathbf{k}_N \hookleftarrow U(\mathcal{K})$. *The probability that* $\exists (i, j, x_1, x_2) \in [N]^2 \times \{0,1\}^L \times \{0,1\}^L$ *such that* $\mathsf{PRF}_{\mathbf{k}_i}(x_1) = \mathsf{PRF}_{\mathbf{k}_j}(x_2)$ *is negligible.*

Proof. We first describe a challenger algorithm $\mathcal{C}$. In the first stage, $\mathcal{C}$ samples $\mathbf{k}_1, \ldots, \mathbf{k}_N \hookleftarrow U(\mathcal{K})$, samples N uniform functions $U_1, \ldots, U_N : \{0,1\}^L \to \{0,1\}^M$ and samples a challenge bit $b \hookleftarrow U(\{0,1\})$. In the second phase, $\mathcal{C}$ waits for queries $x \in \{0,1\}^L$. If $b = 1$, it answers with $(\mathsf{PRF}_{\mathbf{k}_1}(x), \ldots, \mathsf{PRF}_{\mathbf{k}_N}(x))$. On the other hand, if $b = 0$, it responds with $(U_1(x), \ldots, U_N(x))$. By a standard hybrid argument, no PPT adversary $\mathcal{A}$ can guess the bit b with non-negligible advantage under the assumption that PRF is a PRF family and $N = \mathsf{poly}(\lambda)$. Consider the following adversary $\mathcal{A}^*$ that queries $\mathcal{C}$ on the entire set $\{0,1\}^L$. Denote the response to query x as $(y_{1,x}, \ldots, y_{N,x})$. Now, $\mathcal{A}^*$ outputs $b^* = 1$ if there exists (i, j, x_1, x_2) such that $y_{i,x_1} = y_{j,x_2}$. Otherwise, $\mathcal{A}^*$ outputs $b^* = 0$. Note that, if $b = 0$, the probability that $\mathcal{A}^*$ outputs $b^* = 1$ is equal to

$$1 - \prod_{k=1}^{2^L N} \left(1 - \frac{(k-1)}{2^M} \right)$$

which is negligible since $2^L N = \mathsf{poly}(\lambda)$ and $2^M = 2^{\mathsf{poly}(\lambda)}$. Therefore, under the assumption that PRF is a PRF family, the probability that $\mathcal{A}^*$ outputs $b^* = 1$ when $b = 1$ is also negligible. □

Lemma 5. *Our construction provides strong exculpability in the random oracle model assuming that: (i) The $\mathsf{SIS}_{n,m,p,2\sqrt{m}}$ problem is hard; (ii) Parameters (m, n, p, q) are chosen so that the BLMR PRF is pseudo-random; (iii) Π_1 and Π_2 are ZK and HVZK, respectively; (iv) The protocols underlying Π_1 and Π_2 are arguments of knowledge.*

Recall that a successful adversary returns coin_1 and coin_2 such that $PK_{\mathcal{U}^*} = \mathsf{Identify}(PK_\mathcal{B}, \mathsf{coin}_1, \mathsf{coin}_2)$ for honest user $\mathcal{U}^*$. This implies two things:

- First, the two coins have been generated using the public key $PK_{\mathcal{U}^*}$. Indeed, the fact that the identification procedure succeeds implies that these coins share the same serial number $\mathbf{y}_S := (\mathbf{y}_1, \mathbf{y}_2)$. Since the evaluation key of F_{LTF} was sampled in injective mode, the serial number $\mathbf{y}_S$ uniquely determines the value $PK' = \mathbf{y}_2 - H_{\mathsf{UH}}(F_{\mathsf{LTF}}^{-1}(\mathbf{y}_1))$, which underlies both coin_1 and coin_2. Then, the soundness of Π_2 ensures that

$$\mathbf{y}_{T,1} = PK' + \mathsf{FRD}(R_1) \cdot H'_{\mathsf{UH}}(F_{\mathsf{LTF}}^{-1}(\mathbf{y}_1)),$$
$$\mathbf{y}_{T,2} = PK' + \mathsf{FRD}(R_2) \cdot H'_{\mathsf{UH}}(F_{\mathsf{LTF}}^{-1}(\mathbf{y}_1)),$$

  which implies that PK' is the public key $PK_{\mathcal{U}^*}$ pointed to by $\mathsf{Identify}$.
- Second, there exists $d \in \{1, 2\}$ such that $\mathsf{coin}_d = (R_d, \mathbf{y}_{S,d}, \mathbf{y}_{T,d}, \pi_{K,d})$ is *not* the result of a $\mathcal{Q}_{\mathsf{Spend}}$-query w.h.p. To see why, consider the case that coin_1 and coin_2 are both the result of $\mathcal{Q}_{\mathsf{Spend}}$-queries, but do not appear in T_{ds}. This occurs if, when sampling polynomially many seeds, one finds $\mathbf{k}, \mathbf{k}'$ satisfying $\mathsf{PRF}_{\mathbf{k}}(J) = \mathsf{PRF}_{\mathbf{k}'}(J')$ for some $(J, J') \in [0, 2^L - 1]^2$. By Lemma 4, this occurs with negligible probability $\mathsf{negl}_1(\lambda)$.

Proof. Using these two observations, we will prove the strong exculpability of our scheme by defining the following sequence of games. Let ϵ be the probability that $\mathcal{A}$ succeeds against the exculpability of our scheme and let Q_w (resp. Q_s) denote the maximal number of $\mathcal{Q}_{\mathsf{Withdraw}}$ queries (resp. $\mathcal{Q}_{\mathsf{Spend}}$ queries).

Game$_0$: This is exactly the strong exculpability experiment, as defined in Sect. 2. The probability ϵ_0 that $\mathcal{A}$ succeeds in this game is then exactly ϵ.

Game$_{1,0}$: In this game, our reduction $\mathcal{S}$ (acting as a challenger in the strong exculpability experiment) proceeds as in Game$_0$ except that it defines $\mathbf{F}$ as $\bar{\mathbf{A}} \in \mathbb{Z}_p^{n \times m}$, where $\bar{\mathbf{A}}$ is a uniform matrix provided in a $\mathsf{SIS}_{n,m,p,2\sqrt{m}}$ instance. We denote by $\mathbf{e}_{u^*} \in \{0,1\}^m$ the secret key generated by $\mathcal{S}$ for the accused user $PK_{\mathcal{U}^*} = \mathbf{F} \cdot \mathbf{e}_{u^*}$. Note that $\mathcal{A}$ is given black-box access to H_{FS} and $\mathcal{S}$ answers queries to H_{FS} by returning uniformly random elements of $\{-\bar{p}, \ldots, \bar{p}\}^\kappa$. In addition, $\mathcal{S}$ initialises empty lists of honest users $\mathcal{HU}$ and double-spent coins $\mathcal{T}_{\mathsf{ds}}$. As $\bar{\mathbf{A}}$ is distributed as $\mathbf{F}$ in the original setup, the probability that $\mathcal{A}$ succeeds in this game is $\epsilon_{1,0} = \epsilon_0$.

Game$_{1,i}$: For $i \in [1, Q_w]$, this game is defined as Game$_{1,i-1}$, except that $\mathcal{S}$ now answers the i-th $\mathcal{Q}_{\mathsf{Withdraw}}$-query (if any) by running the simulator of Π_1 to simulate the interactive proof generated by the user at this stage. This is done for every user $PK_{\mathcal{U}}$, and not just $PK_{\mathcal{U}^*}$. Any change of behaviour of $\mathcal{A}$ can thus be straightforwardly used against the zero-knowledge property of Π_1. We therefore have $\epsilon_{1,i-1} - \mathsf{Adv}_{ZK}^{\Pi_1}(\mathcal{A}) \leq \epsilon_{1,i}$ for all $i \in [1, Q_w]$.

Game$_{1,Q_w+i}$: For $i \in [1, Q_s]$, this game is defined as Game$_{1,Q_w+i-1}$, except that $\mathcal{S}$ now answers the i-th $\mathcal{Q}_{\mathsf{Spend}}$-query (if any) by running the simulator of Π_2 to simulate the non-interactive argument generated by the spender at this stage. This can be done (using only the user's public key $PK_{\mathcal{U}}$) by applying the standard technique of programming the random oracle H_{FS} on new inputs, which only requires the statistical HVZK property of Π_2. The simulation fails whenever the random oracle H_{FS} needs to be programmed at an input that it was previously queried on. However, this happens with negligible probability at most $\mathtt{Coll}_H := (Q_S + Q_H)/2^\lambda$, where Q_H is the total number of queries made by $\mathcal{A}$ to H_{FS} and the denominator 2^λ is a lower bound on the domain-size of H_{FS}-inputs. Therefore, we can conclude that $\epsilon_{1,Q_w+i-1} - \mathsf{Adv}_{HVZK}^{\Pi_2}(\mathcal{A}) - \mathtt{Coll}_H \leq \epsilon_{1,Q_w+i}$ for all $i \in [1, Q_s]$.

It is important to note that, in Game$_{1,Q_w+Q_s}$, the reduction $\mathcal{S}$ only needs $PK_{\mathcal{U}^*}$ and not $\mathbf{e}_{u^*}$ to simulate the game. This concretely means that the adversary's view is independent of the preimage $\mathbf{e}_{u^*}$ of $PK_{\mathcal{U}^*}$ selected by $\mathcal{S}$. Thanks to [27, Lemma 8], we know that this preimage is not unique: i.e., there exists at least one vector $\mathbf{e} \in \{0,1\}^m \setminus \{\mathbf{e}_{u^*}\}$ such that $\bar{\mathbf{A}} \cdot \mathbf{e}_{u^*} = \bar{\mathbf{A}} \cdot \mathbf{e} \bmod p$ with all but negligible probability. This observation will be crucial in what follows.

Game$_2$: Let Q_H be a polynomial bounding the number of random oracle queries made by $\mathcal{A}$ to H_{FS}. Up until $\mathcal{A}$ terminates, $\mathcal{S}$ answers $\mathcal{A}$'s queries as in the previous games, recording the random oracle queries as $(q_1, q_2, \ldots)$ and the corresponding uniformly distributed responses as $(h_1, h_2, \ldots)$. Our second observation at the beginning of the proof implies that at least one coin coin_d returned by $\mathcal{A}$ is not the result of a $\mathcal{Q}_{\mathsf{Spend}}$-query with overwhelming probability (if none of the coins were generated as a response to $\mathcal{Q}_{\mathsf{Spend}}$-query, then select a random $d \in \{1, 2\}$. Define

$$\pi_{K,d} := \left(\{\mathsf{Comm}_{K,d,j}\}_{j=1}^{\kappa}, \mathsf{Chall}_{K,d}, \{\mathsf{Resp}_{K,d,j}\}_{j=1}^{\kappa} \right),$$

$$\mathsf{Chall}_{K,d} := H_{\mathsf{FS}}\left(\mathsf{par}, R, \mathbf{y}_{S,d}, \mathbf{y}_{T,d}, \{\mathsf{Comm}_{K,d,j}\}_{j=1}^{\kappa} \right).$$

In this game, $\mathcal{S}$ aborts if the above query was not made to H_{FS}. We note that in such a case the proof $\pi_{K,d}$ would only have been acceptable with probability at most $(2\bar{p} + 1)^{-\kappa}$. We then have $\epsilon_{1, Q_w + Q_s} - (2\bar{p} + 1)^{-\kappa} \leq \epsilon_2$.

From now on, we know that there exists an index $i^* \in [Q_H]$ such that the i^*-th H_{FS}-query is used to produce $\mathsf{Chall}_{K,d}$ (i.e., $\mathsf{Chall}_{K,d} = h_{i^*}$) and that $\mathcal{A}$ succeeds in Game_2 with probability $\epsilon_2 \geq \epsilon - Q_w \cdot \mathsf{Adv}_{ZK}^{\Pi_1}(\mathcal{A}) - Q_s(\mathsf{Adv}_{HVZK}^{\Pi_2}(\mathcal{A}) + \mathsf{Coll}_H) - (2\bar{p} + 1)^{-\kappa}$. We then define our last game Game_3 as follows:

1. **Run Game_2 once:** $\mathcal{S}$ runs $\mathcal{A}$ by behaving as in Game_2. If $\mathcal{A}$ fails to win the game, then $\mathcal{S}$ aborts. Otherwise, it records $\text{coin}_d, \pi_{K,d}, \mathsf{Chall}_{K,d}, (q_1, q_2, \dots)$, $(h_1, h_2, \dots), i^*$, sets a variable $\mathsf{fork} = 1$ and proceeds to the next step.

2. **(Search for a 3-fork).** This step is repeated twice. $\mathcal{S}$ runs $\mathcal{A}$ with the same random tape as in the beginning of the first step. In addition, it sends $\mathcal{A}$ the same par as before, giving $\mathcal{A}$ oracle access to H_{FS}. $\mathcal{S}$ allows $\mathcal{A}$ to run until termination, answering queries to H_{FS} as follows:

   – Answer queries $q_1, \dots, q_{i^*-1}$ (which are identical to those of the first run) using the same values $h_1, \dots, h_{i^*-1}$ as before.
   – At the i^*-th query q_{i^*} (which is also the same as the first time $\mathcal{A}$ was run), pick a fresh uniform response h'_{i^*}.
   – For the remaining queries made by $\mathcal{A}$ denoted $q'_{i^*+1}, \dots, q'_{Q_H}$, pick fresh uniform random responses $h'_{i^*+1}, \dots, h'_{Q_H}$.

   If this is the first repetition, $\mathcal{S}$ sets $h_{i^*}^{(2)} = h'_{i^*}$. At the second repetition, it sets $h_{i^*}^{(3)} = h'_{i^*}$. If $\mathcal{A}$ terminates without winning the strong exculpability game, then $\mathcal{S}$ begins the next repetition of this step. If $\mathcal{A}$ terminates and wins the game, denote its output as $(PK'_{\mathcal{B}'}, \text{coin}'_1, \text{coin}'_2)$. As before, let $d' \in \{1, 2\}$ denote the index that was not the result of a $\mathcal{Q}_{\mathsf{Spend}}$-query (picking $d' \in \{1, 2\}$ randomly if neither coin was the result of a spend query). Recall that both coins can be the result of $\mathcal{Q}_{\mathsf{Spend}}$-queries with at most negligible probability $\mathsf{negl}(\lambda)_1$, but if this is the case, $\mathcal{S}$ skips to the next repetition of this step. Denote $\text{coin}'_{d'} = (R'_{d'}, \mathbf{y}'_{S,d'}, \mathbf{y}'_{T,d'}, \pi'_{K,d'})$. Write

$$\pi'_{K,d'} = \left(\{\mathsf{Comm}'_{K,d',j}\}_{j=1}^{\kappa}, \mathsf{Chall}'_{K,d'}, \{\mathsf{Resp}'_{K,d',j}\}_{j=1}^{\kappa} \right).$$

$\mathcal{S}$ skips to the next repetition of this step at this point if

$$\left(R_d, \mathbf{y}_{S,d}, \mathbf{y}_{T,d}, \{\mathsf{Comm}_{K,d,j}\}_{j=1}^{\kappa} \right) \neq \left(R'_{d'}, \mathbf{y}'_{S,d'}, \mathbf{y}'_{T,d'}, \{\mathsf{Comm}'_{K,d',j}\}_{j=1}^{\kappa} \right)$$

or if $h_{i^*} = h'_{i^*}$. Otherwise, $\mathcal{S}$ sets fork $\leftarrow$ fork $+ 1$ and $\pi_K^{(\text{fork}+1)} = \pi'_{K,d'}$.

3. **(Derive SIS solution from 3-fork).** If fork < 3 or, fork $= 3$ but there exists no $j \in [\kappa]$ such that $(h_{i^*}[j], h_{i^*}^{(2)}[j], h_{i^*}^{(3)}[j])$ take three distinct values, then $\mathcal{S}$ terminates outputting $\perp$. Otherwise, $\mathcal{S}$ has access to arguments $\pi_{K,d}, \pi_K^{(2)}, \pi_K^{(3)}$ sharing the same first message which we denote as $\{\text{Comm}_j\}_{j=1}^{\kappa}$. In addition, $\exists j^* \in [\kappa]$ at where $h_{i^*}[j^*], h_{i^*}^{(2)}[j^*], h_{i^*}^{(3)}[j^*]$ take three distinct values in $\{-\bar{p}, \ldots, \bar{p}\}$. Now a witness can be extracted from the transcripts $\pi_{K,d}, \pi_K^{(2)}, \pi_K^{(3)}$ by considering the j^*-th parallel repetition and the special-soundness/extractor of the ZKAoK protocol [35]. We denote this witness as $(\bar{J}, \bar{\mathbf{k}}, \bar{\mathbf{e}}_{u^*})$. If $\bar{\mathbf{e}}_{u^*} = \mathbf{e}_{u^*}$, then $\mathcal{S}$ aborts. Otherwise, $\mathcal{S}$ terminates, outputting $\mathbf{v} := \bar{\mathbf{e}}_{u^*} - \mathbf{e}_{u^*} \in \{-1, 0, 1\}^m$ as a SIS solution.

It then remains to evaluate the probability ϵ_3 that $\mathcal{A}$ succeeds in this last game. We begin by noting that the first and second steps corresponds exactly to the forking algorithm denoted as $F^{\mathcal{A}}$ in Lemma 3. Therefore, a direct application of this forking lemma implies that the variable fork reaches the value fork $= 3$ at the beginning of Step 3 with probability at least

$$\text{frk} := \epsilon_2 \cdot \left(\left(\frac{\epsilon_2}{Q_H} \right)^2 - \frac{3}{(2\bar{p}+1)^{\kappa}} \right).$$

which is non-negligible if ϵ_2 is non-negligible as $1/(2\bar{p}+1)^{\kappa}$ is negligible and Q_H is polynomial. Next, note that $\mathcal{S}$ extracts a witness $(\bar{J}, \bar{\mathbf{k}}, \bar{\mathbf{e}}_{u^*})$ if and only if it does not terminate at, or before the beginning of Step 3. In order to analyse the probability that this occurs, we define three events:

- GF ("Good fork"): This is the event that fork $= 3$ <u>and</u> there exists an index $j^* \in [\kappa]$ such that $(h_{i^*}[j^*], h_{i^*}^{(2)}[j^*], h_{i^*}^{(3)}[j^*])$ is a triple of 3.
- F ("Any fork"): This is the event that fork $= 3$ at the beginning of Step 4.
- GH ("Good hashes"): This is the event that there is an index $j^* \in [\kappa]$ such that $(h_{i^*}[j^*], h_{i^*}^{(2)}[j^*], h_{i^*}^{(3)}[j^*])$ take 3 distinct values.

It is easy to see that $\Pr[\overline{\text{GH}}] = ((6\bar{p}+1)/(2\bar{p}+1)^2)^{\kappa}$ is negligible and that $\Pr[\text{F}] = \text{frk}$. We also have

$$\Pr[\text{F}] \leq \Pr[\text{F}|\text{GH}] \cdot 1 + 1 \cdot \Pr[\overline{\text{GH}}] = \Pr[\text{F}|\text{GH}] + \text{negl}(\lambda).$$

This implies that $\mathcal{S}$ does not abort at the beginning of Step 3 or before with non-negligible probability

$$\Pr[\text{GF}] = \Pr[\text{F} \cap \text{GH}] = \Pr[\text{F}|\text{GH}] \cdot \Pr[\text{GH}] \geq (\text{frk} - \text{negl}(\lambda)) \cdot (1 - \text{negl}(\lambda)).$$

The last step is to evaluate the probability that $\bar{\mathbf{e}}_{u^*} = \mathbf{e}_{u^*}$, leading $\mathcal{S}$ to abort. Here we rely on our previous observation, namely that the adversary's view has been independent of $\mathbf{e}_{u^*}$ since $\text{Game}_{1, Q_w + Q_s}$ and that there is, with overwhelming probability, at least another vector $\bar{\mathbf{e}}_{u^*} \neq \mathbf{e}_{u^*}$ that is a valid secret key for $PK_{\mathcal{U}^*}$. We therefore know that the probability of the event $\bar{\mathbf{e}}_{u^*} \neq \mathbf{e}_{u^*}$ is at least $\frac{1}{2}$. In summary, we get the following bound on the probability ϵ_3 that $\mathcal{A}$ succeeds in Game_3:

$$\epsilon_3 \geq \frac{1}{2} \cdot (\mathsf{frk} - \mathsf{negl}(\lambda)) \cdot (1 - \mathsf{negl}(\lambda))$$

where frk is defined above. Any adversary $\mathcal{A}$ succeeding with non-negligible probability ϵ against the exculpability of our scheme can thus be used to solve the SIS problem, distinguish the BLMR PRF from pseudo-random, or break the zero-knowledge property of Π_1 or Π_2, which completes the proof. $\square$

7   A More Efficient GGM-based Construction

In Sect. 4, we use the BLMR PRF because it allows for a simpler description of the argument of knowledge, as it only requires one rounding per evaluation. Unfortunately, this comes at the price of a super-polynomial modulus q. We can do better by using a PRF obtained by applying the seminal construction of Goldreich, Goldwasser and Micali [23] to the LWR-based PRG of Banerjee et $al.$ [4] for which the LWE-to-LWR reduction of [2] allows the use of a polynomial modulus. This leads to an e-cash construction with $q = \mathsf{poly}(\lambda)$ which still relies on the hardness of standard worst-case lattice problems. Explicitly, the PRF we have in mind relies on the hardness of the $\mathsf{LWR}_{m,m,q,p}$ problem (which is at least as hard as $\mathsf{LWE}_{m',m,q,\alpha'}$ for $m' \geq \frac{\log q}{\log(2\gamma')}m$, $q \geq \gamma' m^2 \alpha' p$ for any $\gamma' \geq 1$ [2]). This PRF uses public parameters $m, p, q, \mathbf{A}_0, \mathbf{A}_1 \in \mathbb{Z}_q^{m \times m}$ where $\mathbf{A}_0, \mathbf{A}_1 \hookleftarrow U(\mathbb{Z}_q^{m \times m})$. The evaluation on seed $\mathbf{k} \in \mathbb{Z}_q^m$ and input $x \in \{0,1\}^L$ is

$$F_{\mathbf{k}}(x) := \left\lfloor \mathbf{A}_{x_L} \cdot \left\lfloor \cdots \cdots \left\lfloor \mathbf{A}_{x_2} \cdot \lfloor \mathbf{A}_{x_1} \cdot \mathbf{k} \rfloor_p \right\rfloor_p \cdots \cdots \right\rfloor_p \right\rfloor_p. \quad (4)$$

When replacing the BLMR PRF with the above in our e-cash construction, it is more convenient to keep the parameters m and n as described in Sect. 4. This allows us to reuse our security proofs without any issues. However, in contrast with the BLMR instantiation, we choose polynomially large p and q such that $q^2 > m^{5/2}p$ in the $\mathsf{ParGen}()$ phase. In addition, the binary public matrices $\mathbf{P}_0, \mathbf{P}_1$ must be replaced by uniformly sampled $\mathbf{A}_0, \mathbf{A}_1 \in \mathbb{Z}_q^{m \times m}$. In the full version [16], we show that this alternative PRF is compatible with the ZK relation $\mathcal{R}^*$ considered in [35], as we did for the BLMR PRF in Sect. 5.1. Combining this with the reasoning in Sect. 5.2 allows us to show that the GGM-based PRF is compatible with the ZKAoKs used in Spend.

7.1   Parameters

We provide in this section some details on the parameters and the complexity of an instantiation of our e-cash system using the GGM-based PRF. Firstly, Theorem 1 states that the security of our construction relies on:

- $\mathsf{LWR}_{m,m,q,p}$ (which is at least as hard as $\mathsf{LWE}_{m',m,q,\alpha'}$ for $m' \geq \frac{\log q}{\log(2\gamma')}m, q \geq \gamma' m^2 \alpha' p$ for any $\gamma' \geq 1$ [2])
- $\mathsf{LWE}_{n_{\mathsf{LTF}},m_{\mathsf{LTF}},q_{\mathsf{LTF}},\alpha}$ with $\alpha = \Theta\left(\frac{\sqrt{n_{\mathsf{LTF}}}}{q_{\mathsf{LTF}}}\right)$, $q_{\mathsf{LTF}} = \Theta(n_{\mathsf{LTF}}^{1+1/\gamma})$ for constant $\gamma < 1$
- $\mathsf{SIS}_{n,m,p,2\sqrt{m}}$
- $\mathsf{SIS}_{n,m_s,q_s,\beta'}$ for $\beta' = \mathcal{O}(\sigma^2 m_s^{1/2}(m_s + \bar{m}))$

and also that we use secure ZKAoKs. Since all moduli will be polynomial, we may safely assume that there is a parameter setting such that the argument system of Yang et al. is a ZKAoK. Additionally, our proof of the clearing property requires use of a signature scheme. Note that we can use the signature scheme of [22] so that the arising assumption is made redundant by the final item listed above. Recall that for our zero-knowledge proofs, we require that q_s, q_{LTF} and p all divide the prime power q. In order to achieve this, we now set $q = q_0^e$ where q_0 is prime and $e > 1$ is a constant integer. Since all moduli are polynomial, we may take $n_{\mathsf{LTF}} = \Theta(m) = \Theta(n \log q) = \tilde{\mathcal{O}}(n)$. Additionally, $m, \bar{m}, m_s, m_{\mathsf{LTF}}, \bar{n}_{\mathsf{LTF}}$ and n' are all $\tilde{\mathcal{O}}(n)$. Note that we will take $\gamma' = 1$ in the LWE-to-LWR reduction result stated above and $\gamma = 1/2$. To comply with hardness results relating standard worst-case lattice problems to SIS [22,29] and LWE [10,31], we require:

$$q^2/p = \tilde{\Omega}(n^{5/2}) \qquad q_{\mathsf{LTF}} = \tilde{\Theta}(n^3) \qquad p = \tilde{\Omega}(n) \qquad q_s = \tilde{\Omega}(\sigma^2 n^2) = \tilde{\Omega}(n^3).$$

Therefore, to base security on worst-case lattice problems, we may take $n, m, n_{\mathsf{LTF}}, \bar{n}_{\mathsf{LTF}}, m_{\mathsf{LTF}}, m_s$ all $\tilde{\mathcal{O}}(\lambda)$, $p = q_0 = \tilde{\mathcal{O}}(\lambda)$ and $q = q_s = q_{\mathsf{LTF}} = q_0^3 = \tilde{\mathcal{O}}(\lambda^3)$. Additional details on the communication costs are provided in the full version of this work.

Acknowledgements. This work is supported by the European Union PROMETHEUS project (Horizon 2020 Research and Innovation Program, grant 780701) and also partly funded by BPI-France in the context of the national project RISQ (P141580). Khoa Nguyen is supported in part by the Gopalakrishnan - NTU PPF 2018, by A*STAR, Singapore under research grant SERC A19E3b0099, and by Vietnam National University HoChiMinh City (VNU-HCM) under grant number NCM2019-18-01.

References

1. Agrawal, S., Boneh, D., Boyen, X.: Efficient lattice (H)IBE in the standard model. In: Gilbert, H. (ed.) EUROCRYPT 2010. LNCS, vol. 6110, pp. 553–572. Springer, Heidelberg (2010). https://doi.org/10.1007/978-3-642-13190-5_28
2. Alwen, J., Krenn, S., Pietrzak, K., Wichs, D.: Learning with rounding, revisited. In: Canetti, R., Garay, J.A. (eds.) CRYPTO 2013. LNCS, vol. 8042, pp. 57–74. Springer, Heidelberg (2013). https://doi.org/10.1007/978-3-642-40041-4_4
3. Banerjee, A., Peikert, C.: New and improved key-homomorphic pseudorandom functions. In: Garay, J.A., Gennaro, R. (eds.) CRYPTO 2014. LNCS, vol. 8616, pp. 353–370. Springer, Heidelberg (2014). https://doi.org/10.1007/978-3-662-44371-2_20

4. Banerjee, A., Peikert, C., Rosen, A.: Pseudorandom functions and lattices. In: Pointcheval, D., Johansson, T. (eds.) EUROCRYPT 2012. LNCS, vol. 7237, pp. 719–737. Springer, Heidelberg (2012). https://doi.org/10.1007/978-3-642-29011-4_42

5. Baum, C., Damgård, I., Lyubashevsky, V., Oechsner, S., Peikert, C.: More efficient commitments from structured lattice assumptions. In: Catalano, D., De Prisco, R. (eds.) SCN 2018. LNCS, vol. 11035, pp. 368–385. Springer, Cham (2018). https://doi.org/10.1007/978-3-319-98113-0_20

6. Belenkiy, M., Chase, M., Kohlweiss, M., Lysyanskaya, A.: Compact E-cash and simulatable VRFs revisited. In: Shacham, H., Waters, B. (eds.) Pairing 2009. LNCS, vol. 5671, pp. 114–131. Springer, Heidelberg (2009). https://doi.org/10.1007/978-3-642-03298-1_9

7. Boneh, D., Lewi, K., Montgomery, H., Raghunathan, A.: Key homomorphic PRFs and their applications. In: Canetti, R., Garay, J.A. (eds.) CRYPTO 2013. LNCS, vol. 8042, pp. 410–428. Springer, Heidelberg (2013). https://doi.org/10.1007/978-3-642-40041-4_23

8. Bootle, J., Lyubashevsky, V., Seiler, G.: Algebraic techniques for short(er) exact lattice-based zero-knowledge proofs. In: Boldyreva, A., Micciancio, D. (eds.) CRYPTO 2019. LNCS, vol. 11692, pp. 176–202. Springer, Cham (2019). https://doi.org/10.1007/978-3-030-26948-7_7

9. Bourse, F., Pointcheval, D., Sanders, O.: Divisible E-cash from constrained pseudorandom functions. In: Galbraith, S.D., Moriai, S. (eds.) ASIACRYPT 2019. LNCS, vol. 11921, pp. 679–708. Springer, Cham (2019). https://doi.org/10.1007/978-3-030-34578-5_24

10. Brakerski, Z., Langlois, A., Peikert, C., Regev, O., Stehlé, D.: On the classical hardness of learning with errors. In: STOC (2013)

11. Camenisch, J., Hohenberger, S., Lysyanskaya, A.: Compact E-cash. In: Cramer, R. (ed.) EUROCRYPT 2005. LNCS, vol. 3494, pp. 302–321. Springer, Heidelberg (2005). https://doi.org/10.1007/11426639_18

12. Canard, S., Pointcheval, D., Sanders, O., Traoré, J.: Divisible E-cash made practical. In: Katz, J. (ed.) PKC 2015. LNCS, vol. 9020, pp. 77–100. Springer, Heidelberg (2015). https://doi.org/10.1007/978-3-662-46447-2_4

13. Chaum, D.: Blind signatures for untraceable payments. In: Chaum, D., Rivest, R.L., Sherman, A.T. (eds.) Advances in Cryptology, pp. 199–203. Springer, Boston, MA (1983). https://doi.org/10.1007/978-1-4757-0602-4_18

14. Damgård, I.: Efficient concurrent zero-knowledge in the auxiliary string model. In: Preneel, B. (ed.) EUROCRYPT 2000. LNCS, vol. 1807, pp. 418–430. Springer, Heidelberg (2000). https://doi.org/10.1007/3-540-45539-6_30

15. Observatoire de l'épargne réglementée. Rapport annuel (2013). https://www.banque-france.fr/sites/default/files/medias/documents/observatoire-de-l-epargne-reglementee-rapport_2013.pdf

16. Deo, A., Libert, B., Nguyen, K., Sanders, O.: Lattice-based E-cash, revisited (full version). IACR Cryptology ePrint Archive 2020/614 (2020)

17. Dodis, Y., Ostrovsky, R., Reyzin, L., Smith, A.: Fuzzy extractors: how to generate strong keys from biometrics and other noisy data. In: SIAM (2008)

18. El Kaafarani, A., Katsumata, S.: Attribute-based signatures for unbounded circuits in the ROM and efficient instantiations from lattices. In: Abdalla, M., Dahab, R. (eds.) PKC 2018. LNCS, vol. 10770, pp. 89–119. Springer, Cham (2018). https://doi.org/10.1007/978-3-319-76581-5_4

19. Esgin, M.F., Zhao, R.K., Steinfeld, R., Liu, J.K., Liu, D.: MatRiCT: efficient, scalable and post-quantum blockchain confidential transactions protocol. In: ACM CCS (2019)
20. Farshim, P., Orlandi, C., Rosie, R.: Security of symmetric primitives under incorrect usage of keys. In: ToSC (2017)
21. Fiat, A., Shamir, A.: How to prove yourself: practical solutions to identification and signature problems. In: Odlyzko, A.M. (ed.) CRYPTO 1986. LNCS, vol. 263, pp. 186–194. Springer, Heidelberg (1987). https://doi.org/10.1007/3-540-47721-7_12
22. Gentry, C., Peikert, C., Vaikuntanathan, V.: Trapdoors for hard lattices and new cryptographic constructions. In: STOC (2008)
23. Goldreich, O., Goldwasser, S., Micali, S.: How to construct random functions. In: FOCS (1984)
24. Kim, S., Wu, D.J.: Watermarking cryptographic functionalities from standard lattice assumptions. In: Katz, J., Shacham, H. (eds.) CRYPTO 2017. LNCS, vol. 10401, pp. 503–536. Springer, Cham (2017). https://doi.org/10.1007/978-3-319-63688-7_17
25. Libert, B., Ling, S., Mouhartem, F., Nguyen, K., Wang, H.: Signature schemes with efficient protocols and dynamic group signatures from lattice assumptions. In: Cheon, J.H., Takagi, T. (eds.) ASIACRYPT 2016. LNCS, vol. 10032, pp. 373–403. Springer, Heidelberg (2016). https://doi.org/10.1007/978-3-662-53890-6_13
26. Libert, B., Ling, S., Nguyen, K., Wang, H.: Zero-knowledge arguments for lattice-based PRFs and applications to E-cash. In: Takagi, T., Peyrin, T. (eds.) ASIACRYPT 2017. LNCS, vol. 10626, pp. 304–335. Springer, Cham (2017). https://doi.org/10.1007/978-3-319-70700-6_11
27. Lyubashevsky, V.: Lattice-based identification schemes secure under active attacks. In: Cramer, R. (ed.) PKC 2008. LNCS, vol. 4939, pp. 162–179. Springer, Heidelberg (2008). https://doi.org/10.1007/978-3-540-78440-1_10
28. Mastercard: Transaction processing rules (2019). https://www.mastercard.us/content/dam/mccom/global/documents/transaction-processing-rules.pdf
29. Micciancio, D., Peikert, C.: Hardness of SIS and LWE with small parameters. In: Canetti, R., Garay, J.A. (eds.) CRYPTO 2013. LNCS, vol. 8042, pp. 21–39. Springer, Heidelberg (2013). https://doi.org/10.1007/978-3-642-40041-4_2
30. Peikert, C., Waters, B.: Lossy trapdoor functions and their applications. In: STOC (2008)
31. Regev, O.: On lattices, learning with errors, random linear codes, and cryptography. In: STOC (2005)
32. Ron, D., Shamir, A.: Quantitative analysis of the full bitcoin transaction graph. In: Sadeghi, A.-R. (ed.) FC 2013. LNCS, vol. 7859, pp. 6–24. Springer, Heidelberg (2013). https://doi.org/10.1007/978-3-642-39884-1_2
33. Visa: Transaction acceptance device guide (2016). https://www.visa.com.pe/dam/VCOM/regional/na/us/partner-with-us/documents/transaction-acceptance-device-guide-tadg.pdf
34. Wee, H.: Dual projective hashing and its applications—lossy trapdoor functions and more. In: Pointcheval, D., Johansson, T. (eds.) EUROCRYPT 2012. LNCS, vol. 7237, pp. 246–262. Springer, Heidelberg (2012). https://doi.org/10.1007/978-3-642-29011-4_16
35. Yang, R., Au, M.H., Zhang, Z., Xu, Q., Yu, Z., Whyte, W.: Efficient lattice-based zero-knowledge arguments with standard soundness: construction and applications. In: Boldyreva, A., Micciancio, D. (eds.) CRYPTO 2019. LNCS, vol. 11692, pp. 147–175. Springer, Cham (2019). https://doi.org/10.1007/978-3-030-26948-7_6

Twisted-PHS: Using the Product Formula to Solve Approx-SVP in Ideal Lattices

Olivier Bernard[1,2]([✉]) and Adeline Roux-Langlois[1]([✉])

[1] Univ Rennes, CNRS, IRISA, Rennes, France
{olivier.bernard,adeline.roux-langlois}@irisa.fr
[2] Thales, Gennevilliers, Laboratoire CHiffre, Gennevilliers, France

Abstract. Approx-SVP is a well-known hard problem on lattices, which asks to find short vectors on a given lattice, but its variant restricted to ideal lattices (which correspond to ideals of the ring of integers $\mathcal{O}_K$ of a number field K) is still not fully understood. For a long time, the best known algorithm to solve this problem on ideal lattices was the same as for arbitrary lattice. But recently, a series of works tends to show that solving this problem could be easier in ideal lattices than in arbitrary ones, in particular in the quantum setting.

Our main contribution is to propose a new "twisted" version of the PHS (by Pellet-Mary, Hanrot and Stehlé 2019) algorithm, that we call Twisted-PHS. As a minor contribution, we also propose several improvements of the PHS algorithm. On the theoretical side, we prove that our Twisted-PHS algorithm performs at least as well as the original PHS algorithm. On the practical side though, we provide a full implementation of our algorithm which suggests that much better approximation factors are achieved, and that the given lattice bases are a lot more orthogonal than the ones used in PHS. This is the first time to our knowledge that this type of algorithm is completely implemented and tested for fields of degrees up to 60.

Keywords: Ideal lattices · Approx-SVP · PHS algorithm

1 Introduction

Lattice-based cryptography is one of the most promising post-quantum solution to build cryptographic constructions, as shown by the large number of lattice-based submissions to the recent NIST post-quantum competition. Among those submissions, and the other recent more advanced constructions, several hard problems are used to build the security proofs, such as the Learning With Errors (LWE) problem [Reg05], its ring [SSTX09,LPR10] or module [LS15] variants (respectively Ring-LWE and Module-LWE) or the NTRU problem [HPS98]. In particular the Ring variant of the Learning With Errors problem is widely used as it seems to allow a nice trade-off between security and efficiency. Indeed, it is defined in a ring, usually $R = \mathbb{Z}/\langle x^n + 1 \rangle$ for n a power of 2, whose

© International Association for Cryptologic Research 2020
S. Moriai and H. Wang (Eds.): ASIACRYPT 2020, LNCS 12492, pp. 349–380, 2020.
https://doi.org/10.1007/978-3-030-64834-3_12

structure allows constructions having a much better efficiency than if based on
unstructured problems like LWE. Concerning its hardness, there exists quantum
worst-case to average case reductions [SSTX09, LPR10, PRS17] from the approx
Shortest Vector Problem on ideal-lattices (Approx-id-SVP) to the Ring-LWE
problem.

Approx-SVP is a well-known hard problem on lattices, which asks to find short
vectors on a given lattice, but its variant restricted to ideal lattices (corresponding to ideals of the ring of integers R of a number field K) is still not fully understood. For a long time, the best known algorithm to solve this problem on ideal
lattices was the same as for arbitrary lattices. The best trade-off in this case is
given by Schnorr's hierarchy [Sch87], which allows to reach an approximation fac-
tor $2^{\tilde{O}(n^\alpha)}$ in time $2^{\tilde{O}(n^{1-\alpha})}$, for $\alpha \in (0,1)$, using the BKZ algorithm. But recently,
a series of works [CGS14, EHKS14, BS16, CDPR16, CDW17, DPW19, PHS19a]
tends to show that solving this problem could be easier in ideal lattices than
in arbitrary ones, in particular in the quantum setting.

Hardness of Approx-SVP on Ideal Lattices. This series of works starts
with a claimed result [CGS14] of a quantum polynomial-time attack against a
scheme named Soliloquy, which solves the Approx-SVP problem on a principal
ideal lattice. The algorithm has two steps: the first one is solving the Principal
Ideal Problem (PIP), and finds a generator of the ideal, the second one is solving a Closest-Vector Problem (CVP) in the log-unit lattice to find the shortest
generator of the ideal. On one hand, the results of [EHKS14, BS16] on describing a quantum algorithm to compute class groups and then solve PIP in arbitrary degree number fields allow to have a quantum polynomial-time algorithm
for the first step. On the other hand, a work by Cramer et al. [CDPR16] provides a full proof of the correctness of the algorithm described by [CGS14], and
then concludes that there exists a polynomial-time quantum algorithm which
solve Approx-SVP on ideal lattices for an approximation factor $2^{\tilde{O}(\sqrt{n})}$. In 2017,
Cramer, Ducas and Wesolowski [CDW17] show how to use the Stickelberger lat-
tice to generalize this result to any ideal lattice in prime power cyclotomic fields.
The practical impact of their result was evaluated by the authors of [DPW19] by
running extensive simulations. They conclude that the CDW algorithm should
beat BKZ-300 for cyclotomic fields of degree larger than 24000.

In parallel, Pellet-Mary, Hanrot and Stehlé [PHS19a] proposed an extended
version of [CDPR16, CDW17] which is now proven for any number fields K.
The main feature of their algorithm, that we call PHS, is to use an exponential
amount of preprocessing, depending only on K, in order to efficiently combine the
two principal resolution steps of [CDW17], namely the CPMP (*Close Principal
Multiple Problem*) and the SGP (*Shortest Generator Problem*). Combining these
two steps in a single CVP instance provides some guarantee that the output of
the CPMP solver has a generator which is "not much larger" than its shortest
non-zero vector. Hence, the PHS algorithm in a number field K of degree n and
discriminant Δ_K is split in two phases, given $\omega \in [0, 1/2]$:

1. The preprocessing phase builds a specific lattice, depending only on the
   field K, together with some hint allowing to efficiently solve Approx-CVP

instances. This phase runs in time $2^{\tilde{O}(\log|\Delta_K|)}$ and outputs a hint $\mathcal{V}$ of bit-size $2^{\tilde{O}(\log^{1-2\omega}|\Delta_K|)}$.

2. The query phase reduces each Approx-id-SVP challenge to an Approx-CVP instance in this fixed lattice. It takes as inputs any ideal of $\mathcal{O}_K$, whose algebraic norm has bit-size bounded by $2^{\text{poly}(\log|\Delta_K|)}$, the hint $\mathcal{V}$, and runs in time $2^{\tilde{O}(\log^{1-2\omega}|\Delta_K|)} + \mathsf{T}_{\mathsf{Su}}(K)$. It outputs a non-zero element x of the ideal which solves Approx-SVP with an approximation factor $2^{\tilde{O}(\log^{\omega+1}|\Delta_K|/n)}$.

The term $\mathsf{T}_{\mathsf{Su}}(K)$ denotes the running time for computing S-unit groups which can then be used to compute class groups, unit groups, and class group discrete logarithms [BS16]. In the quantum world, $\mathsf{T}_{\mathsf{Su}}(K) = \tilde{O}(\ln|\Delta_K|)$ is polynomial, as shown in [BS16], building upon [EHKS14]. In the classical world, it remains subexponential in $\ln|\Delta_K|$, i.e. $\mathsf{T}_{\mathsf{Su}}(K) = \exp\tilde{O}(\ln^{\alpha}|\Delta_K|)$, where $\alpha = 1/2$ for prime power cyclotomic fields [BEF+17], and $\alpha = 2/3$ in the general case [BF14], being recently lowered to $3/5$ by Gélin [Gél17].

Forgetting about the preprocessing cost, the query phase beats the traditional Schnorr's hierarchy [Sch87] when $\log|\Delta_K| \leq \tilde{O}(n^{1+\varepsilon})$ with $\varepsilon = 1/3$ in the quantum case, and $\varepsilon = 1/11$ in the classical case [PHS19a, Fig. 5.3]. It should be noted however that these bounds on the discriminant are not uniform as the approximation factor varies, e.g. for an approximation factor set to $2^{\sqrt{n}}$, the time complexity of the PHS algorithm asymptotically beats Schnorr's hierarchy only in the quantum case and only for $\varepsilon \leq 1/6$.

Our Contribution. Our main contribution is to propose a new "twisted" version of the PHS [PHS19a] algorithm, that we call Twisted-PHS. As a minor contribution, we also propose several improvements of the PHS algorithm, in a optimized version described in Sect. 3.3. On the theoretical side, we prove that our Twisted-PHS algorithm performs at least as well as the original PHS algorithm, using the same CVP solver using a preprocessing hint by Laarhoven [Laa16].

On the practical side though, we provide a full implementation of our algorithm, which suggests that much better approximation factors are achieved and that the given lattice bases are much more orthogonal than the ones used in [PHS19a]. To our knowledge, this is the first time that this type of algorithm is completely implemented and tested for fields of degrees up to 60. As a point of comparison, experiments of [PHS19a] constructed the log-S-unit lattice for cyclotomic fields of degrees at most 24, all but the last two being principal [PHS19a, Fig. 4.1]. We shall also mention the extensive simulations performed by [DPW19] using the Stickelberger lattice in prime power cyclotomic fields. Adapting these results to our construction is not immediate, as we need *explicit* S-units to compute our lattice. This is left for future work.

We explain our experiments in Sect. 5, where we evaluate three algorithms: the original PHS algorithm, as implemented in [PHS19b]; our optimized version Opt-PHS (Sect. 3.3), and our new twisted variant Tw-PHS (Sect. 4). We target two families of number fields, namely non-principal cyclotomic fields $\mathbb{Q}(\zeta_m)$ of prime conductors $m \in [\![23, 71]\!]$, and NTRU Prime fields $\mathbb{Q}(z_q)$ where z_q is a root of $x^q - x - 1$, for $q \in [\![23, 47]\!]$ prime. These correspond to the range of what

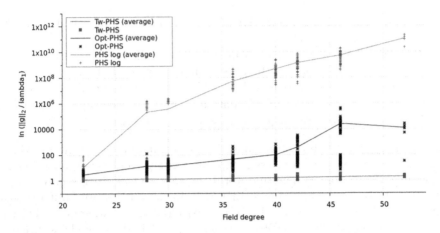

Fig. 1. Approximation factors reached by Tw-PHS, Opt-PHS and PHS for cyclotomic fields of conductors 23, 29, 31, 37, 41, 43, 47 and 53 (in log scale).

is feasible in a reasonable amount of time in a classical setting. For cyclotomic fields, we managed to compute S-units up to $\mathbb{Q}(\zeta_{71})$ for all factor bases in less than a day, and all log-S-unit lattice variants up to $\mathbb{Q}(\zeta_{61})$. For NTRU Prime fields, we managed all computations up to $\mathbb{Q}(z_{47})$.

Experiments. We chose to perform three experiments to test the performances of our Twisted-PHS algorithm, and to compare it with the two other algorithms:

- We first evaluate the *geometric characteristics* of the lattice output by the preprocessing phase: the root Hermite factor δ_0, the orthogonality defect δ, and the average vector basis angle θ_{avg}, as described in details in Sect. 2.5. The last one seems difficult to interpret as it gives similar results in all cases, but the two other seem to show that the lattice output by Twisted-PHS is of better quality than in the two other cases. It shows significantly better root Hermite factor and orthogonality defect than any other lattice.
- For our second experiment, we evaluate *the Gram-Schmidt log norms* of each produced lattice. We propose two comparisons, the first one is before and after BKZ reduction to see the evolution of the norms in each case: it shows that the two curves are almost identical for Twisted-PHS but not for the other PHS variants. The second one is between the lattices output by the different algorithms, after BKZ reduction. The experiments emphasises that the decrease of the log norms seems much smaller in the twisted case than in the two other. Those two observations seem to corroborate the fact that the Twisted-PHS lattice is already quite orthogonal.
- Finally, we implemented all three algorithms from end to end and used them on numerous challenges to estimate their practically achieved *approximation factors*. This is to our knowledge the first time that these types of algorithms are completely run on concrete examples. The results of the experiments, shown in Fig. 1, suggest that the approximation factor reached by our

algorithm increases very slowly with the dimension, in a way that could reveal subexponential or even better. We think that this last feature would be particularly interesting to prove.

Technical Overview. We first quickly recall the principle of the PHS algorithm described in [PHS19a], which is split in two phases. The first phase consists in building a lattice that depends only on the number field K and allowing to express any Approx-id-Svp instance in K as an Approx-Cvp instance in the lattice. This preprocessing chooses a factor base FB, and builds an associated lattice consisting in the diagonal concatenation of some log-unit related lattice and the lattice of relations in the class group Cl_K between ideals of FB, with explicit generators. It then computes a hint of constrained size for the lattice to facilitate forthcoming Approx-Cvp queries. Concretely, they suggest to use Laarhoven's algorithm [Laa16], which for any $\omega \in [0, 1/2]$ outputs a hint $\mathcal{V}$ of bit-size bounded by $2^{\tilde{O}(\log^{1-2\omega}|\Delta_K|)}$ that allows to deliver answers for approximation factors $\tilde{O}(\log|\Delta_K|^\omega)$ in time bounded by the bit-size of $\mathcal{V}$ [Laa16, Cor. 1–2]. The second phase reduces the resolution of Approx-id-Svp to a single call to an Approx-Cvp oracle in the lattice output by the preprocessing phase, for any challenge ideal $\mathfrak{b}$ in the maximal order of K. The main idea of this reduction is to multiply the principal ideal output by the ClDL of $\mathfrak{b}$ on FB by ideals in FB until a "better" principal ideal is reached, i.e. having a short generator.

Our first contribution is to propose three improvements of the PHS algorithm. The first one consists in expliciting a candidate for the isometry used in the first preprocessing phase to build the lattice, and to use its geometric properties to derive a smaller lattice dimension, while still guaranteeing the same proven approximation factor. The last two respectively modify the composition of the factor base and the definition of the target vector in a way that significantly improves the approximation factor experimentally achieved by the second phase of the algorithm. Although these improvements do not modify the core of PHS algorithm and have no impact on the asymptotics, they nevertheless are of importance in practice, as shown by our experiments in Sect. 5.

We now explain our main contribution, called Twisted-PHS, which is based on the PHS algorithm. As in PHS algorithm, our algorithm relies on the so-called *log-S-unit lattice* with respect to a collection FB of prime ideals, called the factor base. This lattice captures local informations on FB, not only on (infinite) embeddings, to reduce a close principal multiple of a target ideal $\mathfrak{b}$ to a principal ideal containing $\mathfrak{b}$ which is guaranteed to have a somehow short generator. The main feature of our algorithm is to use the *Product Formula* to describe this log-S-unit lattice. This induces two major changes in PHS algorithm:

1. The first one is twisting the $\mathfrak{p}$-adic valuations by $\ln \mathcal{N}(\mathfrak{p})$, giving weight to the fact that using a relation increasing the valuations at big norm ideals costs more than a relation involving smaller norm ideals.
2. The second one is projecting the target directly inside the log-S-unit lattice and not only into the unit log-lattice corresponding to fundamental units.

In fact, the way our twisted version uses S-units with respect to FB to reduce the solution of the ClDL problem can be viewed as a natural generalization of the way classical algorithms reduce principal ideal generators using regular units.

Adding weights $\ln\mathcal{N}(\mathfrak{p})$ to integer valuations at any prime ideal $\mathfrak{p}$ intuitively allows to make a more relevant combination of the S-units we use to reduce the output of the ClDL, quantifying the fact that increasing valuations at big norm prime ideals costs more than increasing valuations at small norm prime ideals. Besides, the product formula induces the possibility to project elements on the whole log-S-unit lattice instead of projecting only on the subspace corresponding to the log-unit lattice. As a consequence, it maintains inside the lattice the size and the algebraic norm logarithm of the S-units. At the end, the CVP solver in this alternative lattice combines more efficiently the goal of minimizing the algebraic norm for the CPMP while still guaranteeing a small size for the SGP solution in the obtained principal multiple.

In Sect. 4, we describe two versions of our Twisted-PHS algorithm. The first one, composed by $\mathcal{A}_{\text{tw-pcmp}}^{(\text{Laa})}$ and $\mathcal{A}_{\text{tw-query}}^{(\text{Laa})}$ is proven to perform at least as well as the original PHS algorithm with the same CVP solver using a preprocessing hint by Laarhoven. But in practice, we propose two alternative algorithms $\mathcal{A}_{\text{tw-pcmp}}^{(\text{bkz})}$ and $\mathcal{A}_{\text{tw-query}}^{(\text{np})}$ with the following differences. Algorithm $\mathcal{A}_{\text{tw-pcmp}}^{(\text{bkz})}$ performs a minimal reduction step of the lattice as sole lattice preprocessing to smooth the input basis. Algorithm $\mathcal{A}_{\text{tw-query}}^{(\text{np})}$ resorts to Babai's Nearest Plane algorithm for the CVP solver role. Experimental evidence in Sect. 5 suggest that these algorithms perform remarkably well, because the twisted description of the log-S-unit lattice seems much more orthogonal than expected. Proving this property would remove, in a quantum setting, the only part that is not polynomial in $\ln|\Delta_K|$.

2   Preliminaries

Notations. A vector is designated by a bold letter $\mathbf{v}$, its i-th coordinate by v_i and its ℓ_p-norm, $p \in \mathbb{N}^* \cup \{\infty\}$, by $\|\mathbf{v}\|_p$. As a special case, the n-dimensional vector whose coefficients are all 1's is written $\mathbf{1}_n$. All matrices will be given using *row* vectors, $\mathcal{D}_{\mathbf{v}}$ is the diagonal matrix with coefficients v_i on the diagonal, I_n is the identity and $\mathbf{1}_{n \times n}$ denotes the square matrix of dimension n filled with 1's.

2.1   Number Fields, Ideals and Class Groups

In this paper, K always denotes a number field of degree n over $\mathbb{Q}$ and $\mathcal{O}_K$ its maximal order. The algebraic trace and norm of $\alpha \in K$, resp. denoted by $\text{Tr}(\alpha)$ and $\mathcal{N}(\alpha)$, are defined as the trace and determinant of the endomorphism $x \mapsto \alpha x$ of K, viewed as a $\mathbb{Q}$-vector space. The discriminant of K is written Δ_K and can be defined, for any $\mathbb{Z}$-basis $\omega_1, \ldots, \omega_n$ of $\mathcal{O}_K$, as $\det\big(\text{Tr}(\omega_i\omega_j)\big)_{i,j}$. Most complexities of number theoretic algorithms depend on $\ln|\Delta_K|$.

The fractional ideals of K are designated by gothic letters, like $\mathfrak{b}$, and form a multiplicative group $\mathcal{I}_K$. The class group Cl_K of K is the quotient group of $\mathcal{I}_K$

with its subgroup of principal ideals $\mathcal{P}_K \stackrel{\text{def}}{:=} \{\langle\alpha\rangle,\ \text{for all } \alpha \in K\}$. The class group is a finite group, whose order h_K is called the class number of K. For any ideal $\mathfrak{b} \in \mathcal{I}_K$, the class of $\mathfrak{b}$ in Cl_K is denoted by $[\mathfrak{b}]$.

We will specifically target two families of number fields, widely used in cryptography [Pei16]: cyclotomic fields $\mathbb{Q}(\zeta_m)$, where ζ_m is a primitive m-th root of unity, and NTRU Prime [BCLV17] fields $\mathbb{Q}(z_q)$, where z_q is a root of $x^q - x - 1$ for q prime. Both families have discriminants of order n^n. More exactly, for cyclotomic fields $\mathcal{O}_{\mathbb{Q}(\zeta_m)} = \mathbb{Z}[\zeta_m]$, so we have [Was97, Pr. 2.7]:
$$\Delta_{\mathbb{Q}(\zeta_m)} = (-1)^{\varphi(m)/2} \frac{m^{\varphi(m)}}{\prod_{p \mid m} p^{\varphi(m)/(p-1)}}.$$

For NTRU Prime fields, the siuation is marginally more involved, as $\mathbb{Z}[z_q]$ is maximal if and only if its discriminant $D_0 = q^q - (q-1)^{q-1}$ [Swa62, Th. 2] is squarefree [Kom75, Th. 4]: $\Delta_{\mathbb{Q}(z_q)} = \prod_{p \mid D_0} p^{v_p(D_0) \bmod *2}$, where $p^{v_p(D_0)}$ divides exactly D_0. Note however that there is strong evidence that such D_0's are generically squarefree, say with probability roughly 0.99 [BMT15, Conj. 1.1]. Actually, we checked that the conductor of $\mathbb{Z}[z_q]$ is not divisible by any of the first 10^6 primes for all $q \leq 1000$ outside the set $\{257, 487\}$, for which $59^2 \mid D_0$.

2.2   The Product Formula

Let (r_1, r_2) be the signature of K with $n = r_1 + 2r_2$. The real embeddings of K are numbered from σ_1 to σ_{r_1}, whereas the complex embeddings come in pairs $(\sigma_j, \overline{\sigma}_j)$ for $j \in [\![r_1 + 1, r_2]\!]$.

Each embedding σ of K into $\mathbb{C}$ induces an archimedean absolute value $|\cdot|_\sigma$ on K, such that for $\alpha \in K$, $|\alpha|_\sigma = |\sigma(\alpha)|$; two complex conjugate embeddings yield the same absolute value. Thus, it is common to identify the set $\mathcal{S}_\infty$ of infinite places of K with the embeddings of K into $\mathbb{C}$ up to conjugation, so that $\mathcal{S}_\infty = \{\sigma_1, \dots, \sigma_{r_1}, \sigma_{r_1+1}, \dots, \sigma_{r_1+r_2}\}$. The completion of K with respect to the absolute value induced by an infinite place $\sigma \in \mathcal{S}_\infty$ is denoted by K_σ; it is $\mathbb{R}$ (resp. $\mathbb{C}$) for real places (resp. complex places).

Likewise, let $\mathfrak{p}$ be a prime ideal of $\mathcal{O}_K$ above $p \in \mathbb{Z}$ of residue degree f. For $\alpha \in K$, the largest power of $\mathfrak{p}$ that divides $\langle\alpha\rangle$ is called the valuation of α at $\mathfrak{p}$, and denoted by $v_\mathfrak{p}(\alpha)$; this defines a non-archimedean absolute value $|\cdot|_\mathfrak{p}$ on K such that $|\alpha|_\mathfrak{p} = p^{-v_\mathfrak{p}(\alpha)}$. This absolute value can also be viewed as induced by any of the f embeddings of K into its $\mathfrak{p}$-adic completion $K_\mathfrak{p} \subseteq \mathbb{C}_p$, which is an extension of $\mathbb{Q}_p$ of degree f. Hence, the set $\mathcal{S}_0$ of finite places of K is specified by the infinite set of prime ideals of $\mathcal{O}_K$, and Ostrowski's theorem for number fields ([Con, Th. 3], [Nar04, Th. 3.3]) states that all non archimedean absolute values on K are obtained in this way, up to equivalence.

Probably the most interesting thing is that these absolute values are tied together by the following product formula ([Con, Th. 4], [Nar04, Th. 3.5]):

$$\prod_{\sigma \in \mathcal{S}_\infty} |\alpha|_\sigma^{[K_\sigma : \mathbb{R}]} \cdot \prod_{\mathfrak{p} \in \mathcal{S}_0 \supset p\mathbb{Z}} |\alpha|_\mathfrak{p}^{[K_\mathfrak{p} : \mathbb{Q}_p]} \left(= \mathcal{N}(\alpha) \cdot \prod_{\mathfrak{p} \in \mathcal{S}_0} \mathcal{N}(\mathfrak{p})^{-v_\mathfrak{p}(\alpha)} \right) = 1. \quad (21)$$

As all but finitely many of the $|\alpha|_v$'s, for $v \in \mathcal{S}_\infty \cup \mathcal{S}_0$, are 1, their product is really a finite product. Note that the $\mathcal{S}_\infty$ part is $|\mathcal{N}(\alpha)|$, and each term of the $\mathcal{S}_0$ part can be written as $\mathcal{N}(\mathfrak{p})^{-v_{\mathfrak{p}}(\alpha)}$. This formula is actually a natural generalization to number fields of the innocuous looking product formula for $r \in \mathbb{Q}$, written as: $|r| \cdot \prod_{p \text{ prime}} p^{-v_p(r)} = 1$.

2.3 Unit Groups

A more thorough version of this section is given in the full version [BR20, § 2.3]. Let $\mathcal{O}_K^\times$ be the multiplicative group of units of $\mathcal{O}_K$, i.e. the group of all elements of K of algebraic norm ± 1, and let $\mu(\mathcal{O}_K^\times)$ be its torsion subgroup of roots of unity of K. Classically, the logarithmic embedding from K to $\mathbb{R}^{r_1+r_2}$ is defined as [Coh93, Def. 4.9.6]: $\mathrm{Log}_\infty \alpha = ([K_\sigma : \mathbb{R}] \cdot \ln|\sigma(\alpha)|)_{\sigma \in \mathcal{S}_\infty}$. Actually, it will be more convenient to use a *flat* logarithmic embedding from K to $\mathbb{R}^{r_1+2r_2}$, as in [PHS19a, BDPW20], and defined as follows:

$$\overline{\mathrm{Log}}_\infty\, \alpha = \Big(\{\ln|\sigma_i(\alpha)|\}_{i \in [\![1,r_1]\!]}, \{\ln|\sigma_{r_1+j}(\alpha)|, \ln|\overline{\sigma}_{r_1+j}(\alpha)|\}_{j \in [\![1,r_2]\!]} \Big). \quad (22)$$

Dirichlet's unit theorem [Nar04, Th. 3.13] states that $\mathcal{O}_K^\times$ is a finitely generated abelian group of rank $\nu = r_1 + r_2 - 1$. Further, its image $\overline{\mathrm{Log}}_\infty\, \mathcal{O}_K^\times$ under the flat logarithmic embedding is a lattice, called the *log-unit lattice*, which spans H_0, defined as $\mathcal{L}_0 \cap \mathbb{R}_0^n$, i.e. the intersection of the trace zero hyperplane of $\mathbb{R}^n$ and of $\mathcal{L}_0 = \{\mathbf{y} \in \mathbb{R}^n : y_{r_1+2j-1} = y_{r_1+2j}, j \in [\![1,r_2]\!]\}$: there exist fundamental torsion-free elements $\varepsilon_1, \ldots, \varepsilon_\nu \in \mathcal{O}_K^\times$ such that:

$$\mathcal{O}_K^\times \simeq \mu(\mathcal{O}_K^\times) \times \varepsilon_1^{\mathbb{Z}} \times \cdots \times \varepsilon_\nu^{\mathbb{Z}}. \quad (23)$$

Let $\Lambda_K = (\mathrm{Log}_\infty \varepsilon_i)_{1 \le i \le \nu}$ be any $\mathbb{Z}$-basis of $\mathrm{Log}_\infty \mathcal{O}_K^\times$. The regulator of K, written R_K, quantifies the density of the unit group in K. It is defined as the absolute value of the determinant of $\Lambda_K^{(j)}$, where $\Lambda_K^{(j)}$ is the submatrix of Λ_K without the j-th coordinate, for any $j \in [\![1, r_1 + r_2]\!]$.

On the S-unit Group. The S-unit group generalizes the unit group $\mathcal{O}_K^\times$ by allowing inverses of elements whose valuations are non zero exactly over a chosen finite set of primes of $\mathcal{S}_0$. Let FB $= \{\mathfrak{p}_1, \ldots, \mathfrak{p}_k\}$ be such a factor basis, and let $\mathcal{O}_{K,\mathrm{FB}}^\times$ denote the S-unit group of K with respect to FB. Formally, we have $\mathcal{O}_{K,\mathrm{FB}}^\times = \{\alpha \in K : \exists e_1, \ldots, e_k \in \mathbb{Z}, \langle \alpha \rangle = \prod \mathfrak{p}_j^{e_j}\}$. Similarly, we define a flat S-logarithmic embedding [Nar04, §3, p. 98] from K to $\mathcal{L} = \mathcal{L}_0 \times \mathbb{R}^k$ by:

$$\overline{\mathrm{Log}}_{\infty,\mathrm{FB}}\, \alpha = \Big(\overline{\mathrm{Log}}_\infty\, \alpha, \{-v_{\mathfrak{p}}(\alpha) \cdot \ln \mathcal{N}(\mathfrak{p})\}_{\mathfrak{p} \in \mathrm{FB}} \Big). \quad (24)$$

From the product formula (21), the image of $\mathcal{O}_{K,\mathrm{FB}}^\times$ lies in $H = \mathcal{L} \cap \mathbb{R}_0^{n+k}$, the trace zero hyperplane of $\mathcal{L}$. This fact is used to prove the following theorem:

Theorem 2.1 (Dirichlet-Chevalley-Hasse [Nar04, Th. III.3.12]). *The S-unit group is a finitely generated abelian group of rank* $\sharp\mathcal{S}_\infty + \sharp\mathrm{FB} - 1$. *Further, the* image $\overline{\mathrm{Log}}_{\infty,\mathrm{FB}}\left(\mathcal{O}_{K,\mathrm{FB}}^{\times}/\mu(\mathcal{O}_K^{\times})\right)$ is a lattice which spans the $(\nu+k)$-dimensional space H: there exist fundamental torsion-free S-units $\eta_1,\ldots,\eta_k \in \mathcal{O}_{K,\mathrm{FB}}^{\times}$ st.:

$$\mathcal{O}_{K,\mathrm{FB}}^{\times} \simeq \mu(\mathcal{O}_K^{\times}) \times \varepsilon_1^{\mathbb{Z}} \times \cdots \times \varepsilon_{\nu}^{\mathbb{Z}} \times \eta_1^{\mathbb{Z}} \times \cdots \times \eta_k^{\mathbb{Z}}.$$

Let $\widetilde{\Lambda}_{K,\mathrm{FB}} = \left(\{\overline{\mathrm{Log}}_{\infty,\mathrm{FB}}\,\varepsilon_i\}, \{\overline{\mathrm{Log}}_{\infty,\mathrm{FB}}\,\eta_j\}\right)$ be a row basis of $\overline{\mathrm{Log}}_{\infty,\mathrm{FB}}\,\mathcal{O}_{K,\mathrm{FB}}^{\times}$, which will be called the *log-S-unit lattice*. Using that $\overline{\mathrm{Log}}_{\infty,\mathrm{FB}}\,\varepsilon_i$ is uniformly zero on coordinates corresponding to finite places, the shape of $\widetilde{\Lambda}_{K,\mathrm{FB}}$ is:

$$\widetilde{\Lambda}_{K,\mathrm{FB}} \overset{\mathrm{def}}{:=} \left[\begin{array}{c|c} \widetilde{\Lambda}_K & 0 \\ \hline \begin{matrix} \mathrm{Log}_{\infty}\,\eta_1 \\ \vdots \\ \mathrm{Log}_{\infty}\,\eta_k \end{matrix} & \left(-v_{\mathfrak{p}_j}(\eta_i)\ln\mathcal{N}(\mathfrak{p}_j)\right)_{1\leq i,j\leq k} \end{array} \right]. \tag{25}$$

Similarly, Theorem 2.1 allows to define the S-regulator $R_{K,\mathrm{FB}}$ of K wrpt. FB as the absolute value of any of the (r_1+r_2+k) minors of any row basis $\Lambda_{K,\mathrm{FB}}$ of $\mathrm{Log}_{\infty,\mathrm{FB}}\mathcal{O}_{K,\mathrm{FB}}^{\times}$. The value of $R_{K,\mathrm{FB}}$ is given by the following proposition:

Proposition 2.2. *Let $h_K^{(\mathrm{FB})}$ the cardinal of the subgroup $\mathrm{Cl}_K^{(\mathrm{FB})}$ of Cl_K generated by classes of ideals in* FB. *Then, the S-regulator $R_{K,\mathrm{FB}}$ can be written as:* $R_{K,\mathrm{FB}} = h_K^{(\mathrm{FB})} R_K \prod_{\mathfrak{p}\in\mathrm{FB}} \ln\mathcal{N}(\mathfrak{p})$.

The proof is given in the full version. We stress that the S-regulator could not be consistently defined anymore if these twistings by the $\ln\mathcal{N}(\mathfrak{p})$'s were removed, as in this case, the property that all columns sum to 0 disappears. Finally, the volume of the log-S-unit lattice is tied to $R_{K,\mathrm{FB}}$ by the following proposition, which generalizes [BDPW20, Lem. A.1], and that we also prove in [BR20]:

Proposition 2.3. *Under the flat S-logarithmic embedding, the log-S-unit lattice has volume:* $\mathrm{Vol}\left(\overline{\mathrm{Log}}_{\infty,\mathrm{FB}}\,\mathcal{O}_{K,\mathrm{FB}}^{\times}\right) = \sqrt{n+k} \cdot 2^{-r_2/2} \cdot h_K^{(\mathrm{FB})} R_K \prod_{\mathfrak{p}\in\mathrm{FB}} \ln\mathcal{N}(\mathfrak{p})$. *Using an empty factor basis, it implies* $\mathrm{Vol}\left(\overline{\mathrm{Log}}_{\infty}\,\mathcal{O}_K^{\times}\right) = \sqrt{n} \cdot 2^{-r_2/2} \cdot R_K$.

2.4   Algorithmic Number Theory

This section is split into Sect. 2.4 and Sect. 2.5 in the full version [BR20]. The former recalls useful number theoretic bounds and relations, such as the *analytic class number formula*, allowing to bound $h_K R_K$, Bach's bound on the algebraic norm of class group generators , and the *Prime Ideal Theorem* on the density of prime ideals . All rely on the *Generalized Riemann Hypothesis* (GRH). We only recall problem definitions discussed in the latter, the most essential being the CIDL.

Problem 2.4 (Class Group Discrete Logarithm (ClDL) [BS16]**).** Given a set FB of prime ideals generating a subgroup $\text{Cl}_K^{(\text{FB})}$ of Cl_K, and a fractional ideal $\mathfrak{b}$ st. $[\mathfrak{b}] \in \text{Cl}_K^{(\text{FB})}$, output $\alpha \in K$ and $v_i \in \mathbb{Z}$ st. $\langle \alpha \rangle = \mathfrak{b} \cdot \prod_{\mathfrak{p}_i \in \text{FB}} \mathfrak{p}_i^{v_i}$.

Problem 2.5 (Close Principal Multiple Problem (CPMP) [CDW17, § 2.2]**).** Given a fractional ideal $\mathfrak{b}$, output a "reasonably small" integral ideal $\mathfrak{c}$ such that $[\mathfrak{c}] = [\mathfrak{b}]^{-1}$.

Problem 2.6 (Shortest Generator Problem (SGP)). Given $\mathfrak{a} = \langle \alpha \rangle$, principal ideal generated by some $\alpha \in K$, find the shortest $\alpha' \in \mathfrak{a}$ such that $\mathfrak{a} = \langle \alpha' \rangle$.

2.5 Lattices Geometry and Hard Problems

Let L be a lattice. For any $p \in \mathbb{N}^* \cup \{\infty\}$ and $1 \leq i \leq \dim L$, the i-th minimum $\lambda_i^{(p)}(L)$ of L for the ℓ_p-norm is the minimum radius $r > 0$ such that $\{\mathbf{v} \in L : \|\mathbf{v}\|_p \leq r\}$ has rank i [NV10, Def. 2.13]. For any $\mathbf{t}$ in the span of L, the distance between $\mathbf{t}$ and L is $\text{dist}_p(\mathbf{t}, L) = \inf_{\mathbf{v} \in L} \|\mathbf{t} - \mathbf{v}\|_p$, and the *covering radius* of L wrpt. ℓ_p-norm is $\mu_p(L) = \sup_{\mathbf{t} \in L \otimes \mathbb{R}} \text{dist}_p(\mathbf{t}, L)$. For the euclidean norm, we omit $p = 2$ most of the time.

A fractional ideal $\mathfrak{b}$ of K can be seen, under the canonical embedding, as a full rank lattice in $\mathbb{R}^n$, called an *ideal lattice*, of volume $\sqrt{|\Delta_K|} \cdot \mathcal{N}(\mathfrak{b})$. The arithmetic-geometric mean inequality, using that $|\mathcal{N}(\alpha)| \geq \mathcal{N}(\mathfrak{b})$ for all $\alpha \in \mathfrak{b}$, and the Minkowski's inequality [NV10, Th. 2.4] imply:

$$\mathcal{N}(\mathfrak{b})^{1/n} \leq \lambda_1^{(\infty)}(\mathfrak{b}) \leq \sqrt{|\Delta_K|}^{1/n} \mathcal{N}(\mathfrak{b})^{1/n} \tag{26}$$

$$\sqrt{n} \cdot \mathcal{N}(\mathfrak{b})^{1/n} \leq \lambda_1^{(2)}(\mathfrak{b}) \leq \sqrt{n} \cdot \sqrt{|\Delta_K|}^{1/n} \mathcal{N}(\mathfrak{b})^{1/n} \tag{27}$$

More precisely, $\lambda_1(\mathfrak{b}) \leq (1 + o(1)) \sqrt{2n/\pi e} \cdot \text{Vol}^{1/n}(\mathfrak{b})$, and the Gaussian Heuristic for full rank random lattices [NV10, Def. 2.8] predicts $\lambda_1(\mathfrak{b}) \approx \sqrt{n/2\pi e} \cdot \text{Vol}^{1/n}(\mathfrak{b})$ on average. In the case of ideal lattices, this yields a pretty good estimation of the shortness of vectors, even if $\lambda_1(\mathfrak{b})$ is not known precisely.

We will consider the following algorithmic lattice problems. Both problems can be readily restricted to ideal lattices under the labels Approx-id-SVP and Approx-id-CVP.

Problem 2.7 (Approximate Shortest Vector Problem (Approx-SVP) [NV10, Pb. 2.2]**).** Given a lattice L and an approximation factor $\gamma \geq 1$, find a vector $\mathbf{v} \in L$ such that $\|\mathbf{v}\| \leq \gamma \cdot \lambda_1(L)$.

Problem 2.8 (Approximate Closest Vector Problem (Approx-CVP) [NV10, Pb. 2.5]**).** Given a lattice L, a target $\mathbf{t} \in L \otimes \mathbb{R}$ and an approximation factor $\gamma \geq 1$, find a vector $\mathbf{v} \in L$ such that $\|\mathbf{t} - \mathbf{v}\| \leq \gamma \cdot \text{dist}(\mathbf{t}, L)$.

Actually, it will be more convenient to work with a slightly modified version of Approx-CVP, where the output is required to be at distance absolutely bounded by some B, independently of the target distance to the lattice. By abuse of terminology, we still call this variant Approx-CVP.

Evaluating the Quality of a Lattice Basis. Let $B = (\mathbf{b}_1, \ldots, \mathbf{b}_n)$ be a basis of a full rank n-dimensional lattice L, and let the Gram-Schmidt Orthogonalization of B be $\text{GSO}(B) = (\mathbf{b}_1^\star, \ldots, \mathbf{b}_n^\star)$. Approximation algorithms usually attempt to compute a *good* basis of the given lattice, i.e. whose vectors are as short and as orthogonal as possible. These lattice reduction algorithms, such as LLL [LLL82] or BKZ [CN11], try to limit the decrease of the Gram-Schmidt norms $\|\mathbf{b}_i^\star\|$: intuitively, a wide gap in this sequence reveals that $\mathbf{b}_i$ is far from orthogonal to $\langle \mathbf{b}_1, \ldots, \mathbf{b}_{i-1} \rangle$. Evaluating the quality of a lattice basis is actually a tricky task that depends partly on the targeted problem (see e.g. [Xu13]). We will use the following geometric metrics:

1. the root-Hermite factor δ_0 is widely used to measure the performance of lattice reduction algorithms [NS06, GN08, CN11], especially for solving SVP-like problems: $\delta_0^n(B) = \frac{\|\mathbf{b}_1\|}{\text{Vol}^{1/n} L}$. Experimental evidence suggest that on average, LLL achieves $\delta_0^{\text{LLL}} \approx 1.02$ [NS06, GN08] and BKZ with block size b achieves $\delta_0^{\text{BKZ}_b} \approx \left(\frac{b}{2\pi e} (\pi b)^{1/b} \right)^{1/(2b-2)}$ for $b \geq 50$ [Che13, CN11].
2. the normalized orthogonality defect δ [MG02, Def. 7.5] captures the global quality of the basis, not just of the first vector, and is especially useful for CVP-like problems e.g. if the lattice possesses abnormally short vectors: $\delta^n(B) = \frac{\prod_{i=1}^n \|\mathbf{b}_i\|}{\text{Vol} L}$. For purely orthogonal bases $\delta = 1$, and its smallest possible value is $\left(\prod_i \lambda_i(L)/\text{Vol} L \right)^{1/n} \leq \sqrt{1 + \frac{n}{4}}$ by Minkowski's second theorem [NV10, Th. 2.5].
3. the minimum vector basis angle, defined as [Xu13, Eq. (15)]: $\theta_{\min}(B) = \min_{1 \leq i < j \leq n} \min\{\theta_{ij}, \pi - \theta_{ij}\}$ for $\theta_{ij} = \frac{\arccos\langle \mathbf{b}_i, \mathbf{b}_j \rangle}{\|\mathbf{b}_i\| \|\mathbf{b}_j\|}$. We propose to consider the mean vector basis angle $\theta_{\text{avg}}(B)$, which averages over all $\min\{\theta_{ij}, \pi - \theta_{ij}\}$.

3 The PHS Algorithm

This section describes the PHS algorithm for solving Approx-id-SVP, as introduced by Pellet-Mary, Hanrot and Stehlé in [PHS19a], and discusses several improvements. The PHS algorithm extends the techniques from [CDPR16, CDW17] to any number field K and is split in two phases:

1. the preprocessing phase $\mathcal{A}_{\text{pre-proc}}$, described in Sect. 3.1, builds a specific lattice together with some hint allowing to efficiently solve Approx-CVP instances;
2. the query phase $\mathcal{A}_{\text{query}}$, detailed in Sect. 3.2, reduces each Approx-id-SVP challenge to an Approx-CVP instance in this fixed lattice.

More precisely, under the GRH and several heuristic assumptions detailed in [PHS19a, H. 1–6], they prove the following theorem:

Theorem 3.1 ([PHS19a, Th. 1.1]). *Let $\omega \in [0, 1/2]$ and K be a number field of degree n and discriminant Δ_K with a known basis of $\mathcal{O}_K$. Under some conjectures and heuristics, there exist two algorithms $\mathcal{A}_{\text{pre-proc}}$ and $\mathcal{A}_{\text{query}}$ such that:*

- *Algorithm $\mathcal{A}_{\text{pre-proc}}$ takes as input $\mathcal{O}_K$, runs in time $2^{\tilde{O}(\log|\Delta_K|)}$ and outputs a hint $\mathcal{V}$ of bit-size $2^{\tilde{O}(\log^{1-2\omega}|\Delta_K|)}$;*
- *Algorithm $\mathcal{A}_{\text{query}}$ takes as inputs any ideal $\mathfrak{b}$ of $\mathcal{O}_K$, whose algebraic norm has bit-size bounded by $2^{\text{poly}(\log|\Delta_K|)}$, and the hint $\mathcal{V}$ output by $\mathcal{A}_{\text{pre-proc}}$, runs in time $2^{\tilde{O}(\log^{1-2\omega}|\Delta_K|)} + T_{S_U}(K)$, and outputs a non-zero element $x \in \mathfrak{b}$ such that $\|x\|_2 \le 2^{\tilde{O}(\log^{\omega+1}|\Delta_K|/n)} \cdot \lambda_1(\mathfrak{b})$.*

We start by describing the preprocessing phase $\mathcal{A}_{\text{pre-proc}}$ in Sect. 3.1, then the query phase together in Sect. 3.2. We thereafter discuss several algorithmic and theoretic minor improvements in Sect. 3.3.

3.1 Preprocessing of the Number Field

From a number field K and a size parameter $\omega \in [0, 1/2]$, the preprocessing phase consists in building and preparing a lattice L_{phs} that depends only on the number field K and allows to express any Approx-id-SVP instance in K as an Approx-CVP instance in L_{phs}. The most significant part of this preprocessing is devoted to the computation of a hint of constrained size that can be used to facilitate those forthcoming Approx-CVP queries.

We first define the lattice which is used in [PHS19a], discuss how the authors derive its dimension from volume considerations, and then expose the full pre-processing algorithm.

Definition of the Lattice L_{phs}. Let $\text{FB} = \{\mathfrak{p}_1, \dots, \mathfrak{p}_k\}$ be a set of prime ideals generating the class group Cl_K. The lattice L_{phs} proposed in [PHS19a, § 3.1] consists in the diagonal concatenation of some log-unit related lattice and the lattice of relations in Cl_K between ideals of FB, with explicit generators. Formally, it is generated by the $(\nu + k)$ rows of the following square matrix:

$$B_{L_{\text{phs}}} \stackrel{\text{def}}{:=} \begin{bmatrix} c \cdot B_\Lambda & 0 \\ \hline c \cdot f_{H_0}(\mathbf{h}_{\eta_1}^{(0)}) & \\ \vdots & \ker f_{\text{FB}} = \left(-v_{\mathfrak{p}_j}(\eta_i)\right)_{1 \le i,j \le k} \\ c \cdot f_{H_0}(\mathbf{h}_{\eta_k}^{(0)}) & \end{bmatrix}, \tag{31}$$

- where f_{H_0} is an isometry from $H_0 \subset \mathbb{R}^n$ to $\mathbb{R}^\nu$, where H_0 is the intersection of the span $\mathcal{L}_0$ of $\overline{\text{Log}}_\infty \mathcal{O}_K$, i.e. $\mathcal{L}_0 = \{\mathbf{y} \in \mathbb{R}^n : y_{r_1+2i-1} = y_{r_1+2i}, i \in [\![1, r_2]\!]\}$, and of the trace zero hyperplane $\mathbb{R}_0^n = \mathbf{1}_n^\perp$;
- the matrix B_Λ is a row basis of $f_{H_0}(\overline{\text{Log}}_\infty \mathcal{O}_K^\times)$;
- the bottom right part of $B_{L_{\text{phs}}}$ generates the lattice of all relations in Cl_K between ideals of FB, i.e. is the kernel of $f_{\text{FB}} : (e_1, \dots, e_k) \in \mathbb{Z}^k \mapsto \prod_j [\mathfrak{p}_j]^{e_j}$;

- each row basis vector $\mathbf{v}_i = (v_{i1}, \ldots, v_{ik})$ of $\ker \mathfrak{f}_{FB}$ is associated to $\eta_i \in K$ such that $\langle \eta_i \rangle \cdot \prod_j \mathfrak{p}_j^{v_{ij}} = \mathcal{O}_K$, thus $v_{ij} = -v_{\mathfrak{p}_j}(\eta_i)$, and $\mathbf{h}_{\eta_i}^{(0)} = \pi_{H_0}(\overline{\mathrm{Log}}_\infty \eta_i)$, where π_{H_0} is the projection on H_0 in $\mathbb{R}^n$;
- c is a scaling parameter whose value depends on f_{H_0} (set later to $n^{3/2}/k$).

The condition that the factor base generates Cl_K guarantees that for any challenge ideal there exists a solution to the ClDL on FB. It can be relaxed to some extent to generate only a small index subgroup of Cl_K like in [CDW17]. As we discuss in more details in [BR20, § 3.1], the choice of the isometry f_{H_0} is actually not innocuous, and we exhibit in Sect. 3.3 a candidate with nice properties.

Finally, we detail in the full version a simpler formalism, viewing L_{phs} as generated by the images of the fundamental elements generating $\mathcal{O}_{K,FB}^\times$ under the following isomorphism between $\mathcal{O}_{K,FB}^\times / \mu(\mathcal{O}_K^\times)$ and $L_{phs} \subsetneq \mathbb{R}^\nu \times \mathbb{Z}^k$:

$$\varphi_{phs}(\alpha) = \left(c \cdot f_{H_0} \circ \pi_{H_0}(\overline{\mathrm{Log}}_\infty \alpha), \{-v_{\mathfrak{p}_i}(\alpha)\}_{1 \le i \le k} \right). \tag{32}$$

Volume of L_{phs} and Cardinality of FB. It remains to derive an explicit value for the cardinality k of the factor base FB. As detailed in the full version [BR20]:

$$\mathrm{Vol} L_{phs} = c^\nu \cdot \frac{\sqrt{n}}{2^{r_2/2}} \cdot h_K R_K. \tag{33}$$

The idea is then to choose k such that $\mathrm{Vol}^{1/(\nu+k)} = O(1)$, e.g. by taking $(\nu + k) = \ln \mathrm{Vol} L_{phs}$. Using the analytic class number formula as pointed in Sect. 2.4, and using the fact that c will be later set to $n^{3/2}/k$, $\mathrm{Vol} L_{phs}$ is asymptotically bounded by $\exp \tilde{O}(\ln|\Delta_K| + n \ln \ln|\Delta_K|)$; therefore, $(\nu + k)$ can be set to:

$$\nu + k = \max\{\nu + \log h_K, \ln|\Delta_K| + n \ln \ln|\Delta_K|\}. \tag{34}$$

The $\log h_K$ part is there as a sufficient but not necessary condition ensuring that Cl_K can be generated by $k \ge \log h_K$ ideals [PHS19a, Lem. 2.7]. As $h_K \le \tilde{O}(\sqrt{|\Delta_K|})$, we remark that the second term dominates, so the maximum in the above formula can be ignored; in the associated code [PHS19b], $(k + \nu)$ is explicitly set to $\lfloor \ln|\Delta_K| \rfloor$. We stress that in practice the dimension of L_{phs} is quite sensitive to small changes in the value of c or the targeted root volume. We refer to Sect. 3.3 for more details and examples.

Preprocessing Algorithm. Algorithm 3.1 details the complete preprocessing procedure that, from a number field and some precomputation size parameter, chooses a factor base FB, builds the associated matrix $B_{L_{phs}}$, and processes L_{phs} in order to facilitate Approx-CVP queries.

The dimension k of the factor base and the scaling factor c are set in step 1 as in the published code [PHS19b]. Steps 2 and 3 are a concise version of [PHS19a, Alg. 3.1, st. 1–5]; it basically enlarges a generating set of Cl_K of size $k' \le \log h_K$ by picking $(k - k')$ random prime ideals of bounded norms. The crucial point is to invoke the prime ideal theorem to show that taking a bound which is polynomial in k and $\log|\Delta_K|$ [PHS19a, Cor. 2.10] is actually sufficient.

Algorithm 3.1. PHS Preprocessing $\mathcal{A}_{\text{pre-proc}}$

Input: A number field K of degree n and a parameter $\omega \in [0, 1/2]$.
Output: The basis $B_{L_{\text{phs}}}$ with the preimages $\mathcal{O}_{K,\text{FB}}^{\times}$ of its rows, and Laarhoven's
              hint $\mathcal{V}(L_{\text{phs}})$.

1: Set $k = \left(\lfloor \ln|\Delta_K| \rfloor - \nu \right)$ and $c = \left(n^{3/2}/k\right)$.
2: Compute $\text{Cl}_K = \left\langle [\mathfrak{p}_1], \ldots, [\mathfrak{p}_{k'}] \right\rangle$, with $k' \leq \log h_K$.
3: Randomly extend $\{\mathfrak{p}_1, \ldots, \mathfrak{p}_{k'}\}$ by prime ideals of bounded norm to get FB = $\{\mathfrak{p}_1, \ldots, \mathfrak{p}_k\}$.
4: Compute fundamental elements $\varepsilon_1, \ldots, \varepsilon_\nu, \eta_1, \ldots, \eta_k$ of $\mathcal{O}_{K,\text{FB}}^{\times}$ as in Th. 2.1.
5: Create the matrix $B_{L_{\text{phs}}}$ whose rows are $\varphi_{\text{phs}}(\varepsilon_1), \ldots, \varphi_{\text{phs}}(\eta_k)$ as defined in Eq. (31).
6: Use Laarhoven's algorithm to compute a hint $\mathcal{V} = \mathcal{V}(L_{\text{phs}})$ of size $2^{\tilde{O}(\log^{1-2\omega}|\Delta_K|)}$.
7: **return** $\left(\mathcal{O}_{K,\text{FB}}^{\times}, B_{L_{\text{phs}}}, \mathcal{V}(L_{\text{phs}})\right)$.

The last step consists in preprocessing L_{phs} in order to solve Approx-CVP instances efficiently. As noted in [PHS19a, p. 6], the problem is easy without any constraint on the size of the output hint. To guarantee a hint size that is not exceeding the query phase time, they suggest to use Laarhoven's algorithm [Laa16], which outputs a hint $\mathcal{V}$ of bit-size bounded by $2^{\tilde{O}((\nu+k)^{1-2\omega})}$, i.e. $2^{\tilde{O}(\log^{1-2\omega}|\Delta_K|)}$ using $(\nu + k) = \tilde{O}(\log|\Delta_K|)$, allowing to deliver the answer for approximation factors $(\nu + k)^\omega$ in time bounded by the bit-size of $\mathcal{V}$ [Laa16, Cor. 1–2].

3.2   Query Phase: Solving id-Svp Using the Preprocessing

This section describes the query phase $\mathcal{A}_{\text{query}}$ of PHS algorithm; for any challenge ideal $\mathfrak{b} \subseteq K$ having a polynomial description in $\log|\Delta_K|$, it reduces the resolution of Approx-id-SVP in $\mathfrak{b}$ to a single call to an Approx-CVP oracle in L_{phs} as output by the preprocessing phase.

The main idea of this reduction is to multiply the principal ideal output by the ClDL of $\mathfrak{b}$ on FB by ideals in FB until a "better" principal ideal is reached, i.e. having a short generator. In L_{phs}, it translates into adding vectors of L_{phs} to some target vector derived from $\mathfrak{b}$ until the result is short, hence into solving a CVP instance. This is formalized in Algorithm 3.2, which rewrites [PHS19a, Alg. 3.2] to take into account our change of conventions in the definition of L_{phs} and the choice of Laarhoven's algorithm as the Approx-CVP oracle [Laa16, § 4.2].

Note that the output of the ClDL in step 1 is a S-unit if and only if $\mathfrak{b}$ is only divisible by prime ideals in the factor base. Each exponent v_i can be expressed as $v_i = v_{\mathfrak{p}_i}(\alpha) - v_{\mathfrak{p}_i}(\mathfrak{b})$. Then, the target defined in step 2 can be viewed as a drifted by β image of α in L_{phs}; using the formalism we introduced in Eq. (32), it writes simply as $\mathbf{t} = \varphi_{\text{phs}}(\alpha) + \mathbf{b}_{\text{phs}}$, where $\mathbf{b}_{\text{phs}} = (0, \ldots, 0, \beta, \ldots, \beta)$ is non zero only on the k last coordinates. We stress that the role of $\mathbf{b}_{\text{phs}}$ in the definition of the target serves a unique purpose: guarantee that $\alpha/s \in \mathfrak{b}$. In practice, this is not an anecdotic condition, and choosing carefully β has a significant impact on the length of the output, as we will see in Sect. 3.3. The rest of the proof of correctness, quality and running time of Algorithm 3.2 is recalled in the full version.

Algorithm 3.2. PHS Query $\mathcal{A}_{\mathsf{query}}$

Input: A challenge $\mathfrak{b}$, $\mathcal{A}_{\mathsf{pre\text{-}proc}}(K, \omega) = \left(\mathcal{O}_{K,\mathrm{FB}}^{\times}, B_{L\mathsf{phs}}, \mathcal{V}\right)$, and $\beta > 0$ st. for any $\mathbf{t}$, the
Approx-CVP oracle using $\mathcal{V}(L_{\mathsf{phs}})$ outputs $\mathbf{w} \in L_{\mathsf{phs}}$ with $\|\mathbf{t} - \mathbf{w}\|_{\infty} \leq \beta$.
Output: A short element $x \in \mathfrak{b} \setminus \{0\}$.
1: Solve the ClDL for $\mathfrak{b}$ on FB, i.e. find $\alpha \in K$ st. $\langle \alpha \rangle = \mathfrak{b} \cdot \prod_{\mathfrak{p}_i \in \mathrm{FB}} \mathfrak{p}_i^{v_i}$.
2: Define the target as $\mathbf{t} = \left(c \cdot f_{H_0} \circ \pi_{H_0}\left(\overline{\mathrm{Log}}_{\infty}\, \alpha\right), \{-v_i + \beta\}_{1 \leq i \leq k}\right)$.
3: Use the Approx-CVP solver with $\mathcal{V}(L_{\mathsf{phs}})$ to output $\mathbf{w} \in L_{\mathsf{phs}}$ st. $\|\mathbf{t} - \mathbf{w}\|_{\infty} \leq \beta$.
4: Compute $s = \varphi_{\mathsf{phs}}^{-1}(\mathbf{w}) \in \mathcal{O}_{K,\mathrm{FB}}^{\times}$, using the preimages of $B_{L\mathsf{phs}}$ rows.
5: **return** α/s.

3.3   Optimizing PHS Parameters

In this section, we propose three improvements of the PHS algorithm. The first one consists in expliciting a candidate for f_{H_0} and using its geometric properties to derive a smaller lattice dimension, while still guaranteeing the same proven approximation factor. The last two respectively modify the composition of the factor base and the definition of the target vector in a way that drastically improves the approximation factor experimentally achieved by $\mathcal{A}_{\mathsf{query}}$.

Although these improvements do not modify the core of PHS algorithm and have no impact on the asymptotics, they nevertheless are of importance in practice, as we will see in Sect. 5.

Expliciting the Isometry: Towards Smaller Factor Bases. We exhibit explicitly a candidate for the isometry f_{H_0} going from $H_0 = \mathbb{R}_0^n \cap \mathcal{L}_0 \subseteq \mathbb{R}^n$ to $\mathbb{R}^{\nu}$ and evaluate its effect on the infinity norm. It allows to lower the value of c in Algorithm 3.2 from $n\sqrt{n}/k$ to $n(1 + \ln n)/k$, inducing a smaller $\mathrm{Vol}L_{\mathsf{phs}}$, and in turn implies using a smaller factor base for the same proven approximation factor. We define the isometry f_{H_0} as the linear map represented by $\overline{\mathrm{GSO}}^{\mathrm{T}}(M_{H_0})$, with:

$$M_{H_0} \overset{\text{def}}{:=} \nu \begin{pmatrix} \overset{\nu+1}{\overbrace{\begin{matrix} -1 & 1 & & & \\ & -1 & 1 & & \\ & & \ddots & \ddots & \\ & & & -1 & 1 \end{matrix}}} \end{pmatrix} \cdot \begin{pmatrix} \overset{r_1}{\overbrace{\quad}} \overset{2r_2}{\overbrace{\qquad\qquad}} \\ r_1\left\{ \begin{matrix} I_{r_1} & & \\ \hline & \frac{1}{2} & \frac{1}{2} \\ r_2\left\{ \begin{matrix} & \frac{1}{2} & \frac{1}{2} \\ & & \ddots \\ & & & \frac{1}{2} & \frac{1}{2} \end{matrix}\right. \end{matrix}\right. \end{pmatrix}. \quad (35)$$

Actually, M_{H_0} is simply a basis of $\mathbb{R}_0^n \cap \mathcal{L}_0$ in $\mathbb{R}^n$, constituted of vectors that are orthogonal to $\mathbf{1}_n$ and to each of the r_2 independent vectors $\mathbf{v}_j$, $j \in [\![1, r_2]\!]$, that sends any $\mathbf{y} \in \mathcal{L}_0$ to $\mathbf{0}$ by substracting y_{r_1+2j} from its copy y_{r_1+2j-1} and forgetting every other coordinate.

We prove that this isometry verifies $\forall \mathbf{h} \in H_0, \|\mathbf{h}\|_\infty \leq (1 + \ln n) \cdot \|f_{H_0}(\mathbf{h})\|_\infty$ [BR20, Pr. 3.2]. Hence, as fully explained in [BR20, § 3.3], we can choose:

$$c = \max\left(1, \frac{(1 + \ln n)n}{\sum_{\mathfrak{p} \in \mathrm{FB}} \ln \mathcal{N}(\mathfrak{p})}\right). \tag{36}$$

We quantify the gain obtained by this new value of c using several experiments, all described and discussed in the full version of this paper [BR20, Tab. 3.1–2].

Lowering the Factor Base Weight. Second, we suggest choosing the k elements of the factor base as the k prime ideals of least possible norm, instead of randomly picking them up to some polynomial bound. As discussed in the full version, this incidentally lowers the approximation factor, which depends on $\prod_{\mathfrak{p} \in \mathrm{FB}} \mathcal{N}(\mathfrak{p})$.

Formally, this only modifies step 3 of Algorithm 3.1 as follows. Let $\{\mathfrak{p}_1, \ldots, \mathfrak{p}_{k'}\}$ be a generating set of Cl_K, with $k' \leq \log h_K$, as obtained by the previous step 2. As in Algorithm 3.1, using the prime ideal theorem yields that we can choose some bound B polynomial in k and $\log|\Delta_K|$ such that the set of prime ideals of norm bounded by B contains at least k elements. Then, we order this set by increasing norms, choosing an arbitrary permutation for isonorm ideals, and remove ideals that were already present in $\{\mathfrak{p}_1, \ldots, \mathfrak{p}_{k'}\}$. It remains to extract the first $(k - k')$ elements to obtain our factor base.

There is one issue to consider, namely adapting the justification of [PHS19a, H. 4], relying on L_{phs} being a "somehow random" lattice to derive that $\mu_\infty(L_{\mathrm{phs}})$ is close to $\lambda_1^{(\infty)}(L_{\mathrm{phs}})$. We discuss this in more details for Heuristic 4.8 in Sect. 4.2. Moreover, in practice, it is always possible to empirically upper bound the infinity covering radius of L_{phs} to verify that this heuristic holds. For example, as described in [PHS19a, § 4.1]: take sufficiently many random samples $\mathbf{t}_i$ in the span of L_{phs} from a continuous Gaussian distribution of sufficiently large deviation; solve Approx-CVP for the ℓ_2-norm for each of them to obtain vectors $\mathbf{w}_i \in L_{\mathrm{phs}}$ close to $\mathbf{t}_i$; finally, majorate $\mu_\infty(L_{\mathrm{phs}})$ by $\max_i \|\mathbf{t}_i - \mathbf{w}_i\|_\infty$. Then, if the expected heuristic behaviour is too far from this estimate, we could still replace one ideal of FB by an ideal of bigger norm and iterate the process.

Minimizing the Target Drift. Our last suggested improvement modifies the definition of the target vector to take into account the fact that valuations at prime ideals are integers. Hence, the condition enforcing $\alpha/s \in \mathfrak{b}$, which was written as $\forall \mathfrak{p} \in \mathrm{FB}, v_\mathfrak{p}(\alpha) - v_\mathfrak{p}(s) \geq 0$, can be replaced by the equivalent requirement that $\forall \mathfrak{p} \in \mathrm{FB}, v_\mathfrak{p}(\alpha) - v_\mathfrak{p}(s) > -1$. Intuitively, this reduces the valuations at prime ideals of the output element by one on average, hence lowering the approximation factor bound. Formally, using the notations of Algorithm 3.2, we only modify the definition of the target $\mathbf{t}$ in step 2 of Algorithm 3.2. For any $0 < \varepsilon < 1$, let $\widetilde{\beta} = (\beta - 1 + \varepsilon)$ and let $\widetilde{\mathbf{b}}_{\mathrm{phs}} = (0, \ldots, 0, \widetilde{\beta}, \ldots, \widetilde{\beta})$ with non zero values only on the k last coordinates. The modified target is defined as:

$$\widetilde{\mathbf{t}} = \varphi_{\mathrm{phs}}(\alpha) + \widetilde{\mathbf{b}}_{\mathrm{phs}} = \left(c \cdot f_{H_0} \circ \pi_{H_0}(\overline{\mathrm{Log}}_\infty \alpha), \{-v_i + \widetilde{\beta}\}_{1 \leq i \leq k}\right). \tag{37}$$

The remaining steps of Algorithm 3.2 stay unchanged. We have to prove that the output is still correct, i.e. that $\alpha/s \in \mathfrak{b}$, where $\mathbf{w} = \varphi_{\mathsf{phs}}(s) \in L_{\mathsf{phs}}$ verifies $\|\tilde{\mathbf{t}} - \mathbf{w}\|_\infty \leq \beta$. This is done in the following Proposition 3.2, which adapts [PHS19a, Th. 3.3] to benefit from all the improvements of this section. Its proof is moved to [BR20, Pr. 3.5].

Though this adjustment might seem insignificant at first sight, we stress that the induced gain is of order $\prod_{\mathfrak{p} \in \mathrm{FB}} \mathcal{N}(\mathfrak{p})^{1/n}$, which is roughly subexponential in n, and that its impact is very noticeable experimentally. In fact, the quality of the output is so sensitive to this $\tilde{\beta}$ that we implemented a dichotomic strategy to find, for each challenge $\mathfrak{b}$, the smallest possible translation $\tilde{\beta}$ that must be applied to $\varphi_{\mathsf{phs}}(\alpha)$ to ensure $(\alpha/s) \in \mathfrak{b}$.

Proposition 3.2. *Given access to an Approx-*CVP *oracle that, on any input, output* $\mathbf{w} \in L_{phs}$ *at infinity distance at most* β*, the modified algorithm* $\mathcal{A}_{query}$ *using the isometry* f_{H_0} *defined in Eq. (35), the value c defined in Eq. (36), and for any* $0 < \varepsilon < 1$*, the modified target* $\tilde{\mathbf{t}}$ *defined in Eq. (37), computes* $x \in \mathfrak{b} \setminus \{0\}$ *such that:* $\|x\|_2 \leq \sqrt{n} \cdot \mathcal{N}(\mathfrak{b})^{1/n} \cdot \exp\left[\frac{(\beta + \lfloor 2\beta - 1 \rfloor) \cdot \sum_{\mathfrak{p} \in \mathrm{FB}} \ln \mathcal{N}(\mathfrak{p})}{n}\right].$

4   Twisted-PHS Algorithm

Our main contribution is to propose a twisted version of the PHS algorithm. The main modification is to use the natural description of the log-S-unit lattice given in Eq. (25) that is deduced from the product formula of Eq. (21).

On the theoretical side, we prove that our twisted-PHS algorithm performs at least as well as the original PHS algorithm with the same CVP solver using a preprocessing hint by Laarhoven. More precisely:

Theorem 4.1. *Let* $\omega \in [0, 1/2]$ *and* K *be a number field of degree* n *and discriminant* Δ_K*. Assume that a basis of* $\mathcal{O}_K$ *is known. Under GRH and heuristics Heuristic 4.8 and 4.9, there exist two algorithms* $\mathcal{A}_{tw\text{-}pcmp}^{(Laa)}$ *and* $\mathcal{A}_{tw\text{-}query}^{(Laa)}$ *such that:*

- *Algorithm* $\mathcal{A}_{tw\text{-}pcmp}^{(Laa)}$ *takes as input* $\mathcal{O}_K$*, runs in time* $2^{\tilde{O}(\log|\Delta_K|)}$ *and outputs a hint* $\mathcal{V}$ *of bit-size* $2^{\tilde{O}(\log^{1-2\omega}|\Delta_K|)}$*;*
- *Algorithm* $\mathcal{A}_{tw\text{-}query}^{(Laa)}$ *takes as inputs any ideal* $\mathfrak{b}$ *of* $\mathcal{O}_K$*, whose algebraic norm has bit-size bounded by* $2^{\mathrm{poly}(\log|\Delta_K|)}$*, and the hint* $\mathcal{V}$ *output by* $\mathcal{A}_{tw\text{-}pcmp}^{(Laa)}$*, runs in time* $2^{\tilde{O}(\log^{1-2\omega}|\Delta_K|)} + T_{Su}(K)$*, and outputs a non-zero element* $x \in \mathfrak{b}$ *such that* $\|x\|_2 \leq 2^{\tilde{O}(\log^{\omega+1}|\Delta_K|/n)} \cdot \lambda_1(\mathfrak{b})$*.*

All the results of this section are fully proven in the full version [BR20, §4].

On the practical side though, experimental evidence given in Sect. 5 suggest that we achieve much better approximation factors than expected, and that the given lattice bases are a lot more orthogonal than the ones used in [PHS19a]. Thus, in practice, we propose two alternative algorithms $\mathcal{A}_{tw\text{-}pcmp}^{(bkz)}$ and $\mathcal{A}_{tw\text{-}query}^{(np)}$:

the former applies a minimal reduction strategy as sole lattice preprocessing, and the latter resorts to Babai's Nearest Plane algorithm for the CVP solver role.

4.1   Preprocessing of the Number Field

As for the PHS algorithm, the preprocessing phase consists, from a number field K and a size parameter $\omega \in [0, 1/2]$, in building and preparing a lattice L_{tw} that depends only on the number field and allows to express any Approx-id-SVP instance in K as an Approx-CVP instance in L_{tw}.

Theoretically, the only difference between the original PHS preprocessing and ours resides in the lattice definition and in the factor base elaboration. Its most significant part still consists in computing a hint of constrained size to facilitate forthcoming Approx-CVP queries. In practice though, we replace this hint computation by merely a few rounds of BKZ with small block size (see Sect. 5). In a quantum setting this removes the only part that is not polynomial in $\ln|\Delta_K|$, and in a classical setting avoids the dominating exponential part.

Defining the Lattice L_{tw}: A Full-Rank Version of the log-S-unit Lattice. Let FB $= \{\mathfrak{p}_1, \ldots, \mathfrak{p}_k\}$ be a set of prime ideals generating the class group Cl_K. The lattice L_{tw} used by our twisted-PHS algorithm is basically the log-S-unit lattice $\overline{Log}_{\infty, FB} \mathcal{O}_{K,FB}^{\times}$ wrpt. FB under the flat logarithmic embedding, to which we apply an isometric transformation to obtain a full-rank lattice in $\mathbb{R}^{\nu+k}$.

Formally, L_{tw} is defined as the lattice generated by the images of the fundamental elements generating the S-unit group $\mathcal{O}_{K,FB}^{\times}$, as given by Theorem 2.1, under the following map φ_{tw} from K to $\mathbb{R}^{\nu+k}$:

$$\varphi_{tw}(\alpha) = f_H \circ \pi_H\left(\overline{Log}_{\infty, FB}\, \alpha\right), \tag{41}$$

- where f_H is an isometry from $H \subset \mathbb{R}^{n+k}$ to $\mathbb{R}^{\nu+k}$, with H the intersection of the trace zero hyperplane $\mathbb{R}_0^{n+k} = \mathbf{1}_{n+k}^{\perp}$, and of the span of $\overline{Log}_{\infty, FB}\, \mathcal{O}_{K,FB}^{\times}$, i.e. $\mathcal{L} = \{\mathbf{y} \in \mathbb{R}^{n+k} : y_{r_1+2i-1} = y_{r_1+2i}, i \in [\![1, r_2]\!]\}$;
- π_H is the projection on H, in particular it is the identity on the S-unit group.

This map naturally inherits from the homomorphism properties of $\overline{Log}_{\infty, FB}$, i.e. $\varphi_{tw}(\alpha\alpha') = \varphi_{tw}(\alpha) + \varphi_{tw}(\alpha')$ and $\forall \lambda \in \mathbb{Z}$, $\varphi_{tw}(\alpha^{\lambda}) = \lambda \cdot \varphi_{tw}(\alpha)$, and also defines an isomorphism between $\mathcal{O}_{K,FB}^{\times}/\mu(\mathcal{O}_K^{\times})$ and L_{tw}.

The isometry f_H must be carefully chosen in order to control its effect on the ℓ_∞-norm. Nevertheless, it should be seen as a technicality allowing to work with tools designed for full-rank lattices. Formally, let f_H be the linear map represented by $\overline{GSO}^T(M_H)$, which denotes the transpose of the Gram-Schmidt orthonormalization of the following matrix:

$$M_H \overset{\text{def}}{:=} \begin{pmatrix} \begin{bmatrix} -1 & 1 & & \\ & -1 & 1 & \\ & & \ddots & \ddots \\ & & & -1 & 1 \end{bmatrix} \end{pmatrix} \cdot \begin{pmatrix} \begin{matrix} I_{r_1} & & & & \\ & \frac{1}{2} & \frac{1}{2} & & \\ & \frac{1}{2} & \frac{1}{2} & & \\ & & & \ddots & \\ & & & \frac{1}{2} & \frac{1}{2} \\ & & & & I_k \end{matrix} \end{pmatrix}. \tag{42}$$

Actually, M_H is simply a basis of $\mathbb{R}_0^{n+k} \cap \mathcal{L}$ in $\mathbb{R}^{n+k}$, constituted of vectors that are orthogonal to $\mathbf{1}_{n+k}$ and to each of the r_2 independent vectors $\mathbf{v}_j, j \in [\![1, r_2]\!]$ that sends any $\mathbf{y} \in \mathcal{L}$ to $\mathbf{0}$ by substracting y_{r_1+2j} from its copy y_{r_1+2j-1} and forgetting every other coordinate. Hence, graphically, a row basis of L_{tw} is:

$$B_{L\text{tw}} \overset{\text{def}}{:=} \begin{bmatrix} \widetilde{\Lambda}_K & 0 \\ \hline \overline{\text{Log}}_\infty \eta_1 & \\ \vdots & \left(-v_{\mathfrak{p}_j}(\eta_i) \ln \mathcal{N}(\mathfrak{p}_j) \right)_{1 \le i,j \le k} \\ \overline{\text{Log}}_\infty \eta_k & \end{bmatrix} \cdot \overline{\text{GSO}}^{\mathsf{T}}(M_H), \tag{43}$$

where the first part is the basis $\widetilde{\Lambda}_{K,\text{FB}}$ of $\overline{\text{Log}}_{\infty,\text{FB}}\, \mathcal{O}_{K,\text{FB}}^\times$ defined in Sect. 2.3.

Volume of L_{tw} and Optimal Factor Base Choice. First, we evaluate the volume of $L_{\text{tw}} = f_H\left(\overline{\text{Log}}_{\infty,\text{FB}}\, \mathcal{O}_{K,\text{FB}}^\times\right)$. As the isometry f_H stabilizes the span of the log-S-unit lattice, it preserves its volume, which is given by Proposition 2.3. Using that ideal classes of FB generate the class group, hence $h_K^{(\text{FB})} = h_K$, yields:

$$\text{Vol} L_{\text{tw}} = \sqrt{n+k} \cdot 2^{-r_2/2} \cdot h_K R_K \prod_{1 \le i \le k} \ln \mathcal{N}(\mathfrak{p}_i). \tag{44}$$

Certainly, the volume of L_{tw} is growing with the log norms of the factor base prime ideals, but a remarkable property is that this growth is at first slower than the lattice density increase induced by the bigger dimension. The meaning of this is that we can enlarge the factor base to densify our lattice up to an optimal point, after which including new ideals become counter-productive.

Formally, let $V_{k'}$ denote the *reduced* volume $\text{Vol}^{1/(\nu+k')} L_{\text{tw}}$ for a factor base of size $k' \ge k_0$, where k_0 is the number of generators of Cl_K. We have:

$$V_{k'+1} = V_{k'} \cdot \left(\sqrt{1 + \frac{1}{n+k'}} \cdot \frac{\ln \mathcal{N}(\mathfrak{p}_{k'+1})}{V_{k'}} \right)^{1/(\nu+k'+1)}. \tag{45}$$

This shows that $V_{k'+1} < V_{k'}$ is equivalent to $\ln \mathcal{N}(\mathfrak{p}_{k'+1}) < V_{k'} \big/ \sqrt{1 + \frac{1}{n+k'}}$. Using this property, Algorithm 4.1 outputs a factor base maximizing the density of L_{tw}.

First, for a fixed factor base of size k, we compare the reduced volume V_k of L_{tw} with the reduced volume of L_{phs}, denoted $V_{\mathrm{phs}} \overset{\mathrm{not}}{:=} \left(\sqrt{\frac{n}{2r_2}} \cdot h_K R_K \right)^{1/(\nu+k)}$.

Lemma 4.2. *We have:* $\dfrac{V_k}{V_{\mathrm{phs}}} \leq \dfrac{e^{1/ne}}{k} \cdot \sum_{\mathfrak{p} \in \mathrm{FB}} \ln \mathcal{N}(\mathfrak{p})$.

This means that the gap between the reduced volume of the twisted lattice and the reduced volume of the untwisted lattice evolves roughly as the arithmetic mean of the $\ln \mathcal{N}(\mathfrak{p})$. We stress that this bound is valid for *any* k.

Although the reduced volume significantly decreases in the first loop iterations, reaching precisely the minimum value can be very gradual, so that it might be clever to early abort the loop in Algorithm 4.1 when the gradient is too low, or truncate the output to at most $k' = \tilde{O}(\ln|\Delta_K|)$. We quantify the fact that the density loss is at most constant in the worst case in the following result.

Lemma 4.3. *Let* $k' = C(\ln|\Delta_K| + n \ln \ln|\Delta_K|)$. *Let* V_{min} *be the minimum reduced volume output by* $\mathcal{A}_{\mathrm{tw\text{-}FB}}$, *and suppose* V_{min} *is reached for some* $k > k'$, *then* $V_{k'} \leq e^{1/C + 1/ne} \cdot V_{min}$.

Proposition 4.4. *Algorithm* $\mathcal{A}_{\mathrm{tw\text{-}FB}}$ *terminates in time* $\mathrm{T}_{Su}(K) + \mathrm{poly}(\ln|\Delta_K|)$ *and outputs a factor base of size* $k = \mathrm{poly}(\ln|\Delta_K|)$ *using* $B = \mathrm{poly}(\ln|\Delta_K|)$.

In practice, experiments of Sect. 5 report that the dimensions of the factor bases output by $\mathcal{A}_{\mathrm{tw\text{-}FB}}$ are significantly smaller than those showed in [BR20, Tab. 3.1–2] for the (optimized) PHS algorithm, so that Lemma 4.3 is never triggered.

Algorithm 4.1. Tw-PHS Factor Base Choice $\mathcal{A}_{\mathrm{tw\text{-}FB}}$

Input: A number field K of degree n.
Output: An optimal factor base FB generating Cl_K that minimizes $\mathrm{Vol}^{1/(\nu+k)} L_{\mathrm{tw}}$.
1: Compute $\mathrm{Cl}_K = \langle [\mathfrak{q}_1], \dots, [\mathfrak{q}_{k_0}] \rangle$, with $k_0 \leq \log h_K$.
2: Compute $\mathcal{P}(B) = \{\mathfrak{p}_i : \mathcal{N}(\mathfrak{p}_i) \leq B\} \setminus \{\mathfrak{q}_1, \dots, \mathfrak{q}_{k_0}\}$ ordered by increasing norms, where B is chosen st. $\pi_K(B) = \mathrm{poly}(\ln|\Delta_K|) \geq k_0$.
3: FB $\leftarrow \{\mathfrak{q}_1, \dots, \mathfrak{q}_{k_0}\}$.
4: $i \leftarrow 0$.
5: **while** $\ln \mathcal{N}(\mathfrak{p}_{i+1}) < V_{k_0+i} \big/ \sqrt{1 + \frac{1}{n+k_0+i}}$ **do**
6:       Add $\mathfrak{p}_{i+1}$ to FB.
7:       $i \leftarrow i + 1$.
8: **end while**
9: **return** FB.

Preprocessing Algorithm. Algorithm 4.2 details the complete preprocessing procedure that, from a number field and some precomputation size parameter, chooses a factor base FB, builds the associated matrix $B_{L\mathsf{tw}}$, and processes L_{tw} in order to facilitate Approx-CVP queries.

Algorithm 4.2. Tw-PHS Preprocessing $\mathcal{A}_{\mathsf{tw-pcmp}}$

Input: A number field K of degree n and a parameter $\omega \in [0, 1/2]$ or $\mathfrak{b}$.
Output: The basis $B_{L\mathsf{tw}}$ with the preimages $\mathcal{O}^{\times}_{K,\mathrm{FB}}$ of its rows, and Laarhoven's
          hint $\mathcal{V}(L_{\mathsf{tw}})$.
1: Get an optimal factor base FB $= \mathcal{A}_{\mathsf{tw-FB}}(K)$ of size $k = \sharp\mathrm{FB}$. If needed, truncate
    the output to $k = \tilde{O}(\ln|\Delta_K|)$ as in Lem. 4.3.
2: Compute fundamental elements $\varepsilon_1, \ldots, \varepsilon_\nu, \eta_1, \ldots, \eta_k$ of $\mathcal{O}^{\times}_{K,\mathrm{FB}}$ as in Th. 2.1.
3: Create $B_{L\mathsf{tw}}$, whose rows are $\varphi_{\mathsf{tw}}(\varepsilon_1), \ldots, \varphi_{\mathsf{tw}}(\eta_k)$ as defined in Eq. (43).
4: Use Laarhoven's algorithm to compute a hint $\mathcal{V} = \mathcal{V}(L_{\mathsf{tw}})$ of size $2^{\tilde{O}(\log^{1-2\omega}|\Delta_K|)}$.
5: (or) Use a BKZ of small block size to reduce the basis of L_{tw}.
6: **return** $\left(\mathcal{O}^{\times}_{K,\mathrm{FB}}, B_{L\mathsf{tw}}, \mathcal{V}(L_{\mathsf{tw}})\right)$.

This Tw-PHS preprocessing differs from the original PHS preprocessing given in Algorithm 3.1 on two aspects: the factor base, output by $\mathcal{A}_{\mathsf{tw-FB}}$ in step 1 and which is essentially much smaller in practice, and the new twisted lattice in step 3.

The last two alternative steps consists in preprocessing L_{tw} in order to solve Approx-CVP instances efficiently. Theoretically, we retain in step 4 the same approach as in step 6 of the original PHS preprocessing Algorithm 3.1, that guarantees a hint size not exceeding the query phase time using Laarhoven's algorithm [Laa16]. This outputs a hint $\mathcal{V}$ of bit size bounded by $2^{\tilde{O}(\nu+k)^{1-2\omega}}$, i.e. $2^{\tilde{O}(\log^{1-2\omega}|\Delta_K|)}$ using $(\nu + k) = \tilde{O}(\log|\Delta_K|)$, allowing to deliver the answer for approximation factors $(\nu + k)^\omega$ in time bounded by the bit size of $\mathcal{V}$ [Laa16, Cor. 1–2]. This theoretic version will be denoted by $\mathcal{A}^{(\mathrm{Laa})}_{\mathsf{tw-pcmp}}$.

Nevertheless, in practice the twisted lattice output by Algorithm 4.2 incidentally appears to be a lot more orthogonal than expected. That's the reason why we suggest to replace the exponential step 4 of Algorithm 4.2 by step 5, which performs some polynomial lattice reduction using a small block size BKZ. In a quantum setting this removes the only part that is not polynomial in $\ln|\Delta_K|$, and in a classical setting avoids the dominating exponential part. This practical version will be denoted by $\mathcal{A}^{(\mathrm{bkz})}_{\mathsf{tw-pcmp}}$.

4.2   Query Phase

This section describes the query phase $\mathcal{A}_{\mathsf{tw-query}}$ of the Tw-PHS algorithm. As for the query phase of the original PHS algorithm, it reduces the resolution of Approx-id-SVP in $\mathfrak{b}$, for any challenge ideal $\mathfrak{b} \subseteq K$ having a polynomial description in $\log|\Delta_K|$, to a single call to an Approx-CVP oracle in L_{tw} as output by the preprocessing phase. The main idea of this reduction remains to multiply the principal ideal generator output by the ClDL of $\mathfrak{b}$ on FB by elements of $\mathcal{O}^{\times}_{K,\mathrm{FB}}$ until we reach a principal ideal having a short generator. This translates into adding vectors of L_{tw} to some target vector derived from $\mathfrak{b}$ until the result is short, hence into solving a CVP instance in the log-S-unit lattice L_{tw}.

The essential difference of the Tw-PHS version lies in the definition of this target, which is adapted in order to benefit from the twisted description of the log-S-unit lattice. This is formalized in Algorithm 4.3.

Note that the output of the ClDL in step 1 is not a S-unit unless $\mathfrak{b}$ is divisible only by prime ideals of FB. For each i, $v_i = v_{\mathfrak{p}_i}(\alpha) - v_{\mathfrak{p}_i}(\mathfrak{b})$. For convenience and without any loss of generality we shall assume that $\mathfrak{b}$ is coprime with all elements of the factor base, i.e. $\forall \mathfrak{p} \in \mathrm{FB}$, $v_{\mathfrak{p}}(\mathfrak{b}) = 0$. In that case, the target in step 2 writes naturally as $\mathbf{t} = \varphi_{\mathrm{tw}}(\alpha) + f_H(\mathbf{b}_{\mathrm{tw}})$. This target definition calls a few comments. First, the output of the ClDL is projected on the whole log-S-unit lattice instead of only on the log-unit sublattice, hence maintaining its length and algebraic norm logarithms in the instance scope. Thus, the way our algorithm uses S-units to reduce the solution of the ClDL problem can be seen as a smooth generalization of the way traditional SGP solvers use regular units to reduce the solution of the PIP as in [CDPR16]. Second, the sole purpose of the drift by $\mathbf{b}_{\mathrm{tw}}$ is to ensure that $\alpha/s \in \mathfrak{b}$. Adapting its definition to the twisted setting is slightly tedious and deferred to the next paragraph. The most notable novelty is that we force the use of a drift that is $inside$ the log-S-unit lattice span. This somehow captures and compensates for the perturbation induced on infinite places for correcting negative valuations on finite places using S-units.

Finally, as already mentioned, L_{tw} seems much more orthogonal $in\ practice$ than expected, so that we advise to resort to Babai's Nearest Plane algorithm for solving Approx-CVP in L_{tw}, instead of using Laarhoven's query phase with the precomputed hint. We only keep Laarhoven's algorithm to theoretically prove the correctness and complexity of our new algorithm. The theoretical and practical versions of $\mathcal{A}_{\mathrm{tw\text{-}query}}$ are respectively denoted by $\mathcal{A}^{(\mathrm{Laa})}_{\mathrm{tw\text{-}query}}$ and $\mathcal{A}^{(\mathrm{np})}_{\mathrm{tw\text{-}query}}$.

Algorithm 4.3. Tw-PHS Query $\mathcal{A}_{\mathrm{tw\text{-}query}}$

Input: Challenge $\mathfrak{b}$, $\mathcal{A}_{\mathrm{tw\text{-}pcmp}}(K,\omega) = (\mathcal{O}^{\times}_{K,\mathrm{FB}}, B_{L\mathrm{tw}}, \mathcal{V})$, and $\widetilde{\beta} > 0$ st. for any $\mathbf{t}$, the
          Approx-CVP oracle using $\mathcal{V}(L_{\mathrm{tw}})$ outputs $\mathbf{w} \in L_{\mathrm{tw}}$ with $\|f_H^{-1}(\mathbf{t} - \mathbf{w})\|_{\infty} \leq \widetilde{\beta}$.

Output: A short element $x \in \mathfrak{b} \setminus \{0\}$.

1: Solve the ClDL for $\mathfrak{b}$ on FB, i.e. find $\alpha \in K$ st. $\langle \alpha \rangle = \mathfrak{b} \cdot \prod_{\mathfrak{p}_i \in \mathrm{FB}} \mathfrak{p}_i^{v_i}$.

2: Define the target $\mathbf{t}$ as $f_H^{-1}(\mathbf{t}) = \pi_H\left(\overline{\mathrm{Log}}_{\infty}\, \alpha, \{-v_i \ln \mathcal{N}(\mathfrak{p}_i)\}_{1 \leq i \leq k}\right) + \mathbf{b}_{\mathrm{tw}}$, where the
    drift $\mathbf{b}_{\mathrm{tw}} \in H$ will be defined in Eq. (46).

3: Solve Approx-CVP with $\mathcal{V}(L_{\mathrm{tw}})$ to get $\mathbf{w} \in L_{\mathrm{tw}}$ st. $\|f_H^{-1}(\mathbf{t} - \mathbf{w})\|_{\infty} \leq \widetilde{\beta}$.

4: (or) Use Babai's Nearest Plane to get $\mathbf{w} \in L_{\mathrm{tw}}$ st. $\|f_H^{-1}(\mathbf{t} - \mathbf{w})\|_{\infty}$ is small.

5: Compute $s = \varphi_{\mathrm{tw}}^{-1}(\mathbf{w}) \in \mathcal{O}^{\times}_{K,\mathrm{FB}}$, using the preimages of the rows of $B_{L\mathrm{tw}}$.

6: **return** α/s.

We now detail explicitly our target choice, from which we deduce the correctness and the output quality of Algorithm 4.3, as fully proven in [BR20].

Definition of the Target Vector. Recall that we assumed that $\mathfrak{b}$ is coprime with FB, hence $f_H^{-1}(\mathbf{t}) = \pi_H\left(\overline{\mathrm{Log}}_{\infty,\mathrm{FB}}\,\alpha\right) + \mathbf{b}_{\mathrm{tw}}$, for some $\mathbf{b}_{\mathrm{tw}} \in H$ that must ensure $\alpha/s \in \mathfrak{b}$, for $s = \varphi_{\mathrm{tw}}^{-1}(\mathbf{w})$ and when $\|f_H^{-1}(\mathbf{t} - \mathbf{w})\|_\infty \leq \widetilde{\beta}$. Indexing coordinates by places, we exhibit $\mathbf{b}_{\mathrm{tw}} = \left(\{b_\sigma\}_{\sigma \in \mathcal{S}_\infty \cup \overline{\mathcal{S}}_\infty}, \{b_\mathfrak{p}\}_{\mathfrak{p} \in \mathrm{FB}}\right)$, where:

$$\begin{cases} b_\sigma = -\frac{k}{n}\left(\frac{\ln\mathcal{N}(\mathfrak{b})}{n+k} + \widetilde{\beta}\right) + \frac{1}{n}\sum_{\mathfrak{p} \in \mathrm{FB}} \ln\mathcal{N}(\mathfrak{p}) & \text{for } \sigma \in \mathcal{S}_\infty \cup \overline{\mathcal{S}}_\infty, \\ b_\mathfrak{p} = \widetilde{\beta} - \ln\mathcal{N}(\mathfrak{p}) + \frac{\ln\mathcal{N}(\mathfrak{b})}{n+k} & \text{for } \mathfrak{p} \in \mathrm{FB}. \end{cases} \tag{46}$$

It is easy to verify that all coordinates sum to 0, i.e. $\mathbf{b}_{\mathrm{tw}} \in H$. We now explain this choice, first showing that under the above hypotheses, Algorithm 4.3 is correct.

Proposition 4.5. *Given access to an Approx-CVP oracle that on any input $\mathbf{t}$, outputs $\mathbf{w} \in L_{\mathrm{tw}}$ st. $\|f_H^{-1}(\mathbf{t} - \mathbf{w})\|_\infty \leq \widetilde{\beta}$, $\mathcal{A}_{\mathrm{tw\text{-}query}}$ outputs $x \in \mathfrak{b} \setminus \{0\}$.*

The proof of Proposition 4.5 also quantifies the intuition that the output element has smaller valuations at big norm prime ideals. In particular, strictly positive valuations occur only for ideals st. $\ln\mathcal{N}(\mathfrak{p}) \leq \widetilde{\beta}$. This has a very valuable consequence: estimating the ℓ_∞-norm covering radius of L_{tw} allows to control the prime ideal support of any optimal solution. Hence, even if the Approx-CVP cannot reach $\mu_\infty(L_{\mathrm{tw}})$, it is possible to confine the algebraic norm of each query output by *not* including in FB the prime ideals whose log-norm would *in fine* exceed $\mu_\infty(L_{\mathrm{tw}})$, and at which the optimal solution provably has a null valuation. Roughly speaking, this is what $\mathcal{A}_{\mathrm{tw\text{-}FB}}$ tends to achieve in Algorithm 4.1.

Translating Infinite Coordinates. As already mentionned, one important novelty consists in forcing the drift used to ensure $\alpha/s \in \mathfrak{b}$ to be *inside* the log-S-unit span. The underlying intuition is that "correcting" negative valuations at finite primes should only involve S-units. We modelize this by splitting the weight of the $b_\mathfrak{p}$'s evenly across the infinite places coordinates, hence obtaining Eq. (46). This heuristically presumes that S-units absolute value logarithms are generically balanced on infinite places. Let us summarize our target definition:

$$\mathbf{t} = f_H\left(\left\{\alpha_\sigma - \frac{1}{n}\left[k\widetilde{\beta} + \ln\mathcal{N}(\mathfrak{b}) - \sum_{\mathfrak{p} \in \mathrm{FB}} \ln\mathcal{N}(\mathfrak{p})\right]\right\}_\sigma, \left\{\alpha_\mathfrak{p} + \widetilde{\beta} - \ln\mathcal{N}(\mathfrak{p})\right\}_{\mathfrak{p} \in \mathrm{FB}}\right). \tag{47}$$

Quality of the Output of $\mathcal{A}_{\mathrm{tw\text{-}query}}^{(\mathrm{Laa})}$. To bound the quality of the output of Algorithm 4.3, the general idea is that minimizing the distance of our target to the twisted lattice directly minimizes the $\mathfrak{p}$-adic absolute values $-v_\mathfrak{p}(\alpha)\ln\mathcal{N}(\mathfrak{p})$ instead of minimizing the valuations $v_\mathfrak{p}(\alpha)$ independently of $\ln\mathcal{N}(\mathfrak{p})$.

This makes use of the following log-S-unit lattice structure lemma, adapting its log-unit lattice classical equivalent [PHS19a, Lem. 2.11–12], [CDPR16, § 6.1]:

Lemma 4.6. *For* $\alpha \in K$, *let* $\mathbf{h}_\alpha \stackrel{\mathrm{def}}{:=} \pi_H\big(\overline{\mathrm{Log}}_{\infty,\mathrm{FB}}\,\alpha\big)$. *Decompose* $\langle\alpha\rangle$ *on* FB *as* $\mathfrak{b} \cdot \prod_{\mathfrak{p}\in\mathrm{FB}} \mathfrak{p}^{v_\mathfrak{p}(\alpha)}$, *with* $\mathfrak{b}$ *coprime to* FB. *Then* $\overline{\mathrm{Log}}_{\infty,\mathrm{FB}}\,\alpha = \mathbf{h}_\alpha + \frac{\ln\mathcal{N}(\mathfrak{b})}{n+k}\cdot\mathbf{1}_{n+k}$. *Furthermore, the length of* α *is bounded by:*

$$\|\alpha\|_2 \leq \sqrt{n}\cdot\mathcal{N}(\mathfrak{b})^{1/(n+k)}\cdot\exp\Big[\max_{1\leq j\leq n}(\mathbf{h}_\alpha)_j\Big].$$

Note that using the max of the coordinates of $\mathbf{h}_\alpha$ instead of its ℓ_∞-norm norm acknowledges for the fact that logarithms of small infinite valuations can become large negatives that should be ignored when evaluating the length of α.

Theorem 4.7. *Given access to an Approx-*CVP *oracle that on any input* $\mathbf{t}$, *outputs* $\mathbf{w} \in L_{\mathrm{tw}}$ *st.* $\|f_H^{-1}(\mathbf{t}-\mathbf{w})\|_\infty \leq \widetilde{\beta}$, $\mathcal{A}_{\mathrm{tw\text{-}query}}$ *computes* $x \in \mathfrak{b}\setminus\{0\}$ *such that*

$$\|x\|_2 \leq \sqrt{n}\cdot\mathcal{N}(\mathfrak{b})^{1/n}\cdot\exp\left[\frac{(n+k)\widetilde{\beta}-\sum_{\mathfrak{p}\in\mathrm{FB}}\ln\mathcal{N}(\mathfrak{p})}{n}\right].$$

This outperforms the bound of Proposition 3.2 if $(n+k)\cdot\widetilde{\beta} \leq 2\beta \cdot \sum_{\mathfrak{p}\in\mathrm{FB}}\ln\mathcal{N}(\mathfrak{p})$. In particular, this is implied by Lemma 4.2 if $\widetilde{\beta}/\beta \approx V_k/V_{\mathrm{phs}}$ for $k \geq n$. We will see that under some reasonable heuristics, this is indeed the case when using the *same* factor base, and that experiments suggest a much broader gap. One intuitive reason for this behaviour is that the covering radius of our twisted lattice grows at a slower pace than the log-norm of the prime ideals of FB.

Heuristic Evaluation of $\widetilde{\beta}$**.** Proving the second part of Theorem 4.1 necessitates to evaluate $\widetilde{\beta}$. This evaluation rely on several heuristics that adapt heuristics [PHS19a, H. 4–6]. We argue that the arguments developed in [PHS19a, §4] to support these heuristics can be transposed to our setting, as fully discussed in the full version, and both heuristics are validated by experiments in Sect. 5.

Heuristic 4.8 (Adapted from [PHS19a, H. 4]). The ℓ_∞-norm covering radius of L_{tw} is $O\big(\mathrm{Vol}^{1/(\nu+k)}L_{\mathrm{tw}}\big)$. Likewise, $\mu_2(L_{\mathrm{tw}}) = O\big(\sqrt{\nu+k}\cdot\mathrm{Vol}^{1/(\nu+k)}L_{\mathrm{tw}}\big)$.

This assumption relies on L_{tw} to behave like a random lattice. Heuristically, prime ideals of FB represent uniform random classes in Cl_K, and S-units archimedean absolute value logarithms are likely to be uniform in $\mathbb{R}^n/\overline{\mathrm{Log}}_\infty\,\mathcal{O}_K^\times$.

Heuristic 4.9 (Adapted from [PHS19a, H. 5–6]). With non-negligible probability over the input target vector $\mathbf{t}$, the vector $\mathbf{w}$ output by Laarhoven's algorithm satisfies $\|f_H^{-1}(\mathbf{t}-\mathbf{w})\|_\infty \leq O\big(\ln(n+k)/\sqrt{n+k}\big)\cdot\|\mathbf{t}-\mathbf{w}\|_2$.

This heuristic conveys the idea that coefficients of the output of Laarhoven's algorithm are somehow balanced, so that $\|\mathbf{w}\|_2 \approx \sqrt{n+k}\cdot\|f_H^{-1}(\mathbf{w})\|_\infty$. In our setting, this is justified by assuming $\mathbf{t}$ is uniformly distributed in $\big(\mathbb{R}\otimes L_{\mathrm{tw}}\big)/L_{\mathrm{tw}}$, and can be randomized by multiplying $\mathfrak{b}$ by small ideals coprime to FB.

5   Experimental Data

This is the first time to our knowledge that this type of algorithm is completely implemented and tested for fields of degrees up to 60. As a point of comparison, the experiments of [PHS19a] constructed the log-S-unit lattice L_{phs} for cyclotomic fields of degrees at most 24 and $h_K \leq 3$, all but the last two being principal [PHS19a, Fig. 4.1].

Hardware and Library Description. All S-units and class group computations, for the log-S-unit lattice description and the ClDL resolution, were performed using MAGMA v2.24-10 [BCP97].[1] The BKZ reductions and CVP/SVP computations used fplll v5.3.2 [The16]. All other parts of the experiments rely on SAGEMATH v9.0 [The20]. All the sources and scripts are available as supplementary material on https://github.com/ob3rnard/Twisted-PHS. The experiments took less than a week on a server with 36 cores and 768 GB RAM.

Targeted Algorithms. We evaluate three algorithms: the original PHS algorithm, as implemented in [PHS19b]; our optimized version Opt-PHS described in Sect. 3.3, and our new twisted variant Tw-PHS, which is described in Sect. 4. This yields three different lattices, respectively denoted by L_{phs}, L_{opt} and L_{tw}. Note that there are a few differences between [PHS19a] and its implementation in [PHS19b], but we chose to stick to the provided implementation as much as possible.

In order to separate the improvements due to $\mathcal{A}_{tw\text{-}FB}$ outputting smaller factor bases from those purely induced by our specific use of the product formula to describe the log-S-unit lattice, we also built lattices $L_{phs}^{(0)}$ and $L_{opt}^{(0)}$ corresponding to PHS and Opt-PHS algorithms, but using the *same* factor base as L_{tw}.

Number Fields. As announced in Sect. 2.1, we consider two families of number fields, namely non-principal cyclotomic fields $\mathbb{Q}(\zeta_m)$ of prime conductors $m \in [\![23, 71]\!]$, and NTRU Prime fields $\mathbb{Q}(z_q)$ where z_q is a root of $x^q - x - 1$, for $q \in [\![23, 47]\!]$ prime. These correspond to the range of what is feasible in a reasonable amount of time, as the asymptotics of $T_{Su}(K)$ rapidly speak in a classical setting.

For cyclotomic fields, we managed to compute S-units up to $\mathbb{Q}(\zeta_{71})$ for all factor bases in less than a day, and all log-S-unit lattice variants up to $\mathbb{Q}(\zeta_{61})$. For NTRU Prime fields, we managed all computations up to $\mathbb{Q}(z_{47})$.

BKZ Reductions and CVP *Solving.* We applied the same reduction strategy to all of our lattices. Namely, lattices of dimension less than 60 were HKZ reduced, while lattices of greater dimension were reduced using at most 300 loops of BKZ with block size 40. This yields reasonably good bases for a small computational cost [CN11, p. 2]. Note the loop limit was in practice never hit.

For CVP computations, we applied with these reduced bases Babai's Nearest Plane algorithm, as described in [Gal12, § 18.1, Alg. 26].

---

[1] Note that SAGEMATH is significantly faster than MAGMA for computing class groups, but behaves surprisingly poorly when it comes to computing S-units.

Precision Issues. Choosing the right bit precision for floating point arithmetic in the experiments is particularly tricky. We generically used at most 500 bits of precision in our experiments (corresponding to the lattice volume logarithm in base 2 plus some extra margin). There are two notable exceptions:

1. The S-units wrpt. FB can have *huge* coefficients. Computing the absolute values of their embeddings must then be performed at very high precision. All our lattice constructions were conducted using 10000 bits of precision.
2. Computing the target involves the challenge and the ClDL solution, whose coefficients are potentially *huge* rational numbers, up 2^{25000} for e.g. $\mathbb{Q}(\zeta_{53})$. As above, we adjust the precision in order to obtain sensible values.

In all cases, once in the log space the resulting high precision data can be rounded back to the generic precision before lattice reduction or CVP computations.

5.1   Geometric Characteristics

First, we evaluated the geometric characteristics of each produced lattice, using indicators recalled in Sect. 2.5, namely: the root Hermite factor δ_0, the orthogonality defect δ, and the minimum $\theta_{\min}$ (resp. average θ_{avg}) vector basis angle. Each of these indicators is declined before and after BKZ reduction to compare their evolution. We also evaluated experimentally the relevance of Heuristic 4.8 and 4.9, according to the protocol we detailed in the full version [BR20]. Example results are given in Table 1 for NTRU Prime fields, aside the lattices dimension $d = \nu + k$ and reduced volume $V^{1/d}$. Extensive data can be found in the full version [BR20, Tab. B.1–2] for both cyclotomic and NTRU primes fields.

Table 1. Geometric characteristics of log-S-unit lattices for NTRU Prime field $\mathbb{Q}(z_{47})$.

		d	$V^{1/d}$	δ_0		δ		$\theta_{\min}$		θ_{avg}		μ_2	μ_∞	$\|\cdot\|_\infty/\|\cdot\|_2$	
				–	bkz	–	bkz	–	bkz	–	bkz			Real	Heuristic 4.9
$\mathbb{Q}(z_{47})$	L_{tw}	40	4.576	0.913	0.913	1.650	1.358	49	60	82	84	11.04	5.607	0.632	0.519
	$L_{\text{opt}}^{(0)}$	40	6.231	0.938	0.938	4.628	1.915	37	57	81	81	16.59	8.398	0.658	0.583
	$L_{\text{phs}}^{(0)}$	40	12.06	0.951	0.951	7.908	1.946	38	55	81	81	30.85	15.50	0.662	0.583
	L_{opt}	129	1.376	0.981	0.981	6.189	3.632	21	56	80	83	6.575	2.925	0.696	0.427
	L_{phs}	180	1.309	0.989	0.989	10.15	4.527	31	53	80	83	8.022	2.882	0.704	0.387

Orthogonality Indicators. We first remark that the minimum and average vector basis angles seem difficult to interpret. They are slightly better for the NTRU Prime field but it is harder to extract a general tendency for cyclotomic fields.

After a light BKZ reduction, twisted lattices show significantly better root Hermite factor and orthogonality defect than any other log-S-unit lattice representations, *even* when the lattices have the same dimension, i.e. when the same factor base is used. Second, the evolution of the orthogonality defect before and after the reduction is more restricted in the twisted case than in the others. In particular, we observe that the BKZ-reduced versions of $L_{opt}^{(0)}$ and $L_{phs}^{(0)}$ have *bigger* orthogonality defects than the *unreduced* L_{tw}. This last observation is true for all NTRU Prime fields we tested except $\mathbb{Q}(z_{23})$.

These two phenomenons (better values and small variations) are particularly clear for NTRU Prime fields. We remark that in this case, the twisted version of the log-S-unit lattice fully expresses, since for NTRU Prime fields most factor base elements have distinct norms. On the contrary, factor bases for our targeted cyclotomic fields are composed of one (or two, as for $\mathbb{Q}(\zeta_{59})$) Galois orbits whose elements all have the same norm. Finally, we stress that reducing L_{tw} lattices is much faster in practice than reducing $L_{opt}^{(0)}$ and $L_{phs}^{(0)}$. This is corroborated by the graphs of the Gram-Schmidt log norms in Sect. 5.2.

5.2   Plotting Gram-Schmidt Log Norms

For our second experiment, we evaluate the Gram-Schmidt norms of each produced lattice. We propose two comparisons, the first one is before and after BKZ reduction to see the evolution of the norms in each case at iso factor bases in Fig. 2, and the second one is between the different lattices (after BKZ reduction) in Fig. 3. Again, extensive data for other examples can be found in [BR20, § B.2] for both cyclotomic fields and NTRU Prime fields.

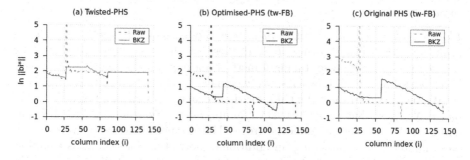

Fig. 2. Log-S-unit lattices for $\mathbb{Q}(\zeta_{59})$: Gram-Schmidt log norms before and after BKZ reduction at iso factor base $\mathcal{A}_{tw\text{-}FB}(K)$ for: (a) L_{tw}; (b) $L_{opt}^{(0)}$; (c) $L_{phs}^{(0)}$.

We first remark that in Fig. 2 the two curves, before and after BKZ reduction, are almost superposed for the Twisted-PHS lattice. This does not seem to be the case for the two other PHS variants we consider here.

Since the volume of L_{tw} is bigger, by roughly the average log norm of the factor base elements by Lemma 4.2, the Gram-Schmidt log norms of our bases have bigger values. The important phenomenon to consider is how these log norms decrease. Figure 3 emphasises that the decrease of the Gram-Schmidt log norms is very limited in the twisted case, compared to other cases (with iso factor base on the left, and the original algorithms on the right), where the decrease of the log norms seems significant. This observation seems to corroborate the fact that the twisted-PHS lattice is already quite orthogonal.

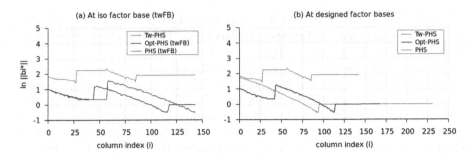

Fig. 3. Log-S-unit lattices for $\mathbb{Q}(\zeta_{59})$: Gram-Schmidt log norms after BKZ reduction: (a) at iso factor base $\mathcal{A}_{\text{tw-FB}}(K)$; (b) at designed factor bases.

Finally, we note that both phenomenons do not depend on the lattices having the same dimension.

5.3   Approximation Factors

We implemented all three algorithms from end to end and used them on numerous challenges to estimate their practically achieved approximation factors. This is to our knowledge the first time that these types of algorithms are completely run on concrete examples.

Ideal SVP *challenges and* ClDL *computations.* For each targeted field, we chose 50 prime ideals $\mathfrak{b}$ of prime norm q. Indeed, these are the most interesting ideals: in the extreme opposite case, taking $\mathfrak{b}$ inert of norm q^n implies that q reaches the lower bound of Eq. (27), as $\|q\|_2 = \sqrt{n} \cdot q$, hence the id-SVP solution is trivial.

We then tried to solve the ClDL for these challenges wrpt. all targeted factor bases. We stress that, using MAGMA, S-units computations for the ClDL become harder as the norm of the challenge grows. This is especially true when the factor base inflates, hence providing an additional motivation for taking as small as possible factor bases. Therefore, we restricted ourselves to challenges of norms around 100 bits. Computing the ClDL solutions for these challenges revealed much harder than computing S-units on all factor bases, which contain only relatively small prime ideals. As a consequence, we were able to compute the ClDL step only up to $\mathbb{Q}(\zeta_{53})$ (partially) and $\mathbb{Q}(z_{47})$.

Query Algorithm. We exclusively used Babai's Nearest Plane algorithm on the BKZ reduced bases of all log-S-unit lattices to solve the Approx-CVP instances. Actually, the hardest computational task was to compute the output α/s, which necessitates a multi-exponentiation over huge S-units. As a particular point of interest, we stress that using directly the drift proposed in [PHS19a] would be especially unfair. Hence, for a challenge $\mathfrak{b}$, the target drifts $\mathbf{b}_{\text{phs}}$, $\widetilde{\mathbf{b}}_{\text{phs}}$ and $\mathbf{b}_{\text{tw}}$ were all minimized using an iterative dichotomic approach on β and $\widetilde{\beta}$, taking a bigger value if the output $x \notin \mathfrak{b}$, and a smaller value if $x \in \mathfrak{b}$. After 5 iterations, the shortest x that verified $x \in \mathfrak{b}$ is returned.

Results. Figure 1 and 4 report the obtained approximation factors. Note that for these dimensions, it is still possible to *exactly* solve id-SVP in the Minkowski space, so that these graphs show *real* approximation factors. We stress that we used a logarithmic scale to represent on the same graphs the performances of the Twisted-, Opt-PHS and PHS algorithms. The figures suggest that the approximation factor reached by our algorithm increases very slowly with the dimension, in a way that could reveal subexponential or even better. This feature would be particularly interesting to prove.

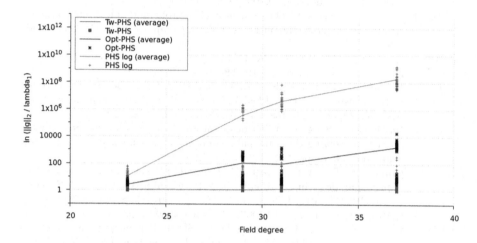

Fig. 4. Approximation factors reached by Tw-PHS, Opt-PHS and PHS for NTRU Prime fields of degrees 23, 29, 31 and 37 (in log scale).

As a final remark, we point out that increasing the factor base for our Twisted-PHS algorithm has very little impact on the quality of the output. This is expected, since the log norm of the prime ideals constrain the valuation of the output, as in the proof of Proposition 4.5 [BR20]. On the contrary, increasing the factor base for the PHS and Opt-PHS variants clearly sabotages the quality of their output, as their lattice description is blind to these prime norms.

Acknowledgements. We thank Thomas Ricosset for valuable discussions on the geometry of lattices. Part of this work was performed while the first author was visiting Alice Pellet-Mary and Damien Stehlé at LIP, ENS Lyon for six weeks. This work is supported by the European Union PROMETHEUS project (Horizon 2020 Research and Innovation Program, grant 780701).

References

[BCLV17] Bernstein, D.J., Chuengsatiansup, C., Lange, T., van Vredendaal, C.: NTRU prime: reducing attack surface at low cost. In: Adams, C., Camenisch, J. (eds.) SAC 2017. LNCS, vol. 10719, pp. 235–260. Springer, Cham (2018). https://doi.org/10.1007/978-3-319-72565-9_12

[BCP97] Bosma, W., Cannon, J., Playoust, C.: The Magma algebra system. I. The user language. J. Symbolic Comput. **24**(3–4), 235–265 (1997). Computational algebra and number theory (London, 1993)

[BDPW20] de Boer, K., Ducas, L., Pellet-Mary, A., Wesolowski, B.: Random Self-reducibility of Ideal-SVP via Arakelov Random Walks. Cryptology ePrint Archive, Report 2020/297 (2020)

[BEF+17] Biasse, J.-F., Espitau, T., Fouque, P.-A., Gélin, A., Kirchner, P.: Computing generator in cyclotomic integer rings. In: Coron, J.-S., Nielsen, J.B. (eds.) EUROCRYPT 2017. LNCS, vol. 10210, pp. 60–88. Springer, Cham (2017). https://doi.org/10.1007/978-3-319-56620-7_3

[BF14] Biasse, J., Fieker, C.: Subexponential class group and unit group computation in large degree number fields. LMS J. Comput. Math. **17**(A), 385–403 (2014)

[BMT15] Boyd, D.W., Martin, G., Thom, M.: Squarefree values of trinomial discriminants. LMS J. Comput. Math. **18**(1), 148–169 (2015)

[BR20] Bernard, O., Roux-Langlois, A.: Twisted-PHS: Using the Product Formula to Solve Approx-SVP in Ideal Lattices (full version). Cryptology ePrint Archive, Report 2020/1081 (2020). https://eprint.iacr.org

[BS16] Biasse, J.-F., Song, F.: Efficient quantum algorithms for computing class groups and solving the principal ideal problem in arbitrary degree number fields. In: SODA, pp. 893–902. SIAM (2016)

[CDPR16] Cramer, R., Ducas, L., Peikert, C., Regev, O.: Recovering short generators of principal ideals in cyclotomic rings. In: Fischlin, M., Coron, J.-S. (eds.) EUROCRYPT 2016. LNCS, vol. 9666, pp. 559–585. Springer, Heidelberg (2016). https://doi.org/10.1007/978-3-662-49896-5_20

[CDW17] Cramer, R., Ducas, L., Wesolowski, B.: Short stickelberger class relations and application to ideal-SVP. In: Coron, J.-S., Nielsen, J.B. (eds.) EUROCRYPT 2017. LNCS, vol. 10210, pp. 324–348. Springer, Cham (2017). https://doi.org/10.1007/978-3-319-56620-7_12

[CGS14] Campbell, P., Groves, M., Shepherd, D.: Soliloquy: a cautionary tale (2014). http://docbox.etsi.org/Workshop/2014/201410_CRYPTO/ S07_Systems_and_Attacks/S07_Groves_Annex.pdf

[Che13] Chen, Y.: Réduction de réseau et sécurité concrète du chiffrement complètement homomorphe. Ph.D. thesis, Paris 7 (2013)

[CN11] Chen, Y., Nguyen, P.Q.: BKZ 2.0: better lattice security estimates. In: Lee, D.H., Wang, X. (eds.) ASIACRYPT 2011. LNCS, vol. 7073, pp. 1–20. Springer, Heidelberg (2011). https://doi.org/10.1007/978-3-642-25385-0_1

[Coh93] Cohen, H.: A Course in Computational Algebraic Number Theory. Graduate Texts in Mathematics, vol. 138. Springer, Heidelberg (1993)

[Con] Conrad, K.: Ostrowski for number fields. In Expository papers on Algebraic Number Theory. https://kconrad.math.uconn.edu/blurbs/gradnumthy/ ostrowskinumbfield.pdf

[DPW19] Ducas, L., Plançon, M., Wesolowski, B.: On the shortness of vectors to be found by the ideal-SVP quantum algorithm. In: Boldyreva, A., Micciancio, D. (eds.) CRYPTO 2019. LNCS, vol. 11692, pp. 322–351. Springer, Cham (2019). https://doi.org/10.1007/978-3-030-26948-7_12

[EHKS14] Eisenträger, K., Hallgren, S., Kitaev, A.Y., Song, F.: A quantum algorithm for computing the unit group of an arbitrary degree number field. In: STOC, pp. 293–302. ACM (2014)

[Gal12] Galbraith, S.D.: Mathematics of Public Key Cryptography. Cambridge University Press, Cambridge (2012)

[Gél17] Gélin, A.: Calcul de groupes de classes d'un corps de nombres et applications à la cryptologie. Ph.D. thesis, UPMC Paris 6 (2017)

[GN08] Gama, N., Nguyen, P.Q.: Predicting lattice reduction. In: Smart, N. (ed.) EUROCRYPT 2008. LNCS, vol. 4965, pp. 31–51. Springer, Heidelberg (2008). https://doi.org/10.1007/978-3-540-78967-3_3

[HPS98] Hoffstein, J., Pipher, J., Silverman, J.H.: NTRU: a ring-based public key cryptosystem. In: Buhler, J.P. (ed.) ANTS 1998. LNCS, vol. 1423, pp. 267–288. Springer, Heidelberg (1998). https://doi.org/10.1007/BFb0054868

[Kom75] Komatsu, K.: Integral bases in algebraic number fields. Journal für die reine und angewandte Mathematik **1975**(278–279), 137–144 (1975)

[Laa16] Laarhoven, T.: Sieving for closest lattice vectors (with preprocessing). In: Avanzi, R., Heys, H. (eds.) SAC 2016. LNCS, vol. 10532, pp. 523–542. Springer, Cham (2017). https://doi.org/10.1007/978-3-319-69453-5_28

[LLL82] Lenstra, A.K., Lenstra, H.W., Lovász, L.: Factoring polynomials with rational coefficients. Math. Ann. **261**, 515–534 (1982)

[LPR10] Lyubashevsky, V., Peikert, C., Regev, O.: On ideal lattices and learning with errors over rings. In: Gilbert, H. (ed.) EUROCRYPT 2010. LNCS, vol. 6110, pp. 1–23. Springer, Heidelberg (2010). https://doi.org/10.1007/978-3-642-13190-5_1

[LS15] Langlois, A., Stehlé, D.: Worst-case to average-case reductions for module lattices. Des. Codes Crypt. **75**(3), 565–599 (2014). https://doi.org/10.1007/s10623-014-9938-4

[MG02] Micciancio, D., Goldwasser, S.: Complexity of Lattice Problems. The Springer International Series in Engineering and Computer Science, vol. 671. Springer, Boston (2002). https://doi.org/10.1007/978-1-4615-0897-7

[Nar04] Narkiewicz, W.: Elementary and Analytic Theory of Algebraic Numbers. Springer Monographs in Mathematics. Springer, Heidelberg (2004). https://doi.org/10.1007/978-3-662-07001-7

[NS06] Nguyen, P.Q., Stehlé, D.: LLL on the average. In: Hess, F., Pauli, S., Pohst, M. (eds.) ANTS 2006. LNCS, vol. 4076, pp. 238–256. Springer, Heidelberg (2006). https://doi.org/10.1007/11792086_18

[NV10] Nguyen, P.Q., Vallée, B. (eds.): The LLL Algorithm. Information Security and Cryptography. Springer, Heidelberg (2010). https://doi.org/10.1007/978-3-642-02295-1

[Pei16] Peikert, C.: A decade of lattice cryptography. Found. Trends Theor. Comput. Sci. **10**(4), 283–424 (2016)

[PHS19a] Pellet-Mary, A., Hanrot, G., Stehlé, D.: Approx-SVP in ideal lattices with pre-processing. In: Ishai, Y., Rijmen, V. (eds.) EUROCRYPT 2019. LNCS, vol. 11477, pp. 685–716. Springer, Cham (2019). https://doi.org/10.1007/978-3-030-17656-3_24

[PHS19b] Pellet-Mary, A., Hanrot, G., Stehlé, D.: Published code of "Approx-SVP in Ideal Lattices with Pre-processing" (2019). https://apelletm.github.io/code/code-approx-ideal-svp.zip/

[PRS17] Peikert, C., Regev, O., Stephens-Davidowitz, N.: Pseudorandomness of ring-LWE for any ring and modulus. In: STOC, pp. 461–473. ACM (2017)

[Reg05] Regev, O.: On lattices, learning with errors, random linear codes, and cryptography. In: STOC, pp. 84–93. ACM (2005)

[Sch87] Schnorr, C.: A hierarchy of polynomial time lattice basis reduction algorithms. Theor. Comput. Sci. **53**, 201–224 (1987)

[SSTX09] Stehlé, D., Steinfeld, R., Tanaka, K., Xagawa, K.: Efficient public key encryption based on ideal lattices. In: Matsui, M. (ed.) ASIACRYPT 2009. LNCS, vol. 5912, pp. 617–635. Springer, Heidelberg (2009). https://doi.org/10.1007/978-3-642-10366-7_36

[Swa62] Swan, R.G.: Factorization of polynomials over finite fields. Pacific J. Math. **12**(3), 1099–1106 (1962)

[The16] The FPLLL development team: FPLLL, a lattice reduction library (2016). https://github.com/fplll/fplll

[The20] The Sage Developers: SageMath, the Sage Mathematics Software System (Version 9.0) (2020). https://www.sagemath.org

[Was97] Washington, L.C.: Introduction to Cyclotomic Fields. Graduate Texts in Mathematics, vol. 83. Springer, New York (1997). https://doi.org/10.1007/978-1-4612-1934-7

[Xu13] Xu, P.: Experimental quality evaluation of lattice basis reduction methods for decorrelating low-dimensional integer least squares problems. EURASIP J. Adv. Signal Process. **137–165**, 2013 (2013)

Simpler Statistically Sender Private Oblivious Transfer from Ideals of Cyclotomic Integers

Daniele Micciancio and Jessica Sorrell[✉]

University of California San Diego, San Diego, USA
{daniele,jlsorrel}@cs.ucsd.edu

Abstract. We present a two-message oblivious transfer protocol achieving statistical sender privacy and computational receiver privacy based on the RLWE assumption for cyclotomic number fields. This work improves upon prior lattice-based statistically sender-private oblivious transfer protocols by reducing the total communication between parties by a factor $\mathcal{O}(n \log q)$ for transfer of length $O(n)$ messages.

Prior work of Brakerski and Döttling uses transference theorems to show that either a lattice or its dual must have short vectors, the existence of which guarantees lossy encryption for encodings with respect to that lattice, and therefore statistical sender privacy. In the case of ideal lattices from embeddings of cyclotomic integers, the existence of one short vector implies the existence of many, and therefore encryption with respect to either a lattice or its dual is guaranteed to "lose" more information about the message than can be ensured in the case of general lattices. This additional structure of ideals of cyclotomic integers allows for efficiency improvements beyond those that are typical when moving from the generic to ideal lattice setting, resulting in smaller message sizes for sender and receiver, as well as a protocol that is simpler to describe and analyze.

1 Introduction

Oblivious transfer (OT) is a cryptographic primitive first introduced by Rabin [Rab05]. An OT protocol is carried out between two parties: a sender and a receiver. For our purposes, the sender possesses exactly two messages (binary strings), and the receiver possesses a bit corresponding to the sender's message that it wishes to receive. The protocol should satisfy security properties for both sender and receiver as well as a correctness property: the receiver should obtain the message corresponding to its bit with high probability while learning

Research supported in part by the National Science Foundation (NSF) under grant CNS-1936703, and by the Simons Foundation. Any opinions, findings, and conclusions or recommendations expressed in this material are those of the author(s) and do not necessarily reflect the views, position or policy of the Government.

S. Moriai and H. Wang (Eds.): ASIACRYPT 2020, LNCS 12492, pp. 381–407, 2020.
https://doi.org/10.1007/978-3-030-64834-3_13

essentially nothing about the other message, and the sender should be unable to guess the receiver's bit with noticeable advantage.

There are a variety of models for the parties involved in an OT protocol, as well as notions of security. In the semi-honest setting, the parties may be assumed to follow the protocol exactly, whereas in the malicious setting we require security even when either or both parties may deviate from the protocol. Using zero-knowledge proofs [GMW87], it is in fact possible to transform a semi-honest OT protocol into one secure against malicious parties, but given the overhead of this transformation, we will be interested in constructing malicious OT directly.

One of the strongest definitions of security we might hope to satisfy with our OT protocol is universally composable (UC) security. This definition requires that for any amount of deviation from the protocol, the outputs of both parties can still be efficiently simulated, even in an environment in which a variety of protocols are concurrently executed. This notion can already be achieved from standard lattice assumptions [PVW08], but requires a trusted third party to generate a common reference string during setup that may only be used a bounded number of times before this trusted setup must again be invoked. More recently, it has been shown how to compile an OT protocol satisfying a much weaker notion of security into one satisfying UC security [DGH+20]. This weaker notion requires computational privacy for the receiver against a cheating sender, and only requires that a cheating receiver should not be able to output both of the sender's messages in their entirety. This compiler could potentially be used to give a UC-secure oblivious transfer protocol from lattice assumptions with a common reference string usable for an unbounded number of executions, but the compiled protocols are fairly complex and inefficient. In any case, it is known that a common reference string (and therefore a trusted third party) is required for any UC-secure OT protocol [CF01], and so other notions of security must be adopted in settings where no trusted party can be assumed.

Another notion, statistically sender-private OT (SSP OT), was introduced in [NP01,AIR01] and requires simulation security only against a cheating receiver, adopting a relaxed notion of computational security against a cheating sender. No setup is required to achieve this notion of security, and many constructions have been given from number theoretic assumptions [Kal05,HK12,BGI+17]. In recent years, SSP OT constructions based on conjectured quantum-secure cryptographic assumptions have also begun to appear in the literature [BD18, DGI+19], and [BGI+17] used with the results of [GH19] or [BDGM19].

Oblivious transfer has myriad uses in cryptography, and perhaps most notably is complete for secure multiparty computation (MPC) [Kil88,IPS09]. Since the security guarantees of the cryptographic constructions built from oblivious transfer depend very much on the properties of the underlying OT protocol, it is important to consider which cryptographic tasks motivate the study of SSP OT specifically. Badrinarayanan et al. [BGI+17] used SSP OT to construct witness-indistinguishable arguments for NP, for which statistical sender privacy is required in the proof of zero knowledge. Jain et al. [JKKR17] showed that two-round SSP OT is sufficient to construct two-round delayed-input interactive arguments for NP that guarantee witness-indistinguishability, witness-hiding, and distributional weak zero-knowledge against delayed-input verifiers, though a computational notion of sender privacy also suffices for their constructions. Badrinarayanan et al. [BGJ+18] subsequently showed that such arguments can be used to compile a three-round semi-malicious MPC protocol into a four-round malicious MPC protocol. SSP OT has been used in constructions of three-round concurrent MPC [BGJ+17], two-message non-malleable commitments [KS17], and two-message witness-indistinguishable proof systems [KKS18]. It also has applications in fully-homomorphic encryption (FHE), as shown by Ostrovsky, Paskin-Cherniavsky, and Paskin-Cherniavsky [OPP14], in their construction of statistically circuit private FHE from SSP OT and any FHE scheme.

1.1 Related Work

To compare prior work on statistically sender private two-round oblivious transfer, we will first need to introduce some convenient vocabulary for referring to the communication complexity of these protocols. We will be interested in the communication *rate* of existing protocols – the fractional bits of information transferred from sender to receiver per bit of communication in the protocol. Somewhat more quantitatively, the *overall rate* of a protocol that transfers a π bit message to the receiver, requires ν bits of receiver communication and τ bits of sender communication is $\frac{\pi}{\nu+\tau}$. It is sometimes useful to distinguish between the contribution of the receiver's communication to the overall rate and the sender's. We refer to the former (π/ν) as the *upload rate*, and the latter (π/τ) as the *download rate*. Our protocol has (upload, download and overall) rate $O(1/\log(\lambda))$.

The first statistically sender private two-round oblivious transfer protocol based on lattice assumptions was given by [BD18], and we take this work as a starting point for our OT protocol. Brakerski and Döttling [BD18] gave a very nice generalization of an existing regularity lemma for lattices, and showed how to use this lemma along with duality properties of lattices to achieve statistically sender private OT with download rate $1/\log(\lambda)$ (similar to our protocol) but much worse upload (and overall) rate $1/(\lambda \cdot \mathsf{polylog}(\lambda))$.

There has since been significant progress in low-communication oblivious transfer from the Learning with Errors (LWE) assumption. Döttling et al. [DGI+19] give a constant-rate SSP OT scheme via their construction of trapdoor hash functions. They use these functions to build download rate-$(1 - O(1/\lambda))$ semi-honest OT, but with upload rate still inversely proportional to λ. They then observe that, for very long (polynomial in λ) messages, the upload rate (and therefore their overall rate) can be brought up to $1 - O(1/\lambda)$ by amortization. The sender's $\mathsf{poly}(\lambda)$-length strings may be divided up into blocks, and each block can be transferred using the receiver's first message. To achieve statistical sender privacy, they leverage a result from [BGI+17], which gives a generic transformation from semi-honest OT with rate above $1/2$ to statistically sender private OT with constant rate. Though this improves on our protocol's

$O(1/\log \lambda)$ overall rate, we observe that similar amortization may be applied to our protocol to achieve a constant upload rate by reuse of the receiver's first message, provided that the sender's messages are strings of length at least $\tilde{O}(n)$ (see Sect. 2.1, Lemma 1). However, many of the previously described applications of SSP OT do not call for polynomially large sender messages, and so the amortization method of [DGI+19] is not applicable.

Furthermore, for applications requiring long sender messages in which statistical sender privacy can be relaxed to computational privacy, a different approach to amortization can be applied to both protocols. The receiver's first message is unchanged, but the sender will use the receiver's message to instead send one of two keys for a constant-rate symmetric encryption scheme, e.g., using a pseudorandom generator or a stream cipher. The sender may encrypt each of its two $\mathrm{poly}(\lambda)$-length messages under their respective keys, and send these ciphertexts as well. The receiver can then recover the key corresponding to its choice bit, and use this key to decrypt the longer message. The other key will be statistically hidden, by the SSP property of the OT protocol, however the sender's security will be reduced to that of the symmetric encryption scheme.

Badrinarayanan et al. [BGI+17] also give a construction of constant rate SSP OT from any linear homomorphic encryption system with rate greater than $1/2$. Such a homomorphic encryption system was later given by Gentry and Halevi [GH19], building off the GSW [GSW13] cryptosystem. Applied to the construction of [BGI+17], their compressible FHE scheme allows compression of both the sender's and receiver's communication, but to achieve constant rate, the receiver must need super-linearly (in the security parameter) many $O(\lambda)$-length messages from the receiver. Concurrent work by Brakerski et al. [BDGM19] also gives a rate-1 FHE scheme based on a batched version [PVW08,BGH13] of the Regev [Reg05] encryption scheme. [BDGM19] also achieves high rate FHE via compression of multiple ciphertexts into a single ciphertext, and so will similarly require settings in which the sender's messages are of length polynomial in the security parameter to realize the benefit of compression.

1.2 Our Contribution

We give a simple, module lattice-based oblivious transfer protocol which improves over the overall rate of similar protocols [BD18] beyond the typical savings achieved when restricting to module lattices, saving a factor $O(\lambda \log \lambda)$. We compare our protocol to other lattice-based SSP OT protocols in two natural settings: a single execution of the protocol and λ parallel executions. We show that for applications requiring at most $O(\lambda)$ messages of length $O(\lambda)$, we achieve the best known overall rate for SSP OT, giving significant improvements in both asymptotic and concrete parameters. Our protocol is also comparatively simple and efficient, requiring only a constant number of polynomial multiplications (see Sect. 4 for a more thorough comparison of the communication and computational complexity of this work with those of other SPP OT protocols).

1.3   Techniques

A lossy encryption scheme [KN08, PVW08] is a public-key encryption scheme that admits the generation of "lossy" public keys – public keys under which encryption statistically hides the encrypted message. The works of Peikert et al. [PVW08] and Hemenway et al. [HLOV11] show that, in fact, lossy encryption is equivalent to statistically sender private 2-round oblivious transfer.

Brakerski and Döttling [BD18] demonstrate one method for achieving such lossy encryption for lattice-based schemes, by showing that a single basis for a lattice can serve as both a lossy and lossless public key. In their OT protocol, the receiver sends a matrix $\mathbf{A}$, defining a q-ary lattice $\Lambda_q(\mathbf{A})$. The sender then encodes a string with respect to $\Lambda_q(\mathbf{A})$, and a second string with respect to the dual lattice $\Lambda_q^*(\mathbf{A})$. They show that for any valid $\mathbf{A}$, for a definition of validity that is efficiently verifiable, encoding with respect to at least one of $\Lambda_q(\mathbf{A})$ or $\Lambda_q^*(\mathbf{A})$ will statistically hide a constant fraction of the encoded string. The partially hidden string, given its encoding, will have sufficient min-entropy for the application of a randomness extractor, yielding a uniformly random one-time pad that can mask one of the sender's messages.

To provide some intuition as to why encoding with respect to both primal and dual lattices guarantees one of the two encodings will be somewhat lossy, we now describe their encoding method informally and at a high level. Encoding a string m with respect to a lattice Λ consists of injectively mapping m to a lattice point $\mathbf{x} \in \Lambda$, and perturbing this lattice point by discrete Gaussian error $\mathbf{e}$ to produce a new point $\mathbf{t} = \mathbf{x} + \mathbf{e}$. Because $\mathbf{e}$ is drawn from a discrete Gaussian, a maximum likelihood decoding of $\mathbf{t}$ will identify the vector $\mathbf{x}' \in \Lambda$ that minimizes $\|\mathbf{e}\|_2 = \|\mathbf{t} - \mathbf{x}'\|_2$, and given a short basis for Λ^*, this can be done efficiently.

To see why such an encoding could be lossy for some lattices, consider the result of maximum likelihood decoding when $\|\mathbf{e}\|_2$ is much larger than the minimum distance λ_1 of the lattice, $\lambda_1(\Lambda) = \min_{\mathbf{v} \in \Lambda} \|\mathbf{v}\|_2$. In this case, there will be several candidate lattice points $\mathbf{x}'$ that correspond to similarly probable values for $\mathbf{e}$. This means that the most probable $\mathbf{x}'$ is not overwhelmingly likely to be correct – there is some entropy in at least one dimension of $\mathbf{x}$, given $\mathbf{t}$.

That one of Λ and Λ^* must contain enough short vectors to guarantee sufficient min-entropy for extraction follows in principle from a transference theorem of Banaszczyk [Ban93]. This theorem implies that for a lattice Λ of rank n, there must be at least n linearly independent vectors in $\Lambda \cup \Lambda^*$ of euclidean length no more than $\sqrt{n}$. So if Λ has no vectors of length less than $\sqrt{n}$, Λ^* must have a basis $\mathbf{B}$ for which $\max_{\mathbf{v} \in \mathbf{B}} \|\mathbf{v}\|_2 \leq \sqrt{n}$. In this case, for a large enough Gaussian, encoding with respect to Λ^* will be highly lossy. Less conditional min-entropy can be guaranteed in the more balanced case, however, when there may be a few short vectors in both Λ and Λ^*. Statistical privacy for the sender is therefore limited by this intermediate case.

We show that applying these same principles restricted to ideal lattices for ideals of cyclotomic integers guarantees more lossiness in the worst case for the sender. The structure of these ideal lattices ensures that Λ must either have many short vectors or none at all, limiting the extent to which Λ and Λ^* can be

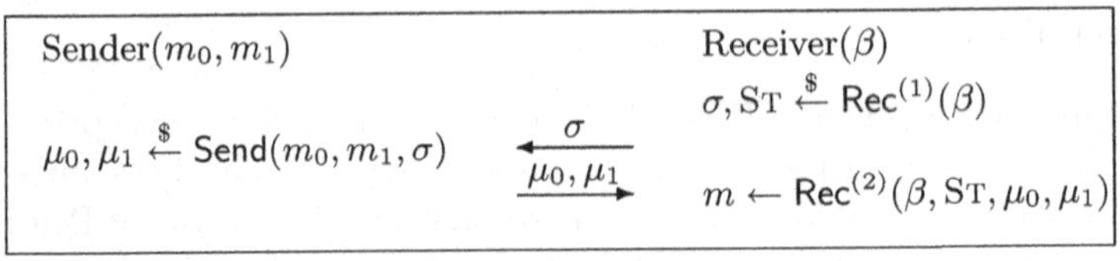

$$\begin{array}{ll}
\text{Sender}(m_0, m_1) & \text{Receiver}(\beta) \\
& \sigma, \text{ST} \xleftarrow{\$} \text{Rec}^{(1)}(\beta) \\
\mu_0, \mu_1 \xleftarrow{\$} \text{Send}(m_0, m_1, \sigma) & \\
\xleftarrow{\sigma} & \\
\xrightarrow{\mu_0, \mu_1} & m \leftarrow \text{Rec}^{(2)}(\beta, \text{ST}, \mu_0, \mu_1)
\end{array}$$

Fig. 1. Two-message oblivious transfer protocol.

adversarially balanced by a cheating receiver. We exploit this structure to give a simpler statistically sender private OT protocol with smaller message sizes, yielding improvements in efficiency beyond those that are expected when moving from a generic lattice to ideal lattice scheme. The receiver's message, which dominates the communication complexity of [BD18], is reduced from $\mathcal{O}(n^2 \log^2 n)$ to $\mathcal{O}(n \log n)$ bits (see Fig. 5), giving a $\mathcal{O}(\log n)$ factor improvement on top of the $\mathcal{O}(n)$ improvements typical of ideal lattice schemes. This is asymptotically modest, but as shown in Fig. 6, yields significantly improved concrete parameters for lattice-based statistically sender secure oblivious transfer, even compared to other subsequent works.

2 Preliminaries

2.1 Oblivious Transfer

A *two-message oblivious transfer protocol*, OT, comprises three algorithms:

$$\text{OT} = (\text{Rec}^{(1)}, \text{Send}, \text{Rec}^{(2)})$$

which are executed by two parties: a sender and a receiver. The protocol proceeds in stages as shown in Fig. 1. (All algorithms additionally take a security parameter 1^λ as input, but we suppress this for notational convenience.) At the outset, the sender is given inputs $m_0, m_1 \in \{0,1\}^n$ for some fixed $n = \text{poly}(\lambda)$, and the receiver is given input bit $\beta \in \{0,1\}$. The receiver runs $\text{Rec}^{(1)}$ on its input $\beta \in \{0,1\}$. $\text{Rec}^{(1)}$ then outputs a message σ to the sender, and some state information ST to be passed to $\text{Rec}^{(2)}$. On receiving σ, the sender runs $\text{Send}(m_0, m_1, \sigma)$, which outputs a message pair (μ_0, μ_1) to be transmitted to the receiver. In the final step, the receiver runs $\text{Rec}^{(2)}(\beta, \text{ST}, \mu)$ which returns a message in $\{0,1\}^n \cup \{\bot\}$.

We will be exclusively interested in two-message oblivious transfer protocols satisfying the following security and correctness properties.

Definition 1 (Correctness). *An* $\text{OT} = (\text{Rec}^{(1)}, \text{Send}, \text{Rec}^{(2)})$ *protocol is correct if for any pair of messages* m_0, m_1 *and bit* $b \in \{0,1\}$,

$$\Pr[\text{Rec}^{(2)}(\text{Send}(m_0, m_1, \text{Rec}^{(1)}(b))) = m_b] \geq 1 - \epsilon$$

for some negligible function $\epsilon(n) = n^{-\omega(1)}$.

Definition 2 (Statistical sender privacy). *An* $\mathsf{OT} = (\mathsf{Rec}^{(1)}, \mathsf{Send}, \mathsf{Rec}^{(2)})$ *protocol is* statistically sender private *if there exists a potentially computationally unbounded extractor* Ext *such that for any receiver message* σ, $\mathsf{Ext}(\sigma)$ *outputs a bit* $b \in \{0, 1\}$ *such that for any pair of messages* (m_0, m_1) *the two distributions*

$$\{\mathsf{Send}(\sigma, m_0, m_1)\} \approx_\Delta \{\mathsf{Send}(\sigma, m_b, m_b)\}$$

are statistically close.

Computational sender privacy is defined similarly, replacing statistical closeness $\approx_\Delta$ with computational indistinguishability. The main difference between sender privacy and full simulation security is that sender privacy does not require the bit b to be efficiencly computable from σ. So, sender privacy can be described as a form of security with respect to a computationally unbounded simulator. For this reason, *statistical* security is perhaps a more natural requirement for the sender, and we do not consider computational sender privacy, except when discussing length extension techniques below.

Definition 3 (Computational receiver privacy). *An* $\mathsf{OT} = (\mathsf{Rec}^{(1)}, \mathsf{Send}, \mathsf{Rec}^{(2)})$ *protocol is* computationally receiver private *if the distributions* $\mathsf{Rec}^{(1)}(0)$ *and* $\mathsf{Rec}^{(1)}(1)$ *are computationally indistinguishable, i.e., for any (potentially cheating, probabilistic polynomial time) sender* S^*

$$|\Pr[S^*(\sigma) = 1 \mid \sigma \leftarrow \mathsf{Rec}^{(1)}(1)] - \Pr[S^*(\sigma) = 1 \mid \sigma \leftarrow \mathsf{Rec}^{(1)}(0)]| < \epsilon$$

for some negligible function $\epsilon(n) = n^{-\omega(1)}$.

Notice also that the sender security with efficient simulator (i.e., the ability to efficiently extract the bit b from the receiver message σ) is clearly at odds with receiver security. In fact, two round protocols cannot achieve full simulation security, and goind beboynd sender privacy requires adding more communication rounds to the protocol.

As discussed in the introduction, it is possible to generically boost the upload rate of a statistically sender private oblivious transfer protocol from $1/\mathsf{poly}(\lambda)$ to a constant. Let $n(\lambda) \in \mathsf{poly}(\lambda)$, and let $\mathsf{OT} = (\mathsf{Rec}^{(1)}, \mathsf{Send}, \mathsf{Rec}^{(2)})$ be a statistically sender private oblivious transfer protocol with sender messages $m_0, m_1 \in \{0, 1\}^n$. Let $\ell(n) \in \mathsf{poly}(n)$. The protocol $\mathsf{OT}_\ell = (\mathsf{Rec}_\ell^{(1)}, \mathsf{Send}_\ell, \mathsf{Rec}_\ell^{(2)})$, described in Fig. 2, transfers length $\ell(n)$ strings by reusing the output of $\mathsf{Rec}^{(1)}$ to execute ℓ/n parallel repetitions of the Send and $\mathsf{Rec}^{(2)}$ subroutines.

Lemma 1 (Parallel OT execution). *Let* $\mathsf{OT} = (\mathsf{Rec}^{(1)}, \mathsf{Send}, \mathsf{Rec}^{(2)})$ *be a statistically sender private oblivious transfer protocol with sender messages* $m_0, m_1 \in \{0, 1\}^n$, *upload rate* v, *and download rate* δ. *Then for* $\ell(n) \in \mathsf{poly}(n)$, *the protocol* $\mathsf{OT}_\ell = (\mathsf{Rec}_\ell^{(1)}, \mathsf{Send}_\ell, \mathsf{Rec}_\ell^{(2)})$ *of Fig. 2 is a statistically sender private oblivious transfer protocol with sender messages* $m_0, m_1 \in \{0, 1\}^{\ell(n)}$, *upload rate* $v\ell/n$, *and download rate* δ.

Algorithm 1 $\mathsf{Rec}_\ell^{(1)}$ Input: $\beta \in \{0,1\}$

$\sigma, \mathrm{ST} \leftarrow \mathsf{Rec}^{(1)}(\beta)$
return σ

Algorithm 2 Send_ℓ Input: $m_0, m_1 \in \{0,1\}^\ell, \sigma$

$m_0^{(1)} \| m_0^{(2)} \| \ldots \| m_0^{(\ell/n)} \leftarrow m_0$ Divide m_0 into blocks of length n
$m_1^{(1)} \| m_1^{(2)} \| \ldots \| m_1^{(\ell/n)} \leftarrow m_0$ Divide m_1 into blocks of length n
for $i \in \{1, \ldots, \ell/k\}$ **do**
    $\mu_0^{(i)}, \mu_1^{(i)} \leftarrow \mathsf{Send}(\sigma, m_0^{(i)}, m_1^{(i)})$
return $\{\mu_0^{(i)}, \mu_1^{(i)}\}_{i=1}^{\ell/n}$

Algorithm 3 $\mathsf{Rec}_\ell^{(2)}$ Input: $\beta, \mathrm{ST}, (\mu_0, \mu_1)$

---

for $i \in \{1, \ldots, \ell/n\}$ **do**
    $m^{(i)} \leftarrow \mathsf{Rec}^{(2)}(\beta, \mathrm{ST}, \mu_0^{(i)}, \mu_1^{(i)})$
return $m^{(1)} \| m^{(2)} \| \ldots \| m^{(\ell/n)}$ Concatenate the $m^{(i)}$s

---

Fig. 2. Amortization of upload rate for an OT protocol for transfer of a single, $\mathsf{poly}(\lambda)$-length message.

Proof. The output of Send_ℓ is by definition the same length as that of Send, while the sender's messages are of length $\ell(n)$, and so the upload rate is $\upsilon\ell/n$. Both the output of Send_ℓ and the length of the sender's messages have increased by a factor ℓ/n compared to Send, and so the upload rate remains the same. Statistical sender privacy is preserved for a setting of $\ell(n) \in \mathsf{poly}(n)$, by a hybrid argument on the distributions of $(\mu_0^{(1)}, \mu_0^{(2)}, \ldots, \mu_0^{(\ell/n)})$ and $(\mu_1^{(1)}, \mu_1^{(2)}, \ldots, \mu_1^{(\ell/n)})$.

It is also possible to generically boost a statistically sender private OT protocol to one with constant overall rate, by trading statistical sender privacy for computational. Given a statistically sender private OT protocol $\mathsf{OT} = (\mathsf{Rec}^{(1)}, \mathsf{Send}, \mathsf{Rec}^{(2)})$ and a pseudorandom generator G with sufficiently large stretch, the protocol $\mathsf{OT_G} = (\mathsf{Rec}_\mathsf{G}^{(1)}, \mathsf{Send}_\mathsf{G}, \mathsf{Rec}_\mathsf{G}^{(2)})$ shown in Fig. 3 will have constant overall rate.

Lemma 2 (OT Length extension). *Let* $\mathsf{OT} = (\mathsf{Rec}^{(1)}, \mathsf{Send}, \mathsf{Rec}^{(2)})$ *be a statistically sender private oblivious transfer protocol with sender messages* $m_0, m_1 \in \{0,1\}^n$, *upload rate* υ, *and download rate* δ. *Let* $\ell(n) \in \mathsf{poly}(n)$ *and* G *be a pseudorandom generator with stretch* $\ell(n)$. *Then protocol* $\mathsf{OT_G} = (\mathsf{Rec}_\mathsf{G}^{(1)}, \mathsf{Send}_\mathsf{G}, \mathsf{Rec}_\mathsf{G}^{(2)})$ *of Fig. 3 is an oblivious transfer protocol with computational privacy for both sender and receiver, sender messages* $m_0, m_1 \in \{0,1\}^{\ell(n)}$, *upload rate* $\upsilon\ell/n$, *and download rate at least* $(1 - n/\delta\ell)$.

Algorithm 4 $\text{Rec}_G^{(1)}$ Input: $\beta \in \{0, 1\}$

$\sigma, \text{ST} \leftarrow \text{Rec}^{(1)}(\beta)$
return σ

Algorithm 5 Send_G   Input: $m_0, m_1 \in \{0, 1\}^\ell, \sigma$

$s_0 \| s_1 \leftarrow \{0, 1\}^{2\ell}$
$\mu_0, \mu_1 \leftarrow \text{Send}(s_0, s_1, \sigma)$
$\text{mask}_0 \leftarrow G(s_0)$
$\text{mask}_1 \leftarrow G(s_1)$
return $(\mu_0, \mu_1, m_0 \oplus \text{mask}_0, m_1 \oplus \text{mask}_1)$

Algorithm 6 $\text{Rec}_G^{(2)}$ Input: β, ST, $(\mu_0, \mu_1, m_0 \oplus \text{mask}_0, m_1 \oplus \text{mask}_1)$

$s \leftarrow \text{Rec}^{(2)}(\mu_0, \mu_1)$
$\text{mask} \leftarrow G(s)$
return $\text{mask} \oplus \mu_\beta$

Fig. 3. Length extension of an OT protocol for transfer of a single, $\text{poly}(\lambda)$-length message

Proof. The upload rate can be shown to be $v\ell/n$ as in Lemma 1. The output of Send_G has increased over that of Send by an additive factor of ℓ, and therefore the download rate is $\frac{\ell}{\ell + n/\delta} \geq 1 - n/\delta\ell$. The seed $s_{1-\beta}$ is statistically hidden from the receiver, and so $m_{1-\beta}$ is computationally hidden, with security reducing to the security of the pseudorandom generator G that was used as its mask.

2.2   Entropy and Extractors

For random variables X, Y, the *conditional min-entropy* of X conditioned on Y is

$$\mathbf{H}_\infty(X \mid Y) := -\log \max_{x,y} \Pr[X = x \mid Y = y].$$

[ILL89] show that a weak conditional min-entropy source X, along with a uniformly random seed s, can be used to generate an output distribution ϵ-close to the uniform distribution, even given the seed s and the possibly correlated value Y.

Definition 4 ((k, m, ϵ)-strong extractor). *A function* $E : \{0, 1\}^l \times \mathcal{X} \rightarrow \{0, 1\}^m$ *is a (k, m, ϵ)-strong extractor (with seed length l) if for all random variables X over $\mathcal{X}$ and Y over $\mathcal{Y}$ such that $\mathbf{H}_\infty(X \mid Y) \geq k$, and for S uniform* on $\{0,1\}^l$, the statistical distance

$$\Delta((\mathsf{E}(S,X),S,Y),(U_m,S,Y)) \leq \epsilon,$$

where U_m is the uniform distribution over $\{0,1\}^m$.

There are many constructions of such (k,m,ϵ)-strong extractors, all with varying seed lengths, codomain sizes, and runtimes. To ensure that our protocol's runtime is not asymptotically dominated by the application of the randomness extractor, we make use of a particular extractor from modified Toeplitz matrices, given by [Hay11]. This choice is more carefully justified in Sect. 3.5.

Theorem 1 ([Hay11]). *For any $n, k \leq n$, and $\epsilon > 0$, the following family of modified Toeplitz matrices over $\mathbb{F}_q$ is a (k, m, ϵ)-strong extractor, for $m = k - 2\log(1/\epsilon)$, seed length $l = \log q(n-1)$, and input space $\mathcal{X} = \mathbb{F}_q^n$, running in time $\mathcal{O}(n\log n)$.*

The seed s selects a matrix $\mathbf{M}$ from the (implicitly defined) family as follows. Sample $n-1$ elements $x_i \in \mathbb{F}_q$ using s. Define the matrix $\mathbf{X} \in \mathbb{F}_q^{m \times n-m}$ by $\mathbf{X}_{i,j} = x_{n-m-j+i}$. Let $\mathbf{I}_m$ be the m-dimensional identity matrix. Then the matrix $\mathbf{M}$ is

$$\mathbf{M} = [\mathbf{X} \mid \mathbf{I}].$$

2.3 Lattices and Gaussian Measures

We write $[\mathbf{x}, \mathbf{y}]$ to indicate horizontal concatenation of vectors (or matrices) $\mathbf{x}$ and $\mathbf{y}$, and $(\mathbf{x}, \mathbf{y})$ to indicate vertical concatenation.

We define a *lattice* as a discrete additive subgroup of the space $\mathbb{R}^n$. A full-rank lattice of dimension n is generated as all $\mathbb{Z}$-linear combinations of a set of n linearly independent basis vectors in $\mathbb{R}^n$. When a basis $\mathbf{B} = [\mathbf{b}_1, \ldots, \mathbf{b}_n]$ is specified, we write the lattice generated by $\mathbf{B}$ as

$$\Lambda(\mathbf{B}) = \{\mathbf{B}^t \mathbf{z} : \mathbf{z} \in \mathbb{Z}^n\}$$

The ith successive minimum of a lattice Λ, for $1 \leq i \leq n$, is defined as

$$\lambda_i(\Lambda) = \min\{\lambda \in \mathbb{R}_{\geq 0} : \mathrm{rank}(\lambda\mathcal{B} \cap \Lambda) = i\}$$

where $\lambda\mathcal{B}$ denotes the ball of radius λ centered on the origin. The *dual lattice* of Λ is the set of vectors in $\mathbb{R}^n$ with integer inner product with all vectors of Λ, and is denoted Λ^*.

$$\Lambda^* := \{\mathbf{x} \in \mathbb{R}^n \mid \forall \mathbf{y} \in \Lambda : \langle \mathbf{x}, \mathbf{y} \rangle \in \mathbb{Z}\}$$

The Gaussian function $\rho_s : \mathbb{R}^n \to (0,1]$ is $\rho_s(\mathbf{x}) = \exp(-\pi(\|\mathbf{x}\|/s)^2)$. We denote the Gaussian sum on a set $X \subset \mathbb{R}^n$ as $\rho_s(X) = \sum_{\mathbf{x} \in X} \rho_s(\mathbf{x})$. The *smoothing parameter* of a lattice, denoted by $\eta_\epsilon(\Lambda)$, is the smallest $s \in \mathbb{R}$ such that $\rho_{1/s}(\Lambda^*) \leq 1 + \epsilon$. We write $D_{\Lambda,s}$ to indicate the *discrete Gaussian distribution* of parameter s over the points of lattice Λ, so that $D_{\Lambda,s}(\mathbf{x}) = \rho_s(\mathbf{x})/\rho_s(\Lambda)$.

We call a random variable X or its distribution *subgaussian* over $\mathbb{R}$ of parameter s if its tails are dominated by a Gaussian of parameter s, so that

$$\Pr\{|X| \geq t\} \leq 2e^{-\pi t^2/s^2} \text{ for all } t \geq 0.$$

A subgaussian variable X with parameter $s > 0$ satisfies

$$\mathbb{E}[e^{2\pi t X}] \leq e^{\pi s^2 t^2}, \text{ for all } t \in \mathbb{R}.$$

The distribution $D_{\Lambda,s}$ is subgaussian with parameter s for any lattice Λ and $s > 0$, $s \in \mathbb{R}$. A random vector $\mathbf{x}$ of dimension n is subgaussian of parameter s if for all unit vectors $\mathbf{u} \in \mathbb{R}^n$, its one-dimensional marginals $\langle \mathbf{u}, \mathbf{x} \rangle$ are also subgaussian of parameter s. This extends to random matrices, where $\mathbf{X}^{m \times n}$ is subgaussian of parameter s if for all unit vectors $\mathbf{u} \in \mathbb{R}^m$, $\mathbf{v} \in \mathbb{R}^n$, $\mathbf{u}^t \mathbf{X} \mathbf{v}$ is subgaussian of parameter s. It follows immediately from these definitions that the concatenation of independent subgaussian vectors, all with parameter s, interpreted as either a vector or matrix, is also subgaussian with parameter s.

We will need the following tail bound on the length of a vector sampled from $D_{\Lambda,s}$.

Lemma 3 ([Ban93]). *For any n-dimensional lattice Λ and $s > 0$, a point sampled from $D_{\Lambda,s}$ has Euclidean norm at most $s\sqrt{n}$, except with probability at most 2^{-2n}.*

We will also need the following bounds on the smoothing parameter of any lattice Λ.

Lemma 4 ([MR04]). *For any n-dimensional lattice Λ, the smoothing parameter $\eta_{2^{-2n}}(\Lambda) \leq \sqrt{n}/\lambda_1(\Lambda^*)$.*

Lemma 5 ([MR04]). *For any n-dimension lattice Λ, and $\epsilon > 0$,*

$$\eta_\epsilon(\Lambda) \leq \sqrt{\frac{\ln(2n(1 + 2/\epsilon))}{\pi}}.$$

It follows from the above that for $\epsilon = 2^{-n}$, $\eta_\epsilon(\mathbb{Z}) \leq \sqrt{n}$.

The Poisson summation formula allows us to relate the Gaussian measure over a lattice to that over its dual.

Lemma 6 (Poisson summation formula). *For any lattice $\Lambda \subset \mathbb{R}^n$ and any complex-valued function $f : \mathbb{R}^n \to \mathbb{C}$, $f(\Lambda) = \frac{1}{\det(\Lambda)} \hat{f}(\Lambda^*)$.*

For $f = \rho_s$, it immediately follows from the above and the observation that $\hat{\rho}_s = s^n \rho_{1/s}$, that $\rho_s(\Lambda) = \frac{s^n}{\det(\Lambda)} \rho_{1/s}(\Lambda^*)$.

The following lemma of [BD18] gives a lower bound on the Gaussian measure over a lattice in terms of its successive minima.

Lemma 7. *For any n-dimensional lattice Λ, $k \in \mathbb{Z}$, $k \leq n$,*

$$\rho_s(\Lambda) \geq (s/\lambda_k(\Lambda))^k.$$

Cyclotomic Integers and Module Lattices. Our protocol makes use of the structure of ideal lattices over cyclotomic integers. Let ζ_{2n} be a primitive $2n$th root of unity, for n a power of 2. We denote by $\Phi_{2n}(X)$ the $2n$th cyclotomic polynomial

$$\Phi_{2n}(X) = \prod_{i \in \mathbb{Z}_{2n}^*} (X - \omega_{2n}^i) = X^n + 1,$$

which is the minimal polynomial of ζ_{2n}, i.e. the lowest degree monic polynomial with coefficients in $\mathbb{Q}$ having ζ_{2n} as a root.

Our protocol operates on elements of the ring $\mathcal{R} = \mathbb{Z}[X]/(\Phi_{2n}(X))$, and we write $\mathcal{R}_q$ to indicate the quotient ring $\mathcal{R}/q\mathcal{R}$. We embed elements of $\mathcal{R}$ into $\mathbb{Z}^n$ via the *coefficient embedding*, denoted σ, which takes an element $a \in \mathcal{R}$ to its coefficient vector. This embedding induces a geometry on $\mathcal{R}$, so that for any norm $\|\cdot\|$ defined on $\mathbb{Z}^n$, and any $a \in \mathcal{R}$, we take $\|a\| = \|\sigma(a)\|$. An ideal $\mathcal{I} \subset \mathcal{R}$ embeds under σ as a lattice in $\mathbb{Z}^n$. Such a lattice $\Lambda = \sigma(\mathcal{I})$ is called an *ideal lattice*.

We may also use σ to embed k-dimensional vectors over $\mathcal{R}$ into $\mathbb{Z}^{nk}$ by applying σ element-wise, so that for $\mathbf{y} \in \mathcal{R}^k$, $\sigma(\mathbf{y}) = (\sigma(y_1), \ldots, \sigma(y_l))$. Let $\mathbf{A} \in \mathcal{R}_q^{l \times k}$ be generators of an $\mathcal{R}$ module $\mathbf{M} \subset \mathcal{R}^k$. Then we may define the *module lattice* $\Lambda = \sigma(\mathbf{M})$, suppressing the embedding notation, as

$$\Lambda(\mathbf{A}) = \{\mathbf{y} \in \mathcal{R}^k : \mathbf{y} = \mathbf{A}^t\mathbf{x}, \ \mathbf{x} \in \mathcal{R}^l\}$$

We will also want to define two q-ary lattices in terms of $\mathbf{A} \in \mathcal{R}_q^{l \times k}$:

$$\Lambda_q(\mathbf{A}) = \{\mathbf{y} \in \mathcal{R}^k : \mathbf{y} = \mathbf{A}^t\mathbf{x} \bmod q\mathcal{R}, \ \mathbf{x} \in \mathcal{R}^l\}$$

$$\text{and } \Lambda_q^\perp(\mathbf{A}) = \{\mathbf{x} \in \mathcal{R}^k : \mathbf{A}\mathbf{x} = 0 \bmod q\mathcal{R}\}.$$

Note that

$$\Lambda_q^\perp(\mathbf{A})^* = \mathcal{R}_q^k + \{\tfrac{1}{q}\mathbf{A}^t\mathbf{s} : \mathbf{s} \in \mathcal{R}_q^k\} = \tfrac{1}{q}\Lambda(\mathbf{A}).$$

We will rely heavily on the following lemma on the successive minima of module lattices over a ring of cyclotomic integers. This is a well-established result (see, for instance, [FP11]), but we re-prove it here for completeness.

Lemma 8. *Let Λ be a module lattice over $\mathcal{R}$. Then $\lambda_1(\Lambda) = \lambda_2(\Lambda) = \cdots = \lambda_n(\Lambda)$.*

Proof. Let $\mathbf{y} \in \mathcal{R}^k$, $\sigma(\mathbf{y}) \in \Lambda$, such that $\|\mathbf{y}\|_2 = \lambda_1(\Lambda)$. Then taking $\mathbf{y}^{(i)} = X^i\mathbf{y}$ for all $0 \leq i < n$, the multiplicative structure of $\mathcal{R}$ gives $\|\mathbf{y}^{(i)}\|_2 = \|X^i\mathbf{y}\|_2 = \|\mathbf{y}\|_2 = \lambda_1$. Suppose the $\mathbf{y}^{(i)}$ are not linearly independent. Then there exist $\alpha_0, \ldots, \alpha_{n-1} \in \mathbb{Z}$ such that

$$\alpha_0\mathbf{y} + \alpha_1 X\mathbf{y} + \cdots + \alpha_{n-1}X^{n-1}\mathbf{y} = (\alpha_0 + \alpha_1 X + \cdots + \alpha_{n-1}X^{n-1})\mathbf{y} = \mathbf{0} \in \mathcal{R}^k.$$

However, $\mathcal{R}$ is a Dedekind domain, and so this cannot be the case. Therefore the $\mathbf{y}^{(i)}$ and $\mathbf{y}$ are linearly independent and all of length λ_1.

The following is a corollary of Lemmata 8 and 7, taking $k = n$ in Lemma 7.

Corollary 1. *For any m-dimensional module lattice Λ over $\mathcal{R}$,*

$$\rho_s(\Lambda) \geq (s/\lambda_1(\Lambda))^n.$$

The following lemma follows from techniques of [BD18] and [CDLP14].

Lemma 9. *Let $\Lambda' \subseteq \Lambda \subseteq \mathbb{Z}^n$ be lattices, and let S be a symmetric set such that $\forall \mathbf{u} \in \Lambda$, $\mathbf{u}$ can be written uniquely as a sum $\mathbf{u} = \mathbf{x} + \mathbf{s}$, where $\mathbf{x} \in \Lambda'$ and $\mathbf{s} \in S$. Let $\mathbf{t} \in \mathbb{Z}^n$ and let $\sigma \in \mathbb{R}$. Then*

$$\frac{\rho_\sigma(\Lambda' + \mathbf{t})}{\rho_\sigma(\Lambda + \mathbf{t})} \leq \frac{1}{\rho_\sigma(S)}.$$

Proof.

$$\rho_\sigma(\Lambda + \mathbf{t}) = \sum_{\mathbf{x} \in \Lambda'} \sum_{\mathbf{s} \in S} \rho_\sigma(\mathbf{x} + \mathbf{t} + \mathbf{s})$$

$$= \sum_{\mathbf{x} \in \Lambda'} \sum_{\mathbf{s} \in S} \frac{1}{2}(\rho_\sigma(\mathbf{x} + \mathbf{t} + \mathbf{s}) + \rho_\sigma(\mathbf{x} + \mathbf{t} - \mathbf{s}))$$

$$= \sum_{\mathbf{x} \in \Lambda'} \sum_{\mathbf{s} \in S} \frac{1}{2}(e^{-\pi\|\mathbf{x}+\mathbf{t}+\mathbf{s}\|^2/\sigma^2} + e^{-\pi\|\mathbf{x}+\mathbf{t}-\mathbf{s}\|^2/\sigma^2})$$

$$= \sum_{\mathbf{x} \in \Lambda'} \sum_{\mathbf{s} \in S} e^{-\pi\|\mathbf{x}+\mathbf{t}\|^2/\sigma^2} e^{-\pi\|\mathbf{s}\|^2/\sigma^2}(e^{-2\pi\langle\mathbf{x}+\mathbf{t},\mathbf{s}\rangle/\sigma^2} + e^{2\pi\langle\mathbf{x}+\mathbf{t},\mathbf{s}\rangle/\sigma^2})$$

$$\geq \sum_{\mathbf{x} \in \Lambda'} \rho_\sigma(\mathbf{x} + \mathbf{t}) \sum_{\mathbf{s} \in S} \rho_\sigma(\mathbf{s})$$

$$= \rho_\sigma(\Lambda' + \mathbf{t})\rho_\sigma(S).$$

All proofs of correctness and security for our protocol hold for general cyclotomic rings of integers, beyond just power of 2 cyclotomics, by considering the canonical embedding of ring elements rather than the coefficient embedding described above. For the sake of simplicity, however, we restrict the description and analysis of the protocol to rings of integers for power of 2 cyclotomics only. In this case, one embedding gives a scaled isometry of the other, so either resulting lattice will have the structural properties we will require for lossy encryption. Other cyclotomic rings will give lattices that are distorted under the two choices of embedding, and so if other concerns force the use of this protocol in an alternative cyclotomic ring, the canonical embedding can be used instead.

2.4 Ring-LWE

The computational receiver privacy of our oblivious transfer protocol will rely on the RingLWE assumption for cyclotomic integers. Informally, it assumes that any probabilistic polynomial time adversary should have only negligible advantage distinguishing the RingLWE distribution described below from the uniform distribution over matrices with equivalent parameters.

Definition 5 (RingLWE). *Let $\mathcal{R}$ be the mth cyclotomic ring of dimension $n = \varphi(m)$. Let $q \in \mathbb{Z}_{>0}$ and χ be a sub-Gaussian distribution over $\mathcal{R}$ with parameter αq. The RingLWE$_{q,\alpha}$ problem is to distinguish between independent samples of the form $(\mathbf{a}, \mathbf{s}\mathbf{a} + \mathbf{e})$ for $s \leftarrow \chi$ fixed across samples, $\mathbf{a} \leftarrow \mathcal{R}_q^k$, and $\mathbf{e} \leftarrow \chi^k$, and the same number of samples of the form $(\mathbf{r}_0, \mathbf{r}_1)$, where each sample is chosen uniformly at random from $\mathcal{R}_q^k \times \mathcal{R}_q^k$.*

Theorem 2 ([PRS17]). *Let $K = \mathbb{Q}(\zeta_{2n})$ for n a power of 2, and let $\mathcal{R}$ be the ring of integers of K. Let $\alpha = \alpha(n) \in (0,1)$, and let $q = q(n) \geq 2$ be an integer such that $\alpha q \geq 2\sqrt{n}$. There is a polynomial-time quantum reduction from K-SIVP$_\gamma$ to (average-case, decision) RingLWE$_{q,\alpha}$ for any $\gamma \leq \max\{\omega(\sqrt{n\log n}/\alpha), \sqrt{2}n\}$.*

3   Oblivious Transfer Protocol

We now present our OT protocol. In the following, let $\mathcal{R}$ denote the ring of integers of the $2n$-th cyclotomic number field for some n a power of 2. Take $q = \text{poly}(n)$ to be prime, $q \equiv 1 \mod 2n$. Let s, σ_0, σ_1 be Gaussian parameters and E be a $(\frac{3n}{2}, n, \epsilon)$-strong extractor for $\epsilon = 2^{-n/4}$, with seed length $l = 2n \log q - 1$, which is guaranteed to exist by Theorem 1. Lastly, take the sender's messages $m_0, m_1 \in \{0,1\}^n$, with m_0 encoded as an element of $\mathcal{R}_2$ and $\alpha \in \mathbb{Z}$ a parameter to be specified.

The protocol is described in Fig. 4 and works as follows. The sender, on input two messages m_0, m_1, waits for the transmission of a matrix $\mathbf{A} \in \mathcal{R}_q^{2\times 3}$ from the receiver. Upon receiving $\mathbf{A}$, it uses this matrix to encrypt the two messages (in two different ways), and sends the resulting ciphertexts to the sender. The receiver, depending on the bit b, chooses the matrix $\mathbf{A}$ in such a way that it can decrypt either the first or the second message. It sends the matrix $\mathbf{A}$ to the sender, and when the sender returns the two ciphertexts, it uses $\mathbf{A}$ to decrypt the ciphertext of its choice.

Informally (and made formal in Sect. 3.3), the sender's privacy is preserved because one of the two sender encodings is statistically hidden. Identifying $\mathbf{x} + \Lambda_q^\perp[\mathbf{A}, \mathbf{I}]$ with $[\mathbf{A}, \mathbf{I}]\mathbf{x} \mod q$ for any $\mathbf{x} \in \mathbb{R}_q^5$ gives a bijective correspondence. So if the lattice $\Lambda_q^\perp[\mathbf{A}, \mathbf{I}]$ has many vectors that are short compared to the parameter of the Gaussian from which $\mathbf{x}_0$ is sampled, then following the intuition from Sect. 1.3, computing $[\mathbf{A}, \mathbf{I}]\mathbf{x}_0$ is a lossy encoding of $\mathbf{x}_0$. If it has enough short vectors, it will in fact lose (almost) *all* information about $\mathbf{x}_0$, so that the result is uniformly distributed over $\mathcal{R}_q^2$, hiding m_0. On the other hand, if $\Lambda_q[\mathbf{A}, \mathbf{I}] = \Lambda_q^\perp([\mathbf{I}, -\mathbf{A}^t])$ has many short vectors, then the same argument says that $[\mathbf{I}, -\mathbf{A}^t](\mathbf{x}_1, \mathbf{x}_2)$ is a lossy encoding of $\mathbf{x}_1$ and $\mathbf{x}_2$. For our settings of parameters, not all information about these vectors is lost, however, and so we use a randomness extractor applied to $\mathbf{x}_2$ to get a random mask, hiding m_1.

Algorithm 7 $\mathsf{Rec}^{(1)}$	**Algorithm 8** Send
Input: $b \in \{0,1\}$	Input: $\mathbf{A} \in \mathcal{R}_q^{2\times 3}$, $m_0, m_1 \in \mathcal{R}_2$

$$
\begin{array}{ll}
\textbf{if } b = 0 \textbf{ then} & \mathbf{x}_0 \xleftarrow{\$} D_{\mathcal{R},\sigma_0}^5 \\
\quad \mathbf{a} \xleftarrow{\$} \mathcal{R}_q^3 & \mu_0 \leftarrow 2[\mathbf{A},\mathbf{I}]\mathbf{x}_0 + \begin{bmatrix} 0 \\ m_0 \end{bmatrix} \mod q \\
\quad z \xleftarrow{\$} D_{\mathcal{R},s} & \\
\quad \mathbf{e} \xleftarrow{\$} D_{\mathcal{R},s}^3 & \mathbf{x}_1 \xleftarrow{\$} D_{\mathcal{R},\sigma_1}^3 \\
\quad \mathbf{b} = z \cdot \mathbf{a} + \mathbf{e} & \mathbf{x}_2 \xleftarrow{\$} D_{\mathcal{R},\sigma_1}^2 \\
\quad \mathbf{A} \leftarrow [\mathbf{a},\mathbf{b}]^t & \mathbf{c} \leftarrow \alpha \cdot (\mathbf{x}_1 - \mathbf{A}^t \mathbf{x}_2) \mod q \\
\quad \textbf{return } (\mathbf{A}, z) & r \leftarrow \{0,1\}^l \\
\textbf{else} & \mu_1 \leftarrow (\mathbf{c}, r, \mathsf{E}(r, \mathbf{x}_2 \mod q) \oplus m_1) \\
\quad \bar{\mathbf{a}} \xleftarrow{\$} \mathcal{R}_q^2 & \textbf{return } (\mu_0, \mu_1) \\
\quad \mathbf{r} \xleftarrow{\$} D_{\mathcal{R},s}^2 & \\
\quad \mathbf{R} \xleftarrow{\$} D_{\mathcal{R},s}^{2\times 2} & \\
\quad \mathbf{A} \leftarrow [\bar{\mathbf{a}} \mid \frac{q-1}{\alpha}\mathbf{I} + \bar{\mathbf{a}}\mathbf{r}^t + \mathbf{R}] & \\
\quad \textbf{return } (\mathbf{A}, \mathbf{r}) &
\end{array}
$$

Algorithm 9 $\mathsf{Rec}^{(2)}$ Input: $b \in \{0,1\}$, ST, (μ_0, μ_1)

$$
\begin{array}{l}
\textbf{if } b = 0 \textbf{ then} \\
\quad z \leftarrow \mathrm{ST} \\
\quad m \leftarrow ([-z, 1]\mu_0 \mod q) \mod 2 \\
\textbf{else} \\
\quad (\mathbf{c}, r, \tau) \leftarrow \mu_1 \\
\quad \mathbf{r} \leftarrow \mathrm{ST} \\
\quad \mathbf{y} \leftarrow -(([\mathbf{r}, -\mathbf{I}] \cdot \mathbf{c}) \mod q) \mod \alpha \\
\quad m \leftarrow \mathsf{E}(r, \mathbf{y}) \oplus \tau \\
\textbf{return } m
\end{array}
$$

Fig. 4. Oblivious Transfer Protocol. In $\mathsf{Rec}^{(1)}$, the receiver generates a matrix along with auxiliary information that allows decoding of one of the sender's two messages. In Send, the sender encodes its first message to be decodable with high probability if $A \leftarrow \mathsf{Rec}^{(1)}(0)$, and the second message so as to be decodable with high probability if $A \leftarrow \mathsf{Rec}^{(1)}(1)$. In the last stage, $\mathsf{Rec}^{(2)}$, the receiver decodes whichever of the sender's messages corresponds to its bit.

3.1 Correctness

In this section, we show that the OT protocol above satisfies our definition of correctness. The proof follows a standard argument for correctness of RingLWE cryptosystems, using concentration bounds to show that with high probability, the noise introduced by encryption does not exceed the threshold required for decoding.

Lemma 10. *If $s = 2\sqrt{n}$, $\sigma_0 \leq q/8\omega(\sqrt{(4ns^2 + 1)\log n})$ and $\sigma_1 \leq \alpha/2\omega$ $(\sqrt{\log n})$ for α a power of 2 so that $\alpha \mid q - 1$ and $\alpha \leq \sqrt{q-1}/s$, the protocol is correct.*

Proof. Since the entries of $\mathbf{e}$ and z are chosen with gaussian distribution of parameter s, with all but negligible probability, $\beta_0 = \|[\mathbf{e}^t, -z]\|_2 < s\sqrt{4n}$. Similarly, the rows of $[\mathbf{r}, \mathbf{R}^t]$ have norm bounded by $\beta_1 < s\sqrt{3n}$ except with negligible probability, and we assume that both inequalities hold in the following.

We first consider the case that $b = 0$. In this case $\mathsf{Rec}(0, (\mu_0, \mu_1))$ computes

$$[-z, 1]\mu_0 = 2[\mathbf{e}^t, -z, 1]\mathbf{x}_0 + m_0 \pmod{q}$$

which equals m_0 modulo 2, as long as $\|[\mathbf{e}^t, -z, 1]\mathbf{x}_0\|_\infty < (q-1)/4$. Since the entries of $\mathbf{x}_0$ are subgaussian of parameter σ_0, the entries of $[\mathbf{e}^t, -z, 1]\mathbf{x}_0$ have subgaussian distribution of parameter

$$\sigma_0\sqrt{\beta_0^2 + 1} < \sigma_0\sqrt{4ns^2 + 1}.$$

So with all but negligible probability,

$$\|[\mathbf{e}^t, -z, 1]\mathbf{x}_0\|_\infty < \sigma_0\omega(\sqrt{(4ns^2 + 1)\log n}) \le (q-1)/4.$$

We now consider the case that $b = 1$. The receiver will successfully recover $m_1 = \tau \oplus \mathsf{E}(r, \mathbf{x}_2)$ if $\mathbf{y} = \mathbf{x}_2$. By definition, before reduction modulo α, the vector $\mathbf{y} \pmod{q}$ equals

$$
\begin{aligned}
-(([\mathbf{r}, -\mathbf{I}] \cdot \mathbf{c}) &= -\alpha([\mathbf{r}, -\mathbf{I}]\mathbf{x}_1 - [\mathbf{r}, -\mathbf{I}]\mathbf{A}^t\mathbf{x}_2) \\
&= -\alpha([\mathbf{r}, -\mathbf{I}]\mathbf{x}_1) - [(q-1)\mathbf{I} + \alpha\mathbf{R}^t]\mathbf{x}_2 \\
&= (((1-q)\mathbf{x}_2 - \alpha([\mathbf{r}, -\mathbf{I}]\mathbf{x}_1 + \mathbf{R}^t\mathbf{x}_2)) \\
&= (\mathbf{x}_2 - \alpha([\mathbf{r}, -\mathbf{I}, \mathbf{R}^t](\mathbf{x}_1, \mathbf{x}_2))) \pmod{q}.
\end{aligned}
$$

So, $\mathbf{y} = ((\mathbf{x}_2 - \alpha\mathbf{v}) \bmod q) \bmod \alpha$ for some vector

$$\mathbf{v} = [\mathbf{r}, -\mathbf{I}, \mathbf{R}^t](\mathbf{x}_1, \mathbf{x}_2).$$

We will show that, with high probability, $\|\mathbf{v}\|_\infty < (q-1)/(2\alpha)$ and $\|\mathbf{x}_2\|_\infty \le \alpha/2$. It follows that, since $\mathbf{v}$ is an integer vector, we also have $\|\mathbf{v}\|_\infty \le (q-1)/(2\alpha) - 1$, and

$$\|\mathbf{x}_2 - \alpha\mathbf{v}\|_\infty \le \|\mathbf{x}_2\|_\infty + \alpha\|\mathbf{v}\|_\infty \le \frac{\alpha}{2} + \frac{q-1}{2} - \alpha < \frac{q}{2}.$$

So, the computation of $\mathbf{y}$ recovers $\mathbf{v}$ over the integers, and $\mathbf{y} = \mathbf{v} \bmod \alpha = \mathbf{x}_2 \bmod \alpha = \mathbf{x}_2$.

Both $\mathbf{x}_1$ and $\mathbf{x}_2$ are drawn from a discrete Gaussian of parameter σ_1 and so, by an argument analogous to that of the previous case, the entries of $\mathbf{v}$ have subgaussian distribution of parameter

$$\sigma_1\sqrt{\beta_1^2 + 1} < \sigma_1\sqrt{3ns^2 + 1}.$$

Then with all but negligible probability we can bound the ℓ_∞ norm of the result by

$$\|\mathbf{v}\|_\infty < \sigma_1 \sqrt{3ns^2 + 1} \cdot \omega(\sqrt{\log n})$$
$$\leq \frac{\alpha\sqrt{3ns^2 + 1}}{2}$$
$$\leq \frac{q - 1}{2\alpha}.$$

We can also bound the coefficients of $\mathbf{x}_2$ by $\sigma_1 \cdot \omega(\sqrt{\log n}) \leq \alpha/2$ so the output is correct except with negligible probability.

3.2   Computational Receiver Privacy

Here we show that the receiver enjoys computational privacy. This follows immediately from the pseudorandomness of RingLWE.

Lemma 11. *Let* $q = \text{poly}(n)$ *be prime,* $q \equiv 1 \mod 2n$. *Take* $s > 2\sqrt{n}$. *Then, the distributions* $\text{Rec}^1(0)$ *and* $\text{Rec}^1(1)$ *are computationally indistinguishable under standard* RingLWE *assumptions.*

Proof. We show that the distribution of matrix $\mathbf{A}$ computed by both $\text{Rec}^1(0)$ and $\text{Rec}^1(1)$ is pseudorandom. For $\text{Rec}^1(0)$, $\mathbf{A}^t = [\mathbf{a}, z\mathbf{a} + \mathbf{e}]$ is just the RingLWE distribution with gaussian parameter $s \geq 2\sqrt{n}$. For $\text{Rec}^1(1)$, $[\bar{\mathbf{a}}, \bar{\mathbf{a}}\mathbf{r}^t + \mathbf{R}]$ is also the RingLWE distribution with secret $\mathbf{r}$ and noise $\mathbf{R}$. So, it is indistinguishable from the uniform distribution under standard RingLWE assumptions. Adding $[\mathbf{0}, \frac{q-1}{\alpha}\mathbf{I}]$ maps the uniform distribution to itself. So, it preserves indistinguishability.

3.3   Statistical Sender Privacy

Finally, we show statistical privacy for the sender. Recall that statistical privacy requires that for all inputs $\mathbf{A}$, one of the sender's two messages must be statistically hidden. As previously described, we wish to consider two cases: one in which $\Lambda_q^\perp([\mathbf{A}, \mathbf{I}])$ has many short vectors, and one in which $\Lambda_q([\mathbf{A}, \mathbf{I}])$ does, formalized in such a way that these cases are exhaustive and give the necessary guarantees on lossiness. To that end, we actually analyze the following two cases: one in which the smoothing parameter of $\Lambda_q^\perp([\mathbf{A}, \mathbf{I}])$ is small compared to σ_0 ($\Lambda_q^\perp([\mathbf{A}, \mathbf{I}])$ has many short vectors), and the other in which the smoothing parameter is large ($\Lambda_q([\mathbf{A}, \mathbf{I}])$ has short vectors). In the first case, the sender's first message m_0 must be statistically hidden, and in the second, m_1 must be.

Theorem 3. *Assume* $\sigma_0\sigma_1 \geq 8q\sqrt{5n}\omega(\sqrt{\log n})$ *and* $\sigma_1 \leq q/\sqrt{n}$. *Then there exists an unbounded extractor* Ext *taking as input an element of* $\mathcal{R}^{2\times 3}$ *and outputting a bit* b, *such that for all* $\mathbf{A} \in \mathcal{R}^{2\times 3}$, *letting* $b \leftarrow \text{Ext}(\mathbf{A})$, *it holds for all* $m_0, m_1 \in \mathcal{R}_2$,

$$\text{Send}(\mathbf{A}, m_0, m_1) \approx_\Delta \text{Send}(\mathbf{A}, m_b, m_b).$$

Proof. We consider two propositions, at least one of which must be true of $\Lambda(\mathbf{A})$, and show that in each case, one of m_0 or m_1 must be statistically hidden. It follows that we can change either m_0 to m_1 or m_1 to m_0, without affecting the distribution by a noticeable amount.

First consider the case $\sigma_0 > \eta_\epsilon(\Lambda_q^\perp([\mathbf{A}, \mathbf{I}])) \cdot \omega(\sqrt{\log n})$. If this is the case, $[\mathbf{A}, \mathbf{I}]\mathbf{x}_0$ is statistically close to uniform. Since q is odd, multiplying by 2 and adding $(0, m_0)$ is a bijection, and preserves the uniform distribution. So, μ_0 is independent of m_0. Clearly, μ_1 is also independent of m_0.

Next we consider the case $\eta_\epsilon(\Lambda_q^\perp([\mathbf{A}, \mathbf{I}])) \geq \sigma_0/2\omega(\sqrt{\log n})$. We show that $\mathbf{x}_2$ (mod q) must have high min-entropy $H_\infty(\mathbf{x}_2 \mid \mathbf{c}) \geq 3n/2$ even when conditioned on $\mathbf{c}$. So, the output of the seeded extractor E is (statistically close to) a uniformly random n-bit mask, and m_1 is statistically hidden. Notice that the conditional distribution of $(\mathbf{x}_1, \mathbf{x}_2)$ given $\mathbf{c}$ is precisely D_{C,σ_1} where

$$C = (\mathbf{c}/\alpha, \mathbf{0}) + \Lambda_q^\perp([\mathbf{I}, -\mathbf{A}^t]) = (\mathbf{c}/\alpha, \mathbf{0}) + \Lambda_q([\mathbf{A}, \mathbf{I}]).$$

Since $\eta_\epsilon(\Lambda_q^\perp([\mathbf{A}, \mathbf{I}])) \geq \sigma_0/2\omega(\sqrt{\log n})$ by assumption, and $\Lambda_q^*([\mathbf{A}, \mathbf{I}])) = \frac{1}{q}\Lambda_q^\perp([\mathbf{A}, \mathbf{I}])$, we have

$$\lambda_1(\Lambda_q([\mathbf{A}, \mathbf{I}])) \leq \frac{q\sqrt{5n}}{\eta_\epsilon(\Lambda_q^\perp([\mathbf{A}, \mathbf{I}]))} \leq \frac{2q\sqrt{5n} \cdot \omega(\sqrt{\log n})}{\sigma_0}.$$

Therefore from Corollary 1 we have that

$$\rho_{\sigma_1}(\Lambda_q([\mathbf{A}, \mathbf{I}])) \geq \left(\frac{\sigma_1}{\lambda_1}\right)^n \geq \left(\frac{\sigma_0\sigma_1}{2q\sqrt{5n} \cdot \omega(\sqrt{\log n})}\right)^n \geq 4^n.$$

For any $\mathbf{c}$ and $\mathbf{x}^*$, let $X = \{(\mathbf{x}_1, \mathbf{x}_2) \in C \mid \mathbf{x}_2 = \mathbf{x}^* \pmod q\}$, and notice that X is a coset $\mathbf{t} + q\mathcal{R}^5$ for some $\mathbf{t} \in C$. Let S be the set of coset representatives of $\Lambda_q([\mathbf{A}, \mathbf{I}])/q\mathcal{R}^5$ obtained by a "centered" reduction (so that all representative have coefficients in the range $(-q/2, q/2)$, recalling that q is odd). Note that S is a symmetric set and that any point $\mathbf{u} \in \Lambda_q([\mathbf{A}, \mathbf{I}])$ can be uniquely written as the sum $\mathbf{u} = \mathbf{x} + \mathbf{s}$, where $\mathbf{x} \in q\mathcal{R}^5$ and $\mathbf{s} \in S$. We may then use Lemma 9 to conclude that

$$\Pr\{(\mathbf{x}_2 = \mathbf{x}^*) \bmod q \mid (\mathbf{x}_1, \mathbf{x}_2) \leftarrow D_{C,\sigma_1}\}$$
$$= \frac{\rho_{\sigma_1}(X)}{\rho_{\sigma_1}(C)} \leq \frac{1}{\rho_{\sigma_1}(S)}.$$

A vector $\mathbf{u}$ sampled from a discrete gaussian over $\Lambda_q([\mathbf{A}, \mathbf{I}])$ of parameter σ_1 must have $\|\mathbf{u}\|_\infty < q/2$ with probability at least $1 - 2^{-5n}$, so we have that

$$\rho_{\sigma_1}(S) \geq (1 - 2^{-5n}) \cdot \rho_{\sigma_1}(\Lambda_q([\mathbf{A}, \mathbf{I}])) \geq (1 - 2^{-5n}) \cdot 4^n > 2^{2n-1}.$$

Therefore $\frac{1}{\rho_{\sigma_1}(S)} \leq 2^{-2n+1}$, and so $H_\infty(\mathbf{x}_2 \bmod q \mid \mathbf{c}) \geq 3n/2$.

Finally, we must argue that there exists an unbounded extractor Ext that, on input $\mathbf{A}$, correctly identifies which of the cases above holds with its output b. We first observe that approximating the value of the smoothing parameter $\eta_\epsilon(\Lambda_q^\perp([\mathbf{A}, \mathbf{I}]))$ to within a factor $(1 + o(1))$ can be done in deterministic

$2^{O(n)}$polylog$(1/\epsilon)$ time and $2^{O(n)}$ space, as shown by Chung et al. [CDLP14]. Then the extractor that on input $\mathbf{A}$, runs the algorithm of [CDLP14], outputs 0 if $\eta_\epsilon(\Lambda_q^\perp([\mathbf{A}, \mathbf{I}])) < \sigma_0/2\omega(\sqrt{\log n})$, and 1 otherwise, will satisfy our definition of statistical sender privacy.

3.4   Parameters

It remains to fix values for parameters that satisfy the competing demands of security and correctness. These require that

$$\sigma_0 \leq q/8\omega(\sqrt{(4ns^2 + 1)\log n}),$$

$$\sigma_1 \leq \alpha/2\omega(\sqrt{\log n}),$$

$$\alpha \leq \sqrt{q-1}/s,$$

and

$$\sigma_0\sigma_1 \geq 8q\sqrt{5n} \cdot \omega(\sqrt{\log n})$$

Letting $\gamma(n) \in \omega(\sqrt{\log n})$, a possible setting of parameters is $q \in \Theta(n^4\gamma^6(n))$, $s = 2\sqrt{n}$, $\alpha \in \Theta(n^{1.5}\gamma^3(n))$, $\sigma_0 \in \Theta(n^3\gamma^5(n))$ and $\sigma_1 \in \Theta(n^{1.5}\gamma^2(n))$.

3.5   Choice of Extractor

A reader already familiar with existing regularity lemmas for lattices may wonder about the use of a generic randomness extractor for producing a uniformly random string from $\mathbf{x}_2$. In the given protocol, $\mathbf{x}_2 \in \mathcal{R}^2$ is sampled from a discrete Gaussian with parameter σ_1, but the generic extractor cannot exploit this additional information about its input. If we instead sampled a matrix $\bar{\mathbf{A}}$ uniformly at random from $\mathcal{R}_q^{k \times l}$, and took $\mathbf{A} = [\mathbf{I}_k, \bar{\mathbf{A}}]$, then with overwhelming probability the distribution induced by $\mathbf{Ax}$ is statistically close to uniform over $\mathcal{R}_q^k$, for $\mathbf{x}$ sampled from $D_{\mathcal{R}^{k+l},\sigma}$ with $\sigma > 2nq^{k/(l+k)+2/n(l+k)}$, by a theorem of Lyubashevsky, et al. [LPR13]. This approach is arguably more natural, as it consists solely of ring operations and makes use of the distribution from which $\mathbf{x}_2$ is drawn.

However $\mathbf{x}_2$ comprises two elements of $\mathcal{R}$, which forces $l = k = 1$. Correctness and receiver security for the protocol require that $\sigma_1 < \sqrt{q}/\sqrt{n}\omega(\sqrt{\log n})$, and so σ_1 is not large enough to guarantee negligible distance from uniformity over $\mathcal{R}_q$. We may instead consider taking $k = 1, l = 4$, sampling $\mathbf{A} = [1, \bar{\mathbf{A}}] \in \mathcal{R}^5$, and using $\mathbf{A}(\mathbf{x}_1, \mathbf{x}_2)$ as the mask for plaintext message m_1, however the Toeplitz matrix construction applied directly to $\mathbf{x}_2$ proves to be comparably efficient, without imposing additional constraints on parameter choices. The Toeplitz matrix sampled by the extractor is an element of $\mathbb{F}_q^{n \times 2n}$, and because this Toeplitz matrix multiplication can be performed at least as efficiently as polynomial multiplication of two degree $2n$ polynomials, there is no clear reason to prefer the more "natural" approach to the use of a more generic extractor.

4   Comparison to Related Protocols

In this section, we provide comparisons of our protocol to existing lattice-based SSP OT protocols. Specifically, we present the asymptotic and concrete parameters required by [BD18, DGI+19, GH19], and this work, as well as communication and computational complexity for all protocols. We remark that, when transferring sufficiently long messages, in the computational setting, both the computational and communication costs of any OT protocol can be reduced to linear in the message length using standard techniques. Namely, one can use the OT protocol on two random (fixed length) strings $\mathbf{x}_0, \mathbf{x}_1 \in \{0, 1\}^n$, and then use these random strings to encrypt the actual messages using a pseudorandom generator or stream cipher. So, for a meaningful comparison, we fix the length of the messages to be transfered to the security parameter n. So, we give comparisons in two representative settings which naturally arise in applications of SSP OT: a single execution of the protocol, and $O(n)$ parallel executions, all with sender messages of length n.

We note that the first setting is particularly unfavorable for SSP OT constructions that make use of compressible FHE. These protocols look more attractive in applications that require $\mathsf{poly}(n)$ simultaneous transfers. When many parallel OTs are required by an application, the receiver can compress fully-homomorphic encryptions of multiple bits and send the resulting compressed ciphertext along with a public key to the sender. The sender can then decompress the ciphertexts, homomorphically select the message corresponding to each of the encrypted bits, compress the resulting encryptions of its messages, and send a single compressed ciphertext to the receiver. But in the setting of a single execution of an OT protocol with $O(n)$-length sender messages, these constructions cannot take full advantage of the compressibility of the FHE scheme. In these cases, it should be possible for the sender to use a (not necessarily homomorphic) encryption scheme with more compact ciphertexts, by using key switching techniques. But even this will not improve the upload rate, however, which is the dominant contribution to the overall rate for these protocols.

The second comparison of these protocols is in a context closer to that of their applications [BGJ+18, JKKR17, BGI+17]. In these applications, linearly many parallel OT executions are required, and so the FHE-based OT schemes can actually make use of their compressibility. The $O(n^2)$ bits to be transferred in this case still fall short of allowing the amortization necessary for these protocols to achieve constant overall rate.

When executing multiple OT instances, our protocol allows a small saving, reducing the receiver communication complexity from 6 to 5 ring elements, but still achieving inverse logarithmic rate $1/O(\log n)$. So, if the number of parallel executions is very large (e.g., transferring $\Omega(n^3)$ bits), constant rate OT protocols would achieve better communication complexity than ours, by a logarithmic factor. However, this comes at a very high computational cost, as the amortization/compression only helps in reducing the communication complexity – the time and space (memory) complexity of those amortized protocols would be higher than ours by a much larger polynomial factor.

In summary, in a typical application setting, our protocol achieves much better communication and computational complexity than previous work. Communication is improved by at least a $O(n \log n)$ factor in the single execution setting, resulting in several orders of magnitude improvement in practice. Even when n parallel executions are considered, we sill achieve at least $O(\log n)$ improvement in communication, and, in many cases, much more than that. When it comes to running time, our protocol outperforms previous work by a large marging both in theory and in practice. We remark that considering n parallel OT executions only helps to reduce the communication complexity of previous protocols, and their running time still scales linearly (or worse, due to the overhead of compression/decompression) with the number of executions.

In our comparison, we focus on the communication complexity, as this parameter can be estimated in a way that is largely independent of the computational/implementation model, and a precise comparison can be carried out without the need to implement previous protocols, none of which have been implemented because clearly not practical. But it should be clear from our pseudocode, that our protocol would also be much faster than previous work, both asymptotically (by polynomial, typically quadratic $O(n^2)$ factors) and in practice (by several orders of magnitude.) See the next two sections for details.

4.1 Single Execution

The following table (Fig. 5) compares asymptotic parameters, communication, and computational complexity for a single execution of the OT protocol. Much of the complexity of related protocols comes from the matrix multiplications that are required by key generation (in the case of [BD18, DGI+19, BDGM19]) or by compression (in the case of [GH19]). So, we express the asymptotic complexity in terms of the matrix multiplication exponent $\omega \leq 3$. However, asymptotically faster matrix multiplication algorithms are likely to be only of theoretical interest, and for practical purposes, one should consider the value $\omega = 3$.

Our algorithm achieves quasi-constant $O(1/\log n)$ communication rate already in the single execution setting, improving other protocols by a superlinear $O(n \log n)$ factor. Some previous protocol [DGI+19, BDGM19] achieve similar sender communication, but much higher communication from the receiver, which dominates the total communication cost.

The improvement in running time is even bigger. Our protocol essentially requires just a constant number of ring operations, which can be implemented (both in theory and in practice) in quasi-linear time $O(n \log n)$. The previous protocol achieving the best asymptotic complexity is that of [BD18], which has running time $O(n^\omega) > O(n^{2.3})$. This is already a substantial $\Omega(n^{1.3})$ theoretical improvement, But in practice, for $\omega = 3$, the improvement is almost quadratic $O(n^2)$, and with a protocol that is also arguably simpler and easier to implement. The other protocols are slower than ours by a quadratic factor $O(n^2)$ or worse. For typical values of the security parameter n (in the hundreds) this is easily estimated to be a running time improvement by several orders of magnitude.

Scheme	Modulus q	Receiver Comm. (bits)	Sender Comm. (bits)	Overall Rate	Operations
[BD18]	$\Theta(n^3 \log^{2.5} n \cdot \gamma(n))$	$\Theta(n^2 \log^2 n)$	$\Theta(n \log^2 n)$	$\Theta(1/n \log^2 n)$	$\Theta(n^\omega)$
[DGI+19]	$\boldsymbol{\Theta(n^{2.5})}$	$\Theta(n^2 \log^2 n)$	$\boldsymbol{\Theta(n \log n)}$	$\Theta(1/n \log^2 n)$	$\Theta(n^3 \log n)$
[GH19]	$\Omega(n^{17.5} \log^{10} n)$	$\Theta(n^2 \log^2 n)$	$\Theta(n^2 \log n)$	$\Theta(1/n \log^2 n)$	$\Omega(n^{1+\omega})$
[BDGM19]	$\Theta(n^{2.5} \log^2 n)$	$\Theta(n^2 \log^2 n)$	$\boldsymbol{\Theta(n \log n)}$	$\Theta(1/n \log^2 n)$	$\Omega(n^3 \log^2 n)$
This work	$\Theta(n^4 \gamma^6(n))$	$\boldsymbol{\Theta(n \log n)}$	$\boldsymbol{\Theta(n \log n)}$	$\boldsymbol{\Theta(1/\log n)}$	$\boldsymbol{\Theta(n \log n)}$

Fig. 5. Comparison of Oblivious Transfer asymptotic parameters in the single execution setting. Compared to prior work, our protocol reduces receiver communication by at least a factor $\mathcal{O}(n \log n)$, while matching the best prior sender communication. Our protocol also improves computational efficiency, requiring at least a factor n fewer operations than prior work. The symbol ω above indicates the matrix multiplication constant, and γ may be taken to be any function in $\omega(\sqrt{\log n})$. (The best parameters within each column are in bold face.)

To make the comparison more tangible, we propose a concrete setting of parameters achieving ~ 120 bits of security for the receiver, and compare to the statistically sender private OT protocols of [BD18, DGI+19, BDGM19], and [GH19] with similar concrete security. (Security for the sender holds in a strong statistical sense, and can be easily estimated without making any computational assumption.) Following standard practice, the parameters of Fig. 6 were chosen based on the security estimates of the LWE security estimator [APS15].

Note that both [DGI+19] and [BDGM19] have impressively low sender communication, due to rounding techniques that enable the receiver to correctly recover its chosen message given only some auxiliary information from the sender along with a single bit per bit of message. The concrete overall rate of these (and other prior) protocols is dominated by the receiver's communication though, and so the savings in download rate achievable by [DGI+19] and [BDGM19] are lost when total communication is considered. On the other hand, our protocol's receiver communication is both asymptotically and concretely balanced with the sender's communication, giving an overall rate several orders of magnitude higher than prior work.

4.2 $O(n)$ Parallel Executions

Here we compare the parameters and efficiency of lattice-based SSP OT protocols for applications requiring $O(n)$ parallel executions of the protocol. In this setting, the compressibility of [GH19] can be utilized to obtain the same receiver and sender communication achieved in the single execution setting $(\Theta(n^2 \log^2 n))$, as the receiver can now pack encryptions of all n of its choice bits into a single ciphertext, and all n^2 of the sender's bits may be similarly packed.

Scheme	dim. n	$\log q$	Receiver Comm. (KB)	Sender Comm. (KB)	Msg. Length $|m_b|$ (KB)	Overall Rate
[BD18]	900	40	3.24×10^5	190	.113	1.5×10^{-7}
[DGI$^+$19]	512	23	14000	2	.064	4.6×10^{-6}
[GH19]	6800	255	3.8×10^8	1.5×10^6	.85	2.2×10^{-9}
[BDGM19]	640	29	20000	2	.08	4×10^{-6}
This work	2048	64	100	115	.256	$\mathbf{1.2 \times 10^{-3}}$

Fig. 6. Concrete parameters achieving 120 bits of receiver security. Compared to prior work, our protocol achieves the best overall rate by several orders of magnitude for a single execution of the protocol.

The compressibility of [BDGM19] is also now reflected in the sender communication. Their FHE scheme gives packed ciphertext lengths that are asymptotically $\max\{n \log q, \ell\}$, where ℓ is the total bit-length of the plaintext messages, and so the length of the plaintext messages dominates the sender communication in the parallel execution setting. However, the receiver is still required to send a large compression key comprising $n \log q$ encryptions with ciphertext size $n^2 \log q$, and so the overall rate of the OT protocol based on [BDGM19] will be dominated by this key.

Because we are considering n parallel but independent executions of an OT protocol, rather than a single execution with large ($\mathsf{poly}(n)$) sender messages, the amortization required to achieve constant overall rate for the trapdoor hash function-based protocol of [DGI+19] is not possible. Similarly, our protocol and that of [BD18] require $\mathsf{poly}(n)$-length sender messages to achieve an improved amortized upload rate. For these protocols, the parameters and complexities given below (Fig. 7) are simply those for running the base protocol n times in parallel.

The last table (Fig. 8) shows the concrete parameters for n parallel executions of each OT protocol. Again we observe that the comparatively high upload rate of our protocol leads to a much better overall rate for applications requiring n parallel OTs.

Scheme	Modulus q	Receiver Comm. (bits)	Sender Comm. (bits)	Overall Rate	Operations
[BD18]	$\Theta(n^3 \log^{2.5} n \cdot \gamma(n))$	$\Theta(n^3 \log^2 n)$	$\Theta(n^2 \log^2 n)$	$\Theta(1/n \log^2 n)$	$\Theta(n^{1+\omega})$
[DGI$^+$19]	$\boldsymbol{\Theta(n^{2.5})}$	$\Theta(n^3 \log^2 n)$	$\Theta(n^2 \log n)$	$\Theta(1/n \log n)$	$\Theta(n^5)$
[GH19]	$\Omega(n^{27.5} \log^{15} n)$	$\Theta(n^2 \log^2 n)$	$\Theta(n^2 \log n)$	$\Theta(1/\log^2 n)$	$\Omega(n^{2+\omega})$
[BDGM19]	$\Theta(n^{4.5} \log^2 n)$	$\Theta(n^3 \log^2 n)$	$\boldsymbol{\Theta(n^2)}$	$\Theta(1/n \log^2 n)$	$\Omega(n^5 \log^2 n)$
This work	$\Theta(n^4 \gamma^6(n))$	$\boldsymbol{\Theta(n^2 \log n)}$	$\Theta(n^2 \log n)$	$\boldsymbol{\Theta(1/\log n)}$	$\boldsymbol{\Theta(n^2 \log n)}$

Fig. 7. Comparison of asymptotic parameters. Compared to prior work, our protocol improves in overall rate by at least a $\log n$ factor, and reduces the computational complexity by at least a factor n for n parallel executions of the SSP OT protocol. The symbol ω above indicates the matrix multiplication constant, and γ may be taken to be any function in $\omega(\sqrt{\log n})$. (The best parameters in each column are in bold face.)

Scheme	dim. n	$\log q$ (bits)	Receiver Comm. (KB)	Sender Comm. (KB)	Msg. Length $\lvert m_b \rvert$ (KB)	Overall Rate
[BD18]	900	40	2.92×10^8	190	102	1.5×10^{-7}
[DGI$^+$19]	512	23	7.17×10^6	1024	33	4.6×10^{-6}
[GH19]	11000	1240	2.3×10^{10}	1.8×10^7	15125	6.6×10^{-7}
[BDGM19]	1300	54	8.0×10^8	220	211	2.6×10^{-7}
This work	2048	64	204800	235520	525	**.0012**

Fig. 8. Concrete parameters achieving 120 bits of receiver security. Compared to prior work, our protocol achieves the best overall rate by several orders of magnitude for n parallel repetitions of the protocol.

Acknowledgements. We would like to thank Nicholas Genise and Daniel Kongsgaard for helpful conversations, and anonymous reviewers for useful suggestions.

References

[AIR01] Aiello, B., Ishai, Y., Reingold, O.: Priced oblivious transfer: how to sell digital goods. In: Pfitzmann, B. (ed.) EUROCRYPT 2001. LNCS, vol. 2045, pp. 119–135. Springer, Heidelberg (2001). https://doi.org/10.1007/3-540-44987-6_8

[APS15] Albrecht, M.R., Player, R., Scott, S.: On the concrete hardness of learning with errors. Cryptology ePrint Archive, Report 2015/046 (2015). http://eprint.iacr.org/2015/046

[Ban93] Banaszczyk, W.: New bounds in some transference theorems in the geometry of numbers (1993)

[BD18] Brakerski, Z., Döttling, N.: Two-message statistically sender-private OT from LWE. In: Beimel, A., Dziembowski, S. (eds.) TCC 2018, Part II. LNCS, vol. 11240, pp. 370–390. Springer, Cham (2018). https://doi.org/10.1007/978-3-030-03810-6_14

[BDGM19] Brakerski, Z., Döttling, N., Garg, S., Malavolta, G.: Leveraging linear decryption: rate-1 fully-homomorphic encryption and time-lock puzzles. In: Hofheinz, D., Rosen, A. (eds.) TCC 2019, Part II. LNCS, vol. 11892, pp. 407–437. Springer, Cham (2019). https://doi.org/10.1007/978-3-030-36033-7_16

[BGH13] Brakerski, Z., Gentry, C., Halevi, S.: Packed ciphertexts in LWE-based homomorphic encryption. In: Kurosawa, K., Hanaoka, G. (eds.) PKC 2013. LNCS, vol. 7778, pp. 1–13. Springer, Heidelberg (2013). https://doi.org/10.1007/978-3-642-36362-7_1

[BGI+17] Badrinarayanan, S., Garg, S., Ishai, Y., Sahai, A., Wadia, A.: Two-message witness indistinguishability and secure computation in the plain model from new assumptions. In: Takagi, T., Peyrin, T. (eds.) ASIACRYPT 2017, Part III. LNCS, vol. 10626, pp. 275–303. Springer, Cham (2017). https://doi.org/10.1007/978-3-319-70700-6_10

[BGJ+17] Badrinarayanan, S., Goyal, V., Jain, A., Khurana, D., Sahai, A.: Round optimal concurrent MPC via strong simulation. In: Kalai, Y., Reyzin, L. (eds.) TCC 2017, Part I. LNCS, vol. 10677, pp. 743–775. Springer, Cham (2017). https://doi.org/10.1007/978-3-319-70500-2_25

[BGJ+18] Badrinarayanan, S., Goyal, V., Jain, A., Kalai, Y.T., Khurana, D., Sahai, A.: Promise zero knowledge and its applications to round optimal MPC. In: Shacham, H., Boldyreva, A. (eds.) CRYPTO 2018, Part II. LNCS, vol. 10992, pp. 459–487. Springer, Cham (2018). https://doi.org/10.1007/978-3-319-96881-0_16

[CDLP14] Chung, K.-M., Dadush, D., Liu, F.-H., Peikert, C.: On the lattice smoothing parameter problem. In: Proceedings of the Annual IEEE Conference on Computational Complexity (2014)

[CF01] Canetti, R., Fischlin, M.: Universally composable commitments. In: Kilian, J. (ed.) CRYPTO 2001. LNCS, vol. 2139, pp. 19–40. Springer, Heidelberg (2001). https://doi.org/10.1007/3-540-44647-8_2

[DGH+20] Döttling, N., Garg, S., Hajiabadi, M., Masny, D., Wichs, D.: Two-round oblivious transfer from CDH or LPN. In: Canteaut, A., Ishai, Y. (eds.) EUROCRYPT 2020, Part II. LNCS, vol. 12106, pp. 768–797. Springer, Cham (2020). https://doi.org/10.1007/978-3-030-45724-2_26

[DGI+19] Döttling, N., Garg, S., Ishai, Y., Malavolta, G., Mour, T., Ostrovsky, R.: Trapdoor hash functions and their applications. In: Boldyreva, A., Micciancio, D. (eds.) CRYPTO 2019, Part III. LNCS, vol. 11694, pp. 3–32. Springer, Cham (2019). https://doi.org/10.1007/978-3-030-26954-8_1

[FP11] Fukshansky, L., Petersen, K.: On well-rounded ideal lattices (2011)

[GH19] Gentry, C., Halevi, S.: Compressible FHE with applications to PIR. In: Hofheinz, D., Rosen, A. (eds.) TCC 2019, Part II. LNCS, vol. 11892, pp. 438–464. Springer, Cham (2019). https://doi.org/10.1007/978-3-030-36033-7_17

[GMW87] Goldreich, O., Micali, S., Wigderson, A.: How to play any mental game or a completeness theorem for protocols with honest majority. In: Aho, A (ed.) 19th ACM STOC, New York City, NY, USA, 25–27 May 1987, pp. 218–229. ACM Press (1987)

[GSW13] Gentry, C., Sahai, A., Waters, B.: Homomorphic encryption from learning with errors: conceptually-simpler, asymptotically-faster, attribute-based. In: Canetti, R., Garay, J.A. (eds.) CRYPTO 2013, Part I. LNCS, vol. 8042, pp. 75–92. Springer, Heidelberg (2013). https://doi.org/10.1007/978-3-642-40041-4_5

[Hay11] Hayashi, M.: Exponential decreasing rate of leaked information in universal random privacy amplification. IEEE Trans. Inf. Theory **57**(6), 3989–4001 (2011)

[HK12] Halevi, S., Kalai, Y.T.: Smooth projective hashing and two-message oblivious transfer. J. Cryptol. **25**(1), 158–193 (2012)

[HLOV11] Hemenway, B., Libert, B., Ostrovsky, R., Vergnaud, D.: Lossy encryption: constructions from general assumptions and efficient selective opening chosen ciphertext security. In: Lee, D.H., Wang, X. (eds.) ASIACRYPT 2011. LNCS, vol. 7073, pp. 70–88. Springer, Heidelberg (2011). https://doi.org/10.1007/978-3-642-25385-0_4

[ILL89] Impagliazzo, R., Levin, L.A., Luby, M.: Pseudo-random generation from one-way functions (extended abstracts). In: 21st ACM STOC, Seattle, WA, USA, 15–17 May 1989, pp. 12–24. ACM Press (1989)

[IPS09] Ishai, Y., Prabhakaran, M., Sahai, A.: Secure arithmetic computation with no honest majority. In: Reingold, O. (ed.) TCC 2009. LNCS, vol. 5444, pp. 294–314. Springer, Heidelberg (2009). https://doi.org/10.1007/978-3-642-00457-5_18

[JKKR17] Jain, A., Kalai, Y.T., Khurana, D., Rothblum, R.: Distinguisher-dependent simulation in two rounds and its applications. In: Katz, J., Shacham, H. (eds.) CRYPTO 2017, Part II. LNCS, vol. 10402, pp. 158–189. Springer, Cham (2017). https://doi.org/10.1007/978-3-319-63715-0_6

[Kal05] Kalai, Y.T.: Smooth projective hashing and two-message oblivious transfer. In: Cramer, R. (ed.) EUROCRYPT 2005. LNCS, vol. 3494, pp. 78–95. Springer, Heidelberg (2005). https://doi.org/10.1007/11426639_5

[Kil88] Kilian, J.: Founding crytpography on oblivious transfer. In: Proceedings of the Twentieth Annual ACM Symposium on Theory of Computing, STOC 1988, pp. 20–31. ACM, New York (1988)

[KKS18] Kalai, Y.T., Khurana, D., Sahai, A.: Statistical witness indistinguishability (and more) in two messages. In: Nielsen, J.B., Rijmen, V. (eds.) EUROCRYPT 2018, Part III. LNCS, vol. 10822, pp. 34–65. Springer, Cham (2018). https://doi.org/10.1007/978-3-319-78372-7_2

[KN08] Kol, G., Naor, M.: Cryptography and game theory: designing protocols for exchanging information. In: Canetti, R. (ed.) TCC 2008. LNCS, vol. 4948, pp. 320–339. Springer, Heidelberg (2008). https://doi.org/10.1007/978-3-540-78524-8_18

[KS17] Khurana, D., Sahai, A.: How to achieve non-malleability in one or two rounds. In: Umans, C (ed.) 58th FOCS, Berkeley, CA, USA, 15–17 October 2017, pp. 564–575. IEEE Computer Society Press (2017)

[LPR13] Lyubashevsky, V., Peikert, C., Regev, O.: A toolkit for ring-LWE cryptography. In: Johansson, T., Nguyen, P.Q. (eds.) EUROCRYPT 2013. LNCS, vol. 7881, pp. 35–54. Springer, Heidelberg (2013). https://doi.org/10.1007/978-3-642-38348-9_3

[MR04] Micciancio, D., Regev, O.: Worst-case to average-case reductions based on Gaussian measures. In: 45th FOCS, Rome, Italy, 17–19 October 2004, pp. 372–381. IEEE Computer Society Press (2004)

[NP01] Naor, M., Pinkas, B.: Efficient oblivious transfer protocols. In: Rao Kosaraju, S. (ed.) 12th SODA, Washington, DC, USA, 7–9 January 2001, pp. 448–457. ACM-SIAM (2001)

[OPP14] Ostrovsky, R., Paskin-Cherniavsky, A., Paskin-Cherniavsky, B.: Maliciously circuit-private FHE. In: Garay, J.A., Gennaro, R. (eds.) CRYPTO 2014, Part I. LNCS, vol. 8616, pp. 536–553. Springer, Heidelberg (2014). https://doi.org/10.1007/978-3-662-44371-2_30

[PRS17] Peikert, C., Regev, O., Stephens-Davidowitz, N.: Pseudorandomness of ring-LWE for any ring and modulus. In: Hatami, A., McKenzie, P., King, V. (ed.) 49th ACM STOC, Montreal, QC, Canada, 19–23 June 2017, pp. 461–473. ACM Press (2017)

[PVW08] Peikert, C., Vaikuntanathan, V., Waters, B.: A framework for efficient and composable oblivious transfer. In: Wagner, D. (ed.) CRYPTO 2008. LNCS, vol. 5157, pp. 554–571. Springer, Heidelberg (2008). https://doi.org/10.1007/978-3-540-85174-5_31

[Rab05] Rabin, M.O.: How to exchange secrets with oblivious transfer. Harvard University Technical report 81 (2005). talr@watson.ibm.com 12955 Accessed 21 Jun 2005

[Reg05] Regev, O.: On lattices, learning with errors, random linear codes, and cryptography. In: Gabow, H.N., Fagin, R. (eds.) 37th ACM STOC, Baltimore, MA, USA, 22–24 May 2005, pp. 84–93. ACM Press (2005)

Isogeny-Based Cryptography

Cryptographic Group Actions and Applications

Navid Alamati[1(✉)], Luca De Feo[2], Hart Montgomery[3], and Sikhar Patranabis[4]

[1] University of Michigan, Ann Arbor, USA
alamati@umich.edu
[2] IBM Research Zürich, Rüschlikon, Switzerland
feo@zurich.ibm.com
[3] Fujitsu Laboratories of America, Sunnyvale, USA
hmontgomery@us.fujitsu.com
[4] ETH Zürich, Zürich, Switzerland
sikharpatranabis@gmail.com

Abstract. Isogeny-based assumptions have emerged as a viable option for quantum-secure cryptography. Recent works have shown how to build efficient (public-key) primitives from isogeny-based assumptions such as CSIDH and CSI-FiSh. However, in its present form, the landscape of isogenies does not seem very amenable to realizing new cryptographic applications. Isogeny-based assumptions often have unique efficiency and security properties, which makes building new cryptographic applications from them a potentially tedious and time-consuming task.

In this work, we propose a new framework based on group actions that enables the easy usage of a variety of isogeny-based assumptions. Our framework generalizes the works of Brassard and Yung (Crypto'90) and Couveignes (Eprint'06). We provide new definitions for group actions endowed with natural hardness assumptions that model isogeny-based constructions amenable to group actions such as CSIDH and CSI-FiSh.

We demonstrate the utility of our new framework by leveraging it to construct several primitives that were not previously known from isogeny-based assumptions. These include smooth projective hashing, dual-mode PKE, two-message statistically sender-private OT, and Naor-Reingold style PRF. These primitives are useful building blocks for a wide range of cryptographic applications.

We introduce a new assumption over group actions called *Linear Hidden Shift* (LHS) assumption. We then present some discussions on the security of the LHS assumption and we show that it implies symmetric KDM-secure encryption, which in turn enables many other primitives that were not previously known from isogeny-based assumptions.

Keywords: Isogenies · Group actions

1 Introduction

The recent advancements in quantum computing [Aar13, AAB+19] represent one of the most worrisome developments for cryptographers. Practical (and scalable)

© International Association for Cryptologic Research 2020
S. Moriai and H. Wang (Eds.): ASIACRYPT 2020, LNCS 12492, pp. 411–439, 2020.
https://doi.org/10.1007/978-3-030-64834-3_14

quantum computers pose a threat to the security of most commonly used cryptosystems today [Gro96, Sho97]. In response to this threat, there has been a surge of interest in developing post-quantum replacements for existing cryptography standards. Notably, NIST has started a competition to determine new standards for post-quantum cryptosystems [CJL+16].

Many of the candidate constructions for post-quantum cryptography are based on lattice assumptions [Reg05, LPR10], including the key exchange and signature candidates in the NIST competition [AASA+19]. The lack of diversity in post-quantum cryptosystems could be a potential problem in the future: what if a big advance in lattice cryptanalysis necessitates impractically large parameters for lattice-based cryptosystems, or, in the worst case, a quantum attack invalidates all of lattice-based cryptography? While there are some candidate non-lattice-based constructions, some of which are quite efficient [ELPS18, MBD+18], the landscape of post-quantum cryptography would change dramatically if lattice-based systems were rendered inefficient by advances in lattice cryptanalysis.

1.1   Isogeny-Based Cryptography

A promising non-lattice-based candidate for post-quantum secure cryptosystems is isogeny-based cryptography. The study of isogeny-based cryptography was initiated by Couveignes [Cou06] in 1997, but began in earnest in the late 2000s with several new ideas around collision-resistant hashing [CLG09], key exchange [RS06, Sto10], signatures [Sto09], and key escrow [Tes06]. Isogeny-based cryptography became much more popular after the introduction of the SIDH key exchange scheme [JD11, DJP14], the first practical post-quantum scheme based on isogenies, and a precursor to the NIST competition candidate SIKE [AKC+17].

One of the most recent additions to the isogeny portfolio is CSIDH [CLM+18], an efficient variant of the original key-exchange proposal of Couveignes, Rostovtsev, and Stolbunov. CSIDH spurred a fair amount of new research in isogeny-based schemes, notably signatures [DG19, BKV19], and will be a key focus of this work. Indeed, among all isogeny-based assumptions, CSIDH, its predecessors, and its derivatives are the only ones that can be interpreted in the framework of group actions.

Known Primitives from Isogeny-Based Assumptions. There exist many primitives from isogeny-based assumptions, which can be broadly categorized into those obtained from an isogeny-based group action, and those which are not related to a group action.

Known constructions from isogeny-based group actions include public-key encryption and non-interactive key exchange (both static and ephemeral) [CLM+18], (efficient) interactive zero-knowledge protocols and signatures [DG19, BKV19], multi-round UC-secure oblivious transfer against passive corruptions [dOPS18], and threshold signatures [DM20].

Known constructions not related to group actions include primitives such as public-key encryption [JD11, AKC+17], ephemeral key exchange [JD11], (efficient) interactive zero-knowledge protocols and signatures [DJP14, YAJ+17,

GPS17], collision-resistant hash functions [CLG09], multi-round UC-secure oblivious transfer against passive corruptions [BOB18, dOPS18, Vit19], and verifiable delay functions [DMPS19].

1.2 Cryptographic Group Actions

In order to simplify the presentation and understanding of certain isogeny-based constructions, some prior works have chosen to use *group actions* as an abstraction for them, including even the first presentations [Cou06].

Informally, a group action is a mapping of the form $\star : G \times X \to X$, where G is a group and X is a set, such that for any $g_1, g_2 \in G$ and any $x \in X$, we have

$$g_1 \star (g_2 \star x) = (g_1 g_2) \star x.$$

From a cryptographic point of view, we can endow group actions with various hardness properties. For instance, a *one-way* group action [BY91] is endowed with the following property: given randomly chosen set elements $x_1, x_2 \in X$, it is hard to find a group element $g \in G$ such that $g \star x_1 = x_2$ (assuming such a g exists). Similarly, one could define a *weak pseudorandom* group action with following property: given a randomly chosen secret group element $g \in G$, an adversary that sees many tuples of the form $(x_i, g \star x_i)$ cannot distinguish them from tuples of the form (x_i, u_i) where each x_i and u_i are sampled uniformly from X.[1] We refer to group actions endowed with such hardness properties as *cryptographic group actions*.

As an example, we note that a simple cryptographic group action is implied by the DDH assumption. If we set $X = \mathbb{H}$ (where $\mathbb{H}$ is some group of prime order p), and $G = \mathbb{Z}_p^*$, then the mapping $z \star h \mapsto h^z$ where $\star : \mathbb{Z}_p^* \times \mathbb{H} \to \mathbb{H}$ is a weak pseudorandom group action assuming that the DDH assumption holds over $\mathbb{H}$. We note that here the "set" $\mathbb{H}$ is actually structured. However, there exist candidate quantum-resistant cryptographic group actions where the set may not be a group.

Cryptographic group actions have received substantially less attention compared to traditional group-theoretic assumptions. Nonetheless, there have been a small number of works studying various candidate cryptographic group actions [GS10, JQSY19] and their hardness properties [BY91, GPSV18]. In terms of public-key primitives, these works have demonstrated that cryptographic group actions endowed with some hardness properties imply PKE and noninteractive key exchange (NIKE).

However, this leaves open a number of questions about the cryptographic utility of group actions. For instance, what are the capabilities of cryptographic group actions in terms of constructing public-key primitives richer than PKE and NIKE? Can we hope to construct from group actions (endowed with hardness properties such as weak pseudorandomness) all (or most) of the primitives that

---

[1] We note that sampling directly from the uniform distribution over the set X may not be possible in certain cases. We elaborate more on this later.

we can achieve from, say, the DDH assumption [Bon98]? Or are cryptographic group actions barely more powerful than NIKE?

In terms of cryptographic capabilities, group-theoretic assumptions have been studied extensively over the past couple of decades. At present, we have a reasonably comprehensive understanding of what is (and is not) constructible from the most commonly encountered group-theoretic assumptions such as DLOG, CDH, and DDH (barring a few breakthrough results using novel non-black-box techniques, e.g., [DG17]). The cryptographic capabilities of these assumptions have also been explained from the point of view of their underlying algebraic structure [AMPR19]. On the other hand, our understanding of the cryptographic capabilities of group actions is still somewhat limited.

So, in our opinion, an important question is the following: what primitives can we build from cryptographic group actions? We believe that it is important to understand the cryptographic capabilities of group actions given that they capture the algebraic structure underlying some candidate post-quantum cryptographic assumptions, namely isogeny-based cryptography amenable to group actions.

1.3 Cryptographic Group Actions and Isogenies

In a nutshell, an isogeny is a morphism of elliptic curves, i.e., a map from a curve to another curve that preserves the group structure. The central objects of study in isogeny-based cryptography are *isogeny graphs*, i.e., graphs whose vertices represent elliptic curves, and whose edges represent isogenies between them. There is a large variety of isogeny graphs, depending on which kinds of curves and isogenies are chosen. One such choice would be *complex multiplication graphs*, which arise from so-called *horizontal* isogenies of complex multiplication elliptic curves; indeed, these graphs are isomorphic to Cayley graphs of *quadratic imaginary class groups*, and thus present a natural group action.

One of the key objects associated with an elliptic curve is its *endomorphism ring*. In the cases that interest us here, this ring is known to be isomorphic to an imaginary quadratic order $\mathcal{O}$, i.e., a 2-dimensional $\mathbb{Z}$-lattice and a subring of an imaginary quadratic number field $\mathbb{Q}(\sqrt{D})$. An elliptic curve with endomorphism ring isomorphic to a given $\mathcal{O}$ is said to have *complex multiplication (CM) by $\mathcal{O}$*.

The celebrated theory of complex multiplication establishes a correspondence between the *ideal classes* of $\mathcal{O}$ and the isogenies between elliptic curves with CM by $\mathcal{O}$. More precisely, it defines a regular abelian group action

$$\mathrm{Cl}\left(\mathcal{O}\right) \times \mathcal{E}_k\left(\mathcal{O}\right) \to \mathcal{E}_k\left(\mathcal{O}\right)$$

of the *class group* $\mathrm{Cl}\left(\mathcal{O}\right)$ on the set $\mathcal{E}_k\left(\mathcal{O}\right)$ of elliptic curves, defined over a field k, with CM by $\mathcal{O}$. Moreover, each element of $\mathrm{Cl}\left(\mathcal{O}\right)$ corresponds to a unique class of isogenies, which can be leveraged to evaluate the group action. We refer the reader to [De 17, Sut19] for more details.

Unfortunately, the correspondence between isogenies and the CM group action becomes less than ideal when we start contemplating algorithmic properties. Indeed, a natural requirement for a cryptographic group action is that given *any* group element $g \in G$ and a set element $x \in X$, computing $g \star x$ can be done efficiently. However this does not hold for the CM group action, which can be evaluated efficiently only for a small subset of group elements.

The usual workaround adopted in isogeny-based cryptography is to represent elements of $\mathrm{Cl}(\mathcal{O})$ as $\mathbb{Z}$-linear combinations of a fixed set of "low norm" generators $\mathfrak{g}_i$ for which evaluating the group action is efficient, i.e., as $\mathfrak{a} = \prod_{i=1}^{\ell} \mathfrak{g}_i^{a_i}$. Then, evaluating the action is efficient as long as the exponents a_i are polynomial in the security parameter.

This trick is not devoid of consequences: group elements do not have a unique representation, sampling uniformly in the group may not be possible in general, and even testing equality becomes tricky. We will capture the limitations of this framework in our definition of a *Restricted Effective Group Action (REGA)*.

To illustrate the severe limitations of an REGA, we refer to SeaSign [DG19], which is the Fiat-Shamir transform of an interactive authentication protocol based on CSIDH. To prove the knowledge of a secret $s \in G$ s.t. $y = s \star x$, the basic idea is to first commit to $r \star x$ for some random r, and then reveal $s^{-b}r$ depending on a bit b sent by the challenger. While it is straightforward to prove that this protocol is zero-knowledge when the elements of G have unique representation and are sampled uniformly, the proof breaks down for CSIDH. To fix this issue, SeaSign uses a rejection sampling technique [Lyu09], which considerably increases parameters and signing/verification time.

An alternative fix is to compute the group structure of $\mathrm{Cl}(\mathcal{O})$, in the form of a *relation lattice* of the low norm generators. This restores the ability to represent uniquely and to sample uniformly the elements of the group. This is the approach taken by the isogeny-based signature CSI-FiSh [BKV19], which precomputes the group structure of CSIDH-512.

While it is clear that the approach taken by CSI-FiSh to build a full-fledged cryptographic group action greatly extends the capabilities of isogeny-based cryptography, recent results [Pei20, BS20] showed quantum attacks against CSIDH for certain choices of parameters. Unfortunately, computing the group structure of a significantly larger class group seems out of reach today, owing to the subexponential complexity of the classical algorithms available. This limitation will go away once quantum computers become powerful enough to apply Shor's algorithms to this group order computation, but until then we believe that REGAs can be a fundamental tool to construct post-quantum cryptographic protocols based on isogenies.

Bilinear maps gained popularity in cryptography partly because works such as [BF01, GPS08] presented them in a generic, easy-to-use manner that abstracted out the mathematical details underlying the Weil or Tate pairings. Similarly, an easy-to-use abstraction for isogeny-based assumptions might make them more accessible to cryptographers.

1.4 Our Contributions

We improve the state of the art of cryptographic group actions and isogeny-based cryptography in three main ways:

- We formally define many notions of cryptographic group actions endowed with natural hardness properties such as *one-wayness, weak unpredictability*, and *weak pseudorandomness*. We then show how certain isogeny-based assumptions can be modeled using our definitions.
- We show several applications of cryptographic group actions (based on our definitions above) which were not previously known from isogeny-based assumptions. These include smooth projective hashing, dual-mode PKE, two-message statistically sender-private OT, and Naor-Reingold style PRF.
- We introduce a new assumption over cryptographic group actions called *linear hidden shift* (LHS) assumption. We then present some discussions on the security of the LHS assumption and we show that it implies symmetric KDM-secure encryption, which in conjunction with PKE implies many powerful primitives that were not previously known from isogeny-based assumptions.

In addition, we also show that a homomorphic primitive with certain properties implies a cryptographic group action. We expand on our contributions in more details below.

Effective Group Action. We begin by introducing some new definitions for group actions endowed with hardness properties. Our first new definition is that of an *effective* group action (EGA). This models the standard notion of cryptographic group actions. Section 2 presents the formal definitions for effective group actions and the associated axioms of mathematical structure. While our definitions bear some resemblance to existing works, they are more amenable to cryptographic constructions in the post-quantum setting. Much of the early work on cryptographic group actions [BY91, Cou06] either predates the major advances in quantum cryptanalysis like Shor's algorithm [Sho97] or did not focus on post-quantum applications.

Suppose we consider a set X and a group G, with an associated group action $\star : G \times X \to X$. We informally define the following cryptographic effective group actions endowed with natural hardness properties:

- One-way EGA: given a pair of set elements $(x, g \star x)$ where $x \leftarrow X$ and $g \leftarrow G$ are sampled uniformly at random, there is no PPT adversary that can recover g.
- Weak Unpredictable EGA: given polynomially many tuples of the form $(x_i, g \star x_i)$ where $g \leftarrow G$ and each $x_i \leftarrow X$ are sampled uniformly at random, there is no PPT adversary that can compute $g \star x^*$ for a given challenge $x^* \leftarrow X$.
- Weak Pseudorandom EGA: there is no PPT adversary that can distinguish tuples of the form $(x_i, g \star x_i)$ from (x_i, u_i) where $g \leftarrow G$ and each $x_i, u_i \leftarrow X$ are sampled uniformly at random.

We also note that CSI-FiSh [BKV19] can be modeled as an effective group action defined above (plausibly as a weak pseudorandom effective group action).

Restricted Effective Group Action. Our definition of EGA does not capture isogeny-based assumptions such as CSIDH [CLM+18], where we cannot compute the group action operation $\star$ efficiently for all $g \in G$.

To address this, we introduce the notion of a *restricted* effective group action (REGA). The basic idea is the following: in an REGA, as we mentioned before, it is not possible to efficiently compute the group action $\star$ for all group elements $g \in G$: instead, the group action is efficiently computable for some small subset of G. Note that we can still "simulate" the effect of a general group action by computing the group action on a sequence of different elements from this subset. While restricted EGAs are considerably less efficient than EGAs with respect to certain applications, they present an easy-to-use abstraction for CSIDH and related assumptions. This makes REGAs useful for building cryptographic protocols from such assumptions. We note that REGAs can be endowed with the same hardness properties as EGAs (such as one-wayness, weak unpredictability, and weak pseudorandomness).

New Constructions. One of the main contribution of our paper is new constructions from our definition of (R)EGA, which can then be concretely instantiated from isogeny-based assumptions. We refer to Fig. 1 for an overview of our results. Specifically, we show the following constructions from any weak pseudorandom (R)EGA:

- Universal and smooth projective hashing, proposed by Cramer and Shoup [CS02], is a useful primitive with many applications, including CCA-secure PKE in the standard model [CS02], password authenticated key-exchange (PAKE) [GL03], privacy-preserving protocols [BPV12], and many others. We show how to construct a universal and smooth projective hash from any weak pseudorandom (R)EGA. To our knowledge, this is the first smooth projective hash function from isogeny-based assumptions. In particular, this also implies the first standard-model CCA-secure encryption scheme from isogenies. Previously known CCA-secure encryption schemes from group action based on isogenies [CLM+18] required random oracles.
- Dual-mode PKE, which was introduced in [PVW08], has numerous applications such as UC-secure round-optimal OT protocols in the common reference string model against actively corrupt receivers and senders. Such OT protocols are in turn sufficient to construct UC-secure round-optimal multi-party computation (MPC) protocols for general functionalities [GS18] in the same security model. In this work, we show how to build a dual-mode PKE from any weak pseudorandom (R)EGA. In particular, this implies the first round-optimal OT and MPC protocols from isogeny-based assumptions. Previously known constructions of OT from isogenies [BOB18, dOPS18, Vit19] were neither round optimal nor UC secure against active corruptions.
- We next show how to build two-message statistically sender-private OT (SSP-OT) [NP01] in the *plain model* from any weak pseudorandom (R)EGA. For this result, we rely on our construction of smooth projective hashing and techniques from [HK12]. This primitive has many cryptographic applications

such as non-malleable commitments [KS17], two-round witness indistinguishable proofs with private-coin verifier [JKKR17,BGI+17,KKS18], and three-message statistical receiver-private OT in the plain model [GJJM20]. To our knowledge, these primitives were not previously known from isogeny-based assumptions.

- We construct Naor-Reingold style PRFs from any weak pseudorandom (R)EGA. Our construction, when based on EGA (and not REGA), results in a PRF that requires a single group action operation. Our construction in the case of REGA requires a linear number of group action operations. This essentially follows from the efficiency restrictions inherent to our definitions of REGA.

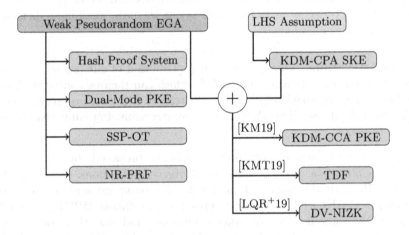

Fig. 1. Overview of our results and implications

Linear Hidden Shift Assumption. We introduce a new assumption over cryptographic group actions that we call the *Linear Hidden Shift* (LHS) assumption and we provide some discussions on its security. We describe the assumption informally below.

For a vector of group elements $\mathbf{g} \in G^n$ and a binary vector $\mathbf{s} \in \{0,1\}^n$, let $\langle \mathbf{g}, \mathbf{s} \rangle$ denote the subset product $\prod_{i=1}^n g_i^{s_i}$. Informally, the LHS assumption states that for any m that is polynomial in the security parameter, the following holds:

$$\{(x_i, \mathbf{g}_i, (\langle \mathbf{g}_i, \mathbf{s} \rangle) \star x_i)\}_{i \in [m]} \overset{c}{\approx} \{(x_i, \mathbf{g}_i, u_i)\}_{i \in [m]},$$

where $\mathbf{g}_i \leftarrow G^n$, $\mathbf{s} \leftarrow \{0,1\}^n$, $x_i \leftarrow X$ and $u_i \leftarrow X$ (all sampled independently).

The LHS assumption is sufficient to realize symmetric KDM-CPA secure encryption, and enables us to realize many cryptographic applications such as trapdoor functions and designated-verifier NIZK, which were previously not known from isogeny-based assumptions. We believe that the LHS assumption is of independent interest and may have other cryptographic applications.

We present some discussions o the security of the LHS assumption. In particular, we first show a *search to decision reduction*: namely, that the decision variant of the LHS assumption mentioned above is *equivalent* to its search variant, which states that no PPT adversary can recover the binary vector $\mathbf{s}$. Next, we show that in certain settings an additive variant of the LHS assumption is equivalent to the weak pseudorandom EGA if $G = \mathbb{Z}_N^*$ and the vectors $\mathbf{g}_i$ are sampled from a structured distribution. Based on this evidence, it appears likely that the LHS assumption holds with respect to some of the known group-action based isogenies.

KHwPRF and Cryptographic Group Actions. A key-homomorphic weak PRF (KHwPRF) [NPR99, BLMR13] is a generic primitive with algebraic structure and is known to imply many cryptosystems that we know how to build from the DDH assumption [AMPR19, AMP19]. We show that any KHwPRF with a *cyclic* output group implies a weak unpredictable group action.

On EGA and Homomorphic Primitives. Recent works [AMPR19, AMP19] have shown that generic primitives (such as weak PRFs) endowed with group homomorphisms imply a large class of cryptographic applications. A natural question to ask is whether such homomorphic primitives can be built in a generic manner from EGA/REGA? This does not seem likely in light of the fact that the authors of [AMP19] ruled out the existence of a few post-quantum secure primitives with "exact" homomorphisms over abelian groups.

This observation seems to have implications for the class of primitives that one can hope to build from EGA/REGA. One such primitive is collision-resistant hash function (CRHF). In particular, the main techniques we currently know of constructing CRHF from generic assumptions either rely on group homomorphism [IKO05] or one-way functions with certain properties [HL18]. This makes it difficult to realize CRHF from EGA/REGA by leveraging known techniques. Note that this does not apply to known constructions of CRHF from non-group-action based isogeny assumptions (such as [CLG09]), which are not covered by our framework.

1.5   Notation

For any positive integer n, we use $[n]$ to denote the set $\{1, \ldots, n\}$. We use λ for the security parameter. For a finite set S, we use $s \leftarrow S$ to sample uniformly from the set S. For a probability distribution $\mathcal{D}$ on a finite set S, we use $s \xleftarrow{s} \mathcal{D}$ to sample from $\mathcal{D}$. We use the notations $\overset{s}{\approx}$ and $\overset{c}{\approx}$ to denote statistical and computational indistinguishably, respectively. Finally, for random variables X and Y, $H_\infty(X|Y)$ denotes the min-entropy of X conditioned on Y.

1.6 Paper Outline

The rest of the paper is organized as follows. Section 2 introduces our group action-based framework and the definitions of EGA and REGA. Section 3 describes our construction of smooth projective hashing from weak pseudorandom EGA/REGA. Section 4 introduces the LHS assumption, presents some discussion on its security and shows how to construct symmetric KDM-secure encryption from it. Due to space constraints, the remaining material is presented in the full version of the paper.

2 Cryptographic Group Actions

In this section we present our definitions of cryptographic group actions. As we mentioned before, we use the definitions of Brassard and Yung [BY91] and Couveignes [Cou06] as starting points and aim to provide solid, modern definitions that allow for easy use of isogenies in cryptographic protocols. We begin by recalling the definition of a group action.

Definition 1. (Group Action) *A group G is said to act on a set X if there is a map $\star : G \times X \to X$ that satisfies the following two properties:*

1. *Identity: If e is the identity element of G, then for any $x \in X$, we have $e \star x = x$.*

2. *Compatibility: For any $g, h \in G$ and any $x \in X$, we have $(gh) \star x = g \star (h \star x)$.*

We may use the abbreviated notation $(G, X, \star)$ to denote a group action.

Remark 1. If $(G, X, \star)$ is a group action, for any $g \in G$ the map $\pi_g : x \mapsto g \star x$ defines a permutation of X.

Properties of Group Actions. We consider group actions that satisfy one or more of the following properties:

1. Transitive: A group action $(G, X, \star)$ is said to be *transitive* if for every $x_1, x_2 \in X$, there exists a group element $g \in G$ such that $x_2 = g \star x_1$. For such a transitive group action, the set X is called a *homogeneous space* for G.
2. Faithful: A group action $(G, X, \star)$ is said to be *faithful* if for each group element $g \in G$, either g is the identity element or there exists a set element $x \in X$ such that $x \neq g \star x$.
3. Free: A group action $(G, X, \star)$ is said to be *free* if for each group element $g \in G$, g is the identity element if and only if there exists some set element $x \in X$ such that $x = g \star x$.
4. Regular: A group action $(G, X, \star)$ is said to be *regular* if it is *both* free *and* transitive. For such a regular group action, the set X is called a *principal homogeneous space* for the group G, or a *G-torsor*.

Remark 2. Typically group action-based cryptography has focused on regular actions. If a group action is regular, then for any $x \in X$, the map $f_x : g \mapsto g \star x$ defines a bijection between G and X; in particular, if G (or X) is finite, then we must have $|G| = |X|$.

2.1 Effective Group Actions

We define an effective group action (EGA) as follows.

Definition 2. (Effective Group Action) *A group action* $(G, X, \star)$ *is* effective *if the following properties are satisfied:*

1. *The group G is finite and there exist efficient (PPT) algorithms for:*
   (a) *Membership testing, i.e., to decide if a given bit string represents a valid group element in G.*
   (b) *Equality testing, i.e., to decide if two bit strings represent the same group element in G.*
   (c) *Sampling, i.e., to sample an element g from a distribution $\mathcal{D}_G$ on G. In this paper, We consider distributions that are statistically close to uniform.*
   (d) *Operation, i.e., to compute gh for any $g, h \in G$.*
   (e) *Inversion, i.e., to compute g^{-1} for any $g \in G$.*
2. *The set X is finite and there exist efficient algorithms for:*
   (a) *Membership testing, i.e., to decide if a bit string represents a valid set element.*
   (b) *Unique representation, i.e., given any arbitrary set element $x \in X$, compute a string $\hat{x}$ that canonically represents x.*
3. *There exists a distinguished element $x_0 \in X$, called the* origin, *such that its bit-string representation is known.*
4. *There exists an efficient algorithm that given (some bit-string representations of) any $g \in G$ and any $x \in X$, outputs $g \star x$.*

Computational Assumptions. We define certain computational assumptions pertaining to group actions.

Definition 3. (One-Way Group Action) *A group action* $(G, X, \star)$ *is said to be* one-way *if the family of efficiently computable functions* $\{f_x : G \to X\}_{x \in X}$ *is one-way, where* $f_x : g \mapsto g \star x$.

Definition 4. (Weak Unpredictable Group Action) *A group action* $(G, X, \star)$ *is said to be* weakly unpredictable *if the family of (efficiently computable) permutations* $\{\pi_g : X \to X\}_{g \in G}$ *is weakly unpredictable, where* $\pi_g : x \mapsto g \star x$.

Definition 5. (Weak Pseudorandom Group Action) *A group action* $(G, X, \star)$ *is said to be* weakly pseudorandom *if the family of (efficiently computable) permutations* $\{\pi_g : X \to X\}_{g \in G}$ *is weakly pseudorandom, where* $\pi_g : x \mapsto g \star x$.

In the full version of the paper, we provide a more formal treatment by describing notions of one-wayness, weak unpredictability, and weak pseudorandomness that are additionally parameterized by distributions over the group G and the set X. One may view the aforementioned definitions as special cases, where both the distributions are assumed to be uniform (or statistically close to uniform).

In what follows, we will focus on group actions where G is abelian and the action is regular. We will characterize them by the computational assumption and their effectivity properties, and we assume that they are abelian and regular unless stated otherwise. Therefore, an OW-EGA/wU-EGA/wPR-EGA will be a one-way/weak unpredictable/weak pseudorandom abelian regular effective group action. Note that Couveignes used the terminology *Hard Homogeneous Space* for wU-EGA, and *Very Hard Homogeneous Space* for wPR-EGA [Cou06]; subsequent literature on isogeny-based cryptography has mostly followed his conventions [DKS18, CLM+18].

Generic Attacks. All known generic attacks against cryptographic group actions are attacks against the one-wayness. Given a pair $(x, g \star x)$, Stolbunov [Sto12] called the problem of finding g the *Group Action Inverse Problem (GAIP)*. The best known classical algorithm for GAIP is a meet-in-the-middle graph walk technique dating back to Pohl [Poh69], with a low-memory variant by Galbraith, Hess and Smart [GHS02], both running in time $O(\sqrt{|G|})$.

Childs, Jao, and Soukharev [CJS14] pointed out that GAIP can be formulated as a *hidden shift problem*, and thus it can be solved by Kuperberg's quantum algorithm and its variants [Kup05, Reg04, Kup13], provided a quantum oracle to evaluate the group action. All these algorithms have subexponential complexity between $\exp(\sqrt{\log N})$ and $L_N(1/2)$.

In the context of isogenies, there is a sizable literature on both classical and quantum attacks [Gal99, GS13, BIJ18, BS20, Pei20]. Little is known in terms of non-generic attacks: a recent result gives an attack against pseudorandomness which applies to some isogeny-based group actions, but not to CSIDH and related constructions [CSV20].

Alternative Axioms. In some circumstances, it is useful to strengthen or weaken the definition of EGA by slightly modifying the set of axioms. Here we list the most important variants.

- Uncertified EGA: Brassard and Yung [BY91] consider group actions without the *Set Membership Testing* axiom. They call *certified* those group actions that have *Set Membership Testing*, and *uncertified* those that do not. It is easy to construct examples of uncertified actions, see, e.g., [BY91, §6.2]. Here, unless otherwise stated, all actions will be certified.
- Hashable OW-EGA: In an OW-EGA, one can efficiently sample from X as follows: first sample $g \leftarrow \mathcal{D}_G$ using the *Group Sampling* axiom, then output $g \star x_0$. However in some applications it is useful to sample from X in a way that does not automatically reveal the group action inverse.
  In a *Hashable OW-EGA*, the existence of the *origin* x_0 is replaced with a *Hashing to the Set* axiom, stating that there exists an efficient sampler

$H : [N] \rightarrow X$ (where the integer N depends on the security parameter) such that for any adversary $\mathcal{A}$

$$\Pr[\mathcal{A}(i,j) \star H(i) = H(j)] \leq \mathrm{negl}(\lambda),$$

for $i, j \leftarrow [N]$.

2.2 Restricted Effective Group Actions

An EGA is a useful abstraction, but sometimes it is too powerful in comparison to what is achievable in practice. A *Restricted Effective Group Action* (REGA) is a weakening of EGA, where we can only evaluate the action of a generating set of small cardinality.

Definition 6. (Restricted Effective Group Action) *Let* $(G, X, \star)$ *be a group action and let* $\mathbf{g} = (g_1, \ldots, g_n)$ *be a (not necessarily minimal) generating set for* G. *The action is said to be* $\mathbf{g}$-*restricted effective, if the following properties are satisfied:*

- G *is finite and* $n = \mathrm{poly}(\log(|G|))$.
- *The set* X *is finite and there exist efficient algorithms for:*
    1. *Membership testing, i.e., to decide if a bit string represents a valid set element.*
    2. *Unique representation, i.e., to compute a string* $\hat{x}$ *that canonically represents any given set element* $x \in X$.
- *There exists a distinguished element* $x_0 \in X$, *called the* origin, *such that its bit-string representation is known.*
- *There exists an efficient algorithm that given any* $i \in [n]$ *and any bit string representation of* $x \in X$, *outputs* $g_i \star x$ *and* $g_i^{-1} \star x$.

Although an REGA is limited to evaluations of the form $g_i \star x$, this is actually enough to evaluate the action of many, and potentially all elements of G without even needing axioms on the effectivity of G.

A *word on* $(g_1, \ldots, g_n)$ is a finite sequence $\sigma \in \{g_1, \ldots, g_n, g_1^{-1}, \ldots, g_n^{-1}\}^*$, to which we canonically associate an element of G by

$$\sigma = \sigma_1 \sigma_2 \cdots \sigma_\ell \mapsto \prod_{i=1}^{\ell} \sigma_i.$$

By hypothesis, any element of G can be represented by a word on $\mathbf{g}$, however this representation may not be unique, nor equality needs to be efficiently testable. From the definition of a $\mathbf{g}$-REGA, it is clear that the action on $x \in X$ of any word of polynomial length on $\mathbf{g}$ can be computed in polynomial time.

When G is abelian, words on $\mathbf{g}$ can be rewritten as vectors in $\mathbb{Z}^n$, canonically mapped to G by

$$(a_1, \ldots, a_n) \mapsto \prod_{i=1}^{n} g_i^{a_i}.$$

It follows from the axioms of REGA that the action of a vector $\mathbf{a} \in \mathbb{Z}^n$ can be efficiently evaluated on any $x \in X$ as long as $\|\mathbf{a}\|$ is polynomial in $\log(|G|)$, where $\| \cdot \|$ is any L^p-norm.

Protocols built on REGA will need to sample elements from G that are statistically close to uniform and for which the group action is efficiently computable. Prior works suggest sampling from a distribution $\mathcal{D}_G$ on the words on $\mathbf{g}$ in the non-abelian case, or from a distribution on vectors in $\mathbb{Z}^n$ in the abelian case. Classic choices in the latter case are balls of fixed radius in L^∞-norm [CLM+18], in L^1-norm [NOTT20], in weighted infinity norms [Sto12, MR18], or discrete Gaussian distributions [DG19]. The latter is plausibly sufficient for applications that require group elements to be sampled from distributions statistically close to uniform [DG19].

2.3 Known-Order Effective Group Action

As a strengthening of EGA, we may assume that the group structure of G is known. By "known order" we mean that a minimal list of generators $\mathbf{g} = (g_1, \ldots, g_n)$ together with their orders $(m_1, \ldots, m_n)$ is known, which in turn is equivalent to a decomposition

$$G \simeq \mathbb{Z}_{m_1} \oplus \cdots \oplus \mathbb{Z}_{m_n}.$$

An important special case is when G is cyclic, i.e., $G = \langle g \rangle \simeq \mathbb{Z}/m\mathbb{Z}$.

Denote by $\mathcal{L}$ the lattice $m_1\mathbb{Z} \oplus \cdots \oplus m_n\mathbb{Z}$, the map $\phi : \mathbb{Z}^n/\mathcal{L} \to G$ defined as

$$(a_1, \ldots, a_n) \mapsto \prod_{i=1}^{n} g_i^{a_i}$$

is an effective isomorphism, its inverse being a generalized discrete logarithm. If $(G, X, \star)$ is an EGA, then it is easy to verify that $(\mathbb{Z}^n/\mathcal{L}, X, \star)$ is an EGA through ϕ. We may just use $\mathbb{Z}^n/\mathcal{L}$ as the standard representation for G.

Definition 7. (Known-order Effective Group Action) *A known-order effective group action (KEGA) is an EGA $(\mathbb{Z}^n/\mathcal{L}, X, \star)$ where the lattice $\mathcal{L}$ is given by the tuple $(m_1, \ldots, m_n)$.*

It may look like we "lose some cryptography" when we replace the group G by its isomorphic image $\mathbb{Z}^n/\mathcal{L}$. However, we stress that the main purpose of cryptography based on group actions is to design protocols that do not rely on discrete log assumptions. Thus, as soon as the group structure of G is known, KEGA is a more appropriate tool to design protocols, owing to its simplicity. For examples of protocols that require the KEGA setting, see [DM20].

Furthermore, KEGA and abelian EGA are quantumly equivalent. Indeed, given any abelian group G, Shor's algorithm and its generalization [Sho97, CM01] precisely compute an isomorphism $G \simeq \mathbb{Z}_{m_1} \oplus \cdots \oplus \mathbb{Z}_{m_n}$ (along with a minimal set of generators) in quantum polynomial time.

Remark 3. An REGA of known order is not automatically a KEGA, indeed the list of generators **g** of a REGA need not be minimal. As an extreme example, consider the case where $G = \langle g_1 \rangle$ is cyclic, and $\mathbf{g} = (g_1, \ldots, g_n)$. Any element of G can be uniquely represented as an integer in $\mathbb{Z}_{m_1}$, however this representation does not lead to an efficiently computable group action. What is needed is an efficient algorithm to convert between the "minimal" representation $G \simeq \mathbb{Z}/\mathcal{L}$, and products of small powers of $(g_1, \ldots, g_n)$. In some instances, this conversion is possible via lattice reduction techniques [BKV19].

3 Hash Proof System

In this section, we demonstrate how to construct universal and smooth projective hashing schemes (also known as hash proof systems or projective hash functions) from any weak pseudorandom effective group action. We begin by recalling the definition of a universal projective hashing scheme as in [CS02].

Definition 8. (Universal Projective Hashing) *Let $\Lambda : K \times \Sigma \to \Gamma$ be an efficiently computable function, and let $L \subset \Sigma$. In addition, let $\alpha : K \to P$ be a "projection" function. We say that the tuple $\Pi = (\Lambda, K, P, \Sigma, \Gamma, L)$ is a universal projective hash function if the following properties hold:*

- **Samplability:** *There exist efficient algorithms to sample uniformly from Σ and from K. In addition, there exists an efficient algorithm to sample uniformly from L along with a witness w that proves membership in L.*
- **Subset Membership Problem:** *If $\sigma_0 \leftarrow L$ and $\sigma_1 \leftarrow \Sigma$ then $\sigma_0 \overset{c}{\approx} \sigma_1$.*
- **Projective Evaluation:** *There exists an efficient algorithm* ProjEval *such that for any* hk $\in K$ *and any* $\sigma \in L$ *with membership witness w, we have*

$$\mathsf{ProjEval}(\alpha(\mathsf{hk}), w) = \Lambda(\mathsf{hk}, \sigma).$$

- **Universality:** *Π is said to be ε-universal if for any $\sigma \in \Sigma \setminus L$, if* hk $\leftarrow K$ *it holds that*

$$H_\infty\big(\Lambda(\mathsf{hk}, \sigma) \,\big|\, (\alpha(\mathsf{hk}), \sigma)\big) \geq \log(\varepsilon^{-1}).$$

Universality$_2$ and Smoothness. We also recall two stronger notions of security for projective hash proof systems, namely universality$_2$ and smoothness, as described in [CS02].

- Universality$_2$: A hash proof system $\Pi = (\Lambda, K, P, \Sigma, \Gamma, L)$ is said to be ε-universal$_2$ if for any $\sigma, \sigma^* \in \Sigma$ such that $\sigma \in \Sigma \setminus (L \cup \{\sigma^*\})$, if hk $\leftarrow K$ it holds that

$$H_\infty\big(\Lambda(\mathsf{hk}, \sigma) \,\big|\, (\alpha(\mathsf{hk}), \sigma, \sigma^*, \Lambda(\mathsf{hk}, \sigma^*))\big) \geq \log(\varepsilon^{-1}).$$

- Smoothness: A hash proof system $\Pi = (\Lambda, K, P, \Sigma, \Gamma, L)$ is said to be smooth if for any $\sigma \in \Sigma \setminus L$, if hk $\leftarrow K$ and $\gamma \leftarrow \Gamma$ it holds that

$$\big(\alpha(\mathsf{hk}), \sigma, \Lambda(\mathsf{hk}, \sigma)\big) \approx_s \big(\alpha(\mathsf{hk}), \sigma, \gamma\big).$$

We now show how to construct a universal hash proof system from any weak pseudorandom EGA.

Construction. Let $(G, X, \star)$ be a weak pseudorandom EGA and let $\ell = \omega(\log \lambda)$ be an integer. Additionally, let $\bar{x}_0 \leftarrow X$ and $\bar{x}_1 \leftarrow X$ be publicly available set elements. We define the input space Σ as

$$\Sigma = \left\{ (x_0, x_1) \in X^2 : \exists (g_0, g_1) \in G^2 \text{ s.t. } x_0 = g_0 \star \bar{x}_0, \; x_1 = g_1 \star \bar{x}_1 \right\}.$$

By the regularity of the group action, this is equivalent to defining $\Sigma = X^2$. We also define the subset $L \subset \Sigma$ as

$$L = \left\{ (x_0, x_1) \in X^2 : \exists g \in G \text{ s.t. } x_0 = g \star \bar{x}_0, \; x_1 = g \star \bar{x}_1 \right\},$$

where the group element g is the witness for membership in L. In addition, we let $\Gamma = X^\ell$ and $K = G^\ell \times \{0, 1\}^\ell$, and we define the hash function $\Lambda : K \times \Sigma \to \Gamma$ to be

$$\Lambda\big((\mathbf{h}, \mathbf{b}), (x_0, x_1)\big) = (h_1 \star x_{b_1}, \ldots, h_\ell \star x_{b_\ell}),$$

where $\mathbf{h} = (h_1, \ldots, h_\ell)$ and $\mathbf{b} = (b_1, \ldots, b_\ell)$. We set the projection space to be $P = X^\ell$, and we define the projection function $\alpha : K \to P$ as

$$\alpha(\mathbf{h}, \mathbf{b}) = (h_1 \star \bar{x}_{b_1}, \ldots, h_\ell \star \bar{x}_{b_\ell}).$$

Subset Membership Problem. We state and prove the following lemma.

Lemma 1. *If $(G, X, \star)$ is a weak pseudorandom EGA, we have $\sigma_0 \overset{c}{\approx} \sigma_1$ where $\sigma_0 \leftarrow L$ and $\sigma_1 \leftarrow \Sigma$.*

Proof. By the weak pseudorandomness of group action we have

$$(\bar{x}_0, \bar{x}_1, g \star \bar{x}_0, g \star \bar{x}_1) \overset{c}{\approx} (\bar{x}_0, \bar{x}_1, x_0, x_1),$$

where $g \leftarrow G$ and $\bar{x}_1, x_0, x_1$ are all sampled uniformly and independently from X. It is easy to see that the "left" tuple corresponds to a uniformly sampled member $\sigma_0 \in L$ and the "right" tuple corresponds to a uniformly sampled element $\sigma_1 \in \Sigma$ (because the action is regular), as required.

Projective Evaluation. We define $\mathsf{ProjEval} : X^\ell \times G \to X^\ell$ as

$$\mathsf{ProjEval}(\mathbf{y}, g) = (g \star y_1, \ldots, g \star y_\ell),$$

where $\mathbf{y} = (y_1, \ldots, y_\ell)$ and g is the witness. Let $(x_0, x_1) = (g \star \bar{x}_0, g \star \bar{x}_1)$ be a member of L with witness g, and let $\mathbf{y} = \alpha(\mathbf{h}, \mathbf{b})$ for some hash key $(\mathbf{h}, \mathbf{b}) \in K$. The algorithm $\mathsf{ProjEval}$ satisfies the projective evaluation property by observing that

$$
\begin{aligned}
\mathsf{ProjEval}\big(\alpha(\mathbf{h}, \mathbf{b}), g\big) &= (g \star y_1, \ldots, g \star y_\ell) \\
&= (g \star (h_1 \star \bar{x}_{b_1}), \ldots, g \star (h_\ell \star \bar{x}_{b_\ell})) \\
&= (h_1 \star (g \star \bar{x}_{b_1}), \ldots, h_\ell \star (g \star \bar{x}_{b_\ell})) \\
&= (h_1 \star x_{b_1}, \ldots, h_\ell \star x_{b_\ell}) \\
&= \Lambda\big((\mathbf{h}, \mathbf{b}), (x_0, x_1)\big).
\end{aligned}
$$

Universality. We now establish the universality property (as defined in [CS02]) via the following lemma.

Lemma 2. *If $(G, X, \star)$ is a weak pseudorandom EGA, then the projective hash function is $2^{-\ell}$-universal.*

Proof. Let $(x_0, x_1) \in \Sigma \setminus L$ be an arbitrary non-member, and let $(\mathbf{h}, \mathbf{b}) \leftarrow K$ be a randomly chosen hash key. We need to show that

$$H_\infty\big(\Lambda((\mathbf{h}, \mathbf{b}), (x_0, x_1))\big|(\bar{x}_0, \bar{x}_1, x_0, x_1, \alpha(\mathbf{h}, \mathbf{b}))\big) = \ell.$$

First, observe that there exists $g_0 \neq g_1$ such that $(x_0, x_1) = (g_0 \star \bar{x}_0, g_1 \star \bar{x}_1)$ because $(x_0, x_1) \notin L$. In addition, let $\mathbf{y} = \alpha(\mathbf{h}, \mathbf{b})$, i.e., for each $i \in [\ell]$ we have $y_i = h_i \star \bar{x}_{b_i}$. By the regularity of the group action, for each $i \in [\ell]$ there exists $d_{i,0} \in G$ and $d_{i,1} \in G$ such that

$$d_{i,0} \star \bar{x}_0 = d_{i,1} \star \bar{x}_1 = y_i.$$

In other words, given the tuple $(\bar{x}_0, \bar{x}_1, x_0, x_1, y_i)$, the bit b_i in the hash-key component (h_i, b_i) has full entropy. On the other hand, we have

$$h_i \star x_{b_i} = h_i \star (g_{b_i} \star \bar{x}_{b_i}) = g_{b_i} \star (h_i \star \bar{x}_{b_i}) = g_{b_i} \star y_i.$$

Since $g_0 \neq g_1$, it follows that given the tuple $(\bar{x}_0, \bar{x}_1, x_0, x_1, y_i)$, the set element $h_i \star x_{b_i} = g_{b_i} \star y_i$ has one bit of entropy (even in the view of a computationally unbounded adversary). By extending the same argument, we get

$$H_\infty\big(\{h_i \star x_{b_i}\}_{i \in [\ell]}\big|(\bar{x}_0, \bar{x}_1, x_0, x_1, \{y_i\}_{i \in [\ell]})\big) = \ell,$$

as desired. This completes the proof of Lemma 2.

The aforementioned lemmas yield the following theorem.

Theorem 1. *There exists a construction of a $2^{-\ell}$-universal projective hash function for any $\ell > 0$ from any weak pseudorandom EGA.*

Remark 4. Our construction and proof work in essentially the same way from a restricted EGA provided that we can sample group elements from a distribution that is *statistically* close to uniform over the group G while retaining the ability to efficiently compute the action. We note that this is plausibly the case with respect to the instantiation of restricted EGA from CSIDH and other similar isogeny-based assumptions (see [DG19] for more details).

Remark 5. In the aforementioned description of the HPS scheme, the hardness of the language membership problem crucially relies on the fact that the group element h such that $x_1 = h \star x_0$ is computationally hidden from the adversary. Note that most applications of HPS typically assume a trusted setup. For applications that necessarily require an untrusted setup, our proposed HPS can still be used, albeit from a hashable EGA.

Universal₂ and Smooth Projective Hashing. Based on known reductions from Section 2.1 of [CS02], Theorem 1 implies the following corollary.

Corollary 1. *Let* $(G, X, \star)$ *be any weak pseudorandom EGA. Assuming the existence of an injective function* $f : X^\ell \to \{0,1\}^m$ *for some* $m = \omega(\log \lambda)$ *and the existence of a pairwise independent hash function* $H : X^\ell \to \{0,1\}$ *for some* $\ell = \omega(\log \lambda)$, *there exists a* $2^{-\ell}$-universal₂ *projective hash function and a smooth projective hash function, respectively.*

Further Applications. Universal₂ and smooth projective hashing imply CCA-secure PKE [CS02]. In addition, smooth projective hashing additionally implies password authenticated key-exchange [GL03], privacy-preserving protocols [BPV12], and many other cryptographic primitives. Hence, our construction allows all of these primitives to be constructed from any weak pseudorandom (R)EGA.

4   Linear Hidden Shift (LHS) Assumption

In this section we introduce a hardness assumption called Linear Hidden Shift (LHS) problem and describe its cryptographic applications.

Notation. Unless stated otherwise, we use $+$ to denote the group operation, and we assume that e denotes the identity element of the group. For a binary vector $\mathbf{s} \in \{0,1\}^n$ and a group element $h \in G$, we use $h \cdot \mathbf{s}$ to denote a vector of group elements whose ith component is $s_i \cdot h$. For a vector of group elements $\mathbf{g} \in G^n$ and a binary vector $\mathbf{s} \in \{0,1\}^n$, we use $\langle \mathbf{g}, \mathbf{s} \rangle$ to denote $s_1 \cdot g_1 + \cdots + s_n \cdot g_n$ where $+$ denotes the group operation (we remark that although the notation resembles an inner product, we do *not* necessarily have an inner product space).

Given a group action $\star : G \times X \to X$, the action naturally extends to the direct product group G^n for any positive integer n. So if $\mathbf{g} \in G^n$ and $\mathbf{x} \in X^n$ are two vectors of group elements and set elements respectively, we use $\mathbf{g} \star \mathbf{x}$ to denote a vector of set element whose ith component is $g_i \star x_i$.

Below, we formally state the search and decision versions of the assumption. Later, we show a simple *search to decision* reduction for the LHS assumption.

Definition 9. (Search Linear Hidden Shift) *Let* $\star : G \times X \to X$ *be a regular group action, and let* $n = \text{poly}(\lambda)$ *be a parameter. We say that (search) LHS problem is hard over* $(G, X, \star)$ *if for any* $m = \text{poly}(\lambda)$ *and for any PPT attacker* $\mathcal{A}$, *we have*

$$\Pr\left[\mathcal{A}\Big(\big\{(x_i, \mathbf{g}_i, (\langle \mathbf{g}_i, \mathbf{s} \rangle) \star x_i)\big\}_{i \in [m]}\Big) \text{ outputs } \mathbf{s}\right] \leq \text{negl}(\lambda),$$

where $\mathbf{g}_i \leftarrow G^n$, $\mathbf{s} \leftarrow \{0,1\}^n$, $x_i \leftarrow X$ *(all sampled independently), and the probability is taken over all random coins in the experiment.*

Definition 10. (Decision Linear Hidden Shift) *Let* $\star : G \times X \to X$ *be a group action, and let* $n = \text{poly}(\lambda)$ *be a parameter. We say that LHS assumption holds over* $(G, X, \star)$ *if for any* $m = \text{poly}(\lambda)$ *we have*

$$\{(x_i, \mathbf{g}_i, (\langle \mathbf{g}_i, \mathbf{s} \rangle) \star x_i)\}_{i \in [m]} \quad \overset{c}{\approx} \quad \{(x_i, \mathbf{g}_i, u_i)\}_{i \in [m]},$$

where $\mathbf{g}_i \leftarrow G^n$, $\mathbf{s} \leftarrow \{0,1\}^n$, $x_i \leftarrow X$ *and* $u_i \leftarrow X$ *(all sampled independently).*

We naturally extend the notation $\langle \mathbf{g}, \mathbf{s} \rangle$ to matrices, i.e., for a matrix $\mathbf{M} \in G^{n \times \ell}$ and a binary vector $\mathbf{s} \in \{0,1\}^n$, we use $\mathbf{s}^t \mathbf{M}$ to denote a vector whose ith component is $\langle \mathbf{m}_i, \mathbf{s} \rangle$ where $\mathbf{m}_i$ is the ith column of $\mathbf{M}$.

Search to Decision Reduction. Using the notation described above the search LHS problem can be stated as the problem of recovering $\mathbf{s}$ given a tuple of the form $(\mathbf{x}, \mathbf{M}, \mathbf{Ms} \star \mathbf{x})$ where $\mathbf{x} \leftarrow X^n$ and $\mathbf{M} \leftarrow G^{m \times n}$. Similarly, the decision LHS problem states that

$$(\mathbf{x}, \mathbf{M}, \mathbf{Ms} \star \mathbf{x}) \quad \overset{c}{\approx} \quad (\mathbf{x}, \mathbf{M}, \mathbf{u}),$$

where $\mathbf{u} \leftarrow X^n$ and $m \gg n$. Now we show a simple search to decision reduction for LHS problem, which is similar to the reductions in [IN96, MM11] for (generalized) knapsack functions.

Lemma 3. (Search to Decision) *Let* $\mathcal{A}$ *be a distinguisher that distinguishes between LHS samples of the form* $(\mathbf{x}, \mathbf{M}, \mathbf{Ms} \star \mathbf{x})$ *and all-random tuple with probability* $1 - \text{negl}(\lambda)$. *There exists a PPT attacker* $\mathcal{A}'$ *that recovers* $\mathbf{s}$ *from an instance of search LHS problem with probability* $1 - \text{negl}(\lambda)$.

Proof. Given an instance of a search problem $(\mathbf{x}, \mathbf{M}, \mathbf{y})$ where $\mathbf{y} = \mathbf{Ms} \star \mathbf{x}$ for some (unknown) vector $\mathbf{s}$, the attacker $\mathcal{A}'$ does the following for each $i \in [n]$: it samples a column vector $\mathbf{r} \leftarrow G^m$, and let $\mathbf{R}_i$ be a matrix whose ith column is $\mathbf{r}$ while *all other* columns are identical to the corresponding columns of $\mathbf{M}$ (so $\mathbf{R}_i$ and $\mathbf{M}$ only differ in the ith column). $\mathcal{A}'$ runs $\mathcal{A}$ on the tuple $(\mathbf{x}, \mathbf{R}_i, \mathbf{y})$. If $\mathcal{A}$ outputs "LHS samples," $\mathcal{A}'$ sets s_i to be zero. Otherwise, $\mathcal{A}'$ sets s_i to be 1.

Observe that if s_i were zero, then $(\mathbf{x}, \mathbf{R}_i, \mathbf{y})$ is distributed as LHS samples because $\mathbf{R}_i \mathbf{s} = \mathbf{Ms}$. On the other hand, if $s_i = 1$ then $(\mathbf{x}, \mathbf{R}_i, \mathbf{y})$ is a random tuple because the action is regular and hence the distribution of $\mathbf{R}_i \mathbf{s} \star \mathbf{x}$ is uniform and independent of $\mathbf{y}$.

Remark 6. We note that the reduction above also works if the group action is *restricted* (where we can only evaluate the action of a set of small cardinality), provided that it is possible to sample a group element from a distribution that is statistically close to uniform.

4.1   Symmetric KDM-CPA Security from LHS

We describe a *symmetric* encryption scheme that satisfies KDM-CPA security (for projection functions) based on the LHS assumption. Our construction follows the blueprint of [BHHO08]. Let $\star : G \times X \to X$ be a group action such that LHS holds. We assume that all parties have access to a *public fixed* non-identity group element $h \in G$. Our construction of symmetric-key bit encryption $\Pi = (\mathsf{Gen}, \mathsf{Enc}, \mathsf{Dec})$ scheme is as follows:

- $\mathsf{Gen}(1^\lambda)$: To generate a secret key, sample a binary vector $\mathbf{s} \leftarrow \{0,1\}^n$.
- $\mathsf{Enc}(\mathbf{s}, b \in \{0,1\})$: Sample $\mathbf{g} \leftarrow G^n$, $x \leftarrow X$, and output

$$\mathsf{ct} = \big(x, \mathbf{g}, (b \cdot h + \langle \mathbf{g}, \mathbf{s} \rangle) \star x\big).$$

- $\mathsf{Dec}(\mathbf{s}, \mathsf{ct} = (x, \mathbf{g}, y))$: Output 0 if $y = \langle \mathbf{g}, \mathbf{s} \rangle \star x$, otherwise output 1.

Lemma 4. *The scheme Π above is CPA secure.*

Proof. We sketch a simple proof. Notice that a tuple of $m = \mathrm{poly}(\lambda)$ ciphertexts encrypting m (arbitrary) bits $\{b_i\}_{i \in [m]}$ in the scheme above has the form $\{x_i, \mathbf{g}_i, (b_i \cdot h) \star y_i\}_{i \in [m]}$ where $\{x_i, \mathbf{g}_i, y_i\}_{i \in [m]}$ are LHS samples. Therefore, by the LHS assumption we have

$$\{x_i, \mathbf{g}_i, (b_i \cdot h) \star y_i\}_{i \in [m]} \quad \overset{c}{\approx} \quad \{x_i, \mathbf{g}_i, (b_i \cdot h) \star u_i\}_{i \in [m]},$$

where each u_i is a random set element. It follows that encryptions of $\{b_i\}_{i \in [m]}$ are indistinguishable from a (truly) random tuple, as required.

Lemma 5. *The scheme Π is KDM secure with respect to projection functions.*

Proof. Observe that encryptions of all bits of the secret key have the form $(\mathbf{x}, \mathbf{M}, (\mathbf{Ms} + h \cdot \mathbf{s}) \star \mathbf{x})$, where $\mathbf{x} \leftarrow X^n$, $\mathbf{M} \leftarrow G^{n \times n}$ and the action is applied componentwise. By a simple rearrangement we have

$$\big(\mathbf{x}, \mathbf{M}, (\mathbf{Ms} + h \cdot \mathbf{s}) \star \mathbf{x}\big) = \big(\mathbf{x}, \mathbf{M}, (\mathbf{M} + h \cdot \mathbf{I})\mathbf{s} \star \mathbf{x}\big).$$

Similarly, it is straightforward to see that encryptions of $\{1 - s_i\}_{i \in [n]}$ have the form

$$(\mathbf{x}', \mathbf{M}', (\mathbf{M}'\mathbf{s} + h \cdot (1 - \mathbf{s})) \star \mathbf{x}'),$$

where $\mathbf{1}$ is the all-one vector. By a simple rearrangement we have

$$\big(\mathbf{x}', \mathbf{M}', (\mathbf{M}'\mathbf{s} + h \cdot (1 - \mathbf{s})) \star \mathbf{x}'\big) = \big(\mathbf{x}', \mathbf{M}', [(\mathbf{M}' - h \cdot \mathbf{I})\mathbf{s} + h \cdot \mathbf{1}] \star \mathbf{x}'\big).$$

Clearly, if $\mathbf{M}$ (resp., $\mathbf{M}'$) is a uniform matrix, then $\mathbf{M}_1 := \mathbf{M} + h \cdot \mathbf{I}$ (resp., $\mathbf{M}_2 := \mathbf{M}' - h \cdot \mathbf{I}$) is also a uniform matrix. Given $2n$ samples of LHS challenges of the form $\{(\mathbf{x}_j, \mathbf{M}_j, \mathbf{y}_j)\}_{j \in [2]}$ where either $\{\mathbf{y}_j = \mathbf{M}_j \mathbf{s} \star \mathbf{x}_j\}_{j \in [2]}$ or $\{\mathbf{y}_j\}_{j \in [2]}$ are truly random vectors of set elements, the reduction simulates encryptions of projection functions of the secret key by computing $(\mathbf{x}_1, \mathbf{M}_1 - h \cdot \mathbf{I}, \mathbf{y}_1)$ and $(\mathbf{x}_2, \mathbf{M}_2 + h \cdot \mathbf{I}, (h \cdot \mathbf{1}) \star \mathbf{y}_2)$. By the LHS assumption it follows that

$$\left(\mathbf{x}, \mathbf{M}, (\mathbf{M} + h \cdot \mathbf{I})\mathbf{s} \star \mathbf{x}\right) \overset{c}{\approx} (\mathbf{x}, \mathbf{M}, \mathbf{u}),$$

$$\left(\mathbf{x}', \mathbf{M}', (\mathbf{M}'\mathbf{s} + h \cdot (\mathbf{1} - \mathbf{s})) \star \mathbf{x}'\right) \overset{c}{\approx} (\mathbf{x}', \mathbf{M}', \mathbf{u}'),$$

where $\mathbf{u} \leftarrow X^n$ and $\mathbf{u}' \leftarrow X^n$ are uniform vectors of set elements. Therefore, encryptions of all projection functions of secret key are indistinguishable from tuples of truly random elements. On the other hand, by Lemma 4 we know that encryptions of zero are indistinguishable from truly random tuples. It follows that

$$\left(\{\mathsf{Enc}(\mathbf{s}, s_i)\}_{i \in [n]}, \{\mathsf{Enc}(\mathbf{s}, 1 - s_i)\}_{i \in [n]}\right) \overset{c}{\approx} \{\mathsf{Enc}(\mathbf{s}, 0)\}_{i \in [2n]},$$

as required. Indistinguishability of multiple encryptions of a projection function of the secret key from random tuples follows from a standard hybrid argument, and the proof is complete.

Instantiation from Restricted EGA. Notice that the reduction above does *not* work in case of a *restricted* EGA because the relation lattice (i.e., the group structure) is not known. However, it is possible to show that an alternative version of the scheme described above is KDM-CPA secure in case of a restricted EGA (for which the LHS assumption holds). Therefore, it is possible to realize symmetric KDM-CPA encryption from a *restricted* EGA provided that we can sample group elements from a distribution over the group G that is statistically close to uniform while retaining the ability to compute the action efficiently. Note that this is plausibly true for the restricted EGAs implied by CSIDH and other similar isogeny-based assumptions [DG19].

- $\mathsf{Gen}(1^\lambda)$: To generate a secret key, sample a binary vector $\mathbf{s} \leftarrow \{0,1\}^n$.
- $\mathsf{Enc}(\mathbf{s}, b \in \{0,1\})$: Sample $\mathbf{g} \leftarrow G^n$, $x \leftarrow X$, and $u \leftarrow X$. If $b = 0$, output the ciphertext $\mathsf{ct} = (x, \mathbf{g}, \langle \mathbf{g}, \mathbf{s} \rangle \star x)$. Otherwise, output $\mathsf{ct} = (x, \mathbf{g}, u)$.
- $\mathsf{Dec}(\mathbf{s}, \mathsf{ct} = (x, \mathbf{g}, y))$: Output 0 if $y = \langle \mathbf{g}, \mathbf{s} \rangle \star x$, otherwise output 1.

Lemma 6. *If $(G, X, \star)$ is a restricted EGA that satisfies the LHS assumption, the construction above is KDM-CPA secure.*

Proof. Observe that an encryption of 0 corresponds to an LHS sample while an encryption of 1 corresponds to a random tuple, so it is easy to see that the construction above is CPA secure based on the LHS assumption. The argument for KDM security is quite similar to the search to decision reduction for the LHS assumption (Lemma 4), and hence we omit the details.

Implications. Using the general amplification of [App14], one can transform a symmetric-key KDM-secure scheme (with respect to projection functions) to a symmetric-key KDM-secure scheme with respect to circuits of a priori bounded size. Therefore, one can construct a symmetric-key KDM-secure scheme (with respect to bounded circuits) based on the LHS assumption. In a recent work, Lombardi *et al.* [LQR+19] showed a construction of reusable designated-verifier NIZK (DV-NIZK) argument for NP assuming *any* PKE and a symmetric-key KDM-secure scheme. Hence, any PKE along with the LHS assumption implies reusable DV-NIZK arguments for NP.

In the same vein, Kitagawa and Matsuda [KM19] showed a construction of KDM-CCA PKE assuming PKE, DV-NIZK, and symmetric-key KDM security with respect to projection functions. Therefore, any PKE along with the LHS assumption implies KDM-CCA PKE.

Furthermore, Kitagawa *et al.* [KMT19] showed a construction of trapdoor function (with adaptive one-wayness) from a randomness-recovering symmetric-key KDM-secure scheme and a PKE scheme with pseudorandom ciphertexts. By plugging in their result, we obtain trapdoor functions with adaptive one-wayness based the LHS assumption and any wPR-(R)EGA.

Remark 7. We note that although our definition of the LHS assumption uses a fresh x_i per each sample, almost all of the results in this section would still be valid if we use a fixed (but randomly chosen) $x \in X$ across all LHS samples.

4.2   On the Security of LHS Assumption

In what follows we provide some insights on the security of the LHS assumption. We consider an additive variant of the LHS assumption, which we call it LHS(+), where $G = \mathbb{Z}_N^*$ and the product term $\mathbf{Ms}$ is computed by a *subset sum* over the columns of $\mathbf{M}$. We show that in this setting the LHS assumption is equivalent to the weak pseudorandomness for (effective) group actions provided that $\mathbf{M}$ is a structured matrix. We describe an attack that breaks the search/decision LHS assumption in certain settings, and explain how such attacks can be avoided.

LHS(+) Assumption. Let $(G, X, \star)$ be an EGA such that $G = \mathbb{Z}_N^*$ and $\varphi(N)/N \geq 1 - \text{negl}(\lambda)$. Consider the following *additive* variant of the LHS assumption

$$(\mathbf{x}, \mathbf{M}, \mathbf{Ms} \star \mathbf{x}) \overset{c}{\approx} (\mathbf{x}, \mathbf{Ms}, \mathbf{u}),$$

where $\mathbf{Ms}$ is computed over $(\mathbb{Z}_N, +)$, i.e., subset sum over the columns of $\mathbf{M}$ modulo N. We show that if $\mathbf{M}$ is a structured "rank" 1 matrix (instead of a uniformly chosen matrix), the additive LHS assumption is equivalent to the weak pseudorandomness of the $(G, X, \star)$.

Let $\overline{\mathbf{M}} = \mathbf{a} \otimes \mathbf{b}$ where $\mathbf{a} \leftarrow \mathbb{Z}_N^m$ and $\mathbf{b} \leftarrow \mathbb{Z}_N^n$ are two randomly chosen vectors of group elements and $\otimes$ denotes the "tensor product" with respect to $\mathbb{Z}_N^*$. To put it differently, the ij^{th} entry of $\overline{\mathbf{M}}$ is equal to $a_i \cdot b_j$ where $\cdot$ denotes the multiplication modulo N. First, observe that $\overline{\mathbf{M}}\mathbf{s} = \mathbf{a} \otimes b^*$ where $b^* = \mathbf{b}^t\mathbf{s}$.

In addition, if n is an integer such that $n > \log(N) + \omega(\log(\lambda))$, then by the leftover hash lemma b^* is distributed uniformly and independent of others. Furthermore, given any $\mathbf{M}$ with the aforementioned structure, one can compute two vectors $\mathbf{a}$ and $\mathbf{b}$ such that $\mathbf{M} = \mathbf{a} \otimes \mathbf{b}$. Consider the rows of LHS(+) assumption, which have the following form:

$$(x_1, a_1 \otimes \mathbf{b}, (a_1 \cdot b^*) \star x_1),$$
$$(x_2, a_2 \otimes \mathbf{b}, (a_2 \cdot b^*) \star x_2),$$
$$\vdots$$
$$(x_m, a_m \otimes \mathbf{b}, (a_m \cdot b^*) \star x_m).$$

For each $i \in [m]$, compute $y_i = a_i \star x_i$. So, given an instance of the LHS(+) problem one can compute the following:

$$(y_1, b^* \star y_1), (y_2, b^* \star y_2), \ldots, (y_m, b^* \star y_m).$$

Therefore, LHS(+) assumption is equivalent to the weak pseudorandomness for EGA in the aforementioned setting (the proof for the other direction is similar).

Attacks on LHS. To analyze the quantum security of LHS assumption, it is reasonable to assume that discrete logarithms are easy in the group G. Then, the LHS problem becomes essentially a linear algebra one. For example, if G is cyclic of order q, we can rewrite all elements of G as their discrete log to a fixed basis, the subset product $\langle \mathbf{g}, \mathbf{s} \rangle$ becomes the standard inner product over $(\mathbb{Z}_q)^n$, and LHS becomes similar to LWE [Reg05], with the main difference that the algebraic structure is hidden by the group action, rather than by noise.

It is then evident that both decision and search LHS can be solved by breaking the one-wayness of the group action, recovering a list of tuples $(\mathbf{a}_i, \langle \mathbf{a}_i, \mathbf{s} \rangle)$, and then using linear algebra over $\mathbb{Z}_q$. The same blueprint also applies to non-cyclic groups. To the best of our knowledge, this is the most efficient generic attack on the LHS assumption.

However, some instantiations may offer easier paths to attack LHS: isogenies are an interesting example. The recent work of Castryck, Sotáková and Vercauteren [CSV20] shows that some instantiations of group actions from isogenies are not pseudorandom EGAs. While it is not evident how breaking pseudorandomness could help solve LHS, their technique is actually more powerful. Indeed, it provides an efficient algorithm to compute some quadratic characters of the group G, directly on its isomorphic representation on X. More precisely, for a fixed quadratic character χ of the class group $\mathrm{Cl}(\mathcal{O})$, on input a pair $(x, y) \in X^2$ such that $y = g \star x$, their algorithm outputs $\chi(g) = \pm 1$.

We can use this algorithm to solve LHS as follows. Define $f : G \to \{0, 1\}$ as $f = (1 - \chi)/2$. For any tuple $(x_i, \mathbf{g}_i = (g_i^{(1)}, \ldots, g_i^{(n)}), \langle \mathbf{g}_i, \mathbf{s} \rangle \star x_i)$ we compute the following

$$\left(f(g_i^{(1)}), \ldots, f(g_i^{(n)}), f(\langle \mathbf{g}_i, \mathbf{s} \rangle)\right).$$

After we collect enough tuples, we obtain a linear system over $\mathbb{Z}_2$, which we solve to recover $\mathbf{s}$. This is analogous to the attack on the discrete logarithm equivalent of LHS using Legendre symbols, and applies to any other group action where the group G has low order characters which can be "read" on X.

Castryck *et al.*'s attack does not apply against CSIDH, because the class group associated to it has no quadratic characters. Even for instantiations where class groups do have quadratic characters, e.g., isogeny schemes based on ordinary elliptic curves, it is easy to block the attack by restricting G to the subgroup of squares inside $\mathrm{Cl}\,(\mathcal{O})$.

References

[AAB+19]   Arute, F., et al.: Quantum supremacy using a programmable superconducting processor. Nature **574**(7779), 505–510 (2019)

[Aar13]   Aaronson, S.: Quantum Computing Since Democritus. Cambridge University Press, Cambridge (2013)

[AASA+19]   Alagic, G., et al.: Status report on the first round of the NIST postquantum cryptography standardization process. US Department of Commerce, National Institute of Standards and Technology (2019)

[AKC+17]   Azarderakhsh, R., et al.: Supersingular Isogeny Key Encapsulation, Vladimir Soukharev (2017)

[AMP19]   Alamati, N., Montgomery, H., Patranabis, S.: Symmetric primitives with structured secrets. In: Boldyreva, A., Micciancio, D. (eds.) CRYPTO 2019, Part I. LNCS, vol. 11692, pp. 650–679. Springer, Cham (2019). https://doi.org/10.1007/978-3-030-26948-7_23

[AMPR19]   Alamati, N., Montgomery, H., Patranabis, S., Roy, A.: Minicrypt primitives with algebraic structure and applications. In: Ishai, Y., Rijmen, V. (eds.) EUROCRYPT 2019, Part II. LNCS, vol. 11477, pp. 55–82. Springer, Cham (2019). https://doi.org/10.1007/978-3-030-17656-3_3

[App14]   Applebaum, B.: Key-dependent message security: generic amplification and completeness. J. Cryptol. **27**(3), 429–451 (2014)

[BF01]   Boneh, D., Franklin, M.: Identity-based encryption from the Weil pairing. In: Kilian, J. (ed.) CRYPTO 2001. LNCS, vol. 2139, pp. 213–229. Springer, Heidelberg (2001). https://doi.org/10.1007/3-540-44647-8_13

[BGI+17]   Badrinarayanan, S., Garg, S., Ishai, Y., Sahai, A., Wadia, A.: Two-message witness indistinguishability and secure computation in the plain model from new assumptions. In: Takagi, T., Peyrin, T. (eds.) ASIACRYPT 2017, Part III. LNCS, vol. 10626, pp. 275–303. Springer, Cham (2017). https://doi.org/10.1007/978-3-319-70700-6_10

[BHHO08]   Boneh, D., Halevi, S., Hamburg, M., Ostrovsky, R.: Circular-secure encryption from decision Diffie-Hellman. In: Wagner, D. (ed.) CRYPTO 2008. LNCS, vol. 5157, pp. 108–125. Springer, Heidelberg (2008). https://doi.org/10.1007/978-3-540-85174-5_7

[BIJ18]   Biasse, J.-F., Iezzi, A., Jacobson Jr., M.J.: A note on the security of CSIDH. In: Chakraborty, D., Iwata, T. (eds.) INDOCRYPT 2018. LNCS, vol. 11356, pp. 153–168. Springer, Cham (2018). https://doi.org/10.1007/978-3-030-05378-9_9

[BKV19]   Beullens, W., Kleinjung, T., Vercauteren, F.: CSI-FiSh: efficient isogeny based signatures through class group computations. In: Galbraith, S.D., Moriai, S. (eds.) ASIACRYPT 2019, Part I. LNCS, vol. 11921, pp. 227–247. Springer, Cham (2019). https://doi.org/10.1007/978-3-030-34578-5_9

[BLMR13] Boneh, D., Lewi, K., Montgomery, H., Raghunathan, A.: Key homomorphic PRFs and their applications. In: Canetti, R., Garay, J.A. (eds.) CRYPTO 2013, Part I. LNCS, vol. 8042, pp. 410–428. Springer, Heidelberg (2013). https://doi.org/10.1007/978-3-642-40041-4_23

[BOB18]   Barreto, P., Oliveira, G., Benits, W.: Supersingular isogeny oblivious transfer. Cryptology ePrint Archive, Report 2018/459 (2018). https://eprint.iacr.org/2018/459

[Bon98]   Boneh, D.: The decision Diffie-Hellman problem. In: Buhler, J.P. (ed.) ANTS 1998. LNCS, vol. 1423, pp. 48–63. Springer, Heidelberg (1998). https://doi.org/10.1007/BFb0054851

[BPV12]   Blazy, O., Pointcheval, D., Vergnaud, D.: Round-optimal privacy-preserving protocols with smooth projective hash functions. In: Cramer, R. (ed.) TCC 2012. LNCS, vol. 7194, pp. 94–111. Springer, Heidelberg (2012). https://doi.org/10.1007/978-3-642-28914-9_6

[BS20]   Bonnetain, X., Schrottenloher, A.: Quantum security analysis of CSIDH. In: Canteaut, A., Ishai, Y. (eds.) EUROCRYPT 2020, Part II. LNCS, vol. 12106, pp. 493–522. Springer, Cham (2020). https://doi.org/10.1007/978-3-030-45724-2_17

[BY91]   Brassard, G., Yung, M.: One-way group actions. In: Menezes, A.J., Vanstone, S.A. (eds.) CRYPTO 1990. LNCS, vol. 537, pp. 94–107. Springer, Heidelberg (1991). https://doi.org/10.1007/3-540-38424-3_7

[CJL+16] Chen, L., et al.: Report on post-quantum cryptography, vol. 12. US Department of Commerce, National Institute of Standards and Technology (2016)

[CJS14]   Childs, A., Jao, D., Soukharev, V.: Constructing elliptic curve isogenies in quantum subexponential time. J. Math. Cryptol. 8(1), 1–29 (2014)

[CLG09]   Charles, D.X., Lauter, K.E., Goren, E.Z.: Cryptographic hash functions from expander graphs. J. Cryptol. 22(1), 93–113 (2009)

[CLM+18] Castryck, W., Lange, T., Martindale, C., Panny, L., Renes, J.: CSIDH: an efficient post-quantum commutative group action. In: Peyrin, T., Galbraith, S. (eds.) ASIACRYPT 2018, Part III. LNCS, vol. 11274, pp. 395–427. Springer, Cham (2018). https://doi.org/10.1007/978-3-030-03332-3_15

[CM01]   Cheung, K.K.H., Mosca, M.: Decomposing finite abelian groups. Quantum Inf. Comput. 1(3), 26–32 (2001)

[Cou06]   Couveignes, J.-M.: Hard homogeneous spaces. Cryptology ePrint Archive, Report 2006/291 (2006). http://eprint.iacr.org/2006/291

[CS02]   Cramer, R., Shoup, V.: Universal hash proofs and a paradigm for adaptive chosen ciphertext secure public-key encryption. In: Knudsen, L.R. (ed.) EUROCRYPT 2002. LNCS, vol. 2332, pp. 45–64. Springer, Heidelberg (2002). https://doi.org/10.1007/3-540-46035-7_4

[CSV20]   Castryck, W., Sotáková, J., Vercauteren, F.: Breaking the decisional Diffie-Hellman problem for class group actions using genus theory. In: Micciancio, D., Ristenpart, T. (eds.) CRYPTO 2020, Part II. LNCS, vol. 12171, pp. 92–120. Springer, Cham (2020). https://doi.org/10.1007/978-3-030-56880-1_4

[De 17]   De Feo, L.: Mathematics of isogeny based cryptography (2017)

[DG17]   Döttling, N., Garg, S.: Identity-based encryption from the Diffie-Hellman assumption. In: Katz, J., Shacham, H. (eds.) CRYPTO 2017, Part I. LNCS, vol. 10401, pp. 537–569. Springer, Cham (2017). https://doi.org/10.1007/978-3-319-63688-7_18

[DG19]   De Feo, L., Galbraith, S.D.: SeaSign: compact isogeny signatures from class group actions. In: Ishai, Y., Rijmen, V. (eds.) EUROCRYPT 2019, Part III. LNCS, vol. 11478, pp. 759–789. Springer, Cham (2019). https://doi.org/10.1007/978-3-030-17659-4_26

[DJP14]   De Feo, L., Jao, D., Plût, J.: Towards quantum-resistant cryptosystems from supersingular elliptic curve isogenies. J. Math. Cryptol. **8**(3), 209–247 (2014)

[DKS18]   De Feo, L., Kieffer, J., Smith, B.: Towards practical key exchange from ordinary isogeny graphs. In: Peyrin, T., Galbraith, S. (eds.) ASIACRYPT 2018, Part III. LNCS, vol. 11274, pp. 365–394. Springer, Cham (2018). https://doi.org/10.1007/978-3-030-03332-3_14

[DM20]   De Feo, L., Meyer, M.: Threshold schemes from isogeny assumptions. In: Kiayias, A., Kohlweiss, M., Wallden, P., Zikas, V. (eds.) PKC 2020, Part II. LNCS, vol. 12111, pp. 187–212. Springer, Cham (2020). https://doi.org/10.1007/978-3-030-45388-6_7

[DMPS19] De Feo, L., Masson, S., Petit, C., Sanso, A.: Verifiable delay functions from supersingular isogenies and pairings. In: Galbraith, S.D., Moriai, S. (eds.) ASIACRYPT 2019, Part I. LNCS, vol. 11921, pp. 248–277. Springer, Cham (2019). https://doi.org/10.1007/978-3-030-34578-5_10

[dOPS18] de Saint Guilhem, C.D., Orsini, E., Petit, C., Smart, N.P.: Secure oblivious transfer from semi-commutative masking. Cryptology ePrint Archive, Report 2018/648 (2018). https://eprint.iacr.org/2018/648

[ELPS18] Eaton, E., Lequesne, M., Parent, A., Sendrier, N.: QC-MDPC: a timing attack and a CCA2 KEM. In: Lange, T., Steinwandt, R. (eds.) PQCrypto 2018. LNCS, vol. 10786, pp. 47–76. Springer, Cham (2018). https://doi.org/10.1007/978-3-319-79063-3_3

[Gal99]   Galbraith, S.D.: Constructing isogenies between elliptic curves over finite fields. LMS J. Comput. Math. **2**, 118–138 (1999)

[GHS02]   Galbraith, S.D., Hess, F., Smart, N.P.: Extending the GHS Weil descent attack. In: Knudsen, L.R. (ed.) EUROCRYPT 2002. LNCS, vol. 2332, pp. 29–44. Springer, Heidelberg (2002). https://doi.org/10.1007/3-540-46035-7_3

[GJJM20] Goyal, V., Jain, A., Jin, Z., Malavolta, G.: Statistical zaps and new oblivious transfer protocols. In: Canteaut, A., Ishai, Y. (eds.) EUROCRYPT 2020, Part III. LNCS, vol. 12107, pp. 668–699. Springer, Cham (2020). https://doi.org/10.1007/978-3-030-45727-3_23

[GL03]   Gennaro, R., Lindell, Y.: A framework for password-based authenticated key exchange. In: Biham, E. (ed.) EUROCRYPT 2003. LNCS, vol. 2656, pp. 524–543. Springer, Heidelberg (2003). https://doi.org/10.1007/3-540-39200-9_33

[GPS08]   Galbraith, S.D., Paterson, K.G., Smart, N.P.: Pairings for cryptographers. Discret. Appl. Math. **156**(16), 3113–3121 (2008). Applications of Algebra to Cryptography

[GPS17] Galbraith, S.D., Petit, C., Silva, J.: Identification protocols and signature schemes based on supersingular isogeny problems. In: Takagi, T., Peyrin, T. (eds.) ASIACRYPT 2017, Part I. LNCS, vol. 10624, pp. 3–33. Springer, Cham (2017). https://doi.org/10.1007/978-3-319-70694-8_1

[GPSV18] Galbraith, S., Panny, L., Smith, B., Vercauteren, F.: Quantum equivalence of the DLP and CDHP for group actions. Cryptology ePrint Archive, Report 2018/1199 (2018). https://eprint.iacr.org/2018/1199

[Gro96] Grover, L.K.: A fast quantum mechanical algorithm for database search. In: 28th ACM STOC, pp. 212–219. ACM Press, May 1996

[GS10] Grigoriev, D., Shpilrain, V.: Authentication schemes from actions on graphs, groups, or rings. Ann. Pure Appl. Logic **162**(3), 194–200 (2010)

[GS13] Galbraith, S.D., Stolbunov, A.: Improved algorithm for the isogeny problem for ordinary elliptic curves. Appl. Algebra Eng. Commun. Comput. **24**(2), 107–131 (2013)

[GS18] Garg, S., Srinivasan, A.: Two-round multiparty secure computation from minimal assumptions. In: Nielsen, J.B., Rijmen, V. (eds.) EUROCRYPT 2018, Part II. LNCS, vol. 10821, pp. 468–499. Springer, Cham (2018). https://doi.org/10.1007/978-3-319-78375-8_16

[HK12] Halevi, S., Kalai, Y.T.: Smooth projective hashing and two-message oblivious transfer. J. Cryptol. **25**(1), 158–193 (2012)

[HL18] Holmgren, J., Lombardi, A.: Cryptographic hashing from strong one-way functions (or: one-way product functions and their applications). In: Thorup, M. (ed.) 59th FOCS, pp. 850–858. IEEE Computer Society Press, October 2018

[IKO05] Ishai, Y., Kushilevitz, E., Ostrovsky, R.: Sufficient conditions for collision-resistant hashing. In: Kilian, J. (ed.) TCC 2005. LNCS, vol. 3378, pp. 445–456. Springer, Heidelberg (2005). https://doi.org/10.1007/978-3-540-30576-7_24

[IN96] Impagliazzo, R., Naor, M.: Efficient cryptographic schemes provably as secure as subset sum. J. Cryptol. **9**(4), 199–216 (1996)

[JD11] Jao, D., De Feo, L.: Towards quantum-resistant cryptosystems from supersingular elliptic curve isogenies. In: Yang, B.-Y. (ed.) PQCrypto 2011. LNCS, vol. 7071, pp. 19–34. Springer, Heidelberg (2011). https://doi.org/10.1007/978-3-642-25405-5_2

[JKKR17] Jain, A., Kalai, Y.T., Khurana, D., Rothblum, R.: Distinguisher-dependent simulation in two rounds and its applications. In: Katz, J., Shacham, H. (eds.) CRYPTO 2017, Part II. LNCS, vol. 10402, pp. 158–189. Springer, Cham (2017). https://doi.org/10.1007/978-3-319-63715-0_6

[JQSY19] Ji, Z., Qiao, Y., Song, F., Yun, A.: General linear group action on tensors: a candidate for post-quantum cryptography. In: Hofheinz, D., Rosen, A. (eds.) TCC 2019, Part I. LNCS, vol. 11891, pp. 251–281. Springer, Cham (2019). https://doi.org/10.1007/978-3-030-36030-6_11

[KKS18] Kalai, Y.T., Khurana, D., Sahai, A.: Statistical witness indistinguishability (and more) in two messages. In: Nielsen, J.B., Rijmen, V. (eds.) EUROCRYPT 2018, Part III. LNCS, vol. 10822, pp. 34–65. Springer, Cham (2018). https://doi.org/10.1007/978-3-319-78372-7_2

[KM19] Kitagawa, F., Matsuda, T.: CPA-to-CCA transformation for KDM security. In: Hofheinz, D., Rosen, A. (eds.) TCC 2019, Part II. LNCS, vol. 11892, pp. 118–148. Springer, Cham (2019). https://doi.org/10.1007/978-3-030-36033-7_5

[KMT19] Kitagawa, F., Matsuda, T., Tanaka, K.: CCA security and trapdoor functions via key-dependent-message security. In: Boldyreva, A., Micciancio, D. (eds.) CRYPTO 2019, Part III. LNCS, vol. 11694, pp. 33–64. Springer, Cham (2019). https://doi.org/10.1007/978-3-030-26954-8_2

[KS17] Khurana, D., Sahai, A.: How to achieve non-malleability in one or two rounds. In: Umans, C. (ed.) 58th FOCS, pp. 564–575. IEEE Computer Society Press, October 2017

[Kup05] Kuperberg, G.: A subexponential-time quantum algorithm for the dihedral hidden subgroup problem. SIAM J. Comput. **35**(1), 170–188 (2005)

[Kup13] Kuperberg, G.: Another subexponential-time quantum algorithm for the dihedral hidden subgroup problem. In: Severini, S., Brandao, F. (eds.) 8th Conference on the Theory of Quantum Computation, Communication and Cryptography (TQC 2013). Leibniz International Proceedings in Informatics (LIPIcs), Dagstuhl, Germany, vol. 22, pp. 20–34. Schloss Dagstuhl-Leibniz-Zentrum fuer Informatik (2013)

[LPR10] Lyubashevsky, V., Peikert, C., Regev, O.: On ideal lattices and learning with errors over rings. In: Gilbert, H. (ed.) EUROCRYPT 2010. LNCS, vol. 6110, pp. 1–23. Springer, Heidelberg (2010). https://doi.org/10.1007/978-3-642-13190-5_1

[LQR+19] Lombardi, A., Quach, W., Rothblum, R.D., Wichs, D., Wu, D.J.: New constructions of reusable designated-verifier NIZKs. In: Boldyreva, A., Micciancio, D. (eds.) CRYPTO 2019, Part III. LNCS, vol. 11694, pp. 670–700. Springer, Cham (2019). https://doi.org/10.1007/978-3-030-26954-8_22

[Lyu09] Lyubashevsky, V.: Fiat-Shamir with aborts: applications to lattice and factoring-based signatures. In: Matsui, M. (ed.) ASIACRYPT 2009. LNCS, vol. 5912, pp. 598–616. Springer, Heidelberg (2009). https://doi.org/10.1007/978-3-642-10366-7_35

[MBD+18] Melchor, C.A., Blazy, O., Deneuville, J.-C., Gaborit, P., Zémor, G.: Efficient encryption from random quasi-cyclic codes. IEEE Trans. Inf. Theory **64**(5), 3927–3943 (2018)

[MM11] Micciancio, D., Mol, P.: Pseudorandom knapsacks and the sample complexity of LWE search-to-decision reductions. In: Rogaway, P. (ed.) CRYPTO 2011. LNCS, vol. 6841, pp. 465–484. Springer, Heidelberg (2011). https://doi.org/10.1007/978-3-642-22792-9_26

[MR18] Meyer, M., Reith, S.: A faster way to the CSIDH. In: Chakraborty, D., Iwata, T. (eds.) INDOCRYPT 2018. LNCS, vol. 11356, pp. 137–152. Springer, Cham (2018). https://doi.org/10.1007/978-3-030-05378-9_8

[NOTT20] Nakagawa, K., Onuki, H., Takayasu, A., Takagi, T.: l_1-norm ball for CSIDH: optimal strategy for choosing the secret key space. Cryptology ePrint Archive, Report 2020/181 (2020)

[NP01] Naor, M., Pinkas, B.: Efficient oblivious transfer protocols. In: Rao Kosaraju, S. (ed.) 12th SODA, pp. 448–457. ACM-SIAM, January 2001

[NPR99] Naor, M., Pinkas, B., Reingold, O.: Distributed pseudo-random functions and KDCs. In: Stern, J. (ed.) EUROCRYPT 1999. LNCS, vol. 1592, pp. 327–346. Springer, Heidelberg (1999). https://doi.org/10.1007/3-540-48910-X_23

[Pei20] Peikert, C.: He gives C-sieves on the CSIDH. In: Canteaut, A., Ishai, Y. (eds.) EUROCRYPT 2020, Part II. LNCS, vol. 12106, pp. 463–492. Springer, Cham (2020). https://doi.org/10.1007/978-3-030-45724-2_16

[Poh69] Pohl, I.: Bidirectional and heuristic search in path problems. Technical report 104, Stanford Linear Accelerator Center, Stanford, California (1969)

[PVW08] Peikert, C., Vaikuntanathan, V., Waters, B.: A framework for efficient and composable oblivious transfer. In: Wagner, D. (ed.) CRYPTO 2008. LNCS, vol. 5157, pp. 554–571. Springer, Heidelberg (2008). https://doi. org/10.1007/978-3-540-85174-5_31

[Reg04] Regev, O.: A subexponential time algorithm for the dihedral hidden subgroup problem with polynomial space. arXiv:quant-ph/0406151, June 2004

[Reg05] Regev, O.: On lattices, learning with errors, random linear codes, and cryptography. In: Gabow, H.N., Fagin, R. (eds.) 37th ACM STOC, pp. 84–93. ACM Press, May 2005

[RS06] Rostovtsev, A., Stolbunov, A.: Public-Key Cryptosystem Based On Isogenies. Cryptology ePrint Archive, Report 2006/145 (2006). http://eprint. iacr.org/2006/145

[Sho97] Shor, P.W.: Polynomial-time algorithms for prime factorization and discrete logarithms on a quantum computer. SIAM J. Comput. **26**(5), 1484–1509 (1997)

[Sto09] Stolbunov, A.: Reductionist security arguments for Public-Key cryptographic schemes based on group action. In: Mjølsnes, S.F. (ed.) Norsk informasjonssikkerhetskonferanse (NISK) (2009)

[Sto10] Stolbunov, A.: Constructing public-key cryptographic schemes based on class group action on a set of isogenous elliptic curves. Adv. Math. Commun. **4**(2), 215 (2010)

[Sto12] Stolbunov, A.: Cryptographic schemes based on isogenies (2012)

[Sut19] Sutherland, A.: Elliptic curves. Massachusetts Institute of Technology: MIT OpenCourseWare (2019). https://math.mit.edu/classes/18. 783/2019/lectures.html

[Tes06] Teske, E.: An elliptic curve trapdoor system. J. Cryptol. **19**(1), 115–133 (2006)

[Vit19] Vitse, V.: Simple oblivious transfer protocols compatible with supersingular isogenies. In: Buchmann, J., Nitaj, A., Rachidi, T. (eds.) AFRICACRYPT 2019. LNCS, vol. 11627, pp. 56–78. Springer, Cham (2019). https://doi.org/10.1007/978-3-030-23696-0_4

[YAJ+17] Yoo, Y., Azarderakhsh, R., Jalali, A., Jao, D., Soukharev, V.: A postquantum digital signature scheme based on supersingular isogenies. In: Kiayias, A. (ed.) FC 2017. LNCS, vol. 10322, pp. 163–181. Springer, Cham (2017). https://doi.org/10.1007/978-3-319-70972-7_9

B-SIDH: Supersingular Isogeny
Diffie-Hellman Using Twisted Torsion

Craig Costello[(✉)]

Microsoft Research, Redmond, USA
craigco@microsoft.com

Abstract. This paper explores a new way of instantiating isogeny-based cryptography in which parties can work in both the $(p + 1)$-torsion of a set of supersingular curves and in the $(p - 1)$-torsion corresponding to the set of their quadratic twists. Although the isomorphism between a given supersingular curve and its quadratic twist is not defined over $\mathbb{F}_{p^2}$ in general, restricting operations to the x-lines of both sets of twists allows all arithmetic to be carried out over $\mathbb{F}_{p^2}$ as usual. Furthermore, since supersingular twists always have the same $\mathbb{F}_{p^2}$-rational j-invariant, the SIDH protocol remains unchanged when Alice and Bob are free to work in both sets of twists.

This framework lifts the restrictions on the shapes of the underlying prime fields originally imposed by Jao and De Feo, and allows a range of new options for instantiating isogeny-based public key cryptography. These include alternatives that exploit Mersenne and Montgomery-friendly primes, as well as the possibility of significantly reducing the size of the primes in the Jao-De Feo construction at no known loss of asymptotic security. For a given target security level, the resulting public keys are smaller than the public keys of all of the key encapsulation schemes currently under consideration in the NIST post-quantum standardisation effort.

The best known attacks against the instantiations proposed in this paper are the classical path finding algorithm due to Delfs and Galbraith and its quantum adapation due to Biasse, Jao and Sankar; these run in respective time $O(p^{1/2})$ and $O(p^{1/4})$, and are essentially memory-free. The upshot is that removing the big-O's and obtaining concrete security estimates is a matter of costing the circuits needed to implement the corresponding isogeny. In contrast to other post-quantum proposals, this makes the security analysis of B-SIDH rather straightforward.

Searches for friendly parameters are used to find several primes that range from 237 to 256 bits, which all offer a conjectured security comparable to the 434-bit prime used to target NIST level 1 security in the SIKE proposal. One noteworthy example is a 247-bit prime for which Alice's secret isogeny is 7901-smooth and Bob's secret isogeny is 7621-smooth.

Keywords: Post-quantum cryptography · Supersingular isogenies · SIDH · SIKE · Quadratic twists

© International Association for Cryptologic Research 2020
S. Moriai and H. Wang (Eds.): ASIACRYPT 2020, LNCS 12492, pp. 440–463, 2020.
https://doi.org/10.1007/978-3-030-64834-3_15

1   Introduction

The best known attacks against Jao and De Feo's SIDH protocol [23] try to recover either Alice's secret 2^m-isogeny $\phi_A \colon E_0 \to E_A$, or Bob's secret 3^n-isogeny $\phi_B \colon E_0 \to E_B$, and both of these problems are instances of the *supersingular isogeny problem*: given a finite field K and two supersingular elliptic curves E, E' defined over K such that $\#E = \#E'$, compute an isogeny $\phi \colon E \to E'$. For the cases of interest where $K = \mathbb{F}_{p^2}$ and p is a large prime, the best known classical algorithm for solving the supersingular isogeny problem is the Delfs-Galbraith algorithm [14], which requires $O(p^{1/2})$ isogeny operations to find a collision (of walks from E and E') in the graph of size $O(p)$. However, the special isogenies computed in SIDH above give rise to appreciably easier instances of the supersingular isogeny problem; they are of a fixed, known degree close to $p^{1/2}$, and this allows for a classical meet-in-the-middle attack that, asymptotically, requires only $O(p^{1/4})$ isogeny operations [23, §5]. Roughly speaking, the difference between the difficulty of the isogeny problems that arise in SIDH and that of the general supersingular isogeny problem is due to the fact that Alice and Bob only take about half as many steps as the diameters of each of their graphs. In other words, the number of possible destination nodes for the secret walks of Alice and Bob is close to the square root of the total number of nodes in the graph.

   Jao and De Feo chose primes of the form $p = 2^m 3^n - 1$ and half-length walks so that Alice and Bob can both compute their isogenies using arithmetic in $\mathbb{F}_{p^2}$; they represent each isomorphism class by a supersingular elliptic curve $E/\mathbb{F}_{p^2}$ with group order $\#E(\mathbb{F}_{p^2}) = (p+1)^2 = (2^m 3^n)^2$, which facilitates a full $\mathbb{F}_{p^2}$-rational 2^m-torsion and full $\mathbb{F}_{p^2}$-rational 3^n-torsion. When all of the subgroups of order 2^m and 3^n are $\mathbb{F}_{p^2}$-rational, so are the corresponding isogeny computations.

   A first observation that sets the scene for this work is that in general there are two choices of $\mathbb{F}_{p^2}$-rational elliptic curve groups corresponding to every node in the supersingular isogeny graph: those whose group orders are $(p+1)^2$, and those whose group orders are $(p-1)^2$. Although curves from these two sets are not isomorphic (or even isogenous!) to one another over $\mathbb{F}_{p^2}$, they do become isomorphic over $\mathbb{F}_{p^4}$, and therefore share the same j-invariant in $\mathbb{F}_{p^2}$ [38, Proposition III.1.4]. Indeed, for any curve whose group order is $(p+1)^2$, its *quadratic twist* over $\mathbb{F}_{p^2}$ has group order $(p-1)^2$.

   The main point of this paper is to exploit the fact that the SIDH protocol does not have to restrict to working in one of the two sets of quadratic twists: it can stay in $\mathbb{F}_{p^2}$ while working in *both* the $(p+1)$-torsion *and* the $(p-1)$-torsion. Moreover, Alice and Bob can work in the torsion corresponding to opposite sets of quadratic twists with no change to the protocol. Optimised Montgomery arithmetic [30] in the SIDH setting only needs the x-coordinates of points [23] and the A coefficient of the curve [11], and as such is entirely *twist-agnostic*; in other words, the twisting morphism (which only alters y-coordinates and the B coefficient) leaves x-coordinates and A coefficients unchanged, so the lifting to $\mathbb{F}_{p^4}$ described above becomes a mere theoretical technicality that is not visible in cryptographic implementations – see Sect. 3.

The price to pay for working with both twists is that at least one of Alice or Bob must now perform walks comprised of steps in multiple ℓ-isogeny graphs, i.e. switching between multiple values of ℓ. This changes the underlying hardness assumption for one or both parties, but (as is discussed in Sect. 4) there is no known reason to believe that switching between many ℓ's makes the resulting SIDH problems any easier, so long as the number of destination nodes remain roughly the same size as in the Jao-De Feo instantiation.

Allowing torsion from both sets of twists unlocks a number of new options and trade-offs for isogeny-based public key cryptography; many examples are given in Sect. 5 to illustrate these possibilities. At a high level, these options fall into two categories: the first is where Alice gets to computes significantly faster 2^m-isogenies (than in existing SIDH/SIKE implementations) at the expense of a heavy slowdown on Bob's side; the second, and perhaps the more interesting, is the possibility of halving the sizes of the underlying fields at no known loss of asymptotic security. Furthermore, this possibility gives rise to the number of secret walks (i.e. possible destination nodes) for both Alice and Bob being very close to the total number of nodes in the graph.

Concrete instantiations of smaller primes are put forward in Sect. 5. For example, B-SIDHp247 uses a 247-bit prime to achieve roughly the same conjectured security as the 434-bit SIKE prime to target NIST's security category 1 [22]. The public keys for B-SIDHp247 are 186 bytes, which are a little over half the size of the 330-byte uncompressed public keys of SIKEp434, and are still smaller than the 196-byte keys that are obtained in SIKEp434 when compression is enabled.

1.1 Naming

The instantiation proposed in this paper is dubbed B-SIDH[1] in order to distinguish it from the original Jao-De Feo SIDH instantiation, and to avoid muddying the waters in the case that future cryptanalysis weakens any variants described herein. Although switching between multiple ℓ-isogeny graphs during a secret isogeny computation does not decrease security in any known way, it may turn out that using torsion with many prime factors is a bad idea, or that decreasing p relative to the degrees of the secret isogenies is a bad idea. Of course, it may also turn out that the one (or both) of the converse statements is true, but in any case it should be emphasised that the instantiations proposed in this paper rely on *different security assumptions* than SIDH and SIKE – see Sect. 4.

1.2 Performance vs. SIDH

There are no performance claims made in this paper, except in the scenarios where Alice's performance will clearly be improved (over her performance in the

---

[1] Pronounced "B-side", in reference to the analogy between the set of supersingular curves of cardinality $(p-1)^2$ and the less popular, sometimes forgotten 'flip-side' of a record.

SIDH/SIKE setting at a comparable security level) thanks to a faster underlying prime, but where it should be reiterated that Bob will almost always suffer a collossal slowdown. The main takeaway of this paper is that the primes and the public keys in the optimal scenarios of Sect. 5 are significantly smaller than the SIDH/SIKE counterparts. Moreover, these public keys will remain smaller even when compression techniques [2,10,31,45] are applied to the SIDH and SIKE public keys. If the ECC+SIDH/SIKE hybrid is used as in [11], these gaps will widen further.

In order to make the performance of the proposed approach competitive with that of SIDH/SIKE, the main research obstacles that arise are (i) finding faster methods of computing ℓ-isogenies for the sizes of ℓ that arise in Sect. 5, and (ii) finding primes p for which both $p + 1$ and $p - 1$ have large enough factors that are as smooth as possible.

The first preprint of this paper left both (i) and (ii) as open avenues for future work, but in the time that has passed since that version went online, progress has been made in both directions. In regards to (i), a leap forward was recently made by Bernstein, De Feo, Leroux and Smith [4]: for P a point of prime order ℓ in $E(\mathbb{F}_q)$, they give an algorithm for evaluating the quotient isogeny ϕ with $\ker(\phi) = \langle P \rangle$ at a point $Q \in E(\mathbb{F}_q)$ using only $\tilde{O}(\sqrt{\ell})$ operations in $\mathbb{F}_q$. This is a huge improvement over the conventional algorithms for isogeny computations that all computed Vélu's formulas [43] using $\tilde{O}(\ell)$ operations in $\mathbb{F}_q$. The authors of [4] note that their algorithm implies an asymptotic speedup for B-SIDH as the security level increases, and give several software implementations that illustrate the (rather large) performance improvements that can be expected for the sizes of isogenies needed in this paper. They note, however, that their implementations are not constant-time, and that "it is too early to guess what the final performance of constant-time B-SIDH will be on top of our ℓ-isogeny algorithm" [4, §A.4].

Regarding (ii), this version of the paper puts forward much better parameters than those in the prior version(s); this is a result of improved search techniques and more compute time – see Sect. 5.

1.3 Related Work

A few days after a preprint of this paper went online, Matsuo sent us his non-peer-reviewed Japanese article [28] from March 2019 that had previously proposed the idea of working in both quadratic twists simultaneously. However, his execution of the idea is very different from that in this paper. In particular, Matsuo did not lift the restriction of Alice and Bob computing their respective 2^m and 3^n isogenies, and his search for primes p such that $2^m \mid p + 1$ and $3^n \mid p - 1$ (or vice versa) forces huge cofactors which produces primes that are, for the most part, either the same size or are larger than their original SIDH counterparts. A crucial difference in this work is allowing at least one of the two parties to compute secret isogenies whose composite degrees have many prime factors, which gives way to a range of new possibilities.

Comments on an earlier version of this paper revealed that De Feo should be credited as the first to mention the idea of exploiting quadratic twists in the realm of SIDH/SIKE. In his habilitation thesis (dated December 2018), De Feo writes [15, p. 50]: *"One particular trick in CSIDH that is completely absent in SIDH is using the quadratic twist to perform part of the computations. I have thought of this for a while, and I see no fundamental reason why it should not work for SIDH, if it was not for the fact that finding suitable parameters seems computationally unfeasible. My favorite example is $p = 17$, so $p^2 - 1 = 2^5 3^2$; if it were possible to find large primes with similar properties, the gain would be spectacular"*.

Section 3 not only confirms De Feo's intuition that there is no obstruction to the use of quadratic twists, it shows that quadratic twists can be used out-of-the-box inside the twist-agnostic SIDH framework. The purpose of Sect. 5 is to start paving the way towards the types of large primes De Feo envisioned, and while it remains to be seen whether the practical gains can be *spectacular*, the work he recently coauthored [4] will almost certainly play a part of any gains that are afforded by the instantiations explored herein.

2   Twist-Agnostic SIDH

The parameter that governs the security of Jao and De Feo's supersingular isogeny Diffie-Hellman (SIDH) protocol is the large prime p. As soon as p is chosen, a set of roughly $\lfloor p/12 \rfloor$ elements is defined: these are the entire set of supersingular j-invariants over $\overline{\mathbb{F}}_p$, and they are the nodes on the graphs that Alice and Bob walk on during the protocol. Alice and Bob share this set of nodes, but their graphs have different edges that depend on the degrees of their secret isogenies. Following [23], for any prime $\ell \nmid p$, there are $\ell + 1$ isogenies (counting multiplicities, and up to isomorphism) of degree ℓ that eminate from a given supersingular isomorphism class. Moreover, Pizer [33,34] showed that this gives rise to a connected $(\ell+1)$-regular multigraph that satisfies the Ramanujan property and thus has optimal expansion properties.

2.1   Rational $(p + 1)$-torsion

The prime p also governs the efficiency of SIDH, where Alice and Bob both compute isogenies whose degrees are of the form ℓ^e. In theory, Alice and Bob could choose any value of ℓ they like (so long as their individual choices of ℓ are coprime), but it is more efficient if the ℓ^e-torsion is defined over $\mathbb{F}_{p^2}$. Observing that the smallest primes ℓ give rise to the most efficient ℓ^e-isogenies, Jao and De Feo construct the prime p to guarantee this rationality condition by setting $p = f \cdot 2^m 3^n - 1$ (allowing for a small *cofactor* f), and representing nodes in the graph by elliptic curves $E/\mathbb{F}_{p^2}$ with

$$E(\mathbb{F}_{p^2}) \quad \cong \quad \mathbb{Z}_{p+1} \times \mathbb{Z}_{p+1}. \tag{1}$$

For any $r \in \mathbb{Z}$ with $r \mid p + 1$, the entire r-torsion $E[r] \cong \mathbb{Z}_r \times \mathbb{Z}_r$ is then contained in $E(\mathbb{F}_{p^2})$. With p chosen as above, it follows that the full 2^m-torsion $E[2^m] \cong \mathbb{Z}_{2^m} \times \mathbb{Z}_{2^m}$, and the full 3^n-torsion $E[3^n] \cong \mathbb{Z}_{3^n} \times \mathbb{Z}_{3^n}$, are both $\mathbb{F}_{p^2}$-rational. Since every (separable) isogeny $\phi: E \to E'$ of degree d is in one-to-one correspondence with a kernel subgroup of order d [38, Proposition III.4.12], and each such isogeny is computed using rational functions of the input curve and the given kernel subgroup [43], it follows that if both of these inputs are $\mathbb{F}_{p^2}$-rational, then so is the isogeny computation.

2.2 SIDH

With $p = f \cdot 2^m 3^n - 1$ as above, the SIDH protocol specifies the following public parameters: a starting supersingular curve $E_0/\mathbb{F}_{p^2}$, a basis $\{P_A, Q_A\}$ for $E[2^m] \cong \mathbb{Z}_{2^m} \times \mathbb{Z}_{2^m}$, and a basis $\{P_B, Q_B\}$ for $E[3^n] \cong \mathbb{Z}_{3^n} \times \mathbb{Z}_{3^n}$. To generate her public key, Alice chooses two secret integers $(\alpha_A, \beta_A) \in \mathbb{Z}_{2^m} \times \mathbb{Z}_{2^m}$ such that her secret point $S_A = [\alpha_A]P_A + [\beta_A]Q_A$ is of order 2^m. She then composes m 2-isogenies to give her secret 2^m-isogeny $\phi_A: E_0 \to E_A$, where $E_A = E_0/\langle S_A \rangle$. Along the way, she moves the basis points P_B and Q_B through the isogeny computation, eventually obtaining their images under ϕ_A. Her public key is then $\mathrm{PK}_A = (E_A, \phi_A(P_B), \phi_A(Q_B))$. On Bob's side, he chooses $(\alpha_B, \beta_B) \in \mathbb{Z}_{3^n} \times \mathbb{Z}_{3^n}$, computes his secret point $S_B = [\alpha_B]P_B + [\beta_B]Q_B$, and then uses it to compute his secret 3^n-isogeny $\phi_B: E_0 \to E_B$ (via n consecutive 3-isogenies), such that $E_B = E_0/\langle S_B \rangle$. His public key is $\mathrm{PK}_B = (E_B, \phi_B(P_A), \phi_B(Q_A))$.

Upon receiving PK_B, Alice uses her secret integers to compute a new secret point $S'_A = [\alpha_A]\phi_B(P_A) + [\beta_A]\phi_B(Q_A)$ of order 2^m on E_B, and then uses it to compute the 2^m-isogeny $\phi'_A: E_B \to E_B/\langle S'_A \rangle$. Bob uses his secret integers and PK_A to compute the point $S'_B = [\alpha_B]\phi_A(P_B) + [\beta_B]\phi_A(Q_B)$ of order 3^n on E_A, and then uses it to compute the 3^n-isogeny $\phi'_B: E_A \to E_A/\langle S'_B \rangle$. Both parties then compute the same shared secret as the j-invariant of their respective image curves $E_B/\langle S'_A \rangle$ and $E_A/\langle S'_B \rangle$, since $E_B/\langle S'_A \rangle \cong E_A/\langle S'_B \rangle$ [23].

2.3 Twist-Agnostic Isogenies

Jao and De Feo exploited the fact that all of the arithmetic in the above computations can be performed on the Kummer line of the associated curves, i.e. in $E/\{\pm 1\}$ rather than E, and furthermore that this arithmetic is particularly efficient if the curves are in Montgomery form [30]

$$E_{(A,B)}: By^2 = x^3 + Ax^2 + x.$$

Henceforth, $E_{(A,B)}$ or E will be used instead of $E_{(A,B)}/\{\pm 1\}$ or $E/\{\pm 1\}$ for simplicity, and unless explicitly stated, y-coordinates will be ignored (using '—'). Furthermore, the B coefficients of Montgomery curves can also be ignored in the SIDH framework [11]; they are merely used to specify which quadratic twist we are working on and are not needed in optimised explicit formulas. In other words, optimised explicit formulas for Montgomery arithmetic ignore B and y and work irrespective of quadratic twist.

Isogenies of composite degree $L = \prod_{i=1}^{k} \ell_i^{e_i}$ can be computed as the composition of e_1 isogenies of degree ℓ_1, followed by e_2 isogenies of degree ℓ_2, and so on. Conventional isogeny algorithms evaluate prime degree ℓ-isogenies in $\tilde{O}(\ell)$ field operations [9,43], whereas the recent Bernstein-De Feo-Leroux-Smith [4] algorithm computes the same result using only $\tilde{O}(\sqrt{\ell})$ field operations; both of these algorithms are already optimised within the twist-agnostic Montgomery framework above. Generally speaking, it follows that for a given target security level (i.e. for a given size of L – see Sect. 4), the most efficient L-isogenies will correspond to the smoothest values of L.

3   Using Torsion from the Quadratic Twists

Let $E/\mathbb{F}_{p^n}$ be an elliptic curve, let t_n be the trace of the p^n-power Frobenius endomorphism, and recall that (i) E is supersingular if and only if t_n is a multiple of p [38, Exercise V.5.10(a)], and that (ii) $\#E(\mathbb{F}_{p^n}) = p^n + 1 - t_n$ with $|t_n| \leq 2\sqrt{p^n}$ [38, Theorem V.1.1]. When $n = 1$, there is only one possible value of t_1 that is a multiple of p such that $|t_1| \leq 2\sqrt{p}$, i.e. $t_1 = 0$, and thus it follows that $E/\mathbb{F}_p$ is supersingular if and only if $\#E(\mathbb{F}_p) = p + 1$. In other words, there is only one possible group order for supersingular elliptic curves over $\mathbb{F}_p$.

The first observation that sets the scene for this work is that there are multiple possibilities for t_2 that correspond to $E/\mathbb{F}_{p^2}$ being supersingular: taking $t_2 \in \{-2p, -p, 0, p, 2p\}$ satisfies (i) and (ii). Of particular interest in the present context are the two possibilities $t_2 = -2p$ and $t_2 = 2p$. All known instantiations of SIDH and SIKE fall into the former case by default. They define a starting supersingular curve $E_0/\mathbb{F}_p$ and lift to work in $E_0(\mathbb{F}_{p^2})$; since $E_0(\mathbb{F}_p) \mid E_0(\mathbb{F}_{p^2})$ and $\#E_0(\mathbb{F}_p) = p + 1$, it must be that $\#E_0(\mathbb{F}_{p^2}) = p^2 + 1 + 2p = (p + 1)^2$ and hence that $t_2 = -2p$.

Upon starting on a curve with $t_2 = -2p$, a choice has seemingly been made among the possibilities for t_2; two elliptic curves are $\mathbb{F}_{p^2}$-isogenous if and only if they have the same group order over $\mathbb{F}_{p^2}$ [41, Theorem 1(c)], so computing $\mathbb{F}_{p^2}$-rational isogeny walks means walking on curves with the same number of points as $E_0/\mathbb{F}_{p^2}$. However, any curve with $t_2 = -2p$ corresponds to the *quadratic twist* of a curve with $t_2 = 2p$, meaning that they not only become isogenous over $\mathbb{F}_{p^4}$, they become isomorphic over $\mathbb{F}_{p^4}$. Moreover, as we saw in Sect. 2.3, optimised isogeny arithmetic works correctly independently of the quadratic twist, so the explicit formulas that are used on the curves with $t_2 = -2p$ can also be used to work on the curves with $t_2 = 2p$.

It is crucial to note that even though two quadratic twists are not isomorphic over $\mathbb{F}_{p^2}$, they will still have the same j-invariant in $\mathbb{F}_{p^2}$ [38, Proposition 1.4(b)]. Put another way, every node in the supersingular isogeny graph can actually be represented by two different $\mathbb{F}_{p^2}$-isomorphism classes: those with $t_2 = -2p$ and the same group structure as $E/\mathbb{F}_{p^2}$ in (1), or those with $t_2 = 2p$ and with group structure

$$E^t(\mathbb{F}_{p^2}) \cong \mathbb{Z}_{p-1} \times \mathbb{Z}_{p-1}.$$

Every such supersingular curve with group structure $\mathbb{Z}_{p-1} \times \mathbb{Z}_{p-1}$ is the *quadratic twist* of a supersingular curve with group structure $\mathbb{Z}_{p+1} \times \mathbb{Z}_{p+1}$, and vice versa. Moreover, in the same way that any factor r of $p+1$ gave rise to a full rational r-torsion in $E(\mathbb{F}_{p^2})$, any factor s of $p-1$ gives rise to a full rational s-torsion in $E^t(\mathbb{F}_{p^2})$.

For Alice and Bob to freely work with points coming from the $(p+1)$-torsion and the $(p-1)$-torsion, it appears that the entire protocol must be lifted to $\mathbb{F}_{p^4}$. While this is technically true, the lifting will ultimately not be visible in an optimised implementation[2].

The point and isogeny formulas ignore the y-coordinates of points and the B coefficients of Montgomery curves, and this is where all the twisting arithmetic happens. The upshot is that while the protocol will be lifted to $\mathbb{F}_{p^4}$, where $E(\mathbb{F}_{p^4}) \cong E^t(\mathbb{F}_{p^4}) \cong \mathbb{Z}_{p^2-1} \times \mathbb{Z}_{p^2-1}$, Alice and Bob are still in a position to work entirely in $\mathbb{F}_{p^2}$ as usual. They can then choose a secret kernel point whose order divides $p+1$, or whose order divides $p-1$, or (more generally) whose order divides the product p^2-1.

To make this concrete, let B be a square in $\mathbb{F}_{p^2}$, let γ be a non-square in $\mathbb{F}_{p^2}$, take $\mathbb{F}_{p^4} = \mathbb{F}_{p^2}(\delta)$ with $\delta^2 = \gamma$, and write

$$E_{A,B} \colon By^2 = x^3 + Ax^2 + x \qquad \text{and} \qquad E^t_{A,\gamma B} \colon \gamma By^2 = x^3 + Ax^2 + x$$

as models [3] for $E/\mathbb{F}_{p^2}$ and $E^t/\mathbb{F}_{p^2}$. The map

$$\sigma \colon E_{A,\gamma B}(\mathbb{F}_{p^4}) \to E_{A,B}(\mathbb{F}_{p^4}), \qquad (x,y) \mapsto (x, \delta y) \tag{2}$$

is a group isomorphism that leaves x-coordinates unchanged.

Write $f(x) = x^3 + Ax^2 + x$. For any $u \in \mathbb{F}_{p^2}$, either (i) $f(u)$ is a square in $\mathbb{F}_{p^2}^*$, in which case $(u, \sqrt{f(u)/B})$ is a point in $E_{A,B}(\mathbb{F}_{p^2})$, (ii) $f(u)$ is a non-square in $\mathbb{F}_{p^2}^*$, in which case $f(u)/(\gamma B)$ is a square, and $(u, \sqrt{f(u)/(\gamma B)})$ is a point in $E_{A,\gamma B}(\mathbb{F}_{p^2})$, or (iii) $f(u) = 0$, in which case $(u,0)$ is one of the three 2-torsion points (on both $E_{A,B}$ and $E_{A,uB}$).

Let $P_1 = (u_1, -)$ be a point corresponding to case (i), let $P_2 = (u_2, -)$ be a point corresponding to case (ii), and suppose $\phi_1 \colon E_{A,B} \to E_{A,B}/\langle P_1 \rangle$ and $\phi_2 \colon E_{A,\gamma B} \to E_{A,\gamma B}/\langle P_2 \rangle$. It does not make sense to evaluate ϕ_1 at P_2 or ϕ_2 at P_1 (these points do not even lie on $\mathbb{F}_{p^2}$-isogenous curves, let alone the same curve), but this is fixed by lifting to $\mathbb{F}_{p^4}$ and precomposing with the twisting morphisms. Setting $\phi'_1 = (\phi_1 \circ \sigma)$ and $\phi'_2 = (\phi_2 \circ \sigma^{-1})$ gives the isogenies $\phi'_1 \colon E_{A,\gamma B} \to E_{A,B}/\langle \sigma(P_2) \rangle$ and $\phi'_2 \colon E_{A,B} \to E_{A,\gamma B}/\langle \sigma^{-1}(P_1) \rangle$, which are well-defined over $\mathbb{F}_{p^4}$.

The key observation from (2) is that $\sigma \colon (x, -) \mapsto (x, -)$ and $\sigma^{-1} \colon (x, -) \mapsto (x, -)$ induce the identity map when working on the corresponding Kummer

---

[2] This is reminiscent of Bernstein's twist-agnostic Curve25519 construction. He also uses a quadratic extension field in the specification of the Curve25519 function [3, Theorem 2.1], but this extension is a technicality that is not seen in the implementation.

[3] The idea works analogously for more general (i.e. short Weierstrass) elliptic curves, but all of the instantiations discussed in this paper allow for Montgomery form.

lines, so the twisting morphisms can simply be ignored in the implementation. Thus, Alice can take her secret points from the $(p + 1)$-torsion of $E_{A,B}(\mathbb{F}_{p^2})$ and Bob can take his secret points from the $(p - 1)$-torsion of $E_{A,\gamma B}$, and the implementation of the SIDH protocol can otherwise remain unchanged.

3.1 B-SIDH in a Nutshell

Henceforth, for a given prime p, M and N will be used to denote the two coprime degrees of Alice and Bob's secret isogenies (e.g. in the traditional setup with $p = 2^m 3^n - 1$ described above, we have $M = 2^m$ and $N = 3^n$). Alice's degree M will always be defined such that $M \mid p + 1$, and Bob's will be N such that $N \mid p - 1$.

Since M and N must be coprime, the even one will always be chosen according to whichever of $p + 1$ and $p - 1$ is the multiple of 4; otherwise, the remaining factors of $p+1$ and $p-1$ are necessarily coprime. The efficacy of the construction in this paper is closely tied to the *smoothness* of M and N (see Sect. 2.3), so obtaining B-SIDH-friendly parameters boils down to searching for primes p such that $p + 1$ and $p - 1$ both contain factors that are large enough to reach a target security level, but smooth enough to be efficiently computable.

3.2 Handling Large ℓ-degree Isogenies

The sizes of ℓ that are encountered in this paper are significantly larger than those in previous works, so it is important to look for ways that such isogenies can be sped up in practice. As mentioned in Sect. 1, Bernstein, De Feo, Leroux and Smith [4] recently gave a drastic improvement for the computation of large prime-degree isogenies: ℓ-isogenies now require only $\tilde{O}(\sqrt{\ell})$ field operations, rather than $\tilde{O}(\ell)$ field operations. The two possibilities below were written in an earlier version of this paper that predates [4], but nevertheless are still worth mentioning, since it is currently unclear how a constant-time variant of [4] performs in practice, i.e., exactly how large ℓ would need to be for such a variant to reign supreme over prior methods or over the more obvious optimisations below. Moreover, either or both of these techniques could be used in conjunction with the algorithm in [4] to give even faster B-SIDH isogenies in practice.

Parallelisation. Let P be a point of order $\ell = 2d + 1$. The algorithm in [9] requires the first d multiples $\{[i]P\}_{1 \le i \le d}$ of the input point, which is what makes ℓ-isogeny computations become rather expensive for large ℓ. However, this process parallelises almost perfectly: for t processors, $\lceil t/2 \rceil$ steps of the Montgomery ladder are used to compute $[i]P$ for $1 \le i \le t$. The i-th processor can then compute $[i + jt]P$ as the differential sum of $[i + (j-1)t]P$, $[t]P$, and $[i + (j-2)t]P$ for $1 \le j \le \lceil d/t \rceil$. After the initial phase that assigns the three values to each processor, no communication is required between the processors until the end, where the subproducts (which were independently accumulated in the same manner as [9, §5]) can all be collected and multiplied together. In the case of computing image points, then one final squaring and one final multiplication are used to finish the routine [9, Theorem 1]; in the case of computing image curves, then $\log(\ell)$ final multiplications and squarings are required [29]. Note that this parallelisation can be exploited across any of the prime degree isogenies that are large enough to make it worthwhile.

Precomputation. Assume Bob is tasked with large prime degree isogenies and he is the one generating ephemeral public keys. The runtime of his public key generation procedure can be improved if storage permits a significant offline precomputation. For example, if his largest prime-degree isogeny is an ℓ-isogeny, he could precompute all of the $\ell+1$ possible image curve/point triples (see Sect. 2.2), and at runtime he could simply select the triple corresponding to his secret key.

4   Security Analysis

There are two main changes to the usual computational isogeny problems underlying SIDH and SIKE [16, Problems 5.1–5.4] that are implicit in this paper. The first is that the isogeny walks now use multiple values of ℓ; the vertex set of a given graph stays fixed, but the edges now change between successive steps. The second is that the walks are no longer *half-length* (i.e. around half the bitlength of p); lowering the size of the primes relative to the length of the walks means that other avenues of attack become relevant with respect to the usual meet-in-the-middle attacks[4]. This section studies the implications of these changes with respect to known attacks from the literature.

4.1   Multiple Edge Sets

Based on current knowledge, there is no reason to believe that a walk consisting of many different prime degree isogenies makes the underlying problem appreciably easier than that of a walk in a fixed ℓ-isogeny graph, provided the number of possible destination nodes is around the same size. When computing L-isogenies with $L = \prod \ell_i^{e_i}$, the number of cyclic subgroups of order L inside any given group $E(\mathbb{F}_{p^2})$ is $\prod(\ell_i + 1)\ell_i^{e_i-1}$, and so long as this is around the same size as $(\ell+1)\ell^{e-1}$, the difficulty of recovering an L-isogeny appears to be no easier than that of recovering an ℓ^e-isogeny. The generalisation of the problems underlying

---

[4] Comments on an earlier version of this paper illustrated some confusion over whether or not torsion point attacks [32] become relevant in this setting. Note that these attacks only become relevant when either (i) Alice and Bob's isogeny degrees are extremely unbalanced, e.g. when one is greater than the square of the other, or (ii) when a secret isogeny degree is *much* larger than the size of the prime p. It is important to stress that neither (i) or (ii) is proposed in this paper, and moreover, that it is unclear how one could possibly achieve (i) or (ii) while working in the proposed framework. The secret isogeny degrees M and N must both be coprime and their product must divide $p^2 - 1$, so their being balanced (i.e. $M \approx N$) immediately rules out one of them being much larger than p.

SIDH to isogenies of multiple degrees has already been considered in prior works (e.g. [32], [19, §2.3], and [7]), where the same conclusion was drawn (or the same assumption was made).

4.2 Security of Non-commutative vs. Commutative Schemes

There are currently two main umbrellas of isogeny-based public-key cryptography under public scrutiny: those like SIDH [23] and SIKE [22] where the curves involved have non-commutative endomorphism rings, and those like CRS [13,36] and CSIDH [6] where the associated endomorphism rings are commutative. It is important to note that, while there are similarities between the instantiations herein and CSIDH (like the use of many different prime isogeny degrees in the same secret computation), this paper falls entirely under the non-commutative umbrella. This means B-SIDH inherits two security virtues from SIDH: the first is that it is seemingly immune to Kuperberg's algorithm [25], meaning that the best known quantum algorithms are exponential (see Sect. 4.4); the second is that it lends itself to regular algorithms and therefore more simple constant-time implementations. On the other hand, it inherits the same drawback as SIDH of being susceptible to active attacks [18], so requires the same transformations that were used in the SIKE proposal – see [22].

4.3 Classical Cryptanalysis

When $L = \prod \ell_i^{e_i} \approx p^{1/2}$, as in the original SIDH proposal, the *meet-in-the-middle* or *claw-finding* algorithms [16, §5.3] stand alone as the best known attacks against SIDH and SIKE. However, the most interesting instantiations proposed in this paper have $L \gg p^{1/2}$, and as L tends towards p, algorithms other than the meet-in-the-middle attacks become relevant. In what follows it will be assumed that $L \approx p$, since this is the extreme case where the alternative attack avenues are most relevant. The underlying problem is to find the isogeny $\phi \colon E_1 \to E_2$ of degree L, where $E_1/\mathbb{F}_{p^2}$ and $E_2/\mathbb{F}_{p^2}$ are supersingular.

Claw-Finding Algorithms. Let $L_1 \approx L_2 \approx p^{1/2}$ with $L_1 L_2 = L$. The claw-finding algorithm cited by Jao and De Feo [23, §5.2] uses $O(L_1)$ time to compute a table of all of the curves L_1-isogenous to E_1, and stores them using $O(L_1)$ memory. It then proceeds by trying one L_2-isogeny at a time, this time emanating from E_2, until a match is found in the table and the problem is solved; this stage requires $O(L_2)$ time and essentially no memory. It follows that the claw-finding algorithm runs in $O(p^{1/2})$ time and requires $O(p^{1/2})$ memory.

Adj, Cervantes-Vázquez, Chi-Domínguez, Menezes and Rodríguez-Henríquez [1] argued that the van Oorschot-Wiener (vOW) parallel collision finding algorithm [42] has a lower overall cost for finding ϕ, and thus should be used to assess the security of SIDH and SIKE. Their implementation confirmed that the original vOW runtime analysis [42] is sharp in the context of finding the isogeny ϕ. If w is the number of entries that can be stored in the table above, m is the number of processors running in parallel, and t is the time taken to compute L_1 and L_2 isogenies, then the vOW algorithm finds ϕ in expected runtime $T = \frac{2.5}{m} \cdot \left(\frac{p^{3/4}}{w^{1/2}} \right) \cdot t$. Adj et al. conclude that $w > 2^{80}$ is infeasible, so conduct their analysis by setting $w = 2^{80}$. With this choice of w, it helps to point out that for $p = 2^{160}$, the runtime of vOW (on one processor) is $T = 2.5 \cdot t \cdot p^{1/2}$; thus, when $p \gg 2^{160}$, the vOW runtime is $T \gg p^{1/2}$.

Random Walk Algorithms for Any Path. There are two styles of applicable random walk algorithms that can be used to solve the general supersingular isogeny problem: both Pollard rho [35] and Delfs-Galbraith [14] find *some* path between E_1 and E_2. The former finds an isogeny between E_1 and E_2 by taking two pseudo-random walks in the graph of size $O(p)$; the number of steps required until these two walks collide is $O(p^{1/2})$ by the birthday paradox. The latter algorithm, which is preferred in practice (see [14, §4] or [5]), uses two self-avoiding random walks to find paths from each curve to two subfield curves, $\tilde{E}_1/\mathbb{F}_p$ and $\tilde{E}_2/\mathbb{F}_p$, and then connects these two subfield curves. Since there are $O(p^{1/2})$ subfield curves in the graph of size $O(p)$, the first step requires $O(p^{1/2})$ steps, and since connecting the two subfield curves requires $O(p^{1/4})$ steps [14], the entire algorithm takes $O(p^{1/2})$ steps to find an isogeny connecting E_1 and E_2. Like vOW, the Delfs-Galbraith algorithm parallelises perfectly, but unlike vOW, it does not have large storage requirements.

Both of these algorithms are likely to terminate with a path that is not the secret path corresponding to ϕ. However, since E_1 is typically a special curve with a known endomorphism ring $\text{End}(E_1)$, it is prudent to assume that this can be used to modify the path into the correct one via the techniques discussed at length in [18, §4].

4.4 Quantum Cryptanalysis

The best known quantum algorithm for solving SIDH and SIKE instances is, asymptotically, Tani's algorithm [40]. Roughly speaking, as $p \to \infty$, Tani's algorithm solves the claw-finding problem for secret isogenies of degree $O(p^{1/2})$ in time $O(p^{1/6})$ on a quantum computer. Translating to the setting of isogenies of degree $L \approx p$, this would give an $O(p^{1/3})$ quantum claw-finding algorithm; note that recent work of Jaques and Schanck [24] shows that (even under the assumption of a large amount of quantum resources) the concrete complexity of Tani's algorithm is much closer to the classical claw-finding complexity. Nevertheless, when $L \approx p$, Tani's algorithm is no longer the superior algorithm for solving the corresponding isogeny problem. In [5], Biasse, Jao and Sankar give a quantum algorithm for the general supersingular isogeny problem (in characteristic p) that runs in time $O(p^{1/4})$. Their algorithm is essentially the Delfs-Galbraith algorithm (from above) ported to the quantum setting; they use Grover's algorithm [20] to get a quadratic speedup from $O(p^{1/2})$ to $O(p^{1/4})$ on the phase that finds the two supersingular subfield curves $\tilde{E}_1/\mathbb{F}_p$ and $\tilde{E}_2/\mathbb{F}_p$, and then develop a subexponential algorithm (based on the Childs-Jao-Soukharev subexponential algorithm [8] for the ordinary case) to connect the subfield path. The memory requirements of this algorithm are small; Biasse, Jao and Sankar define a set of N isogenies of degree 3^λ, where $\lambda \in O(\log(p))$ is chosen large enough so that this set contains a walk that passes through a subfield curve with probability $1/2$. As long as there are enough (i.e. $O(\log(p))$) qubits to encode such a path, then this algorithm succeeds with probability $1/4$ [5, Proposition 2].

As in the classical algorithms, since $\mathrm{End}(E_1)$ is typically known, the path obtained by the above process can presumably be modified into the path corresponding to ϕ at no additional asymptotic cost.

4.5 Security Summary

When $\phi\colon E_1 \to E_2$ is an isogeny between two supersingular curves $E_1/\mathbb{F}_{p^2}$ and $E_2/\mathbb{F}_{p^2}$ of degree $L = \prod_{i=1}^{k} \ell_i^{e_i} \approx p$, the best known classical algorithm for finding ϕ is the Delfs-Galbraith algorithm [14]; it runs in $O(p^{1/2})$ time and (unlike claw-finding or vOW) does not have large storage requirements. Applying Grover's speedup to the Delfs-Galbraith algorithm also gives the best known quantum algorithm [5]; it requires $O(\log(p))$ qubits, run in time $O(p^{1/4})$, and does not have large storage requirements. In the classical case, Delfs-Galbraith parallelises perfectly, where as Grover's algorithm is well-known to give a $\sqrt{m}$ speedup when parallelised across m quantum processors [44].

5   Searching for Friendly Instances

This section presents a variety of example primes for which the approach in this paper becomes interesting in practice. Recall from Sect. 2.3 and Sect. 3.1 that the most interesting primes are those where $M \mid p+1$ and $N \mid p-1$ are both large enough to reach a requisite security level and are as smooth as possible.

At a high level, the methods of searching for these primes fall into three categories:

- **Fast, pre-existing primes.** These are primes that are already popular in the classical ECC literature, e.g. Mersenne and Ridinghood primes: here a large power of 2 typically divides $p+1$, which is an upshot of p being cherry-picked to support fast finite field arithmetic. In the present context, it also means that Alice can compute 2^m-isogenies as usual, meaning that she obtains a speedup over typical SIDH/SIKE isogenies due solely to the faster underlying arithmetic. On the other hand, the scarcity of these primes means that $p-1$ is unlikely to be smooth, so Bob's isogenies tend to be a lot worse than the 3^n-isogenies he computes in SIDH/SIKE. Examples of these primes are given in Sect. 5.1.
- **Extended Euclidean algorithm.** The first method of searching for new primes involves taking a and b coprime, e.g. $a = 2^u$ and $b = 3^v$, using the extended Euclidean algorithm to find integers s and t such that $st < 0$ and $as + bt = 1$, and then sieving over integer values of k until the (unique) integer

lying between $|2a(s - kb)|$ and $|2b(s + ka)|$ is prime. Alice and Bob can then take $M = a \cdot |s - kb|$ and $N = b \cdot |s + ka|$ and have a large part (i.e., around half in the balanced case) of their isogeny product being a small prime power. Examples found with this technique are in Sect. 5.2.

- **Primes of the form** $p = 2x^n - 1$. The second method of searching for friendly instances involves fixing n as a very small integer (e.g. $n = 6$), and searching over $x \in \mathbb{Z}$ until $p = 2x^n - 1$ is prime. Restricting x to be B-smooth guarantees that $p + 1$ is B-smooth, and the factorisation of $p - 1 = 2(x^n - 1)$ for certain values of n increases the likelihood that $p - 1$ is also smooth. This method is arguably the most successful in terms of giving both Alice and Bob fast isogenies, and it is detailed in Sect. 5.3.

The most interesting examples from Sect. 5.2 and Sect. 5.3 are collected and compared in Sect. 5.4.

5.1 Fast Primes: Accelerating Alice, Burdening Bob

Many fast primes are of the form

$$p = 2^m \cdot c - 1, \tag{3}$$

which allow Alice to compute 2^m-isogenies just like she would in SIDH. However, unlike the primes in SIDH where $c = 3^n \approx 2^m$, the values of c that are of interest here are when c is either chosen to facilitate faster field arithmetic in $\mathbb{F}_{p^2}$, is much smaller than 2^m so that p is smaller than usual, or both. Here Alice's computations will benefit from the faster field arithmetic, but Bob's computations become significantly slower due to his isogenies no longer being 3^n-isogenies, but rather $(\prod \ell_i^{e_i})$-isogenies. Depending on the efficacy of the methods in Sect. 3.2, in almost all such cases the factor slowdown incurred on Bob's side will be much worse than the factor speedup enjoyed by Alice, meaning that the runtime of one protocol instance will be significantly slower in general. However, there are real-world scenarios where such a trade-off would be welcomed. One such scenario is in TLS, where servers are oftentimes performing orders of magnitude more runs of the protocol than an individual client is; here slowdowns on the client side could be tolerated (or even unnoticed) to afford a speedup to the server. An example of the opposite scenario, i.e. when the priority becomes the client's performance, is in the arena of lightweight cryptography (e.g. IoT); here it is often the case that resource-constrained devices are communicating with a relatively unconstrained sever.

Mersenne Primes. Putting $c = 1$ into (3) yields Mersenne primes, for which only $m \in \{127, 521\}$ are of interest in this paper. With $m = 521$, write the factorisation $p - 1 = 2^{521} - 2 = 2 \cdot 3 \cdot 5^2 \cdot 11 \cdot \ldots \cdot q_1 \cdot q_2 \cdot q_3 \cdot \ldots$, where $q_1 = 7623851$ (23 bits), $q_2 = 34110701$ (26 bits) and $q_3 = 2400573761$ (32 bits). Alice can use 2^e-isogenies for any $e \leq m$, and can subsequently scale her security up and down over the same field (e.g. to match the security of any of the SIKE instances). On

Bob's side, he can compute L-isogenies for any $L \mid p-1$, e.g. with $L = \prod_{\ell_i \leq q_n} \ell_i^{e_i}$, he can take $n = 1$ to match SIKEp434, $n = 2$ to match SIKEp503, and $n = 3$ to match SIKEp610. Taking $m = 127$ is too small to offer any reasonable security in the elliptic curve setting, however combining the security analyses in [17, §4.1] and [12] reveals that B-SIDH construction in the genus-2 setting could achieve good post-quantum security over this smaller Mersenne prime. The factorisation

$$p-1 = 2^{127} - 2 = 2 \cdot 3^3 \cdot 7^2 \cdot 19 \cdot 43 \cdot 73 \cdot 127 \cdot 337 \cdot 5419 \cdot 92737 \cdot 649657 \cdot 77158673929$$

shows that the product of all odd primes up to 649657 (20 bits) could build a genus-2 isogeny that is large enough to obtain 128 bits of classical security and 64 bits of quantum security.

The Ridinghoods. Putting $c = 2^m - 1$ into (3) yields *Ridinghood* primes, which offer fast Karatsuba-style arithmetic in $\mathbb{F}_p$; the most famous of these has $c = 2^{224}$ and underlies Hamburg's Goldilocks curve [21]. Here Alice can meet the security offered by SIKEp434 by computing 2^{224}-isogenies. If Bob is to compute L-isogenies with $L \mid p - 1$, he would need to compute a prime isogeny whose degree is 78 bits in length. However, allowing Bob to work on both sides (by including factors of c) shows that he can meet the same requisite security when L's largest prime factor is only 24 bits. Of the other Ridinghoods with $m \in \{161, 208, 224, 225, 240, 354\}$, the most striking example is with $m = 225$; here the largest prime-degree isogeny needed for Bob to match the security of SIKEp434 is $\ell = 2^{16} + 1$. Note that both of these examples are subject to the caveat in discussed in the paragraph below.

Bob on Both Sides. In the Ridinghood scenarios above, Bob is better off computing isogenies of order $N = N_1 N_2$, where $N \nmid p - 1$ but where $N_1 \mid p + 1$ and $N_2 \mid p - 1$. In this case, general points in $E_{A,B}[N]$ no longer have their x-coordinate in $\mathbb{F}_{p^2}$, but rather in $\mathbb{F}_{p^4}$, and performing arithmetic in $\mathbb{F}_{p^4}$ would hamper the efficiency of the isogeny algorithms significantly. One way to approach this scenario is to instead have Bob use two bases $\langle P_1, Q_1 \rangle = E_{A,B}[N_1]$ and $\langle P_2, Q_2 \rangle = E_{A,\gamma B}[N_2]$, which can both be defined such that all four x-coordinates are in $\mathbb{F}_{p^2}$. His secret keys are then of the form $(s_1, s_2) \in [0, N_1) \times [0, N_2)$, which generate the secret kernels $S_1 = P_1 + [s_1]Q_1$ and $S_2 = P_2 + [s_2]Q_2$. Bob can compute $\phi_1 \colon E_0 \to E_0/\langle S_1 \rangle$ and then $\phi_2 \colon E_0/\langle S_1 \rangle \to (E_0/\langle S_1 \rangle)/\langle \phi_1(S_2) \rangle$, which corresponds to the secret isogeny $\phi_B = (\phi_2 \circ \phi_1)$; his public key is then $(E_B, P'_A, Q'_A) = (\phi_B(E_0), \phi_B(P_A), \phi_B(Q_A))$, which is the same size as usual. On the other side, Alice's public keys must include the images of all four of Bob's basis points under her secret isogeny, so they become between 1.6x and 1.7x larger (if a static-ephemeral version of Diffie-Hellman à la SIKE [22] is used, then the setup would likely be arranged to make the static key the larger key). Computing these extra image points also incurs some additional overhead, but this would still be faster than working with two basis points that are defined over $\mathbb{F}_{p^4}$.

5.2 Searching with the Extended Euclidean Algorithm

This subsection describes the first of two methods used to search for primes that offer interesting B-SIDH instantiations. Both methods can be used to find primes that target any security level, but for concreteness (and based on the security analysis in Sect. 4) the remainder of this paper will focus on finding primes with $p > 2^{230}$ in order to make the classical complexity of Delfs-Galbraith [14] and the quantum complexity of Biasse-Jao-Sankar [5] large enough to reach NIST's security category 1. Moreover, the respective degrees M and N of Alice and Bob's secret isogenies must both be larger than 2^{210} in order to ensure that the classical and quantum claw-finding complexities roughly match those of SIKEp434 [22].

Let $B > 2$ be a given smoothness bound. The idea in this subsection is to search over coprime a and b so that the extended Euclidean algorithm outputs $s \in \mathbb{Z}$ and $t \in \mathbb{Z}$ such that

$$a \cdot s + b \cdot t = 1, \qquad (4)$$

with $|s| < |b/2|$ and $|t| < |a/2|$ [37, Theorem 4.3]. It follows that $|a \cdot s|$ and $|b \cdot t|$ differ by 1 and hence are necessarily coprime. Thus, if the unique integer lying between $2|a \cdot s|$ and $2|b \cdot t|$ is a prime p, and if the inputs a and b are both B-smooth, it follows that $p^2 - 1$ is B-smooth if and only if $s \cdot t$ is B-smooth.

For a fixed (a, b), there are actually an infinite number of pairs satisfying (4), obtained by writing $(s_k, t_k) = (s + kb, t - ka)$ for any $k \in \mathbb{Z}$. It follows that the bounds on the general solutions are

$$|s_k| < |k + 1/2| \cdot |b| \quad \text{and} \quad |t_k| < |k - 1/2| \cdot |a|.$$

For a given input pair (a, b), this gives a precise number of k values that can be tried to produce a prime p below a certain bound w, namely

$$|k| \le \lfloor w/(a \cdot b) \rfloor. \qquad (5)$$

The following examples illustrate how B-SIDH instances that offer interesting trade-offs can be found in this way.

Example 1. Rather than using the 434-bit prime $p = 2^{216}3^{137} - 1$ as in SIKEp434, suppose the size of the desired prime is instead bounded above by $w = 2^{384}$. On input of $a = 2^{186}$ and $b = 3^{115}$ (note that $2^{182} < b < 2^{183}$), the extended Euclidean algorithm produces (s_0, t_0) with $2^{179} < |t_0| < |s_0| < 2^{180}$. (5) reveals that $|k| \le 54324$. Of the $2 \cdot 54324 + 1$ possible values of k, 1149 of them gave rise to a prime (as the unique integer) lying between $2|a \cdot s_k|$ and $2|b \cdot t_k|$, and $k = -4189$ gave rise to the 382-bit prime

$$p := \texttt{0x277AF122D68C175343851A90621232112FB72C2AAB291357}$$
$$\texttt{9000000000000000000000000000000000000000000000001}.$$

with

$$M = 3^{115} \cdot 7 \cdot 13 \cdot 31^2 \cdot 157 \cdot 241 \quad \text{and}$$
$$N = 2^{188} \cdot 11 \cdot 17 \cdot 29 \cdot 73 \cdot 193,$$

which are such that $2^{213} < M < 2^{214} < N < 2^{215}$. With these sizes, the security of the resulting instantiation is comparable to SIKEp434, but with a prime that fits into six 64-bit words, rather than seven. Alice and Bob pay the price of having to do a handful of slightly larger isogenies, but on the other hand *all* of their arithmetic now takes place over a smaller field.

Example 2. Restricting a and b to be powers of primes restricts the number of inputs to the process. The following example was found by instead letting a and b vary over 2^5-smooth numbers. The coprime numbers $a = 2^4 \cdot 3 \cdot 7^{16} \cdot 17^9 \cdot 31^8$ and $b = 11^{18} \cdot 19 \cdot 23^{13}$ yield the 253-bit prime

$$p = \text{0x1935BECE108DC6C0AAD0712181BB1A414E6A8AAA6B510FC29826190FE7EDA80F}$$

with

$$M = 2^4 \cdot 3 \cdot 7^{16} \cdot 17^9 \cdot 31^8 \cdot 311 \cdot 571 \cdot 1321 \cdot 5119 \cdot 6011 \cdot 14207 \cdot 28477 \cdot 76667 \quad \text{and}$$
$$N = 11^{18} \cdot 19 \cdot 23^{13} \cdot 47 \cdot 79 \cdot 83 \cdot 89 \cdot 151 \cdot 3347 \cdot 17449 \cdot 33461 \cdot 51193,$$

which are such that $M > 2^{224}$ and $N > 2^{213}$.

Example 3. Increasing the smoothness bound on a and b to 2^7 found the 255-bit prime

$$p = \text{0x76042798BBFB78AEBD02490BD2635DEC131ABFFFFFFFFFFFFFFFFFFFFFFFFFFFF}$$

with

$$M = 2^{110} \cdot 5 \cdot 7^2 \cdot 67 \cdot 223 \cdot 4229 \cdot 9787 \cdot 13399 \cdot 21521 \cdot 32257 \cdot 47353 \quad \text{and}$$
$$N = 3^{34} \cdot 11 \cdot 17 \cdot 19^2 \cdot 29 \cdot 37 \cdot 53^2 \cdot 97 \cdot 107 \cdot 109 \cdot 131 \cdot 137 \cdot 197 \cdot 199$$
$$\cdot 227 \cdot 251 \cdot 5519 \cdot 9091 \cdot 33997 \cdot 38201,$$

which are such that $M > 2^{215}$ and $N > 2^{212}$.

Example 4. Unbalancing the inputs a and b to the extended Euclidean algorithm can produce the sorts of unbalanced B-SIDH instantiations that are geared towards the scenarios mentioned at the beginning of Sect. 5.1. On input of $a = 2^{216}$ and $b = 3^2 \cdot 5 \cdot 7 \cdot 11^2 \cdot 17 \cdot 29$, the process finds the 255-bit Montgomery-friendly prime

$$p := \text{0x6E052A4E15FFFFFFFFFFFFFFFFFFFFFFFFFFFFFFFFFFFFFFFFFFFFFFFFFFFFFFFF}$$

Here Alice can take $M = 2^{217}$ and Bob can take

$$N = 3^2 \cdot 5 \cdot 7 \cdot 11^2 \cdot 17 \cdot 29 \cdot 67 \cdot 431 \cdot 467 \cdot 607 \cdot 1579 \cdot 24169 \cdot 68947$$
$$\cdot 345229 \cdot 12676847 \cdot 38334727 \cdot 41110859 \cdot 51040879,$$

which is greater than 2^{216}. In this case Alice can expect a large speedup over her analogous isogeny computations in SIDH/SIKE: she can still compute her

2^{216} isogenies exactly as before, but now she is performing arithmetic over a 255-bit prime (instead of the 434-bit prime). Moreover, her public keys are already smaller than the comparable compressed public keys in SIKEp434, i.e., she need not incur the additional compression overhead, which is significant in SIKE [22]. If the above prime was used in the SIKE scenario with the long-term static secret being an N-isogeny, the estimated speedup on the encapsulator side lies somewhere between a factor 2.5 and a factor 3.5.

5.3   Primes of the Form $p = 2x^n - 1$

This subsection focusses on the second method to find primes that are particularly suited to the B-SIDH construction. In terms of a balanced smoothness for both Alice and Bob, it has found the most promising examples to date.

An earlier version of this paper aimed to find primes p such that $p - 1$ and $p + 1$ are minimally smooth by way of Störmer's theorem [39] (see also [26]). For a given smoothness bound B, Störmer's theorem says that are a finite number of integers, x, such that $x - 1$ and $x + 1$ are B-smooth; moreover, it gives a way to find this set in its entirety. If there are t primes up to B, then finding this set of integers amounts to solving all Pell equations of the form $x^2 - Dy^2 = 1$, where D is both squarefree and B-smooth; there are clearly 2^t such D, and therefore 2^t Pell equations to be solved [26]. Unfortunately, the sizes of B for which this task is feasible did not produce any values of x that offer meaningful security (at least, not in the case where the primes are chosen to underlie *elliptic curves*). For example, with $B = 47$, the largest x such that $x - 1$ and $x + 1$ are B-smooth is (the 42-bit integer) $x = 2218993446251$. With $B = 113$, the largest such x is $x = 38632316754147847668001$ (76 bits), and the largest prime such x is $x = 151908300112120373249$ (68 bits); this required solving $2^t = 2^{30}$ Pell equations, and was the largest B exhaustively searched in this work.

Although it was infeasible to extend this method to the sizes of B required to produce $p > 2^{200}$, it did prove useful in showing factorisation patterns that often arose for values in the larger ranges. In particular, the largest prime values were often of the form $p = 2z^n - 1$, with z and n both integers, and where $n > 1$. Indeed, searching for primes of this form has proven to be the most useful method to date, and the reason is best illustrated via an example. With $n = 2$, we can search over B-smooth x such that $p = 2x^2 - 1$ is prime, at which point we are guaranteed that $p + 1$ is B-smooth and we are hoping that $p - 1 = 2x^2 - 2 = 2(x-1)(x+1)$ is also B-smooth. In other words, we are hoping that two values in $O(\sqrt{p})$ are B-smooth. In contrast, a naive search (i.e. a search with $n = 1$) would be hoping to find one value in $O(p)$ that is B-smooth. Under the heuristic assumption that $x-1$ and $x+1$ are uniformly distributed in $O(\sqrt{p})$, and taking into account well-established smoothness probabilities (cf. [27]), it becomes clear that the search with $n = 2$ is far superior.

This same reasoning extends to larger values of n, and it is readily seen that (for a fixed smoothness bound B and desired size of p) the success probability of the search becomes tied to the ratio d/n, where d is the degree of the largest irreducible factor(s) of $x^n - 1 \in \mathbb{Z}[x]$. Larger values of n can be chosen to minimise this ratio, however a larger n means fewer values of x to search over (for a desired size of $p = 2x^n - 1$). Though some examples were found with $n > 6$ (see Sect. 5.3), the *sweet spot* when aiming for primes between 192 and 256 bits proved to be $n = 4$ and $n = 6$.

Searching with $n = 4$. Write $p(x) = 2x^4 - 1$, and let the smoothness bound be B as usual. A search for primes of this form such that $2^{230} < p < 2^{256}$ must look for $x \in [2^{57.5}, 2^{63.75})$. With the computing resources at hand, an exhaustive search of this domain was out of the question. However, one can do better than searching over smooth values of x by observing that

$$p(x) - 1 = 2(x - 1)(x + 1)(x^2 + 1).$$

When inputting B-smooth values of $x \approx 2^{64}$, the hope is to find $x - 1$, $x + 1$ and $x^2 + 1$ as all being B-smooth. Again, under the heuristic assumption that the smoothness probabilities of these values are independent of one another, this naive search is then hoping for two 64-bit numbers ($x - 1$ and $x + 1$) and one 128-bit number ($x^2 + 1$) to be B-smooth.

A better approach is to instead search through values of $x \approx 2^{64}$ such that $x^2 + 1$ necessarily factors into two numbers of at most 2^{64}. This can be achieved by choosing a subset of the primes less than B, say $\{q_1, \ldots, q_t\}$, and solving the equation $x_i^2 + 1 \equiv 0 \bmod q_i$ for each $1 \le i \le t$. These t values of x_i can then be combined using the CRT to give x such that $x^2 + 1 \equiv 0 \bmod (\prod q_i)$. In this case each of the q_i must be such that $q_i \equiv 1 \bmod 4$, so that $x_i^2 + 1 \equiv 0 \bmod q_i$ has a solution. The trick is to keep choosing random subsets of these primes such that the CRT will output values of $x \in [2^{57.5}, 2^{63.75})$; this way, the search is now hoping to stumble on three 64-bit values that are B-smooth, which is far more likely than the naive search above.

Note that each time a subset is chosen, there are 2^t combinations of solutions (corresponding to the t choices of *sign*) that can be checked. Furthermore, the q_i need not be distinct; solutions to $x_i^2 + 1 \equiv \bmod q_i^z$ are computed via Hensel lifting [37, §12.5.2]. The following example, which is perhaps the most striking example in this paper, was found in precisely this manner.

Example 5. With the smoothness bound $B = 2^{13}$, the primes

$$(q_1, \ldots, q_5) = (4481, 4801, 6673, 7537, 7621)$$

gave one of the solutions for $x^2 + 1 \equiv 0 \bmod (q_1 \cdots q_5)$ as $x = 2811207061409479600$ (lifted to $\mathbb{Z}$). Moreover,

$$x = 2^4 \cdot 5^2 \cdot 7 \cdot 23 \cdot 79 \cdot 107 \cdot 307 \cdot 2129 \cdot 7901$$

is also B-smooth, and yields a (247-bit) prime $p = 2x^4 - 1$. Alice and Bob can take

$$M = 2^{17} \cdot 5^8 \cdot 7^4 \cdot 23^4 \cdot 79^4 \cdot 107^4 \cdot 307^4 \cdot 2129^4 \cdot 7901^2 \quad \text{and}$$

$$N = 3 \cdot 11 \cdot 17 \cdot 241 \cdot 349 \cdot 421 \cdot 613 \cdot 983 \cdot 1327 \cdot 1667 \cdot 2969 \cdot 3769$$
$$\cdot 4481 \cdot 4649 \cdot 4801 \cdot 4877 \cdot 5527 \cdot 6673 \cdot 7103 \cdot 7537 \cdot 7621,$$

which are such that $2^{220} < M < 2^{221}$ and $2^{210} < N < 2^{211}$.

Searching with $n = 6$. In the case of $p = 2x^6 - 1$, it was possible to exhaustively search through the full set of x ranging up to $2^{255/6} < 2^{43}$ (though analogous methods to those described above could be applied if $n = 6$ was used to target higher security levels). Interestingly, this did not produce any factorisations of $p - 1$ that were as smooth as Example 5, so none of the below examples below are as good for Bob as that one. However, some very smooth values of x (which favour Alice) did find examples where $B \approx 2^{16}$ was enough to give Bob the requisite security. Three such examples are given below.

Example 6. The 237-bit prime $p = 2 \cdot (2^3 \cdot 3^4 \cdot 17 \cdot 19 \cdot 31 \cdot 37 \cdot 53^2)^6 - 1$ has

$$p - 1 = 2 \cdot 7 \cdot 13 \cdot 43 \cdot 73 \cdot 103 \cdot 269 \cdot 439 \cdot 881 \cdot 883 \cdot 1321 \cdot 5479 \cdot 9181$$
$$\cdot \, 12541 \cdot 15803 \cdot 20161 \cdot 24043 \cdot 34843 \cdot 48437 \cdot 62753 \cdot 72577 \cdot 709153.$$

Example 7. The 247-bit prime $p = 2 \cdot (2^6 \cdot 3^2 \cdot 7^5 \cdot 11 \cdot 17 \cdot 31 \cdot 37)^6 - 1$ has

$$p - 1 = 2 \cdot 13 \cdot 19^2 \cdot 29 \cdot 43 \cdot 79 \cdot 83 \cdot 107 \cdot 643 \cdot 661 \cdot 733 \cdot 1447 \cdot 2347 \cdot 7753$$
$$\cdot \, 28879 \cdot 29527 \cdot 38281 \cdot 64609 \cdot 76651 \cdot 86311 \cdot 228841 \cdot 745309897.$$

Example 8. The 250-bit prime $p = 2 \cdot (5^3 \cdot 101 \cdot 211 \cdot 461 \cdot 2287)^6 - 1$ has

$$p - 1 = 2^4 \cdot 3^2 \cdot 7 \cdot 13 \cdot 37 \cdot 79 \cdot 107 \cdot 109 \cdot 199 \cdot 349 \cdot 433 \cdot 487 \cdot 1607 \cdot 1993 \cdot 3067$$
$$\cdot \, 5701 \cdot 6199 \cdot 6373 \cdot 7883 \cdot 8821 \cdot 11497 \cdot 19507 \cdot 57037 \cdot 78301 \cdot 486839.$$

Larger n. Although setting $n > 6$ shrinks the search space for primes $p = 2x^n - 1$ of a certain size, interesting examples were still found in some cases. These typically have p much larger than the degree of feasible isogenies on Bob's side, so fall back into the umbrella of the types of primes explored in Sect. 5.1 (here there is typically a comfortable enough margin between p and the isogeny degrees that claw-finding goes back to being the best classical attack). For brevity, write ℓ as the largest prime factor of a given $N \mid p - 1$ in each case. The 331-bit prime $p = 2 \cdot (3^2 \cdot 13)^{48} - 1$ has $N > 2^{213}$ with $\ell < 2^{23}$. The 367-bit prime $p = 2 \cdot (3^2 \cdot 127)^{36} - 1$ has $N > 2^{216}$ with $\ell < 2^{22}$. The 354-bit prime $p = 2 \cdot (2 \cdot 5 \cdot 7^3)^{30} - 1$ has $N > 2^{201}$ with $\ell < 2^{23}$. The 362-bit prime $p = 2 \cdot (2 \cdot 11^2 \cdot 17)^{30} - 1$ has $N > 2^{208}$ and the 363-bit $p = 2 \cdot (2^3 \cdot 23^2)^{30} - 1$ with $N > 2^{212}$, both with $\ell < 2^{24}$. The 258-bit prime $p = 2 \cdot (2^3 \cdot 3^2 \cdot 23)^{24} - 1$ has $N > 2^{229}$ with $\ell < 2^{21}$. The 325-bit prime $p = 2 \cdot (2 \cdot 3 \cdot 5 \cdot 13 \cdot 29)^{24} - 1$ has $N > 2^{270}$ with $\ell < 2^{26}$ and $N > 2^{220}$ with $\ell < 2^{21}$. The 250-bit prime $p = 2 \cdot (29 \cdot 31 \cdot 1901)^{12} - 1$ has $N > 2^{211}$ with $\ell < 2^{18}$ and the largest factor of $p - 1$ is 20 bits.

5.4 Summary

For the examples from this section, Table 1 lists the bitlengths of the maximum prime isogeny degrees required by Alice and Bob, runtime complexities of the relevant classical and quantum attacks (written as base-2 logarithms), and the public key sizes of both standalone B-SIDH and a B-SIDH+ECDH hybrid. Following Sect. 4, the runtime of the Delfs-Galbraith (DG) algorithm is taken as

Table 1. Summary of various B-SIDH-friendly primes p. Further explanation in text.

Ex.	p (bits)	$\ell_{\text{Alice}}^{\max}$ (bits)	$\ell_{\text{Bob}}^{\max}$ (bits)	Classical DG	vOW	Quantum BJS	PK (bytes) B-SIDH	Hybrid
1	382	8	8	-	123	-	287*	335*
2	253	17	16	127	123	64	190	222
3	255	16	16	128	122	64	192	224
4	255	2	26	128	125	64	192	224
5	247	13	13	124	120	62	186	217
6	237	6	17	119	125	60	178	208
7	247	6	18	124	125	62	186	217
8	250	12	16	125	122	63	188	219

$p^{1/2}$, the runtime of van Oorschot-Weiner (vOW) is taken as $2.5 \cdot L^{3/4}/2^{40}$ (with L the degree of the respective isogeny), and the runtime of Biasse-Jao-Sankar (BJS) is taken as $p^{1/4}$; concrete runtimes in all three cases could be obtained by multiplying these complexities with the time taken for the corresponding isogeny computations. While the DG and BJS algorithms depend on the size of p, the complexity of the vOW algorithm depends on the number of possible isogenies computed by a given party (see Sect. 4.1). In the larger examples, Bob's use of all of the odd factors of $p - 1$ can be overkill, so in these instances two options for Bob's isogenies and the subsequent vOW runtime estimates are given. For Example 1, the best quantum attack is not BJS (see the analysis in [22] instead), and public keys could be compressed.

Following [11], B-SIDH public keys are three elements of $\mathbb{F}_{p^2}$, and partnering with an ECDH hybrid adds one additional element of $\mathbb{F}_p$ (the x-coordinate of the public key corresponding to a non-supersingular Montgomery curve with a strong ECDLP). It is worth pointing out that the asymptotic runtime of Delfs-Galbraith against B-SIDH matches the asymptotic runtime of Pollard rho [35] against the ECDLP, making the simplicity of the hybrid approach in [11, §8] particularly attractive.

Acknowledgement. Special thanks to Kevin Kane for setting up a cluster of machines that were used to search for parameters.

References

1. Adj, G., Cervantes-Vázquez, D., Chi-Domínguez, J., Menezes, A., Rodríguez-Henríquez, F.: On the cost of computing isogenies between supersingular elliptic curves. In: Cid, C., Jacobson Jr., M. (eds.) SAC 2018. LNCS, vol. 11349, pp. 322–343. Springer, Cham (2018). https://doi.org/10.1007/978-3-030-10970-7_15
2. Azarderakhsh, R., Jao, D., Kalach, K., Koziel, B., Leonardi, C.: Key compression for isogeny-based cryptosystems. In: AsiaPKC, pp. 1–10. Springer (2016)

3. Bernstein, D.J.: Curve25519: new Diffie-Hellman speed records. In: Yung, M., Dodis, Y., Kiayias, A., Malkin, T. (eds.) PKC 2006. LNCS, vol. 3958, pp. 207–228. Springer, Heidelberg (2006). https://doi.org/10.1007/11745853_14

4. Bernstein, D.J., De Feo, L., Leroux, A., Smith, B.: Faster computation of isogenies of large prime degree. In: Fourteenth Algorithmic Number Theory Symposium, ANTS-XIV (2020)

5. Biasse, J.-F., Jao, D., Sankar, A.: A quantum algorithm for computing isogenies between supersingular elliptic curves. In: Meier, W., Mukhopadhyay, D. (eds.) INDOCRYPT 2014. LNCS, vol. 8885, pp. 428–442. Springer, Cham (2014). https://doi.org/10.1007/978-3-319-13039-2_25

6. Castryck, W., Lange, T., Martindale, C., Panny, L., Renes, J.: CSIDH: an efficient post-quantum commutative group action. In: Peyrin, T., Galbraith, S. (eds.) ASIACRYPT 2018. LNCS, vol. 11274, pp. 395–427. Springer, Cham (2018). https://doi.org/10.1007/978-3-030-03332-3_15

7. Cervantes-Vázquez, D., Ochoa-Jiménez, E., Rodríguez-Henríquez, F.: eSIDH: the revenge of the SIDH. Preprint (2020). https://eprint.iacr.org/2020/021

8. Childs, A.M., Jao, D., Soukharev, V.: Constructing elliptic curve isogenies in quantum subexponential time. J. Math. Cryptol. **8**(1), 1–29 (2014)

9. Costello, C., Hisil, H.: A simple and compact algorithm for SIDH with arbitrary degree isogenies. In: Takagi, T., Peyrin, T. (eds.) ASIACRYPT 2017. LNCS, vol. 10625, pp. 303–329. Springer, Cham (2017). https://doi.org/10.1007/978-3-319-70697-9_11

10. Costello, C., Jao, D., Longa, P., Naehrig, M., Renes, J., Urbanik, D.: Efficient compression of SIDH public keys. In: Coron, J.-S., Nielsen, J.B. (eds.) EUROCRYPT 2017. LNCS, vol. 10210, pp. 679–706. Springer, Cham (2017). https://doi.org/10.1007/978-3-319-56620-7_24

11. Costello, C., Longa, P., Naehrig, M.: Efficient algorithms for supersingular isogeny Diffie-Hellman. In: Robshaw, M., Katz, J. (eds.) CRYPTO 2016. LNCS, vol. 9814, pp. 572–601. Springer, Heidelberg (2016). https://doi.org/10.1007/978-3-662-53018-4_21

12. Costello, C., Smith, B.: The supersingular isogeny problem in genus 2 and beyond. In: Ding, J., Tillich, J.-P. (eds.) PQCrypto 2020. LNCS, vol. 12100, pp. 151–168. Springer, Cham (2020). https://doi.org/10.1007/978-3-030-44223-1_9

13. Couveignes, J.M.: Hard homogeneous spaces. Preprint (2006). http://eprint.iacr.org/2006/291

14. Delfs, C., Galbraith, S.D.: Computing isogenies between supersingular elliptic curves over $\mathbb{F}_p$. Des. Codes Cryptogr. **78**(2), 425–440 (2016). https://doi.org/10.1007/s10623-014-0010-1

15. De Feo, L.: Exploring isogeny graphs. Habilitation thesis, December 2018. https://defeo.lu/hdr/

16. De Feo, L., Jao, D., Plût, J.: Towards quantum-resistant cryptosystems from supersingular elliptic curve isogenies. J. Math. Cryptol. **8**(3), 209–247 (2014)

17. Flynn, E.V., Ti, Y.B.: Genus two isogeny cryptography. In: Ding, J., Steinwandt, R. (eds.) PQCrypto 2019. LNCS, vol. 11505, pp. 286–306. Springer, Cham (2019). https://doi.org/10.1007/978-3-030-25510-7_16

18. Galbraith, S.D., Petit, C., Shani, B., Ti, Y.B.: On the security of supersingular isogeny cryptosystems. In: Cheon, J.H., Takagi, T. (eds.) ASIACRYPT 2016. LNCS, vol. 10031, pp. 63–91. Springer, Heidelberg (2016). https://doi.org/10.1007/978-3-662-53887-6_3

19. Galbraith, S.D., Petit, C., Silva, J.: Identification protocols and signature schemes based on supersingular isogeny problems. In: Takagi, T., Peyrin, T. (eds.) ASIACRYPT 2017. LNCS, vol. 10624, pp. 3–33. Springer, Cham (2017). https://doi.org/10.1007/978-3-319-70694-8_1

20. Grover, L.K.: A fast quantum mechanical algorithm for database search. In: STOC 1996, pp. 212–219. ACM (1996)

21. Hamburg, M.: Ed448-goldilocks, a new elliptic curve. IACR Cryptology ePrint Archive 2015/625 (2015)

22. Jao, D., et al.: SIKE: supersingular isogeny key encapsulation (2017). sike.org/

23. Jao, D., De Feo, L.: Towards quantum-resistant cryptosystems from supersingular elliptic curve isogenies. In: Yang, B.-Y. (ed.) PQCrypto 2011. LNCS, vol. 7071, pp. 19–34. Springer, Heidelberg (2011). https://doi.org/10.1007/978-3-642-25405-5_2

24. Jaques, S., Schanck, J.M.: Quantum cryptanalysis in the RAM model: claw-finding attacks on SIKE. In: Boldyreva, A., Micciancio, D. (eds.) CRYPTO 2019. LNCS, vol. 11692, pp. 32–61. Springer, Cham (2019). https://doi.org/10.1007/978-3-030-26948-7_2

25. Kuperberg, G.: A subexponential-time quantum algorithm for the dihedral hidden subgroup problem. SIAM J. Comput. **35**(1), 170–188 (2005)

26. Lehmer, D.H.: On a problem of Störmer. Ill. J. Math. **8**(1), 57–79 (1964)

27. Lenstra, A.K.: Smoothness probability. In: van Tilborg, H.C.A. (ed.) Encyclopedia of Cryptography and Security. Springer, Boston (2005). https://doi.org/10.1007/0-387-23483-7_407

28. Matsuo, K.: SIDH over quadratic twists. In: Proceedings of SCIS 2019 - 2019 Symposium on Cryptography and Information Security, 3B3-1, January 2019. https://www.iwsec.org/scis/2019/

29. Meyer, M., Reith, S.: A faster way to the CSIDH. In: Chakraborty, D., Iwata, T. (eds.) INDOCRYPT 2018. LNCS, vol. 11356, pp. 137–152. Springer, Cham (2018). https://doi.org/10.1007/978-3-030-05378-9_8

30. Montgomery, P.L.: Speeding the Pollard and elliptic curve methods of factorization. Math. Comput. **48**(177), 243–264 (1987)

31. Naehrig, M., Renes, J.: Dual isogenies and their application to public-key compression for isogeny-based cryptography. In: Galbraith, S.D., Moriai, S. (eds.) ASIACRYPT 2019. LNCS, vol. 11922, pp. 243–272. Springer, Cham (2019). https://doi.org/10.1007/978-3-030-34621-8_9

32. Petit, C.: Faster algorithms for isogeny problems using torsion point images. In: Takagi, T., Peyrin, T. (eds.) ASIACRYPT 2017. LNCS, vol. 10625, pp. 330–353. Springer, Cham (2017). https://doi.org/10.1007/978-3-319-70697-9_12

33. Pizer, A.K.: Ramanujan graphs and Hecke operators. Bull. Am. Math. Soc. **23**(1), 127–137 (1990)

34. Pizer, A.K.: Ramanujan graphs. AMS/IP Stud. Adv. Math. **7**, 159–178 (1998)

35. Pollard, J.M.: Monte Carlo methods for index computation (mod p). Math. Comput. **32**(143), 918–924 (1978)

36. Rostovtsev, A., Stolbunov, A.: Public-key cryptosystem based on isogenies. Preprint (2006). https://eprint.iacr.org/2006/145

37. Shoup, V.: A Computational Introduction to Number Theory and Algebra. Cambridge University Press, Cambridge (2009)

38. Silverman, J.H.: The Arithmetic of Elliptic Curves. Graduate Texts in Mathematics, 2nd edn. Springer, New York (2009). https://doi.org/10.1007/978-0-387-09494-6

39. Størmer, C.: Quelques théorèmes sur l'équation de Pell $x^2 - dy^2 = \pm 1$ et leurs applications. Christiania Videnskabens Selskabs Skrifter, Math. Nat. Kl (2), 48 (1897)
40. Tani, S.: Claw finding algorithms using quantum walk. Theor. Comput. Sci. **410**(50), 5285–5297 (2009)
41. Tate, J.: Endomorphisms of abelian varieties over finite fields. Invent. Math. **2**(2), 134–144 (1966). https://doi.org/10.1007/BF01404549
42. van Oorschot, P.C., Wiener, M.J.: Parallel collision search with cryptanalytic applications. J. Cryptol. **12**(1), 1–28 (1999). https://doi.org/10.1007/PL00003816
43. Vélu, J.: Isogénies entre courbes elliptiques. CR Acad. Sci. Paris Sér. AB **273**, A238–A241 (1971)
44. Zalka, C.: Grover's quantum searching algorithm is optimal. Phys. Rev. A **60**(4), 2746 (1999)
45. Zanon, G., Simplício Jr., M.A., Pereira, G.C.C.F., Doliskani, J., Barreto, P.S.L.M.: Faster key compression for isogeny-based cryptosystems. IEEE Trans. Comput. **68**(5), 688–701 (2019)

Calamari and Falafl: Logarithmic (Linkable) Ring Signatures from Isogenies and Lattices

Ward Beullens[1][(✉)], Shuichi Katsumata[2][(✉)], and Federico Pintore[3][(✉)]

[1] imec-COSIC, KU Leuven, Leuven, Belgium
ward.beullens@esat.kuleuven.be
[2] National Institute of Advanced Industrial Science and Technology (AIST),
Tokyo, Japan
shuichi.katsumata@aist.go.jp
[3] Mathematical Institute, University of Oxford, Oxford, UK
federico.pintore@maths.ox.ac.uk

Abstract. We construct efficient ring signatures (RS) from isogeny and lattice assumptions. Our ring signatures are based on a logarithmic OR proof for group actions. We instantiate this group action by either the CSIDH group action or an MLWE-based group action to obtain our isogeny-based or lattice-based RS scheme, respectively. Even though the OR proof has a binary challenge space and therefore requires a number of repetitions which is linear in the security parameter, the sizes of our ring signatures are small and scale better with the ring size N than previously known post-quantum ring signatures. We also construct linkable ring signatures (LRS) that are almost as efficient as the non-linkable variants. The isogeny-based scheme produces signatures whose size is an order of magnitude smaller than all previously known logarithmic post-quantum ring signatures, but it is relatively slow (e.g. 5.5 KB signatures and 79 s signing time for rings with 8 members). In comparison, the lattice-based construction is much faster, but has larger signatures (e.g. 30 KB signatures and 90 ms signing time for the same ring size). For small ring sizes our lattice-based ring signatures are slightly larger than state-of-the-art schemes, but they are smaller for ring sizes larger than $N \approx 1024$.

1 Introduction

Ring signatures (RS), introduced by Rivest, Shamir, and Tauman [27] allow a person to sign a message on behalf of a group of people (called ring), without revealing which person in the ring signed the message. A ring signature is

This work was supported by CyberSecurity Research Flanders with reference number VR20192203 and the Research Council KU Leuven grants C14/18/067 and STG/17/019. Ward Beullens is funded by FWO SB fellowship 1S95620N. Shuichi Katsumata was supported by JST CREST Grant Number JPMJCR19F6 and JSPS KAKENHI Grant Number JP19H01109.

S. Moriai and H. Wang (Eds.): ASIACRYPT 2020, LNCS 12492, pp. 464–492, 2020.
https://doi.org/10.1007/978-3-030-64834-3_16

required to be *unforgeable*, meaning that one cannot produce a signature without having the secret key of at least one person in the ring, and *anonymous*, meaning that it is impossible to learn which person produced the signature. The original motivation behind ring signatures is to allow a whistleblower to leak information without revealing their identity, while still adding credibility to the information by proving that it was leaked by one of the people in the ring. Linkable ring signatures (LRS) are an extension where one can publicly verify whether two messages were signed by the same person or not. This variant has found applications in e-voting and privacy-friendly digital currencies. In both cases, to protect users' privacy it is important to have at disposal a (linkable) ring signature scheme that can efficiently support very large ring sizes.

The security of many known (linkable) ring signatures relies on the hardness of factoring integers or computing discrete logarithms in finite cyclic groups. Unfortunately, these problems can be solved in quantum polynomial time [28], and hence all the schemes based on them would be no longer secure in the presence of adversaries with access to a sufficiently powerful quantum computer. To resolve this issue it is necessary to consider hard problems that resist attacks from quantum computers. Post-quantum ring signature schemes scaling poly-logarithmically with the ring size have been constructed from symmetric cryptographic primitives [11,19] and the hardness of lattice problems [4,15,16,22,29].

1.1   Our Contributions

In this paper, we introduce a logarithmic OR proof for group actions and we then use it to construct concretely efficient logarithmic ring signatures and linkable ring signatures from isogeny and lattice assumptions. Our (linkable) ring signature schemes are realized by first constructing a generic (linkable) ring signature scheme based on a group action that satisfies certain cryptographic properties, and then instantiating this group action by either the CSIDH group action [8] or a MLWE-based group action. This is, to the best of our knowledge, the first concrete construction of (linkable) ring signatures from isogeny-assumptions with logarithmic signature size.

An advantage of our schemes is that the signature size scales very well with the ring size N, even compared to other post-quantum logarithmic (linkable) ring signatures, since the only dependence on N is due to the signatures containing a small number of paths (in the clear) in Merkle trees of depth $\log N$. Therefore, the term in the signature size that depends on $\log N$ is independent of the CSIDH or lattice parameters. All previous works that relied on a hidden path in a Merkle tree had to prove the consistency of a Merkle hash in zero-knowledge. Therefore, the multiplicative factor of $\log N$ was much larger than ours. The very mild dependence on $\log N$ of our schemes can be observed in Fig. 1, where we see that for our lattice-based ring signature scheme a signature for ring size $N = 2048$ is only 17% larger than a signature for ring size $N = 2$.

For efficiency and convenience we chose to implement our (linkable) ring signature scheme with parameter sets from pre-existing signature schemes: for our isogeny instantiations we consider the CSIDH-512 parameter set, used by

CSI-FiSh [6], while for our lattice instantiation we use the Dilithium II parameter set. This allows us to reuse large portions of code from CSIDH, CSI-FiSh, and Dilithium implementations. The signature size and signing speed of our implementations are shown in Fig. 1. The signature size can be estimated as $\log N + 2.7$ KB for the isogeny-based instantiation and as $0.5 \log N + 29$ KB for the lattice-based instantiation. For ring size $N = 8$ our lattice-based instantiation has a signing time of 90 ms, faster than our isogeny-based instantiation (79 s) by almost 3 orders of magnitude.

Table 1 lists the signature size of our ring signatures and those of some other post-quantum ring signatures[1]. Not surprisingly, the signature size of our isogeny-based (linkable) ring signature is very small compared to the other post-quantum proposals. In particular, it is an order of magnitude smaller. However, we should notice that it is hard to make a meaningful comparison between our schemes and schemes which claim different security levels. For the lattice-based instantiations, we compute the signature size for a parameter set that achieves NIST security level II[2] (see the third row in Table 1) to allow for a fair comparison with the work of Esgin et al. [16]. We observe that for small ring sizes our lattice-based signatures are larger than those of Esgin et al., but for ring sizes larger than $N \approx 1024$ our signatures are the smallest.

Since our isogeny scheme is compact and our lattice scheme is fast, we call our schemes, respectively, the "Compact And Linkable Anonymous Message Authentication fRom Isogenies" (Calamari) and the "Fast Authentication with Linkable Anonymity From Lattices" (Falafl). We give the names "Faafl" and "Camari" to the isogeny and lattice (non-linkable) ring signatures, respectively.

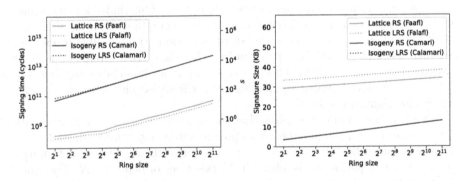

Fig. 1. Signing time (left) and signature size (right) of our isogeny-based and lattice-based (linkable) ring signatures. The left and right scales in the figure of signing time correspond to the isogeny-based and lattice-based schemes, respectively. Signing time is measured on an Intel i5-8400H CPU core.

---

[1] We compare only signature sizes since, to the best of our knowledge, ours is the only post-quantum logarithmic (linkable) ring signature with an implementation.

[2] We used the Dilithium III parameters, 168-bit seeds and commitment randomness, and a challenge space of size 2^{168}, which suffices to achieve NIST level II for low MAXDEPTH.

Table 1. Comparison of the signature size (KB) of some concretely efficient post-quantum ring signature schemes.

	N					Hardness assumption	Security level
	2^1	2^3	2^6	2^{12}	2^{21}		
Calamari	3.5	5.4	8.2	14	23	CSIDH-512	*
Falafl	29	30	32	35	39	MSIS, MLWE	NIST 1
Falafl for 2	49	50	52	55	59	MSIS, MLWE	NIST 2
RAPTOR [23]	~ 2.5	~ 10	81	5161	/	NTRU	100 bits
EZSLL [15,16]	18	19	31	59	148	MSIS, MLWE	NIST 2
KKW [19]	/	/	250	456	/	LowMC	NIST 5

*128 bits of classical security and 60 bits of quantum security [26].

1.2 Technical Overview

Our (linkable) ring signature scheme is based on a generalisation to group actions of the classical sigma protocol for the Graph Isomorphism Problem. Let $\star : G \times \mathcal{X} \to \mathcal{X}$ be a group action and fix $X_0 \in \mathcal{X}$. To prove knowledge of a group element g such that $g \star X_0 = X$, the prover uniformly samples $r \in G$, and sends $R = r \star X$ as commitment. The verifier responds with a random challenge bit c. If $c = 0$ the prover sends $\mathsf{resp} = r + g$, while they send $\mathsf{resp} = r$ if $c = 1$. The verifier checks whether $\mathsf{resp} \star X_0 = R$ when $c = 0$, and whether $\mathsf{resp} \star X = R$ when $c = 1$.

A key observation is that the verification algorithm is independent of X when the challenge bit is 0. This allows us to design the following OR proof for group actions. For some $X_0, X_1, \cdots, X_N \in \mathcal{X}$, the prover wants to prove knowledge of $g \in G$ such that $g \star X_0 = X_I$ for some $I \in \{1, \cdots N\}$. Then they start by simulating a commitment for each X_i with $i \in \{1, \cdots, N\}$, so that they can respond to the challenge $c = 1$, and send these commitments in a random order to the verifier. If the verifier sends $c = 1$, we let the prover respond for all the commitments (and hence I is not leaked). If the verifier sends the challenge bit $c = 0$, the prover can answer the I-th challenge, but not the other challenges, because they do not know group elements g_i such that $g_i \star X_0 = X_i$ for $i \neq I$. Therefore, we let the prover respond only to the I-th challenge. This does not reveal I, because verification is independent of X_I.

More concretely, the prover sends N elements $R_1 = r_1 \star X_1, \cdots, R_N = r_N \star X_N$ in a random order to the verifier, where the r_i are chosen uniformly at random from G. Then, after the verifier sends a challenge bit c, the prover responds with $\mathsf{resp} = r_I + g$ if the challenge bit c is 0, or responds with $r_1, \cdots, r_N$ in case $c = 1$. The verifier checks whether $\mathsf{resp} \star X_0 \in \{R_1, \cdots, R_N\}$ in case $c = 0$ and whether $\{r_1 \star X_1, \cdots, r_N \star X_N\} = \{R_1, \cdots, R_N\}$ in case $c = 1$. Here, note that the commitments are sent in a random order, so the response hides the index I in case $c = 0$.

Since the prover sends N elements $R_1, \cdots, R_N$ as commitment and N group elements $r_1, \cdots, r_N$ as response in case $c = 1$, it looks like the proof size is linear in N, and that there is no improvement over the generic OR proof. However, since the r_i are chosen at random, they can be generated from a pseudorandom number generator (PRG) instead, which reduces the communication cost to just sending a seed as the response in case $c = 1$. Moreover, instead of sending all the R_i we can commit to them using a Merkle tree and only send the root as the commitment. To make verification possible, the prover then sends a path in the Merkle tree to the verifier as part of the response in case $c = 0$. This makes the total proof size logarithmic in N, a clear improvement over generic OR proofs. Furthermore, since for some group actions it is more efficient to compute N group actions $r \star X_i$ with the same element $r \in G$ rather than computing N group actions $r_i \star X_i$ with distinct r_i, in our protocol we set $r_1 = \cdots = r_N = r$. Given that this would break the zero-knowledge property of the Sigma protocol, we replace each R_i by a hiding commitment $\mathsf{Com}(R_i, \mathsf{bits}_i)$, and we let the prover include bits_I in the response in case $c = 0$.

To enlarge the challenge space of the OR proof for group actions, we run parallel executions of it and then we obtain a ring signature scheme by applying the Fiat-Shamir transform to the OR proof. To avoid multi-target attacks similar to those of Dinur and Nadler [12] we made a detailed security proof in the random oracle model, with concrete expressions for the security loss in each step of the proof. This led us to include a unique salt value in each signature and to carefully separate the domain of various calls to the random oracles. We notice that in choosing our concrete parameters, as per usual, we ignore the artificial reduction loss incurred by the rewinding argument of Fiat-Shamir (since no attacks that can exploit this loss are known).

We instantiate the group action $\star$ by either the CSIDH group action or the MLWE group action defined as:

$$\star : R_q^{n+m} \times R_q^m : (\mathbf{s}, \mathbf{e}) \star \mathbf{t} \mapsto \mathbf{A} \star \mathbf{s} + \mathbf{e} + \mathbf{t}$$

where $R_q = \mathbb{Z}_q[X]/(X^d + 1)$ and $\mathbf{A}$ is a matrix belonging to $R_q^{m \times n}$. To achieve one-wayness it is necessary to restrict the domain to $S_\eta^{n+m} \times R_q^m$, where S_η is the set of elements of R_q with coefficients bounded in absolute value by η. In this case we need to use the Fiat-Shamir with aborts technique [24] to ensure that the signatures do not leak the secret key.

In order to obtain a linkable ring signature scheme, we expand our OR proof to an OR proof *with tag* where, given two group actions $\star : G \times \mathcal{X} \to \mathcal{X}$, $\bullet : G \times \mathcal{T} \to \mathcal{T}$ and a list of elements $X_0, X_1, \cdots, X_N \in \mathcal{X}$ and $T_0, T \in \mathcal{T}$, the prover proves knowledge of $g \in G$ such that $g \star X_0 = X_I$ for some $I \in \{1, \cdots, N\}$ and $g \bullet T_0 = T$. This naturally leads to a linkable signature scheme. The signer includes the tag $T = g \bullet T_0$ in the signature and then proves knowledge of g. Two signatures can be linked by checking if the tags are equal (or close with respect to a well defined metric). We require a number of properties from $\star$ and $\bullet$ to make the linkable ring signature secure (see Definition 15). For example, it should not be possible to learn $g \star X_0$ given $g \bullet T_0$, because that would break the anonymity of the linkable ring signature. We give instantiations of $\star$ and $\bullet$ based on the CSIDH group action (where we put $g \bullet X := (2g) \star X$) or based on the hardness of MLWE and MSIS.

Finally, we would like to point out some optimization tricks that allow to further lower the size of the signatures. Since our base protocol (either the OR proof or the OR proof with tag) has a binary challenge, we must execute parallel repetitions to lower the soundness error to make it useable for (linkable) ring signatures. A naive way to accomplish this would be to run the OR proof (with tag) λ-times, where λ is the security parameter. However, since opening to $c = 1$ (which requires communicating only a single seed value) is much cheaper than opening to $c = 0$, we can do much better. Specifically, we choose integers M, K such that $\binom{M}{K} \geq 2^\lambda$ and do $M > \lambda$ executions of the protocol of which exactly K executions are chosen to have challenge bit 0. Setting $K \ll \lambda$, we get a noticeable gain in the signature size. Moreover, since we now only need to open to seed values in most of the parallel runs, we use a *seed tree* to further lower the signature size. Informally, the seed tree generates a number of pseudorandom values and can later disclose an arbitrary subset of them, without revealing information on the remaining values. Further details on our optimization tricks can be found in Sect. 3.4.

Roadmap. In Sect. 2 we provide some necessary preliminaries. In Sect. 3 we first define an *admissible group action*, then we construct a base OR proof for group actions with binary challenge space, which we then extend to a main OR proof with exponential challenge space. Finally we apply the Fiat-Shamir transform to obtain a ring signature scheme. Section 4 follows the same structure: we define an *admissible pair of group actions*, for which we construct an OR proof with tag, which we convert into a linkable ring signature. In Sect. 5 we instantiate the group actions from isogeny and lattice assumptions. Finally, in Sect. 6 we discuss our parameter choices and implementation results, and we draw some conclusions.

2   Preliminaries

A Note on Random Oracles. Throughout the paper, we instantiate several standard cryptographic primitives such as pseudorandom number generators (PRG in short, and denoted by Expand) and commitment schemes by hash functions modeled as a random oracle $\mathcal{O}$. We always assume the input domain of the random oracle is appropriately separated when instantiating several cryptographic primitives by one random oracle. With abuse of notation, we may occasionally write, for example, $\mathcal{O}(\mathsf{Expand}\|\cdot)$ instead of $\mathsf{Expand}(\cdot)$ to make the usage of the random oracle explicit. Here, we identify Expand with a unique string when inputting it to $\mathcal{O}$. Moreover, we denote by $\mathcal{A}^{\mathcal{O}}$ an algorithm $\mathcal{A}$ that has black-box access to $\mathcal{O}$, and we may occasionally omit the superscript $\mathcal{O}$ when the meaning is clear. Finally, for a precise definition of relaxed Sigma protocol in the Random Oracle Model we refer to [5, Sec. 2.1].

2.1 Ring Signatures

In this subsection, we review the definition of ring signatures.

Definition 1 (Ring signature scheme). *A ring signature scheme Π_{RS} consists of four PPT algorithms* (RS.Setup, RS.KeyGen, RS.Sign, RS.Verify) *such that:*

RS.Setup(1^λ) $\rightarrow$ pp : *On input a security parameter 1^λ, it returns public parameters* pp *used by the scheme.*

RS.KeyGen(pp) $\rightarrow$ (vk, sk) : *On input the public parameters* pp, *it outputs a pair of public and secret keys* (vk, sk).

RS.Sign(sk, M, R) $\rightarrow$ σ : *On input a secret key* sk, *a message* M, *and a list of public keys, i.e., a ring,* $R = \{vk_1, \ldots, vk_N\}$, *it outputs a signature σ.*

RS.Verify(R, M, σ) $\rightarrow$ 1/0 : *On input a ring* $R = \{vk_1, \ldots, vk_N\}$, *a message* M, *and a signature σ, it outputs either 1 (accept) or 0 (reject).*

We require a ring signature scheme Π_{RS} to satisfy the following properties: correctness, full anonymity, and unforgeability. Informally, correctness means that verifying a correctly generated signature will always succeed. Anonymity means it should not be possible to learn which secret key was used to produce a signature, even for an adversary that knows the secret keys for all the public keys in the ring. Finally, unforgeability means that it should be impossible to forge a valid signature without knowing a secret key that corresponds to one of the public keys in the ring. For formal security definitions we refer to [5, Sec. 2.2].

2.2 Linkable Ring Signatures

Linkable ring signatures are a variant of ring signatures where anyone can efficiently check if two messages were signed with the same secret key. Below we review the formal definition.

Definition 2 (Linkable ring signature scheme). *A linkable ring signature scheme Π_{LRS} consists of the four PPT algorithms of a ring signature scheme and one additional PPT algorithm* LRS.Link *such that:*

LRS.Link(σ_0, σ_1) $\rightarrow$ 1/0 : *On input two signatures σ_0 and σ_1, it outputs either 1 or 0, where 1 indicates that the signatures were produced with the same secret key.*

In addition to the correctness property, we require a linkable ring signature scheme Π_{LRS} to satisfy linkability, linkable anonymity, and non-frameability. Informally, linkability means that, if an adversary produces more than k signatures with a ring of k (potentially malformed) public keys, then the LRS.Link algorithm will output 1 on at least one pair of signatures. Linkable-anonymity means that an adversary cannot tell which secret key was used to produce a signature. In contrast to the ring signature case, the adversary is not given all the secret keys, otherwise they could use the linkability property to deanonymize the signer. Finally, the non-frameability property says it should be impossible for an adversary to produce a valid signature that links to a signature produced by an honest party. For formal security definitions we refer to [5, Sec. 2.3].

Remark 3 (Unforgeability). We can also require a linkable ring signature to be unforgeable, as defined above for a ring signature. However, it can be shown that unforgeability is implied by linkability and non-frameability.

2.3   Isogenies and Ideal Class Group Actions

Let $\mathbb{F}_p$ be a prime field, with $p \geq 5$, and E a supersingular elliptic curve defined over $\mathbb{F}_p$. The ring $\mathrm{End}_p(E)$ of all endomorphisms of E that are defined over $\mathbb{F}_p$ is isomorphic to an order $\mathcal{O}$ of the field $\mathbb{K} = \mathbb{Q}(\sqrt{-p})$ [8]. The invertible fractional ideals of $\mathcal{O}$ form an abelian group whose quotient by the subgroup of principal fractional ideals is finite, called the *ideal class group* of $\mathcal{O}$ and denoted by $\mathcal{Cl}(\mathcal{O})$. The ideal class group $\mathcal{Cl}(\mathcal{O})$ acts freely and transitively on the set $\mathcal{Ell}_p(\mathcal{O}, \pi)$, which contains all supersingular elliptic curves E over $\mathbb{F}_p$ - modulo isomorphisms defined over $\mathbb{F}_p$ - such that there exists an isomorphism between $\mathcal{O}$ and $\mathrm{End}_p(E)$ mapping $\sqrt{-p} \in \mathcal{O}$ into the Frobenius endomorphism $\pi : (x, y) \mapsto (x^p, y^p)$. We denote this action by $*$. Recently, it has been used to design several cryptographic primitives [6,8,10], whose security proofs rely on (variations of) the Group Action Inverse Problem (GAIP), defined as follows:

Definition 4 (Group Action Inverse Problem (GAIP)). *Let $[E_0]$ be a an element in $\mathcal{Ell}_p(\mathcal{O}, \pi)$, where $p \geq 5$ is an odd prime. Given $[E]$ sampled uniformly at random from $\mathcal{Ell}_p(\mathcal{O}, \pi)$, the GAIP_p problem consists in finding an element $[\mathfrak{a}] \in \mathcal{Cl}(\mathcal{O})$ such that $[\mathfrak{a}] * [E_0] = [E]$.*

For the security of the isogeny-based instantiations of our (linkable) ring signature scheme we will rely on a newly-introduced hard problem, called the Squaring Decisional CSIDH Problem (sdCSIDH in short).

Definition 5 (Squaring Decisional CSIDH (sdCSIDH) Problem). *Let $[E_0]$ be an element in $\mathcal{Ell}_p(\mathcal{O}, \pi)$, where $p \geq 5$ is an odd prime. Given $[\mathfrak{a}]$ sampled uniformly at random from $\mathcal{Cl}(\mathcal{O})$, the $\mathsf{sdCSIDH}_p$ problem consists in distinguishing the two distributions $([\mathfrak{a}] * [E_0], [\mathfrak{a}]^2 * [E_0])$ and $([E], [E'])$, where $[E], [E']$ are both sampled uniformly at random from $\mathcal{Ell}_p(\mathcal{O}, \pi)$.*

In analogy with the classical group-based scenario [3], we assume the above problem is equivalent to the decisional CSIDH problem, recently used in [9,14].

2.4   Lattices

For positive integers n and q, let R and R_q denote the rings $\mathbb{Z}[X]/(X^n + 1)$ and $\mathbb{Z}[X]/(q, X^n + 1)$, respectively. Norms over R are defined through the coefficient vectors of the polynomials, which lie over $\mathbb{Z}^n$. Norms over R_q are defined in the conventional way by uniquely representing coefficients of polynomials in R_q by elements in the range $(-q/2, q/2]$ when q is even and $[-(q-1)/2, (q-1)/2]$ when q is odd (see, for example, [13] for more details).

The hard problems that we rely on for our lattice-based schemes are the *module short integer solution* (MSIS) problem and *module learning with errors* (MLWE) problem, first introduced in [21].

Definition 6 (Module short integer solution Problem). *Let* n, q, k, ℓ, γ *be positive integers. The advantage for the (Hermite normal form) module short integer solution problem* $\mathsf{MSIS}_{n,q,k,\ell,\gamma}$ *for an algorithm* $\mathcal{A}$ *is defined as*

$$\mathsf{Adv}^{\mathsf{MSIS}}_{n,q,k,\ell,\gamma}(\mathcal{A}) = \Pr\left[0 < \|\mathbf{u}\|_\infty \leq \gamma \wedge [\mathbf{A} \mid \mathbf{I}] \cdot \mathbf{u} = \mathbf{0} \mid \mathbf{A} \leftarrow R_q^{k \times \ell}; \mathbf{u} \leftarrow \mathcal{A}(\mathbf{A})\right].$$

Definition 7 (Module learning with errors Problem). *Let* n, q, k, ℓ *be positive integers and* D *a probability distribution over* R_q. *The advantage for the decisional module learning with errors problem* $\mathsf{dMLWE}_{n,q,k,\ell,D}$ *for an algorithm* $\mathcal{A}$ *is defined as*

$$\mathsf{Adv}^{\mathsf{dMLWE}}_{n,q,k,\ell,D}(\mathcal{A}) = |\Pr[\mathcal{A}(\mathbf{A}, \mathbf{As} + \mathbf{e}) \to 1] - \Pr[\mathcal{A}(\mathbf{A}, \mathbf{v}) \to 1]|,$$

where $\mathbf{A} \leftarrow R_q^{k \times \ell}$, $\mathbf{s} \leftarrow D^\ell$, $\mathbf{e} \leftarrow D^k$ *and* $\mathbf{v} \leftarrow R_q^k$.

The advantage for the search *learning with errors problem* $\mathsf{sMLWE}_{n,q,k,\ell,D}$ *is defined analogously to above as the probability that* $\mathcal{A}(\mathbf{A}, \mathbf{v} := \mathbf{As} + \mathbf{e})$ *outputs* $(\tilde{\mathbf{s}}, \tilde{\mathbf{e}})$ *such that* $\mathbf{A}\tilde{\mathbf{s}} + \tilde{\mathbf{e}} = \mathbf{v}$ *and* $(\tilde{\mathbf{s}}, \tilde{\mathbf{e}}) \in \mathsf{Supp}(D^\ell) \times \mathsf{Supp}(D^k)$.

When it is clear from the context, we omit the subscript n and q from above for simplicity. The MLWE assumptions are believed to hold even when D is the uniform distribution over ring elements with infinity norm at most B, say $B \approx 5$, for appropriate choices of n, q, k, ℓ [1]. We write $\mathsf{MLWE}_{k,\ell,B}$ when we consider such distribution. For example, the round-2 NIST candidate signature scheme Dilithium [13] uses such parameters. Looking ahead, we will choose our parameters for MSIS and MLWE in accordance with [13].

2.5   Index-Hiding Merkle Trees

Merkle trees [25] allow to hash a list of elements $A = (a_1, \cdots, a_N)$ into one hash value (often called root). At a later point, one can efficiently prove to a third party that an element a_i was included at a certain position in the list A. In the following, we consider a slight modification of the standard Merkle tree construction, such that one can prove that a single element a_i was included in the tree without revealing its position in the list. Security proofs for the binding and index-hiding properties of our Merkle tree construction can be found in [5, Sec. 2.6].

Formally, the index-hiding Merkle tree technique consists of three algorithms (MerkleTree, getMerklePath, ReconstructRoot) with access to a common collision-resistant hash function $\mathcal{H}_{\mathsf{Coll}} : \{0,1\}^\star \to \{0,1\}^{2\lambda}$ (with λ being the security parameter):

- MerkleTree(A) $\rightarrow$ (root, tree): On input a list of 2^k elements $A = (a_1, \cdots, a_{2^k})$, with $k \in \mathbb{N}$, it constructs a binary tree of height k with $\{l_i = \mathcal{H}_{\mathsf{Coll}}(a_i)\}_{i \in [2^k]}$ as its leaves, and where every internal node h, with children h_{left} and h_{right}, equals the hash of a concatenation of its two children. While it is standard to consider the concatenation $h_{\mathsf{left}} \| h_{\mathsf{right}}$, for index-hiding Merkle trees we consider a variation which consists in ordering the two children according to the lexicographical order (or any other total order on binary strings). We denote by $(h_{\mathsf{left}}, h_{\mathsf{right}})_{\mathsf{lex}}$ this concatenation. The algorithm then outputs the root root of the Merkle tree, as well as a description of the entire tree tree.
- getMerklePath(tree, i) $\rightarrow$ path: On input the description of a Merkle tree tree and an index $i \in [2^k]$, it outputs the list path, which contains the sibling of l_i (i.e. a node, different from l_i, that has the same parent as l_i), as well as the sibling of any ancestor of l_i, ordered by decreasing height.
- ReconstructRoot(a, path) $\rightarrow$ root: On input an element a in the list of elements $A = (a_1, \cdots, a_{2^k})$ and path $= (n_1, \cdots, n_{k-1})$, it outputs a reconstructed root root$' = h_k$, which is calculated by putting $h_0 = \mathcal{H}_{\mathsf{Coll}}(a)$ and defining h_i for $i \in [k]$ recursively as $h_i = \mathcal{H}_{\mathsf{Coll}}((h_{i-1}, n_i)_{\mathsf{lex}})$.

2.6   Seed Tree

We formalize a primitive called *seed tree*, whose purpose is to first generate a number of pseudorandom values and later disclose an arbitrary subset of them, without revealing information on the remaining values. A seed tree is a complete binary tree[3] of λ-bit seed values such that the left (resp. right) child of a seed seed$_h$ is the left (resp. right) half of Expand(seed$\|h$), where Expand is a pseudorandom number generator (PRG). The unique identifier h of the parent seed is appended to separate the input domains of the different calls to the PRG. A sender can efficiently reveal the seed values of a subset of the set of leaves by revealing the appropriate set of internal seeds in the tree. We detail the formal construction of a seed tree below, where Expand : $\{0,1\}^{\lambda + \lceil \log_2(M-1) \rceil} \rightarrow \{0,1\}^{2\lambda}$ is a PRG for any $\lambda, M \in \mathbb{N}$, instantiated by a random oracle $\mathcal{O}$. Then, a seed tree consists of the following four oracle-calling algorithms:

- SeedTree$^{\mathcal{O}}$(seed$_{\mathsf{root}}$, M) $\rightarrow$ $\{\mathsf{leaf}_i\}_{i \in [M]}$: On input a root seed seed$_{\mathsf{root}} \in \{0,1\}^{\lambda}$ and an integer $M \in \mathbb{N}$, it constructs a complete binary tree with M leaves by recursively expanding each seed to obtain its children seeds. Calls are of the form $\mathcal{O}(\mathsf{Expand}\|\mathsf{seed}\|h)$, where $h \in [M-1]$ is a unique identifier for the position of seed in the binary tree.
- ReleaseSeeds$^{\mathcal{O}}$(seed$_{\mathsf{root}}$, $\mathbf{c}$) $\rightarrow$ seeds$_{\mathsf{internal}}$: On input a root seed seed$_{\mathsf{root}} \in \{0,1\}^{\lambda}$, and a challenge $\mathbf{c} \in \{0,1\}^M$, it outputs the list of seeds seeds$_{\mathsf{internal}}$ that covers all the leaves with index i such that $c_i = 1$. Here, we say that a set of nodes F *covers* a set of leaves S if the union of the leaves of the subtrees rooted at each node $v \in F$ is exactly the set S.

---

[3] A *complete* binary tree is a binary tree in which every level, except possibly the last, is completely filled, and all nodes are as far left as possible.

- RecoverLeaves$^{\mathcal{O}}$(seeds$_{internal}$, $\mathbf{c}$) $\rightarrow$ {$\overline{leaf}_i$}$_{i\ s.t.\ c_i=1}$: On input a set seeds$_{internal}$ and a challenge $\mathbf{c} \in \{0,1\}^M$, it computes and outputs all the leaves of the subtrees rooted at the seeds in seeds$_{internal}$.
- SimulateSeeds$^{\mathcal{O}}$($\mathbf{c}$) $\rightarrow$ seeds$_{internal}$: On input a challenge $\mathbf{c} \in \{0,1\}^M$, it identifies the set of nodes covering the leaves with index i such that $c_i = 1$. It then randomly samples a seed from $\{0,1\}^\lambda$ for each of these nodes, and finally outputs the set of these seeds as seeds$_{internal}$.

By construction, the leaves {leaf$_i$}$_{i\ s.t.\ c_i=1}$ output by SeedTree(seed$_{root}$, M) are the same as those output by RecoverLeaves(ReleaseSeeds(seed$_{root}$, $\mathbf{c}$), $\mathbf{c}$) for any $\mathbf{c} \in \{0,1\}^M$. The last algorithm SimulateSeeds can be used to argue that the seeds associated with all the leaves with index i such that $c_i = 0$ are indistinguishable from uniformly random values for a recipient that is only given seeds$_{internal}$ and $\mathbf{c}$. For a formal proof we refer to [5, Lemma 2.11].

3   From Group Actions to Ring Signatures

In this section, our main result consists in showing an efficient OR sigma protocol for group actions. Unlike generic OR sigma protocols, whose proof size grows linearly in N, the proof size of our construction will only grow logarithmically in N. Moreover, the multiplicative overhead in $\log N$ is much smaller (i.e., only the size of a single hash) compared to previous works. To obtain ring signatures, we apply the Fiat-Shamir transform (with aborts) to our OR sigma protocol.

3.1   Admissible Group Actions

Definition 8 (Admissible group action). *Let G be an additive group, S_1, S_2 two symmetric subsets of G, $\mathcal{X}$ a finite set, δ in $[0,1]$ and $D_\mathcal{X}$ a distribution over a set of group actions $\star : G \times \mathcal{X} \rightarrow \mathcal{X}$. We say that $\mathsf{AdmGA} = (G, \mathcal{X}, S_1, S_2, D_\mathcal{X})$ is a δ-admissible group action with respect to $X_0 \in \mathcal{X}$ if the following holds:*

1. *One can efficiently compute $g \star X$ for all $g \in S_1 \cup S_2$ and all $X \in \mathcal{X}$, sample uniformly from S_1, S_2 and $D_\mathcal{X}$, and represent elements of G and $\mathcal{X}$ uniquely.*
2. *The intersection of the sets $S_2 + g$, for $g \in S_1$, is sufficiently large. More formally, let $S_3 = \bigcap_{g \in S_1} S_2 + g$, then*

$$|S_3| = \delta |S_2|.$$

Furthermore, it is efficient to check whether an element $g \in G$ belongs to S_3 and to compute $g \star X$ for all $g \in S_3$, $X \in \mathcal{X}$.
3. *It is difficult to output $g' \in S_2 + S_3$ such that $g' \star X_0 = X$ with non-negligible probability, given $X = g \star X_0$ for some g sampled uniformly from S_1. That is, for any efficient adversary $\mathcal{A}$ we have*

$$\Pr\left[\begin{array}{c|c} g' \in S_2 + S_3, & \star \leftarrow D_\mathcal{X} \\ g' \star X_0 = X & g \leftarrow S_1 \\ & X \leftarrow g \star X_0 \\ & g' \leftarrow \mathcal{A}(\star, X) \end{array}\right] \leq \mathsf{negl}(\lambda).$$

Hereafter, when the context is clear, we omit the description of the group action $\star$ provided to the adversary and implicitly assume the probabilities are taken over the random choice of $\star$.

3.2   From an Admissible Group Action to Base or Sigma Protocol $\Pi_{\Sigma}^{\text{RS-base}}$

Before presenting the main OR sigma protocol used for our ring signature, we present an intermediate *base* OR sigma protocol with a binary challenge space. Looking ahead, our main OR sigma protocol will run the base OR sigma protocol several times to amplify the soundness.

Let $\mathsf{AdmGA} = (G, \mathcal{X}, S_1, S_2, D_{\mathcal{X}})$ be an admissible group action with respect to $X_0 \in \mathcal{X}$, and suppose that $X_1 = s_1 \star X_0, \cdots, X_N = s_N \star X_0$ are N public keys, where the corresponding secret keys $s_1, \cdots, s_N$ are drawn uniformly from S_1. In this section, we give an efficient binary-challenge OR sigma protocol $\Pi_{\Sigma}^{\text{RS-base}} = (P' = (P_1', P_2'), V' = (V_1', V_2'))$ proving knowledge of $(s_I, I) \in S_1 \times [N]$, such that $s_I \star X_0 = X_I$.[4]

We sketch the description of our base OR sigma protocol $\Pi_{\Sigma}^{\text{RS-base}}$. First, the prover samples an element r uniformly from S_2, and computes $R_i = r \star X_i$ for all $i \in [N]$. The prover further samples random bit strings $\{\mathsf{bits}_i\}_{i \in [N]}$ uniformly from $\{0, 1\}^{\lambda}$, and commits to R_i with the random oracle as $\mathsf{C}_i \leftarrow \mathcal{O}(\mathsf{Com} \| R_i \| \mathsf{bits}_i)$. Then, the prover builds a index-hiding Merkle tree with $\mathsf{C}_1, \cdots, \mathsf{C}_N$ as its leaves.[5] Note that this procedure can be done deterministically, by generating randomness by a pseudorandom number generator (PRG) Expand from a short seed seed. The prover sends the root root of the Merkle tree to the verifier, who responds with a uniformly random bit c.

If the challenge bit c is 0, then the prover computes $z = r + s_I$. If $z \notin S_3$, then the prover aborts (this happens with probability $1 - \delta$). Otherwise the prover sends z, the path in the Merkle tree that connects C_I to the root of the tree and the opening bits bits_I for the commitment C_I. The verifier then computes $\tilde{R} = z \star X_0$ and $\tilde{\mathsf{C}} := \mathsf{Com}(\tilde{R}, \mathsf{bits}_I)$, and uses the path to reconstruct the root $\widetilde{\mathsf{root}}$ of the index-hiding Merkle tree. They finally check if $z \in S_3$ and $\widetilde{\mathsf{root}} = \mathsf{root}$.

If the challenge bit c is 1 then the prover reveals r to the verifier, as well as the opening bits bits_i for all $i \in [N]$. This allows the verifier to recompute the index-hiding Merkle tree and to check if its root matches the value of root that they received earlier. Note that in this case, it suffices for the prover to just send seed, since r and the bits_i are derived pseudorandomly from this seed.

A toy protocol is displayed in Fig. 2 and the full protocol is detailed in Fig. 3. In the full protocol, we assume the PRG Expand and the commitment scheme to be instantiated by a random oracle $\mathcal{O}$. We further assume w.l.o.g. that the output length of the random oracle is adjusted appropriately.

---

[4] To be accurate, we prove knowledge of $s_I \in S_2 + S_3$, as we consider "relaxed" special soundness.

[5] For simplicity, we will assume that N is a power of 2. If this is not the case we add additional dummy commitments to make the number of leaves a power of 2.

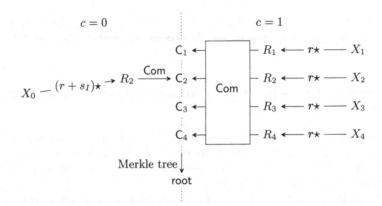

Fig. 2. The base sigma protocol $\Pi_\Sigma^{\text{RS-base}}$ to prove knowledge of (s_I, I) such that $s_I \star X_0 = X_I$ (In the drawing $N = 4$ and $I = 2$). If the challenge bit c is 0, then the left side of the picture is revealed, otherwise the right side of the picture is revealed.

3.3 Security Proof for the Base OR Sigma Protocol $\Pi_\Sigma^{\text{RS-base}}$

The following Theorems 9 and 10 provide the security of $\Pi_\Sigma^{\text{RS-base}}$. For their proofs we refer to [5, Sec. 3.3]

Theorem 9. *Let $\mathcal{O}$ be a random oracle. Define the relation*

$$R = \{((X_1, \cdots, X_N), (s, I)) \mid s \in S_1, X_i \in \mathcal{X}, I \in [N], X_I = s \star X_0\}$$

and the relaxed relation

$$\tilde{R} = \left\{ ((X_1, \cdots, X_N), w) \;\middle|\; \begin{array}{l} X_i \in \mathcal{X} \text{ and} \\ w = (s, I) : s \in S_2 + S_3, I \in [N], X_I = s \star X_0 \text{ or} \\ w = (x, x') : \quad x \neq x', \mathcal{H}_{\text{Coll}}(x) = \mathcal{H}_{\text{Coll}}(x') \text{ or} \\ \qquad\qquad\qquad \mathcal{O}(\text{Com}\|x) = \mathcal{O}(\text{Com}\|x') \end{array} \right\}.$$

Then the OR sigma protocol $\Pi_\Sigma^{\text{RS-base}}$ of Fig. 3 has correctness with probability of aborting $(1 - \delta)/2$ and relaxed special soundness for the relations $(R, \tilde{R})$.[6]

Theorem 10. *The OR sigma protocol $\Pi_\Sigma^{\text{RS-base}}$ of Fig. 3 is non-abort honest-verifier zero-knowledge. More concretely, there exists a simulator Sim such that for any $(\mathsf{X}, \mathsf{W}) \in R$, $\text{chall} \in \mathsf{ChSet}$ and any (computationally unbounded) adversary $\mathcal{A}$ that makes Q queries to the random oracle $\mathcal{O}$, we have*

$$\left| \Pr[\mathcal{A}^{\mathcal{O}}(\tilde{P}^{\mathcal{O}}(\mathsf{X}, \mathsf{W}, \text{chall})) \to 1] - \Pr[\mathcal{A}^{\mathcal{O}}(\mathsf{Sim}^{\mathcal{O}}(\mathsf{X}, \text{chall})) \to 1] \right| \leq \frac{2Q}{2^\lambda}.$$

---

[6] We note that the notion of collision in $\mathcal{O}$ may seem non-standard at this point since the truth table of $\mathcal{O}$ is typically filled in one at a time when queried so it is not clear who is querying the $\mathcal{O}$ right now. However, we observe that this non-standard notion suffices for our (linkable) ring signature application w.l.o.g.

round 1: $P_1'^{\mathcal{O}}((X_1, \cdots, X_N), (s_I, I))$

1: seed $\leftarrow \{0, 1\}^\lambda$ ▷ The only randomness used by the Prover
2: $(r, \text{bits}_1, \cdots, \text{bits}_N) \leftarrow \mathcal{O}(\text{Expand}\|\text{seed})$ ▷ Sample $r \in S_2$ and $\text{bits}_i \in \{0,1\}^\lambda$
3: **for** i from 1 to N **do**
4:      $R_i \leftarrow r \star X_i$
5:      $C_i \leftarrow \mathcal{O}(\text{Com}\|R_i\|\text{bits}_i)$ ▷ Create commitment $C_i \in \{0,1\}^{2\lambda}$
6: $(\text{root}, \text{tree}) \leftarrow \text{MerkleTree}(C_1, \cdots, C_N)$ ▷ Index-hiding Merkle tree
7: Prover sends com $\leftarrow$ root to Verifier.

round 2: $V_1'(\text{com})$

1: $c \leftarrow \{0, 1\}$
2: Verifier sends chall $\leftarrow c$ to Prover.

round 3: $P_2'((s_I, I), \text{chall})$

1: $c \leftarrow$ chall
2: **if** $c = 0$ **then**
3:      $z \leftarrow r + s_I$
4:      **if** $z \notin S_3$ **then**
5:          P aborts the protocol.
6:      path $\leftarrow$ getMerklePath(tree, I)
7:      rsp $\leftarrow (z, \text{path}, \text{bits}_I)$
8: **else**
9:      rsp $\leftarrow$ seed
10: Prover sends rsp to Verifier

Verification: $V_2'^{\mathcal{O}}(\text{com}, \text{chall}, \text{rsp})$

1: $(\text{root}, c) \leftarrow (\text{com}, \text{chall})$
2: **if** $c = 0$ **then**
3:      $(z, \text{path}, \text{bits}) \leftarrow$ rsp
4:      $\widetilde{R} \leftarrow z \star X_0$
5:      $\widetilde{C} \leftarrow \mathcal{O}(\text{Com}\|\widetilde{R}\|\text{bits})$
6:      $\widetilde{\text{root}} \leftarrow \text{ReconstructRoot}(\widetilde{C}, \text{path})$
7:      Verifier outputs accept if $z \in S_3$ and $\widetilde{\text{root}} = \text{root}$, and otherwise outputs reject
8: **else**
9:      Verifier repeats the computation of **round 1** with seed $\leftarrow$ rsp
10:     Verifier outputs accept if the computation results in root, and otherwise outputs reject

Fig. 3. Construction of the base OR sigma protocol $\Pi_\Sigma^{\text{RS-base}} = (P' = (P_1', P_2'), V' = (V_1', V_2'))$, given an admissible group action $\text{AdmGA} = (G, \mathcal{X}, S_1, S_2, D_{\mathcal{X}})$ with respect to $X_0 \in \mathcal{X}$ together with a random group action $\star \leftarrow D_{\mathcal{X}}$. Above, the PRG Expand and the commitment scheme Com are modeled by a random oracle $\mathcal{O}$.

Here $\widetilde{P}$ denotes a non-aborting prover $P' = (P_1', P_2')$ run on (X, W) with challenge fixed as chall. In other words, Sim simulates to $\mathcal{A}$ the view of an honest non-aborting execution of the sigma protocol without using the witness.

3.4 From Base OR Sigma Protocol $\Pi_{\Sigma}^{\text{RS-base}}$ to Main OR Sigma Protocol Π_{Σ}^{RS}

To have an OR sigma protocol where a prover cannot cheat with more than negligible probability, we have to enlarge the challenge space. In this section, we show how to obtain our main OR sigma protocol Π_{Σ}^{RS}, with a large challenge space, from our base OR sigma protocol $\Pi_{\Sigma}^{\text{RS-base}}$ with a binary challenge space. Below, we also incorporate three optimization techniques that lead to a much more efficient protocol compared to simply running $\Pi_{\Sigma}^{\text{RS-base}}$ in parallel λ-times.

Unbalanced Challenge Space $C_{M,K}$. Notice that in $\Pi_{\Sigma}^{\text{RS-base}}$, responding to a challenge with challenge bit $c = 0$ is more costly than responding to the challenge bit $c = 1$ (which requires communicating only a single seed value). Therefore, rather than λ independent executions of $\Pi_{\Sigma}^{\text{RS-base}}$, it is more convenient to choose positive integers M, K such that $\binom{M}{K} \geq 2^{\lambda}$ and do $M > \lambda$ executions of the protocol, of which exactly K are chosen to have challenge bit 0. For example, when targeting 128 bits of security, we can do $M = 250$ executions, out of which $K = 30$ correspond to the challenge bit $c = 0$ (so $M - K = 220$ correspond to $c = 1$). Assuming the cost of responding to the challenge $c = 1$ is negligible, this reduces the response size by roughly a factor 2. Moreover, this optimization makes the response size constant and reduces the probability that the prover needs to abort and restart (which allows for better parameter choices). Below, we denote $C_{M,K}$ as the set of strings in $\{0,1\}^M$ such that exactly K-bits are 0.

Using Seed Tree. Using the unbalanced challenge space, we now run our base OR sigma protocol $\Pi_{\Sigma}^{\text{RS-base}}$ in parallel M times, and in $(M - K) \approx M$ of the runs, we simply output the random seed sampled by $\Pi_{\Sigma}^{\text{RS-base}}$. Here, we use the seed tree (introduced in Sect. 2.6) to optimize this step. In particular, instead of choosing independent seeds for each of the M instances of $\Pi_{\Sigma}^{\text{RS-base}}$, we generate the M seeds using a seed tree. Furthermore, instead of responding with $(M - K)$ seeds, the prover outputs $\text{seeds}_{\text{internal}} \leftarrow \text{ReleaseSeeds}(\text{seed}_{\text{root}}, \mathbf{c})$, where $\mathbf{c}$ is the challenge sampled from $C_{M,K}$. The verifier can then use $\text{seeds}_{\text{internal}}$ along with $\mathbf{c}$ to recover the $(M - K)$ seeds by running RecoverLeaves. This reduces the response length.

Adding Salt. As a final tweak to the standard parallel repetition of sigma protocols, the prover P_1 of the main OR sigma protocol Π_{Σ}^{RS} picks a 2λ bit salt and runs the i-th ($i \in [M]$) instance of $\Pi_{\Sigma}^{\text{RS-base}}$ with the random oracle $\mathcal{O}_i(\cdot) := \mathcal{O}(\text{salt}\|i\|\cdot)$. The prover also salts the seed tree construction. This tweak allows us to prove a tighter security proof for the zero-knowledge property. In practice, this modification does not affect the efficiency of the protocol by much, but it avoids multi-target attacks such as those by Dinur and Nadler [12].

The description of our main OR sigma protocol which incorporates all the above optimizations is depicted in Fig. 4.

Remark 11 (Commitment recoverable). Notice that the underlying base OR sigma protocol $\Pi_\Sigma^{\text{RS-base}}$ is *commitment recoverable*. That is, given the statement X, the challenge chall and the response rsp, there is an efficient deterministic algorithm RecoverCom(X, chall, rsp) that recovers the unique commitment com that leads the verifier to accept. This property allows the signer of a Fiat-Shamir type signature to include the challenge rather than the commitment in a signature, which shortens the signature size. Our main sigma protocol is "almost" commitment recoverable, since one can recover the entire commitment except for the random salt. We use this property in Sect. 3.6.

3.5   Security Proof for the Main OR Sigma Protocol Π_Σ^{RS}

The following Theorems 12 and 13 provide the security of Π_Σ^{RS}. Their proofs can be found in [5, Sec. 3.5]

Theorem 12. *Define the relation R and the relaxed relation $\tilde{R}$ as in Theorem 9. Then the OR sigma protocol Π_Σ^{RS} has correctness with probability of aborting $1 - \delta^K$, high min-entropy and relaxed special soundness for the relations $(R, \tilde{R})$.*

Theorem 13. *The OR sigma protocol Π_Σ^{RS} is non-abort special zero-knowledge. More concretely, there exists a simulator Sim such that, for any $(X, W) \in R$, chall $\in$ ChSet and any (computationally unbounded) adversary $\mathcal{A}$ that makes Q queries of the form salt$\|\cdot$ to the random oracle $\mathcal{O}$ - where salt is the salt value included in the transcript returned by $\tilde{P}$ or Sim, we have*

$$\left| \Pr[\mathcal{A}^{\mathcal{O}}(\tilde{P}^{\mathcal{O}}(X, W, \text{chall})) \rightarrow 1] - \Pr[\mathcal{A}^{\mathcal{O}}(\text{Sim}^{\mathcal{O}}(X, \text{chall})) \rightarrow 1] \right| \leq \frac{3Q}{2^\lambda}.$$

Remark 14. We notice that, for the application of (linkable) ring signatures, it suffices to be able to simulate non-aborting transcripts, because an aborting transcript will never be released by the signer.

3.6   From Main OR Sigma Protocol Π_Σ^{RS} to Ring Signature

We apply the Fiat-Shamir transform [17] to our main OR sigma protocol Π_Σ^{RS} to obtain a ring signature. The resulting scheme is illustrated in Fig. 5, where we also exploit the almost commitment recoverability of Π_Σ^{RS} (see Remark 11). There, $\mathcal{H}_{\text{FS}}$ is a hash function, with range $C_{M,K}$, modeled as a random oracle. The correctness, anonymity, and unforgeability of the ring signature are a direct consequence of the correctness, high min-entropy, non-abort special zero-knowledge, and (relaxed) special soundness property of the underlying OR sigma protocol Π_Σ^{RS}. Since we believe the proofs are folklore (see for example [18, Theorem 4] for some details), we do not provide them (a brief sketch of them can be found in [5, Sec. A.1]).

round 1: $P_1^{\mathcal{O}}((X_1, \cdots, X_N), (s_I, I))$
  1: $\mathsf{seed}_{\mathsf{root}} \leftarrow \{0,1\}^{\lambda}$
  2: $\mathsf{salt} \leftarrow \{0,1\}^{2\lambda}$
  3: $\mathcal{O}'(\cdot) := \mathcal{O}(\mathsf{salt}||\cdot)$
  4: $(\mathsf{seed}_1, \cdots, \mathsf{seed}_M) \leftarrow \mathsf{SeedTree}^{\mathcal{O}'}(\mathsf{seed}_{\mathsf{root}}, M)$
  5: **for** i from 1 to M **do**
  6:     $\mathcal{O}_i(\cdot) := \mathcal{O}(\mathsf{salt}||i||\cdot)$
  7:     $\mathsf{com}_i \leftarrow P_1'^{\mathcal{O}_i}((X_1, \cdots, X_N), (s_I, I); \mathsf{seed}_i)$ $\triangleright$ Run P_1' on randomness seed_i
  8: Prover sends $\mathsf{com} \leftarrow (\mathsf{salt}, \mathsf{com}_1, \cdots, \mathsf{com}_M)$ to Verifier.

round 2: $V_1(\mathsf{com})$
  1: $\mathbf{c} \leftarrow C_{M,K}$
  2: Verifier sends $\mathsf{chall} \leftarrow \mathbf{c}$ to Prover.

round 3: $P_2^{\mathcal{O}}((s_I, I), \mathsf{chall})$
  1: $\mathbf{c} = (c_1, \cdots, c_M) \leftarrow \mathsf{chall}$
  2: **for** i s.t. $c_i = 0$ **do**
  3:     $\mathsf{rsp}_i \leftarrow P_2'((s_I, I), c_i; \mathsf{seed}_i)$ $\triangleright$ Run P_2' on randomness seed_i
  4: $\mathcal{O}'(\cdot) := \mathcal{O}(\mathsf{salt}||\cdot)$
  5: $\mathsf{seeds}_{\mathsf{internal}} \leftarrow \mathsf{ReleaseSeeds}^{\mathcal{O}'}(\mathsf{seed}_{\mathsf{root}}, \mathbf{c})$
  6: Prover sends $\mathsf{rsp} \leftarrow (\mathsf{seeds}_{\mathsf{internal}}, \{\mathsf{rsp}_i\}_{i \text{ s.t. } c_i=0})$ to Verifier

Verification: $V_2^{\mathcal{O}}(\mathsf{com}, \mathsf{chall}, \mathsf{rsp})$
  1: $((\mathsf{salt}, \mathsf{com}_1, \cdots, \mathsf{com}_M), \mathbf{c} = (c_1, \cdots, c_M)) \leftarrow (\mathsf{com}, \mathsf{chall})$
  2: $(\mathsf{seeds}_{\mathsf{internal}}, \{\mathsf{rsp}_i\}_{i \text{ s.t. } c_i=0}) \leftarrow \mathsf{rsp}$
  3: $\mathcal{O}'(\cdot) := \mathcal{O}(\mathsf{salt}||\cdot)$
  4: $\{\mathsf{resp}_i\}_{i \text{ s.t. } c_i=1} \leftarrow \mathsf{RecoverLeaves}^{\mathcal{O}'}(\mathsf{seeds}_{\mathsf{internal}}, \mathbf{c})$
  5: **for** i from 1 to M **do**
  6:     $\mathcal{O}_i(\cdot) := \mathcal{O}(\mathsf{salt}||i||\cdot)$
  7:     Verifier outputs reject if $V_2'^{\mathcal{O}_i}(\mathsf{com}_i, c_i, \mathsf{rsp}_i)$ outputs reject
  8: Verifier outputs accept

Fig. 4. Construction of the main OR sigma protocol $\Pi_{\Sigma}^{\mathsf{RS}} = (P = (P_1, P_2), V = (V_1, V_2))$ based on the base OR sigma protocol $\Pi_{\Sigma}^{\mathsf{RS\text{-}base}} = (P' = (P_1', P_2'), V' = (V_1', V_2'))$. The challenge space is defined as $C_{M,K} := \{\mathbf{c} \in \{0,1\}^M \mid ||\mathbf{c}||_1 = M - K\}$. The seed tree and $\Pi_{\Sigma}^{\mathsf{RS\text{-}base}}$ have access to the random oracle $\mathcal{O}$.

4   From a Pair of Group Actions to Linkable Ring Signatures

In this section we construct a linkable ring signature from a *pair* of group actions, $\star : G \times \mathcal{X} \to \mathcal{X}$ and $\bullet : G \times \mathcal{T} \to \mathcal{T}$, that satisfy certain properties. The proposed linkable ring signature is similar to the ring signature in Sect. 3. In particular, a secret key is a group element $s \in S_1 \subset G$ and the corresponding public key is $s \star X_0 \in \mathcal{X}$ for a fixed public element X_0. To achieve linkability, in this section the signature contains also a tag $T \in \mathcal{T}$, which is obtained as $T = s \bullet T_0$ for

RS.KeyGen(pp)

1: $s \leftarrow S_1$
2: $X \leftarrow s \star X_0$
3: **return** $(vk = X, sk = s)$

RS.Sign(sk, M, R)

1: $(vk_1, \cdots vk_N) \leftarrow R$ ▷ Let vk_I be associated
   to $sk = s_I$.
2: $com = (salt, (com_i)_{i \in [M]}) \leftarrow P_1^{\mathcal{O}}(R, (sk, I))$
3: $chall \leftarrow \mathcal{H}_{FS}(M, R, com)$
4: $rsp \leftarrow P_2^{\mathcal{O}}((sk, I), chall)$
5: **return** $\sigma = (salt, chall, rsp)$

RS.Verify(R, M, σ)

1: $(vk_1, \cdots vk_N) \leftarrow R$
2: $(salt, chall, rsp) \leftarrow \sigma$
3: $com \leftarrow RecoverCom(R, salt, chall, rsp)$
4: **if** $accept = V_2^{\mathcal{O}}(com, chall, rsp) \wedge chall = \mathcal{H}_{FS}(M, R, com)$ **then**
5:     **return** $\top$
6: **else**
7:     **return** $\bot$

Fig. 5. Ring signature Π_{RS} from our main OR sigma protocol Π_{Σ}^{RS} with almost commitment revocability and access to a random oracle $\mathcal{O}$. The setup algorithm RS.Setup(1^λ) outputs a description of an admissible group action $(G, \mathcal{X}, S_1, S_2, D_{\mathcal{X}})$ with respect to a fixed $X_0 \in \mathcal{X}$, together with a random group action $\star \leftarrow D_{\mathcal{X}}$ and as the public parameters pp.

a fixed public element T_0. The signature consists of the tag T, as well as a proof of knowledge of s such that simultaneously $T = s \bullet T_0$ and $s \star X_0$ is a member of the ring of public keys. To check if two signatures are produced by the same party we simply check whether the tags included in the two signatures are "close". Looking ahead, the notion of closeness depends on the underlying algebraic structure used to instantiate the pair of group actions; in the isogeny case, this amounts to checking whether the tags are equal while in the lattice case, this amounts to checking whether the tags are close for the infinity norm.

We require a number of properties from the group actions to make the signature scheme secure. Informally, we need one property per security property of linkable ring signatures (see [5, Sec. 2.3]):

- **Linkability.** It is hard to find secret keys s and s' such that $s' \star X_0 = s \star X_0$ but $s' \bullet T_0 \not\approx s \bullet T_0$. Otherwise, an adversary can use s and s' to sign two messages under the same public key that do not link together.
- **Linkable anonymity.** For a random secret key s, the distributions $(s \star X_0, s \bullet T_0)$ and $(X, T) \leftarrow \mathcal{X} \times \mathcal{T}$ are indistinguishable. Otherwise, an adversary could link the tag to one of the public keys and break anonymity.
- **Non-Frameability.** Given $X = s \star X_0$ and $T = s \bullet T_0$ it is hard to find s' such that $s' \bullet T_0$ is close to T. Otherwise, an adversary can register $s' \star X_0$ as a public key and frame an honest party with public key $s \star X_0$ for signing a message.

4.1   Admissible Pairs of Group Actions

Definition 15 (Admissible pair of group actions). *Let G be an additive group, S_1, S_2 two symmetric subsets of G, $\mathcal{X}$ and $\mathcal{T}$ two finite sets, δ in $[0,1]$, and $D_{\mathcal{X}}$ and $D_{\mathcal{T}}$ distributions over a set of group actions $\star : G \times \mathcal{X} \to \mathcal{X}$ and $\bullet : G \times \mathcal{T} \to \mathcal{T}$, respectively. Finally, let $\mathsf{Link}_{\mathsf{GA}} : \mathcal{T} \times \mathcal{T} \to 1/0$ be an associated efficiently computable function. We say that $\mathsf{AdmPGA} = (G, \mathcal{X}, \mathcal{T}, S_1, S_2, D_{\mathcal{X}}, D_{\mathcal{T}}, \mathsf{Link}_{\mathsf{GA}})$ is a δ-admissible pair of group actions with respect to $(X_0, T_0) \in \mathcal{X} \times \mathcal{T}$ if the following holds:*

1. *One can efficiently compute $g \star X$, $g \bullet T$ for any $g \in S_1 \cup S_2$ and any $(X,T) \in \mathcal{X} \times \mathcal{T}$, sample uniformly from S_1, S_2, $D_{\mathcal{X}}$ and $D_{\mathcal{T}}$, and represent elements of $G, \mathcal{X}$ and $\mathcal{T}$ uniquely.*
2. *For any $T \in \mathcal{T}$, $\mathsf{Link}_{\mathsf{GA}}(T,T) = 1$.*
3. *The intersection of the sets $S_2 + g$, for $g \in S_1$, is large. Let $S_3 = \bigcap_{g \in S_1} S_2 + g$, then*

$$|S_3| = \delta |S_2|.$$

   Furthermore, it is efficient to check whether an element $g \in G$ belongs to S_3, and to compute $g \star X$, $g \bullet T$ for all $g \in S_3, X \in \mathcal{X}, T \in \mathcal{T}$.

4. *For g sampled uniformly from S_1, $(g \star X_0, g \bullet T_0)$ is indistinguishable from (X,T) sampled uniformly from $\mathcal{X} \times \mathcal{T}$:*

$$\{(\star, \bullet, g \star X_0, g \bullet T_0) \,|\, (\star, \bullet, g) \leftarrow D_{\mathcal{X}} \times D_{\mathcal{T}} \times S_1\}$$
$$\approx_c \{(\star, \bullet, X, T) \,|\, (\star, \bullet, X, T) \leftarrow D_{\mathcal{X}} \times D_{\mathcal{T}} \times \mathcal{X} \times \mathcal{T}\}.$$

5. *It is difficult to output $g, g' \in S_2 + S_3$ such that $g \star X_0 = g' \star X_0$ and $\mathsf{Link}_{\mathsf{GA}}(g' \bullet T_0, g \bullet T_0) = 0$. That is, for any efficient adversary $\mathcal{A}$, the following is negligible:*

$$\Pr \left[\begin{array}{c} g, g' \in S_2 + S_3 \\ g \star X_0 = g' \star X_0 \\ \mathsf{Link}_{\mathsf{GA}}(g \bullet T_0, g' \bullet T_0) = 0 \end{array} \middle| \begin{array}{c} (\star, \bullet) \leftarrow D_{\mathcal{X}} \times D_{\mathcal{T}} \\ (g, g') \leftarrow \mathcal{A}(\star, \bullet) \end{array} \right] \leq \mathsf{negl}(\lambda)$$

6. *It is difficult to output $g' \in S_2 + S_3$ such that $\mathsf{Link}_{\mathsf{GA}}(g' \bullet T_0, T) = 1$ with non-negligible probability, given $X = g \star X_0$ and $T = g \bullet T_0$ for some g sampled uniformly from S_1. That is, for any efficient adversary $\mathcal{A}$ we have*

$$\Pr \left[\begin{array}{c} g' \in S_2 + S_3 \\ \mathsf{Link}_{\mathsf{GA}}(g' \bullet T_0, T) = 1 \end{array} \middle| \begin{array}{c} (\star, \bullet, g) \leftarrow D_{\mathcal{X}} \times D_{\mathcal{T}} \times S_1 \\ X \leftarrow g \star X_0 \\ T \leftarrow g \bullet T_0 \\ g' \leftarrow \mathcal{A}(\star, \bullet, X, T) \end{array} \right] \leq \mathsf{negl}(\lambda)$$

Hereafter, when the context is clear, we omit the description of the group actions $\star$ and $\bullet$ provided to the adversary and implicitly assume the probabilities are taken over the random choice of the group actions.

4.2   From an Admissible Pair of Group Actions to Base or Sigma Protocol with Tag

As in Sect. 3, we start by introducing an intermediate *base* OR sigma protocol with tag that has a binary challenge space. The main OR sigma protocol with tag used for our linkable ring signature will run parallel executions of the base OR sigma protocol with tag to amplify the soundness error.

Let $\mathsf{AdmPGA} = (G, \mathcal{X}, \mathcal{T}, S_1, S_2, D_{\mathcal{X}}, D_{\mathcal{T}})$ be a pair of admissible group actions with respect to $(X_0, T_0) \in \mathcal{X} \times \mathcal{T}$, and suppose that $X_1 = s_1 \star X_0, \cdots, X_N = s_N \star X_0$ are N public keys and $T = s_I \bullet T_0$ a tag associated to the I-th user, where the corresponding secret keys $s_1, \cdots, s_N$ are drawn uniformly from S_1. In this section, we introduce an efficient binary-challenge OR sigma protocol with tag $\Pi_{\Sigma}^{\mathsf{LRS\text{-}base}} = (P' = (P_1', P_2'), V' = (V_1', V_2'))$ proving knowledge of $(s_I, I) \in S_1 \times [N]$, such that $s_I \star X_0 = X_I$ and $s_I \bullet T_0 = T$.[7]

We outline the base OR sigma protocol with tag $\Pi_{\Sigma}^{\mathsf{LRS\text{-}base}}$. First, the prover samples an element r uniformly from S_2, and computes $R_i = r \star X_i$ for all $i \in [N]$ and $T' = r \bullet T$. The prover further samples random bit strings bits_i uniformly from $\{0,1\}^{\lambda}$ for $i \in [N]$ and commits R_i as $\mathcal{O}(\mathsf{Com}\|R_i\|\mathsf{bits}_i)$ (or, equivalently, $\mathsf{Com}(R_i, \mathsf{bits}_i)$). Then, the prover builds a index-hiding Merkle tree with $\mathsf{C}_1, \ldots, \mathsf{C}_N$ as its leaves and hashes the root root of the Merkle tree obtaining T' as $h = \mathcal{H}_{\mathsf{Coll}}(T', \mathsf{root})$. Here, the only reason for hashing (T', root) is to lower the communication complexity and it has no impact on the security. Moreover, we note that this whole procedure can be done deterministically, with randomness generated from a seed seed. Finally, the prover sends the hash value h to the verifier, who responds with a uniformly random bit c.

If the challenge bit c is 0, then the prover computes $z = r + s_I$. If $z \notin S_3$, then the prover aborts (this happens with probability $1 - \delta$). Otherwise, the prover sends z, the opening bits bits_I for the commitment C_I, and the path in the index-hiding Merkle tree that connects C_I to the root of the tree. The verifier then computes $\widetilde{R} = z \star X_0$, $\widetilde{T} = z \bullet T_0$ and $\widetilde{\mathsf{C}} = \mathsf{Com}(\widetilde{R}, \mathsf{bits}_I)$, and uses the path to reconstruct the root $\widetilde{\mathsf{root}}$ of the Merkle tree. It finally accepts if and only if h is equal to $\mathcal{H}_{\mathsf{Coll}}(\widetilde{T}, \widetilde{\mathsf{root}})$. If the challenge bit c is 1 then the prover reveals r and the bits_i, for all $i \in [N]$, to the verifier. This allows the verifier to recompute the Merkle tree and $T' = r \bullet T$, and to check if the hash of T' and the obtained root matches the value h received earlier. In this case, it suffices for the prover to just send seed, since r and bits_i are derived pseudorandomly from it. In the full protocol, displayed in Fig. 6, we assume the PRG Expand and the commitment scheme Com to be instantiated by a random oracle $\mathcal{O}$. We further assume w.l.o.g. that the output length of the random oracle is adjusted appropriately.

The following Theorems 16 and 17 provide the security of $\Pi_{\Sigma}^{\mathsf{LRS\text{-}base}}$. Their proofs can be found in [5, Sec. A.2].

---

[7] To be accurate, we prove knowledge of $s_I \in S_2 + S_3$, as we consider "relaxed" special soundness.

round 1: $P_1'^{\mathcal{O}}((X_1, \cdots, X_N, T), (s_I, I))$

1: seed $\leftarrow \{0,1\}^\lambda$ ▷ The only randomness used by the Prover
2: $(r, \mathsf{bits}_1, \cdots, \mathsf{bits}_N) \leftarrow \mathcal{O}(\mathsf{Expand}\|\mathsf{seed})$ ▷ Sample $r \in S_2$ and $\mathsf{bits}_i \in \{0,1\}^\lambda$.
3: $T' \leftarrow r \bullet T$
4: **for** i from 1 to N **do**
5:     $R_i \leftarrow r \star X_i$
6:     $\mathsf{C}_i \leftarrow \mathcal{O}(\mathsf{Com}\|R_i\|\mathsf{bits}_i)$ ▷ Create commitment $\mathsf{C}_i \in \{0,1\}^{2\lambda}$
7: $(\mathsf{root}, \mathsf{tree}) \leftarrow \mathsf{MerkleTree}(\mathsf{C}_1, \cdots, \mathsf{C}_N)$ ▷ Index-hiding Merkle tree
8: $h \leftarrow \mathcal{H}_{\mathsf{Coll}}(T', \mathsf{root})$
9: Prover sends $\mathsf{com} \leftarrow h$ to Verifier.

round 2: $V_1'(\mathsf{com})$

1: $c \leftarrow \{0,1\}$
2: Verifier sends $\mathsf{chall} \leftarrow c$ to Prover.

round 3: $P_2'((s_I, I), \mathsf{chall})$

1: $c \leftarrow \mathsf{chall}$
2: **if** $c = 0$ **then**
3:     $z \leftarrow r + s_I$
4:     **if** $z \notin S_3$ **then**
5:        P aborts the protocol.
6:     $\mathsf{path} \leftarrow \mathsf{getMerklePath}(I, \mathsf{tree})$
7:     $\mathsf{rsp} \leftarrow (z, \mathsf{path}, \mathsf{bits}_I)$
8: **else**
9:     $\mathsf{rsp} \leftarrow \mathsf{seed}$
10: Prover sends rsp to Verifier

Verification: $V_2'^{\mathcal{O}}(\mathsf{com}, \mathsf{chall}, \mathsf{rsp})$

1: $(h, c) \leftarrow (\mathsf{com}, \mathsf{chall})$
2: **if** $c = 0$ **then**
3:     $(z, \mathsf{path}, \mathsf{bits}) \leftarrow \mathsf{rsp}$
4:     $\widetilde{R} \leftarrow z \star X_0$
5:     $\widetilde{\mathsf{C}} = \mathcal{O}(\mathsf{Com}\|\widetilde{R}\|\mathsf{bits})$
6:     $\widetilde{T} \leftarrow z \bullet T_0$
7:     $\widetilde{\mathsf{root}} \leftarrow \mathsf{ReconstructRoot}(\widetilde{\mathsf{C}}, \mathsf{path})$
8:     Verifier outputs **accept** if $z \in S_3$ and $\mathcal{H}_{\mathsf{Coll}}(\widetilde{T}, \widetilde{\mathsf{root}}) = h$, and otherwise outputs **reject**.
9: **else**
10:     Verifier repeats the computation of **round 1** with rsp as seed.
11:     Verifier outputs **accept** iff the computation results in h, and otherwise outputs **reject**.

Fig. 6. Construction of the base OR sigma protocol with tag $\Pi_\Sigma^{\mathsf{LRS\text{-}base}} = (P' = (P_1', P_2'), V' = (V_1', V_2'))$, given an admissible pair of group actions $\mathsf{AdmPGA} = (G, \mathcal{X}, \mathcal{T}, S_1, S_2, D_\mathcal{X}, D_\mathcal{T}, \mathsf{Link}_{\mathsf{GA}})$ with respect to $(X_0, T_0) \in \mathcal{X} \times \mathcal{T}$, together with random group actions $(\star, \bullet) \leftarrow D_\mathcal{X} \times D_\mathcal{T}$. Above, the PRG Expand and the commitment scheme Com are modeled by a random oracle $\mathcal{O}$.

Theorem 16. *Let $\mathcal{O}$ be a random oracle. Define the relation*

$$R = \{((X_1, \cdots, X_N, T), (s, I)) \mid s \in S_1, X_i \in \mathcal{X}, T \in \mathcal{T}, I \in [N], X_I = s \star X_0, T = s \bullet T_0\}$$

and the relaxed relation

$$\tilde{R} = \left\{ ((X_1, \cdots, X_N, T), w) \; \middle| \; \begin{array}{l} \qquad X_i \in \mathcal{X}, T \in \mathcal{T} \text{ and } w \text{ such that :} \\ w = (s, I) : s \in S_2 + S_3, I \in [N], X_I = s \star X_0, T = s \bullet T_0 \\ \qquad\qquad\qquad\qquad or \\ w = (x, x') : \qquad x \neq x', \mathcal{H}_{\mathsf{Coll}}(x) = \mathcal{H}_{\mathsf{Coll}}(x') \text{ or} \\ \qquad\qquad\qquad \mathcal{O}(\mathsf{Com} \| x) = \mathcal{O}(\mathsf{Com} \| x') \end{array} \right\}.$$

Then the base OR sigma protocol with tag $\Pi_{\Sigma}^{\mathsf{LRS\text{-}base}}$ of Fig. 6 has correctness with probability of aborting $(1 - \delta)/2$ and relaxed special soundness for the relations $(R, \tilde{R})$.

Theorem 17. *The OR sigma protocol with tag $\Pi_{\Sigma}^{\mathsf{LRS\text{-}base}}$ of Fig. 6 is non-abort honest-verifier zero-knowledge. More concretely, there exists a simulator* Sim *such that, for any* $(\mathsf{X}, \mathsf{W}) \in R$, chall $\in$ ChSet *and any (computationally unbounded) adversary $\mathcal{A}$ that makes Q queries to the random oracle $\mathcal{O}$, we have*

$$\left| \Pr[\mathcal{A}^{\mathcal{O}}(\tilde{P}^{\mathcal{O}}(\mathsf{X}, \mathsf{W}, \mathsf{chall})) \to 1] - \Pr[\mathcal{A}^{\mathcal{O}}(\mathsf{Sim}^{\mathcal{O}}(\mathsf{X}, \mathsf{chall})) \to 1] \right| \leq \frac{2Q}{2^{\lambda}}.$$

4.3 From Base OR Sigma Protocol with Tag $\Pi_{\Sigma}^{\mathsf{LRS\text{-}base}}$ to Main OR Sigma Protocol with Tag $\Pi_{\Sigma}^{\mathsf{LRS}}$

As in Sect. 3.4, we enlarge the challenge space of our base OR sigma protocol with tag $\Pi_{\Sigma}^{\mathsf{LRS\text{-}base}}$ to obtain our main OR sigma protocol with tag $\Pi_{\Sigma}^{\mathsf{LRS}}$. We also include the same optimization techniques presented in Sect. 3.4. Since the description of our main OR sigma protocol with tag is almost identical to the one depicted in Fig. 4, we omit the details. The only notable difference between $\Pi_{\Sigma}^{\mathsf{RS}}$ from Fig. 4 and $\Pi_{\Sigma}^{\mathsf{LRS}}$ is that in the latter, the statement additionally includes a tag T and runs $\Pi_{\Sigma}^{\mathsf{LRS\text{-}base}}$ as a subroutine instead of $\Pi_{\Sigma}^{\mathsf{RS\text{-}base}}$. Otherwise, the way we transform our base to our main OR sigma protocol is identical. We also note that it is easy to check that our $\Pi_{\Sigma}^{\mathsf{LRS\text{-}base}}$ enjoys almost commitment revocability (see Remark 11). We use this fact when constructing a linkable ring signature in Sect. 4.4.

The following Theorems 18 and 19 provide the security of $\Pi_{\Sigma}^{\mathsf{LRS}}$. We refer to [5, Sec. A.3] for their proofs.

Theorem 18. *Define the relation R and the relaxed relation $\tilde{R}$ as in Theorem 16. Then the OR sigma protocol with tag $\Pi_{\Sigma}^{\mathsf{LRS}}$ has correctness with probability of aborting $1 - \delta^K$, high min-entropy and relaxed special soundness for the relations $(R, \tilde{R})$.*

Theorem 19. *The OR sigma protocol with tag $\Pi_{\Sigma}^{\mathsf{LRS}}$ is non-abort special zero-knowledge. More concretely, there exists a simulator* Sim *such that, for any* $(\mathsf{X}, \mathsf{W}) \in R$, chall $\in$ ChSet *and any (computationally unbounded) adversary $\mathcal{A}$*

that makes Q queries of the form salt$||\cdot$ *to the random oracle $\mathcal{O}$ - where* salt *is the salt value included in the transcript returned by $\widetilde{P}$ or* Sim*, we have:*

$$\left| \Pr[\mathcal{A}^{\mathcal{O}}(\widetilde{P}^{\mathcal{O}}(\mathsf{X}, \mathsf{W}, \mathsf{chall})) \to 1] - \Pr[\mathcal{A}^{\mathcal{O}}(\mathsf{Sim}^{\mathcal{O}}(\mathsf{X}, \mathsf{chall})) \to 1] \right| \leq \frac{3Q}{2^{\lambda}}.$$

4.4   From Main OR Sigma Protocol with Tag $\Pi_{\Sigma}^{\mathsf{LRS}}$ to Linkable Ring Signatures

We apply the Fiat-Shamir transform [17] to our main OR sigma protocol with tag $\Pi_{\Sigma}^{\mathsf{LRS}}$ to obtain a linkable ring signature Π_{LRS}. This is illustrated in Fig. 7, where we also rely on the almost commitment recoverable property of $\Pi_{\Sigma}^{\mathsf{LRS}}$ (see Remark 11). Here, $\mathcal{H}_{\mathsf{FS}}$ is a hash function, with range $C_{M,K}$, modeled as a random oracle. The correctness and security of Π_{LRS} are provided in the following theorem, whose proof can be found in [5, Sec. A.4].

Theorem 20. *Assuming that* AdmPGA *is an admissible pair of group actions (Definition 15) and $\mathcal{H}_{\mathsf{FS}}$ is a collision-resistant hash function, then the linkable ring signature scheme Π_{LRS} in Fig. 7 is correct, linkable, linkable anonymous and non-frameable in the random oracle model.*

LRS.KeyGen(pp)
1: $s \leftarrow S_1$
2: $X := s \star X_0$
3: **return** $(\mathsf{vk} = X, \mathsf{sk} = s)$

LRS.Link(σ_0, σ_1)
1: $(\mathsf{salt}_b, T_b, \mathsf{chall}_b, \mathsf{rsp}_b) \leftarrow \sigma_b$ for $b \in \{0, 1\}$
2: **if** $1 \leftarrow \mathsf{Link}_{\mathsf{GA}}(T_0, T_1)$ **then**
3:     **return** $\top$
4: **else**
5:     **return** $\bot$

LRS.Sign(sk, M, R)
1: $(\mathsf{vk}_1, \cdots \mathsf{vk}_N) \leftarrow \mathsf{R}$ ▷ Let vk_I be associated to $\mathsf{sk} = s_I$.
2: $T := s_I \bullet T_0$
3: $\mathsf{com} = (\mathsf{salt}, (\mathsf{com}_i)_{i \in [M]}) \leftarrow P_1^{\mathcal{O}}((\mathsf{R}, T), (\mathsf{sk}, I))$
4: $\mathsf{chall} \leftarrow \mathcal{H}_{\mathsf{FS}}(\mathsf{M}, (\mathsf{R}, T), \mathsf{com})$
5: $\mathsf{rsp} \leftarrow P_2^{\mathcal{O}}((\mathsf{sk}, I), \mathsf{chall})$
6: **return** $\sigma = (\mathsf{salt}, T, \mathsf{chall}, \mathsf{rsp})$

LRS.Verify(R, M, σ)
1: $(\mathsf{vk}_1, \cdots \mathsf{vk}_N) \leftarrow \mathsf{R}$
2: $(\mathsf{salt}, T, \mathsf{chall}, \mathsf{rsp}) \leftarrow \sigma$
3: $\mathsf{com} \leftarrow \mathsf{RecoverCom}((\mathsf{R}, T), \mathsf{salt}, \mathsf{chall}, \mathsf{rsp})$
4: **if** $\mathsf{accept} = V_2^{\mathcal{O}}(\mathsf{com}, \mathsf{chall}, \mathsf{rsp}) \wedge \mathsf{chall} = \mathcal{H}_{\mathsf{FS}}(\mathsf{M}, (\mathsf{R}, T), \mathsf{com})$ **then**
5:     **return** $\top$
6: **else**
7:     **return** $\bot$

Fig. 7. Linkable ring signature Π_{LRS} from our main OR sigma protocol with tag $\Pi_{\Sigma}^{\mathsf{LRS}}$, with almost commitment revocability and access to a random oracle $\mathcal{O}$. The setup algorithm LRS.Setup(1^{λ}) outputs a description of a pair of admissible group actions $(G, \mathcal{X}, S_1, S_2, D_{\mathcal{X}}, D_{\mathcal{T}})$ with respect to a fixed $(X_0, T_0) \in \mathcal{X} \times \mathcal{T}$, together with random group actions $(\star, \bullet) \leftarrow D_{\mathcal{X}} \times D_{\mathcal{T}}$ as the public parameters pp.

5 Post-quantum Admissible (pair of) Group Actions from Isogeny and Lattice Assumptions

For concrete instantiations of our generic framework for ring signatures (Sect. 3) and linkable ring signatures (Sect. 4), we consider three admissible (pairs of) group actions, based on isogenies between elliptic curves and lattices.

5.1 Isogeny-Based Instantiations

The isogeny-based instantiations we propose exploit the CSIDH paradigm. For the three sets of CSIDH parameters that have been proposed so far - CSIDH-512, CSIDH-1024 and CSIDH-1792 [8,10] - the structure of the corresponding ideal class group $C\ell(\mathcal{O})$ is only known for the first set [6]. We can instantiate our RS and LRS with any CSIDH parameter set regardless of whether the class group is known or not, but the resulting schemes are much more efficient in the former case. We first discuss the case when the structure of $C\ell(\mathcal{O})$ is known.

Known Class Group. For simplicity, we assume that the ideal class group $C\ell(\mathcal{O})$ is cyclic with generator $\mathfrak{g}$ of order cl. Then, the group $\mathbb{Z}_{cl}$ acts freely and transitively on $\mathcal{E}\ell\ell_p(\mathcal{O}, \pi)$ via the group action $\star$ defined as $a \star X := \mathfrak{g}^a * X$ (see Sect. 2.3). In practice, the action of each $a \in \mathbb{Z}_{cl}$ can be computed efficiently when p has a suitable form (in that case the approximate closest vector problem can be solved efficiently in the relation lattice [6]). It can be verified (see [5, Thm. 5.1]) that this group action satisfies all the properties of an admissible group action assuming the hardness of the GAIP_p problem. In this case we have $S_1 = S_2 = S_3 = G$, so $\delta = 1$ and the signing algorithm will never need to abort. Moreover, if we define $\star^2$ to be the group action of $\mathbb{Z}_{cl}$ on $\mathcal{E}\ell\ell_p(\mathcal{O}, \pi)$ defined by $a \star^2 X := (2a) \star X$, then $(\star, \star^2)$ satisfies all the properties of an admissible pair of group actions, assuming the hardness of the GAIP_p and $\mathsf{sdCSIDH}_p$ problem ([5, Thm. 5.1]).

Unknown Class Group. When the structure of the ideal class group $\mathcal{O}$ is not known, computing the action $[\mathfrak{a}] * [E_0]$ of an arbitrary $[\mathfrak{a}] \in C\ell(\mathcal{O})$ on some $[E_0] \in \mathcal{E}\ell\ell_p(\mathcal{O}, \pi)$ has exponential complexity. However, the ideal class action $*$ can still be efficiently computed for a small set of class group elements [8]. In particular, considering p of the form $4\ell_1\ell_2 \cdots \ell_k - 1$, with $\ell_1, \ldots, \ell_k$ small odd primes, a special fractional ideal $\mathfrak{I}_{\ell_i}$ can be associated to each prime ℓ_i. The action of one of these ideals (and their inverses) can be computed very efficiently, since it is determined by an isogeny whose kernel is the unique subgroup of $E_0(\mathbb{F}_p)$ of order ℓ_i. We can thus efficiently compute the action of elements in $C\ell(\mathcal{O})$ of the form $\prod_{i=1}^{k}[\mathfrak{I}_{\ell_i}]^{e_i}$ when the integral exponents e_i are chosen from some small interval $[-B, B]$.

We denote by $\star$ the group action of $\mathbb{Z}^k$ on $\mathcal{E}\ell\ell_p(\mathcal{O}, \pi)$ defined by

$$((e_1, \ldots, e_k), X) \mapsto \prod_{i=1}^{k}[\mathfrak{I}_{\ell_i}]^{e_i} * X.$$

Then it can be verified that, for the sets $S_1 = [-B, B]^k$ and $S_2 = [-B', B']^k$ (with $B' > B$) the group action $\star$ satisfies all the properties of an admissible group action with $\delta = ((2(B' - B) + 1)/(2B' + 1))^k$, assuming the hardness of the GAIP_p problem (see [5, Thm. 5.4]). We note that, for a fixed value of B, the bigger the value of B', the bigger δ, and the smaller the aborting probability of the ring signature scheme. However, a big B' implies high computational costs for the action of elements in S_2 and S_3. Consequently, in concrete instantiations the value of B' must be tuned to balance the two effects. Moreover, if we define $\star^2$ similarly as before, then $(\star, \star^2)$ satisfies all the properties of an admissible pair of group actions, assuming the hardness of the GAIP_p and $\mathsf{sdCSIDH}_p$ problem ([5, Thm. 5.4]).

Remark 21. To avoid using the sdCSIDH hardness assumption, we can formulate an admissible pair of group actions differently. If, considering $\bullet = \star$, we can determine a uniformly random base point T_0 for the tag space such that the element $g \in G$ satisfying $T_0 = g \star X_0$ is unknown to any user, instead of the sdCSIDH hardness assumption we then only require the standard dCSIDH assumption. The drawback is that we require a trusted setup to choose such a T_0. Alternatively, we can look at this as a linkable group signature scheme where the group manager sets $T_0 = t \star X_0$ and remembers t. The group manager can deanonymize any signature because $(-t) \star T$ is the public key of the signer.

Remark 22. Recently, a variant of CSIDH, called CSURF, has been proposed [7]. This work considers the maximal order $\mathcal{O}_{\mathbb{K}}$ and the corresponding set of supersingular elliptic curves $\mathcal{E}\ell\ell_p(\mathcal{O}_{\mathbb{K}}, \pi)$. The action of $\mathcal{C}\ell(\mathcal{O}_{\mathbb{K}})$ on $\mathcal{E}\ell\ell_p(\mathcal{O}_{\mathbb{K}}, \pi)$ can be used in our framework instead of the CSIDH group action.

5.2   Lattice-Based Instantiation

We instantiate an admissible group action (AdmGA) and an admissible pair of group actions (AdmPGA) based on lattices under the MSIS and MLWE assumptions. For the AdmGA, we consider $(G, \mathcal{X})$ to be $(R_q^\ell \times R_q^\ell, R_q^k)$ and $S_b := \{(\mathbf{s}, \mathbf{e}) \in G \mid \|\mathbf{s}\|_\infty, \|\mathbf{e}\|_\infty \leq B_b\}$ for $b \in \{1, 2\}$, where $B_1 < B_2 < q$ are given positive integers. Then, the group action $\star_{\mathbf{A}}$, uniquely defined by a matrix $\mathbf{A} \in R_q^{k \times \ell}$, is defined as $(\mathbf{s}, \mathbf{e}) \star_{\mathbf{A}} \mathbf{w} := (\mathbf{As} + \mathbf{e}) + \mathbf{w}$, for any $\mathbf{w}$ in R_q^k.

We can similarly instantiate the AdmPGA, with the only difference that we have to take care of the tag. To this end, we define $G = R_q^\ell \times R_q^\ell \times R_q^\ell$ and extend S_1, S_2 accordingly, in order to be subsets of G. Then, the group actions $\star_{\mathbf{A}}, \bullet_{\mathbf{B}}$ (where $\mathbf{B} \in R_q^{k \times \ell}$) are defined as $(\mathbf{s}, \mathbf{e}, \tilde{\mathbf{e}}) \star_{\mathbf{A}} \mathbf{w} := (\mathbf{As} + \mathbf{e}) + \mathbf{w}$ and $(\mathbf{s}, \mathbf{e}, \tilde{\mathbf{e}}) \star_{\mathbf{B}} \mathbf{w} := (\mathbf{Bs} + \tilde{\mathbf{e}}) + \mathbf{w}$, for any $\mathbf{w}$ in R_q^k. Finally, for two tags $\mathbf{v}, \mathbf{v}'$, we define $\mathsf{Link}_{\mathsf{GA}}(\mathbf{v}, \mathbf{v}') = 1$ if and only if $\|\mathbf{v} - \mathbf{v}'\|_\infty \leq 2 \cdot (2B_2 - B_1)$. It is an easy calculation checking that our instantiations satisfy the required properties of an AdmGA and AdmPGA, assuming the MSIS and MLWE assumptions (with appropriate parameters). For a formal treatment we refer to [5, Sec. 5.2].

Further Optimization Using Bai-Galbraith [2]. Although we can no longer capture it by our generic construction from admissible (pair of) group actions, we can apply the simple optimization technique of Bai-Galbraith [2], which uses the specific algebraic structure of lattices, to our base OR sigma protocols in Figs. 3 and 6. Effectively, this allows to lower the signature size of our lattice-based (linkable) ring signature scheme with no additional cost. The main observation is that for MLWE, proving knowledge of a short $\mathbf{s} \in R_q^\ell$ indirectly proves knowledge of a short $\mathbf{e} \in R_q^k$ since $\mathbf{e}$ is uniquely defined as $\mathbf{v} - \mathbf{As}$. We incorporate this idea to our base OR sigma protocol by letting the prover only send a short vector $\mathbf{z}$ in R_q^ℓ rather than a short vector $\mathbf{z}$ in $R_q^k \times R_q^\ell$ (for ring signatures) or $\mathbf{z}$ in $R_q^k \times R_q^\ell \times R_q^\ell$ (for linkable ring signatures) as the response. Since $k \approx \ell$, this shortens the response without any actual cost. We believe this optimization is standard by now as it is used by most of the recent proposals for efficient lattice-based signature schemes. Therefore we refer to [5, Appendix B] for the full details. In terms of security, the only difference is that the extracted witness from the base OR sigma protocol will be slightly larger than before. Otherwise, all our proofs in Sects. 3 and 4 are unmodified by this optimization.

6 Parameter Selection, Implementation Results and Conclusions

We implemented the isogeny-based instantiations with known class group and the lattice-based instantiations of our ring signature schemes (standard and linkable). We reuse parameter sets from the pre-existing cryptosystems CSI-FiSh and Dilithium. This allows us to reuse large portions of code from the CSIDH/CSI-FiSh and Dilithium implementations and to rely on earlier work to estimate the concrete security of our parameter choices. We use 128-bit seeds and commitment randomness, and we use 256-bit salts, commitments, and hash values.

Isogeny Parameters. We use the CSIDH-512 prime p, and define our first group action $g \star X$ exactly as in CSI-FiSh. This parameter set was proposed to achieve NIST security level 1. State of the art analysis of this parameter set suggests that it provides 128 bits of classical security and about 60 bits of security against quantum adversaries [26]. We set $M = 247$ and $K = 30$ such that the challenge space consists of binary strings of length $M = 247$ with hamming weight $M - K = 217$. The number of these strings is $\binom{247}{30} \approx 2^{128.1}$.

Lattice Parameters. We use the "medium" parameter set from the NIST PQC candidate Dilithium. More concretely we use the ring $R_q = \mathbb{Z}_q[X]/(X^{256} + 1)$, where $q = 8380417$. The parameters of the MLWE problem are $(k, l) = (3, 4)$ and the coefficients of the LWE secrets are sampled uniformly from $[-6, 6]$. In our implementation we use the optimization by Bai and Galbraith [2]. We chop off $d = 20$ bits of the commitment vector, in such a way that the parameters of the MSIS problem match the parameters of the MSIS problem relevant for the security of the Dilithium scheme. Since we work with binary challenges, the probability that a single rejection sampling check fails is much lower compared to Dilithium. This effect is roughly canceled out by the fact that in our protocol we need a number of parallel checks to succeed all at the same time. The Dilithium "medium" parameters are believed to achieve NIST security level I. Since the lattice signatures are fast, we can afford to have a large number of iterations with a small number of $c = 0$ challenges. This trades signing and verification speed for smaller signatures. Concretely, we set $M = 1749$ and $K = 16$.

6.1   Implementation

For the isogeny-based instantiations we reuse the non-constant-time implementation of the group action CSI-FiSh, which in turn relies on the implementation of the CSIDH group action by Castryck et al. [6,8]. For the lattice-based instantiations we reuse code of the Dilithium NIST submission for arithmetic and packing/unpacking operations. For both instantiations we use cSHAKE to instantiate the random oracles [20]. In the isogeny-based implementation, the performance bottleneck is the evaluation of the CSIDH group action. In the lattice-based implementation the bottleneck is not the lattice arithmetic, but rather the use of symmetric primitives (i.e. hashing, commitments and expanding seeds). This is especially true in the case of large ring sizes since the number of multiplications in R_q is independent of the ring size. The signature sizes and signing times of our implementations are displayed in Fig. 1. Our implementation is publicly available on

$$\text{https://github.com/WardBeullens/Calamari-and-Falafl.}$$

6.2   Conclusions

So far, no *efficient* logarithmic ring signatures have been proven secure in the quantum random oracle model, since the usual multiple rewinding of the adversary in the unforgeability proof is non-trivial in the quantum setting. It remains an interesting open problem to provide security proofs of our schemes in the QROM.

In terms of practical efficiency, we believe the lattice-based implementation can be speed up significantly by using more efficient symmetric primitives and/or by using vectorized implementations. Concerning the isogeny case, we note that, using the larger CSIDH parameters CSIDH-1024 and CSIDH-1792 under the hypothesis that the structure of the ideal class group was know also for them, the signatures sizes would increase with respect to the CSIDH-512 parameters of 0.9 KB or 2.3 KB respectively, independently of the ring size N. This shows that the impact of the CSIDH parameters on the signature size is not dramatic, especially for large N.

References

1. Albrecht, M.R., et al.: Estimate all the LWE, NTRU schemes!. In: Catalano, D., De Prisco, R. (eds.) SCN 2018. LNCS, vol. 11035, pp. 351–367. Springer, Cham (2018). https://doi.org/10.1007/978-3-319-98113-0_19

2. Bai, S., Galbraith, S.D.: An improved compression technique for signatures based on learning with errors. In: Benaloh, J. (ed.) CT-RSA 2014. LNCS, vol. 8366, pp. 28–47. Springer, Cham (2014). https://doi.org/10.1007/978-3-319-04852-9_2

3. Bao, F., Deng, R.H., Zhu, H.F.: Variations of Diffie-Hellman problem. In: Qing, S., Gollmann, D., Zhou, J. (eds.) ICICS 2003. LNCS, vol. 2836, pp. 301–312. Springer, Heidelberg (2003). https://doi.org/10.1007/978-3-540-39927-8_28

4. Baum, C., Lin, H., Oechsner, S.: Towards practical lattice-based one-time linkable ring signatures. In: Naccache, D., et al. (eds.) ICICS 2018. LNCS, vol. 11149, pp. 303–322. Springer, Cham (2018). https://doi.org/10.1007/978-3-030-01950-1_18

5. Beullens, W., Katsumata, S., Pintore, F.: Calamari and Falafl: Logarithmic (Linkable) Ring Signatures from Isogenies and Lattices. In: Cryptology ePrint Archive, Report 2020/646 (2020). https://eprint.iacr.org/2020/646

6. Beullens, W., Kleinjung, T., Vercauteren, F.: CSI-FiSh: efficient isogeny based signatures through class group computations. In: Galbraith, S.D., Moriai, S. (eds.) ASIACRYPT 2019, Part I. LNCS, vol. 11921, pp. 227–247. Springer, Cham (2019). https://doi.org/10.1007/978-3-030-34578-5_9

7. Castryck, W., Decru, T.: CSIDH on the surface. In: Ding, J., Tillich, J.-P. (eds.) PQCrypto 2020. LNCS, vol. 12100, pp. 111–129. Springer, Cham (2020). https://doi.org/10.1007/978-3-030-44223-1_7

8. Castryck, W., Lange, T., Martindale, C., Panny, L., Renes, J.: CSIDH: an efficient post-quantum commutative group action. In: Peyrin, T., Galbraith, S. (eds.) ASIACRYPT 2018, Part III. LNCS, vol. 11274, pp. 395–427. Springer, Cham (2018). https://doi.org/10.1007/978-3-030-03332-3_15

9. Cozzo, D., Smart, N.P.: Sashimi: cutting up CSI-FiSh secret keys to produce an actively secure distributed signing protocol. In: Ding, J., Tillich, J.-P. (eds.) PQCrypto 2020. LNCS, vol. 12100, pp. 169–186. Springer, Cham (2020). https://doi.org/10.1007/978-3-030-44223-1_10

10. De Feo, L., Galbraith, S.D.: SeaSign: compact isogeny signatures from class group actions. In: Ishai, Y., Rijmen, V. (eds.) EUROCRYPT 2019. LNCS, vol. 11478, pp. 759–789. Springer, Cham (2019). https://doi.org/10.1007/978-3-030-17659-4_26

11. Derler, D., Ramacher, S., Slamanig, D.: Post-quantum zero-knowledge proofs for accumulators with applications to ring signatures from symmetric-key primitives. In: Lange, T., Steinwandt, R. (eds.) PQCrypto 2018. LNCS, vol. 10786, pp. 419–440. Springer, Cham (2018). https://doi.org/10.1007/978-3-319-79063-3_20

12. Dinur, I., Nadler, N.: Multi-target attacks on the picnic signature scheme and related protocols. In: Ishai, Y., Rijmen, V. (eds.) EUROCRYPT 2019. LNCS, vol. 11478, pp. 699–727. Springer, Cham (2019). https://doi.org/10.1007/978-3-030-17659-4_24

13. Ducas, L., et al.: CRYSTALS-Dilithium: a lattice-based digital signature scheme. IACR TCHES 2018(1), 238–268 (2018). https://tches.iacr.org/index.php/TCHES/article/view/839

14. El Kaafarani, A., Katsumata, S., Pintore, F.: Lossy CSI-FiSh: efficient signature scheme with tight reduction to decisional CSIDH-512. In: Kiayias, A., Kohlweiss, M., Wallden, P., Zikas, V. (eds.) PKC 2020, Part II. LNCS, vol. 12111, pp. 157–186. Springer, Cham (2020). https://doi.org/10.1007/978-3-030-45388-6_6

15. Esgin, M.F., Steinfeld, R., Liu, J.K., Liu, D.: Lattice-based zero-knowledge proofs: new techniques for shorter and faster constructions and applications. In: Boldyreva, A., Micciancio, D. (eds.) CRYPTO 2019, Part I. LNCS, vol. 11692, pp. 115–146. Springer, Cham (2019). https://doi.org/10.1007/978-3-030-26948-7_5

16. Esgin, M.F., Zhao, R.K., Steinfeld, R., Liu, J.K., Liu, D.: MatRiCT: efficient, scalable and post-quantum blockchain confidential transactions protocol. In: Cavallaro, L., Kinder, J., Wang, X., Katz, J. (eds.) ACM CCS 2019, pp. 567–584. ACM Press, November 2019

17. Fiat, A., Shamir, A.: How to prove yourself: practical solutions to identification and signature problems. In: Odlyzko, A.M. (ed.) CRYPTO 1986. LNCS, vol. 263, pp. 186–194. Springer, Heidelberg (1987). https://doi.org/10.1007/3-540-47721-7_12

18. Groth, J., Kohlweiss, M.: One-out-of-many proofs: or how to leak a secret and spend a coin. In: Oswald, E., Fischlin, M. (eds.) EUROCRYPT 2015, Part II. LNCS, vol. 9057, pp. 253–280. Springer, Heidelberg (2015). https://doi.org/10.1007/978-3-662-46803-6_9

19. Katz, J., Kolesnikov, V., Wang, X.: Improved non-interactive zero knowledge with applications to post-quantum signatures. In: Lie, D., Mannan, M., Backes, M., Wang, X. (eds.) ACM CCS 2018, pp. 525–537. ACM Press, October 2018

20. Kelsey, J., Chang, S., Perlner, R.: SHA-3 derived functions: cSHAKE, KMAC, TupleHash, and ParallelHash. Technical report, National Institute of Standards and Technology (2016)

21. Langlois, A., Stehlé, D.: Worst-case to average-case reductions for module lattices. Des. Codes Crypt. **75**(3), 565–599 (2014). https://doi.org/10.1007/s10623-014-9938-4

22. Libert, B., Ling, S., Nguyen, K., Wang, H.: Zero-knowledge arguments for lattice-based accumulators: logarithmic-size ring signatures and group signatures without trapdoors. In: Fischlin, M., Coron, J.-S. (eds.) EUROCRYPT 2016, Part II. LNCS, vol. 9666, pp. 1–31. Springer, Heidelberg (2016). https://doi.org/10.1007/978-3-662-49896-5_1

23. Lu, X., Au, M.H., Zhang, Z.: Raptor: a practical lattice-based (linkable) ring signature. In: Deng, R.H., Gauthier-Umaña, V., Ochoa, M., Yung, M. (eds.) ACNS 2019. LNCS, vol. 11464, pp. 110–130. Springer, Cham (2019). https://doi.org/10.1007/978-3-030-21568-2_6

24. Lyubashevsky, V.: Fiat-Shamir with aborts: applications to lattice and factoring-based signatures. In: Matsui, M. (ed.) ASIACRYPT 2009. LNCS, vol. 5912, pp. 598–616. Springer, Heidelberg (2009). https://doi.org/10.1007/978-3-642-10366-7_35

25. Merkle, R.C.: A digital signature based on a conventional encryption function. In: Pomerance, C. (ed.) CRYPTO 1987. LNCS, vol. 293, pp. 369–378. Springer, Heidelberg (1988). https://doi.org/10.1007/3-540-48184-2_32

26. Peikert, C.: He gives C-sieves on the CSIDH. In: Canteaut, A., Ishai, Y. (eds.) EUROCRYPT 2020, Part II. LNCS, vol. 12106, pp. 463–492. Springer, Cham (2020). https://doi.org/10.1007/978-3-030-45724-2_16

27. Rivest, R.L., Shamir, A., Tauman, Y.: How to leak a secret. In: Boyd, C. (ed.) ASIACRYPT 2001. LNCS, vol. 2248, pp. 552–565. Springer, Heidelberg (2001). https://doi.org/10.1007/3-540-45682-1_32

28. Shor, P.W.: Algorithms for quantum computation: discrete logarithms and factoring. In: 35th FOCS, pp. 124–134. IEEE Computer Society Press, November 1994

29. Alberto Torres, W.A., et al.: Post-quantum one-time linkable ring signature and application to ring confidential transactions in blockchain (lattice RingCT v1.0). In: Susilo, W., Yang, G. (eds.) ACISP 2018. LNCS, vol. 10946, pp. 558–576. Springer, Cham (2018). https://doi.org/10.1007/978-3-319-93638-3_32

Radical Isogenies

Wouter Castryck, Thomas Decru, and Frederik Vercauteren[⊠]

Imec-COSIC, Leuven, KU, Belgium
{wouter.castryck,thomas.decru,frederik.vercauteren}@kuleuven.be

Abstract. This paper introduces a new approach to computing isogenies called "radical isogenies" and a corresponding method to compute chains of N-isogenies that is very efficient for small N. The method is fully deterministic and completely avoids generating N-torsion points. It is based on explicit formulae for the coordinates of an N-torsion point P' on the codomain of a cyclic N-isogeny $\varphi : E \to E'$, such that composing φ with $E' \to E'/\langle P' \rangle$ yields a cyclic N^2-isogeny. These formulae are simple algebraic expressions in the coefficients of E, the coordinates of a generator P of $\ker \varphi$, and an Nth root $\sqrt[N]{\rho}$, where the radicand ρ itself is given by an easily computable algebraic expression in the coefficients of E and the coordinates of P. The formulae can be iterated and are particularly useful when computing chains of N-isogenies over a finite field $\mathbb{F}_q$ with $\gcd(q - 1, N) = 1$, where taking an Nth root is a simple exponentiation. Compared to the state-of-the-art, our method results in an order of magnitude speed-up for $N \leq 13$; for larger N, the advantage disappears due to the increasing complexity of the formulae. When applied to CSIDH, we obtain a speed-up of about 19% over the implementation by Bernstein, De Feo, Leroux and Smith for the CSURF-512 parameters.

Keywords: Post-quantum cryptography · Isogenies · Tate pairing · CSIDH

1 Introduction

Isogeny-based cryptography is one of the more promising candidates for post-quantum cryptography and although it is slower than lattice-based cryptography, it has the advantage of smaller key and ciphertext sizes. Isogeny-based protocols can be broadly categorized into two families: SIDH and CRS/CSIDH.

SIDH is a key agreement protocol introduced by Jao and De Feo in 2011 [16]. This protocol is based on random walks in isogeny graphs of supersingular elliptic curves E over $\mathbb{F}_{p^2}$, and is reminiscent of the CGL hash function due to Charles, Goren and Lauter from 2009 [8]. The prime p is chosen such that the torsion

This work was supported in part by the Research Council KU Leuven grants C14/18/067 and STG/17/019, by CyberSecurity Research Flanders with reference number VR20192203, and by the Research Foundation Flanders (FWO) through the WOG Coding Theory and Cryptography.

S. Moriai and H. Wang (Eds.): ASIACRYPT 2020, LNCS 12492, pp. 493–519, 2020.
https://doi.org/10.1007/978-3-030-64834-3_17

subgroups $E[2^n]$ and $E[3^m]$ are defined over $\mathbb{F}_{p^2}$, for large exponents n, m. The random walks then correspond to choosing a random point P in $E[2^n]$ or $E[3^m]$ and constructing the isogeny with kernel $\langle P \rangle$, as a composition of isogenies of degree 2 respectively 3.

CRS/CSIDH [7] takes a different approach and computes an action of the ideal-class group $\mathrm{cl}(\mathcal{O})$ of some order $\mathcal{O}$ in an imaginary quadratic field on the set $\mathcal{Ell}_p(\mathcal{O}, t)$ of elliptic curves over a prime field $\mathbb{F}_p$ with $\mathbb{F}_p$-rational endomorphism ring $\mathcal{O}$ and trace of Frobenius t. The idea of using this class group action in cryptography was independently proposed by Couveignes [11] and Rostovtsev-Stolbunov [22] for ordinary elliptic curves. In [7] this idea was ported to the supersingular case, resulting in a speed-up of several orders of magnitude. The computation of the class group action boils down to computing chains of ℓ-isogenies for many small primes ℓ, e.g., for CSIDH-512, ℓ ranges from 3 to 587. This is in stark contrast with SIDH where only 2- and 3-isogenies are used.

In the CSIDH setting, computing an ℓ-isogeny φ from an elliptic curve $E/\mathbb{F}_p$ consists of two steps: first, a generator P of the kernel of φ is computed, i.e. an $\mathbb{F}_p$-rational point of order ℓ, and secondly, given P, an equation for the isogenous curve $E/\langle P \rangle$ is determined.

The most basic approach to solve the first step is to generate a random point $Q \in E(\mathbb{F}_p)$ and to multiply this by the cofactor $\#E(\mathbb{F}_p)/\ell$. Generating a random point is essentially a square root computation at a cost of about $1.5 \log p$ multiplications in $\mathbb{F}_p$, and the multiplication by the cofactor can be done using the Montgomery ladder [2] and takes roughly $11 \log p$ multiplications in $\mathbb{F}_p$. Generating a point of order ℓ is thus a costly operation, even further exacerbated by the fact that multiplication by the cofactor results in the point at infinity $\mathcal{O}_E$ with probability $1/\ell$, which is non-negligible for small ℓ. Note that this also makes the algorithm non-deterministic, negatively affecting constant time implementations. The cost of generating ℓ-torsion points from scratch can be mitigated somewhat by considering a chain of ℓ_i-isogenies for many different primes ℓ_i. Instead of sampling an ℓ_i-torsion point for every ℓ_i-isogeny separately, it is cheaper to sample an $\prod_{i=1}^{k} \ell_i$-torsion point and push it through the isogeny to create a chain of isogenies of respective degrees $\ell_1, \ell_2, \ldots, \ell_k$, multiplying this point with a cofactor that gets smaller in each iteration.

The second step is typically carried out using some form of Vélu's formulae [28], which compute the coefficients of $E/\langle P \rangle$ from the coefficients of E and the coordinates of the scalar multiples of P. Vélu's formulae can also be used to compute the image $\varphi(Q)$ of any point Q under the isogeny. The original implementation of CSIDH uses these formulae on elliptic curves in Montgomery form [7,21], and requires $O(\ell)$ arithmetic operations in $\mathbb{F}_p$ per ℓ-isogeny. Since then many optimizations to CSIDH have been proposed, such as:

- using different forms of elliptic curves, e.g. twisted Edwards curves [18,19] and Hessian curves [12,14];
- adapting Vélu's formulae to only require $\widetilde{O}(\sqrt{\ell})$ operations in $\mathbb{F}_p$ [1] instead of $O(\ell)$;
- changing CSIDH into CSURF to allow the use of very efficient 2-isogenies [6],

– lowering the number of ℓ-isogenies that has to be computed for each ℓ [9,20].

A number of alternative approaches have been considered that avoid the generation of ℓ-torsion points altogether, e.g. by using modular polynomials [3, 13] or division polynomials [3]. This leads to deterministic algorithms which can outperform the above method using Vélu's formulae for small ℓ. Highly optimized approaches exist for 2-isogenies [6] and 3-isogenies [12,14], where the speed-up stems from two ingredients: firstly, an elliptic curve model is chosen that is nicely adapted to 2-torsion (a variant of Montgomery curves) resp. 3-torsion (Hessian curves). The second and main ingredient however is that the coefficients of $E/\langle P \rangle$ can be expressed in terms of the coefficients of E and a single radical of a simple algebraic expression in the coefficients of E. This radical is a square root for 2-isogenies and a cube root for 3-isogenies.

Contributions

The main contribution of this paper is the generalization of the aforementioned special cases of 2- and 3-isogenies to all isogenies of any degree $N \geq 2$.

Concretely, given an elliptic curve E with a point P of order N, one can use Vélu's formulae to compute a defining equation for $E' = E/\langle P \rangle$. We present accompanying formulae which produce a point P' on E' again of order N, such that the composition

$$E \to E' \to E'/\langle P' \rangle \qquad (1)$$

is a cyclic isogeny of degree N^2. These formulae are algebraic expressions in the coefficients of E and the coordinates of P, and one radical (an Nth root) of another algebraic expression in the coefficients of E and the coordinates of P. An important implication of this construction is that the same formulae now apply to E' and P', which allows us to compute chains of N-isogenies of arbitrary length without needing to generate an N-torsion point in every step. In practice, we assume $P = (0,0)$, thereby suppressing its coordinates from the formulae.

More in detail, we proceed as follows: an elliptic curve E over a field K together with a K-rational point P of order $N \geq 4$ can be represented by the Tate normal form

$$E : y^2 + (1 - c)xy - by = x^3 - bx^2 \qquad P = (0,0), \ b,c \in K.$$

We then compute the curve $E' = E/\langle P \rangle$ using Vélu's formulae. The point P' on E' can be constructed as a pre-image of P under the dual isogeny $\hat{\varphi} : E' \to E$, which guarantees that the composition of φ with $E' \to E'/\langle P' \rangle$ is cyclic of order N^2. Our central observation is that P' is defined over $K(b, c, \sqrt[N]{\rho})$ for some $\rho \in K(b,c)$ and we prove that one can take $\rho = t_N(P, -P)$ where t_N denotes the Tate pairing. Indeed, since $\hat{\varphi}(P') = P$ and using the compatibility of the Tate pairing with isogenies, we have

$$t_N(P, -P) = t_N(\hat{\varphi}(P'), -\hat{\varphi}(P')) = t_N(P', -P')^{\deg \hat{\varphi}} = t_N(P', -P')^N,$$

which shows that the field of definition of P' must contain $\sqrt[N]{t_N(P, -P)}$, and we show that this is also sufficient.

The fact that we only require one Nth root explains the name "radical isogenies". By rewriting (E', P') again in Tate normal form with coefficients b' and c', we are ready for another iteration. The formulae we derive in fact express b' and c' directly as elements of $K(b, c, \sqrt[N]{\rho})$.

By specializing to finite fields $\mathbb{F}_q$ with $\gcd(q - 1, N) = 1$, we immediately obtain that the radical $\sqrt[N]{\rho}$ is again defined over $\mathbb{F}_q$, since Nth powering is a field automorphism in this case. We implemented our formulae and considered two application scenarios: firstly, we show that using our formulae, chains of N-isogenies can be computed much faster than using the state-of-the-art methods: for $N = 3, 5, 7$ the best previous approach was to use modular polynomials and we obtain speed-ups of factors 9, 18 and 27. For $N = 11, 13$, the best previous approach was to generate N-torsion points in combination with Vélu's formulae and our radical isogenies outperform this by factors 12 and 5 respectively. Secondly, we implemented a version of CSIDH using radical isogenies for all primes ≤ 13 and obtain a speedup of 19% over the state of the art implementation [1].

Paper organization

Section 2 briefly recaps the necessary background on isogenies, division polynomials, the Tate normal form, the Tate pairing, simple radical extensions, and isogeny-based protocols. Section 3 proves the existence of radical isogeny formulae, while Sect. 4 works out these formulae explicitly for small values of N. Section 5 discusses how our formulae perform when computing chains of N-isogenies, while Sect. 6 reports on an improved implementation of CSIDH using radical isogenies. Finally, Sect. 7 concludes the paper and lists a number of open problems.

2   Background

Throughout this section we let K denote an arbitrary field.

2.1   Isogenies and Vélu's Formulae

Let E and E' be elliptic curves over K. An isogeny $\varphi : E \to E'$ is a non-constant morphism such that $\varphi(\mathcal{O}_E) = \mathcal{O}_{E'}$, where $\mathcal{O}_E, \mathcal{O}_{E'}$ denote the respective points at infinity. The degree of φ is its degree as a morphism and there always exists a dual isogeny $\hat{\varphi} : E' \to E$ such that $\hat{\varphi} \circ \varphi = [\deg(\varphi)]$, where as usual $[\cdot]$ denotes scalar multiplication. The kernel of φ is a finite subgroup of E, more precisely its size is a divisor of $\deg(\varphi)$, where equality holds if and only if φ is separable (which is automatic if $\operatorname{char} K \nmid \deg(\varphi)$). Conversely, given a finite subgroup $C \subset E$, there exists a unique[1] separable isogeny φ having C as its kernel. Concrete formulae for this isogeny were given by Vélu:

Theorem 1. *Let C be a finite subgroup of the elliptic curve*

$$E : y^2 + a_1 xy + a_3 y = x^3 + a_2 x^2 + a_4 x + a_6$$

over K. Fix a partition $C = \{\mathcal{O}_E\} \cup C_2 \cup C^+ \cup C^-$, where C_2 are the order 2 points of C, and C^+ and C^- are such that for any $P \in C^+$ it holds that $-P \in C^-$. Write $S = C^+ \cup C_2$, and for $Q \in S$ define

$$g_Q^x = 3x(Q)^2 + 2a_2 x(Q) + a_4 - a_1 y(Q),$$
$$g_Q^y = -2y(Q) - a_1 x(Q) - a_3,$$

$$u_Q = (g_Q^y)^2, \quad v_Q = \begin{cases} g_Q^x & if \quad 2Q = \mathcal{O}_E, \\ 2g_Q^x - a_1 g_Q^y & else, \end{cases}$$

$$v = \sum_{Q \in S} v_Q, \quad w = \sum_{Q \in S} (u_Q + x(Q) v_Q),$$

$$A_1 = a_1, \quad A_2 = a_2, \quad A_3 = a_3,$$
$$A_4 = a_4 - 5v, \quad A_6 = a_6 - (a_1^2 + 4a_2) - 7w.$$

Then the separable isogeny φ with domain E and kernel C has codomain $E' = E/C$ with Weierstrass equation

$$E' : y^2 + A_1 xy + A_3 y = x^3 + A_2 x^2 + A_4 x + A_6 \tag{2}$$

over $\overline{K}$. Furthermore, for $P \in E$ we can compute the image of P as

$$x(\varphi(P)) = x(P) + \sum_{Q \in C \setminus \{\mathcal{O}_E\}} (x(P + Q) - x(Q))$$

$$y(\varphi(P)) = y(P) + \sum_{Q \in C \setminus \{\mathcal{O}_E\}} (y(P + Q) - y(Q)).$$

Proof. See [28]. ∎

---

[1] Up to post-composition with an isomorphism.

2.2 Division Polynomials

Let E/K be defined by $y^2+a_1xy+a_3y = x^3+a_2x^2+a_4x+a_6$, and let $b_2 = a_1^2+4a_2$, $b_4 = 2a_4 + a_1a_3$, $b_6 = a_3^2 + 4a_6$, $b_8 = a_1^2a_6 + 4a_2a_6 - a_1a_3a_4 + a_2a_3^2 - a_4^2$. For all integers $N \geq 0$, the N-division polynomial is given by

$$\Psi_{E,0} = 0, \quad \Psi_{E,1} = 1, \quad \Psi_{E,2} = 2y+a_1x+a_3, \quad \Psi_{E,N} = t \cdot \prod_{Q \in (E[N] \backslash E[2])/\pm} (x - x(Q)),$$

where $t = N$ if N is odd and $t = \frac{N}{2} \cdot \Psi_{E,2}$ if N is even. By definition, we have that for any non-trivial $P \in E[N]$, $\Psi_{E,N}(P) = 0$. The division polynomials satisfy the following recurrence relation which allows them to be computed efficiently:

$$\Psi_{E,3} = 3x^4 + b_2x^3 + 3b_4x^2 + 3b_6x + b_8$$

$$\frac{\Psi_{E,4}}{\Psi_{E,2}} = 2x^6 + b_2x^5 + 5b_4x^4 + 10b_6x^3 + 10b_8x^2 + (b_2b_8 - b_4b_6)x + (b_4b_8 - b_6^2)$$

$$\Psi_{E,2N+1} = \Psi_{E,N+2}\Psi_{E,N}^3 - \Psi_{E,N-1}\Psi_{E,N+1}^3 \text{ if } N \geq 2$$

$$\Psi_{E,2N} = \frac{\Psi_{E,N}}{\Psi_{E,2}}(\Psi_{E,N+2}\Psi_{E,N-1}^2 - \Psi_{E,N-2}\Psi_{E,N+1}^2) \text{ if } N \geq 3.$$

Note that $\Psi_{E,2}^2 = 4x^3 + (a_1^2 + 4a_2)x^2 + (2a_1a_3 + 4a_4)x + a_3^2 + 4a_6$, i.e. a univariate polynomial in x.

If one is interested in points of exact order N (so not just in $E[N]$), then one can use the reduced N-division polynomial $\psi_{E,N}$ defined as

$$\psi_{E,N} = \frac{\Psi_{E,N}}{\text{lcm}_{d|N,d\neq N}\{\Psi_{E,d}\}}.$$

For all primes ℓ, we have that $\Psi_{E,\ell} = \psi_{E,\ell}$. Note that for $N > 2$, the reduced N-division polynomial of an elliptic curve E is a univariate polynomial in x.

The multiplication by N-map can be expressed explicitly using division polynomials as follows [23, Exercise 3.6]:

$$[N]P = \left(\frac{\phi_{E,N}(P)}{\Psi_{E,N}(P)^2}, \frac{\omega_{E,N}(P)}{\Psi_{E,N}(P)^3}\right), \tag{3}$$

with $\phi_{E,N} = x\Psi_{E,N}^2 - \Psi_{E,N+1}\Psi_{E,N-1}$ and $\omega_{E,N} = \frac{1}{2\Psi_{E,N}}(\Psi_{E,2N} - \Psi_{E,N}(a_1\phi_{E,N} + a_3\Psi_{E,N}^2))$.

2.3 The Tate Normal Form

We will be interested in elliptic curves E over K with a distinguished point $P \in E(K)$ of some finite order N. By translating this point to $(0,0)$ and requiring that the tangent line is horizontal, and with proper scaling, one can easily prove the following lemma; we refer to [25, Lem. 2.1] for further details.

Lemma 2. *Let E be an elliptic curve over K and let $P \in E(K)$ be a point of order $N \geq 4$, then (E, P) is isomorphic to a unique pair of the form*

$$E : y^2 + (1 - c)xy - by = x^3 - bx^2, \qquad P = (0, 0) \tag{4}$$

with $b, c \in K$ and

$$\Delta(b, c) = b^3(c^4 - 8bc^2 - 3c^3 + 16b^2 - 20bc + 3c^2 + b - c) \neq 0 \,.$$

The resulting curve-point pair is said to be in Tate normal form.

Given a Tate normal form, the first few scalar multiples of $P = (0, 0)$ are given by simple expressions in b and c, e.g.

$$2P = (b, bc), \ \ 3P = (c, b - c), \qquad -P = (0, b), \ -2P = (b, 0), \ -3P = (c, c^2) \,.$$

Higher multiples can be computed using (3). Using these multiples, for each $N \geq 4$ one can write down an irreducible polynomial $F_N(b, c) \in \mathbb{Z}[b, c]$ whose vanishing, along with the non-vanishing of $\Delta(b, c)$ and of $F_m(b, c)$ for $4 \leq m < N$, expresses that P has exact order N. For instance, for $N = 4$ we find the equation $F_4(b, c) = c = 0$, by imposing that $3P = -P$. Similarly, for $N = 5$ we find $F_5(b, c) = c - b = 0$ and for $N = 6$ we find $F_6(b, c) = c^2 + c - b = 0$. Further examples can be found in Table 1 below. Alternatively, the polynomial $F_N(b, c)$ can be recovered as a factor of the constant term of the N-division polynomial of the curve (4), when considered over the rational function field $\mathbb{Q}(b, c)$. This is the approach taken in [25, §2], to which we refer for more details.

Remark 3. Up to birational equivalence, $F_N(b, c)$ is a defining polynomial for the modular curve $X_1(N)$. See again [25] for more background.

2.4   The Tate Pairing

Given an elliptic curve E/K and an integer $N \geq 2$, the Tate pairing is a bilinear map

$$t_N : E(K)[N] \times E(K)/NE(K) \to K^*/(K^*)^N : (P_1, P_2) \mapsto t_N(P_1, P_2)$$

which can be computed as follows. Consider a Miller function f_{N,P_1}, i.e., a function on E with divisor $N(P_1) - N(\mathcal{O}_E)$. Let D be a K-rational divisor on E that is linearly equivalent with $(P_2) - (\mathcal{O}_E)$ and whose support is disjoint from $\{P_1, \mathcal{O}_E\}$. Then $t_N(P_1, P_2) = f_{N,P_1}(D)$. If $P_1 \neq P_2$ and the Miller function is normalized, i.e., the leading coefficient of its expansion around $\mathcal{O}_E$ with respect to the uniformizer x/y equals 1 (we are assuming that E is in Weierstrass form), then one can simply compute $t_N(P_1, P_2)$ as $f_{N,P_1}(P_2)$.

For certain instances of K, the Tate pairing is known to be non-degenerate, meaning that for each $P_1 \in E(K)[N] \setminus \{\mathcal{O}_E\}$ there exists a $P_2 \in E(K)/NE(K)$ such that $t_N(P_1, P_2) \neq 1$, and vice versa. Most notably, this is true if $K = \mathbb{F}_q$ is a finite field containing a primitive Nth root of unity ζ_N [15], i.e., for which $N \mid q - 1$.

Another important feature is that the Tate pairing is compatible with isogenies, in the following sense: if $\varphi : E \to E'$ is an isogeny over K then the rule $t_N(\varphi(P_1), P_2') = t_N(P_1, \hat{\varphi}(P_2'))$ applies. In particular we have

$$t_N(\varphi(P_1), \varphi(P_2)) = t_N(P_1, P_2)^{\deg(\varphi)}$$

for all $P_1 \in E(K)[N]$ and $P_2 \in E(K)/NE(K)$. For a proof of this compatibility we refer to [4, Thm. IX.9], which assumes $\zeta_N \in K$, but this condition can be discarded (it is not used in the proof).

2.5   Simple Radical Extensions

Following [10], we say that a field extension $K \subset L$ is simple radical of degree $N \geq 2$ if there exists an $\alpha \in L$ such that (i) $L = K(\alpha)$, (ii) $\rho := \alpha^N \in K$, and (iii) $x^N - \rho \in K[x]$ is irreducible. Property (iii) can be verified easily using the following theorem.

Theorem 4. *Let K be a field, consider an integer $N \geq 2$, and let $\rho \in K^*$. Assume that for all primes $m \mid N$ we have $\rho \notin K^m$. If $4 \mid N$, assume moreover that $\rho \notin -4K^4$. Then the polynomial $x^N - \rho \in K[x]$ is irreducible.*

Proof. See [17, Thm. VI.9.1]. ∎

We will usually write $L = K(\sqrt[N]{\rho})$, although it should be noted that $\sqrt[N]{\rho}$ is only well-defined up to multiplication by ζ_N^i for some $i \in \{0, 1, \ldots, N-1\}$. Apart from this subtlety, we note that the field $K(\sqrt[N]{\rho})$ does not change if we multiply ρ with the Nth power of an element of K^*, or if we raise ρ to some power that is coprime with N.

Remark 1. If $K \subset L$ is simple radical of degree N and if char $K \nmid N$, then the Galois closure of L over K is obtained by adjoining a primitive Nth root of unity ζ_N, and

$$\mathrm{Gal}(L(\zeta_N)/K) = \mathrm{Gal}(L(\zeta_N)/K(\zeta_N)) \rtimes \mathrm{Gal}(L(\zeta_N)/L)$$

where the first factor is cyclic of order N. In particular, if $\zeta_N \in L$ then L is Galois over K with cyclic Galois group. Kummer theory provides a converse statement [24, Lem. 9.13.1].

2.6   CSIDH

We briefly review the CSIDH key agreement protocol, which is our main application of radical isogenies. Let $\mathbb{F}_p$ be a large finite field with $p = c\ell_1\ell_2 \cdots \ell_r - 1$, where the ℓ_i are small distinct primes and where c is some small cofactor. Alice and Bob agree on an order $\mathcal{O} \subset \mathbb{Q}(\sqrt{-p})$ containing $\mathbb{Z}[\sqrt{-p}]$, and they consider the set $\mathscr{E}\!\ell\!\ell_p(\mathcal{O}) = \mathscr{E}\!\ell\!\ell_p(\mathcal{O}, 0)$ of elliptic curves $E/\mathbb{F}_p$ whose endomorphism ring $\mathrm{End}_{\mathbb{F}_p} E$ is isomorphic to $\mathcal{O}$. Such curves are necessarily supersingular, and without loss of generality it can be assumed that the isomorphism $\mathrm{End}_{\mathbb{F}_p} E \cong \mathcal{O}$ identifies the Frobenius endomorphism π_p on E with $\sqrt{-p}$.

To any $E \in \mathcal{E}\ell_p(\mathcal{O})$ and any invertible ideal $\mathfrak{a} \subset \mathcal{O}$ one can, using the above isomorphism, associate the finite subgroup

$$E[\mathfrak{a}] = \bigcap_{\alpha \in \mathfrak{a}} \ker \alpha \subset E.$$

It turns out that the isogenous curve $E/E[\mathfrak{a}]$ is again contained in $\mathcal{E}\ell_p(\mathcal{O})$ and that it depends on the class $[\mathfrak{a}]$ of $\mathfrak{a}$ only; furthermore, this defines a free and transitive action of the ideal-class group $\mathrm{cl}(\mathcal{O})$ on $\mathcal{E}\ell_p(\mathcal{O})$. The key agreement then works as follows: Alice and Bob agree on a starting curve $E \in \mathcal{E}\ell_p(\mathcal{O})$, then both sample a secret ideal-class $[\mathfrak{a}]$ resp. $[\mathfrak{b}]$, compute the isogenous curves $E/E[\mathfrak{a}]$ resp. $E/E[\mathfrak{b}]$, and exchange the outcomes. Both parties can now compute $E/E[\mathfrak{ab}]$ by acting with their own secret ideal-class on the other party's curve.

In order for this to be practical, Alice and Bob should sample $\mathfrak{a}, \mathfrak{b}$ as products of ideals of the form $(\ell_i, \sqrt{-p} - 1)^{e_i}$, whose action corresponds to a chain of $|e_i|$ easy-to-compute ℓ_i-isogenies; this is also true if $e_i < 0$, in which case one considers the equivalent ideal $(\ell_i, \sqrt{-p}+1)^{|e_i|}$. The prime $\ell_i = 2$ requires special treatment: it should be skipped unless $p \equiv 7 \bmod 8$ and $\mathcal{O}$ is the maximal order, in which case one considers $(2, (\sqrt{-p} - 1)/2)$ resp. $(2, (\sqrt{-p} + 1)/2)$ instead of the principal ideals $(2, \sqrt{-p} - 1), (2, \sqrt{-p} + 1)$.

3 Existence of Radical Isogeny Formulae

In this section we prove the existence of radical isogeny formulae, without deriving these formulae explicitly. The explicit derivation for small N, including the cases $N = 2, 3$, is given in the next section. As such, we assume $N \geq 4$ and consider the 'universal' Tate normal curve

$$E : y^2 + (1 - c)xy - by = x^3 - bx^2$$

over the field

$$\mathbb{Q}_N(b, c) := \mathrm{Frac}\, \frac{\mathbb{Q}[b, c]}{(F_N(b, c))},$$

so that the base point $P = (0, 0)$ has order N. Note that $\mathbb{Q}_N(b, c)$ is simply the function field of $X_1(N)$ over $\mathbb{Q}$. Let $\varphi : E \to E'$ be the isogeny with kernel $\langle P \rangle$; for concreteness it can be assumed that the codomain curve E' is given by Eq. (2) provided by Vélu's formulae, although this is not needed for what follows.

Recall that we are interested in those points $P' \in E'$ for which the composition

$$E \xrightarrow{\varphi} E' \to E'/\langle P' \rangle$$

is a cyclic N^2-isogeny. It is easy to check that these points are characterized by the condition

$$\hat{\varphi}(P') = \lambda P \text{ for some } \lambda \in (\mathbb{Z}/N)^*, \tag{5}$$

with $\hat{\varphi} : E' \to E$ the dual of φ. In particular, there are $N\phi(N)$ such points, generating N distinct subgroups of E', where ϕ denotes Euler's totient function.

The points corresponding to $\lambda = 1$ will be called P-distinguished; they can be viewed as a set of canonical generators for these subgroups.

Define

$$\rho := f_{N,P}(-P) \tag{6}$$

where the Miller function $f_{N,P}$ on E is assumed to be normalized, so that ρ is just $t_N(P, -P)$ when considered modulo Nth powers in $\mathbb{Q}_N(b,c)^*$. The main result of this section is:

Theorem 5. *Let $P' \in E'$ be a point satisfying (5). Then the field extension $\mathbb{Q}_N(b,c) \subset \mathbb{Q}_N(b,c)(P')$, obtained by adjoining the coordinates of P', is simple radical of degree N. More precisely, $\mathbb{Q}_N(b,c)(P') = \mathbb{Q}_N(b,c)(\sqrt[N]{\rho})$ for an appropriately chosen Nth root $\sqrt[N]{\rho}$ of $\rho = f_{N,P}(-P)$.*

Proof. The fibre $\hat{\varphi}^{-1}\{\lambda P\}$ decomposes as a union of orbits under the action of the absolute Galois group of $\mathbb{Q}_N(b,c)$, together containing N elements. One of these orbits contains P'. Its number of elements equals the degree of the corresponding closed point, which in turn equals the degree of the extension $\mathbb{Q}_N(b,c) \subset \mathbb{Q}_N(b,c)(P')$. In particular, this extension has degree at most N. On the other hand, by Lemma 6 below, the extension $\mathbb{Q}_N(b,c) \subset \mathbb{Q}_N(b,c)(\sqrt[N]{\rho})$ is of degree precisely N. Therefore, it suffices to prove that $\mathbb{Q}_N(b,c)(P')$ contains an Nth root of ρ.

To this end we consider $\alpha := f_{N,P'}(-P') \in \mathbb{Q}_N(b,c)(P')$, where the Miller function $f_{N,P'}$ is again assumed normalized, and we let μ be such that $\lambda^2\mu \equiv 1 \bmod N$. Modulo Nth powers in $\mathbb{Q}_N(b,c)(P')^*$ we have

$$(\alpha^\mu)^N = t_N(P', -P')^{N\mu} = t_N(\hat{\varphi}(P'), -\hat{\varphi}(P'))^\mu$$
$$= t_N(\lambda P, -\lambda P)^\mu = t_N(P, -P)^{\lambda^2\mu} = \rho,$$

showing that ρ is indeed the Nth power of some element of $\mathbb{Q}_N(b,c)(P')$. ∎

Lemma 6. *The polynomial $x^N - \rho \in \mathbb{Q}_N(b,c)[x]$ is irreducible.*

Proof. According to Theorem 4 it suffices to prove:

(i) for all primes $m \mid N$ we have $\rho \notin \mathbb{Q}_N(b,c)^m$,
(ii) if $4 \mid N$ then $\rho \notin -4\mathbb{Q}_N(b,c)^4$.

Let $p \equiv 1 \bmod 2N$ be a prime number such that $4\sqrt{p} > N^2$. Then the Hasse interval $[p+1-2\sqrt{p}, p+1+2\sqrt{p}]$ contains the integers λN for N consecutive values of λ. At least one of these values satisfies $\gcd(\lambda, N) = 1$. By [27, Thm. 2.4.31] there exists an elliptic curve $\overline{E}/\mathbb{F}_p$ such that $\overline{E}(\mathbb{F}_p) \cong \mathbb{Z}/(\lambda N)$, so in particular $\overline{E}(\mathbb{F}_p)[N^\infty] \cong \mathbb{Z}/(N)$. Without loss of generality we can assume that $\overline{E}$ is in Tate normal form, say with coefficients $\overline{b}, \overline{c} \in \mathbb{F}_p$, and that $\overline{P} = (0,0)$ is a point of order N on $\overline{E}$.

Then, in order to prove (i), assume that $\rho \in \mathbb{Q}_N(b,c)^m$ for some prime divisor $m \mid N$. Since Miller functions are compatible with reduction mod p and with specialization at $\overline{b}, \overline{c} \in \mathbb{F}_p$ (this follows, for instance, from Miller's algorithm), we find that

$$t_N(\overline{P}, [-N/m]\overline{P}) = t_N(\overline{P}, -\overline{P})^{N/m} = 1,$$

in turn implying that $t_N(\overline{Q}, [-N/m]\overline{P}) = 1$ for all $\overline{Q} \in \overline{E}(\mathbb{F}_p)[N]$. This contradicts the non-degeneracy of the Tate pairing over $\mathbb{F}_p$ (which contains all Nth roots of unity by our choice of p). Indeed, $[-N/m]\overline{P}$ is a non-trivial element of $\overline{E}(\mathbb{F}_p)/N\overline{E}(\mathbb{F}_p)$.

As for (ii): if $4 \mid N$ then $p \equiv 1 \bmod 8$, from which it follows that -1 and 4 are 4th powers in $\mathbb{F}_p$, in particular the same holds for -4. As above, if $\rho \in -4\mathbb{Q}_N(b,c)^4$ then we can conclude that

$$t_N(\overline{P}, [-N/4]\overline{P}) = t_N(\overline{P}, -\overline{P})^{N/4} = 1,$$

again contradicting the non-degeneracy of the Tate pairing.   ∎

An immediate consequence of Theorem 5 is that for each point $P' = (x_0', y_0')$ satisfying (5) there exist concrete algebraic formulae

$$x_0'(b, c, \sqrt[N]{\rho}), \qquad y_0'(b, c, \sqrt[N]{\rho}) \tag{7}$$

for its coordinates: these are the radical isogeny formulae we are after. Note that, in order to find these formulae explicitly, it suffices to consider the cases where P' is P-distinguished, i.e., where $\lambda = 1$. Indeed, all other cases are then dealt with by feeding these formulae to the multiplication-by-λ map from (3). Experimentally, it seems that the P-distinguished case yields the simplest formulae.

Remark 2. Our choice of radicand $\rho = f_{N,P}(-P)$ is somewhat arbitrary: any representant of $t_N(P, \mu P)$ for any $\mu \in (\mathbb{Z}/N)^*$ would have worked equally well, with the same proofs. This reflects the fact that scaling ρ by Nth powers, or raising ρ to an exponent that is coprime with N, results in the same simple radical extension.

Given the coordinates of a P-distinguished point P', all other P-distinguished points are found by varying the choice of $\sqrt[N]{\rho}$:

Lemma 7. *Let $\lambda \in (\mathbb{Z}/N)^*$ and consider formulae of the form (7) expressing the coordinates of a point P' such that $\hat{\varphi}(P') = \lambda P$. Then, by varying the choice of the Nth root $\sqrt[N]{\rho}$, i.e., by scaling it with ζ_N^i for $i = 0, 1, \ldots, N-1$, these formulae compute the coordinates of all points P' for which $\hat{\varphi}(P') = \lambda P$.*

Proof. From the proof of Theorem 5 it follows that $\hat{\varphi}^{-1}\{\lambda P\}$ consists of a single Galois orbit, which implies our claim.   ∎

For the applications we have in mind, we want to interpret the formulae (7) in some concrete field K, with the indeterminates b, c replaced by concrete elements $\overline{b}, \overline{c} \in K$. It follows from general principles in algebraic geometry that these specialized formulae continue to produce the coordinates of a point P' defining a cyclic N^2-isogeny, with the possible exception of finitely many field characteristics $p > 0$ and finitely many $(\overline{b}, \overline{c}) \in K^2$. Loosely based on good reduction arguments from the theory of modular curves, we actually believe:

Conjecture 1. *The formulae* (7) *are compatible with specialization to all fields* K *satisfying* char $K \nmid N$ *and to all elements* $\overline{b}, \overline{c} \in K$ *satisfying* $F_N(\overline{b}, \overline{c}) = 0$, $\Delta(\overline{b}, \overline{c}) \neq 0$ *and* $F_m(\overline{b}, \overline{c}) \neq 0$ *for all* $4 \leq m < N$ *(in other words, to all* $\overline{b}, \overline{c}$ *for which* $y^2 + (1 - \overline{c})xy - \overline{b}x = x^3 - \overline{b}x^2$ *is an elliptic curve on which* $\overline{P} = (0, 0)$ *has exact order* N).

It is easy to confirm this conjecture for small values of N, by explicitly factoring the N-division polynomial of E': this is the approach followed in the next section, leading to explicit expressions for the formulae (7). In particular, the above conjecture does not affect any of our conclusions in Sects. 5 and 6, which are based on radical N-isogenies for these small values of N only. But from a purely mathematical point of view, we leave the validity of Conjecture 1 as an interesting open question.

We conclude by recalling that by rewriting (E', P') in Tate normal form, one obtains a curve equation

$$y^2 + (1 - c')xy - b'x = x^3 - b'x^2$$

where now

$$b'(b, c, \sqrt[N]{\rho}), \qquad c'(b, c, \sqrt[N]{\rho}) \tag{8}$$

are certain algebraic expressions in $b, c, \sqrt[N]{\rho}$. The formulae (8) can be applied iteratively, effectively allowing to compute a cyclic N^k-isogeny for arbitrary k without needing to explicitly generate points of order N in each step.

4   Explicit Radical Isogeny Formulae in Low Degree

In this section, we explain how to find concrete formulae of the forms (7) and (8) for small values of N, by factoring the reduced N-division polynomial of E' with the help of Magma [5]. As a by-product, we get a confirmation of Conjecture 1 in these cases. In particular, throughout this section, we work over an arbitrary field K with char $K \nmid N$.

We first deal with the cases $N = 2, 3$, which require to use a different curve model. We note however that the same principles, in particular using the Tate pairing, also applies in these cases.

Case $N = 2$. Since char $K \neq 2$, we can assume that $E : y^2 = x^3 + a_2 x^2 + a_4 x$ for $a_2, a_4 \in K$ and $P = (0, 0)$. A simple calculation shows that the isogenous curve $E/\langle P \rangle$ can be given by

$$E' : y^2 = x^3 - 2a_2 x^2 + (a_2^2 - 4a_4)x .$$

The dual isogeny corresponds to quotienting out $(0, 0)$ on E', so any other point of order 2 on E' is a suitable instance of P'; note that it is automatically P-distinguished. If we define $\rho = a_4$ and $\alpha = \sqrt{\rho}$, then these points are of the form

$$P' = (a_2 + 2\alpha, 0) ,$$

and by translating P' to $(0,0)$, we find the isomorphic model $E' : y^2 = x^3 + a_2'x^2 + a_4'x$, where

$$a_2' = 6\alpha + a_2 \qquad \text{and} \qquad a_4' = 4a_2\alpha + 8a_4. \tag{9}$$

We are now ready to repeat the whole process, since we can divide out by $(0,0)$ again.

Remark 3. We cannot use $f_{2,P}(-P)$ as an instance of ρ in this case, since $P = -P$. Nevertheless, the reader can check that $\rho = a_4$ is a representant of $t_2(P, -P)$.

Case $N = 3$. By requiring that the inflexion point $P = (0,0)$ has a horizontal tangent line, we can assume that $E : y^2 + a_1xy + a_3y = x^3$ for certain $a_1, a_3 \in K$. Vélu's formulae yield

$$E' : y^2 + a_1xy + a_3y = x^3 - 5a_1a_3x - a_1^3a_3 - 7a_3^2$$

as a defining equation for $E/\langle P \rangle$. The 3-division polynomial of E' splits as

$$\Psi_{E',3}(x) = 3(x + a_1^2/3)(x^3 - 9a_1a_3x - a_1^3a_3 - 27a_3^2),$$

and one checks through explicit computation that the linear factor is the kernel polynomial of the dual isogeny. Therefore, any root of the cubic factor is the x-coordinate of a P-distinguished point P'. Letting $\rho = f_{3,P}(-P) = -a_3$ and writing $\alpha = \sqrt[3]{\rho}$, this cubic factor splits as

$$(x + a_1\alpha - 3\alpha^2)(x^2 + (-a_1\alpha + 3\alpha^2)x + a_1^2\alpha^2 - 3a_1a_3 - 9a_3\alpha)$$

(note that it splits completely over $K(\zeta_3)$ in view of Remark 1 and/or Lemma 7). Thus we can take $x_0' = -a_1\alpha + 3\alpha^2$ and then one checks that $y_0' = 4a_3$ is the y-coordinate of the corresponding P-distinguished point $P' = (x_0', y_0')$. Translating P' to $(0,0)$ yields a model

$$E' : y^2 + a_1'xy + a_3'y = x^3,$$

with $a_1' = -6\alpha + a_1$ and $a_3' = 3a_1\alpha^2 - a_1^2\alpha + 9a_3$, and we can repeat. We recall that the simple radical nature of iterated 3-isogenies is not a new observation, see [12,14].

Case $N = 4$. For $N \geq 4$ we switch to the Tate normal form as in Sect. 3. Concretely, for $N = 4$ we have $F_4(b, c) = c = 0$ so we obtain the defining equation $E : y^2 + xy - by = x^3 - bx^2$. From Vélu's formulae we find

$$E' : y^2 + xy - by = x^3 - bx^2 + (-5b^2 + 5b)x + (-3b^3 - 12b^2 + b)$$

as a defining equation for $E/\langle P \rangle$, with reduced 4-division polynomial

$$\psi_{E',4}(x) = 2 \cdot (x + b + 1/2) \cdot (x - 7b) \cdot (x^4 + 4bx^3 + (6b^2 + 24b)x^2 + (4b^3 - 80b^2 + 8b)x + b^4 + 152b^3 - 8b^2 + b).$$

The first linear factor corresponds to the x-coordinate of a generator of the dual isogeny. The second linear factor corresponds to the x-coordinate of a 4-torsion point Q such that $2Q$ is in the kernel of the dual isogeny. Any root of the quartic factor is the x-coordinate of a P-distinguished point P'. Letting $\rho = f_{4,P}(-P) = -b$ and writing $\alpha = \sqrt[4]{\rho}$, one can verify that

$$P' = (4\alpha^3 + 2\alpha^2 + \alpha - b, 2\alpha^3 + \alpha^2 - 8b\alpha - 7b)$$

is such a P-distinguished point. Translating P' to $(0,0)$ we find an isomorphic model of E' given by

$$E' : y^2 + xy - b'y = x^3 - b'x^2, \tag{10}$$

with

$$b' = -\frac{\alpha(4\alpha^2 + 1)}{(2\alpha + 1)^4}$$

This formula can be applied iteratively.

Case $N = 5$. For $N = 5$ we have $F_5(b, c) = b - c = 0$, so we obtain the defining equation $E : y^2 + (1 - b)xy - by = x^3 - bx^2$. Vélu's formulae yield

$$E' : y^2 + (1 - b)xy - by = x^3 - bx^2 - 5b(b^2 + 2b - 1)x - b(b^4 + 10b^3 - 5b^2 + 15b - 1)$$

as a defining equation for the codomain of $\varphi : E \to E/\langle P \rangle$. The 5-division polynomial of E' can be verified to split as

$$
\begin{aligned}
\Psi_{E',5}(x) = 5 \cdot {}& (x^2 + (b^2 - b + 1)x + (b^4 + 3b^3 - 26b^2 - 8b + 1)/5) \\
\cdot {}& (x^5 + 10bx^4 - 5b(b^2 + b - 11)x^3 - 5b(17b^3 + 24b^2 + 46b - 7)x^2 \\
& - 5b(b^5 + 62b^4 + 154b^3 - 65b^2 + 19b - 2)x \\
& - b(b^7 - 19b^6 + 777b^5 - 757b^4 + 755b^3 + 2b^2 + 17b - 1)) \\
\cdot {}& (x^5 - 15bx^4 - 5b(11b^2 - 9b - 1)x^3 - 5b^2(7b^3 + 13b^2 - 13b + 20)x^2 \\
& - 5b^2(2b^5 + 5b^4 + 6b^3 + 196b^2 - 99b + 1)x \\
& - b^2(b^7 + 7b^6 - 62b^5 + 605b^4 - 127b^3 + 1177b^2 + 14b + 1))
\end{aligned}
$$

where the quadratic polynomial factor is the kernel polynomial of the dual isogeny. The roots of the first quintic factor are the x-coordinates of the P-distinguished points. Those of the second quintic factor are the x-coordinates of the points P' for which $\hat{\varphi}(P') = 2P$ (i.e., the doubles of the P-distinguished points). Concretely, letting $\rho = f_{5,P}(-P) = b$ and writing $\alpha = \sqrt[5]{\rho}$, the first quintic factor admits the root

$$x'_0 = 5\alpha^4 + (b - 3)\alpha^3 + (b + 2)\alpha^2 + (2b - 1)\alpha - 2b$$

(with all other roots obtained by scaling α with powers of ζ_5) and then one can check that

$$y_0' = 5\alpha^4 + (b - 3)\alpha^3 + (b^2 - 10b + 1)\alpha^2 + (13b - b^2)\alpha - b^2 - 11b$$

is the y-coordinate of the corresponding P-distinguished point P'. Translating P' to $(0,0)$, we obtain the isomorphic form

$$E' : y^2 + (1 - b')xy - b'y = x^3 - b'x^2,$$

where

$$b' = \alpha \frac{\alpha^4 + 3\alpha^3 + 4\alpha^2 + 2\alpha + 1}{\alpha^4 - 2\alpha^3 + 4\alpha^2 - 3\alpha + 1}$$

and again we can repeat.

Case $N = 6$. For $N = 6$ we have $F_6(b, c) = c^2 + c - b = 0$, so we work with $E : y^2 + (1 - c)xy - (c^2 + c)y = x^3 - (c^2 + c)x^2$. Vélu's formulae yield

$$y^2 + (1 - c)xy - (c^2 + c)y = x^3 - (c^2 + c)x^2$$
$$- (15c^4 + 20c^3 + 5c^2 - 5c)x - (19c^6 + 33c^5 + 18c^4 + 22c^3 + 14c^2 - c)$$

as a model for $E' = E/\langle P \rangle$. Its reduced 6-division polynomial $\psi_{E',6}(x)$ behaves much like in the degree 4 case: there is a unique interesting factor

$$\begin{aligned}
x^6 &+ 6c(2c + 3)x^5 + 3c(20c^3 + 33c^2 + 55c + 37)x^4 \\
&+ 4c(40c^5 + 18c^4 - 237c^3 - 301c^2 - 63c + 28)x^3 \\
&+ 3c(80c^7 - 168c^6 - 1029c^5 - 1028c^4 - 333c^3 - 202c^2 - 93c + 18)x^2 \\
&+ 6c(32c^9 - 192c^8 + 718c^7 + 3131c^6 + 3186c^5 + 847c^4 - 196c^3 - 69c^2 - 22c + 2)x \\
&+ c(64c^{11} - 720c^{10} + 10740c^9 + 38500c^8 + 46773c^7 + 31142c^6 \\
&\qquad\qquad + 17983c^5 + 7506c^4 + 901c^3 + 13c^2 - 18c + 1)
\end{aligned}$$

whose roots are the x-coordinates of the P-distinguished points $P' \in E'$. Letting $\rho = f_{6,P}(-P) = -b^2/c = -c(c + 1)^2$ and writing $\alpha = \sqrt[6]{\rho}$, one checks that

$$x_0' = \frac{6}{c + 1}\alpha^5 + \frac{4}{c + 1}\alpha^4 + 3\alpha^3 + 2\alpha^2 - (3c - 1)\alpha - 2c^2 - 3c$$

is such a root; all other roots are found by scaling α with some power of ζ_6. One then verifies that

$$y_0' = \frac{3c + 9}{c + 1}\alpha^5 + \frac{2c + 6}{c + 1}\alpha^4 - (12c - 3)\alpha^3 - (17c - 1)\alpha^2 - (15c^2 + 19c)\alpha - c^3 - 18c^2 - 16c$$

is the y-coordinate of the corresponding P-distinguished point P'. When writing (E', P') in Tate normal form, we find

$$E' : y^2 + (1 - c')xy - (c'^2 + c')y = x^3 - (c'^2 + c')x^2$$

with

$$c' = \frac{1}{(c+1)(9c+1)^3}((729c^3 + 243c^2 + 243c - 39)\alpha^5 - (108c^2 + 216c - 20)\alpha^4$$
$$- (729c^4 + 729c^3 + 81c^2 - 165c + 10)\alpha^3 + (108c^3 - 36c^2 - 140c + 4)\alpha^2$$
$$+ (729c^5 + 1215c^4 + 486c^3 + 114c^2 + 113c - 1)\alpha - 108c^4 - 36c^3 - 4c^2 - 76c).$$

Once again, this formula can be applied iteratively.

Radical Isogenies of Degree $N \geq 7$. A similar reasoning can be made for $N \geq 7$, but a direct factorization of the reduced N-division polynomial of E' over $\mathbb{Q}_N(b, c)(\sqrt[N]{\rho})$ quickly becomes unwieldy, for several reasons: the coefficients of E' become more involved, the degree of $\psi_{E',N}$ grows quadratically, and both ρ and the base field $\mathbb{Q}_N(b, c)$ become increasingly complicated, see Table 1. For instance, from $N = 7$ onwards it is no longer possible to eliminate one of the variables b, c using the relation $F_N(b, c) = 0$. As long as the modular curve $X_1(N)$ has genus 0, it is possible to get around this by using a different parametrization, see Table 2, but for $N = 11$ and $N \geq 13$ this is no longer the case.

An approach that already works much better is to use number fields, i.e. assign a large enough integer value to b, construct the number field defined by $F_N(b, c) = 0$ and the degree N extension by adjoining $\sqrt[N]{\rho}$. The root of $\psi_{E',N}(x)$ is an expression in c and $\sqrt[N]{\rho}$ with rational coefficients. We know that each such coefficient is a rational function in b, so if b is large enough, this function can be found using lattice reduction. The most effective method is similar to the previous method, but uses p-adic fields instead of number fields. Again we need to choose a "large enough" value for b and a large enough precision with which we represent the p-adic field, to be able to reconstruct the rational function in b. We followed this approach for $N = 13$, since Magma struggles to find the formulae using direct root finding. All formulae for $N = 2, \ldots, 13$ can be found online at https://github.com/KULeuven-COSIC/Radical-Isogenies.

5 Isogeny Chains over Finite Fields

In this section we use our iterable radical isogeny formulae of the form (8) to compute chains of N-isogenies between elliptic curves over finite fields $\mathbb{F}_q$ with char $\mathbb{F}_q \nmid N$; the application to CSIDH is given in Sect. 6. Here we just concentrate on the computation of long chains of N-isogenies for some fixed $N \geq 2$, and address the following two issues. Firstly, the radicand ρ might not admit an Nth root over $\mathbb{F}_q$: in the worst case, this could mean that at every iteration we need to replace the base field with a degree N extension. Secondly, over $\overline{\mathbb{F}}_q$ there are N choices for $\sqrt[N]{\rho}$, hence the question arises which root to take if we want to navigate the N-isogeny graph in a controlled way. We discuss three special cases given by $\gcd(q - 1, N) = 1$, $\gcd(q - 1, N) = N$ and $\gcd(q - 1, N) = 2$.

Table 1. Relations $F_N(b,c) = 0$ and radicands ρ for small $N \geq 4$

N	Polynomial relation $F_N(b,c) = 0$	Radicand $\rho = f_{N,P}(-P)$
4	$c = 0$	$-b$
5	$c - b = 0$	b
6	$c^2 + c - b = 0$	$-b^2/c$
7	$c^3 + cb - b^2 = 0$	b^3/c^2
8	$c^2b - c^2 + 3cb - 2b^2 = 0$	$-b^3/(b-c)$
9	$c^5 + c^4 - c^3b + c^3 - 3c^2b + 3cb^2 - b^3 = 0$	$b^3c^2/(b-c)^2$
10	$c^5 + c^4b + 3c^3b - 3c^2b^2 + c^2b - 2cb^2 + b^3 = 0$	$-b^3c/(c^2 + c - b)$
11	$c^7b + 3c^6b - c^6 - 3c^5b^2 + 6c^5b - 9c^4b^2$ $+ 4c^3b^3 + c^3b^2 - 3c^2b^3 + 3cb^4 - b^5 = 0$	$b^3(b-c)^2/(c^2 + c - b)^2$
12	$c^6 + c^4b + c^4 - 5c^3b - c^2b^3$ $+ 10c^2b^2 - 9cb^3 + 3b^4 = 0$	$-b^4(b-c)/(b^2 - bc - c^3)$
13	$c^{10} - c^9b^2 - 6c^8b^2 + 6c^8b + 5c^7b^3 - 21c^7b^2$ $+ 3c^7b + 24c^6b^3 - 13c^6b^2 + c^6b - 9c^5b^4 +$ $21c^5b^3 - 6c^5b^2 - 15c^4b^4 + 15c^4b^3 + 4c^3b^5 -$ $20c^3b^4 + 15c^2b^5 - 6cb^6 + b^7 = 0$	$b^5(c^2 + c - b)^2/(b^2 - bc - c^3)^2$

Table 2. Modular equations and radicands for low degree isogenies. The parameters r and s are optimised representations of curves with a prescribed N-torsion point from [26]. The transformations $b = rs(r-1)$ and $c = s(r-1)$ can be used to obtain the Tate normal form $E : y^2 + (1-c)xy - by = x^3 - bx^2$, where $P = (0,0)$ is a point of order N expressed by the modular equation.

N	r	s	Modular equation	Radicand ρ
6	A	1	–	$-r^2(A-1)$
7	A	A	–	$r^4(A-1)$
8	$\frac{1}{2-A}$	A	–	$-(r^2s)^2(A-1)$
9	$A^2 - A + 1$	A	–	$r^3s^4(A-1)$
10	$\frac{-A^2}{A^2-3A+1}$	A	–	$-r^5s^9(A-1)(2A-1)^2$
11	$AB + 1$	$1 - A$	$B^2 + (A^2+1)B + A = 0$	$A(rsB)^3$
12	$\frac{2A^2-2A+1}{A}$	$\frac{3A^2-3A+1}{A^2}$	–	$r^4s^3A^{11}(A-1)(2A-1)^2$
13	$1 - AB$	$1 - \frac{AB}{B+1}$	$B^2 + (A^3 + A^2 + 1)B$ $-A^2 - A = 0$	$-r^5B(sA)^3$

5.1   The Case $\gcd(q-1, N) = 1$

The most straightforward case is $\gcd(q-1, N) = 1$, where there is a very natural choice for $\sqrt[N]{\rho}$. Indeed, in this case the map $\mathbb{F}_q \to \mathbb{F}_q : a \mapsto a^N$ is a bijection, so if the starting curve $E : y^2 + (1-c)xy - by = x^3 - bx^2$ is defined over $\mathbb{F}_q$, then so is $\rho(b, c)$ and it admits a unique Nth root which is again defined over $\mathbb{F}_q$. Choosing this instance of $\sqrt[N]{\rho}$ results in new coefficients $b', c' \in \mathbb{F}_q$ and the argument repeats. Moreover, the Nth root can be computed as ρ^μ where μ is such that $\mu N \equiv 1 \bmod (q-1)$. Thus, the condition $\gcd(q-1, N)$ naturally pulls out a chain of N-isogenies whose cost, at least for small N, is dominated by a single $\mathbb{F}_q$-exponentiation at each step.

Lemma 8. *Assume that* $\operatorname{char} \mathbb{F}_q \nmid N$ *and* $\gcd(q-1, N) = 1$, *then* $\operatorname{End}_{\mathbb{F}_q} E$ *is an imaginary quadratic order which is locally maximal at all primes dividing* N, *and our chain of* N-isogenies corresponds to the repeated action of the ideal class $[(N, \pi_q - 1)]$.

Proof. Observe that

$$\ker([N]) \cap \ker(\pi_q - 1) = E(\mathbb{F}_q)[N] = \langle P \rangle,$$

where the last equality follows from $\gcd(q-1, N) = 1$ along with the fact that $P = (0, 0)$ is an $\mathbb{F}_q$-rational point of order N. These properties also imply that

$$\gcd(t^2 - 4q, N) = \gcd((q + 1 - |E(\mathbb{F}_q)|)^2 - 4q, N) = \gcd((q-1)^2, N) = 1$$

with t the trace of Frobenius, showing that $\operatorname{End}_{\mathbb{F}_q} E$ is indeed an imaginary quadratic order which is locally maximal at all primes dividing N; see [29, §4]. Thus the isogeny $E \to E' = E/\langle P \rangle$ is the horizontal isogeny corresponding to the invertible ideal $(N, \pi_q - 1) \subset \operatorname{End}_{\mathbb{F}_q} E$. Since such isogenies do not change the structure of $E(\mathbb{F}_q)$, and since choosing the unique $\mathbb{F}_q$-rational Nth root of ρ clearly produces an $\mathbb{F}_q$-rational point of order N, the reasoning can be repeated and the lemma follows. ∎

Estimating the rough cost of an exponentiation as $1.5 \log q$ multiplications in $\mathbb{F}_q$, our method should be compared with:

(i) generating an $\mathbb{F}_q$-rational N-torsion point and applying (some form of) Vélu's formulae; the main cost in this approach is the generation of the N-torsion point, which consists of generating a random point and multiplying by the cofactor $\#E(\mathbb{F}_q)/N$, taking roughly $11 \log q$ multiplications in $\mathbb{F}_q$; furthermore this procedure has to be repeated with probability $1/N$, which is non-negligible for small N,

(ii) finding an $\mathbb{F}_q$-rational root of $\Phi_N(x, j(E))$, with Φ_N the classical modular polynomial of level N; this roughly amounts to computing x^q modulo the polynomial $\Phi_N(x, j(E))$, whose degree is at least $N + 1$, so we estimate this cost as $1.5(N + 1)^2 \log q$ multiplications in $\mathbb{F}_q$.

However, for growing N it becomes unfair to measure the cost of a radical isogeny by merely an exponentiation in $\mathbb{F}_q$: the algebraic expressions for b' and c'

Table 3. The computational cost of radical N-isogenies over a finite field $\mathbb{F}_q$. The letters $\mathbf{E}, \mathbf{M}, \mathbf{A}$ and $\mathbf{I}$ denote exponentiation, multiplication, addition and inversion respectively. The last column expresses the cost of the multiplications, additions and inversions, relative to the total cost. The percentages are computed from the evaluation of a chain of $10\,000$ horizontal N-isogenies over $\mathbb{F}_p$, where p is the CSURF-512 prime from [6].

	Computational cost	Relative cost of formulae evaluation
3-isogeny	$\mathbf{E} + 6\mathbf{M} + 3\mathbf{A}$	2.2 %
4-isogeny	$\mathbf{E} + 4\mathbf{M} + 3\mathbf{A} + \mathbf{I}$	3.9 %
5-isogeny	$\mathbf{E} + 7\mathbf{M} + 6\mathbf{A} + \mathbf{I}$	4.8%
7-isogeny	$\mathbf{E} + 24\mathbf{M} + 20\mathbf{A} + \mathbf{I}$	10.1%
9-isogeny	$\mathbf{E} + 69\mathbf{M} + 58\mathbf{A} + \mathbf{I}$	20.5%
11-isogeny	$\mathbf{E} + 599\mathbf{M} + 610\mathbf{A} + \mathbf{I}$	67.7%
13-isogeny	$\mathbf{E} + 783\mathbf{M} + 776\mathbf{A} + \mathbf{I}$	71.9%

in terms of $b, c, \sqrt[N]{\rho}$ become increasingly complicated, and the cost of evaluating these expressions quickly overtakes the cost of the exponentiation as shown in Table 3. We also remark that the majority of the multiplications are with small constants coming from the explicit formulae as illustrated in Sect. 4. The size of these constants also grows with N, e.g. for $N = 13$ the constants have a size of up to 14 bits.

A similar overhead is present in approach *(ii)* using modular polynomials (where moreover one is left with the task of determining the correct twist), which seems consistently outperformed by our radical isogeny formulae. As for the basic approach *(i)* using Vélu's formulae, it is shown in Table 4 that for small N, radical isogenies are up to 50 times faster, the main reason being that radical isogenies can be chained without explicitly generating a new N-torsion point on each curve. From $N \approx 15$ onwards, the overhead becomes so large that radical isogenies become less efficient.

5.2   The Case $\gcd(q - 1, N) = N$

At the other extreme, if $N \mid q-1$ then $\mathbb{F}_q$ contains a primitive Nth root of unity ζ_N. As a consequence, if $\rho \in \mathbb{F}_q^*$ admits an Nth root $\sqrt[N]{\rho} \in \mathbb{F}_q$, then all Nth roots are defined over $\mathbb{F}_q$. But the probability that a random $\rho \in \mathbb{F}_q^*$ admits an Nth root in $\mathbb{F}_q$ is $1/N$ only, so one would expect that the base field needs to be extended at most steps of the iteration.

The situation is much better in the following special case: let $q = p^2$ for some prime $p \equiv -1 \bmod N$, so that indeed $N \mid q - 1$, and let $E/\mathbb{F}_q$ be a supersingular elliptic curve, say with $|E(\mathbb{F}_q)| = (p + 1)^2$. Such curves are used in the CGL hash function and in SIDH, but since these rely exclusively on 2 and 3 isogenies which are already heavily optimized, we do not expect any real improvement for these applications. On these curves we have $\pi_q = [-p]$, from which it follows that $E[N] \subset E(\mathbb{F}_q)$. Let $P \in E$ be any point of order N, then we claim that $\rho = f_{N,P}(-P) \in \mathbb{F}_q^*$ is an Nth power, i.e. $t_N(P, -P) = 1$.

Table 4. Clock cycles (using Magma v2.32-2 on an Intel(R) Xeon(R) CPU E5-2630 v2 @ 2.60GHz with 128 GB memory) for an individual step in a horizontal N-isogeny chain, basic Vélu approach vs. (unique) root of the modular polynomial vs. radical isogenies averaged over a chain of 10 000 N-isogenies over the finite field $\mathbb{F}_p$, where p is the CSURF-512 prime from [6]. The probability of failure to sample an N-torsion point for composite N is larger than $1/N$, and the degree of the modular polynomial scales faster for composite numbers, which explain the results for $N = 4, 9$ for the first two methods. * The clock cycles for 4-isogenies for the first two methods are obtained from random 4-isogenies instead of exclusively horizontal ones. Every curve has three 4-isogenous elliptic curves and identifying the correct one would require an additional square-check (see Sect. 5.3).

	Sampling N-torsion	Isogenous curve Vélu	Image of a point	Modular polynomial	Radical isogeny
3-isogeny	50,449,710	38,513	18,860	9,939,840	1,071,612
4-isogeny*	63,693,051	45,093	45,004	29,628,400	1,101,677
5-isogeny	41,519,930	140,968	33,453	19,943,602	1,086,011
7-isogeny	39,049,435	247,526	47,734	34,049,452	1,192,454
9-isogeny	47,994,892	319,695	70,899	76,299,055	1,304,341
11-isogeny	36,755,529	448,043	75,995	76,435,364	3,161,470
13-isogeny	36,252,253	548,833	90,168	147,552,105	3,626,544

To see this, note that the codomain of $\varphi : E \to E' = E/\langle P\rangle$ again satisfies $|E'(\mathbb{F}_q)| = (p+1)^2$ and therefore $E[N] \subset E'(\mathbb{F}_q)$. In particular, any P-distinguished point P' takes coordinates in $\mathbb{F}_q$ and we conclude

$$t_N(P, -P) = t_N(\hat{\varphi}(P'), -\hat{\varphi}(P')) = t_N(P', -P')^N = 1.$$

The argument of course repeats, so in this case one can keep applying our radical isogeny formulae, choosing an Nth root of ρ at each iteration, without ever leaving $\mathbb{F}_q$. A performance comparison with the modular polynomial method *(ii)* from the previous section can be found in Table 5.

5.3   The Case $\gcd(q - 1, N) = 2$

An interesting intermediate case is $\gcd(q - 1, N) = 2$, where an element $\rho \in \mathbb{F}_q^*$ is an Nth power if and only if it is a square. If it is, then it has exactly two Nth roots $\pm\sqrt[N]{\rho}$. If $q \equiv 3 \bmod 4$ then one of these Nth roots is a square and one of them is not; they can be computed as ρ^μ resp. $-\rho^\mu$, where μ is such that $\mu N \equiv 1 \bmod (q-1)/2$.

For $N = 2$, it was observed in [6] that this distinction allows for a controlled navigation of the 2-isogeny graph of supersingular elliptic curves E over a finite prime field $\mathbb{F}_p$ with $p \equiv 7 \bmod 8$. Concretely, such curves come in two types: curves on 'the floor' have endomorphism ring $\mathbb{Z}[\sqrt{-p}]$ and admit a unique $\mathbb{F}_p$-rational point of order 2, while curves on 'the surface' have endomorphism ring $\mathbb{Z}[(1 + \sqrt{-p})/2]$ and have three distinguished $\mathbb{F}_p$-rational points of order 2:

- P^-, whose halves have x-coordinates that are not defined over $\mathbb{F}_p$,
- P_1^+, whose halves are not defined over $\mathbb{F}_p$, but their x-coordinates are,
- P_2^+, whose halves are defined over $\mathbb{F}_p$

Table 5. Clock cycles (using Magma v2.32-2 on an Intel(R) Xeon(R) CPU E5-2630 v2 @ 2.60 GHz with 128 GB memory) for an individual step in an N-isogeny chain, roots of the modular polynomial vs. radical isogenies averaged over a chain of $1\,000$ N-isogenies over finite fields $\mathbb{F}_{p^2}$. The prime $p = 2^{512} + \epsilon$ was chosen per N-isogeny such that $p \equiv -1 \bmod N$ and such that $p \equiv 3 \bmod 4$, so that we could start from $E : y^2 = x^3 + x$; concretely, for $N = 3, 4, 5, 7, 9, 11, 13$ we took $\epsilon = 727, 75, 2743, 7471, 1147, 29607, 1147$ respectively.

	Modular polynomial	Radical isogeny
3-isogeny	397,463,526	7,376,366
4-isogeny	705,256,757	29,128,205
5-isogeny	1,020,128,985	8,988,513
7-isogeny	1,889,168,090	8,973,325
9-isogeny	2,795,301,745	24,966,750
11-isogeny	3,827,699,588	12,707,001
13-isogeny	5,533,476,662	14,563,945

(see Fig. 1). Quotienting out P^- takes us from the surface to the floor, while quotienting out P_1^+ and P_2^+ amounts to traveling along the surface, using the horizontal isogenies corresponding to the respective ideals $(2, (\sqrt{-p} + 1)/2)$, $(2, (\sqrt{-p} - 1)/2)$ of $\mathbb{Z}[(1 + \sqrt{-p})/2]$, see [6, Lem. 5].

Lemma 9. *If the curve point pair (E, P_1^+) resp. (E, P_2^+) is in the form (E, P) with*

$$E : y^2 = x^3 + a_2 x^2 + a_4 x, \qquad P = (0, 0), \ a_2, a_4 \in \mathbb{F}_q$$

as in Sect. 4, then $\rho = a_4$ is a square. Applying the iterative formulae (9) corresponds to the repeated action of $[(2, (\sqrt{-p} + 1)/2)]$ resp. $[(2, (\sqrt{-p} - 1)/2)]$ if one consistently computes $\sqrt{\rho}$ as $-\rho^\mu$ resp. ρ^μ.

Proof. The fact that $\rho = a_4$ is a square follows from the proof of [6, Lem. 3]. From [6, Lem. 4] it follows that selecting $-\rho^\mu$ resp. ρ^μ corresponds to selecting $P_1'^+$ resp. $P_2'^+$ on E', which implies the lemma. Note that the other square root of ρ corresponds to P'^- in both cases, taking us to the floor. ∎

The first observation, namely that ρ is a square, generalizes to all N satisfying $\gcd(p - 1, N) = 2$, where we continue to work over $\mathbb{F}_p$ with $p \equiv 7 \bmod 8$. More precisely, consider a curve E on the surface, let us say in Tate normal form with $P = (0, 0)$ a point of order $N \geq 4$. The cyclic N-isogeny $\varphi : E \to E' = E/\langle P \rangle$ is the composition of a horizontal $N/2$-isogeny, i.e. to another curve on the surface, and either *(i)* a horizontal 2-isogeny or *(ii)* a vertical 2-isogeny. Then we claim that we are in case *(i)* if and only if ρ is a square. To see this, note that we are in case *(i)* if and only if there exists a point $P' \in E'(\mathbb{F}_p)$ such that the composition of φ with $E' \to E'/\langle P' \rangle$ is cyclic of degree N^2. If ρ is a square then the existence of such a point simply follows from our radical isogeny formulae (7). Conversely,

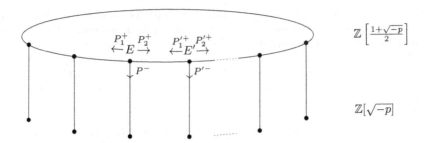

Fig. 1. A connected component of the 2-isogeny graph of supersingular elliptic curves over $\mathbb{F}_p$ with $p \equiv 7 \bmod 8$, highlighting two elliptic curves on the surface together with their three distinguished 2-torsion points and the corresponding 2-isogenies.

if there exists such a point P' then we necessarily have $P = \lambda\hat{\varphi}(P')$ for some $\lambda \in (\mathbb{Z}/N)^*$, and it follows from

$$t_N(P, -P) = t_N(\lambda\hat{\varphi}(P'), -\lambda\hat{\varphi}(P')) = t_N(P', -P')^{N\lambda^2}$$

that ρ is a square.

Unfortunately, it seems harder to generalize the second observation, but based on experiments we conjecture the following statement for $N = 4$, in which case we can take $\mu = (p+1)/8$:

Conjecture 2. *Assume that $N = 4$ and that (E, P) is in Tate normal form*

$$y^2 + xy - by = x^3 - bx^2, \qquad P = (0,0), \ b \in \mathbb{F}_p$$

as above. If the isogeny $E \to E/\langle P\rangle$ is horizontal then $\rho = -b$ is a square. Moreover, applying the iterative formula (10) *corresponds to the repeated action of $[(2, (\sqrt{-p}-1)/2)]^2$ if one consistently computes $\alpha = \sqrt[4]{\rho}$ as $-\rho^\mu$ resp. ρ^μ, depending on whether $p \equiv 7 \bmod 16$ resp. $p \equiv 15 \bmod 16$.*

Note that we have just come to argue why $\rho = -b$ is indeed a square. Also, since $P = (0,0) \in E(\mathbb{F}_p)$, we necessarily have that $2P$ equals P_2^+, the unique point of order 2 whose halves are $\mathbb{F}_p$-rational. As a result, since the isogeny $\varphi : E \to E' = E/\langle P\rangle$ is cyclic and horizontal, it necessarily corresponds to the action of $[(2, (\sqrt{-p}-1)/2)]^2$. Therefore, the main open problem in proving the conjecture is the last claim. So far, we did not succeed in giving a proof, nor did we manage to generalize its statement to larger values of N.

6 Speeding up CSIDH

The core operation in CSIDH [7] is computing a composition of many horizontal isogenies of small prime degree ℓ_i for $i = 1, \ldots, n$, where the ℓ_i are typically consecutive small primes starting from 2 or 3. The exact composition that needs to be computed can be specified as an exponent vector $[e_1, \ldots, e_n]$, where each

$e_i \in [-B_i, B_i]$ indicates how many horizontal isogenies of degree ℓ_i have to be computed. In practice often $B_i = B$ for all i, where B is some fixed small value such that $(2B + 1)^n > 2^{2\lambda}$, with λ the (classical) security parameter. In the previous section, we considered this problem for a single ℓ_i and showed that generating a new ℓ_i-torsion point in every step is expensive.

In CSIDH this problem is (partly) remedied by chaining isogenies of distinct degrees, i.e. computing a horizontal isogeny of degree $N = \prod_{i=1}^{n} \ell_i^{\delta_i}$ where $\delta_i = 1$ if $|e_i| > 1$ and zero otherwise. Without loss of generality we will assume that all $\delta_i = 1$. Instead of generating an ℓ_i-torsion point in every step, one first generates a point Q of order (possibly dividing) N and then pushes Q through the isogeny chain. Denote with $Q_k = \varphi_k(Q)$ with φ_k the isogeny of degree $N_k = \prod_{i=1}^{k} \ell_i$, then if Q had order N at the start, Q_k will have order $M_k = N/N_k$. To generate a point of order ℓ_{k+1} it therefore suffices to compute $[M_k/\ell_{k+1}]Q_k$, which is much cheaper than a full scalar multiplication, certainly for larger k. Note that in practice the original point P does not necessarily have order N, so this procedure might skip a few ℓ_i. This method therefore amortizes the cost of one full scalar multiplication (to generate the initial Q) over the different primes ℓ_i, and only requires a multiplication by $[M_k/\ell_{k+1}]$ in step k. Table 4 shows that pushing a point through an isogeny is a rather cheap operation, and the main costs are still the generation of the initial Q's and the scalar multiplications by $[M_k/\ell_{k+1}]$. Table 4 also shows that excluding the computation of an N-torsion point, computing a radical isogeny of degree N is slower than a simple application of Vélu's formulae.

For the above approach, it is clear that the number of initial Q's that need to be generated is (at least) $\max_i B_i$, so it typically does not make sense to sample the exponent vectors from a very skew box, i.e. to take $B_1 \gg B_n$, even though computing an isogeny of degree ℓ_1 is much cheaper than computing an isogeny of degree ℓ_n. However, using radical isogenies it does make sense to really skew the box since for every prime ℓ_i one only needs to generate one Q.

Implementation

To illustrate this approach, we implemented a variant of CSIDH that also uses radical isogenies to compute the class group action. Our implementation uses Magma v.2.25-2 [5] and is available at https://github.com/KULeuven-COSIC/Radical-Isogenies and builds upon the code from [1]. Concretely, for 128 bits of classical security, consider the field $\mathbb{F}_p$, with p the CSURF-512 prime from [6], i.e.

$$p = 2^3 \cdot 3 \cdot \underbrace{(3 \cdot \ldots \cdot 389)}_{\substack{\text{74 consecutive primes,} \\ \text{skip 347 and 359}}} - 1 \approx 2^{512}.$$

In the implementation of [1], the authors used $B_i = 5$ for all i, however using radical isogenies we propose the skew box

$$I = [-202; 202] \times [-170; 170] \times [-95; 95] \times [-91; 91] \times [-33; 33]$$
$$\times [-29; 29] \times [-6; 6]^{20} \times [-5; 5]^{14} \times [-4; 4]^{10} \times [-3; 3]^{10} \times [-2; 2]^8 \times [-1; 1]^7.$$

These vectors represent the action of classes of ideals of the form

$$\left(2, \frac{\sqrt{-p}-1}{2}\right)^{e_1} (3, \sqrt{-p}-1)^{e_2} (5, \sqrt{-p}-1)^{e_3} \cdots (389, \sqrt{-p}-1)^{e_{75}}$$

on elements from the set of public keys $S_p^- = \{A \in \mathbb{F}_p \mid y^2 = x^3 + Ax^2 - x$ is a supersingular elliptic curve$\}$. The set S_p^- is in 1-to-1 correspondence with $\mathbb{F}_p$-isomorphism classes of supersingular elliptic curves, which allows for a slightly easier key validation than using Montgomery curves. The set I contains approximately 2^{256} integer vectors, and just as in [7], we heuristically assume that these vectors represent the elements in the class group quasi-uniformly.

The first step in computing the class group action is finding a 4-torsion point P, such that if we compute the isogeny $\varphi : E \to E/\langle 2P \rangle$, it holds that $\varphi(P)$ has halves defined over $\mathbb{F}_p$. In accordance with Conjecture 2 and the discussion following it, this implies that the isogeny with kernel $\langle P \rangle$ will then correspond to the action of $\left(2, \frac{\sqrt{-p}-1}{2}\right)^2$. In order to iteratively compute this horizontal $4^{\lfloor e_1/2 \rfloor}$-isogeny, we first swap to the Tate normal form by translating P to $(0, 0)$. After iterating the 4-isogeny formula $\lfloor e_1/2 \rfloor$ times, we perform a vertical isogeny to a Montgomery representation of an elliptic curve on the floor. If e_1 is odd, we do a single horizontal 2-isogeny on the Montgomery curve, as explained in [1].

The rest of the computation is done on Montgomery curves on the floor for two reasons. The first is that arithmetic on Montgomery curves is slightly more efficient than arithmetic on curves represented by elements of S_p^-. The second reason is that, in order to compute 3-, 5-, 7-, 11- and 13-isogenies, we will need to swap between elliptic curves in Tate normal form and Montgomery curves. Computing the Montgomery representation of an elliptic curve is essentially finding a two-torsion point, which in practice means finding a solution to a cubic equation. If a cubic equation has three solutions, the explicit formulae to compute any single one of them require going through a quadratic field extension, even if all solutions are defined over the ground field.[2] An elliptic curve on the floor however, only has one nontrivial two-torsion point. In this case, the cubic equation has exactly one solution over $\mathbb{F}_p$, and the formula to find it does not require field extensions.

We then compute a horizontal 3^{e_2}-isogeny as follows. We first sample a 9-torsion point and swap to the Tate normal form by translating this point to $(0, 0)$. Next, we calculate a $9^{\lfloor e_2/2 \rfloor - 1}$-isogeny iteratively. We perform one last 9-isogeny using Vélu's formulae on the Tate normal form with kernel generator $(0, 0)$, before swapping back to the Montgomery form of this curve. The reason for this choice is that one more iteration of the formulae would be more expensive, since we already know the final 9-torsion point and hence can simply use Vélu's formulae. If e_2 is odd, we will compute this final 3-isogeny together with the ℓ-isogenies for $\ell \geq 17$.

---

[2] This is known as the *casus irreducibilis*, proven by Pierre Wantzel in the first half of the 19th century.

The ℓ^{e_i}-isogenies for $\ell^{e_i} = 5^{e_3}, 7^{e_4}, 11^{e_5}, 13^{e_6}$ are then iteratively computed in a similar manner. We first compute an ℓ-torsion point on a Montgomery curve to swap to the Tate normal form. Next, we iterate the formulae for ℓ-isogenies $e_i - 1$ times, and the final ℓ-isogeny is computed using Vélu's formulae, at which point we go back to the Montgomery representation of the curve. The only noteworthy exception is that if $|e_i| = 1$, we use the original computation of the CSIDH class group action. The reason for this is that swapping to a Tate normal form requires sampling an ℓ-torsion point, which means it is more efficient to perform this action together with the ℓ-isogenies for $\ell \geq 17$.

The rest of the ℓ-isogenies for $\ell \geq 17$ are performed as in [7], where optimizations such as those of [1] can be applied. At the end, we perform one final vertical isogeny to the surface to obtain a public key in S_p^-.

We set the bound to swap to the new formulae of [1] at $\ell > 113$, since this is the threshold where they start outperforming the formulae of [21] in Magma. The box I from which the exponent vectors are sampled was obtained heuristically over a large sample and is near optimal. Over a sample size of $100\,000$ class group actions each, our variant of CSIDH results in a speed-up of 19% over the one from [1]. We do note that this comparison is with respect to the CSIDH-512 parameter version, since the Magma code from [1] based on the CSURF-512 parameters did not seem to work. Since the CSIDH-512 parameters do not allow horizontal 2-isogenies, a small part of our speed-up can be ascribed to the work of [6].

7 Conclusion and Open Problems

Starting from a curve E with an N-torsion point P we have proved the existence of explicit formulae for the isogenous curve $E' = E/\langle P \rangle$ and the coordinates of a point P' on E' of order N, such that the composition of $E \to E' = E/\langle P \rangle$ with $E' \to E'/\langle P' \rangle$ is cyclic of degree N^2. This property implies that the formulae can be used repeatedly to compute chains of N-isogenies without generating N-torsion points in each step of the chain. Furthermore, the formulae, which we have described explicitly for $N \leq 13$, only involve basic arithmetic operations, except for the extraction of an Nth root. We have implemented these formulae and used them in two main applications: computing a chain consisting solely of N-isogenies, where we obtained a speed-up ranging from a factor 29 for $N = 7$ to a factor 5 for $N = 13$, and an improved implementation of CSIDH which is 19% faster than the state of the art implementation.

Open Problems. The following problems remain open and are interesting future work:

- Prove Conjecture 1, stating that our formulae have good reduction wherever there is no obvious obstruction.
- Devise a more efficient method for explicitly finding the radical isogeny formulae to avoid our current approach of factoring N-division polynomials as in Sect. 4, which is a major bottleneck.

- Optimize our formulae, e.g. is it indeed true that the P-distinguished case yields the most compact expressions? Using the relations $\alpha^N = \rho(b,c)$ and $F_N(b,c) = 0$, using different instances of ρ, or using different parametrizations of $X_1(N)$ as in Table 2 or [26], can we rewrite our formulae such that they become more efficient?
- Prove Conjecture 2 on radical isogenies of degree $N = 4$ between supersingular elliptic curves over $\mathbb{F}_p$ with $p \equiv 7 \bmod 8$, and generalize it to larger even values of N.
- Measure the impact of our work on constant-time implementations of CSIDH and on the quantum circuits discussed in [3].

Acknowledgments. We are very grateful to Karl Rubin and Alice Silverberg who provided insights on how an earlier approach to proving Theorem 5 using the theory of modular curves was related to known results. We are also very much indebted to Shahed Sharif whose remarks pointed us in the direction of the more direct approach using Tate pairings presented above. We also thank several other attendants of the online "Workshop on the Mathematics of Post-Quantum Crypto", held during June 6–8, 2020, for further helpful feedback.

References

1. Bernstein, D., De Feo, L., Leroux, A., Smith, B.: Faster computation of isogenies of large prime degree. In: ANTS-XIV. Mathematical Sciences Publishers (2020)
2. Bernstein, D. J., Lange, T.: Montgomery curves and the Montgomery ladder. In: IACR Cryptology ePrint Archive, p. 293 (2017) https://ia.cr/2017/293
3. Bernstein, D.J., Lange, T., Martindale, C., Panny, L.: Quantum circuits for the CSIDH: optimizing quantum evaluation of isogenies. In: Ishai, Y., Rijmen, V. (eds.) EUROCRYPT 2019. LNCS, vol. 11477, pp. 409–441. Springer, Cham (2019). https://doi.org/10.1007/978-3-030-17656-3_15
4. Blake, I.F., Seroussi, G., Smart, N.P. (eds.): Advances in elliptic curve cryptography. London Mathematical Society Lecture Note Series, vol. 317. Cambridge University Press, Cambridge (2005)
5. Bosma, W., Cannon, J., Playoust, C.: The Magma algebra system I: the user language. Journal of Symbolic Computation **24**(3–4), 235–265 (1997)
6. Castryck, W., Decru, T.: CSIDH on the surface. In: Ding, J., Tillich, J.-P. (eds.) PQCrypto 2020. LNCS, vol. 12100, pp. 111–129. Springer, Cham (2020). https://doi.org/10.1007/978-3-030-44223-1_7
7. Castryck, W., Lange, T., Martindale, C., Panny, L., Renes, J.: CSIDH: an efficient post-quantum commutative group action. In: Peyrin, T., Galbraith, S. (eds.) ASIACRYPT 2018. LNCS, vol. 11274, pp. 395–427. Springer, Cham (2018). https://doi.org/10.1007/978-3-030-03332-3_15
8. Charles, D.X., Lauter, K.E., Goren, E.Z.: Cryptographic hash functions from expander graphs. Journal of Cryptology **22**(1), 93–113 (2007). https://doi.org/10.1007/s00145-007-9002-x
9. Chi-Domínguez, J.-J., Rodríguez-Henríquez, F.: Optimal strategies for CSIDH. Adv. Math. Commun. (2019)
10. Conrad, K.: Simple radical extensions. Expository paper. https://kconrad.math.uconn.edu/blurbs/galoistheory/simpleradical.pdf

11. Couveignes, J.M.: Hard homogeneous spaces. IACR Cryptology ePrint Archive, p. 291 (2006) https://ia.cr/2006/291
12. Dang, T., Moody, D.: Twisted Hessian isogenies. IACR Cryptology ePrint Archive, 2019, p. 1003 (2019) https://ia.cr/2019/1003
13. De Feo, L., Kieffer, J., Smith, B.: Towards practical key exchange from ordinary isogeny graphs. In: Peyrin, T., Galbraith, S. (eds.) ASIACRYPT 2018. LNCS, vol. 11274, pp. 365–394. Springer, Cham (2018). https://doi.org/10.1007/978-3-030-03332-3_14
14. Lontouo, P.B.F., Fouotsa, E.: Analogue of Vélu's formulas for computing isogenies over Hessian model of elliptic curves. IACR Cryptology ePrint Archive, 2019, p. 1480 (2019) https://ia.cr/2019/1480
15. Hess, F.: A note on the Tate pairing of curves over finite fields. Archiv der Mathematik **82**, 28–32 (2004)
16. Jao, D., De Feo, L.: Towards quantum-resistant cryptosystems from supersingular elliptic curve isogenies. In: Yang, B.-Y. (ed.) PQCrypto 2011. LNCS, vol. 7071, pp. 19–34. Springer, Heidelberg (2011). https://doi.org/10.1007/978-3-642-25405-5_2
17. Lang, S.: Algebra, volume 211 of Graduate Texts in Mathematics. Springer-Verlag, New York, third ed. (2002) https://doi.org/10.1007/978-1-4613-0041-0
18. Meyer, M., Reith, S.: A faster way to the CSIDH. In: Chakraborty, D., Iwata, T. (eds.) INDOCRYPT 2018. LNCS, vol. 11356, pp. 137–152. Springer, Cham (2018). https://doi.org/10.1007/978-3-030-05378-9_8
19. Moriya, T., Onuki, H., Takagi, T.: How to construct CSIDH on edwards curves. In: Jarecki, S. (ed.) CT-RSA 2020. LNCS, vol. 12006, pp. 512–537. Springer, Cham (2020). https://doi.org/10.1007/978-3-030-40186-3_22
20. Nakagawa, K., Onuki, H., Takayasu, A., Takagi, T.: l_1-norm ball for CSIDH: optimal strategy for choosing the secret key space. IACR Cryptology ePrint Archive, 2020, p. 181 (2020) https://ia.cr/2020/181
21. Renes, J.: Computing isogenies between montgomery curves using the action of $(0, 0)$. In: Lange, T., Steinwandt, R. (eds.) PQCrypto 2018. LNCS, vol. 10786, pp. 229–247. Springer, Cham (2018). https://doi.org/10.1007/978-3-319-79063-3_11
22. Rostovtsev, A., Stolbunov, A.: Public-key cryptosystem based on isogenies. IACR Cryptology ePrint Archive, 2006, p. 145 (2006) https://ia.cr/2006/145.pdf
23. Silverman, J.H.: The Arithmetic of Elliptic Curves. GTM, vol. 106. Springer, New York (2009). https://doi.org/10.1007/978-0-387-09494-6
24. The Stacks project authors. The stacks project (2020) https://stacks.math.columbia.edu
25. Streng., M.: Generators of the group of modular units for $\Gamma_1(N)$ over the rationals. Cornell University arXiv:1503.08127v2 (2019)
26. Sutherland, A.: Constructing elliptic curves over finite fields with prescribed torsion. Mathematics of Computation **81**(278), 1131–1147 (2012)
27. Tsfasman, M.A., Vlăduţ, S.G.: Algebraic-geometric codes, volume 58 of Mathematics and its Applications (Soviet Series). Kluwer Academic Publishers Group, Dordrecht, Translated from the Russian by the authors (1991)
28. Vélu, J.: Isogénies entre courbes elliptiques. Comptes-Rendus de l'Académie des Sciences, Série **I**(273), 238–241 (1971)
29. Waterhouse, W.C.: Abelian varieties over finite fields. Annales scientifiques de l'École Normale Supérieure **2**, 521–560 (1969)

Oblivious Pseudorandom Functions from Isogenies

Dan Boneh[1], Dmitry Kogan[1(✉)], and Katharine Woo[1,2]

[1] Stanford University, Stanford, CA, USA
{dabo,dkogan}@cs.stanford.edu
[2] Princeton University, Princeton, NJ, USA
khwoo@princeton.edu

Abstract. An oblivious PRF, or OPRF, is a protocol between a client and a server, where the server has a key k for a secure pseudorandom function F, and the client has an input x for the function. At the end of the protocol the client learns $F(k, x)$, and nothing else, and the server learns nothing. An OPRF is verifiable if the client is convinced that the server has evaluated the PRF correctly with respect to a prior commitment to k. OPRFs and verifiable OPRFs have numerous applications, such as private-set-intersection protocols, password-based key-exchange protocols, and defense against denial-of-service attacks. Existing OPRF constructions use RSA-, Diffie-Hellman-, and lattice-type assumptions. The first two are not post-quantum secure.

In this paper we construct OPRFs and verifiable OPRFs from isogenies. Our main construction uses isogenies of supersingular elliptic curves over $\mathbb{F}_{p^2}$ and tries to adapt the Diffie-Hellman OPRF to that setting. However, a recent attack on supersingular-isogeny systems due to Galbraith et al. [ASIACRYPT 2016] makes this approach difficult to secure. To overcome this attack, and to validate the server's response, we develop two new zero-knowledge protocols that convince each party that its peer has sent valid messages. With these protocols in place, we obtain an OPRF in the SIDH setting and prove its security in the UC framework.

Our second construction is an adaptation of the Naor-Reingold PRF to commutative group actions. Combining it with recent constructions of oblivious transfer from isogenies, we obtain an OPRF in the CSIDH setting.

1 Introduction

Let $F : \mathcal{K} \times \mathcal{X} \to \mathcal{Y}$ be a secure pseudorandom function (PRF) [30]. An *oblivious PRF*, or *OPRF*, is a protocol between a client who has an input $x \in \mathcal{X}$, and a server who has a key $k \in \mathcal{K}$. At the end of the protocol the client learns $F(k, x)$ and nothing else, and the server learns nothing at all [24,54]. Intuitively, an OPRF needs to be secure against a malicious client who is trying to learn more information about the server's key k, and a malicious server who is trying to

© International Association for Cryptologic Research 2020
S. Moriai and H. Wang (Eds.): ASIACRYPT 2020, LNCS 12492, pp. 520–550, 2020.
https://doi.org/10.1007/978-3-030-64834-3_18

learn more information about the client's input x. Earlier works [24,41] defined an OPRF as the secure computation of the above two-party functionality, and Jarecki et al. [36,37] later gave strong but flexible security definitions for an OPRF in the UC framework [13].

An OPRF is said to be *verifiable* if the server commits to its key k by publishing some public parameters derived from k. At the end of the OPRF protocol, the client should be convinced that the obtained value $y \in \mathcal{Y}$ satisfies $y = F(k, x)$ with respect to the server's committed key k. One benefit of verifiability is that it allows a group of clients to verify that the values they each obtain are all consistent with the same PRF key. Without verifiability, in applications where a client later reveals the obtained value to the server, a malicious server can link values with previous evaluations by using a different key for each evaluation.

Oblivious PRFs have many real-world applications. They are used in private-set-intersection protocols [41,46,47,58–60], in password-management systems [23,37], in adaptive oblivious transfer [41], in de-duplication systems [44], in password-authenticated key exchange [40], and are deployed at Cloudflare to defend against Denial of Service attacks [21]. As a result, there is an ongoing effort to standardize OPRFs at the Crypto Forum Research Group [20].

An OPRF can be built from general secure two-party computation. A much simpler and widely used OPRF, called DH-OPRF, is built from a PRF whose security is based on the Decisional Diffie-Hellman (DDH) assumption in the random-oracle model. Let $\mathbb{G}$ be a cyclic group of prime order q, and let $H : \mathcal{X} \rightarrow \mathbb{G}$ be a hash function. For $k \in \mathbb{Z}_q$ and $x \in \mathcal{X}$, the PRF is defined as $F(k, x) = H(x)^k$. This PRF is secure, assuming DDH holds in $\mathbb{G}$ and H is a random oracle [53]. This PRF then supports the following OPRF protocol: a client computes $H(x)$, blinds it as $u \leftarrow H(x)^r$ for a random $r \xleftarrow{\text{R}} \mathbb{Z}_q$, and sends u to the server. The server responds with $v \leftarrow u^k$. The client then computes the unblinded PRF value $y \leftarrow v^{1/r} = H(x)^k$. Appropriate modifications can make this OPRF verifiable. Security of the resulting OPRF relies on the one-more discrete-log assumption [7]. Jarecki et al. [36,37] showed this OPRF is secure in the Universally Composable framework [13].

Another simple verifiable OPRF in the random-oracle model, called RSA-OPRF, is derived directly from RSA blind signatures [7,17]. Since there are quantum-polynomial-time algorithms for the DDH and RSA problems, neither of these OPRFs is post-quantum secure.

Building an efficient post-quantum secure OPRF is more challenging. One solution is to use a generic post-quantum secure two-party-computation protocol to evaluate a PRF. For example, instantiating Yao's garbled-circuits protocol with a post-quantum-secure oblivious transfer results in a post-quantum-secure two-party computation protocol [11] that can then be used to obliviously evaluate an AES circuit. The downside is that the communication in generic protocols is proportional to the circuit size, which motivates the search for efficient special-purpose OPRF protocols from post-quantum primitives. Albrecht et al. [3] recently proposed an OPRF based on the ring learning-with-errors problem and the short-integer-solution problem in one dimension.

Our Contributions. In this paper we give another path towards a simple post-quantum secure OPRF by constructing several OPRFs from hard problems on isogenies of elliptic curves, in the random-oracle model.

Our first set of constructions operates on supersingular elliptic-curve isogenies over a field $\mathbb{F}_{p^2}$. Starting with a simple idea for an OPRF in the honest-but-curious setting, based on the SIDH key-exchange protocol of De Feo, Jao, and Plût [22], we then show how to elevate this OPRF to the setting of a malicious client and malicious server, and to make the OPRF verifiable. Our security proofs are set in the UC framework [13] in the random-oracle model. We describe our construction using an abstraction we call an *augmentable commitment*, defined in Sect. 2. These commitments abstract away many of the complexities of working with supersingular-curves isogenies, and they may be of independent interest.

To ensure that our OPRF is secure against a malicious client, we construct a zero-knowledge proof of knowledge for proving that the first message the client sends to the server is well formed. Here, a well formed message should contain an elliptic curve, obtained by correctly applying an isogeny to some base curve, together with points on that curve, obtained by applying that same isogeny to predetermined points on the base curve. To secure against a malicious server and obtain a verifiable OPRF, we construct an additional zero-knowledge proof of knowledge for proving that four elliptic curves (E, E_a, E_b, E_{ab}) form an isogeny DDH tuple, where the prover only knows the isogenies $\phi_a \colon E \to E_a$ and $\phi'_a \colon E_b \to E_{ab}$, whereas the isogeny $\phi_a \colon E \to E_a$ is private to the client. Our complete protocol requires up to 2MB of communication for 128-bit security, with the main bottleneck being the cut-and-choose repetitions in our zero-knowledge proofs of knowledge. We describe this protocol, using the language of augmentable commitments, in Sect. 6.

Our second class of OPRF protocols, presented in Sect. 8, builds an OPRF from a commutative group action, such as the one obtained from isogenies of ordinary elliptic curves [19,61] or from isogenies of supersingular curves over $\mathbb{F}_p$ as in CSIDH [14]. Commutative group actions give rise to a generalized Diffie-Hellman problem, yet a construction similar to the DH-OPRF is not currently possible. The reason is that there is no known way to construct a hash function that maps its inputs to uniformly sampled elements in an isogeny class, without learning additional information about the output elements. This additional information would allow the client to evaluate the PRF at any point of its choice from just a single response from the server, breaking the security requirement. Therefore, an OPRF from commutative group actions requires a very different approach.

Our construction makes use of two observations. First, we adapt the Naor-Reingold PRF [54] to the setting of a commutative group action. This requires a new proof of security because the original proof of security in [54] relies on the DDH assumption and its random self-reduction. The difficulty is that the DDH problem for a commutative group action does not have the required random self-reduction. We nevertheless prove PRF security based on the DDH assumption for such group actions; however the security reduction is not as efficient as for DDH over groups. Second, we observe that, similarly to the original PRF construction [54], this group-action variant admits an oblivious evaluation. The resulting OPRF scheme makes use of a 1-out-of-2 oblivious-transfer protocol, but such protocols are already known from isogeny problems [6,51,63,69]. We thus obtain an OPRF from a commutative group action.

Between the two constructions, the supersingular construction is asymptotically more efficient, in the sense that it requires asymptotically less communication between the client and the server. The reason is a sub-exponential quantum algorithm for the discrete-log problem for a commutative group action due to Kuperberg [48,49]. Kuperberg's attack applies to commutative group actions, which underpin our second construction, yet it does not apply to the non-commutative structure of supersingular isogenies over $\mathbb{F}_{p^2}$, which underpin our first construction. As a result, the first construction allows using smaller fields, which results in less communication asymptotically (in the security parameter). Its exponential security also makes it more robust to improvements in attacks. However, the second construction has better (i.e., smaller) constants, and as a result, the second construction is more efficient concretely: 424KB of communication vs. 2MB for the first construction.

1.1   Background and Notation

Let E be a supersingular elliptic curve over $\mathbb{F}_{p^2}$. Recall that every separable degree-d isogeny $\phi: E \to E'$ has a kernel $G = \ker(\phi)$ which is a subgroup of order d of $E(\bar{\mathbb{F}}_p)$. In the special case when G is a cyclic subgroup of $E(\mathbb{F}_{p^2})$, we can succinctly represent G by specifying a generator $K \in E(\mathbb{F}_{p^2})$, where K is an element of the d-torsion of $E(\mathbb{F}_{p^2})$.

We follow de Saint Guilhem, Orsini, Petit, and Smart [63] and use the following notation to represent degree-d isogenies. Recall that the *projective line* $\mathbb{P}_d$ is the set of all equivalence classes $[x:y]$, where $x, y \in \mathbb{Z}/d\mathbb{Z}$, and the ideal generated by x and y is all of $\mathbb{Z}/d\mathbb{Z}$. We specify an isogeny of degree d using an element $k \in \mathbb{P}_d$. For $k = [k_p : k_q] \in \mathbb{P}_d$, and generators P_d, Q_d of the d-torsion $E[d]$, the notation $\langle k \cdot (P_d, Q_d) \rangle$ refers to the order-d cyclic group generated by $k_p P_d + k_q Q_d \in E[d]$.

1.2   Overview of Our Techniques

Our main result is an OPRF from isogenies on supersingular elliptic curves. We briefly summarize the main technical ideas, and refer to Sect. 2–7 for the details.

Let $E/\mathbb{F}_{p^2}$ be a fixed supersingular elliptic curve, and let $N_{\mathsf{K}}, N_{\mathsf{M}}, N_{\mathsf{R}}$ be positive integers such that $E[N_{\mathsf{K}} \times N_{\mathsf{M}} \times N_{\mathsf{R}}]$ is contained in $E(\mathbb{F}_{p^2})$, where $p, N_{\mathsf{K}}, N_{\mathsf{M}}, N_{\mathsf{R}}$ are pairwise relatively prime. Let us derive a PRF $F : \mathcal{K} \times \mathcal{X} \to \mathcal{Y}$ from the SIDH key-exchange protocol of [22]. The PRF makes use of two hash functions $H_1 : \mathcal{X} \to \mathbb{P}_{N_{\mathsf{M}}}$ and $H_2 : \mathcal{X} \times \mathbb{F}_{p^2} \to \mathcal{Y}$, and works as follows:

- The domain is $\mathcal{X}$. For each $x \in \mathcal{X}$ we obtain $m = H_1(x) \in \mathbb{P}_{N_{\mathsf{M}}}$, for which there is a corresponding degree-N_{M} isogeny $\phi_m : E \to E_m$;

- The key space is $\mathcal{K} = \mathbb{P}_{N_K}$. For each $k \in \mathbb{P}_{N_K}$ there is a corresponding degree-N_K isogeny $\phi_k : E \to E_k$;
- Let $\phi : E \to E_{m,k}$ be an isogeny with kernel $\ker(\phi_m) \times \ker(\phi_k)$. Define $F(k, x) = H_2(x, j(E_{m,k}))$.

When H_1 and H_2 are modeled as random oracles, and assuming N_K is sufficiently large (i.e., superpolynomial in the security parameter), this function F is a secure PRF.

To make this PRF into an oblivious PRF between a client and a server, it is tempting to try the following blinding approach (also used in [62,65] in an attempt to construct a blinded version of an earlier undeniable-signature scheme [35]):

- The client has $x \in \mathcal{X}$. It computes $m = H_1(x) \in \mathbb{P}_{N_M}$ which defines the degree-N_M isogeny $\phi_m : E \to E_m$ above. The client chooses a random $r \in \mathbb{P}_{N_R}$, and computes the corresponding degree-N_R isogeny $\phi_r : E \to E_r$. Next, the client constructs an isogeny $\phi_{r,m} : E \to E_{r,m}$ whose kernel is $\ker(\phi_r) \times \ker(\phi_m)$. It sends $E_{r,m}$ to the server, along with four additional points on $E_{r,m}$, as specified in Sect. 3. Two of these four points are computed as $P'_K = \phi_{r,m}(P_K)$ and $Q'_K = \phi_{r,m}(Q_K)$, where $P_K, Q_K \in E$ are some fixed generators of $E[N_K]$.
- The server has the secret key $k \in \mathbb{P}_{N_k}$, and the corresponding isogeny $\phi_k : E \to E_k$. It uses P'_K, Q'_K to construct the curve $E_{r,m,k}$, which is the target of an isogeny acting on E and whose kernel is $\ker(\phi_r) \times \ker(\phi_m) \times \ker(\phi_k)$. It sends $E_{r,m,k}$ back to the client, along with two additional points in $E[N_R]$.
- The client uses its knowledge of ϕ_r to recover the required $E_{m,k}$ using an appropriate dual isogeny $\hat{\phi}' : E_{r,m,k} \to E_{m,k}$. Once the client has $E_{m,k}$, it can obtain the required PRF value $F(k, x)$ since $F(k, x) = H_2(x, j(E_{m,k}))$.

While this is a natural construction for an OPRF, it is unfortunately completely insecure. It is vulnerable to a clever active attack due to Galbraith et al. [27], which was originally used to attack SIDH key exchange where one of the parties uses a static key. In our setting, the attack lets a malicious client send carefully crafted points $P'_K, Q'_K \in E_{r,m}$ that are *not* the images of the fixed points $P_K, Q_K \in E$ under the isogeny $\phi_{r,m} : E \to E_{r,m}$. The client can then learn information about the PRF key k from the server's response. With enough such queries, the client can extract k from the server, thus fully breaking the OPRF.

In the SIDH key-exchange setting, there are several countermeasures against this active attack. Kirkwood et al. [45] suggest an approach, based on the Fujisaki-Okamoto [25] transformation, where the client sends encrypted information to the server. The server decrypts and uses the information from the client to validate the request. However, this approach cannot be used in an OPRF protocol because the information sent from the client reveals m to the server, which violates the OPRF privacy requirement.

Our solution is to have the client prove to the server that the points P'_K and Q'_K are generated correctly without leaking any information about m or r to the server. To do so, we present in Sect. 5 a special-purpose zero-knowledge protocol that allows the client to prove the correctness of the points it sends.

Our protocol develops an idea sketc.hed by Galbraith [26, Section 7.2], and builds on the isogeny-based identification protocol of De Feo et al. [22].

We obtain an OPRF that is secure against a malicious client. To further secure the OPRF against a malicious server, the server needs to somehow prove to the client that its response $E_{r,m,k}$ is consistent with its commitment E_k to the secret key $k \in \mathbb{P}_{N_K}$. In other words, the server needs to prove that $(E, E_{r,m}, E_k, E_{r,m,k})$ form an isogeny DDH tuple, where the server only knows $\phi_k : E \to E_k$ and $\phi'_k : E_{r,m} \to E_{r,m,k}$. A similar protocol is needed in the constructions of [35,62,65] for the purpose of online signature confirmation. However, we cannot use their protocol because they assume the server knows both ϕ_k and $\phi_{r,m} : E \to E_{r,m}$. For us, this would break the OPRF privacy requirement because $\ker(\phi_{r,m})$ reveals information about $m \in \mathbb{P}_{N_M}$.

To address this, we develop in Sect. 6 a zero-knowledge proof of equality that lets the server prove the consistency of its response to the client. A key challenge is to ensure security of the OPRF, meaning that we must prevent the client from abusing the consistency check for extracting information about the key k. The result is a new private-coin protocol, that jointly meets the security requirements of both parties, and is quite different from the [22]-style public-coin protocol.

Our complete verifiable OPRF appears in Protocol 15.

Security Assumptions. Our OPRF construction is based on the hardness of isogeny problems on supersingular curves over a field $\mathbb{F}_{p^2}$ for a prime p of the form $p = f \cdot N_1 \cdot \ldots \cdot N_n - 1$, for relatively prime N_i. Specifically, for our verifiable OPRF, we use $n = 5$ prime powers.

The privacy of the client in our protocol relies on the hardness the Decisional SIDH Isogeny Problem [22,29] adjusted from the standard SIDH setting of $n = 2$ prime powers to our setting of $n = 5$ (similarly to [35,63,65]). The security of the server in our protocol relies on a one-more Diffie-Hellman-type assumption in the SIDH setting. Recently, Merz, Minko, and Petit [52] presented a polynomial-time attack on certain "one-more" SIDH assumptions, introduced in [35,65]. In Sect. 3, we present a new type of one-more SIDH assumption and discuss why it is not susceptible to this attack. Finally, our zero-knowledge proof, designed to prevent the active attack of [27], relies on the hardness of a variant of the Decisional Supersingular Product problem [22]. We discuss the security assumptions in more detail in Sect. 3 and 5.

1.3   Additional Related Work

OPRF from Oblivious-Transfer Extension. An efficient oblivious PRF can be constructed from oblivious-transfer extension [33]. The first works to do so [47,59,60] constructed a one-time OPRF, namely one where the client can only issue a single query to the server. Subsequent work [58] constructs a many-time OPRF from oblivious-transfer extension, but the client must choose all the query points before the OPRF key is generated. These non-adaptive OPRF schemes are sufficient for protocols for private set intersection, and can be post-quantum secure if the underlying 1-out-of-2 oblivious transfer is post-quantum secure. The constructions in this paper give an OPRF which allows the client to select the query points adaptively, at any time after the OPRF key is generated, and supports an exponential size domain.

Blind Signatures. Verifiable OPRFs share resemblance with blind signatures [17]. Both primitives allow a server holding a secret key to provide the client with a "certified" value on blinded input. However, unlike an OPRF, a blind signature does not have to be deterministic, yet it has to be publicly verifiable. Indeed, Jarecki and Liu [41] observed that earlier constructions [12] of oblivious-transfer protocols from unique blind signatures [7,8,17] and, similarly, from blind IBE schemes [31], give rise to OPRFs. None of these constructions are post-quantum secure. Recent works [62,65] constructed variants of blind signatures from supersingular isogenies. As discussed above, the online verification protocols in these schemes require unblinding the message.

2   Augmentable Commitments

In this section we introduce a primitive, called *augmentable commitments*, that makes it easier to describe the OPRF construction and prove its security. This abstraction makes it possible to describe the scheme without cluttering the description with many elliptic curve points.

An augmentable commitment is a commitment scheme where one can commit to a value $x_1 \in \mathcal{X}_1$ to obtain a commitment com. Later, someone else can append $x_2 \in \mathcal{X}_2$ to the commitment com to obtain a new commitment com' to (x_1, x_2). One can also obtain com' by committing in the reverse order, by first committing to $x_2 \in \mathcal{X}_2$, and then appending $x_1 \in \mathcal{X}_1$. We will refer to com' as $[\![x_1, x_2]\!]$. Regular values are append-only, in the sense that, given $[\![x_1, x_2]\!]$, it should be computationally unfeasible to compute $[\![x_2]\!]$ or $[\![x_1', x_2]\!]$. Looking ahead, this "non-malleability" property will provide privacy *for the server* in our OPRF protocol. It prevents the client from learning the value of the OPRF at one point given its evaluation at another.

To hide the contents of the commitment, its creator may include in it a special type of value $r \in \mathcal{R}$, called a *blind*. Such a blinded commitment $[\![r, x_1, x_2]\!]$ can later be *unblinded* to obtain $[\![x_1, x_2]\!]$, which is a binding commitment to x_1 and x_2, but may not be hiding. The blinding property will provide privacy *for the client* in our OPRF protocol, as it will prevent the server from learning the point where the OPRF is being evaluated.

We next define augmentable commitments more precisely and more generally. In the next sections we show how to use augmentable commitments to construct an OPRF scheme and how to construct them from supersingular isogenies.

Definition 1 (Augmentable Commitment Scheme).   An augmentable commitment scheme $\mathcal{G}$ with an *input space* $\mathcal{X} = \mathcal{X}_1 \times \cdots \times \mathcal{X}_{n-1}$, a blinding space $\mathcal{R} := \mathcal{X}_n$, a commitment space $\mathcal{C}$, and a space of representatives $\mathcal{J}$, consists of five algorithms

- Setup$(1^\lambda) \to \mathsf{com}_0 \in \mathcal{C}$. The algorithm takes as input the security parameter and outputs the "empty" commitment com_0.
- Blind$(\mathsf{com}_0 \in \mathcal{C}, r \in \mathcal{R}) \to \mathsf{com} \in \mathcal{C}$. The algorithm takes as input the empty commitment and a blind value r, and creates an initial blinded commitment.
- Append $(\mathsf{com} \in \mathcal{C}, i \in [n-1], x \in \mathcal{X}_i) \to \mathsf{com}' \in \mathcal{C}$. The algorithm takes as input a commitment com, an index of an input space, and an input from that space, and outputs a new commitment. The input commitment com can be the empty commitment com_0, a blinded commitment output by Blind, or a commitment obtained from a previous call to Append.
- Unblind $(\mathsf{com} \in \mathcal{C}, r \in \mathcal{R}) \to \mathsf{com}' \in \mathcal{C}$. The algorithm takes as input a commitment previously blinded with r together with the same blind value r used for blinding, and outputs an unblinded commitment.
- Invariant $(\mathsf{com} \in \mathcal{C}) \to j \in \mathcal{J}$ returns the invariant of a commitment.

For simplicity, we avoid including explicit public parameters in the syntax of the scheme. If the scheme requires the Setup algorithm to set some public parameters, we assume without the loss of generality that they are included in the empty commitment com_0 and in all subsequent commitments.

Note that the Blind step is the only time when an element $r \in \mathcal{R}$ of the blinding space may be committed to.

For brevity, we use the notation $[\![x_1, \ldots, x_t]\!]$ to refer to a commitment to a sequence of elements $x_1 \in \mathcal{X}_{i_1}, \ldots, x_t \in \mathcal{X}_{i_t}$. Specifically, if none of the distinct indices $i_1, \ldots, i_t \in [n-1]$ is the blinding index, we define $\mathsf{com}_j \leftarrow$ Append$(\mathsf{com}_{j-1}, i_j, x_j)$, and set $[\![x_1, \ldots, x_t]\!] := \mathsf{com}_t$. Similarly, if $i_1 = n$ is the index of the blinding space $\mathcal{R} = \mathcal{X}_n$, we define $\mathsf{com}_1 \leftarrow$ Blind(com_0, x_1), and for $j \in [2, t]$ we define $\mathsf{com}_j \leftarrow$ Append$(\mathsf{com}_{j-1}, x_j)$, and set $[\![x_1, \ldots, x_t]\!] := \mathsf{com}_t$.

For two commitments $c, c' \in \mathcal{C}$, we write $c \sim c'$ if and only if Invariant$(c) =$ Invariant(c').

The commitment scheme must satisfy the following correctness property, which states that (i) commitments to the same set of elements in a different order are equivalent; and (ii) unblinding results in an a commitment to the remaining elements.

Correctness. For every $t \in [n-1]$, every set of *distinct* indices $i_1, \ldots, i_t \in [n-1]$, every set of values $x_j \in \mathcal{X}_{i_j}$, and every $r \in \mathcal{R}$, we require the following.

1. Invariant$([\![x_1, \ldots, x_t]\!])$ is independent of the ordering of $x_1, \ldots, x_t$. Similarly, Invariant$([\![r, x_1, \ldots, x_t]\!])$ is independent of the ordering of $x_1, \ldots, x_t$.
2. Unblind$([\![r, x_1, \ldots, x_t]\!], r) \sim [\![x_1, \ldots, x_t]\!]$.

An augmentable commitment must satisfy the following three security requirements: hiding, weak binding, and one-more unpredictability. We give formal game-based definitions of those properties in the full version of this work

Hiding. The hiding property requires that a random committed element, be it an input or a blind, computationally hides all other committed elements. More specifically, an adversary should not be able to distinguish between a commitment to a set of random values and a commitment to a set of values of his choice, provided that the commitment includes at least one additional random element, that the adversary does not know. This additional element can either be an input element or a blind, i.e., the hiding property holds with respect to both inputs and blinds, with the only difference being that blinds can also be unblinded.

Weak Binding. The binding requirement asks that no efficient adversary can produce a collision between two commitments. We actually only need a weak form of binding, in the sense that the adversary needs to produce a pair of distinct elements that create a collision with noticeable probability over a random choice of a sequence of appended elements.

One-More Unpredictability. In an augmentable commitment scheme, the result of augmenting a secret value to one randomly chosen value should not reveal the result of augmenting that same secret value to other random values. Specifically, consider a game between a challenger and adversary. The challenger chooses a secret input value k and gives the adversary $t + 1$ challenges $m_1, \ldots, m_{t+1}$, each of which is a random input value to the commitment. The solution to the ith challenge is the $\mathsf{Invariant}(\llbracket m_i, k \rrbracket)$ of a commitment to both the challenge value and the challenger's secret value. Finally, the adversary may issue queries to the challenger. Each query consists of an input value m of the adversary's choice, to which the challenger responds with $\mathsf{Invariant}(\llbracket m, k \rrbracket)$, where k is the challenger's secret value. The one-more unpredictability property requires that after issuing at most t queries the adversary should not be able to produce the solution to all $t + 1$ challenges.

Remark 2. de Saint Guilhem et al. [63] introduced an abstraction called *semi-commutative masking structure* that captures both commutative group actions and isogenies on supersingular elliptic curves. Our abstraction of augmentable commitments draws inspiration from theirs and shares some technical similarities with it. One difference is that our abstraction separates regular values, that are append-only, from blinds, that can be removed.

3   Augmentable Commitments from Supersingular Isogenies

In this section we show how to construct an augmentable commitment scheme from supersingular isogenies. We refer to this scheme as $\mathcal{G}_{\mathsf{si}}$. We begin by defining a parameterization algorithm, which we use throughout our construction and our security assumptions.

Definition 3 (Parameterization $p(\lambda, n)$). We define the following deterministic algorithm. On input a security parameter $\lambda \in \mathbb{N}$ and an integer $n \in \mathbb{N}$, compute the first n primes $\ell_1, \ldots, \ell_n$ and choose $e_1, \ldots, e_n$ to be positive integers such that for all $i \in [n]$, $N_i := \ell_i^{e_i} \approx 2^{2\lambda}$. Choose $f \in \mathbb{N}$ to be a cofactor such that $p = f \cdot N_1 \cdot \ldots \cdot N_n - 1$ is a prime. Output $p(\lambda, n) := p$.

For $\lambda \in \mathbb{N}$, and $p(\lambda, n+1) = f \cdot N_1 \cdot \ldots \cdot N_{n+1} - 1$, the input space of the commitment are the projective lines $\mathbb{P}_{N_i}$ for $i \in [n-1]$, and the blinding space is the projective line $\mathbb{P}_{N_n}$. For now, we do not explicitly use the N_{n+1} torsion, and in particular, $\mathbb{P}_{N_{n+1}}$ is not part of the commitment input/blinding spaces. In Sect. 5, we will use this extra torsion to construct zero knowledge proofs on our commitment scheme.

Setup. The input to the setup routine is a security parameter $\lambda \in \mathbb{N}$. It computes $p = p(\lambda, n+1) = f \cdot N_1 \cdot \ldots N_{n+1} - 1$, then chooses E_0 to be a random supersingular elliptic curve over $\mathbb{F}_{p^2}$ such that $E_0(\mathbb{F}_{p^2}) \cong \mathbb{Z}_{N_1}^2 \times \ldots \times \mathbb{Z}_{N_{n+1}}^2 \times \mathbb{Z}_f^2$. Finally, for $i \in [n]$, the setup routine chooses P_i^0, Q_i^0 generators of $E_0[N_i] \cong \mathbb{Z}_{N_i}^2$ and outputs the empty commitment that consists of the curve E_0 and the generators $(P_i^0, Q_i^0)_{i \in [n-1]}$.

Our augmentable commitments take the form $(E, (P_i, Q_i)_{i \in I})$, where $I \subseteq [n]$, representing the curve E by its j-invariant $j(E) \in \mathbb{F}_{p^2}$ using $2 \log p$ bits. (All logarithms in this work have base two.) This defines the curve up to isomorphism, and a canonical curve in that isomorphism class can be efficiently computed. Therefore, before outputting a commitment, each of the algorithms in our construction first computes an isomorphism from the curve it has computed to the canonical curve of the same isomorphism class. It also computes the images of the points in the commitment under this isomorphism [5,28,63]. Thus, any published points are always on the canonical curve. Similarly to SIDH public-key compression [5,18,34], each basis can be represented using $3 \log N_i$ bits. Overall, the size of the commitment is at most $5 \log p$ bits.

Blinding. The Blind algorithm blinds the empty commitment with a blind $r \in \mathbb{P}_{N_n}$ as follows. First, compute a degree N_n isogeny $\phi_r \colon E_0 \to E_r$ where $E_r = E_0 / \langle r \cdot (P_n^0, Q_n^0) \rangle$ and P_n^0, Q_n^0 is a canonical basis for $E_0[N_n]$. Then compute a canonical basis P_n, Q_n for $E_r[N_n]$. This basis, together with the knowledge of the kernel of the dual isogeny $\hat{phi}_r$ is what enables to later unblind the commitment. Finally output the commitment

$$\llbracket r \rrbracket := \Big(E_r,\ (\phi_r(P_j^0),\ \phi_r(Q_j^0))_{j \in [n-1]},\ P_n,\ Q_n \Big).$$

Appending. To append a value $x_t \in \mathbb{P}_{N_j}$ to a commitment $\llbracket r, x_1, \ldots, x_{t-1} \rrbracket = (E, (P_i, Q_i)_{i \in I})$ for some $j \in I \cap [n-1]$, the algorithm Append computes the isogeny $\phi' \colon E \to E'$ with kernel $\langle x_t \cdot (P_j, Q_j) \rangle$. The new commitment is then

$$\llbracket r, x_1, \ldots, x_t \rrbracket = \Big(E',\ (\phi'(P_i),\ \phi'(Q_i))_{i \in I \setminus \{j\}} \Big).$$

As values are added to the commitment, the Append algorithm drops the bases of the corresponding torsion groups from the commitment. However, the commitment tracks the basis for the blinding space throughout, and the Unblind algorithm uses them to remove the blind r.

Unblinding. Algorithm Unblind removes $r \in \mathbb{P}_{N_n}$ from a blinded commitment $\llbracket r, x_1, \ldots, x_t \rrbracket = (E', (P_i', Q_i')_{i \in I})$ by first computing the isogeny $\phi_r \colon E_0 \to E_r$ for

$E_r = E_0 / \langle r \cdot (P_n^0, Q_n^0) \rangle$ together with the canonical basis $P_n, Q_n \in E_r[N_n]$ as in the Blind algorithm above. It then computes a representative $\hat{r} \in \mathbb{P}_{N_n}$ of the kernel $\langle \hat{r} \cdot (P_n, Q_n) \rangle$ for the dual isogeny $\hat{phi}_{r:E_r \to E_0}$. Finally, it computes the unblinding isogeny $\phi : E' \to E$ where $E = E' / \langle \hat{r} \cdot (P_n', Q_n') \rangle$, and outputs (E)—a curve isomorphic to the curve of $[\![x_1, \ldots, x_t]\!]$.

The Invariant of a commitment $(E, (P_i, Q_i)_{i \in I})$ is the j-invariant $j(E) \in \mathbb{F}_{p^2}$.

The full specification of our augmentable-commitment construction $\mathcal{G}_{\text{si}}$ appears in the full version of this work We also prove there that $\mathcal{G}_{\text{si}}$ meets the correctness requirement of Definition 1. We now turn to discussing its security.

Hiding. The hiding property of our construction relies on the following variant of the Decisional Supersingular Isogeny problem.

Problem 4 (Decisional SIDH Isogeny problem). Let $p = p(\lambda, n) = f \cdot N_1 \cdot N_2 \cdot \ldots \cdot N_n - 1$ be as in Definition 3 and $i \in [n]$. The Decisional SIDH Isogeny problem is to distinguish between the following two distributions:

1. $(E, E_\phi, P, Q, \phi(P), \phi(Q))$ where E is a randomly chosen supersingular curve over $\mathbb{F}_{p^2}$, the points $P, Q \in E[(p+1)/N_i]$ are a random basis for the $(p+1)/N_i$-torsion of $E(\mathbb{F}_{p^2})$, ϕ is a random degree-N_i isogeny from E and E_ϕ is the codomain of ϕ.

2. (E, E', P, Q, P', Q') where E, P, and Q are as above, E' is another randomly chosen supersingular curve over $\mathbb{F}_{p^2}$, and the points $P, Q \in E[(p+1)/N_i]$ are a basis for the $(p+1)/N_i$-torsion of $E(\mathbb{F}_{p^2})$ chosen uniformly at random subject to the constraint that $e(P, Q)^{N_i} = e(P', Q')$, where $e(\cdot, \cdot)$ denotes the Weil pairing.

The **Decisional SIDH Isogeny assumption** is that for every constant n and every $i \in [n]$, no efficient algorithm can distinguish between the above two distributions with probability non-negligible in λ.

The DSSI problem was originally introduced by De Feo et al. [22]. In its original form, it is the problem of deciding whether two supersingular curves over $\mathbb{F}_{p^2}$, for $p = \ell_1^{e_1} \cdot \ell_2^{e_2} \cdot f \pm 1$ are $\ell_1^{e_1}$-isogenous to one another. Galbraith and Vercauteren [29, Definition 3] introduced the above variant, in which the distinguisher is also given extra points on each curve. This problem is also discussed in [68,69, Problem 3.4]. Our construction requires using more than 2 large torsions, and in particular we assume the problem to be hard for $n = 5$. A three-prime variant is considered in [35], a four-prime variant in [65], and an n-prime variant appears in [4,63].

Remark 5. Petit [57] showed an attack on "unbalanced" SIDH variants that reveal the action of a secret degree-A isogeny on the B-torsion of the base curve for $B \gg A$. Petit's attack, as well as its recent improvement by Kutas et al. [50], further require that $A \cdot B > p$. Even though our augmentable commitment has a similar imbalance (with $A = N_i$ and $B = \Pi_{j \neq i} N_j$), their second condition

$A \cdot B > p$ does not hold in our case. Therefore, these attacks do not currently apply to our construction.

Remark 6. The requirement that $e(P,Q)^{N_i} = e(P',Q')$ is needed to prevent a simple distinguishing attack based on the Weil pairing. Let $e_m \colon E[m] \times E[m] \to \mu_m$ be the Weil pairing on the m-torsion. Then it holds that [64, Proposition III.8.2]: $e_m(\phi(P),\phi(Q)) = e_m(P,Q)^{\deg(\phi)}$, where the first pairing is computed over E'. The requirement $e(P,Q)^{N_i} = e(P',Q')$ prevents distinguishing via this relation, by making sure it holds in both cases.

In the full version of this work e prove the augmentable commitment scheme $\mathcal{G}_{\mathsf{si}}$ is hiding under the Decisional SIDH Isogeny assumption.

Weak Binding. The binding requirement builds on the conjectured difficulty of efficiently finding a pair of distinct isogenies of the same prime-power degree with the same target curve. The following problem underpins the security of Charles, Lauter, and Goren [16] hash function.

Problem 7 (Supersingular Isogeny Collision problem). Let $p = p(\lambda, n)$ be a prime as in Definition 3, and let ℓ be a different prime. Given a randomly chosen supersingular elliptic curve $E/\mathbb{F}_{p^2}$, find a positive integer k, a supersingular curve $E'/\mathbb{F}_{p^2}$, and two distinct isogenies of degree ℓ^k from E to E'.

The Supersingular Isogeny Collision Assumption states that for every constant n, no efficient adversary solves the above problem with probability non-negligible in λ.

In the full version of this work e prove the our protocol meets the weak-binding requirement under the supersingular-isogeny collision assumption.

One-More Unpredictability. Intuitively, we require that when a secret $K \xleftarrow{\text{R}} E[N_K]$ is chosen at random, then the value $E/\langle M_1, K\rangle$, for a given randomly chosen $M_1 \xleftarrow{\text{R}} E[N_M]$, should not reveal the value $E/\langle M_2, K\rangle$, for another randomly chosen $M_2 \xleftarrow{\text{R}} E[N_M]$.

This kind of assumption appears in the group setting. For example, consider a cyclic group $\mathbb{G}$ of prime order q, and let $\alpha \xleftarrow{\text{R}} \mathbb{Z}_q$ be some secret. The One-More Diffie-Hellman problem [7] requires an adversary to compute the value v^α for $t+1$ randomly chosen values $v \xleftarrow{\text{R}} \mathbb{G}$ while allowing the adversary to make at most t queries to a CDH oracle for α (i.e., an oracle that replies with u^α on a query $u \in \mathbb{G}$). The One-More Diffie-Hellman assumption states that no adversary can solve this problem for any polynomial t with non-negligible probability.

Our starting point is a candidate of the One-More Diffie-Hellman assumption in the SIDH setting, introduced by Srinath and Chandrasekaran [65], called the *One-More SSCDH* assumption. Their candidate assumption stated that given t queries to a SIDH oracle (i.e., an oracle that responds to a query $M \in E[N_M]$ with $E'/\langle M, K\rangle$ for a secret $K \in E[N_K]$), it is computationally infeasible to produce $t+1$ pairs of curves $(E/\langle M\rangle, E/\langle M, K\rangle)$ for $t+1$ distinct $M \in E[N_M]$.

However, this starting point is insecure. First, Merz, Minko, and Petit [52], recently showed a polynomial-time attacks on this assumption. Moreover, this assumption is also vulnerable to the active key-recovery attack on SIDH with static keys [27]. Finally, our security proof requires giving the adversary access to a decision oracle, which opens up the possibility of computation-to-decision reductions for isogeny problems [26, 29, 67]. We now explain each of these attacks and describe how our proposed one-more problem avoids them.

Recent Attacks on One-More SIDH Problems. The attack of Merz, Minko, and Petit [52] exploits a key difference between the One-More DH assumption in the group setting and the OMSSCDH assumption [65]. In the group setting, the adversary needs to produce valid DH tuples for *random* challenges. In contrast, the assumption of Srinath and Chandrasekaran [65] relaxes this requirement and allows the challenges to be *adversarially chosen*. In the group setting, relaxing the random-challenges requirement breaks the one-more hardness: given a single DH tuple (v, v^α), it is easy to produce any number of random-looking DH tuples simply by choosing $\beta \xleftarrow{R} \mathbb{Z}_q$ and computing the DH tuple $(v^\beta, (v^\alpha)^\beta)$.

Even though the simple rerandomization that works in the group setting does not extend to the SIDH setting (due to the requirement that the challenges are all of the form $E/\langle M \rangle$ for $M \in E[N_M]$), Merz et al. devise a polynomial-time attack on the above OMSSCDH assumption by computing short isogenies from a given SIDH tuple. They point out that their polynomial-time attack on OMSSCDH does not translate to a polynomial-time attack on the signature scheme of Srinath and Chandrasekaran [65] nor on the signature scheme of Jao and Soukharev [35] because the challenges in these schemes are outputs of a hash function, modeled as a random oracle. This is consistent with the group setting, where the one-more assumption is only hard for random challenges.

Therefore, to avoid this attack, we provide the adversary in our one-more problem with *random* challenges, rather than allowing it to choose the challenge curves adversarially.

Active Attacks. The aforementioned modification prevents the specialized attack of [52]. However, the resulting problem is still vulnerable to a general active attack on SIDH with static keys due to Galbraith et al. [28]. As discussed in the introduction, by sending a sequence of queries, each of which consists of a curve E' together with a maliciously crafted basis $P_K, Q_K \in E'[N_K]$, an adversary can recover the secret key K. We therefore require the adversary to submit kernels M as its solve queries, rather than arbitrary curves with (possibly malicious) torsion points. This requirement is enforced in the actual protocol using a zero-knowledge proof of knowledge, described in the Sect. 5.

Search-to-Decision Reductions. The security proof of our OPRF requires a stronger variant of a one-more assumption, in which the adversary is given additional access to a decision oracle that allows it to check the validity of solutions throughout its execution. In the group setting, the Gap One-More Diffie-Hellman assumption [36, 42] states that the one-more problem is hard even in the presence of such a decision oracle.

The exact same type of assumption is unsound in the SIDH setting. The issue, as shown by Galbraith and Vercauteren [29], and independently by Thormarker [67], is that the search variant of the isogeny problem can be reduced to its decisional variant. Moreover, as pointed out by Galbraith [26], a similar search-to-decision reduction applies also for the SIDH problem. (We describe this reduction for completeness in the full version of this work) The One-More SIDH problem is thus easy if the adversary is given a full-fledged decision oracle for the SIDH problem. Therefore, we need to formulate a weaker assumption, in which the adversary is given oracle access to a more restrictive decision oracle. Intuitively, we only allow the adversary to check SIDH solutions to the challenges given to it (with respect to the secret key K), rather than make arbitrary SIDH decision queries. This is a much weaker assumption, and in particular, unlike a general SIDH decision oracle, the challenger answering this more restricted form of queries can be efficiently implemented.

Attack Game 8 (Auxiliary One-More SIDH). Let $p = p(\lambda, n) = f \cdot N_1 \cdot \ldots \cdot N_n - 1$ be as in Definition 3 and let $\mathsf{M}, \mathsf{K} \in [n]$ be distinct indices. Consider the following game, played between a challenger and an adversary:

- The challenger chooses a random supersingular curve $E_0/\mathbb{F}_{p^2}$ and a random basis P, Q of $E_0[(p+1)/(N_\mathsf{M} \cdot N_\mathsf{K})]$. It then chooses a random point $K \in E_0(\mathbb{F}_{p^2})$ of order N_K, computes the isogeny $\phi \colon E_0 \to E_0/\langle K \rangle$, and sends E_0, P, Q, and $E_0/\langle K \rangle$ to the adversary.
- The adversary makes a sequence of queries to the challenger, each of which can be one of the following two types:
  - Challenge query: the challenger chooses $M \xleftarrow{\text{R}} E_0[N_\mathsf{M}]$ and sends it to the adversary.
  - Solve query: the adversary submits $V \in E_0[(p+1)/N_\mathsf{K}]$ to the challenger, who computes the isogeny $\phi \colon E_0 \to E'$ with $\ker(\phi) = \langle V, K \rangle$, and sends $j(E') \in \mathbb{F}_{p^2}$, together with $\phi(P), \phi(Q)$ to the adversary.
  - Decision query: the adversary submits a pair (i, j) to the challenger, where i is a positive integer bounded by the number of challenge queries the adversary has made so far, and $j \in \mathbb{F}_{p^2}$. The challenger responds true if $j = j(E_0/\langle M, K \rangle)$, where M is the challenger's response to the ith challenge query, and false otherwise.
- At the end, the adversary outputs a list of distinct pairs, each of the form (i, j) where i is a positive integer bounded by the number of challenge queries, and $j \in \mathbb{F}_{p^2}$.

We call an output-pair (i, j) correct if j is the j-invariant of the curve $E' = E/\langle M, K \rangle$ where M is the challenger's response to the ith challenge query. We say that the adversary wins the game if the number of correct pairs exceeds the number of Solve queries.

The Auxiliary One-More SIDH assumption states that for every constant n and every distinct $\mathsf{M}, \mathsf{K} \in [n]$, every efficient adversary wins the above game with probability negligible in λ.

Remark 9. We allow the adversary to learn the action of the secret isogeny on an auxiliary torsion group $E_0[(p+1)/(N_{\mathsf{M}} \cdot N_{\mathsf{K}})]$. (The construction of Srinath and Chandrasekaran [65, Sec. 4.4] implicitly has this type of leakage, yet their security proof seems to overlook this when reducing to their version of the OMSSCDH assumption.)

It is important that the solve query provides the adversary with the action of the secret isogeny only on this torsion. Disclosing the action of the secret isogeny on $E[N_{\mathsf{K}}]$ would leak the secret. Disclosing the action of the secret isogeny on $E[N_{\mathsf{M}}]$ would allow the adversary to break the one-more assumption, since the adversary would eventually learn the action of ϕ on $E[N_{\mathsf{M}}]$.

In the full version of this work we show that $\mathcal{G}_{\mathsf{si}}$ is one-more unpredictable under the Auxiliary One-More SIDH assumption.

4   Oblivious PRF from Augmentable Commitments

We begin by giving an overview of our construction of an oblivious PRF from augmentable commitments. We do not yet give a formal security definition, so for now, we can think of an OPRF as a two party functionality $(x, k) \mapsto (F(k, x), \perp)$ where F is a pseudorandom function. Intuitively, each execution should allow the user to evaluate the PRF at a single point, while providing privacy for the user's input.

Our basic protocol consists of two-rounds and is somewhat reminiscent of the DH-OPRF protocol in the group setting. Recall that in the group setting, the user, given input x, sends to the server the group element $\mathsf{com} \leftarrow H(x)^r$, which we can view as a commitment to x. The server then computes $\overline{\mathsf{com}} \leftarrow \mathsf{com}^k$ and sends it back to the user, who computes $\mathsf{com}_{\mathsf{out}} \leftarrow \overline{\mathsf{com}}^{1/r}$. Generalizing this protocol to the language of augmentable commitments, we obtain the protocol in Fig. 1.

Handling malicious clients. However, this basic construction has a critical problem. Our augmentable commitment scheme provides a weaker form of "one-more unpredictability", as compared to the One-More Diffie-Hellman assumption in the group setting. Specifically, the one-more-unpredictability adversary needs to submit values, rather than commitments, as its solve queries. In contrast, the group-based one-more DH assumption is stronger, in that it considers more powerful adversaries that can query the one-more challenger on group elements rather than on scalars. (The underlying reason for this security definition is to prevent the active attacks on our isogeny-based instantiation of augmentable commitments, as discussed in the introduction and in Sect. 3). Therefore, our construction requires the user to attach, as part of its message, a zero-knowledge proof of the committed values. We present this proof system in Sect. 5. This protocol is specific for the isogeny-based construction.

Handling malicious servers. In this simple OPRF, the user cannot detect malicious servers that use a different key on each response, or even send arbitrary responses that do not correspond to a well-defined key.

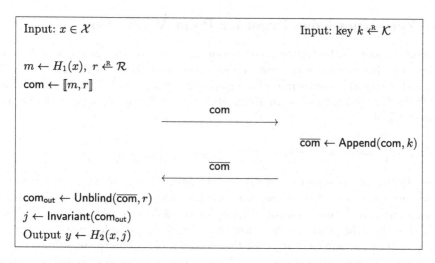

Fig. 1. The basic OPRF protocol from augmentable commitments. Note that, as presented, this basic version is not secure against malicious parties.

A verifiable OPRF provides the user with the following guarantee. On each evaluation of the OPRF, the user obtains, in addition to the output value $y = F(k, x)$, a function descriptor pk. If on two inputs x_1 and x_2 the user obtains two outputs y_1, pk and y_2, pk with a matching function descriptor, there must exist a key k such that $y_1 = F(k, x_1)$ and $y_2 = F(k, x_2)$. The function descriptor therefore commits the server to a particular function for all inputs.

In our verifiable-OPRF construction, the function descriptor is the output y_ϵ of the OPRF on some fixed point ϵ. (We think of ϵ as being outside the "official" domain of the OPRF.) After obliviously evaluating the OPRF on a point x and obtaining output y_x, the user runs λ additional evaluations of the OPRF, each time setting the input at random as either x or ϵ. At the end of the λ evaluations, the user checks that the output of each of the λ evaluations matches either y_ϵ or y_x (consistently with its random choice for that evaluation). If all λ checks pass, the user accepts the output y_x with respect to descriptor y_ϵ.

An issue with the above protocol is that a malicious user may abuse the λ evaluations to evaluate the OPRF on λ additional points, rather than for verification. Learning the value of the OPRF on more than one point from a single instance of the protocol would violate the server's security requirement of the OPRF. To prevent this, we add an additional phase to our protocol: the server first commits to the outputs of the OPRF on the λ verification instances. The user then proves to the server that each of the λ verification inputs is either x or ϵ. (Doing this without revealing x to the server requires an extra layer of blinding.) This provides the server with the assurance that the user would not learn any "extra" values of the OPRF from the verification instances. The server then opens the commitment to the verification outputs, which the client verifies as above. We present this protocol in Sect. 6.

In Sect. 7 we give the full specification (Protocol 15) of our final construction.

5   Zero-Knowledge Proof for Point Verification

A critical part of the OPRF construction is a zero-knowledge proof of knowledge (ZKPK) that lets the client prove to the server that its PRF query is well formed. Using the abstraction of augmentable commitments, what is needed is a ZKPK for the contents of an augmentable commitment, or more generally to the relation:

$$R_{\mathsf{com}} = \left\{ ((\mathsf{com}_0,\ \mathsf{com}_t),\ (x_1,\dots,x_t)) : \begin{array}{l} \mathsf{com}_1 = \mathsf{Blind}(\mathsf{com}_0, x_1) \\ \mathsf{com}_i = \mathsf{Append}(\mathsf{com}_{i-1},\ x_i)\ \forall i \in [2,t] \end{array} \right\}.$$

The ZKPK we construct is specific to the instantiation of augmentable commitment from Sect. 3, and uses some of the algebraic properties of isogenies. Specifically, we design a custom ZKPK for the following relation $\mathcal{R}_{\mathsf{iso}}$. (In the full version of this work we show how the relation $\mathcal{R}_{\mathsf{iso}}$ enables expressing statements about the language R_{com} for the augmentable commitment scheme $\mathcal{G}_{\mathsf{si}}$.)

Let $p = p(\lambda, n+1) = f \cdot N_1 \cdot \ldots \cdot N_{n+1} - 1$ be a prime as in Defintion 3. For clarity, we denote $N_{\mathsf{S}} := N_{n+1}$. Let E be a supersingular elliptic curve defined over $\mathbb{F}_{p^2}$. Define the relation:

$$\mathcal{R}_{\mathsf{iso}} := \left\{ \Big(j(E),\ P_{\mathsf{K}},\ Q_{\mathsf{K}},\ j(E'),\ P'_{\mathsf{K}},\ Q'_{\mathsf{K}},\ d\Big),\ V \right\}, \tag{1}$$

where the *statement* $\Big(j(E),\ P_{\mathsf{K}},\ Q_{\mathsf{K}},\ j(E'),\ P'_{\mathsf{K}},\ Q'_{\mathsf{K}},\ d\Big)$ contains:

- a j-invariant $j(E) \in \mathbb{F}_{p^2}$ of a supersingular elliptic curve $E/\mathbb{F}_{p^2}$,
- points $P_{\mathsf{K}}, Q_{\mathsf{K}} \in E[N_{\mathsf{K}}]$ for some N_{K} relatively prime to N_{S},
- a j-invariant $j(E') \in \mathbb{F}_{p^2}$ of a supersingular elliptic curve $E'/\mathbb{F}_{p^2}$,
- points $P'_{\mathsf{K}}, Q'_{\mathsf{K}} \in E'[N_{\mathsf{K}}]$, and
- a positive integer d relatively prime to N_{S} and N_{K},

The *witness* V is a point of order d in $E(\mathbb{F}_{p^2})$ such that $E' = E/\langle V \rangle$ and the isogeny $\phi: E \to E'$ satisfies $P'_{\mathsf{K}} = \phi(P_{\mathsf{K}})$ and $Q'_{\mathsf{K}} = \phi(Q_{\mathsf{K}})$. Note that by definition, N_{K}, d, and N_{S} all divide $(p+1)$ and are relatively prime.

The Protocol. We design a ZKPK for the relation $\mathcal{R}_{\mathsf{iso}}$ where the verifier (server) has the statement $\Big(j(E),\ P_{\mathsf{K}},\ Q_{\mathsf{K}},\ j(E'),\ P'_{\mathsf{K}},\ Q'_{\mathsf{K}},\ d\Big)$ and the verifier (client) proves knowledge of the witness V. We first describe a protocol that has perfect completeness, constant soundness error, and honest-verifier computational zero knowledge. Repeating the protocol in parallel λ times makes the soundness error negligible. Indeed, the repetitions required in this protocol (as well as in the one in the next section) are responsible for the bulk of the communication in our OPRF construction.

The protocol is based on the idea sketc.hed by Galbraith [26, Sec 7.2], which builds on the isogeny-based identification protocol of De Feo et al. [22].

Remark 10. In the following, when we refer to the prover "committing" to one or more elements, we refer to a standard commitment scheme (as opposed to our augmentable commitment scheme) such as a standard hash-based commitment in the random-oracle model.

First, the prover chooses a random point S of order N_S. The prover then computes an isogeny σ with domain E and kernel $\langle S \rangle$ and an isogeny σ' with domain E' and kernel $\langle \phi(S) \rangle$. Let $\tilde{E}$ and $\tilde{E}'$ be the target curves of the isogenies σ and σ' respectively. For consistency of notation, we denote points on the curve $\tilde{E}$ as $\tilde{P}$, $\tilde{Q}$ etc. Similarly, we denote points on the curve $\tilde{E}'$ as $\tilde{P}'$, $\tilde{Q}'$ etc. The prover can also calculate the isogeny $\tilde{\phi} \colon \tilde{E} \to \tilde{E}'$ using the image of the generator V of ϕ under σ.

The prover chooses a random basis $\tilde{P}_S, \tilde{Q}_S$ of the N_S-torsion subgroup of $\tilde{E}$. The prover then computes the kernel of the dual isogeny $\hat{\sigma}$ and expresses its generator as $s \cdot (\tilde{P}_S, \cdot \tilde{Q}_S)$ for some $s \in \mathbb{P}_{N_S}$. (Note that the kernel of $\hat{\sigma}'$ is then generated by $s \cdot (\tilde{\phi}(\tilde{P}_S), \tilde{\phi}(\tilde{Q}_S))$.)

The prover commits separately to (1) the curve $\tilde{E}$ together with the points $\tilde{P}_S, \tilde{Q}_S$, (2) the curve $\tilde{E}'$ together with the points $\tilde{P}'_S = \tilde{\phi}(\tilde{P}_S), \tilde{Q}'_S = \tilde{\phi}(\tilde{Q}_S)$, (3) the scalar s, (4) a random generator $\tilde{V}$ of $\ker(\tilde{\phi})$, and (5–8) the images of P_K, Q_K under σ and of P'_K, Q'_K under σ'. (Committing to all those elements makes the protocol online-extractable without rewinding, which is necessary for UC security.)

Each execution of the protocol will verify the validity of only one of the two points P'_K and Q'_K according to a random choice made by the verifier. Additionally, according to another random three-way choice of the verifier, the prover will reveal one of three isogenies (i.e., either σ, σ', or $\tilde{\phi}$) along with some points. The following diagram illustrates the commitments opened in each of the three cases where the verifier chooses to verify the validity of the point P'_K:

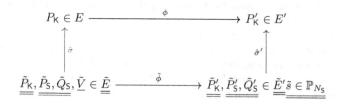

- In the <u>red case</u>, the prover reveals the curve $\tilde{E}$, the random generators $\tilde{P}_S$, $\tilde{Q}_S$ of $\tilde{E}[N_S]$, the element $\tilde{s} \in \mathbb{P}_{N_S}$, and the point $\tilde{P}_K = \sigma(P_K) \in \tilde{E}[N_K]$. The verifier computes the isogeny $\hat{\sigma} \colon \tilde{E} \to \tilde{E}/\langle \tilde{s} \cdot (\tilde{P}_S, s_q \tilde{Q}_S) \rangle$, and checks that $\hat{\sigma}(\tilde{P}_K) = [N_S^2]P_K$, where $[N_S^2]$ is the multiplication by N_S^2 map.
- Similarly, in the <u>green case</u>, the prover reveals the curve $\tilde{E}'$, the random generators $\tilde{P}'_S = \tilde{\phi}(\tilde{P}_S)$, $\tilde{Q}'_S = \tilde{\phi}(\tilde{Q}_S)$ of $\tilde{E}'[N_S]$, the element $\tilde{s} \in \mathbb{P}_{N_S}$, and the point $\tilde{P}'_K = \sigma'(P'_K)$. The verifier computes the isogeny $\hat{\sigma}' \colon \tilde{E}' \to \tilde{E}'/\langle \tilde{s} \cdot (\tilde{P}'_S, \tilde{Q}'_S) \rangle$, and checks that $\hat{\sigma}'(\tilde{P}'_K) = [N_S]P'_K$, where $[N_S]$ is the multiplication by N_S map.
- Finally, in the <u>blue case</u>, the prover reveals the curves $\tilde{E}$ and $\tilde{E}'$, a random generator $\tilde{V}$ of $\ker(\tilde{\phi})$, and the points $\tilde{P}_S, \tilde{Q}_S \in \tilde{E}[N_S]$, $\tilde{P}_K \in \tilde{E}[N_K]$, $\tilde{P}'_K \in \tilde{E}'[N_K]$, and $\tilde{P}'_S, \tilde{Q}'_S \in \tilde{E}'[N_S]$. The verifier computes the isogeny $\tilde{\phi} \colon \tilde{E} \to \tilde{E}/\langle \tilde{V} \rangle$ and checks that $\tilde{\phi}(\tilde{P}_K) = \tilde{P}'_K$, $\tilde{\phi}(\tilde{P}_S) = \tilde{P}'_S$ and $\tilde{\phi}(\tilde{Q}_S) = \tilde{Q}'_S$.

Remark 11. In our protocol, as well as in the security game for the underlying assumption, we specifically choose to reveal the image of only a single generator of the N_K-torsion under the secret random isogeny σ. The reason for this choice is to prevent a distinguishing attack using the Weil pairing. Had we revealed both images $\tilde{P}_K = \sigma(P_K), \tilde{Q}_K = \sigma(Q_K)$, then the verifier would have obtained the two relations $e(\tilde{P}_K, \tilde{V}) = e(P_K, V)^{v \cdot \deg(\sigma)}$ and $e(\tilde{Q}_K, \tilde{V}) = e(Q_K, V)^{v \cdot \deg(\sigma)}$, which would allow to verifier to distinguish V from random. By revealing only one out of the two points $\tilde{P}_K, \tilde{Q}_K$, and by revealing a random generator $v \cdot \sigma(V)$ instead of $\sigma(V)$, the protocol prevents tis pairing attack.

The zero-knowledge property of our protocol is based on the hardness of a variant of the Decisional Supersingular Product problem (DSSP), introduced by De Feo et al. [22]. As our protocol also needs to verify the action of the secret isogeny on the N_K-torsion, we need to slightly strengthen the assumption by giving the adversary additional points. More specifically, we consider the following:

Attack Game 12 (Auxiliary Decisional Supersingular Product). Let $p = p(\lambda, n + 1) = f \cdot N_1 \cdot \ldots \cdot N_{n+1}$ be as in Definition 3. Let E_0 be a supersingular elliptic curve over $\mathbb{F}_{p^2}$ as above. Consider the following game, played between a challenger and an adversary:

- The adversary chooses and sends to the challenger $V_0 \in E(\mathbb{F}_{p^2})$ of order exactly d relatively prime to N_S, and a point $P_K \in E(\mathbb{F}_{p^2})$ of order relatively prime to N_S and d.
- The challenger executes the following steps:
  - choose $c \xleftarrow{\text{R}} \{0, 1\}$, $v \xleftarrow{\text{R}} \mathbb{Z}_d^*$, and a random point $V_1 \in E(\mathbb{F}_{p^2})$ of order d
  - compute a random degree-N_S isogeny $\sigma : E_0 \to E'$
  - send $j(E') \in \mathbb{F}_{p^2}$ and the points $v \cdot \sigma(V_c), \sigma(P_K) \in E'(\mathbb{F}_{p^2})$ to the adversary
- The adversary outputs a bit c'.

We say that the adversary wins if $c' = c$.
The Auxiliary Decisional Supersingular Product Assumption is that for every constant n, the winning probability of every efficient adversary in the above game is negligible.

In the full version of this work we formally define sigma protocols, give the full details of the above protocol, and prove that it is special computational honest-verifier zero knowledge, under the Auxiliary Decisional Supersingular Product assumption. We also discuss how to transform this sigma protocol into a non-interactive zero-knowledge proof of knowledge (NIZKPK) in the random-oracle model using standard techniques.

Concrete Efficiency. We estimate the size of the resulting NIZKPK. In a single execution of the above protocol, the prover sends 8 hash-based commitments in its first message. Of the three possible openings, the "blue" one, that consists of 2 j-invariants and 7 points, is the largest one. The opening also includes 5 random nonces used for the hash-based commitments, each of which is λ-bits long. The size of a j-invariant in $\mathbb{F}_{p^2}$ is $2\log p$ bits. A naive representation of each point over $\mathbb{F}_{p^2}$ would have also been $2\log p$ bits (x-coordinate and a sign bit). However, Azarderakhsh et al. [5] observed that a point in an N_i-torsion can be represented using only $2\log N_i$ bits. Since in our construction $\log N_i \leq \log p/4$, the prover can send all 7 points in less than $4\log p$ bits, and together with the j-invariant, the size of the prover's last message is less than $6\log p$ bits. (In the non-interactive proof, the verifier's only message is a random challenge, which is derived from a random oracle and thus does not increase the size of the proof.) Since each execution of the protocol has soundness error $5/6$, we must repeat the protocol $\lambda/\log(6/5) = 3.8\lambda$ times. Overall, we estimate the size of the proof as $3.8\lambda \cdot (13\lambda + 6\log p)$.

6 Zero-Knowledge Proof of Equality of Isogenies

Recall that to make our OPRF verifiable, the server must convince the verifier that it has evaluated the OPRF consistently with its evaluation on some fixed point. This boils down to proving the commitments satisfy the following relation

$$R_{eq} = \left\{ ((\mathsf{com}_0, \mathsf{com}_1, \overline{\mathsf{com}}_0, \overline{\mathsf{com}}_1), k) \;\middle|\; \begin{array}{c} \mathsf{com}_0, \mathsf{com}_1, \overline{\mathsf{com}}_0, \overline{\mathsf{com}}_1 \in \mathcal{C} \\ k \in \mathcal{K} \\ \overline{\mathsf{com}}_0 = \mathsf{Append}(\mathsf{com}_0, k) \\ \overline{\mathsf{com}}_1 = \mathsf{Append}(\mathsf{com}_1, k) \end{array} \right\}$$

Moreover, the proof must be zero-knowledge, and in particular, the user should not learn any additional information about the key beyond what it already knows from $\overline{\mathsf{com}}_0$ and $\overline{\mathsf{com}}_1$.

The idea behind Protocol 13 below is as follows. The user (verifier) sends to the server λ augmentable commitments, each of which is obtained by appending a random value v_i to either com_1 or com_2, chosen at random. The user saves the values v_i and the random choices $b_i \in \{0, 1\}$.

Next, the server (prover) appends its secret value k to each of the λ commitments, and sends to the user a hash-based commitment $h = H(j_1, \ldots, j_\lambda, s_{\mathsf{out}})$ to their invariants, where $s_{\mathsf{out}} \xleftarrow{\text{R}} \{0, 1\}^\lambda$.

The user then reveals to the server the random values $v_1, \ldots, v_\lambda$, and the server uses them to check that each of the λ commitments received in the first round has indeed been obtained by appending v_i to one of com_1 or com_2. This protects the server against a malicious user that tries to learn additional information about k by sending commitments that are not com_1 or com_2.

Once this check passes, the server sends to the user the opening s_{out} to the hash-based commitment. Finally, the user computes the expected values of the invariants $j'_1, \ldots, j'_\lambda$ as $j'_i = \mathsf{Invariant}(\mathsf{Append}(\overline{\mathsf{com}}_{b_i}, v_i))$ and checks that $h = H(j'_1, \ldots, j'_\lambda, s_{\mathsf{out}})$.

This protocol is generic for augmentable commitments, but we think that its instantiation with the isogeny-based construction of augmentable commitments may be of independent interest.

Protocol 13 (Equality of Appended Values). Let $\mathcal{G}$ be an augmentable commitment scheme with input space $\mathcal{M} \times \mathcal{K} \times \mathcal{V} \times \mathcal{R}$, and commitment space $\mathcal{C}$. Let NIZKPK be a simulation-sound online-extractable proof for the relation R_{com}. Let $H_3 \colon \{0,1\}^* \to \{0,1\}^\lambda$ be a hash function, modeled as random oracle.

Inputs:

- The verifier's inputs are: commitments $\text{com}_0, \text{com}_1, \overline{\text{com}}_0, \overline{\text{com}}_1 \in \mathcal{C}$.
- The prover's inputs are: commitments $\text{com}_0, \text{com}_1, \overline{\text{com}}_0, \overline{\text{com}}_1 \in \mathcal{C}$; a value $k \in \mathcal{K}$ such that $\text{Append}(\text{com}_0, k) = \overline{\text{com}}_0$ and $\text{Append}(\text{com}_1, k) = \overline{\text{com}}_1$.

Evaluation:

- The prover computes and sends to the verifier proofs π_0, π_1, such that for $b = 0, 1$ it holds $\pi_b \leftarrow \text{NIZKPK}[(k)\colon \text{Append}(\text{com}_b, k) = \overline{\text{com}}_b]$.
- The verifier checks the proofs and aborts if either check fails. Else, for $i = 1, \ldots, \lambda$, the verifier samples $v_i \xleftarrow{R} \mathcal{V}$ and $b_i \xleftarrow{R} \{0,1\}$, computes $\text{com}^{(i)} \leftarrow \text{Append}(\text{com}_{b_i}, v_i)$, and sends $(\text{com}^{(1)}, \ldots, \text{com}^{(\lambda)})$ to the prover.
- The prover uses k to compute, for $i = 1, \ldots, \lambda$, the commitment $\overline{\text{com}}^{(i)} \leftarrow \text{Append}(\text{com}^{(i)}, k)$ and the invariant $j_i \leftarrow \text{Invariant}(\overline{\text{com}}^{(i)})$. It then chooses $s_{\text{out}} \xleftarrow{R} \{0,1\}^\lambda$, and sends $h \leftarrow H_3(j_1, \ldots, j_\lambda, s_{\text{out}})$ to the verifier.
- The verifier sends $(b_1, v_1, \ldots, b_\lambda, v_\lambda)$ to the prover.
- The prover, for $i = 1, \ldots, \lambda$, checks that $\text{Invariant}(\text{Append}(\text{com}_{b_i}, v_i)) = \text{Invariant}(\text{com}^{(i)})$. If one of the checks fail, the server aborts. Otherwise, it sends s_{out} to the user.
- The verifier computes the invariants $j_i' = \text{Invariant}(\text{Append}(\overline{\text{com}}_{b_i}, v_i))$ and accepts if $h = H_3(j_1', \ldots, j_\lambda', s_{\text{out}})$.

In the full version of this worke prove the following lemma, which shows the soundness of this protocol, and we prove the zero-knowledge property of this protocol as part of security proof of the full protocol.

Lemma 14. *Suppose that $\mathcal{G}$ is a secure augmentable commitment scheme, and let $\text{com}_0 = \llbracket r_0, m_0 \rrbracket$ and $\text{com}_1 = \llbracket r_1, m_1 \rrbracket$ be two commitments. Then for every efficient prover P^*, the probability that the honest verifier of Protocol 13 accepts on input $(\text{com}_0, \text{com}_1, \overline{\text{com}}_0, \overline{\text{com}}_1) \notin L_{\text{eq}}$ when interacting with prover P^* is negligible. Here L_{eq} is the corresponding language of R_{eq}.*

Concrete Efficiency. We estimate the communication complexity of the protocol. The communication is dominated by the verifier having to send λ augmentable commitments and λ values $v_i \in \mathcal{V}$. The size of each supersingular-isogeny-based augmentable commitment is at most $5 \log p$ bits. Moreover, a commitment that includes $v_i \in \mathcal{V}$ as one of its values does not include a basis for the N_{V}-torsion, which cancels out having to send the v_i values in the next message. Therefore, we can bound the overall communication complexity by $5\lambda \log p$ plus the size of the proofs of knowledge π_0 and π_1.

7   Putting It All Together

We now combine the basic protocol from Sect. 4 with the two protocols from Sect. 5 and 6 to obtain a maliciously secure verifiable OPRF.

Protocol 15 implements the OPRF ideal functionality $\mathcal{F}_{\text{VOPRF}}$ as defined in the full version of this work (That definition is based on [36] with some of the later modifications from [38, 40].)

In the full version of this worke prove the following theorem.

Theorem 16. *Suppose that $\mathcal{G}$ is a secure augmentable commitment scheme. Then Protocol 15 realizes ideal functionality $\mathcal{F}_{\text{VOPRF}}$ in the random-oracle model.*

The main ideas of the proof are as follows. The privacy of the user's input easily follows from the hiding property of the underlying augmentable commitment scheme. The main challenge is to simulate the honest server. To this end, the simulator in the ideal world chooses a random secret key for the honest server, and uses it to simulate the interaction of the real-world adversary with that server. Specifically, each time the environment activates the honest server, the simulator responds to an adversary's message by appending its secret key to the commitment sent by the adversary.

The only way the environment can distinguish this from the real world is to find an inconsistency between the value of the OPRF computed via an honest-user honest-server interaction, and the value of the OPRF computed by the adversary directly as $H_2(x, \text{Invariant}(\llbracket m, k \rrbracket))$ for $m = H_1(x)$. To prevent this inconsistency, whenever the adversary makes this type of query to the random oracle H_2, the simulator evaluates the ideal-world OPRF at point x and programs the random oracle H_2 to the output value of the PRF. However, the ticketing mechanism of the OPRF ideal functionality limits the number of times the simulator can evaluate the ideal-world OPRF by the number of activations of the honest server. The simulation would therefore fail if the adversary correctly predicts the value $\text{Invariant}(\llbracket m, k \rrbracket)$ on a number of points greater than the number of server activations. However, this would violate the one-more unpredictability property of the underlying augmentable commitment scheme.

The full proof appears in the full version of this work

Concrete Efficiency and Parameter Estimation

The communication complexity of the complete OPRF protocol is dominated by the communication complexity of the zero-knowledge proofs. More specifically, the protocol includes 3 NIZKPKs for the relation R_{com}, the size of each of which we have estimated in Sect. 5 to be $3.8\lambda \cdot (13\lambda + 6 \log p)$. In addition, the complete protocol executes the proof-of-equality sub-protocol once. In Sect. 6 we estimated the communication complexity of that sub-protocol as $5\lambda \log p$. Therefore, we can bound the communication complexity of the complete protocol as $73\lambda \log p + 148\lambda^2$.

We set $p(\lambda)$ based on the best known attacks on our assumptions. For standard SIDH problems (including the Decisional SIDH problem and the Decisional

---

Protocol 15 (Augmentable-Commitment Verifiable OPRF). The protocol involves a user U and a server S. The protocol uses:

- An augmentable commitment scheme $\mathcal{G}$ with $m = 3$ values, $n = 1$ blinds, input space $\mathcal{M} \times \mathcal{K} \times \mathcal{V} \times \mathcal{R}$, and commitment space $\mathcal{C}$.
- A simulation-sound online-extractable NIZKPK for the relation R_{com}.
- Hash functions, modeled as random oracles:
  - $H_1 : \{0,1\}^* \cup \{\epsilon\} \to \mathcal{M}$ (where ϵ is a special symbol), used to hash PRF inputs to the input space $\mathcal{M}$ of the commitment scheme,
  - $H_2 : \{0,1\}^* \to \{0,1\}^\ell$, used to hash to the PRF output space,
  - $H_3 : \{0,1\}^* \to \{0,1\}^\lambda$, used in Protocol 13 for proving equality of appended values.

Initialization. On input INIT from the environment, server S:
- chooses $k \xleftarrow{\text{R}} \mathcal{K}$ and stores it,
- computes $m_\epsilon \leftarrow H_1(\epsilon)$, $r_\epsilon \xleftarrow{\text{R}} \mathcal{R}$, and $\mathsf{com}_\epsilon \leftarrow [\![r_\epsilon, m_\epsilon]\!]$.
- computes $\overline{\mathsf{com}}_\epsilon \leftarrow [\![r_\epsilon, m_\epsilon, k]\!]$ and a proof of knowledge of a committed value $\pi_k \leftarrow \mathsf{NIZKPK}[(k) : \mathsf{Append}(\mathsf{com}_\epsilon, k) = \overline{\mathsf{com}}_\epsilon]$,
- stores $\mathsf{pk} = (r_\epsilon, \overline{\mathsf{com}}_\epsilon, \pi_k)$ and outputs (INIT, pk).

Evaluation
- On input (EVAL, S, x), user U proceeds as follows:
  - $m \leftarrow H_1(x)$, $r_m \xleftarrow{\text{R}} \mathcal{R}$, $\mathsf{com}_m \leftarrow [\![r_m, m]\!]$
  - compute proof $\pi_m \leftarrow \mathsf{NIZKPK}[(m, r_m) : \mathsf{com}_m = [\![r_m, m]\!]]$
  - send message (com_m, π_m) to the server
  - store (com_m, r_m)
- On input SERVERCOMPLETE from the environment and message (com_m, π_m) from the user, server S verifies the proof π_m, computes $\overline{\mathsf{com}}_m \leftarrow \mathsf{Append}(\mathsf{com}_m, k)$ and $\pi_m \leftarrow \mathsf{NIZKPK}[(k) : \mathsf{Append}(\mathsf{com}_m, k) = \overline{\mathsf{com}}_m]$, and sends the descriptor $\mathsf{pk} = (r_\epsilon, \overline{\mathsf{com}}_\epsilon, \pi_k)$ and $\overline{\mathsf{com}}_m, \pi_m$ to the user.
- On message $(\mathsf{pk} = (r_\epsilon, \overline{\mathsf{com}}_\epsilon, \pi_k), \overline{\mathsf{com}}_m, \pi_m)$ from the server, user U verifies the proofs π_k, π_m.
- The user and server run Protocol 13, in which the sender proves to the user that there exists a k such that $[\![r_\epsilon, m_\epsilon, k]\!] = \overline{\mathsf{com}}_\epsilon$ and $[\![r_m, m, k]\!] = \overline{\mathsf{com}}_m$.
- At the end of the equality protocol, the user, provided it accepts, computes $j \leftarrow \mathsf{Invariant}(\mathsf{Unblind}(\overline{\mathsf{com}}_m, r_m))$ and $y \leftarrow H_2(x, \mathsf{pk}, j)$ and outputs (EVAL, pk, y).

Supersingular Product problem), the best known attacks are meet-in-the-middle attacks that run in time $O(\sqrt{N_i})$ [55]. Although quantum collision-finding algorithms [66] have a better asymptotic running time of $O(\sqrt[3]{N_i})$, recent work [1,34] suggests that the classical algorithm outperform the quantum ones when attacking SIDH, due to the large memory requirement of the quantum algorithms. One caveat is that our one-more assumption admits a better attack than SIDH: Merz et al. [52] showed an attack on the schemes of [35,65] that runs in time $N_i^{2/5}$. This *exponential-time* attack, unlike the aforementioned *polynomial-time* attack from the same paper [52], also applies to our one-more assumption. We therefore set $N_i \approx 2^{5\lambda/2}$ for λ-bit security. (The torsion used for the zero-knowledge proof does not need to be increased as it is used only within a non-interactive proof.) Overall, for $n = 5$ prime powers, the prime p is 12λ-bits long.

Plugging in $\log p = 12\lambda$ into the expression for the communication complexity we have calculated above, we obtain that the total communication complexity is bounded by $1024\lambda^2$ bits. For $\lambda = 128$, the communication complexity is under 2MB.

8   Naor-Reingold OPRF from an Abelian Group Action

We now turn to constructing an OPRF from an abelian group action, such as the action obtained from isogenies of *ordinary* elliptic curves or from isogenies of supersingular curves over $\mathbb{F}_p$ as in CSIDH [14].

First, we show that the Naor-Reingold PRF [54] can be adapted to work with an abelian group action that satisfies a DDH-like assumption. Second, we show that the technique used to build an OPRF from the Naor-Reingold PRF carries over to the setting of an abelian group action.

A technical difficulty is that the proof of security of the Naor-Reingold PRF in [54] makes use of the random self reduction of the DDH problem in a prime order group. The DDH problem for an arbitrary abelian group action does not have the required random self reduction. We therefore need to give a new security proof for the Naor-Reingold PRF. We are able to prove security based on the DDH assumption for a group action; however the security reduction is not as efficient as the proof of Naor-Reingold in a prime order group.

Recall that an action of a group G on a set X is a map $G \times X \to X$ such that $(gh) \cdot x = g \cdot (h \cdot x)$ for every $g, h \in G$ and $x \in X$, and $e \cdot x = x$ for every $x \in X$, where $e \in G$ is the identity element of G.

Let G be an abelian finite group acting on S transitively and faithfully (we recall the definitions of these properties in the full version of this work, and let $s_0 \in S$ be some fixed element. We define the Naor-Reingold PRF, with key space $\mathcal{K} = G^{n+1}$ and input space $\mathcal{X} = \{0,1\}^n$, as follows:

$$F_{\mathsf{NR}}\Big((k_0, ..., k_n), (x_1, ..., x_n)\Big) = (k_0 k_1^{x_1} k_2^{x_2} \ldots k_n^{x_n}) \cdot s_0. \tag{2}$$

The security of this PRF requires the following group-action variant of the DDH assumption to hold in G:

Definition 17 (Group-Action DDH [19,61]). Let G be an abelian group acting on a set S transitively and faithfully, and let $s \in S$. We say that the *Group-Action DDH assumption* holds in (G, s) if the two distributions

$$\{(a \cdot s,\ b \cdot s,\ (ab) \cdot s) : a, b \xleftarrow{\text{R}} G\} \quad \text{and} \quad \{(a \cdot s,\ b \cdot s,\ c \cdot s) : a, b, c \xleftarrow{\text{R}} G\}$$

are computationally indistinguishable.

Theorem 18. *Suppose that the Group-Action DDH assumption holds in (G, s_0). Then the Naor-Reingold PRF F_{NR} is a secure pseudorandom function.*

Proof sketch. Boneh et al. [9, Sec. 4.1] show that the Naor-Reingold PRF is a special case of the *augmented cascade*. Therefore, to prove that (2) is a secure PRF, it suffices to show that for every polynomially bounded Q, the function

$$P(g, s_1, \ldots, s_Q) = (s_1, \; g \cdot s_1, \ldots, s_Q, \; g \cdot s_Q)$$

is a secure pseudorandom generator (PRG), where $g \in G$ and $s_1, \ldots, s_Q \in S$. This can be done by a simple sequence of $(Q + 1)$ hybrid distributions, where at hybrid i, for $i = 1, \ldots, Q$, the quantity $g \cdot s_i$ is replaced by random element t_i in S. A distinguisher for any pair of consecutive hybrid distributions gives an attack on the Group-Action DDH assumption for (G, s_0). Overall, the reduction incurs a factor of Q loss between an attacker on the PRG and the derived attacker on the Group-Action DDH assumption. The proof of the theorem now follows by [9, Thm. 3].

Next, we observe that because the group G is abelian, we can evaluate F_{NR} obliviously with the following protocol, first described in [24] in a group of prime order.

Protocol 19. *A client that holds input $(x_1, \ldots, x_n) \in \{0, 1\}^n$ and a server that holds input $(k_0, k_1, \ldots, k_n) \in G^{n+1}$ proceed as follows:*

1. *For each $i = 1, \ldots, n$, the server chooses a random r_i in G.*
2. *For each $i = 1, \ldots, n$, the client and server engage in a 1-out-of-2 oblivious-transfer protocol that gives to the client r_i if $x_i = 0$, and $k_i r_i$ if $x_i = 1$. The client stores the output as $b_i \in G$.*
3. *The server sends $s' = (k_0 \prod_{i=1}^{n} r_i^{-1}) \cdot s_0$ to the client.*
4. *The client evaluates $(\prod_{i=1}^{n} b_i) \cdot s'$ to obtain F_{NR} evaluated at $(x_1, \ldots, x_n)$.*

The same security argument from [24, Sec. 5] also applies to this OPRF.

Instantiation from Isogenies. We can now instantiate the above construction using isogenies. Couveignes [19], Rostovtsev and Stolbunov [61] first proposed using a group action on the set of ordinary elliptic curves. More recently, Castryck et al. [14] proposed CSIDH, a construction that uses the set of supersingular elliptic curves defined over a prime field $\mathbb{F}_p$. Whereas the full endomorphism ring of such curves is non-commutative (and therefore does not give rise to a commutative group action), the subring of $\mathbb{F}_p$-*rational* endomorphisms is an order in an imaginary quadratic field, which gives rise to a commutative group action as in the ordinary case. The main advantage of using the CSIDH group action, over using the group action of ordinary curves, is that it is much more efficient.

More specifically, let $\text{Ell}_p(\mathcal{O})$ be the set of supersingular elliptic curves over $\mathbb{F}_p$ whose $\mathbb{F}_p$-rational endomorphism ring $\mathcal{O}$ is an order in an imaginary quadratic field. The class group $\text{Cl}(\mathcal{O})$, which is an abelian group, acts transitively and faithfully on $\text{Ell}_p(\mathcal{O})$. (See the full version of this work or additional background.) For $[\mathfrak{a}_0], \ldots, [\mathfrak{a}_n] \in \text{Cl}(\mathcal{O})$ and $E_0 \in \text{Ell}_p(\mathcal{O})$, let

$$F_{\text{NR}}(([\mathfrak{a}_0], [\mathfrak{a}_1], \ldots, [\mathfrak{a}_n], E_0), (x_1, \ldots, x_n)) = j([\mathfrak{a}_n]^{x_n} \ldots [\mathfrak{a}_1]^{x_1} [\mathfrak{a}_0] \cdot E_0).$$

Assuming the hardness of Group-Action DDH problem in the class group, Theorem 18 then implies that F_{NR} is a PRF. Moreover, instantiating Protocol 19 with the isogeny-based oblivious-transfer protocol of Lai, Galbraith, and de Saint Guilhelm [51], which is secure against malicious adversaries, gives an OPRF protocol from a commutative group action on elliptic curves.

Remark 20. Recently, Castryck, Sotáková, and Vercauteren [15] showed that the DDH problem is easy in ideal-class-group actions when the class number is even. Such groups are therefore unsuited for the above construction. As a countermeasure to their attack, they suggest working with supersingular elliptic curves over $\mathbb{F}_p$ for $p \equiv 3 \pmod 4$, which is already the case for CSIDH [14]. In that setting, the Group-Action DDH problem is conjectured to be hard.

Remark 21. Our construction targets the case of *commutative* group actions. We mention a recent work by Ji et al. [43], that studies the case of *non-commutative* group actions. The above reduction does not seem to carry over to the non-commutative case, which might explain why Ji et al. require a different assumption.

Efficiency. To compute the communication complexity of this instantiation, first assume without loss of generality that $n = \lambda$ (since otherwise we can compose the PRF with a λ-bit hash function). The protocol requires $n = \lambda$ executions of the OT protocol [51]. Each such execution communicates 3 elliptic curves over $\mathbb{F}_p$, 4 encryptions of class-group elements, and an additional λ-bit string. Overall, this adds up to $\lambda \cdot (3 \log p + 4 \cdot \log p/2 + \lambda) = 5\lambda \log p + \lambda^2$ bits.

Kuperberg's algorithm [48,49] for solving the commutative-group-action discrete-log problem, runs in time $\exp(\sqrt{\log(p)})$, which requires setting $p = \Omega(\lambda^2)$. As a result, the overall communication complexity of this protocol is asymptotically $\Omega(\lambda^3)$, compared to $O(\lambda^2)$ communication in the protocol from the previous sections. While the initial CSIDH paper [14] suggested that using a 512-bit prime might be sufficient, recent analysis [10,56] recommends using primes as large as 5280-bits long. This leads to Protocol 19 having communication complexity of 424KB.

9   Conclusions and Open Problems

We constructed two OPRFs from isogenies on elliptic curves. Our main construction of a verifiable OPRF from isogenies on supersingular elliptic curves is based on a new one-more SIDH assumption. Our construction achieves malicious security by virtue of two new zero-knowledge proofs, and introduces a new abstraction called Augmentable Commitments, which may help simplify the exposition of future SIDH-based constructions. We also presented a second construction from commutative group actions.

Future Work. It would be interesting to extend our OPRF to support threshold PRF evaluation, where the PRF key is distributed across multiple servers. Threshold OPRFs [38] have applications to management of passwords and keys [2,32,39]. It would also be good to reduce the communication cost of our zero-knowledge proofs, as that would improve the overall efficiency of the OPRF.

Acknowledgements. We would like to thank David Wu for helpful conversations. We thank Henry Corrigan-Gibbs, Michel Dellepere, and Steven Galbraith for giving helpful suggestions that improved this article. Finally, we would like to thank the anonymous Asiacrypt reviewers for their constructive comments. This work was supported in part by DARPA, NSF, ONR, and the Simons Foundation.

References

1. Adj, G., Cervantes-Vázquez, D., Chi-Dominguez, J.J., Menezes, A., Rodriguez-Henriquez F. (2019) On the Cost of Computing Isogenies Between Supersingular Elliptic Curves. In: Cid, C., Jacobson, Jr. M. (eds.) Selected Areas in Cryptography – SAC 2018. SAC 2018. Lecture Notes in Computer Science, vol 11349. Springer, Cham (2019) https://doi.org/10.1007/978-3-030-10970-7_15
2. Agrawal, S., Miao, P., Mohassel, P., Mukherjee, P.: PASTA: password-based threshold authentication. In: Proceedings of the 2018 ACM SIGSAC Conference on Computer and Communications Security, pp. 2042–2059 (2018)
3. Albrecht, M.R., Davidson, A., Deo, A., Smart, N.P.: Round-optimal verifiable oblivious pseudorandom functions from ideal lattices. Cryptology ePrint Archive, Report 2019/1271 (2019)
4. Azarderakhsh, R., Jalali, A., Jao, D., Soukharev, V.: Practical supersingular isogeny group key agreement. Cryptology ePrint Archive, Report 2019/330 (2019)
5. Azarderakhsh, R., Jao, D., Kalach, K., Koziel, B., Leonardi, C.: Key compression for isogeny-based cryptosystems. In: Proceedings of the 3rd ACM International Workshop on ASIA Public-Key Cryptography, pp. 1–10 (2016)
6. Barreto, P., Oliveira, G., Benits, W.: Supersingular isogeny oblivious transfer. arXiv preprint arXiv:1805.06589 (2018)
7. Bellare, M., Namprempre, C., Pointcheval, D., Semanko, M.: The one-more-RSA-inversion problems and the security of Chaum's blind signature scheme. J. Cryptol. **16**(3), 185–215 (2003)
8. Boldyreva, A.: Threshold signatures, multisignatures and blind signatures based on the gap-diffie-hellman-group signature scheme. In: Desmedt, Y.G. (ed.) PKC 2003. LNCS, vol. 2567, pp. 31–46. Springer, Heidelberg (2003). https://doi.org/10.1007/3-540-36288-6_3
9. Boneh, D., Montogomery, H., Raghunathan, A.: Algebraic pseudorandom functions with improved efficiency from the augmented cascade. In: Proceedings of the 17th ACM Conference on Computer and Communications Security, pp. 131–140 (2010)
10. Bonnetain, X., Schrottenloher, A.: Quantum security analysis of CSIDH. In: Canteaut, A., Ishai, Y. (eds.) EUROCRYPT 2020. LNCS, vol. 12106, pp. 493–522. Springer, Cham (2020). https://doi.org/10.1007/978-3-030-45724-2_17

11. Büscher, N., et al.: Secure two-party computation in a quantum world. ACNS (2020)

12. Camenisch, J., Neven, G., Shelat, A.: Simulatable adaptive oblivious transfer. In: Naor, M. (ed.) EUROCRYPT 2007. LNCS, vol. 4515, pp. 573–590. Springer, Heidelberg (2007). https://doi.org/10.1007/978-3-540-72540-4_33

13. Canetti, R.: Universally composable security: a new paradigm for cryptographic protocols. In: Proceedings 42nd IEEE Symposium on Foundations of Computer Science, pp. 136–145. IEEE (2001)

14. Castryck, W., Lange, T., Martindale, C., Panny, L., Renes, J.: CSIDH: an efficient post-quantum commutative group action. In: Peyrin, T., Galbraith, S. (eds.) ASIACRYPT 2018. LNCS, vol. 11274, pp. 395–427. Springer, Cham (2018). https://doi.org/10.1007/978-3-030-03332-3_15

15. Castryck, W., Sotáková, J., Vercauteren, F.: Breaking the decisional diffie-hellman problem for class group actions using genus theory. CRYPTO (2020)

16. Charles, D.X., Lauter, K.E., Goren, E.Z.: Cryptographic hash functions from expander graphs. J. Cryptol. $22(1)$, 93–113 (2009)

17. Chaum, D.: Blind signatures for untraceable payments. In: Chaum, D., Rivest, R.L., Sherman, A.T. (eds.) Advances in Cryptology, pp. 199–203. Springer, Boston, MA (1983). https://doi.org/10.1007/978-1-4757-0602-4_18

18. Costello, C., Jao, D., Longa, P., Naehrig, M., Renes, J., Urbanik, D.: Efficient compression of SIDH public keys. In: Coron, Jean-Sébastien, Nielsen, Jesper Buus (eds.) EUROCRYPT 2017. LNCS, vol. 10210, pp. 679–706. Springer, Cham (2017). https://doi.org/10.1007/978-3-319-56620-7_24

19. Couveignes, J.M.: Hard homogeneous spaces. Cryptology ePrint Archive, Report 2006/291 (2006)

20. Davidson, A., Sullivan, N., Wood, C.: Oblivious pseudorandom functions (OPRFs) using prime-order groups. Internet-Draft draft-irtf-cfrg-voprf01 (2019)

21. Davidson, A., Goldberg, I., Sullivan, N., Tankersley, G., Valsorda, F.: Privacy pass: bypassing internet challenges anonymously. Proc. Priv. Enhancing Technol. $2018(3)$, 164–180 (2018)

22. De Feo, L., Jao, D., Plût, J.: Towards quantum-resistant cryptosystems from supersingular elliptic curve isogenies. J. Math. Cryptol. $8(3)$, 209–247 (2014)

23. Everspaugh, A., Chatterjee, R., Scott, S., Juels, A., Ristenpart, T.: The Pythia PRF service. In: 24th USENIX Security Symposium (USENIX Security 15), pp. 547–562 (2015)

24. Freedman, M.J., Ishai, Y., Pinkas, B., Reingold, O.: Keyword search and oblivious pseudorandom functions. In: Kilian, J. (ed.) TCC 2005. LNCS, vol. 3378, pp. 303–324. Springer, Heidelberg (2005). https://doi.org/10.1007/978-3-540-30576-7_17

25. Fujisaki, E., Okamoto, T.: Secure integration of asymmetric and symmetric encryption schemes. J. Cryptol. $26(1)$, 80–101 (2013)

26. Galbraith, S.D.: Authenticated key exchange for SIDH. IACR Cryptol. ePrint Archive, Report 2018/266 (2018)

27. Galbraith, S.D., Petit, C., Shani, B., Ti, Y.B.: On the security of supersingular isogeny cryptosystems. In: Cheon, J.H., Takagi, T. (eds.) ASIACRYPT 2016. LNCS, vol. 10031, pp. 63–91. Springer, Heidelberg (2016). https://doi.org/10.1007/978-3-662-53887-6_3

28. Galbraith, S.D., Petit, C., Silva, J.: Identification protocols and signature schemes based on supersingular isogeny problems. J. Cryptol. $33(1)$, 130–175 (2020)

29. Galbraith, S.D., Vercauteren, F.: Computational problems in supersingular elliptic curve isogenies. Quantum Inf. Process. $17(10)$, 265 (2018)

30. Goldreich, O., Goldwasser, S., Micali, S.: How to construct random functions. J. ACM **33**(4), 792–807 (1986)

31. Green, M., Hohenberger, S.: Blind identity-based encryption and simulatable oblivious transfer. In: Kurosawa, K. (ed.) ASIACRYPT 2007. LNCS, vol. 4833, pp. 265–282. Springer, Heidelberg (2007). https://doi.org/10.1007/978-3-540-76900-2_16

32. Harchol, Y., Abraham, I., Pinkas, B.: Distributed SSH key management with proactive RSA threshold signatures. In: Preneel, B., Vercauteren, F. (eds.) ACNS 2018. LNCS, vol. 10892, pp. 22–43. Springer, Cham (2018). https://doi.org/10.1007/978-3-319-93387-0_2

33. Ishai, Y., Kilian, J., Nissim, K., Petrank, E.: Extendingoblivious transfers efficiently. In: Boneh, D. (ed.) CRYPTO 2003. LNCS, vol. 2729, pp. 145–161. Springer, Heidelberg (2003). https://doi.org/10.1007/978-3-540-45146-4_9

34. Jao, D., et al.: SIKE: supersingular isogeny key encapsulation (2017)

35. Jao, D., Soukharev, V.: Isogeny-based quantum-resistant undeniable signatures. In: Mosca, M. (ed.) PQCrypto 2014. LNCS, vol. 8772, pp. 160–179. Springer, Cham (2014). https://doi.org/10.1007/978-3-319-11659-4_10

36. Jarecki, S., Kiayias, A., Krawczyk, H.: Round-optimal password-protected secret sharing and T-PAKE in the password-only model. In: Sarkar, P., Iwata, T. (eds.) ASIACRYPT 2014. LNCS, vol. 8874, pp. 233–253. Springer, Heidelberg (2014). https://doi.org/10.1007/978-3-662-45608-8_13

37. Jarecki, S., Kiayias, A., Krawczyk, H., Xu, J.: Highly-efficient and composable password-protected secret sharing (or: How to protect your bitcoin wallet online). In: 2016 IEEE European Symposium on Security and Privacy (EuroS&P), pp. 276–291. IEEE (2016)

38. Jarecki, S., Kiayias, A., Krawczyk, H., Xu, J.: TOPPSS: cost-minimal password-protected secret sharing based on threshold OPRF. In: Gollmann, D., Miyaji, A., Kikuchi, H. (eds.) ACNS 2017. LNCS, vol. 10355, pp. 39–58. Springer, Cham (2017). https://doi.org/10.1007/978-3-319-61204-1_3

39. Jarecki, S., Krawczyk, H., Resch, J.K.: Updatable oblivious key management for storage systems. In: Proceedings of the 2019 ACM SIGSAC Conference on Computer and Communications Security, pp. 379–393 (2019)

40. Jarecki, S., Krawczyk, H., Xu, J.: OPAQUE: an asymmetric PAKE protocol secure against pre-computation attacks. In: Nielsen, J.B., Rijmen, V. (eds.) EUROCRYPT 2018. LNCS, vol. 10822, pp. 456–486. Springer, Cham (2018). https://doi.org/10.1007/978-3-319-78372-7_15

41. Jarecki, S., Liu, X.: Efficient oblivious pseudorandom function with applications to adaptive OT and secure computation of set intersection. In: Reingold, O. (ed.) TCC 2009. LNCS, vol. 5444, pp. 577–594. Springer, Heidelberg (2009). https://doi.org/10.1007/978-3-642-00457-5_34

42. Jarecki, S., Liu, X.: Fast secure computation of set intersection. In: Garay, J.A., De Prisco, R. (eds.) SCN 2010. LNCS, vol. 6280, pp. 418–435. Springer, Heidelberg (2010). https://doi.org/10.1007/978-3-642-15317-4_26

43. Ji, Z., Qiao, Y., Song, F., Yun, A.: General linear group action on tensors: a candidate for post-quantum cryptography. In: Hofheinz, D., Rosen, A. (eds.) TCC 2019. LNCS, vol. 11891, pp. 251–281. Springer, Cham (2019). https://doi.org/10.1007/978-3-030-36030-6_11

44. Keelveedhi, S., Bellare, M., Ristenpart, T.: Dupless: Server-aided encryption for deduplicated storage. In: 22nd USENIX Security Symposium (USENIX Security 13), pp. 179–194 (2013)

45. Kirkwood, D., Lackey, B.C., McVey, J., Motley, M., Solinas, J.A., Tuller, D.: Failure is not an option: standardization issues for post-quantum key agreement. In: Workshop on Cybersecurity in a Post-Quantum World, p. 21 (2015)

46. Kiss, Á., Liu, J., Schneider, T., Asokan, N., Pinkas, B.: Private set intersection for unequal set sizes with mobile applications. Proc. Priv. Enhancing Technol. **2017**(4), 177–197 (2017)

47. Kolesnikov, V., Kumaresan, R., Rosulek, M., Trieu, N.: Efficient batched oblivious PRF with applications to private set intersection. In: Proceedings of the 2016 ACM SIGSAC Conference on Computer and Communications Security, pp. 818–829 (2016)

48. Kuperberg, G.: A subexponential-time quantum algorithm for the dihedral hidden subgroup problem. SIAM J. Comput. **35**(1), 170–188 (2005)

49. Kuperberg, G.: Another subexponential-time quantum algorithm for the dihedral hidden subgroup problem. arXiv preprint arXiv:1112.3333 (2013)

50. Kutas, P., Martindale, C., Panny, L., Petit, C., Stange, K.E.: Weak instances of SIDH variants under improved torsion-point attacks. In: Cryptology ePrint Archive, Report 2020/633 (2020)

51. Lai, Y.F., Galbraith, S.D., de Saint Guilhem, C.D.: Compact, efficient and UC-secure isogeny-based oblivious transfer. In: Cryptology ePrint Archive, Report 2020/1012 (2020)

52. Merz, S.-P., Minko, R., Petit, C.: Another look at some isogeny hardness assumptions. In: Jarecki, S. (ed.) CT-RSA 2020. LNCS, vol. 12006, pp. 496–511. Springer, Cham (2020). https://doi.org/10.1007/978-3-030-40186-3_21

53. Naor, M., Pinkas, B., Reingold, O.: Distributed pseudo-random functions and KDCs. In: Stern, J. (ed.) EUROCRYPT 1999. LNCS, vol. 1592, pp. 327–346. Springer, Heidelberg (1999). https://doi.org/10.1007/3-540-48910-X_23

54. Naor, M., Reingold, O.: Number-theoretic constructions of efficient pseudo-random functions. J. ACM (JACM) **51**(2), 231–262 (1997)

55. van Oorschot, P.C., Wiener, M.J.: Parallel collision search with cryptanalytic applications. J. Cryptol. **12**(1), 1–28 (1999)

56. Peikert, C.: He gives C-sieves on the CSIDH. In: Canteaut, A., Ishai, Y. (eds.) EUROCRYPT 2020. LNCS, vol. 12106, pp. 463–492. Springer, Cham (2020). https://doi.org/10.1007/978-3-030-45724-2_16

57. Petit, C.: Faster algorithms for isogeny problems using torsion point images. In: Takagi, T., Peyrin, T. (eds.) ASIACRYPT 2017. LNCS, vol. 10625, pp. 330–353. Springer, Cham (2017). https://doi.org/10.1007/978-3-319-70697-9_12

58. Pinkas, B., Rosulek, M., Trieu, N., Yanai, A.: SpOT-light: lightweight private set intersection from sparse OT extension. In: Boldyreva, A., Micciancio, D. (eds.) CRYPTO 2019. LNCS, vol. 11694, pp. 401–431. Springer, Cham (2019). https://doi.org/10.1007/978-3-030-26954-8_13

59. Pinkas, B., Schneider, T., Zohner, M.: Faster private set intersection based on OT extension. In: 23rd USENIX Security Symposium (USENIX Security 14), pp. 797–812 (2014)

60. Pinkas, B., Schneider, T., Zohner, M.: Scalable private set intersection based on OT extension. ACM Trans. Priv. Secur. **21**(2), 7:1–7:35 (2018)

61. Rostovtsev, A., Stolbunov, A.: Public-key cryptosystem based on isogenies. In: Cryptology ePrint Archive, Report 2006/145 (2006)

62. Sahu, R.A., Gini, A., Pal, A.: Supersingular isogeny-based designated verifier blind signature. In: Cryptology ePrint Archive, Report 2019/1498 (2019)

63. de Saint Guilhem, C.D., Orsini, E., Petit, C., Smart, N.P.: Secure oblivious transfer from semi-commutative masking. In: Cryptology ePrint Archive, Report 2018/648 (2018)
64. Silverman, J.: The Arithmetic of Elliptic Curves. Graduate Texts in Mathematics, Springer, New York (2009)
65. Srinath, M.S., Chandrasekaran, V.: Isogeny-based quantum-resistant undeniable blind signature scheme. I. J. Netw. Secur. **20**(1), 9–18 (2018)
66. Tani, S.: Claw finding algorithms using quantum walk. Theor. Comput. Sci. **410**(50), 5285–5297 (2009)
67. Thormarker, E.: Post-quantum cryptography: supersingular isogeny Diffie-Hellman key exchange. Ph.D. thesis, Thesis, Stockholm University (2017)
68. Urbanik, D., Jao, D.: Sok: the problem landscape of SIDH. In: Proceedings of the 5th ACM on ASIA Public-Key Cryptography Workshop, pp. 53–60 (2018)
69. Vitse, V.: Simple oblivious transfer protocols compatible with supersingular isogenies. In: Buchmann, J., Nitaj, A., Rachidi, T. (eds.) AFRICACRYPT 2019. LNCS, vol. 11627, pp. 56–78. Springer, Cham (2019). https://doi.org/10.1007/978-3-030-23696-0_4

SiGamal: A Supersingular Isogeny-Based PKE and Its Application to a PRF

Tomoki Moriya[✉], Hiroshi Onuki, and Tsuyoshi Takagi

Department of Mathematical Informatics, The University of Tokyo, Tokyo, Japan
{tomoki_moriya,onuki,takagi}@mist.i.u-tokyo.ac.jp

Abstract. We propose two new supersingular isogeny-based public key encryptions: SiGamal and C-SiGamal. They were developed by giving an additional point of the order 2^r to CSIDH. SiGamal is similar to ElGamal encryption, while C-SiGamal is a compressed version of SiGamal. We prove that SiGamal and C-SiGamal are IND-CPA secure without using hash functions under a new assumption: the P-CSSDDH assumption. This assumption comes from the expectation that no efficient algorithm can distinguish between a random point and a point that is the image of a public point under a hidden isogeny.

Next, we propose a Naor-Reingold type pseudo random function (PRF) based on SiGamal. If the P-CSSDDH assumption and the CSSDDH* assumption, which guarantees the security of CSIDH that uses a prime p in the setting of SiGamal, hold, then our proposed function is a pseudo random function. Moreover, we estimate that the computational costs of group actions to compute our proposed PRF are about $\sqrt{\frac{8T}{3\pi}}$ times that of the group actions in CSIDH, where T is the Hamming weight of the input of the PRF.

Finally, we experimented with group actions in SiGamal and C-SiGamal. The computational costs of group actions in SiGamal-512 with a 256-bit plaintext message space were about 2.62 times that of a group action in CSIDH-512.

Keywords: Isogeny-based cryptography · Isogenies · CSIDH · Public key encryption

1 Introduction

Public key cryptosystems are important technologies for guaranteeing the security of communication. Currently, RSA [24] and ECC [11,16] are widely used public key cryptosystems. Shor showed, however, that both of them can be broken by using a quantum computer in polynomial time [25]. Thus, we need to develop new cryptosystems that cannot be broken even by using quantum computers (*i.e.*, post-quantum cryptosystems), before actual quantum computers that can break RSA and ECC are developed.

Isogeny-based cryptosystems depend on the computational complexity of the isogeny problem. Because the isogeny problem is considered hard to solve even

© International Association for Cryptologic Research 2020
S. Moriai and H. Wang (Eds.): ASIACRYPT 2020, LNCS 12492, pp. 551–580, 2020.
https://doi.org/10.1007/978-3-030-64834-3_19

Table 1. Comparison of isogeny-based encryption schemes

Schemes	SIKE	SIDH		CSIDH		SÉTA	SiGamal
Hash	Used	Not used	Used	Not used	Used	Not used	Not used
Security	IND-CCA	OW-CPA	IND-CPA	OW-CPA	IND-CPA	OW-CPA	IND-CPA
Assumption	SSCDH	SSDDH	SSCDH	CSSDDH	CSSCDH	RCSSI	P-CSSDDH

by using quantum computers, isogeny-based cryptosystems are considered to be one potential type of post-quantum cryptosystem. In fact, Supersingular Isogeny Key Encapsulation (SIKE) [1] remained a candidate for the standardization of post-quantum cryptography in the NIST second-round competition [19].

There are some isogeny-based key encryption schemes. In 2011, Jao and De Feo proposed an isogeny-based key exchange scheme: Supersingular Isogeny Diffie-Hellman (SIDH) [10]. In 2018, Castryck, Lange, Martindale, Panny, and Renes proposed another isogeny-based key exchange scheme: Commutative Supersingular Isogeny Diffie-Hellman (CSIDH) [3]. Finally, in 2019, de Saint Guilhem, Kutas, Petit, and Javier proposed a public key encryption scheme: Supersingular Encryption from Torsion Attacks (SÉTA) [6]. As far as we know, these key encryptions require hash functions for IND-CPA security.

1.1   Our Results

One of our motivations in this paper is to construct secure schemes under a minimum assumption. Without using hash functions, we propose two new public key encryption schemes based on CSIDH: SiGamal and C-SiGamal. SiGamal is very similar to ElGamal encryption [8], while C-SiGamal is a compressed version of SiGamal. The bit length of a ciphertext in SiGamal is four times the bit length of the prime p in the setting, while the bit length of a ciphertext in C-SiGamal is twice the bit length of the prime p in the setting.

We define two new assumptions: the P-CSSCDH assumption (the Point-Commutative Supersingular Computational Diffie-Hellman assumption) and the P-CSSDDH assumption (the Point-Commutative Supersingular Decisional Diffie-Hellman assumption). These two assumptions come from the idea that it is hard to compute the image point of a given point under a hidden isogeny. The P-CSSCDH assumption is a computational assumption, and the P-CSSDDH assumption is a decisional assumption. We prove that, if the P-CSSCDH assumption holds, then SiGamal and C-SiGamal are OW-CPA secure; furthermore, if the P-CSSDDH assumption holds, then SiGamal and C-SiGamal are IND-CPA secure.

We summarize a comparison of isogeny-based public key encryption schemes in Table 1. Here, we regard SIDH and CSIDH as encryption schemes that use the simple XOR cipher. As shown in this table, only our proposed schemes can achieve IND-CPA security without using hash functions.

Next, we construct a new Naor-Reingold type pseudo random function (PRF) from SiGamal. This PRF is a post-quantum PRF. We prove that the pseudo randomness of this function is guaranteed from the P-CSSDDH and CSSDDH* assumptions. The CSSDDH* assumption guarantees the security of CSIDH that uses a prime p in the setting of SiGamal. This PRF needs to compute group actions many times. We estimate, by using approximations, that the computational costs of our proposed PRF are $\sqrt{\frac{8T}{3\pi}}$ times that of a group action in SiGamal, where T is the Hamming weight of the input of the PRF.

Finally, to evaluate the proposed key encryption schemes, we implemented group actions in SiGamal and C-SiGamal and measured their computational costs. In our experiment, the computational costs of group actions in SiGamal and C-SiGamal that send 256-bit plaintexts were about 2.62 times that of a group action in CSIDH-512. Furthermore, we implemented t times group actions to evaluate the proposed PRF. Our approximation was roughly correct.

Organization. We explain important mathematical concepts and algorithms in Sect. 2.1 to 2.4. We explain public key encryption in Sect. 2.5. In Sect. 2.6, we explain the PRF. Then, we propose SiGamal in Sect. 3 and C-SiGamal in Sect. 4. In Sect. 5, we propose a new isogeny-based PRF. In Sect. 6, we show our experimentation results, and in Sect. 7, we conclude this paper.

2 Preliminaries

2.1 Basic Mathematical Concepts

Here, we explain the basic mathematical concepts behind isogeny-based cryptography.

Elliptic Curves. Let $\mathbb{L}$ be a field, and let $\mathbb{L}'$ be an algebraic extension field of $\mathbb{L}$. First, an *elliptic curve* E defined over $\mathbb{L}$ is a nonsingular algebraic curve that is defined over $\mathbb{L}$ and has genus one. Denote by $E(\mathbb{L}')$ the $\mathbb{L}'$-rational points of the elliptic curve E. Here, $E(\mathbb{L}')$ is an abelian group [27, III. 2]. Next, a *supersingular elliptic curve* E over a finite field $\mathbb{L}$ of characteristic p is defined as an elliptic curve that satisfies $\#E(\mathbb{L}) \equiv 1 \pmod{p}$, where $\#E(\mathbb{L})$ is the cardinality of $E(\mathbb{L})$. Furthermore, let $\mathbb{L}$ be a field whose characteristic is odd. Then, an elliptic curve E defined by the following equation is called a *Montgomery curve*:

$$E: bY^2Z = X^3 + aX^2Z + XZ^2 \quad (a, b \in \mathbb{L} \text{ and } b(a^2 - 4) \neq 0).$$

Let E and E' be elliptic curves defined over $\mathbb{L}$. Define an *isogeny* $\phi: E \to E'$ over $\mathbb{L}'$ as a rational map over $\mathbb{L}'$ that is a non-zero group homomorphism from $E(\overline{\mathbb{L}})$ to $E'(\overline{\mathbb{L}})$, where $\overline{\mathbb{L}}$ is the algebraic closure of $\mathbb{L}$. A separable isogeny satisfying $\# \ker \phi = \ell$ is called an *ℓ-isogeny*. Denote by $\mathrm{End}_{\mathbb{L}'}(E)$ the endomorphism ring of E over $\mathbb{L}'$, and represent it as $\mathrm{End}_p(E)$ when $\mathbb{L}'$ is a prime field $\mathbb{F}_p$. Note also that an isogeny $\phi: E \to E'$ defined over $\mathbb{L}'$ is called an *isomorphism* over $\mathbb{L}'$ if it has the inverse isogeny over $\mathbb{L}'$.

If G is a finite subgroup of $E(\overline{\mathbb{L}})$, then there exists an isogeny $\phi\colon E \to E'$ such that its kernel is G and E' is unique up to an $\overline{\mathbb{L}}$-isomorphism [27, Proposition III.4.12]. This isogeny can be efficiently calculated by using Vélu formulas [29]. We denote a representative of E' by E/G.

Next, we define the *j-invariant* of a Montgomery curve $E\colon bY^2Z = X^3 + aX^2Z + XZ^2$ ($a, b \in \mathbb{L}$ and $b(a^2 - 4) \neq 0$) by the following equation:

$$j(E) := \frac{256(a^2 - 3)^3}{a^2 - 4}.$$

It is known that the j-invariants of two elliptic curves are the same if and only if the elliptic curves are $\overline{\mathbb{L}}$-isomorphic.

Finally, we define $E[k]$ ($k \in \mathbb{Z}_{>0}$) as the k-torsion subgroup of $E(\overline{\mathbb{L}})$. For an endomorphism ϕ of E, we sometimes denote $\ker \phi$ by $E[\phi]$.

Ideal Class Groups. Let $\mathbb{L}$ be a number field, and $\mathcal{O}$ be an order in $\mathbb{L}$. A *fractional ideal* $\mathfrak{a}$ of $\mathcal{O}$ is a non-zero $\mathcal{O}$-submodule of $\mathbb{L}$ that satisfies $\alpha\mathfrak{a} \subset \mathcal{O}$ for some $\alpha \in \mathcal{O} \setminus \{0\}$. Moreover, an *invertible fractional ideal* $\mathfrak{a}$ of $\mathcal{O}$ is defined as a fractional ideal of $\mathcal{O}$ that satisfies $\mathfrak{a}\mathfrak{b} = \mathcal{O}$ for some fractional ideal $\mathfrak{b}$ of $\mathcal{O}$. The fractional ideal $\mathfrak{b}$ can be represented as $\mathfrak{a}^{-1}$. If a fractional ideal $\mathfrak{a}$ is contained in $\mathcal{O}$, then it is called an *integral ideal* of $\mathcal{O}$. Let $J(\mathcal{O})$ be a set of integral ideals of $\mathcal{O}$.

Next, let $I(\mathcal{O})$ specifically be a set of invertible fractional ideals of $\mathcal{O}$. $I(\mathcal{O})$ is then an abelian group derived from the multiplication of ideals with the identity $\mathcal{O}$. Let $P(\mathcal{O})$ be a subgroup of $I(\mathcal{O})$ defined by $P(\mathcal{O}) = \{\mathfrak{a} \mid \mathfrak{a} = \alpha\mathcal{O} \text{ (for some } \alpha \in \mathbb{L}^{\times})\}$. We call the abelian group $\mathrm{cl}(\mathcal{O})$ defined by $I(\mathcal{O})/P(\mathcal{O})$ the *ideal class group* of $\mathcal{O}$. Denote by $[\mathfrak{a}]$ an element of $\mathrm{cl}(\mathcal{O})$ that is an equivalence class of $\mathfrak{a}$.

Notation. The $\mathbb{F}_p$-endomorphism ring $\mathrm{End}_p(E)$ of a supersingular elliptic curve E defined over $\mathbb{F}_p$ is isomorphic to an order in an imaginary quadratic field [7]. Denote by $\mathcal{Ell}_p(\mathcal{O})$ the set of $\mathbb{F}_p$-isomorphism classes of any elliptic curve E whose $\mathbb{F}_p$-endomorphism ring $\mathrm{End}_p(E)$ is isomorphic to $\mathcal{O}$.

2.2 Group Action of Ideal Class Group

In this subsection, we explain an important group action that is a main part of our proposed encryption system. First, Waterhouse gave the following theorem.

Theorem 1 ([30, Theorem 4.5]). *Let $\mathcal{O}$ be an order of an imaginary quadratic field and E be an elliptic curve defined over $\mathbb{F}_p$. If $\mathcal{Ell}_p(\mathcal{O})$ contains the $\mathbb{F}_p$-isomorphism class of supersingular elliptic curves, then the action of the ideal class group $\mathrm{cl}(\mathcal{O})$ on $\mathcal{Ell}_p(\mathcal{O})$,*

$$\mathrm{cl}(\mathcal{O}) \times \mathcal{Ell}_p(\mathcal{O}) \longrightarrow \mathcal{Ell}_p(\mathcal{O})$$
$$([\mathfrak{a}], E) \longmapsto E/E[\mathfrak{a}],$$

is free and transitive, where $\mathfrak{a}$ is an integral ideal of $\mathcal{O}$, and $E[\mathfrak{a}]$ is the intersection of the kernels of elements in $\mathfrak{a}$.

In general, we cannot efficiently compute the group action in Theorem 1. Castryck, Lange, Martindale, Panny, and Renes, however, proposed a method for computing this group action efficiently in a special case [3]. They focused on the action of $\mathrm{cl}(\mathbb{Z}[\pi_p])$ on $\mathcal{Ell}_p(\mathbb{Z}[\pi_p])$, where π_p is the p-Frobenius map over elliptic curves. In [3], they proved the following theorem.

Theorem 2 ([3, **Proposition 8**]). *Let p be a prime satisfying $p \equiv 3$ (mod 8). Let E be a supersingular elliptic curve defined over $\mathbb{F}_p$. Then, $\mathrm{End}_p(E) \cong \mathbb{Z}[\pi_p]$ holds if and only if there exists $a \in \mathbb{F}_p$ such that E is $\mathbb{F}_p$-isomorphic to a Montgomery curve $Y^2 Z = X^3 + aX^2 Z + XZ^2$, where π_p is the p-Frobenius map. Moreover, if such an a exists, then it is unique.*

In other words, a Montgomery curve that belongs to an $\mathbb{F}_p$-isomorphism class $E/E[\mathfrak{a}]$ is unique. Denote this Montgomery curve by $[\mathfrak{a}]E$.

Let the prime p be $4 \cdot \ell_1 \cdots \ell_n - 1$, where the $\ell_1, \ldots, \ell_n$ are small distinct odd primes. Let integral ideals $\mathfrak{l}_i$ $(i = 1, \ldots, n)$ in $\mathbb{Z}[\pi_p]$ be $(\ell_i, \pi_p - 1)$ and integral ideals $\overline{\mathfrak{l}_i}$ $(i = 1, \ldots, n)$ in $\mathbb{Z}[\pi_p]$ be $(\ell_i, \pi_p + 1)$. Because $\pi_p^2 + p = 0$ over supersingular elliptic curves defined over $\mathbb{F}_p$, it is easy to verify that $[\mathfrak{l}_i]^{-1} = [\overline{\mathfrak{l}_i}]$ over such elliptic curves. The actions of $[\mathfrak{l}_i]$ and $[\overline{\mathfrak{l}_i}]$ are efficiently computed by Theorem 1 and Vélu formulas on Montgomery curves [15]. Therefore, an action of $[\mathfrak{l}_1]^{e_1} \cdots [\mathfrak{l}_n]^{e_n} \in \mathrm{cl}(\mathbb{Z}[\pi_p])$ can be efficiently computed, where $e_1, \ldots, e_n$ are integers whose absolute values are small. According to the discussion in [3], from some heuristic assumptions, it holds that

$$\#\mathrm{cl}(\mathbb{Z}[\pi_p]) \approx \#\{[\mathfrak{l}_1]^{e_1} \cdots [\mathfrak{l}_n]^{e_n} \mid e_1, \ldots, e_n \in \{-m, \ldots, m\}\},$$

where m is the smallest number that satisfies $2m + 1 \geq \sqrt[2n]{p}$, and we call m a key bound. Therefore, it suffices to consider the action of $[\mathfrak{l}_1]^{e_1} \cdots [\mathfrak{l}_n]^{e_n}$, instead of the action of a random element of $\mathrm{cl}(\mathbb{Z}[\pi_p])$. Algorithm 1 specifies this sequence of group actions.

In this paper, we extend this computational method for our proposed scheme. In our scheme, we use a prime p that satisfies $p = 2^r \cdot \ell_1 \cdots \ell_n - 1$, where $r \geq 3$ and the $\ell_1, \ldots, \ell_n$ are small distinct odd primes. Therefore, we need the following theorem.

Theorem 3 ([2, **Proposition 3**]). *Let $p > 3$ be a prime that satisfies $p \equiv 3$ (mod 4), and let E be a supersingular elliptic curve defined over $\mathbb{F}_p$. If $\mathrm{End}_p(E) \cong \mathbb{Z}[\pi_p]$ holds, then there exists $a \in \mathbb{F}_p$ such that E is $\mathbb{F}_p$-isomorphic to $Y^2 Z = X^3 + aX^2 Z + X^2 Z$. Moreover, if such an a exists, then it is unique.*

From Theorem 3, even if we use a prime $p = 2^r \cdot \ell_1 \cdots \ell_n - 1$, we can compute the action of $\mathrm{cl}(\mathbb{Z}[\pi_p])$ in the same way as that proposed in [3] (*i.e.*, Algorithm 1).

Moreover, we consider mapping points in E to $[\mathfrak{a}]E$ by an isogeny whose kernel is $E[\mathfrak{a}]$. Because we use isogenies to compute $[\mathfrak{a}]E$, it is easy to map a point $P \in E$ to $[\mathfrak{a}]E$. In general, however, the image of P is not unique since

Algorithm 1. Evaluation of a class group action [3]

Input: $a \in \mathbb{F}_p$ such that $E\colon Y^2 Z = X^3 + aX^2 Z + XZ^2$ is supersingular, and a list of integers $(e_1, \ldots, e_n)$

Output: A Montgomery coefficient of $[\mathfrak{l}_1^{e_1} \cdots \mathfrak{l}_n^{e_n}]E$

1: **while** some $e_i \neq 0$ **do**
2:     Sample a random $x \in \mathbb{F}_p$
3:     $x(P) \leftarrow x$
4:     Set $s \leftarrow +1$ if $x^3 + ax^2 + x$ is a square in $\mathbb{F}_p$, else $s \leftarrow -1$
5:     Let $S = \{i \mid \text{sign}(e_i) = s\}$
6:     **if** $S = \emptyset$ **then**
7:         Go to line 2
8:     **end if**
9:     $k \leftarrow \prod_{i \in S} \ell_i$, $x(P) \leftarrow x(((p+1)/k)P)$
10:    **for all** $i \in S$ **do**
11:        $x(Q) \leftarrow x((k/\ell_i)P)$
12:        **if** $Q \neq (0:1:0)$ **then**
13:            Compute an ℓ_i-isogeny $\phi\colon E_a \rightarrow E_{a'}$ with $\ker \phi = \langle Q \rangle$
14:            $a \leftarrow a'$, $x(P) \leftarrow x(\phi(P))$, $k \leftarrow k/\ell_i$, $e_i \leftarrow e_i - s$
15:        **end if**
16:    **end for**
17: **end while**
18: **return** a

---

there are various isogenies $E \rightarrow [\mathfrak{a}]E$ whose kernels are $E[\mathfrak{a}]$. In particular, in general, the image of P over the isogeny $E \rightarrow [\mathfrak{a}]E \rightarrow [\mathfrak{a}][\mathfrak{b}]E$ and that of P over the isogeny $E \rightarrow [\mathfrak{b}]E \rightarrow [\mathfrak{a}][\mathfrak{b}]E$ are not same. The following theorem guarantees that the image of P is unique up to $\{\pm 1\}$.

Theorem 4. *Let E be a supersingular elliptic curve defined over $\mathbb{F}_p$. Let $\Phi_{[\mathfrak{a}],(F)}$ denote an isogeny $\phi\colon F \rightarrow [\mathfrak{a}]F$ such that $\ker \phi = F[\mathfrak{a}]$. If the following isogenies are defined over $\mathbb{F}_p$, then they satisfy the following equations:*

$$\Phi_{[\mathfrak{b}],([\mathfrak{a}]E)} \circ \Phi_{[\mathfrak{a}],(E)} = [\pm 1] \circ \Phi_{[\mathfrak{a}],([\mathfrak{b}]E)} \circ \Phi_{[\mathfrak{b}],(E)}.$$

To prove Theorem 4, we need the following lemma.

Lemma 1. *Let E_1 and E_2 be supersingular elliptic curves defined over $\mathbb{F}_p$. Let G be a finite subgroup of $E_1(\overline{\mathbb{F}_p})$ defined over $\mathbb{F}_p$ (i.e., $\pi_p(G) = G$). Let $\phi\colon E_1 \rightarrow E_2$ and $\psi\colon E_1 \rightarrow E_2$ be separable isogenies defined over $\mathbb{F}_p$. If $\ker \phi = \ker \psi = G$, then $\phi = \psi$, or $\phi = [-1] \circ \psi$.*

Proof. From [9, Theorem 9.6.18], there are unique isogenies $\lambda_1\colon E_2 \rightarrow E_2$ and $\lambda_2\colon E_2 \rightarrow E_2$ defined over $\mathbb{F}_p$ such that $\psi = \lambda_1 \circ \phi$ and $\phi = \lambda_2 \circ \psi$. Furthermore, from the uniqueness of isogenies in [9, Theorem 9.6.18], it holds that $\lambda_1 = \lambda_2^{-1}$. Therefore, λ_2 is an automorphism of E_2 defined over $\mathbb{F}_p$.

Next, from [27, Theorem III.10.1], if $j(E_2) \neq 0$ and $j(E_2) \neq 1728$, then there are no automorphisms other than $[\pm 1]$. Therefore, we have $\lambda_2(x, y) = (x, \pm y) = $

$[\pm 1](x, y)$. Since E_2 is supersingular, if $j(E_2) = 0$, then $p \equiv 2 \pmod 3$, and if $j(E_2) = 1728$, then $p \equiv 3 \pmod 4$. Therefore, from [27, Theorem III.10.1], even if $j(E_2) = 0$ or $j(E_2) = 1728$, there are no automorphisms defined over $\mathbb{F}_p$ other than $[\pm 1]$, and we have $\lambda_2(x, y) = (x, \pm y) = [\pm 1](x, y)$. □

Now, we can prove Theorem 4.

Proof of Theorem 4. From Lemma 1, it suffices to show that

$$\ker\left(\Phi_{[\mathfrak{b}],([\mathfrak{a}]E)} \circ \Phi_{[\mathfrak{a}],(E)}\right) = \ker\left(\Phi_{[\mathfrak{a}],([\mathfrak{b}]E)} \circ \Phi_{[\mathfrak{b}],(E)}\right).$$

Indeed, this holds from [30, Proposition 3.12]. □

As shown above, the image of $P \in E$ under the isogeny defined by the integral ideal $\mathfrak{a}$ in $\mathrm{End}(E)$ is unique up to $[\pm 1]$. We denote this equivalence class of two points by $\mathfrak{a}P$. Note that, even if $[\mathfrak{a}] = [\mathfrak{a}']$, it does not always hold that $\mathfrak{a}P = \mathfrak{a}'P$. In fact, when $[\mathfrak{a}][\bar{\mathfrak{a}}] = [1]$, we have $\mathfrak{a}\bar{\mathfrak{a}}P = N(\mathfrak{a})P$, where $N(\mathfrak{a})$ is the norm of $\mathfrak{a}$.

All elements of $J(\mathbb{Z}[\pi_p])$ appearing in this paper are defined by $(\alpha)\mathfrak{l}_1^{e_1} \cdots \mathfrak{l}_n^{e_n}$, where α is an integer. An equivalence class $(\alpha)\mathfrak{l}_1^{e_1} \cdots \mathfrak{l}_n^{e_n} P$ is a class of images of αP under the isogeny defined by $\mathfrak{l}_1^{e_1} \cdots \mathfrak{l}_n^{e_n}$.

2.3 CSIDH

CSIDH (Commutative Supersingular Isogeny Diffie-Hellman) is a Diffie-Hellman-type key exchange scheme [3]. It is based on actions of the ideal class group $\mathrm{cl}(\mathbb{Z}[\pi_p])$ on $\mathcal{Ell}_p(\mathbb{Z}[\pi_p])$.

The exact scheme is as follows. Suppose that Alice and Bob want to share a shared key denoted by $\mathrm{SK}_{\mathrm{shared}}$.

Setup. Let p be a prime that satisfies $p = 4 \cdot \ell_1 \cdots \ell_n - 1$, where $\ell_1, \ldots, \ell_n$ are small distinct odd primes. Then, let p and $E_0 : Y^2 Z = X^3 + XZ^2$ be public parameters.

Key generation. Randomly choose an integer vector $(e_1, \ldots, e_n)$ from $\{-m, \ldots, m\}^n$. Define $[\mathfrak{a}] = [\mathfrak{l}_1^{e_1} \cdots \mathfrak{l}_n^{e_n}] \in \mathrm{cl}(\mathbb{Z}[\pi_p])$. Then, calculate the action of $[\mathfrak{a}]$ on E_0 and the Montgomery coefficient $a \in \mathbb{F}_p$ of $[\mathfrak{a}]E_0 : Y^2 Z = X^3 + aX^2 Z + XZ^2$. The integer vector $(e_1, \ldots, e_n)$ is the secret key, and $a \in \mathbb{F}_p$ is the public key.

Key exchange. Alice and Bob have pairs of keys, $([\mathfrak{a}], a)$ and $([\mathfrak{b}], b)$, respectively. Alice calculates the action $[\mathfrak{a}][\mathfrak{b}]E_0$. Bob calculates the action $[\mathfrak{b}][\mathfrak{a}]E_0$. Denote the Montgomery coefficient of $[\mathfrak{a}][\mathfrak{b}]E_0$ by $\mathrm{SK}_{\mathrm{Alice}}$ and that of $[\mathfrak{b}][\mathfrak{a}]E_0$ by $\mathrm{SK}_{\mathrm{Bob}}$.

From the commutativity of $\mathrm{cl}(\mathbb{Z}[\pi_p])$ and Theorem 2, $\mathrm{SK}_{\mathrm{Alice}} = \mathrm{SK}_{\mathrm{Bob}}$ holds. This value is the shared key $\mathrm{SK}_{\mathrm{shared}}$.

CSIDH is secure under the following assumption.

Definition 1 (Commutative Supersingular Decisional Diffie-Hellman assumption (CSSDDH assumption)). *Let p be a prime that satisfies $p = 4 \cdot \ell_1 \cdots \ell_n - 1$, where $\ell_1, \ldots \ell_n$ are small distinct odd primes. Let E_0 be the elliptic* *curve* $Y^2Z = X^3 + XZ^2$ *and* $[\mathfrak{a}]$, $[\mathfrak{b}]$, *and* $[\mathfrak{c}]$ *be random elements of* $\mathrm{cl}(\mathbb{Z}[\pi_p])$. *Set* λ *as the bit length of* p.

The CSSDDH assumption holds if, for any efficient algorithm (e.g., any probabilistic polynomial time (PPT) algorithm) $\mathcal{A}$,

$$\left| \Pr \left[b = b^* \left| \begin{array}{l} [\mathfrak{a}], [\mathfrak{b}], [\mathfrak{c}] \leftarrow \mathrm{cl}(\mathbb{Z}[\pi_p]), \ b \xleftarrow{\$} \{0,1\}, \\ F_0 := [\mathfrak{a}][\mathfrak{b}]E_0, \ F_1 := [\mathfrak{c}]E_0, \\ b^* \leftarrow \mathcal{A}(E_0, [\mathfrak{a}]E_0, [\mathfrak{b}]E_0, F_b) \end{array} \right. \right] - \frac{1}{2} \right| < \mathrm{negl}(\lambda).$$

Remark 1. In the above definition, we sample elements of $\mathrm{cl}(\mathbb{Z}[\pi_p])$ by taking $(e_1, \ldots, e_n)$ uniformly from $\{-m, \ldots, m\}^n$ that represents $[\mathfrak{l}_1^{e_1} \cdots \mathfrak{l}_n^{e_n}] \in \mathrm{cl}(\mathbb{Z}[\pi_p])$. This is not a uniform sampling method from $\mathrm{cl}(\mathbb{Z}[\pi_p])$. For instance, refer to [21].

2.4 Pohlig-Hellman Algorithm [23]

Pohlig and Hellman proposed an algorithm in 1978 to solve the discrete logarithm problem [23]. The Pohlig-Hellman algorithm indicates that, if a cyclic group G has smooth order, then the discrete logarithm problem over G can be efficiently solved. In this subsection, we explain this algorithm to solve the discrete logarithm problem over $\mathbb{Z}/2^r\mathbb{Z}$.

Let μ be an element of $\mathbb{Z}/2^r\mathbb{Z}$, and P be a generator of $\mathbb{Z}/2^r\mathbb{Z}$. Let $\mu_0, \ldots, \mu_{r-1}$ be numbers in $\{0,1\}$ that satisfy $\mu = \sum_{j=0}^{r-1} \mu_j 2^j$. For given P and μP, we want to compute μ efficiently.

Step 0: First, we compute $2^{r-1} \cdot \mu P$. If $\mu_0 = 0$, then $2^{r-1} \cdot \mu P = 0$, while if $\mu_0 = 1$, then $2^{r-1} \cdot \mu P \neq 0$. Therefore, we can obtain the value of μ_0 by computing $2^{r-1} \cdot \mu P$.

Step i ($1 \leq i \leq r-1$): Define $\mu^{(i)} = \mu - \sum_{j=0}^{i-1} \mu_j 2^j$. From the definition of $\mu_0, \ldots, \mu_{r-1}$, it is clearly true that $\mu^{(i)} = \sum_{j=i}^{r-1} \mu_j 2^j$. We thus compute $\mu^{(i)} P = \mu P - \sum_{j=0}^{i-1} \mu_j 2^j P$. Furthermore, we compute $2^{r-i-1} \cdot \mu^{(i)} P$. If $\mu_i = 0$, then $2^{r-i-1} \cdot \mu^{(i)} P = 0$, while if $\mu_i = 1$, then $2^{r-i-1} \cdot \mu^{(i)} P \neq 0$. Therefore, we can obtain the value of μ_i by computing $2^{r-i-1} \cdot \mu^{(i)} P$.

As a result, from the $r-1$ steps above, we obtain the value of μ.

Algorithm 2 is the Pohlig-Hellman algorithm for points in Montgomery curves.

2.5 Public Key Encryption

In this subsection, we introduce the definition and security of public key encryption.

Algorithm 2. The Pohlig-Hellman algorithm for Montgomery curves

---

Input: $a \in \mathbb{F}_p$ such that $E: Y^2 Z = X^3 + aX^2 Z + XZ^2$ is supersingular, and x-coordinates of points $P, Q \in E$ that have order 2^r and satisfy $Q \in \langle P \rangle$

Output: μ or $2^r - \mu$ such that $P = \mu Q$

1: $x(P_0) \leftarrow x(P)$
2: $x(Q_0) \leftarrow x(Q)$
3: **for all** $i \in \{1, \dots, r-2\}$ **do**
4:      $x(P_i) \leftarrow x(2P_{i-1})$
5:      $x(Q_i) \leftarrow x(2Q_{i-1})$
6: **end for**
7: $M \leftarrow 1$
8: **for all** $i \in \{2, \dots, r-1\}$ **do**
9:      $x(R) \leftarrow x(MQ_{r-i})$
10:     **if** $x(P_{r-i}) \neq x(R)$ **then**
11:         $M \leftarrow M + 2^i$
12:     **end if**
13: **end for**
14: **return** M

Definition of Public Key Encryption

Definition 2 (Public key encryption (PKE)). *An algorithm $\mathcal{P}(\lambda)$ is called a public key encryption scheme (i.e., a PKE scheme) if it consists of the following algorithms that can be computed efficiently (e.g., PPT algorithms):* KeyGen, Enc, Dec.

KeyGen: *Given a security parameter λ as input, output public keys* **pk**, *secret keys* **sk**, *and a plaintext message space $\mathcal{M}$.*
Enc: *Given a plaintext $\mu \in \mathcal{M}$ and* **pk**, *output a ciphertext c.*
Dec: *Given c and* **sk**, *output a plaintext $\tilde{\mu}$.*

Definition 3 (Correctness). *If a public key encryption scheme $\mathcal{P}(\lambda)$ holds for any plaintexts μ, i.e.,*

$$\mathsf{Dec}(\mathsf{Enc}(\mu, \mathbf{pk}), \mathbf{sk}) = \mu,$$

then $\mathcal{P}(\lambda)$ is correct.

Security of Public Key Encryption. Here, we introduce some security definitions.

Definition 4 (OW-CPA security). *Let $\mathcal{P}$ be a public key encryption with a plaintext message space $\mathcal{M}$. We say that $\mathcal{P}$ is OW-CPA secure if, for any efficient adversary $\mathcal{A}$,*

$$\Pr\left[\mu = \mu^* \;\middle|\; \begin{array}{l} (\mathbf{pk}, \mathbf{sk}) \leftarrow \mathsf{KeyGen}(\lambda),\ \mu \xleftarrow{\$} \mathcal{M}, \\ c \leftarrow \mathsf{Enc}(\mathbf{pk}, \mu),\ \mu^* \leftarrow \mathcal{A}(\mathbf{pk}, c) \end{array}\right] < \mathrm{negl}(\lambda),$$

where $\mu \xleftarrow{\$} \mathcal{M}$ means that μ is uniformly and randomly sampled from $\mathcal{M}$.

Definition 5 (IND-CPA security). *Let $\mathcal{P}$ be a public key encryption with a plaintext message space $\mathcal{M}$. We say that $\mathcal{P}$ is IND-CPA secure if, for any efficient adversary $\mathcal{A}$,*

$$\left| \Pr\left[b = b^* \;\middle|\; \begin{array}{l} (\mathbf{pk}, \mathbf{sk}) \leftarrow \mathsf{KeyGen}(\lambda), \; \mu_0, \mu_1 \leftarrow \mathcal{A}(\mathbf{pk}), \\ b \xleftarrow{\$} \{0,1\}, \; c \leftarrow \mathsf{Enc}(\mathbf{pk}, \mu_b), \\ b^* \leftarrow \mathcal{A}(\mathbf{pk}, c) \end{array} \right] - \frac{1}{2} \right| < \mathrm{negl}(\lambda).$$

Definition 6 (IND-CCA security). *Let $\mathcal{P}$ be a public key encryption with a plaintext message space $\mathcal{M}$. We say that $\mathcal{P}$ is IND-CCA secure if, for any efficient adversary $\mathcal{A}$,*

$$\left| \Pr\left[b = b^* \;\middle|\; \begin{array}{l} (\mathbf{pk}, \mathbf{sk}) \leftarrow \mathsf{KeyGen}(\lambda), \; \mu_0, \mu_1 \leftarrow \mathcal{A}^{O(\cdot)}(\mathbf{pk}), \\ b \xleftarrow{\$} \{0,1\}, \; c \leftarrow \mathsf{Enc}(\mathbf{pk}, \mu_b), \\ b^* \leftarrow \mathcal{A}^{O(\cdot)}(\mathbf{pk}, c) \end{array} \right] - \frac{1}{2} \right| < \mathrm{negl}(\lambda),$$

where $O(\cdot)$ is a decryption oracle that outputs $\mathsf{Dec}(\mathbf{sk}, c^*)$ for all $c^* \neq c$.

Natural ElGamal-Like PKE Based on CSIDH. We explain a natural way of constructing a PKE based on CSIDH without using hash functions.

KeyGen: Let p be a prime that satisfies $p = 4 \cdot \ell_1 \cdots \ell_n - 1$, where $\ell_1, \ldots, \ell_n$ are small distinct odd primes. Let E_0 be an elliptic curve $Y^2 Z = X^3 + X Z^2$. Alice takes random integers $e_1, \ldots, e_n$, defines $[\mathfrak{a}] = [\mathfrak{l}_1^{e_1} \cdots \mathfrak{l}_n^{e_n}] \in \mathrm{cl}(\mathbb{Z}[\pi_p])$, and then computes $E_1 := [\mathfrak{a}] E_0$. Alice publishes (E_0, E_1) as public keys and keeps $(e_1, \ldots, e_n)$ as a secret key. Let $\{0,1\}^{\log_2 p}$ be a plaintext message space $\mathcal{M}$.

Enc: Let μ be a plaintext in $\mathcal{M}$. Bob takes random integers $e_1', \ldots, e_n'$, defines $[\mathfrak{b}] = [\mathfrak{l}_1^{e_1'} \cdots \mathfrak{l}_n^{e_n'}]$ in $\mathrm{cl}(\mathbb{Z}[\pi_p])$, and computes a point $E_3 := [\mathfrak{b}] E_0$, $E_4 := [\mathfrak{b}] E_1$. Let the Montgomery coefficient of E_4 be S. Then, Bob computes $c := \mu \oplus S$ and sends (E_3, c) to Alice as a ciphertext.

Dec: Alice computes $[\mathfrak{a}] E_3$ and gets the Montgomery coefficient of $[\mathfrak{a}] E_3$, which is S. Alice then computes $c \oplus S$ as a plaintext.

It is trivial that $c \oplus S = \mu$, and this key encryption scheme is thus correct.

Theorem 5. *This key exchange scheme is not IND-CPA secure.*

Proof. Let (E_3, c) be a ciphertext of a plaintext μ_b, where $b = 0, 1$. An adversary $\mathcal{A}$ computes $\mu_0 \oplus c$ and $\mu_1 \oplus c$. Note that the probability that a random elliptic curve defined over $\mathbb{F}_p$ becomes supersingular is exponentially small. If $\mu_{b'} \oplus c$ represents a supersingular elliptic curve, then $b = b'$ holds with high probability. Therefore, $\mathcal{A}$ can guess b, and the scheme is not IND-CPA secure. □

By using an entropy-smoothing hash function H, however, we can construct an IND-CPA secure scheme under the CSSDDH assumption (Definition 1). In this scheme, the ciphertext is $(E_3, \mu \oplus H(S))$ instead of $(E_3, \mu \oplus S)$. Refer to [26, §3.4] for the details.

2.6   Pseudo Random Function

In this subsection, we explain the pseudo random function (PRF).

Definition of PRF. Below is the definition of the basic PRF.

Definition 7 (Pseudo random functions). *Let $f^{(s)} \colon \{0,1\}^t \to \{0,1\}^{t'}$ be a function indexed by $s \in S_{\mathrm{Key}}$, where S_{Key} is a set of keys. A family of functions $\mathcal{F} = \{f^{(s)} \mid s \in S_{\mathrm{Key}}\}$ is called a pseudo random function family if it satisfies two properties:*

1. *There is an efficient algorithm to compute $f_s(x)$ from given s and x.*
2. *For any efficient adversary $\mathcal{A}$ that makes $\mathrm{poly}(\lambda)$ queries to the oracle,*

$$\left| \Pr\left[b = b^* \;\middle|\; \begin{array}{l} b \xleftarrow{\$} \{0,1\}, \ \mathbf{pk} \xleftarrow{\$} S_{\mathrm{PubKey}}, \\ f_0 \xleftarrow{\$} \mathcal{F}, \ f_1 \xleftarrow{\$} \mathcal{R}, \ b^* \leftarrow \mathcal{A}^{f_b(\cdot)}(\mathbf{pk}) \end{array} \right] - \frac{1}{2} \right| < \mathrm{negl}(\lambda),$$

where $\mathcal{R}$ is a set of functions mapping from $\{0,1\}^t$ to $\{0,1\}^{t'}$, λ is a bit length of p, and S_{PubKey} is a set of public keys.

Naor-Reingold PRF. Naor and Reingold proposed an efficient PRF under the Decisional Diffie-Hellman assumption (DDH assumption) [18].

Definition 8 (Naor-Reingold PRF). *Let p be a prime, let q be a prime divisor of $p - 1$ that satisfies $p \approx q$, and let g be an element of $(\mathbb{F}_p)^\times$ whose order is q. The set $\{p, q, g\}$ is a public key. Take $a_0, \dots, a_t$ from $(\mathbb{F}_q)^\times$ as secret keys. Define a function $f_{\{a_0,\dots,a_t\}} \colon \{0,1\}^t \to \langle g \rangle$:*

$$f_{\{a_0,\dots,a_t\}}((x_1,\dots,x_t)) := g^{a_0 \prod_{i=1}^{t} a_i^{x_i}}.$$

If the DDH assumption holds, this function is a PRF [18, Theorem 4.1], and it is called the Naor-Reingold PRF.

3   SiGamal

In this section, we explain the first proposed scheme: SiGamal.

3.1   Overview

The main idea of this scheme is to send plaintexts by using isogenies. Alice publishes (E_0, P_0), where E_0 is an elliptic curve, and P_0 is a point of E_0. Bob computes an isogeny $\phi \colon E_0 \to E_0'$ and a point $\mu\phi(P_0)$, where μ is a plaintext. If Alice can learn $\phi(P_0)$ in some way, then she gets μ by solving the discrete logarithm problem.

Algorithm 3. Evaluation of a class group action with a point P_0

Input: $a \in \mathbb{F}_p$ such that $E\colon Y^2 Z = X^3 + aX^2 Z + XZ^2$ is supersingular, the x-coordinate of a point P_0 of E, and a list of integers $(\alpha, e_1, \ldots, e_n)$

Output: A Montgomery coefficient of $[\mathfrak{l}_1^{e_1} \cdots \mathfrak{l}_n^{e_n}]E$, and the x-coordinate of $(\alpha)\mathfrak{l}_1^{e_1} \cdots \mathfrak{l}_n^{e_n} P_0$

1: $P_0 \leftarrow \alpha P_0$
2: **while** some $e_i \neq 0$ **do**
3:     Sample a random $x \in \mathbb{F}_p$
4:     $x(P) \leftarrow x$
5:     Set $s \leftarrow +1$ if $x^3 + ax^2 + x$ is a square in $\mathbb{F}_p$, else $s \leftarrow -1$
6:     Let $S = \{i \mid \operatorname{sign}(e_i) = s\}$
7:     **if** $S = \emptyset$ **then**
8:         Go to line 2
9:     **end if**
10:     $k \leftarrow \prod_{i \in S} \ell_i$, $x(P) \leftarrow x(((p+1)/k)P)$
11:     **for all** $i \in S$ **do**
12:         $x(Q) \leftarrow x((k/\ell_i)P)$
13:         **if** $Q \neq (0:1:0)$ **then**
14:             Compute an ℓ_i-isogeny $\phi\colon E_a \to E_{a'}$ with $\ker \phi = \langle Q \rangle$
15:             $a \leftarrow a'$, $x(P) \leftarrow x(\phi(P))$, $k \leftarrow k/\ell_i$, $x(P_0) \leftarrow x(\phi(P_0))$, $e_i \leftarrow e_i - s$
16:         **end if**
17:     **end for**
18: **end while**
19: **return** $a, x(P_0)$

SiGamal achieves this in a similar way to ElGamal encryption [8]. The main diagram of SiGamal is as follows.

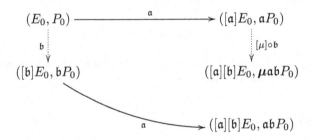

3.2   Encryption Scheme of SiGamal

In this subsection, we explain the scheme of SiGamal in precise detail.

KeyGen: Let p be a prime that satisfies $p = 2^r \cdot \ell_1 \cdots \ell_n - 1$, where $\ell_1, \ldots, \ell_n$ are small distinct odd primes. Let E_0 be the elliptic curve $Y^2 Z = X^3 + XZ^2$, and P_0 be a random point in $E_0(\mathbb{F}_p)$ of order 2^r. Alice takes random integers $\alpha, e_1, \ldots, e_n$, defines $\mathfrak{a} = (\alpha)\mathfrak{l}_1^{e_1} \cdots \mathfrak{l}_n^{e_n} \in J(\mathbb{Z}[\pi_p])$, and computes $E_1 := [\mathfrak{a}]E_0$ and $P_1 := \mathfrak{a}P_0$, where α is a uniformly random element of $(\mathbb{Z}/2^r\mathbb{Z})^\times$.

Alice then publishes (E_0, P_0) and (E_1, P_1) as public keys, and she keeps $(\alpha, e_1, \ldots, e_n)$ as a secret key. Let $\{0, 1\}^{r-2}$ be a plaintext message space.

Enc: Let $\mu \in \{0, 1\}^{r-2}$ be a plaintext. Bob embeds μ in $(\mathbb{Z}/2^r\mathbb{Z})^\times$ via $\mu \mapsto 2\mu + 1 \in (\mathbb{Z}/2^r\mathbb{Z})^\times$. Bob takes random integers $\beta, e_1', \ldots, e_n'$ and defines $\mathfrak{b} = (\beta)\mathfrak{l}_1^{e_1'} \cdots \mathfrak{l}_n^{e_n'} \in J(\mathbb{Z}[\pi_p])$, where β is a uniformly random element of $(\mathbb{Z}/2^r\mathbb{Z})^\times$. Next, Bob computes $(2\mu + 1)P_1$, $E_3 := [\mathfrak{b}]E_0$, $P_3 := \mathfrak{b}P_0$, $E_4 := [\mathfrak{b}]E_1$, and $P_4 := \mathfrak{b}((2\mu + 1)P_1)$. Bob then sends (E_3, P_3, E_4, P_4) to Alice as a ciphertext.

Dec: Alice computes $\mathfrak{a}P_3$ and solves the discrete logarithm problem over $\mathbb{Z}/2^r\mathbb{Z}$ for $\mathfrak{a}P_3$ and P_4 by using the Pohlig-Hellman algorithm. Let M be the solution of this computation. If the most significant bit of M is 1, then Alice changes M to $2^r - M$. Finally, Alice computes $(M - 1)/2$ as a plaintext $\tilde{\mu}$.

Remark 2. In the above scheme, any point is described by its x-coordinate. For instance, to be precise, Bob sends $(E_3, x(P_3), E_4, x(P_4))$ to Alice.

Remark 3. For computing a group action, we use Algorithm 3.

Remark 4. In this paper, we construct SiGamal based on CSIDH key exchange [3]. Similarly, we can construct SiGamal based on SIDH key exchange [10] according to [13]. In that case, we take a prime p satisfying $p = 2^r 3^{e_A} 5^{e_B} - 1$, where $3^{e_A} \approx 5^{e_B}$.

Moreover, we can construct SiGamal based on CSURF [2]. In the CSURF algorithm, we need to compute 2-isogenies. Therefore, we embed a plaintext μ in a subgroup of order ℓ^r, where ℓ is an odd prime.

Theorem 6. *SiGamal is correct.*

Proof. By Theorem 4, $\mathfrak{a}P_3$ is $\mathfrak{b}P_1$ or $-\mathfrak{b}P_1$. Therefore, Alice gets $2\mu + 1$ or $2^r - (2\mu + 1)$. Since the bit length of μ is less than $r - 2$, the most significant bit of $2\mu + 1$ is always 0. Thus, if the most significant bit of M is 1, then $M = 2^r - (2\mu + 1)$. Therefore, after adjusting this, Alice gets $2\mu + 1$ as M. Hence, $\tilde{\mu} = \mu$, and SiGamal is correct. $\square$

3.3   Security of SiGamal

In this subsection, we prove the security of SiGamal.

First, we define new assumptions: the P-CSSCDH assumption and the P-CSSDDH assumption. These assumptions are based on the idea that it is hard to compute the image of a fixed point under a hidden isogeny. In [6,28], problems of computing images over isogenies in SIDH settings are considered hard to solve. Petit provided a method for computing an isogeny between two given elliptic curves in an SIDH setting by using image points of sufficiently large degree under the isogeny [22]. Because the isogeny problem is hard, the problem of computing image points in the SIDH setting is considered hard. When we translate these problems into those in the CSIDH setting, the P-CSSCDH assumption and the P-CSSDDH assumption are one of natural constructions of assumptions. Therefore, we consider these new assumptions below to be correct.

Definition 9 (Points-Commutative Supersingular Isogeny Computational Diffie-Hellman assumption (P-CSSCDH assumption)). *Let p be a prime that satisfies $p = 2^r \cdot \ell_1 \cdots \ell_n - 1$, where $\ell_1, \ldots \ell_n$ are small distinct odd primes. Let E_0 be the elliptic curve $Y^2 Z = X^3 + X Z^2$, P_0 be a uniformly random point in $E_0(\mathbb{F}_p)$ of order 2^r, and $\mathfrak{a}$ and $\mathfrak{b}$ be random elements of $J(\mathbb{Z}[\pi_p])$. Set λ as the bit length of p.*

The P-CSSCDH assumption holds if, for any efficient algorithm $\mathcal{A}$,

$$\Pr\left[\; \mathfrak{a}\mathfrak{b}P_0 = P^* \;\middle|\; \begin{array}{l} P_0 \xleftarrow{\$} E_0(\mathbb{F}_p)_{\text{order } 2^r}, \; \mathfrak{a}, \mathfrak{b} \leftarrow J(\mathbb{Z}[\pi_p]), \\ P^* \leftarrow \mathcal{A}(E_0, P_0, [\mathfrak{a}]E_0, \mathfrak{a}P_0, [\mathfrak{b}]E_0, \mathfrak{b}P_0, [\mathfrak{a}][\mathfrak{b}]E_0) \end{array} \right] < \text{negl}(\lambda).$$

Definition 10 (Points-Commutative Supersingular Isogeny Decisional Diffie-Hellman assumption (P-CSSDDH assumption)). *Let p be a prime that satisfies $p = 2^r \cdot \ell_1 \cdots \ell_n - 1$, where $\ell_1, \ldots \ell_n$ are small distinct odd primes. Let E_0 be the elliptic curve $Y^2 Z = X^3 + X Z^2$, P_0 be a uniformly random point in $E_0(\mathbb{F}_p)$ of order 2^r, and $\mathfrak{a}$ and $\mathfrak{b}$ be random elements of $J(\mathbb{Z}[\pi_p])$ whose norms are odd. Furthermore, let Q be a uniformly random point of order 2^r in $([\mathfrak{a}][\mathfrak{b}]E_0)(\mathbb{F}_p)$. Set λ as the bit length of p.*

The P-CSSDDH assumption holds if, for any efficient algorithm $\mathcal{A}$,

$$\left| \Pr\left[\; b = b^* \;\middle|\; \begin{array}{l} P_0 \xleftarrow{\$} E_0(\mathbb{F}_p)_{\text{order } 2^r}, \; \mathfrak{a}, \mathfrak{b} \leftarrow J(\mathbb{Z}[\pi_p]), \; b \xleftarrow{\$} \{0,1\}, \\ Q \xleftarrow{\$} ([\mathfrak{a}][\mathfrak{b}]E_0)(\mathbb{F}_p)_{\text{order } 2^r}, \; R_0 := \mathfrak{a}\mathfrak{b}P_0, \; R_1 := Q, \\ b^* \leftarrow \mathcal{A}(E_0, P_0, [\mathfrak{a}]E_0, \mathfrak{a}P_0, [\mathfrak{b}]E_0, \mathfrak{b}P_0, [\mathfrak{a}][\mathfrak{b}]E_0, R_b) \end{array} \right] - \frac{1}{2} \right| < \text{negl}(\lambda).$$

Remark 5. An equivalence class $\mathfrak{a}\mathfrak{b}P_0$ is uniquely determined from

$$E_0, P_0, [\mathfrak{a}]E_0, \mathfrak{a}P_0, [\mathfrak{b}]E_0, \mathfrak{b}P_0, [\mathfrak{a}][\mathfrak{b}]E_0.$$

Now, we prove this fact.

Let $\mathfrak{a}$, $\mathfrak{a}'$, $\mathfrak{b}$, and $\mathfrak{b}'$ be elements of $J(\mathbb{Z}[\pi_p])$ such that $[\mathfrak{a}] = [\mathfrak{a}']$, $[\mathfrak{b}] = [\mathfrak{b}']$, $\mathfrak{a}P_0 = \mathfrak{a}'P_0$, $\mathfrak{b}P_0 = \mathfrak{b}'P_0$, and the norms of $\mathfrak{a}$, $\mathfrak{a}'$, $\mathfrak{b}$, and $\mathfrak{b}'$ are coprime to the order of P_0. Now, we prove that $\mathfrak{a}\mathfrak{b}P_0 = \mathfrak{a}'\mathfrak{b}'P_0$. From the definition of an ideal class group, there exist $\alpha, \beta \in \mathbb{Q}(\pi_p)^\times$ such that $\mathfrak{a} = \mathfrak{a}'\alpha$ and $\mathfrak{b} = \mathfrak{b}'\beta$. Then, $\alpha(P_0) = \pm P_0$ holds because the norms of $\mathfrak{a}$ and $\mathfrak{a}'$ are coprime to the order of P_0, and $\mathfrak{a}P_0 = \mathfrak{a}'P_0$. Similarly, $\beta(P_0) = \pm P_0$. Therefore, $\mathfrak{a}\mathfrak{b}P_0 = \mathfrak{a}'\mathfrak{b}'\alpha\beta P_0 = \mathfrak{a}'\mathfrak{b}'P_0$.

Remark 6. In the above definitions, we sample elements of $J(\mathbb{Z}[\pi_p])$ by taking $(\alpha, e_1, \ldots, e_n)$ uniformly from $(\mathbb{Z}/2^r\mathbb{Z})^\times \times \{-m, \ldots, m\}^n$ that represents $\alpha \mathfrak{l}_1^{e_1} \cdots \mathfrak{l}_n^{e_n} \in J(\mathbb{Z}[\pi_p])$.

Next, we prove the security of SiGamal under the above assumptions.

Theorem 7. *If the P-CSSCDH assumption holds, then SiGamal is OW-CPA secure.*

Proof. Assume that SiGamal is not OW-CPA secure. In that case, there exists an efficient algorithm (adversary) $\mathcal{A}'$ that, with high probability, outputs a hidden plaintext μ from

$$(E_0, P_0, [a]E_0, aP_0), ([b]E_0, bP_0, [a][b]E_0, (2\mu + 1)abP_0).$$

Now, we construct a new algorithm $\mathcal{A}$ that outputs abP_0 from

$$(E_0, P_0), ([a]E_0, aP_0), ([b]E_0, bP_0), [a][b]E_0$$

with high probability (*i.e.*, $\omega\left(\frac{1}{\text{poly}(\lambda)}\right)$). Taking a random point Q of order 2^r from $[a][b]E_0$, we compute

$$\mu := \mathcal{A}'((E_0, P_0, [a]E_0, aP_0), ([b]E_0, bP_0, [a][b]E_0, Q)).$$

Here, $Q = (2\mu + 1)abP_0$ holds with high probability. Note that $2\mu + 1$ belongs to $(\mathbb{Z}/2^r\mathbb{Z})^\times$. From Q and μ, we compute $\frac{1}{2\mu+1}Q$. That is, algorithm $\mathcal{A}$ outputs $\frac{1}{2\mu+1}Q$, which is abP_0 with high probability.

It is clear that $\mathcal{A}$ is an efficient algorithm. Therefore, the P-CSSCDH assumption does not hold.   □

Theorem 8. *If the P-CSSDDH assumption holds, then SiGamal is IND-CPA secure.*

Proof. Assume that SiGamal is not IND-CPA secure. In that case, there exists an efficient algorithm (adversary) $\mathcal{A}'$ judging whether a given ciphertext was encrypted from μ_0 or μ_1. Denote the advantage of $\mathcal{A}'$ (*i.e.*, the left side of the inequality in Definition 5) by $\text{Adv}_{\mathcal{A}'}(\lambda)$. Note that $\text{Adv}_{\mathcal{A}'}(\lambda) = \omega\left(\frac{1}{\text{poly}(\lambda)}\right)$.

Now, we construct a new algorithm $\mathcal{A}$ that outputs b, with a probability of $\omega\left(\frac{1}{\text{poly}(\lambda)}\right) + \frac{1}{2}$, from

$$E_0, P_0, [a]E_0, aP_0, [b]E_0, bP_0, [a][b]E_0, R_b,$$

where $R_0 = abP_0$, and $R_1 = Q$. Taking $\tilde{b} \in \{0, 1\}$ uniformly at random, we compute $(2\mu_{\tilde{b}} + 1)R_b$. Let

$$b^* := \mathcal{A}'((E_0, P_0, [a]E_0, aP_0), ([b]E_0, bP_0, [a][b]E_0, (2\mu_{\tilde{b}} + 1)R_b)).$$

If $\tilde{b} = b^*$, then $\mathcal{A}$ outputs 0, while if $\tilde{b} \neq b^*$, $\mathcal{A}$ outputs 1.

Next, we discuss the probability that $\mathcal{A}$ outputs the correct b. If $b = 0$, then $b^* = \tilde{b}$ with a probability of $\text{Adv}_{\mathcal{A}'}(\lambda) + \frac{1}{2}$ or $-\text{Adv}_{\mathcal{A}'}(\lambda) + \frac{1}{2}$. If $b = 1$, then the adversary $\mathcal{A}'$ cannot get any information about $\mu_{\tilde{b}}$ since $(2\mu_{\tilde{b}} + 1)R_b$ is a uniformly random point. Therefore, if $b = 1$, $b^* \neq \tilde{b}$ with a probability of $\frac{1}{2}$. Consequently, the probability that $\mathcal{A}$ outputs the correct b is

$$\frac{1}{2}\left(\pm\text{Adv}_{\mathcal{A}'}(\lambda) + \frac{1}{2} + \frac{1}{2}\right) = \pm\frac{1}{2}\text{Adv}_{\mathcal{A}'}(\lambda) + \frac{1}{2} = \omega\left(\frac{1}{\text{poly}(\lambda)}\right) + \frac{1}{2}.$$

Therefore, as algorithm $\mathcal{A}$ is an efficient algorithm, the P-CSSDDH assumption does not hold.   □

Note that SiGamal is not IND-CCA secure, because anyone can easily compute a ciphertext of a plaintext $3\mu+1$: $([\mathfrak{b}]E_0, \mathfrak{b}P_0, [\mathfrak{b}]E_1, 3(2\mu+1)\mathfrak{b}P_1)$ from the ciphertext of a plaintext μ: $([\mathfrak{b}]E_0, \mathfrak{b}P_0, [\mathfrak{b}]E_1, (2\mu+1)\mathfrak{b}P_1)$.

Remark 7. In the SiGamal scheme, Bob can omit sending $[\mathfrak{a}][\mathfrak{b}]E_0$ in the ciphertext $([\mathfrak{b}]E_0, \mathfrak{b}P_0, [\mathfrak{a}][\mathfrak{b}]E_0, (2\mu+1)\mathfrak{a}\mathfrak{b}P_0)$. Note that Bob sends only the x-coordinate of $(2\mu+1)\mathfrak{a}\mathfrak{b}P_0$. When Bob omits sending $[\mathfrak{a}][\mathfrak{b}]E_0$, it is hard to compute the ciphertext of a plaintext $3\mu+1$ from that of a plaintext μ, because the elliptic curve $[\mathfrak{a}][\mathfrak{b}]E_0$ is hidden. The question of whether SiGamal with hidden $[\mathfrak{a}][\mathfrak{b}]E_0$ is IND-CCA secure is an open problem.

Remark 8. SiGamal is attacked by computing a group element $[\mathfrak{a}]$ from E_0 and $[\mathfrak{a}]E_0$. This method of attack is the same as that for CSIDH. Therefore, the security level of SiGamal is the same as that of CSIDH for the same security parameter.

4   C-SiGamal (Compressed-SiGamal)

In this section, we explain the second proposed scheme: C-SiGamal, which is a compressed version of SiGamal. The bit length of a ciphertext in C-SiGamal is half that of a ciphertext in SiGamal, but the scheme of C-SiGamal is a little bit more complicated than that of SiGamal.

4.1   Encryption Scheme of C-SiGamal

In this subsection, we explain the scheme of C-SiGamal in precise detail.

Let E be a supersingular elliptic curve $Y^2Z = X^3 + aX^2Z + XZ^2$. Let P_E be a point in E such that $P_E = \ell_1 \cdots \ell_n \tilde{P}_E$, where $\tilde{P}_E$ is the point in $E(\mathbb{F}_p)$ that has the largest x-coordinate in $\{-2, -3, \ldots, -p+1\}$ among points whose orders are divisible by 2^r. We use this point to construct C-SiGamal. The reason why we define $\tilde{P}_E$ as above is explained in Appendix A.

The scheme of C-SiGamal is as follows.

KeyGen: Let p be a prime that satisfies $p = 2^r \cdot \ell_1 \cdots \ell_n - 1$, where $\ell_1, \ldots, \ell_n$ are small distinct odd primes. Let E_0 be the elliptic curve $Y^2Z = X^3 + XZ^2$, and P_0 be a random point in $E_0(\mathbb{F}_p)$ of order 2^r. Alice takes random integers $\alpha, e_1, \ldots, e_n$, defines $\mathfrak{a} = (\alpha)\mathfrak{l}_1^{e_1} \cdots \mathfrak{l}_n^{e_n} \in J(\mathbb{Z}[\pi_p])$, and computes $E_1 := [\mathfrak{a}]E_0$ and $P_1 := \mathfrak{a}P_0$. Alice then publishes (E_0, P_0) and (E_1, P_1) as public keys, and keeps $(\alpha, e_1, \ldots, e_n)$ as a secret key. Let $\{0,1\}^{r-2}$ be a plaintext message space.

Enc: Let μ be a plaintext. Bob takes random integers $\beta, e'_1, \ldots, e'_n$, defines $\mathfrak{b} = (\beta)\mathfrak{l}_1^{e'_1} \cdots \mathfrak{l}_n^{e'_n}$ in $J(\mathbb{Z}[\pi_p])$, and computes $E_3 := [\mathfrak{b}]E_0$, $P_3 := \mathfrak{b}P_0$, $E_4 := [\mathfrak{b}]E_1$, and $P_4 := \mathfrak{b}P_1$. Bob computes $(2\mu+1)P_{E_4}$ and gets μ^* satisfying $(2\mu+1)P_{E_4} = \mu^*P_4$ by using the Pohlig-Hellman algorithm. Bob then computes $P'_3 := \mu^*P_3$ and sends (E_3, P'_3) to Alice as a ciphertext.

Dec: Alice computes $E_4 = [a]E_3$ and aP_3'. Alice then solves the discrete logarithm problem over $\mathbb{Z}/2^r\mathbb{Z}$ for aP_3' and P_{E_4} by using the Pohlig-Hellman algorithm. Let M be the solution of this computation. If the most significant bit of M is 1, then Alice changes M to $2^r - M$. Finally, Alice computes $(M-1)/2$ as a plaintext $\tilde{\mu}$.

The main diagram of C-SiGamal is as follows.

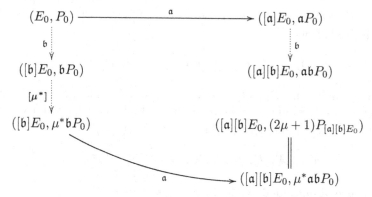

Theorem 9. *C-SiGamal is correct.*

Proof. The proof of this theorem is similar to that of Theorem 6.   □

4.2   Security of C-SiGamal

In this subsection, we prove the security of C-SiGamal.

Theorem 10. *If the P-CSSCDH assumption holds, then C-SiGamal is OW-CPA secure.*

Proof. Assume that C-SiGamal is not OW-CPA secure. In that case, there is an efficient algorithm (adversary) $\mathcal{A}'$ that, with high probability, outputs a hidden plaintext μ from

$$(E_0, P_0, [a]E_0, aP_0), ([b]E_0, \mu^*bP_0).$$

Now, we construct a new algorithm $\mathcal{A}$ that outputs abP_0 from

$$(E_0, P_0), ([a]E_0, aP_0), ([b]E_0, bP_0), [a][b]E_0$$

with high probability (*i.e.*, $\omega\left(\frac{1}{\text{poly}(\lambda)}\right)$). Taking a random element ν in $(\mathbb{Z}/2^r\mathbb{Z})^\times$ and the point $P_{[a][b]E_0}$ in $[a][b]E_0$, we compute

$$\mu := \mathcal{A}'((E_0, P_0, [a]E_0, aP_0), ([b]E_0, \nu bP_0)).$$

Here, $(2\mu+1)P_{[a][b]E_0} = \nu abP_0$ holds with high probability. Then, we compute $\frac{2\mu+1}{\nu}P_{[a][b]E_0}$. That is, algorithm $\mathcal{A}$ outputs $\frac{2\mu+1}{\nu}P_{[a][b]E_0}$, which is abP_0 with high probability.

It is clear that $\mathcal{A}$ is an efficient algorithm. Therefore, the P-CSSCDH assumption does not hold.   □

Theorem 11. *If the P-CSSDDH assumption holds, then C-SiGamal is IND-CPA secure.*

Proof. Assume that C-SiGamal is not IND-CPA secure. In that, there exists an efficient algorithm (adversary) $\mathcal{A}'$ judging whether a given ciphertext was encrypted from μ_0 or μ_1. Denote the advantage of $\mathcal{A}'$ (*i.e.*, the left side of the inequality in Definition 5) by $\mathrm{Adv}_{\mathcal{A}'}(\lambda)$. Note that $\mathrm{Adv}_{\mathcal{A}'}(\lambda) = \omega\left(\frac{1}{\mathrm{poly}(\lambda)}\right)$.

Now, we construct a new algorithm $\mathcal{A}$ that outputs b, with a probability of $\omega\left(\frac{1}{\mathrm{poly}(\lambda)}\right) + \frac{1}{2}$, from

$$E_0, P_0, [\mathfrak{a}]E_0, \mathfrak{a}P_0, [\mathfrak{b}]E_0, \mathfrak{b}P_0, [\mathfrak{a}][\mathfrak{b}]E_0, R_b,$$

where $R_0 = \mathfrak{a}\mathfrak{b}P_0$, and $R_1 = Q$. Taking the point $P_{[\mathfrak{a}][\mathfrak{b}]E_0}$ in $[\mathfrak{a}][\mathfrak{b}]E_0$ and $\tilde{b} \in \{0,1\}$ uniformly at random, we compute a point $(2\mu_{\tilde{b}} + 1)R_b$ and a value $\mu_{\tilde{b}}^* \in (\mathbb{Z}/2^r\mathbb{Z})^\times$ such that $\mu_{\tilde{b}}^* P_{[\mathfrak{a}][\mathfrak{b}]E_0} = (2\mu_{\tilde{b}} + 1)R_b$. Then, let

$$b^* := \mathcal{A}'((E_0, P_0, [\mathfrak{a}]E_0, \mathfrak{a}P_0), ([\mathfrak{b}]E_0, \mu_{\tilde{b}}^*\mathfrak{b}P_0)).$$

If $\tilde{b} = b^*$, then $\mathcal{A}$ outputs 0, while if $\tilde{b} \neq b^*$, $\mathcal{A}$ outputs 1.

Next, we discuss the probability that $\mathcal{A}$ outputs the correct b. If $b = 0$, then $b^* = \tilde{b}$ with a probability of $\mathrm{Adv}_{\mathcal{A}'}(\lambda) + \frac{1}{2}$ or $-\mathrm{Adv}_{\mathcal{A}'}(\lambda) + \frac{1}{2}$. If $b = 1$, then the adversary $\mathcal{A}'$ cannot get any information about $\mu_{\tilde{b}}$ because $(2\mu_{\tilde{b}} + 1)R_b$ is a uniformly random point and $\mu_{\tilde{b}}^*$ is a uniformly random value. Therefore, if $b = 1$, then $b^* \neq \tilde{b}$ with a probability of $\frac{1}{2}$. Consequently, the probability that $\mathcal{A}$ outputs the correct b is

$$\frac{1}{2}\left(\pm\mathrm{Adv}_{\mathcal{A}'}(\lambda) + \frac{1}{2} + \frac{1}{2}\right) = \pm\frac{1}{2}\mathrm{Adv}_{\mathcal{A}'}(\lambda) + \frac{1}{2} = \omega\left(\frac{1}{\mathrm{poly}(\lambda)}\right) + \frac{1}{2}.$$

As algorithm $\mathcal{A}$ is an efficient algorithm, the P-CSSDDH assumption does not hold. $\square$

Finally, note that C-SiGamal is not IND-CCA secure for the same reason that SiGamal is not.

4.3 Comparing Key Size of Each Scheme

In this subsection, we compare the key sizes of CSIDH, SiGamal, and C-SiGamal. The result of comparison is shown in Table 2, where p is a prime in the setting of each scheme, and r is an exponent of a prime factor 2 of $p + 1$.

From this table, the bit length of a ciphertext in SiGamal is twice that of a ciphertext in CSIDH; however, that of a ciphertext in C-SiGamal is the same as that of a ciphertext in CSIDH. Therefore, though C-SiGamal is more complicated than SiGamal, the cost of sending ciphertexts in C-SiGamal is as small as that in CSIDH.

Table 2. Comparison of key sizes of CSIDH, SiGamal, and C-SiGamal

	CSIDH	SiGamal	C-SiGamal
Sizes of plaintexts $(2^r \| (p+1))$	–	$r-2$	$r-2$
Alice's public key	$2\log_2 p$	$4\log_2 p$	$4\log_2 p$
Bob's public key (ciphertext)	$2\log_2 p$	$4\log_2 p$	$\mathbf{2\log_2 p}$

5 Naor-Reingold Type PRF Based on SiGamal

In this section, we propose a new Naor-Reingold type pseudo random function based on SiGamal. This type of PRF can be realized by using CSIDH in a similar way to [18, Construction 4.2]. In this construction, we need a family of pairwise independent hash functions because the output of this function is a supersingular elliptic curve. However, by using SiGamal, we can construct a Naor-Reingold type PRF without using hash functions.

5.1 Definition of Our Proposed PRF

Definition 11. *Let a prime p satisfy $p = 2^r \ell_1 \cdots \ell_n - 1$, where $\ell_1, \ldots, \ell_n$ are small distinct odd primes. Let E_0 be the supersingular elliptic curve $Y^2 Z = X^3 + X Z^2$, and P_0 be a point of order 2^r in $E_0(\mathbb{F}_p)$. Let $\mathfrak{a}_0, \ldots, \mathfrak{a}_t$ be random integral ideals of $\mathbb{Z}[\pi_p]$ whose norms are odd. Denote by $\mathfrak{A}$ the set $(\mathfrak{a}_0, \ldots, \mathfrak{a}_t)$.*
We define the function $f_{p,E_0,P_0,\mathfrak{A}} : \{0,1\}^t \to \{0,1\}^{r-2} = \{0, \ldots, 2^{r-2} - 1\}$ as follows. From $x = (x_1, \ldots, x_t) \in \{0,1\}^t$, $f_{p,E_0,P_0,\mathfrak{A}}$ outputs ν_x, where ν_x is the value in $\{0,1\}^{r-2}$ satisfying

$$\mathfrak{a}_0 \prod_{i=1}^{t} \mathfrak{a}_i^{x_i} P_0 = (2\nu_x + 1) P_{[\mathfrak{a}_0] \prod_{i=1}^{t} [\mathfrak{a}_i]^{x_i} E_0}.$$

The function defined in Definition 11 is a pseudo random function over the P-CSSDDH assumption and the CSSDDH* assumption. First, we define the CSSDDH* assumption. This assumption is essentially the same as the CSSDDH assumption (Definition 1). The difference between the CSSDDH assumption and the CSSDDH* assumption is the setting of the prime p.

Definition 12 (CSSDDH* assumption). *Let p be a prime that satisfies $p = 2^r \cdot \ell_1 \cdots \ell_n - 1$, where $\ell_1, \ldots \ell_n$ are small distinct odd primes. Let E_0 be the elliptic curve $Y^2 Z = X^3 + X Z^2$, and $[\mathfrak{a}], [\mathfrak{b}],$ and $[\mathfrak{c}]$ be random elements of $\mathrm{cl}(\mathbb{Z}[\pi_p])$. Set λ as the bit length of p.*
The CSSDDH assumption holds if, for any efficient algorithm $\mathcal{A}$,*

$$\left| \Pr\left[b = b^* \middle| \begin{array}{l} [\mathfrak{a}], [\mathfrak{b}], [\mathfrak{c}] \leftarrow \mathrm{cl}(\mathbb{Z}[\pi_p]), \ b \xleftarrow{\$} \{0,1\}, \\ F_0 := [\mathfrak{a}][\mathfrak{b}]E_0, \ F_1 := [\mathfrak{c}]E_0, \\ b^* \leftarrow \mathcal{A}(E_0, [\mathfrak{a}]E_0, [\mathfrak{b}]E_0, F_b) \end{array} \right] - \frac{1}{2} \right| < \mathrm{negl}(\lambda).$$

Next, we prove that the function defined in Definition 11 is a pseudo random function.

Theorem 12. *If the P-CSSDDH assumption and the CSSDDH* assumption hold, the function defined in Definition 11 is a pseudo random function.*

Before proving Theorem 12, we prove the following lemmas.

Lemma 2. *Let a prime p satisfy $p = 2^r \ell_1 \cdots \ell_n - 1$, where $\ell_1, \ldots, \ell_n$ are small distinct odd primes, and let λ be the bit length of p. If the P-CSSDDH assumption and the CSSDDH* assumption hold, for any efficient adversary $\mathcal{A}$,*

$$\left| \Pr \left[b = b^* \middle| \begin{array}{l} P_0 \xleftarrow{\$} E_0(\mathbb{F}_p)_{\text{order } 2^r}, \; \mathfrak{a}, \mathfrak{b}, \mathfrak{c} \leftarrow J(\mathbb{Z}[\pi_p]), \\ b \xleftarrow{\$} \{0,1\}, \; F_0 := [\mathfrak{a}][\mathfrak{b}]E_0, \; R_0 := \mathfrak{a}\mathfrak{b}P_0, \\ F_1 := [\mathfrak{c}]E_0, \; R_1 := \mathfrak{c}P_0, \\ b^* \leftarrow \mathcal{A}(E_0, P_0, [\mathfrak{a}]E_0, \mathfrak{a}P_0, [\mathfrak{b}]E_0, \mathfrak{b}P_0, F_b, R_b) \end{array} \right] - \frac{1}{2} \right| < \mathrm{negl}(\lambda).$$

Proof. For simplicity, let $S_{\mathrm{p}} := \{E_0, P_0, [\mathfrak{a}]E_0, \mathfrak{a}P_0, [\mathfrak{b}]E_0, \mathfrak{b}P_0\}$. From the P-CSSDDH assumption,

$$\left| \Pr\left[\mathcal{A}(S_{\mathrm{p}}, [\mathfrak{a}][\mathfrak{b}]E_0, \mathfrak{a}\mathfrak{b}P_0) = 1\right] - \Pr\left[\mathcal{A}(S_{\mathrm{p}}, [\mathfrak{a}][\mathfrak{b}]E_0, k\mathfrak{a}\mathfrak{b}P_0) = 1 \,\middle|\, k \xleftarrow{\$} (\mathbb{Z}/2^r\mathbb{Z})^\times\right] \right| < \mathrm{negl}(\lambda).$$

Note that $\mathfrak{a}P_0$, $\mathfrak{b}P_0$, and $\mathfrak{c}P_0$ are uniformly random points in $([\mathfrak{a}]E_0)(\mathbb{F}_p)_{\text{order } 2^r}$, $([\mathfrak{b}]E_0)(\mathbb{F}_p)_{\text{order } 2^r}$, and $([\mathfrak{c}]E_0)(\mathbb{F}_p)_{\text{order } 2^r}$, respectively. From the CSSDDH* assumption,

$$\left| \Pr\left[\mathcal{A}(A_{\mathrm{p}}, [\mathfrak{a}][\mathfrak{b}]E_0, k\mathfrak{a}\mathfrak{b}P_0) = 1 \,\middle|\, k \xleftarrow{\$} (\mathbb{Z}/2^r\mathbb{Z})^\times\right] - \Pr\left[\mathcal{A}(S_{\mathrm{p}}, [\mathfrak{c}]E_0, \mathfrak{c}P_0) = 1\right] \right| < \mathrm{negl}(\lambda).$$

Therefore,

$$\left| \Pr\left[\mathcal{A}(S, [\mathfrak{a}][\mathfrak{b}]E_0, \mathfrak{a}\mathfrak{b}P_0) = 1\right] - \Pr\left[\mathcal{A}(S, [\mathfrak{c}]E_0, \mathfrak{c}P_0) = 1\right] \right| < 2 \cdot \mathrm{negl}(\lambda).$$

This inequality is equivalent to what we want to prove.   □

Lemma 3. *Let a prime p satisfy $p = 2^r \ell_1 \cdots \ell_n - 1$, where $\ell_1, \ldots, \ell_n$ are small distinct odd primes, let λ be the bit length of p, and let v be a small integer such that $v = \mathrm{poly}(\lambda)$. If the P-CSSDDH assumption and the CSSDDH* assumption hold, for any efficient adversary $\mathcal{A}$,*

$$\left| \Pr \left[b = b^* \middle| \begin{array}{l} P_0 \xleftarrow{\$} E_0(\mathbb{F}_p)_{\text{order } 2^r}, \; b \xleftarrow{\$} \{0,1\}, \\ \mathfrak{a}, \mathfrak{b}_1, \ldots, \mathfrak{b}_v, \mathfrak{c}_1, \ldots, \mathfrak{c}_v \leftarrow J(\mathbb{Z}[\pi_p]), \; F_0^{(i)} := [\mathfrak{a}][\mathfrak{b}_i]E_0, \\ R_0^{(i)} := \mathfrak{a}\mathfrak{b}_i P_0, \; F_1^{(i)} := [\mathfrak{c}_i]E_0, \; R_1^{(i)} := \mathfrak{c}_i P_0, \\ b^* \leftarrow \mathcal{A}(E_0, P_0, [\mathfrak{a}]E_0, \mathfrak{a}P_0, \{[\mathfrak{b}_i]E_0, \mathfrak{b}_i P_0, F_b^{(i)}, R_b^{(i)}\}_{i=1,\ldots,v}) \end{array} \right] - \frac{1}{2} \right| < \mathrm{negl}(\lambda).$$

Proof. For simplicity, let $S_p := \{E_0, P_0, [\mathfrak{a}]E_0, \mathfrak{a}P_0\}$. From Lemma 2, for any efficient adversary $\mathcal{A}'$,

$$|\Pr[\mathcal{A}'(S_p, [\mathfrak{b}]E_0, \mathfrak{b}P_0, [\mathfrak{a}][\mathfrak{b}]E_0, \mathfrak{a}\mathfrak{b}P_0) = 1] - \Pr[\mathcal{A}'(S_p, [\mathfrak{b}]E_0, \mathfrak{b}P_0, [\mathfrak{c}]E_0, \mathfrak{c}P_0) = 1]| < \mathrm{negl}(\lambda).$$

Therefore, for any $j \in \{1, \ldots, v\}$,

$$|\Pr[\mathcal{A}(S_p, DH_j, R_j) = 1] - \Pr[\mathcal{A}(S_p, DH_{j-1}, R_{j-1}) = 1]| < \mathrm{negl}(\lambda),$$

where DH_j is the set $\{[\mathfrak{b}_i]E_0, \mathfrak{b}_iP_0, [\mathfrak{a}][\mathfrak{b}_i]E_0, \mathfrak{a}\mathfrak{b}_iP_0 \mid i = 1, \ldots, j\}$, and R_j is the set $\{[\mathfrak{b}_i]E_0, \mathfrak{b}_iP_0, [\mathfrak{c}_i]E_0, \mathfrak{c}_iP_0 \mid i = j+1, \ldots, v\}$. We have

$$|\Pr[\mathcal{A}(S_p, DH_v, R_v) = 1] - \Pr[\mathcal{A}(S_p, DH_0, R_0) = 1]|$$

$$\leq \sum_{j=1}^{v} |\Pr[\mathcal{A}(S_p, DH_j, R_j) = 1] - \Pr[\mathcal{A}(S_p, DH_{j-1}, R_{j-1}) = 1]|$$

$$< v \cdot \mathrm{negl}(\lambda).$$

This inequality is equivalent to what we want to prove. $\square$

Now, we prove Theorem 12.

Proof of Theorem 12. This proof is similar to that of [18, Theorem 4.1].

Let $\mathcal{A}$ be an efficient adversary. Let a prime p satisfy $p = 2^r \ell_1 \cdots \ell_n - 1$, where $\ell_1, \ldots, \ell_n$ are small distinct odd primes. Let E_0 be the supersingular elliptic curve $Y^2Z = X^3 + XZ^2$. Now, we prove

$$\left| \Pr\left[b = b^* \middle| \begin{array}{l} P_0 \xleftarrow{\$} E_0(\mathbb{F}_p)_{\text{order } 2^r}, \ b \xleftarrow{\$} \{0,1\}, \\ \mathfrak{A} \leftarrow J(\mathbb{Z}[\pi_p])^{t+1}, \ f_0 := f_{p,E_0,P_0,\mathfrak{A}}, \\ f_1 \xleftarrow{\$} \mathcal{R}, \ b^* \leftarrow \mathcal{A}^{f_b(\cdot)}(p, E_0, P_0) \end{array} \right] - \frac{1}{2} \right| < \mathrm{negl}(\lambda),$$

where $\mathcal{R}$ is a set of functions mapping from $\{0,1\}^t$ to $\{0,1\}^{r-2}$, and λ is a bit length of p.

Let $\mathfrak{a}, \mathfrak{b}_1, \ldots, \mathfrak{b}_v, \mathfrak{c}_1, \ldots, \mathfrak{c}_v$ be random elements of $J(\mathbb{Z}[\pi_p])$ whose norms are odd. Let $F_0^{(j)} := [\mathfrak{a}][\mathfrak{b}_j]E_0$, $R_0^{(j)} := \mathfrak{a}\mathfrak{b}_jP_0$, $F_1^{(j)} := [\mathfrak{c}_j]E_0$, and $R_1^{(j)} := \mathfrak{c}_jP_0$. Let the queries asked by $\mathcal{A}$ be $x^{(1)}, \ldots, x^{(u)}$. We define an efficient adversary $\mathcal{A}'$ as follows.

1. Receive $S_{p,b} := (p, E_0, P_0, [\mathfrak{a}]E_0, \mathfrak{a}P_0, \{[\mathfrak{b}_j]E_0, \mathfrak{b}_jP_0, F_b^{(j)}, R_b^{(j)}\}_{j=1,\ldots,u})$, where b is 0 or 1.
2. Take a random element J from $\{1, \ldots, t\}$.
3. Take random elements $\mathfrak{a}_{J+1}, \ldots, \mathfrak{a}_t$ from $J(\mathbb{Z}[\pi_p])$ whose norms are odd.
4. Give (p, E_0, P_0) to $\mathcal{A}$.
5. For the query $x^{(u')}$, reply with

$$\left(\prod_{i=J+1,\ldots,t} [\mathfrak{a}_i]^{x_i^{(u')}} F_b^{(j)}, \ \prod_{i=J+1,\ldots,t} \mathfrak{a}_i^{x_i^{(u')}} R_b^{(j)} \right) \quad (\text{if } x_J^{(u')} = 1),$$

$$\left(\prod_{i=J+1,\ldots,t} [\mathfrak{a}_i]^{x_i^{(u')}} [\mathfrak{b}_j]E_0, \ \prod_{i=J+1,\ldots,t} \mathfrak{a}_i^{x_i^{(u')}} \mathfrak{b}_jP_0 \right) \quad (\text{if } x_J^{(u')} = 0),$$

where $u' = 1, \ldots, u$, and

$$j = j(u') = \min \{u'' \mid (x_1^{(u'')}, \ldots, x_{J-1}^{(u'')}) = (x_1^{(u')}, \ldots, x_{J-1}^{(u')})\}.$$

6. Output whatever $\mathcal{A}$ outputs.

From Lemma 3, it holds that, for any $i = 1, \ldots, t$,

$$|\Pr[\mathcal{A}'(S_{p,0}) = 1 \mid J = i] - \Pr[\mathcal{A}'(S_{p,1}) = 1 \mid J = i]| < \mathrm{negl}(\lambda).$$

By the definition of $\mathcal{A}'$,

$$\Pr[\mathcal{A}'(S_{p,1}) = 1 \mid J = i] = \Pr[\mathcal{A}'(S_{p,0}) = 1 \mid J = i+1],$$
$$\Pr[\mathcal{A}'(S_{p,0}) = 1 \mid J = 1] = \Pr[\mathcal{A}^{f_0(\cdot)}(p, E_0, P_0) = 1],$$
$$\Pr[\mathcal{A}'(S_{p,1}) = 1 \mid J = v] = \Pr[\mathcal{A}^{f_1(\cdot)}(p, E_0, P_0) = 1].$$

Therefore,

$$\left| \Pr[\mathcal{A}^{f_0(\cdot)}(p, E_0, P_0) = 1] - \Pr[\mathcal{A}^{f_1(\cdot)}(p, E_0, P_0) = 1] \right|$$
$$= |\Pr[\mathcal{A}'(S_{p,0}) = 1 \mid J = 1] - \Pr[\mathcal{A}'(S_{p,1}) = 1 \mid J = t]|$$
$$\leq \sum_{J=1}^{t} |\Pr[\mathcal{A}'(S_{p,0}) = 1 \mid J = i] - \Pr[\mathcal{A}'(S_{p,1}) = 1 \mid J = i]|$$
$$< t \cdot \mathrm{negl}(\lambda).$$

This inequality is equivalent to what we want to prove.   □

5.2   Evaluating Cost of Computing Our Proposed PRF

In this subsection, we discuss the cost of computing our proposed PRF.

It seems that the main cost of computing our proposed PRF is the cost of computing group actions T times, where T is the Hamming weight of an input (i.e., the number of 1s contained in the bit string of input is T). However, the cost of the calculations can be reduced by adding integer vectors before computing group actions. We show that the cost of group actions for the PRF is about $\sqrt{\frac{8T}{3\pi}}$ times that of an original group action under some approximations.

From [12], the cost of group actions are evaluated approximately by the L^1-norm of an integer vector $(e_1, \ldots, e_n)$. Therefore, if we compute these actions straightforwardly, the cost is about

$$\sum_{k=1}^{T} \sum_{j=1}^{n} \mathrm{E}\left[|i| \;\middle|\; i \xleftarrow{\$} \{-m, \ldots, m\}\right] = Tn \cdot \frac{1}{2m+1} \sum_{i=-m}^{m} |i| = \frac{Tnm(m+1)}{2m+1},$$

where $\mathrm{E}[X]$ is the expected value of a random value X. However, if we consider that $\mathfrak{l}_i \overline{\mathfrak{l}_i} P = \ell_i P$, we can reduce the number of computations of isogenies. How much it costs to compute group actions T times is not trivial.

The expected value of the L^1-norm of the integer vector of T times group actions is

$$\sum_{j=1}^{n} E\left[\left|\sum_{i=1}^{T} m_i\right| \;\middle|\; m_1, \ldots, m_T \xleftarrow{\$} \{-m, \ldots, m\}\right].$$

From the Central Limit Theorem, when $T \to \infty$,

$$\Pr\left[\sum_{i=1}^{T} m_i = s \;\middle|\; m_1, \ldots, m_T \xleftarrow{\$} \{-m, \ldots, m\}\right] \approx \frac{1}{\sqrt{2\pi T\sigma^2}} \exp\left(-\frac{s^2}{2T\sigma^2}\right),$$

where $\sigma^2 = E[\, i^2 \mid i \xleftarrow{\$} \{-m, \ldots, m\}] = \frac{m(m+1)}{3}$. Based on this equation, we approximate as follows.

$$E\left[\left|\sum_{i=1}^{T} m_i\right| \;\middle|\; m_1, \ldots, m_T \xleftarrow{\$} \{-m, \ldots, m\}\right] \approx \sum_{s=-\infty}^{\infty} \frac{|s|}{\sqrt{2\pi T\sigma^2}} \exp\left(-\frac{s^2}{2T\sigma^2}\right),$$

$$\approx \int_{-\infty}^{\infty} \frac{|s|}{\sqrt{2\pi T\sigma^2}} \exp\left(-\frac{s^2}{2T\sigma^2}\right) ds,$$

$$= \sqrt{\frac{2Tm(m+1)}{3\pi}}.$$

The expected value we want is about $n\sqrt{\frac{2Tm(m+1)}{3\pi}}$. Note that the expected value of the L^1-norm of an integer vector of one group action is $\frac{nm(m+1)}{2m+1}$. In conclusion, the cost of our proposed PRF when the Hamming weight of input is T is about

$$\sqrt{\frac{2Tm(m+1)}{3\pi}} \cdot \frac{2m+1}{m(m+1)} \approx \sqrt{\frac{8T}{3\pi}}$$

times that of a group action in SiGamal.

This result was confirmed in our experiment in Subsect. 6.3.

Remark 9. Our discussion in this subsection focuses on a non-constant time algorithm of group actions. When we use a constant time algorithm (*e.g.*, algorithms proposed in [4,14,20]), this discussion does not hold.

6   Experimentation

In this section, we show the results of our experimentation to estimate the computational costs of our proposed schemes. We fixed the security levels of all schemes to the security level of CSIDH-512. In other words, we chose primes that satisfied the condition that their bit lengths were about 512 in all experiments. Our source codes of MAGMA are published on http://tomoriya.work/code.html.

6.1   Parameters

In this subsection, we propose two parameters for SiGamal and C-SiGamal: (p_{128}, P_{128}) for the case when the plaintext message space is $\{0,1\}^{128}$ and (p_{256}, P_{256}) for the case when the plaintext message space is $\{0,1\}^{256}$. Let the bit lengths of p_{128} and p_{256} be about 512 to adapt the security level of SiGamal and C-SiGamal to that of CSIDH-512.

$(\boldsymbol{p_{128}, P_{128}})$. Let p_{128} be a prime $2^{130} \cdot \ell_1 \cdots \ell_{60} - 1$, where ℓ_1 through ℓ_{59} are the smallest distinct odd primes, and ℓ_{60} is 569. The bit length of p_{128} is 522. Set a key bound m_{128} over p_{128} as 10. Finally, let a point P_{128} of order 2^{130} in $E_0(\mathbb{F}_{p_{128}})$ be $\ell_1 \cdots \ell_{60} \tilde{P}_{128}$, where $\tilde{P}_{128}$ is a point whose x-coordinate is 331.

$(\boldsymbol{p_{256}, P_{256}})$. Let p_{256} be a prime $2^{258} \cdot \ell_1 \cdots \ell_{43} - 1$, where ℓ_1 through ℓ_{42} are the smallest distinct odd primes, and ℓ_{43} is 307. The bit length of p_{256} is 515. Set a key bound m_{258} over p_{258} as 32. Finally, let a point P_{256} of order 2^{258} in $E_0(\mathbb{F}_{p_{256}})$ be $\ell_1 \cdots \ell_{43} \tilde{P}_{256}$, where $\tilde{P}_{256}$ is a point whose x-coordinate is 199.

Table 3. Computational costs of group actions

Parameters	(p_{128}, P_{128})	(p_{256}, P_{256})	CSIDH-512
Bit lengths of primes	522	515	512
M	511,531	866,000	328,301
S	158,849	302,400	116,953
a	480,134	838,330	332,933
Total	662,617	1,149,836	438,510

6.2   Computational Costs of SiGamal and C-SiGamal

In this subsection, we show the results of our experiment on SiGamal and C-SiGamal. The schemes of SiGamal and C-SiGamal consist of group actions, scalar multiplications, and the Pohlig-Hellman algorithm. The computational complexity of scalar multiplications is $O(r)$, and that of the Pohlig-Hellman algorithm is $O(r^2)$. Their computational costs have a little effect on all computational costs of SiGamal and C-SiGamal.

We implemented group actions of $\mathrm{cl}(\mathbb{Z}[\pi_p])$ over p_{128}, p_{256}, and, as a reference value, p_0. Here, p_0 is a prime proposed in the original CSIDH paper [3]: a prime $4\ell_1 \cdots \ell_{74} - 1$ such that $\ell_1 \ldots \ell_{73}$ are the smallest distinct odd primes and $\ell_{74} = 587$, and the key bound m_0 is 5. We implemented Algorithm 3 over p_{128} and p_{256} and Algorithm 1 over p_0 according to [15]. Then, for each case, we measured the average computational cost over 50,000 trials. Refer to [17, Appendix A.1] for the computational costs of each formula for the Montgomery curves. The results are listed in Table 3, in which we denote field multiplication by **M**, field squaring by **S**, and field addition, subtraction, or doubling by **a**. The quantity "total" means the total number of $\tilde{M}$, where $1\mathbf{S} = 0.8\mathbf{M}$, and $1\mathbf{a} = 0.05\mathbf{M}$.

Remark 10. There are techniques for improving the efficiency of group actions in CSIDH, such as SIMBA [14], optimal addition chains for scalar multiplications [4], and key space optimization [12]. These techniques can be adapted to SiGamal and C-SiGamal.

Next, we implemented the schemes of SiGamal and C-SiGamal. We used Algorithm 2 for the Pohlig-Hellman algorithm in our experiments. The result is shown in Table 4. The computational costs of the encryption algorithms of C-SiGamal over p_{128} were about 108% higher than that of two group actions, and those over p_{256} were about 117% higher than that of two group actions. Moreover, that of the decryption algorithms of SiGamal and C-SiGamal over p_{128} were about 116% higher than that of one group action, and those over p_{256} were about 134% higher than that of one group action.

Table 4. Computational costs of SiGamal and C-SiGamal (numbers of **M**)

Parameters	(p_{128}, P_{128})		(p_{256}, P_{256})	
A bit length of plaintexts	128		256	
Schemes	SiGamal	C-SiGamal	SiGamal	C-SiGamal
Key generation	663,411		1,154,035	
Encryption	1,327,899	1,434,944	2,306,317	2,703,339
Decryption	761,058	768,602	1,538,498	1,545,253

From Table 3, the computational cost of a group action over (p_{256}, P_{256}) was about 2.62 times that of a group action of CSIDH-512. Therefore, SiGamal and C-SiGamal need more computation than CSIDH. However, when we use CSIDH for secure communication, we need to use hash functions since a shared key in CSIDH is a supersingular elliptic curve. If these hash functions are attacked, the communication is less secure, even if CSIDH is not broken. In fact, the ElGamal like encryption based on CSIDH in Subsect. 2.5 is not IND-CPA secure without using hash functions. In comparison, when we use SiGamal or C-SiGamal, the security of communication is guaranteed by the security of SiGamal or C-SiGamal. Moreover, bit lengths of shared keys in CSIDH are determined by the security parameter (*i.e.*, the bit length of the prime p) and hash functions, while bit lengths of plaintexts in SiGamal and C-SiGamal are determined by r. Because the only condition that r satisfies is $r < \log_2 p$, bit lengths of plaintexts in SiGamal and C-SiGamal are determined relatively freely. In summary, SiGamal and C-SiGamal are less efficient than CSIDH; however, SiGamal and C-SiGamal are superior to CSIDH in terms of security and functionality.

6.3   Computational Costs of Our Proposed PRF

In this subsection, we show the result of our experiment with our proposed PRF. We measured the computational costs of $T = 128$ and 256 times group

Table 5. Computational costs of T times group actions over (p_{128}, P_{128})

	$T = 128$	$T = 256$	$T = 1$
Computational costs	7,196,112	10,184,430	662,617
(Costs of T times)/(Costs of one time)	10.860	15.370	1
$\sqrt{\dfrac{8T}{3\pi}}$ (in Subsect. 5.2)	10.424	14.741	–

actions over $(p_{128}, P_{0,(128)})$. These costs are close to the computational costs of our proposed PRF, where T is the Hamming weight of an input. Moreover, we computed the value of the computational costs of T times group actions divided by that of one time group action, and we compared them with the approximation $\sqrt{\frac{8T}{3\pi}}$ in Subsect. 5.2.

All of the results are shown in Table 5. As can be seen, the approximation $\sqrt{\frac{8T}{3\pi}}$ has some precision.

7   Conclusion

We proposed new isogeny-based public key encryptions: SiGamal and C-SiGamal. We developed SiGamal by giving CSIDH additional points of order 2^r, where $r - 2$ is the bit length of a plaintext. The scheme of SiGamal is similar to that of ElGamal encryption, while C-SiGamal is a compressed version of SiGamal. These schemes do not use hash functions.

In addition, we proved that, if the new P-CSSCDH assumption holds, then SiGamal and C-SiGamal are OW-CPA secure, and if the new P-CSSDDH assumption holds, then SiGamal and C-SiGamal are IND-CPA secure.

Next, we constructed an isogeny-based Naor-Reingold type PRF from SiGamal. We showed that if the P-CSSDDH assumption and the CSSDDH* assumption hold, then our proposed function is a PRF. Furthermore, we estimated the computational cost of the PRF when the Hamming weight of an input is T. In our discussion, the computational cost is about $\sqrt{\frac{8T}{3\pi}}$ times that of a group action in SiGamal.

Finally, we experimented with group actions in SiGamal and C-SiGamal and measured their computational costs. The costs of these group actions in SiGamal and C-SiGamal with $r = 258$ were about 2.62 times that of a group action in CSIDH-512. Moreover, we experimented with T times group actions, and we confirmed the approximated value $\sqrt{\frac{8T}{3\pi}}$.

7.1   Future Work

CSIDH also has an algorithm that uses Edwards curves [17]; however, it is not obvious how to implement SiGamal and C-SiGamal on Edwards curves because, in [17], $p \equiv 3 \pmod 8$ is crucial. It will be a future work for us to realize SiGamal and C-SiGamal with Edwards curves.

Another important direction for future work will be developing high-level schemes (*e.g.*, homomorphic encryptions, an oblivious PRF) based on SiGamal and C-SiGamal.

Acknowlegements. This work was supported by JST CREST Grant Number JPMJCR14D6, Japan.

Appendix A   Generating Points of order 2^r

In this section, we explain the properties of points in Montgomery curves. These properties give us an efficient method for generating points of order 2^r for C-SiGamal.

Definition 13. *Let E be a Montgomery curve defined over a field $\mathbb{K}$ and $P = (X : Y : Z)$ be a point in $E(\overline{\mathbb{K}}) \setminus \{(0 : 1 : 0)\}$. Define the function $x \colon E \to \overline{\mathbb{K}}$ as $x(P) := X/Z$, and define the function $y \colon E \to \overline{\mathbb{K}}$ as $y(P) := Y/Z$.*

Proposition 1. *Let p be a prime satisfying $p \equiv 3 \pmod 4$ and E be a supersingular Montgomery curve defined over $\mathbb{F}_p$ satisfying $\mathrm{End}_p(E) \cong \mathbb{Z}[\pi_p]$. If a point $P \in E$ belongs to $E[\pi_p - 1] \setminus E[2]$, then*

$$x(P) \in (\mathbb{F}_p^\times)^2 \iff P \in 2E[\pi_p - 1].$$

If a point $P \in E$ belongs to $E[\pi_p + 1] \setminus E[2]$, then

$$x(P) \notin (\mathbb{F}_p^\times)^2 \iff P \in 2E[\pi_p + 1].$$

Proof. We prove the case that $P \in E[\pi_p - 1] \setminus E[2]$. The other case can be proven in a similar way.

Assume that $P \in 2E[\pi_p - 1]$. Let Q be a point in $E[\pi_p - 1]$ such that $P = 2Q$. From doubling formulas of Montgomery curves,

$$x(P) = \frac{(x(Q)^2 - 1)^2}{4y(Q)^2}.$$

Since $x(Q), y(Q) \in \mathbb{F}_p$, $x(P)$ belongs to $(\mathbb{F}_p)^2$. Note that $(0 : 0 : 1)$ is a point of order 2. We have $x(P) \in (\mathbb{F}_p^\times)^2$.

Conversely, assume that $P \notin 2E[\pi_p - 1]$. First, we assume $E = E_0$ (*i.e.*, $E \colon Y^2 Z = X^3 + XZ^2$). Take $x' \in \mathbb{F}_p^\times$ such that $x'^2 + 1 \notin (\mathbb{F}_p^\times)^2$. Note that x' exists since, if it does not exist, all elements in $\mathbb{F}_p^\times$ belong to $(\mathbb{F}_p^\times)^2$. Define a point $Q = (x_1, y_1) \in E$ as $Q := (x', \sqrt{x'(x'^2 + 1)})$. If Q does not belong to $E[\pi_p - 1]$, we retake $-x'$ as x'. Now, $x_1 \notin (\mathbb{F}_p^\times)^2$ holds because $x_1^2 + 1 \notin (\mathbb{F}_p^\times)^2$ and $x_1^3 + x_1 \in (\mathbb{F}_p^\times)^2$. Therefore, by the previous paragraph, $Q \notin 2E[\pi_p - 1]$. Define a point $R = (x_2, y_2) \in E$ as $R := P - Q$. By considering the order of R, we have $R \in 2E[\pi_p - 1]$. Since x_2 and $y_2^2 = x_2^3 + x_2$ belong to $(\mathbb{F}_p^\times)^2$, it holds that $x_2^2 + 1 \in (\mathbb{F}_p^\times)^2$. From the addition formulas of Montgomery curves,

$$x(P) = \left(\frac{y_2 - y_1}{x_2 - x_1}\right)^2 - x_1 - x_2 = \frac{\left(\sqrt{x_1(x_2^2 + 1)} - \sqrt{x_2(x_1^2 + 1)}\right)^2}{(x_2 - x_1)^2}.$$

Since $x_1, x_1^2 + 1 \notin (\mathbb{F}_p^\times)^2$ and $x_2, x_2^2 + 1 \in (\mathbb{F}_p^\times)^2$, it holds that $x_1(x_2^2 + 1)$ and $x_2(x_1^2 + 1)$ are not in $(\mathbb{F}_p^\times)^2$. For any $d \notin \mathbb{F}_p^2$, we can write $\mathbb{F}_{p^2} = \mathbb{F}_p(\sqrt{d})$. Therefore, there exists $\alpha \in \mathbb{F}_p$ such that

$$\sqrt{x_1(x_2^2 + 1)} - \sqrt{x_2(x_1^2 + 1)} = \alpha\sqrt{d}.$$

Then, we have $\alpha \neq 0$ since an easy calculation shows that $\alpha = 0$ if and only if $x_1 x_2 = 1$ or $x_1 = x_2$. Therefore, it holds that $x(P) \notin (\mathbb{F}_p^\times)^2$.

Next, we prove the general case. By Theorem 1, there exists an ideal class $[\mathfrak{a}] \in \mathrm{cl}(\mathbb{Z}[\pi_p])$ such that $E = E_0/E_0[\mathfrak{a}]$. We can take a representative $\mathfrak{a}$ as an integral ideal prime to $\pi_p - 1$. This means that there is an isogeny $\varphi : E_0 \to E$ defined over $\mathbb{F}_p$ whose degree is prime to $p + 1$. Then, the isogeny φ induces a bijection from $E_0[\pi_p - 1]$ to $E[\pi_p - 1]$, and maps $2E_0[\pi_p - 1]$ onto $2E[\pi - 1]$. Furthermore, by a formula of isogenies with odd degree between Montgomery curves (e.g., see Theorem 1 in [5]), we have $x(P) \in (\mathbb{F}_p^\times)^2$ if and only if $x(\varphi(P)) \in (\mathbb{F}_p^\times)^2$ for $P \in E_0[\pi - 1]$. Therefore, the general case follows from the case of E_0. □

Define $p = 2^r \ell_1 \cdots \ell_n - 1$, where $\ell_1, \ldots, \ell_n$ are small distinct odd primes, and $r \geq 3$. From the law of quadratic reciprocity, $2, \ell_1, \ldots, \ell_n$ are all square in $\mathbb{F}_p$. Therefore, according to Proposition 1, points in $E(\mathbb{F}_p)$ whose x-coordinates are products of these primes belong to $2E[\pi_p - 1]$. Therefore, we need to exclude these points to generate a point of order 2^r in $E(\mathbb{F}_p)$. Conversely, points in $E(\mathbb{F}_p)$ whose x-coordinates are -1 times products of $2, \ell_1, \ldots, \ell_n$ do not belong to $2E[\pi_p - 1]$. Therefore, to generate points of order 2^r in $E(\mathbb{F}_p)$, it is convenient to take x-coordinates of points from -2 to $-p + 1$.

References

1. Azarderakhsh, R., et al.: Supersingular isogeny key encapsulation. Submission to the NIST Post-Quantum Standardization Project (2017)
2. Castryck, W., Decru, T.: CSIDH on the surface. In: Ding, J., Tillich, J.-P. (eds.) PQCrypto 2020. LNCS, vol. 12100, pp. 111–129. Springer, Cham (2020). https://doi.org/10.1007/978-3-030-44223-1_7
3. Castryck, W., Lange, T., Martindale, C., Panny, L., Renes, J.: CSIDH: an efficient post-quantum group action. In: Peyrin, T., Galbraith, S. (eds.) ASIACRYPT 2018. LNCS, vol. 11274, pp. 395–427. Springer, Cham (2018). https://doi.org/10.1007/978-3-030-03332-3_15
4. Cervantes-Vázquez, D., Chenu, M., Chi-Domínguez, J.-J., De Feo, L., Rodríguez-Henríquez, F., Smith, B.: Stronger and faster side-channel protections for CSIDH. In: Schwabe, P., Thériault, N. (eds.) LATINCRYPT 2019. LNCS, vol. 11774, pp. 173–193. Springer, Cham (2019). https://doi.org/10.1007/978-3-030-30530-7_9

5. Costello, C., Hisil, H.: A simple and compact algorithm for SIDH with arbitrary degree isogenies. In: Takagi, T., Peyrin, T. (eds.) ASIACRYPT 2017. LNCS, vol. 10625, pp. 303–329. Springer, Cham (2017). https://doi.org/10.1007/978-3-319-70697-9_11

6. de Saint Guilhem, C.D., Kutas, P., Petit, C., Silva, J.: SÉTA: supersingular encryption from torsion attacks. IACR Cryptology ePrint Archive, 2019:1291 (2019). https://ia.cr/2019/1291

7. Delfs, C., Galbraith, S.D.: Computing isogenies between supersingular elliptic curves over $\mathbb{F}_p$. Designs, Codes and Cryptography, pp. 425–440 (2016)

8. ElGamal, T.: A public key cryptosystem and a signature scheme based on discrete logarithms. IEEE Trans. Inf. Theory **31**(4), 469–472 (1985)

9. Galbraith, S.D.: Mathematics of Public Key Cryptography. Cambridge University Press, Cambridge (2012)

10. Jao, D., De Feo, L.: Towards quantum-resistant cryptosystems from supersingular elliptic curve isogenies. In: Yang, B.-Y. (ed.) PQCrypto 2011. LNCS, vol. 7071, pp. 19–34. Springer, Heidelberg (2011). https://doi.org/10.1007/978-3-642-25405-5_2

11. Koblitz, N.: Elliptic curve cryptosystems. Math. Comput. **48**, 203–209 (1987)

12. Kohei, N., Hiroshi, O., Atsushi, T., Tsuyoshi, T.: L_1-norm ball for CSIDH: optimal strategy for choosing the secret key space. IACR Cryptology ePrint Archive, 2020:181 (2020). https://ia.cr/2020/181

13. Leonardi, C.: A note on the ending elliptic curve in SIDH. IACR Cryptology ePrint Archive, 2020:262 (2020). https://ia.cr/2020/262

14. Meyer, M., Campos, F., Reith, S.: On lions and elligators: an efficient constant-time implementation of CSIDH. In: Ding, J., Steinwandt, R. (eds.) PQCrypto 2019. LNCS, vol. 11505, pp. 307–325. Springer, Cham (2019). https://doi.org/10.1007/978-3-030-25510-7_17

15. Meyer, M., Reith, S.: A faster way to the CSIDH. In: Chakraborty, D., Iwata, T. (eds.) INDOCRYPT 2018. LNCS, vol. 11356, pp. 137–152. Springer, Cham (2018). https://doi.org/10.1007/978-3-030-05378-9_8

16. Miller, V.S.: Use of elliptic curves in cryptography. In: Williams, H.C. (ed.) CRYPTO 1985. LNCS, vol. 218, pp. 417–426. Springer, Heidelberg (1986). https://doi.org/10.1007/3-540-39799-X_31

17. Moriya, T., Onuki, H., Takagi, T.: How to construct CSIDH on Edwards curves. In: Jarecki, S. (ed.) CT-RSA 2020. LNCS, vol. 12006, pp. 512–537. Springer, Cham (2020). https://doi.org/10.1007/978-3-030-40186-3_22

18. Naor, M., Reingold, O.: Number-theoretic constructions of efficient pseudo-random functions. J. ACM (JACM) **51**(2), 231–262 (2004)

19. National Institute of Standards and Technology. Post-quantum cryptography standardization, December 2016. https://csrc.nist.gov/Projects/Post-Quantum-Cryptography/Post-Quantum-Cryptography-Standardization

20. Onuki, H., Aikawa, Y., Yamazaki, T., Takagi, T.: A faster constant-time algorithm of CSIDH keeping two points (short paper). In: Attrapadung, N., Yagi, T. (eds.) IWSEC 2019. LNCS, vol. 11689, pp. 23–33. Springer, Cham (2019). https://doi.org/10.1007/978-3-030-26834-3_2

21. Onuki, H., Takagi, T.: On collisions related to an ideal class of order 3 in CSIDH. In: Aoki, K., Kanaoka, A. (eds.) IWSEC 2020. LNCS, vol. 12231, pp. 131–148. Springer, Cham (2020). https://doi.org/10.1007/978-3-030-58208-1_8

22. Petit, C.: Faster algorithms for isogeny problems using torsion point images. In: Takagi, T., Peyrin, T. (eds.) ASIACRYPT 2017. LNCS, vol. 10625, pp. 330–353. Springer, Cham (2017). https://doi.org/10.1007/978-3-319-70697-9_12

23. Pohlig, S., Hellman, M.: An improved algorithm for computing logarithms over $GF(p)$ and its cryptographic significance. IEEE Trans. Inf. Theory **24**(1), 106–110 (1978)
24. Rivest, R.L., Shamir, A., Adleman, L.: A method for obtaining digital signatures and public-key cryptosystems. Commun. ACM **21**, 120–126 (1978)
25. Shor, P.W.: Algorithms for quantum computation: discrete logarithms and factoring. In: Proceedings 35th Annual Symposium on Foundations of Computer Science, pp. 124–134. IEEE (1994)
26. Shoup, V.: Sequences of games: a tool for taming complexity in security proofs. IACR Cryptology ePrint Archive, 2004:332 (2004). https://ia.cr/2004/332
27. Silverman, J.H.: The Arithmetic of Elliptic Curves. GTM, vol. 106. Springer, New York (2009). https://doi.org/10.1007/978-0-387-09494-6
28. Taraskin, O., Soukharev, V., Jao, D., LeGrow, J.: An isogeny-based password-authenticated key establishment protocol. IACR Cryptology ePrint Archive, 2018:886 (2018). https://ia.cr/2018/886
29. Vélu, J.: Isogénies entre courbes elliptiques, pp. 305–347. CR Acad. Sci. Paris, Séries A (1971)
30. Waterhouse, W.C.: Abelian varieties over finite fields. In: Annales scientifiques de l'École Normale Supérieure, pp. 521–560 (1969)

Quantum Algorithms

Estimating Quantum
Speedups for Lattice Sieves

Martin R. Albrecht[1], Vlad Gheorghiu[2], Eamonn W. Postlethwaite[1(✉)],
and John M. Schanck[2(✉)]

[1] Information Security Group, Royal Holloway, University of London, Egham, UK
eamonn.postlethwaite.2016@rhul.ac.uk
[2] Institute for Quantum Computing, University of Waterloo, Waterloo, Canada
jschanck@uwaterloo.ca

Abstract. Quantum variants of lattice sieve algorithms are routinely
used to assess the security of lattice based cryptographic constructions.
In this work we provide a heuristic, non-asymptotic, analysis of the cost of
several algorithms for near neighbour search on high dimensional spheres.
These algorithms are key components of lattice sieves. We design quantum circuits for near neighbour search algorithms and provide software
that numerically optimises algorithm parameters according to various
cost metrics. Using this software we estimate the cost of classical and
quantum near neighbour search on spheres. For the most performant
near neighbour search algorithm that we analyse we find a small quantum
speedup in dimensions of cryptanalytic interest. Achieving this speedup
requires several optimistic physical and algorithmic assumptions.

1 Introduction

Sieving algorithms for the shortest vector problem (SVP) in a lattice have
received a great deal of attention recently [1,2,8,17,33,40]. The attention mostly
stems from lattice based cryptography, as many attacks on lattice based cryptographic constructions involve finding short lattice vectors [3,36,39].

Lattice based cryptography is thought to be secure against quantum adversaries. None of the known algorithms to solve SVP (to a small approximation
factor) do so in subexponential time, but this is not to say that there is no gain
to be had given a large quantum computer. Lattice sieve algorithms use near
neighbour search (NNS) as a subroutine; near neighbour search algorithms use

The full version can be found at https://eprint.iacr.org/2019/1161. The research of
MA was supported by EPSRC grants EP/S020330/1, EP/S02087X/1, by the European
Union Horizon 2020 Research and Innovation Program Grant 780701 and Innovate UK
grant AQuaSec; the research of EP was supported by the EPSRC and the UK govern-
ment as part of the Centre for Doctoral Training in Cyber Security at Royal Holloway,
University of London (EP/P009301/1). VG and JS were supported by NSERC and
CIFAR. IQC is supported in part by the Government of Canada and the Province of
Ontario.

S. Moriai and H. Wang (Eds.): ASIACRYPT 2020, LNCS 12492, pp. 583–613, 2020.
https://doi.org/10.1007/978-3-030-64834-3_20

black box search as a subroutine; and Grover's quantum search algorithm [25] gives a square root improvement to the query complexity of black box search. A black box search that is expected to take $\Theta(N)$ queries on classical hardware will take $\Theta(\sqrt{N})$ queries on quantum hardware using Grover's algorithm.

Previous work has analysed the effect of quantum search on the query complexity of lattice sieves [34,35]. Of course, one must implement the queries efficiently in order to realise the improvement in practice. Recent work has given concrete quantum resource estimates for the black box search problems involved in key recovery attacks on AES [23,28] and preimage attacks on SHA-2 and SHA-3 [4]. In this work, we give explicit quantum circuits that implement the black box search subroutines of several quantum lattice sieves. Our quantum circuits are efficient enough to yield a cost improvement in dimensions of cryptanalytic interest. However, for the most performant sieve that we analyse the cost improvement is small and several barriers stand in the way of achieving it.

Outline and Contributions. We start with some preliminaries in Sect. 2. In particular, we discuss the "XOR and Population Count" operation (henceforth popcount), which is our primary optimisation target. The popcount operation is used to identify pairs of vectors that are likely to lie at a small angle to each other. It is typically less expensive than a full inner product computation.

In Sect. 3 we introduce and analyse a filtered quantum search procedure. We present our quantum circuit for popcount in Sect. 4. In Sect. 5 we provide a heuristic analysis of the probability that popcount successfully identifies pairs of vectors that are close to each other. This analysis may be of independent interest; previous work [2,17] has relied largely on experimental data for choosing popcount parameters.

In Sect. 6, we rederive the overall cost of the NNS subroutines of three lattice sieves. Our cost analysis exposes the impact of the popcount parameters so that we can numerically optimise these in parallel with the sieve parameters. We have chosen to profile the Nguyen–Vidick sieve [40], the bgj1 specialisation [2] of the Becker–Gama–Joux sieve [9], and the Becker–Ducas–Gama–Laarhoven sieve [8]. We have chosen these three sieves as they are, respectively, the earliest and most conceptually simple, the most performant yet implemented, and the fastest known asymptotically.

Finally, we optimise the cost of classical and quantum search under various cost metrics to produce Fig. 2 of Sect. 7. We conclude by discussing barriers to obtaining the reported quantum advantages in NNS, the relationship between SVP and NNS, and future work. Both the data produced, and the source code used to compute it, are available at https://github.com/jschanck/eprint-2019-1161. We consider our software a contribution in its own right; it is documented, easily extensible and allows for the inclusion of new nearest neighbour search strategies and cost models.

Interpretation. Quantum computation seems to be more difficult than classical computation. As such, there will likely be some minimal dimension, a crossover point, below which classical sieves outperform quantum ones. Our estimates give non-trivial crossover points for the sieves we consider. Yet, our results do not rule out the relevance of quantum sieves to lattice cryptanalysis. The crossover points that we estimate are well below the dimensions commonly thought to achieve 128 bits of security against quantum adversaries. However, our initial logical circuit level analysis (Fig. 2, q: depth-width) is optimistic. It ignores the costs of quantum random access memory and quantum error correction.

To illustrate the potential impact of error correction, we apply a cost model developed by Gidney and Ekerå to our quantum circuits. The Gidney–Ekerå model was developed as part of a recent analysis of Shor's algorithm [20]. In the Gidney–Ekerå model, the crossover point for the NNS algorithm underlying the Becker–Ducas–Gama–Laarhoven sieve [8] is dimension 312. In this dimension, the classical and quantum variants both perform $2^{119.0}$ operations and need at least $2^{78.3}$ bits of (quantum accessible) random access memory. A large cost improvement is obtained asymptotically, but for cryptanalytically relevant dimensions the improvement is tenuous. Between dimensions 352 and 824 our estimate for the quantum cost grows from appoximately 2^{128} to approximately 2^{256}. In dimension 352 this is an improvement of a factor of $2^{1.8}$ over our estimate for the classical cost. In dimension 824 the improvement is by a factor of $2^{14.4}$.

We caution that a memory constraint would significantly reduce the range of cryptanalytically relevant dimensions. For instance, an adversary with no more than 2^{128} bits of quantum accessible classical memory is limited to dimension 544 and below. In these dimensions we estimate a cost improvement of no more than a factor of $2^{13.6}$ at the logical circuit level and no more than $2^{7.1}$ in the Gidney–Ekerå metric.

A depth constraint would also reduce the range of cryptanalytically relevant dimensions. The quantum algorithms that we consider would be more severely affected by a depth constraint than their classical counterparts, due to the poor parallisability of Grover's algorithm.

2   Preliminaries

2.1   Models of Computation

We describe quantum algorithms as circuits using the Clifford+T gate set, but we augment this gate set with a table lookup operation (qRAM). We describe classical algorithms as programs for RAM machines (random access memory machines).

Clifford+T+qRAM Quantum Circuits. Quantum circuits can be described at the *logical layer*, wherein an array of n qubits encodes a unit vector in $(\mathbb{C}^2)^{\otimes n}$, or at the *physical layer*, wherein the state space may be much larger. Ignoring qubit initialisation and measurement, a circuit is a sequence of unitary operations, one per unit time. Each unitary in the sequence is constructed by parallel composition of gates. At most one gate can be applied to each qubit per time step. The Clifford+T gate set

$$\mathbf{H} = \frac{1}{\sqrt{2}} \begin{pmatrix} 1 & 1 \\ 1 & -1 \end{pmatrix}, \quad \mathbf{S} = \begin{pmatrix} 1 & 0 \\ 0 & i \end{pmatrix}, \quad \mathbf{CNOT} = \begin{pmatrix} 1 & 0 & 0 & 0 \\ 0 & 1 & 0 & 0 \\ 0 & 0 & 0 & 1 \\ 0 & 0 & 1 & 0 \end{pmatrix}, \quad \mathbf{T} = \begin{pmatrix} 1 & 0 \\ 0 & e^{i\pi/4} \end{pmatrix},$$

is commonly used to describe circuits at the logical layer due to its relationship with some quantum error correcting codes. This gate set is universal for quantum computation when combined with qubit initialisation (of $|0\rangle$ and $|1\rangle$ states) and measurement in the computational basis.

In addition to Clifford+T gates, we allow unit cost table lookups in the form of qRAM (quantum access to classical RAM). The difference between RAM and qRAM is that qRAM can construct arbitrary superpositions of table entries. Suppose that $(R_0, \ldots, R_{2^n-1})$ are registers of a classical RAM and that each register encodes an ℓ bit binary string. We allow our Clifford+T circuits access to these registers in the form of an $(n + \ell)$ qubit qRAM gate that enacts

$$\sum_{j=0}^{2^n-1} \alpha_j |j\rangle |x\rangle \xrightarrow{qRAM} \sum_{j=0}^{2^n-1} \alpha_j |j\rangle |x \oplus R_j\rangle. \tag{1}$$

Here $\sum_j \alpha_j |j\rangle$ is a superposition of addresses and x is an arbitrary ℓ bit string.

Quantum access to classical RAM is a powerful resource, and the algorithms we describe below fail to achieve an advantage over their classical counterparts when qRAM is not available. We discuss qRAM at greater length in Sect. 7.

RAM Machines. We describe classical algorithms in terms of random access memory machines. For comparability with the Clifford+T gate set, we will work with a limited instruction set, e.g. {NOT, AND, OR, XOR, LOAD, STORE}. For comparability with qRAM, LOAD and STORE act on ℓ bit registers.

Cost. The cost of a RAM program is the number of instructions that it performs. One can similarly define the *gate cost* of a quantum circuit to be the number of gates that it performs. Both metrics are reasonable in isolation, but it is not clear how one should compare the two. Jaques and Schanck recommend that quantum circuits be assigned a cost in the unit of RAM instructions to account for the role that classical computers play in dispatching gates to quantum memories [29]. They also recommend that the identity gate be assigned unit cost to account for error correction. The *depth-width cost* of a quantum circuit is the total number of gate operations that it performs when one includes identity gates in the count.

2.2   Black Box Search

A predicate on $\{0, 1, \ldots, N-1\}$ is a function $f : \{0, 1, \ldots, N-1\} \to \{0, 1\}$. The kernel, or set of roots, of f is $\mathrm{Ker}(f) = \{x : f(x) = 0\}$. We write $|f|$ for $|\mathrm{Ker}(f)|$. A black box search algorithm finds a root of a predicate without exploiting any structure present in the description of the predicate itself. Of course, black box search algorithms can be applied when structure is known, and we will often use structure such as "f has M roots" or "f is expected to have no more than M roots" in our analyses. We will also use the fact that the set of predicates on any given finite set can be viewed as a Boolean algebra. We write $f \cup g$ for the predicate with kernel $\mathrm{Ker}(f) \cup \mathrm{Ker}(g)$ and $f \cap g$ for the predicate with kernel $\mathrm{Ker}(f) \cap \mathrm{Ker}(g)$.

Exhaustive Search. An exhaustive search evaluates $f(0)$, $f(1)$, $f(2)$, and so on until a root of f is found. The order does not matter so long as each element of the search space is queried at most once. If f is a uniformly random predicate with M roots, then this process has probability $1 - \binom{N-M}{j}/\binom{N}{j} \geq 1 - (1 - M/N)^j$ of finding a root during j evaluations of f. This is true even if M is not known.

Filtered Search. If f is expensive to evaluate, we may try to decrease the cost of exhaustive search by applying a search filter. We say that a predicate g is a filter for f if $f \neq g$ and $|f \cap g| \geq 1$. We say that g recognises f with a false positive rate of

$$\rho_f(g) = 1 - \frac{|f \cap g|}{|g|},$$

and a false negative rate of

$$\eta_f(g) = 1 - \frac{|f \cap g|}{|f|}.$$

A filtered search evaluates $g(0), f(0), g(1), f(1), g(2), f(2)$, and so on until a root of $f \cap g$ is found. The evaluation of $f(i)$ can be skipped when i is not a root of g, which may reduce the cost of filtered search below that of exhaustive search.

Quantum Search. Grover's quantum search algorithm is a black box search algorithm that provides a quadratic advantage over exhaustive search in terms of query complexity. Suppose that f is a predicate with M roots. Let $\mathbf{D}$ be any unitary transformation that maps $|0\rangle$ to $\frac{1}{\sqrt{N}} \sum_i |i\rangle$, let $\mathbf{R}_0 = \mathbf{I}_N - 2|0\rangle\langle 0|$ and let $\mathbf{R}_f$ be the unitary $|x\rangle \mapsto (-1)^{f(x)}|x\rangle$. Measuring $\mathbf{D}|0\rangle$ yields a root of f with probability M/N. Grover's quantum search algorithm amplifies this to probability ≈ 1 by repeatedly applying the unitary $\mathbf{G}(f) = \mathbf{D}\mathbf{R}_0\mathbf{D}^{-1}\mathbf{R}_f$ [25]. Suppose that j repetitions are applied. The analysis in [25] shows that measuring the state $\mathbf{G}(f)^j \mathbf{D}|0\rangle$ yields a root of f with probability $\sin^2((2j+1) \cdot \theta)$ where $\sin^2(\theta) = M/N$. Assuming $M \ll N$, the probability of success is maximised at $j \approx \frac{\pi}{4}\sqrt{N/M}$ iterations. Boyer, Brassard, Høyer, and Tapp (BBHT) show that a constant success probability can be obtained after $O(\sqrt{N/M})$ iterations.

The same complexity can be obtained when M is not known. One simply runs the algorithm repeatedly with j chosen uniformly from successively larger intervals. The following lemma contains the core observation.

Lemma 1 (Lemma 2 of [12]). *Suppose that measuring $\mathbf{D}|0\rangle$ would yield a root of f with probability $\sin^2(\theta)$. Fix a positive integer m. Let j be chosen uniformly from $\{0, \ldots, m-1\}$. The expected probability that measuring $\mathbf{G}(f)^j\mathbf{D}|0\rangle$ yields a root of f is $\frac{1}{m}\sum_{j=0}^{m-1}\sin^2((2j+1)\cdot\theta) = \frac{1}{2} - \frac{\sin(4m\theta)}{4m\sin(2\theta)}$. If $m > 1/\sin(2\theta)$ then this quantity is at least $1/4$.*

The complete strategy is made precise by [12, Theorem 3].

Amplitude Amplification. Brassard, Høyer, Mosca, and Tapp observed that the $\mathbf{D}$ subroutine of Grover's algorithm can be replaced with any algorithm that finds a root of f with positive probability [13]. This generalisation of Grover's algorithm is called amplitude amplification. Let $\mathbf{A}$ be a quantum algorithm that makes no measurements and let p be the probability that measuring $\mathbf{A}|0\rangle$ yields a root of f. Let $\mathbf{G}(\mathbf{A}, f) = \mathbf{A}\mathbf{R}_0\mathbf{A}^{-1}\mathbf{R}_f$, where $\mathbf{R}_0$ and $\mathbf{R}_f$ are as in Grover's algorithm. Let θ be such that $\sin^2(\theta) = p$. Suppose that j iterations of $\mathbf{G}(\mathbf{A}, f)$ are applied to $\mathbf{A}|0\rangle$. The analysis in [13] shows that measuring the state $\mathbf{G}(\mathbf{A}, f)^j\mathbf{A}|0\rangle$ yields a root of f with probability $\sin^2((2j+1)\cdot\theta)$. The BBHT strategy for handling an unknown number of roots generalises to an unknown p.

2.3   Lattice Sieving and Near Neighbour Search on the Sphere

A Euclidean lattice of rank m and dimension d is an abelian group generated by integer sums of $m \leq d$ linearly independent vectors in $\mathbb{R}^d$. In this paper we only consider full rank lattices, i.e. $m = d$. The shortest vector problem in a lattice Λ is the problem of finding a non-zero $v \in \Lambda$ of minimal Euclidean norm. Norms in this work are Euclidean and denoted $\|\cdot\|$. The angular distance of $u, v \in \mathbb{R}^d$ is denoted $\theta(u, v) = \arccos(\langle u, v \rangle / \|u\|\|v\|)$, $\arccos(x) \in [0, \pi]$.

A lattice sieve takes as input a list of lattice points, $L \subset \Lambda$, and searches for integer combinations of these points that are short. If the initial list is sufficiently large, SVP can be solved by performing this process recursively. Each point in the initial list can be sampled at a cost polynomial in d [31]. Hence the initial list can be sampled at a cost of $|L|^{1+o(1)}$.

Sieves that combine k points at a time are called k-sieves. The sieves that we consider in this paper are 2-sieves. They take integer combinations of the form $u \pm v$ with $u, v \in L$ and $u \neq \pm v$. If $\|u \pm v\| \geq \max\{\|u\|, \|v\|\}$ then we say that (u, v) is a reduced pair, else it is a reducible pair.

We analyse 2-sieves under the heuristic that the points in L are independent and identically distributed (i.i.d.) uniformly in a thin spherical shell. This heuristic was introduced by Nguyen and Vidick in [40]. As a further simplification, we assume that the shell is very thin and normalise such that $L \subset \mathcal{S}^{d-1}$, the unit sphere in $\mathbb{R}^d$. As such, (u, v) are reducible if and only if $\theta(u, v) < \pi/3$. The popcount filter, introduced in Sect. 2.4, acts as a first approximation to $\theta(\cdot, \cdot)$.

When we model L as a subset of $\mathcal{S}^{d-1}$, we can translate some lattice sieves into the language of (angular) near neighbour search on the sphere. For example, the Nguyen–Vidick sieve [40], which checks all pairs in L for reducibility, becomes[1] Algorithm 1 with $\theta = \pi/3$.

Algorithm 1. AllPairSearch

Input: A list $L = (v_1, v_2, \ldots v_N) \subset \mathcal{S}^{d-1}$ of N points. Parameter $\theta \in (0, \pi/2)$.
Output: A list of pairs $(u, v) \in L \times L$ with $\theta(u, v) \leq \theta$.

1: **function** AllPairSearch$(L; \theta)$
2:     $L' \leftarrow \emptyset$
3:     **for** $1 \leq i < N$ **do**
4:         $L_i \leftarrow (v_{i+1}, \ldots, v_N)$
5:         Search L_i for any number of u that satisfy $\theta(u, v_i) \leq \theta$.
6:         For each such u found, add (u, v_i) to L'.
7:         If $|L'| \geq N$, **return** L'.
8:     **return** L'

2.4   The popcount Filter

Charikar's locality sensitive hashing (LSH) scheme [15] is a family of hash functions $\mathcal{H}$, defined on $\mathcal{S}^{d-1}$, for which

$$\Pr_{h \leftarrow \mathcal{H}}[h(u) = h(v)] = 1 - \frac{\theta(u, v)}{\pi}. \tag{2}$$

The hash function family is defined by

$$\mathcal{H} = \left\{ u \mapsto \mathrm{sgn}(\langle r, u \rangle) : r \in \mathcal{S}^{d-1} \right\},$$

where $\mathrm{sgn}(x) = 1$ if $x \geq 0$ and $\mathrm{sgn}(x) = 0$ if $x < 0$. Equation 2 follows from the fact that $\theta(u, v)/\pi$ is the probability that uniformly random u and v lie in opposite hemispheres.

Charikar observed that one can estimate $\theta(u, v)/\pi$ by choosing a random hash function $h = (h_1, \ldots, h_n) \in \mathcal{H}^n$ and measuring the Hamming distance between $h(u) = (h_1(u), \ldots, h_n(u))$ and $h(v) = (h_1(v), \ldots, h_n(v))$. Each bit $h_i(u) \oplus h_i(v)$ is Bernoulli distributed with parameter $p = \theta(u, v)/\pi$. In the limit of large n, the normalised Hamming weight $wt(h(u) \oplus h(v))/n$ converges to a normal distribution with mean p and standard deviation $\sqrt{p(1-p)/n}$.

In the sieving literature, the process of filtering a $\theta(\cdot, \cdot)$ test using a threshold on the value of $wt(h(u) \oplus h(v))$ is known as the "XOR and population count

---

[1] This is slightly imprecise. The analogy with the Nguyen–Vidick sieve is completed only when Algorithm 1 is wrapped in a procedure that takes each $(u, v) \in L'$ and maps it to $(u \pm v)/\|u \pm v\|$, and then recurses.

trick" [2,17,18]. Functions in $\mathcal{H}^n$ are also used in Laarhoven's HashSieve [33]. We write $\text{popcount}_{k,n}(u, v; h)$ for a search filter of this type

$$\text{popcount}_{k,n}(u, v; h) = \begin{cases} 0 & \text{if } \sum_{i=1}^n h_i(u) \oplus h_i(v) \leq k, \\ 1 & \text{otherwise.} \end{cases}$$

When the n hash functions are fixed we write $\text{popcount}_{k,n}(u, v)$. The threshold, k, is chosen based on the desired false positive and false negative rates. Heuristically, if one's goal is to detect points at angle at most θ, one should take $k/n \approx \theta/\pi$. If $k/n \ll \theta/\pi$ then the false negative rate will be large, and many neighbouring pairs will be missed. An important consequence of missing potential reductions is that the N required to iterate Algorithms 1, 3, 4 increases. In Sect. 6 this increase is captured in the quantity $\ell(k, n)$. If $k/n \gg \theta/\pi$ then the false positive rate will be large, and the full inner product test will be applied often. We calculate these false positive and negative rates in Sect. 5. These calculations and the fact that popcount is significantly cheaper than an inner product makes popcount a good candidate for use as a filter under the techniques of Sect. 2.2. Furthermore it is the filter used in the most performant sieves to date [2,17].

2.5 Geometric Figures on the Sphere

Our analysis of the popcount filter requires some basic facts about the size of some geometric figures on the sphere. We measure the volume of subsets of $\mathcal{S}^{d-1} = \{v \in \mathbb{R}^d : \|v\| = 1\}$ using the $(d-1)$ dimensional spherical probability measure[2] μ^{d-1}. The spherical cap of angle θ about $u \in \mathcal{S}^{d-1}$ is $\mathcal{C}^{d-1}(u, \theta) = \{v \in \mathcal{S}^{d-1} : \theta(u, v) \leq \theta\}$. The measure of a spherical cap is

$$C_d(u, \theta) := \mu^{d-1}(\mathcal{C}^{d-1}(u, \theta)) = \frac{1}{\sqrt{\pi}} \frac{\Gamma(\frac{d}{2})}{\Gamma(\frac{d-1}{2})} \int_0^\theta \sin^{d-2}(t) \, dt.$$

We will often interpret $C_d(u, \theta)$ as the probability that v drawn uniformly from $\mathcal{S}^{d-1}$ satisfies $\theta(u, v) \leq \theta$. We denote the density of the event $\theta(u, v) = \theta$ by

$$A_d(u, \theta) := \frac{\partial}{\partial \theta} C_d(u, \theta) = \frac{1}{\sqrt{\pi}} \frac{\Gamma(\frac{d}{2})}{\Gamma(\frac{d-1}{2})} \sin^{d-2}(\theta).$$

Note that $C_d(u, \theta)$ does not depend on u, so we may write $C_d(\theta)$ and $A_d(\theta)$ without ambiguity. The wedge formed by the intersection of two caps is $\mathcal{W}^{d-1}(u, \theta_u, v, \theta_v) = \mathcal{C}^{d-1}(u, \theta_u) \cap \mathcal{C}^{d-1}(v, \theta_v)$. The measure of a wedge only depends on $\theta = \theta(u, v)$, θ_u, and θ_v, so we denote it

$$W_d(\theta, \theta_u, \theta_v) = \mu^{d-1}(\mathcal{W}^{d-1}(u, \theta_u, v, \theta_v)).$$

We will often interpret $W_d(\theta, \theta_u, \theta_v)$ as the probability that w drawn uniformly from $\mathcal{S}^{d-1}$ satisfies $\theta(u, w) \leq \theta_u$ and $\theta(v, w) \leq \theta_v$. Note that $\theta \geq \theta_u + \theta_v \Rightarrow W_d(\theta, \theta_u, \theta_v) = 0$. An integral representation of $W_d(\theta, \theta_u, \theta_v)$ is given in Appendix A of the full version.

---

[2] By "probability measure" we mean that $\mu^{d-1}(\mathcal{S}^{d-1}) = 1$.

3   Filtered Quantum Search

A filter can reduce the cost of a search because a classical computer can branch to avoid evaluating an expensive predicate. A quantum circuit cannot branch inside a Grover search in this way. Nevertheless, a filter can be used to reduce the cost of a quantum search.

The idea is to apply amplitude amplification to a Grover search. The inner Grover search prepares the uniform superposition over roots of the filter, g. The outer amplitude amplification searches for a root of f among the roots of g. We present pseudocode for this strategy in Algorithm 2.

If $|g|$ and $|f \cap g|$ are known, then we can choose the number of iterations of the inner Grover search and the outer amplitude amplification optimally. When these quantities are not known, we can attempt to guess them as in the BBHT algorithm. In our applications, we have some information about $|g|$ and $|f \cap g|$, which we can use to fine-tune a BBHT-like strategy.

Proposition 1 gives the cost of Algorithm 2 when we know *1.* a lower bound, Q, on the size of $|f \cap g|$, and *2.* the value of $|g|$ up to relative error γ. In essence, when a filter with a low false positive rate is used to search a space with few true positives, Algorithm 2 can be tuned such that it finds a root of f with probability at least $1/14$ and at a cost of roughly $\frac{\gamma}{2}\sqrt{N/Q}$ iterations of $\mathbf{G}(g)$.

Algorithm 2. FilteredQuantumSearch

Input: A predicate f and a filter g defined on $\{0, \dots, N-1\}$. Integer parameters m_1 and m_2.
Output: A root of f or $\perp$.
1: **function** FilteredQuantumSearch($f, g; m_1, m_2$)
2:     Sample integers j and k with $0 \le j < m_1$ and $0 \le k < m_2$ uniformly at random.
3:     Let $\mathbf{A}_j = \mathbf{G}(g)^j \mathbf{D}$.
4:     Let $\mathbf{B}_k = \mathbf{G}(\mathbf{A}_j, f \cap g)^k$.
5:     Prepare the state $|\psi\rangle = \mathbf{B}_k \mathbf{A}_j |0\rangle$.
6:     Let r be the result of measuring $|\psi\rangle$ in the computational basis.
7:     **if** $f(r) = 0$ **then**
8:         **return** r
9:     **return** $\perp$

If we know that the the inner Grover search succeeds with probability $x < 1$, we can compensate with a factor of $\sqrt{1/x}$ more iterations of the outer amplitude amplification. We do not know x. However, in our applications, we do know that the value of θ for which $\sin^2(\theta) = |g|/N$ will be fairly small, e.g. $\theta < 1/10$. The following technical lemma shows that, when θ is small, we may assume that $x = 1/5$ with little impact on the overall cost of the search.

Let j and $\mathbf{A}_j$ be as in Algorithm 2. Let $p_\theta(j)$ be the probability that measuring $\mathbf{A}_j|0\rangle$ would yield a root of g. For any $x \in (0,1)$, there is some probability $q_x(m_1)$ that the choice of j is insufficient, i.e. that $p_\theta(j) < x$. We expect to repeat Algorithm 2 a total of $(1 - q_x(m_1))^{-1}$ times to avoid this type of failure.

Lemma 2. *Fix $\theta \in [0, \pi/2]$ and $x \in [0, 1)$. Let $p_\theta, q_x : \mathbb{R} \to \mathbb{R}$ be defined by $p_\theta(j) = \sin^2((2j+1) \cdot \theta)$ and $q_x(m) = \frac{1}{m} |\{j \in \mathbb{Z} : 0 \leq j < m, p_\theta(j) < x\}|$. If $m > \frac{\pi}{4\theta}$, then*

$$q_x(m) < \frac{3 \arcsin(\sqrt{x})}{\pi - \arcsin(\sqrt{x})} + \frac{6\theta}{\pi}.$$

Proof. Observe that $p_\theta(j) < x$ when $|(2j+1)\theta \bmod \pi| < \arcsin(\sqrt{x})$. Let I_0 be the interval $[0, \arcsin(\sqrt{x}))$. For integers $t \geq 1$ let $I_t = (t\pi - \arcsin(\sqrt{x}), t\pi + \arcsin(\sqrt{x}))$. Let $c = c(m)$ be the largest integer for which $[0, (2m-1) \cdot \theta)$ intersects I_c. The quantity $mq_x(m)$ counts the number of non-negative integers $i < m$ for which $(2i+1) \cdot \theta$ lies in $I_0 \cup I_1 \cup \cdots \cup I_c$. This is no more than $(c+1) + \lfloor (2c+1) \arcsin(\sqrt{x})/(2\theta) \rfloor$. It follows that $q_x(m) < (c+1)/m + (2c+1) \arcsin(\sqrt{x})/2m\theta$. Note that $2m\theta > (2m-1)\theta > c\pi - \arcsin(\sqrt{x})$ and $(c+1)/m < 2\theta/\pi + 1/m$. Hence $q_x(m) < (2c+1) \arcsin(\sqrt{x})/(c\pi - \arcsin(\sqrt{x})) + 2\theta/\pi + 1/m$. Moreover, $q_x(m) > q_x(m-1)$ when $(2m-1) \cdot \theta$ lies in I_c, and $q_x(m) < q_x(m-1)$ otherwise. The upper bound on $q_x(m)$ that we have derived is decreasing as a function of c. Hence the claim holds when $c \geq 1$. Finally, when $m = \frac{\pi}{4\theta}$ and $c = 0$ we have $q_x(m) < 2 \arcsin(\sqrt{x})/\pi + 4\theta/\pi$ and $q_x(m)$ is decreasing until $c = 1$. $\square$

There are situations in which filtering is not effective, e.g. when the false positive rate of g is very high, when evaluting g is not much less expensive than evaluating f, or when f has a very large number of roots. In these cases, other algorithms will outperform Algorithm 2. We remark on these below. Proposition 1 optimises the choice of m_1 and m_2 in Algorithm 2 for a large class of filters that are typical of our applications.

Proposition 1. *Suppose that f and g are predicates on a domain of size N and that g is a filter for f. Let $Q \in \mathbb{R}$ be such that $1 \leq Q \leq |f \cap g|$. Let P and γ be real numbers such that $P/\gamma \leq |g| \leq \gamma P$. If $\gamma P/N < 1/100$ and $\gamma Q/P < 1/4$, then there are parameters m_1 and m_2 for Algorithm 2 such that Algorithm 2 finds a root of f with probability at least $1/14$ and has a cost that is dominated by $\approx \frac{\gamma}{2}\sqrt{N/Q}$ times the cost of $\mathbf{G}(g)$ or by $\approx \frac{2}{3}\sqrt{\gamma P/Q}$ times the cost of $\mathbf{R}_{f \cap g}$.*

Proof. Fix $x \in (0, 1)$. We will analyse Algorithm 2 with respect to the parameters $m_1 = \left\lceil \frac{\pi}{4}\sqrt{\gamma N/P} \right\rceil$ and $m_2 = \left\lceil \sqrt{\gamma P/3xQ} \right\rceil$. Let θ_g be such that $\sin^2(\theta_g) = |g|/N$. Let j and k be chosen as in Algorithm 2. Let $p = p_{\theta_g}(j)$ and $q = q_x(m_1)$ be defined as in Lemma 2. Note that since $|g|/N < \gamma P/N < 1/100$ we can use $6\theta_g/\pi < 1/5$ in applying Lemma 2. Let $\theta_h(j)$ be such that $\sin^2(\theta_h(j)) = p \cdot |f \cap g|/|g|$. With probability at least $1 - q$ we have $p \geq x$, which implies that $\sin(\theta_h(j)) > \sqrt{xQ/\gamma P}$. Since $\gamma Q/P < 1/4 \Rightarrow \sin^2(\theta_h(j)) < 1/4$, then $\cos(\theta_h(j)) > \sqrt{3/4}$. Thus $1/\sin(2\theta_h(j)) < \sqrt{\frac{\gamma P}{3xQ}} \leq m_2$. By Lemma 1 measuring $\mathbf{G}(\mathbf{A}_j, f \cap g)^k \mathbf{A}_j |0\rangle$ yields a root of $f \cap g$ with probability at least $1/4$. It follows that Algorithm 2 succeeds with probability at least $(1-q)/4$.

The algorithm evaluates $\mathbf{G}(g)$ exactly $k \cdot j + 1$ times and evaluates $\mathbf{G}(g)^{-1}$ exactly $k \cdot j$ times. The expected value of $2kj + 1$ is $c_1(x) \cdot \gamma \cdot \sqrt{N/Q}$ where

$c_1(x) \approx (\pi/8)/\sqrt{3x}$. Likewise the algorithm evaluates $\mathbf{R}_{f \cap g}$ exactly k times, which is $c_2(x) \cdot \sqrt{\gamma P/Q}$ in expectation where $c_2(x) \approx (1/2)/\sqrt{3x}$. Taking $x = 1/5$, and applying the upper bound on $q_x(m_1)$ from Lemma 2, we have $(1 - q_x(m_1))/4 \geq 1/14$, $c_1(x) \approx 1/2$ and $c_2(x) \approx 2/3$. $\qquad\qquad\square$

Remark 1. When $\gamma P/N \geq 1/100$ or $\gamma Q/P \geq 1/4$ there are better algorithms. If both inequalities hold then classical search finds a root of f quickly. If $\gamma Q/P \geq 1/4$ then finding a root of f is not much harder than finding a root of g, so one can search on g directly. If $\gamma P/N \geq 1/100$ then the filter has little effect and one can search on f directly.

Remark 2. It is helpful to understand when we can ignore the cost of $\mathbf{R}_{f \cap g}$ in Proposition 1. Roughly speaking, if evaluating f is c times more expensive than evaluating g, then the cost of calls to $\mathbf{G}(g)$ will dominate when $N > c^2 |g|$. In a classical filtered search the cost of evaluating g dominates when $N > c |g|$.

4   Circuits for popcount

Consider a program for $\mathrm{popcount}_{k,n}(u, v)$. This program loads u and v from specified memory addresses, computes $h(u)$ and $h(v)$, computes the Hamming weight of $h(u) \oplus h(v)$, and checks whether it is less than or equal to k. Recall $h(u)$ is defined by n inner products. If the popcount procedure is executed many times for each u, then it may be reasonable to compute $h(u)$ once and store it in memory. Moreover, if u is fixed for many sequential calls to the procedure, then it may be reasonable to cache $h(u)$ between calls. The algorithms that we consider in Sect. 6 use both of these optimisations.

In this section we describe RAM programs and quantum circuits that compute $\mathrm{popcount}_{k,n}(u, \cdot)$ for a fixed u. These circuits have the value of $h(u)$ hardcoded. They load $h(v)$ from memory, compute the Hamming weight of $h(u) \oplus h(v)$, and check whether the Hamming weight is less than or equal to k. We ignore the initial, one time, cost of computing $h(u)$ and $h(v)$.

4.1   Quantum Circuit for popcount

Loading $h(v)$ costs a single qRAM gate. Computing $h(u) \oplus h(v)$ can then be done in-place using a sequence of $\mathbf{X}$ gates that encode $h(u)$. The bulk of the effort is in computing the Hamming weight. For that we use a tree of in-place adders. The final comparison is also computed with an adder, although only one bit of the output is needed. See Fig. 1 for a full description of the circuit.

We use the Cuccaro–Draper–Kutin–Petrie adder [16], with "incoming carry" inputs, to compute the Hamming weight. We argue in favour of this choice of adder in Appendix C of the full version. We use the Häner–Roetteler–Svore [26] carry bit circuit for implementing the comparison.

We will later use popcount within filtered quantum searches by defining predicates of the form $g(i) = \mathrm{popcount}_{k,n}(u, v_i)$, $i \in \{1, \ldots, N\}$. To simplify that later discussion, we cost the entire Grover iteration $\mathbf{G}(g) = \mathbf{D}\mathbf{R}_0\mathbf{D}^{-1}\mathbf{R}_g$ here. In Appendix B of the full version we introduce the (possibly multiply controlled) Toffoli gate and discuss the Toffoli count for $\mathbf{G}(g)$, which in turn gives the $\mathbf{T}$ count for $\mathbf{G}(g)$.

The Cost of $\mathbf{R}_g$. The $\mathbf{R}_g$ subroutine is computed by running the popcount circuit in Fig. 1 and then uncomputing the addition tree and $\mathbf{X}$ gates. The circuit uses in-place i bit adders[3] for $i \in \{1, \dots, \ell-1\}$. The width of the circuit is given in Appendix B of the full version. The depth of the circuit is

$$\text{depth} = 2 + d(\text{CARRY}) + \sum_{i=1}^{\ell-1} 2 \cdot d(\text{ADD}_i), \qquad (3)$$

where $d(\cdot)$ denotes the depth of its argument. The factor of 2 accounts for uncomputation of the ADD_i circuits. The CARRY circuit is only cost once as the carry bit is computed directly into the $|-\rangle$ state during the CARRY circuit itself. The summand 2 accounts for the $\mathbf{X}$ gates used to compute, and later uncompute, $h(u) \oplus h(v)$.

The Cost of $\mathbf{D}\mathbf{R}_0\mathbf{D}^{-1}$. Recall that $\mathbf{D}$ can be any circuit that maps $|0\rangle$ to the uniform distribution on the domain of the search predicate. While there is no serious difficulty in sampling from the uniform distribution on $\{0, \dots, N-1\}$ for any integer N, when costing the circuit we assume that N is a power of two. In this case $\mathbf{D}$ is simply $\log_2 N$ parallel $\mathbf{H}$ gates. The reflection $\mathbf{R}_0$ is implemented as a multiply controlled Toffoli gate that targets an ancilla initialised in the $|-\rangle$ state. We use Maslov's multiply controlled Toffoli from [37]. The depth and width of $\mathbf{D}\mathbf{R}_0\mathbf{D}^{-1}$ are both $O(\log N)$; our software calculates the exact value.

4.2   RAM Program for popcount

Recall that we use a RAM instruction set that consists of simple bit operations and table lookups. A Boolean circuit for popcount is schematically similar to Fig. 1. Let $\ell = \lceil \log_2 n \rceil$. Loading $h(v)$ has cost 1. Computing $h(v) \oplus h(w)$ takes n XOR instructions and has depth 1. Following [41, Table. II], with $c_{FA} = 5$ the number of instructions in a full adder, $(n - \ell - 1)c_{FA} + \ell$ lower bounds the instruction cost of computing the Hamming weight and comparing it with a fixed k. This has depth $(\ell - 1)(\delta_{\text{sum}} + \delta_{\text{carry}}) + 1$. We assume $\delta_{\text{sum}} = \delta_{\text{carry}} = 1$. Thus, the overall instruction count is $6n - 4\ell - 5$ and the overall depth is 2ℓ.

4.3   Cost of Inner Products

The optimal popcount parameters will depend on the cost of a computing an inner product in dimension d. The cost of one inner product is amortised over

---

[3] An in-place i bit quantum adder takes two i bit inputs, initialises an ancilla qubit in the $|0\rangle$ state, and returns the addition result in an $i + 1$ bit register that includes the new ancilla and overlaps with i bits of the input.

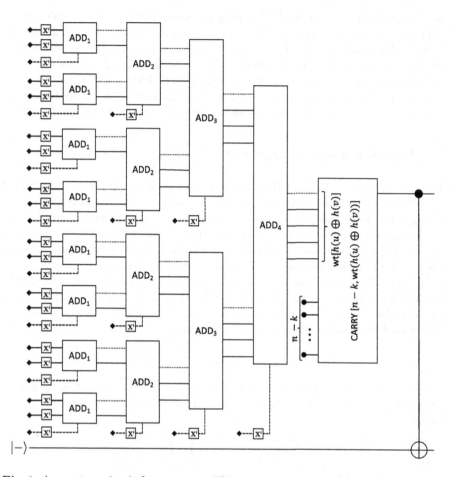

Fig. 1. A quantum circuit for popcount. This circuit computes $h(u) \oplus h(v)$ for a fixed n bit $h(u)$, computes the Hamming weight of $h(u) \oplus h(v)$, and checks whether the Hamming weight is less than or equal to k. Here $n = 2^\ell - 1 = 31$. The input qubits are represented as lines ending with a black diamond. The dashed lines represent incoming carry inputs, and the dotted lines represent carry outputs. Not all of the output wires are drawn. For space efficiency, some of the input qubits are fed into the incoming carry qubits of the adders (dashed lines). The $\mathbf{X}^i$ mean that gate $\mathbf{X}$ is applied to input qubit i if bit i of $h(u)$ is 1. The circuit uses a depth $\ell - 1$ binary tree of full bit adders from [16], where ADD_i denotes an i bit full adder. The output $wt(h(u) \oplus h(v))$ from the tree of adders together with the binary representation of the number $n - k$ are finally fed into the input of the CARRY circuit from [26], which computes the carry bit of $n - k + wt(h(u) \oplus h(v))$ (the carry bit will be 0 if $wt(h(u) \oplus h(v)) \leq k$, and 1 otherwise). The final **CNOT** is for illustration only. In actuality, the carry bit is computed directly into an ancilla that is initialised in the $|-\rangle = (|0\rangle - |1\rangle)/\sqrt{2}$ state, so we can obtain the needed phase kickback. The tree of adders and the initial $\mathbf{X}$ gates, but not the CARRY circuit, are run in reverse to clean up scratch space and return the inputs to their initial state. The uncomputation step is not depicted here.

many popcounts, and a small change in the popcount parameters will quickly suppress the ratio of inner products to popcounts (see Remark 2). Hence we only need a rough estimate for the cost of an inner product. We assume 32 bits of precision are sufficient. We then assume schoolbook multiplication is used for scalar products, which costs approximately 32^2 AND instructions. We then assume the cost of a full inner product is approximately $32^2\,d$, i.e. we ignore the cost of the final summation, assuming it is dwarfed by the ANDs.[4]

5   The Accuracy of popcount

Here we give an analysis of the popcount technique based on some standard simplifying assumptions. We are particularly interested in the probability that a popcount filter identifies a random pair of points as potential neighbours. We are also interested in the probability that a pair of actual neighbours are not identified as potential neighbours, i.e. the false negative rate. Our software computes all of the quantities in this section to high precision.

Let $P_{k,n}(u,v)$ be the probability that $\mathrm{popcount}_{k,n}(u,v;h) = 0$ for a uniformly random h (recall $\mathrm{popcount}_{k,n}(u,v;h) = 0$ if u, v pass the filter). In other words, let $h = (h_1, \ldots, h_n)$ be a collection of independent random variables that are distributed uniformly on the sphere, and define

$$P_{k,n}(u,v) = 1 - \mathbb{E}\left[\mathrm{popcount}_{k,n}(u,v;h)\right].$$

The hyperplane defined by h_i separates u and v with probability $\theta(u,v)/\pi$, and $\mathrm{popcount}_{k,n}(u,v;h) = 0$ if no more than k of the hyperplanes separate u and v. Hence,

$$P_{k,n}(u,v) = \sum_{i=0}^{k} \binom{n}{i} \cdot \left(\frac{\theta(u,v)}{\pi}\right)^i \cdot \left(1 - \frac{\theta(u,v)}{\pi}\right)^{n-i}.$$

Note that $P_{k,n}(u,v)$ depends only on the angle between u and v, so it makes sense to define $P_{k,n}(\theta)$. The main heuristic in our analysis of popcount is that $P_{k,n}(u,v)$ is a good approximation to the probability that $\mathrm{popcount}_{k,n}(u,v;h) = 0$ for *fixed* h and *varying* u and v. Under this assumption, all of the quantities in question can be determined by integrating $P_{k,n}(u,v)$ over different regions of the sphere.

Let $\hat{P}_{k,n}$ denote the event that $\mathrm{popcount}_{k,n}(u,v;h) = 0$ for uniformly random u, v, and h. Let $\hat{R}_\theta$ be the event that $\theta(u,v) \leq \theta$. Recall that $\Pr[\hat{R}_\theta] = C_d(\theta)$, and observe that $\Pr[\hat{R}_\theta]$ is a cumulative distribution with associated density

---

[4] We also tested the effect of assuming 8-bit inner products are sufficient. As expected, this reduces all costs by a factor of two to four and thus does not substantially alter our relative results.

$A_d(\theta) = \frac{\partial}{\partial \theta} C_d(\theta)$. We find, letting $\mathcal{S} = \mathcal{S}^{d-1}$ for some implicit d,

$$
\begin{aligned}
\Pr[\hat{P}_{k,n}] &= \int_{\mathcal{S}} \int_{\mathcal{S}} P_{k,n}(u,v) \, d\mu(v) \, d\mu(u) \\
&= \int_{\mathcal{S}} \left(\int_0^{\pi} P_{k,n}(\theta) \cdot A_d(\theta) \, d\theta \right) d\mu(u) \\
&= \int_0^{\pi} P_{k,n}(\theta) \cdot A_d(\theta) \, d\theta.
\end{aligned}
\tag{4}
$$

Let u, v such that $\theta(u,v) \leq \varphi$ be neighbours. The false negative rate is $1 - \Pr[\hat{P}_{k,n} \mid \hat{R}_\varphi]$. The quantity $\Pr[\hat{P}_{k,n} \wedge \hat{R}_\varphi]$ can be calculated by changing the upper limit of integration in Eq. 4. It follows that

$$
1 - \Pr[\hat{P}_{k,n} \mid \hat{R}_\varphi] = 1 - \frac{1}{C_d(\varphi)} \int_0^{\varphi} P_{k,n}(\theta) \cdot A_d(\theta) \, d\theta.
\tag{5}
$$

In Sect. 6 we consider u and v that are uniformly distributed in a cap of angle $\beta < \pi/2$, rather than the uniformly distributed on the sphere. Let $\hat{B}_{w,\beta}$ be the event that u and v are uniformly distributed in a cap of angle β about w. We have

$$
\begin{aligned}
\Pr[\hat{B}_{w,\beta}] &= \int_{\mathcal{S}} \int_{\mathcal{S}} \mathbb{1} \left\{ w \in \mathcal{W}^{d-1}(u,\beta,v,\beta) \right\} \, d\mu(v) \, d\mu(u) \\
&= \int_0^{2\beta} W_d(\theta,\beta,\beta) \cdot A_d(\theta) \, d\theta.
\end{aligned}
\tag{6}
$$

In the second line we have used the fact that $\beta < \pi/2$ and $W(\theta,\theta_1,\theta_2)$ is zero when $\theta \geq \theta_1 + \theta_2$. The quantity $\Pr[\hat{B}_{w,\beta} \wedge \hat{R}_\varphi]$ can be computed by changing the upper limit of integration in Eq. 6 from 2β to $\min\{2\beta, \varphi\}$. We note that $\hat{B}_{w,\beta}$ has no dependence on w and therefore may also be written $\hat{B}_\beta$. The conditional probability that $\texttt{popcount}_{k,n}(u,v;h) = 0$, given that u,v are uniformly distributed in a cap B_β, $\Pr[\hat{P}_{k,n} \mid \hat{B}_\beta]$, can be computed using Eq. 6 and

$$
\Pr[\hat{P}_{k,n} \wedge \hat{B}_\beta] = \int_0^{2\beta} P_{k,n}(\theta) \cdot W_d(\theta,\beta,\beta) \cdot A_d(\theta) \, d\theta.
\tag{7}
$$

The quantity $\Pr[\hat{P}_{k,n} \wedge \hat{B}_\beta \wedge \hat{R}_\varphi]$ can be computed by changing the upper limit of integration in Eq. 7 from 2β to $\min\{2\beta, \varphi\}$. The false negative rate for $\texttt{popcount}$ when restricted to a cap is $1 - \Pr[\hat{P}_{k,n} \mid \hat{B}_{w,\beta} \wedge \hat{R}_\varphi]$.

6 Tuning popcount for NNS

We now use the circuit sizes from Sect. 4 and the probabilities from Sect. 5 to optimise $\texttt{popcount}$ for use in NNS algorithms. Our analysis is with respect to points sampled independently from the uniform distribution on the sphere.

We further restrict our attention to *list-size preserving* parameterisations, which take an input list of size N and return an output list of (expected) size N.

We use the notation for events introduced in Sect. 5. In particular, we write $\hat{R}_\theta$ for the event that a uniformly random pair of vectors are neighbours, i.e. that they lie at angle less than or equal to θ of one another; $\hat{P}_{k,n}$ for the event that popcount identifies a uniformly random pair of vectors as potential neighbours; $\hat{B}_\beta$ for the event that a uniformly random pair of vectors lie in a uniformly random cap of angle β; and $\hat{B}_{w,\beta}$ for the same event except we highlight the cap is centred on w. Throughout this section we use $\text{popcount}_{k,n}(u, \cdot)$, for various fixed u, as a filter for the search predicate $\theta(u, \cdot) \leq \theta$. We write $\eta(k, n)$ for the false negative rate of popcount. We assume that $\theta(u, v) \leq \theta$ is computed using an inner product test. Throughout this section, c_1 represents the instruction cost of the inner product test from Sect. 4.3, $c_2(k, n)$ the instruction cost of popcount from Sect. 4.2, q_1 the quantum cost of the reflection $\mathbf{R}_{f \cap g}$, and $q_2(k, n)$ the quantum cost of $\mathbf{G}(g)$ from Sect. 4.1. We note that c_1, q_1 have a dependence on d that we suppress. We write $q_0(m)$ for the number of $\mathbf{G}(g)$ iterations that are applied during a quantum search on a set of size m.

Our goal is to minimise the cost of list-size preserving NNS algorithms as a function of the input list size, the popcount parameters k and n, and the other NNS parameters. In a list of N points there are $\binom{N}{2}$ ordered pairs. We expect $\binom{N}{2} \cdot \Pr[\hat{R}_\theta] = \binom{N}{2} \cdot C_d(\theta)$ of these to be neighbours, and we expect a $1 - \eta(k, n)$ fraction of neighbours to be detected by popcount. List-size preserving parmaterisations that use a popcount filter must therefore take an input list of size at least

$$\ell(k, n) = \frac{2}{1 - \eta(k, n)} \cdot \frac{1}{C_d(\theta)}. \tag{8}$$

The optimised costs reported in Fig. 2 typically use popcount parameters for which $\ell(k, n) \in (2/C_d(\pi/3), 4/C_d(\pi/3))$. Here we assume that list-size preserving parameterisations take $N = \ell(k, n)$. Note that $\eta(k, n) = 1 - \Pr[\hat{P}_{k,n} \mid \hat{R}_\theta]$ when the search is over a set of points uniformly distributed on the sphere, and $\eta(k, n) = 1 - \Pr[\hat{P}_{k,n} \mid \hat{R}_\theta \wedge \hat{B}_\beta]$ when the search is over a set of points uniformly distributed in a cap of angle β (left implicit).

In each of the quantum analyses, we apply Proposition 1 with $\gamma = 1$, $P = |g|$ and $Q = 1$ to estimate $q_0(m)$. We assume that filtered quantum search succeeds with probability 1 instead of probability at least $1/14$, as guaranteed by Proposition 1. In practice, one will not know $|g|$ and one will therefore take $\gamma > 1$. Our use of $\gamma = 1$ is a systematic underestimate of the true cost of the search. There may be searches where our lower bound of $Q = 1$ on $|f \cap g|$ is too pessimistic. However, the probability of success in filtered quantum search decreases quadratically with $Q/|f \cap g|$ if $Q > |f \cap g|$. In Sects. 6.1 and 6.3 we expect $|f \cap g| \approx 2$ so the effect of taking $Q = 1$ is negligible. In Sect. 6.2, where Q may be larger, an optimistic analysis using the expected value of Q makes negligible savings in dimension 512 and small savings in dimension 1024. This analysis does not decrement Q when a neighbour is found in, then removed from, a search space and ignores the quadratic decrease in success probability.

6.1   AllPairSearch

As a warmup, we optimise AllPairSearch. Asymptotically its complexity is $2^{(0.415...+o(1))d}$ classically and $2^{(0.311...+o(1))d}$ quantumly. We describe implementations of Line 5 of Algorithm 1 based on filtered search and filtered quantum search, and optimise popcount relative to these implementations.

Filtered Search. Suppose that Line 5 applies $\mathtt{popcount}_{k,n}(v_i, \cdot)$ to each of v_{i+1} through v_N and then applies an inner product test to each vector that passes. With an input list of size $N = \ell(k, n)$, we expect this implementation to test all $\binom{N}{2}$ pairs before finding N neighbouring pairs. Moreover, we expect the popcount filter to identify $\binom{N}{2} \cdot \Pr[\hat{P}_{k,n}]$ potential neighbours, and to perform an equal number of inner product tests. The optimal parameters are obtained by minimising

$$\left(c_1 \cdot \Pr[\hat{P}_{k,n}] + c_2(k, n)\right) \cdot \binom{\ell(k, n)}{2}. \tag{9}$$

Filtered Quantum Search. Suppose that Line 5 is implemented using the search routine Algorithm 2. Specifically, we take the predicate f to be $\theta(v_i, \cdot) \leq \theta$ with domain L_i. We take the filter g to be $\mathtt{popcount}_{k,n}(v_i, \cdot)$. Each call to the search routine returns at most one neighbour of v_i. To find all detectable neighbours of v_i in L_i we must repeat the search $|f \cap g|$ times. This is expected to be $|L_i| \cdot \Pr[\hat{P}_{k,n} \wedge \hat{R}_\theta]$. Known neighbours of v_i can be removed from L_i to avoid a coupon collector scenario. We consider an implementation in which searches are repeated until a search fails to find a neighbour of v_i.

We expect to call the search subroutine $|L_i| \cdot \Pr[\hat{P}_{k,n} \wedge \hat{R}_\theta] + 1$ times in iteration i. Proposition 1 with $P = |L_i| \cdot \Pr[\hat{P}_{k,n}]$, $Q = 1$, and $\gamma = 1$ gives $q_0(|L_i|) = \frac{1}{2}\sqrt{|L_i|}$ iterations of $\mathbf{G}(g)$. As i ranges from 1 to $N - 1$ the quantity $|L_i|$ takes each value in $\{1, \ldots, N - 1\}$. Our proposed implementation therefore performs an expected

$$\sum_{j=1}^{N-1} \frac{1}{2}\sqrt{j}\left(j \cdot \Pr[\hat{P}_{k,n} \wedge \hat{R}_\theta] + 1\right)$$

$$= \Pr[\hat{P}_{k,n} \wedge \hat{R}_\theta]\left(\frac{1}{5}N^{5/2} + \frac{1}{4}N^{3/2}\right) + \frac{1}{3}N^{3/2} + O(\sqrt{N}) \tag{10}$$

applications of $\mathbf{G}(g)$; the expansion is obtained by the Euler–Maclaurin formula. When $N = \ell(k, n)$ we expect $N \cdot \Pr[\hat{P}_{k,n} \wedge \hat{R}_\theta] = 2 + O(1/N)$. The right hand side of Eq. 10 is then $\frac{11}{15}N^{3/2} + O(\sqrt{N})$.

Proposition 1 also provides an estimate for the rate at which reflections about the true positives, $\mathbf{R}_{f \cap g}$ are performed. With P and Q as above, we find that $\mathbf{R}_{f \cap g}$ is performed at roughly $p(k, n) = \sqrt{\Pr[\hat{P}_{k,n}]}$ the rate of calls to $\mathbf{G}(g)$. The optimal popcount parameters (up to some small error due to the $O(\sqrt{N})$

term in Eq. 10) are obtained by minimising the total cost

$$\frac{11}{15}\left(q_1 p(k,n) + q_2(k,n)\right) \cdot \ell(k,n)^{3/2}. \tag{11}$$

6.2   RandomBucketSearch

One can improve AllPairSearch by *bucketing* the search space such that vectors in the same bucket are more likely to be neighbours [33]. For example, one could pick a hemisphere H and divide the list into $L_1 = L \cap H$ and $L_2 = L \backslash L_1$. These lists would be approximately half the size of the original and the combined cost of AllPairSearch within L_1 and then within L_2 would be half the cost of an AllPairSearch within L. However, this strategy would fail to detect the expected θ/π fraction of neighbours that lie in opposite hemispheres.

Becker, Gama, and Joux [9] present a very efficient generalisation of this strategy. They propose bucketing the input list into subsets of the form $\{v \in L : \text{popcount}_{k,n}(0, v; h) = 0\}$ with varying choices of h. This bucketing strategy is applied recursively until the buckets are of a minimum size. Neighbouring pairs are then found by an AllPairSearch.

A variant of the Becker–Gama–Joux algorithm that uses buckets of the form $L \cap \mathcal{C}^{d-1}(f, \theta_1)$, with randomly chosen f and fixed θ_1, was proposed and implemented in [2]. This variant is sometimes called bgj1. Here we call it RandomBucketSearch. This algorithm has asymptotic complexity $2^{(0.349...+o(1))d}$ classically [2] and $2^{(0.301...+o(1))d}$ quantumly.[5] This is worse than the Becker–Gama–Joux algorithm, but RandomBucketSearch is conceptually simple and still provides an enormous improvement over AllPairSearch. Pseudocode is presented in Algorithm 3.

Description of Algorithm 3. The algorithm takes as input a list of N points uniformly distributed on the sphere. A random bucket centre f is drawn uniformly from $\mathcal{S}^{d-1}$ in each of the t iterations of the outer loop. The choice of f defines a bucket in Line 5, $L_f = L \cap \mathcal{C}^{d-1}(f, \theta_1)$, which is of expected size $N \cdot C_d(\theta_1)$. For each $v_j \in L_f$, the inner loop searches a set $L_{f,j} \subset L_f$ for neighbours of v_j. The quantity $|L_{f,j}|$ takes each value in $\{1, \ldots, |L_f| - 1\}$ as v_j ranges over L_f. The inner loop is identical to the loop in AllPairSearch apart from indexing and the fact that elements of L_f are known to be in the cap $\mathcal{C}^{d-1}(f, \theta_1)$.

A bucket L_f is expected to contain $\binom{N}{2} \cdot \Pr[\hat{R}_\theta \wedge \hat{B}_{f,\theta_1}]$ neighbouring pairs. Only a $1 - \eta(k, n)$ fraction of these are expected to be identified by the popcount filter. When $\theta_1 > \theta$ it is reasonable to assume that $\Pr[\hat{R}_\theta \wedge \hat{B}_{f,\theta_1}] \approx C_d(\theta) \cdot W_d(\theta, \theta_1, \theta_1)$. We use this approximation. The expected number of neighbouring

---

[5] The asymptotic quantum complexity is calculated, similarly to the classical complexity [2], using the asymptotic value of $W_d(\theta, \theta_1, \theta_1)$ given in [8]. Let $N = 1/C_d(\pi/3)$ and $t(\theta_1) = 1/W_d(\pi/3, \theta_1, \theta_1)$. The exponent $0.3013\ldots$ is obtained by minimising $t(\theta_1)\left(N + (NC_d(\theta_1))^{3/2}\right)$ with respect to θ_1.

Algorithm 3. RandomBucketSearch

Input: A list $L = (v_1, v_2, \ldots v_N) \subset \mathcal{S}^{d-1}$ of N points. Parameters $\theta, \theta_1 \in (0, \pi/2)$ and $t \in \mathbb{Z}_+$.

Output: A list of pairs $(u, v) \in L \times L$ with $\theta(u, v) \leq \theta$.

1: **function** RandomBucketSearch($L; \theta, \theta_1, t$)
2:    $L' \leftarrow \emptyset$
3:    **for** $1 \leq i \leq t$ **do**
4:        Sample f uniformly on $\mathcal{S}^{d-1}$
5:        $L_f \leftarrow L \cap \mathcal{C}^{d-1}(f, \theta_1)$
6:        **for** j such that $v_j \in L_f$ **do**
7:            $L_{f,j} \leftarrow \{v_k \in L_f : j < k \leq N\}$
8:            Search $L_{f,j}$ for any number of u that satisfy $\theta(v_j, u) \leq \theta$
9:            For each such u found, add (v_j, u) to L'.
10:           If $|L'| \geq N$, **return** L'.
11:   **return** L'

---

pairs in L_f that are detected by the popcount filter is therefore approximately $\binom{N}{2} \cdot (1 - \eta(k, n)) \cdot C_d(\theta) \cdot W_d(\theta, \theta_1, \theta_1)$. When $N = \ell(k, n)$ this is $N \cdot W_d(\theta, \theta_1, \theta_1)$. If all detectable neighbours are found by the search routine then the algorithm is list-size preserving when $N = \ell(k, n)$ and $t = 1/W_d(\theta, \theta_1, \theta_1)$.

We can now derive optimal popcount parameters for various implementations of Line 8.

Filtered Search. Suppose that Line 8 of Algorithm 3 applies $\text{popcount}_{k,n}(v_j, \cdot)$ to each element of $L_{f,j}$ and then applies an inner product test to each vector that passes. This implementation applies popcount tests to all $\binom{|L_f|}{2} \approx \binom{N \cdot C_d(\theta_1)}{2}$ pairs of elements in L_f and finds all of the neighbouring pairs that pass. In the process it applies inner product tests to a $p(\theta_1, k, n) = \Pr[\hat{P}_{k,n} \mid \hat{B}_{f,\theta_1}]$ fraction of pairs. The cost of populating buckets in one iteration of Line 5 is $c_1 \cdot \ell(k, n)$. The cost of all searches on Line 8 is $(c_1 \cdot p(\theta_1, k, n) + c_2(k, n)) \cdot \binom{N C_d(\theta_1)}{2}$. With the list-size preserving parameters N and t given above, the optimal θ_1, k, and n can be obtained by minimising the total cost

$$\frac{c_1 \cdot \ell(k, n) + (c_1 \cdot p(\theta_1, k, n) + c_2(k, n)) \cdot \binom{\ell(k,n) \cdot C_d(\theta_1)}{2}}{W_d(\theta, \theta_1, \theta_1)}. \tag{12}$$

Filtered Quantum Search. Suppose that Line 8 is implemented using the search routine Algorithm 2. We take the predicate f to be $\theta(v_j, \cdot) \leq \theta$ with domain $L_{f,j}$. We take the filter g to be $\text{popcount}_{k,n}(v_j, \cdot)$. Each call to the search routine returns at most one neighbour of v_j. To find all detectable neighbours of v_j in $L_{f,j}$ we must repeat the search several times. Known neighbours of v_j can be removed from $L_{f,j}$ to avoid a coupon collector scenario. Proposition 1 with $P = |L_{f,j}| \cdot \Pr[\hat{P}_{k,n} \mid \hat{B}_{f,\theta_1}]$, $Q = 1$, and $\gamma = 1$ gives us that the number of $\mathbf{G}(g)$ iterations in a search on a set of size $|L_{f,j}|$ is $q_0(|L_{f,j}|) = \frac{1}{2}\sqrt{|L_{f,j}|}$.

We consider an implementation of Line 8 in which searches are repeated until a search fails to find a neighbour of v_j. With $N = \ell(k, n)$, the set L_f is of expected size $\ell(k, n) \cdot C_d(\theta_1)$ and contains an expected $\ell(k, n) \cdot W_d(\theta, \theta_1, \theta_1)$ neighbouring pairs detectable by popcount. The set $L_{f,j}$ is expected to contain a proportional fraction of these pairs. As such, we expect to call the search subroutine $|L_{f,j}| \cdot r(\theta_1, k, n) + 1$ times in iteration j where

$$r(\theta_1, k, n) = \frac{N \cdot W_d(\theta, \theta_1, \theta_1)}{\binom{|L_f|}{2}} \approx \frac{2\, W_d(\theta, \theta_1, \theta_1)}{\ell(k, n) \cdot C_d(\theta_1)^2}.$$

The inner loop makes an expected

$$\sum_{j=1}^{|L_f|-1} \frac{1}{2} \sqrt{j}\, (j \cdot r(\theta_1, k, n) + 1)$$

applications of $\mathbf{G}(g)$. This admits an asymptotic expansion similar to that of Eq. 10. If we assume that $|L_f|$ takes its expected value of $\ell(k, n) \cdot C_d(\theta_1)$, then the inner loop makes

$$q_3(\theta_1, k, n) \cdot (\ell(k, n) \cdot C_d(\theta_1))^{3/2}$$

applications of $\mathbf{G}(g)$, where

$$q_3(\theta_1, k, n) = \frac{2\, W_d(\theta, \theta_1, \theta_1)}{5\, C_d(\theta_1)} + \frac{1}{3}.$$

Proposition 1 also provides an estimate for the rate at which reflections about the true positives, $\mathbf{R}_{f \cap g}$ are performed. With P and Q as above, we find that $\mathbf{R}_{f \cap g}$ is applied at roughly $p(\theta_1, k, n) = \sqrt{\Pr[\hat{P}_{k,n} \mid \hat{B}_{f,\theta_1}]}$ the rate of $\mathbf{G}(g)$ iterations. The total cost of searching for neighbouring pairs in L_f is therefore

$$s(\theta_1, k, n) = (q_1 \cdot p(\theta_1, k, n) + q_2(k, n)) \cdot q_3(\theta_1, k, n) \cdot \left(\ell(k, n) \cdot C_d(\theta_1)\right)^{3/2}. \tag{13}$$

Populating L_f has a cost of $c_1 \cdot \ell(k, n)$. With the list-size preserving t given above, the optimal parameters θ_1, k, and n can be obtained by minimising the total cost

$$\frac{c_1 \cdot \ell(k, n) + s(\theta_1, k, n)}{W_d(\theta, \theta_1, \theta_1)}. \tag{14}$$

6.3   ListDecodingSearch

The optimal choice of θ_1 in RandomBucketSearch balances the cost of $N \cdot t$ cap membership tests against the cost of all calls to the search subroutine. It can be seen that reducing the cost of populating the buckets would allow us to choose a smaller θ_1, which would reduce the cost of searching within each bucket.

Algorithm 4, ListDecodingSearch, is due to Becker, Ducas, Gama, and Laarhoven [8]. Its complexity is $2^{(0.292\ldots+o(1))d}$ classically and $2^{(0.265\ldots+o(1))d}$ quantumly [34,35]. Like RandomBucketSearch, it computes a large number of list-cap intersections. However, these list-cap intersections involve a structured list—the list-cap intersections in RandomBucketSearch involve the inherently unstructured input list.

Algorithm 4. ListDecodingSearch

Input: A list $L = (v_1, v_2, \ldots v_N) \subset \mathcal{S}^{d-1}$ of N. Parameters $\theta, \theta_1, \theta_2 \in (0, \pi/2)$ and $t \in \mathbb{Z}_+$.
Output: A list of pairs $(u, v) \in L \times L$ with $\theta(u, v) \leq \theta$.

1: **function** ListDecodingSearch($L; \theta, \theta_1, \theta_2, t$)
2:     Sample a random product code F of size t
3:     Initialise an empty list L_f for each $f \in F$
4:     **for** $1 \leq i \leq N$ **do**
5:         $F_i \leftarrow F \cap \mathcal{C}^{d-1}(v_i, \theta_2)$
6:         Add v_i to L_f for each f in F_i
7:     **for** $1 \leq j < N$ **do**
8:         $F_j \leftarrow F \cap \mathcal{C}^{d-1}(v_j, \theta_1)$
9:         **for** $f \in F_j$ **do**
10:             $L_{f,j} \leftarrow \{v_k \in L_f : j < k \leq N\}$
11:         $L_{F,j} \leftarrow \coprod_{f \in F_j} L_{f,j}$ (disjoint union)
12:         Search $L_{F,j}$ for any number of u that satisfy $\theta(v_j, u) \leq \theta$
13:         For each such u found, add (v_j, u) to L'.
14:         If $|L'| \geq N$, **return** L'.
15:     **return** L'

Description of Algorithm 4. The algorithm first samples a t point *random product code* F. See [8] for background on random product codes. In our analysis, we treat F as a list of uniformly random points on $\mathcal{S}^{d-1}$. A formal statement is given as [8, Theorem 5.1], showing that such a heuristic is essentially true, up to a subexponential loss on the probability of finding the intend pairs.

The first loop populates t buckets that have as centres the points f of F. Bucket L_f stores elements of L that lie in the cap of angle θ_2 about f. Each bucket is of expected size $N \cdot C_d(\theta_2)$.

The second loop iterates over $v_j \in L$ and searches for neighbours of v_j in the disjoint union of buckets with centres within an angle θ_1 of v_j. The set F_j constructed on Line 8 contains an expected $t \cdot C_d(\theta_1)$ bucket centres. The disjoint union of certain elements from the corresponding buckets, denoted $L_{F,j}$, is of expected size $(N - j) \cdot C_d(\theta_2) \cdot t \cdot C_d(\theta_1)$. We note that by simplifying and assuming the expected size of $L_{F,j}$ is $N \cdot C_d(\theta_2) \cdot t \cdot C_d(\theta_1)$ the costs given below are never wrong by more than a factor of two.

Suppose that w is a neighbour of v_j, so $\theta(v_j, w) \leq \theta$. The measure of the wedge formed by a cap of angle θ_1 about v_j and a cap of angle θ_2 about w is at least $W_d(\theta, \theta_1, \theta_2)$. Assuming that the points of a random product code are indistinguishable from points sampled uniformly on the sphere, the probability that some $f \in F_j$ contains w is at least $t \cdot W_d(\theta, \theta_1, \theta_2)$.

The second loop is executed N times. Iteration j searches $L_{F,j}$ for neighbours of v_j. With $N = \ell(k, n)$ there are expected to be N detectable neighbouring pairs in L. With $t = 1/W_d(\theta, \theta_1, \theta_2)$ we expect that each neighbouring pair is of the form (v_j, w) with $w \in L_{F,j}$.

The angles θ_1, θ_2 relate to the spherical cap parameters α, β respectively in [8], and are such that $\theta_1 \geq \theta_2$. Optimal time complexity is achieved when $\theta_1 = \theta_2$.

We have omitted the list decoding mechanism by which list-cap intersections are computed. In our analysis we assume that the cost of a list-cap intersection such as $F_i = F \cap \mathcal{C}^{d-1}(v_i, \theta_2)$ is proportional to $|F_i|$, but independent of $|F|$, i.e. we are in the "efficient list-decodability regime" of [8, Section 5.1] and may take their parameter $m = \log d$. In particular, we assume that in the cost of $O(\log(d) \cdot |F_i|)$ inner products and $|F|^{O(1/\log(d))}$ other operations, as stated in [8, Lemma 5.1], the first cost dominates. In [8] these costs relate to $O(m \cdot M \cdot \mathcal{C}_n(\alpha))$ and $O(nB + mB \log B)$ respectively. We therefore assume the cost of forming $F_i = F \cap \mathcal{C}^{d-1}(v_i, \theta_2)$ is $\log(d) \cdot |F_i|$ inner product tests.

Filtered Search. Suppose that the implementation of Line 12 of Algorithm 4 applies $\mathrm{popcount}_{k,n}(v_j, \cdot)$ to each element of $L_{F,j}$ and then applies an inner product test to each vector that passes. This implementation applies $\mathrm{popcount}$ tests to all $N \cdot C_d(\theta_2) \cdot t \cdot C_d(\theta_1)$ elements of $L_{F,j}$ and finds all of the neighbours of v_j that pass. Note that $w \in L_{F,j}$ implies that there exists some $f \in F$ such that both v_j and w lie in a cap of angle θ_1 around f. Inner product tests are applied to a $p(\theta_1, k, n) \geq \Pr[\hat{P}_{k,n} \mid \hat{B}_{f,\theta_1}]$ fraction of all pairs.[6]

The cost of preparing all t buckets in the first loop is $c_1 \cdot N \cdot t \cdot C_d(\theta_2)$. The cost of constructing the search spaces in the second loop is $c_1 \cdot N \cdot t \cdot C_d(\theta_1)$. Each search has a cost of $|L_{F,j}|$ $\mathrm{popcount}$ tests and $|L_{F,j}| \cdot p(\theta_1, k, n)$ inner product tests. With the list-size preserving parameterisation given above, the optimal θ_1, θ_2, k, and n can be obtained by minimising the total cost

$$\frac{\ell(k, n)}{W_d(\theta, \theta_1, \theta_2)} \Big(c_1 \cdot C_d(\theta_1) + c_1 \cdot C_d(\theta_2)$$

$$+ \big(c_1 \cdot p(\theta_1, k, n) + c_2(k, n) \big) \cdot \ell(k, n) \cdot C_d(\theta_1) \cdot C_d(\theta_2) \Big). \quad (15)$$

Filtered Quantum Search. Suppose that Line 12 is implemented using Algorithm 2. We take the predicate f to be $\theta(v_j, \cdot) \leq \theta$ with domain $L_{F,j}$. We take the filter g to be $\mathrm{popcount}_{k,n}(v_j, \cdot)$. Each call to the search routine returns at

---

[6] The inequality is because v_j and w may be contained in multiple buckets, $L_{f,j}$.

most one neighbour of v_j. Known neighbours of v_j can be removed from $L_{F,j}$ to avoid a coupon collector scenario. Proposition 1 with $P = |L_{F,j}| \cdot \Pr[\hat{P}_{k,n} \mid \hat{B}_{f,\theta_2}]$, $Q = 1$, and $\gamma = 1$ gives us that the number of $\mathbf{G}(g)$ iterations in a search on a set of size $|L_{F,j}|$ is $q_0(|L_{F,j}|) \approx \frac{1}{2}\sqrt{|L_{F,j}|}$.

Assuming that computing $F_j = F \cap C(v_j, \theta_1)$ has a cost of $c_1|F_j|$, the N iterations of Lines 5 and 8 have a total cost of

$$c_1 \cdot N \cdot t \cdot (C_d(\theta_1) + C_d(\theta_2)) \tag{16}$$

Each search applies an expected

$$q_0(|L_{F,j}|) \approx \frac{1}{2}\sqrt{N \cdot C_d(\theta_1) \cdot t \cdot C_d(\theta_2)}$$

applications of $\mathbf{G}(g)$. Reflections about the true positives, $\mathbf{R}_{f \cap g}$, are performed at roughly $p(\theta_1, k, n) = \sqrt{\Pr[\hat{P}_{k,n} \mid B_{f,\theta_1}]}$ the rate of $\mathbf{G}(g)$ iterations. We consider an implementation of Line 8 in which searches are repeated until a search fails to find a neighbour of v_j. With the list-size preserving parameters given above, we expect to perform two filtered quantum searches per iteration of the second loop. The optimal parameters can be obtained by minimising the total cost

$$\ell(k,n)\left(c_1 \frac{C_d(\theta_1) + C_d(\theta_2)}{W_d(\theta, \theta_1, \theta_2)} + (q_1 p(\theta_1, k, n) + q_2(k, n))\sqrt{\frac{\ell(k,n)C_d(\theta_1)C_d(\theta_2)}{W_d(\theta, \theta_1, \theta_2)}}\right).$$

7   Cost Estimates

Our software numerically optimises the cost functions in Sects. 6.1, 6.2 and 6.3 with respect to several classical and quantum cost metrics. The classical cost metrics that we consider are: c (unit cost), which assigns unit cost to popcount; c (RAM), which uses the classical circuits of Sect. 4. The quantum cost metrics that we consider are: q (unit cost), which assigns unit cost to a Grover iteration; q (depth-width), which assigns unit cost to every gate (including the identity) in the quantum circuits of Sect. 4; q (gates), which assigns unit cost only to the non-identity gates; q (T count), which assigns unit cost only to T gates; and q (GE19), which is described in Sect. 7.1.

We stress that our software, and Fig. 2, give *estimates* for the cost of each algorithm. These estimates are neither upper bounds nor lower bounds. As we mention above, we have systematically omitted and underestimated some costs. For instance, we have omitted the list decoding mechanism in our costing of Algorithm 4. We have approximated other costs. For instance, the cost that we assign to an inner product in Sect. 4.3. We have also not explored the entire optimisation space. We only consider values of the popcount parameter n that are one less than a power of two. Moreover, following the discussion in Sect. 2.4, we set $k = \lfloor n/3 \rfloor$.

While we have omitted and approximated some costs, we have tried to ensure that these omissions and approximations will ultimately lead our software to *underestimate* of the total cost of the algorithm. For instance, if our inner product cost is accurate, our optimisation procedure ensures that we satisfy Remark 2 and can ignore costs relating to $\mathbf{R}_{f \cap g}$.

Our results are presented in Fig. 2. We also plot the leading term of the asymptotic complexity of the respective algorithms as these are routinely referred to in the literature. The source code, and raw data for all considered cost metrics, is available at https://github.com/jschanck/eprint-2019-1161.

7.1   Barriers to a Quantum Advantage

As expected, our results in Fig. 2 indicate that quantum search provides a substantial savings over classical search asymptotically. Our plots fully contain the range of costs from 2^{128} to 2^{256} that are commonly thought to be cryptanalytically interesting. Modest cost improvements are attained in this range.

The range of parameters in which a sieve could conceivably be run, however, is much narrower. If one assumes a memory density of one petabyte per gram (2^{53} bits per gram), a 2^{140} bit memory would have a mass comparable with that of the Moon. Supposing that a 2-sieve stores $1/C_d(\pi/3)$ vectors, and that each vector is $\log_2(d)$ bits, an adversary with a 2^{140} bit memory could only run a sieve in dimension 608 or lower. The potential cost improvement in dimension 608 is smaller than the potential cost improvement in, say, dimension 1000. The potential cost improvement that can be actualised is likely smaller still.

We expect that our cost estimates are underestimates. However, the quantum advantage could grow, shrink, or even be eliminated if our underestimates do not affect quantum and classical costs equally. In this section, we list several reasons to think that the advantage might shrink or disappear.

Error Correction Overhead. By using the depth-width metric for quantum circuits, we assume that dispatching a logical gate to a logical qubit costs one RAM instruction. In practice, however, the cost depends on the error correcting code that is used for logical qubits. This cost may be significant.

Gidney and Ekerå have estimated the resources required to factor a 2048 bit RSA modulus using Shor's algorithm on a surface code based quantum computer [20]. Under a plausible assumption on the physical qubit error rate, they calculate that a factoring circuit with $2^{12.6}$ logical qubits and depth 2^{31} requires a distance $\delta = 27$ surface code. Each logical qubit is encoded in $2\delta^2 = 1458$ physical qubits, and the error tracking routine applies at least $\delta^2 = 729$ bit instructions, per logical qubit per layer of logical circuit depth, to read its input.

In general, a circuit of depth D and width W requires a distance $\delta = \Theta(\log(DW))$ surface code. To perform a single logical gate, classical control hardware dispatches several instructions to each of the $\Theta(\log^2(DW))$ physical qubits. The classical control hardware also performs a non-trivial error tracking routine between logical gates, which takes measurement results from half of the

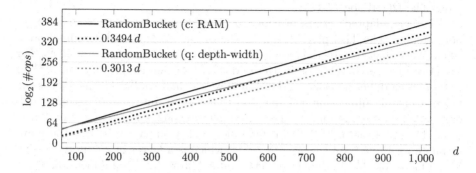

RandomBucketSearch. Comparing c: (RAM) with q: (depth-width), and the leading terms of the asymptotic complexities.

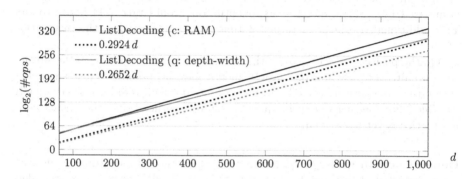

ListDecodingSearch. Comparing c: (RAM) with q: (depth-width), and the leading terms of the asymptotic complexities.

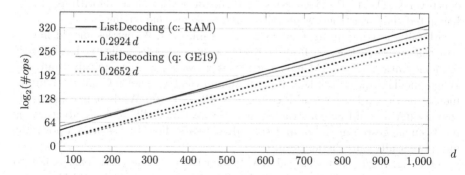

ListDecodingSearch. Comparing c: (RAM) with q: (GE19), and the leading terms of the asymptotic complexities.

Fig. 2. Quantum ("q") and classical ("c") resource estimates for NNS search.

physical qubits as input.[7] Consequently, the cost of surface code computation grows like $\Omega(DW \log^2(DW))$.

We have adapted scripts provided by Gidney and Ekerå to estimate δ for our circuits. The last plot of Fig. 2 shows the cost of ListDecodingSearch when every logical gate (including the identity) is assigned a cost of δ^2. For ListDecodingSearch the cost in the Gidney–Ekerå metric grows from 2^{128} to 2^{256} between dimensions 352 and 824, and we calculate a 2^{128} bit memory is sufficient to run in dimension 544. We find that the advantage of quantum search over classical search is a factor of $2^{1.8}$ in dimension 352, a factor of $2^{7.1}$ in dimension 544, and a factor of $2^{14.4}$ in dimension 824. Compare this with the naïve estimate for the advantage, $2^{0.292d-0.265d}$, which is a factor of $2^{9.5}$ in dimension 352, a factor of $2^{14.7}$ in dimension 544, and a factor of $2^{22.5}$ in dimension 824.

One should also note that error correction for the surface code sets a natural clock speed, which Gidney and Ekerå estimate at one cycle per microsecond. Gidney and Ekerå estimate that their factoring circuit, the cost of which is dominated by a single modular exponentiation, would take 7.44 hours to run. This additional overhead in terms of time is not refelected in the instruction count.

On the positive side, the cost estimate used in Fig. 2 is specific to the surface code architecture. Significant improvements may be possible. Gottesman has shown that an overhead of $\Theta(1)$ physical qubits per logical qubit is theoretically possible [22]. Whether this technique offers lower overhead than the surface code in practice is yet to be seen.

Dependence on qRAM. Quantum accessible classical memories are used in many quantum algorithms. For example, they are used in black box search algorithms [25], in collision finding algorithms [14], and in some algorithms for the the dihedral hidden subgroup problem [32]. The use of qRAM is not without controversy [11,24]. Previous work on quantum lattice sieve algorithms [34,35] has noted that constructing practical qRAM seems challenging.

Morally, looking up an ℓ bit value in a table with 2^n entries should have a cost that grows at least with $n + \ell$. Recent results [5,6,38] indicate that realistic implementations of qRAM have costs that grow much more quickly than this. When ancillary qubits are kept to a minimum, the best known Clifford+T implementation of a qRAM has a **T** count of $4 \cdot (2^n - 1)$ [6]. While it is conceivable that a qRAM could be constructed at lower cost on a different architecture, as has been suggested in [21], a unit cost qRAM gate should be seen as a powerful, and potentially unrealistic, resource.

One can argue that classical RAMs also have a large cost. This is not to say that classical and quantum RAMs have the same cost. A qRAM can be used to construct an arbitrary superposition over the elements of a memory. This process relies on quantum interference and necessarily takes as long as a worst case memory access time. This is in contrast with classical RAM, where

---

[7] For a thorough introduction to how logical gates are performed on the surface code see [19], and for more advanced techniques see e.g. [27].

careful programming and attention to a computer's caches can mask the fact that accessing an N bit memory laid out in a 3-dimensional space necessarily takes $\Omega(N^{1/3})$ time.

If the cost of a qRAM gate is equivalent to $\Theta(N^{1/3})$ Clifford+T gates, then the asymptotic cost of quantum AllPair search is $2^{(0.380\ldots+o(1))d}$, the asymptotic cost of quantum RandomBucket search is $2^{(0.336\ldots+o(1))d}$, and the asymptotic cost of quantum ListDecoding search is $2^{(0.284\ldots+o(1))d}$. If memory is constrained to two dimensions, and qRAM costs $\Theta(N^{1/2})$ Clifford+T gates, the quantum asymptotics match the classical RAM asymptotics.

Quantum Sampling Routines. We have assumed that $\mathbf{D}$ in Sect. 4.1 (the uniform sampling subroutine in Grover's algorithm) is implemented using parallel $\mathbf{H}$ gates. This is the smallest possible circuit that might implement $\mathbf{D}$, and may be a significant underestimate. In Line 12 of Algorithm 4 we must construct a superposition (ideally uniform) over $\{k : v_k \in L_{F,j}\}$. The set $L_{F,j}$ is presented as a disjoint union of smaller sets. Copying the elements of these smaller sets to a flat array would be more expensive than our estimate for the cost of search. While we do not expect the cost of sampling near uniformly from $L_{F,j}$ to be large, it could easily exceed the cost of popcount.

7.2   Relevance to SVP

The NNS algorithms that we have analysed are closely related to lattice sieves for SVP. While the asymptotic cost of NNS algorithms are often used as a proxy for the asymptotic cost of solving SVP, we caution the reader against making this comparison in a non-asymptotic setting. On the one hand, our estimates might lead one to underestimate the cost of solving SVP:

- the costs given in Fig. 2 represent one iteration of NNS within a sieve, while sieve algorithms make $\mathsf{poly}(d)$ iterations;
- the costs given in Fig. 2 do not account for all of the subroutines within each NNS algorithm.

On the other hand, our estimates might lead one to overestimate the cost of solving SVP:

- it is a mistake to conflate the cost of NNS in dimension d with the cost of SVP in dimension d. The "dimensions for free" technique of [17] can be used to solve SVP in dimension d by calling an NNS routine polynomially many times in dimension $d' < d$. Our analysis seamlessly applies to dimension d';
- there are heuristics that exploit structure present in applications to SVP not captured in our general setting, e.g. the vector space structure allowing both $\pm u$ to be tested for the cost of u, and keeping the vectors sorted by length.

7.3   Future Work

The sieving techniques considered here are not exhaustive. While it would be relatively easy to adapt our software to other 2-sieves, like the cross polytope sieve [10], future work might consider k-sieves such as [7,30].

Future work might also address the barriers to a quantum advantage discussed in Sect. 7.1. Two additional barriers are worth mentioning here. First, as Grover search does not parallelise well, one might consider depth restrictions for classical and quantum circuits. Second, our estimates might be refined by including some of the classical subroutines, present in both the classical and quantum variants of the same sieve, that we have ignored, e.g. the cost of sampling lattice vectors or the cost of list-decoding in Algorithm 4. Any cost increase will reduce the range of cryptanalytically relevant dimensions, giving fewer dimensions to overcome quantum overheads.

Finally, our estimates should be checked against experiments. Our analysis of Algorithm 3 recommends a database of size $N(d) \approx 2/C_d(\pi/3)$, while the largest sieving experiments to date [2] runs Algorithm 3 with a database of size $N'(d) = 3.2 \cdot 2^{0.2075d}$ up to dimension $d = 127$. There is a factor of 8 gap between $N'(127)$ and $N(127)$. A factor of two can be explained by the fact that [2] treats each database entry u as $\pm u$. It is possible that the remaining factor of four can be explained by the other heuristics used in [2]. As d increases, $N(d)$ and $N'(d)$ continue to diverge, so future work could attempt to determine more accurately the required list size.

Acknowledgements. We thank Léo Ducas for helpful discussions regarding ListDecodingSearch.

References

1. Ajtai, M., Kumar, R., Sivakumar, D.: A sieve algorithm for the shortest lattice vector problem. In: 33rd ACM STOC, pp. 601–610. ACM Press, July 2001
2. Albrecht, M.R., Ducas, L., Herold, G., Kirshanova, E., Postlethwaite, E.W., Stevens, M.: The general sieve kernel and new records in lattice reduction. In: Ishai, Y., Rijmen, V. (eds.) EUROCRYPT 2019, Part II. LNCS, vol. 11477, pp. 717–746. Springer, Cham (2019). https://doi.org/10.1007/978-3-030-17656-3_25
3. Alkim, E., Ducas, L., Pöppelmann, T., Schwabe, P.: Post-quantum key exchange - a new hope. In: Holz, T., Savage, S. (eds.) USENIX Security 2016, pp. 327–343. USENIX Association, August 2016
4. Amy, M., Di Matteo, O., Gheorghiu, V., Mosca, M., Parent, A., Schanck, J.: Estimating the cost of generic quantum pre-image attacks on SHA-2 and SHA-3. In: Avanzi, R., Heys, H. (eds.) SAC 2016. LNCS, vol. 10532, pp. 317–337. Springer, Cham (2017). https://doi.org/10.1007/978-3-319-69453-5_18
5. Arunachalam, S., Gheorghiu, V., Jochym-O'Connor, T., Mosca, M., Srinivasan, P.V.: On the robustness of bucket brigade quantum ram. New J. Phys. **17**(12), 123010 (2015). http://stacks.iop.org/1367-2630/17/i=12/a=123010

6. Babbush, R., et al.: Encoding electronic spectra in quantum circuits with linear T complexity. Phys. Rev. X **8**, 041015 (2018). https://link.aps.org/doi/10.1103/PhysRevX.8.041015
7. Bai, S., Laarhoven, T., Stehlé, D.: Tuple lattice sieving. LMS J. Comput. Math. **19**(A), 146–162 (2016)
8. Becker, A., Ducas, L., Gama, N., Laarhoven, T.: New directions in nearest neighbor searching with applications to lattice sieving. In: Krauthgamer, R. (ed.) 27th SODA, pp. 10–24. ACM-SIAM, January 2016
9. Becker, A., Gama, N., Joux, A.: Speeding-up lattice sieving without increasing the memory, using sub-quadratic nearest neighbor search. Cryptology ePrint Archive, Report 2015/522 (2015). http://eprint.iacr.org/2015/522
10. Becker, A., Laarhoven, T.: Efficient (ideal) lattice sieving using cross-polytope LSH. In: Pointcheval, D., Nitaj, A., Rachidi, T. (eds.) AFRICACRYPT 2016. LNCS, vol. 9646, pp. 3–23. Springer, Cham (2016). https://doi.org/10.1007/978-3-319-31517-1_1
11. Bernstein, D.J.: Cost analysis of hash collisions: Will quantum computers make sharcs obsolete? In: Workshop Record of SHARCS 2009: Special-purpose Hardware for Attacking Cryptographic Systems (2009). http://cr.yp.to/papers.html#collisioncost
12. Boyer, M., Brassard, G., Høyer, P., Tapp, A.: Tight bounds on quantum searching. Fortschritte der Physik **46**(4–5), 493–505 (1998). https://onlinelibrary.wiley.com/doi/abs/10.1002/
13. Brassard, G., Hoyer, P., Mosca, M., Tapp, A.: Quantum amplitude amplification and estimation. Contemp. Math. **305**, 53–74 (2002). https://arxiv.org/abs/quant-ph/0005055
14. Brassard, G., Høyer, P., Tapp, A.: Quantum cryptanalysis of hash and claw-free functions. SIGACT News **28**(2), 14–19 (1997). http://doi.acm.org/10.1145/261342.261346
15. Charikar, M.: Similarity estimation techniques from rounding algorithms. In: 34th ACM STOC, pp. 380–388. ACM Press, May 2002
16. Cuccaro, S.A., Draper, T.G., Kutin, S.A., Moulton, D.P.: A new quantum ripple-carry addition circuit (2004). arXiv:quant-ph/0410184
17. Ducas, L.: Shortest vector from lattice sieving: a few dimensions for free. In: Nielsen, J.B., Rijmen, V. (eds.) EUROCRYPT 2018. LNCS, vol. 10820, pp. 125–145. Springer, Cham (2018). https://doi.org/10.1007/978-3-319-78381-9_5
18. Fitzpatrick, R., et al.: Tuning GaussSieve for speed. In: Aranha, D.F., Menezes, A. (eds.) LATINCRYPT 2014. LNCS, vol. 8895, pp. 288–305. Springer, Cham (2015). https://doi.org/10.1007/978-3-319-16295-9_16
19. Fowler, A.G., Mariantoni, M., Martinis, J.M., Cleland, A.N.: Surface codes: towards practical large-scale quantum computation. Phys. Rev. A **86**, 032324 (2012). https://link.aps.org/doi/10.1103/PhysRevA.86.032324
20. Gidney, C., Ekerå, M.: How to factor 2048 bit RSA integers in 8 hours using 20 million noisy qubits (2019). https://arxiv.org/abs/1905.09749
21. Giovannetti, V., Lloyd, S., Maccone, L.: Quantum random access memory. Phys. Rev. Lett. **100**, 160501 (2008). http://link.aps.org/doi/10.1103/PhysRevLett.100.160501
22. Gottesman, D.: Fault-tolerant quantum computation with constant overhead (2013). https://arxiv.org/abs/1310.2984

23. Grassl, M., Langenberg, B., Roetteler, M., Steinwandt, R.: Applying Grover's algorithm to AES: quantum resource estimates. In: Takagi, T. (ed.) PQCrypto 2016. LNCS, vol. 9606, pp. 29–43. Springer, Cham (2016). https://doi.org/10.1007/978-3-319-29360-8_3

24. Grover, L., Rudolph, T.: How significant are the known collision and element distinctness quantum algorithms. Quantum Info. Comput. **4**, 201–206 (2004)

25. Grover, L.K.: Quantum mechanics helps in searching for a needle in a haystack. Phys. Rev. Lett. **79**, 325–328 (1997). http://link.aps.org/doi/10.1103/PhysRevLett.79.325

26. Häner, T., Roetteler, M., Svore, K.M.: Factoring using 2n + 2 qubits with toffoli based modular multiplication. Quantum Info. Comput. **17**(7–8), 673–684 (2017). http://dl.acm.org/citation.cfm?id=3179553.3179560

27. Horsman, C., Fowler, A.G., Devitt, S., Meter, R.V.: Surface code quantum computing by lattice surgery. New J. Phys. **14**(12), 123011 (2012). http://stacks.iop.org/1367-2630/14/i=12/a=123011

28. Jaques, S., Naehrig, M., Roetteler, M., Virdia, F.: Implementing Grover oracles for quantum key search on AES and LowMC. Cryptology ePrint Archive, Report 2019/1146 (2019). https://eprint.iacr.org/2019/1146

29. Jaques, S., Schanck, J.M.: Quantum cryptanalysis in the RAM model: claw-finding attacks on SIKE. In: Boldyreva, A., Micciancio, D. (eds.) CRYPTO 2019. LNCS, vol. 11692, pp. 32–61. Springer, Cham (2019). https://doi.org/10.1007/978-3-030-26948-7_2

30. Kirshanova, E., Mårtensson, E., Postlethwaite, E.W., Moulik, S.R.: Quantum algorithms for the approximate k-list problem and their application to lattice sieving. In: Galbraith, S.D., Moriai, S. (eds.) ASIACRYPT 2019. LNCS, vol. 11921, pp. 521–551. Springer, Cham (2019). https://doi.org/10.1007/978-3-030-34578-5_19

31. Klein, P.N.: Finding the closest lattice vector when it's unusually close. In: Shmoys, D.B. (ed.) 11th SODA, pp. 937–941. ACM-SIAM, January 2000

32. Kuperberg, G.: Another subexponential-time quantum algorithm for the Dihedral Hidden Subgroup Problem. In: Theory of Quantum Computation, Communication and Cryptography - TQC 2013, pp. 20–34. LIPIcs 22 (2013). http://drops.dagstuhl.de/opus/volltexte/2013/4321

33. Laarhoven, T.: Sieving for shortest vectors in lattices using angular locality-sensitive hashing. In: Gennaro, R., Robshaw, M. (eds.) CRYPTO 2015. LNCS, vol. 9215, pp. 3–22. Springer, Heidelberg (2015). https://doi.org/10.1007/978-3-662-47989-6_1

34. Laarhoven, T.: Search problems in cryptography: from fingerprinting to lattice sieving. Ph.D. thesis, Department of Mathematics and Computer Science, proefschrift, February 2016

35. Laarhoven, T., Mosca, M., van de Pol, J.: Solving the shortest vector problem in lattices faster using quantum search. In: Gaborit, P. (ed.) PQCrypto 2013. LNCS, vol. 7932, pp. 83–101. Springer, Heidelberg (2013). https://doi.org/10.1007/978-3-642-38616-9_6

36. Lindner, R., Peikert, C.: Better key sizes (and attacks) for LWE-based encryption. In: Kiayias, A. (ed.) CT-RSA 2011. LNCS, vol. 6558, pp. 319–339. Springer, Heidelberg (2011). https://doi.org/10.1007/978-3-642-19074-2_21

37. Maslov, D.: Advantages of using relative-phase Toffoli gates with an application to multiple control Toffoli optimization. Phys. Rev. A **93**(2), 022311 (2016)

38. Matteo, O.D., Gheorghiu, V., Mosca, M.: Fault tolerant resource estimation of quantum random-access memories (2019). arXiv:1902.01329v1

39. Micciancio, D., Regev, O.: Lattice-based cryptography. In: Bernstein, D.J., Buchmann, J., Dahmen, E. (eds.) Post-Quantum Cryptography, pp. 147–191. Springer, Heidelberg (2009). https://doi.org/10.1007/978-3-540-88702-7_5
40. Nguyen, P.Q., Vidick, T.: Sieve algorithms for the shortest vector problem are practical. J. Math. Cryptol. **2**(2), 181–207 (2008)
41. Parhami, B.: Efficient hamming weight comparators for binary vectors based on accumulative and up/down parallel counters. IEEE Trans. Circ. Syst. **56-II**(2), 167–171 (2009). https://doi.org/10.1109/TCSII.2008.2010176

A Combinatorial Approach to Quantum Random Functions

Nico Döttling[1](✉), Giulio Malavolta[2](✉), and Sihang Pu[1](✉)

[1] CISPA Helmholtz Center for Information Security, Saarbrücken, Germany
{doettling,sihang.pu}@cispa.saarland
[2] Max Planck Institute for Security and Privacy, Bochum, Germany
giulio.malavolta@hotmail.it

Abstract. Quantum pseudorandom functions (QPRFs) extend the classical security of a PRF by allowing the adversary to issue queries on input superpositions. Zhandry [Zhandry, FOCS 2012] showed a separation between the two notions and proved that common construction paradigms are also quantum secure, albeit with a new ad-hoc analysis. In this work we revisit the question of constructing QPRFs and propose a new method starting from small-domain (classical) PRFs: At the heart of our approach is a new domain-extension technique based on bipartite expanders. Interestingly, our analysis is almost entirely classical.

As a corollary of our main theorem, we obtain the first (approximate) key-homomorphic quantum PRF based on the quantum intractability of the learning with errors problem.

1 Introduction

Pseudorandom functions (PRFs) are one of the fundamental building blocks of modern cryptography. PRFs were introduced in the seminal work of Goldreich, Goldwasser and Micali [13] answering the question of how to build a function that is indistinguishable from a random function. Loosely speaking, a PRF guarantees that no efficient algorithm, with oracle access to such a function, can distinguish it from a truly random function. PRFs have been shown to be an invaluable tool in the design of cryptographic primitives (such as block ciphers and message authentication codes) and are by now a well-understood object: After the tree-based construction of [13], PRFs have been build from pseudorandom synthesizers [19] and directly from many hard problems [2,7,11,18,20–22].

However, when considering the more delicate quantum settings, the study of the hardness of PRFs is still at its infancy. Before delving into the details of this primitive, some clarification is needed as one can define the quantum security of a PRFs in two ways:

1. The PRF is secure against a quantum machine that can only issue classical queries to the function (although the internal state of the adversary is quantum).

© International Association for Cryptologic Research 2020
S. Moriai and H. Wang (Eds.): ASIACRYPT 2020, LNCS 12492, pp. 614–632, 2020.
https://doi.org/10.1007/978-3-030-64834-3_21

2. The PRF is secure against a quantum machine that is allowed to query it on input superposition states and is given as a response the superposition of the corresponding outputs, i.e., it can issue *quantum queries*. This setting is the focus of our work and we refer to it as *quantum security*.

The first setting is commonly referred to as *post-quantum security* and it involves the use of hard problems that are conjectured to be intractable even for quantum computers, but this aspect typically does not further affect the analysis of known construction paradigms. On the other hand, the latter setting has been shown to require a fundamentally different approach: In his pioneer work, Zhandry [27] gave a separation between the two models, i.e., he constructed a PRF that is post-quantum secure but provably not quantum secure. On the positive side, he showed that the generic constructions of [13] and [19] are also quantum secure, albeit with a completely different analysis. He also provided a quantum analysis of the PRFs of [2], which assumes the post-quantum hardness of the learning with errors problem [24].

Beyond the theoretical interest, quantum security gives a more conservative model to analyze the hardness of PRFs in a world with quantum machines. As an example, if PRF is used as a message authentication code (MAC) by some quantum computer, then it is reasonable to assume that an adversary might be able to obtain the function output when evaluated on some input superposition. In this case, MACs based on post-quantum secure PRFs might not be secure anymore. Boneh and Zhandry in their work[8] studied this problem and constructed the first message authentication codes against quantum chosen message attack. They also showed that a quantum secure PRF is sufficient for constructing a quantum secure MAC. Unfortunately, the current landscape of quantum PRFs is rather unsatisfactory: Current techniques to analyze hardness of PRFs in the quantum settings are geared towards specific constructions. As a result, only a handful of quantum-secure schemes are known.

1.1   What Makes QPRFs Challenging?

At the heart of Zhandry's separation result [27] is the observation that quantum algorithms can detect *hidden linear structures*. This problem is also present when we extend the domain of truly random functions. Assume that $f : \{0,1\}^\lambda \rightarrow \{0,1\}^\lambda$ is a uniformly random function and $H : \{0,1\}^{2\lambda} \rightarrow \{0,1\}^\lambda$ is a random linear function and therefore a universal hash function [9]. The function $x \mapsto f(H(x))$ can easily be shown to be *statistically indistinguishable* from a truly random function for any classical distinguisher with oracle access to this function. However, using the algorithm of Boneh and Lipton [6] one can efficiently find elements in the kernel of H via superposition queries to $f(H(\cdot))$. Given an element z in the kernel of H, $f(H(x))$ can be distinguished from a truly random function $g : \{0,1\}^{2\lambda} \rightarrow \{0,1\}^\lambda$ by two classical queries, as it holds for any $x \in \{0,1\}^{2\lambda}$ that $f(H(x + z)) = f(H(x))$. Such a collision, however, happens only with exponentially small probability for a random g.

What this shows is that the advantage of superposition adversaries over classical adversaries goes far beyond their computational advantage. Superposition adversaries can learn strictly more about the structure of a function it is given oracle access to than a classical (even unbounded) adversary ever could.

1.2 Our Results

In this work we explore a different route and we propose a new approach to construct QPRFs. Our construction is based on the framework of Döttling and Schröder [12], which in turn builds on earlier ideas of PRF domain extension [4, 16] and constructions of adaptively secure PRFs from non-adaptively secure ones [3].

At the heart of our approach is a domain extension technique based on bipartite expander graphs, which crucially allows us to reduce the quantum hardness of our PRF to the classical (post-quantum) hardness of a small-domain PRF. Specifically, we will prove the following theorem.

Theorem 1 (Informal). *For any q let* $\mathsf{PRF}_q : \mathcal{K} \times \mathcal{Y} \to \mathcal{Z}$ *be a (post-quantum) classically secure PRF with (small) domain* $\mathcal{Y}_q$ *and let* $\Gamma(x, j)$ *be a suitable expander mapping from a vertex* x *to its* j*-th degree neighbor, where the expander* Γ *has degree* D_i*. Then*

$$F(K, x) = \bigoplus_{i=1}^{\omega(\log \lambda)} \bigoplus_{j \in [D_i]} \mathsf{PRF}_{2^i}(K_{2^i}, \Gamma(x, j)),$$

where $K = (K_{2^1}, \ldots, K_{2^i}, \ldots, K_{2^{\omega(\log \lambda)}})^1$, *is a quantum PRF.*

This gives an alternative and (arguably) conceptually simpler approach to constructing QPRFs. An interesting aspect of our result is that our analysis concerns almost exclusively the classical settings and quantum security is achieved by a simple observation: The crux of our analysis will consist in reducing the classical hardness of the PRF to that of a small domain PRF, which is also trivially quantum secure since the attacker can query the full domain. This result can be seen as a compiler which converts any post-quantum secure PRF into a QPRF at a moderate overhead and without having to go through the (expensive) GGM construction of [27].

As an additional result, we obtain a new implication: Assuming the quantum-intractability of the learning with errors problem, then there exists a quantum (almost) key-homomorphic PRF.

Quantum Key-Homomorphic PRF. Key-homomorphic PRFs were introduced by Boneh et al. [5] and have applications in the context of proxy-re-encryption and related key security. In a nutshell, for key-homomorphic PRFs

---

[1] Note that we could XOR them from $\log \lambda$ to $\omega(\log \lambda)$, but for simplicity, we still use the range from 1 to $\omega(\log \lambda)$.

the key-space is a group and it holds for all x that $PRF(K_1 + K_2, x) = PRF(K_1, x) + PRF(K_2, x)$. Key-homomorphic PRFs give rise to a very natural protocol for a distributed PRF. Boneh et al. showed that the function

$$\mathsf{PRF}_{\mathsf{KH}}(\mathbf{k}, x) = \left\lfloor \prod_{i=1}^{\ell} \mathbf{A}_{x_i} \cdot \mathbf{k} \right\rceil_p ,$$

where $\mathbf{A}_0$ and $\mathbf{A}_1$ are two random public matrices in $\mathbb{Z}_q^{m \times m}$, is additively key-homomorphic (ignoring a small error) over the vector space $\mathbb{Z}_q^m$. The function is pseudorandom under the learning with errors assumption, which is conjectured to be intractable also for quantum computers. Then a simple application of our compiler shows us that

$$F(K, x) = \sum_{i=1}^{\omega(\log \lambda)} \sum_{j \in [D_i]} \mathsf{PRF}_{\mathsf{KH}}(K_{2^i}, \Gamma(x, j)) \bmod p$$

is a quantum key-homomorphic PRF.

1.3   Technical Overview

We start by providing a technical outline of our results. As mentioned above, we use the framework of [12] to construct our QPRFs. This framework has two steps, a domain extension step and a combiner step. The domain extension step takes a *small domain* PRF with domain size $\mathsf{poly}(q)$ and constructs from it a q-bounded PRF on a large domain, e.g. $\{0, 1\}^\lambda$. A PRF is called q-bounded if security is only guaranteed for adversaries which make at most q queries. An important aspect about this step is that the small domain PRF can be evaluated in time (essentially) independent of q.

The second step, or combiner step, combines a small number of bounded PRFs which have the same domain. The key idea here is to set the bounds in an exponentially increasing way. More specifically, if $\mathsf{PRF}_q(K_q, x)$ are q-bounded PRFs, we combine them into a function F via

$$F(K, x) = \bigoplus_{i=1}^{t} \mathsf{PRF}_{2^i}(K_{2^i}, x)$$

where $K = (K_1, \ldots, K_{2^t})$. We will choose the parameter t to be slightly super-logarithmic in the security parameter λ. We claim that if $\mathsf{PRF}_q(K_q, x)$ is a q-bounded QPRF as long as q is polynomial, then $F(K, x)$ is an (unbounded) QPRF. We will briefly argue how this can be established. Fix a BQP distinguisher $\mathcal{A}$ against the QPRF security of F. Since this distinguisher is efficient, there is a polynomial upper bound q on the number of superposition queries $\mathcal{A}$ will make. Given such a distinguisher we will, choose $i^* = \lceil \log(q) \rceil \leqslant t$ and construct a BQP distinguisher $\mathcal{A}'$ against the 2^{i^*}-bounded security of $\mathsf{PRF}_{2^{i^*}}$. Notice that since $2^{i^*} \leqslant 2q$ and q is polynomial it holds that 2^{i^*} is also polynomial. The distinguisher $\mathcal{A}'$ gets q-bounded superposition access to an oracle

$\mathcal{O}$ which computes either $\mathsf{PRF}_{2^{i*}}$ or a uniformly random function f. Given a superposition query $\sum |x\rangle$ by $\mathcal{A}$, $\mathcal{A}'$ submits this query to its oracle $\mathcal{O}$ obtaining a superposition state $\sum |x\rangle |\mathcal{O}(x)\rangle$. Now, $\mathcal{A}'$ can convert this state into

$$\sum |x\rangle |\mathcal{O}(x) \oplus \bigoplus_{i \neq i^*} \mathsf{PRF}_{2^i}(K_{2^i}, x)\rangle$$

via a local quantum computation and forwards this state to $\mathcal{A}$. In the end, $\mathcal{A}'$ outputs whatever $\mathcal{A}$ outputs. Now notice that if $\mathcal{O}(\cdot)$ computes $\mathsf{PRF}_{2^{i*}}(K_{2^{i*}}, \cdot)$, then $\mathcal{A}'$ perfectly simulated superposition access to $F(K, \cdot)$ to $\mathcal{A}$. On the other hand, if $\mathcal{O}(\cdot)$ computes a truly random function, then $\mathcal{O}(x) \oplus \bigoplus_{i \neq i^*} \mathsf{PRF}_{2^i}(K_{2^i}, x)$ is also a truly random function. Consequently, $\mathcal{A}'$ distinguishes $\mathsf{PRF}_{2^{i*}}$ from uniform with the same advantage that $\mathcal{A}$ distinguishes F from uniform.

The more challenging aspect of our approach is the construction of a q-bounded QPRF from a small domain PRF. As outlined in Sect. 1.1, even domain extension techniques that are statistically secure against classical adversaries might be completely insecure against a superposition adversary. We circumnavigate this problem by adopting a *perfectly secure* domain extension technique. We can then use a Lemma by Zhandry [27] which states that any classical $2q$-uniform function is identically distributed to a uniform function from the view of a q-bounded superposition adversary.

It turns out that we can realize perfectly secure domain extension using *highly unbalanced expander graphs* via constructions that have previously been used to construct space-efficient k-independent functions [10]. In a nutshell, a highly unbalanced expander is a bipartite graph Γ where the set of left vertices $[N]$ can be made super-polynomially large, the set of right vertices $[L]$ is only polynomially large, and the degree D is poly-logarithmic. Moreover, such graphs have a unique neighbor expansion property in the sense that it holds for any subset $S \subset [N]$ of left-vertices not larger than a (polynomial) bound Q that there exists a vertex v in $\Gamma(S) \subset [L]$ (the neighborhood of S) which has a unique neighbor in S. A construction of such graphs was provided by Guruswami, Umans and Vadhan [14].

Equipped with such a graph Γ, we can now extend a random function f defined on *the small domain* [L] to a Q-bounded random function g defined on the large domain $[N]$ as via a simple *tabulation function*. For a left vertex $x \in [N]$ and an index $j \in [D]$, let $\Gamma(x, j) \in [L]$ be the j-th neighbor of x. Define the function g by

$$g(x) = \bigoplus_{j \in [D]} f(\Gamma(x, j)).$$

We claim that if f is a uniformly random function, then g is a Q-uniform function, i.e. it holds for any pairwise distinct $x_1, \ldots, x_Q \in [N]$ that $g(x_1), \ldots, g(x_Q)$ are independent and uniformly random. To see this note that by the unique neighbor expansion property of Γ, as the set $S = \{x_1, \ldots, x_Q\}$ is of size Q there exists a vertex $v \in \Gamma(S)$ which has a unique neighbor x_{i^*} in S. In other words, there is an index $j^* \in [D]$ such that the term $f(\Gamma(x_{i^*}, j^*))$ only appears in

$$g(x_{i^*}) = \bigoplus_{j \in [D]} f(\Gamma(x_{i^*}, j)),$$

but not in any other $g(x_i)$ for $i \neq i^*$. Since $f(\Gamma(x_{i^*}, j^*))$ is uniformly random and independent of all the $g(x_i)$, it follows that $g(x_{i^*})$ is uniformly random and independent of all the $g(x_i)$. We can repeat this argument recursively arguing that the $g(x_1), \ldots, g(x_Q)$ are uniformly random and independent. Now assume that $Q = 2q$. We claim that if PRF is a post-quantum PRF with (polynomially-sized) domain $[L]$, then it holds that

$$F(K, x) = \bigoplus_{j \in [D]} \mathsf{PRF}(K, \Gamma(x, j))$$

is a q-bounded QPRF on the large domain $[N]$. To argue security, assume that $\mathcal{A}$ is a q-bounded BQP distinguisher which distinguishes F from a truly random function. We will first replace PRF with a truly random function f and argue security via the post-quantum security of PRF. Specifically, if $\mathcal{A}$ could distinguish these two cases we can construct a post-quantum distinguisher $\mathcal{A}'$ against the PRF security of PRF. $\mathcal{A}'$ is given access to an oracle $\mathcal{O}$ and proceeds as follows. It first queries $\mathcal{O}$ on every possible input obtaining the entire function table of $\mathcal{O}$. This can be performed efficiently as the domain of $\mathcal{O}$ is of size L, which is polynomial. Now, $\mathcal{A}'$ can give $\mathcal{A}$ superposition access to the function $\mathcal{O}'(x) = \bigoplus_{j \in [D]} \mathcal{O}(\Gamma(x, j))$ via a local quantum computation, since it knows the entire function table of $\mathcal{O}$. Consequently, if $\mathcal{A}$ distinguishes $F(K, x)$ from a function $F'(x) = \bigoplus_{j \in [D]} f(\Gamma(x, j))$ where f is a truly random function, then $\mathcal{A}'$ distiguishes PRF from a truly random function. Finally, as $F'(x) = \bigoplus_{j \in [D]} f(\Gamma(x, j))$ is a $2q$-uniform function, we can argue that since $\mathcal{A}$ is q-bounded it is identically distributed to a uniformly random function from the view of $\mathcal{A}$ via a Lemma by Zhandry [27]. This concludes the overview.

From a conceptual perspective, the main reason why our proof is simpler than, e.g., Zhandry's proof for QPRF security of the GGM construction [27], stems from the fact that the above reduction $\mathcal{A}'$ can query the entire function table of the small domain PRF PRF and simulate a quantum oracle for $\mathcal{A}$ locally.

2   Applications

In this section we discuss the possible applications of quantum secure PRFs.

2.1   Quantum Secure MACs

Classically, any pseudorandom function can be used to implement message authentication codes (MAC). Moreover, for quantum adversaries, we can use post-quantum secure PRFs to protect classical messages. However, what if the quantum adversary has the ability to query superpositions of messages? In this situation, the entire chosen message game would be held in the quantum environment which needs stronger version of security. For instance, considering a random oracle H, if the adversary can only issue classical queries, after learning q queries she does not learn any additional information at other inputs; but if she can issue quantum queries, then she might get information on all inputs simultaneously, even with just a single query.

Boneh and Zhandry [8] defined a quantum chosen message attack game to model the security of any MAC scheme in the quantum setting. First, quantum queries need to be explicitly modeled as the adversary could be entangled with the queries. We denote the adversary's state just prior to issuing a signing query by $\Sigma_{m,x,y}\psi_{m,x,y}|m, x, y\rangle$ and the signing oracle performs the following transformation,

$$\Sigma_{m,x,y}\psi_{m,x,y}|m, x, y\rangle \rightarrow \Sigma_{m,x,y}\psi_{m,x,y}|m, x \oplus S(k, m; r), y\rangle,$$

where r is a random string and $S(k, m; r)$ is the signing algorithm of a MAC scheme. Then we say that the adversary wins this game if she can generate $q+1$ valid classical message-tag pairs after issuing q quantum chosen message queries. The formal definition of quantum secure MACs is given as follows [2].

Definition 1. *A MAC system is existentially unforgeable under a quantum chosen message attack (EUF-qCMA) if no adversary can win the quantum MAC game with non-negligible advantage in λ.*

Boneh and Zhandry [8] also showed that a quantum secure pseudorandom function gives rise to the quantum-secure MAC, namely $S(k, m) = \mathsf{PRF}(k, m)$.

Theorem 2 ([8]). *If* $\mathsf{PRF} : \mathcal{K} \times \mathcal{X} \rightarrow \mathcal{Y}$ *is a quantum-secure pseudorandom function and $1/|\mathcal{Y}|$ is negligible, then $S(k, m) = \mathsf{PRF}(k, m)$ is a EUF-qCMA-secure MAC.*

Therefore, the Theorem 2 implies that a quantum secure PRF is sufficient to give us a quantum secure MAC.

2.2   Pseudorandom Quantum States

Pseudorandom states (or pseudorandom quantum states, denoted as PRS), are a set of random states $\{|\phi_k\rangle\}$ that is indistinguishable from Haar random quantum states. In [17], Ji et al. generalizes the definition of pseudorandomness in the classical case to the quantum setting:

Definition 2 (Pseudorandom states). *Let κ be the security parameter. Let $\mathcal{H}$ be a Hilbert space and $\mathcal{K}$ the key space, both parameterized by κ. A keyed family of quantum states $\{|\phi_k\rangle \in S(\mathcal{H}_{k \in \mathcal{K}})\}$ is pseudorandom, if the following two conditions hold:*

---

[2] Recently, blind-unforgeable, a stronger security notion for qMAC is defined in [1]. It implies EUF-qCMA notion and can also be satisfied by quantum secure PRF.

1. *Efficient generation.* There is a polynomial-time quantum algorithm G that generates state $|\phi_k\rangle$ on input k. That is, for all $k \in \mathcal{K}, G(k) = |\phi_k\rangle$.
2. *Pseudorandomness.* Any polynomially many copies of $|\phi_k\rangle$ with the same random $k \in \mathcal{K}$ is computationally indistinguishable from the same number of copies of a Haar random state. More precisely, for any efficient quantum algorithm $\mathcal{A}$ and any $m \in \mathsf{poly}(\kappa)$,

$$| \Pr_{k \leftarrow \mathcal{K}}[\mathcal{A}(|\phi_k\rangle^{\otimes m}) = 1] - \Pr_{|\psi\rangle \leftarrow \mu}[\mathcal{A}(|\psi\rangle^{\otimes m}) = 1]| = \mathsf{negl}(\kappa)$$

where μ is the Haar measure on $S(\mathcal{H})$.

Moreover, they also show that any quantum secure PRF could be used to construct PRS as follows.

Theorem 3 ([17]). *For any QPRF PRF : $\mathcal{K} \times \mathcal{X} \to \mathcal{X}$, the family of states $\{|\phi_k\rangle\}_{k \in \mathcal{K}}$,*

$$|\phi_k\rangle = \frac{1}{\sqrt{N}} \sum_{x \in \mathcal{X}} \omega_N^{\mathsf{PRF}_k(x)} |x\rangle,$$

is a PRS.

Finally, PRS can be immediately used to construct a private-key quantum money scheme [17].

3   Preliminaries

We denote by $\lambda \in \mathbb{N}$ the security parameter, by $\mathsf{poly}(\lambda)$ any function that is bounded by a polynomial in λ, and by $\mathsf{negl}(\lambda)$ any function that is negligible in the security parameter. We abbreviate computational indistinguishability of two distributions by $\approx_c$. The set of N elements is always written as $[N]$. We also denote as $\mathcal{D}^{\mathcal{O}}$ a distinguisher $\mathcal{D}$ access to an oracle $\mathcal{O}$ via classical queries and $\mathcal{A}^{|\mathcal{O}\rangle}$ via quantum queries.

3.1   Quantum Computing

We recall some basic facts about quantum computing.

Fact 1 ([23]). *Any classical efficiently computable function f can be implemented efficiently by a quantum computer. Furthermore, any function that has an efficient classical algorithm computing it can be implemented efficiently as a quantum-accessible oracle.*

Fact 2 ([28]). *For any sets $\mathcal{X}$ and $\mathcal{Y}$, we can efficiently 'construct' a random oracle from $\mathcal{X}$ to $\mathcal{Y}$ capable of handling q quantum queries, where q is a polynomial. More specifically, the behavior of any quantum algorithm making at most q queries to a $2q$-wise independent function is identical to its behavior when the queries are made to a random function.*

A more formal statement of Fact 2 is given in the following.

Theorem 4 ([28]). *Let A be a quantum algorithm making q quantum queries to an oracle $H : \mathcal{X} \to \mathcal{Y}$. If we draw H from some weight assignment D^3, then for every z, the quantity $\Pr_{H \leftarrow\$ D}[A^H(\cdot) = z]$ is a linear combination of the quantities $\Pr_{H \leftarrow\$ D}[H(x_i) = r_i, \forall i \in \{1, \ldots, 2q\}]$ for all possible settings of the x_i and r_i.*

This is proved in [28] and immediately implies that, if two weight assignments on oracles, D_1 and D_2, are $2q$-wise equivalent, then any q query quantum algorithm behaves the same under both weight assignments, since for all $2q$ pairs (x_i, r_i) it holds that

$$\Pr_{H \leftarrow\$ D_1}[H(x_i) = r_i, \forall i \in \{1, \ldots, 2q\}] = \Pr_{H \leftarrow\$ D_2}[H(x_i) = r_i, \forall i \in \{1, \ldots, 2q\}].$$

3.2 Pseudorandom Functions

We recall definition of classical pseudorandom functions [13].

Definition 3 (Pseudorandom Functions). *Let $\mathcal{X}_\lambda$ and $\mathcal{Y}_\lambda$ be two finite sets depending on λ. We say that an efficiently computable keyed function $\mathsf{PRF} : \mathcal{K}_\lambda \times \mathcal{X}_\lambda \to \mathcal{Y}_\lambda$ with key-space $\mathcal{K}_\lambda$ is a pseudorandom function (PRF), if it holds for every PPT oracle adversary $\mathcal{A}$ that*

$$|\Pr[\mathcal{A}^{\mathsf{PRF}(K,\cdot)}(1^\lambda) = 1] - \Pr[\mathcal{A}^R(1^\lambda) = 1]| \leqslant \mathsf{negl}(\lambda),$$

where $K \leftarrow\$ \mathcal{K}_\lambda$ and $R : \mathcal{X}_\lambda \to \mathcal{Y}_\lambda$ is a randomly chosen function. Moreover, if $|\mathcal{X}| \leqslant \mathsf{poly}(\lambda)$, then we say that PRF is a small-domain PRF, otherwise we call PRF a large-domain PRF.

If $\mathcal{A}$ is a quantum machine, then we say that the PRF is *post-quantum secure*. Note that $\mathcal{A}$ is restricted to issue only classical queries, but its computation can be quantum. We now recall the notion of q-bounded PRF [12]. The difference between q-bounded PRF and PRF is just the former can only send at most q distinct queries. As in [12], our only restriction is that the runtime of the function depends polynomially on λ and $\log(q)$.

Definition 4 (Bounded Pseudorandom Functions). *Let $\mathcal{X}_\lambda$ and $\mathcal{Y}_\lambda$ be finite sets. A keyed function $F_q : \mathcal{K}_q \times X_\lambda \to \mathcal{Y}_\lambda$ parameterized by a parameter q is a q-bounded pseudorandom function (bPRF), if F_q is computable in time $\mathsf{poly}(\lambda, \log(q))$ and if it holds for all efficiently computable $q^* = q(\lambda) \leqslant \mathsf{poly}(\lambda)$ and all q^*-query distinguishers $\mathcal{D}$ (i.e. send at most q^* distinct queries) that*

$$|\Pr[\mathcal{D}^{F_q(K,\cdot)}(1^\lambda) = 1] - \Pr[\mathcal{D}^R(1^\lambda) = 1]| \leqslant \mathsf{negl}(\lambda),$$

where $K \leftarrow\$ \mathcal{K}_q$ and $R : \mathcal{X}_\lambda \to \mathcal{Y}_\lambda$ is a randomly chosen function.

---

[3] A weight assignment on a set X is a function $D : X \to R$ such that $\sum_x D(x) = 1$. As an example, and the way we use it in our work, it could model a probability distribution.

Quantum Pseudorandom Functions. We define quantum PRFs in the following. Roughly speaking, we say a pseudorandom function PRF is quantum-secure if no efficient quantum adversary $\mathcal{A}$ making quantum queries can distinguish between a random function R and the function PRF. By quantum query we mean that the adversary $\mathcal{A}$ can send a quantum superposition to the oracle and receive a the corresponding quantum superposition of the function evaluation in return.

Definition 5 (Quantum-secure Pseudorandom Functions). *A pseudorandom function* PRF $: \mathcal{K}_\lambda \times \mathcal{X}_\lambda \to \mathcal{Y}_\lambda$ *is quantum-secure if no efficient quantum adversary $\mathcal{A}$ making quantum queries can distinguish between a truly random function R and the function* PRF$(K, \cdot)$ *for a random $K \leftarrow\!\!\$\, \mathcal{K}_\lambda$. Specifically, for keyed function* PRF $: \mathcal{K}_\lambda \times \mathcal{X}_\lambda \to \mathcal{Y}_\lambda$ *with key-space $\mathcal{K}_\lambda$, we say it is a quantum-secure pseudorandom function (QPRF) if it holds for every efficient quantum adversary $\mathcal{A}$ that*

$$|\Pr[\mathcal{A}^{|\mathsf{PRF}(K,\cdot)\rangle}(1^\lambda) = 1] - \Pr[\mathcal{A}^{|R\rangle}(1^\lambda) = 1]| \leqslant \mathsf{negl}(\lambda),$$

where $K \leftarrow\!\!\$\, \mathcal{K}_\lambda$ and $R : \mathcal{X}_\lambda \to \mathcal{Y}_\lambda$ is a randomly chosen function.

We also define the notion of q-bounded quantum PRFs in a similar spirit as above.

Definition 6 (Bounded Quantum-secure Pseudorandom Functions). *Let $\mathcal{X}_\lambda$ and $\mathcal{Y}_\lambda$ be finite sets. A keyed function $F_q : \mathcal{K}_q \times X_\lambda \to \mathcal{Y}_\lambda$ parameterized by a parameter q is a q-bounded quantum-secure pseudorandom function (bQPRF), if F_q is computable in time $\mathsf{poly}(\lambda, \log(q))$ and if it holds for all efficiently computable $q^* = q(\lambda) \leqslant \mathsf{poly}(\lambda)$ and all q^*-query quantum adversary $\mathcal{A}$ (i.e. send at most q^* distinct quantum queries) that*

$$|\Pr[\mathcal{A}^{|F_q(K,\cdot)\rangle}(1^\lambda) = 1] - \Pr[\mathcal{A}^{|R\rangle}(1^\lambda) = 1]| \leqslant \mathsf{negl}(\lambda),$$

where $K \leftarrow\!\!\$\, K_q$ and $R : \mathcal{X}_\lambda \to \mathcal{Y}_\lambda$ is a randomly chosen function.

4 Bipartite Expanders

Expanders are highly connected sparse graphs, which are significantly useful in computer science, and there is a rich body of work on constructions and properties of expanders (see, e.g., [15] and references therein). We recall the definitions of bipartite graphs and expanders in the following.

Definition 7 (Bipartite Graph). *A bipartite graph with N left-vertices, L right-vertices, and D left-degrees is specified by a function $\Gamma : [N] \times [D] \to [L]$, where $\Gamma(x, j)$ denotes the j-th neighbor of x. For a set $S \subseteq [N]$, we denote as $\Gamma(S)$ its set of neighbors $\{\Gamma(x, j) : x \in S, j \in [D]\}$.*

Definition 8 (Bipartite Expander). *A bipartite graph $\Gamma : [N] \times [D] \to [L]$ is a $(\leqslant Q, A)$ expander if for all $S \subseteq [N]$ with $|S| \leqslant Q$, it has: $|\Gamma(S)| \geqslant A \cdot |S|$, where A is expansion factor.*

We are only interested in highly unbalanced expanders with $N \gg L$. An explicit construction (i.e., where $\Gamma(\cdot, \cdot)$ is computable in polynomial time) of such an expander has been shown in [14]. We recall here the theorem.

Theorem 5 ([14]). *For all constants* $\alpha > 0$: *for every* $N \in \mathbb{N}, Q \leqslant N$, *and* $\xi > 0$, *there is an explicit* $(\leqslant Q, (1 - \xi)D)$ *expander* $\Gamma : [N] \times [D] \rightarrow [L]$ *with degree* $D = O\left(((\log N)(\log Q)/\xi)^{1+1/\alpha}\right)$ *and* $L \leqslant D^2 \cdot Q^{1+\alpha}$. *Moreover,* D *and* L *are powers of* 2.

4.1   Q-unique Expanders

In our construction, we need a $(\leqslant Q, (1 - \xi)D)$ expander to be *Q-unique*, which means in every subset of left-vertices with size not greater than Q, there must exist a vertex with a unique neighbor (i.e., this unique neighbor is connected to only one vertex). This property is defined in [10] as constructing functions where every subset S of inputs of size at most Q contains an input that has many unique neighbors. It is formalized as:

Definition 9 (*Q-unique* **Expander**). *A* $(\leqslant Q, (1 - \xi)D)$ *expander* $\Gamma : [N] \times [D] \rightarrow [L]$ *is Q-unique if for all* $S \subseteq [N], |S| \leqslant Q$, *there exists a* $x \in S$ *such that* $|\Gamma(\{x\}) \backslash \Gamma(S \backslash \{x\})| > l \geqslant 0$ *holds.*

Note l in Definition 9 is a way to measure *uniqueness* of a expander: The greater the l is, the more unique neighbors an input can have. In our construction, we only need $l = 0$ which means (at least) one unique neighbor would be sufficient for us. Moreover, there is also a concept of *Q-wise-independence*:

Definition 10 (*Q-wise-independence*). *Let* Q *be a positive integer and let* $\mathcal{F}$ *be a family of functions from* $\mathcal{Y}$ *to* $\mathcal{Z}$. *We say that* $\mathcal{F}$ *is a Q-wise-independent family of functions if, for every choice of* $l \leqslant Q$ *distinct keys* $y_1, \ldots, y_l$ *and arbitrary values* $z_1, \ldots, z_l$, *then, for* f *selected uniformly at random from* $\mathcal{F}$ *we have that*

$$\Pr[f(y_1) = z_1, \ldots, f(y_l) = z_l] = |\mathcal{Z}|^{-l}.$$

The existence of such *Q-unique* expanders is showed as follows.

Theorem 6. *Given any* $(\leqslant Q, (1 - \xi)D)$ *expander* $\Gamma : [N] \times [D] \rightarrow [L]$ *from Definition 8, if* $\xi < 1/2$, *then expander* Γ *is Q-unique for* $l = 0$.

Proof. First we want to show that there must exist a vertex in $\Gamma(S)$ with degree at most one, when $\xi < 1/2$. Assume towards contradiction that every vertex in $\Gamma(S)$ has degree at least 2 when $\xi < 1/2$. Then the number of edges between S and $\Gamma(S)$ is at least two times as $|\Gamma(S)|$. By Definition 7, we have that

$$D \cdot |S| \geqslant 2 \cdot |\Gamma(S)|.$$

Next, by Definition 8, we have $|\Gamma(S)| \geqslant (1 - \xi)D \cdot |S|$ (in which $(1 - \xi)D$ is expansion factor), therefore

$$D \cdot |S| \geqslant 2(1 - \xi)D \cdot |S|$$
$$1 \geqslant 2(1 - \xi)$$
$$\xi \geqslant 1/2,$$

which is a contradiction since there is $\xi < 1/2$. It follows that if $\xi < 1/2$, then there exists one vertex in $\Gamma(S)$ with degree less than or equal to 1. However, we already know that the degree cannot be zero since it's in the neighbors set. Therefore it must be 1. This completes the proof.   □

Now we will state a useful lemma here. In his seminal paper [25], Siegel showed how a Q-*unique* expander can be combined with a small domain random function to obtain a Q-*wise-independent* function. We use a light variation of Siegel's technique here. It is also used by works [26] and [10].

Lemma 1. *Let* $\Gamma : [N] \times [D] \to [L]$ *be a Q-unique expander, let* $f : [L] \to \{0,1\}^\lambda$ *be a uniformly random function and let* $h : [N] \to \{0,1\}^\lambda$ *be defined by*

$$h(x) = \bigoplus_{j \in [D]} f(\Gamma(x,j)).$$

Then h is a Q-wise-independent function.

4.2   Parameters

Typically, goals in constructing an unbalanced bipartite expander are to maximize the expansion factor A, minimize the degree D, and minimize the size L of the right-hand side ($L \leqslant N$). Although we do not care about the concrete expansion factor A in this work, we still expect a small L (to highly extend domains of PRFs) and small D (to reduce computational overheads). By Theorem 5 we can fix a domain size $N = 2^\lambda$ and a bound $Q = \mathsf{poly}(\lambda)$ and get an explicit expander $\Gamma : [N] \times [D] \to [L]$ where $D = \mathsf{poly}(\log(N), \log(Q))$ and $L = \mathsf{poly}(D, Q)$. Consequently, the degree D is essentially independent of Q and L is of size at most polynomial in Q.

5   Our Quantum Pseudorandom Function

In this section, we present our construction for a quantum PRF from bipartite expanders. First we show how to construct a perfectly secure (or *loseless*) domain extender which takes as input a small-domain classical (post-quantum) PRF and outputs a q-bounded quantum PRF with large domain. Second we show a combiner that turns a family of q-bounded quantum PRFs into a standard quantum PRF. Note that our proof of security is tight: If a quantum adversary $\mathcal{A}$ can distinguish a quantum PRF F from truly random function R with advantage ϵ, then there exists an adversary $\mathcal{A}'$ which can distinguish a small-domain PRF from a truly random function (issuing only classical queries) with the same advantage ϵ.

5.1 Domain Extension

In the following we present a new domain extension technique based on bipartite expanders. Our compiler is shown below.

Construction 1. *Let* $\mathsf{PRF} : \mathcal{K}_q \times \mathcal{Y} \to \mathcal{Z}$ *be a keyed function with key space* $\mathcal{K}_q$. *Let* $\Gamma : \{0,1\}^\lambda \times [D] \to \{0,1\}^l$ *be a* $(\leqslant 2q, (1 - \xi)D)$ *expander with* $\xi \in (0, 1/2)$. *We define the keyed function* $F_q : \mathcal{K}_q \times \mathcal{X} \to \mathcal{Z}$ *with key space* $\mathcal{K}_q$ *by*

$$F_q(K, x) = \bigoplus_{j \in [D]} \mathsf{PRF}(K, \Gamma(x, j)),$$

where $K \leftarrow_\$ \mathcal{K}_q$, $D = \mathsf{poly}(\lambda)$, $l = \mathcal{O}(\log(\lambda))$, *and* $\mathcal{X} : \{0,1\}^\lambda, \mathcal{Y} : \{0,1\}^l, \mathcal{Z} : \{0,1\}^m$.

The following theorem states that the function F_q is a q-bounded quantum PRF.

Theorem 7. *Let* PRF *and* F_q *be as in Construction 1. If* PRF *is a post-quantum (classically secure) PRF, then* F_q *is a* q-bounded quantum PRF. More specifi-cally, if there exists a* $q^* \leqslant \mathsf{poly}(\lambda)$ *and a* q^*-query quantum adversary $\mathcal{A}$ *that distinguishes* F_{q^*} *from a truly random function* $R : \mathcal{X} \to \mathcal{Z}$ *with advantage* ϵ, *then there exists an efficient quantum adversary* $\mathcal{A}'$ *with essentially the same runtime as* $\mathcal{A}$ *that distinguish* PRF *from a truly random function* $R' : \mathcal{Y} \to \mathcal{Z}$ *with advantage at least* ϵ.

Before delving into the proof of the main theorem, we state the following useful lemma. Loosely speaking, we show that if a small-domain PRF is post-quantum secure[4] (where the adversary is allowed to issue only classical queries), then such a PRF is also quantum secure. Intuitively, this holds because an adversary can query classically the full domain of the PRF in polynomial time. We stress that the counterexample of [27] does not apply in these settings, since we consider only PRFs with small (poly-sized) domain.

Lemma 2. *Let* PRF *be a small-domain and post-quantum secure PRF as defined in Definition 3, then* PRF *is also quantum-secure as defined in Definition 5. Specifically, if there exists an efficient quantum adversary* $\mathcal{A}$ *which can make quantum queries to distinguish* $\mathsf{PRF} : \mathcal{K} \times \mathcal{Y} \to \mathcal{Z}$ *from truly random function* $R : \mathcal{Y} \to \mathcal{Z}$ *with advantage* ϵ, *where* $|\mathcal{Y}| \leqslant \mathsf{poly}(\lambda)$, *then there exists an efficient quantum adversary* $\mathcal{A}'$ *(with essentially the same runtime as* $\mathcal{A}$*) that can only make classical queries to distinguish from* PRF *and* $\mathcal{R}$ *with advantage* ϵ.

Proof. Assume that there exists an efficient (i.e., running in polynomial time) quantum adversary $\mathcal{A}$ who is able to distinguish PRF from a random function $R : \mathcal{Y} \to \mathcal{Z}$ with advantage ϵ (given quantum oracle access to PRF). We can con-struct a quantum adversary $\mathcal{A}'$ who only sends classical queries and breaks the

---

[4] Any small domain PRF built from symmetric primitives is post-quantum secure as long as underling symmetric assumptions are post-quantum secure.

security of PRF with the same advantage. From Fact 1, any classical efficiently computable function f can be efficiently implemented by quantum computer, thus we are able to efficiently implement a quantum circuit which computes transformation U_f on quantum computers. Specifically, given input states $|x, y\rangle$, where x corresponds to 'data' register and y corresponds to 'target' register, the quantum circuit corresponding to U_f would transform it into $|x, y \oplus f(x)\rangle$, i.e., $U_f|x, y\rangle = |x, y \oplus f(x)\rangle$. For notational convenience, we also use $U_f|x\rangle$ to denote the state of "target" register after passing through the circuit corresponding to U_f.

> **Quantum Adversary** $\mathcal{A}'(1^\lambda)$:
> Obtain function table of $T(x)$ by querying $\mathcal{O}'$ classically;
> Construct the quantum circuit corresponding to U_T;
> $b' \leftarrow \mathcal{A}^{|\mathcal{O}(|y\rangle)\rangle}$;
> Output b'.
> **Classical Oracle** $\mathcal{O}'(x)$:
> Return $T(x)$.
> **Quantum Oracle** $\mathcal{O}(|y\rangle)$:
> Return $U_T|y\rangle$.

Recall that given the description of T, then U_T is efficiently computable. Furhtermore, $\mathcal{A}'$ issues only polynomially-many queries, since PRF has a small domain. We can conclude that $\mathcal{A}'$ is efficient. Consider the case where $T(x) = \mathsf{PRF}(K, x)$, for uniformly chosen $K \leftarrow_\$ \mathcal{K}$, then O is identically distributed to PRF. On the other hand, if $T(x) = R(x)$ then O is identically distributed to a truly random function. Thus it holds that

$$|\Pr[\mathcal{A}'^{\mathsf{PRF}(K, \cdot)}(1^\lambda) = 1] - \Pr[\mathcal{A}'^R(1^\lambda) = 1]| = |\Pr[\mathcal{A}^{|\mathsf{PRF}(K, \cdot)\rangle}(1^\lambda) = 1] - \Pr[\mathcal{A}^{|R\rangle}(1^\lambda) = 1]|$$
$$= \epsilon,$$

which completes the proof.   □

We are now in the position of proving the main theorem of this section.

Proof (of Theorem 7). Let $\mathcal{A}$ be a q-query quantum adversary with advantage ϵ against F_q. We are going to construct an adversary $\mathcal{A}'$ with the same advantage against PRF. Consider the following sequence of hybrids.

- **Hybrid$_0$**: This is defined exactly as the real experiment where $\mathcal{A}$ has oracle access to a function

$$F_0(x) = \bigoplus_{j \in [D]} \mathsf{PRF}(K, \Gamma(x, j)),$$

where K is uniformly sampled from $\mathcal{K}, x \in \mathcal{X}$ and $\Gamma : \mathcal{X} \times [D] \to \mathcal{Y}$ is a $(\leqslant 2q, (1 - \xi)D)$ expander as in Construction 1. $\mathcal{A}$ can send at most q distinct quantum queries.

- **Hybrid$_1$**: This experiment is defined as Hybrid$_0$ except that we replace PRF with a truly random function $R : \mathcal{Y} \to \mathcal{Z}$. That is, the adversary $\mathcal{A}$ has oracle access to a function

$$F_1(x) = \bigoplus_{j \in [D]} R(\Gamma(x, j)),$$

where R_j is a function uniformly sampled from $\mathcal{Y}$ to $\mathcal{Z}$.
- **Hybrid$_2$**: This is the ideal experiment where $\mathcal{A}$ has oracle access to a truly random function

$$F_2(x) = R(x)$$

which is uniformly sampled from $\mathcal{X}$ to $\mathcal{Z}$.

Since F_0 and F_2 are in real and ideal experiment, respectively, it holds that

$$|\Pr[\mathcal{A}^{|F_0\rangle}(1^\lambda) = 1] - \Pr[\mathcal{A}^{|F_2\rangle}(1^\lambda) = 1]| = \epsilon.$$

Similarly, we can define two other advantages as:

$$|\Pr[\mathcal{A}^{|F_0\rangle}(1^\lambda) = 1] - \Pr[\mathcal{A}^{|F_1\rangle}(1^\lambda) = 1]| = \epsilon_0,$$
$$|\Pr[\mathcal{A}^{|F_1\rangle}(1^\lambda) = 1] - \Pr[\mathcal{A}^{|F_2\rangle}(1^\lambda) = 1]| = \epsilon_1.$$

We first show that $\epsilon_1 = 0$. By Construction 1 we have $\xi \in (0, 1/2)$, thus we know the expander $\Gamma : \{0,1\}^\lambda \times [D] \to \{0,1\}^l$ is *2q-unique* by Theorem 6. By Lemma 1, we know that for all distinct $(x_1, \ldots, x_{2q}) \in \mathcal{X}^{2q}$, the outputs $F_1(x_1), \ldots, F_1(x_{2q})$ are distributed independently and uniformly at random, that is, $Pr[F_1(x_1) = r_1, \ldots, F_1(x_{2q}) = r_{2q}]$ equals to 2^{-2qm}.

Then by Theorem 4, we have

$$\Pr[\mathcal{A}^{|F_1\rangle}(1^\lambda) = 1] = \Pr[\mathcal{A}^{|F_2\rangle}(1^\lambda) = 1],$$

since for all $2q$ pairs (x_i, r_i), it holds that

$$\Pr[F_1(x_i) = r_i, \forall i \in \{1, \ldots, 2q\}] = 2^{-2qm}$$
$$= \Pr[F_2(x_i) = r_i, \forall i \in \{1, \ldots, 2q\}].$$

This means that $\epsilon_1 = 0$. By triangle inequality we have

$$\epsilon_0 = |\Pr[\mathcal{A}^{|F_0\rangle}(1^\lambda) = 1] - \Pr[\mathcal{A}^{|F_1\rangle}(1^\lambda) = 1]|$$
$$\geqslant |\Pr[\mathcal{A}^{|F_0\rangle}(1^\lambda) = 1] - \Pr[\mathcal{A}^{|F_2\rangle}(1^\lambda) = 1]| - |\Pr[\mathcal{A}^{|F_1\rangle}(1^\lambda) = 1] - \Pr[\mathcal{A}^{|F_2\rangle}(1^\lambda) = 1]|$$
$$= \epsilon - \epsilon_1$$
$$= \epsilon.$$

We are left with constructing an adversary that can distinguish a small-domain PRF from a truly random function with advantage ϵ_0. First we allow such an adversary to issue quantum oracle queries. Since we could use Toffoli gates to simulate any classical circuits in quantum settings, without losing generality, let $U_\oplus$ be a quantum circuit to compute $U_\oplus |x_1, \ldots, x_D, y\rangle \to |x_1, \ldots, x_D, y + (x_1 \oplus \cdots \oplus x_D)\rangle$ and U_{Γ_j} be another one to compute $U_{\Gamma_j} |x, y\rangle \to |x, y + \Gamma(x, j)\rangle$. The adversary $\mathcal{A}''$ is defined in the following.

Quantum Adversary $\mathcal{A}''(1^\lambda)$:

For each $j \in [D]$ construct the circuit

U_{Γ_j};

$b' \leftarrow \mathcal{A}^{|\mathcal{O}(|x\rangle\rangle\rangle}$;

Output b'.

Quantum Oracle $\mathcal{O}''(|x\rangle)$:

Return $U_T|x\rangle$.

Quantum Oracle $\mathcal{O}(|x\rangle)$:

Return $U_\oplus|\mathcal{O}''(U_{\Gamma_1}|x\rangle), \ldots, \mathcal{O}''(U_{\Gamma_D}|x\rangle)\rangle$.

Note that $\mathcal{A}$ makes at most q distinct quantum queries ($q \leqslant \mathrm{poly}(\lambda)$), thus $\mathcal{A}''$ is an efficient quantum adversary running in polynomial time. First assume that $T(x) = \mathsf{PRF}(K, x)$ for $K \leftarrow_\$ \mathcal{K}_q$, then the oracle $\mathcal{O}$ in $\mathcal{A}''$'s simulation is identically distributed to $F_0(x)$. On the other hand, if $T(x) = R(x)$ is a uniformly random function, $\mathcal{O}$ computes $\bigoplus_{j=1}^D R(\Gamma(x, j))$ which is F_1. Therefore we have

$$| \Pr[\mathcal{A}''^{|\mathsf{PRF}(K, \cdot)\rangle}(1^\lambda) = 1] - \Pr[\mathcal{A}''^{|R(\cdot)\rangle}(1^\lambda) = 1]| = | \Pr[\mathcal{A}^{|F_0\rangle}(1^\lambda) = 1] - \Pr[\mathcal{A}^{|F_1\rangle}(1^\lambda) = 1]|$$

$$= \epsilon_0$$

$$\geqslant \epsilon.$$

By Lemma 2 we know that there exists an adversary $\mathcal{A}'$ with the same advantage ϵ, which issues only classical queries, since the PRF has a small (poly-sized) domain. This completes the proof. $\qquad\square$

5.2 Unbounded Queries

Finally, we show that the combiner of [12] allows us to remove the restriction on the query bound of our quantum PRF. The innovation of our paper is that we lift the analysis to the quantum settings.

Construction 2. *Let $\omega(\log(\lambda))$ be a slightly super-logarithmic upperbound. For a given parameter q, let $F_q : \mathcal{K}_q \times \mathcal{X} \to \mathcal{Z}$ be a keyed function with corresponding key space $\mathcal{K}_q$. Define the function $F : \mathcal{K} \times \mathcal{X} \to \mathcal{Z}$ with key space $\mathcal{K} = \prod_{i=1}^{\omega(\log(\lambda))} \mathcal{K}_{2^i}$ by*

$$F(K, x) = \bigoplus_{i=1}^{\omega(\log(\lambda))} F_{2^i}(K_{2^i}, x),$$

where $K_{2^i} \leftarrow_\$ \mathcal{K}_{2^i}$ for $i = 1, \ldots, \omega(\log(\lambda))$ and $K = (K_{2^i})_{i=1,\ldots,\omega(\log(\lambda))}$.

Theorem 8. *Let F_q and F be as in Construction 2. If F_q is a q-bounded quantum PRF, then F is a quantum PRF. Specifically, if $\mathcal{A}$ is an efficient quantum adversary against F with advantage ϵ that makes at most $q' = \mathrm{poly}(\lambda)$ distinct quantum queries, then there exists an q^*-query quantum adversary $\mathcal{A}'$ (with essentially the same runtime as $\mathcal{A}$) with advantage ϵ against F_{q^*}, where $q^* = 2^{\lceil \log(q') \rceil} \leqslant 2q' = \mathrm{poly}(\lambda)$.*

Proof. Let $\mathcal{A}$ be an efficient quantum adversary which can send quantum superpositions to distinguish F from a truly random function R with advantage ϵ, then we can construct an efficient q^*-query quantum adversary $\mathcal{A}'$ to distinguish F_q from R for some q. Since $q' = \text{poly}(\lambda)$, we have $\log(q') \leqslant \omega(\log(\lambda))$ thus $2^1 \leqslant q^* = 2^{\lceil \log(q') \rceil} \leqslant \text{poly}(\lambda) < 2^{\omega(\log(\lambda))}$ for sufficient large λ.

> **Bounded Quantum Adversary $\mathcal{A}'(1^\lambda)$:**
> Set i^* as $\lceil \log(q') \rceil$;
> Generate K_{2^i} for $i \in \{1, \ldots, \omega(\log(\lambda))\} \backslash i^*$;
> $b' \leftarrow \mathcal{A}^{|\mathcal{O}(|x\rangle)\rangle}$;
> Output b'.
> **Quantum oracle $\mathcal{O}'(|x\rangle)$:**
> Return $U_T|x\rangle$.
> **Quantum oracle $\mathcal{O}(|x\rangle)$:**
> Return $U_\oplus |F_{2^1}, \ldots \mathcal{O}'(|x\rangle), \ldots F_{2^{\omega(\log(\lambda))}}\rangle$.

Where $\mathcal{O}'(|x\rangle)$ is the i^*-th element in $\{1, \ldots, \omega(\log(\lambda))\}$ and we write $F_{2^i}(K_i, x)$ as F_{2^i} to simplify the notation. Observe that $q' \leqslant 2^{\lceil \log(q') \rceil} = q^* \leqslant \text{poly}(\lambda)$ thus $\mathcal{A}'$ is able to run $\mathcal{A}$ as a black box and q' queries can be handled by $\mathcal{A}'$. Then we consider distributions of different $T(x)$. If $T(x) = F_{2^{i^*}}(K, x)$ for uniformly randomized $K \leftarrow_\$ K_{2^{i^*}}$, then oracle $\mathcal{O}$ is identically distributed to $F(K, x)$ for $K \leftarrow_\$ \mathcal{K}$. Otherwise, if $T(x) = R(x)$, then the distribution of oracle $\mathcal{O}$ should be uniform since O' and other F_{2^i} are independent, thus it will be identically distributed to $R(x)$. Therefore it holds that

$$|\Pr[\mathcal{A}'^{|F_{2^{i^*}}\rangle}(1^\lambda) = 1] - \Pr[\mathcal{A}'^{|R\rangle}(1^\lambda) = 1]| = |\Pr[\mathcal{A}^{|F\rangle}(1^\lambda) = 1] - \Pr[\mathcal{A}^{|R\rangle}(1^\lambda) = 1]|$$
$$= \epsilon.$$

which completes the proof. $\qquad\qquad\qquad\qquad\qquad\qquad\qquad\qquad\qquad\qquad\square$

References

1. Alagic, G., Majenz, C., Russell, A., Song, F.: Quantum-access-secure message authentication via blind-unforgeability. In: Canteaut, A., Ishai, Y. (eds.) EUROCRYPT 2020, Part III. LNCS, vol. 12107, pp. 788–817. Springer, Cham (2020). https://doi.org/10.1007/978-3-030-45727-3_27
2. Banerjee, A., Peikert, C., Rosen, A.: Pseudorandom functions and lattices. In: Pointcheval, D., Johansson, T. (eds.) EUROCRYPT 2012. LNCS, vol. 7237, pp. 719–737. Springer, Heidelberg (2012). https://doi.org/10.1007/978-3-642-29011-4_42
3. Berman, I., Haitner, I.: From non-adaptive to adaptive pseudorandom functions. In: Cramer, R. (ed.) TCC 2012. LNCS, vol. 7194, pp. 357–368. Springer, Heidelberg (2012). https://doi.org/10.1007/978-3-642-28914-9_20
4. Berman, I., Haitner, I., Komargodski, I., Naor, M.: Hardness preserving reductions via cuckoo hashing. In: Sahai, A. (ed.) TCC 2013. LNCS, vol. 7785, pp. 40–59. Springer, Heidelberg (2013). https://doi.org/10.1007/978-3-642-36594-2_3

5. Boneh, D., Lewi, K., Montgomery, H., Raghunathan, A.: Key homomorphic PRFs and their applications. In: Canetti, R., Garay, J.A. (eds.) CRYPTO 2013, Part I. LNCS, vol. 8042, pp. 410–428. Springer, Heidelberg (2013). https://doi.org/10.1007/978-3-642-40041-4_23

6. Boneh, D., Lipton, R.J.: Quantum cryptanalysis of hidden linear functions. In: Coppersmith, D. (ed.) CRYPTO 1995. LNCS, vol. 963, pp. 424–437. Springer, Heidelberg (1995). https://doi.org/10.1007/3-540-44750-4_34

7. Boneh, D., Montgomery, H.W., Raghunathan, A.: Algebraic pseudorandom functions with improved efficiency from the augmented cascade. In: Al-Shaer, E., Keromytis, A.D., Shmatikov, V. (eds.) ACM CCS 2010: 17th Conference on Computer and Communications Security, Chicago, Illinois, USA, 4–8 October 2010, pp. 131–140. ACM Press (2010). https://doi.org/10.1145/1866307.1866323

8. Boneh, D., Zhandry, M.: Quantum-secure message authentication codes. In: Johansson, T., Nguyen, P.Q. (eds.) EUROCRYPT 2013. LNCS, vol. 7881, pp. 592–608. Springer, Heidelberg (2013). https://doi.org/10.1007/978-3-642-38348-9_35

9. Carter, L., Wegman, M.N.: Universal classes of hash functions (extended abstract). In: STOC, pp. 106–112. ACM (1977)

10. Christiani, T., Pagh, R., Thorup, M.: From independence to expansion and back again. In: Servedio, R.A., Rubinfeld, R. (eds.) 47th Annual ACM Symposium on Theory of Computing, Portland, OR, USA, 14–17 June 2015, pp. 813–820. ACM Press (2015). https://doi.org/10.1145/2746539.2746620

11. Dodis, Y., Yampolskiy, A.: A verifiable random function with short proofs and keys. In: Vaudenay, S. (ed.) PKC 2005. LNCS, vol. 3386, pp. 416–431. Springer, Heidelberg (2005). https://doi.org/10.1007/978-3-540-30580-4_28

12. Döttling, N., Schröder, D.: Efficient pseudorandom functions via on-the-fly adaptation. In: Gennaro, R., Robshaw, M. (eds.) CRYPTO 2015, Part I. LNCS, vol. 9215, pp. 329–350. Springer, Heidelberg (2015). https://doi.org/10.1007/978-3-662-47989-6_16

13. Goldreich, O., Goldwasser, S., Micali, S.: How to construct random functions (extended abstract). In: 25th Annual Symposium on Foundations of Computer Science, Singer Island, Florida, 24–26 October 1984, pp. 464–479. IEEE Computer Society Press (1984). https://doi.org/10.1109/SFCS.1984.715949

14. Guruswami, V., Umans, C., Vadhan, S.: Unbalanced expanders and randomness extractors from Parvaresh-Vardy codes. J. ACM (JACM) 56(4), 20 (2009)

15. Hoory, S., Linial, N., Wigderson, A.: Expander graphs and their applications. Bull. Am. Math. Soc. 43(4), 439–561 (2006)

16. Jain, A., Pietrzak, K., Tentes, A.: Hardness preserving constructions of pseudorandom functions. In: Cramer, R. (ed.) TCC 2012. LNCS, vol. 7194, pp. 369–382. Springer, Heidelberg (2012). https://doi.org/10.1007/978-3-642-28914-9_21

17. Ji, Z., Liu, Y.-K., Song, F.: Pseudorandom quantum states. In: Shacham, H., Boldyreva, A. (eds.) CRYPTO 2018, Part III. LNCS, vol. 10993, pp. 126–152. Springer, Cham (2018). https://doi.org/10.1007/978-3-319-96878-0_5

18. Lewko, A.B., Waters, B.: Efficient pseudorandom functions from the decisional linear assumption and weaker variants. In: Al-Shaer, E., Jha, S., Keromytis, A.D. (eds.) ACM CCS 2009: 16th Conference on Computer and Communications Security, Chicago, Illinois, USA, 9–13 November 2009, pp. 112–120. ACM Press (2009). https://doi.org/10.1145/1653662.1653677

19. Naor, M., Reingold, O.: Synthesizers and their application to the parallel construction of pseudo-random functions. In: 36th Annual Symposium on Foundations of Computer Science, Milwaukee, Wisconsin, 23–25 October 1995, pp. 170–181. IEEE Computer Society Press (1995). https://doi.org/10.1109/SFCS.1995.492474

20. Naor, M., Reingold, O.: Number-theoretic constructions of efficient pseudo-random functions. In: 38th Annual Symposium on Foundations of Computer Science, Miami Beach, Florida, 19–22 October 1997, pp. 458–467. IEEE Computer Society Press (1997). https://doi.org/10.1109/SFCS.1997.646134

21. Naor, M., Reingold, O.: On the construction of pseudo-random permutations: Luby-Rackoff revisited (extended abstract). In: 29th Annual ACM Symposium on Theory of Computing, El Paso, TX, USA, 4–6 May 1997, pp. 189–199. ACM Press (1997). https://doi.org/10.1145/258533.258581

22. Naor, M., Reingold, O., Rosen, A.: Pseudo-random functions and factoring (extended abstract). In: 32nd Annual ACM Symposium on Theory of Computing, Portland, OR, USA, 21–23 May 2000, pp. 11–20. ACM Press (2000). https://doi.org/10.1145/335305.335307

23. Nielsen, M.A., Chuang, I.: Quantum computation and quantum information (2002)

24. Regev, O.: On lattices, learning with errors, random linear codes, and cryptography. In: Gabow, H.N., Fagin, R. (eds.) 37th Annual ACM Symposium on Theory of Computing, Baltimore, MA, USA, 22–24 May 2005, pp. 84–93. ACM Press (2005). https://doi.org/10.1145/1060590.1060603

25. Siegel, A.: On universal classes of extremely random constant-time hash functions. SIAM J. Comput. **33**(3), 505–543 (2004)

26. Thorup, M.: Simple tabulation, fast expanders, double tabulation, and high independence. In: 54th Annual Symposium on Foundations of Computer Science, Berkeley, CA, USA, 26–29 October 2013, pp. 90–99. IEEE Computer Society Press (2013). https://doi.org/10.1109/FOCS.2013.18

27. Zhandry, M.: How to construct quantum random functions. In: 53rd Annual Symposium on Foundations of Computer Science, New Brunswick, NJ, USA, 20–23 October 2012, pp. 679–687. IEEE Computer Society Press (2012). https://doi.org/10.1109/FOCS.2012.37

28. Zhandry, M.: Secure identity-based encryption in the quantum random oracle model. In: Safavi-Naini, R., Canetti, R. (eds.) CRYPTO 2012. LNCS, vol. 7417, pp. 758–775. Springer, Heidelberg (2012). https://doi.org/10.1007/978-3-642-32009-5_44

Improved Classical and Quantum Algorithms for Subset-Sum

Xavier Bonnetain[1], Rémi Bricout[2,3], André Schrottenloher[3(✉)], and Yixin Shen[4]

[1] Institute for Quantum Computing, Department of Combinatorics and Optimization, University of Waterloo, Waterloo, ON, Canada
[2] Sorbonne Université, Collège Doctoral, 75005 Paris, France
[3] Inria, Paris, France
andre.schrottenloher@inria.fr
[4] Université de Paris, IRIF, CNRS, 75006 Paris, France

Abstract. We present new classical and quantum algorithms for solving random subset-sum instances. First, we improve over the Becker-Coron-Joux algorithm (EUROCRYPT 2011) from $\widetilde{\mathcal{O}}\left(2^{0.291n}\right)$ down to $\widetilde{\mathcal{O}}\left(2^{0.283n}\right)$, using more general representations with values in $\{-1, 0, 1, 2\}$. Next, we improve the state of the art of quantum algorithms for this problem in several directions. By combining the Howgrave-Graham-Joux algorithm (EUROCRYPT 2010) and quantum search, we devise an algorithm with asymptotic running time $\widetilde{\mathcal{O}}\left(2^{0.236n}\right)$, lower than the cost of the quantum walk based on the same classical algorithm proposed by Bernstein, Jeffery, Lange and Meurer (PQCRYPTO 2013). This algorithm has the advantage of using *classical* memory with quantum random access, while the previously known algorithms used the quantum walk framework, and required *quantum* memory with quantum random access.

We also propose new quantum walks for subset-sum, performing better than the previous best time complexity of $\widetilde{\mathcal{O}}\left(2^{0.226n}\right)$ given by Helm and May (TQC 2018). We combine our new techniques to reach a time $\widetilde{\mathcal{O}}\left(2^{0.216n}\right)$. This time is dependent on a heuristic on quantum walk updates, formalized by Helm and May, that is also required by the previous algorithms. We show how to partially overcome this heuristic, and we obtain an algorithm with quantum time $\widetilde{\mathcal{O}}\left(2^{0.218n}\right)$ requiring only the standard classical subset-sum heuristics.

Keywords: Subset-sum · Representation technique · Quantum search · Quantum walk · List merging

1 Introduction

We study the *subset-sum problem*, also known as *knapsack problem*: given n integers $\mathbf{a} = (a_1, \ldots a_n)$, and a target integer S, find an n-bit vector $\mathbf{e} = (e_1, \ldots e_n) \in \{0, 1\}^n$ such that $\mathbf{e} \cdot \mathbf{a} = \sum_i e_i a_i = S$. The *density* of the knapsack instance is defined as $d = n/(\log_2 \max_i a_i)$, and for a random instance $\mathbf{a}$, it is related to the number of solutions that one can expect.

© International Association for Cryptologic Research 2020
S. Moriai and H. Wang (Eds.): ASIACRYPT 2020, LNCS 12492, pp. 633–666, 2020.
https://doi.org/10.1007/978-3-030-64834-3_22

The decision version of the knapsack problem is NP-complete [16]. Although certain densities admit efficient algorithms, related to lattice reduction [27,28], the best algorithms known for the knapsack problem when the density is close to 1 are exponential-time, which is why we name these instances "hard" knapsacks. This problem underlies some cryptographic schemes aiming at post-quantum security (see *e.g.* [29]), and is used as a building block in some quantum hidden shift algorithms [7], which have some applications in quantum cryptanalysis of isogeny-based [11] and symmetric cryptographic schemes [9].

In this paper, we focus on the case where $d = 1$, where expectedly a single solution exists. Instead of naively looking for the solution **e** via exhaustive search, in time 2^n, Horowitz and Sahni [20] proposed to use a meet-in-the-middle approach in $2^{n/2}$ time and memory. The idea is to find a collision between two lists of $2^{n/2}$ subknapsacks, *i.e.* to merge these two lists for a single solution. Schroeppel and Shamir [37] later improved this to a 4-list merge, in which the memory complexity can be reduced down to $2^{n/4}$.

The Representation Technique. At EUROCRYPT 2010, Howgrave-Graham and Joux [21] (HGJ) proposed a heuristic algorithm solving *random* subset-sum instances in time $\widetilde{\mathcal{O}}\left(2^{0.337n}\right)$, thereby breaking the $2^{n/2}$ bound. Their key idea was to represent the knapsack solution ambiguously as a sum of vectors in $\{0,1\}^n$. This *representation technique* increases the search space size, allowing to merge more lists, with new arbitrary constraints, thereby allowing for a more time-efficient algorithm. The time complexity exponent is obtained by numerical optimization of the list sizes and constraints, assuming that the individual elements obtained in the merging steps are well-distributed. This is the standard heuristic of classical and quantum subset-sum algorithms. Later, Becker, Coron and Joux [3] (BCJ) improved the asymptotic runtime down to $\widetilde{\mathcal{O}}\left(2^{0.291n}\right)$ by allowing even more representations, with vectors in $\{-1,0,1\}^n$.

The BCJ representation technique is not only a tool for subset-sums, as it has been used to speed up generic decoding algorithms, classically [4,31,32] and quantumly [22]. Therefore, the subset-sum problem serves as the simplest application of representations, and improving our understanding of the classical and quantum algorithms may have consequences on these other generic problems.

Quantum Algorithms for the Subset-Sum Problem. Cryptosystems based on hard subset-sums are natural candidates for post-quantum cryptography, but to understand precisely their security, we have to study the best generic algorithms for solving subset-sums. The first quantum time speedup for this problem was obtained in [6], with a quantum time $\widetilde{\mathcal{O}}\left(2^{0.241n}\right)$. The algorithm was based on the HGJ algorithm. Later on, [18] devised an algorithm based on BCJ, running in time $\widetilde{\mathcal{O}}\left(2^{0.226n}\right)$. Both algorithms use the corresponding classical merging structure, wrapped in a quantum walk on a Johnson graph, in the MNRS quantum walk framework [30]. However, they suffer from two limitations.

First, both use the model of *quantum memory with quantum random-access* (QRAQM), which is stronger than the standard quantum circuit model, as it allows unit-time lookups in superposition of all the qubits in the circuit.

The QRAQM model is used in most quantum walk algorithms to date, but its practical realizations are still unclear. With a more restrictive model, i.e., *classical memory with quantum random-access* (QRACM), no quantum time speedup over BCJ was previously known. This is not the case for some other hard problems in post-quantum cryptography, *e.g.* heuristic lattice sieving for the Shortest Vector Problem, where the best quantum algorithms to date require only QRACM [25].

Second, both use a conjecture (implicit in [6], made explicit in [18]) about quantum walk updates. In short, the quantum walk maintains a data structure, that contains a merging tree similar to HGJ (resp. BCJ), with lists of smaller size. A quantum walk step is made of updates that changes an element in the lowest-level lists, and requires to modify the upper levels accordingly, *i.e.*, to track the partial collisions that must be removed or added. In order to be efficient, the update needs to run in polynomial time. Moreover, the resulting data structure shall be a function of the lowest-level list, and not depend on the path taken in the walk. The conjecture states that it should be possible to guarantee sound updates without impacting the time complexity exponent. However, it does not seem an easy task and the current literature on subset-sums lacks further justification or workarounds.

Contributions. In this paper, we improve classical and quantum subset-sum algorithms based on representations. We write these algorithms as sequences of "merge-and-filter" operations, where lists of subknapsacks are first merged with respect to an arbitrary constraint, then *filtered* to remove the subknapsacks that cannot be part of a solution.

First, we propose a more time-efficient classical subset-sum algorithm based on representations. We have two classical improvements: we revisit the previous algorithms and show that some of the constraints they enforced were not needed, and we use more general distributions by allowing "2"s in the representations. Overall, we obtain a better time complexity exponent of 0.283.

Most of our contributions concern quantum algorithms. As a generic tool, we introduce *quantum filtering*, which speeds up the filtering of representations with a quantum search. We use this improvement in all our new quantum algorithms.

We give an improved quantum walk based on quantum filtering and our extended $\{-1, 0, 1, 2\}$ representations. Our best runtime exponent is 0.216, under the quantum walk update heuristic of [18]. Next, we show how to overcome this heuristic, by designing a new data structure for the vertices in the quantum walk, and a new update procedure with guaranteed time. We remove this heuristic from the previous algorithms [6,18] with no additional cost. However, we find that removing it from our quantum walk increases its cost to 0.218.

In a different direction, we devise a new quantum subset-sum algorithm based on HGJ, with time $\widetilde{\mathcal{O}}\left(2^{0.236n}\right)$. It is the first quantum time speedup on subset-sums that is *not* based on a quantum walk. The algorithm performs instead a depth-first traversal of the HGJ tree, using quantum search as its only building block. Hence, by construction, it does not require the additional heuristic of [18] *and* it only uses *classical memory with quantum random-access*, giving also the first quantum time speedup for subset-sum in this memory model.

A summary of our contributions is given in Table 1^1. All these complexity exponents are obtained by numerical optimization. Our code is available at https://github.com/xbonnetain/optimization-subset-sum.

Table 1. Previous and **new** algorithms for subset-sum, classical and quantum, with time and memory exponents rounded upwards. We note that the removal of Heuristic 2 in [6,18] comes from our new analysis in Sect. 6.4. QW: Quantum Walk. QS: Quantum Search. CF: Constraint filtering (not studied in this paper). QF: Quantum filtering.

Time exp.	Memory exp.	Representations	Memory model	Techniques	Requires Heur. 2	Reference
Classical						
0.3370	0.3113	$\{0,1\}$	RAM			[21]
0.2909	0.2909	$\{-1,0,1\}$	RAM			[3]
0.287		$\{-1,0,1\}$	RAM	CF		[36]
0.2830	**0.2830**	$\{-1,0,1,2\}$	RAM			Sect. 2.5
Quantum						
0.241	0.241	$\{0,1\}$	QRAQM	QW	No	[6] + Sect. 6.4
0.226	0.226	$\{-1,0,1\}$	QRAQM	QW	No	[18] + Sect. 6.4
0.2356	**0.2356**	$\{0,1\}$	**QRACM**	QS + QF	No	Sect. 4.3
0.2156	**0.2110**	$\{-1,0,1,2\}$	QRAQM	QW + QF	Yes	Sect. 5.3
0.2182	**0.2182**	$\{-1,0,1,2\}$	QRAQM	QW + QF	No	Sect. 6.4

Outline. In Sect. 2, we study classical algorithms. We review the representation technique, the HGJ algorithm and introduce our new $\{-1,0,1,2\}$ representations to improve over [3]. In Sect. 3, we move to the quantum setting, introduce some preliminaries and the previous quantum algorithms for subset-sum. In Sect. 4, we present and study our new quantum algorithm based on HGJ and quantum search. We give different optimizations and time-memory trade-offs. In Sect. 5, we present our new quantum algorithm based on a quantum walk. Finally, in Sect. 6 we show how to overcome the quantum walk update conjecture, up to a potential increase in the update cost. We conclude, and give a summary of our new results in Sect. 7.

2   List Merging and Classical Subset-Sum Algorithms

In this section, we remain in the classical realm. We introduce the standard subset-sum notations and heuristics and give a new presentation of the HGJ algorithm, putting an emphasis on the *merge-and-filter* operation. We introduce our extended $\{-1,0,1,2\}$ representations and detail our improvements over BCJ.

---

[1] After this work, Alexander May has informed us that the thesis [14] contains unpublished results using more symbols, with the best exponent of 0.2871 obtained with the symbol set $\{-2,-1,0,1,2\}$.

2.1   Notations and Conventions

Hereafter and in the rest of the paper, all time and memory complexities, classical and quantum, are exponential in n. We use the soft-O notation $\tilde{\mathcal{O}}$ which removes polynomial factors in n, and focus on the asymptotic exponent, relative to n. We use negl(n) for any function that vanishes inverse-exponentially in n. We often replace asymptotic exponential time and memory complexities (*e.g.* $\tilde{\mathcal{O}}(2^{\alpha n})$) by their exponents (*e.g.* α). We use capital letters (*e.g.* L) and corresponding letters (*e.g.* ℓ) to denote the same value, in $\log_2$ and relatively to n: $\ell = \log_2(L)/n$.

Definition 1 (Entropies and multinomial functions). *We define the following functions:*

Hamming Entropy: $h(x) = -x \log_2 x - (1-x) \log_2(1-x)$

Binomial: $\mathrm{bin}(\omega, \alpha) = h(\alpha/\omega)\omega$

2-way Entropy: $g(x, y) = -x \log_2 x - y \log_2 y - (1 - x - y) \log_2(1 - x - y)$

Trinomial: $\mathrm{trin}(\omega, \alpha, \beta) = g(\alpha/\omega, \beta/\omega)\omega$

3-way Entropy: $f(x, y, z) = -x \log_2 x - y \log_2 y - z \log_2 z - $
$$(1 - x - y - z) \log_2(1 - x - y - z)$$

Quadrinomial: $\mathrm{quadrin}(\omega, \alpha, \beta, \gamma) = f(\alpha/\omega, \beta/\omega, \gamma/\omega)\omega$

Property 1 (Standard approximations). We have the following approximations, asymptotically in n:

$$\mathrm{bin}(\omega, \alpha) \simeq \tfrac{1}{n} \log_2 \binom{\omega n}{\alpha n} \quad ; \quad \mathrm{trin}(\omega, \alpha, \beta) \simeq \tfrac{1}{n} \log_2 \binom{\omega n}{\alpha n, \beta n}$$
$$\mathrm{quadrin}(\omega, \alpha, \beta, \gamma) \simeq \tfrac{1}{n} \log_2 \binom{\omega n}{\alpha n, \beta n, \gamma n}$$

Definition 2 (Distributions of knapsacks). *A* knapsack *or* subknapsack *is a vector* $\mathbf{e} \in \{-1, 0, 1, 2\}^n$. *The set of* $\mathbf{e}$ *with* αn *"-1", $(\alpha + \beta - 2\gamma)n$ "1", γn "2" and $(1 - 2\alpha - \beta + \gamma)n$ "0" is denoted* $D^n[\alpha, \beta, \gamma]$. *If* $\gamma = 0$, *we may omit the third parameter. This coincides with the notation* $D^n[\alpha, \beta]$ *from [18].*

Note that we always add vectors *over the integers*, and thus, the sum of two vectors of $D^n[*, *, *]$ may contain unwanted symbols $-2, 3$ or 4.

Property 2 (Size of knapsack sets). We have:

$$\tfrac{1}{n} \log_2 |D^n[0, \beta, 0]| \simeq h(\beta) \quad ; \quad \tfrac{1}{n} \log_2 |D^n[\alpha, \beta, 0]| \simeq g(\alpha, \alpha + \beta)$$
$$\tfrac{1}{n} \log_2 |D^n[\alpha, \beta, \gamma]| \simeq f(\alpha, \alpha + \beta - 2\gamma, \gamma) \ .$$

Subset-sum. The problem we will solve is defined as follows:

Definition 3 (Random subset-sum instance of weight $n/2$). *Let* $\mathbf{a}$ *be chosen uniformly at random from* $(\mathbb{Z}_N)^n$, *where* $N \simeq 2^n$. *Let* $\mathbf{e}$ *be chosen uniformly at random from* $D^n[0, 1/2, 0]$. *Let* $t = \mathbf{a} \cdot \mathbf{e} \pmod{N}$. *Then* $(\mathbf{a}, t)$ *is a random subset-sum instance. A solution is a vector* $\mathbf{e}'$ *such that* $\mathbf{a} \cdot \mathbf{e}' = t \pmod{N}$.

Sampling. Throughout this paper, we assume that we can classically sample uniformly at random from $D^n[\alpha, \beta, \gamma]$ in time $\text{poly}(n)$. (Since αn, βn and γn will in general not be integer, we suppose to have them rounded to the nearest integer.) This comes from an efficient bijection between representations and integers (see Appendix A in the full version of the paper [8]). In addition, we can efficiently produce the uniform superposition of vectors of $D^n[\alpha, \beta, \gamma]$, using $\text{poly}(n)$ quantum gates, and we can perform a quantum search among representations.

2.2   Merging and Filtering

In all subset-sum algorithms studied in this paper, we repeatedly sample vectors with certain distributions $D^n[*, *, *]$, then combine them. Let $D_1 = D^n[\alpha_1, \beta_1, \gamma_1]$, $D_2 = D^n[\alpha_2, \beta_2, \gamma_2]$ be two input distributions and $D = D^n[\alpha, \beta, \gamma]$ be a target. Given two lists $L_1 \in D_1^{|L_1|}$ and $L_2 \in D_2^{|L_2|}$, we define:

- the *merged list* $L = L_1 \bowtie_c L_2$ containing all vectors $\mathbf{e} = \mathbf{e_1} + \mathbf{e_2}$ such that: $\mathbf{e_1} \in L_1, \mathbf{e_2} \in L_2, (\mathbf{e_1} + \mathbf{e_2}) \cdot \mathbf{a} = s \mod M$, $s \leq M$ is an arbitrary integer and $M \approx 2^{cn}$ (we write $L_1 \bowtie_c L_2$ because s is an arbitrary value, whose choice is without incidence on the algorithm)
- the *filtered list* $L^f = (L \cap D) \subseteq L$, containing the vectors with the target distribution of $1, -1, 2$ (the target D will always be clear from context).

In general, L is exponentially bigger than L^f and does not need to be written down, as vectors can be filtered on the fly. The algorithms then repeat the merge-and-filter operation on multiple levels, moving towards the distribution $D^n[0, 1/2]$ while increasing the bit-length of the modular constraint, until we satisfy $\mathbf{e} \cdot \mathbf{a} = t \mod 2^n$ and obtain a solution. Note that this merging-and-filtering view that we adopt, where the merged list is repeatedly sampled before an element passes the filter, has some similarities with the ideas developed in the withdrawn article [15].

The standard subset-sum heuristic assumes that vectors in L^f are drawn independently, uniformly at random from D. It simplifies the complexity analysis of both classical and quantum algorithms studied in this paper. Note that this heuristic, which is backed by experiments, actually leads to provable probabilistic algorithms in the classical setting (see [3, Theorem 2]). We adopt the version of [18].

Heuristic 1. *If input vectors are uniformly distributed in $D_1 \times D_2$, then the filtered pairs are uniformly distributed in D (more precisely, among the subset of vectors in D satisfying the modular condition).*

Filtering Representations. We note $\ell = (1/n) \log_2 |L|$, and so on for ℓ_1, ℓ_2, ℓ^f. By Heuristic 1, the average sizes of L_1, L_2, L and L^f are related by:

- $\ell = \ell_1 + \ell_2 - c$
- $\ell^f = \ell + \text{pf}$, where pf is negative and $2^{\text{pf}n}$ is the probability that a pair $(\mathbf{e_1}, \mathbf{e_2})$, drawn uniformly at random from $D_1 \times D_2$, has $(\mathbf{e_1} + \mathbf{e_2}) \in D$.

In particular, the occurrence of collisions in L^f is a negligible phenomenon, unless ℓ^f approaches $(\log_2 |D|/n) - c$, which is the maximum number of vectors in D with constraint c. For a given random knapsack problem, with high probability, the size of any list built by sampling, merging and filtering remains very close to its average (by a Chernoff bound and a union bound on all lists).

Here, pf depends only on D_1, D_2 and D. Working with this *filtering probability* is especially useful for writing down our algorithm in Sect. 4. We give its formula for $\{0,1\}$ representations below. Two similar results for $\{-1,0,1\}$ and $\{-1,0,1,2\}$ can be found in the full version of the paper [8].

Lemma 1. (Filtering HGJ-style representations). *Let* $\mathbf{e_1} \in D^n[0,\alpha]$ *and* $\mathbf{e_2} \in D^n[0,\beta]$ *be drawn uniformly at random. The probability that* $\mathbf{e_1} + \mathbf{e_2} \in D^n[0,\alpha + \beta]$ *is 0 if* $\alpha + \beta > 1$, *and* $2^{\mathsf{pf}_1(\alpha,\beta)n}$ *otherwise, with*

$$\mathsf{pf}_1(\alpha,\beta) = \mathrm{bin}\,(1 - \alpha, \beta) - h(\beta) = \mathrm{bin}\,(1 - \beta, \alpha) - h(\alpha)\ .$$

Proof. The probability that a $\mathbf{e_1} + \mathbf{e_2}$ survives the filtering is:

$$\binom{n - \alpha n}{\beta n} \Big/ \binom{n}{\beta n} = \binom{n - \beta n}{\alpha n} \Big/ \binom{n}{\alpha n}\ .$$

Indeed, given a choice of αn bit positions among n, the other βn bit positions must be compatible, hence chosen among the $(1 - \alpha)n$ remaining positions. By taking the $\log_2$, we obtain the formula for the filtering probability.   □

Time Complexity of Merging. Classically, the time complexity of the merge-and-filter operation is related to the size of the *merged list*.

Lemma 2 (Classical merging with filtering). *Let L_1 and L_2 be two sorted lists stored in classical memory with random access. In $\log_2$, relatively to n, and discarding logarithmic factors, merging and filtering L_1 and L_2 costs a time* $\max(\min(\ell_1, \ell_2), \ell_1 + \ell_2 - c)$ *and memory* $\max(\ell_1, \ell_2, \ell^f)$, *assuming that we must store the filtered output list.*

Proof. Assuming sorted lists, there are two symmetric ways to produce a stream of elements of $L_1 \bowtie_c L_2$: we can go through the elements of L_1, and for each one, find the matching elements in L_2 by dichotomy search (time $\ell_1 + \max(0, \ell_2 - c)$) or we can exchange the role of L_1 and L_2. Although we do not need to store $L_1 \bowtie_c L_2$, we need to examine all its elements in order to filter them.   □

2.3 Correctness of the Algorithms

While the operation of *merging and filtering* is the same as in previous works, our complexity analysis differs [3,6,18,21]. We enforce the constraint that the final list contains a single solution, hence if it is of size $2^{n\ell_0}$, we constrain $\ell_0 = 0$. Next, we limit the sizes of the lists so that they do not contain duplicate vectors: these are *saturation constraints*. A list of size $2^{n\ell}$, of vectors sampled from a distribution D, with a constraint of cn bits, has the constraint: $\ell \leq \frac{1}{n}\log_2|D| - c$. This says that there are not more than $|D|/2^{cn}$ vectors $\mathbf{e}$ such that $\mathbf{e} \cdot \mathbf{a} = r$ (mod 2^{cn}) for the (randomly chosen) arbitrary constraint r.

Previous works focus on the solution vector $\mathbf{e}$ and compute the number of *representations* of $\mathbf{e}$, that is, the number of ways it can be decomposed as a sum: $\mathbf{e} = \mathbf{e}_1 + \ldots + \mathbf{e}_t$ of vectors satisfying the constraints on the distributions. Then, they compare this with the probability that a given representation passes the arbitrary constraints imposed by the algorithm. As their lists contains all the subknapsacks that fulfill the constraint, this really reflects the number of duplicates, and it suffices to enforce that the number of representations is equal to the inverse probability that a representation fulfills the constraint. If the two lists we merge are not of maximal size, the size of the merged list is the number of elements that fulfill the corresponding distribution times the probability that such an element is effectively the sum of two elements in the initial lists.

The two approaches are strictly equivalent, as the probability that the sum of two subknapsacks is valid is exactly the number of representations of the sum, divided by the number of pairs of subknapsacks.

2.4   The HGJ Algorithm

We start our study of classical subset-sum by recalling the algorithm of Howgrave-Graham and Joux [21], with the corrected time complexity of [3]. The algorithm builds a merging tree of lists of subknapsacks, with four levels, numbered 3 down to 0. Level j contains 2^j lists. In total, 8 lists are merged together into one.

Level 3. We build 8 lists denoted $L_0^3 \ldots L_7^3$. They contain *all* subknapsacks of weight $\frac{n}{16}$ on $\frac{n}{2}$ bits, either left or right:

$$\begin{cases} L_{2i}^3 = D^{n/2}[0, 1/8] \times \{0^{n/2}\} \\ L_{2i+1}^3 = \{0^{n/2}\} \times D^{n/2}[0, 1/8] \end{cases}$$

From Property 2, these level-3 lists have size $\ell_3 = h(1/8)/2$. As the positions set to 1 cannot interfere, these is no filtering when merging L_{2i}^3 and L_{2i+1}^3.

Level 2. We merge the lists pairwise with a (random) constraint on $c_2 n$ bits, and obtain 4 filtered lists. The size of the filtered lists plays a role in the memory complexity of the algorithm, but the time complexity depends on the size of the unfiltered lists.

In practice, when we say "with a constraint on $c_j n$ bits", we assume that given the subset-sum objective t modulo 2^n, random values r_i^j such that $\sum_i r_i^j = t \bmod 2^{c_j n}$ are selected at level j, and the r_i^j have $c_j n$ bits only. Hence, at this step, we have selected 4 integers on $c_2 n$ bits $r_0^1, r_1^1, r_2^1, r_3^1$ such that $r_0^1 + r_1^1 + r_2^1 + r_3^1 = t \bmod 2^{c_2 n}$. The 4 level-2 lists $L_0^2, L_1^2, L_2^2, L_3^2$ have size $\ell_2 = (h(1/8) - c_2)$, they contain subknapsacks of weight $\frac{n}{8}$ on n bits.

Remark 1. The precise values of these r_i are irrelevant, since they cancel out each other in the end. They are selected at random during a run of the algorithm, and although there could be "bad" values of them that affect significantly the computation, this is not expected to happen.

Level 1. We merge the lists pairwise with $(c_1 - c_2)n$ new bits of constraint, ensuring that the constraint is compatible with the previous ones. We obtain two filtered lists L_0^1, L_1^1, containing subknapsacks of weight $n/4$. They have size:

$$\ell_1 = 2\ell_2 - (c_1 - c_2) + \mathsf{pf}_1 (1/8, 1/8)$$

where $\mathsf{pf}_1 (1/8, 1/8)$ is given by Lemma 1.

Level 0. We find a solution to the subset-sum problem with the complete constraint on n bits. This means that the list L^0 must have expected length $\ell_0 = 0$. Note that there remains $(1 - c_1)n$ bits of constraint to satisfy, and the filtering term is similar as before, so:

$$\ell_0 = 2\ell_1 - (1 - c_1) + \mathsf{pf}_1 (1/4, 1/4) \ .$$

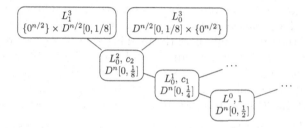

Fig. 1. The HGJ algorithm (duplicate lists are omitted)

By Lemma 2, the time complexity of this algorithm is determined by the sizes of the unfiltered lists: $\max (\ell_3, 2\ell_3 - c_2, 2\ell_2 - (c_1 - c_2), 2\ell_1 - (1 - c_1))$. The memory complexity depends of the sizes of the filtered lists: $\max (\ell_3, \ell_2, \ell_1)$. By a numerical optimization, one obtains a time exponent of $0.337n$.

2.5   The BCJ Algorithm and Our Improvements

The HGJ algorithm uses representations to increase artificially the search space. The algorithm of Becker, Coron and Joux [3] improves the runtime exponent down to 0.291 by allowing even more freedom in the representations, which can now contain "−1"s. The "−1"s have to cancel out progressively, to ensure the validity of the final knapsack solution.

We improve over this algorithm in two different ways. First, we relax the constraints $\ell_j + c_j = g(\alpha_j, 1/2^{j+1})$ enforced in [3], as only the inequalities $\ell_j + c_j \leqslant g(\alpha_j, 1/2^{j+1})$ are necessary: they make sure the lists are not larger than the number of distinct elements they can contain. This idea was also implicitly used in [13], in the context of syndrome decoding. When optimizing the parameters under these new constraints, we bring the asymptotic time exponent down to $0.289n$.

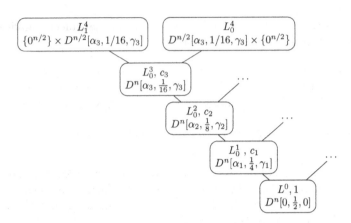

Fig. 2. Our improved algorithm (duplicate lists are omitted).

$\{-1, 0, 1, 2\}$ *representations.* Next, we allow the value "2" in the subknapsacks. This allows us to have more representations for the final solution from the same initial distributions. Indeed, in BCJ, if on a bit the solution is the sum of a "−1" and two "1"s, then it can only pass the merging steps if we first have the "−1" that cancels a "1", and then the addition of the second "1". When allowing "2"s, we can have the sum of the two "1's and then at a later step the addition of a "−1". The algorithm builds a merging tree with five levels, numbered 4 down to 0. Level j contains 2^j lists. In total, 16 lists are merged together into one.

Level 4. We build 16 lists $L_0^4 \dots L_{15}^4$. They contain complete distributions on $\frac{n}{2}$ bits, either left or right, with $\frac{n}{32} + \frac{\alpha_3 n}{2} - \gamma_3 n$ "1", $\frac{\alpha_3 n}{2}$ "−1" and $\frac{\gamma_3 n}{2}$ "2":

$$\begin{cases} L_{2i}^4 = D^{n/2}[\alpha_3, 1/16, \gamma_3] \times \{0^{n/2}\} \\ L_{2i+1}^4 = \{0^{n/2}\} \times D^{n/2}[\alpha_3, 1/16, \gamma_3] \end{cases}$$

As before, this avoids filtering at the first level. These lists have size: $\ell_4 = f(\alpha_3, 1/16 + \alpha_3 - 2\gamma_3, \gamma_3)/2$.

Level 3. We merge into 8 lists $L_0^3 \dots L_7^3$, with a constraint on c_3 bits. As there is no filtering, these lists have size: $\ell_3 = f(\alpha_3, 1/16 + \alpha_3 - 2\gamma_3, \gamma_3) - c_3$.

Level 2. We now merge and filter. We force a target distribution $D^n[\alpha_2, 1/8, \gamma_2]$, with α_2 and γ_2 to be optimized later. There is a first filtering probability p_2. We have $\ell_2 = 2\ell_3 - (c_2 - c_3) + p_2$.

Level 1. Similarly, we have: $\ell_1 = 2\ell_2 - (c_1 - c_2) + p_1$.

Level 0. We have $\ell_0 = 2\ell_1 - (1 - c_1) + p_0 = 0$, since the goal is to obtain one solution in the list L_0.

With these constraints, we find a time $\tilde{\mathcal{O}}\left(2^{0.2830n}\right)$ (rounded upwards) with the following parameters:

$\alpha_1 = 0.0340, \alpha_2 = 0.0311, \alpha_3 = 0.0202, \gamma_1 = 0.0041, \gamma_2 = 0.0006, \gamma_3 = 0.0001$

$c_1 = 0.8067, c_2 = 0.5509, c_3 = 0.2680, p_0 = -0.2829, p_1 = -0.0447, p_2 = -0.0135$

$\ell_1 = 0.2382, \ell_2 = 0.2694, \ell_3 = 0.2829, \ell_4 = 0.2755$

Remark 2 (On numeric optimizations). All algorithms since HGJ, including quantum ones, rely on (nonlinear) numeric optimizations. Their correctness is easy to check, since the obtained parameters satisfy the constraints, but there is no formal proof that the parameters are indeed optimal for a given constraint set. The same goes for all algorithms studied in this paper. In order to gain confidence in our results, we tried many different starting points and several equivalent rewriting of the constraints.

Remark 3 (Adding more symbols). In general, adding more symbols ("−2"s, "3"s, *etc.*) can only increase the parameter search space and improve the optimal time complexity. However, we expect that the improvements from adding more symbols will become smaller and smaller, while the obtained constraints will become more difficult to write down and the parameters harder to optimize. Note that adding "−1"s decreases the time complexity exponent by 0.048, while adding "2"s decreases it only by 0.006.

Remark 4 (On the number of levels). Algorithms based on merging-and-filtering, classical and quantum, have a number of levels (say, 4 or 5) which must be selected before writing down the constraints. The time complexity is a decreasing function of the number of levels, which quickly reaches a minimum. In all algorithms studied in this paper, adding one more level does not change the cost of the upper levels, which will remain the most expensive.

3   Quantum Preliminaries and Previous Work

In this section, we recall some preliminaries of quantum computation (quantum search and quantum walks) that will be useful throughout the rest of this paper. We also recall previous quantum algorithms for subset-sum. As we consider all our algorithms from the point of view of asymptotic complexities, and neglect polynomial factors in n, a high-level overview is often enough, and we will use quantum building blocks as black boxes. The interested reader may find more details in [35].

3.1   Quantum Preliminaries

All the quantum algorithms considered in this paper run in the quantum circuit model, with quantum random-access memory, often denoted as qRAM. "Baseline" quantum circuits are simply built using a universal gate set. Many quantum algorithms use qRAM access, and require the circuit model to be augmented with the so-called "qRAM gate". This includes subset-sum, lattice sieving and generic decoding algorithms that obtain time speedups with respect to their classical counterparts. Given an input register $1 \leq i \leq r$, which represents the index of a memory cell, and many quantum registers $|x_1, \ldots x_r\rangle$, which represent stored data, the qRAM gate fetches the data from register x_i:

$$|i\rangle |x_1, \ldots x_r\rangle |y\rangle \mapsto |i\rangle |x_1, \ldots x_r\rangle |y \oplus x_i\rangle \ .$$

We will use the terminology of [24] for the qRAM gate:

- If the input i is classical, then this is the plain quantum circuit model (with classical RAM);
- If the x_j are classical, we have *quantum-accessible classical memory* (QRACM)
- In general, we have *quantum-accessible quantum memory* (QRAQM)

All known quantum algorithms for subset-sum with a quantum time speedup over the best classical one require QRAQM. For comparison, speedups on heuristic lattice sieving algorithms exist in the QRACM model [23,26], including the best one to date [25]. While no physical architecture for quantum random access has been proposed that would indeed produce a constant or negligible overhead in time, some authors [24] consider the separation meaningful. If we assign a cost $\mathcal{O}(N)$ to a QRACM query of N cells, then we can replace it by *classical* memory. Subset-sum algorithms were studied in this setting by Helm and May [19].

Quantum Search. One of the most well-known quantum algorithms is Grover's unstructured search algorithm [17]. We present here its generalization, amplitude amplification [12].

Lemma 3 (Amplitude amplification, from [12]). *Let $\mathcal{A}$ be a reversible quantum circuit, f a computable boolean function over the output of $\mathcal{A}$, O_f its implementation as a quantum circuit, and a be the initial success probability of $\mathcal{A}$, that is, the probability that $O_f \mathcal{A} |0\rangle$ outputs "true". There exists a quantum reversible algorithm that calls $\mathcal{O}\left(\sqrt{1/a}\right)$ times $\mathcal{A}$, $\mathcal{A}^\dagger$ and O_f, uses as many qubits as $\mathcal{A}$ and O_f, and produces an output that passes the test f with probability greater than $\max(a, 1-a)$.*

This is known to be optimal when the functions are black-box oracles [5].

As we will use quantum search as a subprocedure, we make some remarks similar to [33, Appendix A.2] and [10, Sect. 5.2] to justify that, up to additional polynomial factors in time, we can consider it runs with no errors and allows to return all the solutions efficiently.

Remark 5 (Error in a sequence of quantum searches). Throughout this paper, we will assume that a quantum search in a search space of size S with T solutions runs in exact time $\sqrt{S/T}$. In practice, there is a constant overhead, but since S and T are always exponential in n, the difference is negligible. Furthermore, this is a probabilistic procedure, and it will return a wrong result with a probability of the order $\sqrt{T/S}$. As we can test if an error occurs, we can make it negligible by redoing the quantum search polynomially many times.

Remark 6 (Finding all solutions). Quantum search returns a solution among the T possibilities, selected uniformly at random. Finding all solutions is then an instance of the coupon collector problem with T coupons [34]; all coupons are collected after on average $\mathcal{O}(T \log(T))$ trials. However, *in the QRACM model*, which is assumed in this paper, this logarithmic factor disappears. We can run the search of Lemma 3 with a new test function that returns 0 if the output of $\mathcal{A}$ is incorrect, *or* if it is correct but has already been found. The change to the runtime is negligible, and thus, we collect all solutions with only $\mathcal{O}(T)$ searches.

Quantum Walks. Quantum walks can be seen as a generalization of quantum search. They allow to obtain polynomial speedups on many unstructured problems, with sometimes optimal results (*e.g.* Ambainis' algorithm for element distinctness [1]). In this paper, we consider walks in the MNRS framework [30].

Let $G = (V, E)$ be an undirected, connected, regular graph, such that some vertices of G are "marked". Let ϵ be the fraction of marked vertices, that is, a random vertex has a probability ϵ of being marked. Let δ be the spectral gap of G, which is defined as the difference between its two largest eigenvalues.

In a *classical* random walk on G, we can start from any vertex and reach the stationary distribution in approximately $\frac{1}{\delta}$ random walk steps. Then, such a random vertex is marked with probability ϵ. Assume that we have a procedure Setup that samples a random vertex to start with in time S, Check that verifies if a vertex is marked or not in time C and Update that performs a walk step in time U, then we will have found a marked vertex in expected time: $S + \frac{1}{\epsilon}\left(\frac{1}{\delta}U + C\right)$.

Quantum walks reproduce the same process, except that their internal state is not a vertex of G, but a superposition of vertices. The walk starts in the uniform superposition $\sum_{v \in V} |v\rangle$, which must be generated by the Setup procedure. It repeats $\sqrt{1/\epsilon}$ iterations that, similarly to amplitude amplification, move the amplitude towards the marked vertices. An update produces, from a vertex, the superposition of its neighbors. Each iteration does not need to repeat $\frac{1}{\delta}$ vertex updates and, instead, takes a time equivalent to $\sqrt{1/\delta}$ updates to achieve a good mixing. Thanks to the following theorem , we will only need to specify the setup, checking and update unitaries.

Theorem 1 (Quantum walk on a graph (adapted from [30])). *Let $G = (V, E)$ be a regular graph with spectral gap $\delta > 0$. Let $\epsilon > 0$ be a lower bound on the probability that a vertex chosen randomly of G is marked. For a random walk on G, let S, U, C be the setup, update and checking cost. Then there exists a quantum algorithm that with high probability finds a marked vertex in time*

$$\mathcal{O}\left(S + \frac{1}{\sqrt{\epsilon}}\left(\frac{1}{\sqrt{\delta}}U + C\right)\right).$$

3.2 Solving Subset-Sum with Quantum Walks

In 2013, Bernstein, Jeffery, Lange and Meurer [6] constructed quantum subset sum algorithms inspired by Schroeppel-Shamir [37] and HGJ [21]. We briefly explain the idea of their quantum walk for HGJ. The graph G that they consider is a product Johnson graph. We recall formal definitions from [22].

Definition 4 (Johnson graph). *A Johnson graph $J(N, R)$ is an undirected graph whose vertices are the subsets of R elements among a set of size N, and there is an edge between two vertices S and S' iff $|S \cap S'| = R - 1$, in other words, if S' can be obtained from S by replacing an element. Its spectral gap is given by $\delta = \frac{N}{R(N-R)}$.*

Theorem 2 (Cartesian product of Johnson graphs [22]). *Let $J^m(N, R)$ be defined as the cartesian product of m Johnson graphs $J(N, R)$, i.e., a vertex in $J^m(N, R)$ is a tuple of m subsets $S_1, \ldots S_m$ and there is an edge between $S_1, \ldots S_m$ and $S_1', \ldots S_m'$ iff all subsets are equal at all indices except one index i, which satisfies $|S_i \cap S_i'| = R - 1$. Then it has $\binom{N}{R}^m$ vertices and its spectral gap is greater than $\frac{1}{m} \frac{N}{R(N-R)}$.*

In [6], a vertex contains a product of 8 sublists $L_0'^3 \subset L_0^3, \ldots, L_7'^3 \subset L_7^3$ of a smaller size than the classical lists: $\ell < \ell_3$. There is an edge between two vertices if we can transform one into the other by replacing only one element in one of the sublists. The spectral gap of such a graph is (in $\log_2$, relative to n) $-\ell$.

In addition, each vertex has an internal data structure which reproduces the HGJ merging tree, from level 3 to level 0. Since the initial lists are smaller, the list L^0 is now of expected size $8(\ell - \ell_3)$ (in $\log_2$, relative to n), *i.e.*, the walk needs to run for $4(\ell_3 - \ell)$ steps. Each step requires $\ell/2$ updates.

In the Setup procedure, we simply start from all choices for the sublists and build the tree by merging and filtering. Assuming that the merged lists have decreasing sizes, the setup time is ℓ. The vertex is marked if it contains a solution at level 0. Hence, checking if a vertex is marked takes time $\mathsf{C} = 1$, but the update procedure needs to ensure the consistency of the data structure. Indeed, when updating, we remove an element $\mathbf{e}$ from one of the lists $L_i'^3$ and replace it by a $\mathbf{e}'$ from L_i^3. We then have to track all subknapsacks in the upper levels where $\mathbf{e}$ intervened, to remove them, and to add the new collisions where $\mathbf{e}'$ intervenes.

Assuming that the update can run in poly(n), an optimization with the new parameter ℓ yields an exponent 0.241. In [6], the parameters are such that on average, a subknapsack intervenes only in a single sum at the next level. The authors propose to simply limit the number of elements to be updated at each level, in order to guarantee a constant update time.

Quantum Walk Based on BCJ. In [18], Helm and May quantize, in the same way, the BCJ algorithm. They add "-1" symbols and a new level in the merging tree data structure, reaching a time exponent of 0.226. But they remark that this result depends on a conjecture, or a heuristic, that was implicit in [6].

Heuristic 2 (Helm-May). *In these quantum walk subset-sum algorithms, an update with expected constant time U can be replaced by an update with exact time U without affecting the runtime of the algorithm, up to a polynomial factor.*

Indeed, it is easy to construct "bad" vertices and edges for which an exact update, *i.e.* the complete reconstruction of the merging tree, will take exponential time: by adding a single new subknapsack $\mathbf{e}$, we find an exponential number of pairs $\mathbf{e} + \mathbf{e}'$ to include at the next level. So we would like to update only a few elements among them. But in the MNRS framework, the data structure of a vertex must depend solely on the vertex itself (*i.e.* on the lowest-level lists in the merging tree). And if we do as proposed in [6], we add a dependency on the path that lead to the vertex, and lose the consistency of the walk.

In a related context, the problem of "quantum search with variable times" was studied by Ambainis [2]. In a quantum search for some x such that $f(x) = 1$, in a set of size N, if the time to evaluate f on x is always 1, then the search requires time $\mathcal{O}\left(\sqrt{N}\right)$. Ambainis showed that if the elements have different evaluation times $t_1, \ldots t_N$, then the search now requires $\widetilde{\mathcal{O}}(\sqrt{t_1^2 + \ldots + t_N^2})$, the geometric mean of $t_1, \ldots t_N$. As quantum search can be seen as a particular type of quantum walk, this shows that Heuristic 2 is wrong in general, as we can artificially create a gap between the geometric mean and expectation of the update time U; but also, that it may be difficult to actually overcome. In this paper, we will obtain different heuristic and non-heuristic times.

4   Quantum Asymmetric HGJ

In this section, we give the first quantum algorithm for the subset-sum problem, *in the QRACM model*, with an asymptotic complexity smaller than BCJ.

4.1   Quantum Match-and-Filter

We open this section with some technical lemmas that replace the classical merge-and-filter Lemma 2. In this section, we will consider a merging tree as in the HGJ algorithm, but this tree will be built using quantum search. The following lemmas bound the expected time of merge-and-filter *and* match-and-filter operations performed quantumly, in the QRACM model. This will have consequences both in this section and in the next one.

First, we remark that we can use a much more simple data structure than the ones in [1,6]. In this data structure, we store pairs $\mathbf{e}, \mathbf{e} \cdot \mathbf{a}$ indexed by $\mathbf{e} \cdot \mathbf{a}$ mod M for some $M \simeq 2^m$.

Definition 5 (Unique modulus list). *A unique modulus list is a qRAM data structure $\mathcal{L}(M)$ that stores at most M entries $(\mathbf{e}, \mathbf{e} \cdot \mathbf{a})$, indexed by $\mathbf{e} \cdot \mathbf{a}$ mod M, and supports the following operations:*

- *Insertion: inserts the entry $(\mathbf{e}, \mathbf{e} \cdot \mathbf{a})$ if the modulus is not already occupied;*
- *Deletion: deletes $(\mathbf{e}, \mathbf{e} \cdot \mathbf{a})$ (not necessary in this section)*
- *Query in superposition: returns the superposition of all entries $(\mathbf{e}, \mathbf{e} \cdot \mathbf{a})$ with some modular condition on $\mathbf{e} \cdot \mathbf{a}$, e.g. $\mathbf{e} \cdot \mathbf{a} = t$ mod M' for some t and some modulus M'.*

Note that all of these operations, *including* the query in superposition of all the entries with a given modulus, cost $\mathcal{O}(1)$ qRAM gates only. For the latter, we need only some Hadamard gates to prepare the adequate superposition of indices. Furthermore, the list remains sorted by design.

Next, we write a lemma for quantum *matching* with filtering, in which one of the lists is not written down. We start from a unitary that produces the uniform superposition of the elements of a list L_1, and we wrap it into an amplitude amplification, in order to obtain a unitary that produces the uniform superposition of the elements of the merged-and-filtered list.

Lemma 4 (Quantum matching with filtering). *Let L_2 be a list stored in QRACM (with the* unique modulus list *data structure of Definition 5). Assume given a unitary U that produces in time t_{L_1} the uniform superposition of $L_1 = x_0, \ldots x_{2^m-1}$ where $x_i = (\mathbf{e_i}, \mathbf{e_i} \cdot \mathbf{a})$. We merge L_1 and L_2 with a modular condition of cn bits and a filtering probability p. Let L be the merged list and L^f the filtered list. Assume $|L^f| \geq 1$. Then there exists a unitary U' producing the uniform superposition of L^f in time: $\mathcal{O}\left(\frac{t_{L_1}}{\sqrt{p}} \max(\sqrt{2^{cn}/|L_2|}, 1)\right)$.*

Notice that this is also the time complexity to produce a single random element of L^f. If we want to produce and store the whole list L^f, it suffices to multiply this complexity by the number of elements in L^f (*i.e.* $p|L_1||L_2|/2^{cn}$). We would obtain: $\mathcal{O}\left(t_{L_1}\sqrt{p}\max\left(|L_1|\sqrt{\frac{|L_2|}{2^{cn}}}, \frac{|L_1||L_2|}{2^{cn}}\right)\right)$.

Proof. Since L_2 is stored in a unique modulus list, all its elements have distinct moduli. Note that the *expected* sizes of L and L^f follow from Heuristic 1. Although the number of iterations of quantum search should depend on the *real* sizes of these lists, the concentration around the average is so high (given by Chernoff bounds) that the error remains negligible if we run the search with the expected number of iterations. We separate three cases.

- If $|L_2| < 2^{cn}$, then we have no choice but to make a quantum search on elements of L_1 that match the modular constraint and pass the filtering step, in time: $\mathcal{O}\left(t_{L_1}\sqrt{\frac{2^{cn}}{L_2 p}}\right)$.
- If $|L_2| > 2^{cn}$ but $|L_2| < 2^{cn}/p$, an element of L_1 will always pass the modular constraint, with more than one candidate, but in general all these candidates will be filtered out. Given an element of L_1, producing the superposition of these candidates is done in time 1, so finding the one that passes the filter, if there is one, takes time $\sqrt{|L_2|/2^{cn}}$. Next, we wrap this in a quantum search to find the "good" elements of L_1 (passing the two conditions), with $\mathcal{O}\left(\sqrt{2^{cn}/pL_2}\right)$ iterations. The total time is:

$$\mathcal{O}\left(\sqrt{\frac{2^{cn}}{L_2 p}} \times \left(\sqrt{|L_2|/2^{cn}} \times t_{L_1}\right) = \frac{t_{L_1}}{\sqrt{p}}\right).$$

- If $|L_2| > 2^{cn}/p$, an element of L_1 yields on average more than one filtered candidate. Producing the superposition of the modular candidates is done in time $\mathcal{O}(1)$ thanks to the data structure, then finding the superposition of filtered candidates requires $1/\sqrt{p}$ iterations. The total time is: $\mathcal{O}(t_{L_1}/\sqrt{p})$.

The total time in all cases is: $\mathcal{O}\left(\frac{t_{L_1}}{\sqrt{p}}\max(\sqrt{2^{cn}/|L_2|}, 1)\right)$. Note that classically, the coupon collector problem would have added a polynomial factor, but this is not the case here thanks to QRACM (Remark 6). □

In the QRACM model, we have the following corollary for merging and filtering two lists of equal size. This result will be helpful in Sect. 4.3 and 5.

Corollary 1. *Consider two lists L_1, L_2 of size $|L_1| = |L_2| = |L|$ exponential in n. We merge L_1 and L_2 with a modular condition of cn bits, and filter with a probability p. Assume that $2^{cn} < |L|$. Then L^f can be written down in quantum time:* $\mathcal{O}\left(\sqrt{p}\frac{|L|^2}{2^{cn}}\right)$.

Proof. We do a quantum search to find each element of L^f. We have $t_{L_1} = \mathcal{O}(1)$ since it is a mere QRACM query, and we use Lemma 4.   □

4.2 Revisiting HGJ

We now introduce our new algorithm for subset-sum in the QRACM model.

Our starting point is the HGJ algorithm. Similarly to [33], we use a merging tree in which the lists at a given level may have different sizes. Classically, this does not improve the time complexity. However, quantumly, we will use quantum filtering. Since our algorithm does not require to write data in superposition, only to read from classical registers with quantum random access, we require only QRACM instead of QRAQM.

In the following, we consider that all lists, except L_0^3, L_0^2, L_0^1, L^0, are built with classical merges. The final list L^0, containing (expectedly) a single element, and a branch leading to it, are part of a nested quantum search. Each list L_0^3, L_0^2, L_0^1, L^0 corresponds either to a search space, the solutions of a search, or both. We represent this situation on Fig. 3. Our procedure runs as follows:

1. (Classical step): build the *intermediate lists* L_1^3, L_1^2, L_1^1 and store them using a *unique modulus list* data structure (Definition 5).
2. (Quantum step): do a quantum search on L_0^3. To test a vector $\mathbf{e} \in L_0^3$:
   - Find $\mathbf{e}_3 \in L_1^3$ such that $\mathbf{e} + \mathbf{e}_3$ passes the $c_0^2 n$-bit modular constraint (assume that there is at most one such solution). There is no filtering here.
   - Find $\mathbf{e}_2 \in L_1^2$ such that $(\mathbf{e} + \mathbf{e}_3) + \mathbf{e}_2$ passes the additional $(c^1 - c_0^2)n$-bit constraint.
   - If it also passes the filtering step, find $\mathbf{e}_1 \in L_1^1$ such that $(\mathbf{e} + \mathbf{e}_3 + \mathbf{e}_2) + \mathbf{e}_1$ is a solution to the knapsack problem (and passes the filter).

Structural constraints are imposed on the tree, in order to guarantee that there exists a knapsack solution. The only difference between the quantum and classical settings is in the optimization goal: the final time complexity.

Structural Constraints. We now introduce the variables and the structural constraints that determine the shape of the tree in Fig. 3. The asymmetry happens both in the weights at level 0 and at the constraints at level 1 and 2. We write $\ell_i^j = (\log_2 |L_i^j|)/n$. With the lists built classically, we expect a symmetry to be respected, so we have: $\ell_2^3 = \ell_3^3$, $\ell_4^3 = \ell_5^3 = \ell_6^3 = \ell_7^3$, $\ell_2^2 = \ell_3^2$. We also tweak the left-right split at level 0: lists from L_2^3 to L_7^3 have a standard balanced left-right split; however, we introduce a parameter r that determines the proportion of

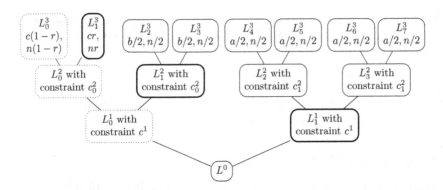

Fig. 3. Quantum HGJ algorithm. Dotted lists are search spaces (they are not stored). Bold lists are stored in QRACM. In Sect. 4.3, L_2^2 and L_3^2 are also stored in QRACM.

positions set to zero in list L_0^3: in L_0^3, the vectors weigh $cn(1 - r)$ on a support of size $n(1 - r)$, instead of $cn/2$ on a support of size $n/2$. In total we have $c + b + 2a = \frac{1}{2}$, as the weight of the solution is supposed to be exactly $n/2$.

Then we note that:

- The lists at level 3 have a maximal size depending on the corresponding weight of their vectors:

$$\ell_0^3 \le h(c)(1 - r), \quad \ell_1^3 \le h(c)r, \quad \ell_2^3 = \ell_3^3 \le h(b)/2, \quad \ell_4^3 \le h(a)/2$$

- The lists at level 2 cannot contain more representations than the filtered list of all subknapsacks of corresponding weight:

$$\ell_0^2 \le h(c) - c_0^2, \quad \ell_1^2 \le h(b) - c_0^2, \quad \ell_2^2 = \ell_3^2 \le h(a) - c_1^2$$

- Same at levels 1 and 0: $\ell_0^1 \le h(c + b) - c^1, \quad \ell_1^1 \le h(2a) - c^1$
- The merging at level 2 is exact (there is no filtering):

$$\ell_0^2 = \ell_0^3 + \ell_1^3 - c_0^2, \quad \ell_1^2 = \ell_2^3 + \ell_3^3 - c_0^2, \quad \ell_2^2 = \ell_4^3 + \ell_5^3 - c_1^2, \quad \ell_3^2 = \ell_6^3 + \ell_7^3 - c_1^2,$$

- At level 1, with a constraint $c^1 \ge c_0^2, c_1^2$ that subsumes the previous ones:

$$\ell_0^1 = \ell_0^2 + \ell_1^2 - c^1 + c_0^2 + \mathsf{pf}_1(b, c) \ , \qquad \ell_1^1 = \ell_2^2 + \ell_3^2 - c^1 + c_1^2 + \mathsf{pf}_1(a, a)$$

- And finally at level 0: $\ell^0 = 0 = \ell_0^1 + \ell_1^1 - (1 - c^1) + \mathsf{pf}_1(b + c, 2a)$

Classical Optimization. All the previous constraints depend on the problem, not on the computation model. Now we can get to the time complexity in the classical setting, that we want to minimize:

$$\max\left(\ell_4^3, \ell_2^3, \ell_1^3, \ell_2^3 + \ell_3^3 - c_0^2, \ell_4^3 + \ell_5^3 - c_1^2, \ell_2^2 + \ell_3^2 - c^1 + c_1^2, \right.$$
$$\left. \ell_0^3 + \max(\ell_1^3 - c_0^2, 0) + \max(\ell_1^2 - c^1 + c_0^2, 0) + \max(\mathsf{pf}_1(b, c) + \ell_1^1 - (1 - c^1), 0)\right) \ .$$

The last term corresponds to the exhaustive search on ℓ_0^3. In order to keep the same freedom as before, it is possible that an element of L_0^3 matches against *several* elements of L_1^3, all of which yield a potential solution that has to be matched against L_1^2, etc. Hence for each element of L_0^3, we find the expected $\max(\ell_1^3 - c_0^2, 0)$ candidates matching the constraint c_0^2. For each of these candidates, we find the expected $\max(\ell_1^2 - c^1 + c_0^2, 0)$ candidates matching the constraint c^1. For each of these candidates, if it passes the filter, we search for a collision in L_1^1; this explains the $\max(\mathsf{pf}_1(b, c) + \ell_1^1 - (1 - c^1), 0)$ term. In the end, we check if the final candidates pass the filter on the last level.

We verified that optimizing the classical time under our constraints gives the time complexity of HGJ.

Quantum Optimization. The time complexity for producing the intermediate lists is unchanged. The only difference is the way we find the element in L_0^3 that will lead to a solution, which is a nested sequence of quantum searches.

- We can produce the superposition of all elements in L_0^2 in time

$$t_2 = \frac{1}{2} \max(c_0^2 - \ell_1^3, 0)$$

- By Lemma 4, we can produce the superposition of all elements in L_0^1 in time

$$t_2 - \frac{1}{2}\mathsf{pf}_1(b, c) + \frac{1}{2} \max\left(c^1 - c_0^2 - \ell_1^2, 0\right)$$

- Finally, we expect that there are $\left(\ell_0^3 + \ell_1^2 - c^1 + c_0^2 + \mathsf{pf}_1(b, c)\right)$ elements in L_0^1, which gives the number of iterations of the quantum search.

The time of this search is:

$$\frac{1}{2}\left(\ell_0^1 + \max(c_0^2 - \ell_1^3, 0) - \mathsf{pf}_1(b, c) + \max\left(c^1 - c_0^2 - \ell_1^2, 0\right)\right)$$

and the total time complexity is:

$$\max\left(\ell_4^3, \ell_2^3, \ell_1^3, \ell_2^3 + \ell_3^3 - c_0^2, \ell_4^3 + \ell_5^3 - c_1^2, \ell_2^2 + \ell_3^2 - c^1 + c_1^2,\right.$$
$$\left.\frac{1}{2}\left(\ell_0^1 + \max(c_0^2 - \ell_1^3, 0) - \mathsf{pf}_1(b, c) + \max\left(c^1 - c_0^2 - \ell_1^2, 0\right)\right)\right)$$

We obtain a quantum time complexity exponent of 0.2374 with this method (the detailed parameters are given in Table 2).

4.3 Improvement via Quantum Filtering

Let us keep the tree structure of Fig. 3 and its structural constraints. The final quantum search step is already made efficient with respect to the filtering of representations, as we only pay half of the filtering term $\mathsf{pf}_1(b, c)$. However, we can look towards the *intermediate lists* in the tree, *i.e.*, L_1^3, L_1^2, L_1^1. The merging at the first level is exact: due to the left-right split, there is no filtering of representations, hence the complexity is determined by the size of the output list. However, the construction of L_1^1 contains a filtering step. Thus, we can use Corollary 1 to produce the elements of L_1^1 faster and reduce the time complexity from: $\ell_2^2 + \ell_3^2 - c^1 + c_1^2$ to: $\ell_2^2 + \ell_3^2 - c^1 + c_1^2 + \frac{1}{2}\mathsf{pf}_1\,(a,a)$. By optimizing with this time complexity, we obtain a time exponent 0.2356 (the detailed parameters are given in Table 2). The corresponding memory is 0.2356 (given by the list L_1^3).

Table 2. Optimization results for the quantum asymmetric HGJ algorithm (in $\log_2$ and relative to n), rounded to four digits. The time complexity is an upper bound.

Variant	Time	a	b	c	ℓ_0^3	ℓ_1^3	ℓ_2^3	ℓ_4^3	ℓ_0^2	ℓ_0^1
Classical	0.3370	0.1249	0.11	0.1401	0.3026	0.2267	0.25	0.2598	0.3369	0.3114
Section 4.2	0.2374	0.0951	0.0951	0.2146	0.4621	0.2367	0.2267	0.2267	0.4746	0.4395
Section 4.3	0.2356	0.0969	0.0952	0.2110	0.4691	0.2356	0.2267	0.2296	0.4695	0.4368

Remark 7 (More improvements). We have tried increasing the tree depth or changing the tree structure, but it does not seem to bring any improvement. In theory, we could allow for more general representations involving "−1" and "2". However, computing the filtering probability, when merging two lists of subknapsacks in $D^n[\alpha, \beta, \gamma]$ with *different distributions* becomes much more technical. We managed to compute it for $D^n[\alpha, \beta]$, but the number of parameters was too high for our numerical optimizer, which failed to converge.

4.4   Quantum Time-Memory Tradeoff

In the original HGJ algorithm, the lists at level 3 contain full distributions $D^{n/2}[0, 1/8]$. By reducing their sizes to a smaller exponential, one can still run the merging steps, but the final list L^0 is of expected size exponentially small in n. Hence, one must redo the tree many times. This general time-memory tradeoff is outlined in [21] and is also reminiscent of Schroeppel and Shamir's algorithm [37], which can actually be seen as repeating $2^{n/4}$ times a merge of lists of size $2^{n/4}$, that yields $2^{-n/4}$ solutions on average.

Asymmetric Tradeoff. The tradeoff that we propose is adapted to the QRACM model. It consists in increasing the asymmetry of the tree: we reduce the sizes of the intermediate lists L_1^3, L_1^2, L_1^1 in order to use less memory; this in turn increases the size of L_0^3, L_0^2 and L_0^1 in order to ensure that a solution exists. We find that this tradeoff is close to the time-memory product curve $TM = 2^{n/2}$, and actually slightly better (the optimal point when $m = 0.2356$ has $TM = 2^{0.4712n}$). This is shown on Fig. 4. At $m = 0$, we start at $2^{n/2}$, where L_0^3 contains all vectors of Hamming weight $n/2$.

Fact 1. *For any memory constraint* $m \leq 0.2356$ *(in* $\log_2$ *and proportion of* n*), the optimal time complexity in the quantum asymmetric HGJ algorithm of Sect. 4.3 is lower than* $\tilde{\mathcal{O}}\left(2^{n/2-m}\right)$.

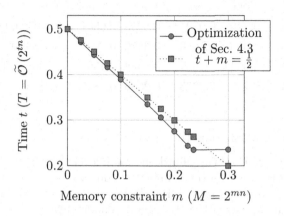

Fig. 4. Quantum time-memory tradeoff of the asymmetric HGJ algorithm

Improving the QRACM Usage. In trying to reduce the quantum or quantum-accessible hardware used by our algorithm, it makes sense to draw a line between QRACM and classical RAM, *i.e.*, between the part of the memory that is actually accessed quantumly, and the memory that is used only classically. We now try to enforce the constraint only on the QRACM, using possibly more RAM. In this context, we cannot produce the list L_1^1 via quantum filtering. The memory constraint on lists L_1^3, L_1^2, L_1^1 still holds; however, we can increase the size of lists $L_4^3, L_5^3, L_6^3, L_7^3, L_2^2, L_3^2$.

Fact 2. *For any QRACM constraint* $m \leq 0.2356$*, the optimal time complexity obtained by using more RAM is always smaller than the best optimization of Sect. 4.3.*

The difference remains only marginal, as can be seen in Table 3, but it shows a tradeoff between quantum and classical resources.

5   New Algorithms Based on Quantum Walks

In this section, we improve the algorithm by Helm and May [18] based on BCJ and the MNRS quantum walk framework. Our algorithm is a quantum walk on a product Johnson graph, as in Sect. 3.2. There are two new ideas involved.

Table 3. Time-memory tradeoffs (QRACM) for three variants of our asymmetric HGJ algorithm, obtained by numerical optimization, and rounded upwards. The last variant uses more classical RAM than the QRACM constraint.

QRACM	Section 4.2		Section 4.3		With more RAM	
bound	Time	Memory	Time	Memory	Time	Memory
0.0500	0.4433	0.0501	0.4433	0.0501	0.4412	0.0650
0.1000	0.3896	0.1000	0.3896	0.1000	0.3860	0.1259
0.1500	0.3348	0.1501	0.3348	0.1501	0.3301	0.1894
0.3000	0.2374	0.2373	0.2356	0.2356	0.2373	0.2373

5.1   Asymmetric 5th Level

In our new algorithm, we can afford one more level than BCJ. We then have a 6-level merging tree, with levels numbered 5 down to 0. Lists at level i all have the same size ℓ_i, *except at level 5*. Recall that the merging tree, and all its lists, is the additional data structure attached to a node in the Johnson graph. In the original algorithm of [18], there are 5 levels, and a node is a collection of 16 lists, each list being a subset of size ℓ_4 among the $g(1/16 + \alpha_3, \alpha_3)/2$ vectors having the right distribution.

In our new algorithm, at level 5, we separate the lists into "left" lists of size ℓ_5^l and "right" lists of size ℓ_5^r. The quantum walk will only be performed on the left lists, while the right ones are full enumerations. Each list at level 4 is obtained by merging a "left" and a "right" list. The left-right-split at level 5 is then asymmetric: vectors in one of the left lists L_5^l are sampled from $D^{\eta n}[\alpha_4, 1/32, \gamma_4] \times \{0^{(1-\eta)n}\}$ and the right lists L_5^r contain *all* the vectors from $\{0^{\eta n}\} \times D^{(1-\eta)n}[\alpha_4, 1/32, \gamma_4]$. This yields a new constraint: $\ell_5^r = f(1/32 + \alpha_4 - 2\gamma_4, \alpha_4, \gamma_4)(1-\eta)$.

While this asymmetry does not bring any advantage classically, it helps in reducing the update time. We enforce the constraint $\ell_5^r = c_4$, so that for each element of L_5^l, there is on average one matching element in L_5^r. So updating the list L_4 at level 4 is done on average time 1. Then we also have $\ell_4 = \ell_5^l$.

With this construction, ℓ_5^r and ℓ_5^l are actually unneeded parameters. We only need the constraints $c_4(= \ell_5^r) = f(1/32 + \alpha_4 - 2\gamma_4, \alpha_4, \gamma_4)(1-\eta)$ and $\ell_4(= \ell_5^l) \le f(1/32 + \alpha_4 - 2\gamma, \alpha_4, \gamma_4)\eta$. The total setup time is now:

$$S = \max \left(\underbrace{c_4, \ell_4}_{\text{Lv. 5 and 4}} , \underbrace{2\ell_4 - (c_3 - c_4)}_{\text{Level 3}}, \underbrace{2\ell_3 - (c_2 - c_3)}_{\text{Level 2}}, \underbrace{2\ell_2 - (c_1 - c_2)}_{\text{Level 1}}, \right.$$
$$\left. \underbrace{\ell_1 + \max(\ell_1 - (1 - c_1), 0)}_{\text{Level 0}} \right)$$

and the expected update time for level 5 (inserting a new element in a list L_5^l at the bottom of the tree) and at level 4 (inserting a new element in L_4) is 1.

The spectral gap of the graph is $\delta = -\ell_5^l$ and the proportion of marked vertices is $\epsilon = -\ell_0$.

Saturation Constraints. In the quantum walk, we have $\ell_0 < 0$, since we expect only some proportion of the nodes to be marked (to contain a solution). This proportion is hence ℓ_0. The saturation constraints are modified as follows:

$$\ell_5^l \leq \tfrac{\ell_0}{16} + f(\tfrac{1}{32} + \alpha_4 - 2\gamma_4, \alpha_4, \gamma_4)\eta, \qquad \ell_4 \leq \tfrac{\ell_0}{16} + f(\tfrac{1}{32} + \alpha_4 - 2\gamma_4, \alpha_4, \gamma_4) - c_4$$
$$\ell_3 \leq \tfrac{\ell_0}{8} + f(\tfrac{1}{16} + \alpha_3 - 2\gamma_3, \alpha_3, \gamma_3) - c_3, \quad \ell_2 \leq \tfrac{\ell_0}{4} + f(\tfrac{1}{8} + \alpha_2 - 2\gamma_2, \alpha_2, \gamma_2) - c_2$$
$$\ell_1 \leq \tfrac{\ell_0}{2} + f(1/4 + \alpha_1 - 2\gamma_1, \alpha_1, \gamma_1) - c_1$$

Indeed, the *classical* walk will go through a total of $-\ell_0$ trees before finding a solution. Hence, it needs to go through $-\ell_0/16$ different lists at level 5 (and 4), which is why we need to introduce ℓ_0 in the saturation constraint: there must be enough elements, not only in L_5^l, but in the whole search space that will be spanned by the walk. These constraints ensure the existence of marked vertices in the walk.

5.2   Better Setup and Updates Using Quantum Search

Along the lines of Lemma 4 and Corollary 1, we now show how to use a quantum search to speed up the Setup and Update steps in the quantum walk. As the structure of the graph is unchanged, we still have $\epsilon = -\ell_0$ and a spectral gap $\delta = -\ell_5^l$.

Setup. Let $p_i, (1 \leq i \leq 3)$ be the filtering probabilities at level i, *i.e.*, the (logarithms of the) probabilities that an element that satisfies the modulo condition resp. at level i also has the desired distribution of 0s, 1s, -1s and 2s, and appears in list L_i. Notice that $p_i \leq 0$. Due to the left-right split, there is no filtering at level 4.

We use quantum filtering (Corollary 1) to speed up the computation of lists at levels 3, 2 and 1 in the setup, reducing in general a time $2\ell - c$ to $2\ell - c + \mathsf{p}f/2$. It does not apply for level 0, since L_0 has a negative expected size. At this level, we will simply perform a quantum search over L_1. If there is too much constraint, *i.e.*, $(1 - c_1) > \ell_1$, then for a given element in L_1, there is on average less than one modular candidate. If $(1 - c_1) < \ell_1$, there is on average more than one (although less than one with the filter) and we have to do another quantum search on them all. This is why the setup time at level 0, in full generality, becomes $(\ell_1 + \max(\ell_1 - (1 - c_1), 0))/2$. The setup time can thus be improved to:

$$S = \max\Bigg(\underbrace{c_4, \ell_4}_{\text{Lv. 5 and 4}}, \underbrace{2\ell_4 - (c_3 - c_4) + p_3/2}_{\text{Level 3}}, \underbrace{2\ell_3 - (c_2 - c_3) + p_2/2}_{\text{Level 2}},$$
$$\underbrace{2\ell_2 - (c_1 - c_2) + p_1/2}_{\text{Level 1}}, \underbrace{(\ell_1 + \max(\ell_1 - (1 - c_1), 0))/2}_{\text{Level 0}} \Bigg) .$$

Update. Our update will also use a quantum search. First of all, recall that the updates of levels 5 and 4 are performed in (expected) time 1. Having added an element in L_4, we need to update the upper level. There are on average

$\ell_4 - (c_3 - c_4)$ candidates satisfying the modular condition. To avoid a blowup in the time complexity, we forbid to have more than one element inserted in L_3 on average, which means: $\ell_4 - (c_3 - c_4) + p_3 \leq 0 \iff \ell_3 \leq \ell_4$. We then find this element, if it exists, with a quantum search among the $\ell_4 - (c_3 - c_4)$ candidates.

Similarly, as at most one element is updated in L_3, we can move on to the upper levels 2, 1 and 0 and use the same argument. We forbid to have more than one element inserted in L_2 on average: $\ell_3 - (c_2 - c_3) + p_2 \leq 0 \iff \ell_2 \leq \ell_3$, and in L_1: $\ell_1 \leq \ell_2$. At level 0, a quantum search may not be needed, hence a time $\max(\ell_1 - (1 - c_1), 0)/2$. The expected update time becomes:

$$U = \max \left(0, \underbrace{(\ell_4 - (c_3 - c_4))/2}_{\text{Level 3}}, \underbrace{(\ell_3 - (c_2 - c_3))/2}_{\text{Level 2}}, \right.$$
$$\left. \underbrace{(\ell_2 - (c_1 - c_2))/2}_{\text{Level 1}}, \underbrace{(\ell_1 - (1 - c_1))/2}_{\text{Level 0}} \right).$$

5.3 Parameters

Using the following parameters, we found an algorithm that runs in time $\widetilde{\mathcal{O}}\left(2^{0.2156n}\right)$:

$$\ell_0 = -0.1916, \ell_1 = 0.1996, \ell_2 = 0.2030, \ell_3 = 0.2110, \ell_4(= \ell_5^l) = 0.2110$$
$$c_1 = 0.6190, c_2 = 0.4445, c_3 = 0.2506, c_4(= \ell_5^r) = 0.0487$$
$$\alpha_1 = 0.0176, \alpha_2 = 0.0153, \alpha_3 = 0.0131, \alpha_4 = 0.0087$$
$$\gamma_1 = 0.0019, \gamma_2 = \gamma_3 = \gamma_4 = 0, \eta = 0.8448$$

There are many different parameters that achieve the same time. The above set achieves the lowest memory that we found, at $\widetilde{\mathcal{O}}\left(2^{0.2110n}\right)$. Note that time and memory complexities are different in this quantum walk, contrary to previous works, since the update procedure has now a (small) exponential cost.

Remark 8. (Time-memory tradeoffs). Quantum walks have a natural time-memory tradeoff which consists in reducing the vertex size. Smaller vertices have a smaller chance of being marked, and the walk goes on for a longer time. This is also applicable to our algorithms, but requires a re-optimization with a memory constraint.

6   Mitigating Quantum Walk Heuristics for Subset-Sum

In this section, we provide a modified quantum walk NEW-QW for any quantum walk subset-sum algorithm QW, including [6,18] and ours, that will no longer rely on Heuristic 2. In NEW-QW, the Johnson graph is the same, but the vertex data structure and the update procedure are different (Sect. 6.2). It allows us to guarantee the update time, at the expense of losing some marked vertices. In Sect. 6.3, we will show that most marked vertices in QW remain marked.

6.1   New Data Structure for Storing Lists

The main requirement of the vertex data structure is to store lists of subknapsacks with modular constraints in QRAQM. For each list, we will use two data structures. The first one is the combination of a hash table and a skip list given in [1] (abbreviated *skip list* below) and the second one is a *Bucket-modulus list* data structure, adapted from Definition 5, that we define below.

Hash Table and Skip List. We use the data structure of [1] to store lists of entries $(\mathbf{e}, \mathbf{e} \cdot \mathbf{a})$, sorted by knapsack value $\mathbf{e} \cdot \mathbf{a}$. The data structure for M entries, that we denote $\mathcal{SL}(M)$, uses $\widetilde{\mathcal{O}}(M)$ qRAM memory cells and supports the following operations: inserting an entry in the list, deleting an entry from the list and producing the uniform superposition of entries in the list. All these operations require time $\mathsf{polylog}(M)$.

We resort to this data structure because the proposal of "radix trees" in [6] is less detailed. It is defined relatively to a choice of $\mathsf{polylog}(M) = \mathrm{poly}(n)$ hash functions selected from a family of independent hash functions of the entries (we refer to [1] for more details). For a given choice of hash functions, the insertion or deletion operations can fail. Thus, the data structure is equipped with a superposition of such choices. Instead of storing $\mathcal{SL}(M)$, we store: $\sum_h |h\rangle \, |\mathcal{SL}_h(M)\rangle$ where $\mathcal{SL}_h$ is the data structure flavored with the choice of hash functions h. Insertions and deletions are performed depending on h. This allows for a globally negligible error: if sufficiently many hash functions are used, the insertion and deletion of *any element* add a global error vector of amplitude $o(2^{-n})$ *regardless of the current state of the data*. The standard "hybrid argument" from [5] and [1, Lemma 5] can then be used in the context of an MNRS quantum walk.

Proposition 1. ([1], **Lemma 5, adapted**). *Consider an MNRS quantum walk with a "perfect" (theoretical) update unitary U, managing data structures, and an "imperfect" update unitary U' such that, for any basis state $|x\rangle$:*

$$U' |x\rangle = U |x\rangle + |\delta_x\rangle$$

where $|\delta_x\rangle$ is an error vector of amplitude bounded by $o(2^{-n})$ for any x. Then running the walk with U' instead of U, after T steps, the final "imperfect" state $|\psi'\rangle$ deviates from the "perfect" state $|\psi\rangle$ by: $\| |\psi'\rangle - |\psi\rangle \| \le o(2^{-n}T)$.

This holds as a general principle: in the update unitary, any perfect procedure can be replaced by an imperfect one as long as its error is negligible (with respect to the total number of updates) *and data-independent*. In contrast, the problem with Heuristic 2 is that a generic constant-time update induces data-dependent errors (bad cases) that do not seem easy to overcome.

Bucket-modulus List. Let $B = \mathrm{poly}(n)$ be a "bucket size" that will be chosen later. The bucket-modulus list is a tool for making our update time data-independent: it limits the number of vectors that can have a given modulus (where moduli are of the same order as the list size).

Definition 6. (Bucket-modulus list). *A Bucket-modulus list* $\mathcal{BL}(B, M)$ *is a qRAM data structure that stores at most* $B \times M$ *entries* $(\mathbf{e}, \mathbf{e} \cdot \mathbf{a})$, *with at most* B *entries sharing the same modulus* $\mathbf{e} \cdot \mathbf{a} \mod M$. *Thus,* $\mathcal{BL}(B, M)$ *contains* M *"buckets". Buckets are indexed by moduli, and kept sorted. It supports the following operations:*

- *Insertion: insert* $(\mathbf{e}, \mathbf{e} \cdot \mathbf{a})$. *If the bucket at index* $\mathbf{e} \cdot \mathbf{a} \mod M$ *contains* B *elements, empty the bucket. Otherwise, sort it using a simple sorting circuit.*
- *Deletion: remove an entry from the corresponding bucket.*
- *Query in superposition: similar as in Definition 5.*

In our new quantum walks, each list will be stored in a skip list $\mathcal{SL}(M)$ associated with a bucket-modulus $\mathcal{BL}(B, M)$. Each time we insert or delete an element from $\mathcal{SL}(M)$, we update the bucket-modulus list accordingly, according to the following rules.

Upon deletion of an element $\mathbf{e}$ in $\mathcal{SL}(M)$, let $\mathbf{e} \cdot \mathbf{a} = T \mod M$, there are three cases for $\mathcal{BL}(B, M)$:

- If $|\{\mathbf{e}' \in \mathcal{SL}(M), \mathbf{e}' \cdot \mathbf{a} = T\}| > B + 1$, then bucket number T in $\mathcal{BL}(B, M)$ stays empty;
- If $|\{\mathbf{e}' \in \mathcal{SL}(M), \mathbf{e}' \cdot \mathbf{a} = T\}| = B + 1$, then removing $\mathbf{e}$ makes the number of elements reach the bound B, so we add them all in the bucket at index T;
- If $|\{\mathbf{e}' \in \mathcal{SL}(M), \mathbf{e}' \cdot \mathbf{a} = T\}| \leq B$, then we remove $\mathbf{e}$ from its bucket.

Upon insertion of an element $\mathbf{e}$ in $\mathcal{SL}(M)$, there are also three cases for $\mathcal{BL}(B, M)$:

- If $|\{\mathbf{e}' \in \mathcal{SL}(M), \mathbf{e}' \cdot \mathbf{a} = T\}| = B$, then we empty the bucket at index T;
- If $|\{\mathbf{e}' \in \mathcal{SL}(M), \mathbf{e}' \cdot \mathbf{a} = T\}| < B$, then we add $\mathbf{e}$ to the bucket at index T in $\mathcal{BL}(B, M)$;
- If $|\{\mathbf{e}' \in \mathcal{SL}(M), \mathbf{e}' \cdot \mathbf{a} = T\}| > B$, then the bucket is empty and remains empty.

In all cases, there are at most B insertions or deletions in a single bucket. Note that $\mathcal{BL}(B, M) \subseteq \mathcal{SL}(M)$ but that some elements of $\mathcal{SL}(M)$ will be dropped.

Remark 9. The mapping from a skip list of size M (considered as perfect), which does not "forget" any of its elements, to a corresponding bucket-modulus list with M buckets, which forgets some of the previous elements, is deterministic. Given a skip list L, a corresponding bucket modulus list L' can be obtained by inserting all elements of L into an empty bucket modulus list.

6.2 New Data Structure for Vertices

The algorithms that we consider use multiple levels of merging. However, we will focus only on a single level. Our arguments can be generalized to any constant number of merges (with an increase in the polynomial factors involved). Recall that the product Johnson graph on which we run the quantum walk is unchanged, only the data structure is adapted.

In the following, we will consider the merging of two lists L_l and L_r of subknapsacks of respective sizes ℓ_l and ℓ_r, with a modular constraint c and a filtering probability pf. The merged list is denoted $L^c = L_l \bowtie_c L_r$ and the filtered list is denoted L^f. We assume that pairs $(\mathbf{e_1}, \mathbf{e_2})$ in L^c must satisfy $(\mathbf{e_1} + \mathbf{e_2}) \cdot \mathbf{a} = 0 \mod 2^{cn}$ (the generalization to any value modulo any moduli is straightforward).

On the positive side, our new data structure can be updated, *by design*, with a fixed time that is data-independent. On the negative side, we will not build the complete list L^f, and miss some of the solutions. As we drop a fraction of the vectors, some nodes that were previously marked will potentially appear unmarked, but this fraction is polynomial at most. We defer a formal proof of this fact to Sect. 6.3 and focus on the runtime.

We will focus on the case where $\ell_l = \ell_r$ and either L_l or L_r are updated, which happens at all levels in our quantum walk, except the first level. Because there is no filtering at the first level, it is actually much simpler to study with the same arguments. In previous quantum walks, we had $\ell^c = 2\ell - c \leq \ell$, *i.e.* $\ell \leq c$; now we will have $2\ell - c \geq \ell$ and $2\ell - c + \mathsf{pf} \leq \ell$.

Recall that our heuristic time complexity analysis assumes an update time $(\ell - c)/2$. Indeed, the update of an element in L_l or L_r modifies on average $(\ell - c)$ elements in $L_l \bowtie_c L_r$, among which we expect at most one filtered pair $(\mathbf{e_1}, \mathbf{e_2})$ (by the inequality $2\ell - c + \mathsf{pf} \leq \ell$). We find this solution with a quantum search. In the following, we modify the data structure of vertices in order to guarantee the best update time possible, up to additional polynomial factors. We will see however that it does not reach $(\ell - c)/2$. We now define our intermediate lists and sublists, before giving the update procedure and its time complexity.

Definitions. Both lists L_l, L_r are of size $M \simeq 2^{\ell n}$. We store them in skip lists. In both L_r and L_l, for each $T \leq M$, we expect on average only one element $\mathbf{e}$ such that $\mathbf{e} \cdot \mathbf{a} = T \mod M$. We introduce two *Bucket-modulus lists* (Definition 6) $L'_l(B, M)$ and $L'_r(B, M)$ that we will write as L'_l and L'_r for simplicity, indexed by $\mathbf{e} \cdot \mathbf{a} \mod M$, with an arbitrary bound $B = \mathrm{poly}(n)$ for the bucket sizes. They are attached to L_l and L_r as detailed in Sect. 6.1. When an element in L_l or L_r is modified, they are modified accordingly.

In L'_l and L'_r, we consider the sublists of subknapsacks having the same modulo $C \mod 2^{cn}$, and we denote by $L'_{l,C}$ and $L'_{r,C}$ these sublists. They can be easily considered separately since the vectors are sorted by knapsack weight. By design of the bucket-modulus lists, $L'_{l,C}$ and $L'_{r,C}$ both have size at most $B2^{(\ell-c)n}$. We have:

$$L'_l \bowtie_c L'_r = \bigcup_{0 \leq C \leq 2^{cn}-1} L'_{l,C} \times L'_{r,C} .$$

Next, we have a case disjunction to make. The most complicated case is when $2\ell - 2c + \mathsf{pf} > 0$, that is, each product $L'_{l,C} \times L'_{r,C}$ for a given C yields more than one filtered pair on average. In that case, we define sublists $L'_{l,C,i}$ of $L'_{l,C}$ and sublists $L'_{r,C,j}$ of $L'_{r,C}$ using a new arbitrary modular constraint, so that each of these sublists is of size $-\mathsf{pf}/2$ (at most). There are $\ell - c + \mathsf{pf}/2$ sublists (exactly). The rationale of this cut is that a product $L'_{l,C,i} \times L'_{r,C,j}$ for a given i,j now yields on average a single filtered pair (or less). When $2\ell - 2c + \mathsf{pf} \leq 0$, we don't perform this last cut and consider the product $L'_{l,C} \times L'_{r,C}$ immediately. By a slight abuse of notation, we denote: $(L'_{l,C,i} \times L'_{r,C,j})^f$ the set of filtered pairs from $L'_{l,C,i} \times L'_{r,C,j}$, and we have:

$$L^f = \bigcup_{0 \leq C \leq 2^{cn}-1} \bigcup_{i,j} (L'_{l,C,i} \times L'_{r,C,j})^f .$$

Algorithm 1. Update algorithm: given L_l, L_r of size ℓ, we insert or delete an element in L_l and update the filtered list L^f accordingly. We focus here on the case $2\ell - 2c + \mathsf{pf} > 0$.

Data: skip lists for L_l, L_r, L^f, bucket-modulus lists L'_l, L'_r
1:   ▷ The bucket-modulus list for L^f will be updated later
Input: an insertion/deletion instruction for L_l
Output: updates L_l, L'_l, L^f accordingly
2: Insert or delete in L_l ▷ only one element to update
3: Update the bucket-modulus structure L'_l ▷ at most B elements to update
4: **for** each element **e** to insert/delete in L'_l **do**   ▷ $B = \mathrm{poly}(n)$ iterations
5:     Select its corresponding sublist $L'_{l,C,i}$
6:     Let $L''_{l,C,i} = L'_{l,C,i} \cup \{e\}$ or $L'_{l,C,i} \backslash \{e\}$
7:     **for** each sublist $L'_{r,C,j}$ **do**   ▷ $\ell - c + \mathsf{pf}/2$ iterations
8:         Estimate $s = |(L'_{l,C,i} \times L'_{r,C,j})^f|$ ▷ time $\widetilde{\mathcal{O}}\left(B \times 2^{-\mathsf{pf}n/2}\right)$
9:         Estimate $s' = |(L''_{l,C,i} \times L'_{r,C,j})^f|$ ▷ time $\widetilde{\mathcal{O}}\left(B \times 2^{-\mathsf{pf}n/2}\right)$
                              ▷ In the case of an insertion, $s' \geq s$ and $s' \leq s$ for a deletion
10:        **if** $s > B$ and $s' \leq B$
                    ▷ The removal of **e** makes the number of filtered pairs acceptable
11:            **then** $L^f \leftarrow L^f \cup (L''_{l,C,i} \times L'_{r,C,j})^f$
12:        **if** $s > B$ and $s' > B$
13:            **then** do nothing
14:        **if** $s \leq B$ and $s' > B$
                              ▷ The insertion of **e** overflows the filtered pairs
15:            **then** remove all $(L'_{l,C,i} \times L'_{r,C,j})^f$ from L^f
16:        **if** $s \leq B$ and $s' \leq B$
17:            **then** update L^f with the (at most) B new or removed pairs
18:    **end for**
19: **end for**

Algorithm and Complexity. Algorithm 1 details our update procedure. We now compute its time complexity and explain why it remains data-independent.

Recall that we want to avoid the "bad cases" where an update goes on for too long: this is the case where an update in L_l (or L_r) creates too many updates in L^f. In Algorithm 1, we avoid this by deliberately limiting the number of elements that can be updated. We can see that L^f will be smaller than the "perfect" one for two reasons: • the bucket-modulus data structure loses some vectors, since the buckets are dropped when they overflow. • filtered pairs are lost. Indeed, the algorithm ensures that in L^f, at most B solutions $\mathbf{e}_l + \mathbf{e}_r$ come from a cross-product $L'_{l,C,i} \times L'_{r,C,j}$.

This makes the update procedure *history-independent* and its time complexity *data-independent*. Indeed:

Lemma 5. *The state of the data structures L_l, L_r, L^f after Algorithm 1 depends only on L_l, L_r, L^f before and on the element that was inserted/deleted.*

We omit a formal proof, as it follows from our definition of the bucket-modulus list and of Algorithm 1.

Lemma 6. *With a good choice of B, Algorithm 1 runs with a data-independent error in $o(2^n)$. The time complexity of Algorithm 1 is $\widetilde{\mathcal{O}}\left(2^{(\ell-c)n}\right)$ and an update modifies $\widetilde{\mathcal{O}}\left(2^{\max(\ell-c+\mathsf{pf}/2,0)n}\right)$ elements in the filtered list L^f at the next level (respectively $\ell - c$ and $\max(\ell - c + \mathsf{pf}/2, 0)$ in log scale).*

Proof. We check step by step the time complexity of Algorithm 1:

- Insertion and deletion from the skip list for L_l is done in $\mathrm{poly}(n)$, with a global error that can be omitted.
- The bucket-modulus list L'_l is updated in time $\mathcal{O}(B) = \mathrm{poly}(n)$ without errors. At most B elements must be inserted or removed.
- For each insertion or removal in L'_l, we select the corresponding sublist $L'_{l,C,i}$ (or simply $L'_{l,C}$ if $2\ell - 2c + \mathsf{pf} \leq 0$). We look at the sublists $L'_{r,C,j}$ and we estimate the number of filtered pairs in the products $L'_{l,C,i} \times L'_{r,C,j}$ (of size $-\mathsf{pf}$), checking whether it is smaller or bigger than B. We explain in [8, Appendix C] how to do that reversibly in time $\widetilde{\mathcal{O}}\left(B \times 2^{-\mathsf{pf}n/2}\right)$ ($-\mathsf{pf}/2$ in log scale). There are $\ell - c + \mathsf{pf}/2$ classical iterations, thus the total time is $\ell - c$.
- Depending whether we have found more or less than B filtered pairs, we will have to remove or to add all of them in L^f. This means that $B \times 2^{(\ell-c+\mathsf{pf}/2)n}$ insertion or deletion instructions will be passed over to L^f.

There are two sources of data-independent errors: first, the skip list data structure (see Sect. 6.1). Second, the procedure of [8, Appendix C]. Both can be made exponentially small at the price of a polynomial overhead. Note that B will be set in order to get a sufficiently small probability of error (see the next section), and can be a global $\mathcal{O}(n)$. However, the polynomial overhead of our update unitary grows with the number of levels. □

6.3   Fraction of Marked Vertices

Now that we have computed the update time of NEW-QW, it remains to compute its fraction ϵ_{new} of marked vertices. We will show that $\epsilon_{new} = \epsilon \left(1 - \frac{1}{\text{poly}(n)}\right)$ with overwhelming probability on the random subset-sum instance, where ϵ is the previous fraction in QW.

Consider a marked vertex in QW. There is a path in the data structure leading to the solution, hence a constant number of subknapsacks $\mathbf{e}_1, \dots, \mathbf{e}_t$ such that the vertex will remain marked *if and only* if none of them is "accidentally" discarded by our new data structure. Thus, if G is the graph of the walk, we want to upper bound:

$$\Pr_{v \in G} \left(\begin{array}{c} v \text{ is marked in QW and} \\ \text{not marked in NEW-QW} \end{array} \right) \leq \sum_{\mathbf{e}_i, 1 \leq i \leq t} \Pr_{v \in G} \left(\begin{array}{c} \mathbf{e}_i \in v \text{ in QW} \\ \mathbf{e}_i \notin v \text{ in NEW-QW} \end{array} \right).$$

We focus on some level in the tree, on a list L of average size $2^{\ell n}$, and on a single vector $\mathbf{e}_0$ that must appear in L. Subknapsacks in L are taken from $\mathcal{B} \subseteq D^n[\alpha, \beta, \gamma]$. We study the event that $\mathbf{e}_0$ is accidentally discarded from L. This can happen for two reasons:

- we have $|\{\mathbf{e} \in L, \mathbf{e} \cdot \mathbf{a} = \mathbf{e}_0 \cdot \mathbf{a} \mod 2^{\ell n}\}| > B$: the vector is dropped at the bucket-modulus level;
- at the next level, there are more than B pairs from some product of lists $L'_{l,C,i} \times L'_{r,C,j}$ to which the vector $\mathbf{e}_0$ belongs, that will pass the filter.

We remark the following to make our computations easier.

Fact 3. *We can replace the L from our new data structure NEW-QW by a list of exact size $2^{\ell n}$, which is a sublist from the list L in QW.*

At successive levels, our new data structure discards more and more vectors. Hence, the actual lists are smaller than in QW. However, removing a vector $\mathbf{e}$ from a list, if it does not unmark the vertex, does not increase the probability of unmarking it at the next level, since $\mathbf{e}$ does not belong to the unique solution.

Fact 4. *When a vertex in NEW-QW is sampled uniformly at random, given a list L at some merging level, we can assume that the elements of L are sampled uniformly at random from their distribution $\mathcal{B}$ (with a modular constraint).*

This fact translates Heuristic 1 as a global property of the Johnson graph. At the first level, nodes contain lists of exponential size which are sampled without replacement. However, when sampling with replacement, the probability of collisions is exponentially low. Thus, we can replace $\Pr_{v \in G}$ by $\Pr_{v \in G'}$ where G' is a "completed" graph containing all lists sampled uniformly at random with replacement. This adds only a negligible number of vertices and does not impact the probability of being discarded.

Number of Vectors Having the Same Modulus. Let $N \simeq 2^n$ and M be a divisor of N. Given a particular $\mathbf{e}_0 \in \mathcal{B}$ and a vector $\mathbf{a} \in \mathbb{Z}_N^n$,

$$\text{For } \mathbf{e} \in \mathcal{B}, \text{ define } X_{\mathbf{e}}(a) = \begin{cases} 1 & \text{if } \mathbf{e} \cdot \mathbf{a} = \mathbf{e}_0 \cdot \mathbf{a} \pmod{M} \\ 0 & \text{otherwise} \end{cases}$$

We prove the following Lemma in the full version of the paper [8].

Lemma 7. *If* $|\mathcal{B}| \gg M \simeq |L|$, *then for a* $1 - \text{negl}(n)$ *proportion of* $\mathbf{a} \in \mathbb{Z}_N^n$, *and with an appropriate* $B = \mathcal{O}(n)$:

$$\Pr_{\mathbf{e}_1,\cdots,\mathbf{e}_{|L|} \sim Unif(\mathcal{B})} \left[\sum_{i=1}^{|L|} X_{\mathbf{e}_i}(\mathbf{a}) < B - 1 \right] > 1 - \frac{1}{\text{poly}(n)} \tag{1}$$

For the number of filtered pairs, we use the fact that the vectors at each level are sampled uniformly at random from their distribution. If this is the case, then a Chernoff bound (similar to the proof of Lemma 7) limits the deviation of the number of filtered pairs in $L'_{l,C,i} \times L'_{r,C,j}$ from its expectation (which is 1 by construction): the probability that there are more than $B + 1$ pairs is smaller than $e^{-(B+1)/3}$. By taking a sufficiently big $B = \mathcal{O}(n)$, we can take a union bound over all products of lists $L'_{l,C,i} \times L'_{r,C,j}$ in which $\mathbf{e}_0$ intervenes. We also take a union bound over the intermediate subknapsacks that we are considering. The loss of vertices remains inverse polynomial.

6.4 Time Complexities Without Heuristic 2

Previous quantum subset-sum algorithms [6,18] have the same time complexities without Heuristic 2, as they fall in parameter ranges where the bucket-modulus data structure is enough. However, this is not the case of our new quantum walk. We keep the same set of constraints and optimize with a new update time. Although using the extended $\{-1, 0, 1, 2\}$ representations brings an improvement, neither do the fifth level, nor the left-right split. This simplifies our constraints. Let $\widehat{\max}(\cdot) = \max(\cdot, 0)$. The guaranteed update time becomes:

$$\mathsf{U} = \widehat{\max}\Big(\underbrace{\ell_3 - (c_2 - c_3)}_{\text{Level 2}}, \underbrace{\widehat{\max}(\ell_3 - (c_2 - c_3) + \frac{p_2}{2}) + \widehat{\max}(\ell_2 - (c_1 - c_2))}_{\substack{\text{Number of elements} \\ \text{to update at level 1}}},$$

$$\underbrace{\frac{1}{2}\Big(\widehat{\max}\Big(\ell_3 - (c_2 - c_3) + \frac{p_2}{2}\Big) + \widehat{\max}\Big(\ell_2 - (c_1 - c_2) + \frac{p_1}{2}\Big) + \widehat{\max}(\ell_1 - (1 - c_1))\Big)}_{\text{Final quantum search among all updated elements}} \Big)$$

We obtain the time exponent 0.2182 (rounded upwards) with the following parameters (rounded). The memory exponent is 0.2182 as well.

$$\ell_0 = -0.2021, \ell_1 = 0.1883, \ell_2 = 0.2102, \ell_3 = 0.2182, \ell_4 = 0.2182$$
$$c_3 = 0.2182, c_2 = 0.4283, c_1 = 0.6305, p_0 = -0.2093, p_1 = -0.0298, p_2 = -0.0160$$
$$\alpha_1 = 0.0172, \alpha_2 = 0.0145, \alpha_3 = 0.0107, \gamma_1 = 0.0020$$

7   Conclusion

In this paper, we proposed improved classical and quantum heuristic algorithms for subset-sum, building upon several new ideas. First, we used extended representations ($\{-1, 0, 1, 2\}$) to improve the current best classical and quantum algorithms. In the quantum setting, we showed how to use a quantum search to speed up the process of *filtering* representations, leading to an overall improvement on existing work. We built an "asymmetric HGJ" algorithm that uses a nested quantum search, leading to the first quantum speedup on subset-sum in the model of *classical memory with quantum random access*. By combining all our ideas, we obtained the best quantum walk algorithm for subset-sum in the MNRS framework. Although its complexity still relies on Heuristic 2, we showed how to partially overcome it and obtained the first quantum walk that requires only the classical subset-sum heuristic, and the best to date for this problem.

Open Questions. We leave as open the possibility to use representations with "−1"s (or even "2"s) in a quantum asymmetric merging tree, as in Sect. 4.3. Another question is how to bridge the gap between heuristic and non-heuristic quantum walk complexities. In our work, the use of an improved vertex data structure seems to encounter a limitation, and we may need a more generic result on quantum walks, similar to [2]. Finally, it would be of interest to study representations with a larger set of integers.

Acknowledgments. The authors want to thank André Chailloux, Stacey Jeffery, Antoine Joux, Frédéric Magniez, Alexander May, Amaury Pouly, Nicolas Sendrier for helpful discussions and comments. Thanks to Zhenzhen Bao and the anonymous CRYPTO and ASIACRYPT referees for their detailed comments. This project has received funding from the European Research Council (ERC) under the European Union's Horizon 2020 research and innovation programme (grant agreement no. 714294 - acronym QUASYModo). Research also supported in part by the ERA-NET Cofund in Quantum Technologies project QuantAlgo and the French ANR Blanc project RDAM.

References

1. Ambainis, A.: Quantum walk algorithm for element distinctness. SIAM J. Comput. **37**(1), 210–239 (2007)
2. Ambainis, A.: Quantum search with variable times. Theory Comput. Syst. **47**(3), 786–807 (2010)
3. Becker, A., Coron, J.-S., Joux, A.: Improved generic algorithms for hard knapsacks. In: Paterson, K.G. (ed.) EUROCRYPT 2011. LNCS, vol. 6632, pp. 364–385. Springer, Heidelberg (2011). https://doi.org/10.1007/978-3-642-20465-4_21
4. Becker, A., Joux, A., May, A., Meurer, A.: Decoding random binary linear codes in $2^{n/20}$: how $1 + 1 = 0$ improves information set decoding. In: Pointcheval, D., Johansson, T. (eds.) EUROCRYPT 2012. LNCS, vol. 7237, pp. 520–536. Springer, Heidelberg (2012). https://doi.org/10.1007/978-3-642-29011-4_31
5. Bennett, C.H., Bernstein, E., Brassard, G., Vazirani, U.V.: Strengths and weaknesses of quantum computing. SIAM J. Comput. **26**(5), 1510–1523 (1997)

6. Bernstein, D.J., Jeffery, S., Lange, T., Meurer, A.: Quantum algorithms for the subset-sum problem. In: Gaborit, P. (ed.) PQCrypto 2013. LNCS, vol. 7932, pp. 16–33. Springer, Heidelberg (2013). https://doi.org/10.1007/978-3-642-38616-9_2
7. Bonnetain, X.: Improved low-qubit hidden shift algorithms. CoRR (2019)
8. Bonnetain, X., Bricout, R., Schrottenloher, A., Shen, Y.: Improved classical and quantum algorithms for subset-sum. IACR Cryptol. ePrint Arch., vol. 168 (2020). https://eprint.iacr.org/2020/168
9. Bonnetain, X., Naya-Plasencia, M.: Hidden shift quantum cryptanalysis and implications. In: Peyrin, T., Galbraith, S. (eds.) ASIACRYPT 2018. LNCS, vol. 11272, pp. 560–592. Springer, Cham (2018). https://doi.org/10.1007/978-3-030-03326-2_19
10. Bonnetain, X., Naya-Plasencia, M., Schrottenloher, A.: Quantum security analysis of AES. IACR Trans. Symmetric Cryptol. **2019**(2), 55–93 (2019)
11. Bonnetain, X., Schrottenloher, A.: Quantum security analysis of CSIDH. In: Canteaut, A., Ishai, Y. (eds.) EUROCRYPT 2020. LNCS, vol. 12106, pp. 493–522. Springer, Cham (2020). https://doi.org/10.1007/978-3-030-45724-2_17
12. Brassard, G., Hoyer, P., Mosca, M., Tapp, A.: Quantum amplitude amplification and estimation. Contemp. Math. **305**, 53–74 (2002)
13. Bricout, R., Chailloux, A., Debris-Alazard, T., Lequesne, M.: Ternary syndrome decoding with large weight. In: Paterson, K.G., Stebila, D. (eds.) SAC 2019. LNCS, vol. 11959, pp. 437–466. Springer, Cham (2020). https://doi.org/10.1007/978-3-030-38471-5_18
14. Böhme, E.: Verbesserte Subset-Sum Algorithmen. Master's thesis, Ruhr Universität Bochum (2011)
15. Esser, A., May, A.: Better sample - random subset sum in $2^{0.255n}$ and its impact on decoding random linear codes. CoRR abs/1907.04295 (2019), withdrawn
16. Garey, M.R., Johnson, D.S.: Computers and Intractability: A Guide to the Theory of NP-Completeness. Freeman, W.H. (1979)
17. Grover, L.K.: A fast quantum mechanical algorithm for database search. In: Proceedings of the Twenty-Eighth Annual ACM Symposium on the Theory of Computing 1996, pp. 212–219. ACM (1996)
18. Helm, A., May, A.: Subset sum quantumly in 1.17^n. In: TQC. LIPIcs, vol. 111, pp. 5:1–5:15. Schloss Dagstuhl - Leibniz-Zentrum fuer Informatik (2018)
19. Helm, A., May, A.: The power of few qubits and collisions – subset sum below Grover's bound. In: Ding, J., Tillich, J.-P. (eds.) PQCrypto 2020. LNCS, vol. 12100, pp. 445–460. Springer, Cham (2020). https://doi.org/10.1007/978-3-030-44223-1_24
20. Horowitz, E., Sahni, S.: Computing partitions with applications to the knapsack problem. J. ACM **21**(2), 277–292 (1974)
21. Howgrave-Graham, N., Joux, A.: New generic algorithms for hard knapsacks. In: Gilbert, H. (ed.) EUROCRYPT 2010. LNCS, vol. 6110, pp. 235–256. Springer, Heidelberg (2010). https://doi.org/10.1007/978-3-642-13190-5_12
22. Kachigar, G., Tillich, J.-P.: Quantum information set decoding algorithms. In: Lange, T., Takagi, T. (eds.) PQCrypto 2017. LNCS, vol. 10346, pp. 69–89. Springer, Cham (2017). https://doi.org/10.1007/978-3-319-59879-6_5
23. Kirshanova, E., Mårtensson, E., Postlethwaite, E.W., Moulik, S.R.: Quantum algorithms for the approximate k-list problem and their application to lattice sieving. In: Galbraith, S.D., Moriai, S. (eds.) ASIACRYPT 2019. LNCS, vol. 11921, pp. 521–551. Springer, Cham (2019). https://doi.org/10.1007/978-3-030-34578-5_19

24. Kuperberg, G.: Another subexponential-time quantum algorithm for the dihedral hidden subgroup problem. In: TQC. LIPIcs, vol. 22, pp. 20–34. Schloss Dagstuhl - Leibniz-Zentrum fuer Informatik (2013)

25. Laarhoven, T.: Search problems in cryptography. Ph.D. thesis, PhD thesis, Eindhoven University of Technology (2015)

26. Laarhoven, T., Mosca, M., van de Pol, J.: Finding shortest lattice vectors faster using quantum search. Des. Codes Cryptogr. **77**(2–3), 375–400 (2015)

27. Lagarias, J.C., Odlyzko, A.M.: Solving low-density subset sum problems. In: FOCS, pp. 1–10. IEEE Computer Society (1983)

28. Lyubashevsky, V.: The parity problem in the presence of noise, decoding random linear codes, and the subset sum problem. In: Chekuri, C., Jansen, K., Rolim, J.D.P., Trevisan, L. (eds.) APPROX/RANDOM -2005. LNCS, vol. 3624, pp. 378–389. Springer, Heidelberg (2005). https://doi.org/10.1007/11538462_32

29. Lyubashevsky, V., Palacio, A., Segev, G.: Public-key cryptographic primitives provably as secure as subset sum. In: Micciancio, D. (ed.) TCC 2010. LNCS, vol. 5978, pp. 382–400. Springer, Heidelberg (2010). https://doi.org/10.1007/978-3-642-11799-2_23

30. Magniez, F., Nayak, A., Roland, J., Santha, M.: Search via quantum walk. SIAM J. Comput. **40**(1), 142–164 (2011)

31. May, A., Meurer, A., Thomae, E.: Decoding Random Linear Codes in $\tilde{\mathcal{O}}(2^{0.054n})$. In: Lee, D.H., Wang, X. (eds.) ASIACRYPT 2011. LNCS, vol. 7073, pp. 107–124. Springer, Heidelberg (2011). https://doi.org/10.1007/978-3-642-25385-0_6

32. May, A., Ozerov, I.: On computing nearest neighbors with applications to decoding of binary linear codes. In: Oswald, E., Fischlin, M. (eds.) EUROCRYPT 2015. LNCS, vol. 9056, pp. 203–228. Springer, Heidelberg (2015). https://doi.org/10.1007/978-3-662-46800-5_9

33. Naya-Plasencia, M., Schrottenloher, A.: Optimal merging in quantum k-xor and k-sum algorithms. In: Canteaut, A., Ishai, Y. (eds.) EUROCRYPT 2020. LNCS, vol. 12106, pp. 311–340. Springer, Cham (2020). https://doi.org/10.1007/978-3-030-45724-2_11

34. Newman, D.J., Shepp, L.: The double dixie cup problem. Am. Math. Mon. **67**(1), 58–61 (1960)

35. Nielsen, M.A., Chuang, I.: Quantum computation and quantum information (2002)

36. Ozerov, I.: Combinatorial Algorithms for Subset Sum Problems. Ph.D. thesis, Ruhr Universität Bochum (2016)

37. Schroeppel, R., Shamir, A.: A $T = O(2^{n/2})$, $S = O(2^{n/4})$ algorithm for certain NP-complete problems. SIAM J. Comput. **10**(3), 456–464 (1981)

Security Limitations of Classical-Client Delegated Quantum Computing

Christian Badertscher[1] , Alexandru Cojocaru[2] , Léo Colisson[3](✉) ,
Elham Kashefi[2,3], Dominik Leichtle[3] , Atul Mantri[4], and Petros Wallden[2]

[1] IOHK, Zurich, Switzerland
christian.badertscher@iohk.io
[2] School of Informatics, University of Edinburgh,
10 Crichton Street, Edinburgh EH8 9AB, UK
a.d.cojocaru@sms.ed.ac.uk, ekashefi@inf.ed.ac.uk, petros.wallden@ed.ac.uk
[3] Laboratoire d'Informatique de Paris 6 (LIP6), Sorbonne Université,
4 Place Jussieu, 75252 Paris CEDEX 05, France
{leo.colisson,dominik.leichtle}@lip6.fr
[4] Joint Center for Quantum Information and Computer Science (QuICS),
University of Maryland, College Park, USA
amantri@umd.edu

Abstract. Secure delegated quantum computing allows a computationally weak client to outsource an arbitrary quantum computation to an
untrusted quantum server in a privacy-preserving manner. One of the
promising candidates to achieve classical delegation of quantum computation is classical-client remote state preparation ($\mathsf{RSP_{CC}}$), where a client
remotely prepares a quantum state using a classical channel. However,
the privacy loss incurred by employing $\mathsf{RSP_{CC}}$ as a sub-module is unclear.
In this work, we investigate this question using the Constructive Cryptography framework by Maurer and Renner [MR11]. We first identify
the goal of $\mathsf{RSP_{CC}}$ as the construction of ideal RSP resources from classical channels and then reveal the security limitations of using $\mathsf{RSP_{CC}}$.
First, we uncover a fundamental relationship between constructing ideal
RSP resources (from classical channels) and the task of cloning quantum states. Any classically constructed ideal RSP resource must leak to
the server the full classical description (possibly in an encoded form) of
the generated quantum state, even if we target computational security
only. As a consequence, we find that the realization of common RSP
resources, without weakening their guarantees drastically, is impossible
due to the no-cloning theorem. Second, the above result does not rule
out that a specific $\mathsf{RSP_{CC}}$ protocol can replace the quantum channel at
least in some contexts, such as the Universal Blind Quantum Computing (UBQC) protocol of Broadbent et al. [BFK09]. However, we show
that the resulting UBQC protocol cannot maintain its proven composable security as soon as $\mathsf{RSP_{CC}}$ is used as a subroutine. Third, we show
that replacing the quantum channel of the above UBQC protocol by the
$\mathsf{RSP_{CC}}$ protocol QFactory of Cojocaru et al. [CCKW19] preserves the
weaker, game-based, security of UBQC.

© International Association for Cryptologic Research 2020
S. Moriai and H. Wang (Eds.): ASIACRYPT 2020, LNCS 12492, pp. 667–696, 2020.
https://doi.org/10.1007/978-3-030-64834-3_23

Keywords: Remote state preparation · Blind quantum computing

1   Introduction

The expected rapid advances in quantum technologies in the decades to come are likely to further disrupt the field of computing. To fully realize the technological potential, remote access, and manipulation of data must offer strong privacy and integrity guarantees and currently available quantum cloud platform designs have still a lot of room for improvement.

There is a large body of research that exploits the client-server setting defined in [Chi05] to offer different functionalities, including secure delegated quantum computation [BFK09, MF13, DFPR14, Bro15a, Mah18a, Fit17], verifiable delegated quantum computation [ABOE08, RUV12, FK17, HM15, Bro15b, FHM18, TMM+18, Mah18b, GKK19, Vid20], secure multiparty quantum computation [KP17, KMW17, KW17], and quantum fully homomorphic encryption [BJ15, DSS16]. It turns out that one of the central building blocks for most of these protocols is secure *remote state preparation* (RSP) that was first defined in [DKL12]. At a high level, RSP resources enable a client to remotely prepare a quantum state on the server side and are, therefore, the natural candidate to replace quantum channel resources in a modular fashion. These resources further appear to enable a large ecosystem of composable protocols [DKL12, DFPR14], including in particular the *Universal Blind Quantum Computation* (UBQC) [BFK09] protocol used to delegate a computation to a remote quantum server who has no knowledge of the ongoing computation.

However, in most of the above-mentioned works, the users and providers do have access to quantum resources to achieve their goals, in particular to quantum channels in addition to classical communication channels. This might prove to be challenging for some quantum devices, e.g. those with superconducting qubits, and in general, it also restricts the use of these quantum cloud services to users with suitable quantum technology.

Motivated by these practical constraints, [CCKW18] introduced a protocol mimicking this remote state preparation resource over a purely *classical* channel (under the assumption that the learning-with-error (LWE) problem is computationally hard for quantum servers). This is a cryptographic primitive between a fully classical client and a server (with a quantum computer). By the end of the interactive protocol the client has "prepared" remotely on the server's lab, a quantum state (typically a single qubit $|+_\theta\rangle := \frac{1}{\sqrt{2}}(|0\rangle + e^{i\theta}|1\rangle)$). This protocol further enjoys some important privacy guarantees concerning the prepared state. The important role of such a classical RSP primitive as part of larger protocols – most notably in their role in replacing quantum channels between client and server – stems from their ability to make the aforementioned protocols available to classical users, in particular clients without quantum-capable infrastructure on their end. It is therefore of utmost importance to develop an understanding of this primitive, notably its security guarantees when composed in larger contexts such as in [GV19].

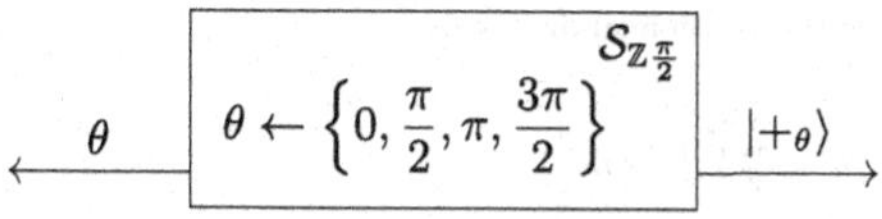

Fig. 1. Ideal resource $\mathcal{S}_{\mathbb{Z}_{\frac{\pi}{2}}}$

In this paper, we initiate the study of analyzing classical remote state-preparation from first principles. We thereby follow the Constructive Cryptography (CC) framework [MR11,Mau11] to provide a clean treatment of the RSP primitive from a composable perspective. (Note that the framework is also referred to as Abstract Cryptography (AC) in earlier works.) Armed with such a definition, we then investigate the limitations and possibilities of using classical RSP both in general and in more specific contexts.

1.1 Overview of Our Contributions

In this work, we cover the security of RSP$_\mathsf{CC}$, the class of remote state preparation protocols which only use a classical channel, and the use-case that corresponds to its arguably most important application: Universal Blind Quantum Computing (UBQC) protocols with a completely classical client. The UBQC protocol can be divided in two stages: first, the client needs to send random $|+_\theta\rangle$ (with $\theta \in \{0, \frac{\pi}{4}, \ldots, \frac{7\pi}{4}\}$) to the server, and after this initial quantum interaction, the communication is purely classical. In this work, we analyze the security of UBQC$_\mathsf{CC}$, the family of protocols where a protocol in RSP$_\mathsf{CC}$ is used to replace the initial quantum interaction from the original quantum-client UBQC protocol. An example of an RSP resource is the $\mathcal{S}_{\mathbb{Z}_{\frac{\pi}{2}}}$ resource where $\mathbb{Z}_{\pi/2} = \{0, \pi/2, \pi, 3\pi/2\}$ depicted in Fig. 1 outputting the quantum state $|+_\theta\rangle$ on its right interface, and the classical description of this state, θ, on its left interface.

In Sect. 3, we show a wide-ranging limitation to the universally composable guarantees that any protocol in the family RSP$_\mathsf{CC}$ can achieve. The limitation follows just from the relation between (i) the notion of classical realization and (ii) a property we call describability – which roughly speaking measures how leaky an RSP resource is, i.e. what amount of information about the classical description of the final state can be extracted by an unbounded malicious server. We emphasize that even if this specific property is an information-theoretic notion, our final impossibility result also targets computational security. The limitation directly affects the amount of additional leakage on the classical description of the quantum state. In this way, it rules out a wide set of desirable resources, even against computationally bounded distinguishers.

Theorem 1 (Security Limitations of RSP$_\mathsf{CC}$). *Any RSP resource, realizable by an RSP$_\mathsf{CC}$ protocol with security against quantum polynomial-time distinguishers, must leak an encoded, but complete description of the generated quantum state to the server.*

The importance of Theorem 1 lies in the fact that it is drawing a connection between the composability of an RSP$_\mathsf{CC}$ protocol – a *computational* notion

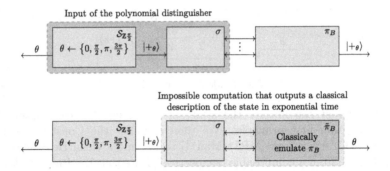

Fig. 2. Idea of the proof of impossibility of composable RSP$_{CC}$, exemplified by the $\mathcal{S}_{\mathbb{Z}\frac{\pi}{2}}$ primitive from Fig. 1. $\tilde{\pi}_B$ runs the same computations as π_B by emulating it. In this way, the classical description of the quantum state can be extracted.

– with the statistical leakage of the ideal functionality it is constructing – an *information-theoretic* notion. This allows us to use fundamental physical principles such as no-cloning or no-signaling in the security analysis of *computationally* secure RSP$_{CC}$ protocols. As one direct application of this powerful tool, we show that secure implementations of the ideal resource in Fig. 1 give rise to the construction of a quantum cloner, and are hence impossible.

Proof Sketch. While Theorem 1 applies to much more general RSP resources having arbitrary behavior at its interfaces and targeting any output quantum state, for simplicity we exemplify the main ideas of our proof for the ideal resource $\mathcal{S}_{\mathbb{Z}\frac{\pi}{2}}$. The composable security of a protocol realizing $\mathcal{S}_{\mathbb{Z}\frac{\pi}{2}}$ implies, by definition, the existence of a simulator σ which turns the right interface of the ideal resource into a completely classical interface as depicted in Fig. 2. Running the protocol of the honest server with access to this classical interface allows the distinguisher to reconstruct the quantum state $|+_\theta\rangle$ the simulator received from the ideal resource. Since the distinguisher also has access to θ via the left interface of the ideal resource, it can perform a simple measurement to verify the consistency of the state obtained after interacting with the simulator. By the correctness of the protocol, the obtained quantum state $|+_\theta\rangle$ must therefore indeed comply with θ. We emphasize that this consistency check can be performed efficiently, i.e. by *polynomially-bounded* quantum distinguishers.

Since the quantum state, $|+_\theta\rangle$, is transmitted from σ to the distinguisher over a classical channel, the ensemble of exchanged classical messages must contain a complete encoding of the description of the state, θ. A (possibly computationally unbounded) algorithm can hence extract the actual description of the state using a classical emulation of the honest server. This property of the ideal resource is central to our proof technique, we call it *describability*.   □

Having a full description of the quantum state produced by $\mathcal{S}_{\mathbb{Z}\frac{\pi}{2}}$ would allow us to clone it, a procedure prohibited by the no-cloning theorem. We conclude that the resource $\mathcal{S}_{\mathbb{Z}\frac{\pi}{2}}$ cannot be constructed from a classical channel only.

One could attempt to modify the ideal resource, to incorporate such an extensive leakage, which is necessary as the above proof implies. However, this yields an ideal resource that is not a useful idealization or abstraction of the real world (because it is fully leaky, i.e. reveals to a malicious server the full classical description of the state) which puts in question whether they are at all useful in a composable analysis. Indeed, ideal resources are typically described in a way that it is obvious that they are secure (i.e. in a perfect, ideal sense), and we can then claim that a protocol is secure because it is (for any computationally bounded distinguisher) indistinguishable from the perfectly secure resource. Consider for example constructions of composite protocols that utilize a (non-leaky) ideal resource as a sub-module, say that leaks only the size of an encrypted message. These constructions require a fresh security analysis if the sub-module is replaced by any leaky version of it (like a resource leaking a specific encrypted form of the real message), but since the modified resource is very specific and not trivially secure, it appears that this replacement does not give any benefit compared to directly using the implementation as a subroutine and then examining the composable security of the combined protocol as a whole. This latter way is therefore examined next.

More precisely, we might still be able to use $\mathsf{RSP_{CC}}$ protocols as a subroutine in other, specific protocols, and expect the overall protocol to still construct a useful ideal functionality. The protocol family $\mathsf{UBQC_{CC}}$ is such an application. Unfortunately, as we show in Sect. 4, $\mathsf{UBQC_{CC}}$ fails to provide the expected composable security guarantees once classical remote state preparation is used to replace the quantum channel from client to server (where composable security for UBQC refers to the goal of achieving the established ideal functionality of [DFPR14] which we recall in Sect. 4). This holds even if the distinguisher is computationally bounded.

Theorem 3 (Impossibility of $\mathsf{UBQC_{CC}}$). *No $\mathsf{RSP_{CC}}$ protocol can replace the quantum channel in the UBQC protocol while preserving composable security.*

Proof Sketch. To prove the impossibility of $\mathsf{UBQC_{CC}}$ protocol we show that there does not exist any simulator that can be attached to the ideal UBQC functionality to emulate the behavior of concrete $\mathsf{UBQC_{CC}}$ protocol. This $\mathsf{UBQC_{CC}}$ uses any $\mathsf{RSP_{CC}}$ protocol as a subroutine in the UBQC protocol of [BFK09] to enable the delegation of quantum computation with a completely classical-client. The proof proceeds in three steps. Firstly, we realize that the possibility of a composable $\mathsf{UBQC_{CC}}$ protocol, which delegates arbitrary quantum computation, can be reduced to the possibility of any composable $\mathsf{UBQC_{CC}}$ protocol that delegates single-qubit quantum computation. The latter protocol is much simpler to analyze. Next, we present a connection between the single-qubit $\mathsf{UBQC_{CC}}$ and the RSP functionality. This step allows us to employ the toolbox we developed for our previous result (Theorem 1). Finally, we show that the existence of a simulator for such an RSP functionality (that leaks the classical description, even in the form of an encoded message) would violate the no-signaling principle. Therefore, via this series of reduction, we show that the UBQC functionality, as defined in [DFPR14], cannot be realized with only a classical channel by any $\mathsf{UBQC_{CC}}$ protocol of this kind (the one which uses RSP functionality to replace quantum channel in UBQC protocol). □

In Sect. 5, we show that the protocol family $\mathsf{RSP_{CC}}$ contains protocols with reasonably restricted leakage that can be used as subroutines in specific applications resulting in combined protocols that offer a decent level of security. Specifically, we prove the blindness property of QF-UBQC, a concrete $\mathsf{UBQC_{CC}}$ protocol that consists of the universal blind quantum computation (UBQC) protocol of [BFK09] and the specific LWE-based remote state preparation ($\mathsf{RSP_{CC}}$) protocol from [CCKW19]. This yields the first provably secure $\mathsf{UBQC_{CC}}$ protocol from standard assumptions with a classical RSP protocol as a subroutine.

Theorem 4 (Game-Based Security of QF-UBQC). *The universal blind quantum computation protocol with a classical client* $\mathsf{UBQC_{CC}}$ *that combines the* $\mathsf{RSP_{CC}}$ *protocol of* [CCKW19] *and the* UBQC *protocol of* [BFK09] *is blind in the game-based setting. We call this protocol* QF-UBQC.

The statement of Theorem 4 can be summarized as follows: No malicious (but computationally bounded) server in the QF-UBQC protocol could distinguish between two runs of the protocol performing different computations. This holds even when it is the adversary that chooses the two computations that it will be asked to distinguish. The security is achieved in the plain model, i.e., without relying on additional setup such as a measurement buffer. The protocol itself is a combination of UBQC with the QFactory protocol. For every qubit that the client would transmit to the server in the original UBQC protocol, QFactory is invoked as a subprocedure to the end of remotely preparing the respective qubit state on the server over a classical channel.

Proof Sketch. By a series of games, we show that the real protocol on a single qubit is indistinguishable from a game where the adversary guesses the outcome of a hidden coin flip. We generalize this special case to the full protocol on arbitrary quantum computation with a polynomial number of qubits by induction over the size of the computation.   □

1.2   Related Work

While $\mathsf{RSP_{CC}}$ was first introduced in [CCKW18] (under a different terminology), (game-based) security was only proven against weak (honest-but-curious) adversaries. Security against malicious adversaries was proven for a modified protocol in [CCKW19], where a verifiable version of $\mathsf{RSP_{CC}}$ was also given, but security was not proven in full generality. This protocol, called *QFactory*, is the basis of the positive results in this work. It is important to note that [CCKW19] only shows the (game-based) security of QFactory whereas, in this work, we prove the (game-based) security of a classical-client delegated quantum computing protocol that uses QFactory as a subroutine. QFactory was also used as a sub-module by [Zha20] to design a blind quantum computing scheme with a succinct quantum client. In parallel [GV19] gave another protocol that offers a stronger notion of *verifiable* $\mathsf{RSP_{CC}}$ and proved the security of their primitive in the CC framework.

The security analysis, however, requires the assumption of a *measurement buffer* resource in addition to the classical channel to construct a verifiable RSP$_{CC}$. The ideal functionality of the measurement buffer takes from Alice a classical message x and from Bob a classical message ξ corresponding to the measurement operation along with a quantum state ρ, respectively, and outputs the measurement outcome $\xi(x,\rho)$ to both Alice and Bob. Bob also receives the post-measurement quantum state. Our result confirms that this measurement buffer resource is a strictly non-classical assumption.

In the information-theoretic setting with perfect security (leaking at most the input size), the question of secure delegation of quantum computation with a completely classical client was first considered in [MK14]. The authors showed a negative result by presenting a *scheme-dependent* impossibility proof. This was further studied in [DK16, ACGK19] which showed that such a classical delegation would have implications in computational complexity theory. To be precise, [ACGK19] conjecture that such a result is unlikely by presenting an oracle separation between BQP and the class of problems that can be classically delegated with perfect security (which is equivalent to the complexity class NP/POLY ∩ coNP/POLY as proven by [AFK87]). On the other hand, a different approach to secure delegated quantum computation with a completely classical client, without going via the route of RSP$_{CC}$, was also developed in [MDMF17] where the server is computationally unbounded and in [Mah18a, Bra18] with the computationally bounded server. The security was analyzed for the overall protocol (rather than using a module to replace quantum communication). It is worth noting that [MDMF17] is known to be not composable secure in the Constructive Cryptography framework [Man19].

2 Preliminaries

We assume basic familiarity with quantum computing, for a detailed introduction, see [NC00] (in this paper we only deal with finite dimensional Hilbert spaces).

2.1 The Constructive Cryptography Framework

There exists a few frameworks [BOM04, Unr04, Unr10, MR11] for general composability in the quantum world. We chose to use the Constructive Cryptography (CC) framework mostly because its abstraction levels allow having a result that is independent of any universal quantum computation model. Also, using CC is a common approach to analyze both classical as well as quantum primitives, and their composable security guarantees in general and in related works including [DFPR14, MK13, DK16, GV19]. However, our results should be easy to port to other general composable frameworks.

The Constructive Cryptography (CC) framework (also sometimes referred to as the Abstract Cryptography (AC) framework) introduced by Maurer and

Renner [MR11] is a top-down and axiomatic approach, where the desired functionality is described as an (ideal) *resource* S with a certain input-output behavior independent of any particular implementation scheme. A resource has some interfaces $\mathcal{I}$ corresponding to the different parties that could use the resource. In our case, we will have only two interfaces corresponding to Alice (the client) and Bob (the server), therefore $\mathcal{I} = \{A, B\}$. Resources are not just used to describe the desired functionality (such as a perfect state preparation resource), but also to model the assumed resources of a protocol (e.g., a communication channel). The second important notion is the *converter* which, for example, is used to define a protocol. Converters always have two interfaces, an inner and an outer one, and the inner interface can be connected to the interface of a resource. When we denote by $\pi_A \mathcal{R} \pi_B$ we refer to connecting the inner interfaces of π_A and π_B to the interfaces A and B of the resource $\mathcal{R}$.

To characterize the distance between two resources (and therefore the security), we use the so-called *distinguishers*. We then say that two resources S_1 and S_2 are indistinguishable (within ε), and denote it as $S_1 \approx_\varepsilon S_2$, if no distinguisher can distinguish between S_1 and S_2 with an advantage greater than ε. In the following, we will mostly focus on quantum polynomial-time (QPT) distinguishers.

Central to Constructive Cryptography is the notion of a secure construction of an (ideal) resource S from an assumed resource $\mathcal{R}$ by a protocol (specified as a pair of converters). We directly state the definition for the special case we are interested in, namely in two-party protocols between a client A and a server B, where A is always considered to be honest. The definition can therefore be simplified as follows:

Definition 1 (See [Mau11,MR11]**).** *Let $\mathcal{I} = \{A, B\}$ be a set of two interfaces (A being the left interface and B the right one), and let $\mathcal{R}, S$ be two resources. Then, we say that for the two converters π_A, π_B, the protocol $\pi := (\pi_A, \pi_B)$ (securely) constructs S from $\mathcal{R}$ within ε, or that $\mathcal{R}$ realizes S within ε if the following two conditions are satisfied:*

1. Availability (i.e. correctness):

$$\pi_A \mathcal{R} \pi_B \approx_\varepsilon S \vdash \tag{1}$$

(where $\vdash$ represents a filter, i.e. a trivial converter that enforces honest/correct behavior, and $A \approx_\varepsilon B$ means that no quantum polynomial-time (QPT) distinguisher can distinguish between A and B (given black-box access to A or B) with an advantage better than ε)
2. Security: there exists $\sigma \in \Sigma$ (called a simulator) such that:

$$\pi_A \mathcal{R} \approx_\varepsilon S \sigma \tag{2}$$

We also extend this definition when ε is a function $\varepsilon : \mathbb{N} \to \mathbb{R}$: we say that S is ε-classically-realizable if for any $n \in \mathbb{N}$, S is $\varepsilon(n)$-realizable.

In our work, we instantiate a general model of computation to capture general quantum computations within converters which ensures that they follow the laws of quantum physics (e.g., excluding that the input-output behavior is signaling). Indeed, without such a restriction, we could not base our statements on results from quantum physics, because an arbitrary physical reality may not respect them, such as cloning of quantum states, signaling, and more. More specifically, in this work, we assume that any converter that interacts classically on its inner interface and outputs a single quantum message on its outer interface can be represented as a sequence of quantum instruments (which is a generalization of CPTP maps taking into account both quantum and classical outputs, see [DL70]) and constitutes the most general expression of allowed quantum operations. More precisely, this model takes into account interactive converters (and models the computation in sequential dependent stages). This is similar to if one would in the classical world instantiate the converter by a sequence of classical Turing machines (passing state to each other) [Gol01].

2.2   Notation

We denote by $\mathbb{Z}_{\frac{\pi}{2}}$ the set of the 4 angles $\{0, \frac{\pi}{2}, \pi, \frac{3\pi}{2}\}$, and $\mathbb{Z}_{\frac{\pi}{4}} = \{0, \frac{\pi}{4}, ..., \frac{7\pi}{4}\}$ the similar set of 8 angles. If ρ is a quantum state, $[\rho]$ is the *classical* representation (as a density matrix) of this state. We also denote the quantum state $|+_\theta\rangle :=$ $\frac{1}{\sqrt{2}}(|0\rangle + e^{i\theta}|1\rangle)$, where $\theta \in \mathbb{Z}_{\frac{\pi}{4}}$, and for any angle θ, $[\theta]$ will denote $[|+_\theta\rangle\langle+_\theta|]$, i.e. the classical description of the density matrix corresponding to $|+_\theta\rangle$. For a protocol $\mathcal{P} = (P_1, P_2)$ with two interacting algorithms P_1 and P_2 denoting the two participating parties, let $\langle P_1, P_2 \rangle$ denote the execution of the two algorithms, exchanging messages. We use the notation $\mathcal{C}$ to denote the *classical channel* resource, that just forwards classical messages between the two parties.

3   Impossibility of Composable Classical RSP

In this section, we first define what RSP tries to achieve in terms of resources and subsequently quantify the amount of information that an ideal RSP resource must leak to the server. One would expect that, against a computationally bounded distinguisher, the resource can express clear privacy guarantees (i.e. a small amount of leakage), but we prove that it cannot be the case.

The reason is as follows: assuming that there exists a simulator making the ideal resource indistinguishable from the real protocol, we can exploit this fact to construct an algorithm that can classically describe the quantum state given by the ideal resource. It is not difficult to verify that there could exist an inefficient algorithm (i.e. with exponential run-time) that achieves such a task. We show that even a computationally bounded distinguisher can distinguish the real protocol from the ideal protocol whenever a simulator's strategy is independent of the classical description of the quantum state. This would mean that for an RSP protocol to be composable there must exist a simulator that possesses at least a classical transcript encoding the description of a quantum state. This fact coupled with the quantum no-cloning theorem implies that the most meaningful and natural RSP resources cannot be realized from a classical channel alone. We finally conclude the section by looking at the class of imperfect (describable) RSP resources which avoid the no-go result at the price of being "fully-leaky", not standard, and having an unfortunately unclear composable security.

3.1   Remote State Preparation and Describable Resources

We first introduce, based on the standard definition in the Constructive Cryptography framework, the notion of *correctness* and *security* of a two-party protocol which constructs (realizes) a resource from a *classical* channel $\mathcal{C}$.

Definition 2 (Classically-Realizable Resource). *An ideal resource $\mathcal{S}$ is said to be ε-classically-realizable if it is realizable from a classical channel in the sense of Definition 1.*

A simple ideal prototype that captures the goal of a RSP protocol could be phrased as follows: the resource outputs a quantum state (chosen from a set of states) on one interface and a classical description of that state on the other interface to the client. For our purposes, this view is too narrow and we want to generalize this notion. For instance, a resource could accept some inputs from the client or interact with the server, and it may still be possible to use this resource to come up with a quantum state and its description. More precisely, if there is an efficient way to convert the client and server interfaces to comply with the basic prototype above, then such a resource can be understood as RSP resource, too. To make this idea formal, we need to introduce some converters that witness this:

1. A converter $\mathcal{A}$ will output, after interacting with the ideal resource, a classical description $[\rho]$ which is one of the following:
   (a) A density matrix (positive and with trace 1) corresponding to a quantum state ρ.
   (b) The null matrix, which is useful to denote the fact that we detected some deviation that should not happen in an honest run.
2. A converter $\mathcal{Q}$, whose goal is to output a quantum state ρ' as close as possible to the state ρ output by $\mathcal{A}$.
3. A converter $\mathcal{P}$, whose goal is to output a classical description $[\rho']$ of a quantum state ρ' which is close to ρ (cf. Definition 3).

An RSP must meet two central criteria:

1. Accuracy of the classical description of the obtained quantum state: We require that the quantum state ρ described by $\mathcal{A}$'s output is close to $\mathcal{Q}$'s output ρ'. This is to be understood in terms of the trace distance.
2. Purity of the obtained quantum state: Since the RSP resource aims to replace a noise-free quantum channel, it is desirable that the quantum state output by $\mathcal{Q}$ admit a high degree of purity, i.e. more formally, that $\mathrm{Tr}\left(\rho'^{2}\right)$ be close to one. Since ρ' is required to be close to ρ, this implies a high purity of ρ as well.

It turns out that these two conditions can be unified and equivalently captured requiring that the quantity $\text{Tr}(\rho\rho')$ is close to one. A rigorous formulation of this claim and its proof is provided in the full version of this work [BCC+20].

An RSP resource (together with $\mathcal{A}$ and $\mathcal{Q}$) can also be seen as a resource whose accuracy can be easily *tested*. For example, if such a resource outputs a state ρ', instead of $|\phi\rangle$ (i.e. $[\rho] = [|\phi\rangle\langle\phi|]$), then one way to verify this behavior would be to measure ρ' by doing a projection on $|\phi\rangle$. This test would pass with probability $p_s := \langle\phi|\rho'|\phi\rangle$, and therefore if the resource outputs correct state (i.e. if $\rho' = |\phi\rangle\langle\phi|$), the test will always succeed. However, when ρ' is far from $|\phi\rangle\langle\phi|$, this test is unlikely to pass, and we will have $p_s < 1$. We can then generalize this same idea for arbitrary (eventually not pure) states by remarking that $p_s = \langle\phi|\rho'|\phi\rangle = \text{Tr}(|\phi\rangle\langle\phi|\rho') = \text{Tr}(\rho\rho')$. Indeed, this last expression corresponds exactly to the probability of outputting E_0 when measuring the state ρ' according to the POVM $\{E_0 := \rho, E_1 := I - \rho\}$, and since the classical description of ρ is known, it is possible to perform this POVM and test the (average) accuracy of the resource. When ρ is pure, the expression is equal to the (squared) fidelity between ρ and ρ'. This motivates the following definition, which characterizes the set of RSP resources.

Definition 3 (RSP resources). *A resource S is said to be ε-remote state preparation resource (or equivalently, a* remote state preparation resource within ε *with respect to converters $\mathcal{A}$ and $\mathcal{Q}$) if the following three conditions hold: (1) both converters output a single message at the outer interface, where the output $[\rho]$ of $\mathcal{A}$ is classical and is either a density matrix or the null matrix, and the output ρ' of $\mathcal{Q}$ can be any quantum state of same dimension as ρ; (2) the equation:*

$$\underset{([\rho],\rho')\leftarrow\mathcal{A}S\vdash\mathcal{Q}}{\mathbb{E}}[\,\text{Tr}(\rho\rho')\,] \geq 1 - \varepsilon \tag{3}$$

is satisfied, where the probability is taken over the randomness of $\mathcal{A}$, S and $\mathcal{Q}$, and finally, (3) for all the possible outputs $[\rho]$ of $([\rho], \rho') \leftarrow \mathcal{A}S \vdash \mathcal{Q}$, if we define $E_0 = \rho$, $E_1 = I - \rho$, then the POVM $\{E_0, E_1\}$ must be efficiently implementable by any distinguisher.

Describable Resources. So far, we have specified that a resource qualifies as an RSP resource if, when all parties follow the protocol, we know how to compute a quantum state on the right interface and classical description of a "close" state on the other interface. A security-related question now is, if it is also possible to extract (possibly inefficiently) from the right interface a *classical* description of a quantum state that is close to the state described by the client. If we find a converter $\mathcal{P}$ doing this, we would call the (RSP) resource *describable*. The following definition captures this.

Definition 4 (Describable Resource). *Let S be a resource and $\mathcal{A}$ a converter outputting a single classical message $[\rho]$ on its outer interface (either equal to a density matrix or the null matrix). Then we say that $(S, \mathcal{A})$ is ε-describable (or, equivalently, that S is describable within ε with respect to $\mathcal{A}$) if there exists a* *(possibly unbounded) converter $\mathcal{P}$ (outputting a single classical message $[\rho']$ on its outer interface representing a density matrix) such that:*

$$\mathop{\mathbb{E}}_{([\rho],[\rho'])\leftarrow\mathcal{ASP}} [\operatorname{Tr}(\rho\rho')] \geq 1 - \varepsilon \tag{4}$$

(the expectation is taken over the randomness of $\mathcal{S}$, $\mathcal{A}$ and $\mathcal{P}$).

Reproducible Converters. In the proof of our first result, we will encounter a crucial decoding step. Roughly speaking, the core of this decoding step is the ability to convert the classical interaction with a client, which can be seen as an arbitrary encoding of a quantum state, back into an explicit representation of the state prepared by the server. The ability of such a conversion can be phrased by the following definition.

Definition 5 (Reproducible Converter). *A converter π is said to be reproducible if there exists a converter $\tilde{\pi}$ such that the following holds*

$$\mathcal{C}\pi \approx_0^{\mathcal{D}^u} \mathcal{C}\tilde{\pi}\mathcal{T}, \tag{5}$$

where $\tilde{\pi}$, possibly inefficient converter, outputs only a classical message $[\rho']$ at its right interface, and $\mathcal{T}$ takes as input on its inner interface a classical description, $[\rho']$, of a quantum state ρ' and reproduces the exact same quantum state ρ'. The indistinguishability requirement is with respect to any unbounded distinguisher $D \in \mathcal{D}^u$ and the subscript "0" refers to perfect indistinguishability. Since $\mathcal{C}$ represents classical channel and is a neutral resource, the above condition can be equivalently written as $\pi \approx_0^{\mathcal{D}^u} \tilde{\pi}\mathcal{T}$. This is pictorially represented in Fig. 3.

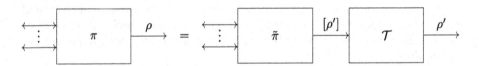

Fig. 3. Reproducible converter.

Classical Communication and Reproducibility. We see that in general, being reproducible is a property that stands in conflict with the quantum no-cloning theorem. More precisely, the ability to reproduce implies that there is a way to extract knowledge of a state sufficient to clone it. However, whenever communication is classical, quite the opposite is true. This is formalized in the following lemma. Intuitively, it says that in principle it is always possible to compute the exact description of the state from the classical transcript and the *quantum instruments* (circuit) used to implement the action of the converter. The following statement is proven in the full version of this work [BCC+20].

Lemma 1. *Let* $\pi = (\pi_i)_i$ *be a converter, where* π_i *are quantum instruments corresponding to the successive rounds of the protocol* π. *Then* π *is reproducible if (i) it receives and transmits only classical messages from the inner interfaces, and (ii) it outputs at the end a quantum state on the outer interface.*

3.2 Classically-Realizable RSP are Describable

In this section we show our main result about remote state preparation resources, which interestingly links a constructive notion (*composability*) concerning a computational notion with an information-theoretic property (*describability*). As a consequence, we obtain the *impossibility* of non-describable RSP$_{CC}$ composable protocols (secure against *computationally bounded* distinguishers). While this connection does not rule out all the possible RSP resources, it shows that most *useful* RSP resources are impossible. Indeed, the describable property is usually not desirable, as it implies an unbounded adversary could learn the description of the state it received from an ideal resource. To illustrate this theorem, we will see in the Sect. 3.3 some examples showing how this result can be used to prove the impossibility of classical protocols implementing some specific resources, and in Sect. 3.4 we give a brief outline how "imperfect" resources could escape the impossibility result.

Theorem 1 (Classically-Realizable RSP are Describable). *If an ideal resource* S *is both an* ε_1-*remote state preparation with respect to some* A *and* Q *and* ε_2-*classically-realizable (including against only polynomially bounded distinguishers), then it is* $(\varepsilon_1 + 2\varepsilon_2)$-*describable with respect to* A. *In particular, if* $\varepsilon_1 = \mathsf{negl}(n)$ *and* $\varepsilon_2 = \mathsf{negl}(n)$, *then* S *is describable within a negligible error* $\varepsilon_1 + 2\varepsilon_2 = \mathsf{negl}(n)$.

Proof. Let S be an ε_1-remote state preparation resource with respect to (A, Q) which is ε_2-classically-realizable. Then there exist π_A, π_B, σ, such that:

$$\mathop{\mathbb{E}}_{([\rho],\rho') \leftarrow AS\vdash Q}[\operatorname{Tr}(\rho\rho')] \geq 1 - \varepsilon_1 \tag{6}$$

$$\pi_A C \pi_B \approx_{\varepsilon_2} S \vdash \tag{7}$$

and

$$\pi_A C \approx_{\varepsilon_2} S\sigma \tag{8}$$

Now, using (7), we get:

$$A\pi_A C \pi_B Q \approx_{\varepsilon_2} AS \vdash Q \tag{9}$$

So it means that we can't distinguish between $AS \vdash Q$ and $A\pi_A C\pi_B Q$ with an advantage better than ε_2 (i.e. with probability better than $\frac{1}{2}(1 + \varepsilon_2)$). But, if we construct the following distinguisher, that runs $([\rho], \rho') \leftarrow AS \vdash Q$, and then measures ρ' using the POVM $\{E_0, E_1\}$ (possible because this POVM is assumed to be efficiently implementable by distinguishers in $\mathcal{D}$), with $E_0 = [\rho]$ and $E_1 = I - [\rho]$ (which is possible because we know the classical description of ρ, which is positive and smaller than I, even when $[\rho] = 0$), we will measure E_0

with probability $1 - \varepsilon_1$. So it means that by replacing $\mathcal{AS} \vdash \mathcal{Q}$ with $\mathcal{A}\pi_A \mathcal{C}\pi_B \mathcal{Q}$, the overall probability of measuring E_0 needs to be close to $1 - \varepsilon_1$. More precisely, we need to have:

$$\mathop{\mathbb{E}}_{([\rho],\rho') \leftarrow \mathcal{A}\pi_A \mathcal{C}\pi_B \mathcal{Q}} [\operatorname{Tr}(\rho\rho')] \geq 1 - \varepsilon_1 - \varepsilon_2 \tag{10}$$

Indeed, if the above probability is smaller than $1 - \varepsilon_1 - \varepsilon_2$, then we can define a distinguisher that outputs 0 if it measures E_0, and 1 if it measures E_1, and his probability of distinguishing the two distributions would be equal to:

$$\frac{1}{2} \mathop{\mathbb{E}}_{([\rho],\rho') \leftarrow \mathcal{AS}\vdash\mathcal{Q}} [\operatorname{Tr}(\rho\rho')] + \frac{1}{2} \mathop{\mathbb{E}}_{([\rho],\rho') \leftarrow \mathcal{A}\pi_A \mathcal{C}\pi_B \mathcal{Q}} [\operatorname{Tr}((I - \rho)\rho')] \tag{11}$$

$$> \frac{1}{2} ((1 - \varepsilon_1) + 1 - (1 - \varepsilon_1 - \varepsilon_2)) = \frac{1}{2}(1 + \varepsilon_2) \tag{12}$$

So this distinguisher would have an advantage greater than ε_2, which is in contradiction with Eq. (9).

Using a similar argument and Eq. (7), we have:

$$\mathop{\mathbb{E}}_{([\rho],\rho') \leftarrow \mathcal{AS}\sigma\pi_B \mathcal{Q}} [\operatorname{Tr}(\rho\rho')] \geq 1 - \varepsilon_1 - 2\varepsilon_2 \tag{13}$$

We will now use $\pi_B \mathcal{Q}$ to construct a $\mathcal{B}$ that can describe the state given by the ideal resource. To do that, because $\pi_B \mathcal{Q}$ interacts only classically with the inner interface and outputs a single quantum state on the outer interface, then according to Lemma 1, $\pi_B \mathcal{Q}$ is reproducible, i.e. there exists a $\mathcal{B}$ such that $\pi_B \mathcal{Q} \approx_0 \mathcal{BT}$. Note that here $\mathcal{B}$ is not efficient anymore. Of course, the proof does apply when the distinguisher is polynomially bounded. Therefore, we have:

$$\mathop{\mathbb{E}}_{([\rho],\rho') \leftarrow \mathcal{AS}\sigma\mathcal{BT}} [\operatorname{Tr}(\rho\rho')] \geq 1 - \varepsilon_1 - 2\varepsilon_2 \tag{14}$$

$\mathcal{T}$ could be omitted as it only converts the classical description $[\rho']$ into ρ'. After defining $\mathcal{P} = \sigma\mathcal{B}$, we have that $\mathcal{S}$ is $(\varepsilon_1 + 2\varepsilon_2)$-describable. $\qquad\square$

3.3   RSP Resources Impossible to Realize Classically

In the last section, we proved that if an RSP functionality is classically-realizable (secure against polynomial quantum distinguishers), then this resource is describable by an unbounded adversary having access to the right interface of that resource.

Our main result in the previous section directly implies that as long as there exists *no unbounded* adversary that, given access to the right interface, can find the classical description given on the left interface, then the RSP resource is *impossible* to classically realize (against QPT distinguishers). Very importantly, this no-go result shows that the *only* type of RSP resources that can be classically realized are the ones that *leak* on the right interface enough information to allow a (possibly unbounded) adversary to determine the classical description given on the left interface. From a security point of view, this property is highly non-desirable, as the resource must leak the *secret description* of the state at least in *some representation*. In this section, we present some of these RSP resources that are impossible to realize classically. The proofs of all results from this section can be found in the full version of this work [BCC+20].

Definition 6 (Ideal Resource $\mathcal{S}_{\mathbb{Z}\frac{\pi}{2}}$). $\mathcal{S}_{\mathbb{Z}\frac{\pi}{2}}$ *is the verifiable* RSP *resource (RSP which does not allow any deviation from the server), that receives no input, that internally picks a random* $\theta \leftarrow \mathbb{Z}\frac{\pi}{2}$, *and that sends* θ *on the left interface, and* $|+_\theta\rangle$ *on the right interface as shown in Fig. 1.*

Lemma 2. *There exists a universal constant* $\eta > 0$, *such that for all* $0 \le \varepsilon < \eta$ *the resource* $\mathcal{S}_{\mathbb{Z}\frac{\pi}{2}}$ *is not* ε-*classically-realizable.*

Next, we describe a verifiable remote state preparation RSP_V, a variant of $\mathcal{S}_{\mathbb{Z}\frac{\pi}{2}}$, introduced in [GV19]. Unlike $\mathcal{S}_{\mathbb{Z}\frac{\pi}{2}}$, in RSP_V, the dishonest server can make the resource abort and the client can partially choose the basis of the output state. However, similar to the $\mathcal{S}_{\mathbb{Z}\frac{\pi}{2}}$, we prove that classically-realizable RSP_V is also not possible.

Definition 7 (Ideal Resource RSP_V, See [GV19]). *The ideal verifiable remote state preparation resource,* RSP_V, *takes an input* $W \in \{X, Z\}$ *on the left interface, but no honest input on the right interface. The right interface has a filtered functionality that corresponds to a bit* $c \in \{0, 1\}$. *When* $c = 1$, RSP_V *outputs error message* ERR *on both the interfaces, otherwise:*

1. *if* $W = Z$ *the resource picks a random bit* b *and outputs* $b \in \mathbb{Z}_2$ *to the left interface and a computational basis state* $|b\rangle\langle b|$ *to the right interface;*
2. *if* $W = X$ *the resource picks a random angle* $\theta \in \mathbb{Z}\frac{\pi}{4}$ *and outputs* θ *to the left interface and a quantum state* $|+_\theta\rangle\langle+_\theta|$ *to the right interface.*

Corollary 1. *There exists a universal constant* $\eta > 0$, *such that for all* $0 \le \varepsilon < \eta$ *the resource* RSP_V *is not* ε-*classically-realizable.*

Remark 1. Note that our impossibility of classically-realizing RSP_V does not contradict the result of [GV19]. Specifically, in their work they make use of an additional assumption of the so-called measurement buffer, see section Sect. 1.2. However, we show that it is impossible to realize this measurement buffer resource with a protocol interacting purely classically, therefore the measurement buffer recreates a quantum channel. Additionally, this method has a second drawback: the server can put a known state as the input of the measurement buffer, and if the dishonest server passes the test (an event that occurs with probability $\frac{1}{n}$), then he can check that the state has not been changed, leading to polynomial security (a polynomially bounded distinguisher can distinguish between the ideal and the real world). As in CC, the security of the whole protocol is the sum of the security of the inner protocols, any protocol using this RSP as a sub-module will not be asymptotically secure (against QPT distinguisher).

3.4   Accepting the Limitations: Fully Leaky RSP Resources

As explained in the previous section, Theorem 1 rules out all resources that are impossible to be *describable* with unbounded power, and that the only type of classically-realizable RSP resources would be the one leaking the full classical description of the output quantum state to an unbounded adversary, which we will refer to as being *fully-leaky* RSP. Fully-leaky RSP resources can be separated into two categories:

1. If the RSP is describable in quantum polynomial time, then the adversary can get the full description in polynomial time. This is not an interesting case as the useful properties that we know from quantum computations (such as UBQC) cannot be preserved if such a resource is employed to prepare the quantum states.
2. If the RSP is only describable using unbounded power, then these *fully-leaky* RSP resources are not trivially insecure, but their universally composable security remains unclear. Indeed, it defeats the purpose of aiming at a nice ideal resource where the provided security should be clear "by definition" and it becomes hard to quantify the impact of this additional leakage when composed with other protocols. A possible remedy would be to show restricted composition following [JM17] which we discuss in the full version of this work [BCC+20], where we also present a concrete resource that falls into this second category, i.e., one that leaks an encoding of the classical description of the final state that is not trivially decodable.

4   Impossibility of Composable Classical-Client UBQC

In the previous section, we showed that it was impossible to get a (useful) composable $\mathsf{RSP_{CC}}$ protocol. A (weaker) RSP protocol, however, could still be used internally in other protocols, hoping for the overall protocol to be composably secure. To this end, we analyze the composable security of a well-known delegated quantum computing protocol, universal blind quantum computation (UBQC), proposed in [BFK09]. The UBQC protocol allows a semi-quantum client, Alice, to delegate an arbitrary quantum computation to a (universal) quantum server Bob, in such a way that her input, the quantum computation, and the output of the computation are information-theoretically hidden from Bob. The protocol requires Alice to be able to prepare single qubits of the form $|+_\theta\rangle$, where $\theta \in \mathbb{Z}\frac{\pi}{4}$ and send these states to Bob at the beginning of the protocol, the rest of the communication between the two parties being classical. We define the family of protocols $\mathsf{RSP_{CC}^{8-states}}$ as the RSP protocols that classically delegate the preparation of an output state $|+_\theta\rangle$, where $\theta \in \mathbb{Z}\frac{\pi}{4}$. That is, without loss of generality, we assume a pair of converters P_A, P_B such that the resource $R := P_A C P_B$ has the behavior of the prototype RSP resource except with negligible probability. Put differently, we assume we have an (except with negligible error) *correct* RSP protocol, but we make *no assumption about the security* of this protocol. Therefore, one can directly instantiate the quantum interaction with the $\mathsf{RSP_{CC}^{8-states}}$

at the first step as shown in Protocol 1. While UBQC allows for both quantum and classical outputs and inputs, given that we want to remove the quantum interaction in favor of a completely classical interaction, we only focus on the classical input and classical output functionality of UBQC in the remaining of the paper.

Protocol 1. UBQC with $\mathsf{RSP}_{\mathsf{CC}}^{\mathsf{8-states}}$ (See [BFK09])

- **Client's classical input:** An n-qubit unitary U that is represented as set of angles $\{\phi\}_{i,j}$ of a one-way quantum computation over a brickwork state/cluster state [MDF17], of the size $n \times m$, along with the dependencies X and Z obtained via flow construction [DK06].
- **Client's classical output:** The measurement outcome $\bar{s}$ corresponding to the n-qubit quantum state, where $\bar{s} = \langle 0| U |0\rangle$.

1. Client and Server runs $n \times m$ different instances of $\mathsf{RSP}_{\mathsf{CC}}^{\mathsf{8-states}}$ (in parallel) to obtain $\theta_{i,j}$ on client's side and $|+_{\theta_{i,j}}\rangle$ on server's side, where $\theta_{i,j} \leftarrow \mathbb{Z}_{\frac{\pi}{4}}$, $i \in \{1, \cdots, n\}$, $j \in \{1, \cdots, m\}$
2. Server entangles all the qubits, $n \times (m-1)$ received from $\mathsf{RSP}_{\mathsf{CC}}^{\mathsf{8-states}}$, by applying controlled-Z gates between them in order to create a graph state $\mathcal{G}_{n \times m}$
3. For $j \in [1, m]$ and $i \in [1, n]$
   (a) Client computes $\delta_{i,j} = \phi'_{i,j} + \theta_{i,j} + r_{i,j}\pi$, $r_{i,j} \leftarrow \{0, 1\}$, where $\phi'_{i,j} = (-1)^{s^X_{i,j}}\phi_{i,j} + s^Z_{i,j}\pi$ and $s^X_{i,j}$ and $s^Z_{i,j}$ are computed using the previous measurement outcomes and the X and Z dependency sets. Client then sends the measurement angle $\delta_{i,j}$ to the Server.
   (b) Server measures the qubit $|+_{\theta_{i,j}}\rangle$ in the basis $\{|+_{\delta_{i,j}}\rangle, |-_{\delta_{i,j}}\rangle\}$ and obtains a measurement outcome $s_{i,j} \in \{0, 1\}$. Server sends the measurement result to the client.
   (c) Client computes $\bar{s}_{i,j} = s_{i,j} \oplus r_{i,j}$.
4. The measurement outcome corresponding to the last layer of the graph state ($j = m$) is the outcome of the computation.

Note that Protocol 1 is based on measurement-based model of quantum computing (MBQC). This model is known to be equivalent to the quantum circuit model (up to polynomial overhead in resources) and does not require one to perform quantum gates on their side to realize arbitrary quantum computation. Instead, the computation is performed by an (adaptive) sequence of single-qubit projective measurements that steer the information flow across a highly entangled resource state. Intuitively, UBQC can be seen as a distributed MBQC where the measurements are performed by the server whereas the classical update of measurement bases is performed by the client. Since the projective measurements in quantum physics, in general, are probabilistic in nature and therefore, the client needs to update the measurement bases (and classically inform the server about the update) based on the outcomes of the earlier measurements to ensure the correctness of the computation. Roughly speaking, this information flow is captured by the X and Z dependencies. For more details, we refer the reader to [RB01, Nie06].

Next, we show that the Universal Blind Quantum Computing protocol [BFK09], which is proven to be secure in the Constructive Cryptography
framework [DFPR14], cannot be proven composably secure (for the same ideal
resource) when the quantum interaction is replaced with $\mathsf{RSP_{CC}}$ (this class of
protocol is denoted as $\mathsf{UBQC_{CC}}$). We also give an outlook that the impossibility
proof also rules out weaker ideal resources.

4.1   Impossibility of Composable $\mathsf{UBQC_{CC}}$ on 1 Qubit

To prove that there exists no $\mathsf{UBQC_{CC}}$ protocol, we will first focus on the simpler
case when the computation is described by a single measurement angle. The
resource that performs a blind quantum computation on one qubit ($\mathcal{S}_{UBQC1}$) is
defined as below:

Definition 8 (Ideal resource of single-qubit UBQC (See [DFPR14])). *The
definition of the ideal resource $\mathcal{S}_{UBQC1}$, depicted in Fig. 4, achieves blind quantum computation specified by a single angle ϕ. The input (ξ, ρ) is filtered when
$c = 0$. The ξ can be any deviation (specified for example using the classical
description of a CPTP map) that outputs a classical bit, and which can depend
on the computation angle ϕ and some arbitrary quantum state ρ.*

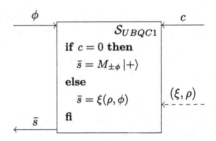

Fig. 4. Ideal resource $\mathcal{S}_{UBQC1}$ for UBQC with one angle, with a filtered (dashed) input.
In the case of honest server the output $\bar{s} \in \{0, 1\}$ is computed by measuring the qubits
$|+\rangle$ in the $\{|+_\phi\rangle, |-_\phi\rangle\}$ basis. On the other hand if $c = 1$ any malicious behavior of
server can be captured by (ξ, ρ), i.e. the output $\bar{s}$ is computed by applying the CPTP
map ξ on the input ϕ and on another auxiliary state ρ chosen by the server.

Theorem 2 (No-go composable classical-client single-qubit UBQC). *Let
(P_A, P_B) be a protocol interacting only through a classical channel $\mathcal{C}$, such that
$(\theta, \rho_B) \leftarrow (P_A \mathcal{C} P_B)$ with $\theta \in \mathbb{Z}_{\frac{\pi}{4}}$, and such that (by correctness) the trace dis-
tance between ρ_B and $|+_\theta\rangle \langle+_\theta|$ is negligible with overwhelming probability. Then,
if we define π_A and π_B as the UBQC protocol on one qubit that makes use of
(P_A, P_B) as a sub-protocol to replace the quantum channel (as pictured in Fig. 5),
(π_A, π_B) is not composable, i.e. there exists no simulator σ such that:*

$$\pi_A \mathcal{C} \pi_B \approx_\varepsilon \mathcal{S}_{UBQC1} \vdash^{c=0}, \qquad \pi_A \mathcal{C} \approx_\varepsilon \mathcal{S}_{UBQC1} \sigma \qquad (15)$$

for some negligible $\varepsilon = \mathsf{negl}(n)$.

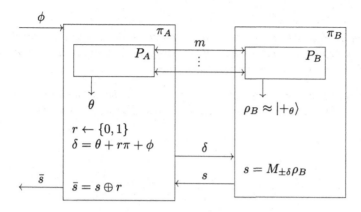

Fig. 5. UBQC with one qubit when both Alice and Bob follows the protocol honestly (see Protocol 1)

Proof. In order to prove this theorem, we will proceed by contradiction. Let us assume that there exists (P_A, P_B), and a simulator σ having the above properties. Then, for the same resource $\mathcal{S}_{UBQC1}$ we consider a different protocol $\pi' = (\pi'_A, \pi'_B)$ that realizes it, but using a different filter $\vdash^\sigma$ and a different simulator σ':

$$\pi'_A \mathcal{C} \pi'_B \approx_\varepsilon \mathcal{S}_{UBQC1} \vdash^\sigma \tag{16}$$

$$\pi'_A \mathcal{C} \approx_\varepsilon \mathcal{S}_{UBQC1} \sigma' \tag{17}$$

More specifically, the new filter $\vdash^\sigma_{UBQC1}$ will depend on σ defined in Eq. (15). Then our main proof can be described in the following steps:

1. We first show in Lemma 3 that $\mathcal{S}_{UBQC1}$ is also ε-classically-realizable by (π'_A, π'_B) with the filter $\vdash^\sigma$.
2. We then prove in Lemma 4 that the resource $\mathcal{S}_{UBQC1}$ is an RSP within $\mathsf{negl}(n)$, with respect to some well chosen converters $\mathcal{A}$ and $\mathcal{Q}$ (see Fig. 6) and this new filter $\vdash^\sigma$.
3. Then, we use the main result about RSP (Theorem 1) to show that $\mathcal{S}_{UBQC1}$ is describable within $\mathsf{negl}(n)$ with respect to $\mathcal{A}$ (Corollary 2).
4. Finally, in Lemma 6 we prove that if $\mathcal{S}_{UBQC1}$ is describable then we could achieve *superluminal signaling*, a contradiction.

The above sequence of statements concludes the proof. □

In the following, we give a brief overview of the above-mentioned statements needed to conclude Theorem 2. The proofs of these statements are given in the full version of this work [BCC+20].

Definition 9. *Let $\pi' = (\pi'_A, \pi'_B)$ the protocol realizing $\mathcal{S}_{UBQC1}$ described in the following way (as pictured Fig. 6):*

- $\pi'_A = \pi_A$ *(Fig. 5)*
- π'_B: *runs* P_B, *obtains a state* ρ_B, *then uses the angle* δ *received from its inner interface to compute* $\tilde{\rho} := R_Z(-\delta)\rho_B$, *and finally outputs* $\tilde{\rho}$ *on its outer interface and* $s := 0$ *on its inner interface.*

Then we define $\vdash^\sigma = \sigma\pi'_B$ *depicted in Fig. 7 (with* σ *being the simulator from Eq. (15) above). We further let the converters* $\mathcal{A}$ *and* $\mathcal{Q}$ *be as described in Fig. 6.*

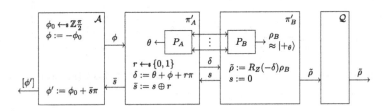

Fig. 6. Definition of $\mathcal{A}$, π'_A, π'_B and $\mathcal{Q}$.

Lemma 3. *If* $\mathcal{S}_{UBQC1}$ *is* ε*-classically-realizable by* (π_A, π_B) *with the filter* $\vdash^{c=0}$ *then* $\mathcal{S}_{UBQC1}$ *is also* ε*-classically-realizable by* (π'_A, π'_B) *with the filter* $\vdash^\sigma$.

Lemma 4. *If* $\mathcal{S}_{UBQC1}$ *is* $\mathsf{negl}(n)$*-classically-realizable with* $\vdash^{c=0}$ *then* $\mathcal{S}_{UBQC1}$ *is an* $\mathsf{negl}(n)$*-remote state preparation resource with respect the converters* $\mathcal{A}$ *and* $\mathcal{Q}$ *and filter* $\vdash^\sigma$ *defined in Fig. 6.*

Now, using our main Theorem 1 we obtain directly that if $\mathcal{S}_{UBQC1}$ is classically-realizable and RSP with respect to filter $\vdash^\sigma$, then it is also describable:

Corollary 2. *If* $\mathcal{S}_{UBQC1}$ *is* $\mathsf{negl}(n)$*-classically-realizable with respect to filter* $\vdash^{c=0}$ *then* $\mathcal{S}_{UBQC1}$ *is* $\mathsf{negl}(n)$*-describable with respect to the converter* $\mathcal{A}$ *described above.*

We further need a technical observation:

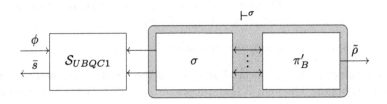

Fig. 7. Description of $\vdash^\sigma$

Lemma 5. *Let* $\Omega = \{[\rho_i]\}$ *be a set of (classical descriptions of) density matrices, such that* $\forall i \neq j$, $\mathrm{Tr}(\rho_i \rho_j) \leq 1 - \eta$. *Then let* $([\rho], [\tilde{\rho}])$ *be two random variables (representing classical description of density matrices), such that* $[\rho] \in \Omega$ *and* $\underset{([\rho],[\tilde{\rho}])}{\mathbb{E}} [\mathrm{Tr}(\rho\tilde{\rho})] \geq 1 - \varepsilon$, *with* $\eta > 6\sqrt{\varepsilon}$. *Then, if we define the following "rounding" operation that rounds* $\tilde{\rho}$ *to the closest* $\tilde{\rho}_r \in \Omega$:

$$[\tilde{\rho}_r] := \mathrm{Round}_\Omega([\tilde{\rho}]) := \underset{[\tilde{\rho}_r]\in\Omega}{\arg\max} \mathrm{Tr}(\tilde{\rho}_r\tilde{\rho}) \tag{18}$$

Then we have:

$$\underset{([\rho],[\tilde{\rho}])}{\Pr} [\mathrm{Round}_\Omega([\tilde{\rho}]) = [\rho]] \geq 1 - \sqrt{\varepsilon} \tag{19}$$

In particular, if $\varepsilon = \mathsf{negl}(n)$, *and* $\eta \neq 0$ *is a constant,* $\Pr[\mathrm{Round}_\Omega([\tilde{\rho}]) = [\rho]] \geq 1 - \mathsf{negl}(n)$.

We state the last step of this sequence for which we give the proof here.

Lemma 6. $\mathcal{S}_{UBQC1}$ *cannot be* $\mathsf{negl}(n)$-*describable with respect to converter* $\mathcal{A}$.

Proof. If we assume that $\mathcal{S}_{UBQC1}$ is $\mathsf{negl}(n)$-describable, then there exists a converter $\mathcal{P}$ (outputting $[\tilde{\rho}]$) such that:

$$\underset{([\rho],[\tilde{\rho}])\leftarrow\mathcal{A}\mathcal{S}_{UBQC1}\mathcal{P}}{\mathbb{E}} [\mathrm{Tr}(\rho\tilde{\rho})] \geq 1 - \mathsf{negl}(n) \tag{20}$$

We define the set $\Omega := \{[|+_{\theta'}\rangle\langle+_{\theta'}|] \mid \theta' \in \{0, \pi/4, ..., 7\pi/4\}\}$. For simplicity, we will denote in the following $[\theta] \doteq [|+_\theta\rangle\langle+_\theta|]$.

In the remaining of the proof, we are going to use the converters $\mathcal{A}$ and $\mathcal{P}$ together with the ideal resource $\mathcal{S}_{UBQC1}$, to construct a 2-party setting that would achieve signaling, which would end our contradiction proof. More specifically, we will define a converter D running on the right interface of $\mathcal{S}_{UBQC1}$ which will manage to recover the ϕ_0 chosen randomly by $\mathcal{A}$.

As shown in Fig. 8, if we define C as $C := \mathcal{A}\mathcal{S}_{UBQC1}$ and D the converter described above, then the setting can be seen equivalently as: C chooses as random ϕ_0 and D needs to output $\phi_0 \bmod \pi$. This is however impossible, as no message is sent from $\mathcal{S}_{UBQC1}$ to its right interface (as seen in Fig. 8) (and thus no message from C to D), and therefore guessing ϕ_0 is forbidden by the no-signaling principle [GRW80].

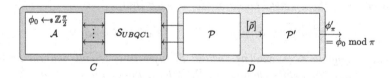

Fig. 8. Illustration of the no-signaling argument

We define $\mathcal{P}'$ as the converter that, given $[\tilde{\rho}]$ from the outer interface of $\mathcal{P}$ computes $[\tilde{\phi}] = \mathrm{Round}_\Omega([\tilde{\rho}])$ and outputs $\tilde{\phi}_\pi = \tilde{\phi} \bmod \pi$ (as depicted in Fig. 8). We will now prove that $\tilde{\phi}_\pi = \phi_0 \bmod \pi$ with overwhelming probability.

All elements in Ω are different pure states, and in finite number, so there exist a constant $\eta > 0$ respecting the first condition of Lemma 5. Moreover from Eq. (20) we have that $\mathcal{S}_{UBQC1}$ is ε-describable with $\varepsilon = \mathsf{negl}(n)$, so we also have (for large enough n), $\eta > 6\sqrt{\varepsilon}$. Therefore, from Lemma 5, we have that:

$$\Pr_{([\rho],[\tilde{\rho}]) \leftarrow \mathcal{A}\mathcal{S}_{UBQC1}\mathcal{P}} [\, \mathrm{Round}_\Omega([\tilde{\rho}]) = [\rho]\,] \geq 1 - \mathsf{negl}(n) \tag{21}$$

But using the definition of converter $\mathcal{A}$, we have: $[\rho] = [\phi']$, where $\phi' = \phi_0 + \bar{s}\pi$, and hence $\phi' \bmod \pi = \phi_0 \bmod \pi$. Then, using the definition of $\mathcal{P}'$, Eq. (21) is equivalent to:

$$\Pr_{([\phi'],\tilde{\phi}_\pi) \leftarrow \mathcal{A}\mathcal{S}_{UBQC1}\mathcal{P}\mathcal{P}'} [\, \tilde{\phi}_\pi = \phi_0 \bmod \pi\,] \geq 1 - \mathsf{negl}(n) \tag{22}$$

However, as pictured in Fig. 8, this can be seen as a game between $C = \mathcal{A}\mathcal{S}_{UBQC1}$ and $D = \mathcal{P}\mathcal{P}'$, where, as explained before, C picks a $\phi_0 \in \mathbb{Z}_{\frac{\pi}{2}}$ randomly, and D needs to output $\phi_0 \bmod \pi$. From Eq. (22) D wins with overwhelming probability, however, we know that since there is no information transfer from C to D, the probability of winning this game better than $1/2$ (guessing the bit at random) would imply signaling. $\qquad\square$

4.2   Impossibility of Composable $\mathsf{UBQC_{CC}}$ on Any Number of Qubits

We saw in Theorem 2 that it is not possible to implement a composable classical-client UBQC protocol performing a computation on a single qubit. In this section, we prove that this result generalizes to the impossibility of $\mathsf{UBQC_{CC}}$ on computations using an arbitrary number of qubits. The proof which can be found in the full version of this work [BCC+20] works by reducing the general case to the single-qubit case from the previous section.

Theorem 3 (No-go Composable Classical-Client UBQC). *Let (P_A, P_B) be a protocol interacting only through a classical channel $\mathcal{C}$, such that $(\theta, \rho_B) \leftarrow (P_A \mathcal{C} P_B)$ with $\theta \in \mathbb{Z}_{\frac{\pi}{4}}$, and such that the trace distance between ρ_B and $|+_\theta\rangle\langle+_\theta|$ is negligible with overwhelming probability. Then, if we define (π_A^G, π_B^G) as the UBQC protocol on any fixed graph G (with at least one output qubit, that uses (P_A, P_B) as a sub-protocol to replace the quantum channel, (π_A^G, π_B^G) is not composable, i.e. there exists no simulator σ such that:*

$$\pi_A^G \mathcal{C} \pi_B^G \approx_\varepsilon \mathcal{S}_{UBQC} \vdash^{c=0}, \qquad \pi_A^G \mathcal{C} \approx_\varepsilon \mathcal{S}_{UBQC}\sigma \tag{23}$$

for some negligible $\varepsilon = \mathsf{negl}(n)$, where $\mathcal{S}_{UBQC}$ is a trivial generalization of $\mathcal{S}_{UBQC1}$ to multiple qubits (defined in [DFPR14] under the notation $\mathcal{S}^{blind}$) for which an additional leakage l^{ψ_A} is send to the server, which is (at least in our case) equal to the size of the graph state.

5   Game-Based Security of QF-UBQC

While we know from Theorem 3 that classical-client UBQC (UBQC$_{CC}$) cannot be proven secure in a fully composable setting, there is hope that it remains possible with a weaker definition of security. And indeed, in this section we show that UBQC$_{CC}$ is possible in the *game-based setting* by implementing it using a combination of the known quantum-client UBQC Protocol 1 [BFK09] and 8-states QFactory Protocol [CCKW19]. We start with giving a formal definition of the game-based security of UBQC$_{CC}$.

Definition 10 (Blindness of UBQC$_{CC}$). *A UBQC$_{CC}$ protocol $\mathcal{P} = (P_C, P_S)$ is said to be (computationally) blind if no (computationally bounded) malicious server can distinguish between runs of the protocol with adversarially chosen measurement patterns on the same MBQC graph.*

In formal terms, $\mathcal{P}$ is said to be (computationally) blind if and only if for any quantum-polynomial-time adversary A it holds that

$$\Pr\left[c' = c \;\middle|\; (\phi^{(1)}, \phi^{(2)}) \leftarrow A, \, c \leftarrow\!\$ \, \{0,1\}, \, \left\langle P_C(\phi^{(c)}), A \right\rangle, \, c' \leftarrow A \right] \leq \frac{1}{2} + \mathrm{negl}(\lambda),$$

where λ is the security parameter, and $\left\langle P_C(\phi^{(c)}), A \right\rangle$ denotes the interaction of the two algorithms $P_C(\phi^{(c)})$ and A.

Remark 2. Although, Definition 10 is written using the terminology of measurement-based model. It doesn't compromise the generality, as the model is universal and can be easily translated into a circuit model, because the measurement pattern and unitary operators are in a one-to-one mapping.

5.1   Implementing Classical-Client UBQC with QFactory

The UBQC protocol from [BFK09], where the quantum interaction is replaced by a RSP$_{CC}^{8-\text{states}}$ protocol, is shown in Protocol 1. In this section, we replace the RSP$_{CC}^{8-\text{states}}$ protocol with a concrete protocol proposed in [CCKW19]. This protocol, known by the name of 8-states QFactory (we consider the case where abort occurs with negligible probability) exactly emulates the capability of RSP$_{CC}^{8-\text{states}}$. The resulting protocol contains a QFactory instance for each qubit that would have been generated on the client's side. The keys to all QFactory instances are generated entirely independently by the client.

Unfortunately, considering the results from Sect. 4 there is no hope that the composable security of any UBQC$_{CC}$ may be achieved. Nonetheless, letting go of composability, we can prove the game-based security for this specific combination of protocols. This leads us to the main theorem of this section.

Theorem 4 (Game-based Blindness of QF-UBQC). *The protocol resulting from combining the quantum-client UBQC protocol with QFactory is a (computationally) blind implementation of UBQC$_{CC}$ in the game-based model according to Definition 10. We call this protocol QF-UBQC.*

The proof of Theorem 4 which will be given in the remainder of this section and follows two main ideas:

1. Every angle used in the UBQC protocol has only eight possible values, and can, therefore, be described by three bits. In the protocol, the first bit is the one for which QFactory *cannot* guarantee blindness. Fortunately, the additional one-time padding in UBQC allows analyzing the blindness of the protocol independently of the blindness of exactly this first bit. Therefore, it suffices to rely on the blindness of the last two bits which is conveniently guaranteed by QFactory and the hardness of LWE.
2. To analyze the leakage about the last two bits during a QFactory run, it is sufficient to notice that the leakage is equal to a ciphertext under an LWE-based encryption scheme. The semantic security of this encryption scheme and the hardness assumption for LWE guarantee that this leakage is negligible and can be omitted.

In more detail, the 8-states QFactory protocol which is used here consists of two combined runs of 4-states QFactory, each contributing with a single bit (hidden from the server) to the three-bit encoding of the angles used in the UBQC protocol. The formulae for how these angles from the 4-states protocol are combined in the 8-states protocol can be found in [CCKW19]. If the basis bit B_1 is the hidden bit of the first 4-states QFactory instance and basis B_1' the hidden bit of the second instance, then we obtain:

$$L_1 = B_2' \oplus B_2 \oplus [B_1 \cdot (s_1 \oplus s_2)], \; L_2 = B_1' \oplus [(B_2 \oplus s_2) \cdot B_1], \; L_3 = B_1, \quad (24)$$

where $L = L_1 L_2 L_3 \in \{0,1\}^3$ is the description of the output state $|+_{L\frac{\pi}{4}}\rangle$, s_1, s_2 are computed by the server, and

$$B_2 = f(\mathsf{sk}, B_1, y, b), \qquad B_2' = f(\mathsf{sk}', B_1', y', b') \quad (25)$$

for some function f, QFactory secret keys $\mathsf{sk}, \mathsf{sk}'$, and server-chosen values y, b, y', b'.

The two 4-states QFactory instances now leak the ciphertext of B_1 and B_1', respectively. Given the semantic security of the encryption, after a run of 8-states QFactory, L_2 and L_3 remain hidden, while the blindness of L_1 cannot be guaranteed by QFactory. This fact is going to be crucial. Due to space constraints, we give here the security proof for the single-qubit case. By induction, the security proof can be extended to apply to UBQC for MBQC computations on a polynomial number of qubits. The proof is given in the full version of this work [BCC+20].

Lemma 7 (Blindness in the single-qubit case). *The protocol resulting from combining the quantum-client UBQC protocol with (8-states) QFactory is a (computationally) blind implementation of UBQC$_{\mathsf{CC}}$ in the game-based model for MBQC computations on a single qubit.*

Proof. We start with the real protocol, describing the adaptive blindness of QFactory combined with single-qubit UBQC. In the following, we denote the set of possible angles by $M = \{j\pi/4, j = 0, \ldots, 7\}$. The encryption scheme that appears in Game 1 is the semantically secure public-key encryption scheme from [Reg09]. The two key pairs are generated independently on the challenger's side.

GAME 1:

Adversary		Challenger
1 : Choose $\phi^{(1)}, \phi^{(2)} \in M$	$\xrightarrow{\phi^{(1)}, \phi^{(2)}}$	$c \xleftarrow{\$} \{0,1\}$
2 :		$B_1, B_1' \xleftarrow{\$} \{0,1\}$
3 :	$\xleftarrow{\text{pk, pk}', \; \text{Enc}^{\text{pk}}(B_1), \text{Enc}^{\text{pk}'}(B_1')}$	Generate key pairs $(\text{sk}, \text{pk}), (\text{sk}', \text{pk}')$
4 :	$\xrightarrow{y, b, y', b', s_1, s_2}$	$B_2 = f(\text{sk}, B_1, y, b), \; B_2' = f(\text{sk}', B_1', y', b')$
5 :		$L_1 = B_2' \oplus B_2 \oplus [B_1 \cdot (s_1 \oplus s_2)]$
6 :		$L_2 = B_1' \oplus [(B_2 \oplus s_2) \cdot B_1]$
7 :		$L_3 = B_1$
8 :		$r \xleftarrow{\$} \{0,1\}$
9 :	$\xleftarrow{\delta}$	$\delta = \phi^{(c)} + L_3\pi/4 + L_2\pi/2 + L_1\pi + r\pi$
10 :	$\xrightarrow{s}$	
	Compute guess	
11 : $c' \in \{0,1\}$	$\xrightarrow{c'}$	Check $c' = c$?

In the following, instead of repeating the redundant parts of subsequent games, we only present incremental modifications to Game 1. Any line that is not explicitly written is assumed to be identical to the previous game.

Since s is never used by the challenger, we can remove it from the protocol without distorting the success probability of the adversary. Next, we remove L_1 from the protocol and from the calculation of δ. L_1 is only used in the calculation of δ, which can be expressed as $\delta = \phi^{(c)} + L_3\pi/4 + L_2\pi/2 + (L_1 + r)\pi$. Since r is a uniform binary random variable with unique use in this line, $(L_1 + r)$ is still uniform over $\{0,1\}$ and hence removing L_1 leaves the distribution of the protocol outcome unchanged.

GAME 2:

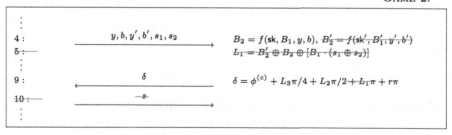

The next step introduces a (negligible) distortion to the success probability of the adversary. By the semantic security of the employed encryption scheme, no quantum-polynomial-time adversary can notice if the plaintext is replaced by pure randomness except with negligible probability, even if information about the original plaintext is leaked on the side. Therefore, replacing B_1' in the encryption by independent randomness cannot lead to a significant change in the adversary's success probability. Further, since ciphertexts of independent randomness can be equally generated by the adversary herself (having the public key), we can remove the encryption of B_1' from the protocol altogether.

GAME 3:

3 : $\overleftarrow{pk, pk', \mathrm{Enc}^{pk}(B_1), \mathrm{Enc}^{pk'}(B_1')}$ Generate key pairs $(\mathsf{sk}, \mathsf{pk}), (\mathsf{sk}', \mathsf{pk}')$

Next, note that B_1' perfectly one-time pads the value of L_2. This breaks the dependency of L_2 on B_2, s_2 and B_1. It does not change the distribution of L_2, if L_2 is instead directly sampled uniformly from $\{0,1\}$. Since B_2 is unused, we remove it in the following game, and y, b, y', b', s_1, s_2 can be ignored.

GAME 4:

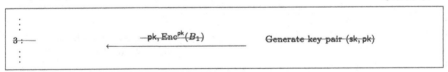

By the same argument as for the transition from Game 2 to Game 3, we remove the encryption of B_1 from the following game. This introduces at most a negligible change in the success probability of the adversary.

Finally, since the encryption scheme is not in use anymore, we can also remove the key generation and the message containing the public key without affecting the adversary's success probability.

GAME 5:

3 :— $\overleftarrow{\text{pk, Enc}^{pk}(B_1)}$ Generate key pair (sk, pk)

We now see that δ is a uniformly random number, L_2, L_3, and r being i.i.d. uniform bits. Therefore, the calculation and the message containing δ can be removed from the protocol without affecting the adversary.

GAME 6:

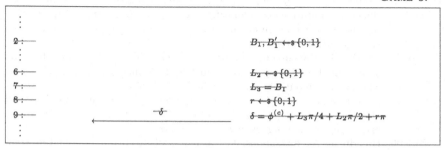

In Game 6, the inputs of the adversary are ignored by the challenger. Therefore, the computation angles $\phi^{(1)}$, $\phi^{(2)}$ can equally be removed from the protocol:

GAME 7:

Adversary		Challenger
1 : ~~Choose $\phi^{(1)}, \phi^{(2)} \in M$~~	$\xrightarrow{~~~\phi^{(1)}, \phi^{(2)}~~~}$	$c \leftarrow\!\!\text{\$}\, \{0, 1\}$
11 : Compute guess $c' \in \{0, 1\}$	$\xrightarrow{\quad c' \quad}$	Check $c' = c$?

Game 7 exactly describes the adversary's uninformed guess of the outcome of an independent bit flip. Therefore, by a simple information-theoretic argument, any strategy for the adversary will lead to a success probability of exactly $1/2$. The proof is concluded by a standard hybrid argument [BCC+20].   □

Acknowledgments. The authors thank Céline Chevalier, Omar Fawzi, Daniel Jost, and Luka Music for very useful discussions and the anonymous reviewers of ASIACRYPT 2020 for their comments and suggestions that greatly improved this work. LC also thanks M.T. This work has been supported in part by grant FA9550-17-1-0055, by the European Union's H2020 Programme under grant agreement number ERC-669891, and by the French ANR Project ANR-18-CE39-0015 (CryptiQ). EK acknowledges support from the EPSRC Verification of Quantum Technology grant (EP/N003829/1), the EPSRC Hub in Quantum Computing and Simulation (EP/T001062/1), and the UK Quantum Technology Hub: NQIT grant (EP/M013243/1). LC and DL gratefully acknowledge support from the French ANR project ANR-18-CE47-0010 (QUDATA). LC, EK, and DL acknowledge funding from the EU Flagship Quantum Internet Alliance (QIA) project. AM gratefully acknowledges funding from the AFOSR MURI project "Scalable Certification of Quantum Computing Devices and Networks". This work was partly done while AM was at the University of Edinburgh, UK supported by EPSRC Verification of Quantum Technology grant (EP/N003829/1).

References

[ABOE08] Aharonov, D., Ben-Or, M., Eban, E.: Interactive proofs for quantum computations. arXiv preprint arXiv:0810.5375 (2008)

[ACGK19] Aaronson, S., Cojocaru, A., Gheorghiu, A., Kashefi, E.: Complexity-theoretic limitations on blind delegated quantum computation. In: 46th International Colloquium on Automata, Languages, and Programming (ICALP 2019) (2019)

[AFK87] Abadi, M., Feigenbaum, J., Kilian, J.: On hiding information from an oracle. In: Proceedings of the Nineteenth Annual ACM Symposium on Theory of Computing, pp. 195–203. ACM (1987)

[BCC+20] Badertscher, C., et al.: Security limitations of classical-client delegated quantum computing. Cryptology ePrint Archive, Report 2020/818 (2020). https://eprint.iacr.org/2020/818 (full version)

[BFK09] Broadbent, A., Fitzsimons, J., Kashefi, E.: Universal blind quantum computation. In: 50th Annual IEEE Symposium on Foundations of Computer Science, FOCS 2009, pp. 517–526. IEEE (2009)

[BJ15] Broadbent, A., Jeffery, S.: Quantum homomorphic encryption for circuits of low T-gate complexity. In: Gennaro, R., Robshaw, M. (eds.) CRYPTO 2015. LNCS, vol. 9216, pp. 609–629. Springer, Heidelberg (2015). https://doi.org/10.1007/978-3-662-48000-7_30

[BOM04] Ben-Or, M., Mayers, D.: General security definition and composability for quantum & classical protocols. arXiv preprint quant-ph/0409062 (2004)

[Bra18] Brakerski, Z.: Quantum FHE (almost) as secure as classical. In: Shacham, H., Boldyreva, A. (eds.) CRYPTO 2018. LNCS, vol. 10993, pp. 67–95. Springer, Cham (2018). https://doi.org/10.1007/978-3-319-96878-0_3

[Bro15a] Broadbent, A.: Delegating private quantum computations. Can. J. Phys. 93(9), 941–946 (2015)

[Bro15b] Broadbent, A.: How to verify a quantum computation. arXiv preprint arXiv:1509.09180 (2015)

[CCKW18] Cojocaru, A., Colisson, L., Kashefi, E., Wallden, P.: On the possibility of classical client blind quantum computing. arXiv preprint arXiv:1802.08759 (2018)

[CCKW19] Cojocaru, A., Colisson, L., Kashefi, E., Wallden, P.: QFactory: classically-instructed remote secret qubits preparation. In: Galbraith, S.D., Moriai, S. (eds.) ASIACRYPT 2019. LNCS, vol. 11921, pp. 615–645. Springer, Cham (2019). https://doi.org/10.1007/978-3-030-34578-5_22

[Chi05] Childs, A.M.: Secure assisted quantum computation. Quantum Inf. Comput. 5(6), 456–466 (2005)

[DFPR14] Dunjko, V., Fitzsimons, J.F., Portmann, C., Renner, R.: Composable security of delegated quantum computation. In: Sarkar, P., Iwata, T. (eds.) ASIACRYPT 2014. LNCS, vol. 8874, pp. 406–425. Springer, Heidelberg (2014). https://doi.org/10.1007/978-3-662-45608-8_22

[DK06] Danos, V., Kashefi, E.: Determinism in the one-way model. Phys. Rev. A 74(5), 052310 (2006)

[DK16] Dunjko, V., Kashefi, E.: Blind quantum computing with two almost identical states. arXiv preprint arXiv:1604.01586 (2016)

[DKL12] Dunjko, V., Kashefi, E., Leverrier, A.: Blind quantum computing with weak coherent pulses. Phys. Rev. Lett. 108(20), 200502 (2012)

[DL70] Davies, E.B., Lewis, J.T.: An operational approach to quantum probability. Commun. Math. Phys. 17(3), 239–260 (1970)

[DSS16] Dulek, Y., Schaffner, C., Speelman, F.: Quantum homomorphic encryption for polynomial-sized circuits. In: Robshaw, M., Katz, J. (eds.) CRYPTO 2016. LNCS, vol. 9816, pp. 3–32. Springer, Heidelberg (2016). https://doi.org/10.1007/978-3-662-53015-3_1

[FHM18]   Fitzsimons, J.F., Hajdušek, M., Morimae, T.: Post hoc verification of quantum computation. Phys. Rev. Lett. **120**(4), 040501 (2018)

[Fit17]   Fitzsimons, J.F.: Private quantum computation: an introduction to blind quantum computing and related protocols. NPJ Quantum Inf. **3**(1), 23 (2017)

[FK17]   Fitzsimons, J.F., Kashefi, E.: Unconditionally verifiable blind quantum computation. Phys. Rev. A **96**(1), 012303 (2017)

[GKK19]   Gheorghiu, A., Kapourniotis, T., Kashefi, E.: Verification of quantum computation: an overview of existing approaches. Theory Comput. Syst. **63**(4), 715–808 (2019)

[Gol01]   Goldreich, O.: Foundations of Cryptography. Cambridge University Press, Cambridge (2001)

[GRW80]   Ghirardi, G.C., Rimini, A., Weber, T.: A general argument against superluminal transmission through the quantum mechanical measurement process. Lettere al Nuovo Cimento (1971–1985) **27**, 293–298 (1980)

[GV19]   Gheorghiu, A., Vidick, T.: Computationally-secure and composable remote state preparation. In: 2019 IEEE 60th Annual Symposium on Foundations of Computer Science (FOCS), pp. 1024–1033 (2019)

[HM15]   Hayashi, M., Morimae, T.: Verifiable measurement-only blind quantum computing with stabilizer testing. Phys. Rev. Lett. **115**(22), 220502 (2015)

[JM17]   Jost, D., Maurer, U.: Context-restricted indifferentiability: generalizing UCE and implications on the soundness of hash-function constructions. IACR Cryptology ePrint Archive 2017:461 (2017)

[KMW17]   Kashefi, E., Music, L., Wallden, P.: The quantum cut-and-choose technique and quantum two-party computation. arXiv preprint arXiv:1703.03754 (2017)

[KP17]   Kashefi, E., Pappa, A.: Multiparty delegated quantum computing. Cryptography **1**(2), 12 (2017)

[KW17]   Kashefi, E., Wallden, P.: Garbled quantum computation. Cryptography **1**(1), 6 (2017)

[Mah18a]   Mahadev, U.: Classical homomorphic encryption for quantum circuits. In: Thorup, M. (ed.) 59th IEEE Annual Symposium on Foundations of Computer Science, FOCS 2018, Paris, France, 7–9 October 2018, pp. 332–338. IEEE Computer Society (2018)

[Mah18b]   Mahadev, U.: Classical verification of quantum computations. In: Thorup, M. (ed.) 59th IEEE Annual Symposium on Foundations of Computer Science, FOCS 2018, Paris, France, 7–9 October 2018, pp. 259–267. IEEE Computer Society (2018)

[Man19]   Mantri, A.: Secure delegated quantum computing, Ph.d. thesis (2019)

[Mau11]   Maurer, U.: Constructive cryptography – a new paradigm for security definitions and proofs. In: Mödersheim, S., Palamidessi, C. (eds.) TOSCA 2011. LNCS, vol. 6993, pp. 33–56. Springer, Heidelberg (2012). https://doi.org/10.1007/978-3-642-27375-9_3

[MDF17]   Mantri, A., Demarie, T.F., Fitzsimons, J.F.: Universality of quantum computation with cluster states and (X, Y)-plane measurements. Sci. Rep. **7**, 42861 (2017)

[MDMF17]   Mantri, A., Demarie, T.F., Menicucci, N.C., Fitzsimons, J.F.: Flow ambiguity: a path towards classically driven blind quantum computation. Phys. Rev. X **7**(3), 031004 (2017)

[MF13]   Morimae, T., Fujii, K.: Blind quantum computation protocol in which alice only makes measurements. Phys. Rev. A **87**(5), 050301 (2013)

[MK13] Morimae, T., Koshiba, T.: Composable security of measuring-alice blind quantum computation. arXiv preprint arXiv:1306.2113 (2013)

[MK14] Morimae, T., Koshiba, T.: Impossibility of perfectly-secure delegated quantum computing for classical client. arXiv preprint arXiv:1407.1636 (2014)

[MR11] Maurer, U., Renner, R.: Abstract cryptography. In: Innovations in Computer Science. Citeseer (2011)

[NC00] Nielsen, M.A., Chuang, I.: Quantum Computation and Quantum Information. Cambridge University Press, Cambridge (2000)

[Nie06] Nielsen, M.A.: Cluster-state quantum computation. Rep. Math. Phys. **57**(1), 147–161 (2006)

[RB01] Raussendorf, R., Briegel, H.J.: A one-way quantum computer. Phys. Rev. Lett. **86**(22), 5188 (2001)

[Reg09] Regev, O.: On lattices, learning with errors, random linear codes, and cryptography. J. ACM (JACM) **56**(6), 34 (2009)

[RUV12] Reichardt, B.W., Unger, F., Vazirani, U.: A classical leash for a quantum system: command of quantum systems via rigidity of CHSH games. arXiv preprint arXiv:1209.0448 (2012)

[TMM+18] Takeuchi, Y., Mantri, A., Morimae, T., Mizutani, A., Fitzsimons, J.F.: Resource-efficient verification of quantum computing using Serfling's bound. arXiv preprint arXiv:1806.09138 (2018)

[Unr04] Unruh, D.: Simulatable security for quantum protocols. arXiv preprint quant-ph/0409125 (2004)

[Unr10] Unruh, D.: Universally composable quantum multi-party computation. In: Gilbert, H. (ed.) EUROCRYPT 2010. LNCS, vol. 6110, pp. 486–505. Springer, Heidelberg (2010). https://doi.org/10.1007/978-3-642-13190-5_25

[Vid20] Vidick, T.: Verifying quantum computations at scale: a cryptographic leash on quantum devices. Bull. Am. Math. Soc. **57**(1), 39–76 (2020)

[Zha20] Zhang, J.: Succinct blind quantum computation using a random oracle. arXiv, abs/2004.12621 (2020)

Quantum Circuit Implementations
of AES with Fewer Qubits

Jian Zou[1,2], Zihao Wei[3,4], Siwei Sun[3,4(✉)], Ximeng Liu[1,2], and Wenling Wu[5]

[1] Mathematics and Computer Science of Fuzhou University,
Fuzhou, Fujian Province, China
fzuzoujian15@163.com, snbnix@gmail.com
[2] Key Lab of Information Security of Network Systems (Fuzhou University),
Fujian Province, China
[3] State Key Laboratory of Information Security,
Institute of Information Engineering, Chinese Academy of Sciences, Beijing, China
weizihao@iie.ac.cn, siweisun.isaac@gmail.com
[4] School of Cyber Security,
University of Chinese Academy of Sciences, Beijing, China
[5] Institute of Software, Chinese Academy of Sciences, Beijing, China
wwl@tca.iscas.ac.cn

Abstract. We propose some quantum circuit implementations of AES with the following improvements. Firstly, we propose some quantum circuits of the AES S-box and S-box^{-1}, which require fewer qubits than prior work. Secondly, we reduce the number of qubits in the zig-zag method by introducing the S-box^{-1} operation in our quantum circuits of AES. Thirdly, we present a method to reduce the number of qubits in the key schedule of AES. While the previous quantum circuits of AES-128, AES-192, and AES-256 need at least 864, 896, and 1232 qubits respectively, our quantum circuit implementations of AES-128, AES-192, and AES-256 only require 512, 640, and 768 qubits respectively, where the number of qubits is reduced by more than 30%.

Keywords: AES · S-box · S-box^{-1} · Quantum circuit · Circuit complexity

1 Introduction

In the post-quantum era, we need to study the security of cryptographic systems against quantum attackers. In fact, many cryptographic schemes turn out to be less secure against attacks based on quantum computing. Some asymmetric cryptographic primitives face devastating attacks due to Shor's algorithm [24]. In contrast, the impact of quantum computing on secret-key cryptography seems to be less severe. Most of the existing works are based on Grover's algorithm [12] and Simon's algorithm [25]. Grover's algorithm can solve the search problem with quadratic speed-up, while Simon's algorithm can find the hidden period with polynomially many quantum queries. In such attacks, the corresponding quantum oracle of the target cipher has to be implemented. Due to

© International Association for Cryptologic Research 2020
S. Moriai and H. Wang (Eds.): ASIACRYPT 2020, LNCS 12492, pp. 697–726, 2020.
https://doi.org/10.1007/978-3-030-64834-3_24

the importance of AES, it is one of the most studied ciphers [3,11,15,17,18] in the context of efficient synthesis of quantum circuits. These implementations can be potentially used in some quantum attacks against symmetric-key primitives involving AES [4,9,13,16]. In this paper, we construct some quantum circuits of AES with fewer qubits, and the techniques involved may provide more flexible qubit and circuit depth trade-offs for the quantum circuits of AES.

A quantum oracle for any classical vectorial Boolean function can be constructed with the Clifford + T gate set, which consists of the Hadamard gate (H), Phase gate (S), controlled-NOT gate (CNOT), and non-clifford T gate. There are some works on synthesizing optimal reversible circuits, such as reversible Boolean functions. Shende et al. [22] considered the synthesis of 3-bit reversible logic circuits using NOT gate, CNOT gate, and Toffoli gate. Golubitsky et al. [10] proposed an optimal 4-bit reversible circuits composed with NOT gate, CNOT gate, Toffoli gate, and the 4-bit Toffoli gate. The goal of synthesizing the optimal quantum circuit implementation is to reduce the circuit depth and number of qubits [3,11,17,18]. According to our current understanding of fault-tolerant quantum computing, the metric of T-depth is probably the most important. However, before practical quantum computers are built, the method for reducing the cost with respect to the number of qubits is also very meaningful, and it may provides more flexible qubit and depth trade-offs.

Recently, the construction of efficient quantum circuits of AES has attracted much attention. In [8], Datta et al. presented a reversible implementation of AES. In [15], Jaques et al. proposed a method to minimize the depth-times-width cost metric for quantum circuits of AES. In [11], Grassl et al. proposed a quantum circuit of AES aiming at the lowest possible number of qubits. In [17], Kim et al. showed some time-memory trade-offs for key search on AES. In [3], Almazrooie et al. presented a new quantum circuit of AES-128. By utilizing the classical algebraic structure of the S-box [5], Langenberg et al. in [18] showed a new way to construct the quantum circuit of AES's S-box, based on which Langenberg et al. proposed an efficient quantum circuit of AES-128. Compared to Almazrooie et al.'s and Grassl et al.'s estimates, the circuit proposed by Langenberg et al. could reduce the number of qubits and Toffoli gates simultaneously. Langenberg et al.'s work shows that we can construct an improved quantum circuit of AES by constructing a more efficient classical circuit of AES.

There are several works on how to reduce the gate number of AES in the classical setting [1,7,14,19,28]. In [14], Itoh and Tsujii proposed the tower field architecture for calculating multiplicative inverse in $\mathbb{F}_2$, which was a powerful technique for designing compact hardware implementation of S-box. By using the tower field technique, Canright in [7] showed an efficient method for computing the multiplicative inverse of the input. In [6], Boyar and Peralta proposed a depth 16 circuit for the S-box in AES by using the tower field implementation.

Contribution. Firstly, we propose an improved quantum circuit for the S-box^{-1} of AES based on the improved classical circuit of the inverse of the AES S-box [28,29]. Also, by exploiting some useful linear relationship, we propose some improved qubit-depth trade-offs for the quantum circuits of S-box/S-box^{-1} of AES. The improvements of the S-box and its inverse lead to corresponding improvements of the quantum circuits of the round function and the key-schedule algorithm of AES. Taking AES-128 as an example, we can generate W_{4i} by XORing $SubWord(RotWord(W_{4i-1}))$, $Rcon(i/s)$, W_{4i-1}, W_{4i-5}, $W4_{4i-9}$ to W_{4i-13} (for $4 \leq i \leq 10$). In other words, we can obtain W_{4i} without introducing new qubits or cleaning up W_{4i-13} (for $4 \leq i \leq 10$). That is, our quantum circuit for the key schedules of AES-128/-192/-256 need 128/192/256 qubit, and 6 ancillas qubits, which require fewer qubits than the previous works [3,11,15,18].

Secondly, we propose an improved zig-zag method with fewer qubits. To compute the output of the AES round function, we need 256 qubits to store the 128 qubits input and the 128 qubits output of the round function. In other words, we need at least 256 qubits in the zig-zag method. By using our quantum circuits of AES's S-box and S-box^{-1}, we propose an improved zigzag method for AES-128/-192/-256 with 256 qubits, which matches the minimum values. That is, our improved zig-zag method require 256/256/256 qubits for AES-128/-192/-256, while the prior work needed at least 528/656/656 qubits for AES-128/-192/-256, respectively.

We summarize the quantum resources to implement AES in Table 1. The # Toffoli/CNOT/NOT means the number of Toffoli gates, CNOT gates, and NOT gates, and # qubits means the number of qubits. We will adopt the same notations in the following tables. As shown in Table 1, our quantum circuit implementations of AES require fewer qubits than the prior works. Also, our quantum circuits of AES-128/-256 can obtain the best trade-off of $T \cdot M$, where T is the Toffoli depth and M is the number of qubits.

Table 1. Summary of the quantum resources to implement AES

Algorithm	# qubits	Toffoli depth	# Toffoli	# CNOT	# NOT	$T \cdot M$	Source
AES-128	984	12672	151552	166548	1456	12469248	[11]
	976	not reported	150528	192832	1370	not reported	[3]
	864	1880	16940	107960	1570	1624320	[18]
	512	2016	19788	128517	4528	1032192	Sect. 6.1
AES-192	1112	11088	172032	189432	1608	12329856	[11]
	896	1640	19580	125580	1692	1469440	[18]
	640	2022	22380	152378	5128	1294080	Sect. 6.2
AES-256	1336	14976	215040	233836	1943	20007936	[11]
	1232	2160	23760	151011	1992	2661120	[18]
	768	2292	26774	177645	6103	1760256	Sect. 6.2

Remark. In this work, the Toffoli-count and Toffoli-depth are involved in our metric. A more fine-grained and accurate approach is to implement the entire circuit with the Clifford+T set, count the number of T gate, and measure the T-depth as was done in [15]. In [15], the quantum circuit was implemented with Q# [26] and the cost of the quantum circuit was estimated by the resource esti-mator of Q#. However, it seems that there are some issues with the resource estimator (see https://github.com/microsoft/qsharp-runtime/issues/192). So we do not use it here.

Outline. In Sect. 2, we present the definitions of some quantum gates. Sect. 3 not only makes a brief introduction to AES, but also shows the algebraic structures of AES's S-box/S-box^{-1}. In Sect. 4, we propose our improved quantum circuits of AES's S-box and S-box^{-1}. Section 5 shows our improved ideas for the zig-zag method and the key schedule of AES. In Sect. 6, we show our improved quantum circuit implementations of AES. We conclude this paper in Sect. 7.

2   Notations

The classical circuits allow wires to be joined together, such as $a = a \oplus b$ and $a = a \wedge b$. Obviously these operations are not reversible and not unitary. Different from the classical circuits, quantum circuits shall be reversible and unitary, which can be constructed by replacing classical gates with quantum gates. For example, we shall simulate AND gates with the Toffoli gate, while a XOR gate can be simulated with the CNOT gate.

Some prior works [2] showed that the quantum circuit consisting only of Clifford gates were not advantageous over classical computing. In other words, we shall adopt some non-Clifford gates (i.e. Toffoli gate) to obtain the quantum benefit. Also, some works [23,27] showed the Toffoli gate and Clifford gates were universal. That is, we can implement any quantum computation by these gates. As shown in [20], the Clifford groups are much cheaper than the Toffoli gate (or T-gate). As a result, [11,17,18] defined the Toffoli depth as the time cost of the algorithm, while the memory cost is the total number of logical qubits required to perform the quantum algorithm. Similar to [11,17,18], we define the time and memory cost of our quantum circuit implementation of AES as follows.

Definition 1. *A unit of quantum computational time cost is defined as the time for running a nonparallelizable logical Toffoli gate.*

Definition 2. *The space cost of the quantum circuit is defined as the number of logical qubits for the entire quantum computational.*

Apart from the two definitions, we also clarify three kinds of qubits to avoid the confusions.

1. **Data qubits** are written as the input message, such as the round key or the input plaintext.
2. **Ancilla qubits** (or called garbage qubits) are initialized qubits those assist certain operation, which get written unwanted information after a certain operation. Note that we shall clean up the ancilla qubits at the end of the quantum circuit.

3. **Output qubits** contain the output information of a certain operation. Note that we do not need to clean up the output qubits.

Based on the definitions of three types of qubits, we adopt the following two strategies to reduce the number of qubits. First, we shall avoid applying the Toffoli gate to ancilla qubits, because these wires shall be cleaned up. However, we do not need to clean up the output qubits. As a result, we shall apply the Toffoli gates to output qubits to avoid involving them in the cleanup process. Second, some ancilla qubits remained idle until the end of the quantum circuit. By uncomputing these wires, we can reuse these ancilla qubits instead of introducing new ancilla qubits, which can reduce the number of qubits.

3   The AES Block Cipher

AES [21] is a family of iterative block ciphers based on the SPN structure. Its members with 128-bit, 192-bit, and 256-bit keys are denoted as AES-128 (10-round), AES-192 (12-round), and AES-256 (14-round), respectively. We will show the round function and key schedule of AES in the following. We refer the reader to [21] for the full description of AES.

3.1   Specification of AES

The AES round function consists the following four operations: **AddRound-Key ∘ MixColumns ∘ ShiftRows ∘ SubBytes**, where

- **AddRoundKey** exclusive-ors each round key to the state;
- **SubBytes** is the only non-linear transformation in AES, which applies an 8-bit S-box to the 16 bytes of the state in parallel. The algebraic structure of S-box is shown in Sect. 3.2.
- **ShiftRows** cyclically rotates the cells of the i-th row to the left by i-byte (for $0 \leq i \leq 3$).
- **MixColumns** does a linear transformation on each column of the state with the MDS matrix

$$M = \begin{bmatrix} 0 \times 02 & 0 \times 03 & 0 \times 01 & 0 \times 01 \\ 0 \times 01 & 0 \times 02 & 0 \times 03 & 0 \times 01 \\ 0 \times 01 & 0 \times 01 & 0 \times 02 & 0 \times 03 \\ 0 \times 03 & 0 \times 01 & 0 \times 01 & 0 \times 01 \end{bmatrix}.$$

Similar to the encryption procession of AES, the decryption process of AES also consists of four operations **AddRoundKey ∘ InvMC ∘ InvShiftRows ∘ InvSubBytes**, where

- **AddRoundKey** exclusive-ors the round key to the state;
- **InvSubBytes** is the inverse operation of SubBytes;
- **InvShiftRows** cyclically rotates the cells of the i-th row to the right by i-byte (for $0 \leq i \leq 3$).

- **InvMC** does a linear transformation on each column with the MDS matrix

$$M^{-1} = \begin{bmatrix} 0 \times 0E & 0 \times 0B & 0 \times 0D & 0 \times 09 \\ 0 \times 09 & 0 \times 0E & 0 \times 0B & 0 \times 0D \\ 0 \times 0D & 0 \times 09 & 0 \times 0E & 0 \times 0B \\ 0 \times 0B & 0 \times 0D & 0 \times 09 & 0 \times 0E \end{bmatrix}.$$

The key schedules of AES-128/-192/-256 are described in Algorithm 1 and Algorithm 2. The parameters s and t used in the key schedules of AES-128 are $s = 4$, $t = 43$, while AES-192 adopts $s = 6$, $t = 51$.

Algorithm 1. The key schedules of AES-128 and AES-192

For $i = s$ till $i = t$ do
If $i \equiv 0 \mod s$, then
$\qquad W_i = W_{i-s} \oplus \mathbf{SubWord}(\mathbf{RotWord}(W_{i-1})) \oplus \mathbf{Rcon}(i/s)$;
else $W_i = W_{i-s} \oplus W_{i-1}$.

Algorithm 2. The key schedules of AES-256

For $i = 8$ till $i = 59$ do
If $i \equiv 0 \mod 8$, then
$\qquad W_i = W_{i-8} \oplus \mathbf{SubWord}(\mathbf{RotWord}(W_{i-1})) \oplus \mathbf{Rcon}(i/8)$;
If $i \equiv 4 \mod 8$, then
$\qquad W_i = W_{i-8} \oplus \mathbf{SubWord}(W_{i-1})$;
else $W_i = W_{i-8} \oplus W_{i-1}$.

The operations **RotWord**, **Rcon** and **SubWord** used in Algorithm 1 and Algorithm 2 are explained as follows.

- **RotWord** cyclically rotates the four bytes to the left by 1-byte;
- **Rcon** exclusive-ors the constant to each byte of the word;
- **SubWord** applies an S-box operation to each byte of the word.

3.2   The Algebraic Structures of the S-Box of AES

There are several ways to implement the S-box of AES. In [5], Boyar and Peralta showed an efficient way to compute AES's S-box by using the tower field architecture. Since we do not find a circuit with fewer AND gate than the classical circuit proposed by Boyar and Peralta [5], we adopt their classical circuit to construct our quantum circuit of AES's S-box in the Sect. 4. Their circuit represents AES's S-box as $S(x) = B_S \cdot F_S(U_S \cdot x)$, where the matrix U_S takes $x_0, x_1, \cdots, x_7$ as input and outputs $x_7, y_1, \cdots, y_{21}$.

$$
\begin{array}{llll}
y_{14} = x_3 \oplus x_5, & y_{13} = x_0 \oplus x_6, & y_9 = x_0 \oplus x_3, & y_8 = x_0 \oplus x_5, \\
t_0 = x_1 \oplus x_2, & y_1 = t_0 \oplus x_7, & y_4 = y_1 \oplus x_3, & y_{12} = y_{13} \oplus y_{14}, \\
y_2 = y_1 \oplus x_0, & y_5 = y_1 \oplus x_6, & y_3 = y_5 \oplus y_8, & t_1 = x_4 \oplus y_{12}, \\
y_{15} = t_1 \oplus x_5, & y_{20} = t_1 \oplus x_1, & y_6 = y_{15} \oplus x_7, & y_{10} = y_{15} \oplus t_0, \\
y_{11} = y_{20} \oplus y_9, & y_7 = x_7 \oplus y_{11}, & y_{17} = y_{10} \oplus y_{11}, & y_{19} = y_{10} \oplus y_8, \\
y_{16} = t_0 \oplus y_{11}, & y_{21} = y_{13} \oplus y_{16}, & y_{18} = x_0 \oplus y_{16}.
\end{array}
$$

The function $F_S : \mathbb{F}_2^{22} \to \mathbb{F}_2^{18}$ takes $x_7, y_1, \cdots, y_{21}$ as input and outputs $z_0, z_1, \cdots, z_{17}$.

$$
\begin{array}{llll}
t_2 = y_{12} \cdot y_{15}, & t_3 = y_3 \cdot y_6, & t_4 = t_3 \oplus t_2, & t_5 = y_4 \cdot x_7, \\
t_6 = t_5 \oplus t_2, & t_7 = y_{13} \cdot y_{16}, & t_8 = y_5 \cdot y_1, & t_9 = t_8 \oplus t_7, \\
t_{10} = y_2 \cdot y_7, & t_{11} = t_{10} \oplus t_7, & t_{12} = y_9 \cdot y_{11}, & t_{13} = y_{14} \cdot y_{17}, \\
t_{14} = t_{13} \oplus t_{12}, & t_{15} = y_8 \cdot y_{10}, & t_{16} = t_{15} \oplus t_{12}, & t_{17} = t_4 \oplus y_{20}, \\
t_{18} = t_6 \oplus t_{16}, & t_{19} = t_9 \oplus t_{14}, & t_{20} = t_{11} \oplus t_{16}, & t_{21} = t_{17} \oplus t_{14}, \\
t_{22} = t_{18} \oplus y_{19}, & t_{23} = t_{19} \oplus y_{21}, & t_{24} = t_{20} \oplus t_{18}, & \\
t_{25} = t_{21} \oplus t_{22}, & t_{26} = t_{21} \cdot t_{23}, & t_{27} = t_{24} \oplus t_{26}, & t_{28} = t_{25} \cdot t_{27}, \\
t_{29} = t_{28} \oplus t_{22}, & t_{30} = t_{23} \oplus t_{24}, & t_{31} = t_{22} \oplus t_{26}, & t_{32} = t_{31} \cdot t_{30}, \\
t_{33} = t_{32} \oplus t_{24}, & t_{34} = t_{23} \oplus t_{33}, & t_{35} = t_{27} \oplus t_{33}, & t_{36} = t_{24} \cdot t_{35}, \\
t_{37} = t_{36} \oplus t_{34}, & t_{38} = t_{27} \oplus t_{36}, & t_{39} = t_{29} \cdot t_{38}, & t_{40} = t_{25} \oplus t_{39}, \\
t_{41} = t_{40} \oplus t_{37}, & t_{42} = t_{29} \oplus t_{33}, & t_{43} = t_{29} \oplus t_{40}, & t_{44} = t_{33} \oplus t_{37}, \\
t_{45} = t_{42} \oplus t_{41}, & z_0 = t_{44} \cdot y_{15}, & z_1 = t_{37} \cdot y_6, & z_2 = t_{33} \cdot x_7, \\
z_3 = t_{43} \cdot y_{16}, & z_4 = t_{40} \cdot y_1, & z_5 = t_{29} \cdot y_7, & z_6 = t_{42} \cdot y_{11}, \\
z_7 = t_{45} \cdot y_{17}, & z_8 = t_{41} \cdot y_{10}, & z_9 = t_{44} \cdot y_{12}, & z_{10} = t_{37} \cdot y_3, \\
z_{11} = t_{33} \cdot y_4, & z_{12} = t_{43} \cdot y_{13}, & z_{13} = t_{40} \cdot y_5, & z_{14} = t_{29} \cdot y_2, \\
z_{15} = t_{42} \cdot y_9, & z_{16} = t_{45} \cdot y_{14}, & z_{17} = t_{41} \cdot y_8. &
\end{array}
$$

The matrix B_S takes $z_0, z_1, \cdots, z_{17}$ as input and outputs $s_0, s_1, \cdots, s_7$.

$$
\begin{array}{llll}
t_{46} = z_{15} \oplus z_{16}, & t_{47} = z_{10} \oplus z_{11}, & t_{48} = z_5 \oplus z_{13}, & t_{49} = z_9 \oplus z_{10}, \\
t_{50} = z_2 \oplus z_{12}, & t_{51} = z_2 \oplus z_5, & t_{52} = z_7 \oplus z_8, & t_{53} = z_0 \oplus z_3, \\
t_{54} = z_6 \oplus z_7, & t_{55} = z_{16} \oplus z_{17}, & t_{56} = z_{12} \oplus t_{48}, & t_{57} = t_{50} \oplus t_{53}, \\
t_{58} = z_4 \oplus t_{46}, & t_{59} = z_3 \oplus t_{54}, & t_{60} = t_{46} \oplus t_{57}, & t_{61} = z_{14} \oplus t_{57}, \\
t_{62} = t_{52} \oplus t_{58}, & t_{63} = t_{49} \oplus t_{58}, & t_{64} = z_4 \oplus t_{59}, & t_{65} = t_{61} \oplus t_{62}, \\
t_{66} = z_1 \oplus t_{63}, & s_0 = t_{59} \oplus t_{63}, & s_6 = \overline{t_{56} \oplus t_{62}}, & s_7 = \overline{t_{48} \oplus t_{60}}, \\
t_{67} = t_{64} \oplus t_{65}, & s_3 = t_{53} \oplus t_{66}, & s_4 = t_{51} \oplus t_{66}, & s_5 = t_{47} \oplus t_{65}, \\
s_1 = \overline{t_{64} \oplus s_3}, & s_2 = \overline{t_{55} \oplus t_{67}}. & &
\end{array}
$$

3.3 Our Improved Classical Circuit of the S-Box^{-1} of AES

By using the tower technique, we propose an improved implementation of the S-box^{-1} (see in Table 2), which can be used to construct our quantum circuit of AES's S-box^{-1}. We can express AES's S-box^{-1} as $S^{-1}(x) = B' \cdot F'(U' \cdot x)$, where the matrix $U' \in F_2^{8 \times 22}$ takes $x_0, x_1, \cdots, x_7$ as input and outputs $y_0, y_1, \cdots, y_{21}$, where $U_i = x_i$ (for $0 \leq i \leq 7$).

$$
\begin{array}{llll}
y_5 = \overline{U_1}, & y_4 = U_5 \oplus U_0, & y_{13} = U_2 \oplus y_5, & y_6 = y_4 \oplus y_{13}, \\
y_9 = y_5 \oplus y_4, & y_{20} = U_4 \oplus y_4, & y_{18} = \overline{U_6}, & y_2 = y_6 \oplus y_{18}, \\
t_0 = U_1 \oplus U_0, & y_7 = U_4 \oplus t_0, & y_{17} = y_6 \oplus y_7, & y_{16} = U_7 \oplus t_0, \\
y_3 = y_2 \oplus y_{16}, & y_{15} = y_5 \oplus y_7, & y_{11} = y_9 \oplus y_{17}, & y_{19} = y_{17} \oplus y_{16}, \\
t_1 = U_3 \oplus t_0, & y_1 = y_{20} \oplus t_1, & y_{14} = y_3 \oplus y_1, & y_{12} = U_2 \oplus t_1, \\
y_0 = y_2 \oplus y_{12}, & y_{10} = y_{14} \oplus y_{12}, & y_8 = y_1 \oplus y_0, & y_{21} = U_7 \oplus y_{12}.
\end{array}
$$

The non-linear function $F' : \mathbb{F}_2^{22} \to \mathbb{F}_2^{18}$ takes $y_0, y_1, \cdots, y_{21}$ as input and outputs $z_0, z_1, \cdots, z_{17}$.

$$t_2 = y_7 \cdot y_3, \quad t_3 = y_{17} \cdot y_{16}, \quad t_4 = y_6 \cdot y_2, \quad t_5 = y_{15} \cdot y_{14},$$
$$t_6 = y_{13} \cdot y_{12}, \quad t_7 = y_{11} \cdot y_{10}, \quad t_8 = y_5 \cdot y_1, \quad t_9 = y_9 \cdot y_8,$$
$$t_{10} = y_4 \cdot y_0, \quad t_{11} = t_2 \oplus t_3, \quad t_{12} = t_4 \oplus t_3, \quad t_{13} = t_5 \oplus t_6,$$
$$t_{14} = t_5 \oplus t_7, \quad t_{15} = t_8 \oplus t_9, \quad t_{16} = t_{10} \oplus t_9, \quad t_{17} = t_{11} \oplus t_{13},$$
$$t_{18} = t_{17} \oplus y_{21}, \quad t_{19} = t_{12} \oplus t_{14}, \quad t_{20} = t_{19} \oplus y_{20}, \quad t_{21} = t_{15} \oplus t_{13},$$
$$t_{22} = t_{21} \oplus y_{19}, \quad t_{23} = t_{16} \oplus t_{14}, \quad t_{24} = t_{23} \oplus y_{18},$$
$$t_{25} = t_{18} \oplus t_{20}, \quad t_{26} = t_{20} \cdot t_{24}, \quad t_{27} = t_{22} \oplus t_{26}, \quad t_{28} = t_{25} \cdot t_{27},$$
$$t_{29} = t_{18} \oplus t_{28}, \quad t_{30} = t_{22} \oplus t_{24}, \quad t_{31} = t_{18} \oplus t_{26}, \quad t_{32} = t_{30} \cdot t_{31},$$
$$t_{33} = t_{22} \oplus t_{32}, \quad t_{34} = t_{24} \oplus t_{33}, \quad t_{35} = t_{27} \oplus t_{33}, \quad t_{36} = t_{22} \cdot t_{35},$$
$$t_{37} = t_{36} \oplus t_{34}, \quad t_{38} = t_{27} \oplus t_{36}, \quad t_{39} = t_{29} \cdot t_{38}, \quad t_{40} = t_{39} \oplus t_{25},$$
$$t_{41} = t_{33} \oplus t_{37}, \quad t_{42} = t_{33} \oplus t_{29}, \quad t_{43} = t_{37} \oplus t_{40}, \quad t_{44} = t_{42} \oplus t_{43},$$
$$t_{45} = t_{29} \oplus t_{40}, \quad z_{17} = y_3 \cdot t_{33}, \quad z_{16} = y_{16} \cdot t_{41}, \quad z_{15} = y_2 \cdot t_{37},$$
$$z_{14} = y_{12} \cdot t_{43}, \quad z_{13} = y_{14} \cdot t_{42}, \quad z_{12} = y_{10} \cdot t_{44}, \quad z_{11} = y_1 \cdot t_{29},$$
$$z_{10} = y_8 \cdot t_{45}, \quad z_9 = y_0 \cdot t_{40}, \quad z_8 = y_7 \cdot t_{33}, \quad z_7 = y_{17} \cdot t_{41},$$
$$z_6 = y_6 \cdot t_{37}, \quad z_5 = y_{13} \cdot t_{43}, \quad z_4 = y_{15} \cdot t_{42}, \quad z_3 = y_{11} \cdot t_{44},$$
$$z_2 = y_5 \cdot t_{29}, \quad z_1 = y_9 \cdot t_{45}, \quad z_0 = y_4 \cdot t_{40}.$$

The matrix B' takes $z_0, z_1, \cdots, z_{17}$ as input and outputs $s_0, s_1, \cdots, s_7$.

$$t_{46} = z_5 \oplus z_3, \quad t_{47} = z_6 \oplus t_{46}, \quad t_{48} = z_8 \oplus t_{47}, \quad t_{49} = z_{17} \oplus z_{11},$$
$$t_{50} = t_{48} \oplus t_{49}, \quad t_{51} = z_{16} \oplus z_{10}, \quad s_5 = t_{50} \oplus t_{51}, \quad t_{52} = z_{15} \oplus z_{12},$$
$$t_{53} = z_{15} \oplus z_9, \quad s_2 = t_{50} \oplus t_{53}, \quad t_{54} = z_{16} \oplus z_{13}, \quad t_{55} = t_{52} \oplus t_{54},$$
$$s_7 = t_{48} \oplus t_{55}, \quad t_{56} = z_2 \oplus z_1, \quad t_{57} = z_2 \oplus z_0, \quad s_0 = t_{46} \oplus t_{57},$$
$$t_{58} = s_2 \oplus t_{56}, \quad t_{59} = z_5 \oplus z_4, \quad t_{60} = z_8 \oplus z_7, \quad s_3 = t_{58} \oplus t_{60},$$
$$t_{61} = z_{14} \oplus z_{11}, \quad t_{62} = t_{51} \oplus t_{52}, \quad s_4 = t_{61} \oplus t_{62}, \quad t_{63} = s_5 \oplus t_{59},$$
$$t_{64} = t_{55} \oplus s_0, \quad t_{65} = t_{58} \oplus t_{63}, \quad s_6 = t_{64} \oplus t_{65}, \quad t_{66} = s_2 \oplus s_7,$$
$$t_{67} = s_4 \oplus t_{65}, \quad s_1 = t_{66} \oplus t_{67}.$$

Table 2. Summary of the resources to implement AES's S-box^{-1}

Algorithm	# XOR/XNOR	XOR3	# NAND	# AND	# NOR	# NOT	Source
S-box	96	0	0	36	0	0	[19]
	80	0	34	0	6	0	[7]
	83	0	0	32	0	0	[5]
	81	0	0	32	0	0	[1]
	69	0	33	0	8	0	[28]
	51	9	33	0	8	0	[28]
S-box^{-1}	87	0	0	34	0	0	[1]
	81	0	34	0	0	6	[7]
	82	0	0	32	0	4	Sect. 3.3

4   The Quantum Circuits for the Basic AES Operations

4.1   Quantum Circuits for Three Linear Transformations of AES

As pointed out in [11], the three linear transformations of AES can be implemented with the CNOT gates as follows. We just adopt their quantum circuit of three linear transformations in our quantum circuits of AES.

1. **AddRoundKey:** The AddRoundKey transformation xors 128-bit roundkey to the state, which can be executed with 128 CNOT gates in parallel.
2. **ShiftRows:** Since the ShiftRows transformation just permutes the order of the sixteen bytes of AES, we do not need any quantum gates to execute these operations.
3. **MixColumns:** The MixColumns transformation operates a column (32 bits) at a time, which can be specified with a 32×32 matrix. The resultant circuit of MixColumns has 277 CNOT gates with a total depth of 39, which can be estimated by an LUP-decomposition [11].

In the following, we present our improved quantum circuit implementations of AES's S-box and S-box^{-1}. The details of our implementation of AES S-box and S-box^{-1} are available at https://github.com/Asiacrypt2020submission370/aes/.

4.2   Improved Quantum Circuit Implementations of AES's S-Box

In this subsection, we propose some improved quantum circuit implementations of AES's S-box. Our quantum circuit of AES's S-box considers the following two cases: $|x\rangle|0^a\rangle \longrightarrow |x\rangle|S(x)\rangle|0^{a-8}\rangle$ and $|x\rangle|b\rangle|0^{a-8}\rangle \longrightarrow |x\rangle|S(x)\oplus b\rangle|0^{a-8}\rangle$. Note that the prior works [11,18] only considered $|x\rangle|0^a\rangle \longrightarrow |x\rangle|S(x)\rangle|0^{a-8}\rangle$.

Firstly, we improve the quantum circuit sending $|x\rangle|0^8\rangle$ to $|x\rangle|S(x)\rangle$. In this part, we propose an improved quantum circuit of AES's S-box, which requires fewer qubits than the prior work. In detail, our quantum circuit of AES's S-box requires only 6 ancilla qubits, which maps $|x\rangle|0^{14}\rangle$ to $|x\rangle|S(x)\rangle|0^6\rangle$. The prior work needed at least 16 ancilla qubits to compute the Sbox, which maps $|x\rangle|0^{24}\rangle$ to $|x\rangle|S(x)\rangle|0^{16}\rangle$. Our improved quantum circuits of AES's S-box adopt the following two new observations, which are based on the algebraic structures of the S-box (see Sect. 3.2).

Observation 1. *As shown in Sect. 3.2, the 18 values of $z_0, \cdots, z_{17}$ can be obtained with the knowledge of $t_{29}, t_{33}, t_{37}, t_{40}, t_{41}, t_{42}, t_{43}, t_{44}, t_{45}$ and $x_7, y_0, \cdots, y_{17}$, where $y_0, \cdots, y_{17}$ are the linear combination of $x_0, x_1, \cdots, x_7$. Besides, $t_{41}, t_{42}, t_{43}, t_{44}, t_{45}$ can be obtained by the linear combination of $t_{29}, t_{33}, t_{37}, t_{40}$. In other words, we can obtain $z_0, \cdots, z_{17}$ only with the knowledge of $t_{29}, t_{33}, t_{37}, t_{40}$ and $x_0, x_1, \cdots, x_7$.*

Observation 2. *The $s_0, s_1, \cdots, s_7$ can be obtained by a linear combination of $z_0, \cdots, z_{17}$ as follows, where $\bar{s}$ applies the NOT operation on s.*

$$s_0 = z_3 \oplus z_4 \oplus z_6 \oplus z_7 \oplus z_9 \oplus z_{10} \oplus z_{15} \oplus z_{16},$$

$$\overline{s_1} = z_0 \oplus z_1 \oplus z_6 \oplus z_7 \oplus z_9 \oplus z_{10} \oplus z_{15} \oplus z_{16},$$

$$\overline{s_2} = z_0 \oplus z_2 \oplus z_6 \oplus z_8 \oplus z_{12} \oplus z_{14} \oplus z_{15} \oplus z_{17},$$

$$s_3 = z_0 \oplus z_1 \oplus z_3 \oplus z_4 \oplus z_9 \oplus z_{10} \oplus z_{15} \oplus z_{16},$$

$$s_4 = z_1 \oplus z_2 \oplus z_4 \oplus z_5 \oplus z_9 \oplus z_{10} \oplus z_{15} \oplus z_{16},$$

$$s_5 = z_0 \oplus z_2 \oplus z_3 \oplus z_4 \oplus z_7 \oplus z_8 \oplus z_{10} \oplus z_{11} \oplus z_{12} \oplus z_{14} \oplus z_{15} \oplus z_{16},$$

$$\overline{s_6} = z_4 \oplus z_5 \oplus z_7 \oplus z_8 \oplus z_{12} \oplus z_{13} \oplus z_{15} \oplus z_{16},$$

$$\overline{s_7} = z_0 \oplus z_2 \oplus z_3 \oplus z_5 \oplus z_{12} \oplus z_{13} \oplus z_{15} \oplus z_{16}.$$

The above two observations explore the linear relationship between different parameters in the algebraic structure of AES's S-box. According to Observation 1, we can obtain $z_0, \cdots, z_{17}$ with the knowledge of $t_{29}, t_{33}, t_{37}, t_{40}$ and $x_0, x_1, \cdots, x_7$. Obviously, we can obtain $t_{29}, t_{33}, t_{37}, t_{40}$ by storing all t_i (for $2 \leq i \leq 40$), which requires 39 ancilla qubits (see in Sect. 3.2). Algorithm 3 can output $t_{29}, t_{33}, t_{37}, t_{40}$ with 6 ancilla qubits by reusing some ancilla qubits.

As shown in our Algorithm 3 can be constructed with 6 ancilla qubit, 17 Tofoli gates, and 93 CNOT gates, while our previous Algorithm 3 required 6 ancilla qubits, 21 Toffoli gates, and 109 CNOT gates to calculate the same values. There are several t_i can be computed in parallel as follows. First, we can compute t_7 and t_9 in parallel. Second, we can compute t_2 and t_{18} in parallel. Third, t_{29} and t_{37} can also computed in parallel. To sum up, the Toffoli depth of Algorithm 3 is 14.

Since Algorithm 3 need to recompute t_{36} and t_2, we can obtain a new depth-qubit tradeoff of Algorithm 3 as follows. First, we observe that our new Algorithm 3 shall compute t_{36} three times. If we introduce a new ancilla qubit to store t_{36}, we do not need to recompute t_{36}. That is, we can save two Toffoli gates and two Toffoli depth by storing t_{36} in a new ancilla qubit. Second, our new Algorithm 3 need to compute t_2 twice. If we introduce a new ancilla qubit to store t_2, we can save one Toffoli gates and one Toffoli depth. That is, we can obtain a new depth-qubit tradeoff i of our new Algorithm 3 with $14 - i$ Toffoli depth, $6 + i$ ancilla qubits, $17 - (i + 1)$ Toffoli gates, and $93 + (i + 1)$ CNOT gates (for $1 \leq i \leq 2$).

Algorithm 3. Output t_{29}, t_{33}, t_{37}, t_{40} of S-box with 6 ancilla qubits

---

Input, $U[i] = x[i]$; (for $0 \leq i \leq 7$);
Input $T[j] = 0$; (for $0 \leq j \leq 5$);
1: $U[0] = U[0] \oplus U[6]$;
2: $U[6] = U[6] \oplus U[2] \oplus U[4] \oplus U[5]$;
3: $T[0] = (U[0] \cdot U[6]) \oplus T[0]$;
4: $T[1] = T[1] \oplus T[0]$;
5: $U[1] = U[1] \oplus U[2] \oplus U[7]$;
6: $U[2] = U[2] \oplus U[1] \oplus U[4] \oplus U[5] \oplus U[6]$;
7: $T[1] = (U[1] \cdot U[2]) \oplus T[1]$;
8: $U[0] = U[0] \oplus U[1] \oplus U[2] \oplus U[3]$;
9: $U[6] = U[6] \oplus U[1] \oplus U[7]$;
10: $T[2] = (U[0] \cdot U[6]) \oplus T[2]$;
11: $T[3] = T[3] \oplus T[2]$;
12: $U[5] = U[5] \oplus U[3]$;
13: $U[0] = U[0] \oplus U[2] \oplus U[4] \oplus U[6] \oplus U[7]$;
14: $T[3] = (U[5] \cdot U[0]) \oplus T[3]$;
15: $T[1] = T[1] \oplus T[3]$;
16: $U[0] = U[0] \oplus U[3] \oplus U[4]$;
17: $T[1] = T[1] \oplus U[0]$;
18: $U[0] = U[0] \oplus U[1] \oplus U[2] \oplus U[6] \oplus U[7]$;

19: $U[6] = U[6] \oplus U[7]$;
20: $T[0] = (U[0] \cdot U[6]) \oplus T[0]$;
21: $U[0] = U[0] \oplus U[2] \oplus U[5]$;
22: $U[5] = U[5] \oplus U[0] \oplus U[3] \oplus U[4]$;
23: $T[4] = (U[0] \cdot U[5]) \oplus T[4]$;
24: $T[3] = T[3] \oplus T[4]$;
25: $U[0] = U[0] \oplus U[1] \oplus U[3]$;
26: $U[5] = U[5] \oplus U[7]$;
27: $T[3] = (U[0] \cdot U[5]) \oplus T[3]$;
28: $U[1] = U[1] \oplus U[2] \oplus U[4] \oplus U[5] \oplus U[6]$;
29: $T[3] = T[3] \oplus U[1]$;
30: $U[1] = U[1] \oplus U[2] \oplus U[4] \oplus U[6]$;
31: $U[0] = U[0] \oplus U[2]$;
32: $T[2] = (U[1] \cdot U[0]) \oplus T[2]$;
33: $T[0] = T[0] \oplus T[2]$;
34: $T[2] = T[2] \oplus T[4]$;
35: $U[0] = U[0] \oplus U[1] \oplus U[2] \oplus U[3] \oplus U[5]$;
36: $U[5] = U[5] \oplus U[7]$;
37: $T[4] = (U[0] \cdot U[5]) \oplus T[4]$;
38: $U[2] = U[2] \oplus U[3] \oplus U[4] \oplus U[5] \oplus U[6]$;
39: $T[0] = T[0] \oplus U[2]$;
40: $U[1] = U[1] \oplus U[3] \oplus U[5] \oplus U[7]$;
41: $T[2] = (U[1] \cdot U[7]) \oplus T[2]$;
42: $U[0] = U[0] \oplus U[2] \oplus U[4] \oplus U[6] \oplus U[7]$;
43: $T[2] = T[2] \oplus U[0]$;

44: $T[4] = (T[1] \cdot T[3]) \oplus T[4]$;
45: $T[1] = T[1] \oplus T[0]$;
46: $T[4] = T[4] \oplus T[2]$;
47: $T[5] = (T[1] \cdot T[4]) \oplus T[5]$;
48: $T[5] = T[5] \oplus T[0]$;
49: $T[1] = T[1] \oplus T[0] \oplus T[5]$;
50: $T[4] = T[4] \oplus T[2] \oplus T[0]$;
51: $T[5] = T[5] \oplus T[4]$;
52: $T[1] = (T[0] \cdot T[5]) \oplus T[1]$;
53: $T[3] = T[3] \oplus T[2]$;
54: $T[2] = (T[3] \cdot T[4]) \oplus T[2]$;
55: $T[4] = (T[0] \cdot T[5]) \oplus T[4]$;
56: $T[3] = (T[2] \cdot T[4]) \oplus T[3]$;
57: $T[4] = (T[0] \cdot T[5]) \oplus T[4]$;
58: $T[5] = T[5] \oplus T[4]$;
59: $U[3] = U[3] \oplus U[2] \oplus U[4] \oplus U[5] \oplus U[6]$;
60: $U[4] = U[4] \oplus U[0] \oplus U[3] \oplus U[7]$;
61: $U[2] = U[2] \oplus U[6]$;
62: $U[5] = U[5] \oplus U[7]$;
63: $U[6] = U[6] \oplus U[0] \oplus U[1] \oplus U[3] \oplus U[4] \oplus U[5]$;
64: Output $U[0] = y_1 9$, $U[1] = y_4$, $U[2] = y_2$, $U[3] = y_5$, $U[4] = y_{14}$, $U[5] = y_6$, $U[6] = y_{21}$, $U[7] = x_7$ and $T[0] = t_{24}$, $T[1] = t_{37}$, $T[2] = t_2 9$, $T[3] = t_{40}$, $T[4] = t_2 7$, $T[5] = t_3 3$.

Note that Langenberg *et al.* in [18] also utilized the linear relationship between z_i and s_j (for $0 \leq i \leq 17$ and $0 \leq j \leq 7$) to reduce the number of Toffoli gates. However, they did not explore the whole linear relationship like Observation 2. As a result, they needed to introduce a new ancilla qubit Z in their work. According to Observation 2, we can construct Algorithm 4 for AES's S-box with the output of Algorithm 3.

Algorithm 4. Compute AES's S-box, when the output qubits are zero.

Input $T[0] = t_{29}$, $T[1] = t_{37}$, $T[2] = t_{40}$, $T[3] = t_{33}$, $T[4] = t_{24}$, $T[5] = t_{27}$;
Input $U[0] = y_5$, $U[1] = y_{19}$, $U[2] = y_{14}$, $U[3] = y_2$, $U[4] = y_6$, $U[5] = y_{21}$, $U[6] = y_4$, $U[7] = x_7$;
1: $U[1] = U[1] \oplus U[0] \oplus U[4] \oplus U[2]$;
2: $T[3] = T[3] \oplus T[1]$;
3: $S[5] = (T[3] \cdot U[1]) \oplus S[5]$;
4: $S[6] = S[6] \oplus S[5]$;
5: $U[1] = U[1] \oplus U[0] \oplus U[4] \oplus U[2]$;
6: $T[3] = T[3] \oplus T[1]$;
7: $S[2] = (T[2] \cdot U[2]) \oplus S[2]$;
8: $S[5] = S[2] \oplus S[5]$;
9: $S[2] = S[2] \oplus S[6]$;
10: $S[4] = (T[1] \cdot U[5]) \oplus S[4]$;
11: $S[1] = S[1] \oplus S[4]$;
12: $S[3] = S[3] \oplus S[4]$;
13: $U[5] = U[5] \oplus U[7]$;
14: $T[1] = T[1] \oplus T[5]$;
15: $S[7] = (T[1] \cdot U[5]) \oplus S[7]$;
16: $S[1] = S[1] \oplus S[7]$;
17: $S[3] = S[3] \oplus S[7]$;
18: $S[4] = S[4] \oplus S[7]$;
19: $U[5] = U[5] \oplus U[7]$;
20: $T[1] = T[1] \oplus T[5]$;
21: $S[7] = (T[5] \cdot U[7]) \oplus S[7]$;

22: $S[2] = S[2] \oplus S[7]$;
23: $S[5] = S[5] \oplus S[7]$;
24: $S[6] = S[6] \oplus S[7]$;
25: $U[1] = U[1] \oplus U[3] \oplus U[0] \oplus U[4] \oplus U[5] \oplus U[6]$;
26: $S[7] = (T[2] \cdot U[1]) \oplus S[7]$;
27: $S[2] = S[2] \oplus S[7]$;
28: $S[4] = S[4] \oplus S[7]$;
29: $S[5] = S[5] \oplus S[7]$;
30: $U[1] = U[1] \oplus U[3] \oplus U[0] \oplus U[4] \oplus U[5] \oplus U[6]$;
31: $U[2] = U[2] \oplus U[3]$;
32: $T[3] = T[3] \oplus T[2]$;
33: $S[7] = (T[3] \cdot U[2]) \oplus S[7]$;
34: $S[2] = S[2] \oplus S[7]$;
35: $S[5] = S[5] \oplus S[7]$;
36: $U[2] = U[2] \oplus U[3]$;
37: $T[3] = T[3] \oplus T[2]$;
38: $S[7] = (T[3] \cdot U[3]) \oplus S[7]$;
39: $S[6] = S[6] \oplus S[7]$;
40: $U[6] = U[6] \oplus U[3] \oplus U[2]$;
41: $T[2] = T[3] \oplus T[2]$;
42: $S[0] = (T[2] \cdot U[6]) \oplus S[0]$;
43: $S[4] = S[4] \oplus S[0]$;
44: $S[6] = S[6] \oplus S[0]$;
45: $S[7] = S[7] \oplus S[0]$;

46: $U[6] = U[6] \oplus U[3] \oplus U[2]$;
47: $T[2] = T[3] \oplus T[2]$;
48: $U[1] = U[1] \oplus U[0] \oplus U[4] \oplus U[2] \oplus U[5]$;
49: $S[0] = (T[3] \cdot U[1]) \oplus S[0]$;
50: $S[1] = S[1] \oplus S[0]$;
51: $S[2] = S[2] \oplus S[0]$;
52: $S[3] = S[3] \oplus S[0]$;
53: $S[4] = S[4] \oplus S[0]$;
54: $S[5] = S[5] \oplus S[0]$;
55: $S[6] = S[6] \oplus S[0]$;
56: $U[1] = U[1] \oplus U[0] \oplus U[4] \oplus U[2] \oplus U[5]$;
57: $U[3] = U[7] \oplus U[3] \oplus U[0] \oplus U[4] \oplus U[5] \oplus U[6] \oplus U[1]$;
58: $T[5] = T[5] \oplus T[2]$;
59: $S[0] = (T[5] \cdot U[3]) \oplus S[0]$;
60: $S[2] = S[2] \oplus S[0]$;
61: $S[5] = S[5] \oplus S[0]$;
62: $S[6] = S[6] \oplus S[0]$;
63: $U[3] = U[7] \oplus U[3] \oplus U[0] \oplus U[4] \oplus U[5] \oplus U[6] \oplus U[1]$;
64: $T[5] = T[5] \oplus T[2]$;
65: $U[3] = U[7] \oplus U[3] \oplus U[2] \oplus U[5] \oplus U[6]$;
66: $T[5] = T[5] \oplus T[2] \oplus T[1] \oplus T[3]$;
67: $S[0] = (T[5] \cdot U[3]) \oplus S[0]$;
68: $S[3] = S[3] \oplus S[0]$;
69: $S[4] = S[4] \oplus S[0]$;
70: $S[5] = S[5] \oplus S[0]$;
71: $S[6] = S[6] \oplus S[0]$;
72: $U[3] = U[7] \oplus U[3] \oplus U[2] \oplus U[5] \oplus U[6]$;
73: $T[5] = T[5] \oplus T[2] \oplus T[1] \oplus T[3]$;
74: $U[2] = U[2] \oplus U[3] \oplus U[4]$;
75: $T[5] = T[5] \oplus T[1]$;
76: $S[0] = (T[5] \cdot U[2]) \oplus S[0]$;
77: $S[5] = S[5] \oplus S[0]$;

78: $U[2] = U[2] \oplus U[3] \oplus U[4]$;
79: $T[5] = T[5] \oplus T[1]$;
80: $U[1] = U[1] \oplus U[3] \oplus U[4] \oplus U[2]$;
81: $S[0] = (T[1] \cdot U[1]) \oplus S[0]$;
82: $S[2] = S[2] \oplus S[0]$;
83: $S[6] = S[6] \oplus S[0]$;
84: $S[7] = S[7] \oplus S[0]$;
85: $U[1] = U[1] \oplus U[3] \oplus U[4] \oplus U[2]$;
86: $U[1] = U[1] \oplus U[2]$;
87: $T[5] = T[5] \oplus T[2]$;
88: $S[0] = (T[5] \cdot U[1]) \oplus S[0]$;
89: $S[2] = S[2] \oplus S[0]$;
90: $U[1] = U[1] \oplus U[2]$;
91: $T[5] = T[5] \oplus T[2]$;
92: $T[5] = T[5] \oplus T[2] \oplus T[1] \oplus T[3]$;
93: $S[0] = (T[5] \cdot U[4]) \oplus S[0]$;
94: $S[1] = S[1] \oplus S[0]$;
95: $S[3] = S[3] \oplus S[0]$;
96: $S[4] = S[4] \oplus S[0]$;
97: $S[5] = S[5] \oplus S[0]$;
98: $S[6] = S[6] \oplus S[0]$;
99: $S[7] = S[7] \oplus S[0]$;
100: $T[5] = T[5] \oplus T[2] \oplus T[1] \oplus T[3]$;
101: $U[1] = U[1] \oplus U[4] \oplus U[2]$;
102: $T[3] = T[3] \oplus T[1]$;
103: $S[2] = (T[3] \cdot U[1]) \oplus S[2]$;
104: $U[1] = U[1] \oplus U[4] \oplus U[2]$;
105: $T[3] = T[3] \oplus T[1]$;
106: $S[5] = (T[5] \cdot U[1]) \oplus S[5]$;
107: Compute $\overline{S[1]}$; $\overline{S[2]}$; $\overline{S[6]}$; $\overline{S[7]}$;
108: Adopt Algorithm 3 to set $T[i] = 0$ (for $0 \leq i \leq 5$) and $U[j] = x_j$ (for $0 \leq j \leq 7$);
109: Output $S[0]$, $S[1]$, $S[2]$, $S[3]$, $S[4]$, $S[5]$, $S[6]$, $S[7]$.

We can obtain the time and memory cost of Algorithm 4 as follows.

1. It needs 18 Toffoli gates and 140 CNOT gates to obtain z_i for $1 \leq i \leq 17$.
2. Since Algorithm 4 adopt Algorithm 3 twice to clean up the ancilla qubits, we can obtain a new depth-qubit trade-off i of Algorithm 4 as follows.

a. When $i = 0$, Algorithm 4 can compute the output of S-box with 6 ancilla qubits, 52 Toffoli gates, 326 CNOT gates, and 4 NOT gates. The Toffoli depth of Algorithm 4 in this case is $2 \times 14 + 13 = 41$.
b. When $1 \leq i \leq 2$, Algorithm 4 can compute the output of S-box with $6 + i$ ancilla qubits, $52 - 2(i + 1)$ Toffoli gates, $326 + 2(i + 1)$ CNOT gates, 4 NOT gates. The Toffoli depth of Algorithm 4 in this case is $41 - 2i$.

Next, we improve the quantum circuit sending $|x\rangle|b\rangle$ to $|x\rangle|S(x) \oplus b\rangle$. In this part, we propose a new quantum circuit of AES's S-box, which maps $|x\rangle|b\rangle|0^7\rangle$ to $|x\rangle|S(x) \oplus b\rangle|0^7\rangle$ with the output of Algorithm 3. Since the qubits encoding b are not necessarily zero, we cannot adopt Algorithm 4 directly. According to Observation 2, this problem can be solved by introducing a new ancilla qubit Z, which can be used to store each z_i. After filling Z with z_i, we just XOR Z to s_j according to linear relationship in Observation 2. Note that we shall clean up Z each time so as to store new z_i.

Since this Algorithm 5 is similar to Algorithm 4, we just give a brief description of Algorithm 5 in the following pseudo code.

Algorithm 5. Compute AES's S-box, when output qubits are not zero.

Input: the output of Algorithm 3;
1: $Z = Toffoli(t_{41}, y_{10}, Z)$;
2: $S[2] = CNOT(S[2], Z)$;
3: $S[5] = CNOT(S[5], Z)$;
4: $S[6] = CNOT(S[6], Z)$;
5: $Z = Toffoli(t_{41}, y_{10}, Z)$;
6: $Z = Toffoli(t_{29}, y_2, Z)$;
7: $S[2] = CNOT(S[2], Z)$;
8: $S[5] = CNOT(S[5], Z)$;
9: $Z = Toffoli(t_{29}, y_2, Z)$;
10: $Z = Toffoli(t_{37}, y_6, Z)$;
11: $S[1] = CNOT(S[1], Z)$;
12: $S[3] = CNOT(S[3], Z)$;
13: $S[4] = CNOT(S[4], Z)$;
14: $Z = Toffoli(t_{37}, y_6, Z)$;
15: $Z = Toffoli(t_{44}, y_{15}, Z)$;
16: $S[1] = CNOT(S[1], Z)$;
17: $S[2] = CNOT(S[2], Z)$;
18: $S[3] = CNOT(S[3], Z)$;
19: $S[5] = CNOT(S[5], Z)$;
20: $S[7] = CNOT(S[7], Z)$;
21: $Z = Toffoli(t_{44}, y_{15}, Z)$;
22: $Z = Toffoli(t_{33}, x_7, Z)$;
23: $S[2] = CNOT(S[2], Z)$;
24: $S[4] = CNOT(S[4], Z)$;
25: $S[5] = CNOT(S[5], Z)$;
26: $S[7] = CNOT(S[7], Z)$;
27: $Z = Toffoli(t_{33}, x_7, Z)$;
28: $Z = Toffoli(t_{29}, y_7, Z)$;
29: $S[4] = CNOT(S[4], Z)$;
30: $S[6] = CNOT(S[6], Z)$;
31: $S[7] = CNOT(S[7], Z)$;
32: $Z = Toffoli(t_{29}, y_7, Z)$;
33: $Z = Toffoli(t_{43}, y_{13}, Z)$;
34: $S[2] = CNOT(S[2], Z)$;
35: $S[5] = CNOT(S[5], Z)$;
36: $S[6] = CNOT(S[6], Z)$;
37: $S[7] = CNOT(S[7], Z)$;
38: $Z = Toffoli(t_{43}, y_{13}, Z)$;
39: $Z = Toffoli(t_{40}, y_5, Z)$;
40: $S[6] = CNOT(S[6], Z)$;
41: $S[7] = CNOT(S[7], Z)$;
42: $Z = Toffoli(t_{40}, y_5, Z)$;
43: $Z = Toffoli(t_{43}, y_{16}, Z)$;
44: $S[0] = CNOT(S[0], Z)$;
45: $S[3] = CNOT(S[3], Z)$;
46: $S[5] = CNOT(S[5], Z)$;
47: $S[7] = CNOT(S[7], Z)$;
48: $Z = Toffoli(t_{43}, y_{16}, Z)$;
49: $Z = Toffoli(t_{40}, y_1, Z)$;
50: $S[0] = CNOT(S[0], Z)$;
51: $S[3] = CNOT(S[3], Z)$;
52: $S[4] = CNOT(S[4], Z)$;
53: $S[5] = CNOT(S[5], Z)$;
54: $S[6] = CNOT(S[6], Z)$;
55: $Z = Toffoli(t_{40}, y_1, Z)$;
56: $Z = Toffoli(t_{42}, y_{11}, Z)$;
57: $S[0] = CNOT(S[0], Z)$;
58: $S[1] = CNOT(S[1], Z)$;
59: $S[2] = CNOT(S[2], Z)$;
60: $Z = Toffoli(t_{42}, y_{11}, Z)$;
61: $Z = Toffoli(t_{45}, y_{17}, Z)$;
62: $S[0] = CNOT(S[0], Z)$;
63: $S[1] = CNOT(S[1], Z)$;
64: $S[5] = CNOT(S[5], Z)$;
65: $S[6] = CNOT(S[6], Z)$;
66: $Z = Toffoli(t_{45}, y_{17}, Z)$;
67: $Z = Toffoli(t_{44}, y_{12}, Z)$;
68: $S[0] = CNOT(S[0], Z)$;
69: $S[1] = CNOT(S[1], Z)$;
70: $S[3] = CNOT(S[3], Z)$;
71: $S[4] = CNOT(S[4], Z)$;
72: $Z = Toffoli(t_{44}, y_{12}, Z)$;
73: $Z = Toffoli(t_{37}, y_3, Z)$;
74: $S[0] = CNOT(S[0], Z)$;
75: $S[1] = CNOT(S[1], Z)$;
76: $S[3] = CNOT(S[3], Z)$;
77: $S[4] = CNOT(S[4], Z)$;
78: $S[5] = CNOT(S[5], Z)$;
79: $Z = Toffoli(t_{37}, y_3, Z)$;
80: $Z = Toffoli(t_{42}, y_9, Z)$;
81: $S[0] = CNOT(S[0], Z)$;
82: $S[1] = CNOT(S[1], Z)$;
83: $S[2] = CNOT(S[2], Z)$;
84: $S[3] = CNOT(S[3], Z)$;
85: $S[4] = CNOT(S[4], Z)$;
86: $S[5] = CNOT(S[5], Z)$;
87: $S[6] = CNOT(S[6], Z)$;
88: $S[7] = CNOT(S[7], Z)$;
89: $Z = Toffoli(t_{42}, y_9, Z)$;
90: $Z = Toffoli(t_{45}, y_{14}, Z)$;
91: $S[0] = CNOT(S[0], Z)$;
92: $S[1] = CNOT(S[1], Z)$;
93: $S[3] = CNOT(S[3], Z)$;
94: $S[4] = CNOT(S[4], Z)$;
95: $S[5] = CNOT(S[5], Z)$;
96: $S[6] = CNOT(S[6], Z)$;
97: $S[7] = CNOT(S[7], Z)$;
98: $Z = Toffoli(t_{45}, y_{14}, Z)$;
99: $S[5] = Toffoli(t_{33}, y_4, S[5])$;
100: $S[2] = Toffoli(t_{41}, y_8, S[2])$;
101: Compute $\overline{S[1]}$; $\overline{S[2]}$; $\overline{S[6]}$; $\overline{S[7]}$;
102: Adopt Algorithm 3 to set $T[i] = 0$ (for $0 \leq i \leq 5$) and $U[j] = x_j$ (for $0 \leq j \leq 7$);
103: Output $S[0]$, $S[1]$, $S[2]$, $S[3]$, $S[4]$, $S[5]$, $S[6]$, $S[7]$.

Similar to Algorithm 4, we can obtain the time and memory cost of Algorithm 5 as follows

1. Algorithm 5 calculates each z_i (for $0 \leq i \leq 17$) in the same order as Algorithm 4. That is, Algorithm 5 needs the same cost to compute each t_i and y_j as Algorithm 4.

2. Since z_{11} (or z_{17}) only appears in S_5 (or S_2) (see in Observation 2), we can store z_{11} (or z_{17}) in S_5 (or S_2) without affecting the other output qubits. In other words, we can compute z_{11} and z_{17} in parallel with other z_i. Because we do not need to store z_{11} and z_{17} in Z, we just need to clean up Z sixteen times so as to store new z_i. That is, Algorithm 5 needs 34 Toffoli gates to calculate each z_i (for $0 \leq i \leq 17$).
3. Algorithm 5 shall adopt Algorithm 3 twice to compute S-box and clean up these ancilla qubits.

Similar to Algorithm 4, We can obtain a new depth-qubit trade-off i of Algorithm 5 as follows.

1. When $i = 0$, Algorithm 5 can compute the output of S-box with 7 ancilla qubits, 68 Toffoli gates, 352 CNOT gates, 4 NOT gates, and 60 Toffoli depth.
2. When $1 \leq i \leq 2$, we can compute S-box with $7+i$ ancilla qubits, $68 - 2(i+1)$ Toffoli gates, $352 + 2(i + 1)$ CNOT gates, 4 NOT gates, and $60 - 2i$ Toffoli depth.

4.3   Improved Quantum Circuit Implementation of the S-Box^{-1}

Here we propose an new quantum circuit of AES's S-box$^-1$ with 7 ancilla qubits, which maps $|x\rangle|S(x)\rangle|0^7\rangle$ to $|x \oplus S^{-1}(S(x))\rangle|S(x)\rangle|0^7\rangle = |0^8\rangle|S(x)\rangle|0^7\rangle$. We can adopt our quantum circuit of S-box^{-1} to remove some state values. We will use this property to improve the zig-zag method. Our quantum circuit of AES's S-box^{-1} benefits from the following observations, which are based on our improved classical circuit of AES's S-box^{-1}.

Observation 3. *The 18-bit $z_0, \cdots, z_{17}$ for computing S-box^{-1} can be obtained with the knowledge of $t_{29}, t_{33}, t_{37}, t_{40}, t_{41}, t_{42}, t_{43}, t_{44}, t_{45}$ and $y_0, \cdots, y_{21}$. Note that $y_0, \cdots, y_{21}$ are the linear combination of $x_0, \cdots, x_7$. Besides, $t_{41}, t_{42}, t_{43}, t_{44}, t_{45}$ can be obtained by the linear combination of $t_{29}, t_{33}, t_{37}, t_{40}$. That is, we can obtain $z_0, \cdots, z_{17}$ with the knowledge of $t_{29}, t_{33}, t_{37}, t_{40}$ and $x_0, \cdots, x_7$.*

Observation 4. *The 8-bit output of S-box^{-1} $s_0, \cdots, s_7$ can be seen as a linear combination of the 18-bit $z_0, \cdots, z_{17}$ as follows.*

$$s_0 = z_0 \oplus z_2 \oplus z_3 \oplus z_5$$
$$s_1 = z_1 \oplus z_2 \oplus z_4 \oplus z_5 \oplus z_{13} \oplus z_{14} \oplus z_{16} \oplus z_{17}$$
$$s_2 = z_3 \oplus z_5 \oplus z_6 \oplus z_8 \oplus z_9 \oplus z_{11} \oplus z_{15} \oplus z_{17}$$
$$s_3 = z_1 \oplus z_2 \oplus z_3 \oplus z_5 \oplus z_6 \oplus z_7 \oplus z_9 \oplus z_{11} \oplus z_{15} \oplus z_{17}$$
$$s_4 = z_{10} \oplus z_{11} \oplus z_{12} \oplus z_{14} \oplus z_{15} \oplus z_{16}$$
$$s_5 = z_3 \oplus z_5 \oplus z_6 \oplus z_8 \oplus z_{10} \oplus z_{11} \oplus z_{16} \oplus z_{17}$$
$$s_6 = z_0 \oplus z_1 \oplus z_3 \oplus z_4 \oplus z_9 \oplus z_{10} \oplus z_{12} \oplus z_{13}$$
$$s_7 = z_3 \oplus z_5 \oplus z_6 \oplus z_8 \oplus z_{12} \oplus z_{13} \oplus z_{15} \oplus z_{16}$$

According to Observation 3, we can obtain $z_0, \cdots, z_{17}$ by $t_{29}, t_{33}, t_{37}, t_{40}$ and $x_0, \cdots, x_7$. We propose Algorithm 6 to compute the $t_{29}, t_{33}, t_{37}, t_{40}$. As shown in Algorithm 6, we can compute the $z_0, \cdots, z_{17}$ of the S-box^{-1} with 6 ancilla qubits, 17 Toffoli gates, 110 CNOT gates and 12 NOT gates.

Algorithm 6. Compute t_{29}, t_{33}, t_{37}, t_{40} of S-box^{-1} with 6 ancilla qubits

Input $U[0] = x_7,\ U[1] = x_6,\ U[2] = x_5,\ U[3] = x_4,$
$U[4] = x_3,\ U[5] = x_2,\ U[6] = x_1\ U[7] = x_0;$
Input $T[j] = 0;$ (for $0 \leq j \leq 5$);

1: $U[7] = \overline{U[7] \oplus U[3]};$
2: $U[6] = U[6] \oplus U[5] \oplus U[4] \oplus U[3] \oplus U[1] \oplus U[0];$
3: $T[0] = (U[6] \cdot U[7]) \oplus T[0];$
4: $T[2] = T[2] \oplus T[0];$
5: $U[5] = \overline{U[5] \oplus U[3] \oplus U[2]};$
6: $U[7] = U[7] \oplus U[6] \oplus U[5] \oplus U[4] \oplus U[3] \oplus U[2] \oplus U[1];$

7: $T[0] = (U[5] \cdot U[7]) \oplus T[0];$
8: $T[1] = T[1] \oplus T[0];$
9: $U[7] = \overline{U[7] \oplus U[2] \oplus U[0]};$
10: $U[6] = U[6] \oplus U[5] \oplus U[4] \oplus U[3] \oplus U[2] \oplus U[0];$
11: $U[6] = \overline{U[6]};$
12: $T[2] = (U[6] \cdot U[7]) \oplus T[2];$
13: $T[3] = T[3] \oplus T[2];$
14: $U[5] = U[5] \oplus U[6] \oplus U[2] \oplus U[1];$
15: $U[7] = U[7] \oplus U[6] \oplus U[5] \oplus U[4] \oplus U[3] \oplus U[2] \oplus U[1];$

16: $T[0] = (U[5] \cdot U[7]) \oplus T[0];$
17: $T[2] = (U[5] \cdot U[7]) \oplus T[2];$
18: $U[7] = U[7] \oplus U[3] \oplus U[4];$
19: $U[5] = \overline{U[5] \oplus U[7] \oplus U[1] \oplus U[0]};$
20: $T[1] = (U[5] \cdot U[7]) \oplus T[1];$
21: $T[3] = (U[5] \cdot U[7]) \oplus T[3];$
22: $U[5] = U[5] \oplus U[6] \oplus U[3] \oplus U[0];$
23: $U[7] = U[7] \oplus U[5] \oplus U[2] \oplus U[1] \oplus U[0];$
24: $T[0] = (U[5] \cdot U[7]) \oplus T[0];$
25: $U[7] = \overline{U[7] \oplus U[5] \oplus U[3] \oplus U[1] \oplus U[0]};$
26: $U[1] = \overline{U[1] \oplus U[7]};$
27: $T[1] = (U[7] \cdot U[1]) \oplus T[1];$
28: $U[1] = U[1] \oplus U[7] \oplus U[6] \oplus U[3];$
29: $U[4] = \overline{U[4] \oplus U[3] \oplus U[2] \oplus U[1]};$
30: $T[2] = (U[1] \cdot U[4]) \oplus T[2];$
31: $U[5] = \overline{U[5] \oplus U[3] \oplus U[2] \oplus U[1]};$
32: $U[6] = U[6] \oplus U[4];$
33: $T[3] = (U[6] \cdot U[5]) \oplus T[3];$

34: $U[7] = U[7] \oplus U[3] \oplus U[4] \oplus U[1] \oplus U[0];$
35: $T[0] = T[0] \oplus U[7];$
36: $U[5] = U[5] \oplus U[3];$
37: $T[1] = T[1] \oplus U[5];$
38: $U[7] = U[7] \oplus U[4] \oplus U[1];$
39: $T[2] = T[2] \oplus U[7];$
40: $U[6] = U[6] \oplus U[3] \oplus U[4] \oplus U[1];$
41: $T[3] = T[3] \oplus U[6];$
42: $T[4] = (T[1] \cdot T[3]) \oplus T[4];$
43: $T[3] = T[3] \oplus T[2];$
44: $T[4] = T[4] \oplus T[0];$
45: $T[5] = T[5] \oplus T[2];$
46: $T[5] = (T[3] \cdot T[4]) \oplus T[5];$
47: $T[4] = T[4] \oplus T[0];$
48: $T[4] = T[4] \oplus T[2];$
49: $T[3] = T[3] \oplus T[2];$
50: $T[5] = T[5] \oplus T[4];$
51: $T[4] = (T[5] \cdot T[2]) \oplus T[4];$
52: $T[2] = (T[1] \cdot T[3]) \oplus T[2];$
53: $T[1] = T[0] \oplus T[1];$
54: $T[0] = (T[1] \cdot T[2]) \oplus T[0];$
55: $T[1] = (T[0] \cdot T[4]) \oplus T[1];$
56: $T[4] = T[4] \oplus T[2];$
57: $T[2] = T[2] \oplus T[5];$
58: $T[3] = T[3] \oplus T[2];$
59: $T[4] = T[4] \oplus T[3];$
60: $U[7] = \overline{U[7] \oplus U[6] \oplus U[5] \oplus U[2] \oplus U[1]};$
61: $U[5] = U[5] \oplus U[7] \oplus U[3] \oplus U[2] \oplus U[1] \oplus U[0];$
62: $U[5] = \overline{U[5]};$
63: $U[6] = U[6] \oplus U[3] \oplus U[4] \oplus U[1];$
64: $U[0] = U[0] \oplus U[5] \oplus U[3] \oplus U[7];$
65: $U[3] = U[6] \oplus U[5] \oplus U[3] \oplus U[4] \oplus U[1];$
66: $U[2] = \overline{U[6] \oplus U[5] \oplus U[3] \oplus U[4] \oplus U[2] \oplus U[0]};$
67: Output $U[0] = y_7,\ U[1] = y_5,\ U[2] = y_4,\ U[3] = y_6,\ U[4] = y_1,\ U[5] = y_2,\ U[6] = y_0,\ U[7] = y_3;$
and $T[0] = t_{29},\ T[1] = t_{40},\ U[6] = t_{33},\ T[3] = t_{34},\ T[4] = t_{37},\ T[5] = t_{35}.$

As shown in the above, we can obtain the 14 outputs of Algorithm 6 with 7 ancilla qubits, 17 Toffoli gates, 110 CNOT gates and 12 NOT gates. The Toffoli depth of Algorithm 6 is 14, because we can compute some t_i in parallel as follows. First, we can compute the two t_6 in parallel. Second, we can compute the two t_7 in parallel. Third, we can compute the t_8 and t_{10} in parallel.

Similar to Algorithm 3, we can obtain a new depth-qubit trade-off of Algorithm 6 by introducing more ancilla qubits. Note that Algorithm 6 need to compute t_6, t_7, t_{26} twice. If we introduce 3 more ancilla qubits to store these values, we do not need to recompute t_6, t_7, t_{26} again. That is, we can obtain a new depth-qubit trade-off of Algorithm 6, which needs $7+i$ ancilla qubits, $17-i$ Toffoli gates, $110+i$ CNOT gates and 12 NOT gates (for $0 \leq i \leq 3$). The Toffoli depth of this new trade-off Algorithm 6 is 13 (for $1 \leq i \leq 3$).

After obtaining the 14-bit output of Algorithm 6, we can construct Algorithm 7 by using Observation 4. Since our algorithm for S-box^{-1} can not make sure the output bits are zero, we shall introduce a new ancilla qubit Z to store each z_i in this algorithm.

Algorithm 7. Compute the 8-bit output of the S-box^{-1} of AES

Input $T[0] = t_{29}$, $T[1] = t_{40}$, $T[2] = t_{33}$,
$T[3] = t_{34}$, $T[4] = t_{37}$, $T[5] = t_{35}$;
Input $U[0] = y_7$, $U[1] = y_5$, $U[2] = y_4$,
$U[3] = y_6$, $U[4] = y_1$, $U[5] = y_2$, $U[6] = y_0$,
$U[7] = y_3$.
1: $Z = (T[1] \cdot U[2]) \oplus Z$;
2: $S[0] = S[0] \oplus Z$;
3: $S[6] = S[6] \oplus Z$;
4: $Z = (T[1] \cdot U[2]) \oplus Z$;
5: $T[0] = T[0] \oplus T[1]$;
6: $U[2] = U[2] \oplus U[1]$;
7: $Z = (T[0] \cdot U[2]) \oplus Z$;
8: $S[1] = S[1] \oplus Z$;
9: $S[3] = S[3] \oplus Z$;
10: $S[6] = S[6] \oplus Z$;
11: $Z = (T[0] \cdot U[2]) \oplus Z$;
12: $T[0] = T[0] \oplus T[1]$;
13: $U[2] = U[2] \oplus U[1]$;
14: $Z = (T[0] \cdot U[1]) \oplus Z$;
15: $S[0] = S[0] \oplus Z$;
16: $S[1] = S[1] \oplus Z$;
17: $S[3] = S[3] \oplus Z$;
18: $Z = (T[0] \cdot U[1]) \oplus Z$;
19: $T[4] = T[4] \oplus T[1] \oplus T[0] \oplus T[2]$;
20: $U[2] = U[2] \oplus U[3] \oplus U[1] \oplus U[0]$;
21: $Z = (T[4] \cdot U[2]) \oplus Z$;
22: $S[0] = S[0] \oplus Z$;
23: $S[2] = S[2] \oplus Z$;
24: $S[3] = S[3] \oplus Z$;
25: $S[5] = S[5] \oplus Z$;
26: $S[6] = S[6] \oplus Z$;
27: $S[7] = S[7] \oplus Z$;
28: $Z = (T[4] \cdot U[2]) \oplus Z$;
29: $T[4] = T[4] \oplus T[1] \oplus T[0] \oplus T[2]$;
30: $U[2] = U[2] \oplus U[3] \oplus U[1] \oplus U[0]$;
31: $T[0] = T[0] \oplus T[2]$;
32: $U[1] = U[1] \oplus U[0]$;
33: $Z = (T[0] \cdot U[1]) \oplus Z$;
34: $S[1] = S[1] \oplus Z$;
35: $S[6] = S[6] \oplus Z$;
36: $Z = (T[0] \cdot U[1]) \oplus Z$;
37: $T[0] = T[0] \oplus T[2]$;
38: $U[1] = U[1] \oplus U[0]$;
39: $T[4] = T[4] \oplus T[1]$;
40: $U[3] = U[3] \oplus U[2]$;
41: $Z = (T[4] \cdot U[3]) \oplus Z$;
42: $S[0] = S[0] \oplus Z$;
43: $S[1] = S[1] \oplus Z$;
44: $S[2] = S[2] \oplus Z$;
45: $S[3] = S[3] \oplus Z$;
46: $S[5] = S[5] \oplus Z$;
47: $S[7] = S[7] \oplus Z$;
48: $Z = (T[4] \cdot U[3]) \oplus Z$;
49: $T[4] = T[4] \oplus T[1]$;
50: $U[3] = U[3] \oplus U[2]$;
51: $Z = (T[4] \cdot U[3]) \oplus Z$;
52: $S[2] = S[2] \oplus Z$;

53: $S[3] = S[3] \oplus Z$;
54: $S[5] = S[5] \oplus Z$;
55: $S[7] = S[7] \oplus Z$;
56: $Z = (T[4] \cdot U[3]) \oplus Z$;
57: $Z = (T[2] \cdot U[0]) \oplus Z$;
58: $S[2] = S[2] \oplus Z$;
59: $S[5] = S[5] \oplus Z$;
60: $S[7] = S[7] \oplus Z$;
61: $Z = (T[2] \cdot U[0]) \oplus Z$;
62: $Z = (T[1] \cdot U[6]) \oplus Z$;
63: $S[2] = S[2] \oplus Z$;
64: $S[3] = S[3] \oplus Z$;
65: $S[6] = S[6] \oplus Z$;
66: $Z = (T[1] \cdot U[6]) \oplus Z$;
67: $T[1] = T[1] \oplus T[0]$;
68: $U[6] = U[6] \oplus U[4]$;
69: $Z = (T[1] \cdot U[6]) \oplus Z$;
70: $S[4] = S[4] \oplus Z$;
71: $S[5] = S[5] \oplus Z$;
72: $S[6] = S[6] \oplus Z$;
73: $Z = (T[1] \cdot U[6]) \oplus Z$;
74: $T[1] = T[1] \oplus T[0]$;
75: $U[6] = U[6] \oplus U[4]$;
76: $Z = (T[0] \cdot U[4]) \oplus Z$;
77: $S[2] = S[2] \oplus Z$;
78: $S[3] = S[3] \oplus Z$;
79: $S[4] = S[4] \oplus Z$;
80: $S[5] = S[5] \oplus Z$;
81: $Z = (T[0] \cdot U[4]) \oplus Z$;
82: $T[4] = T[4] \oplus T[1] \oplus T[0] \oplus T[2]$;
83: $U[7] = U[7] \oplus U[6] \oplus U[5] \oplus U[4]$;
84: $Z = (T[4] \cdot U[7]) \oplus Z$;
85: $S[4] = S[4] \oplus Z$;
86: $S[6] = S[6] \oplus Z$;
87: $S[7] = S[7] \oplus Z$;
88: $Z = (T[4] \cdot U[7]) \oplus Z$;
89: $T[4] = T[4] \oplus T[1] \oplus T[0] \oplus T[2]$;
90: $U[7] = U[7] \oplus U[6] \oplus U[5] \oplus U[4]$;
91: $T[0] = T[0] \oplus T[2]$;
92: $U[7] = U[7] \oplus U[4]$;
93: $Z = (T[0] \cdot U[7]) \oplus Z$;
94: $S[1] = S[1] \oplus Z$;
95: $S[6] = S[6] \oplus Z$;
96: $S[7] = S[7] \oplus Z$;
97: $Z = (T[0] \cdot U[7]) \oplus Z$;
98: $T[0] = T[0] \oplus T[2]$;
99: $U[7] = U[7] \oplus U[4]$;
100: $T[1] = T[1] \oplus T[4]$;
101: $U[6] = U[6] \oplus U[5]$;
102: $Z = (T[1] \cdot U[6]) \oplus Z$;
103: $S[1] = S[1] \oplus Z$;
104: $S[4] = S[4] \oplus Z$;
105: $Z = (T[1] \cdot U[6]) \oplus Z$;
106: $T[1] = T[1] \oplus T[4]$;
107: $U[6] = U[6] \oplus U[5]$;
108: $Z = (T[4] \cdot U[5]) \oplus Z$;
109: $S[2] = S[2] \oplus Z$;

110: $S[3] = S[3] \oplus Z$;
111: $S[4] = S[4] \oplus Z$;
112: $S[7] = S[7] \oplus Z$;
113: $Z = (T[4] \cdot U[5]) \oplus Z$;
114: $T[4] = T[4] \oplus T[2]$;
115: $U[7] = U[7] \oplus U[5]$;
116: $Z = (T[4] \cdot U[7]) \oplus Z$;
117: $S[1] = S[1] \oplus Z$;
118: $S[4] = S[4] \oplus Z$;
119: $S[5] = S[5] \oplus Z$;
120: $S[7] = S[7] \oplus Z$;
121: $Z = (T[4] \cdot U[7]) \oplus Z$;
122: $T[4] = T[4] \oplus T[2]$;
123: $U[7] = U[7] \oplus U[5]$;
124: $Z = (T[2] \cdot U[7]) \oplus Z$;

125: $S[1] = S[1] \oplus Z$;
126: $S[2] = S[2] \oplus Z$;
127: $S[3] = S[3] \oplus Z$;
128: $S[5] = S[5] \oplus Z$;
129: $Z = (T[2] \cdot U[7]) \oplus Z$;
130: $T[4] = T[4] \oplus T[2]$;
131: $U[0] = U[0] \oplus U[3]$;
132: $S[3] = (T[4] \cdot U[0]) \oplus S[3]$;
133: $T[4] = T[4] \oplus T[2]$;
134: $U[0] = U[0] \oplus U[3]$;
135: Adopt the Algorithm 6 to set $T[i] = 0$ (for $0 \le i \le 5$) and $U[j] = x_j$ (for $0 \le j \le 7$);
136: Output $S[0]$, $S[1]$, $S[2]$, $S[3]$, $S[4]$, $S[5]$, $S[6]$, $S[7]$.

The time and space cost of Algorithm 7 can be computed as follows. First, Algorithm 7 needs 35 Toffoli gates and 115 CNOT gates to compute each z_i for $0 \le i \le 17$. Second, Algorithm 7 needs to adopt Algorithm 6 twice to compute S-box^{-1} and clean up the ancilla qubits, which set $T[i] = 0$ and $U[j] = x_j$ for $0 \le i \le 5$ and $0 \le j \le 7$. To sum up, Algorithm 7 can output S-box^{-1} with 7 ancilla qubits, 69 Toffoli gates, 335 CNOT and 24 NOT gates. The depth of Algorithm 7 is 62. Given more ancilla qubits, we can also propose a new depth-qubit trade-off of Algorithm 7, which needs $7 + i$ ancilla qubits, $69 - 2i$ Toffoli gates, $335 + 2i$ CNOT, and 24 NOT gates (for $0 \le i \le 3$). The Toffoli depth of the above algorithm is 60 (for $1 \le i \le 3$).

5   Our Strategies for the Zig-Zag Method and the Key Schedule of AES

5.1   Zig-Zag Method with Improved Depth-Qubit Trade-Offs

The prior quantum circuit of AES [3,11,18] adopted the zig-zag method to reduce the number of qubits. As shown in Fig. 1, the prior zig-zag method needed 512 qubits by reusing some qubits. However, they could not remove the Round 4, Round 7 and Round 9, unless the entire process was reversed. The reason for this drawback is that the prior work only considered the encryption algorithm in their zig-zag method. That is, they should know Round $i - 1$ so as to remove Round i. In this subsection, we propose an improved zig-zag method (see in Fig. 2), which just needs 256 qubits. We can achieve this goal by applying our quantum circuit of S-box^{-1} in our zig-zag method.

Denote the j-th output of the 16 S-box in Round i as s_j^i (for $0 \le j \le 15$), while the j-th byte of Round $i - 1$ is denoted as r_j^{i-1} (for $0 \le j \le 15$). Given $|r^{i-1}\rangle|0^{128}\rangle$, we can explain how to obtain Round i and remove Round $i - 1$ within these 256 qubits.

1. Given $|r^{i-1}\rangle$, we can compute the first r bytes of s_0^i, s_1^i, $\cdots$, s_{r-1}^i with our Algorithm 4. We can store s_0^i, s_1^i, $\cdots$, s_{r-1}^i in the first $8 \cdot r$ qubits of $|0^{128}\rangle$, while the left $|0^{128-8 \cdot r}\rangle$ qubits can be used for ancilla qubits. We can choose r to obtain a improved depth-qubits trade-off for our quantum circuit.

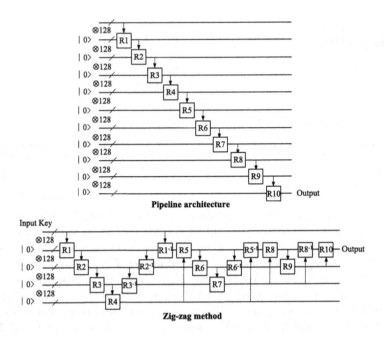

Fig. 1. Comparison between the pipeline architecture and the zig-zag method. The round i is indicated by R_i, while R_i^{-1} means to remove the round i.

2. After computing $s_0^i, \cdots, s_{r-1}^i$, we can remove the first r bytes in Round $i-1$ by using our Algorithm 7. That is, we can compute $|s_j^i\rangle|r_j^{i-1}\rangle|0^7\rangle \xrightarrow{Algorithm\ 7} |s_j^i\rangle|r_j^{i-1} \oplus Sbox^{-1}(s_j^i)\rangle|0^7\rangle$ for $0 \leq j \leq r-1$). Note that we can still use the left $|0^{128-8\cdot r}\rangle$ qubits as ancilla qubits. Since $r_j^{i-1} = Sbox^{-1}(s_j^i)$, we have $|s_j^i\rangle|r_j^{i-1} \oplus Sbox^{-1}(s_j^i)\rangle|0^7\rangle = |s_j^i\rangle|0^8\rangle|0^7\rangle$

3. These re-zero $|0^{8\cdot r}\rangle$ in Round $i-1$ can be used as ancilla qubits for obtaining $s_r^i, s_{r+1}^i, \cdots, s_{15}^i$ and removing the left $16-r$ bytes in Round $i-1$.

4. After computing the 16 bytes of $s_0^i, s_1^i, \cdots, s_{15}^i$, we can compute the 16 bytes of Round i by computing $AK \circ MC \circ SR(S_i)$, where S_i is the 16 bytes output of the S-box in Round i, and AK, MC and SR are the abbreviations for AddRoundKey, MixColumns and ShiftRows.

After generating Round i, we can compute Round $i+1$ and remove Round i in a similar way. We can assign the newly calculated Round $i+1$ to these 128 re-initialized zero qubits of Round $i-1$. We can compute the ciphertext of AES-128 by repeating the above operation 10 times. Obviously, we can construct the zig-zag method for AES-192/-256 with 256 qubits in a similar way, where the prior zig-zag method needs 656 qubits for AES-192/-256 both.

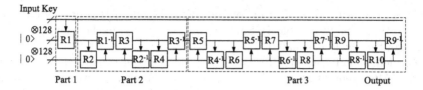

Fig. 2. Our method for improving the zig-zag method. The round i is indicated by R_i, while R_i^{-1} means to remove the round i.

5.2 Improved Quantum Circuits for the Key Schedule of AES

In this subsection, we propose some improved quantum circuit implementations for the key schedule of AES-128/-192/-256.

Our Strategy for the Key Schedule of AES-128. Our quantum circuit for the key-schedule of AES-128 only requires 128 qubits, while the prior works needed at least 224 qubits. We can achieve this improvement by combining our quantum circuit of S-box (Algorithm 5) with the property proposed by Langenberg *et al.* [18] (see Table 3).

We take W_{16} as an example to explain Table 3, where $W_{16} : W_{15}, W_{11}, W_7, W_3$. It means W_{16} can be computed with the knowledge of W_{15}, W_{11}, W_7, and W_3. According to Algorithm 1, we can rewrite W_{16} as $W_{16} = W_{15} \oplus W_{11}W_7 \oplus W_3 \oplus SubWord(RotWord(W_{15})) \oplus Rcon(4)$. We can obtain the other W_i in Table 3 similarly.

According to Table 3, we can compute all W_j (for $4 \leq i \leq 43$) with these ten 32-bit W_{4i+3} (for $1 \leq i \leq 10$). In [11], Grassl *et al.* just stored these ten 32-bit W_{4i+3} (for $1 \leq i \leq 10$) with $32 \times 10 = 320$ qubits to generate each roundkey of AES-128. In [18], Langenberg *et al.* showed that they could generate all round keys of AES-128 with 224 qubits by reusing some qubits as follows. After computing seven 32-qubit words $W_7, W_{11}, W_{15}, W_{19}, W_{23}, W_{27}, W_{31}$, they just cleaned up W_7 so as to assign W_{32} to these 32 re-zero qubits. Then they could compute W_{33}, W_{34} and W_{35} one by one with the knowledge of $W_{19}, W_{23}, W_{27}, W_{31}$. Obviously, they could compute the left round-keys similarly.

When the output qubits were not zero, Langenberg *et al.* could not apply their quantum circuit of S-box to compute AES's S-box. As a result, they should remove W_7 to generate W_{32}. Based on Algorithm 5, our improved quantum circuit for the key schedule of AES-128 can be explained as follows.

1 As shown in Sect. 6, we can generate four 32-qubit words $W_7, W_{11}, W_{15}, W_{19}$ in the 128 zero qubits.
2 Since we have no zero qubits left, we shall remove $W_7, W_{11}, W_{15}, W_{19}$ to generate new W_{4i+3} (for $5 \leq i \leq 10$). In detail, we can compute W_{20} by XORing $SubWord(RotWord(W_{19})), Rcon(5), W_{19}, W_{11}, W_{15}$ to W_7. We shall adopt Algorithm 5 to compute SubWord, because the output qubits are not zero. As a result, we can assign the newly calculated W_{20} to W_7 without introducing new qubits.

3 After generating W_{20}, we can compute W_{21}, W_{22} and W_{23} one by one with W_{11}, W_{15}, W_{19} (see Table 3). Since we only store W_{23} in the memory, we can assign the newly calculated W_{20+j} to W_{20+j-1} (for $1 \leq j \leq 3$).

4 The left round keys W_i (for $24 \leq i \leq 43$) can be generated in a similar way. After generating W_{4i-1}, W_{4i-5}, W_{4i-9}, and W_{4i-13}, we can assign the newly calculated W_{4i} to W_{4i-13} (for $5 \leq i \leq 10$) without introducing new qubits. After computing W_{4i}, we can generate W_{4i+1}, W_{4i+2}, W_{4i+3} as follows: $W_{4i+1} = W_{4i} \oplus W_{4i-1} \oplus W_{4i-9}$, $W_{4i+2} = W_{4i+1} \oplus W_{4i-1} \oplus W_{4i-5}$, $W_{4i+3} = W_{4i+2} \oplus W_{4i-1}$. We can assign the newly calculated W_{4i+j} to W_{4i+j-1} (for $1 \leq j \leq 3$).

Our Strategy for the Key Schedule of AES-192 and AES-256. Similar to AES-128, we can obtain a property for AES-192 (or AES-256) in Table 4 (or Table 5).

The quantum circuit for the key schedule of AES-192 is similar to AES-128. After generating W_{11}, W_{17}, W_{23}, W_{29}, W_{35} and W_{41} in the 192 qubits, we can compute W_{42} by xoring $SubWord(RotWord(W_{41}))$, $Rcon(7)$, W_{35}, W_{17} to W_{11}. Then we can compute the round-key W_{42+j} (for $1 \leq j \leq 5$) one by one with the knowledge of W_{42+j-1}, W_{17}, W_{23}, W_{29}, W_{35} and W_{41}. Obviously, we can compute left round keys for AES-192 in a similar way. To sum up, we can compute the 12 round-key of AES-192 with 192 qubits.

The quantum circuit for the key schedule of AES-256 can be constructed as follows. After generating the eight round-keys W_{11}, W_{15}, W_{19}, W_{23}, W_{27}, W_{31}, W_{35} and W_{39} in the quantum memory, we can compute W_{40} for AES-256 by XORing $SubWord(RotWord(W_{39}))$, $Rcon(5)$, W_{35}, W_{27}, W_{19} to W_{11}. Then we can compute the round-key W_{40+j} ($1 \leq j \leq 3$) for Round 10 one by one with the knowledge of W_{39}, W_{35}, W_{27}, W_{19}. Similar to W_{40}, we can obtain the left round key W_{44}, W_{48}, W_{52}, and W_{56} without introducing new qubits. To sum up, we can compute the 14 round-key of AES-256 with 256 qubits.

Table 3. The keys required to construct each round-key of AES-128.

$W_4 : W_3, W_0$	$W_5 : W_4, W_1$	$W_6 : W_5, W_2$	$W_7 : W_6, W_3$
$W_8 : W_7, W_3, W_2, W_1$	$W_9 : W_8, W_7, W_3, W_2$	$W_{10} : W_7, W_3$	$W_{11} : W_{10}, W_7$
$W_{12} : W_{11}, W_7, W_2$	$W_{13} : W_{12}, W_{11}, W_3$	$W_{14} : W_{13}, W_{11}, W_7$	$W_{15} : W_{14}, W_{11}$
$W_{16} : W_{15}, W_{11}, W_7, W_3$	$W_{17} : W_{16}, W_{15}, W_7$	$W_{18} : W_{17}, W_{15}, W_{11}$	$W_{19} : W_{18}, W_{15}$
$W_{20} : W_{19}, W_{15}, W_{11}, W_7$	$W_{21} : W_{20}, W_{19}, W_{11}$	$W_{22} : W_{21}, W_{19}, W_{15}$	$W_{23} : W_{22}, W_{19}$
$W_{24} : W_{23}, W_{19}, W_{15}, W_{11}$	$W_{25} : W_{24}, W_{23}, W_{15}$	$W_{26} : W_{25}, W_{23}, W_{19}$	$W_{27} : W_{26}, W_{23}$
$W_{28} : W_{27}, W_{23}, W_{19}, W_{15}$	$W_{29} : W_{28}, W_{27}, W_{19}$	$W_{30} : W_{29}, W_{27}, W_{23}$	$W_{31} : W_{30}, W_{27}$
$W_{32} : W_{31}, W_{27}, W_{23}, W_{19}$	$W_{33} : W_{32}, W_{31}, W_{23}$	$W_{34} : W_{33}, W_{31}, W_{27}$	$W_{35} : W_{34}, W_{31}$
$W_{36} : W_{35}, W_{31}, W_{27}, W_{23}$	$W_{37} : W_{36}, W_{35}, W_{27}$	$W_{38} : W_{37}, W_{35}, W_{31}$	$W_{39} : W_{38}, W_{35}$
$W_{40} : W_{39}, W_{35}, W_{31}, W_{27}$	$W_{41} : W_{40}, W_{39}, W_{31}$	$W_{42} : W_{41}, W_{39}, W_{35}$	$W_{43} : W_{42}, W_{39}$

Table 4. The keys required to construct round-key of AES-192.

$W_6 : W_5, W_0$	$W_7 : W_6, W_1$	$W_8 : W_7, W_2$
$W_9 : W_8, W_3$	$W_{10} : W_9, W_4$	$W_{11} : W_{10}, W_5$
$W_{12} : W_{11}, W_1, W_2, W_3, W_4, W_5$	$W_{13} : W_{12}, W_{11}, W_2, W_3, W_4, W_5$	$W_{14} : W_{13}, W_{11}, W_3, W_4, W_5$
$W_{15} : W_{14}, W_{11}, W_4, W_5$	$W_{16} : W_{15}, W_{11}, W_5$	$W_{17} : W_{16}, W_{11}$
$W_{18} : W_{17}, W_{11}, W_2, W_4$	$W_{19} : W_{18}, W_{17}, W_3, W_5$	$W_{20} : W_{19}, W_{17}, W_{11}, W_4$
$W_{21} : W_{20}, W_{17}, W_5$	$W_{22} : W_{21}, W_{17}, W_{11}$	$W_{23} : W_{22}, W_{17}$
$W_{24} : W_{23}, W_{17}, W_3, W_4$	$W_{25} : W_{24}, W_{23}, W_4, W_5$	$W_{26} : W_{25}, W_{23}, W_{17}, W_{11}, W_5$
$W_{27} : W_{26}, W_{23}, W_{11}$	$W_{28} : W_{27}, W_{23}, W_{17}$	$W_{29} : W_{28}, W_{23}$
$W_{30} : W_{29}, W_{23}, W_4$	$W_{31} : W_{30}, W_{29}, W_5$	$W_{32} : W_{31}, W_{29}, W_{23}, W_{17}, W_{11}$
$W_{33} : W_{32}, W_{29}, W_{17}$	$W_{34} : W_{33}, W_{29}, W_{23}$	$W_{35} : W_{34}, W_{29}$
$W_{36} : W_{35}, W_{29}, W_{11}, W_5$	$W_{37} : W_{36}, W_{35}, W_{11}$	$W_{38} : W_{37}, W_{35}, W_{29}, W_{23}, W_{17}$
$W_{39} : W_{38}, W_{35}, W_{29}$	$W_{40} : W_{39}, W_{35}, W_{29}$	$W_{41} : W_{40}, W_{35}$
$W_{42} : W_{41}, W_{35}, W_{17}, W_{11}$	$W_{43} : W_{42}, W_{41}, W_{17}$	$W_{44} : W_{43}, W_{41}, W_{35}, W_{29}, W_{23}$
$W_{45} : W_{44}, W_{41}, W_{35}$	$W_{46} : W_{45}, W_{41}, W_{35}$	$W_{47} : W_{46}, W_{41}$
$W_{48} : W_{47}, W_{41}, W_{23}, W_{17}$	$W_{49} : W_{48}, W_{47}, W_{23}$	$W_{50} : W_{49}, W_{47}, W_{41}, W_{35}, W_{29}$
$W_{51} : W_{50}, W_{47}, W_{41}$		

Table 5. The keys required to construct round-key of AES-256.

$W_8 : W_7, W_0$	$W_9 : W_8, W_1$	$W_{10} : W_9, W_2$	$W_{11} : W_{10}, W_3$
$W_{12} : W_{11}, W_4$	$W_{13} : W_{12}, W_5$	$W_{14} : W_{13}, W_6$	$W_{15} : W_{14}, W_7$
$W_{16} : W_{15}, W_{11}, W_3, W_2, W_1$	$W_{17} : W_{16}, W_{11}, W_3, W_2$	$W_{18} : W_{17}, W_{11}, W_3$	$W_{19} : W_{18}, W_{11}$
$W_{20} : W_{19}, W_{15}, W_7, W_6, W_5$	$W_{21} : W_{20}, W_{15}, W_7, W_6$	$W_{22} : W_{21}, W_{15}, W_7$	$W_{23} : W_{22}, W_{15}$
$W_{24} : W_{23}, W_{19}, W_{11}, W_2$	$W_{25} : W_{24}, W_{19}, W_3$	$W_{26} : W_{25}, W_{19}, W_{11}$	$W_{27} : W_{26}, W_{19}$
$W_{28} : W_{27}, W_{23}, W_{15}, W_6$	$W_{29} : W_{28}, W_{23}, W_7$	$W_{30} : W_{29}, W_{23}, W_{15}$	$W_{31} : W_{30}, W_{23}$
$W_{32} : W_{31}, W_{27}, W_{19}, W_{11}, W_3$	$W_{33} : W_{32}, W_{31}, W_{11}$	$W_{34} : W_{33}, W_{27}, W_{19}$	$W_{35} : W_{34}, W_{27}$
$W_{36} : W_{35}, W_{31}, W_{23}, W_{15}, W_7$	$W_{37} : W_{36}, W_{35}, W_{15}$	$W_{38} : W_{37}, W_{31}, W_{23}$	$W_{39} : W_{38}, W_{31}$
$W_{40} : W_{39}, W_{35}, W_{27}, W_{19}, W_{11}$	$W_{41} : W_{40}, W_{39}, W_{19}$	$W_{42} : W_{41}, W_{35}, W_{27}$	$W_{43} : W_{42}, W_{35}$
$W_{44} : W_{43}, W_{39}, W_{31}, W_{23}, W_{15}$	$W_{45} : W_{44}, W_{43}, W_{23}$	$W_{46} : W_{45}, W_{39}, W_{31}$	$W_{47} : W_{46}, W_{39}$
$W_{48} : W_{47}, W_{43}, W_{35}, W_{27}, W_{19}$	$W_{49} : W_{48}, W_{47}, W_{27}$	$W_{50} : W_{49}, W_{43}, W_{35}$	$W_{51} : W_{50}, W_{43}$
$W_{52} : W_{51}, W_{47}, W_{39}, W_{31}, W_{23}$	$W_{53} : W_{52}, W_{51}, W_{31}$	$W_{54} : W_{53}, W_{47}, W_{39}$	$W_{55} : W_{54}, W_{47}$
$W_{56} : W_{55}, W_{51}, W_{43}, W_{35}, W_{27}$	$W_{57} : W_{56}, W_{55}, W_{35}$	$W_{58} : W_{57}, W_{51}, W_{43}$	$W_{59} : W_{58}, W_{51}$

6 Improved Quantum Circuit Implementations of AES

6.1 Our Improved Quantum Circuit of AES-128

As shown in Fig. 2, we can divide our quantum circuit of AES-128 into three parts. Part 1 only contains Round 1, which does not need the S-box^{-1} operation. Part 2 contains Round 2, Round 3 and Round 4. Part 3 contains the left 6 rounds, which shall use Algorithm 5 to compute the round-keys.

After denoting r_i^j and s_i^{j+1} as the i-th byte of Round j and the S-box operations in Round $j + 1$ (for $0 \le j \le 9$ and $0 \le i \le 15$), the time and memory cost of each parts can be computed as follows.

The Time and Space Cost of Part 1. We just compute Round 1 and remove Round 0 in Part 1 (see in Fig. 3).

1. We can obtain Round 0 by implementing at most 128 Pauli-X gates (or called NOT gate) on the input keys W_0, W_1, W_2, W_3.

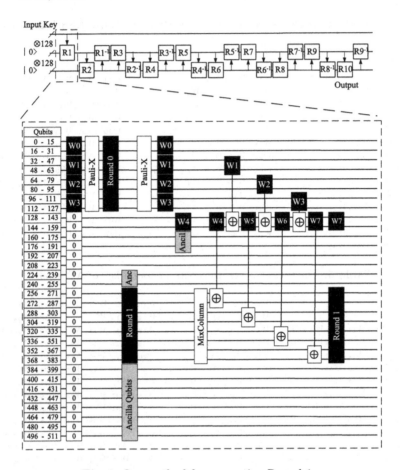

Fig. 3. Our method for computing Round 1.

2. We can adopt Algorithm 4 in parallel to compute s_i^1 (for $0 \leq i \leq 15$), because we have 384 zero qubits (from the 128 to 511 qubits in initial state in Fig. 3). Since we need 128 qubits to store these 16 bytes s_i^1 (for $0 \leq i \leq 15$), we have $384 - 128 = 256$ qubits left for ancilla qubits. In other words, we can obtain a depth-qubit trade-off $i = 2$ for these 16 S-box operations. That is, we can implement these 16 S-box operations with 128 ancilla qubits, 736 Toffoli gates and 5,312 CNOT gates. The Toffoli depth of these 16 S-box operations is $41 - 4 = 37$, because we can implement the 16 S-box in parallel.

3. After obtaining s_i^1 (for $0 \leq i \leq 15$), we can apply at most 128 NOT gates to Round 0 so as to obtain W_0, W_1, W_2, W_3 again. Then we can compute the round-key W_4, W_5, W_6, W_7 for Round 1 with the knowledge of W_0, W_1, W_2, W_3. Similar to step 2, we can obtain a depth-qubit trade-off $i = 2$ for these 4 S-box operations for W_4, because we have 224 ancilla qubits left. That is, we need 184 Toffoli gates and 1328 CNOT gates to implement these 4 S-box operations. The Toffoli depth of this operation is 37.

4. We not only require $3 \times 32 = 96$ CNOT gates and 1 NOT gate to produce W_4, W_5, W_6, W_7, but also need 128 CNOT gates to implement the AddRoundKey operation. In addition, we still need $277 \times 4 = 1108$ CNOT gates to implement 4 times MixColumns operations.

To sum up, we can implement Part 1 with 920 Toffoli gates, 7,972 CNOT gates, and 337 NOT gates. Since the 16 S-box in Round 1 and W_4 cannot be implemented in parallel, the Toffoli depth of the above operation is 74.

The Time and Space Cost of Part 2. Part 2 contains three similar rounds from Round 2 to Round 4.

In the following, we show the time and memory cost of computing Round 4 and removing Round 3, which can be divided into 5 phases (see in Fig. 4).

1. We can compute $s_0^4, \cdots, s_7^4$ in Round 4 and the first two bytes S-box operations of W_{16}, which requires 80 qubits to store these 10 bytes output of S-box. Since we have 160 zero qubits (the 224–255 and 384–511 qubits in state0 in Fig. 4), we have $160 - 80 = 80$ qubits left for ancilla qubits. As a result, we can obtain a depth-qubit trade-off $i = 2$ for these 10 S-box operations. That is, we can implement these 10 S-box operations with 80 ancilla qubits, 460 Toffoli gates, 3320 CNOT gates and 40 NOT gates. The Toffoli depth of these 10 S-box operations is 37.

2. We can remove $r_0^3, \cdots, r_7^3$ in Round 3 by adopting Algorithm 7. Since we have 80 zero qubits (the 240–255 and 448–511 qubits in state1 in Fig. 4), we can obtain a depth-qubit trade-off $i = 3$ for these 8 S-box^{-1} operations. That is, we can implement these 8 S-box^{-1} operations with 80 ancilla qubits, 504 Toffoli gates, 2728 CNOT gates and 192 NOT gates. The Toffoli depth of the 8 S-box^{-1} operations is 60.

3. We can compute $s_8^4 \cdots, s_{15}^4$ in Round 4 and the last two bytes of W_{16}, which requires 80 qubits to store these 10 bytes output of S-box. Since we have 144 zero qubits (the 240–319 and 448–511 qubits in state2 in Fig. 4), we have $144 - 80 = 64$ qubits left for ancilla qubits. In other words, we can obtain the depth-qubit trade-off $i = 1$ (and $i = 0$) for the first 4 S-box (the left 6 S-box) operations. That is, we can implement the first 4 S-box operations with $4 * 7 = 28$ ancilla qubits, 192 Toffoli gates, 1320 CNOT gates and 16 NOT gates, while the left 6 S-box operations can be implemented with 36 ancilla qubits, 312 Toffoli gates, 1956 CNOT gates and 24 NOT gates. To sum up, we can implement these 10 S-box operations with 64 ancilla qubits, 504 Toffoli gates, 3276 CNOT gates and 40 NOT gates. The Toffoli depth of these 10 S-box operations is 41.

4. We can remove the $r_8^3, \cdots, r_{15}^3$ in Round 3 by adopting Algorithm 7. Since we have 64 zero qubits here (the 256–319 qubits in state3 in Fig. 4), we can obtain a depth-qubit trade-off $i = 1$ for these 8 S-box^{-1} operations. That is, we can implement these 8 S-box^{-1} operations with 64 ancilla qubits, 544 Toffoli gates, 2688 CNOT gates and 192 NOT gates. The Toffoli depth of the 8 S-box^{-1} operations is 61.

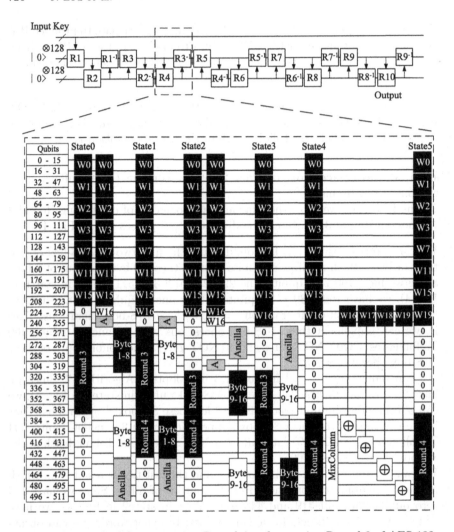

Fig. 4. Our method for computing Round 4 and removing Round 3 of AES-128.

5. We shall implement the MixColumns and AddRoundKey operations so as to obtain Round 4. The MixColumns operation for 128-bit state requires $277 \times 4 = 1108$ CNOT operations. According to the round-key algorithm of AES-128, after the SubWord operation, we still need $32 \times 8 = 256$ CNOT gates and 1 NOT gate to compute W_{16}, W_{17}, W_{18}, W_{19}. As a result, we can implement the AddRoundKey with $256+128 = 384$ CNOT gates and 1 NOT gate.

To sum up, we need 2012 Toffoli gates, 13504 CNOT gates and 465 NOT gates to obtain Round 4 and remove Round 3. The Toffoli depth of the above five steps is 199. Since the time and memory cost of the left two rounds in Part

2 is similar to the above operation, we just provide some results and ignore the details. First, we require 1928 Toffoli gates, 13556 CNOT gates and 465 NOT gates to obtain Round 3 and remove Round 2. The Toffoli depth of this transformation is 194. Second, we require 1968 Toffoli gates, 13548 CNOT gates and 465 NOT gates to obtain Round 2 and remove Round 1, while the Toffoli depth is 157.

The Time and Space Cost of Part 3. Part 3 contains 6 similar rounds operations. In the following, we will show the time and memory cost of obtaining Round 5 and removing Round 4.

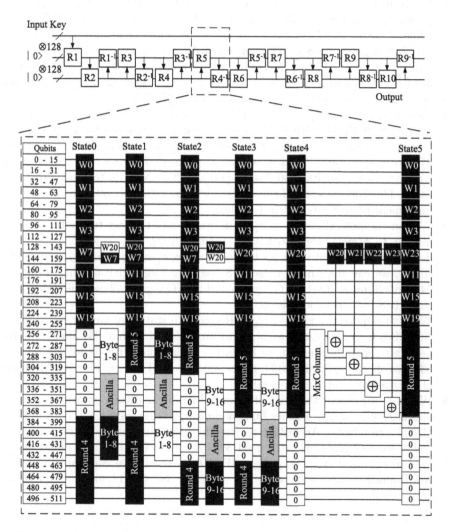

Fig. 5. Our method for computing Round 5 and removing Round 4 of AES-128.

Then we can compute the time and memory cost of the other rounds in Part 3 in a similar way. As shown in Fig. 5, we can divide the above transformation into 5 phases.

1. We can compute the $s_0^5, \cdots, s_7^5$ in Round 5 and the first two S-box operations of W_{20}. Since we have 128 zero bits (from the 256 to 383 qubits in state0 in Fig. 5), we have $128 - 64 = 64$ qubits left for ancilla qubits, because we need $|0\rangle^{\otimes 64}$ qubits to store $s_0^5, \cdots, s_7^5$. Since Algorithm 4 and Algorithm 5 require 6 and 7 ancilla qubits respectively, we need $6 \times 8 + 2 \times 7 = 62$ qubits to run Algorithm 4 eight times and Algorithm 5 twice in parallel. Then we have $64 - 48 - 14 = 2$ ancilla qubits left, which can introduce one more ancilla qubit for the first 2 S-box of W_{20}. That is, we can implement the first 2 S-box of W_{20} with 16 ancilla qubits, 128 Toffoli gates, 706 CNOT gates and 8 NOT gates, while the 8 S-box of Round 5 can be implemented with 48 ancilla qubits, 416 Toffoli gates, 2608 CNOT gates and 32 NOT gates. To sum up, we can implement these 10 S-box operations with 64 ancilla qubits, 544 Toffoli gates, 3314 CNOT gates and 40 NOT gates. The Toffoli depth of these 10 S-box operations is 56, which is determined by Algorithm 5.

2. We can remove the $r_0^4, \cdots, r_7^4$ in Round 4 by computing eight times S-box^{-1} operations with Algorithm 7. Since we have 64 qubits left for ancilla qubits (see in state1 in Fig. 5), we can obtain a depth-qubit trade-off $i = 1$ for these 8 S-box^{-1} operations. That is, we can implement these 8 S-box^{-1} operations with 64 ancilla qubits, 536 Toffoli gates, 2696 CNOT gates and 192 NOT gates. The Toffoli depth of these 8 S-box^{-1} operations is 60, because we can implement these 8 S-box^{-1} in parallel.

3. We can compute the $s_8^5, \cdots, s_{15}^5$ in Round 5 and the last two bytes of W_{20}. Similar to Step 1, we also have 2 ancilla qubits left, which can obtain a depth-qubit trade-off $i = 1$ for the last 2 S-box operations in W_{20}. Similar to step 1, we can implement these 10 S-box operations with 64 ancilla qubits, 544 Toffoli gates, 3264 CNOT gates and 40 NOT gates. The Toffoli depth of these 10 S-box operations is 56.

4. We shall remove the $r_8^4, \cdots, r_{15}^4$ of Round 4 in state3 by implementing eight times S-box^{-1} operations with Algorithm 7. Since we have 64 ancilla qubits here, we can implement these 8 S-box^{-1} operations with 64 ancilla qubits, 536 Toffoli gates, 2696 CNOT gates and 192 NOT gates. The Toffoli depth of the 8 S-box^{-1} operation is 60.

5. We shall implement the MixColumns and AddRoundKey operations so as to obtain Round 5. The 4 times MixColumns operation requires $277 \times 4 = 1108$ CNOT operations. According to the key algorithm of AES-128, after the $SubWord$ operation, we still need $32 \times 8 = 256$ CNOT gates and 1 NOT gate to compute $W_{20}, W_{21}, W_{22}, W_{23}$. As a result, we can implement the AddRoundKey operation with $256 + 128 = 384$ CNOT gates and 1 NOT gate.

Table 6. The quantum resource for AES-128 AES-192 and AES-256.

Algorithm	Operation	Toffoli depth	# Toffoli	# CNOT	# NOT
AES-128	Obtain Round 1 and Remove Round 0	74	920	7972	337
	Obtain Round 2 and Remove Round 1	157	1968	13548	465
	Obtain Round 3 and Remove Round 2	194	1928	13529	465
	Obtain Round 4 and Remove Round 3	199	2012	13504	465
	Obtain Round 5 and Remove Round 4	232	2160	13512	465
	Obtain Round 6 and Remove Round 5	232	2160	13512	465
	Obtain Round 7 and Remove Round 6	232	2160	13512	465
	Obtain Round 8 and Remove Round 7	232	2160	13512	465
	Obtain Round 9 and Remove Round 8	232	2160	13512	468
	Obtain Round 10 and Remove Round 9	232	2160	12404	468
	Sum of 10 rounds	2016	19788	128517	4528
AES-192	Obtain Round 1 and Remove Round 0	74	920	7940	81
	Obtain Round 2 and Remove Round 1	97	1744	12132	448
	Obtain Round 3 and Remove Round 2	97	2080	13908	465
	Obtain Round 4 and Remove Round 3	157	1928	13620	465
	Obtain Round 5 and Remove Round 4	157	1744	12260	448
	Obtain Round 6 and Remove Round 5	157	1968	13676	465
	Obtain Round 7 and Remove Round 6	194	1928	13529	465
	Obtain Round 8 and Remove Round 7	194	1928	13573	448
	Obtain Round 9 and Remove Round 8	199	2012	13472	465
	Obtain Round 10 and Remove Round 9	232	2160	13284	465
	Obtain Round 11 and Remove Round 10	232	1808	12228	448
	Obtain Round 12 and Remove Round 11	232	2160	12756	465
	Sum of 12 rounds	2022	22380	152378	5128
AES-256	Obtain Round 1 and Remove Round 0	37	736	6568	64
	Obtain Round 2 and Remove Round 1	97	1774	12152	465
	Obtain Round 3 and Remove Round 2	97	1774	12152	464
	Obtain Round 4 and Remove Round 3	97	1774	12344	465
	Obtain Round 5 and Remove Round 4	97	2080	13684	464
	Obtain Round 6 and Remove Round 5	157	1928	13588	465
	Obtain Round 7 and Remove Round 6	157	1968	13548	464
	Obtain Round 8 and Remove Round 7	194	1928	13461	465
	Obtain Round 9 and Remove Round 8	199	2012	13536	464
	Obtain Round 10 and Remove Round 9	232	2160	13544	465
	Obtain Round 11 and Remove Round 10	232	2160	13544	464
	Obtain Round 12 and Remove Round 11	232	2160	13544	465
	Obtain Round 13 and Remove Round 12	232	2160	13544	464
	Obtain Round 14 and Remove Round 13	232	2160	12436	465
	Sum of 14 rounds	2292	26774	177645	6103

That is, we need 2160 Toffoli gates, 13512 CNOT gates, 465 NOT gates to obtain Round 5 and remove Round 4, while the Toffoli depth is 232. We can compute the time and space cost of the left 5 rounds in Part 3 in a similar way. However, different rounds of AES-128 require different cost in the AddRoundKey operation. According to the key schedule of AES-128, we need $256 \times 3 = 768$ CNOT gates and $1 \times 3 = 3$ NOT gate to generate the 3 round-keys of Round 6, Round 7 and Round 8, while the round-key of Round 9 and Round 10 require $256 \times 2 = 512$ CNOT gates and $4 \times 2 = 8$ NOT gates.

The time and memory cost of our quantum circuit of AES-128 can be obtained by summing Part 1, Part 2 and Part 3. All in all, our quantum circuit of AES-128 needs 512 qubits, 19788 Toffoli gates, 128517 CNOT gates and 4528 NOT gates. The Toffoli depth of our quantum circuit of AES-128 is 2016 (see in Table 6).

6.2   Quantum Circuit Implementations of AES-192 and AES-256

Since our quantum circuit implementation of AES-192 and AES-256 are similar to AES-128, we just show the conclusions and omit the details (see in Table 6). Our quantum circuit of AES-192 requires 640 qubits, 22380 Toffoli gates, 152378 CNOT gates and 5128 NOT gates. The Toffoli depth of our quantum circuit implementation of AES-192 is 2022. Our quantum circuit of AES-256 requires 768 qubits, 26774 Toffoli gates, 177645 CNOT gates and 6103 NOT gates. The Toffoli depth of our quantum circuit implementation of AES-256 is 2292.

7   Conclusion

In this paper, we propose some improved quantum circuit implementations of AES. In the future, there are still several research directions. First, we can explore some possible time-space trade-offs for our quantum circuit of AES by using Kim *et al.*'s work. Second, we can explore some improved quantum circuits for the other construction, such as the Feistel-SPN. Third, we can explore some improved quantum circuits of the S-box of the other block cipher, such as SM4 and Camellia.

Acknowledgments. We would like to thank anonymous referees for their helpful comments and suggestions. Jian Zou is supported by the National Natural Science Foundation of China (No. 61902073). Zihao Wei and Siwei Sun are supported by the National Key Research and Development Program of China (Grant No. 2018YFA0704704), the Chinese Major Program of National Cryptography Development Foundation (Grant No. MMJJ20180102), the National Natural Science Foundation of China (61772519, 61802400), and the Youth Innovation Promotion Association of Chinese Academy of Sciences. Wenling Wu is supported by the National Natural Science Foundation of China (No. 61672509).

References

1. Circuit minimization team (CMT). http://www.cs.yale.edu/homes/peralta/CircuitStuff/CMT.html
2. Aaronson, S., Gottesman, D.: Improved simulation of stabilizer circuits. CoRR quant-ph/0406196 (2004)
3. Almazrooie, M., Samsudin, A., Abdullah, R., Mutter, K.N.: Quantum reversible circuit of AES-128. Quantum Inf. Process. **17**(5), 1–30 (2018). https://doi.org/10.1007/s11128-018-1864-3

4. Bonnetain, X., Naya-Plasencia, M., Schrottenloher, A.: Quantum security analysis of AES. IACR Trans. Symmetric Cryptol. **2019**(2), 55–93 (2019)
5. Boyar, J., Peralta, R.: A new combinational logic minimization technique with applications to cryptology. In: Festa, P. (ed.) SEA 2010. LNCS, vol. 6049, pp. 178–189. Springer, Heidelberg (2010). https://doi.org/10.1007/978-3-642-13193-6_16
6. Boyar, J., Peralta, R.: A small depth-16 circuit for the AES s-box. In: Gritzalis, D., Furnell, S., Theoharidou, M. (eds.) Information Security and Privacy Research-27th IFIP TC 11 Information Security and Privacy Conference, SEC 2012, Heraklion, Crete, Greece, June 4–6, 2012. Proceedings. IFIP Advances in Information and Communication Technology, vol. 376, pp. 287–298. Springer (2012). https://doi.org/10.1007/978-3-642-30436-1_24
7. Canright, D.: A very compact S-box for AES. In: Rao, J.R., Sunar, B. (eds.) CHES 2005. LNCS, vol. 3659, pp. 441–455. Springer, Heidelberg (2005). https://doi.org/10.1007/11545262_32
8. Datta, K., Shrivastav, V., Sengupta, I., Rahaman, H.: Reversible logic implementation of AES algorithm. In: Proceedings of the 8th International Conference on Design and Technology of Integrated Systems in Nanoscale Era, DTIS 2013, March 26–28, Abu Dhabi, UAE, pp. 140–144. IEEE (2013)
9. Dong, X., Sun, S., Shi, D., Gao, F., Wang, X., Hu, L.: Quantum collision attacks on AES-like hashing with low quantum random access memories. In: Advances in Cryptology-ASIACRYPT 2020-the 26th Annual International Conference on the Theory and Application of Cryptology and Information Security (2020)
10. Golubitsky, O., Maslov, D.: A study of optimal 4-bit reversible Toffoli circuits and their synthesis. IEEE Trans. Comput. **61**(9), 1341–1353 (2012)
11. Grassl, M., Langenberg, B., Roetteler, M., Steinwandt, R.: Applying Grover's algorithm to AES: quantum resource estimates. In: Takagi, T. (ed.) PQCrypto 2016. LNCS, vol. 9606, pp. 29–43. Springer, Cham (2016). https://doi.org/10.1007/978-3-319-29360-8_3
12. Grover, L.K.: A fast quantum mechanical algorithm for database search. In: Miller, G.L. (ed.) Proceedings of the Twenty-Eighth Annual ACM Symposium on the Theory of Computing, Philadelphia, Pennsylvania, USA, May 22–24, pp. 212–219. ACM (1996)
13. Hosoyamada, A., Sasaki, Yu.: Finding hash collisions with quantum computers by using differential trails with smaller probability than birthday bound. In: Canteaut, A., Ishai, Y. (eds.) EUROCRYPT 2020. LNCS, vol. 12106, pp. 249–279. Springer, Cham (2020). https://doi.org/10.1007/978-3-030-45724-2_9
14. Itoh, T., Tsujii, S.: A fast algorithm for computing multiplicative inverses in gf(2m̂) using normal bases. Inf. Comput. **78**(3), 171–177 (1988)
15. Jaques, S., Naehrig, M., Roetteler, M., Virdia, F.: Implementing Grover oracles for quantum key search on AES and LowMC. In: Canteaut, A., Ishai, Y. (eds.) EUROCRYPT 2020. LNCS, vol. 12106, pp. 280–310. Springer, Cham (2020). https://doi.org/10.1007/978-3-030-45724-2_10
16. Kaplan, M., Leurent, G., Leverrier, A., Naya-Plasencia, M.: Quantum differential and linear cryptanalysis. IACR Trans. Symmetric Cryptol. **2016**(1), 71–94 (2016)
17. Kim, P., Han, D., Jeong, K.C.: Time-space complexity of quantum search algorithms in symmetric cryptanalysis: applying to AES and SHA-2. Quantum Inf. Process. **17**(12), 339 (2018)
18. Langenberg, B., Pham, H., Steinwandt, R.: Reducing the cost of implementing AES as a quantum circuit. IACR Cryptol. ePrint Arch. **2019**, 854 (2019)

19. Mentens, N., Batina, L., Preneel, B., Verbauwhede, I.: A systematic evaluation of compact hardware implementations for the Rijndael S-Box. In: Menezes, A. (ed.) CT-RSA 2005. LNCS, vol. 3376, pp. 323–333. Springer, Heidelberg (2005). https://doi.org/10.1007/978-3-540-30574-3_22

20. Nielsen, M.A., Chuang, I.L.: Quantum Computation and Quantum Information (10th Anniversary edition). Cambridge University Press, Cambridge (2016)

21. NIST: Specification for the advanced encryption standard (AES), federal information processing standards publication, vol. 197 (2001)

22. Shende, V.V., Prasad, A.K., Markov, I.L., Hayes, J.P.: Synthesis of reversible logic circuits. IEEE Trans. CAD Integr. Circuits Syst. **22**(6), 710–722 (2003)

23. Shi, Y.: Both Toffoli and controlled-not need little help to do universal quantum computing. Quantum Inf. Comput. **3**(1), 84–92 (2003)

24. Shor, P.W.: Polynomial-time algorithms for prime factorization and discrete logarithms on a quantum computer. SIAM J. Comput. **26**(5), 1484–1509 (1997)

25. Simon, D.R.: On the power of quantum computation. SIAM J. Comput. **26**(5), 1474–1483 (1997)

26. Svore, K.M., et al.: Q#: Enabling scalable quantum computing and development with a high-level DSL. In: Proceedings of the Real World Domain Specific Languages Workshop, RWDSL@CGO 2018, Vienna, Austria, February 24, pp. 7:1–7:10 (2018)

27. Toffoli, T.: Reversible computing. In: de Bakker, J., van Leeuwen, J. (eds.) ICALP 1980. LNCS, vol. 85, pp. 632–644. Springer, Heidelberg (1980). https://doi.org/10.1007/3-540-10003-2_104

28. Wei, Z., Sun, S., Hu, L., Wei, M., Boyar, J., Peralta, R.: Scrutinizing the tower field implementation of the $\mathbb{F}_{2^8}$ inverter - with applications to AES, camellia, and SM4. IACR Cryptol. ePrint Arch. **2019**, 738 (2019)

29. Wei, Z., Sun, S., Hu, L., Wei, M., Peralta, R.: Searching the space of tower field implementations of the $\mathbb{F}_{2^8}$ inverter-with applications to AES, Camellia, and SM4. Int. J. Inf. Comput. Secur. (IJICS) (2020)

Quantum Collision Attacks on AES-Like Hashing with Low Quantum Random Access Memories

Xiaoyang Dong[1], Siwei Sun[2,3](✉), Danping Shi[2,3], Fei Gao[4], Xiaoyun Wang[1,5], and Lei Hu[2,3]

[1] Institute for Advanced Study, Beijing National Research Center for Information Science and Technology, Tsinghua University, Beijing, China
{xiaoyangdong,xiaoyunwang}@tsinghua.edu.cn
[2] State Key Laboratory of Information Security, Institute of Information Engineering, Chinese Academy of Sciences, Beijing, China
siweisun.isaac@gmail.com
[3] School of Cyber Security, University of Chinese Academy of Sciences, Beijing, China
{shidanping,hulei}@iie.ac.cn
[4] State Key Laboratory of Networking and Switching Technology, Beijing University of Posts and Telecommunications, Beijing, China
gaof@bupt.edu.cn
[5] Key Laboratory of Cryptologic Technology and Information Security, Ministry of Education, Shandong University, Jinan, China

Abstract. At EUROCRYPT 2020, Hosoyamada and Sasaki proposed the first dedicated quantum attack on hash functions—a quantum version of the rebound attack exploiting differentials whose probabilities are too low to be useful in the classical setting. This work opens up a new perspective toward the security of hash functions against quantum attacks. In particular, it tells us that the search for differentials should not stop at the classical birthday bound. Despite these interesting and promising implications, the concrete attacks described by Hosoyamada and Sasaki make use of large quantum random access memories (qRAMs), a resource whose availability in the foreseeable future is controversial even in the quantum computation community. Without large qRAMs, these attacks incur significant increases in time complexities. In this work, we reduce or even avoid the use of qRAMs by performing a quantum rebound attack based on differentials with non-full-active super S-boxes. Along the way, an MILP-based method is proposed to systematically explore the search space of useful truncated differentials with respect to rebound attacks. As a result, we obtain improved attacks on AES-MMO, AES-MP, and the first classical collision attacks on 4- and 5-round Grøstl-512. Interestingly, the use of non-full-active super S-box differentials in the analysis of AES-MMO gives rise to new difficulties in collecting enough starting points. To overcome this issue, we consider attacks involving two message blocks to gain more degrees of freedom, and we successfully compress the qRAM demand of the collision attacks on AES-MMO and AES-MP (EUROCRYPT

© International Association for Cryptologic Research 2020
S. Moriai and H. Wang (Eds.): ASIACRYPT 2020, LNCS 12492, pp. 727–757, 2020.
https://doi.org/10.1007/978-3-030-64834-3_25

2020) from 2^{48} to a range from 2^{16} to 0, while still maintaining a comparable time complexity. To the best of our knowledge, these are the first dedicated quantum attacks on hash functions that slightly outperform Chailloux, Naya-Plasencia, and Schrottenloher's generic quantum collision attack (ASIACRYPT 2017) in a model where large qRAMs are not available. This work demonstrates again how a clever combination of classical cryptanalytic technique and quantum computation leads to improved attacks, and shows that the direction pointed out by Hosoyamada and Sasaki deserves further investigation.

Keywords: Quantum computation · qRAM · Collision attacks · Rebound attacks · AES-like hashing · MILP

1   Introduction

Shor's seminal work [44] showed that a sufficiently large quantum computer allows to factor numbers and compute discrete logarithms in polynomial time, which can be devastating to many public-key schemes in use today. To prepare for the future, the public-key cryptography community and standardization bodies have put substantial effort in the research of post-quantum public-key cryptography. In particular, NIST has initiated a process to solicit, evaluate, and standardize one or more quantum-resistant public-key cryptographic algorithms [41]. In contrast, the research on how quantum computation would change the landscape of the security of symmetric-key cryptography seems to be less active. For almost twenty years, it was generally believed that the quadratic speedup in an exhaustive search attack due to Grover's algorithm [16] is the only advantage an attacker equipped with a quantum computer would have when attacking symmetric-key ciphers, and thus doubling the key length addresses the concern.

This naive view started to change with the initial work of Kuwakado and Morii, who showed that the classically provable secure Even-Mansour cipher and the three-round Feistel network can be broken in polynomial time with the help of a quantum computer [28,29]. Several years later, more generic constructions were broken [25,32]. Almost all these attacks enjoying exponential speedups rely on Simon's algorithm [45] to find a key-dependent hidden period, where accesses to the quantum superposition oracle of the keyed primitives are necessary. This is a quite strong requirement, and sometimes its practical relevance is questioned. Therefore, attacks with higher complexities are still meaningful if they do not need to make online queries to superposition oracles of keyed primitives [2,18].

When we apply quantum algorithms to keyless primitives, online queries are not needed since all computations are public and can be done offline. Classical algorithms find collisions of an n-bit ideal hash function with time complexity $O(2^{n/2})$. In the quantum setting, BHT algorithm [6] finds collisions with a query complexity of $O(2^{n/3})$ if an $O(2^{n/3})$-qubit quantum random access memory (qRAM) is available [6]. However, it is generally admitted that the difficulty of fabricating large qRAMs is enormous [13,14], and thus quantum algorithms (even with relatively higher time complexities) using less or no qRAMs are preferable. Chailloux, Naya-Plasencia, and Schrottenloher first overcome the $O(2^{n/2})$

classical bound without using large qRAMs [7]. This algorithm has a time complexity of $O(2^{2n/5})$, with quantum memory of $O(n)$ and a classical memory of $O(2^{n/5})$. Also, quantum algorithms for the generalized birthday problem (or the k-XOR problem) in settings with or without large qRAMs can be found in [15,39].

The above mentioned attacks on hash functions are generic in the sense that they do not exploit any internal characteristics of the targets. In fact, before year 2020, no dedicated quantum attack is seen in the open literature, in stark contrast to the line of cryptanalytic research targeting keyed primitives in the quantum setting, where attempts to escalate dedicated attacks are plentiful (e.g., differential and linear attacks [26], impossible differential attacks [47], meet-in-the-middle attacks [4,19], slide attacks [3,10], etc.). The first dedicated quantum attack on hash functions was presented at EUROCRYPT 2020 by Hosoyamada and Sasaki [20], showing that differentials whose probability is too low to be useful in the classical setting may be exploited in quantum attacks. They applied a quantum version of the rebound attack on AES-MMO and Whirlpool, and gave the first quantum collision attack on AES-MMO.

Our Contribution. Motivated by the fact that the availability of large qRAMs is controversial [1,13,14], we try to lower the qRAM requirements of Hosoyamada and Sasaki's attacks [20]. With the application of non-full-active super S-box techniques [42], we can significantly reduce (or even avoid) the use of qRAMs. Along the way, we propose an MILP-based method to systematically explore the search space of useful differential trails with respect to rebound attacks, which is of independent interest. With the help of this method, we find differentials leading to improved attacks in both the classical and quantum settings. For example, we present the first classical collision attacks on 4-round and 5-round Grøstl-512, where the complexity of the 4-round attack is significantly better than previously known best attacks on 3-round Grøstl-512. Also, we obtain improved semi-free-start collision attacks on Grøstl-256.

In the analysis of AES-MMO and AES-MP, the differentials we find leading to non-full-active super S-boxes for the inbound phase cannot generate enough starting points to produce a collision due to the probabilistic nature of the outbound phase of the attack. To overcome this difficulty, we consider two blocks of messages, execute rebound attacks on the second message block, and borrow degrees of freedom from the first one. As a result, we successfully compress the qRAM demand from 2^{48} to a range from 2^{16} to 0, while still maintaining a comparable time complexity. Hosoyamada and Sasaki's work [20] tells us that certain worthless truncated differential trails in the classical setting are exploitable in the quantum setting. Our work further enlarges the space of quantumly exploitable truncated differential trails by considering collisions produced by two-block messages, where trails unable to generate enough starting points during the inbound phase of a single-block rebound collision attack are included. We believe this observation will inspire new attacks on hash functions in the quantum setting. Moreover, in a model without large qRAMs, Hosoyamada and Sasaki's attacks are inferior to the generic attack by Chailloux, Naya-Plasencia, and Schrottenloher [7]:

> "*However, in the setting that a small quantum computer of polynomial size and exponential large classical memory is available, our rebound attack is lower than the best attack by Chailloux et al. (see [20, Sect. 1.1, Page 6])*"

To the best of our knowledge, our work is the first dedicated quantum attack on hash functions that slightly surpasses the generic quantum collision attack [7] in a model where large qRAMs are not available. In the quantum time-space scenario, our attacks also gain improvements. For example, the attack without qRAM on 7-round AES-MMO needs a time complexity of $2^{45.8}$. If we have S quantum computers in parallel, we will find the collision with time $2^{45.8}/\sqrt{S}$. In the same setting, Hosoyamada and Sasaki [20]'s attack needs about $2^{59.5}/\sqrt{S}$ time complexity. A summary of our attacks on AES-MMO, AES-MP, and Grøstl is given in Table 1.

Table 1. Classical and quantum collision attacks on AES-MMO, AES-MP, Grøstl. Q-Model I and II are quantum settings with qRAM and without qRAM, respectively.

Settings	Attack	Rounds	Time	c-Memory	qRAM	Source
Collision attacks on AES-MMO and AES-MP						
Classic	Dedicated	5	2^{56}	2^4	0	[33]
	Dedicated	6	2^{56}	2^{32}	0	[12,30]
Q-Model I	Dedicated	7	$2^{42.50}$	0	2^{48}	[20]
	Dedicated	7	$2^{45.4}$	0	2^{16}	Section 4
	Generic	all	2^{56}	0	2^{16}	[6]
	Generic	all	$2^{42.66}$	0	$2^{42.66}$	[6]
Q-Model II	Dedicated	7	$2^{59.5}$	0	0	[20]
	Dedicated	7	$2^{45.8}$	0	0	Section 5
	Generic	all	$2^{51.2}$	$2^{25.6}$	0	[7]
Collision attacks on Grøstl-512						
Classic	Dedicated	3	2^{192}	2^{64}	0	[43]
	Dedicated	4	2^{128}	2^{64}	0	Section 6
	Dedicated	5	2^{240}	2^{64}	0	Section 6
Q-Model I	Dedicated	4	$2^{88.4}$	0	2^{16}	Section 6
	Dedicated	5	$2^{200.4}$	0	2^{16}	Section 6
	Generic	all	2^{248}	0	2^{16}	[6]
	Generic	all	$2^{170.7}$	0	$2^{170.7}$	[6]
Q-Model II	Dedicated	4	$2^{89.3}$	0	0	Section 6
	Dedicated	5	$2^{201.3}$	0	0	Section 6
	Generic	all	2^{205}	$2^{102.4}$	0	[7]
Semi-free-start collision attacks on Grøstl-256						
Classic	Dedicated	6	2^{120}	2^{64}	0	[43]
	Dedicated	6	2^{112}	2^{64}	0	Section 6
Q-Model II	Dedicated	6	$2^{92.8}$	0	0	Section 7
	Generic	6	$2^{102.4}$	$2^{51.2}$	0	[7]

Organization. Section 2 gives a brief introduction of AES-like hashing, quantum computation, and qRAMs. We describe the classical technique for collision attacks on hash functions with the rebound technique, and show how to search for useful truncated differential trails with non-full-active super S-boxes by MILP with multiple objectives in Sect. 3. This is followed by Sect. 4, to Sect. 7, which present our improved attacks on AES-MMO, AES-MP, and Grøstl. Section 8 concludes the paper.

2 Preliminaries

In this section, we give a brief introduction of AES-like hashing and quantum computation, and familiarize the readers with the functionalities of quantum random access memories (qRAMs).

2.1 AES-Like Hashing

To be concrete, we first recall the round function of AES-128 [8]. It operates on a 16-byte state arranged into a rectangular shape and contains four major transformations as illustrated in Fig. 1: SubBytes (SB), ShiftRows (SR), MixColumns (MC), and AddRoundKey (AK). The parameters like the numbers of rows and columns, the sizes of the cells, the order of the transformations, and the roles played by the rows and columns can be altered by making compatible changes to the operations involved to produce new designs, which are loosely called as AES-like round functions. In this paper, we assume the MixColumns is to multiply an MDS matrix to each column of the state.

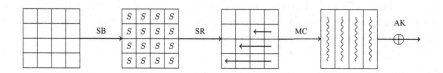

Fig. 1. The round function of AES

By using (keyed) permutations with AES-like round functions in certain hashing modes, compression functions (denoted as CF) can be constructed. For example, the MD, MMO, and MP hashing modes [35, Section 9.4] are illustrated in Fig. 2. Plugging such compression functions into the Merkle-Damgård construction [9,36], one arrives at AES-like hashings. Concrete designs include AES-MMO, AES-MP, and Grøstl [11], which are the main targets of this work.

2.2 Quantum Computation and Quantum RAM

The states of an n-qubit quantum system can be described as unit vectors in $\mathbb{C}^{2^n}$ under the orthonormal basis $\{|0\cdots00\rangle, |0\cdots01\rangle, \cdots, |1\cdots11\rangle\}$, alternatively written as $\{|i\rangle : 0 \le i < 2^n\}$. Quantum algorithms are typically realized

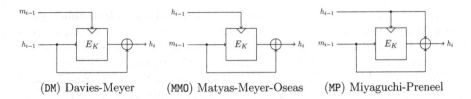

(DM) Davies-Meyer   (MMO) Matyas-Meyer-Oseas   (MP) Miyaguchi-Preneel

Fig. 2. Common Hashing Modes

by manipulating the state of an n-qubit system through a series of unitary transformations and measurements, where all unitary transformations can be implemented as a sequence of single-qubit and two-qubit transformations, which are called quantum gates in the standard quantum circuit model [40]. The efficiency of a quantum algorithm is quantified in terms of the amount of quantum gates used.

Superposition Oracles for Classical Circuit. Given a Boolean function $f : \mathbb{F}_2^n \to \mathbb{F}_2$. The superposition oracle of f is the unitary transformation $\mathcal{U}_f$ acting on an $(n+1)$-qubit system sending a standard basis vector $|x, y\rangle$ to $|x, y \oplus f(x)\rangle$, where $x \in \mathbb{F}_2^n$ and $y \in \mathbb{F}_2$. As a linear operator, $\mathcal{U}_f$ acts on superposition states as

$$\mathcal{U}_f \left(\sum_{x \in \mathbb{F}_2^n} a_i |x\rangle |0\rangle \right) = \sum_{x \in \mathbb{F}_2^n} a_i |x\rangle |f(x)\rangle. \tag{1}$$

Note that $\mathcal{U}_f$ can be implemented efficiently in the quantum circuit model as long as there is an efficient classical circuit that computes f. To build the quantum circuit of $\mathcal{U}_f$, we first construct an efficient reversible circuit of f and substitute quantum gates for each of the reversible gates involved.

Grover's Algorithm. Given a search space of 2^n elements, say $\{x : x \in \mathbb{F}_2^n\}$, and a Boolean function or predicate $f : \mathbb{F}_2^n \to \mathbb{F}_2$, the best classical algorithm with a black-box access to f requires about 2^n evaluations of the black-box oracle to identify x such that $f(x) = 1$ with probability one (For the sake of simplicity, we assume that there is only one such x). In the quantum setting, Grover's algorithm solves the same problem with about $O(\sqrt{2^n})$ calls to a quantum oracle $\mathcal{U}_f$ that outputs $\sum_x a_x |x\rangle |y \oplus f(x)\rangle$ upon input of $\sum_x a_x |x\rangle |y\rangle$. Starting with a uniform superposition

$$|\psi\rangle = \frac{1}{\sqrt{2^n}} \sum_{x \in \mathbb{F}_2^n} |x\rangle,$$

by applying the Hadamard transformation $H^{\otimes n}$ to $|0\rangle^{\otimes n}$. Then Grover's algorithm iteratively apply the unitary transformation $(2 |\psi\rangle \langle\psi| - I)\mathcal{U}_f$ to $|\psi\rangle$ such that the amplitudes of those values x with $f(x) = 1$ are amplified. Then a final measurement gives a value x of interest with an overwhelming probability [16].

One caveat here: complexity can be hidden in the complexity of constructing the oracle circuit employed by Grover's algorithm. The speedup of the search would be illusory unless the oracle circuit can be implemented efficiently. Therefore, it is important to have a clear view on what resources it takes to implement the oracle. For example, a large qRAM is necessary if it requires a large qRAM to implement the oracle efficiently.

Quantum Amplitude Amplification. Let $\mathcal{P} = |j_0\rangle \langle j_0| + \cdots + |j_{s-1}\rangle \langle j_{s-1}|$ be a projector with $\{|j_0\rangle, \cdots, |j_{s-1}\rangle\} \subseteq \{|0\rangle, \cdots, |2^n - 1\rangle\}$, and $\mathcal{A}$ be a unitary operator such that $\mathcal{A}|0\rangle = \alpha|\phi_P\rangle + \beta|\phi_P^{\perp}\rangle$, where $\mathcal{P}|\phi_P\rangle = |\phi_P\rangle$ and $\mathcal{P}|\phi_P^{\perp}\rangle = 0$. Then there exists a quantum algorithm that requires exclusively $\lfloor \frac{\pi}{4\theta} - \frac{1}{2} \rfloor$ calls to $\mathcal{U}_P$, $\mathcal{U}_P^{\dagger}$, $\mathcal{A}$, and $\mathcal{A}^{\dagger}$, after a final measurement, to produce a quantum state close to $|\psi_P\rangle$, where $\sin(\theta) = |\alpha|$, and the effect of the unitary operator $\mathcal{U}_P$ on base vectors satisfying $\mathcal{U}_P|x\rangle|y\rangle = |x\rangle|y \oplus 1\rangle$ if $|x\rangle \in \{|j_0\rangle, \cdots, |j_{s-1}\rangle\}$ and $\mathcal{U}_P|x\rangle|y\rangle = |x\rangle|y\rangle$ otherwise [5].

The quantum amplitude amplification can be regarded as a generalization of Grover's algorithm in which $\mathcal{A}$ is restricted to produce an equal superposition of all basis vectors. Similarly, when analyzing the complexity of the quantum amplitude amplification, we should take into account the complexities for implementing $\mathcal{U}_P$ and $\mathcal{A}$.

Quantum Random Access Memories (qRAM). A quantum random access memory (qRAM) is a quantum analogue of a classical random access memory (RAM), which uses n-qubit to address any quantum superposition of 2^n memory cells. Given a list of classical data $L = \{x_0, \cdots, x_{2^n-1}\}$ with $x_i \in \mathbb{F}_2^m$, the qRAM for L is modeled as an unitary transformation $\mathcal{U}_{qRAM}^L$ such that

$$\mathcal{U}_{qRAM}^L : |i\rangle_{\text{Addr}} \otimes |y\rangle_{\text{Out}} \mapsto |i\rangle_{\text{Addr}} \otimes |y \oplus x_i\rangle_{\text{Out}}, \tag{2}$$

where $i \in \mathbb{F}_2^n$, $y \in \mathbb{F}_2^m$, and $|\cdot\rangle_{\text{Addr}}$ and $|\cdot\rangle_{\text{Out}}$ may be regarded as the address and output registers respectively. Therefore, we can access any quantum superposition of the data cells by using the corresponding superposition of addresses:

$$\mathcal{U}_{qRAM}^L \left(\sum_i a_i |i\rangle \otimes |y\rangle \right) = \sum_i a_i |i\rangle \otimes |y \oplus x_i\rangle. \tag{3}$$

For the time being, it is unknown how a working qRAM (at least for large qRAMs) can be built. Nevertheless, this disappointing fact does not stop researchers from working in a model where large qRAMs are available, in the same spirit that people started to work on classical and quantum algorithms long before a classical or quantum computer had been built. From another perspective, the absence of large qRAMs and the fact that a qRAM of size $O(n)$ can be simulated with a quantum circuit of size $O(n)$ makes it quite meaningful to conduct research in an attempt to reduce or even avoid the use of qRAM in quantum algorithms.

3   MILP Models for the Rebound Attack

For the sake of concreteness, we restrict our discussion to collision attacks on AES-MMO, which is standardized by Zigbee and used by many multi-party computation protocols [17, 27] due to its efficiency. Assume that there is a differential trail for E_K with probability p whose input and output differences share a common value Δ. Given around $1/p$ pairs of input messages with difference Δ, we expect one pair $(m, m \oplus \Delta)$ follows this differential trail: $E_K(m) \oplus E_K(m \oplus \Delta) = \Delta$. If this is the case, the differences of the outputs of the MMO construction is

$$(m \oplus E_K(m)) \oplus (m \oplus \Delta \oplus E_K(m \oplus \Delta)) = \Delta \oplus \Delta = 0, \tag{4}$$

that is, a collision. Since K is known in hash functions, it is possible to generate many data pairs which confirm to one particular segment (typically the most difficult part) of the desired trail. Then these pairs are tested to find one fulfilling the remaining part of the trail. This is the basic strategy employed by the so-called rebound attack proposed by Mendel, Rechberger, Schläffer and Thomsen [31, 33].

In a rebound attack, the target primitive and thus the differential trail covering it is split into three parts. An inbound part is placed at the middle surrounded by two outbound parts. By utilizing the degrees of freedom of the inbound part, many data pairs conforming to the differential of the inbound part (named as inbound differential) can be constructed deterministically or with a very high probability. Then these data pairs, named as *starting points*, are propagated through the outbound parts to find pairs respecting the outbound differential by chance. Among many improvements and extensions of the rebound attacks [22–24, 38], the super S-box technique [12, 30] and the non-full-active super S-box technique [42] are most relevant to our work.

3.1   The Full-Active and Non-Full-Active Super S-Box Techniques

In the context of rebound attacks on AES-MMO, the super S-box technique enlarges the inbound part by one more round than previous analysis by identifying four non-interfering $\mathbb{F}_2^{32} \to \mathbb{F}_2^{32}$ permutations across two consecutive AES rounds and regarding them as four super S-boxes. Initially, when using the super S-box technique for the inbound phase, researchers only considered differentials activating all cells of the super S-boxes, and we refer the reader to Fig. 3 for an example, where one of the four super S-boxes involved in the inbound phase (surround by the dashed line) is highlighted. To generate starting points under this configuration (full-active super S-box) with complexity one on average, one has to store a table $\mathbb{L}_{\Delta_{in}}$ whose entry $\mathbb{L}_{\Delta_{in}}[\Delta_{out}]$ at index Δ_{out} contains the pairs respecting the differential $(\Delta_{in}, \Delta_{out})$ of the super S-box [12, 30]. Since the memory of $\mathbb{L}_{\Delta_{in}}$ is released after the analysis for one particular input difference Δ_{in} is done, we only need the memory to store one copy of $\mathbb{L}_{\Delta_{in}}$.

In [42], Sasaki, Wang, Sakiyama, and Ohta found that by using differentials with non-full active super S-boxes, the memory complexity of the inbound phase

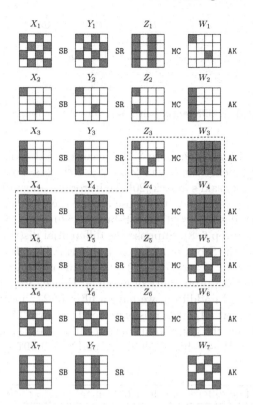

Fig. 3. The differential trail used in Hosoyamada and Sasaki's quantum collision attack on 7-round `AES-MMO` [20] with its inbound part and one of the super S-boxes highlighted

can be significantly reduced. This is because typically data pairs compatible with a given differential with a non-full-active super S-box can be built up progressively by working on 8-bit values. We refer the reader to [42] for more details. In what follows, we describe how to generate data pairs respecting a given differential with a non-full-active super S-box through a concrete example shown in Fig. 4. This is also a differential we actually used in our improved attacks on `AES-MMO`.

First, we precompute the differential distribution table `DDT` of the small S-box in table $\mathbb{T}$ using Algorithm 1 and load it into random access memories. As shown in Fig. 4, given the truncated differential of the super S-box $\texttt{SSB} = \texttt{SB} \circ \texttt{MC} \circ \texttt{SB}$, we can generate data pairs conforming to a given differential $(\Delta A, \Delta D)$ for $\texttt{SSB}$ by enumerating $(A[0], \beta) \in \mathbb{F}_2^{11}$ with Algorithm 2. We remember an easy property for `MC` when understanding Algorithm 2.

Property 1. $\texttt{MC} \cdot (X[0], X[1], X[2], X[3])^T = (Y[0], Y[1], Y[2], Y[3])^T$ can be used to fully determine the remaining unknowns if any four of $X[0], \cdots, X[3], Y[0], \cdots, Y[3]$ are known.

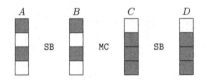

Fig. 4. A differential with non-full-active super S-box

Note that in Algorithm 2, there are 3 DDT accesses to determine a combination of $(A[2], C[1], C[2])$, hence, we have $2 \times 2 \times 2 = 8$ choices. Following the strategy of Hosoyamada and Sasaki's attack [20], we introduce an auxiliary 3-bit variable β to specify which combination to choose among the 8 choices. The complexity of Algorithm 2 includes $2 + 2 = 4$ small S-boxes evaluations (Step 1 and Step 19) and 3 DDT accesses (Step 6–8). Suppose the differential distribution of the S-box is similar to that of the S-box of AES, i.e., 4-uniform. Therefore, it returns a pair when accessing $\mathbb{T}$ with $(\delta_{in}, \delta_{out}) \in \mathbb{F}_2^8 \times \mathbb{F}_2^8$ with probability of about $\frac{1}{2}$, and returns empty also with probability of about $\frac{1}{2}$. Hence, Step 6–8 of Algorithm 2 act as a filter of 2^{-3}. In addition, we have a filter of 2^{-8} in Step 19. Therefore, by traversing the 11-bit $(A[0], \beta)$, it is expected to return $(2^8 \times 2^3 \times 2^{-3} \times 2^{-8}=)$ 1 pair which conforms the given input-output differences $(\Delta A, \Delta D)$ of SSB. The total complexity is $2^{11} \cdot 4$ S-box evaluations and $2^{11} \cdot 3$ DDT accesses.

Algorithm 1. The differential distribution table of S with data pairs

---

1 Let $\mathbb{T}$ be an empty dictionary
2 **for** $\delta_{\text{IN}} \in \mathbb{F}_2^8$ **do**
3   **for** $x \in \mathbb{F}_2^8$ **do**
4          $x' \leftarrow x \oplus \delta_{in}$, $y \leftarrow S(x)$, $y' \leftarrow S(x')$, $\delta_{out} \leftarrow y \oplus y'$
5   **if** $x \le x'$ **then**
6 | Insert (x, x', y, y') into $\mathbb{T}[(\delta_{in}, \delta_{out})]$
7   **end**
8   **end**
9 **end**
10 **return** $\mathbb{T}$

We consider a more general scenario: a column state A with d c-bit cells is mapped to $D = \text{SB} \circ \text{MC} \circ \text{SB}(A)$, where SB is a parallel application of d $c \times c$ small S-boxes and $\text{MC} : \mathbb{F}_{2^c}^d \rightarrow \mathbb{F}_{2^c}^d$ is a linear transformation with branch number $d + 1$. Assume that a differential of the super S-box $\text{SSB} = \text{SB} \circ \text{MC} \circ \text{SB}$ leads to s non-active $c \times c$ S-boxes, and thus we have $2d - s$ small active S-boxes. To generate a pair respecting a given differential $(\Delta A, \Delta D)$ for the SSB, we perform the following steps:

1. Guess $d - s$ cells of (A, D) (the guessed positions must be selected within the active cells of (A, D)).

Algorithm 2. Generating data pairs for non-full-active super S-box

---

Input: The differential $(\Delta A, \Delta D)$, $A[0]$, and a 3-bit index $\beta = (\beta_0, \beta_1, \beta_2)$
Output: Data A such that $\mathrm{SSB}(A) \oplus \mathrm{SSB}(A \oplus \Delta A) = \Delta D$

1 $B[0] = S(A[0])$, $B'[0] = S(A[0] \oplus \Delta A[0])$, $\Delta B[0] = B[0] \oplus B'[0]$
2 /* Together with 3 non-active bytes in $(\Delta B, \Delta C)$, 4 bytes of
    differences are known in total.   */
3 According to Property 1, we get $\Delta B[2]$ and $\Delta C[1,2,3]$

4 /* Determine the pairs through accessing DDT   */
5 /* We obtain values with probability of 2^{-3} */
6 $(A[2], A'[2], B[2], B'[2]) \leftarrow \mathbb{T}[(\Delta A[2], \Delta B[2])]$
7 $(C[1], C'[1], D[1], D'[1]) \leftarrow \mathbb{T}[(\Delta C[1], \Delta D[1])]$
8 $(C[2], C'[2], D[2], D'[2]) \leftarrow \mathbb{T}[(\Delta C[2], \Delta D[2])]$

9 /* Pick combinations of $(A[2], C[1], C[2])$ by β: $\beta_0 \cdot \Delta A[2] = 0$ if $\beta_0 = 0$
    and $\beta_0 \cdot \Delta A[2] = \Delta A[2]$ if $\beta_0 = 1$ */
10 $A[2] = A[2] \oplus \beta_0 \cdot \Delta A[2]$, $A'[2] = A[2] \oplus \Delta A[2]$;
11 $B[2] = B[2] \oplus \beta_0 \cdot \Delta B[2]$, $B'[2] = B[2] \oplus \Delta B[2]$;
12 $C[1] = C[1] \oplus \beta_1 \cdot \Delta C[1]$, $C'[1] = C[1] \oplus \Delta C[1]$;
13 $D[1] = D[1] \oplus \beta_1 \cdot \Delta D[1]$, $D'[1] = D[1] \oplus \Delta D[1]$;
14 $C[2] = C[2] \oplus \beta_2 \cdot \Delta C[2]$, $C'[2] = C[2] \oplus \Delta C[2]$;
15 $D[2] = D[2] \oplus \beta_2 \cdot \Delta D[2]$, $D'[2] = D[2] \oplus \Delta D[2]$.

16 /* $B[0]$, $B[2]$, $C[1]$, and $C[2]$ are known   */
17 With Property 1, all the values of B and C are known

18 /* Among the 5 active S-boxes, only the S-box with $(\Delta C[3], \Delta D[3])$ is
    not considered, which acts as a filter.   */
19 if $S(C[3]) \oplus S(C[3] \oplus \Delta C[3]) = \Delta D[3]$ /* probability of 2^{-8} */
20 then
21     $\mid$ return $A \leftarrow \mathrm{SB}^{-1}(B)$ together with $A \oplus \Delta A$
22 end

---

2. Compute the values of $d - s$ cells of (B, C) from the guessed $d - s$ cells of (A, D). Compute the differences of $d - s$ active cells of $(\Delta B, \Delta C)$.

3. Combining with the s non-active cells of $(\Delta B, \Delta C)$, we get $(d - s) + s = d$ cells with known differences among the input-output differences of MC. By Property 1, we know all the differences in the truncated differential.

4. Since $d - s$ cells of (B, C) have been determined, we need an additional s cells to determine all other cells of (B, C) through MC. Therefore, we compute another s cells through s DDT accesses. Here, similar to Algorithm 2, an s-bit auxiliary variable β is needed to specify which combination to choose among the 2^s choices. In Algorithm 2, ($s =$)3-bit β is needed.

5. Combining with the $d - s$ cells of (B, C) in Step 2 and s cells by accessing DDT, we know d cells of (B, C). By Property 1, we derive the remaining d cells.

6. Now, there are

$$\underbrace{(2d-s)}_{\text{All active S-boxes}} - \underbrace{(d-s)}_{\text{Guessed}} - \underbrace{s}_{\text{Fixed by DDT}} = d - s$$

unused active Sboxes, which are used as a $2^{-(d-s)c}$-bit filter. In Algorithm 2, it is a filter of $2^{-(d-s)c} = 2^{-(4-3)\times 8} = 2^{-8}$. Once it passes the filter, we obtain the full (A, D) and (A', D') conform to the differential of the SSB.

The complexity of the whole procedure is s DDT accesses and $4(d-s)$ S-boxes evaluations $(2(d-s)$ in step 2 and $2(d-s)$ in step 6). We have to repeat for $2^{(d-s)c} \times 2^s$ times to traverse the initial guesses and s-bit auxiliary variable β to find one pair on average, which need about $2^{(d-s)c+s} \cdot s$ DDT accesses and $2^{(d-s)c+s} \cdot 4(d-s)$ small S-box evaluations. Suppose one DDT access is equivalent to one S-box evaluation, hence the total time complexity is in classical setting:

$$2^{(d-s)c+s} \cdot (s + 4(d-s)) \quad \text{S-box evaluations.} \tag{5}$$

In quantum setting, we use Grover's algorithm to accelerate the procedures with time complexity (including uncomputing):

$$2 \cdot \frac{\pi}{4} \cdot \sqrt{2^{(d-s)c+s}} \cdot (s + 4(d-s)) \quad \text{S-box evaluations,} \tag{6}$$

with 2^{16} qRAM to store the DDT. We refer the readers to Sect. 4 and 5 to find the detailed definitions and implementations of quantum oracles for the application of Grover's algorithm. From the Eq. (5) and (6), we see that the dominating part is $2^{(d-s)c}$ (in this paper, $c = 8$), hence, we will maximize s by our MILP model in order to reduce the complexity to compute the non-full-active super S-box.

3.2   Searching for Exploitable Differentials in Classical and Quantum Attacks with MILP

Following recent MILP based approach for automatic cryptanalysis [37,46], we propose an MILP model with *multiple optimization objectives* whose solution space captures the set of exploitable differentials with respect to rebound attacks in both the classical and quantum settings. Let us now clarify the variables, constraints, and objective functions.

Variables and Constraints. For an R-round primitive, we first introduce an integral variable l, which determines the inbound part from round $l+1$ to round $l+2$, and the outbound part with a backward chunk from round l to round 0 and a forward chunk from round $l+3$ to round $R-1$.

Then, we introduce a set of 0–1 variables x_j for all cells of the states involved, where $x_j = 1$ if and only if the corresponding cell is differentially active. These variables model the truncated differential trails of the target, and the constraints imposed on them are the same as [37].

To capture the probability of the trails, we also introduce a set of 0–1 variables w_j for each cell of the states right before (in the backward chunk) or after (in the forward chunk) the MC operations. Concretely, in the backward chunk, given MC with differentially active input-output cells, $w_j = 1$ if and only if the corresponding input cell of the MC is *differentially inactive*. Similarly, in the forward chunk, given MC with differentially active input-output cells, $w_j = 1$ if and only if the corresponding output cell of the MC is *differentially inactive*. Therefore, the probability of the truncated differential trail for the outbound phase can be calculated as $2^{-c \cdot \sum w_j}$, where c is the cell size in bits and the sum of w_j is taken over the scope of the outbound part.

The Objective Functions. To minimize the time complexity of the outbound phase (including the cancellation introduced by Eq. (4)), our first priority objective function is to minimize

$$\sum_{\text{Outbound}} w_j + \sum_{\text{Round 0}} x_j.$$

According to the discussion of Sect. 3.1, the complexity for analyzing one super S-box is minimized when the number of inactive small S-boxes is maximized. Assuming we have h super S-boxes, let s_i $(0 \le i < h)$ denote the number of inactive small S-boxes in the corresponding super S-box. We set our second priority objective function to maximize the *minimal* of $\{s_0, s_1, ..., s_{h-1}\}$, i.e., the objective function is

$$\texttt{maximize} : \min \{s_0, s_1, ..., s_{h-1}\}.$$

Note that this type of objective can be realized in MILP by maximizing λ with the constraints $\lambda \le s_j$ for $0 \le j < h - 1$.

Remark. Since in all of our attacks we have enough degrees of freedom potentially borrowed from other message blocks, we do not care about the degrees of freedom provided by the inbound differential.

4   Quantum Collision Attacks on 7-Round AES-MMO and AES-MP with Low qRAM

Before we dive into the details of the attack with low qRAM, we would like to give some high-level remarks on the difference between our attack and Hosoyamada and Sasaki's attack [20]. The differentials used in [20] and our attack are presented in Fig. 3 and Fig. 5, respectively. We can see that both differentials cover seven rounds of AES, and the probabilities of the segments of the differentials covering the outbound phases are both 2^{-801}. The main difference appears

---

[1] In Fig. 5, the differential transition from Z_5 to W_5 needs a two-byte condition, whose probability is about 2^{-16}. Eight-byte differences in ΔX_1 and ΔW_7 have to be equal, which holds with probability 2^{-64}.

in the inbound phases: The differential employed by Hosoyamada and Sasaki (see Fig. 3) activates all cells of the super S-boxes involved in the inbound phase while the differential we used gives rise to non-full-active super S-boxes. This discrepancy is the core reason for the reduction of the qRAM usage and brings some technical difficulties preventing us from applying Hosoyamada and Sasaki's attack directly.

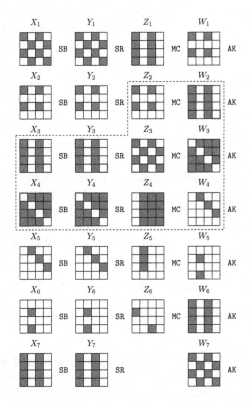

Fig. 5. The differential trail used in our quantum collision attack on 7-round AES-MMO

Since the differential probability of the outbound phase is 2^{-80}, we have to generate about 2^{80} starting points to find a collision. If we follow Hosoyamada and Sasaki's strategy and try to produce a collision for $h = \mathrm{CF}(m, IV)$ with one message block by a rebound attack based on the differential given in Fig. 5, we are doomed to fail due to an inherent shortage of enough starting points. Let us look at the differential trail (see Fig. 5) for the inbound part. There are $2^{8\times4}$ possibilities for ΔZ_2 and $2^{8\times3}$ possibilities for ΔW_4. Therefore, we expect to have totally $2^{8\times4} \times 2^{8\times3} = 2^{56} < 2^{80}$ starting points when the subkeys are fixed by the IV. In contrast, Hosoyamada and Sasaki's trail (see Fig. 3) can create as many as $2^{8\times8} \times 2^{8\times3} = 2^{88} > 2^{80}$ starting points that conforming with the inbound differential.

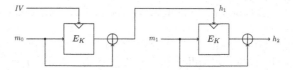

Fig. 6. The framework of the collision attacks with two message blocks

To address this issue, we consider collisions produced by a pair of two-block messages (m_0, m_1) and (m_0, m'_1) whose hash values are computed according to Fig. 6. The rebound attack happens at the second message block, and the degrees of freedom for generating starting points is replenished by varying the first message block m_0. To be more specific, we can generate about $2^{24} \times 2^{56} = 2^{80}$ starting points after go through 2^{24} different m_0's, among which we expect to find one starting point fulfilling the outbound differential and thus leading to a collision.

4.1 A Low-qRAM Quantum Collision Attack on 7-Round AES-MMO

Similar to [20], at the core of our attack is the application of Grover's algorithm to a search space where the interested elements are marked by an efficiently computable Boolean function F. Now, let us proceed to define our F.

For the convenience of discussion, we call the instantiated input-output difference pair $(\Delta_{in}, \Delta_{out}) \in \mathbb{F}_2^{32} \times \mathbb{F}_2^{24}$ for $(\Delta X_3, \Delta Y_4)$ with regard to Fig. 5 the inbound differential. The goal of the inbound phase of a rebound attack is to generate data pairs respecting the inbound differential. We define

$$F : \mathbb{F}_2^{24} \times \mathbb{F}_2^{32} \times \mathbb{F}_2^{24} \times \mathbb{F}_2^3 \to \mathbb{F}_2 \qquad (7)$$

in a way such that $F(m_0, \Delta_{in}, \Delta_{out}, \alpha) = 1$ if and only if the starting point computed with $(m_0, \Delta_{in}, \Delta_{out})$ and indexed by $\alpha = (\alpha_0, \alpha_1, \alpha_2) \in \mathbb{F}_2^3$ fulfills the outbound differential.[2] Note that we can set the search space of m_0 to be the most significant 24 bits, with its remaining bits set to 0. Therefore, if $F(m_0, \Delta_{in}, \Delta_{out}, \alpha) = 1$, we can produce two messages m_1 and m'_1 with the help of Algorithm 2 such that

$$\text{CF}(m_1, \text{CF}(m_0, IV)) = \text{CF}(m'_1, \text{CF}(m_0, IV)),$$

where m_1 and m'_1 are obtained from the starting point indexed by α. Given $(m_0, \Delta_{in}, \Delta_{out}, \alpha)$, $F(m_0, \Delta_{in}, \Delta_{out}, \alpha)$ can be computed in the classical world by the following approach:

---

[2] Note that given $(m_0, \Delta_{in}, \Delta_{out})$, we can derive the input-output differences for the four SSB. If there exists one input-output pair for each SSB, there will be $(2 \cdot 2 \cdot 2 \cdot 2)/2 = 8$ choices for starting points. Therefore, Hosoyamada and Sasaki [20] introduced a 3-bit α to specify which starting point to choose. We also adopt this strategy in our definition of F.

1. Compute $h_1 = \mathrm{CF}(m_0, IV)$, which is treated as the master key for the second block encryption.
2. Compute the differential $(\Delta X_3^{(i)}, \Delta Y_4^{(i)})$ for each super S-box $\mathrm{SSB}^{(i)}$ ($0 \leq i < 4$) from the inbound differential $(\Delta_{in}, \Delta_{out})$. Note that the differential trail for $\mathrm{SSB}^{(0)}$ with input difference $\Delta X_3^{(0)}$ and output difference $\Delta Y_4^{(0)}$ is highlighted in Fig. 5.
3. Solve the non-full active super S-box $\mathrm{SSB}^{(0)}$ to obtain $X_3^{(0)}$ such that

$$\mathrm{SSB}^{(0)}(X_3^{(0)} \oplus \Delta X_3^{(0)}) \oplus \mathrm{SSB}^{(0)}(X_3^{(0)}) = \Delta Y_4^{(0)}.$$

If $\alpha_0 = 0$, pick $\min\{X_3^{(0)}, X_3^{(0)} \oplus \Delta X_3^{(0)}\}$ as the new value for $X_3^{(0)}$. Else, pick $\max\{X_3^{(0)}, X_3^{(0)} \oplus \Delta X_3^{(0)}\}$ as the new value for $X_3^{(0)}$. Similarly, we obtain $X_3^{(1)}$, $X_3^{(2)}$. For the pair $(X_3^{(3)}, X_3^{(3)} \oplus \Delta X_3^{(3)})$, we always pick the bigger one as $X_3^{(3)}$. We can build the starting point

$$X_3 = (X_3^{(0)}, X_3^{(1)}, X_3^{(2)}, X_3^{(3)})$$

according to the index α.
4. If the starting point $(X_3, X_3 \oplus \Delta X_3)$ obtained in step 3 respects the outbound differential, $F(m_0, \Delta_{in}, \Delta_{out}, \alpha)$ returns 1, otherwise it returns 0.

Therefore, by applying Grover's search with the quantum oracle $\mathcal{U}_F$ which maps $|m_0, \Delta_{in}, \Delta_{out}, \alpha\rangle |y\rangle$ to $|m_0, \Delta_{in}, \Delta_{out}, \alpha\rangle |y \oplus F(m_0, \Delta_{in}, \Delta_{out}, \alpha)\rangle$, we can find a collision with around $\frac{\pi}{4} \cdot \sqrt{2^{83}}$ queries. To estimate the overall complexity, we need to be clear on the complexity incurred by $\mathcal{U}_F$.

4.2 Implementation of the Quantum Oracle $\mathcal{U}_F$

Similar to [20], we need some additional functions to implement $\mathcal{U}_F$. First, we define $G^{(i)}$, which marks the values of one byte of $X_3^{(i)}$ and a 3-bit index β leading to solutions (compatible data pairs) for the given differential $(\Delta X_3^{(i)}, \Delta Y_4^{(i)})$ of the super S-box $\mathrm{SSB}^{(i)}$ and an initial message block m_0 when Algorithm 2 or its variants are applied. For example, $G^{(0)}(m_0, \Delta X_3^{(0)}, \Delta Y_4^{(0)}, X_3^{(0)}[0], \beta) = 1$ if and only if we pass the check in Step 19 of Algorithm 2 upon input of $(m_0, \Delta X_3^{(0)}, \Delta Y_4^{(0)}, X_3^{(0)}[0], \beta)$. Note that, since $G^{(0)}$ is just to mark the correct 11-bit $(X_3^{(i)}[0], \beta)$ for a given $(m_0, \Delta X_3^{(0)}, \Delta Y_4^{(0)})$, we can return $G^{(0)} = 1$ once it passes the check in Step 19 of Algorithm 2.

Since the computation of $G^{(i)}$ in the classical setting uses the table $\mathbb{T}$ computed by Algorithm 1, implementing a quantum oracle of $G^{(i)}$ requires qRAMs. The implementation of the quantum oracle $\mathcal{U}_{G^{(0)}}$ of $G^{(0)}$ is presented in Algorithm 3.

For $0 \leq i < 3$, we use the function $D^{(i)}$ to compute the actual input-output data pair respecting the differential of the super S-box $\mathrm{SSB}^{(i)}$ with the knowledge of one byte of $X_3^{(i)}[0]$ and β obtained by executing Grover search on $G^{(i)}$. $D^{(i)}$ is

---

Algorithm 3. Implementation of $\mathcal{U}_{G^{(0)}}$

Input: $|m_0, \Delta X_3^{(0)}, \Delta Y_4^{(0)}; X_3^{(0)}[0], \beta\rangle\, |y\rangle$ with $\beta = (\beta_0, \beta_1, \beta_2) \in \mathbb{F}_2^3$

Output: $|m_0, \Delta X_3^{(0)}, \Delta Y_4^{(0)}; X_3^{(0)}[0], \beta\rangle\, |y \oplus G^{(0)}(m_0, \Delta X_3^{(0)}, \Delta Y_4^{(0)}; X_3^{(0)}[0], \beta)\rangle$

1 Compute $h_1 = \mathtt{CF}(m_0, IV)$

2 Apply the quantum circuit of Step 1-19 Algorithm 2 with input;   /* Requires 2^{16} qRAMSs */

3 **if** *It passes the check in Step 19 of Algorithm 2* **then**
4 $\quad$ **return** $|m_0, \Delta X_3^{(0)}, \Delta Y_4^{(0)}; X_3^{(0)}[0], \beta\rangle\, |y \oplus 1\rangle$
5 **else**
6 $\quad$ **return** $|m_0, \Delta X_3^{(0)}, \Delta Y_4^{(0)}; X_3^{(0)}[0], \beta\rangle\, |y\rangle$
7 **end**

---

just to replay a full version of Algorithm 2 and outputs $\min\{X_3^{(i)}, X_3^{(i)} \oplus \Delta X_3^{(i)}\}$ upon input

$$(m_0, \Delta X_3^{(i)}, \Delta Y_4^{(i)}, X_3^{(i)}[0], \beta; \alpha_i = 0),$$

and outputs $\max\{X_3^{(i)}, X_3^{(i)} \oplus \Delta X_3^{(i)}\}$ upon input

$$(m_0, \Delta X_3^{(i)}, \Delta Y_4^{(i)}, X_3^{(i)}[0], \beta; \alpha_i = 1),$$

such that $\mathtt{SSB}^{(i)}(X_3^{(i)}) \oplus \mathtt{SSB}^{(i)}(X_3^{(i)} \oplus \Delta X_3^{(i)}) = \Delta Y_4^{(i)}$. In addition, $D^{(3)}$ is defined differently. It always returns the smaller one of $X_3^{(3)}$ and $X_3^{(3)} \oplus \Delta X_3^{(3)}$ upon the input $(m_0, \Delta X_3^{(i)}, \Delta Y_4^{(i)}, X_3^{(i)}[0], \beta)$, such that

$$\mathtt{SSB}^{(3)}(X_3^{(3)}) \oplus \mathtt{SSB}^{(3)}(X_3^{(3)} \oplus \Delta X_3^{(3)}) = \Delta Y_4^{(3)}.$$

Finally, the oracle $\mathcal{U}_F$ can be constructed by using $\mathcal{U}_{G^{(i)}}$ and the quantum circuits of $D^{(i)}$ which is presented in Algorithm 4.

Complexity Analysis. To produce fair and comparable results, the assumptions made by Hosoyamada and Sasaki [20] are inherited in our complexity analysis:

- The complexity of the computation of 7-round $\mathtt{AES}$ is approximated by $16 \times 7 + 4 \times 7 = 140$ S-box computations.
- The complexity of one access to the qRAM storing a table is equivalent to one S-box computation.
- The complexity of the resolution of the linear equation involving $\mathtt{MC}$ with four knowns and four unknowns is equivalent to one $\mathtt{MC}$ operation and is ignored.
- One inverse Sbox is about two Sboxes [21].
- Uncomputing is taken into account.

First of all, in our attack, the differential distribution table with 2^{16} classical data for the S-box is precomputed (see Algorithm 1) and loaded into a qRAM in advance, which is accessed by the quantum circuits for $G^{(i)}$ and $D^{(i)}$.

Algorithm 4. Implementation of $\mathcal{U}_F$.

Input: $|m_0, \Delta_{in}, \Delta_{out}; \alpha\rangle |y\rangle$, with $\alpha = (\alpha_0, \alpha_1, \alpha_2) \in \mathbb{F}_2^3$
Output: $|m_0, \Delta_{in}, \Delta_{out}; \alpha\rangle |y \oplus F(m_0, \Delta_{in}, \Delta_{out}; \alpha)\rangle$

1 Compute $h_1 = \text{CF}(m_0, IV)$.

2 **for** $i \in \{0, 1, 2\}$ **do**

3 $\quad$ Compute the corresponding differential $\Delta X_3^{(i)} \to \Delta Y_4^{(i)}$ for $\text{SSB}^{(i)}$ from $(\Delta_{in}, \Delta_{out})$.

4 $\quad$ Run Grover search on the function $G^{(i)}(m_0, \Delta X_3^{(i)}, \Delta Y_4^{(i)}; \cdot) : \mathbb{F}_2^{11} \to \mathbb{F}_2$. Let $X_3^{(i)}[0] \in \mathbb{F}_2^8$ and $\beta^{(i)} \in \mathbb{F}_2^3$ be the output.

5 $\quad$ Run $D^{(i)}(m_0, \Delta X_3^{(i)}, \Delta Y_4^{(i)}, X_3^{(i)}[0], \beta^{(i)}, \alpha_i)$. Let $X_3^{(i)}$ be the output.

6 **end**

7 Compute the corresponding differential $\Delta X_3^{(3)} \to \Delta Y_4^{(3)}$ for $\text{SSB}^{(3)}$ from $(\Delta_{in}, \Delta_{out})$.

8 Run Grover search on the function $G^{(3)}(m_0, \Delta X_3^{(0)}, \Delta Y_4^{(3)}; \cdot) : \mathbb{F}_2^{11} \to \mathbb{F}_2$. Let $X_3^{(3)}[0] \in \mathbb{F}_2^8$ and $\beta^{(3)} \in \mathbb{F}_2^3$ be the output.

9 Run $D^{(3)}(m_0, \Delta X_3^{(3)}, \Delta Y_4^{(3)}, X_3^{(3)}[0], \beta^{(3)})$. Let $X_3^{(3)}$ be the output.

10 /* Create starting points derived from $(m_0, \Delta_{in}, \Delta_{out}; \alpha)$ */

11 $X \leftarrow (X_3^{(0)}, \cdots X_3^{(3)})$

12 $X' \leftarrow (X_3^{(0)} \oplus \Delta X_3^{(0)}, \cdots, X_3^{(3)} \oplus \Delta X_3^{(3)})$

13 **if** (X, X') *fulfills the outbound differential* **then**

14 $\quad$ **return** $|m_0, \Delta_{in}, \Delta_{out}, \alpha\rangle |y \oplus 1\rangle$

15 **else**

16 $\quad$ **return** $|m_0, \Delta_{in}, \Delta_{out}, \alpha\rangle |y\rangle$

17 **end**

Complexity of the Grover Search on $G^{(i)}$. Applying Grover algorithm to $G^{(i)}$ given $(m_0, \Delta X_3^{(i)}, \Delta Y_4^{(i)})$ to find a 11-bit value $(X_3^{(i)}[0], \beta^{(i)})$ requires $\frac{\pi}{4}\sqrt{2^{8+3}} \approx 2^{5.15}$ queries to the oracle $\mathcal{U}_{G^{(i)}}$[3]. According to the analysis of Algorithm 2, one query to $\mathcal{U}_{G^{(i)}}$ takes about $s = 3$ qRAM accesses and $4(d-s) = 4(4-3) = 4$ S-box evaluations, the overall complexity can be estimated as $2 \times 2^{5.15} \times (3+4) \times \frac{1}{140} \approx 2^{1.83}$ 7-round AES computations.

Complexity of $D^{(i)}$. $D^{(i)}$ is just to replay a full version of Algorithm 2. In Step 1–19 of Algorithm 2, it needs $s + 4(d-s) = 3 + 4(4-3) = 7$ S-boxes evaluations. In Step 21, since all the 5 active bytes are known before, we just compute the last 3 inactive Sboxes (see Fig. 4) to determine a conforming pair for the $\text{SSB}^{(i)}$. Hence, totally $7 + 3 = 10$ Sboxes evaluations are needed, which is about $2 \times \frac{10}{140} \approx 2^{-2.8}$ 7-round AES computations.

---

[3] Supplementary Material C of the full version of the paper at https://eprint.iacr.org/2020/1030 discusses the Grover search on small space.

Complexity of $\mathcal{U}_F$. In Algorithm 4, Step 1 needs one 7-round AES computation; Step 2–9 need $4 \times (2^{1.83} + 2^{-2.8}) \approx 2^{3.88}$ 7-round AES computations. In Step 13, according to Fig. 5, we need to compute backward for 2 rounds and forward for 3 rounds from the starting point (X, X'). Therefore, $2 \times 2 \times 16 = 64$ inverse Sboxes and $2 \times 3 \times 16 = 96$ Sboxes are needed, which are equal to $2 \times \frac{64 \times 2 + 96}{140} = 3.2$ 7-round AES computations. Totally, the complexity of $\mathcal{U}_F$ is $1 + 2^{3.88} + 3.2 \approx 2^{4.24}$ 7-round AES computations. Supplementary Material D of the full version of the paper at https://eprint.iacr.org/2020/1030 discusses the success probability of $\mathcal{U}_F$.

Complexity to Find a Collision. To identify an 83-bit value $(m_0, \Delta_{in}, \Delta_{out}, \alpha) \in \mathbb{F}_2^{24} \times \mathbb{F}_2^{32} \times \mathbb{F}_2^{24} \times \mathbb{F}_2^3$ with Grover search such that $F(m_0, \Delta_{in}, \Delta_{out}, \alpha) = 1$ requires about $\frac{\pi}{4} \times \sqrt{2^{83}}$ queries to $\mathcal{U}_F$. Therefore, the complexity to find a collision is $\frac{\pi}{4} \times \sqrt{2^{83}} \times 2^{4.24} = 2^{45.4}$ 7-round AES computations.

5   Quantum Attacks on 7-Round AES-MMO Without qRAM

The qRAM dependence of the previous attack comes from the qRAM dependence of $\mathcal{U}_{G^{(i)}}$ and $D^{(i)}$. To get rid of the qRAMs, we re-implement $\mathcal{U}_{G^{(i)}}$ and $D^{(i)}$ without using the DDT stored in qRAMs, while keep their functional behavior unchanged. In this section, we introduce two method to reduced qRAMs to zero.

Method 1. The idea is simple: given a differential of an 8×8 S-box, data pairs are generated by on-line search instead of table lookups. Since the methods for re-implementing $\mathcal{U}_{G^{(i)}}$ and $D^{(i)}$ are similar, we only give the details of the implementation of $\mathcal{U}_{G^{(0)}}$ in Algorithm 5. The complexity analysis of this new attack is given in the following.

Complexity of the Grover Search on $G^{(i)}$. Applying Grover's algorithm to $G^{(i)}$ given $(m_0, \Delta X_3^{(i)}, \Delta Y_4^{(i)})$ to find a 11-bit value $(X_3^{(i)}[0], \beta^{(i)})$ requires $\frac{\pi}{4}\sqrt{2^{8+3}} \approx 2^{5.15}$ queries to the oracle $\mathcal{U}_{G^{(i)}}$. According to Algorithm 5, the complexity of one query to $U_{G^{(i)}}$ is dominated by Step 6–8, which is about $3 \cdot \frac{\pi}{4} \cdot \sqrt{2^8} \cdot (\frac{1}{140}) = 2^{-1.89}$ 7-round AES. Hence, the total complexity of the Grover search on $G^{(i)}$ is about $2 \times 2^{5.15} \times 2^{-1.89} = 2^{4.27}$ 7-round AES.

Complexity of $D^{(i)}$. With $(X_3^{(i)}[0], \beta^{(i)})$, $D^{(i)}$ outputs the pair respecting the differential of the super S-box on-line. The implementation of $D^{(i)}$ is similar to $G^{(i)}$, with Step 12–14 of Algorithm 5 replaced by outputting X_3^i according to α_i (please refer the definitions of $D^{(i)}$ in Sect. 4.2 for details). The complexity of $D^{(i)}$ is also bounded by Step 6–8 of Algorithm 5. The complexity is about $2 \times 2^{-1.89} = 2^{0.89}$ 7-round AES.

Complexity of $\mathcal{U}_F$. The implementation of $\mathcal{U}_F$ without qRAM is obtained by replacing $G^{(i)}$ and $D^{(i)}$'s with their no-qRAM versions (Algorithm 4). The complexity of one query to $\mathcal{U}_F$ is about $4 \times (2^{4.27} + 2^{-0.89}) + 1 + 3.2 \approx 2^{6.384}$ 7-round AES computations.

Algorithm 5. Implementation of $\mathcal{U}_{G^{(0)}}$ without using qRAMs

Input: $|m_0, \Delta X_3^{(0)}, \Delta Y_4^{(0)}; X_3^{(0)}[0], \beta\rangle |y\rangle$ with $\beta = (\beta_0, \beta_1, \beta_2) \in \mathbb{F}_2^3$
Output: $|m_0, \Delta X_3^{(0)}, \Delta Y_4^{(i)}; X_3^{(0)}[0], \beta\rangle |y \oplus G^{(0)}(m_0, \Delta X_3^{(0)}, \Delta Y_4^{(i)}; X_8^{(0)}[0], \beta)\rangle$

1 /* Please look back to Figure 5   */
2 $Z_3^{(0)}[0] \leftarrow S(X_3^{(0)}[0])$
3 $\Delta Z_3^{(0)}[0] \leftarrow S(X_3^{(0)}[0] \oplus \Delta X_3^{(0)}[0]) \oplus S(X_3^{(0)}[0])$

4 Solving the system of equations $\text{MC}(\Delta Z_3^{(0)}) = \Delta W_3^{(0)}$ with the knowledge of
  $\Delta Z_3^{(0)}[0]$ and $\Delta Z_3^{(0)}[1] = \Delta Z_3^{(0)}[3] = \Delta W_3^{(0)}[0] = 0$

5 Let $g_j : \mathbb{F}_2^8 \times \mathbb{F}_2^8 \times \mathbb{F}_2 \times \mathbb{F}_2^8 \to \mathbb{F}_2$ be a Boolean function such that
  $g_j(\delta_{in}, \delta_{out}, \beta_j = 0, x) = 1$ if and only if $S(x) \oplus S(x \oplus \delta_{in}) = \delta_{out}$ and
  $x \leq x \oplus \delta_{in}$, and $g_j(\delta_{in}, \delta_{out}, \beta_j = 1, x) = 1$ if and only if
  $S(x) \oplus S(x \oplus \delta_{in}) = \delta_{out}$, and $x > x \oplus \delta_{in}$.

6 Run the Grover search on the function $g_0(\Delta X_3^{(0)}[2], \Delta Y_3^{(0)}[2], \beta_0; \cdot) : \mathbb{F}_2^8 \to \mathbb{F}_2$.
  Let $X_3^{(0)}[2]$ be the output.
7 Run the Grover search on the function $g_1(\Delta X_4^{(0)}[1], \Delta Y_4^{(0)}[1], \beta_1; \cdot) : \mathbb{F}_2^8 \to \mathbb{F}_2$.
  Let $X_4^{(0)}[1]$ be the output.
8 Run the Grover search on the function $g_2(\Delta X_4^{(0)}[2], \Delta Y_4^{(0)}[2], \beta_2; \cdot) : \mathbb{F}_2^8 \to \mathbb{F}_2$.
  Let $X_4^{(0)}[2]$ be the output.

9 Compute $Z_3^{(0)}[2]$, $W_3^{(0)}[2]$ and $W_3^{(0)}[3]$;   /* $Z_3^{(0)}[0]$ is known */
10 Solve the equation $\text{MC}(Z_3^{(0)}) = W_3^{(0)}$ for $W_3^{(0)}[3]$ and compute $X_4^{(0)}[3]$

11 **if** $S(X_4^{(0)}[3] \oplus \Delta W_3^{(0)}[3]) \oplus S(X_4^{(0)}[3]) = \Delta Y_4^{(0)}[3]$ **then**
12 $\quad$ **return** $|m_0, \Delta_{in}, \Delta_{out}, \alpha\rangle |y \oplus 1\rangle$
13 **else**
14 $\quad$ **return** $|m_0, \Delta_{in}, \Delta_{out}, \alpha\rangle |y\rangle$
15 **end**

Complexity to Find a Collision. To identify an 83-bit value $(m_0, \Delta_{in}, \Delta_{out}, \alpha) \in \mathbb{F}_2^{24} \times \mathbb{F}_2^{32} \times \mathbb{F}_2^{24} \times \mathbb{F}_2^3$ with Grover search such that $F(m_0, \Delta_{in}, \Delta_{out}, \alpha) = 1$ requires about $\frac{\pi}{4} \times \sqrt{2^{83}}$ queries to $\mathcal{U}_F$. Therefore, the complexity to find a collision is $\frac{\pi}{4} \times \sqrt{2^{83}} \times 2^{6.384} = 2^{47.584}$ 7-round AES computations.

Method 2. At FSE 2020, Bonnetain, Naya-Plasencia and Schrottenloher [4] introduced a quantum circuit that fulfilled the functionality of DDT. The cost is equivalent to 2 Sboxes computations and 22 ancilla qubits. In this section, we use this idea to implement $\mathcal{U}_F$ without qRAMs. The complexity is quit similar to Algorithm 4, since when one DDT access is needed, we just replace it by 2 Sbox evaluations. The updated complexity of $G^{(i)}$ is $2s + 4(d - s) = 6 + 4 = 10$ Sbox evaluations. Therefore, applying Grover's algorithm to $G^{(i)}$ costs $2 \times 2^{5.15} \times 10 \times \frac{1}{140} \approx 2^{2.34}$ 7-round AES. The complexity of $D^{(i)}$ is about $2 \times \frac{13}{140} \approx 2^{-2.43}$ 7-round AES. Hence, the complexity of $\mathcal{U}_F$ becomes $1 + 4 \times (2^{2.34} + 2^{-2.43}) + 3.2 \approx 2^{4.66}$

7-round AES. Totally, we need $\frac{\pi}{4} \times \sqrt{83} \times 2^{4.66} \approx 2^{45.8}$ 7-round AES computations with 22 ancilla qubits.

6   Collision Attacks on Grøstl-512

Grøstl is a SHA3 finalist hash function. It comes with two versions: Grøstl-256 and Grøstl-512, with the trailing digits signifying the sizes of the outputs in bits. The structure of Grøstl-$\frac{n}{2}$ with two message blocks is depicted in Fig. 7, where P and Q are two n-bit AES-like permutations. Before it outputs the hash value, an output transformation based on P and a truncation $\Omega : \mathbb{F}_2^n \to \mathbb{F}_2^{n/2}$ are applied to h_2. We refer the reader to [11] for more details of the design.

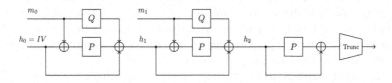

Fig. 7. Grøstl-$\frac{n}{2}$ with two message blocks

The best known collision attack on Grøstl-512 reaches 3 rounds [43]. Based on differentials found by MILP technique, we present the first classical and dedicated quantum collision attacks on 4-round and 5-round Grøstl-512. To facilitate our discussion, we use the alternative but equivalent description of Grøstl introduced by [34], which is illustrated in Fig. 8. Let P^- and Q^- be the AES-like permutations with their last MB operations removed. We have the following equivalent description of Grøstl. For $1 \leq i \leq t$, we set

$$v_0 = \text{MB}^{-1}(IV),$$
$$v_i = P^-(\text{MB}(v_{i-1}) \oplus m_{i-1}) \oplus Q^-(m_{i-1}) \oplus v_{i-1},$$
$$h = \Omega(\text{MB}(v_t)).$$

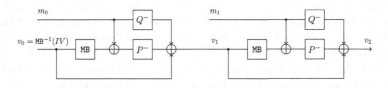

Fig. 8. An alternative description of Grøstl-$\frac{n}{2}$ with two message blocks

6.1   Exploitable Differential Trails of Grøstl-512

The differential trails we used in our collision attacks on Grøstl-512 are inspired by Mendel, Rijmen and Schläffer's collision attack on 4-round Grøstl-256 [34]. In [34], a random difference is injected through m_0 to create a fully differentially active chaining value v_1. Then a sequence of local rebound attacks is performed to cancel the differences in the chaining values "column" by "column", which eventually leads to a full collision. The differential trails employed to trigger such cancellations are shown in Fig. 11 in the Supplementary Material A of the full version of the paper at https://eprint.iacr.org/2020/1030.

However, if we adopt a series of similar differential trails in the attack on 4-round Grøstl-512, we end up with impossible differentials (see Fig. 12 in the Supplementary Material A of the full version of the paper for examples) such that the cancellation of the last "column" never happens. To overcome this difficulty, we have to cancel multiple "columns" at once during the rebound attack over the final message block, which increases the time complexity significantly. To minimize the complexity penalty due to the multiple-column cancellation, we apply the MILP model to the last two steps to find two truncated differential trails to cancel the differences in the last two chaining values before the collision. The identified trails are depicted in Fig. 13 in the full version of the paper, where in the last step we attempt to cancel 16 active bytes at once, and the numbers of inactive S-boxes for the 16 super S-boxes SSB of the inbound phase (see Fig. 9) are given as $(s_0, s_1, \cdots, s_{15}) = (7, 7, 6, 7, 7, 7, 5, 3, 4, 4, 4, 4, 4, 4, 5, 7)$.

6.2   Classical and Quantum Collision Attacks on 4-Round Grøstl-512

Based on the differential trails given in Fig. 13 in Supplementary Material A of the full version of the paper, a classical collision attack on 4-round Grøstl-512 can be constructed. The strategy of the attack generally follows the strategy of [34] with a critical difference at the initial difference injection. The attack of [34] starts with an arbitrary fully active chaining value v_1. In our attack, we impose additional conditions on the fully active chaining value v_1. We now clarify these conditions.

From Fig. 13 of the full version of the paper we can see that for a fixed initial pair of message blocks (m_0, m_0'), the difference of the cells of the chaining states v_i keeps unchanged throughout the entire attack unless they are canceled. Therefore, to force the chaining values following the specified differential trails for the last two-column cancellation, we can pretest some cells of Δv_1, which are marked by blue cells in Fig. 13, and the required differential transformation is depicted in Fig. 9.

Specifically, we introduce some conditions on some active bytes (marked by blue) within some columns in the chaining values. For example, in v_{i-1} of Fig. 13, there are 10 blue bytes. In the first column of v_{i-1}, the two active blue bytes have to meet the condition for the differential propagation:

$$(0, *, 0, *, 0, 0, 0, 0, 0)^T \xrightarrow{\text{MB}} (*, *, *, *, 0, *, *, *)^T.$$

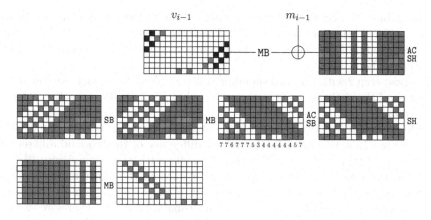

Fig. 9. The inbound phase of the last step of the collision attack on `Grøstl-512`. The gray and blue bytes are active, but there are conditions on blue bytes. The green bytes are inactive due to the conditions imposed on the blue cells. (Color figure online)

Similar conditions for other blue bytes in the other 4 columns are also needed. For randomly selected pair (m_0, m_0'), the output difference Δv_1 meets the conditions in the blue bytes with probability $2^{-8 \times 5} = 2^{-40}$. Hence, with 2^{40} (m_0, m_0') pairs, we are expected to find one correct pair.

In summary, this attack starts with a fully differentially active v_1 fulfilling the required conditions by injecting a random difference at m_0, repeats local rebound-like attacks over the subsequent message blocks to cancel the differences column by column until there are only two differentially active columns, and a final rebound attack is employed to cancel the last two active columns as a whole. The colliding pair is of the form: $M = (m_0, m_1, \cdots, m_t)$ and $M' = (m_0', m_1, \cdots, m_t)$, that is, only the starting message block m_0 has a difference. The procedure of the attack is outlined in the following.

1. Choose arbitrary 2^{40} message blocks m_0, m_0' and compute the difference $\Delta v_1 = v_1 \oplus v_1'$ with conditions on five columns satisfied in the blue bytes. Since the probability is 2^{-40} for a random pair (m_0, m_0'), we are expected to find one right pair.
2. Perform rebound attacks over the message block m_1. Note that the input difference Δ_{in} of the inbound phase is fixed due to Δv_1, and the output difference Δ_{out} of the inbound phase has 8 active cells as shown in Fig. 13. Using the full-active-super S-box technique[4], we can generate $2^0 \times 2^{64} = 2^{64}$ messages m_1 (starting points) such that the pair $(m_1 \oplus \text{MB}(v_1), m_1 \oplus \text{MB}(v_1'))$ respect the given inbound differential. With regards to the outbound differential, the truncated differential $(8 \to 8 \to 8)$ given in Fig. 13 holds with

---

[4] There are at least one full-active super S-box among the 16 ones, which bounds the memory complexity in this step in classical setting. Hence, we do not need the non-full-active super S-box technique here. The non-full-active super S-box technique is only used in the quantum attack versions.

probability 1, and the 8-bytes cancellation due to the feed-forward exclusive-or happens with probability 2^{-64}. Therefore, we expect one of 2^{64} starting points to fulfill the one-column local collision, and the time complexity of this step is about 2^{64}.

3. Repeat step 2 with the corresponding differential trails to inactivate the differences of the chaining values column by column until only two active columns remain.

4. Eliminate the last two active columns with the same strategy of step 2. Since there are 16 active bytes in the output difference of the inbound differential, we can obtain $2^{16\times8} = 2^{128}$ starting points with time complexity 2^{128} by using the super S-box technique. With regard to the outbound differential, the truncated differential $16 \rightarrow 16 \rightarrow 16$ holds with probability 1, and the two-column cancellation happens with probability 2^{-128}. Therefore, we can obtain the desired collision with 2^{128} starting points.

The time complexity of the attack is dominated by Step 4 of the above procedure, which is about 2^{128}. The storage of the super-Sbox leads to a memory complexity of 2^{64}. Finally, we find a collision for the 4-round Grøstl-512 with about 16 message blocks. A quantum version of the same attack on 4-round Grøstl-512 with or without qRAMs can be constructed based on the same method given in Sect. 4 and Sect. 5, and we refer the reader to Supplementary Material B of the full version of the paper at https://eprint.iacr.org/2020/1030 for the details.

6.3 Classical and Quantum Collision Attacks on 5-Round Grøstl-512

The 4-round collision attack can be extended to a 5-round collision attack shown in Fig. 14 in Supplementary Material A of the full version of the paper, where the probabilities of the outbound phases of the rebound attacks are 2^{-56} and 2^{-112} (the last step). When a local rebound attack fails to produce the local collision on a column, we will perform the same attack on the next message block until the desire difference cancellations occur. Therefore, how many message blocks are used in the attack is unknown before we reach a full collision. We briefly summarize the attack on 5-round Grøstl-512 below:

1. Choose arbitrary message blocks m_0, m_0' and compute the difference $\Delta v_1 = v_1 \oplus v_1'$ until the required conditions on the blue cells are satisfied. We are expected to find one correct pair after 2^{40} repetitions.

2. Perform rebound attacks over the message block m_1. Note that the input difference Δ_{in} of the inbound phase is fixed due to Δv_1, and the output difference Δ_{out} of the inbound phase has 8 active cells. Using the full-active super S-box technique, we can generate $2^0 \times 2^{64} = 2^{64}$ messages m_1 (starting points). With regards to the outbound differential, the truncated differential $(128 \rightarrow 64 \rightarrow 8 \rightarrow 1 \rightarrow 8 \rightarrow 8)$ holds with probability 2^{-56}, and the 8-bytes cancellation due to the feed-forward exclusive-or happens with probability 2^{-64}. Therefore, we can obtain the desired difference for the chaining value

with probability $2^{64} \times 2^{-56} \times 2^{-64} = 2^{-56}$ with 2^{64} time complexity. If we are failed to get the desired difference, we perform the same attack over the next message block with the chaining values produced previously. We will succeed in canceling the 8-byte difference after about 2^{56} additional message blocks are processed.

3. Repeat step 2 with the corresponding differential trails to inactivate the differences of the chaining values column by column until only two active columns remain.

4. Eliminate the last two active columns with the same strategy of step 2. The success probability of the local rebound attack performed in this step is different from others. Since there are 16 active bytes in the output difference of the inbound differential, we can obtain $2^{16 \times 8} = 2^{128}$ starting points with time complexity 2^{128} by using the super S-box technique. With regard to the outbound differential, the truncated differential trail $88 \rightarrow 96 \rightarrow 16 \rightarrow 2 \rightarrow 16 \rightarrow 16$ holds with probability 2^{-112}, and the two-column cancellation happens with probability 2^{-128}. Therefore, we can obtain the desired collision with probability $2^{128} \times 2^{-112} \times 2^{-128} = 2^{-112}$ with 2^{128} time complexity (within this step). If we fail to get the collision, repeating Step 4 with about 2^{112} additional message blocks will achieve the collision.

The time complexity of the attack is dominated by step 4, which can be estimated as $2^{112} \times 2^{128} = 2^{240}$. The storage of the super S-box leads to a memory complexity of 2^{64}. Finally, we find a collision with about 2^{112} message blocks. A quantum version of the same attack can be constructed, which is quite similar to the attack given in Supplementary Material B of the full version of the paper. We repeat a quantum version of Step 4 for 2^{112} times to find a collision. The time complexity of the quantum attack with 2^{16} qRAMs is $2^{88.37} \times 2^{112} = 2^{200.4}$, and the time complexity of the quantum attack without qRAMs is $2^{89.3} \times 2^{112} = 2^{201.3}$.

7   Semi-Free-Start Collision Attacks on Grøstl-256

So far, the best collision attack on 6-round Grøstl-256 is a semi-free-start collision attack with time complexity 2^{120} and memory complexity 2^{64}. Based on the truncated differential trail covering 6-round Grøstl-256 found by the MILP technique, which is depicted in Fig. 10, we can improve this attack in both the classical and quantum settings.

The Classical Attack. Two rebound attacks are applied to P and Q separately. The inbound phase of the rebound attack on P begins at P_2 and ends at P_4. There are $2^{56} \times 2^{56} = 2^{112}$ input-output differences in total, and we expect to find 2^{112} starting points with 2^{112} time complexity based on the super S-box technique. In the outbound phase, the probability for fulfilling the outbound truncated differential trail is $2^{-48} \times 2^{-48} = 2^{-96}$. Therefore, we can produce $2^{112} \times 2^{-96} = 2^{16}$ pairs respecting the 6-round truncated differential covering

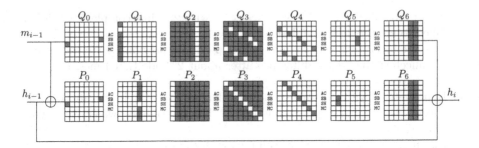

Fig. 10. Differential trail of the compression function of 6-round `Grøstl-256`

P with time complexity 2^{112}. Similarly, performing a rebound attack with time complexity 2^{112} over Q generates 2^{16} pairs respecting the truncated differential trail covering Q. Combining the results of the two rebound attacks, we obtain $2^{16} \times 2^{16} = 2^{32}$ quartets $((P_0, P_0'), (Q_0, Q_0'))$, among which we expect to identify $2^{32} \times 2^{-16} \times 2^{-16} = 1$ quartet such that $\Delta Q_0 = \Delta P_0$ and $\Delta P_6 = \Delta Q_6$. This leads to a semi-free-start collision with $m_{i-1} = Q_0$, $m_{i-1}' = Q_0'$, and $h_{i-1} = Q_0 \oplus P_0 = Q_0' \oplus P_0'$. The time complexity of the attack about 2^{112}, and we need 2^{64} memory to apply the super S-box technique.

The Quantum Attack Without qRAMs. The quantum attack is also based on the differential trails shown in Fig. 10. Given an inbound differential $(\Delta_{in}^P, \Delta_{out}^P) \in \mathbb{F}_2^{56} \times \mathbb{F}_2^{56}$ for the permutation P. If there is a starting point respecting the given inbound differential, then one can generate 2^7 different starting points, which are indexed by $\alpha_P \in \mathbb{F}_2^7$. We define $F_P : \mathbb{F}_2^{56} \times \mathbb{F}_2^{56} \times \mathbb{F}_2^7 \to \mathbb{F}_2$ such that $F_P(\Delta_{in}^P, \Delta_{out}^P, \alpha_P) = 1$ if and only if there is a starting point respecting the inbound differential $(\Delta_{in}^P, \Delta_{out}^P)$ and the particular starting point indexed by α_P also conforming with the outbound differential of P. The probability of the outbound phase is $2^{-48-48} = 2^{-96}$. Therefore, given $(\Delta_{in}^P, \Delta_{out}^P, \alpha_P)$, $F_P(\cdot)$ return 1 with probability of $2^{-96-7} = 2^{-103}$.

Applying Grover algorithm with certainty to the quantum oracle $\mathcal{U}_{F_P}$ which is constructed without qRAM with similar techniques shown in previous sections, we can obtain a superposition

$$|\rho\rangle = \frac{1}{\sqrt{\{x \in \mathbb{F}_2^{119} : F_P(x) = 1\}}} \sum_{F_P(x)=1} |x\rangle, \qquad (8)$$

where $\sqrt{\{x \in \mathbb{F}_2^{119} : F_P(x) = 1\}} \approx \sqrt{2^{56} \times 2^{56} \times 2^7 \times 2^{-103}} \approx \sqrt{2^{16}}$.

As shown in the generalized version of Algorithm 2, given parameters ($d = 8, c = 8, s$), where s is the sum of the non-active bytes of the input-output differential of the non-full-active super S-box, we have to traverse $2^{(d-s)c+s}$ to find the conforming pair of super S-box (an s-bit auxiliary variable to specify which value to choose within the pair obtained by accessing s DDT). To find a conforming pair for the super S-box, we also define a similar $G^{(i)}$ as defined in

Algorithm 5. According to the Eq. (6), the time complexity to implement $G^{(i)}$ is about $4(d-s)+s$, with s DDT accesses and $4(d-s)$ small Sbox evaluations. Here, we only considering the attack without storing DDT in qRAM. Hence, s DDT accesses become s implementations of Grover algorithm to find a conforming pair for the s S-boxes. Hence, the time complexity to search on $U_{G^{(i)}}$ using Grover algorithm is about

$$2 \cdot \frac{\pi}{4} \cdot \sqrt{2^{(d-s)c+s}} \cdot (4(d-s) + s \cdot (\frac{\pi}{4} \cdot \sqrt{2^c})), \text{ S-box evaluations.} \qquad (9)$$

Considering the non-full-active super S-boxes in Fig. 10, the sum of non-active Sboxes in each SSB is $s = 2$. Hence, to find a conforming pair with given input and output differences of SSB, the time complexity is about $2^{31.27}$ S-box evaluations according to Eq. (9), which is about $2^{31.27}/768 = 2^{21.68}$ 6-round Grøstl-256 without qRAM.

When applying Grover algorithm to setup F_P, we need about $\frac{\pi}{4} \cdot \sqrt{2^{96+7}} \cdot 8 \cdot 2^{21.68} \approx 2^{75.8}$ 6-round Grøstl-256 without qRAM to get the desired superposition in Eq. (8).

Similarly, applying Grover search to F_Q, where $F_P(\Delta_{in}^Q, \Delta_{out}^Q, \alpha_Q) = 1$ if and only if there is a starting point respecting the inbound differential $(\Delta_{in}^Q, \Delta_{out}^Q)$ and the particular starting point indexed by α_Q also conforming with the outbound differential of Q. With the same complexity of the first Grover search, we obtain a superposition

$$|\varrho\rangle = \frac{1}{\sqrt{\{x \in \mathbb{F}_2^{119} : F_Q(x) = 1\}}} \sum_{F_Q(x)=1} |x\rangle, \qquad (10)$$

where $\sqrt{\{x \in \mathbb{F}_2^{119} : F_Q(x) = 1\}} \approx \sqrt{2^{56} \times 2^{56} \times 2^7 \times 2^{-103}} \approx \sqrt{2^{16}}$.

Now, we are ready to perform the amplitude amplification with $\mathcal{A}$ being the unitary operator sending $|0\rangle$ to $|\rho\rangle \otimes |\varrho\rangle$ and projector $\sum_{x \in \mathbb{C}} |x\rangle \langle x|$, where $\mathbb{C}$ is the set of all $(\Delta_{in}^Q, \Delta_{out}^Q, \alpha_Q; \Delta_{in}^P, \Delta_{out}^P, \alpha_P) \in \mathbb{F}_2^{238}$ such that the starting points due to $(\Delta_{in}^Q, \Delta_{out}^Q, \alpha_Q)$ and $(\Delta_{in}^P, \Delta_{out}^P, \alpha_P)$ produce a semi-free-start collision. As shown in Fig. 10, the probability that $\Delta Q_0 = \Delta P_0$ and $\Delta Q_6 = \Delta P_6$, which lead a collision, is about $2^{-16} \times 2^{-16} = 2^{-32}$. The complexity to find a collision without qRAM is $\sqrt{2^{32}} \cdot 2 \cdot 2^{75.8} \approx 2^{92.8}$ 6-round Grøstl-256.

8 Conclusion

In this work, we show that the amount of qRAMs required by the quantum attacks on AES-MMO and AES-MP proposed by Hosoyamada and Sasaki can be significantly reduced with only a slight increase in the time complexity. This is achieved by performing a quantum version of the rebound attack based on the non-full-active super S-box technique. Along the way, we find that the non-full-active super S-box analysis can be partially automated with the MILP approach, which is of independent interest, leading to improved attacks on Grøstl in both the classical and quantum settings. To the best our knowledge, our attacks are the first dedicated quantum collision attack on hash functions that slightly out-perform Chailloux, Naya-Plasencia, and Schrottenloher's generic attack (ASI-ACRYPT 2017) in a model where large qRAMs are not available.

Acknowledgments. We thank the anonymous reviewers for their helpful and detailed comments. This work is supported by the National Key Research and Development Program of China (Grant No. 2018YFA0704701, 2018YFA0704704), the Major Program of Guangdong Basic and Applied Research (Grant No. 2019B030302008), Major Scientific and Techological Innovation Project of Shandong Province, China (Grant No. 2019JZZY010133), the Chinese Major Program of National Cryptography Development Foundation (No. MMJJ20180101, MMJJ20180102), and the National Natural Science Foundation of China (No. 61902207, 61772519, 61802400).

References

1. Arunachalam, S., Gheorghiu, V., Jochym-O'Connor, T., Mosca, M., Srinivasan, P.V.: On the robustness of bucket brigade quantum RAM. In: TQC 2015, Brussels, Belgium, 20–22 May 2015, pp. 226–244 (2015)
2. Bonnetain, X., Hosoyamada, A., Naya-Plasencia, M., Sasaki, Y., Schrottenloher, A.: Quantum attacks without superposition queries: the offline Simon's algorithm. In: Galbraith, S.D., Moriai, S. (eds.) ASIACRYPT 2019, Part I. LNCS, vol. 11921, pp. 552–583. Springer, Cham (2019). https://doi.org/10.1007/978-3-030-34578-5_20
3. Bonnetain, X., Naya-Plasencia, M., Schrottenloher, A.: On quantum slide attacks. In: Paterson, K.G., Stebila, D. (eds.) SAC 2019. LNCS, vol. 11959, pp. 492–519. Springer, Cham (2020). https://doi.org/10.1007/978-3-030-38471-5_20
4. Bonnetain, X., Naya-Plasencia, M., Schrottenloher, A.: Quantum security analysis of AES. IACR Trans. Symmetric Cryptol. **2019**(2), 55–93 (2019)
5. Brassard, G., Hoyer, P., Mosca, M., Tapp, A.: Quantum amplitude amplification and estimation. Contemp. Math. **305**, 53–74 (2002)
6. Brassard, G., Høyer, P., Tapp, A.: Quantum cryptanalysis of hash and claw-free functions. In: Lucchesi, C.L., Moura, A.V. (eds.) LATIN 1998. LNCS, vol. 1380, pp. 163–169. Springer, Heidelberg (1998). https://doi.org/10.1007/BFb0054319
7. Chailloux, A., Naya-Plasencia, M., Schrottenloher, A.: An efficient quantum collision search algorithm and implications on symmetric cryptography. In: Takagi, T., Peyrin, T. (eds.) ASIACRYPT 2017, Part II. LNCS, vol. 10625, pp. 211–240. Springer, Cham (2017). https://doi.org/10.1007/978-3-319-70697-9_8
8. Daemen, J., Rijmen, V.: The Design of Rijndael: AES - The Advanced Encryption Standard. Information Security and Cryptography. Springer, Heidelberg (2002). https://doi.org/10.1007/978-3-662-04722-4
9. Damgård, I.B.: A design principle for hash functions. In: Brassard, G. (ed.) CRYPTO 1989. LNCS, vol. 435, pp. 416–427. Springer, New York (1990). https://doi.org/10.1007/0-387-34805-0_39
10. Dong, X., Dong, B., Wang, X.: Quantum attacks on some Feistel block ciphers. Des. Codes Cryptogr. **88**(6), 1179–1203 (2020)
11. Gauravaram, P., et al.: Grøstl - a SHA-3 candidate. In: Symmetric Cryptography, 11–16 January 2009 (2009)
12. Gilbert, H., Peyrin, T.: Super-sbox cryptanalysis: improved attacks for AES-like permutations. In: Hong, S., Iwata, T. (eds.) FSE 2010. LNCS, vol. 6147, pp. 365–383. Springer, Heidelberg (2010). https://doi.org/10.1007/978-3-642-13858-4_21

13. Giovannetti, V., Lloyd, S., Maccone, L.: Architectures for a quantum random access memory. Phys. Rev. A **78**(5), 052310 (2008)
14. Giovannetti, V., Lloyd, S., Maccone, L.: Quantum random access memory. Phys. Rev. Lett. **100**(16), 160501 (2008)
15. Grassi, L., Naya-Plasencia, M., Schrottenloher, A.: Quantum algorithms for the k-xor problem. In: Peyrin, T., Galbraith, S. (eds.) ASIACRYPT 2018, Part I. LNCS, vol. 11272, pp. 527–559. Springer, Cham (2018). https://doi.org/10.1007/978-3-030-03326-2_18
16. Grover, L.K.: A fast quantum mechanical algorithm for database search. In: Proceedings of the Twenty-Eighth Annual ACM Symposium on the Theory of Computing, Philadelphia, Pennsylvania, USA, 22–24 May 1996, pp. 212–219 (1996)
17. Guo, C., Katz, J., Wang, X., Yu, Y.: Efficient and secure multiparty computation from fixed-key block ciphers. IACR Cryptology ePrint Archive 2019, 74 (2019)
18. Hosoyamada, A., Sasaki, Y.: Cryptanalysis against symmetric-key schemes with online classical queries and offline quantum computations. In: Smart, N.P. (ed.) CT-RSA 2018. LNCS, vol. 10808, pp. 198–218. Springer, Cham (2018). https://doi.org/10.1007/978-3-319-76953-0_11
19. Hosoyamada, A., Sasaki, Y.: Quantum Demiric-Selçuk meet-in-the-middle attacks: applications to 6-round generic Feistel constructions. In: Catalano, D., De Prisco, R. (eds.) SCN 2018. LNCS, vol. 11035, pp. 386–403. Springer, Cham (2018). https://doi.org/10.1007/978-3-319-98113-0_21
20. Hosoyamada, A., Sasaki, Y.: Finding hash collisions with quantum computers by using differential trails with smaller probability than birthday bound. In: Canteaut, A., Ishai, Y. (eds.) EUROCRYPT 2020, Part II. LNCS, vol. 12106, pp. 249–279. Springer, Cham (2020). https://doi.org/10.1007/978-3-030-45724-2_9
21. Jaques, S., Naehrig, M., Roetteler, M., Virdia, F.: Implementing Grover oracles for quantum key search on AES and LowMC. In: Canteaut, A., Ishai, Y. (eds.) EUROCRYPT 2020. LNCS, vol. 12106, pp. 280–310. Springer, Cham (2020). https://doi.org/10.1007/978-3-030-45724-2_10
22. Jean, J., Naya-Plasencia, M., Peyrin, T.: Improved rebound attack on the finalist Grøstl. In: Canteaut, A. (ed.) FSE 2012. LNCS, vol. 7549, pp. 110–126. Springer, Heidelberg (2012). https://doi.org/10.1007/978-3-642-34047-5_7
23. Jean, J., Naya-Plasencia, M., Peyrin, T.: Multiple limited-birthday distinguishers and applications. In: Lange, T., Lauter, K., Lisoněk, P. (eds.) SAC 2013. LNCS, vol. 8282, pp. 533–550. Springer, Heidelberg (2014). https://doi.org/10.1007/978-3-662-43414-7_27
24. Jean, J., Naya-Plasencia, M., Schläffer, M.: Improved analysis of ECHO-256. In: Miri, A., Vaudenay, S. (eds.) SAC 2011. LNCS, vol. 7118, pp. 19–36. Springer, Heidelberg (2012). https://doi.org/10.1007/978-3-642-28496-0_2
25. Kaplan, M., Leurent, G., Leverrier, A., Naya-Plasencia, M.: Breaking symmetric cryptosystems using quantum period finding. In: Robshaw, M., Katz, J. (eds.) CRYPTO 2016, Part II. LNCS, vol. 9815, pp. 207–237. Springer, Heidelberg (2016). https://doi.org/10.1007/978-3-662-53008-5_8
26. Kaplan, M., Leurent, G., Leverrier, A., Naya-Plasencia, M.: Quantum differential and linear cryptanalysis. IACR Trans. Symmetric Cryptol. **2016**(1), 71–94 (2016)
27. Keller, M., Orsini, E., Scholl, P.: MASCOT: faster malicious arithmetic secure computation with oblivious transfer. In: Proceedings of the 2016 ACM SIGSAC Conference on Computer and Communications Security, Vienna, Austria, 24–28 October 2016, pp. 830–842 (2016)

28. Kuwakado, H., Morii, M.: Quantum distinguisher between the 3-round Feistel cipher and the random permutation. In: Proceedings of the ISIT 2010, Austin, Texas, USA, 13–18 June 2010, pp. 2682–2685 (2010)

29. Kuwakado, H., Morii, M.: Security on the quantum-type Even-Mansour cipher. In: ISITA 2012, Honolulu, HI, USA, 28–31 October 2012, pp. 312–316 (2012)

30. Lamberger, M., Mendel, F., Rechberger, C., Rijmen, V., Schläffer, M.: Rebound distinguishers: results on the full whirlpool compression function. In: Matsui, M. (ed.) ASIACRYPT 2009. LNCS, vol. 5912, pp. 126–143. Springer, Heidelberg (2009). https://doi.org/10.1007/978-3-642-10366-7_8

31. Lamberger, M., Mendel, F., Schläffer, M., Rechberger, C., Rijmen, V.: The rebound attack and subspace distinguishers: application to whirlpool. J. Cryptol. **28**(2), 257–296 (2015)

32. Leander, G., May, A.: Grover meets Simon – quantumly attacking the FX-construction. In: Takagi, T., Peyrin, T. (eds.) ASIACRYPT 2017, Part II. LNCS, vol. 10625, pp. 161–178. Springer, Cham (2017). https://doi.org/10.1007/978-3-319-70697-9_6

33. Mendel, F., Rechberger, C., Schläffer, M., Thomsen, S.S.: The rebound attack: cryptanalysis of reduced whirlpool and. In: Dunkelman, O. (ed.) FSE 2009. LNCS, vol. 5665, pp. 260–276. Springer, Heidelberg (2009). https://doi.org/10.1007/978-3-642-03317-9_16

34. Mendel, F., Rijmen, V., Schläffer, M.: Collision attack on 5 rounds of Grøstl. In: Cid, C., Rechberger, C. (eds.) FSE 2014. LNCS, vol. 8540, pp. 509–521. Springer, Heidelberg (2015). https://doi.org/10.1007/978-3-662-46706-0_26

35. Menezes, A., van Oorschot, P.C., Vanstone, S.A.: Handbook of Applied Cryptography. CRC Press (1996)

36. Merkle, R.C.: A certified digital signature. In: Brassard, G. (ed.) CRYPTO 1989. LNCS, vol. 435, pp. 218–238. Springer, New York (1990). https://doi.org/10.1007/0-387-34805-0_21

37. Mouha, N., Wang, Q., Gu, D., Preneel, B.: Differential and linear cryptanalysis using mixed-integer linear programming. In: Wu, C.-K., Yung, M., Lin, D. (eds.) Inscrypt 2011. LNCS, vol. 7537, pp. 57–76. Springer, Heidelberg (2012). https://doi.org/10.1007/978-3-642-34704-7_5

38. Naya-Plasencia, M.: How to improve rebound attacks. In: Rogaway, P. (ed.) CRYPTO 2011. LNCS, vol. 6841, pp. 188–205. Springer, Heidelberg (2011). https://doi.org/10.1007/978-3-642-22792-9_11

39. Naya-Plasencia, M., Schrottenloher, A.: Optimal merging in quantum k-xor and k-sum algorithms. IACR Cryptology ePrint Archive 2019, 501 (2019). https://eprint.iacr.org/2019/501

40. Nielsen, M.A., Chuang, I.L.: Quantum Computation and Quantum Information, 10th Anniversary edn. Cambridge University Press (2016)

41. NIST: The post quantum project. https://csrc.nist.gov/projects/post-quantum-cryptography

42. Sasaki, Y., Li, Y., Wang, L., Sakiyama, K., Ohta, K.: Non-full-active super-sbox analysis: applications to ECHO and Grøstl. In: Abe, M. (ed.) ASIACRYPT 2010. LNCS, vol. 6477, pp. 38–55. Springer, Heidelberg (2010). https://doi.org/10.1007/978-3-642-17373-8_3

43. Schläffer, M.: Updated differential analysis of grøstl. Grøstl website, January 2011 (2011)

44. Shor, P.W.: Algorithms for quantum computation: discrete logarithms and factoring. In: 35th Annual Symposium on Foundations of Computer Science, Santa Fe, New Mexico, USA, 20–22 November 1994, pp. 124–134 (1994)

45. Simon, D.R.: On the power of quantum computation. SIAM J. Comput. **26**(5), 1474–1483 (1997)
46. Sun, S., Hu, L., Wang, P., Qiao, K., Ma, X., Song, L.: Automatic security evaluation and (related-key) differential characteristic search: application to SIMON, PRESENT, LBlock, DES(L) and other bit-oriented block ciphers. In: Sarkar, P., Iwata, T. (eds.) ASIACRYPT 2014, Part I. LNCS, vol. 8873, pp. 158–178. Springer, Heidelberg (2014). https://doi.org/10.1007/978-3-662-45611-8_9
47. Xie, H., Yang, L.: Quantum impossible differential and truncated differential cryptanalysis. CoRR abs/1712.06997 (2017). http://arxiv.org/abs/1712.06997

Authenticated Key Exchange

Fuzzy Asymmetric Password-Authenticated Key Exchange

Andreas Erwig[1], Julia Hesse[2], Maximilian Orlt[1], and Siavash Riahi[1(✉)]

[1] Technische Universität Darmstadt, Darmstadt, Germany
{andreas.erwig,maximilian.orlt,siavash.riahi}@tu-darmstadt.de
[2] IBM Research, Zurich, Switzerland
jhs@zurich.ibm.com

Abstract. Password-Authenticated Key Exchange (PAKE) lets users with passwords exchange a cryptographic key. There have been two variants of PAKE which make it more applicable to real-world scenarios:

- *Asymmetric* PAKE (aPAKE), which aims at protecting a client's password even if the authentication server is untrusted, and
- *Fuzzy* PAKE (fPAKE), which enables key agreement even if passwords of users are noisy, but "close enough".

Supporting fuzzy password matches eases the use of higher entropy passwords and enables using biometrics and environmental readings (both of which are naturally noisy).

Until now, both variants of PAKE have been considered only in separation. In this paper, we consider both of them simultaneously. We introduce the notion of *Fuzzy Asymmetric PAKE* (fuzzy aPAKE), which protects against untrusted servers *and* supports noisy passwords. We formulate our new notion in the Universal Composability framework of Canetti (FOCS'01), which is the preferred model for password-based primitives. We then show that fuzzy aPAKE can be obtained from oblivious transfer and some variant of robust secret sharing (Cramer et al, EC'15). We achieve security against malicious parties while avoiding expensive tools such as non-interactive zero-knowledge proofs. Our construction is round-optimal, with message and password file sizes that are independent of the schemes error tolerance.

1   Introduction

In a world of watches interacting with smartphones and our water kettle negotiating with the blinds in our house, communicating devices are ubiquitous. Developments in user-centric technology are rapid, and they call for authentication methods that conveniently work with, e.g., biometric scans, human-memorable passwords or fingerprints derived from environmental readings.

Password-authenticated Key Exchange (PAKE) protocols [BM92,BPR00, BMP00,KOY01,GL03,KV11,CDVW12,BBC+13,CHK+05] are the cryptographic answer to this need. They solve the problem of establishing a secure communication channel between two users who share nothing but a low-entropy

© International Association for Cryptologic Research 2020
S. Moriai and H. Wang (Eds.): ASIACRYPT 2020, LNCS 12492, pp. 761–784, 2020.
https://doi.org/10.1007/978-3-030-64834-3_26

string, often simply called *password*. Two interesting variants of PAKE protocols that are known from the literature are *asymmetric* PAKE [BM93, GMR06, JKX18, BJX19] which aims at protecting the user's password even if his password file at some server is stolen, and *fuzzy* PAKE [DHP+18] which can tolerate some errors in the password. The former is useful in settings where authentication servers store thousands of user accounts and the server cannot be fully trusted. The latter introduces a usability aspect to PAKE protocols used by humans trying to remember passwords exactly. Furthermore, fuzzy PAKE broadens applicability of PAKE to the fuzzy setting and thereby allows using environmental readings or biometrics as passwords.

This work is the first to consider a combination of both PAKE variants. Namely, we introduce the notion of *fuzzy asymmetric PAKE* (fuzzy aPAKE). This new primitive allows a client and an untrusted server to authenticate to each other using a password, and both parties are guaranteed to derive the same cryptographic key as long as their passwords are within some predefined distance (in some predefined metric). Consider a client authenticating to a server using his fingerprint scan. In this setting, asymmetric PAKE protocols would not work since subsequent scans do not match exactly. Fuzzy PAKE, on the other hand, would require the server to store the fingerprint (or at least some template of it that uniquely identifies the person) in the clear, which is unacceptable for sensitive and ephemeral personal data that is biometrics. Fuzzy asymmetric PAKE, as introduced in this paper, is the only known cryptographic solution that applies to this setting: it works with fuzzy authentication data *and* does not reveal this authentication data to the server.

Why is This Hard? Given that there is a lot of literature about both asymmetric PAKE and fuzzy cryptography, one could ask whether existing techniques could be used to obtain fuzzy aPAKE. As explained already in [DHP+18], techniques from fuzzy cryptography such as information reconciliation [BBR88] or fuzzy extractors [DRS04] cannot be used with passwords of low entropy. Essentially, these techniques lose several bits of their inputs, which is acceptable when inputs have high entropy, but devastating in case of passwords.

Looking at techniques for asymmetric PAKE, all of them require some kind of password hardening such as hashing [GMR06, HL19, PW17], applying a PRF [JKX18] or a hash proof system [BJX19]. Unfortunately, such functions destroy all notions of closeness of their inputs by design. Further, it is unclear how to define a fuzzy version of, e.g., an oblivious PRF as used in [JKX18] that is not simply a constant function. While such definitions exist for "fuzzy" cryptographic hashing (e.g., robust property-preserving hashing [BLV19]), these functions either do not provide useful error correction or already their description leaks too much information about the password of the client. Overall, there seems to be no candidate asymmetric PAKE which can be made fuzzy.

Regarding more naive approaches, it is tempting to try to apply generic techniques for multi-party computation to obtain a fuzzy PAKE such as garbled circuits [Yao86]. The circuit would be created w.r.t some function of the password $h \leftarrow H(\mathsf{pw})$. The user's input would be pw'. Now the circuit finds all passwords close enough to pw' and outputs the shared key if one of these passwords yield h. Despite the inefficiency of this approach, it is unclear how to actually write down the circuit. As shown in [Hes19], h needs to be the output of some idealized assumption such as a programmable random oracle, and thus has no representation as a circuit.

Our Contributions. In this paper, we give the first formal definition of fuzzy asymmetric PAKE. Our definition is in the Universal Composability framework of Canetti [Can01], which is the preferred model for PAKE protocols (cf., e.g., [JKX18] for reasons). Essentially, we take the aPAKE functionality from [GMR06] (in a revised version due to [Hes19]) and equip it with fuzzy password matching (taken from the fuzzy PAKE functionality $\mathcal{F}_{\mathsf{fPAKE}}$ from [DHP+18]). Our resulting functionality $\mathcal{F}_{\mathsf{faPAKE}}$ is flexible in two ways: it can be optionally equipped with a mutual key confirmation (often called *explicit authentication*), and, just as $\mathcal{F}_{\mathsf{fPAKE}}$, $\mathcal{F}_{\mathsf{faPAKE}}$ can be parametrized with arbitrary metrics for distance, arbitrary thresholds and arbitrary adversarial leakage. Thus, our model is suitable to analyze protocols for a wide range of applications, from tolerating only few language-specific typos in passwords [CWP+17] to usage of noisy biometric scans of few thousand bits length.

We then give two constructions for fuzzy asymmetric PAKE. Our first construction $\mathit{\Pi}_{\mathsf{faPAKE}}$ uses error-correcting codes (ECC)[1] and oblivious transfer (OT) as efficient building blocks. $\mathit{\Pi}_{\mathsf{faPAKE}}$ works for Hamming distance and can correct $\mathcal{O}(\log(n))$ errors in n-bit passwords. Let us now give more details on $\mathit{\Pi}_{\mathsf{faPAKE}}$.

The idea of our protocol is to first encode a cryptographic key and store it at the server, in a file together with random values to hide the codeword. The exact position of the codeword in the file is dictated by the password. A client holding a close enough password is thus able to retrieve almost the whole codeword correctly and can thus decode the session key given the error correction capabilities of the encoding. An attacker stealing the password file, however, cannot simply decode since the file contains too much randomness. To remove this randomness, he is bound to decode subsets of the file until he finds two subsets which decode to the same session key. Since decoding can be assumed to be as expensive as hashing, the effort of an off-line dictionary attack on the password file follows from a purely combinatorial argument on the parameters of the scheme (i.e., password size and error correction threshold).

To bound the client to one password guess per run of the protocol (which is the common security requirement for PAKE), we employ an n-times 1-out-of-2 OT scheme. Each OT lets the client choose either the true or the random part of the codeword for each of the n password bits (here we assume that the codeword is from $\mathbb{F}^n$ for some large field $\mathbb{F}$). Further, we apply randomization techniques to keep a client from collecting parts of the password file over several runs of the protocol.

---

[1] More precisely, we use a variant of *Robust Secret Sharing*, which can be instantiated with some class of error-correcting codes. However, since most readers are presumably more familiar with the latter, we describe our constructions in terms of codes.

A plus of our protocol is that it elegantly circumvents usage of expensive techniques such as non-interactive zero-knowledge proofs to ensure security against a malicious server. Indeed, a malicious server could make the client reconstruct the session key regardless of her password by entering only the true codeword in the OT. Such attacks would be devastating in applications where the client uses the session key to encrypt her secrets and sends them to the bogus server. Thus, the client needs a means to check correct behavior of the server. We achieve this by letting the server send his transcript of the current protocol run (e.g., the full password file) to the client, symmetrically encrypted with the session key. The client decrypts and checks whether the server executed the protocol with a password close enough to his own. Crucially, a corrupted client can only decrypt (and thus learn the server's secrets) if he holds a close enough password, since otherwise he will not know the encryption key.

Our proof of security is in the UC model and thus our protocol features composability guarantees and security even in the presence of adversarially-chosen passwords. As shown in [Hes19], strong idealized assumptions are necessary in order to achieve security in the UC model in case of asymmetric PAKE protocols. The reason lies in the adaptive nature of a server compromise attack (an adversary stealing the password file), against which our fuzzy version of asymmetric PAKE should also provide some protection. And indeed, our proof is in the generic group model and additionally requires encryption to be modeled as an ideal cipher. Both assumptions provide our simulator with the power to monitor off-line password guesses (*observability*) of the environment as well as to adjust a password file to contain a specific password even after having revealed the file (*programmability*)[2]. As a technicality, usage of the generic group model requires the client to perform decoding *in the exponent*. We give an example of a code that is decodable in the exponent.

Our second construction Π_{transf} is a "naive" approach of building fuzzy aPAKE from aPAKE. Namely, for a given pw, a server could simply store a list of, say, k hashes $H(pw')$ for all pw' close enough to pw. Then, client and server execute k times an aPAKE protocol, with the client entering the same password every time and the server entering all hashes one by one. The fully secure protocol would need to protect against malicious behavior, e.g., by having both parties prove correct behavior. Unfortunately, this approach has two drawbacks. First, it does not scale asymptotically and has huge password files and communication overhead depending not only on the fuzziness threshold but also on the size of the password. Second, we show that Π_{transf} cannot be considered a secure fuzzy aPAKE, but has slightly weaker security guarantees.

On the plus side, Π_{transf} is already practical (and sufficiently secure) for applications where only few passwords should let the client pass. Facebook's authentication protocol, for example, is reported to correct capitalization of the first

---

[2] We mention that already the fuzzy PAKE construction for Hamming distance from [DHP+18] relies on both the ideal cipher and random oracle model. Usage of the generic group model (together with a random oracle) has been recently shown useful in constructing strongly secure aPAKEs [BJX19].

letter [Ale15], resulting in only two hashes to be stored in the password file. As analyzed in [CAA+16,CWP+17], correcting few common typographical mistakes as, e.g., accidental caps lock, increases usability significantly more than it decreases security. For such applications, our protocol Π_{transf} is a good choice.

1.1   Roadmap

In Sect. 2 we give a definition of our main building blocks, error-correcting codes which are decodable in the exponent. In Sect. 3, we provide the formal definition of fuzzy aPAKE and discuss the design of our functionality. Our fuzzy aPAKE protocol can be found in Sect. 4. Our naive approach of building faPAKE from aPAKE can be found in Sect. 5. Efficiency is considered in Sect. 6.

2   Preliminaries

2.1   Robust Secret Sharing in the Exponent

An l-out-of-n secret sharing scheme allows to share a secret value s into n shares $(s_1, \cdots, s_n)$ in such a way that given at least l of these shares, the secret can be reconstructed. Simultaneously, any tuple of shares smaller than l is distributed independently of s. *Robust secret sharing* (RSS) [CDD+15] improves upon secret sharing schemes in the presence of malicious shares. Intuitively, an $(n, l-1, r)_q$-RSS is an l-out-of-n secret sharing scheme which allows the presence of up to $n - r$ corrupted shares. In detail the reconstruction of the secret is reliable for an n-tuple input $(\hat{s}_1, \cdots, \hat{s}_n)$ of r different secret shares s_i and $n - r$ random values a_i even if the positions of the correct shares are unknown.

We recall the definition of RSS as stated in [DHP+18]. For a vector $c \in \mathbb{F}_q^n$ and a set $A \subseteq [n]$, we denote with c_A the projection $\mathbb{F}_q^n \to \mathbb{F}_q^{|A|}$, i.e., the subvector $(c_i)_{i \in A}$.

Definition 1. *Let $\lambda \in \mathbb{N}$, q a λ-bit prime, $\mathbb{F}_q$ a finite field and $n, l, r \in \mathbb{N}$ with $l < r \leq n$. An $(n, l, r)_q$ robust secret sharing scheme (RSS) consists of two probabilistic algorithms* Share $: \mathbb{F}_q \to \mathbb{F}_q^n$ *and* Rec $: \mathbb{F}_q^n \to \mathbb{F}_q$ *with the following properties:*

- l-privacy: *for any $s, s' \in \mathbb{F}_q, A \subset [n]$ with $|A| \leq l$, the projections c_A of $c \xleftarrow{\$} $ Share(s) and c'_A of $c' \xleftarrow{\$} $ Share(s') are identically distributed.*
- r-robustness: *for any $s \in \mathbb{F}_q, A \subset [n]$ with $|A| \geq r$, any c output by Share(s), and any $\tilde{c}$ such that $c_A = \tilde{c}_A$, it holds that Rec$(\tilde{c}) = s$.*

We now introduce a variant of RSS which produces shares that are hidden in the exponent of some group G, and which features a reconstruction algorithm that can handle shares in the exponent. At the same time we sacrifice absolute correctness of Rec and allow for a negligible error in the definition of robustness.

Definition 2 (Robust Secret Sharing in the Exponent). *Let* $\lambda \in \mathbb{N}$, q *a* λ-*bit prime,* $\mathbb{F}_q$ *a finite field and* $n, l, r \in \mathbb{N}$ *with* $l < r \leq n$. *Let* $RSS = (\mathsf{Share}', \mathsf{Rec}')$ *be a* $(n, l, r)_q$ *robust secret sharing scheme and let* $G = \langle g \rangle$ *be a cyclic group of prime order* q. *An* $(n, l, r)_q$ *robust secret sharing scheme in the exponent (RSSExp) with respect to* G *consists of two probabilistic algorithms* $\mathsf{Share} : \mathbb{F}_q \to G^n$ *and* $\mathsf{Rec} : G^n \to G$ *which are defined as follows:*

- $\mathsf{Share}(s)$: *On input a secret value* $s \leftarrow \mathbb{F}_q$, *obtain secret shares* $(s_1, \cdots, s_n) \leftarrow \mathsf{Share}'(s)$ *and output* $(g^{s_1}, \cdots, g^{s_n})$.
- $\mathsf{Rec}(g^{\hat{s}_1}, \cdots, g^{\hat{s}_n})$: *On input* n *group elements, this algorithm outputs* $g^{\hat{s}}$, *where* $\hat{s} \leftarrow \mathsf{Rec}'(\hat{s}_1, \cdots, \hat{s}_n)$.

Further, an (n, l, r)-*RSSExp scheme fulfills the following properties:*

- *l-privacy: as in Definition 1.*
- *r-robustness: for any* $s \in \mathbb{F}_q$, $A \subset [n]$ *with* $|A| \geq r$, *any* c *output by* $\mathsf{Share}(s)$, *and any* $\tilde{c}$ *such that* $c_A = \tilde{c}_A$, *it holds that* $\mathsf{Rec}(\tilde{c}) = g^s$ *with overwhelming probability in* n.

Note that any (n, l, r)-RSSExp scheme trivially fulfills the l-privacy property. In the next part of this section we show how to achieve r-robustness.

Instantiations of RSSExp. In [DHP+18], it is shown how to construct an RSS scheme from any *maximum distance separable* (MDS) code. An $(n + 1, k)_q$ MDS code is a linear q-ary code of length n and rank k, which can correct up to $\lfloor (n - k + 1)/2 \rfloor$ errors. We refer to [Rot06] for a more in depth introduction to linear codes.

Concretely, [DHP+18] propose to use Reed-Solomon codes, which are closely related to Shamir's secret sharing scheme [MS81]. In general, we are not aware of any RSS scheme that is not also an MDS code. For this reason, we focus now on decoding algorithms of linear codes.

Which Decoding Alorithm Works Also in the Exponent? In the following Lemma we show that it is possible to build an $(n, l - 1, l + t, g)$-RSSExp scheme from an l-out-of-$(l + 2t)$ Shamir's secret sharing scheme.

Lemma 1. *Let* $n, l \in \mathbb{N}$ *and* $(\mathsf{Share}', \mathsf{Rec}')$ *be an* l-*out-of-*n *Shamir's secret sharing scheme with* $n = l + 2t$ *for some* t *and* $t \cdot l = \mathcal{O}(n \log n)$, $G = \langle g \rangle$ *a cyclic group of order* q. *Further let* Share *be the algorithm that outputs* $g^{\mathsf{Share}'(s)}$ *on input* $s \in \mathbb{F}_q$. *Then there exists an algorithm* Rec *using* $\mathrm{poly}(n) \cdot \mathcal{O}(\log q)$ *group operations such that* $(\mathsf{Share}, \mathsf{Rec})$ *is an* $(n, l - 1, l + t)$-*RSSExp scheme with respect to* G.

Proof. $(l - 1)$-privacy of l-out-of-n Shamir's secret sharing scheme is shown in [DHP+18], Lemma 5, and can be directly applied to the case where shares are lifted to the exponent of some group. Let Rec be the "unique decoding by randomized enumeration" algorithm defined by Canetti and Goldwasser [CG99] (essentially, the algorithm decodes random subsets of shares until it finds redundancy), but applied to shares in the exponent using, e.g., Lagrange interpolation. Peikert [Pei06] shows in his Proposition 2.1 that, if $t < (n+1-l)/2$ (i.e., the number of errors allows for unique decoding) and $t \cdot l = \mathcal{O}(n \log n)$, then Rec succeeds with overwhelming probability in n and requires $poly(n) \cdot \mathcal{O}(\log q)$ group operations. Since $n = l + 2t$, it holds that $t < (n+1-l)/2$ and hence $(l+t)$-robustness is achieved.

3   Security Model

We now present our security definition for asymmetric fuzzy password authenticated key exchange (Π_{faPAKE}). Our functionality combines the fuzzy PAKE functionality $\mathcal{F}_{\mathsf{fPAKE}}$ from [DHP+18] with the asymmetric PAKE functionality $\mathcal{F}_{\mathsf{apwKE}}$ [GMR06] (with revisions due to [Hes19]). In order to capture the notion of fuzziness in our model, we say that a key exchange using passwords pw and pw' is successful if $d(pw, pw') \leq \delta$, where d is an arbitrary distance function and δ a fixed threshold. $\mathcal{F}_{\mathsf{fPAKE}}$ can be parametrized with arbitrary functions $hdist()$ such as Hamming distance or edit distance.

Roles: In this work we consider an asymmetric setting, namely a client $\mathcal{P}_C$ and a server $\mathcal{P}_S$. Each party executes different code. In this setting $\mathcal{P}_C$ uses a password pw while $\mathcal{P}_S$ has access to some value denoted by FILE, which is generated from a password pw' but does not immediately reveal pw'. The goal of $\mathcal{P}_C$ is convincing $\mathcal{P}_S$ that $d(pw, pw') \leq \delta$, while $\mathcal{P}_S$ only has access to FILE (and does not have access to pw').

Modeling Adversarial Capabilities: The standard security requirement for PAKE is that an attacker is bound to one password guessing attempt per run of the protocol. This resistance to off-line dictionary attacks is also featured by our functionality $\mathcal{F}_{\mathsf{faPAKE}}$ via the TESTPWD interface that can be called by the adversary only once per session. Since we are in the setting of asymmetric PAKE, however, the adversary can also gain access to the password file FILE by compromising the server. Such a compromise is essentially a corruption query with the effect that a part of the internal state of the server is leaked to the adversary. However, opposed to standard corruption, the adversary is not allowed to control the party or modify its internal state. $\mathcal{F}_{\mathsf{faPAKE}}$ provides an interface for server compromise named STEALPWDFILE. As a consequence of such a query (which, as natural for corruption queries, can only be asked by the adversary upon getting instructions from the environment), a dictionary attack becomes possible. Such an attack is reflected in $\mathcal{F}_{\mathsf{faPAKE}}$ by the OFFLINETESTPWD interface, which allows an unbounded number of password guesses. Accounting for protocols that allow precomputation of, e.g., hash tables of the form $H(\mathsf{pw})$, $\mathcal{F}_{\mathsf{faPAKE}}$ accepts OFFLINETESTPWD queries already *before* STEALPWDFILE was issued. $\mathcal{F}_{\mathsf{faPAKE}}$ silently stores these guesses in the form of (OFFLINE, pw) records. Upon STEALPWDFILE, $\mathcal{F}_{\mathsf{faPAKE}}$ sends the client's pw_C to the adversary in case a record

(OFFLINE, pw_C) exists. This models the fact that the adversary learns the client's password from his precomputated values only upon learning the password file, i.e., compromising the server[3]. Besides offline password guesses, the adversary can use FILE of the compromised server to run a key exchange session with the user. This is captured within the IMPERSONATE interface.

All these interfaces were already present in aPAKE functionalities in the literature. The key difference of $\mathcal{F}_{\text{faPAKE}}$ is now that all these interfaces apply fuzzy matching when it comes to comparing passwords. Namely, $\mathcal{F}_{\text{faPAKE}}$ is parametrized with two thresholds δ and γ. δ is the "success threshold", for which it is guaranteed that passwords within distance δ enable a successful key exchange. On the other hand, γ can be seen as the "security threshold", with $\gamma \geq \delta$. Guessing a password within range γ does not enable the adversary to successfully exchange a key, but it might provide him with more information than just "wrong guess". Following [DHP+18], we enable weakenings of $\mathcal{F}_{\text{faPAKE}}$ in terms of leakage from adversarial interfaces (cf. Fig. 2). Here, the adversary, in addition to learning whether or not his password guess was close enough, is provided with the output of different leakage functions L_c, L_m and L_f. Essentially, he learns $L_c(\text{pw}, \text{pw}')$ if his guess was within range δ of the other password, L_m if it was within range $\gamma > \delta$ and L_f if it was further away than γ. $\mathcal{F}_{\text{faPAKE}}$ can be instantiated with any thresholds γ, δ and arbitrary functions L_c, L_m, L_f. Looking ahead, the additional threshold γ enables us to prove security of constructions using building blocks such as error-correcting codes, which come with a "gray zone" where reliable error correction is not possible, but also the encoded secret is not information-theoretically hidden. While guessing a password in this gray zone does not enable an attacker to reliably compute the same password as the client, security is still considered to be compromised since some information about the honest party's password (and thus her key) might be leaked. To keep the notion flexible, we allow describing the amount of leakage with $L_m(\cdot, \cdot)$ and mark the record `compromised` to model partial leakage of the key.

Naturally, one would aim for δ and γ to be close, where $\delta = \gamma$ offers optimal security guarantees in terms of no special adversarial leakage if passwords are only $\delta + 1$ apart (an equivalent formulation would be to set $L_m = L_f$). $\mathcal{F}_{\text{faPAKE}}$ is strongest if $L_f = L_m = L_c = \bot$. Below we provide examples of nontrivial leakage functions, verbatim taken from [DHP+18].

Since in a fuzzy aPAKE protocol the password file stored at the server needs to allow for fuzzy matching, files are required to store the password in a structured or algebraic form. An adversary stealing the file could now attempt to alter the file to contain a different (still unknown) password. This kind of attack does not seem to constitute a real threat, since the attacker basically just destroyed the file and cannot use it anymore to impersonate the server towards the corresponding client. To allow for efficient protocols, we therefore choose to incorpo-

---

[3] Recent PAKE protocols [JKX18,BJX19] have offered resistance against so-called precomputation attacks, where an attacker should not be able to pre-compute any values that can be used in the dictionary attack. Our protocols do not offer such guarantees.

rate malleability of password files into our functionality $\mathcal{F}_{\mathsf{faPAKE}}$ by allowing the adversary to present a function f within an IMPERSONATE query. The impersonation attack is then carried out with $f(pw)$ instead of pw, where pw denotes the server's password.

Figure 1 depicts $\mathcal{F}_{\mathsf{faPAKE}}$ with the set of leakage functions from the second example below, namely leaking whether the password is close enough to derive a common cryptographic key.

Examples of Leakage Functions.

1. *No leakage.* The strongest option is to provide no feedback at all to the adversary. We define $\mathcal{F}_{\mathsf{faPAKE}}^N$ to be the functionality described in Fig. 1, except that TESTPWD, IMPERSONATE, OFFLINETESTPWD and STEALPWDFILE use the check depicted in Fig. 2 with

$$L_c^N(\mathsf{pw}, \mathsf{pw}') = L_m^N(\mathsf{pw}, \mathsf{pw}') = L_f^N(\mathsf{pw}, \mathsf{pw}') = \perp.$$

2. *Correctness of guess.* The basic functionality $\mathcal{F}_{\mathsf{faPAKE}}$, described in Fig. 1, leaks the correctness of the adversary's guess. That is, in the language of Fig. 2,

$$L_c(\mathsf{pw}, \mathsf{pw}') = \text{"correct guess"},$$
$$\text{and} \quad L_m(\mathsf{pw}, \mathsf{pw}') = L_f(\mathsf{pw}, \mathsf{pw}') = \text{"wrong guess"}.$$

3. *Matching positions ("mask").* Assume the two passwords are strings of length n over some finite alphabet, with the jth character of the string pw denoted by $\mathsf{pw}[j]$. We define $\mathcal{F}_{\mathsf{faPAKE}}^M$ to be the functionality described in Fig. 1, except that TESTPWD, IMPERSONATE, OFFLINETESTPWD and STEALPWDFILE use the check depicted in Fig. 2, with L_c and L_m that leak the indices at which the guessed password differs from the actual one when the guess is close enough (we will call this leakage the *mask* of the passwords). That is,

$$L_c^M(\mathsf{pw}, \mathsf{pw}') = (\{j \text{ s.t. } \mathsf{pw}[j] = \mathsf{pw}'[j]\}, \text{"correct guess"}),$$
$$L_m^M(\mathsf{pw}, \mathsf{pw}') = (\{j \text{ s.t. } \mathsf{pw}[j] = \mathsf{pw}'[j]\}, \text{"wrong guess"})$$
$$\text{and} \quad L_f^M(\mathsf{pw}, \mathsf{pw}') = \text{"wrong guess"}.$$

4. *Full password.* The weakest definition—or the strongest leakage—reveals the entire actual password to the adversary *if the password guess is close enough.* We define $\mathcal{F}_{\mathsf{faPAKE}}^P$ to be the functionality described in Fig. 1, except that TESTPWD, IMPERSONATE, OFFLINETESTPWD and STEALPWDFILE use the check depicted in Fig. 2, with

$$L_c^P(\mathsf{pw}, \mathsf{pw}') = L_m^P(\mathsf{pw}, \mathsf{pw}') = \mathsf{pw} \text{ and } L_f^P(\mathsf{pw}, \mathsf{pw}') = \text{"wrong guess"}.$$

4   Fuzzy aPAKE from Secret Sharing

We now describe our protocol for fuzzy aPAKE with Hamming distance as metric for closeness of passwords. The very basic structure of our protocol is as follows:

The functionality $\mathcal{F}_{\mathsf{faPAKE}}$ is parameterized by a security parameter λ and tolerances $\delta \leq \gamma$. It interacts with an adversary $\mathcal{S}$ and a client and a server party $\mathcal{P} \in \{\mathcal{P}_C, \mathcal{P}_S\}$ via the following queries:

Password Registration

- On $(\textsc{StorePwdFile}, \mathsf{sid}, \mathcal{P}_C, \mathsf{pw})$ from $\mathcal{P}_S$, if this is the first $\textsc{StorePwdFile}$ message, record $(\textsc{file}, \mathcal{P}_C, \mathcal{P}_S, \mathsf{pw})$ and mark it **uncompromised**.

Stealing Password Data

- On $\boxed{(\textsc{StealPwdFile}, \mathsf{sid})}$ from $\mathcal{S}$, if there is no record $(\textsc{file}, \mathcal{P}_C, \mathcal{P}_S, \mathsf{pw})$, return "no password file" to $\mathcal{S}$. Otherwise, if the record is marked **uncompromised**, mark it **compromised**; regardless, for all records $(\textsc{offline}, \mathsf{pw}')$ set $d \leftarrow d(\mathsf{pw}, \mathsf{pw}')$ and do:
  - If $d \leq \delta$, send ("correct guess", pw') to $\mathcal{S}$;

  If no such pw' is recorded, return "password file stolen" to $\mathcal{S}$.
- On $(\textsc{OfflineTestPwd}, \mathsf{sid}, \mathsf{pw}')$ from $\mathcal{S}$, do:
  - If there is a record $(\textsc{file}, \mathcal{P}_C, \mathcal{P}_S, \mathsf{pw})$ marked **compromised**, then set $d \leftarrow d(\mathsf{pw}, \mathsf{pw}')$ and do:
    * If $d \leq \delta$, mark record **compromised** and send "correct guess" to $\mathcal{S}$;
    * If $d > \delta$, mark record **interrupted** and send "wrong guess" to $\mathcal{S}$.
  - Else, record $(\textsc{offline}, \mathsf{pw}')$

Password Authentication

- On $(\textsc{UsrSession}, \mathsf{sid}, \mathsf{ssid}, \mathcal{P}_S, \mathsf{pw}')$ from $\mathcal{P}_C$, send $(\textsc{UsrSession}, \mathsf{sid}, \mathsf{ssid}, \mathcal{P}_C, \mathcal{P}_S)$ to $\mathcal{S}$. Also, if this is the first $\textsc{UsrSession}$ message for ssid, record $(\mathsf{ssid}, \mathcal{P}_C, \mathcal{P}_S, \mathsf{pw}')$ and mark it **fresh**.
- On $(\textsc{SrvSession}, \mathsf{sid}, \mathsf{ssid})$ from $\mathcal{P}_S$, retrieve $(\textsc{file}, \mathcal{P}_C, \mathcal{P}_S, \mathsf{pw})$ and send $(\textsc{SrvSession}, \mathsf{sid}, \mathsf{ssid}, \mathcal{P}_C, \mathcal{P}_S)$ to $\mathcal{S}$. Also, if this is the first $\textsc{SrvSession}$ message for ssid, record $(\mathsf{ssid}, \mathcal{P}_S, \mathcal{P}_C, \mathsf{pw})$ and mark it **fresh**.

Active Session Attacks

- On $(\textsc{TestPwd}, \mathsf{sid}, \mathsf{ssid}, \mathcal{P}, \mathsf{pw}')$ from $\mathcal{S}$, if there is a record $(\mathsf{ssid}, \mathcal{P}, \mathcal{P}', \mathsf{pw})$ marked **fresh**, then set $d \leftarrow d(\mathsf{pw}, \mathsf{pw}')$ and do:
  - If $d \leq \delta$, mark record **compromised** and send "correct guess" to $\mathcal{S}$;
  - If $d > \delta$, mark record **interrupted** and send "wrong guess" to $\mathcal{S}$.
- On $(\textsc{Impersonate}, \mathsf{sid}, \mathsf{ssid}, f)$ from $\mathcal{S}$, if there is a record $(\mathsf{ssid}, \mathcal{P}_C, \mathcal{P}_S, \mathsf{pw})$ marked **fresh** and a record $(\textsc{file}, \mathcal{P}_C, \mathcal{P}_S, \mathsf{pw}')$ marked **compromised**, then set $d \leftarrow d(\mathsf{pw}, f(\mathsf{pw}'))$ and do:
  - If $d \leq \delta$, mark record **compromised** and send "correct guess" to $\mathcal{S}$;
  - If $d > \delta$, mark record **interrupted** and send "wrong guess" to $\mathcal{S}$.

Key Generation and Implicit Authentication

- On $(\textsc{NewKey}, \mathsf{sid}, \mathsf{ssid}, \mathcal{P}, \mathsf{k})$ from $\mathcal{S}$ where $|\mathsf{k}| = \lambda$ or $\mathsf{k} = \bot$, if there is a record $(\mathsf{ssid}, \mathcal{P}, \mathcal{P}', \mathsf{pw})$ not marked **completed**, do:
  - If the record is marked **compromised**, or either $\mathcal{P}$ or $\mathcal{P}'$ is corrupted, send $(\mathsf{sid}, \mathsf{ssid}, \mathsf{k})$ to $\mathcal{P}$.
  - Else if the record is marked **fresh**, $(\mathsf{sid}, \mathsf{ssid}, \mathsf{k}')$ was sent to $\mathcal{P}'$, and at that time there was a record $(\mathsf{ssid}, \mathcal{P}', \mathcal{P}, \mathsf{pw})$ with $d(\mathsf{pw}, \mathsf{pw}') \leq \delta$ marked **fresh**, send $(\mathsf{sid}, \mathsf{ssid}, \mathsf{k}')$ to $\mathcal{P}$.
  - Else if $\mathsf{k} \neq \bot$, the record is marked **fresh**, $(\mathsf{sid}, \mathsf{ssid}, \mathsf{k}')$ was sent to $\mathcal{P}'$, and at that time there was a record $(\mathsf{ssid}, \mathcal{P}', \mathcal{P}, \mathsf{pw})$ with $d(\mathsf{pw}, \mathsf{pw}') \leq \delta$ marked **fresh**, send $(\mathsf{sid}, \mathsf{ssid}, \mathsf{k}')$ to $\mathcal{P}$.
  - Else, pick $\mathsf{k}'' \xleftarrow{\$} \{0,1\}^\lambda$ and send $(\mathsf{sid}, \mathsf{ssid}, \mathsf{k}'')$ to $\mathcal{P}$.

  Finally, mark $(\mathsf{ssid}, \mathcal{P}, \mathcal{P}', \mathsf{pw})$ **completed**.

Fig. 1. Ideal functionality $\mathcal{F}_{\mathsf{faPAKE}}$. Framed queries can only be asked upon getting instructions from $\mathcal{Z}$.

- If $d \leq \delta$, mark the record compromised and reply to S with $L_c(\mathsf{pw}, \mathsf{pw}')$;
- If $\delta < d \leq \gamma$, mark the record compromised and reply to S with $L_m(\mathsf{pw}, \mathsf{pw}')$;
- If $\gamma < d$, mark the record interrupted and reply to S with $L_f(\mathsf{pw}, \mathsf{pw}')$.

Fig. 2. Modified distance checks to allow for different leakage to be used in TESTPWD, OFFLINETESTPWD, IMPERSONATE and STEALPWDFILE. In STEALPWDFILE, record marking is skipped.

we let the server encode a cryptographic key K using an error-correcting code[4]. The resulting codeword (different parts of codeword are depicted as white circles in the illustration below) is then transmitted to the client, who decodes to obtain the key.

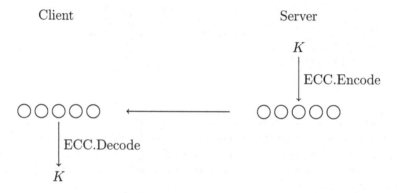

To make the retrieval of the cryptographic key password-dependent, the server stores the codeword together with randomness (depicted as grey circles below) in a password file. The position of the true codeword values in the file are dictated by the password bits. For example, in the illustration below, the server uses the password 01110. For this, we require the encoding algorithm to output codewords whose dimension matches the number of password bits. Now instead of getting the full password file, the client can choose to see only one value per column (either a part of the codeword or a random value). Technically, this is realized by employing a n-time 1-out-of-2 oblivious transfer (OT) protocol[5], where $n = 5$ is the password size of our toy example. The oblivious part is crucial to keep the server from learning the client's password. With this approach, passwords within the error correction threshold of the password used by the server are sufficient to let the client decode the cryptographic key. In the illustration below, the client uses password 11110, letting him obtain 4/5

---

[4] Formally, we will define our scheme using the more general concept of robust secret sharing. However, for this overview it will be convenient to use the terminology of error-correcting codes.

[5] The protocol is not restricted by 1-out-of-2 OT, but can use 1-out-of-n OT for any $n \in \mathbb{N}$. In this work we consider $n = 2$, but in practice $n > 2$ might be useful to reduce the number of wrong shares (e.g. $n = 2^7$ in case of ASCII encoding).

of the codeword correctly. Furthermore, an adversary stealing the password file is now faced with the computationally expensive task of finding the codeword within the file. Generalized to an $(n - 2t)$-out-of-n RSS, the naive approach of finding $n - 2t$ shares of the codeword by taking random subsets succeeds with probability $1/2^{n-2t}$ (as there are $\binom{n}{2t}$ "good" choices containing shares only, and $\binom{n}{2t} \cdot 2^{n-2t}$ choices overall). Here, n is the password size and t the number of errors that the fuzzy aPAKE protocol allows in passwords.

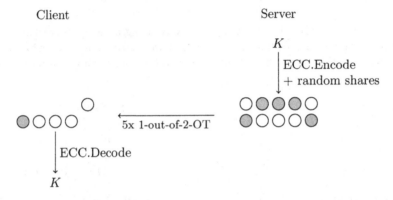

The above protocol can only be used to derive a single cryptographic key. Further, it is prone to a malicious client who could send pw and pw $\oplus 1^n$ in two subsequent runs and obtain the full password file. The solution is randomization of the password file in each run of the protocol. This is straightforward for linear secret sharing.

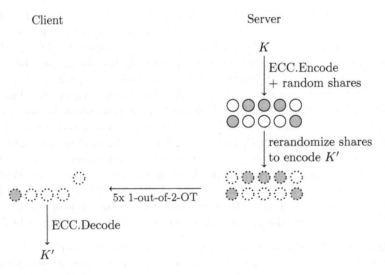

Unfortunately, the above protocol cannot be proven UC secure. As already mentioned before, UC-secure asymmetric PAKE protocols require an idealized assumption to reveal password guesses against the file to the adversary [Hes19].

Furthermore, we need to require that a password file does not fix the password that is contained in it, in order to prove security in the presence of adaptive server compromise attacks. To remedy the situation, we let the server store the password file in the exponent of a publicly known large group and prove security of our construction in the generic group model [Sho97]. As a consequence, the client now needs to perform decoding in the exponent. We summarize in Sect. 2 which known decoding techniqes work also in the exponent, and detail in Sect. 6 how this affects the parameter choices of our scheme.

To complete our high-level protocol description, we now consider malicious behavior of client and server in the above protocol. Firstly, we observe that the client cannot cheat apart from using a different password in the OT (which does not constitute an attack) or outputting a wrong cryptographic key (which also does not constitute an attack). Things look differently when we consider a malicious server. The server could, e.g., deviate from the protocol by entering only correct codeword parts in the OT, making the key exchange succeed regardless of the password the client is using. To prevent such attacks, we let the server prove correct behavior by encrypting his view of the protocol run under the symmetric key K'. The view consists of the randomized password file as well as g^{pw}. A client being able to derive K' can now check whether the server indeed holds a password pw close enough to his own, and whether the transmitted password file parts match the password file created with pw. The formal description of our protocol can be found in Fig. 3.

It is worth noting the similarity of our protocol to the fuzzy PAKE from RSS/ECC of [DHP+18]. Namely, the overall idea is the same (server choosing and encoding K, sending it to the client who can decode if and only if his password is close enough). Essentially, both protocols transmit the codeword *encrypted* with the password, using a symmetric cipher that tolerates errors in the password - let us call this a *fuzzy symmetric cipher*. [DHP+18] uses the following fuzzy symmetric cipher: XOR the codeword (the message) with cryptographic keys derived from the individual password bits. These cryptographic keys are exchanged using PAKE on individual password bits. Unfortunately, this approach does not work in the asymmetric setting, since the server would have to store the password in the clear to access its individual bits. For the asymmetric case, one has to come up with a fuzzy cipher that works with a key that is some function of the password. This function needs to have two properties: hide the password sufficiently, and still allow to evaluate distance of its input.

4.1 Security

Theorem 1. *Let $n, l, t \in \mathbb{N}$ with $n = l + 2t$ and (Share, Rec) be an $(n, l-1, l+t)$-RSSExp scheme with respect to a generic group G. Then the protocol depicted in Fig. 3 UC-emulates $\mathcal{F}^P_{faPAKE}$ in the $\mathcal{F}_{IC}, \mathcal{F}^n_{OT}$-hybrid model, with $\gamma = 2t$, $\delta = t$, Hamming distance $d()$ and with respect to static byzantine corruptions and adaptive server compromise.*

We now provide a proof sketch for Theorem 1. The detailed proof can be found in the full version of this paper [EHOR20].

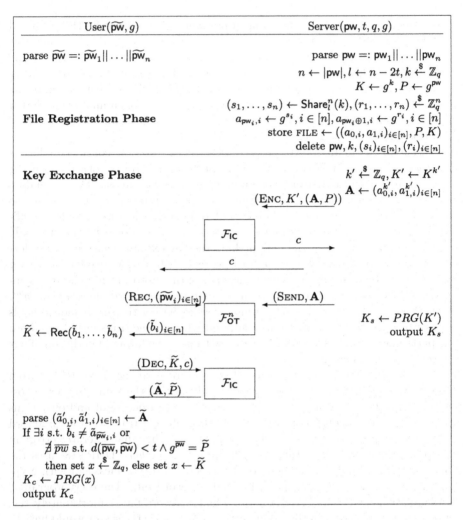

Fig. 3. Protocol Π_{faPAKE} for asymmetric fuzzy PAKE using an n times 1-out-of-2 Oblivious Transfer.

Proof Sketch: The overall proof strategy is to give a simulated transcript and output of the protocol that is indistinguishable from a real protocol execution and runs independently of the parties' passwords. The simulator is allowed to make one password guess per execution (in case of compromised server the simulator can run several offline password guesses). In the following, we describe the different cases of corruption that have to be considered.

– **Honest session:** Apart from the interaction between client and server through the UC-secure OT, the only message that needs to be simulated is one ideal cipher output which is sent from the server to the client and serves as a commitment to the servers values. Since the ideal cipher generates a uniformly random ciphertext from the ciphertext space, the simulator can replace the $\mathcal{F}_{\mathsf{IC}}$ output by a random value as long as the key is unknown. Hence, the simulator runs independently from the passwords of the parties.

- **Corrupted client:** In case of corrupted client, it is crucial to bind the client to submitting all n password bits at once such that the client is not able to adaptively change the password bits based on previous OT outputs. We achieve this by using non-adaptive n times 1-out-of-2 OT executions. Hence, $\mathcal{S}$ is able to query TestPwd on the submitted password bits before it needs to simulate the OT outputs for the client. In case TestPwd returns the server's password, $\mathcal{S}$ can simulate valid OT outputs. Otherwise, $\mathcal{S}$ chooses random outputs which is indistinguishable from the real execution due to the privacy property of the RSSExp scheme.

- **Corrupted server:** Whenever the corrupted server sends the ciphertext that contains the OT inputs and g^{pw}, $\mathcal{S}$ reconstructs pw from the inputs to the ideal cipher and the generic group operations requestes by the environment. $\mathcal{S}$ then checks whether pw is close to the client's password using the TestPwd interface. If so the simulator gets the client's password and can simulate the client. Otherwise the client's behavior is independent of its password. Hence, $\mathcal{S}$ can simulate the client with an arbitrary password that is not close to the server's.

- **Server compromise:** (1) Simulating the password file. $\mathcal{S}$ assembles a table with random group element handles as password file, and a random handle corresponding to g^k. As soon as $\mathcal{Z}$ starts decoding with some subset of these elements by querying the GGM, $\mathcal{S}$ learns these queries. As soon as this subset of elements corresponds to a password, the simulator submits this password to OfflineTestPwd. If the answer includes the server's password, then $\mathcal{S}$ programs the GGM such that the decoding results in the handle of g^k.

  (2) Impersonation attacks. The environment could use a file (e.g., the one obtained from $\mathcal{S}$ or a randomized variant of it) to impersonate the server. For this, the environment has to modify the ciphertext c to encrypt the file. Upon the environment sending an encryption query to $\mathcal{F}_{\mathsf{IC}}$ including an element P at the end of the message to be encrypted, the simulator checks if the GGM contains a tuple (pw, P). If so, $\mathcal{S}$ runs a TestPwd query on pw and learns the client's password $\widetilde{\mathsf{pw}}$ in case pw and $\widetilde{\mathsf{pw}}$ are close[6]. If there is no tuple (pw, P) in the GGM, $\mathcal{S}$ checks whether P was computed from the file (A', P') by the environment sending $f(P')$ to the GGM (and the simulator replying with P). If such a query happened, $\mathcal{S}$ issues an Impersonate query using the same function f.

- **MITM attack on honest session:** Apart from the interaction between client and server through the UC-secure OT, the only message that is sent is one ideal cipher output from the server to the client. Any attempt by $\mathcal{Z}$ to tamper with this message can be detected and hence $\mathcal{S}$ can simulate accordingly.

---

[6] We could alternatively let $\mathcal{S}$ issue an Impersonate query, but since the password is known issueing TestPwd works just as well.

Password Salting. In the UC modeling each protocol session has access to a fresh instantiation of the ideal functionalities. Consequently each protocol session invokes a fresh instantiation of RO or GGM, which return different values when queried on the same input in different sessions. Therefore the password files generated for two users with the same password are different. In practice however the passwords must be salted, i.e. instead of storing the g^{pw}, the server stores $g^{(\mathsf{sid}\|\mathsf{pw})}$ where sid is the respective session identifier. By applying this standard technique of salting in practice, the password files for two clients who use the same password would be different.

Use Cases for Hamming Distance Metric. Although hamming distance is not the most optimal way to measure the distance of two passwords, it is quite suitable for biometric applications. As an example, a server can derive the password file from a client's iris scan or fingerprint such that the client can use this biometric data for authentication. Another example would be wearable or IoT devices. Such devices can measure unique characteristics of the user or environment, such as heart beat patterns and use these measurements for authentication. Our next construction is more suitable for password matching applications where users authenticate themselves with a human memorable password, but might input some characters of the password incorrectly.

5   Fuzzy aPAKE from Standard aPAKE

We now show how to construct a fuzzy aPAKE from asymmetric PAKE. Essentially, the idea is to let the server run an aPAKE protocol with the client multiple times, entering all the passwords that are close to the password he originally registered. For formally defining the protocol, it will be convenient to assume a (possibly probabilistic) function $\mathsf{close}(pw) := \{pw_i | d(\mathsf{pw}, \mathsf{pw}_i) < \delta\}$ that produces a set of all authenticating passwords. For example, for $d(), \delta$ accepting passwords where the first letter's case should be ignored, we would get $\mathsf{close}(\text{holy–moly!}) = \{\text{Holy–moly!, holy–moly!}\}$. When asking to register a password file containing pw, the server stores FILE $:= \{H(\mathsf{pw}_i) | \mathsf{pw}_i \in \mathsf{close}(\mathsf{pw}) \; \forall i = 1, ..., |\mathsf{close}(\mathsf{pw})|\}$ as arbitrarily ordered list of hash values of all authenticating passwords. Let $k := |\text{FILE}|$ be the number of such passwords. Now client and server execute the aPAKE protocol k times, where the client *always* enters his password, and the server enters all values from the password file (in an order determined by a random permutation τ). Then, similar to our protocol Π_{faPAKE}, the server proves honest behavior by encrypting the (permuted) password file under all k keys generated by the aPAKE protocol. The client decrypts and looks for a password file that was generated from a password that is close to his own password. If he finds such a file, he uses the corresponding decryption key (generated from aPAKE) to perform an explicit authentication step with the server. Note that this extra round of explicit authentication cannot be skipped, since otherwise the server would not know which key to output. While the computation on the client side sounds heavy at first sight, if both parties follow the protocol, all but one decryption attempts on the client side will fail. The client can efficiently recognized a failed decryption attempt by searching the decrypted message for the hash of his own password. The protocol is depicted in Fig. 4.

Π_{transf} does not scale asymptotically, neither in the size of the password nor the number of errors. As an example, for correcting only one arbitrary error in an n-bit password, the password file size is already $k = n + 1$. For correcting up to t errors, we get $k := 1 + \sum_{i=1}^{t} \binom{n}{i}$. Note that k determines not only the size of the password file but also the number of aPAKE executions. On the plus side, the construction works with arbitrary metric and distances, does not have a "security gap" between δ and γ and has reasonable computational complexity on both the client and server side.

Unfortunately Π_{transf} cannot be proven secure given the original ideal functionality $\mathcal{F}_{\mathsf{faPAKE}}$, or rather its variant with explicit authentication (see the full version of this paper [EHOR20] for more details). In a nutshell, an attacker tampering with the single aPAKE executions can issue k password guesses using arbitrary passwords from the dictionary. A fuzzy aPAKE as defined within $\mathcal{F}_{\mathsf{faPAKE}}$, however, needs to bound the attacker to use k *close* passwords. To remedy the situation we modify the TESTPWD interface of our $\mathcal{F}_{\mathsf{faPAKE}}$ functionality such that it allows n single password guesses. By single guess we mean that, instead of comparing a guess to all passwords within some threshold of the password of the attacked party (as it is done by $\mathcal{F}_{\mathsf{faPAKE}}$), it is compared to just one password. In case the client is attacked, the functionality compares with the client's password (and allows k such comparisons). In case the server is attacked, comparison is against a randomly chosen password close to the server's password[7]. Overall, the amount of information that the attacker obtains from both TESTPWD interfaces is comparable: they both allow the attacker to exclude k passwords from being "close enough" to authenticate towards an honest party. Stated differently, to go through the whole dictionary D of passwords, with both TESTPWD interfaces an attacker would need to tamper with $|D|/k$ key exchange sessions. We refer the reader to the full version of this paper [EHOR20] for more details regarding the modified functionalities.

We let $\mathcal{F}'_{\mathsf{faPAKE}}$ denote the ideal functionality $\mathcal{F}^{P}_{\mathsf{faPAKE}}$ with interfaces TESTPWD and NEWKEY.

Theorem 2. *Protocol Π_{transf} UC-emulates $\mathcal{F}'_{\mathsf{faPAKE}}$ with arbitrary distance function $d()$ and arbitrary threshold $\delta = \gamma$ in the $(\mathcal{F}_{\mathsf{aPAKE}}, \mathcal{F}_{RO}, \mathcal{F}_{IC})$-hybrid model w.r.t static corruptions and adaptive server compromise and $H()$ denoting calls to $\mathcal{F}_{RO}$.*

We now provide a proof sketch for Theorem 2. The detailed proof can be found in the full version of this paper [EHOR20].

Proof Sketch. We need to consider the following attack scenarios:

---

[7] Programming this randomized behavior into the functionality greatly simplifies proving security of Π_{transf} and does not seem to weaken the functionality compared to one using non-randomized equality checks.

- *Passive attacks*: The environment $\mathcal{Z}$ tries to distinguish uncorrupted real and ideal execution by merely observing transcript and outputs of the protocol, while providing the inputs of both honest parties. Since the outputs of the protocol are random oracle outputs and the transcript consists of a random ciphertext vector $\vec{e}$ output by the ideal cipher, $\mathcal{Z}$ cannot distinguish real outputs from simulated random values unless it queries either the ideal cipher functionality $\mathcal{F}_{IC}$ or the random oracle $\mathcal{F}_{RO}$ with the corresponding inputs. This can be excluded with overwhelming probability since these inputs are uniformly random values of high entropy chosen by honest parties.
- *Active message tampering*: We consider $\mathcal{Z}$ injecting a message into a protocol execution between two honest parties. The only messages being sent in unauthenticated channels are the encryption vector $\vec{e}$ and the explicit authentication message h. Replacing the message h would simply result in two different keys as output for the parties, simulatable by sending $\bot$ via NEWKEY. Tampering with $\vec{e}$ is a bit more tricky. Namely, we have to consider $\mathcal{Z}$ modifying only single components of $\vec{e}$. Tampering with each element of the vector $\vec{e}$ lowers the probability for the parties to output the same key. Hence, the simulator needs to adjust the probability for the parties to output the same key by forcing the functionality to only output the same session key with this exact probability, i.e., the simulator sends $\bot$ via NEWKEY with the inverse probability.
- *(Static) Byzantine corruption*: We consider the case where $\mathcal{Z}$ corrupts one of the parties.
  - In case of corrupted server, given an adversarially computed $\vec{e}$, the simulator extracts all k passwords used by $\mathcal{Z}$ from the server's inputs to $\mathcal{F}_{IC}$ and $\mathcal{F}_{RO}$ and submits them as password guess to $\mathcal{F}'_{faPAKE}$ (via TESTPWD). $\mathcal{S}$ then uses the answers (either "wrong guess" or the client's true password) to continue the simulation faithfully. In case the corrupted server deviates from the protocol (e.g., $\vec{e}$ does not encrypt a set of passwords generated by close(), or sends garbage to the $\mathcal{F}_{aPAKE}$ instance in which the server uses the client's password), the simulator sends $\bot$ via the NEWKEY interface to simulate failure of the key exchange.
  - The case of a corrupted client is handled similarly using the freedom of k individual TESTPWD queries.
- *Server compromise*: The password file is simulated without knowledge of the password by sampling random hash values. The simulator now exploits observability and programmability of the random oracle (that models the hash function) as follows: as soon as $\mathcal{Z}$ wants to compute $H(\mathsf{pw})$, $\mathcal{S}$ submits pw to its OFFLINETESTPWD interface. Upon learning the server's true password, $\mathcal{S}$ programs the random oracle such that the password file contains hash values of all passwords close to pw.
- *Attacking $\mathcal{F}_{aPAKE}$*: While using $\mathcal{F}_{aPAKE}$ as hybrid functionality helps the parties to exchange the key, it gives us a hard time when simulating. Essentially, the simulator has to simulate answers to all adversarial interfaces of each instance of $\mathcal{F}_{aPAKE}$ since $\mathcal{Z}$ is allowed to query them. And $\mathcal{F}_{aPAKE}$ has a lot of them: STEALPWDFILE, TESTPWD, OFFLINETESTPWD and IMPERSONATE.

In a nutshell, OFFLINETESTPWD queries can be answered by querying the corresponding interface at $\mathcal{F}'_{\mathsf{faPAKE}}$. The same holds for STEALPWDFILE and IMPERSONATE, only that they can be queried only once in $\mathcal{F}'_{\mathsf{faPAKE}}$. Our proof thus needs to argue that the one answer provided by $\mathcal{F}_{\mathsf{faPAKE}}$ includes already enough information to simulate answers to all k. The most annoying interface, namely TESTPWD is handled by forwarding each individual TESTPWD guess to $\mathcal{F}'_{\mathsf{faPAKE}}$. This explains why $\mathcal{F}'_{\mathsf{faPAKE}}$ needs to allow k individual password guesses instead of one fuzzy one (as provided by $\mathcal{F}_{\mathsf{faPAKE}}$).

6   Efficiency

Efficiency of Π_{faPAKE}. When instantiated with the statically secure OT from [BDD+17], Π_{faPAKE} is round-optimal and requires each party to send only one message. While 2 consecutive messages are in any case required for the OT, we can conveniently merge the ciphertext sent by the server with his message sent within the OT. In order to compute the total message size, let us first give more details on the OT instantiations that are compatible with Π_{faPAKE} and their communication complexity. Π_{faPAKE} can use any UC-secure protocol for 1-out-of-2 OT with the slight modification that the sender only continues the protocol after having received n input-dependent messages of the client (in UC-secure protocol, the client is usually committed to his input when sending his first message). E.g., one could modify the round-efficient statically secure OT protocol from [BDD+17], Fig. 3, to let the sender Alice wait for receiver Bob to complete the first step of the protocol n times. The protocol requires one round of communication. In total, 3 strings, 1 public key and 2 ciphertexts are send around per 1-out-of-2 OT. For sender inputs from $\mathbb{F}_q^2$ and security parameter λ with $q = 2^\lambda$, the communication complexity of the n-fold 1-out-of-2 OT is then $8\lambda n$ bits. This results in a total message size of $8\lambda n + |c| = 8\lambda n + (2n+1)\lambda \approx 10\lambda n$ bits. For each login attempt of a client, the server needs to perform $2n + 1$ group exponentiations in order to refresh the values in the password file, as well as an encryption of $2n + 1$ group elements. Finally, the server has to perform one PRG execution. Note that the server has to do some additional computations during the initial setup phase of the protocol, however since this phase is only run once, we do not consider its complexity in this section. The client's computation is where our protocol lacks efficiency. Namely, with the naive decoding technique from [CG99], client's computation is only polynomial in $|\mathsf{pw}|$ if the error correction capability δ is not larger than $\log|\mathsf{pw}|$. And still for such δ, going beyond password sizes of, say, 40 bits does not seem feasible.

Efficiency of Π_{transf}. In order to achieve the fuzzy password matching in Π_{transf}, the server is required to store one hash value for each password that lies within distance δ of the original password. As a consequence, the password file size is highly dependent on these threshold parameters. If we consider Hamming distance as done in our first construction, for $\delta = 1$ the password file is of size $\mathcal{O}(n)$. However for $\delta = 2$ it grows to $\mathcal{O}(n^2)$ and for $\delta = 3$ to $\mathcal{O}(n^3)$. Hence,

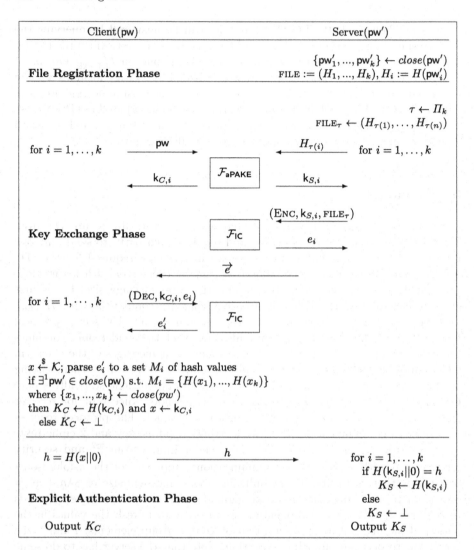

Fig. 4. Protocol Π_{transf} for fuzzy asymmetric PAKE. The parties participate in k executions of the aPAKE protocol. Afterwards they verify if at least one of the produced k keys match and agree on it. We denote $\Pi_n := perm(1, ..., k)$ the set of permutations $[k] \rightarrow [k]$. $close(\mathrm{pw})$ is a function outputting a list of all authenticating passwords (see text for a formal description).

such error tolerance can only be achieved in Π_{transf} at the cost of huge password files. The same correlation to the error tolerance holds for the amount of aPAKE executions in Π_{transf}.

In order to determine the computational complexity of Π_{transf} in terms of required group operations, we chose an instantiation of an aPAKE protocol,

OPAQUE [JKX18], that requires a constant number of group exponentiations. As previously discussed, Π_{transf} requires k aPAKE executions with k being the size of the password file.

Despite its shortcomings when used with Hamming distance, Π_{transf} serves as a good illustration for how to construct a general purpose faPAKE protocol that already has practical relevance. Instantiated with distance and threshold suitable to correct, e.g., capitalization of first letters or transposition of certain digits, we obtain an efficient "almost secure" fuzzy aPAKE scheme.

We present a comparison of the two schemes in Table 1. Π_{transf} is listed twice. First it is compared to Π_{faPAKE} when using Hamming distance. The last row indicates its efficiency for parameters resulting in k authenticating passwords, where k can be as small as 2.

Table 1. Comparison of Π_{faPAKE} and Π_{transf}. We assume n-bit passwords in case of Hamming distance. File size and communication complexity are in bits. The Client and Server column indicate the number of group operations.

	File size	Message size	Thresholds	Metric	Client	Server	Assumption
Π_{faPAKE}	$(2n+2)\lambda$	$10\lambda n$	$2\delta = \gamma$	Hamming	$poly(n) \cdot \mathcal{O}(\log q)$	$\mathcal{O}(n \log q)$	IC, GGM
Π_{transf}	$\mathcal{O}(n^\delta)$	$\mathcal{O}(n^\delta)$	$\delta = \gamma$	Hamming	$\mathcal{O}(n^\delta \log q)$	$\mathcal{O}(n^\delta \log q)$	IC, ROM
Π_{transf}	λk	$\mathcal{O}(k)$	$\delta = \gamma$	arbitrary	$\mathcal{O}(k)$	$\mathcal{O}(k)$	IC, ROM

7   Conclusion

In this paper, we initiated the study of *fuzzy asymmetric PAKE*. Our security notion in the UC framework results from a natural combination of existing functionalities. Protocols fulfilling our definition enjoy strong security guarantees common to all UC-secure PAKE protocols such as protection against off-line attacks and simulatability even when run with adversarially-chosen passwords.

We demonstrate that UC-secure fuzzy aPAKE can be build from OT and Error-Correcting Codes, where fuzziness of passwords is measured in terms of their Hamming distance. Our protocol is inspired by the ideas of [DHP+18] for building a fuzzy *symmetric* PAKE. We also show how to build a (mildly less secure) fuzzy aPAKE from (non-fuzzy) aPAKE. Our construction allows for arbitrary notions of fuzziness and yields efficient, strongly secure and practical protocols for use cases such as, e.g., correction of typical orthographic errors in typed passwords.

Our two constructions nicely show the trade-offs that one can have for fuzzy aPAKE. The "naive" construction from aPAKE has large password file size when used with Hamming distance, but also works for arbitrary closeness notions possibly leading to small password files and practical efficiency. The construction using Error-Correcting Codes is restricted to Hamming distance and $\log(|\mathsf{pw}|)$ error correction threshold. I comes with a computational overhead on the client side, but has only little communication and small password file size. It is worth noting that, for this construction, all efficiency drawbacks could be remedied by finding a more efficient decoding method that works in the exponent. We leave this as well as finding more fuzzy aPAKE constructions as future work. Specifically, no fuzzy aPAKE scheme with *strong* compromise security (as defined in [JKX18]) is known.

Acknowledgments. This work was partly supported by the German Research Foundation (DFG) Emmy Noether Program *FA 1320/1-1*, by the *DFG CRC 1119 CROSS-ING* (project S7), by the German Federal Ministry of Education and Research (BMBF) *iBlockchain project* (grant nr. 16KIS0902), by the German Federal Ministry of Education and Research and the Hessen State Ministry for Higher Education, Research and the Arts within their joint support of the *National Research Center for Applied Cybersecurity ATHENE*, by the VeriSec project 16KIS0634 from the Federal Ministry of Education and Research (BMBF), and by the European Union's Horizon 2020 research and innovation programme under grant agreement No. 786725 – OLYMPUS.

We would like to thank Sophia Yakoubov for helpful discussions on earlier versions of this work.

References

[Ale15]   Muffet, A.: Facebook: password hashing & authentication, presentation at real world crypto (2015)

[BBC+13] Benhamouda, F., Blazy, O., Chevalier, C., Pointcheval, D., Vergnaud, D.: New techniques for SPHFs and efficient one-round PAKE protocols. In: Canetti, R., Garay, J.A. (eds.) CRYPTO 2013, Part I. LNCS, vol. 8042, pp. 449–475. Springer, Heidelberg (2013). https://doi.org/10.1007/978-3-642-40041-4_25

[BBR88]   Bennett, C.H., Brassard, G., Robert, J.-M.: Privacy amplification by public discussion. SIAM J. Comput. **17**(2), 210–229 (1988)

[BDD+17] Barreto, P.S.L.M., David, B., Dowsley, R., Morozov, K., Nascimento, A.C.A.: A framework for efficient adaptively secure composable oblivious transfer in the ROM. CoRR, abs/1710.08256 (2017)

[BJX19]   Bradley, T., Jarecki, S., Xu, J.: Strong asymmetric PAKE based on trapdoor CKEM. In: Boldyreva, A., Micciancio, D. (eds.) CRYPTO 2019, Part III. LNCS, vol. 11694, pp. 798–825. Springer, Cham (2019). https://doi.org/10.1007/978-3-030-26954-8_26

[BLV19]   Boyle, E., LaVigne, R., Vaikuntanathan, V.: Adversarially robust property-preserving hash functions. In: Blum, A. (ed.) ITCS 2019, vol. 124, pp. 16:1–16:20. LIPIcs, January 2019

[BM92]   Bellovin, S.M., Merritt, M.: Encrypted key exchange: password-based protocols secure against dictionary attacks. In: 1992 IEEE Symposium on Security and Privacy, pp. 72–84. IEEE Computer Society Press, May 1992

[BM93]   Bellovin, S.M., Merritt, M.: Augmented encrypted key exchange: a password-based protocol secure against dictionary attacks and password file compromise. In: Denning, D.E., Pyle, R., Ganesan, R., Sandhu, R.S., Ashby, V. (eds.) ACM CCS 1993, pp. 244–250. ACM Press, November 1993

[BMP00] Boyko, V., MacKenzie, P., Patel, S.: Provably secure password-authenticated key exchange using Diffie-Hellman. In: Preneel, B. (ed.) EUROCRYPT 2000. LNCS, vol. 1807, pp. 156–171. Springer, Heidelberg (2000). https://doi.org/10.1007/3-540-45539-6_12

[BPR00] Bellare, M., Pointcheval, D., Rogaway, P.: Authenticated key exchange secure against dictionary attacks. In: Preneel, B. (ed.) EUROCRYPT 2000. LNCS, vol. 1807, pp. 139–155. Springer, Heidelberg (2000). https://doi.org/10.1007/3-540-45539-6_11

[CAA+16] Chatterjee, R., Athayle, A., Akhawe, D., Juels, A., Ristenpart, T.: pASSWORD tYPOS and how to correct them securely. In: 2016 IEEE Symposium on Security and Privacy, pp. 799–818. IEEE Computer Society Press, May 2016

[Can01] Canetti, R.: Universally composable security: a new paradigm for cryptographic protocols. In: 42nd FOCS, pp. 136–145. IEEE Computer Society Press, October 2001

[CDD+15] Cramer, R., Damgård, I.B., Döttling, N., Fehr, S., Spini, G.: Linear secret sharing schemes from error correcting codes and universal hash functions. In: Oswald, E., Fischlin, M. (eds.) EUROCRYPT 2015, Part II. LNCS, vol. 9057, pp. 313–336. Springer, Heidelberg (2015). https://doi.org/10.1007/978-3-662-46803-6_11

[CDVW12] Canetti, R., Dachman-Soled, D., Vaikuntanathan, V., Wee, H.: Efficient password authenticated key exchange via oblivious transfer. In: Fischlin, M., Buchmann, J., Manulis, M. (eds.) PKC 2012. LNCS, vol. 7293, pp. 449–466. Springer, Heidelberg (2012). https://doi.org/10.1007/978-3-642-30057-8_27

[CG99] Canetti, R., Goldwasser, S.: An efficient *threshold* public key cryptosystem secure against adaptive chosen ciphertext attack (extended abstract). In: Stern, J. (ed.) EUROCRYPT 1999. LNCS, vol. 1592, pp. 90–106. Springer, Heidelberg (1999). https://doi.org/10.1007/3-540-48910-X_7

[CHK+05] Canetti, R., Halevi, S., Katz, J., Lindell, Y., MacKenzie, P.: Universally composable password-based key exchange. In: Cramer, R. (ed.) EUROCRYPT 2005. LNCS, vol. 3494, pp. 404–421. Springer, Heidelberg (2005). https://doi.org/10.1007/11426639_24

[CWP+17] Chatterjee, R., Woodage, J., Pnueli, Y., Chowdhury, A., Ristenpart, T.: The TypTop system: personalized typo-tolerant password checking. In: Thuraisingham, B.M., Evans, D., Malkin, T., Xu, D. (eds.) ACM CCS 2017, pp. 329–346. ACM Press, October/November 2017

[DHP+18] Dupont, P.-A., Hesse, J., Pointcheval, D., Reyzin, L., Yakoubov, S.: Fuzzy password-authenticated key exchange. In: Nielsen, J.B., Rijmen, V. (eds.) EUROCRYPT 2018, Part III. LNCS, vol. 10822, pp. 393–424. Springer, Cham (2018). https://doi.org/10.1007/978-3-319-78372-7_13

[DRS04] Dodis, Y., Reyzin, L., Smith, A.: Fuzzy extractors: how to generate strong keys from biometrics and other noisy data. In: Cachin, C., Camenisch, J.L. (eds.) EUROCRYPT 2004. LNCS, vol. 3027, pp. 523–540. Springer, Heidelberg (2004). https://doi.org/10.1007/978-3-540-24676-3_31

[EHOR20] Erwig, A., Hesse, J., Orlt, M., Riahi, S.: Fuzzy asymmetric password-authenticated key exchange. Cryptology ePrint Archive, Report 2020/987 (2020). https://eprint.iacr.org/2020/987

[GL03]   Gennaro, R., Lindell, Y.: A framework for password-based authenticated key exchange. In: Biham, E. (ed.) EUROCRYPT 2003. LNCS, vol. 2656, pp. 524–543. Springer, Heidelberg (2003). https://doi.org/10.1007/3-540-39200-9_33

[GMR06] Gentry, C., MacKenzie, P., Ramzan, Z.: A method for making password-based key exchange resilient to server compromise. In: Dwork, C. (ed.) CRYPTO 2006. LNCS, vol. 4117, pp. 142–159. Springer, Heidelberg (2006). https://doi.org/10.1007/11818175_9

[Hes19] Hesse, J.: Separating standard and asymmetric password-authenticated key exchange. Cryptology ePrint Archive, Report 2019/1064 (2019). https://eprint.iacr.org/2019/1064

[HL19]   Haase, B., Labrique, B.: Aucpace: efficient verifier-based PAKE protocol tailored for the iiot. IACR Trans. Cryptogr. Hardw. Embed. Syst. **2019**(2), 1–48 (2019)

[JKX18] Jarecki, S., Krawczyk, H., Xu, J.: OPAQUE: an asymmetric PAKE protocol secure against pre-computation attacks. In: Nielsen, J.B., Rijmen, V. (eds.) EUROCRYPT 2018, Part III. LNCS, vol. 10822, pp. 456–486. Springer, Cham (2018). https://doi.org/10.1007/978-3-319-78372-7_15

[KOY01] Katz, J., Ostrovsky, R., Yung, M.: Efficient password-authenticated key exchange using human-memorable passwords. In: Pfitzmann, B. (ed.) EUROCRYPT 2001. LNCS, vol. 2045, pp. 475–494. Springer, Heidelberg (2001). https://doi.org/10.1007/3-540-44987-6_29

[KV11]   Katz, J., Vaikuntanathan, V.: Round-optimal password-based authenticated key exchange. In: Ishai, Y. (ed.) TCC 2011. LNCS, vol. 6597, pp. 293–310. Springer, Heidelberg (2011). https://doi.org/10.1007/978-3-642-19571-6_18

[MS81]   McEliece, R.J., Sarwate, D.V.: On sharing secrets and Reed-Solomon codes. Commun. ACM **24**(9), 583–584 (1981)

[Pei06] Peikert, C.: On error correction in the exponent. In: Halevi, S., Rabin, T. (eds.) TCC 2006. LNCS, vol. 3876, pp. 167–183. Springer, Heidelberg (2006). https://doi.org/10.1007/11681878_9

[PW17]   Pointcheval, D., Wang, G.: VTBPEKE: verifier-based two-basis password exponential key exchange. In: Karri, R., Sinanoglu, O., Sadeghi, A.-R., Yi, X. (eds.) ASIACCS 2017, pp. 301–312. ACM Press, April 2017

[Rot06] Roth, R.: Introduction to Coding Theory. Cambridge University Press, New York (2006)

[Sho97] Shoup, V.: Lower bounds for discrete logarithms and related problems. In: Fumy, W. (ed.) EUROCRYPT 1997. LNCS, vol. 1233, pp. 256–266. Springer, Heidelberg (1997). https://doi.org/10.1007/3-540-69053-0_18

[Yao86] Yao, A.C.-C.: How to generate and exchange secrets (extended abstract). In: 27th FOCS, pp. 162–167. IEEE Computer Society Press, October 1986

Two-Pass Authenticated Key Exchange with Explicit Authentication and Tight Security

Xiangyu Liu[1,2], Shengli Liu[1,2,3(✉)], Dawu Gu[1], and Jian Weng[4]

[1] Department of Computer Science and Engineering, Shanghai Jiao Tong University, Shanghai 200240, China
{xiangyu_liu,slliu,dwgu}@sjtu.edu.cn
[2] State Key Laboratory of Cryptology, P.O. Box 5159, Beijing 100878, China
[3] Westone Cryptologic Research Center, Beijing 100070, China
[4] College of Cyber Security, Jinan University, Guangzhou 510632, China
cryptjweng@gmail.com

Abstract. We propose a generic construction of 2-pass authenticated key exchange (AKE) scheme with explicit authentication from key encapsulation mechanism (KEM) and signature (SIG) schemes. We improve the security model due to Gjøsteen and Jager [Crypto2018] to a stronger one. In the strong model, if a replayed message is accepted by some user, the authentication of AKE is broken. We define a new security notion named "IND-mCPA with adaptive reveals" for KEM. When the underlying KEM has such a security and SIG has unforgeability with adaptive corruptions, our construction of AKE equipped with counters as states is secure in the strong model, and stateless AKE without counter is secure in the traditional model. We also present a KEM possessing tight "IND-mCPA security with adaptive reveals" from the Computation Diffie-Hellman assumption in the random oracle model. When the generic construction of AKE is instantiated with the KEM and the available SIG by Gjøsteen and Jager [Crypto2018], we obtain the first practical 2-pass AKE with tight security and explicit authentication. In addition, the integration of the tightly IND-mCCA secure KEM (derived from PKE by Han *et al.* [Crypto2019]) and the tightly secure SIG by Bader *et al.* [TCC2015] results in the first tightly secure 2-pass AKE with explicit authentication in the standard model.

Keywords: Authenticated key exchange · Tight security · Explicit authentication · Two-pass protocol

1 Introduction

Among the primitives, algorithms and protocols in public key cryptography, authenticated key exchange (AKE) [1,4,6–8,11,15,20,22] is by far the most widely deployed one in the real world. For example, TLS [21] implements AKE to

© International Association for Cryptologic Research 2020
S. Moriai and H. Wang (Eds.): ASIACRYPT 2020, LNCS 12492, pp. 785–814, 2020.
https://doi.org/10.1007/978-3-030-64834-3_27

compute shared session keys for peer communication parties. There are several billions of active users in Facebook, Instagram, Wechat, etc., which lead to more than 2^{30} TLS handshakes daily [11]. AKE allows two communication parties to share a session key, which is then used to provide security for the later communications of the two parties. The wide deployment of AKE pushes its security to paramount importance. The security of AKE consists of two aspects. One aspect considers passive adversaries, and it requires the pseudorandomness of the shared session key. The other considers authentication to detect active adversaries. The authentication functionality of AKE guarantees the identification of the parties and the integrity of the messages transmitted during AKE, by detecting message modification, discard, insertion, etc., from adversaries. There are two types of authentication, explicit authentication [1,4,7,11,20] and implicit authentication [6,8,15,16,22]. Implicit authentication detects active attacks in the later communication (after the completion of key exchange), while explicit authentication detects active attacks during the execution of AKE. Explicit authentication enjoys its own advantages. Once the authentication fails, the protocol execution stops and no subsequent messages follow any more, avoiding unnecessary computation and communication.

The security of AKE (also other cryptographic primitives) is achieved by a security reduction under proper security model. Security reduction transforms the ability of a successful adversary $\mathcal{A}$ to an algorithm $\mathcal{B}$ solving a well-known hard problem. If $\mathcal{A}$ wins with probability ϵ, then $\mathcal{B}$ solves the problem with probability ϵ/L. The parameter L is called the security loss factor. If L is a constant (or $O(\lambda)$ with λ security parameter), the security reduction is tight (almost tight). The loose factor L is generally a polynomial of μ, the number of users, and ℓ, the number of executions per user. Given a loose security reduction, the deployment of AKE has to choose a larger security parameter to compensate the loss factor L, resulting in larger elements and slower computations in the execution of AKE. Taking $\mu \approx 2^{30}$ into account, this will lead to a great efficiency loss of AKE. Therefore, pursuing tight security of AKE is not only of theoretical value but also of practical significance.

1.1 Tightly Secure Authenticated Key Exchange

AKE is generally implemented in the multi-user setting, and it is quite possible for an adversary $\mathcal{A}$ to adaptively obtain session keys of some protocol instances and/or long-term secret keys of corrupted users. This is formalized by the reveal and corruption queries of $\mathcal{A}$ in the security model. The security of AKE asks authentication and indistinguishability. Roughly speaking, authentication requires that if a party P_i uses received messages to compute a session key and accepts it, then the messages must be sent from another (unique) party P_j, instead of $\mathcal{A}$. Indistinguishability characterizes the pseudorandomness of the session key, which is successfully generated and accepted by two parties.

A good choice for AKE is the 2-pass signed Diffie-Hellman protocol [7]. It uses a signature (SIG) scheme to provide authentication and a DH-like key encapsulation mechanism (KEM) to provide indistinguishability, where P_i contributes

$pk = g^a$, P_j contributes $C = g^b$ and the session key is $K = g^{ab}$. However, as shown by Gjøsteen and Jager [11], it is hard to achieve tight security due to the following "commitment problem": in the reduction, if the DDH challenge (g^x, g^y, g^z) is embedded in the challenge session, then it can not be revealed, and vice versa. Hence, the reduction algorithm has to guess the challenge session (from $\mu\ell$ sessions) and embed the DDH problem into it. That is reason why many protocols [7,16,18] have a loose factor $L = \mu\ell$ (or quadratic factor $L = \mu^2\ell^2$).

To deal with the "commitment problem", Gjøsteen and Jager [11] suggested to add an extra hash commitment $G(g^a)$ as the first message, resulting in a 3-pass signed DH protocol with tight security.

Up to now, there are only two constructions of AKE [1,11] with tight security and explicit authentication, and both need three passes. One is the 3-pass signed DH protocol in the random oracle model [11], as mentioned above. The other is a 3-pass AKE in the standard model by Bader et al. [1]. This AKE is constructed from a SIG scheme secure against adaptive corruptions (MU-EUF-CMA^{corr} security), a strongly secure one-time SIG and a KEM scheme secure against adaptive corruptions (MU-IND-CPA^{corr} security). The KEM is constructed from two public key encryption schemes, where the ciphertext is two encryptions of the same random encapsulated key. Note that such a KEM is not a good choice for AKE, since the session key is completely determined by the responder.

Over these years, reducing the round complexity and pursuing low-latency key exchange have become a major design criteria [10,13,17,21] by both researchers and practitioners. Compared with 3-pass protocols, 2-pass protocols are clearly more efficient, especially when the transmission time is high. Furthermore, in a 2-pass AKE, any modification of the last (2nd) message can be detected immediately, and no payloads from the initiator follow, which saves computation and communication resources. Hence, a natural question is:

Is it possible to construct 2-pass AKE with explicit authentication and tight security?

1.2   Our Approach

We answer the above question in the affirmative.

Achieving Tight Security. Our generic construction of AKE consists of two building blocks, KEM and SIG. KEM is used to generate the session key, where initiator P_i contributes pk and responder P_j contributes ciphertext C under pk. We rely on KEM's security to guarantee the pseudorandomness of the session key. Meanwhile, every party has a signing key as its long-term secret key, and every transmitted message is signed by SIG, which provides authentication to resist active attacks. See Fig. 1 (a) for the construction.

We solve the "commitment problem" with a tightly IND-mCPA^{reveal} secure KEM. The IND-mCPA^{reveal} security is a new notion, which *allows the adversary to reveal the encapsulated keys from the challenge ciphertexts*. With such a KEM, the reduction algorithm $\mathcal{B}$ can embed challenge ciphertexts to every session of AKE, while keeping the ability of answering reveal queries from $\mathcal{A}$. We also ask

KEM to have *diverse property* (Subsect. 2.3) to make sure that both initiator and responder contribute to the session key. Meanwhile, SIG is required to have tight MU-EUF-CMA^{corr} security, where the adversary can corrupt some users to get their signing keys.

Currently, tight MU-EUF-CMA^{corr} secure SIGs are available [1,11]. To achieve tight security for AKE, the difficulty is constructing KEM with tight IND-mCPA^{reveal} security. As discussed above, it is hard for the traditional DH-like KEM to achieve tight IND-mCPA^{reveal} security, due to the "commitment problem" in the security reduction.

In this paper, we present two KEM schemes that achieve tight IND-mCPA^{reveal} security. Our first proposal is $pk = (g^{x_1}, g^{x_2}), C = g^y, K = H(g^{x_1 y}, g^{x_2 y})$ in the random oracle model[1], which is derived from twin ElGamal PKE [5], and based on the strong twin Diffie-Hellman (st2DH) assumption (which in turn on CDH). Here we explain why tight IND-mCPA^{reveal} security can be achieved in the single user setting. It can be easily extended to the multi-user setting, since $\mathcal{B}$ can embed the 2DH problem into multiple (pk, C) pairs with the help of the random self-reducibility of DDH [9]. In the reduction, given a 2DH challenge tuple (g^{x_1}, g^{x_2}, g^y), $\mathcal{B}$ sets $pk = (g^{x_1}, g^{x_2})$, generates a randomization b and computes the challenge ciphertext as $C = g^{y+b}$. The "commitment problem" is circumvented by $\mathcal{B}$'s simulation of random oracle $H(\cdot)$ and the decision oracle 2DH, which checks whether the inputs are two DDH tuples. If $\mathcal{A}$ has not asked $H(C^{x_1}, C^{x_2})$ before, then the encapsulated key is random to $\mathcal{A}$, and $\mathcal{B}$ just samples a random key k and implicitly set $H(C^{x_1}, C^{x_2}) = k$. If $\mathcal{A}$ has asked $H(C^{x_1}, C^{x_2})$, then $\mathcal{B}$ must have stored item $(C^{x_1}, C^{x_2}, k = H(C^{x_1}, C^{x_2}))$ in the hash list. Hence $\mathcal{B}$ can always resort to the decision oracle $2DH(g^{x_1}, g^{x_2}, C, C^{x_1}, C^{x_2}) = 1$ to locate this item, and return the corresponding k to $\mathcal{A}$. In this way, $\mathcal{B}$ can answer reveal queries from $\mathcal{A}$ correctly, and tight IND-mCPA^{reveal} security follows.

Our second proposal of KEM is derived from the tightly IND-mCCA secure PKE scheme in [14], which has tight IND-mCCA security in the standard model. We prove that IND-mCCA security implies IND-mCPA^{reveal} security with a tight reduction. Note that the two notions are defined in different styles, e.g., the decapsulation oracle in IND-mCCA security cannot decapsulate the challenge ciphertext, while IND-mCPA^{reveal} security allows the challenge encapsulated key to be revealed. Hence, the tight security proof of implication is non-trivial (see Subsect. 2.2 for details).

Perfect Forward Security and KCI Resistance. Our generic construction provides perfect forward security (PFS, a.k.a. perfect forward secrecy [12,16]) and KCI resistance (security against key-compromise impersonation attacks [16]). PFS means that once a party has been corrupted at some moment, then the exchanged session keys completed before the corruption remain hidden from $\mathcal{A}$. KCI resistance assures that sessions, which are established by honest P_i but not controlled by $\mathcal{A}$, remain secure after corruption. In our construction, the long-term secret key is used to sign messages and provide authentication. Hence, the

---

[1] To simplify the description, the hash input does not include pk and C.

exposure of long-term secret key does not give $\mathcal{A}$ any advantages to break the pseudorandomness of the session key. The same analysis applies to KCI resistance.

Dealing with Replay Attacks. Compared with multi-pass AKE, 2-pass AKE inherently open to replay attacks [13]. In a 2-pass AKE protocol, when P_i sends a message msg to P_j, there are only two choices for P_j: compute a session key & accept or reject. If P_j accepts, the message msg can always be replayed to P_j by an adversary (see Fig. 1 (b)). This replay attack contradicts neither the explicit authentication defined by [11], nor the implicit authentication, since msg does originate from P_i and the session key keeps pseudorandom to the adversary. However, it does exhaust the computing & memory resources of P_j and waste bandwidth of the network.

The essence of explicit authentication is to detect active attacks in real time. In this paper, we formalize a stronger security of AKE, by including replay attacks in the active attacks. Meanwhile, we choose an efficient and practical way to prevent replay attacks, by adding counters to identify the freshness of messages, as advised in [13]. Roughly speaking, each party maintains a local counter ctr. Initiator P_i increases its counter ctr_i before it sends $(\text{msg}, \text{ctr}_i)$ to P_j. Responder P_j recognizes the freshness of $(\text{msg}, \text{ctr}_i)$ by checking whether $\text{ctr}_i > \text{ctr}_j$. To respond fresh msg, P_j will synchronize its counter $\text{ctr}_j := \text{ctr}_i$ and send $(\text{msg}', \text{ctr}_j)$ to P_i. The freshness of $(\text{msg}', \text{ctr}_j)$ is recognized by P_i's checking of the synchronization $\text{ctr}_i = \text{ctr}_j$. In this way, any replayed message contradicts either $\text{ctr}_i > \text{ctr}_j$ or $\text{ctr}_i = \text{ctr}_j$, and replay attacks can be detected immediately in our 2-pass AKE (see Fig. 1 (c)).

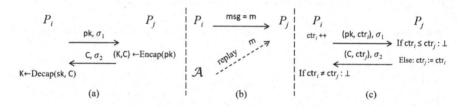

Fig. 1. (a) KEM+SIG construction, (b) replay attacks, and (c) counter measure.

1.3 Our Contribution

We present a security model which is stronger than that in [11]. In our strong model, the adversary breaks authentication as long as a party accepts a replayed message. To detect replay attacks, we introduce counters for each party as its state. The counter will increase after execution of AKE, thus a replayed message will be rejected due to its old counter.

We propose a generic construction of 2-pass AKE from KEM and SIG schemes. We formalize a new security notion, named IND-mCPA^{reveal}, for KEM and show that IND-mCCA security of KEM implies IND-mCPA^{reveal} security. The strong security of our 2-pass AKE (equipped with counter) can be tightly reduced to the IND-mCPA^{reveal} security of KEM and the MU-EUF-CMA^{corr} security of SIG. Taking off counters from AKE results in a stateless AKE, which is tightly secure in the original model of [11].

We give two instantiations of tightly secure 2-pass AKE.

- We present an instantiation of KEM and proved its tight IND-mCPA^{reveal} security based on the CDH assumption in the random oracle model. Together with the signature scheme in [11], we obtain the first practical 2-pass AKE scheme with strong and tight security (and a 2-pass stateless AKE scheme with tight security) from the DDH assumption in the random oracle model.
- When instantiating KEM with the tightly IND-mCCA secure KEM derived from [14] and SIG with the signature scheme in [1], we obtain the first 2-pass AKE scheme with strong and tight security (also a 2-pass stateless AKE scheme with tight security) based on the Matrix-DDH assumption in the standard model.

The comparison of our AKE schemes with other tightly secure AKE schemes with explicit authentication[2] is shown in Table 1.

Table 1. Comparison among tightly secure AKE schemes with explicit authentication. Here "**Comp.**" denotes computation complexity in terms of exponentiations or pairing operations, "**Comm.**" denotes communication complexity in terms of the number of group elements/exponents (identities of users excluded). "**I**" denotes the initiator, "**R**" the responder, "**Sec. Loss**" the security loss factor, "**♯Pass.**" the number of passes in AKE, "RO" the random oracle model, and "Std" the standard model. **Note:** in [BHJ+15]'s AKE, the session key is determined only by the responder.

AKE Scheme	Comp. (I)	Comp. (R)	Comm. (I+R)	Assumption	Sec. Loss	♯Pass.	Model
[GJ18][11]	17	17	12+11	DDH	$O(1)$	3	RO
Ours: AKE$_{\text{DDH}}$	19	18	12+11	DDH	$O(1)$	2	RO
[BHJ+15][1]	22 $O(k^2)$	23 $O(k^2)$	11+9 $(2k^2+4k+5)+(4k+7)$	1-LIN = SXDH $\mathcal{D}_k$-MDDH	$O(\lambda)$	3	Std
Ours: AKE$_{\text{MDDH}}$	37 $O(k^3)$	22 $O(k^3)$	7+8 $(k^2+5k+1)+(4k+4)$	1-LIN = SXDH $\mathcal{D}_k$-MDDH	$O(\lambda)$	2	Std

2   Preliminaries

Let $\lambda \in \mathbb{N}$ denote the security parameter. For $\mu \in \mathbb{N}$, define $[\mu] := \{1, 2, ..., \mu\}$. Denote by $x := y$ the operation of assigning y to x. Denote by $x \xleftarrow{\$} \mathcal{X}$ the

---

[2] Some AKE protocols, like [6] and [22], consider tight security and implicit authentication. In the security model of implicit authentication, $\mathcal{A}$'s advantage is defined by the ability of breaking indistinguishability (with no authentication requirement). Most AKE protocols with implicit authentication are 2-pass. They can be extended to provide explicit authentication via the key confirmation method [16], but with the price of an extra pass and the addition computation of MAC.

operation of sampling x uniformly at random from a set $\mathcal{X}$. For a distribution $\mathcal{D}$, denote by $x \leftarrow \mathcal{D}$ the operation of sampling x according to $\mathcal{D}$. For an algorithm $\mathcal{A}$, denote by $y \leftarrow \mathcal{A}(x; r)$, or simply $y \leftarrow \mathcal{A}(x)$, the operation of running $\mathcal{A}$ with input x and randomness r and assigning the output to y. "PPT" is short for probabilistic polynomial-time, and $\emptyset$ an empty string.

2.1 Digital Signature with Adaptive Corruptions

Definition 1 (SIG). *A signature (SIG) scheme* $\mathsf{SIG} = (\mathsf{Setup}, \mathsf{Gen}, \mathsf{Sign}, \mathsf{Ver})$ *consists of four algorithms.*

- $\mathsf{Setup}(1^\lambda)$: *The setup algorithm takes as input the security parameter* 1^λ *and outputs the public parameter* $\mathsf{pp}_{\mathsf{SIG}}$, *which determines the message space* $\mathcal{M}$, *the signature space* Σ, *and the key space* $\mathcal{VK} \times \mathcal{SK}$.
- $\mathsf{Gen}(\mathsf{pp}_{\mathsf{SIG}})$: *The key generation algorithm takes as input* $\mathsf{pp}_{\mathsf{SIG}}$ *and outputs a pair of keys* $(vk, sk) \in \mathcal{VK} \times \mathcal{SK}$.
- $\mathsf{Sign}(sk, m)$: *The signing algorithm takes as input a signing key* sk *and a message* $m \in \mathcal{M}$, *and outputs a signature* $\sigma \in \Sigma$.
- $\mathsf{Ver}(vk, m, \sigma)$: *The verification algorithm takes as input a verification key* vk, *a message* m *and a signature* σ, *and outputs a binary bit 0/1, indicating whether* (m, σ) *is valid or not.*

Correctness of SIG. For all $\mathsf{pp}_{\mathsf{SIG}} \leftarrow \mathsf{Setup}(1^\lambda)$, $(vk, sk) \leftarrow \mathsf{Gen}(\mathsf{pp}_{\mathsf{SIG}})$, $\sigma \leftarrow \mathsf{Sign}(sk, m)$, it holds that $\mathsf{Ver}(vk, m, \sigma) = 1$.

We recall the security notion existential unforgeability with adaptive corruptions (MU-EUF-CMA^{corr}) by Bader *et al.* in [1].

Definition 2. *A signature scheme* SIG *is MU-EUF-CMA^{corr} secure if for all PPT adversary* $\mathcal{A}$, $\mathsf{Adv}^{\mathsf{m\text{-}corr}}_{\mathsf{SIG},\mu,\mathcal{A}}(\lambda) := \Pr[\mathsf{Exp}^{\mathsf{m\text{-}corr}}_{\mathsf{SIG},\mu,\mathcal{A}}(\lambda) \Rightarrow 1]$ *is negligible (Fig. 2).*

$\mathsf{Exp}^{\mathsf{m\text{-}corr}}_{\mathsf{SIG},\mu,\mathcal{A}}(\lambda)$:	$\mathcal{O}_{\mathrm{SIGN}}(i, m)$:
$\mathsf{pp}_{\mathsf{SIG}} \leftarrow \mathsf{Setup}(1^\lambda)$	$\sigma \leftarrow \mathsf{Sign}(sk_i, m)$
For $i \in [\mu]$: $(vk_i, sk_i) \leftarrow \mathsf{Gen}(\mathsf{pp}_{\mathsf{SIG}})$	$\mathcal{S}_i := \mathcal{S}_i \cup \{(m, \sigma)\}$
$\quad\quad \mathcal{S}_i := \varnothing$ //Record the signing queries	Return σ
$\mathcal{S}^{\mathsf{corr}} := \varnothing$ //Record the corruption queries	
$(i^*, m^*, \sigma^*) \leftarrow \mathcal{A}^{\mathcal{O}_{\mathrm{SIGN}}(\cdot,\cdot), \mathcal{O}_{\mathrm{CORR}}(\cdot)}(\mathsf{pp}_{\mathsf{SIG}}, \mathsf{VKList} := \{vk_i\}_{i \in [\mu]})$	$\mathcal{O}_{\mathrm{CORR}}(i)$:
	$\mathcal{S}^{\mathsf{corr}} := \mathcal{S}^{\mathsf{corr}} \cup \{i\}$
If $i^* \notin \mathcal{S}^{\mathsf{corr}} \wedge (m^*, \cdot) \notin \mathcal{S}_{i^*} \wedge \mathsf{Ver}(vk_{i^*}, m^*, \sigma^*) = 1$: Return 1	Return sk_i
Else: Return 0	

Fig. 2. The MU-EUF-CMA^{corr} security experiment $\mathsf{Exp}^{\mathsf{m\text{-}corr}}_{\mathsf{SIG},\mu,\mathcal{A}}(\lambda)$ of SIG.

2.2   KEM and Its Security in the Multi-user Setting

We review the syntax of KEM and its multi-challenge CCA (IND-mCCA) security. We also define a new security notion, namely IND-mCPA^{reveal}, which will serve our generic construction of AKE. Then we show that IND-mCCA security of KEM implies IND-mCPA^{reveal} security.

Definition 3 (KEM). *A key encapsulation mechanism (KEM) scheme* KEM *= (Setup, Gen, Encap, Decap) consists of four algorithms:*

- Setup(1^λ): *The set up algorithm takes as input* 1^λ *and outputs the public parameter* pp_{KEM}, *which determines the encapsulation key space* $\mathcal{K}$, *the key space* $\mathcal{PK} \times \mathcal{SK}$, *and the ciphertext space* $\mathcal{CT}$.
- Gen(pp_{KEM}): *The key generation algorithm takes as input* pp_{KEM} *and outputs a pair of keys* $(pk, sk) \in \mathcal{PK} \times \mathcal{SK}$.
- Encap(pk): *The encapsulation algorithm takes as input* pk *and outputs an encapsulated key* $K \in \mathcal{K}$ *along with a ciphertext* $C \in \mathcal{CT}$.
- Decap(sk, C): *The decapsulation algorithm takes as input* sk *and a ciphertext* C, *and outputs* K' *with* $K' \in \mathcal{K} \cup \{\bot\}$.

Correctness of KEM. For all $\text{pp}_{\text{KEM}} \leftarrow \text{Setup}(1^\lambda)$, $(pk, sk) \leftarrow \text{Gen}(\text{pp}_{\text{KEM}})$, $(K, C) \leftarrow \text{Encap}(pk)$, it holds that $\text{Decap}(sk, C) = K$.

Definition 4 (IND-mCCA security). *A KEM scheme* KEM *is IND-mCCA secure if for all PPT adversary* $\mathcal{A}$, $\text{Adv}^{\text{m-cca}}_{\text{KEM},\theta,\mathcal{A}}(\lambda) := \left| \Pr[\text{Exp}^{\text{m-cca}}_{\text{KEM},\theta,\mathcal{A}}(\lambda) \Rightarrow 1] - \frac{1}{2} \right|$ *is negligible (Fig. 3).*

IND-mCPA^{reveal} Security. The IND-mCPA security of KEM considers the pseudorandomness of multiple encapsulated keys $\{K \mid (K, C) \leftarrow \text{Encap}(pk_i)\}$, where $\{(pk_i, C)\}$ are the corresponding public keys and challenge ciphertexts. Now consider a stronger attack which allows the adversary to choose any (pk_i, C), even if (pk_i, C) is one of the challenges, and see the (revealed) key K decapsulated from C and sk_i. This defines a stronger security notion IND-mCPA^{reveal}, which asks the pseudorandomness of unrevealed keys. KEM with this security notion fits our AKE protocol.

Definition 5. *A KEM scheme* KEM *is IND-mCPA^{reveal} secure if for all PPT adversary* $\mathcal{A}$, $\text{Adv}^{\text{r-m-cpa}}_{\text{KEM},\theta,\mathcal{A}}(\lambda) := \left| \Pr[\text{Exp}^{\text{r-m-cpa}}_{\text{KEM},\theta,\mathcal{A}}(\lambda) \Rightarrow 1] - \frac{1}{2} \right|$ *is negligible (Fig. 4).*

Note that in $\text{Exp}^{\text{r-m-cpa}}_{\text{KEM},\theta,\mathcal{A}}(\lambda)$, the encapsulation oracle generates tuples $\{(pk_i, C)\}$ as challenges. However, keys decapsulated from $\{(pk_i, C)\}$ can also be revealed. Upon revealed, $\{(pk_i, C)\}$ cannot serve as challenges any more. Meanwhile, each challenge (pk_i, C) will be associated with an independently chosen random bit β. Therefore, IND-mCPA^{reveal} is different from IND-mCCA.

IND-mCCA Implies IND-mCPA^{reveal}. We prove that IND-mCCA security implies IND-mCPA^{reveal} security with a tight reduction.

$\mathsf{Exp}^{\mathsf{m\text{-}cca}}_{\mathsf{KEM},\theta,\mathcal{A}}(\lambda):$	$\mathcal{O}^{\beta}_{\mathrm{ENC}}(i):$
$\mathsf{pp}_{\mathsf{KEM}} \leftarrow \mathsf{Setup}(1^{\lambda})$	$(K,C) \leftarrow \mathsf{KEM.Encap}(pk_i)$
For $i \in [\theta]$: $(pk_i, sk_i) \leftarrow \mathsf{Gen}(\mathsf{pp}_{\mathsf{KEM}})$	$k_0 := K; k_1 \overset{\$}{\leftarrow} \mathcal{K}$
$\mathsf{CList} := \varnothing$ //Records the encapsulation queries	$\mathsf{CList} := \mathsf{CList} \cup \{(pk_i, C)\}$
$\beta \overset{\$}{\leftarrow} \{0,1\}$	Return (k_{β}, C)
$\beta' \leftarrow \mathcal{A}^{\mathcal{O}^{\beta}_{\mathrm{ENC}}(\cdot), \mathcal{O}_{\mathrm{DEC}}(\cdot,\cdot)}(\mathsf{pp}_{\mathsf{KEM}}, \mathsf{PKList} := \{pk_i\}_{i \in [\theta]})$	$\mathcal{O}_{\mathrm{DEC}}(i, C'):$
	If $(pk_i, C') \in \mathsf{CList}$: Return $\perp$
If $\beta' = \beta$: Return 1	$K' \leftarrow \mathsf{KEM.Decap}(sk_i, C')$
Else: Return 0	Return K'

Fig. 3. The IND-mCCA security experiment $\mathsf{Exp}^{\mathsf{m\text{-}cca}}_{\mathsf{KEM},\theta,\mathcal{A}}(\lambda)$ of KEM.

$\mathsf{Exp}^{\mathsf{r\text{-}m\text{-}cpa}}_{\mathsf{KEM},\theta,\mathcal{A}}(\lambda):$	$\mathcal{O}_{\mathrm{ENCAP}}(i):$
$\mathsf{pp}_{\mathsf{KEM}} \leftarrow \mathsf{Setup}(1^{\lambda})$	$(K,C) \leftarrow \mathsf{Encap}(pk_i)$
For $i \in [\theta]$: $(pk_i, sk_i) \leftarrow \mathsf{Gen}(\mathsf{pp}_{\mathsf{KEM}})$	$\beta \overset{\$}{\leftarrow} \{0,1\}; k_0 := K; k_1 \overset{\$}{\leftarrow} \mathcal{K}$
$\mathsf{CList} := \varnothing$ //Records the encapsulation queries	$\mathsf{CList} := \mathsf{CList} \cup \{(pk_i, C, K, \beta)\}$
$\mathsf{RList} := \varnothing$ //Records the reveal queries	Return (k_{β}, C)
$(pk_{i^*}, C^*, \beta') \leftarrow \mathcal{A}^{\mathcal{O}_{\mathrm{ENCAP}}(\cdot), \mathcal{O}_{\mathrm{REVEAL}}(\cdot,\cdot)}(\mathsf{pp}_{\mathsf{KEM}}, \mathsf{PKList} := \{pk_i\}_{u \in [\theta]})$	
	$\mathcal{O}_{\mathrm{REVEAL}}(i, C'):$
If $\exists (pk_{i^*}, C^*, \cdot, \beta) \in \mathsf{CList}$ s.t. $(pk_{i^*}, C^*) \notin \mathsf{RList} \wedge \beta' = \beta$: Return 1	$K' \leftarrow \mathsf{Decap}(sk_i, C')$
Else: Return 0	$\mathsf{RList} := \mathsf{RList} \cup \{(pk_i, C')\}$
	Return K'

Fig. 4. The IND-mCPA^{reveal} security experiment $\mathsf{Exp}^{\mathsf{r\text{-}m\text{-}cpa}}_{\mathsf{KEM},\theta,\mathcal{A}}(\lambda)$ of KEM.

Theorem 1. *If a KEM KEM is IND-mCCA secure, it is also IND-mCPA^{reveal} secure. More precisely, for any PPT adversary $\mathcal{A}$ of advantage $\mathsf{Adv}^{\mathsf{r\text{-}m\text{-}cpa}}_{\mathsf{KEM},\theta,\mathcal{A}}(\lambda)$ in $\mathsf{Exp}^{\mathsf{r\text{-}m\text{-}cpa}}_{\mathsf{KEM},\theta,\mathcal{A}}(\lambda)$, there exists a PPT algorithm $\mathcal{B}$ which has advantage $\mathsf{Adv}^{\mathsf{m\text{-}cca}}_{\mathsf{KEM},\theta,\mathcal{B}}(\lambda)$ in $\mathsf{Exp}^{\mathsf{m\text{-}cca}}_{\mathsf{KEM},\theta,\mathcal{B}}(\lambda)$ such that $\mathsf{Adv}^{\mathsf{r\text{-}m\text{-}cpa}}_{\mathsf{KEM},\theta,\mathcal{A}}(\lambda) \leq 2\mathsf{Adv}^{\mathsf{m\text{-}cca}}_{\mathsf{KEM},\theta,\mathcal{B}}(\lambda).$*

Proof. Given a PPT $\mathcal{A}$ in $\mathsf{Exp}^{\mathsf{r\text{-}m\text{-}cpa}}_{\mathsf{KEM},\theta,\mathcal{A}}(\lambda)$, we construct a PPT algorithm $\mathcal{B}$ in $\mathsf{Exp}^{\mathsf{m\text{-}cca}}_{\mathsf{KEM},\theta,\mathcal{B}}(\lambda)$. Let $\mathcal{C}$ be $\mathcal{B}$'s challenger. Then $\mathcal{C}$ provides two oracles, $\mathcal{O}^{\beta}_{\mathrm{ENC}}(\cdot)$ and $\mathcal{O}_{\mathrm{DEC}}(\cdot,\cdot)$ to $\mathcal{B}$. $\mathcal{B}$ simulates $\mathsf{Exp}^{\mathsf{r\text{-}m\text{-}cpa}}_{\mathsf{KEM},\theta,\mathcal{A}}(\lambda)$ for $\mathcal{A}$ as follows.

1. First $\mathcal{B}$ gets $\mathsf{pp}_{\mathsf{KEM}}$ and a set of public keys $\{pk_i\}_{i \in [\theta]}$ from its own challenger $\mathcal{C}$. Then it sends $\mathsf{pp}_{\mathsf{KEM}}$ and $\mathsf{PKList} := \{pk_i\}_{i \in [\theta]}$ to $\mathcal{A}$. $\mathcal{B}$ also prepares two lists $\mathsf{CList} := \varnothing$ and $\mathsf{RList} := \varnothing$.

2. There are two kinds of oracle queries from $\mathcal{A}$, and $\mathcal{B}$ answers them as follows.
   $\mathcal{O}_{\mathrm{ENCAP}}(i)$: $\mathcal{B}$ asks its own oracle $\mathcal{O}^{\beta}_{\mathrm{ENC}}(i)$ and obtains $(K,C) \leftarrow \mathcal{O}^{\beta}_{\mathrm{ENC}}(i)$.

   Then it sets $k_0 := K$, samples $k_1 \leftarrow \mathcal{K}$, throws a coin $b \overset{\$}{\leftarrow} \{0,1\}$, appends (pk_i, C, K, b) into CList and returns (k_b, C) to $\mathcal{A}$.

   $\mathcal{O}_{\mathrm{REVEAL}}(i, C')$: $\mathcal{B}$ checks whether $(pk_i, C', \cdot, \cdot) \in \mathsf{CList}$. If yes, $\mathcal{B}$ parses the tuple as (pk_i, C', K, b) and returns K to $\mathcal{A}$. Otherwise, $\mathcal{B}$ asks its own oracle $\mathcal{O}_{\mathrm{DEC}}(i, C')$. Let $K' \leftarrow \mathcal{O}_{\mathrm{DEC}}(i, C')$, then $\mathcal{B}$ updates $\mathsf{RList} := \mathsf{RList} \cup \{(pk_i, C')\}$ and returns K' to $\mathcal{A}$.

3. If $\mathcal{A}$ aborts, $\mathcal{B}$ outputs a random bit. Otherwise, $\mathcal{A}$ outputs (pk_{i^*}, C^*, b'). If $\exists (pk_{i^*}, C^*, \cdot, b) \in \mathsf{CList}$ s.t. $(pk_{i^*}, C^*) \notin \mathsf{RList} \wedge b' = b$, $\mathcal{B}$ outputs $\beta' = 0$. Otherwise, it outputs 1.

Let β be the random bit generated by $\mathcal{B}$'s challenger $\mathcal{C}$, then $\mathcal{B}$ wins in $\mathsf{Exp}^{\text{m-cca}}_{\mathsf{KEM},\theta,\mathcal{B}}(\lambda)$ if $\beta' = \beta$. Recall that $\mathcal{O}^{\beta}_{\mathrm{ENC}}(\cdot)$ will always return real keys if $\beta = 0$ and random keys if $\beta = 1$.

Case 1: $\beta = 0$. In this case, the output (K, C) of $\mathcal{O}^0_{\mathrm{ENC}}(i)$ is a real encapsulation pair. $\mathcal{B}$ simulates $\mathcal{O}_{\mathrm{ENCAP}}(i)$ by outputting (k_b, C), where k_b is either a real or a random key with $1/2$ probability. Furthermore, for each $(pk_i, C', K, b) \in \mathsf{CList}$, it holds that $\mathsf{Decap}(sk_i, C') = K$. For simulation of $\mathcal{O}_{\mathrm{REVEAL}}(i, C')$, if there exists $(pk_i, C', K, b) \in \mathsf{CList}$, $\mathcal{B}$ returns K; otherwise $\mathcal{B}$ asks its own oracle $\mathcal{O}_{\mathrm{DEC}}(i, C')$ and returns the output of $\mathcal{O}_{\mathrm{DEC}}(i, C')$ to $\mathcal{A}$. Thus, $\mathcal{B}$ perfectly simulates $\mathsf{Exp}^{\text{r-m-cpa}}_{\mathsf{KEM},\theta,\mathcal{A}}(\lambda)$ for $\mathcal{A}$.

Case 2: $\beta = 1$. In this case, the output (K, C) of $\mathcal{O}^1_{\mathrm{ENC}}(i)$ contains a random key K, which is independent of C. In $\mathcal{B}$'s answer (k_b, C) to $\mathcal{O}_{\mathrm{ENCAP}}(i)$, k_b is a random key, independent from b. Moreover, $\mathcal{B}$'s answer to $\mathcal{O}_{\mathrm{REVEAL}}(i, C')$ does not use b at all. Hence $\mathcal{A}$ learns nothing about b from $\mathcal{O}_{\mathrm{ENCAP}}(i)$ and $\mathcal{O}_{\mathrm{REVEAL}}(i, C')$. Thus, $\Pr[b' = b] = 1/2$ and $\Pr[\beta' = \beta] = 1/2$.

$$\mathsf{Adv}^{\text{m-cca}}_{\mathsf{KEM},\theta,\mathcal{B}}(\lambda) = |\Pr[\beta' = \beta] - 1/2|$$
$$= |\Pr[\beta' = \beta | \beta = 0]\Pr[\beta = 0] + \Pr[\beta' = \beta | \beta = 1]\Pr[\beta = 1] - 1/2|$$
$$= |\frac{1}{2}(\frac{1}{2} + \mathsf{Adv}^{\text{r-m-cpa}}_{\mathsf{KEM},\theta,\mathcal{A}}(\lambda)) + \frac{1}{2} \cdot \frac{1}{2} - \frac{1}{2}| = \frac{1}{2}\mathsf{Adv}^{\text{r-m-cpa}}_{\mathsf{KEM},\theta,\mathcal{A}}(\lambda). \qquad \square$$

2.3 Diverse Property of KEM

We define a property called *diverse property* for KEM, which is useful in the security proof of our AKE.

Definition 6 (Diverse Property). *A KEM scheme* $\mathsf{KEM} = (\mathsf{Setup}, \mathsf{Gen}, \mathsf{Encap}, \mathsf{Decap})$ *has diverse property if for all* $\mathsf{pp}_{\mathsf{KEM}} \leftarrow \mathsf{Setup}(1^\lambda)$, *it holds that:*

$$\Pr\left[\begin{matrix} \tilde{r} \xleftarrow{\$} \tilde{\mathcal{R}}; r, \bar{r} \xleftarrow{\$} \mathcal{R}; (pk, sk) \leftarrow \mathsf{Gen}(\mathsf{pp}_{\mathsf{KEM}}; \tilde{r}); \\ (K, C) \leftarrow \mathsf{Encap}(pk; r); (\bar{K}, \bar{C}) \leftarrow \mathsf{Encap}(pk; \bar{r}) \end{matrix} : K = \bar{K}\right] = 2^{-\Omega(\lambda)},$$

$$\Pr\left[\begin{matrix} \tilde{r}, \tilde{r}' \xleftarrow{\$} \tilde{\mathcal{R}}; r \xleftarrow{\$} \mathcal{R}; \\ (pk, sk) \leftarrow \mathsf{Gen}(\mathsf{pp}_{\mathsf{KEM}}; \tilde{r}); (pk', sk') \leftarrow \mathsf{Gen}(\mathsf{pp}_{\mathsf{KEM}}; \tilde{r}'); \\ (K, C) \leftarrow \mathsf{Encap}(pk; r); (K', C') \leftarrow \mathsf{Encap}(pk'; r) \end{matrix} : K = K'\right] = 2^{-\Omega(\lambda)},$$

where $\tilde{\mathcal{R}}, \mathcal{R}$ *are the randomness spaces in* Gen *and* Encap *respectively.*

2.4 The Strong Twin Diffie-Hellman Assumption

Let GGen be a group generation algorithm such that $\mathcal{G} := (\mathbb{G}, q, g) \leftarrow \mathsf{GGen}(1^\lambda)$, where $\mathbb{G}$ is a cyclic group of prime order q with generator g.

Definition 7. *For any adversary* $\mathcal{A}$, *the advantage of* $\mathcal{A}$ *in solving the Computational Diffie-Hellman (CDH) problem is defined as*

$$\mathsf{Adv}^{\mathsf{CDH}}_{\mathbb{G},\mathcal{A}}(\lambda) := \Pr[(\mathbb{G}, q, g) \leftarrow \mathsf{GGen}(1^\lambda); x, y \xleftarrow{\$} \mathbb{Z}_q : \mathcal{A}(\mathbb{G}, q, g, g^x, g^y) = g^{xy}].$$

Definition 8. *For any adversary $\mathcal{A}$, the advantage of $\mathcal{A}$ in solving the Decisional Diffie-Hellman (DDH) problem is defined as*

$$\mathsf{Adv}^{DDH}_{\mathbb{G},\mathcal{A}}(\lambda) := |\Pr[(\mathbb{G}, q, g) \leftarrow \mathit{GGen}(1^\lambda); x, y \xleftarrow{\$} \mathbb{Z}_q : \mathcal{A}(\mathbb{G}, q, g, g^x, g^y, g^{xy}) = 1]-$$

$$\Pr[(\mathbb{G}, q, g) \leftarrow \mathit{GGen}(1^\lambda); x, y, z \xleftarrow{\$} \mathbb{Z}_q : \mathcal{A}(\mathbb{G}, q, g, g^x, g^y, g^z) = 1]|.$$

In [5], Cash *et al.* proposed the *Strong Twin Diffie-Hellman (strong 2DH or st2DH)* problem, and proved that it is as hard as the CDH problem.

Definition 9. *[5] For any adversary $\mathcal{A}$, its advantage in solving the strong twin Diffie-Hellman problem is defined as* $\mathsf{Adv}^{\mathsf{st2DH}}_{\mathbb{G},\mathcal{A}}(\lambda) :=$

$$\Pr[\mathcal{G} \leftarrow \mathit{GGen}(1^\lambda); x_1, x_2, y \xleftarrow{\$} \mathbb{Z}_q : \mathcal{A}^{2\mathrm{DH}(g^{x_1}, g^{x_2}, \cdot, \cdot, \cdot)}(\mathbb{G}, q, g, g^{x_1}, g^{x_2}, g^y) = (g^{x_1 y}, g^{x_2 y})],$$

where the decision oracle $2\mathrm{DH}(g^{x_1}, g^{x_2}, \cdot, \cdot, \cdot)$ *takes as input* (g^y, g^{z_1}, g^{z_2}) *and outputs 1 if* $(x_1 y = z_1) \wedge (x_2 y = z_2)$ *and 0 otherwise.*

Theorem 2. *[5] For any PPT adversary $\mathcal{A}$ against the strong 2DH problem, there exists a PPT algorithm $\mathcal{B}$ against the CDH problem such that* $\mathsf{Adv}^{\mathsf{st2DH}}_{\mathbb{G},\mathcal{A}}(\lambda) \leq \mathsf{Adv}^{\mathsf{CDH}}_{\mathbb{G},\mathcal{B}}(\lambda) + Q/q$, *where Q is the maximum number of decision oracle queries.*

3   Authenticated Key Exchange Scheme

3.1   Definition of Authenticated Key Exchange

We consider a generic AKE scheme, in which each party maintains a state st_i. If $\mathsf{st}_i = \perp$, the AKE scheme is stateless.

Definition 10 (AKE). *An authenticated key exchange (AKE) scheme* $\mathsf{AKE} = (\mathsf{AKE.Setup}, \mathsf{AKE.Gen}, \mathsf{AKE.Protocol})$ *consists of two probabilistic algorithms and an interactive protocol.*

- $\mathsf{AKE.Setup}(1^\lambda)$: *The setup algorithm takes as input the security parameter 1^λ, and outputs the public parameter* $\mathsf{pp_{AKE}}$.
- $\mathsf{AKE.Gen}(\mathsf{pp_{AKE}}, P_i)$: *The generation algorithm takes as input* $\mathsf{pp_{AKE}}$ *and a party P_i, and outputs a key pair (pk_i, sk_i) and an initial state st_i.*
- $\mathsf{AKE.Protocol}(P_i(\mathsf{res}_i) \rightleftharpoons P_j(\mathsf{res}_j))$: *The protocol involves two parties P_i and P_j, who have access to their own resources,* $\mathsf{res}_i := (sk_i, \mathsf{st}_i, \mathsf{pp_{AKE}}, \{pk_u\}_{u \in [\mu]})$ *and* $\mathsf{res}_j := (sk_j, \mathsf{st}_j, \mathsf{pp_{AKE}}, \{pk_u\}_{u \in [\mu]})$, *respectively. Here μ is the total number of users. After execution, P_i outputs a flag $\Psi_i \in \{\emptyset, \mathbf{accept}, \mathbf{reject}\}$, and a session key k_i (k_i might be empty string $\emptyset$), and P_j outputs (Ψ_j, k_j) similarly. Note that every execution of protocol may lead to update of $\mathsf{st}_i, \mathsf{st}_j$.*

Correctness of AKE. For any distinct and honest parties P_i and P_j, they share the same session key after the execution $\mathsf{AKE.Protocol}(P_i(\mathsf{res}_i) \rightleftharpoons P_j(\mathsf{res}_j))$, i.e., $\Psi_i = \Psi_j = \mathbf{accept}, k_i = k_j \neq \emptyset$.

Definition 11 (Stateless AKE). *In Definition 10, if st_i is set to $\perp$ (i.e., no state involved) for each party P_i, then the AKE becomes a stateless AKE.*

3.2   Security Model of AKE

We will adapt the security model formalized by [1,11,19], which in turn followed the model proposed by Bellare and Rogaway [2]. We also include replay attacks in the security model, leading to a stronger model than those in [1,2,11].

First we will define oracles and their static variables in the model. Then we describe the security experiment and the corresponding security notions.

Oracles. Suppose there are at most μ users $P_1, P_2, ..., P_\mu$, and each user will involve at most ℓ instances. P_i is formalized by a series of oracles, $\pi_i^1, \pi_i^2, ..., \pi_i^\ell$. Oracle π_i^s formalizes P_i's execution of the s-th protocol instance. Since we consider stateful P_i, we have two requirements.

(1) The very first queries to oracles $\pi_i^1, \pi_i^2, ..., \pi_i^\ell$ by the adversary $\mathcal{A}$ must be in chronological order $1, 2, ..., \ell$. That is, for $1 \le s < \ell$, π_i^{s+1} is inaccessible to $\mathcal{A}$ before π_i^s is invoked. However, we stress that it does not eliminate the possibility that $\mathcal{A}$ queries π_i^s, then π_i^{s+1}, and back to $\pi_i^s, \pi_i^{s-1}, ...$ again.
(2) There is a state st_i shared and maintained by $\pi_i^1, \pi_i^2, ..., \pi_i^\ell$.

Each oracle π_i^s has access to P_i's resource $\mathsf{res}_i := (sk_i, \mathsf{st}_i, \mathsf{pp}_{\mathsf{AKE}}, \mathsf{PKList} := \{pk_u\}_{u \in [\mu]})$, where st_i is the state of the time being. π_i^s also has its own variables $\mathsf{var}_i^s := (\mathsf{Pid}_i^s, k_i^s, \varPsi_i^s)$.

- Pid_i^s: The intended communication peer's identity.
- $k_i^s \in \mathcal{K}$: The session key computed by π_i^s. Here $\mathcal{K}$ is the session key space. We assume that $\emptyset \in \mathcal{K}$.
- $\varPsi_i^s \in \{\emptyset, \mathbf{accept}, \mathbf{reject}\}$: $\varPsi_i^s$ indicates whether π_i^s has completed the protocol execution and accepted k_i^s.

At the beginning, $(\mathsf{Pid}_i^s, k_i^s, \varPsi_i^s)$ are initialized to $(\emptyset, \emptyset, \emptyset)$. We declare that $k_i^s \ne \emptyset$ if and only if $\varPsi_i^s = \mathbf{accept}$.

Security Experiment. To define the security notion of AKE, we first formalize the security experiment $\mathsf{Exp}_{\mu,\ell,\mathcal{A}}^{\mathsf{AKE}}(\lambda)$ with the help of the oracles defined above. $\mathsf{Exp}_{\mu,\ell,\mathcal{A}}^{\mathsf{AKE}}(\lambda)$ is a game played between an AKE challenger $\mathcal{C}$ and an adversary $\mathcal{A}$. $\mathcal{C}$ will simulate the executions of the ℓ protocol instances for each of the μ users with oracles π_i^s. See Fig. 5 for the formal description of $\mathsf{Exp}_{\mu,\ell,\mathcal{A}}^{\mathsf{AKE}}(\lambda)$.

Adversary $\mathcal{A}$ may copy, delay, erase, replay, and interpolate the messages transmitted in the network. This is formalized by the query Send to oracle π_i^s. With Send, $\mathcal{A}$ could send arbitrary message to any oracle π_i^s. Then π_i^s will execute the AKE protocol according to the protocol specification for P_i.

We also allow the adversary to observe session keys of its choices. This can be reflected by the Reveal query to oracle π_i^s.

$\mathsf{Corrupt}$ query allows $\mathcal{A}$ to corrupt a party P_i and get its long-term secret key sk_i. With $\mathsf{RegisterCorrupt}$ query, $\mathcal{A}$ can register a new party without public key certification. The public key is then known to all other users.

We introduce Test query to formalize the pseudorandomness of k_i^s. For a Test query to π_i^s, the oracle will return $\perp$ if the session key k_i^s is not generated yet.

$\mathsf{Exp}^{\text{strong}}_{\text{AKE},\mu,\ell,\mathcal{A}}(\lambda)$, $\mathsf{Exp}_{\text{AKE},\mu,\ell,\mathcal{A}}(\lambda)$:	$\mathcal{O}_{\text{AKE}}(\text{query})$:
$\text{pp}_{\text{AKE}} \leftarrow \text{AKE.Setup}(1^\lambda)$	If query=$\mathsf{Send}(i,s,j,\text{msg})$:
For $i \in [\mu]$:	$\quad \text{res}_i := (sk_i, \text{st}_i, \text{pp}_{\text{AKE}}, \text{PKList})$
$\quad (pk_i, sk_i, \text{st}_i) \leftarrow \text{AKE.Gen}(\text{pp}_{\text{AKE}}, P_i)$;	$\quad \text{var}_i^s := (\text{Pid}_i^s, k_i^s, \Psi_i^s)$
$\quad crp_i := 0$ //Corruption variable	$\quad (\text{msg}', \text{st}_i', \text{Pid}_i^s, k_i^s, \Psi_i^s) \leftarrow \pi_i^s(\text{msg}, \text{res}_i, \text{var}_i^s)$
$\text{PKList} := \{pk_i\}_{i\in[\mu]}$	$\quad \text{st}_i := \text{st}_i'$
For $(i,s) \in [\mu] \times [\ell]$:	$\quad$ Let $j := \text{Pid}_i^s$
$\quad b_i^s \overset{\$}{\leftarrow} \{0,1\}$; $\text{Pid}_i^s := k_i^s := \Psi_i^s := \emptyset$;	$\quad$ If $\Psi_i^s = \text{accept} \wedge crp_j = 1$: $\text{Aflag}_i^s := 1$
$\quad \text{Aflag}_i^s := 0$; $\text{Tflag}_i^s := 0$;	$\quad$ Return msg'
$\quad$ //Whether Pid_i^s is corrupted when π_i^s is accepted or tested	If query=$\mathsf{Corrupt}(i)$:
$\quad T_i^s := 0$; $R_i^s := 0$ //Test & Reveal variables	$\quad crp_i := 1$
$(i^*, s^*, b^*) \leftarrow \mathcal{A}^{\mathcal{O}_{\text{AKE}}(\cdot)}(\text{pp}_{\text{AKE}}, \text{PKList})$	$\quad$ Return sk_i
	If query=$\mathsf{RegisterCorrupt}(u, pk_u)$:
$\text{Win}_{\text{Auth}}:=0$	$\quad$ If $u \in [\mu]$: Return $\bot$
$\text{Win}_{\text{Auth}}:=1$, If $\exists(i,s) \in [\mu] \times [\ell]$ s.t.	$\quad \text{PKList} := \text{PKList} \cup \{pk_u\}$
(1) $\Psi_i^s = \text{accept}$ //π_i^s is τ-accepted	$\quad$ Return PKList
(2) $\text{Aflag}_i^s = 0$ //P_j is $\hat{\tau}$-corrupted with $j := \text{Pid}_i^s$ and $\hat{\tau} > \tau$	
(3) (3.1) $\vee$ (3.2) $\vee$ (3.3). Let $j := \text{Pid}_i^s$	If query=$\mathsf{Reveal}(i,s)$:
$\quad$ (3.1) $\nexists t \in [\ell]$ s.t. $\mathsf{Partner}(\pi_i^s \leftarrow \pi_j^t)$	$\quad$ If $\Psi_i^s \neq \text{accept}$: Return $\bot$
$\quad$ (3.2) $\exists t \in [\ell], (j',t') \in [\mu] \times [\ell]$ with $(j,t) \neq (j',t')$ s.t.	$\quad$ Else: $R_i^s := 1$; Return k_i^s
$\qquad \mathsf{Partner}(\pi_i^s \leftarrow \pi_j^t) \wedge \mathsf{Partner}(\pi_i^s \leftarrow \pi_{j'}^{t'})$	
$\boxed{\text{(3.3) } \exists t \in [\ell], (i',s') \in [\mu] \times [\ell] \text{ with } (i,s) \neq (i',s') \text{ s.t.}}$	If query=$\mathsf{Test}(i,s)$:
$\boxed{\qquad \mathsf{Partner}(\pi_i^s \leftarrow \pi_j^t) \wedge \mathsf{Partner}(\pi_{i'}^{s'} \leftarrow \pi_j^t)}$	$\quad$ If $\Psi_i^s \neq \text{accept}$: Return $\bot$
	$\quad$ Let $j := \text{Pid}_i^s$
$\text{Win}_{\text{Ind}}:=0$	$\quad$ If $crp_j = 1$: $\text{Tflag}_i^s := 1$
$(i,s,b^*) := (i^*,s^*,b^*)$; $j := \text{Pid}_i^s$	$\quad T_i^s := 1$; $k_0 := k_i^s$; $k_1 \overset{\$}{\leftarrow} \mathcal{K}$; Return $k_{b_i^s}$
If (1') $T_i^s = 1 \wedge \text{Tflag}_i^s = 0$	
$\quad$ //π_i^s is τ-tested and Pid_i^s is $\hat{\tau}$-corrupt with $\hat{\tau} > \tau$	
(2') $R_i^s = 0$ //π_i^s is ∞-revealed	$\pi_i^s(\text{msg}, \text{res}_i, \text{var}_i^s)$:
(3') If $\exists t \in [\ell]$ s.t. $\mathsf{Partner}(\pi_i^s \leftarrow \pi_j^t)$ then $R_j^t = T_j^t = 0$	//π_i^s executes AKE according to the protocol specification
$\quad$ //If π_i^s is partnered to π_j^t, then π_j^t is ∞-revealed and ∞-tested	If $\text{msg} = \top$:
Then: $\quad$ If $b^* = b_i^s$: $\text{Win}_{\text{Ind}}=1$; Return 1	$\quad \pi_i^s$ is an initiator;
$\qquad\quad$ Else: Return 0	$\quad \pi_i^s$ generates the first message msg' of AKE
Else: $\quad$ Abort	$\qquad$ and updates st_i' and $(\text{Pid}_i^s, k_i^s, \Psi_i^s)$
	If $\text{msg} \neq \top$:
$\mathsf{D\text{-}Partner}(\pi_i^s, \pi_j^t)$: $\quad$ //Checking whether $\mathsf{Partner}(\pi_i^s \leftarrow \pi_j^t)$	$\quad \pi_i^s$ uses msg to generate the next message msg'
If π_i^s is the initiator and $k_i^s = \mathsf{K}(\pi_i^s, \pi_j^t) \neq \emptyset$: Return 1	$\qquad$ and updates st_i' and $(\text{Pid}_i^s, k_i^s, \Psi_i^s)$;
If π_i^s is the responder and $k_i^s = \mathsf{K}(\pi_j^t, \pi_i^s) \neq \emptyset$: Return 1	$\quad$ If msg is the last message of AKE: $\text{msg}' := \emptyset$
Return 0	Return $(\text{msg}', \text{st}_i', \text{Pid}_i^s, k_i^s, \Psi_i^s)$

Fig. 5. The strong security experiment $\mathsf{Exp}^{\text{strong}}_{\text{AKE},\mu,\ell,\mathcal{A}}(\lambda)$ and the security experiment $\mathsf{Exp}_{\text{AKE},\mu,\ell,\mathcal{A}}(\lambda)$ of AKE, with framed part $\boxed{\cdots}$ only in $\mathsf{Exp}^{\text{strong}}_{\text{AKE},\mu,\ell,\mathcal{A}}(\lambda)$.

Otherwise, π_i^s will return k_i^s or a truly random key with half probability. The task of $\mathcal{A}$ is to tell whether the key is the true session key or a random key.

Formally, the queries by $\mathcal{A}$ are described as follows.

– $\mathsf{Send}(i, s, j, \text{msg})$: If $\text{msg} = \top$, it means that $\mathcal{A}$ asks oracle π_i^s to send the first protocol message to P_j. Otherwise, $\mathcal{A}$ impersonates P_j to send message msg to π_i^s. Then π_i^s executes the AKE protocol with msg as P_i does, outputs a message msg', and updates the state st_i and its own variables var_i^s. In formula, $(\text{msg}', \text{st}_i', \text{Pid}_i^s, k_i^s, \Psi_i^s) \leftarrow \pi_i^s(\text{msg}, \text{res}_i, \text{var}_i^s)$. Only the output message msg' is returned to $\mathcal{A}$.

If $\mathsf{Send}(i, s, j, \text{msg})$ is the τ-th query asked by $\mathcal{A}$ and π_i^s changes Ψ_i^s to **accept** after that, then we say that π_i^s is τ-*accepted*.

– $\mathsf{Corrupt}(i)$: $\mathcal{C}$ reveals to $\mathcal{A}$ party P_i's long-term secret key sk_i. After corruption, $\pi_i^1, ..., \pi_i^\ell$ will stop answering any query from $\mathcal{A}$.

If $\mathsf{Corrupt}(i)$ is the τ-th query asked by $\mathcal{A}$, we say that P_i is τ-*corrupted*.

If $\mathcal{A}$ has never asked Corrupt(i), we say that P_i is ∞-*corrupted*.

- RegisterCorrupt(i, pk_i): It means that $\mathcal{A}$ registers a new party P_i $(i > \mu)$. $\mathcal{C}$ distributes (P_i, pk_i) to all users. In this case, we say that P_i is *0-corrupted*.
- Reveal(i, s): The query means that $\mathcal{A}$ asks $\mathcal{C}$ to reveal π_i^s's session key. If $\Psi_i^s \neq$ **accept**, $\mathcal{C}$ returns $\bot$. Otherwise, $\mathcal{C}$ returns the session key k_i^s of π_i^s. If Reveal(i, s) is the τ-th query asked by $\mathcal{A}$, we say that π_i^s is τ-*revealed*. If $\mathcal{A}$ has never asked Reveal(i, s), we say that π_i^s is ∞-*revealed*.
- Test(i, s): If $\Psi_i^s \neq$ **accept**, $\mathcal{C}$ returns $\bot$. Otherwise, $\mathcal{C}$ throws a coin $b_i^s \xleftarrow{\$} \{0, 1\}$, sets $k_0 = k_i^s$, samples $k_1 \xleftarrow{\$} \mathcal{K}$, and returns $k_{b_i^s}$ to $\mathcal{A}$. We require that $\mathcal{A}$ could ask Test(i, s) to each oracle π_i^s only once. If Test(i, s) is the τ-th query asked by $\mathcal{A}$ and $\Psi_i^s =$ **accept**, we say that π_i^s is τ-*tested*. If $\mathcal{A}$ has never asked Test(i, s), we say that π_i^s is ∞-*tested*.

Informally, the pseudorandomness of k_i^s asks that any PPT adversary $\mathcal{A}$, access to Test(i, s), could guess b_i^s with probability no better than $1/2 +$ negl. Yet, we have to exclude some trivial attacks: (1) $\mathcal{A}$ asks Reveal(i, s); (2) $\mathcal{A}$ asked Corrupt(j) before $\Psi_i^s =$ **accept**; (3) $\mathcal{A}$ asks Reveal(j, t); (4) $\mathcal{A}$ asks Test(j, t), given that π_i^s and π_j^t have a successful protocol execution with each other.

Definition 12 (Original Key [19]). *For two oracles π_i^s and π_j^t, the original key, denoted as $\mathsf{K}(\pi_i^s, \pi_j^t)$, is the session key computed by the two peers of the protocol under a passive adversary only, where π_i^s is the initiator.*

Remark 1. We note that $\mathsf{K}(\pi_i^s, \pi_j^t)$ is determined by the identities of P_i and P_j, the internal randomness and the states st_i^s and st_j^t, where st_i^s and st_j^t denote the states when π_i^s and π_j^t are invoked respectively.

Definition 13 (Partner [19]). *Let $\mathsf{K}(\cdot, \cdot)$ denote the original key function. We say that an oracle π_i^s is partnered to π_j^t, denoted as $\mathsf{Partner}(\pi_i^s \leftarrow \pi_j^t)$[3], if one of the following requirements holds:*

- *π_i^s is the initiator and $k_i^s = \mathsf{K}(\pi_i^s, \pi_j^t) \neq \emptyset$, or*
- *π_i^s is the responder and $k_i^s = \mathsf{K}(\pi_j^t, \pi_i^s) \neq \emptyset$.*

For 2-pass AKE, the security model of [11] cannot cover replay attacks. Given $\mathsf{Partner}(\pi_{i'}^{s'} \leftarrow \pi_j^t)$, a successful replay attack means that $\mathcal{A}$ resends to π_i^s the messages, which were sent from π_j^t to $\pi_{i'}^{s'}$, and π_i^s is fooled to compute a session key, i.e., $\mathsf{Partner}(\pi_i^s \leftarrow \pi_j^t)$. Now, we add the formalization of replay attacks (see (3.3) in Fig. 5) in the security model of [11] and define a stronger security notion.

Definition 14 (Strong Security of AKE). *Let μ be the number of users and ℓ the maximum number of protocol executions per user. The strong security experiment $\mathsf{Exp}_{\mathsf{AKE}, \mu, \ell, \mathcal{A}}^{\mathsf{strong}}(\lambda)$ (see Fig. 5) is played between the challenger $\mathcal{C}$ and the adversary $\mathcal{A}$.*

---

[3] The arrow notion $\pi_i^s \leftarrow \pi_j^t$ means π_i^s (not necessarily π_j^t) has computed and accepted the original key.

1. $\mathcal{C}$ *runs* AKE.Setup(1^λ) *to get AKE public parameter* $\mathsf{pp}_{\mathsf{AKE}}$.
2. *For each party* P_i, $\mathcal{C}$ *runs* AKE.Gen$(\mathsf{pp}_{\mathsf{AKE}}, P_i)$ *to get the long-term key pair* (pk_i, sk_i) *and* P_i*'s initial state* st_i. *Then it provides* $\mathcal{A}$ *with the public parameter* $\mathsf{pp}_{\mathsf{AKE}}$ *and public key list* PKList $:= \{pk_i\}_{i\in[\mu]}$.
3. $\mathcal{A}$ *asks* $\mathcal{C}$ Send, Corrupt, RegisterCorrupt, Reveal, *and* Test *queries adaptively.*
4. *At the end of the experiment,* $\mathcal{A}$ *terminates with an output* (i^*, s^*, b^*), *where* b^* *is a guess for* $b_{i^*}^{s^*}$ *of oracle* $\pi_{i^*}^{s^*}$.

Strong Authentication. *Let* $\mathsf{Win}_{\mathsf{Auth}}$ *denote the event that* $\mathcal{A}$ *breaks authentication in the security experiment.* $\mathsf{Win}_{\mathsf{Auth}}$ *happens iff* $\exists (i, s) \in [\mu] \times [\ell]$ *s.t.*

(1) π_i^s *is* τ*-accepted.*
(2) P_j *is* $\hat{\tau}$*-corrupted with* $j := \mathsf{Pid}_i^s$ *and* $\hat{\tau} > \tau$.
(3) *Either (3.1) or (3.2) or (3.3) happens. Let* $j := \mathsf{Pid}_i^s$.
   (3.1) *There is no oracle* π_j^t *that* π_i^s *is partnered to.*
   (3.2) *There exist two distinct oracles* π_j^t *and* $\pi_{j'}^{t'}$, *to which* π_i^s *is partnered.*
   (3.3) *There exist two oracles* $\pi_{i'}^{s'}$ *and* π_j^t *with* $(i', s') \neq (i, s)$, *such that both* π_i^s *and* $\pi_{i'}^{s'}$ *are partnered to* π_j^t.

Remark 2. Given $(1) \wedge (2)$, (3.1) indicates a successful impersonation of P_j, (3.2) suggests one instance of P_i has multiple partners, and (3.3) corresponds to a successful replay attack.

Indistinguishability. *Let* $\mathsf{Win}_{\mathsf{Ind}}$ *denote the event that* $\mathcal{A}$ *breaks indistinguishability in* $\mathsf{Exp}_{\mathsf{AKE},\mu,\ell,\mathcal{A}}^{\mathsf{strong}}(\lambda)$ *above. For simplicity, let* $(i, s, b^*) := (i^*, s^*, b^*)$ *be* $\mathcal{A}$*'s output.* $\mathsf{Win}_{\mathsf{Ind}}$ *happens iff* $b^* = b_i^s$, *and the following conditions are satisfied.*

(1') π_i^s *is* τ*-tested and* Pid_i^s *is* $\tilde{\tau}$*-corrupt with* $\tilde{\tau} > \tau$.
(2') π_i^s *is* ∞*-revealed.*
(3') *If* π_i^s *is partnered to* π_j^t $(j = \mathsf{Pid}_i^s)$, *then* π_j^t *is* ∞*-revealed and* ∞*-tested.*

Note that $\mathsf{Exp}_{\mathsf{AKE},\mu,\ell,\mathcal{A}}^{\mathsf{strong}}(\lambda) \Rightarrow 1$ *iff* $\mathsf{Win}_{\mathsf{Ind}}$ *happens. Hence, the advantage of* $\mathcal{A}$ *is defined as*

$$\mathsf{Adv}_{\mathsf{AKE},\mu,\ell,\mathcal{A}}^{\mathsf{strong}}(\lambda) := \max\{\Pr[\mathsf{Win}_{\mathsf{Auth}}], |\Pr[\mathsf{Win}_{\mathsf{Ind}}] - 1/2|\}$$
$$= \max\{\Pr[\mathsf{Win}_{\mathsf{Auth}}], |\Pr[\mathsf{Exp}_{\mathsf{AKE},\mu,\ell,\mathcal{A}}^{\mathsf{strong}}(\lambda) \Rightarrow 1] - 1/2|\}.$$

An AKE scheme AKE *has strong security if for any PPT adversary* $\mathcal{A}$, *it holds that* $\mathsf{Adv}_{\mathsf{AKE},\mu,\ell,\mathcal{A}}^{\mathsf{strong}}(\lambda)$ *is negligible.*

Remark 3. Indisitinguishability asks the pseudorandomness of the session key shared between P_i and P_j, excluding trivial attacks such like P_j is corrupted, or the session key is tested in P_j, or it is revealed.

Definition 15 (Security of AKE). *The security experiment* $\mathsf{Exp}_{\mathsf{AKE},\mu,\ell,\mathcal{A}}(\lambda)$ *(see Fig. 5) is defined like* $\mathsf{Exp}^{\mathsf{strong}}_{\mathsf{AKE},\mu,\ell,\mathcal{A}}(\lambda)$ *except that (3.3) is eliminated from* $\mathsf{Win}_{\mathsf{Auth}}$. *Similarly, an AKE scheme* AKE *has security if for any PPT adversary* $\mathcal{A}$, *the following advantage is negligible:*

$$\mathsf{Adv}_{\mathsf{AKE},\mu,\ell,\mathcal{A}}(\lambda) := \max\{\Pr[\mathsf{Win}_{\mathsf{Auth}}], |\Pr[\mathsf{Exp}_{\mathsf{AKE},\mu,\ell,\mathcal{A}}(\lambda) \Rightarrow 1] - 1/2|\}.$$

Remark 4 (Perfect Forward Security and KCI Resistance). The security model of AKE supports (perfect) forward security (a.k.a. forward secrecy [12]) (characterized by "π_i^s is τ-tested and Pid_i^s is $\tilde{\tau}$-corrupt with $\tilde{\tau} > \tau$" in $\mathsf{Win}_{\mathsf{Ind}}$). That is, if P_i or its partner P_j has been corrupted at some moment, then the exchanged session keys completed before the corruption remain hidden from the adversary. Meanwhile, π_i^s may be corrupted before $\mathsf{Test}(i,s)$, which provides resistance to key-compromise impersonation (KCI) attacks [16].

4   Generic Construction of AKE and Its Security Proof

4.1   Construction

There are two building blocks in our AKE scheme, namely a $\mathsf{MU\text{-}EUF\text{-}CMA}^{\mathsf{corr}}$ secure signature scheme $\mathsf{SIG} = (\mathsf{SIG.Setup}, \mathsf{SIG.Gen}, \mathsf{SIG.Sign}, \mathsf{SIG.Ver})$ and an $\mathsf{IND\text{-}mCPA}^{\mathsf{reveal}}$ secure KEM scheme $\mathsf{KEM} = (\mathsf{KEM.Setup}, \mathsf{KEM.Gen}, \mathsf{KEM.}$ $\mathsf{Encap}, \mathsf{KEM.Decap})$ with diverse property. Our AKE scheme is shown in Fig. 6.

In our AKE scheme AKE, every party P_i will keep two arrays of static counters as its state, i.e., $\mathsf{st}_i = \{\mathsf{sctr}_{i,0}[j], \mathsf{sctr}_{i,1}[j]\}_{j \in [\mu]}$. Static counters $\mathsf{sctr}_{i,b}[j]$ are initialized to 0s and will record the serial number of protocol instances. Counter $\mathsf{sctr}_{i,0}[j]$ implies that P_i is the initiator and P_j is the responder, while $\mathsf{sctr}_{i,1}[j]$ implies P_j the initiator and P_i the responder. For example, $\mathsf{sctr}_{i,0}[j] = 3$ denotes that P_i has initialized 3 protocol instances with P_j, while $\mathsf{sctr}_{j,1}[i] = 5$ denotes that P_j, as a responder, has 5 protocol instances with P_i.

AKE.Setup(1^λ). $\mathsf{pp}_{\mathsf{SIG}} \leftarrow \mathsf{SIG.Setup}(1^\lambda)$, $\mathsf{pp}_{\mathsf{KEM}} \leftarrow \mathsf{KEM.Setup}(1^\lambda)$. Return $\mathsf{pp}_{\mathsf{AKE}} := (\mathsf{pp}_{\mathsf{SIG}}, \mathsf{pp}_{\mathsf{KEM}})$.
AKE.Gen$(\mathsf{pp}_{\mathsf{AKE}}, P_i)$. $(vk_i, sk_i) \leftarrow \mathsf{SIG.Gen}(\mathsf{pp}_{\mathsf{SIG}})$, $\mathsf{sctr}_{i,0}[u] := 0$; $\mathsf{sctr}_{i,1}[u] := 0$ for $u \in [\mu]$, $\mathsf{st}_i := \{\mathsf{sctr}_{i,0}[u], \mathsf{sctr}_{i,1}[u]\}_{u \in [\mu]}$. Return $((vk_i, sk_i), \mathsf{st}_i)$.
AKE.Protocol$(P_i \rightleftharpoons P_j)$. P_i has access to $\mathsf{res}_i = (sk_i, \mathsf{st}_i, \mathsf{pp}_{\mathsf{AKE}}, \mathsf{PKList} = \{vk_u\}_{u \in [\mu]})$ and P_j has access to $\mathsf{res}_j = (sk_j, \mathsf{st}_j, \mathsf{pp}_{\mathsf{AKE}}, \mathsf{PKList} = \{vk_u\}_{u \in [\mu]})$. As an initiator, P_i invokes $(pk_{\mathsf{KEM}}, sk_{\mathsf{KEM}}) \leftarrow \mathsf{KEM.Gen}(\mathsf{pp}_{\mathsf{KEM}})$, increases its counter with $\mathsf{sctr}_{i,0}[j] := \mathsf{sctr}_{i,0}[j] + 1$, and uses sk_i to sign a signature σ_1 of message $m_1 := (P_i, P_j, \mathsf{sctr}_{i,0}[j], pk_{\mathsf{KEM}})$. Then P_i sends (m_1, σ_1) to P_j.

After P_j obtains (m_1, σ_1), it will verify σ_1 with vk_i and check whether its own counter $\mathsf{sctr}_{j,1}[i]$ is less than ctr contained in $m_1 = (P_i, P_j, \mathsf{ctr}, pk_{\mathsf{KEM}})$. If everything goes well, then P_j takes m_1 as a valid message; otherwise P_j

returns (**reject**, $\emptyset$). If m_1 is valid, P_j stores (m_1, σ_1), encapsulates a key K via $(K, C) \leftarrow \mathsf{KEM.Encap}(pk_{\mathsf{KEM}})$ and synchronizes $\mathsf{sctr}_{j,1}[i] := \mathsf{ctr}$. Then P_j signs $m_1 \| m_2$ with $m_2 := (P_i, P_j, \mathsf{sctr}_{j,1}[i], C)$ via $\sigma_2 \leftarrow \mathsf{SIG.Sign}(sk_j, m_1 \| m_2)$ and sends (m_2, σ_2) to P_i. P_j will accept K as the session key with P_i by returning (**accept**, K).

After P_i obtains (m_2, σ_2), it will verify whether $(m_1 \| m_2, \sigma_2)$ is a valid message-signature pair w.r.t. vk_j. It also checks synchronization of its own counter $\mathsf{sctr}_{i,0}[j]$ and the counter ctr' in $m_2 = (P_i, P_j, \mathsf{ctr}', C)$, i.e., whether $\mathsf{sctr}_{i,0}[j] = \mathsf{ctr}'$. If everything goes well, P_i will take m_2 as a valid message and decapsulate the ciphertext C in m_2 to obtain $K' \leftarrow \mathsf{KEM.Decap}(sk_{\mathsf{KEM}}, C)$. P_i will accept K' as the session key with P_j by returning (**accept**, K'). If m_2 is invalid, P_i returns (**reject**, $\emptyset$).

Correctness. The correctness of AKE follows from the correctness of SIG & KEM and the fact of $\mathsf{sctr}_{i,0}[j] \geq \mathsf{sctr}_{j,1}[i]$. The increasing mode of counters in our AKE is as follows: the initiator P_i always increases the counter $\mathsf{sctr}_{i,0}[j]$, while the responder P_j synchronizes its counter $\mathsf{sctr}_{j,1}[i] := \mathsf{sctr}_{i,0}[j]$ only if the received message m_1 is valid. If m_1 is invalid, $\mathsf{sctr}_{j,1}[i]$ stays the same, so $\mathsf{sctr}_{i,0}[j] > \mathsf{sctr}_{j,1}[i]$. Consequently, $\mathsf{sctr}_{i,0}[j] \geq \mathsf{sctr}_{j,1}[i]$ holds in either case.

We can also construct a stateless AKE scheme $\mathsf{AKE}^{\mathsf{stateless}}$, where all states are removed from the AKE scheme. See Fig. 6.

Remark 5 (Synchronization). A failed execution of AKE does not lead to desynchronization. If m_1 or m_2 is lost (due to the network) or modified by active attacks, then the underlying session fails (i.e., P_i does not accept). In this scenario, it keeps that $\mathsf{sctr}_{i,0}[j] \geq \mathsf{sctr}_{j,1}[i]$, and P_i can launch a new session as the initiator latter and correctness (synchronization) still holds.

Remark 6 (PKI Setting). Our security model simply assumes that each party has access to the public key list. In practice, the users' public keys are registered via certificates from PKI. In some real-world protocols (like TLS [21]), public keys and certificates are also exchanged through the protocol (by sending $(m_1, vk_i, cert_i, \sigma_1)$ and $(m_2, vk_j, cert_j, \sigma_2)$). In this case, σ_1 is a signature of $(m_1, vk_i, cert_i)$, and so is σ_2. (Identities are suggested to be included in the signature to prevent unknown key-share (UKS) attacks [3].)

4.2 Security Proof

Before the proof, we define two sets Sent_i^s and Recv_i^s for π_i^s and event (4) for each $(i, s) \in [\mu] \times [\ell]$ in $\mathsf{Exp}_{\mathsf{AKE}, \mu, \ell, \mathcal{A}}^{\mathsf{strong}}(\lambda)$.

- Sent_i^s: The set collecting messages sent by π_i^s.
- Recv_i^s: The set collecting *valid* messages received and stored by π_i^s. We stress that invalid messages will be discarded and do not appear in Recv_i^s.

AKE.Setup(1^λ):
   $pp_{SIG} \leftarrow$ SIG.Setup(1^λ); $pp_{KEM} \leftarrow$ KEM.Setup(1^λ)
   Return $pp_{AKE} := (pp_{SIG}, pp_{KEM})$

AKE.Gen(pp_{AKE}, P_i):
   $(vk_i, sk_i) \leftarrow$ SIG.Gen(pp_{SIG})
   $st_i := \{sctr_{i,0}[u] := 0, sctr_{i,1}[u] := 0\}_{u \in [\mu]}$
   Return $((vk_i, sk_i),\ st_i\ )$

AKE.Protocol($P_i \rightleftharpoons P_j$):

$P_i(res_i)$
$res_i = (sk_i,\ st_i,\ pp_{AKE}, PKList = \{vk_u\}_{u \in [\mu]})$
   with $st_i = \{sctr_{i,0}[u], sctr_{i,1}[u]\}_{u \in [\mu]}$

$\Psi_i := \emptyset;\ k_i := \emptyset$
$(pk_{KEM}, sk_{KEM}) \leftarrow$ KEM.Gen(pp_{KEM})
$sctr_{i,0}[j] := sctr_{i,0}[j] + 1$
$m_1 := (P_i, P_j,\ sctr_{i,0}[j],\ pk_{KEM})$
$\sigma_1 \leftarrow$ SIG.Sign(sk_i, m_1)
//Update the state
$st_i := \{sctr_{i,0}[u], sctr_{i,1}[u]\}_{u \in [\mu]}$

      $\xrightarrow{\ (m_1, \sigma_1)\ }$

$P_j(res_j)$
$res_j = (sk_j,\ st_j,\ pp_{AKE}, PKList = \{vk_u\}_{u \in [\mu]})$
   with $st_j = \{sctr_{j,0}[u], sctr_{j,1}[u]\}_{u \in [\mu]}$

$\Psi_j := \emptyset;\ k_j := \emptyset$
Parse $m_1 = (P_i, P'_j,\ ctr,\ pk_{KEM})$
If NOT ($P'_j = P_j \wedge ctr > sctr_{j,1}[i]$
      $\wedge$ SIG.Ver(vk_i, m_1, σ_1) = 1):
   $\Psi_j = $ **reject** //m_1 is invalid
Else: //m_1 is valid
   $sctr_{j,1}[i] := ctr;$
   $(K, C) \leftarrow$ KEM.Encap(pk_{KEM});
   $m_2 := (P_i, P_j,\ sctr_{j,1}[i],\ C)$;
   $\sigma_2 \leftarrow$ SIG.Sign($sk_j, m_1 || m_2$);
   $k_j := K;\ \Psi_j = $ **accept**;
   //Update the state
   $st_j := \{sctr_{j,0}[u], sctr_{j,1}[u]\}_{u \in [\mu]}$

Parse $m_2 = (P'_i, P'_j,\ ctr',\ C)$

      $\xleftarrow{\ (m_2, \sigma_2)\ }$ Return (Ψ_j, k_j)

If NOT ($P'_i = P_i \wedge P'_j = P_j\ \wedge sctr_{i,0}[j] = ctr'$
      $\wedge$ SIG.Ver($vk_j, m_1 || m_2, \sigma_2$) = 1):
   $\Psi_i = $ **reject** //m_2 is invalid
Else: //m_2 is valid
   $K' \leftarrow$ KEM.Decap(sk_{KEM}, C);
   $k_i := K';\ \Psi_i = $ **accept**
Return (Ψ_i, k_i)

Fig. 6. Generic construction of AKE and AKE^{stateless} from KEM and SIG, with gray parts only in AKE.

Message Consistency. π_i^s *is message-consistent with* π_j^t *as a responder, if* π_i^s is a responder with $Recv_i^s = \{(m_1, \cdot)\} \neq \varnothing$ and π_j^t is an initiator with $Sent_j^t = \{(m_1, \cdot)\} \neq \varnothing$. π_i^s *is message-consistent with* π_j^t *as an initiator, if* π_i^s is an initiator with $Sent_i^s = \{(m_1, \cdot)\} \neq \varnothing$, $Recv_i^s = \{(m_2, \cdot)\} \neq \varnothing$ and π_j^t is a responder with $Recv_j^t = \{(m_1, \cdot)\} \neq \varnothing$, $Sent_j^t = \{(m_2, \cdot)\} \neq \varnothing$.

Define Event (4) for (i, s)**:** Let $j := Pid_i^s$. If π_i^s is responder, then $\nexists t \in [\ell]$ such that π_i^s is message-consistent with π_j^t as a responder; if π_i^s is an initiator, then $\nexists t \in [\ell]$ such that π_i^s is message-consistent with π_j^t as an initiator.

Claim 1. *For a specific pair (i, s) with $j := \mathsf{Pid}_i^s$, if $\neg(4)$ happens, there exists $t \in [\ell]$ such that π_i^s is not only message-consistent with π_j^t either as a responder or as an initiator, but also $\mathsf{Partner}(\pi_i^s \leftarrow \pi_j^t)$.*

Proof of Claim 1. If $\neg(4)$ happens, then π_i^s must be message-consistent with some π_j^t. Hence π_i^s and π_j^t are executing the protocol following the specification of AKE, and π_i^s must be accepted with k_i^s $(\neq \emptyset)$. According to the correctness of AKE, k_i^s must be the original key, so $\mathsf{Partner}(\pi_i^s \leftarrow \pi_j^t)$. ∎

Claim 2. *For a specific pair (i, s), if (1) π_i^s is accepted; (2) P_j with $j = \mathsf{Pid}_i^s$ is uncorrupted; and (4) happens, then π_i^s can always collect a valid message-signature pair (m, σ) from Sent_i^s and Recv_i^s, such that $\mathsf{SIG.Ver}(vk_j, m, \sigma) = 1$ with $j := \mathsf{Pid}_i^s$. Meanwhile, m must be different from any message m' signed by π_j^t for all $t \in [\ell]$.*

Proof of Claim 2. (1) means π_i^s is accepted, so $\mathsf{Recv}_i^s \neq \emptyset$ and $\mathsf{Sent}_i^s \neq \emptyset$. (2) says P_j is not corrupted yet, so π_j^t is accessible.

Case 1: Responder π_i^s. Let $\mathsf{Recv}_i^s = \{(m_1, \sigma_1)\}$, we have $\mathsf{SIG.Ver}(vk_j, m_1, \sigma_1) = 1$ since m_1 is valid. And for any π_j^t with $\mathsf{Sent}_j^t = \{(m_1', \sigma_1')\} \neq \emptyset$, we know that σ_1' is a signature of m_1' signed with sk_j. Meanwhile, (4) implies $m_1 \neq m_1'$.

Case 2: Initiator π_i^s. Let $\mathsf{Sent}_i^s = \{(m_1, \sigma_1)\}$ and $\mathsf{Recv}_i^s = \{(m_2, \sigma_2)\}$, we have $\mathsf{SIG.Ver}(vk_j, m_1 \| m_2, \sigma_2) = 1$ since m_2 is valid. And for any π_j^t with $\mathsf{Recv}_j^t \neq \emptyset$ and $\mathsf{Sent}_j^t \neq \emptyset$, let $\mathsf{Recv}_j^t = \{(m_1', \sigma_1')\}$ and $\mathsf{Sent}_j^t = \{(m_2', \sigma_2')\}$, then σ_2' is a signature of $m_1' \| m_2'$ signed with sk_j. Similarly, $m_1 \| m_2 \neq m_1' \| m_2'$ by (4). ∎

We analyse $\mathsf{Win}_{\mathsf{Auth}}$ first in the proof of AKE's strong security.

Theorem 3. *Suppose that SIG is $MU\text{-}EUF\text{-}CMA^{\mathsf{corr}}$ secure, KEM is IND-$mCPA^{\mathsf{reveal}}$ secure and has diverse property, then AKE has strong authentication. More precisely, for any PPT adversary $\mathcal{A}$ against AKE, there exists a PPT adversary $\mathcal{B}_{\mathsf{SIG}}$ such that $\Pr[\mathsf{Win}_{\mathsf{Auth}}] \leq 2\mathsf{Adv}_{\mathsf{SIG}, \mu, \mathcal{B}_{\mathsf{SIG}}}^{\mathsf{m\text{-}corr}}(\lambda) + 2^{-\Omega(\lambda)}$.*

Proof. In $\mathsf{Exp}_{\mathsf{AKE}, \mu, \ell, \mathcal{A}}^{\mathsf{strong}}(\lambda)$, $\mathcal{A}$ is allowed to ask Send, Corrupt, RegisterCorrupt, Reveal, and Test queries adaptively. According to the definition, $\mathsf{Win}_{\mathsf{Auth}}$ happens iff $\exists(i, s)$ such that $(1) \wedge (2) \wedge ((3.1) \vee (3.2) \vee (3.3))$ holds, where

(1) π_i^s is τ-accepted;

(2) P_j is $\hat{\tau}$-corrupted with $j := \mathsf{Pid}_i^s$ and $\hat{\tau} > \tau$;

(3.1) $\nexists t \in [\ell]$ s.t. $\mathsf{Partner}(\pi_i^s \leftarrow \pi_j^t)$, where $j := \mathsf{Pid}_i^s$;

(3.2) $\exists\, t \in [\ell], (j', t') \in [\mu] \times [\ell]$ with $(j, t) \neq (j', t')$ s.t. $\mathsf{Partner}(\pi_i^s \leftarrow \pi_j^t) \wedge \mathsf{Partner}(\pi_i^s \leftarrow \pi_{j'}^{t'})$, where $j := \mathsf{Pid}_i^s$;

(3.3) $\exists\, t \in [\ell], (i', s') \in [\mu] \times [\ell]$ with $(i, s) \neq (i', s')$ s.t. $\mathsf{Partner}(\pi_i^s \leftarrow \pi_j^t) \wedge \mathsf{Partner}(\pi_{i'}^{s'} \leftarrow \pi_j^t)$, where $j := \mathsf{Pid}_i^s$;

$$\Pr[\mathsf{Win_{Auth}}] = \Pr_{\exists(i,s)}[(1) \wedge (2) \wedge ((3.1) \vee (3.2) \vee (3.3))]$$

$$\leq \Pr_{\exists(i,s)}[(1) \wedge (2) \wedge (3.1)] + \Pr_{\exists(i,s)}[(1) \wedge (2) \wedge (3.2)] + \Pr_{\exists(i,s)}[(1) \wedge (2) \wedge (3.3)]. \quad (1)$$

Lemma 1. *There exists a PPT algorithm* $\mathcal{B}_{\mathsf{SIG}}$ *such that*

$$\Pr_{\exists(i,s)}[(1) \wedge (2) \wedge (3.1)] \leq \Pr_{\exists(i,s)}[(1) \wedge (2) \wedge (4)] \leq \mathsf{Adv}^{m\text{-}corr}_{SIG,\mu,\mathcal{B}_{SIG}}(\lambda).$$

Proof of Lemma 1. First we prove $\Pr_{\exists(i,s)}[(1) \wedge (2) \wedge (3.1)] \leq \Pr_{\exists(i,s)}[(1) \wedge (2) \wedge (4)]$. This can be done by a proof of $\Pr_{\exists(i,s)}[(1) \wedge (2) \wedge \neg(3.1)] \geq \Pr_{\exists(i,s)}[(1) \wedge (2) \wedge \neg(4)]$. For a specific pair (i,s), if $(1) \wedge (2) \wedge \neg(4)$ happens, according to Claim 1, there exists $t \in [\ell]$ such that $\mathsf{Partner}(\pi_i^s \leftarrow \pi_j^t)$, hence $(1) \wedge (2) \wedge \neg(3.1)$ must happen.

Next we prove that $\Pr_{\exists(i,s)}[(1) \wedge (2) \wedge (4)] \leq \mathsf{Adv}^{m\text{-}corr}_{SIG,\mu,\mathcal{B}_{SIG}}(\lambda)$.

To this end, we construct a PPT algorithm $\mathcal{B}_{\mathsf{SIG}}$ against the MU-EUF-CMA^{corr} security of SIG. Let $\mathcal{C}_{\mathsf{SIG}}$ be the challenger of $\mathcal{B}_{\mathsf{SIG}}$ in $\mathsf{Exp}^{m\text{-}corr}_{SIG,\mu,\mathcal{B}_{SIG}}(\lambda)$. $\mathcal{B}_{\mathsf{SIG}}$ gets a list of verification keys $\{vk_i\}_{i \in [\mu]}$ from $\mathcal{C}_{\mathsf{SIG}}$. $\mathcal{C}_{\mathsf{SIG}}$ also provides $\mathcal{B}_{\mathsf{SIG}}$ with $\mathsf{pp}_{\mathsf{SIG}}$, oracles $\mathcal{O}_{\mathrm{SIGN}}(\cdot,\cdot)$ and $\mathcal{O}_{\mathrm{CORR}}(\cdot)$, where $\mathcal{O}_{\mathrm{SIGN}}(i,m)$ returns a signature with $\sigma \leftarrow \mathsf{SIG.Sign}(sk_i, m)$, and $\mathcal{O}_{\mathrm{CORR}}(i)$ returns the signing key sk_i.

$\mathcal{B}_{\mathsf{SIG}}$ simulates the strong security experiment of AKE for $\mathcal{A}$. First $\mathcal{B}_{\mathsf{SIG}}$ invokes $\mathsf{pp}_{\mathsf{KEM}} \leftarrow \mathsf{KEM.Setup}(1^\lambda)$, sets $\mathsf{pp}_{\mathsf{AKE}} := (\mathsf{pp}_{\mathsf{SIG}}, \mathsf{pp}_{\mathsf{KEM}})$, and sends $\mathsf{pp}_{\mathsf{AKE}}$ and $\mathsf{PKList} := \{vk_i\}_{i \in [\mu]}$ to $\mathcal{A}$. Then $\mathcal{B}_{\mathsf{SIG}}$ answers the queries of $\mathcal{A}$ as follows.

- $\mathsf{Send}(i,s,j,\mathsf{msg})$: $\mathcal{B}_{\mathsf{SIG}}$ answers just like the challenger in $\mathsf{Exp}^{strong}_{AKE,\mu,\ell,\mathcal{A}}(\lambda)$. Whenever there is a message m to be signed with sk_i, $\mathcal{B}_{\mathsf{SIG}}$ asks its own oracle $\mathcal{O}_{\mathrm{SIGN}}(i,m)$ to get the corresponding signature. In this way, $\mathcal{B}_{\mathsf{SIG}}$ answers the Send query perfectly.
- $\mathsf{Corrupt}(i)$: Given i, $\mathcal{B}_{\mathsf{SIG}}$ asks its own oracle $\mathcal{O}_{\mathrm{CORR}}(i)$ to get sk_i. Then it returns sk_i to $\mathcal{A}$.
- $\mathsf{RegisterCorrupt}(u, vk_u)$: $\mathcal{B}_{\mathsf{SIG}}$ registers a new party P_u (0-corrupted) and adds vk_u to PKList. Then $\mathcal{B}_{\mathsf{SIG}}$ returns PKList.
- $\mathsf{Reveal}(i,s)$: $\mathcal{B}_{\mathsf{SIG}}$ answers just like the challenger in the experiment.
- $\mathsf{Test}(i,s)$: $\mathcal{B}_{\mathsf{SIG}}$ answers just like the challenger in the experiment.

In the simulation, $\mathcal{B}_{\mathsf{SIG}}$ checks whether $\exists(i,s)$ such that $(1) \wedge (2) \wedge (4)$ happens. If yes, there exists a τ-accepted oracle π_i^s with $j := \mathsf{Pid}_i^s$. Claim 2 tells us that a valid message-signature pair (m, σ) can be derived from $\mathsf{Sent}_i^s \cup \mathsf{Recv}_i^s = \{(m_1, \sigma_1), (m_2, \sigma_2)\}$, such that $\mathsf{SIG.Ver}(vk_j, m, \sigma) = 1$. $\mathcal{B}_{\mathsf{SIG}}$ then outputs (j, m, σ) as its forgery.

Now $\mathcal{B}_{\mathsf{SIG}}$ simulates the experiment perfectly. Event (2) implies that P_j is not corrupted yet, so $\mathcal{B}_{\mathsf{SIG}}$ never queries $\mathcal{O}_{\mathrm{CORR}}(j)$. And by Claim 2, m must be different from any message signed by π_j^t for all $t \in [\ell]$. Therefore, $\mathcal{B}_{\mathsf{SIG}}$ never queries $\mathcal{O}_{\mathrm{SIGN}}(j,m)$ and m is a fresh message. So if $(1) \wedge (2) \wedge (4)$ happens, $\mathcal{B}_{\mathsf{SIG}}$ wins in $\mathsf{Exp}^{m\text{-}corr}_{SIG,\mu,\mathcal{B}_{SIG}}(\lambda)$, thus $\Pr[(1) \wedge (2) \wedge (4)] \leq \mathsf{Adv}^{m\text{-}corr}_{SIG,\mu,\mathcal{B}_{SIG}}(\lambda)$. ∎

Lemma 2. $\Pr_{\exists(i,s)}[(1) \wedge (2) \wedge (3.2)] = 2^{-\Omega(\lambda)}$.

Proof of Lemma 2. For a specific pair (i, s), if event $(1) \wedge (2) \wedge (3.2)$ happens, then there exist at least two oracles to which π_i^s is partnered. Suppose π_i^s is partnered to two distinct oracles π_j^t and $\pi_{j'}^{t'}$.

Case 1: Responder π_i^s. Let pk_{KEM}, pk'_{KEM} be the public keys of KEM determined by the internal randomness of π_j^t and $\pi_{j'}^{t'}$. On the one hand, $\mathsf{Partner}(\pi_i^s \leftarrow \pi_j^t)$ means $k_i^s = K$, and the original key K is derived from $(K, C) \leftarrow \mathsf{KEM}.\mathsf{Encap}(pk_{\mathsf{KEM}}; r)$; on the other hand, $\mathsf{Partner}(\pi_i^s \leftarrow \pi_{j'}^{t'})$ means $k_i^s = K'$ and K' is derived from $(K', C') \leftarrow \mathsf{KEM}.\mathsf{Encap}(pk'_{\mathsf{KEM}}; r)$. Here r is the internal randomness chosen by π_i^s. This suggests $K = K'$. According to the diverse property of KEM, this occurs with probability $2^{-\Omega(\lambda)}$.

Case 2: Initiator π_i^s. Let pk_{KEM} be the public key of KEM determined by the internal randomness of π_i^s, and r, r' be the randomness chosen by π_j^t and $\pi_{j'}^{t'}$, respectively. Let $(K, C) \leftarrow \mathsf{KEM}.\mathsf{Encap}(pk_{\mathsf{KEM}}; r)$ and $(K', C') \leftarrow \mathsf{KEM}.\mathsf{Encap}(pk_{\mathsf{KEM}}; r')$. Since $\mathsf{Partner}(\pi_i^s \leftarrow \pi_j^t)$ and π_i^s is the initiator, we have $k_i^s = \mathsf{KEM}.\mathsf{Decap}(sk_{\mathsf{KEM}}, C)$. Similarly $\mathsf{Partner}(\pi_i^s \leftarrow \pi_{j'}^{t'})$ implies $k_i^s = \mathsf{KEM}.\mathsf{Decap}(sk_{\mathsf{KEM}}, C')$. By the correctness of KEM, we have $K = k_i^s = K'$, which occurs with probability $2^{-\Omega(\lambda)}$ by the diverse property of KEM.

There are $\mu\ell$ choices for (i, s) and $C_{\mu\ell}^2$ choices for (j, t) and (j', t'). By a union bound, $\Pr_{\exists(i,s)}[(1) \wedge (2) \wedge (3.2)] = \mu\ell \cdot C_{\mu\ell}^2 \cdot 2^{-\Omega(\lambda)} = 2^{-\Omega(\lambda)}$. ∎

Lemma 3. *If there exists an accepted π_i^s with $j := \mathsf{Pid}_i^s$, and P_j is uncorrupted when π_i^s accepts, then there exists a unique π_j^t, which π_i^s is partnered to and message-consistent with, except with probability* $\mathsf{Adv}_{\mathsf{SIG},\mu,\mathcal{B}_{\mathsf{SIG}}}^{\mathsf{m\text{-}corr}}(\lambda) + 2^{-\Omega(\lambda)}$, *i.e.,*
$$\Pr_{\exists(i,s)}[(1) \wedge (2)] - \Pr_{\exists(i,s)}[(1) \wedge (2) \wedge \neg(4) \wedge \neg(3.2)] \leq \mathsf{Adv}_{\mathsf{SIG},\mu,\mathcal{B}_{\mathsf{SIG}}}^{\mathsf{m\text{-}corr}}(\lambda) + 2^{-\Omega(\lambda)}.$$

Proof of Lemma 3. This is done by the total probability rule, Lemmas 1 and 2.

$$\Pr_{\exists(i,s)}[(1) \wedge (2)]$$
$$= \Pr_{\exists(i,s)}[(1) \wedge (2) \wedge (4)] + \Pr_{\exists(i,s)}[(1) \wedge (2) \wedge \neg(4) \wedge (3.2)] + \Pr_{\exists(i,s)}[(1) \wedge (2) \wedge \neg(4) \wedge \neg(3.2)]$$
$$\leq \Pr_{\exists(i,s)}[(1) \wedge (2) \wedge (4)] + \Pr_{\exists(i,s)}[(1) \wedge (2) \wedge (3.2)] + \Pr_{\exists(i,s)}[(1) \wedge (2) \wedge \neg(4) \wedge \neg(3.2)]$$
$$\leq \mathsf{Adv}_{\mathsf{SIG},\mu,\mathcal{B}_{\mathsf{SIG}}}^{\mathsf{m\text{-}corr}}(\lambda) + 2^{-\Omega(\lambda)} + \Pr_{\exists(i,s)}[(1) \wedge (2) \wedge \neg(4) \wedge \neg(3.2)]$$
∎

Lemma 4. $\Pr_{\exists(i,s)}[(1) \wedge (2) \wedge (3.3)] \leq \mathsf{Adv}_{\mathsf{SIG},\mu,\mathcal{B}_{\mathsf{SIG}}}^{\mathsf{m\text{-}corr}}(\lambda) + 2^{-\Omega(\lambda)}$.

Proof of Lemma 4. Suppose that there exists (i, s) such that $(1) \wedge (2) \wedge (3.3)$ holds. That is to say, $\exists (i, s), (i', s'), t$ with $(i, s) \neq (i', s')$ and $j := \mathsf{Pid}_i^s$, such that P_j is uncorrupted, $\mathsf{Partner}(\pi_i^s \leftarrow \pi_j^t)$ and $\mathsf{Partner}(\pi_{i'}^{s'} \leftarrow \pi_j^t)$.

According to Lemma 3, except with probability $\mathsf{Adv}_{\mathsf{SIG},\mu,\mathcal{B}_{\mathsf{SIG}}}^{\mathsf{m\text{-}corr}}(\lambda) + 2^{-\Omega(\lambda)}$, both π_i^s and $\pi_{i'}^{s'}$ must be uniquely partnered to and message-consistent with π_j^t. In this case, $\mathsf{Pid}_i^s = \mathsf{Pid}_{i'}^{s'} = j$. Meanwhile, the message sent by π_j^t contains a unique identity indicating its peer, so $i = i'$.

Given $i = i'$, we have the following fact. Suppose $s' < s$.

Fact 1. Let $\mathsf{st}_i^s = \{\mathsf{sctr}_{i,0}^s[u], \mathsf{sctr}_{i,1}^s[u]\}_{u \in [\mu]}$ and $\mathsf{st}_i^{s'} = \{\mathsf{sctr}_{i,0}^{s'}[u], \mathsf{sctr}_{i,1}^{s'}[u]\}_{u \in [\mu]}$ be the current states when π_i^s and $\pi_{i'}^{s'}$ are invoked. If $\Psi_i^{s'} = \mathbf{accept}$ and $\mathrm{Pid}_i^{s'} = j$, then $\mathsf{sctr}_{i,0}^{s'}[j] < \mathsf{sctr}_{i,0}^s[j]$ and $\mathsf{sctr}_{i,1}^{s'}[j] \leq \mathsf{sctr}_{i,1}^s[j]$.

We then show that the counters in states will make $(1) \wedge (2) \wedge (3.3)$ impossible.

Case 1: Responder π_i^s. Suppose that $((m_2, \sigma_2), \overline{\mathsf{st}}_i^{s'}, ...) \leftarrow \pi_i^{s'}((m_1, \sigma_1), ...)$, where $\overline{\mathsf{st}}_i^{s'} = \{\overline{\mathsf{sctr}}_{i,0}^{s'}[u], \overline{\mathsf{sctr}}_{i,1}^{s'}[u]\}_{u \in [\mu]}$. Let ctr be the counter contained in m_1, then $\mathsf{sctr}_{i,1}^{s'}[j] < \mathsf{ctr} = \overline{\mathsf{sctr}}_{i,1}^{s'}[j]$. By Fact 1 we have $\overline{\mathsf{sctr}}_{i,1}^{s'}[j] \leq \mathsf{sctr}_{i,1}^s[j]$. Consequently $\mathsf{ctr} \leq \mathsf{sctr}_{i,1}^s[j]$, which means $\Psi_i^s = \mathbf{reject}$. This contradicts to $\Psi_i^s = \mathbf{accept}$.

Case 2: Initiator π_i^s. Let (m_2, σ_2) be the message sent by π_j^t. Message m_2 contains a counter ctr and defines a unique partner. $\Psi_i^{s'} = \Psi_i^s = \mathbf{accept}$ means $\mathsf{sctr}_{i,0}^{s'}[j] + 1 = \mathsf{sctr}_{i,0}^s[j] + 1 = \mathsf{ctr}$. By Fact 1 we have $\mathsf{sctr}_{i,0}^{s'}[j] < \mathsf{sctr}_{i,0}^s[j]$, and this leads to a contradiction. ∎

Theorem 3 follows from Eq. (1), Lemmas 1, 2 and 4. □

Theorem 4. *Suppose that* SIG *is MU-EUF-CMA^{corr} secure,* KEM *is IND-mCPA^{reveal} secure and has diverse property, then* AKE *is strongly secure. More precisely, for any PPT adversary $\mathcal{A}$ against* AKE*, there exist PPT adversaries $\mathcal{B}_{\mathsf{SIG}}$ and $\mathcal{B}_{\mathsf{KEM}}$ such that* $\mathsf{Adv}_{\mathsf{AKE},\mu,\ell,\mathcal{A}}^{\mathsf{strong}}(\lambda) \leq 2\mathsf{Adv}_{\mathsf{SIG},\mu,\mathcal{B}_{\mathsf{SIG}}}^{\mathsf{m\text{-}corr}}(\lambda) + \mathsf{Adv}_{\mathsf{KEM},\mu\ell,\mathcal{B}_{\mathsf{KEM}}}^{\mathsf{r\text{-}m\text{-}cpa}}(\lambda) + 2^{-\Omega(\lambda)}$.

Proof. We prove it by three games, Game 0, Game 1 and Game 2.

Game 0. Game 0 is the original game. Thus

$$\Pr[\mathsf{Exp}_{\mathsf{AKE},\mu,\ell,\mathcal{A}}^{\mathsf{strong}}(\lambda) \Rightarrow 1] = \Pr[\mathbf{Game\ 0} \Rightarrow 1]. \tag{2}$$

Game 1. Game 1 is the same as Game 0 except that the experiment will abort if bad happens, where $\mathsf{bad} := \exists(i, s)\ ((1) \wedge (2) \wedge (4))$. In words, bad means there exists an accepted π_i^s such that π_i^s is not message-consistent with any oracle π_j^t. If bad does not happen, Game 0 is identical to Game 1. By the difference lemma and Lemma 1, we have

$$|\Pr[\mathbf{Game\ 1} \Rightarrow 1] - \Pr[\mathbf{Game\ 0} \Rightarrow 1]| \leq \Pr[\mathsf{bad}] \leq \mathsf{Adv}_{\mathsf{SIG},\mu,\mathcal{B}_{\mathsf{SIG}}}^{\mathsf{m\text{-}corr}}(\lambda). \tag{3}$$

Game 2. Game 2 is the same as Game 1 except that D-Partner(π_i^s, π_j^t) in the experiment is changed to a new one, where D-Partner(π_i^s, π_j^t) is the algorithm to check whether π_i^s is partnered to π_j^t.

D-Partner(π_i^s, π_j^t) in Game 1	D-Partner(π_i^s, π_j^t) in Game 2

Initiator π_i^s:
    If $k_i^s = \mathsf{K}(\pi_i^s, \pi_j^t) \neq \emptyset$: Return 1
Responder π_i^s:
    If $k_i^s = \mathsf{K}(\pi_j^t, \pi_i^s) \neq \emptyset$: Return 1
Else: Return 0
	If $\Psi_i^s \neq \mathbf{accept}$: Return 0
	If π_i^s is message-consistent with π_j^t
	    as a responder: Return 1
	If π_i^s is message-consistent with π_j^t
	    as an initiator: Return 1
	Else: Return 0

In Game 2, deciding $\mathsf{Partner}(\pi_i^s \leftarrow \pi_j^t)$ is implemented by simply checking the message consistency between π_i^s and π_j^t. It gets rid of computation of original keys as in Game 1, and this is a preparation for the proof of Lemma 5.

We then prove that the new algorithm D-Partner(π_i^s, π_j^t) has the same functionality as the old one except with probability $2^{-\Omega(\lambda)}$.

Note that D-Partner(π_i^s, π_j^t) is only invoked in testing $(1') \wedge (2') \wedge (3')$. $(1')$ implies the existence of an accepted π_i^s with $j := \mathsf{Pid}_i^s$ and P_j uncorrupted. If bad does not happens, according to Claim 1, there exists $t \in [\ell]$ s.t. $\mathsf{Partner}(\pi_i^s \leftarrow \pi_j^t)$ and π_i^s is message-consistent with π_j^t. So, if π_i^s is uniquely partnered, then $\mathsf{Partner}(\pi_i^s \leftarrow \pi_j^t)$ if and only if π_i^s is message-consistent with π_j^t. Hence, Game 1 and Game 2 are the same unless π_i^s is partnered to multiple oracles, which happens with probability no more than $2^{-\Omega(\lambda)}$ by Lemma 2. Thus,

$$|\Pr[\mathbf{Game\,2} \Rightarrow 1] - \Pr[\mathbf{Game\,1} \Rightarrow 1]| \leq 2^{-\Omega(\lambda)}. \qquad (4)$$

Lemma 5. *There exists a PPT algorithm $\mathcal{B}_{\mathsf{KEM}}$ such that*

$$|\Pr[\mathbf{Game\,2} \Rightarrow 1] - 1/2| \leq \mathsf{Adv}^{\mathsf{r\text{-}m\text{-}cpa}}_{\mathsf{KEM},\mu\ell,\mathcal{B}_{\mathsf{KEM}}}(\lambda). \qquad (5)$$

Proof of Lemma 5. Let (i^*, s^*, b^*) be the output of $\mathcal{A}$. For simplicity, define $(i, s, b^*) := (i^*, s^*, b^*)$ and $j := \mathsf{Pid}_i^s$. Recall that $\mathsf{Exp}^{\mathsf{strong}}_{\mathsf{AKE},\mu,\ell,\mathcal{A}}(\lambda)$ outputs 1 iff $b^* = b_i^s$ under the following conditions.

$(1')$ π_i^s is τ-tested and Pid_i^s is $\tilde{\tau}$-corrupt with $\tilde{\tau} > \tau$.
$(2')$ π_i^s is ∞-revealed.
$(3')$ If $\exists t \in [\ell]$ s.t. π_i^s is partnered to π_j^t, then π_j^t is ∞-revealed and ∞-tested.

Now we construct a PPT algorithm $\mathcal{B}_{\mathsf{KEM}}$ to break KEM's IND-mCPA[reveal] security (Definition 5) by simulating Game 2 for $\mathcal{A}$. $\mathcal{B}_{\mathsf{KEM}}$ first obtains from its challenger $\mathcal{C}_{\mathsf{KEM}}$ the public parameter $\mathsf{pp}_{\mathsf{KEM}}$ of KEM and a list of $\mu\ell$ public keys $\mathsf{PKList}_{\mathsf{KEM}} := \{pk_1, pk_2, ..., pk_{\mu\ell}\}$. Meanwhile, $\mathcal{B}_{\mathsf{KEM}}$ has access to two oracles $\mathcal{O}_{\mathrm{ENCAP}}(\cdot)$ and $\mathcal{O}_{\mathrm{REVEAL}}(\cdot, \cdot)$. See Fig. 7 for $\mathcal{B}_{\mathsf{KEM}}$'s simulation of Game 2.

In the simulation, to send the first message (m_1, σ_1) for π_i^s, $\mathcal{B}_{\mathsf{KEM}}$ can always use public key $pk_{(i-1)\mu+s} \in \mathsf{PKList}_{\mathsf{KEM}}$ as pk_{KEM} in m_1 and sign m_1 with sk_i. Hence $\mathcal{B}_{\mathsf{KEM}}$'s simulation of (m_1, σ_1) is perfect. After receiving a message (m_1, σ_1), to generate (m_2, σ_2) for π_j^t, $\mathcal{B}_{\mathsf{KEM}}$ invokes its oracle $\mathcal{O}_{\mathrm{ENCAP}}(\cdot)$ to generate (K, C) if $pk_{\mathsf{KEM}} \in \mathsf{PKList}_{\mathsf{KEM}}$ (pk_{KEM} is in m_1). In this case, $\mathcal{B}_{\mathsf{KEM}}$ stores $(pk_{\mathsf{KEM}}, K, C)$ into $\overline{\mathsf{CList}}$, but $\mathcal{B}_{\mathsf{KEM}}$ cannot determine the session key k_j^t, since K might be random with half probability. So $\mathcal{B}_{\mathsf{KEM}}$ sets $k_j^t := *$. If

$\mathcal{B}_{\mathsf{KEM}}^{\mathcal{O}_{\mathrm{ENCAP}}(\cdot),\,\mathcal{O}_{\mathrm{REVEAL}}(\cdot,\cdot)}(1^\lambda, \mu, \ell, \mathsf{pp}_{\mathsf{KEM}}, \mathsf{PKList}_{\mathsf{KEM}})$:

//Simulation of **Game 2**

$\mathsf{pp}_{\mathsf{SIG}} \leftarrow \mathsf{SIG.Setup}(1^\lambda)$; $\mathsf{pp}_{\mathsf{AKE}} := (\mathsf{pp}_{\mathsf{SIG}}, \mathsf{pp}_{\mathsf{KEM}})$

For $i \in [\mu]$:

  $(vk_i, sk_i) \leftarrow \mathsf{SIG.Gen}(\mathsf{pp}_{\mathsf{SIG}})$;

  $\mathsf{st}_i := \{\mathsf{sctr}_{i,0}[u] := 0, \mathsf{sctr}_{i,1}[u] := 0\}_{u \in [\mu]}$;

  $crp_i := 0$ //Corruption variable

For $(i,s) \in [\mu] \times [\ell]$:

  $b_i^s \xleftarrow{\$} \{0,1\}$; $\mathsf{Pid}_i^s := k_i^s := \Psi_i^s := \emptyset$; $\mathsf{Sent}_i^s := \mathsf{Recv}_i^s := \varnothing$;

  $\mathsf{Aflag}_i^s := 0$; $\mathsf{Tflag}_i^s := 0$;

  //Whether Pid_i^s is corrupted when π_i^s is accepted/tested

  $T_i^s := 0$; $R_i^s := 0$ //Test & Reveal variables

$\mathsf{PKList} := \{vk_i\}_{i \in [\mu]}$; $\overline{\mathsf{CList}} := \varnothing$

$(i^*, s^*, b^*) \leftarrow \mathcal{A}^{\mathcal{O}_{\mathsf{AKE}}(\cdot)}(\mathsf{pp}_{\mathsf{AKE}}, \mathsf{PKList})$

$\mathcal{B}_{\mathsf{KEM}}$ aborts if bad happens during the simulation

If (i^*, s^*) satisfies $(1') \wedge (2') \wedge (3')$:

  Parses $\overline{\mathsf{CList}}[i^*, s^*] = (pk_{\mathsf{KEM}}, C, K)$;

  Return $(pk_{\mathsf{KEM}}, C, b^*)$

$\mathcal{O}_{\mathsf{AKE}}(\text{query})$:

If query=$\mathsf{Send}(i, s, j, \mathsf{msg} = \top)$: //sim. of initiator π_i^s

  $pk_{\mathsf{KEM}} := pk_{(i-1)\mu+s}$

  $\mathsf{Pid}_i^s := j$; $\mathsf{sctr}_{i,0}[j] := \mathsf{sctr}_{i,0}[j] + 1$

  $m_1 = (i, \mathsf{Pid}_i^s, \mathsf{sctr}_{i,0}[j], pk_{\mathsf{KEM}})$; $\sigma_1 \leftarrow \mathsf{SIG.Sign}(sk_i, m_1)$

  $\mathsf{Sent}_i^s := \{(m_1, \sigma_1)\}$

  Return (m_1, σ_1)

If query=$\mathsf{Send}(j, t, i, \mathsf{msg} \neq \top)$: //sim. of responder π_j^t

  Parse $\mathsf{msg} = (m_1 = (i, \mathsf{Pid}_i^s, \mathsf{ctr}, pk_{\mathsf{KEM}}), \sigma_1)$

  If Not $(\mathsf{Pid}_i^s = j \wedge \mathsf{ctr} > \mathsf{sctr}_{j,1}[i] \wedge \mathsf{SIG.Ver}(vk_i, m_1, \sigma_1) = 1)$:

    $\Psi_j^t := \mathbf{reject}$; Return $\perp$

  $\mathsf{Pid}_j^t := i$; $\mathsf{sctr}_{j,1}[i] := \mathsf{ctr}$

  If $pk_{\mathsf{KEM}} \in \mathsf{PKList}_{\mathsf{KEM}}$:

    $(K, C) \leftarrow \mathcal{O}_{\mathrm{ENCAP}}(pk_{\mathsf{KEM}})$;

    $\overline{\mathsf{CList}}[j, t] := (pk_{\mathsf{KEM}}, C, K)$; $k_j^t := *$

  If $pk_{\mathsf{KEM}} \notin \mathsf{PKList}_{\mathsf{KEM}}$:

    $(K, C) \leftarrow \mathsf{KEM.Encap}(pk_{\mathsf{KEM}})$; $k_j^t := K$

  $\Psi_j^t := \mathbf{accept}$; $\mathsf{Recv}_j^t := \{(m_1, \sigma_1)\}$

  If $crp_i = 1$: $\mathsf{Aflag}_j^t := 1$

  $m_2 := (\mathsf{Pid}_j^t, j, \mathsf{sctr}_{j,1}[i], C)$; $\sigma_2 \leftarrow \mathsf{SIG.Sign}(sk_j, m_1 || m_2)$

  $\mathsf{Sent}_j^t := \{(m_2, \sigma_2)\}$

  Return (m_2, σ_2)

$\mathcal{O}_{\mathsf{AKE}}(\text{query})$:

If query=$\mathsf{Send}(i, s, j, \mathsf{msg} \neq \top)$: //sim. of initiator π_i^s

  Parse $\mathsf{msg} = (m_2 = (\mathsf{Pid}_j^t, j, \mathsf{ctr}, C), \sigma_2)$

  Choose $(m_1, \sigma_1) \in \mathsf{Sent}_i^s$, $pk_{\mathsf{KEM}} \in m_1$

  If NOT $(\mathsf{Pid}_j^t = i \wedge \mathsf{Pid}_i^s = j \wedge \mathsf{ctr} = \mathsf{sctr}_{i,0}[j] \wedge \mathsf{SIG.Ver}(vk_j, m_1 || m_2, \sigma_2) = 1)$:

    $\Psi_i^s := \mathbf{reject}$; Return $\perp$

  //$pk_{\mathsf{KEM}} \in \mathsf{PKList}_{\mathsf{KEM}}$, since m_1 is generated by π_i^s

  If $\exists t \in [\ell]$ s.t. $\overline{\mathsf{CList}}[j, t] = (pk_{\mathsf{KEM}}, C, K)$ for some K:

    $\overline{\mathsf{CList}}[i, s] := (pk_{\mathsf{KEM}}, C, K)$; $k_i^s := *$

  Else:

    $K' \leftarrow \mathcal{O}_{\mathrm{REVEAL}}(pk_{\mathsf{KEM}}, C)$; $k_i^s := K'$

  $\Psi_i^s := \mathbf{accept}$; $\mathsf{Recv}_i^s := \{(m_2, \sigma_2)\}$

  If $crp_j = 1$: $\mathsf{Aflag}_i^s := 1$

  Return $\emptyset$

If query=$\mathsf{Corrupt}(i)$:

  $crp_i := 1$; Return sk_i

If query=$\mathsf{RegisterCorrupt}(u, pk_u)$:

  If $u \in [\mu]$: Return $\perp$

  $\mathsf{PKList} := \mathsf{PKList} \cup \{pk_u\}$; Return PKList

If query=$\mathsf{Reveal}(i, s)$:

  If $\Psi_i^s \neq \mathbf{accept}$: Return $\perp$

  $R_i^s := 1$

  If $k_i^s \neq *$: Return k_i^s

  If $k_i^s = *$: Parse $\overline{\mathsf{CList}}[i, s] = (pk_{\mathsf{KEM}}, C, K)$;

    $K' \leftarrow \mathcal{O}_{\mathrm{REVEAL}}(pk_{\mathsf{KEM}}, C)$; Return K'

If query=$\mathsf{Test}(i, s)$:

  If $\Psi_i^s \neq \mathbf{accept}$: Return $\perp$

  $j := \mathsf{Pid}_i^s$; $T_i^s := 1$

  If $crp_j = 1$: $\mathsf{Tflag}_i^s := 1$

  If $k_i^s \neq *$: $k_0 := k_i^s$; $k_1 \xleftarrow{\$} \mathcal{K}$; Return $k_{b_i^s}$

  Parse $\overline{\mathsf{CList}}[i, s] = (pk_{\mathsf{KEM}}, C, K)$;

  If $k_i^s = * \wedge \exists t \in [\ell]$ s.t. ($\mathsf{D\text{-}Partner}(\pi_i^s, \pi_j^t) = 1 \wedge T_j^t = 1$):

    //$\mathcal{A}$ has asked $\mathsf{Test}(j, t)$ where $\mathsf{Partner}(\pi_i^s \leftarrow \pi_j^t)$

    $K' \leftarrow \mathcal{O}_{\mathrm{REVEAL}}(pk_{\mathsf{KEM}}, C)$;

    $k_0 := K'$; $k_1 \xleftarrow{\$} \mathcal{K}$; Return $k_{b_i^s}$

  Else: Return K

Fig. 7. $\mathcal{B}_{\mathsf{KEM}}$'s simulation of **Game 2**.

$pk_{\mathsf{KEM}} \notin \mathsf{PKList}_{\mathsf{KEM}}$, then m_1 must be forged by $\mathcal{A}$. In this case, $\mathcal{B}_{\mathsf{KEM}}$ can invoke $(K, C) \leftarrow \mathsf{KEM.Encap}(pk_{\mathsf{KEM}})$ and set $k_j^t := K$. Thus in either case, $\mathcal{B}_{\mathsf{KEM}}$'s simulation of (m_2, σ_2) for π_j^t is perfect, just like Game 2 does.

After receiving the last message (m_2, σ_2) for π_i^s, $\mathcal{B}_{\mathsf{KEM}}$ retrieves pk_{KEM} from m_1 and C from m_2 ($pk_{\mathsf{KEM}} \in \mathsf{PKList}_{\mathsf{KEM}}$ since m_1 is generated by $\mathcal{B}_{\mathsf{KEM}}$). If $(pk_{\mathsf{KEM}}, C, K) \in \overline{\mathsf{CList}}$ for some K, then $\mathcal{B}_{\mathsf{KEM}}$ has asked $\mathcal{O}_{\mathrm{ENCAP}}(\cdot)$ to generate (K, C) w.r.t pk_{KEM}, so $\mathcal{B}_{\mathsf{KEM}}$ sets $k_i^s := *$. Otherwise, C is forged by $\mathcal{A}$. In this case, $\mathcal{B}_{\mathsf{KEM}}$ uses its oracle $\mathcal{O}_{\mathrm{REVEAL}}(\cdot, \cdot)$ to reveal the real key K', and sets $k_i^s := K'$. At last, $\mathcal{B}_{\mathsf{KEM}}$ returns $\emptyset$ to $\mathcal{A}$ as Game 2 does.

$\mathcal{B}_{\mathsf{KEM}}$'s simulation makes sure that if $\Psi_i^s = \mathbf{accept}$ and $k_i^s \neq *$, then k_i^s must be the real session key. Hence, upon a $\mathsf{Reveal}(i, s)$ query, $\mathcal{B}_{\mathsf{KEM}}$ will return k_i^s if $k_i^s \neq *$. Otherwise, it will ask $\mathcal{O}_{\mathrm{REVEAL}}(\cdot, \cdot)$ to get the real key and return it to $\mathcal{A}$. Therefore, $\mathcal{B}_{\mathsf{KEM}}$'s answers to Reveal queries are perfect.

Upon a $\mathsf{Test}(i,s)$ query, if $k_i^s \neq *$, then k_i^s is the real session key. If $k_i^s = *$ and $\mathcal{A}$ has asked $\mathsf{Test}(j,t)$, where $\mathsf{Partner}(\pi_i^s \leftarrow \pi_j^t)$, then $\mathcal{B}_{\mathsf{KEM}}$ asks $\mathcal{O}_{\mathrm{REVEAL}}(\cdot,\cdot)$ to get the real session key. In either case, $\mathcal{B}_{\mathsf{KEM}}$ can answer Test queries with the help of the real session key, exactly like Game 2 does. We stress that $\mathcal{B}_{\mathsf{KEM}}$ checks partnership with message consistency, instead of computing the original key. If $k_i^s = *$ and there is no such a partner which has been tested, $\mathcal{B}_{\mathsf{KEM}}$ retrieves $\overline{\mathsf{CList}}[i,s] = (pk_{\mathsf{KEM}}, C, K)$ associated with π_i^s, and returns K to $\mathcal{A}$. This simulation is also perfect, since K is either a real key or a random key with half probability.

Given $\mathcal{A}$'s outputs (i^*, s^*, b^*), let $(i,s,b^*) := (i^*, s^*, b^*)$ and $j := \mathsf{Pid}_i^s$. Condition $(1')$ implies that P_j is uncorrupted when π_i^s is tested (hence accepted). Thus there exists a unique π_j^t to which π_i^s is partnered, and this implies the existence of $\overline{\mathsf{CList}}[i,s] = (pk_{\mathsf{KEM}}, C, K)$. Conditions $(2') \wedge (3')$ said that π_i^s, π_j^t are ∞-revealed, and π_j^t is ∞-tested. Hence $\mathcal{B}_{\mathsf{KEM}}$ has never asked $\mathcal{O}_{\mathrm{REVEAL}}(\cdot,\cdot)$ for (pk_{KEM}, C). Consequently, $\mathcal{B}_{\mathsf{KEM}}$ implicitly sets $b_i^s = \beta$ where β is the random coin chosen by $\mathcal{C}_{\mathsf{KEM}}$. Thus $\mathcal{B}_{\mathsf{KEM}}$ wins as long as $b^* = b_i^s$, and Lemma 5 follows.   ∎

By Eqs. (2), (3), (4), (5), we have

$$\left| \Pr[\mathsf{Exp}_{\mathsf{AKE},\mu,\ell,\mathcal{A}}^{\mathsf{strong}}(\lambda) \Rightarrow 1] - 1/2 \right| \leq \mathsf{Adv}_{\mathsf{SIG},\mu,\mathcal{B}_{\mathsf{SIG}}}^{\mathsf{m\text{-}corr}}(\lambda) + \mathsf{Adv}_{\mathsf{KEM},\mu\ell,\mathcal{B}_{\mathsf{KEM}}}^{\mathsf{r\text{-}m\text{-}cpa}}(\lambda) + 2^{-\Omega(\lambda)}.$$

$$\mathsf{Adv}_{\mathsf{AKE},\mu,\ell,\mathcal{A}}^{\mathsf{strong}}(\lambda) := \max\{\Pr[\mathsf{Win}_{\mathsf{Auth}}], |\Pr[\mathsf{Exp}_{\mathsf{AKE},\mu,\ell,\mathcal{A}}^{\mathsf{strong}}(\lambda) \Rightarrow 1] - 1/2|\}$$
$$\leq 2\mathsf{Adv}_{\mathsf{SIG},\mu,\mathcal{B}_{\mathsf{SIG}}}^{\mathsf{m\text{-}corr}}(\lambda) + \mathsf{Adv}_{\mathsf{KEM},\mu\ell,\mathcal{B}_{\mathsf{KEM}}}^{\mathsf{r\text{-}m\text{-}cpa}}(\lambda) + 2^{-\Omega(\lambda)}. \qquad \square$$

Note that in the strong security of AKE, only the proof of $\Pr[(1) \wedge (2) \wedge (3.3)] \leq \mathsf{Adv}_{\mathsf{SIG},\mu,\mathcal{B}_{\mathsf{SIG}}}^{\mathsf{m\text{-}corr}}(\lambda) + 2^{-\Omega(\lambda)}$ in Lemma 4 makes use of the non-decreasing property of counters in states. For our stateless AKE scheme $\mathsf{AKE}^{\mathsf{stateless}}$, the normal (not strong) security requirement (see Fig. 5) does not need $(1) \wedge (2) \wedge (3.3)$. Therefore, $\mathsf{AKE}^{\mathsf{stateless}}$ can be proved to be secure, and the security proof almost verbatim follows that of Theorems 3 and 4. Hence we have the following corollary.

Corollary 1. *Suppose that* SIG *is MU-EUF-CMA*^{corr} *secure,* KEM *is IND-mCPA*^{reveal} *secure and has diverse property, then our stateless AKE scheme* $\mathsf{AKE}^{\mathsf{stateless}}$ *is secure. More precisely, for any PPT adversary* $\mathcal{A}$ *against* $\mathsf{AKE}^{\mathsf{stateless}}$, *there exist PPT adversaries* $\mathcal{B}_{\mathsf{SIG}}$ *and* $\mathcal{B}_{\mathsf{KEM}}$ *such that*

$$\mathsf{Adv}_{\mathsf{AKE},\mu,\ell,\mathcal{A}}^{\mathsf{stateless}}(\lambda) \leq \mathsf{Adv}_{\mathsf{SIG},\mu,\mathcal{B}_{\mathsf{SIG}}}^{\mathsf{m\text{-}corr}}(\lambda) + \mathsf{Adv}_{\mathsf{KEM},\mu\ell,\mathcal{B}_{\mathsf{KEM}}}^{\mathsf{r\text{-}m\text{-}cpa}}(\lambda) + 2^{-\Omega(\lambda)}.$$

5 Instantiations of AKE with Tight Security

In this section, we present specific constructions of AKE by instantiating the two building blocks KEM and SIG, where KEM has tight IND-mCPA^{reveal} security and diverse property, and SIG has tight MU-EUF-CMA^{corr} security.

5.1 Instantiations of KEM with Tight IND-mCPA^{reveal} Security

We present two KEM schemes. The first one is derived from the twin ElGamal encryption [5] based on the CDH assumption in the RO model. The other is derived from [14] and based on the MDDH assumption in the standard model.

KEM$_{\text{st2DH}}$ from the st2DH Assumption in the RO Model.   Now   we present KEM$_{\text{st2DH}}$, and prove that its IND-mCPA^{reveal} security can be tightly reduced to the st2DH assumption [5], which is in turn to the CDH assumption by Theorem 2, in the random oracle model. See Fig. 8

KEM.Setup(1^λ):	KEM.Encap(pk):
$(\mathbb{G}, q, g) \leftarrow \text{GGen}(1^\lambda)$	Parse $pk = (X_1, X_2)$
$H : \mathbb{G}^2 \to \mathcal{K}$	$y \xleftarrow{\$} \mathbb{Z}_q;\ C := g^y$
Return $\text{pp}_{\text{KEM}} := (\mathbb{G}, q, g, H)$	$K := H(X_1, X_2, C, X_1^y, X_2^y)$
	Return (K, C)
KEM.Gen(pp_{KEM}):	
$x_1, x_2 \xleftarrow{\$} \mathbb{Z}_q$	KEM.Decap(sk, C):
$X_1 := g^{x_1};\ X_2 := g^{x_2}$	Parse $sk = (x_1, x_2)$
$pk := (X_1, X_2);\ sk := (x_1, x_2)$	$K' := H(X_1, X_2, C, C^{x_1}, C^{x_2})$
Return (pk, sk)	Return K'

Fig. 8. KEM$_{\text{st2DH}}$ from the strong twin DH assumption.

Correctness. Correctness is due to $((g^{x_1})^y, (g^{x_2})^y) = ((g^y)^{x_1}, (g^y)^{x_2})$.

Theorem 5. *The KEM scheme* KEM$_{\text{st2DH}}$ *is IND-mCPA^{reveal} secure in the random oracle model. More precisely, for any PPT adversary $\mathcal{A}$ against the IND-mCPA^{reveal} security, there exists a PPT adversary $\mathcal{B}$ solving the st2DH problem such that* $\text{Adv}^{\text{r-m-cpa}}_{\text{KEM}_{\text{st2DH}}, \theta, \mathcal{A}}(\lambda) \leq \text{Adv}^{\text{st2DH}}_{\mathbb{G}, \mathcal{B}}(\lambda) \leq \text{Adv}^{\text{CDH}}_{\mathbb{G}}(\lambda) + 2^{-\Omega(\lambda)}$.

Proof Sketch. We construct a PPT algorithm $\mathcal{B}$ that simulates $\text{Exp}^{\text{r-m-cpa}}_{\text{KEM}_{\text{st2DH}}, \theta, \mathcal{A}}(\lambda)$ to the KEM adversary $\mathcal{A}$, and uses $\mathcal{A}$'s ability to solve the st2DH problem. Due to the space limitation, we sketch the high-level idea of the proof in the single user setting. The formal proof can be found in our full version in ePrint.

Let (g^{x_1}, g^{x_2}, g^y) be the tuple needed to be solved. Intuitively $\mathcal{B}$ will embed (g^{x_1}, g^{x_2}) to the public key, and embed g^y to the challenge ciphertext $C = g^{y+b}$. If $\mathcal{A}$ never asked $H(g^{x_1}, g^{x_2}, C, C^{x_1}, C^{x_2})$, then $k = H(g^{x_1}, g^{x_2}, C, C^{x_1}, C^{x_2})$ is truly random and $\mathcal{A}$ has no advantage at all. If $\mathcal{A}$ ever asked $H(g^{x_1}, g^{x_2}, C, C^{x_1}, C^{x_2})$, then $\mathcal{B}$ can find the answer $(C^{x_1}/g^b, C^{x_2}/g^b)$ to the st2DH problem. The difficult part of $\mathcal{B}$'s simulation is the reveal of encapsulated key $k = H(g^{x_1}, g^{x_2}, C, C^{x_1}, C^{x_2})$ to $\mathcal{A}$, when the secret key (x_1, x_2) and $\log_g C$ are unknown. This difficulty is circumvented by $\mathcal{B}$'s simulation of random oracle $H(\cdot)$ and the decision oracle 2DH. If $\mathcal{A}$ has not asked $H(g^{x_1}, g^{x_2}, C, C^{x_1}, C^{x_2})$ before, $\mathcal{B}$ samples a random key k and implicitly set

$H(g^{x_1}, g^{x_2}, C, C^{x_1}, C^{x_2}) = k$. If $\mathcal{A}$ has asked $H(g^{x_1}, g^{x_2}, C, C^{x_1}, C^{x_2})$, $\mathcal{B}$ must have stored item $((g^{x_1}, g^{x_2}, C, C^{x_1}, C^{x_2}), k)$ in the hash list. Then $\mathcal{B}$ can resort to the decision oracle $2\mathsf{DH}(g^{x_1}, g^{x_2}, C, C^{x_1}, C^{x_2}) = 1$ to locate this item, and return k to $\mathcal{A}$. In this way, $\mathcal{B}$ successfully simulates the reveal oracle to $\mathcal{A}$.

The diverse property of $\mathsf{KEM_{st2DH}}$ is proved in our full version.

$\mathsf{KEM_{MDDH}}$ from the MDDH Assumption in the Standard Model. In [14], Han *et al.* proposed a public key encryption (PKE) scheme based on the MDDH assumption over bilinear groups. The PKE scheme has almost tight IND-mCCA security. In the encryption, the plaintext is masked by K, which can be regarded as an encapsulated key. As a result, from the PKE we can derive an IND-mCCA secure KEM $\mathsf{KEM_{MDDH}}$. The definition of the MDDH assumption and the scheme $\mathsf{KEM_{MDDH}}$ appear in the full version (see ePrint).

Theorem 6 (IND-mCCA Security of $\mathsf{KEM_{MDDH}}$). *Let $\ell' \geq 2k + 1$. If (i) the $\mathcal{D}_{\ell',k}$-MDDH assumption holds over both $\mathbb{G}_1$ and $\mathbb{G}_2$, (ii) $\mathcal{H}$ is a collision-resistant function family, then $\mathsf{KEM_{MDDH}}$ is IND-mCCA secure. More precisely, for any PPT adversary $\mathcal{A}$ who makes at most Q_e times of ENC queries and Q_d times of DEC queries, there exist PPT adversaries $\mathcal{B}_1$, $\mathcal{B}_2$ and $\mathcal{B}_3$, such that*

$$\mathsf{Adv}^{m\text{-}cca}_{\mathsf{KEM_{MDDH}}, \theta, \mathcal{A}}(\lambda) \leq (4\lceil \log Q_e \rceil + \ell' - k + 2) \cdot \left(\mathsf{Adv}^{MDDH}_{\mathcal{D}_{\ell',k}, \mathbb{G}_1, \mathcal{B}_1}(\lambda) + \mathsf{Adv}^{MDDH}_{\mathcal{D}_{\ell',k}, \mathbb{G}_2, \mathcal{B}_2}(\lambda) \right)$$
$$+ \mathsf{Adv}^{cr}_{\mathcal{H}, \mathcal{B}_3}(\lambda) + 2^{-\Omega(\lambda)}.$$

The diverse property of $\mathsf{KEM_{MDDH}}$ can also be easily tested.

5.2 Instantiations of SIG with Tight MU-EUF-CMA^{corr} Security

We review two signature schemes. The first one $\mathsf{SIG_{DDH}}$ was proposed by Gjøsteen and Jager [11] and its MU-EUF-CMA^{corr} security was based on the DDH assumption in the random oracle model. The other one $\mathsf{SIG_{MDDH}}$ was proposed by Bader *et al.* [1] and its MU-EUF-CMA^{corr} security was based one the MDDH assumption over bilinear group but in the standard model.

$\mathsf{SIG_{DDH}}$ from the DDH Assumption in the RO Model. The DDH-based signature scheme $\mathsf{SIG_{DDH}}$ in [11] is shown in our full version, and its MU-EUF-CMA^{corr} security can be tightly reduced to the DDH & CDH assumptions in the random oracle model. See Theorem 7.

Theorem 7. *[11] For any PPT adversary $\mathcal{A}$ against $\mathsf{SIG_{DDH}}$, there exist PPT adversaries $\mathcal{B}_{\mathsf{DDH}}$ and $\mathcal{B}_{\mathsf{CDH}}$ against the DDH and CDH problems such that*

$$\mathsf{Adv}^{m\text{-}corr}_{\mathsf{SIG_{DDH}}, \mu, \mathcal{A}}(\lambda) \leq \mathsf{Adv}^{DDH}_{\mathbb{G}, \mathcal{B}_{\mathsf{DDH}}}(\lambda) + 2\mathsf{Adv}^{CDH}_{\mathbb{G}, \mathcal{B}_{\mathsf{CDH}}}(\lambda) + 2^{-\Omega(\lambda)}.$$

$\mathsf{SIG_{MDDH}}$ from the MDDH Assumption in the Standard Model. The MDDH-based signature scheme $\mathsf{SIG_{MDDH}}$ in [1] is shown in our full version, and its MU-EUF-CMA^{corr} security can be tightly reduced to the MDDH assumption. See Theorem 8.

Theorem 8. *[1] For any PPT adversary $\mathcal{A}$ against $\mathsf{SIG}_{\mathsf{MDDH}}$, there exist PPT adversaries $\mathcal{B}_1$ and $\mathcal{B}_2$ against $\mathcal{D}_k$-MDDH in $\mathbb{G}_1$ and $\mathbb{G}_2$ such that*

$$\mathsf{Adv}^{\mathsf{m\text{-}corr}}_{\mathsf{SIG}_{\mathsf{MDDH}},\mu,\mathcal{A}}(\lambda) \leq \mathsf{Adv}^{\mathsf{MDDH}}_{\mathcal{D}_k,\mathbb{G}_1,\mathcal{B}_1}(\lambda) + 2\lambda \cdot \mathsf{Adv}^{\mathsf{MDDH}}_{\mathcal{D}_k,\mathbb{G}_2,\mathcal{B}_2}(\lambda) + 2/q.$$

5.3 Instantiations of AKE

Following the generic construction of AKE in Fig. 6, if we instantiate the KEM and SIG schemes with $\mathsf{KEM}_{\mathsf{st2DH}}$ and $\mathsf{SIG}_{\mathsf{DDH}}$, then we obtain a practical 2-pass AKE scheme $\mathsf{AKE}_{\mathsf{DDH}}$ ($\mathsf{AKE}^{\mathsf{stateless}}_{\mathsf{DDH}}$) with tight security in the random oracle model.

By Theorems 2, 4, 5, 7, we have the following corollary.

Corollary 2. $\mathsf{AKE}_{\mathsf{DDH}}$ *is strongly secure ($\mathsf{AKE}^{\mathsf{stateless}}_{\mathsf{DDH}}$ is secure) in the random oracle model. More precisely, for any PPT adversary $\mathcal{A}$ against $\mathsf{AKE}_{\mathsf{DDH}}$ ($\mathsf{AKE}^{\mathsf{stateless}}_{\mathsf{DDH}}$), there exist PPT adversaries $\mathcal{B}_{\mathsf{DDH}}$ and $\mathcal{B}_{\mathsf{CDH}}$ against the DDH and CDH problems such that*

$$\mathsf{Adv}_{\mathsf{AKE}^{\mathsf{stateless}}_{\mathsf{DDH}},\mu,\mathcal{A}}(\lambda) \leq \mathsf{Adv}^{\mathsf{strong}}_{\mathsf{AKE}_{\mathsf{DDH}},\mu,\ell,\mathcal{A}}(\lambda) \leq 2\mathsf{Adv}^{\mathsf{DDH}}_{\mathbb{G},\mathcal{B}_{\mathsf{DDH}}}(\lambda) + 5\mathsf{Adv}^{\mathsf{CDH}}_{\mathbb{G},\mathcal{B}_{\mathsf{CDH}}}(\lambda) + 2^{-\Omega(\lambda)}.$$

Similarly, if we instantiate the KEM and SIG schemes with $\mathsf{KEM}_{\mathsf{MDDH}}$ and $\mathsf{SIG}_{\mathsf{MDDH}}$, then we obtain another 2-pass AKE scheme $\mathsf{AKE}_{\mathsf{MDDH}}$ ($\mathsf{AKE}^{\mathsf{stateless}}_{\mathsf{MDDH}}$) with tight security in the standard model.

We refer the reader to our full version for the $\mathsf{AKE}_{\mathsf{DDH}}$ and $\mathsf{AKE}_{\mathsf{MDDH}}$ schemes.

By Theorems 1, 4, 6, 8, we have the following corollary.

Corollary 3. $\mathsf{AKE}_{\mathsf{MDDH}}$ *is strongly secure ($\mathsf{AKE}^{\mathsf{stateless}}_{\mathsf{MDDH}}$ is secure) in the standard model. More precisely, for any PPT adversary $\mathcal{A}$ against $\mathsf{AKE}_{\mathsf{MDDH}}$ ($\mathsf{AKE}^{\mathsf{stateless}}_{\mathsf{MDDH}}$), there exist PPT adversaries $\mathcal{B}_1$, $\mathcal{B}_2$, $\mathcal{B}'_1$, $\mathcal{B}'_2$ and $\mathcal{B}_3$ such that*

$$\mathsf{Adv}_{\mathsf{AKE}^{\mathsf{stateless}}_{\mathsf{MDDH}},\mu,\ell,\mathcal{A}}(\lambda) \leq \mathsf{Adv}^{\mathsf{strong}}_{\mathsf{AKE}_{\mathsf{MDDH}},\mu,\ell,\mathcal{A}}(\lambda) \leq 2^{-\Omega(\lambda)} + 2\mathsf{Adv}^{\mathsf{MDDH}}_{\mathcal{D}_k,\mathbb{G}_1,\mathcal{B}_1}(\lambda) + 4\lambda \cdot \mathsf{Adv}^{\mathsf{MDDH}}_{\mathcal{D}_k,\mathbb{G}_2,\mathcal{B}_2}(\lambda)$$
$$+ 2\mathsf{Adv}^{cr}_{\mathcal{H},\mathcal{B}_3}(\lambda) + (8\lceil \log Q_e \rceil + 2\ell' - 2k + 4) \cdot \left(\mathsf{Adv}^{\mathsf{MDDH}}_{\mathcal{D}_{\ell',k},\mathbb{G}_1,\mathcal{B}'_1}(\lambda) + \mathsf{Adv}^{\mathsf{MDDH}}_{\mathcal{D}_{\ell',k},\mathbb{G}_2,\mathcal{B}'_2}(\lambda)\right).$$

Acknowledgments. This work is supported by National Natural Science Foundation of China (61925207, 61672346, 61932014, 61825203, U1736203, 61732021), Guangdong Major Project of Basic and Applied Basic Research (2019B030302008), and the Guangdong Provincal Science and Technology Project (2017B010111005).

References

1. Bader, C., Hofheinz, D., Jager, T., Kiltz, E., Li, Y.: Tightly-secure authenticated key exchange. In: Dodis, Y., Nielsen, J.B. (eds.) TCC 2015, Part I. LNCS, vol. 9014, pp. 629–658. Springer, Heidelberg (2015). https://doi.org/10.1007/978-3-662-46494-6_26
2. Bellare, M., Rogaway, P.: Entity authentication and key distribution. In: Stinson, D.R. (ed.) CRYPTO 1993. LNCS, vol. 773, pp. 232–249. Springer, Heidelberg (1994). https://doi.org/10.1007/3-540-48329-2_21

3. Blake-Wilson, S., Menezes, A.: Unknown key-share attacks on the station-to-station (STS) protocol. In: Imai, H., Zheng, Y. (eds.) PKC 1999. LNCS, vol. 1560, pp. 154–170. Springer, Heidelberg (1999). https://doi.org/10.1007/3-540-49162-7_12

4. Canetti, R., Krawczyk, H.: Security analysis of IKE's signature-based key-exchange protocol. In: Yung, M. (ed.) CRYPTO 2002. LNCS, vol. 2442, pp. 143–161. Springer, Heidelberg (2002). https://doi.org/10.1007/3-540-45708-9_10

5. Cash, D., Kiltz, E., Shoup, V.: The twin Diffie-Hellman problem and applications. In: Smart, N. (ed.) EUROCRYPT 2008. LNCS, vol. 4965, pp. 127–145. Springer, Heidelberg (2008). https://doi.org/10.1007/978-3-540-78967-3_8

6. Cohn-Gordon, K., Cremers, C., Gjøsteen, K., Jacobsen, H., Jager, T.: Highly efficient key exchange protocols with optimal tightness. In: Boldyreva, A., Micciancio, D. (eds.) CRYPTO 2019, Part III. LNCS, vol. 11694, pp. 767–797. Springer, Cham (2019). https://doi.org/10.1007/978-3-030-26954-8_25

7. Cremers, C., Feltz, M.: Beyond eCK: perfect forward secrecy under actor compromise and ephemeral-key reveal. In: Foresti, S., Yung, M., Martinelli, F. (eds.) ESORICS 2012. LNCS, vol. 7459, pp. 734–751. Springer, Heidelberg (2012). https://doi.org/10.1007/978-3-642-33167-1_42

8. Ding, J., Branco, P., Schmitt, K.: Key exchange and authenticated key exchange with reusable keys based on RLWE assumption. IACR Cryptology ePrint Archive 2019, 665 (2019)

9. Escala, A., Herold, G., Kiltz, E., Ràfols, C., Villar, J.: An algebraic framework for Diffie-Hellman assumptions. In: Canetti, R., Garay, J.A. (eds.) CRYPTO 2013, Part II. LNCS, vol. 8043, pp. 129–147. Springer, Heidelberg (2013). https://doi.org/10.1007/978-3-642-40084-1_8

10. Fischlin, M., Günther, F.: Replay attacks on zero round-trip time: the case of the TLS 1.3 handshake candidates. In: 2017 IEEE European Symposium on Security and Privacy, EuroS&P 2017, Paris, France, 26–28 April 2017, pp. 60–75 (2017)

11. Gjøsteen, K., Jager, T.: Practical and tightly-secure digital signatures and authenticated key exchange. In: Shacham, H., Boldyreva, A. (eds.) CRYPTO 2018, Part II. LNCS, vol. 10992, pp. 95–125. Springer, Cham (2018). https://doi.org/10.1007/978-3-319-96881-0_4

12. Günther, C.G.: An identity-based key-exchange protocol. In: Quisquater, J.-J., Vandewalle, J. (eds.) EUROCRYPT 1989. LNCS, vol. 434, pp. 29–37. Springer, Heidelberg (1990). https://doi.org/10.1007/3-540-46885-4_5

13. Halevi, S., Krawczyk, H.: One-pass HMQV and asymmetric key-wrapping. In: Catalano, D., Fazio, N., Gennaro, R., Nicolosi, A. (eds.) PKC 2011. LNCS, vol. 6571, pp. 317–334. Springer, Heidelberg (2011). https://doi.org/10.1007/978-3-642-19379-8_20

14. Han, S., Liu, S., Lyu, L., Gu, D.: Tight leakage-resilient CCA-security from quasi-adaptive hash proof system. In: Boldyreva, A., Micciancio, D. (eds.) CRYPTO 2019, Part II. LNCS, vol. 11693, pp. 417–447. Springer, Cham (2019). https://doi.org/10.1007/978-3-030-26951-7_15

15. Jin, Z., Zhao, Y.: Generic and practical key establishment from lattice. In: Deng, R.H., Gauthier-Umaña, V., Ochoa, M., Yung, M. (eds.) ACNS 2019. LNCS, vol. 11464, pp. 302–322. Springer, Cham (2019). https://doi.org/10.1007/978-3-030-21568-2_15

16. Krawczyk, H.: HMQV: a high-performance secure Diffie-Hellman protocol. In: Shoup, V. (ed.) CRYPTO 2005. LNCS, vol. 3621, pp. 546–566. Springer, Heidelberg (2005). https://doi.org/10.1007/11535218_33

17. Krawczyk, H., Wee, H.: The OPTLS protocol and TLS 1.3. In: IEEE European Symposium on Security and Privacy, EuroS&P 2016, Saarbrücken, Germany, 21–24 March 2016, pp. 81–96 (2016)
18. LaMacchia, B., Lauter, K., Mityagin, A.: Stronger security of authenticated key exchange. In: Susilo, W., Liu, J.K., Mu, Y. (eds.) ProvSec 2007. LNCS, vol. 4784, pp. 1–16. Springer, Heidelberg (2007). https://doi.org/10.1007/978-3-540-75670-5_1
19. Li, Y., Schäge, S.: No-match attacks and robust partnering definitions: defining trivial attacks for security protocols is not trivial. In: Proceedings of the 2017 ACM SIGSAC Conference on Computer and Communications Security, CCS 2017, Dallas, TX, USA, 30 October–03 November 2017, pp. 1343–1360 (2017)
20. Peikert, C.: Lattice cryptography for the internet. In: Mosca, M. (ed.) PQCrypto 2014. LNCS, vol. 8772, pp. 197–219. Springer, Cham (2014). https://doi.org/10.1007/978-3-319-11659-4_12
21. Rescorla, E.: The transport layer security (TLS) protocol version 1.3. RFC 8446, pp. 1–160 (2018)
22. Xiao, Y., Zhang, R., Ma, H.: Tightly secure two-pass authenticated key exchange protocol in the CK model. In: Jarecki, S. (ed.) CT-RSA 2020. LNCS, vol. 12006, pp. 171–198. Springer, Cham (2020). https://doi.org/10.1007/978-3-030-40186-3_9

Author Index